D1738703

THE PHILOSOPHY OF
HILARY PUTNAM

THE LIBRARY OF LIVING PHILOSOPHERS

Hilary Putnam

THE LIBRARY OF LIVING PHILOSOPHERS
VOLUME XXXIV

THE PHILOSOPHY OF
HILARY PUTNAM

EDITED BY

RANDALL E. AUXIER,
DOUGLAS R. ANDERSON,
AND
LEWIS EDWIN HAHN

SOUTHERN ILLINOIS UNIVERSITY CARBONDALE

CHICAGO, ILLINOIS • OPEN COURT • ESTABLISHED 1887

To order books from Open Court, call 1-800-815-2280, or visit our website at
www.opencourtbooks.com.

Cover and frontispiece photos by Jan-Olav Wedin.

THE PHILOSOPHY OF HILARY PUTNAM

Open Court Publishing Company is a division of Carus Publishing Company,
dba Cricket Media.

Printed and bound in the United States of America.

Library of Congress Cataloging-in-Publication Data

The philosophy of Hilary Putnam / edited by Randall E. Auxier, Douglas R. Anderson, and
Lewis Edwin Hahn, Southern Illinois University Carbondale.
    pages cm. — (Library of living philosophers ; volume XXXIV)
    Summary: "This volume consists of an intellectual autobiography by world-renowned
philosopher Hilary Putnam, 26 critical or descriptive essays, 26 replies by Hilary Putnam,
and a bibliography listing all of Putnam's published writings"— Provided by publisher.
    Includes bibliographical references and index.
    ISBN 978-0-8126-9893-0 (hardback)
    1. Putnam, Hilary. I. Auxier, Randall E., 1961– editor. II. Anderson, Douglas R., editor.
III. Hahn, Lewis Edwin, 1908–2004, editor.
    B945.P874P49 2015
    191—dc23

                                                                    2015003628

The Library of Living Philosophers is published under the sponsorship of Southern Illinois
University Carbondale.

GENERAL INTRODUCTION
TO
THE LIBRARY OF LIVING PHILOSOPHERS

Since its founding in 1938 by Paul Arthur Schilpp, the Library of Living Philosophers has been devoted to critical analysis and discussion of some of the world's greatest living philosophers. The format for the series provides for creating in each volume a dialogue between the critics and the great philosopher. The aim is not refutation or confrontation but rather fruitful joining of issues and improved understanding of the positions and issues involved. That is, the goal is not overcoming those who differ from us philosophically but interacting creatively with them.

The basic idea for the series, according to Professor Schilpp's general introduction to the earlier volumes, came from the late F.C.S. Schiller's essay "Must Philosophers Disagree?" While Schiller may have been overly optimistic about ending "interminable controversies" in this way, it seems clear that directing searching questions to great philosophers about what they really mean or how they might resolve or address difficulties in their philosophies can produce far greater clarity of understanding and more fruitful philosophizing than would otherwise exist.

To Paul Arthur Schilpp's undying credit, he acted on this basic thought in launching the Library of Living Philosophers. The general plan for the volumes has sometimes been altered to fit circumstances, but in ways that have well served the mission of the series. The intellectual autobiographies, or, in a few cases, the biographies, shed a great deal of light on both how the philosophies of the great thinkers developed and the major philosophical movements and issues of their time; and many of our great philosophers seek to orient their outlook not merely to their contemporaries but also to what they find most important in earlier philosophers. The critical perspectives of our distinguished contributors have often stood on their own as landmark studies, widely cited and familiar not only to subsequent specialists, but frequently discussed in their own right as pieces of great philosophy. The bibliography helps to provide ready access to the featured scholar's writings and thought.

There is no reason to alter our historical format or mission for the present century. We are pleased that the success of the Library of Living Philosophers has led to a wider appreciation of the need for dialogue of the type our format creates. We respect the efforts of other academic publishers to employ versions of our format to facilitate pluralistic, meaningful, sharp, constructive, and respectful exchange in philosophical ideas. We are fortunate to have such support from the Open Court Publishing Company, the Edward C. Hegeler Foundation, and the Board of Trustees, College of Liberal Arts, and the Department of Philosophy of Southern Illinois University Carbondale, as to permit us to carry out our purpose with a degree of deliberate thoroughness and comprehensiveness not available to other academic publishers, and we have rededicated ourselves to maintaining the highest standards in scholarship and accuracy anywhere to be found in academic publishing. In recognition of the permanent value that has been accorded our previous volumes, we are committed to keeping our volumes in print and available, and to maintaining our sense of the long-term importance of providing the most reliable source for scholarly analysis by the most distinguished voices of our day about the most important philosophical contributions of the greatest living thinkers.

The Library of Living Philosophers has never construed "philosophy" in a narrow and strictly academic sense. Past volumes have been dedicated both to the leading academic philosophers and to the most visible and influential public philosophers. We renew with each volume our historical orientation to the practice of philosophy as a quest for truth, beauty, and the best life, and we affirm that this quest is a public activity and its results a public possession, both for the present generation and in the future. We seek, with the sober judgment of our Advisory Board, to bring forth volumes on the thought of figures whose ideas have made a genuine difference to the lives of people everywhere. Ideas truly do have consequences, and many of the ideas that have had the broadest impact were indeed best articulated by the figures to whom we have dedicated past volumes. The selfless work of Paul Arthur Schilpp and Lewis Edwin Hahn in realizing this mission stands among the most important scholarly contributions to twentieth-century philosophy. Their judgment regarding how best to pursue the purposes of the Library of Living Philosophers has found constant and continuous confirmation in the reception and ongoing importance accorded this series. Let us continue in their footsteps as well as we may.

RANDALL E. AUXIER

DEPARTMENT OF PHILOSOPHY
SOUTHERN ILLINOIS UNIVERSITY CARBONDALE

FOUNDER'S GENERAL INTRODUCTION*
TO
THE LIBRARY OF LIVING PHILOSOPHERS

According to the late F. C. S. Schiller, the greatest obstacle to fruitful discussion in philosophy is "the curious etiquette which apparently taboos the asking of questions about a philosopher's meaning while he is alive." The "interminable controversies which fill the histories of philosophy," he goes on to say, "could have been ended at once by asking the living philosophers a few searching questions."

The confident optimism of this last remark undoubtedly goes too far. Living thinkers have often been asked "a few searching questions," but their answers have not stopped "interminable controversies" about their real meaning. It is nonetheless true that there would be far greater clarity of understanding than is now often the case if more such searching questions had been directed to great thinkers while they were still alive.

This, at any rate, is the basic thought behind the present undertaking. The volumes of the Library of Living Philosophers can in no sense take the place of the major writings of great and original thinkers. Students who would know the philosophies of such men as John Dewey, George Santayana, Alfred North Whitehead, G. E. Moore, Bertrand Russell, Ernst Cassirer, Karl Jaspers, Rudolf Carnap, Martin Buber, et al., will still need to read the writings of these men. There is no substitute for first-hand contact with the original thought of the philosopher himself. Least of all does this Library pretend to be such a substitute. The Library in fact will spare neither effort nor expense in offering to the student the best possible guide to the published writings of a given thinker. We shall attempt to meet this aim by providing at the end of each volume in our series as nearly complete a bibliography of the published work of the philosopher in question as possible. Nor should one overlook the fact that essays in each volume cannot but finally lead to this same goal. The interpretive and critical discussions of the various

---

*This General Introduction sets forth in the founder's words the underlying conception of the Library. —R. E. A.

phases of a great thinker's work and, most of all, the reply of the thinker himself, are bound to lead the reader to the works of the philosopher himself.

At the same time, there is no denying that different experts find different ideas in the writings of the same philosopher. This is as true of the appreciative interpreter and grateful disciple as it is of the critical opponent. Nor can it be denied that such differences of reading and of interpretation on the part of other experts often leave the neophyte aghast before the whole maze of widely varying and even opposing interpretations. Who is right and whose interpretation shall he accept? When the doctors disagree among themselves, what is the poor student to do? If, in desperation, he decides that all of the interpreters are probably wrong and that the only thing for him to do is to go back to the original writings of the philosopher himself and then make his own decision—uninfluenced (as if this were possible) by the interpretation of anyone else—the result is not that he has actually come to the meaning of the original philosopher himself, but rather that he has set up one more interpretation, which may differ to a greater or lesser degree from the interpretations already existing. It is clear that in this direction lies chaos, just the kind of chaos which Schiller has so graphically and inimitably described.**

It is curious that until now no way of escaping this difficulty has been seriously considered. It has not occurred to students of philosophy that one effective way of meeting the problem at least partially is to put these varying interpretations and critiques before the philosopher while he is still alive and to ask him to act at one and the same time as both defendant and judge. If the world's greatest living philosophers can be induced to cooperate in an enterprise whereby their own work can, at least to some extent, be saved from becoming merely "desiccated lecture-fodder," which on the one hand "provides innocuous sustenance for ruminant professors," and on the other hand gives an opportunity to such ruminants and their understudies to "speculate safely, endlessly, and fruitlessly, about what a philosopher must have meant" (Schiller), they will have taken a long step toward making their intentions more clearly comprehensible.

With this in mind, the Library of Living Philosophers expects to publish at more or less regular intervals a volume on each of the greater among the world's living philosophers. In each case it will be the purpose of the editor of the Library to bring together in the volume the interpretations and criticisms of a wide range of that particular thinker's scholarly contemporaries, each of whom will be given a free hand to discuss the specific phase of the thinker's work that has been assigned to him. All contributed essays will

---

**In his essay "Must Philosophers Disagree?" in the volume of the same title (London: Macmillan, 1934), from which the above quotations were taken.

finally be submitted to the philosopher with whose work and thought they are concerned, for his careful perusal and reply. And, although it would be expecting too much to imagine that the philosopher's reply will be able to stop all differences of interpretation and of critique, this should at least serve the purpose of stopping certain of the grosser and more general kinds of misinterpretations. If no further gain than this were to come from the present and projected volumes of this Library, it would seem to be fully justified.

In carrying out this principal purpose of the Library, the editor announces that (as far as is humanly possible) each volume will contain the following elements:

First, an intellectual autobiography of the thinker whenever this can be secured; in any case an authoritative and authorized biography;

Second, a series of expository and critical articles written by the leading exponents and opponents of the philosopher's thought;

Third, the reply to the critics and commentators by the philosopher himself; and

Fourth, a bibliography of writings of the philosopher to provide a ready instrument to give access to his writings and thought.

PAUL ARTHUR SCHILPP
FOUNDER AND EDITOR, 1939–1981

DEPARTMENT OF PHILOSOPHY
SOUTHERN ILLINOIS UNIVERSITY CARBONDALE

ADVISORY BOARD

TABLE OF CONTENTS

PREFACE

All persons are puzzles until at last we find in some word or act the key to the man, to the woman; straightway all their past words and actions lie in light before us.[1]

—EMERSON

The prefaces to our volumes are rare opportunities to characterize a great mind and a complete human being, together and as a whole, from the standpoint of those who have been privileged to spend extensive time in study of both primary and secondary works, to meet, to converse, and to have carried on extensive correspondence with both the principal subject of the volume and some two dozen of the ablest critics. In the years that it takes to prepare a volume in the Library of Living Philosophers, it is possible, then, for us to reflect upon those qualities of mind that have distinguished a philosopher and which have taken that philosophy, itself, to a level of permanent human significance. Virtues come to the fore, as do challenges and even defects that have been overcome, in this longitudinal kind of study. By the time a philosopher has been elected by our Advisory Board to be treated in a volume, it is obvious to everyone, within the discipline and beyond it, that the philosopher's achievement has been extraordinary.

THE OTHER HALF OF THE STORY

Hilary Putnam, Cogan University Professor Emeritus of Harvard, has always been a model, both personally and intellectually, of numerous humane virtues, and I think the virtues that reveal the most about his achievement are his genuineness and his courage, in several complementary senses of that ancient virtue. But before launching into a consideration of courage, one thing really has to be made clear. Ruth Anna Putnam is an integral part of any story about what they achieved together, in *every* sense. There can really be no discussion of the qualities of Hilary Putnam's mind, his character, his honors and achievements, his insights, and (most importantly) his development, that does not credit from the start the idea that the completed human being is part of a family and, in this case, also half of a marriage,

which explains far more about who he is than one can read in any book or
article he ever wrote, with the possible exception of the Intellectual Autobiography in this volume.

The Putnams came to Southern Illinois University in Carbondale in
2001. The main purpose of their trip was to examine some of the scholarly
papers, correspondence, and ephemera held in Morris Library from the
estate of Samuel Putnam, Hilary's father, who was an important humanist,
translator, scholar, journalist, and activist.[2] At that time, Ruth Anna had not
yet been invited to contribute an essay to the volume—after all, the aim of
the volume is to collect the finest *critics* of a philosopher's thought. Perhaps
the venerable Professor Hahn, who announced the present volume and at
that time had just retired as Editor, assumed, in his delightful, gentlemanly,
and old-fashioned way, that Ruth Anna, distinguished philosopher though
she is, would prefer not to receive such an assignment as to criticize her
husband! Everyone knew that she had some sharp philosophical differences
with Hilary (their philosophical exchanges have not been a private matter).
Still, one would normally not wish to invite devoted partners to square off
for the ages. But on that trip in 2001, Ruth Anna said to me that she did in
fact want to contribute to the volume, and, she said, "I promise to be *critical*!" I do not believe she ever really had any qualms about being critical
of Hilary's ideas, and the invitation would certainly have been forthcoming
even without the promise, but anyone who knows the couple is now smiling.
I think it is important to record that pleasant fact about this moment in history and of the Putnams' lives, for those who would not learn it otherwise.

The point is that Hilary's virtues cannot possibly be separated from
Ruth Anna's. Of course, hypothetically, if anyone were qualified to parse
the modal logic we would need to assess sentences about what might have
been Hilary's character *without* having shared a full life with Ruth Anna,
Hilary would be the person to do it. The trouble is that the posited universe
of discourse is *not* a nearby possible world, and no Kripke frame will provide an accessibility relation. I can almost hear Hilary saying that it is hard
to analyze what cannot even be imagined. Below, then, is a discussion of
Hilary Putnam's courage, and of his genuineness, and how these characters
permeate his intellectual achievements and his life. But these are characters
of a *shared* life, one that never allowed body and mind, action and thought,
fact and value, or Ruth Anna and Hilary to grow apart.

A MOMENT IN TIME

Hilary Putnam spoke to a packed auditorium in Atlanta in 1991. Like Emerson before him, he has spoken to appreciative audiences nearly everywhere,
even if some were a bit quarrelsome. Had he so desired, Putnam surely

could have left teaching and secured a fine living on that circuit alone by the mid-1980s. On this occasion, he spoke on the topic of William James at Emory University on a fall evening. A few of us had the nerve, if not quite the courage (in the mature sense), to ask some pointed questions. There were deep difficulties at that moment in time in the philosophy profession, and these questions were supposed to lay a stumbling block before the speaker. Young people who are experiencing their early disappointments with the world are apt to throw such frustrations back upon the elders, as symbols of the status quo, and they often do so without great discretion. Everyone there was about to receive a benevolent lesson in courage, and in genuineness. The moment contains a key to a puzzle. We shall return to it.

Serving Two Masters

It is not easy to understand courage. It comes in different colors and stripes; it leaves such varied traces. Even Plato struggled to characterize it, offering a number of unsatisfactory answers, most notably that courage, for guardians of the city, at least, is believing what they have been taught by their betters and acting on that teaching without question. Not many people today could accept such a view, especially for our guardians, but then, not many accepted it during Plato's time either, including Plato himself, for all we know. Yet, there is something in Plato's point, as always. We cannot let ourselves lose it altogether.

Others, following Aristotle, point out that courage, as applied to action, is a mean between rashness and cowardice, or, relative to feeling, that it is a kind of resolve about doing one's duty either without excessive fear or in spite of it. There is a permanent insight here as well. The thoughts of Plato and Aristotle set the agenda for the rest of us, and in general that is a fortunate thing, even if it sometimes bedevils us all. Emerson appreciated both Plato and Aristotle. And he learned reverence and wonder, among other places, in Goethe's parlor. Goethe said this:

> Plato relates himself to the world as a blessed spirit, whom it pleases sometimes to stay for a while in the world; he is not so much concerned to come to know the world, because he already presupposes it, as to communicate to it in a friendly way what he brings along with him and what it needs. He penetrates into the depths more in order to fill them with his being than in order to investigate them. He moves longingly to the heights in order to become again a part of his origin. Everything that he utters is related to an eternal One, Good, True, Beautiful, whose demands he strives to enliven in his bosom . . . . Aristotle, on the contrary, stands to the world as a man, an architect. He is only here once and must here make and create. He inquires about the earth, but not farther

than to find a ground . . . . He draws a huge circumference for his building, procures materials from all sides, arranges them, piles them up, and climbs thus in regular form, pyramid fashion to the top; whereas Plato, like an obelisk, indeed like a pointed flame, seeks heaven. When two such men appear, who as it were, share humanity as separate representatives of splendid but not easily reconcilable properties, when they had the fortune to educate themselves fully, to utter their education completely . . . when their works for the best part remain to mankind and are more or less continuously studied and reflected on: it naturally follows that the world, insofar as it is regarded as feeling and thinking, was compelled to surrender itself to one or the other, to recognize one or the other as master, teacher, and leader.[3]

Granting Goethe's point, nevertheless, concerning any matter of real depth, to choose just one of these masters to the *complete* exclusion of the other is to err. Putnam characterizes the age of Aristotle and Plato as the first Enlightenment of the Western world, marking the appearance on the philosophical scene of what he calls "reflective transcendence."[4]

The phrase sounds like something straight from Emerson's journals. Reflective transcendence increases our tolerance for ambiguity, for holding on to creative tension. *Must* we choose between Plato and Aristotle? Emerson would not make a mistake like that any more than Putnam would, at least not during a time of Enlightenment, such as the one Putnam believes we now live in, with the ongoing unfolding of a democratic vision articulated by the pragmatists in North America. Persons are puzzles, Emerson said, but then there comes a moment when the key to the man, or to the woman, is apparent.

WONDER AND REVERENCE

To hold to both Plato and Aristotle as "master, teacher, and leader," Emerson places courage alongside "disinterestedness" and "practical power" as the "three qualities which conspicuously attract the wonder and reverence of mankind."[5]

The first of these involves the ability to look upon desirable things or self-interested courses of action without experiencing any temptation to obtain or follow them. The second is the ability to start with nothing but one's hands, intelligence, and will, combining them to accomplish great purposes that would overwhelm most people. This practical power is especially obvious when, for instance, one needs to win a war or a battle, but also is illustrated in building a city or in *making peace*. These two, then, disinterestedness and practical power, and especially the third quality, courage, attract *wonder and reverence*. Yet, "it is plain that there is no separate essence called courage, no cup or cell in the brain, no vessel in the heart containing drops or atoms that make or give this virtue." Still, "it is the right or healthy state of every man, when he is free to do that which is constitutional to him to do.[6] Such a person is a wonderful presence, in the original sense of the adjective.

Putnam, along with the wise worthies of the American philosophical tradition, avoids simplistic formulas. Here Emerson guides that tradition by making room for the individual enactment of courage in the context of a quality of character, a kind of free constitution, that is social, through and through. He always insisted that it is easier to communicate a "form" than to pass along its "virtue." We can see the adaptation of Plato's tenacious steadfastness in following what our betters have told us to Aristotle's mean, once we remove the merely abstract conviction that there must be an inflexible essence. To grasp Putnam's courage, therefore, requires that we understand how he did what he did *when free to do what was in his constitution to do*—and this was much of the time. We are now in a position to take stock.

BACK IN THE LECTURE HALL

Back in the lecture hall in 1991, this was not Putnam's usual audience. These scholars and teachers were humanistic practitioners of a perennial philosophy, a pursuit of wisdom more than of knowledge. They take the history of philosophy, and not language analysis, to be a course of study more fit to human aspirations and limitations. They have been ill-treated by the dominant models of scientific philosophy. The question was asked: "Are you saying that we wasted the last half century in philosophy?" A pause. The questioner wanted justification for a half century of slights and jeers directed at himself and his intellectual kin; he wanted, quite unreasonably, some apology and admission of a mistake on the part of those who had mocked or ignored James and so many like him.

A FREE CONSTITUTION

For most of his career, Putnam occupied a position of influence, power, even celebrity. Certain kinds of choices are available to persons so situated that are beyond the reach of most people. There is a kind of freedom in it, although the exercise of that freedom comes at a cost, and the freer one is, the higher the cost. A paragraph often attributed to Emerson runs as follows:

> Whatever you do, you need courage. Whatever course you decide upon, there is always someone to tell you that you are wrong. There are always difficulties arising that tempt you to believe your critics are right. To map out a course of action and follow it to an end requires some of the same courage that a soldier needs. Peace has its victories, but it takes brave men and women to win them.[7]

Although Emerson did not write this, it addresses his idea about what inspires reverence and wonder. Note how the epigram folds in the other two qualities that attract wonder and reverence: *disinterestedness* as to being tempted to believe one's critics and *practical power* in achieving a purpose. It is particularly telling in the inclusion of making peace as one of the great demands on our courage.

Putnam grew up among humanistic, broad-minded, politically leftist scholars. Looking at his work during the 1950s, '60s, and '70s in the philosophy of mathematics and physics, followed by important contributions to the philosophy of language, of mind, and of logic, one would not easily detect this broad background. Yet, the ideas of thinking broadly and being committed to act in service of high ideals are lessons that were provided for him from the cradle. Putnam learned ideals as he learned his name; he always knew that people are prone to misuse power and that all kinds of people, especially ordinary people, must struggle for their dignity. He did not come from an especially privileged family, by Western standards, but from one quite dedicated to the deep value of learning. Is this power?

POWER: PRACTICAL AND PRIVILEGED

It could not have been easy for Putnam to understand *his own* power within the professional climate as it unfolded in the second half of the twentieth century. He was and is an unassuming servant of ideas, first and foremost. He had come to his position on his merits more than his pedigree and had achieved prominence on the weight of his work. The ideas themselves must carry the case, in the end, he believed. Wherever one can find sound thinking, one really must follow it and add one's stanza to its long epic. This is the only *entitlement* of anyone deeply devoted to philosophy. It is not a strategy for getting to Harvard. That one person, due merely to situation or circumstance, should receive a more sympathetic or wider hearing than others of equal merit is not the right norm for progress in our thinking. Putnam will regard this as common sense. The fact is, however, that everyone read what Putnam wrote, whether they wanted to or not, both because of the importance of the ideas and because of the influence of the person who penned them. From beyond the candy store window, where most of us stand, one can scarcely distinguish the deserving from the simply fortunate among those within.

One thing that was clear to hungry waifs standing out in the cold was that Putnam was free to change his mind whenever he wanted to, and that seemed like the exercise of privilege. The others who wielded similar influence came to consider Putnam's frequent changes of view a sort of adorable quirk. Daniel Dennett famously took Putnam's first name as a noun for his lexicon:

> hilary, n. (from *hilary term*) A very brief but significant period in the intellectual career of a distinguished philosopher. "Oh, that's what I thought three or four hilaries ago."[8]

Coming from Dennett, whatever their differences on functionalism may be, this is not an attack. It is worth noting that the philosopher must be *distinguished* and the periods, however brief, are *significant*. That means that most philosophers are not really able (or allowed) to have such episodes. Rather, the seriousness of stating one's professional views is something repeated all the way from the Little Ivies down to the community colleges. Below these elite levels, changing one's view is a sign of weakness, at least whenever one looks *across* the profession or *down* from one's own perch. Those in the crystal towers can waffle and waver. In that case, this is the exercise of a prerogative.

The resentment of privilege, on the other hand, also tends to rise from below and converge. In the metaphorical middle, the Purdues and Penn States, the Washington Universities and Universities of Washington of our discipline, to which the unlikely rise and the privileged sink to share large, impersonal departments, there is tremendous pressure to conform to the models established by that upper echelon. Changing one's mind, even "significantly" for the better, casts doubt upon the waffler. Naturally, at the same time, a tiny ripple at Harvard can create a tsunami out in the Great Middle.

MAKING WAVES

It took more fortitude on Putnam's part to handle the response of his mainstream peers (and soon-to-be critics) than to handle the wondering amazement of those on the margins who pursued philosophy by other-than-analytic methods. Many of those latter associated the professional ascendency of language analysis with figures like Putnam himself, although he was never dismissive of any historical approach to philosophy. Still, he was among the pillars of the establishment and a student of Hans Reichenbach, renown both for his personal kindness and his philosophical narrowness. Reverence to accompany our wonder is usually reserved to a later generation, it seems. We cannot distinguish courage from foolhardiness when we are left in its wake.

So it was that Putnam's change of viewpoint finally asked more than the metaphorical middle could forbear. It was Putnam's drift toward—and then full conversion to—pragmatism. He had finally "hilaried" to the point of making himself unacceptable to those who waited upon the slightest Harvard ripple, perceived or real. If there was one thing the world did not need, it was to be reminded of what William James said a century ago or why it was not quite so daft or naïve as we had been told.

Now here was Putnam, enthusiastically reading and defending James—publicly. The abuse of James, especially on the matter of "truth," was something of a sport among the first-generation analytic formalists who followed in the train of Bertrand Russell. The ordinary language philosophers and those who were obsessed with Wittgenstein had no interest in James, but he certainly was passé by any standard. By the second generation (recalling that academic generations are only about twenty-five years in duration), no one bothered even to mock James. Putnam often criticizes, and has long done so, those who spend their graduate school years learning who they *do not* have to read or take seriously. He knew what he criticized first-hand from being more or less constantly surrounded by it. Indeed, he repeated this criticism of narrowness to the surprised crowd gathered in Atlanta in 1991. How can it serve philosophy to substitute jingoism for effort and reflection? Putnam never put up with it. But then, *he* was free to do what was in his constitution to do.

A Long and Winding Road

Being able to change his mind as often as the ideas themselves and concomitant inquiry suggested, Putnam became, at length, a pragmatist. Our debt to history demands that we emphasize that Ruth Anna had been a pragmatist during the full duration of Hilary's quest for uncertainty. If it were not simply beyond the limits of acceptable analogy, one might think of the patience of St. Monica, the latter being the true "patron" of Christian theology. Our story is not quite so dramatic. But there is something to be said for the way human beings learn together, read together, and grow together, intellectually, morally, and spiritually. The order of nature permits accidents, but if anything is *really* knowable, it is that people who share their lives will affect each other's ideas.

I met with Hilary and Ruth Anna a number of times and came to know them in something of the way a student knows benevolent teachers. It was a great privilege to undertake a systematic study of Putnam's full corpus and to begin to teach his writings to graduate students here in the Great Middle. Putnam became the one philosopher I was comfortable defending as the best and most faithful inheritor of the legacy of John Dewey. That is not a statement one makes lightly, when Dewey is the gold standard of philosophical practice. Even the margins have their strict standards of conservation, and indeed, they become all the more stringent as one moves out from the center. They are a centripetal counter-movement to the danger of being slung into nothingness. The pragmatists had been waiting for a deliverer but largely knew him not when he came to be among them. Most were content to let the Romans do their worst. But Putnam is a persuasive man, and he is hard to scare.

WASTING OUR TIME?

And then Putnam said: "I believe that people never waste their time when they are sincerely searching for the truth." It was a question seeking justification by way of accusation in a painful time. In the kindest terms (and Putnam is not always so gentle with questioners), the audience was reminded of the sincerity of those other inquirers. Those gathered were being taught not to focus first on what was worst or merely human about their own movement or any other, but instead upon why they set aside their plows and followed a call to truth, an ἐκκλησία, following after something worth having, if indeed it could be had. It was an answer that aimed at peace; indeed, it did more than merely aim. One looks for some word or act and straightway there is the key to the man, to the woman.

Emerson said: "To be genuine. . . . The difficulty increases with the gifts of the individual. A plough-boy can be, but a minister, an orator, an ingenious thinker how hardly!"[9]

Yes, it must be hard, for an ingenious thinker, but it can be done, especially if that genuineness is in one's constitution, when one is free to follow it, when one is not tempted to believe one's critics, and when one is undertaking a great work, such as sincerely seeking the truth or making peace.

A TIME FOR THE AGES

The Library of Living Philosophers completed seventy-five years of service to Sophia in 2013. Recent times have not been easy in the publishing industry and higher education is in the middle of massive changes. The future is always uncertain but now more than usual. We do not know what is in store, but one thing is beyond dispute: This is the last volume in our series that will bear the distinguished name of Lewis Edwin Hahn. All of us who have had a part in finishing the work he started regard him with wonder and reverence, and we dedicate our efforts to his memory and hope that they will be worthy of his legacy.

RANDALL E. AUXIER

KERRVILLE, TX
MAY 19, 2014

NOTES

1. From the journals, September 1842, in *The Heart of Emerson's Journals*, ed. Bliss Perry (Boston: Houghton Mifflin, 1926), 183.

2. The holdings of the Morris Library in this area are found here: http://archives.lib. siu.edu/index.php?p=collections/controlcard&id=2089&q=putnam (accessed May 6, 2014).

3. Goethe, *Gedenkausgabe der Werke, Briefe und Gespräche*, 24 vols., ed. Ernst Beutler, *Naturwissenschaftliche Schriften, Erster Teil* (Zürich: Artemis-Verlag, 1949), XVI, 346–47. Ernst Cassirer quoted this passage in two places: *Kant's Life and Thought*, trans. James Haden (New Haven: Yale University Press, 1981), 417–18; and, in the essay "The Concept of Philosophy as a Philosophical Problem," trans. Donald Phillip Verene in *Symbol, Myth, and Culture: Essays and Lectures of Ernst Cassirer, 1935–1945*, ed. Donald Phillip Verene (New Haven: Yale University Press, 1979), 50–51. I have used Verene's translation except in two places where the Haden translation contains lines omitted by Cassirer in the essay Verene translated. This work of Goethe's has never been translated in full.

4. Putnam, *Ethics without Ontology* (Cambridge, MA: Harvard University Press, 2004), 92.

5. All passages from Emerson are taken from *The Complete Writings of Ralph Waldo Emerson* (New York: William H. Wise & Co., 1929). This passage is from "Courage" (originally published in *Society and Solitude*, 1870), 697.

6. Emerson, "Courage," 701.

7. This passage comes from the Christian magazine *Young People's Weekly*, and the likely author is either David Caleb Cook (1875–1927) or someone who worked in his missionary organization. It was appropriated by Mary Allette Ayer for one of her motivational books of epigrams in 1908 and from there made its way onto the internet. The story of this passage and how if came to be attributed to Emerson himself is at http://irregulartimes. com/2013/03/03/the-evolution-of-a-quote-misconceived-misattributed-misconstrued/ (accessed May 17, 2014).

8. See http://www.philosophicallexicon.com/ (accessed May 7, 2014). John Heil has defended Putnam's famous changes of position in the entry he wrote for *Blackwell's Companion to Analytic Philosophy*, ed. A. P. Martinich and David Sosa (Malden, MA: Blackwell, 2001), 393–412.

9. This is from Emerson's journals, Boston, August 18, 1832; in *The Heart of Emerson's Journals*, ed. Bliss Perry (Boston: Houghton Mifflin, 1926), 59.

PART ONE

INTELLECTUAL AUTOBIOGRAPHY OF HILARY PUTNAM

In fact, "true-in-L" (as defined by a Tarskian "truth definition) is an expression whose _definiens_ contains _no_ occurrences of the name "L". The word "L", which elsewhere designates a particular language, occurs only _accidentally_ in the expression "true-in-L", just as "cat" occurs only accidentally in "cattle". And since a Tarskian "truth definition" provides no _general_ notion of truth, but only an infinite series of different notions, "true-in-L₁", "true-in-L₂", ..., then Quine's definition of validity, presupposing as it does that ~~Quine~~ Tarski has provided a purely extensional explanation of the predicate "true", likewise provides only an infinite series of different notions of validity, "valid-in-L₁", "valid-in-L₂", etc; and not a single notion "valid" applicable (truly or falsely, but in any case meaningfully) to statements in an arbitrary language

INTELLECTUAL AUTOBIOGRAPHY

I. My Family

My father, Samuel Putnam, came from a family that arrived in the British colony of Virginia in 1647. The family may have been puritan. At any rate, my father's parents and grandparents and great-great-grandparents were Calvinists, although, to their great disgust, my father would have much preferred it if they had been Roman Catholics. (He was not a churchgoer, however.) Here is the genealogical information on the family I have been able to find:

A PUTNAM/PUTMAN FAMILY TREE:

(According to the information on the following site:
http://www.billputman.com), including census records from Ohio and Illinois.)
["+" precedes the name of the paternal ancestor's wife]

William Putnam + Jane Salter or Slater of Chesham, Buckinghamshire, England

begat

Thomas Putnam (1623–after 1650) + Dorothy
Came to Virginia on the *Increase* with their son Thomas in 1647)

who begat

Thomas Putman II (mid-1640s–about 1705?) + (?)
(name also got spelled Putnam, Puttman, and Pitman)
who begat
Zachariah Putman I (1690–1748) + ?
who begat
(Thomas, Mary and) Zachariah Putman II (around 1715–1753) + Margaret

who begat

Henry Putman (1747–1825) + Elizabeth Kendrick
who begat

(11 children, including:)Thomas Putman (1790–1827) + Nancy Grover (1792–1872)
who begat
Zachariah Putman (1824–after 1880) + Mary Ann Whitmer
who begat
(10 children, including:) my grandfather, George B. Putman (August 18, 1865–March 9, 1913)) + my grandmother, Edith Cook (Feb. 4th, 1870–Sept. 2, 1961)

who begat

Glenn, Betty, and Erle Samuel (my father) (Oct, 10,1888–Jan.15,1950) (for some reason my father later always gave his birth year as 1892, but this is wrong!) + Riva Lillian Sampson (Nov. 29. 1883–Dec. 27, 1979)
who begat

ME[1]

My mother, Riva Lillian Sampson, was the daughter of Michael Sampson and Toby[2] (I have not been able to find her maiden name). They were both born in Kovno, in what was then the Grand Duchy of Lithuania (then part of the Russian empire). At some point—probably in the 1880s—they emigrated to Manchester, England, where Michael worked in the sweatshops of the garment industry, as he was to do later in Chicago. I don't know when they moved to Chicago, but my mother was born there in 1893, and she told me that some of her older siblings were born in Manchester.

Neither my father's family nor my mother's family could afford to send their children to college. Yet both of my parents had a thirst for education. My father made friends with the local Catholic priest (in Rossville, Illinois), who taught him Latin and Greek, whence my father's affection for the Roman Catholic church. On the basis of what he learned from the priest, my father received a scholarship to the University of Chicago, but the scholarship didn't pay enough to live on, which caused my father to leave the University after two years. My father was a virtuoso at foreign languages all his life; he told me that at the University he had to insert "mistakes" into his translations from Latin and Greek, or the professor wouldn't believe that they were his own. After leaving the University of Chicago, my father, who had dropped the name "Erle" and called himself simply "Samuel Putnam" as soon as he left Rossville, became a newspaper reporter and then later a translator and writer.

My mother's parents took her out of high school when she reached 16, and found her a job as a stenographer, so she could supplement the family income. (She had many brothers and sisters—I am not sure just how many.) But I know that she found a retired French teacher to teach her French, and I possess a notebook that she kept as a young woman that shows wide reading. (One thing that intrigues me is that my parents were both admirers of Tolstoy and Emerson at age 16.)

So how did a Jewish girl with Yiddish-speaking parents and a "WASP" reporter-translator-writer come to meet? My mother loved to tell the story till the end of her long life. My father had a first marriage of short duration, which ended in an amicable divorce. When the divorce was granted, my father "threw a party" for his friends, including the woman he had just divorced. My mother, who lived just below but had never been introduced to my father, went upstairs to "complain about the noise." Naturally, my father invited her to join the party, and the rest, as they say, is history.

I was born on July 31, 1926, and about six months later my father, equipped with an advance from the publisher Pat Covici, and a contract to translate "all the extant works of François Rabelais," took me and my mother to France. My earliest memories are of my childhood in France, and my first language was French. Originally we lived in Montparnasse, then in Fontenay-aux-Roses, a suburb of Paris, and finally in a beautiful village called Mirmande, near Valence, from which one can see the Rhone Alps, where I went to the one-room schoolhouse for first grade. In 1933 we returned to the United States. I didn't know a word of English when we arrived; according to my father, what I said, as a little boy from the French countryside seeing the New York skyline from the boat, was "écoute mon vieux, quesque à cassée?"[3] After three years in different locations, my family settled in Philadelphia, where we resided until about 1947, and where I stayed on until I graduated from the University of Pennsylvania in 1948. My father's translation of Rabelais appeared in 1929, and was enthusiastically reviewed at the time.[4]

In addition, my father published two biographies, one of Rabelais, and another titled *Marguerite of Navarre, First Modern Woman*, and he edited a little magazine called the *New Review*. The story of those years is told in my father's autobiography *Paris Was Our Mistress* in which I figure mainly as "the baby": e.g., Ford Maddox Ford pushed my baby carriage, Pirandello came to our house in Fontenay-aux-Roses "to see the baby" (I am told that I sat on Pirandello's lap), and so on.

II. COMMUNISM

According to Wikipedia (which credits a book by Peter J. King with the information[5]), "Samuel Putnam, was a journalist and translator who wrote for the *Daily Worker*, a publication of the American Communist Party. As a result of his father's commitment to communism, [Hilary] Putnam had a secular upbringing, although his mother, Riva, was Jewish."[6] This information is not wrong, but it can easily mislead. My father *was* a journalist in Chicago, but totally apolitical at that time. Even during my childhood in France, my father was apolitical. Only in 1936, after our return to America, did my father join the Communist Party, with which he only broke (in utter disillusionment) in 1945.[7] Years later, when I asked him why he became a communist, his answer was unforgettable: "Because I saw world-famous writers starving on the streets of New York." Also, my secular education was just as much a result of my mother's feelings of estrangement from her father as of my father's communism.

In any case, I was the child of communist parents from the age of ten until the age of nineteen. In fact, my first philosophy course (at age twelve!) was a course in "dialectical materialism" taught by my father at the Thomas Jefferson School in Philadelphia (a "workers' school" run by the Communist Party); the text was Friedrich Engels's *Socialism: Utopian and Scientific*.[8] At a time when my Jewish classmates were studying Hebrew and going to religious camps, I was going to meetings of something called "Young Pioneers" (my only memory is of a failed attempt to learn to play the trumpet—it sounded exactly like a foghorn when I blew into it), and going to a summer camp called "Nature Friends," frequented by communists and fellow travelers.

Even at Central High, Philadelphia's renowned academic high school, I remained faithful to my family's communist beliefs until my second or third year, when I became completely disillusioned with Stalinism. (My disillusionment, at that time, was only with Stalinism, not with Marxism.) This came about as a result of books I read then, particularly Köstler's *Darkness at Noon* and Trotsky's *The Revolution Betrayed*. That reading convinced me that the Moscow Trials were a complete frame-up, and that the Soviet Union, far from being the socialist utopia that my parents considered it to be, was a horrible dictatorship.

What appealed to me about communism? As a child growing up in those years, the years of the Spanish Civil War, the years of Munich, the years of the "United Front" in France and elsewhere, my parents' conviction that the communist parties of the world were the only consistent opposition to fascism seemed more than plausible. But my continuing (if often wavering, or flickering almost to extinction) attraction to Marxism was not only based on the struggles against fascism of the 1930s and 1940s (as we interpreted them at that time); it was based on something less bound to current events and struggles.

In a word, what seemed right—in fact, what still seems right to me— about the arguments of communists, and, of course, anti-Stalinist socialists as well, is this: since the late nineteenth century—certainly since the early twentieth century—humankind has possessed the technical know-how and the industrial and agricultural capacity to do the following three things: (1) to make sure that no one in the world suffers from hunger and malnutrition; (2) to provide every one of the world's families with at least minimal housing; (3) to provide every child in the world with an education. What motivates the right sort of socialist—today, that means to me, social democrats who work for gradual improvement and not revolutionaries—is the sense that to accept starvation, homelessness, and illiteracy as "inevitable" is to show a criminal lack of compassion.

III. A PAINFUL ARGUMENT WITH MY FATHER

My father suffered from tuberculosis, which was diagnosed when I was still in elementary school in Philadelphia. At that time, he spent two years at a sanatorium in Saranac Lake, New York. In the end, the only way to halt the spread of his disease (there were no antibiotics against tuberculosis at the time) was to surgically collapse one of his lungs. He bore all this not only without complaint, but with a sense of humor (at least in his letters to my mother and myself from the sanatorium).

In fact, both of my parents were totally uncomplaining and tremendously hard workers. To support the three of us and later to put me through college, my mother worked as a secretary and my father did four book length translations a year (with one lung!), in addition to writing a history of Brazilian literature titled *Marvelous Journey: A Survey of Four Centuries of Brazilian Writing* and many articles (more than 70 on Brazilian literature alone).[9] Among his translations was a highly praised translation of *Don Quixote*. Yet he always found time to talk to me.

My father was the easiest person to get along with I have ever known. He was loved by his friends, of whom he had a great many, a loving parent, and a fascinating talker (all traits he inherited from his mother, my grandmother Edith, by the way). I remember only one noisy argument with him, and the contrast between his demeanor on that occasion was all the more terrifying because it was so unlike him to behave in the way he did.

The argument took place in the autumn of 1944, during my first semester at the University of Pennsylvania. After looking around at the various groups on the socialist left, I decided to join a Trotskyist group. When I told my father he went into a towering rage, and literally told me to get out of the house! As I left, he shouted that I was "an objective agent of the Gestapo"! I stayed for a few days with a friend's parents, and promptly came down with the flu. My mother, who was disgusted with me for upsetting my father, but who loved me too much to see me cast into exile, came to the house where I was staying and brought me home with a high fever, and there I remained, even after I recovered from the flu, although the atmosphere was strained for the next few months.

When I was looking around for a socialist group to join, I also met my only close black friend at that time, Joseph Applegate, who, although less than a year older than I, had graduated from college and was teaching Spanish at one of the Philadelphia high schools. Unlike me, Joe decided not to join any of those groups. In fact, he found them ridiculous.

I dropped out of the University when I joined the Trotskyists (I subsequently made up for the lost year by taking extra courses the next three years), and took a job at the Philadelphia Naval Yard helping to build destroyers, and trying (unsuccessfully) to convert my fellow workers to Trotskyism. By the spring of 1945, I had decided that the Trotskyists were just as bad as the Stalinists, and I left radical politics (until the Vietnam war, many years later). By the end of the year my father too became totally disillusioned with Stalin, and regretted that (in his own words) "out of misguided humility [he] had forced himself to live in the stifling atmosphere of the party line with all its ruthless intolerance for the process of the mind."[10] Did my disillusionment have something to do with that? I like to think so. In any case, it became clear to him that the Party was totally controlled from Moscow, and that he had been a dupe of a tyranny for nearly ten years.

IV. MY EARLY INTERESTS

I had a juvenile interest in philosophy (not counting my father's lectures on "dialectical materialism" at the Thomas Jefferson School), one awakened by reading Will Durant's remarkable *The Story of Philosophy*, and I even started a small philosophy club at Central High School sometime around 1943, but I did not think of pursuing philosophy as a profession until my senior year at the University of Pennsylvania ("Penn"). Prior to that, if I thought of any profession, it was of becoming a writer like my father, or a poet—my favorite poets in high school were Housman and Swinburne, and in college, Auden, MacNeice, and Rilke—or perhaps a mathematician under the influence of Norman Tyson Hamilton, one of my two best friends in high school,[11] and of Bill Turanski, my best friend in college, both of whom planned to—and later did—go on to be mathematicians. When I returned to Penn in 1945 after my experiments in Trotskyism, I took various philosophy courses, but I also took courses taught by Zellig Harris in the new field of "Linguistic Analysis" (one of my fellow students was Noam Chomsky, although my real friendship with Noam began many years later, when he spent a year in Princeton on a fellowship from the Institute for Advanced Study), and courses in German. I fulfilled all the requirements for a major in each of those subjects, although my "official" major was philosophy. I was also active in one student group, the Philomathean Society, which proudly describes itself as "the oldest continuously-existing literary society in the United States" ("Philo" was founded in 1813).

Why was German one of my three "majors" (albeit unofficially)? A natural question, especially since we were still at war with Germany until May of 1945! There were several reasons. One was that Central High School decided to offer a one semester course in German in my senior year (1944)—don't ask me why!—and curiosity led me to take that course. The following summer, I procured two copies of Goethe's *Faust*, one in English and one in German, and (having an apparently congenital love of poetry) I memorized several hundred lines in German, some of which I still remember. So it seemed natural to go on with German at Penn (the German department was staffed by refugees from Germany, who were staunchly anti-Nazi). Secondly, in line with my vague thoughts of becoming a "writer" I had taken a course in the English novel from the chairman of the English Department, the distinguished scholar of Anglo-Saxon, Albert C. Baugh. At a certain point in the semester, Baugh said (the exact words are burned into my memory), "The second volume of *Gulliver's Travels* is the ravings of a madman," and I decided *at that instant* that I wouldn't take any more courses in literature from *that* department. Instead, I decided to take all the literature courses offered by the German Department, which was delighted to have a few students who wished to read Goethe, Schiller, Hölderlin, Rilke and the other great German dramatists and poets in the original language. We did not read any novels that I remember, although "Tur" (my friend Turanski) led me to read the Swiss novelist Friedrich Dürrenmatt on my own.

In the summer of 1946, Joseph Applegate and I decided to see Mexico. As a Spanish teacher, he had enough money to afford such a trip, but I had to ask my parents, who were able to give me $200 for that purpose. I recall that the roundtrip ticket to Mexico City—four nights and five days on the bus, with no breaks—cost $100, and with the remaining $100 I was able to live for the six weeks we were in that city. In 1946, there was not yet any smog in Mexico City—in fact, it must have been one of the most beautiful cities in the Americas. To minimize lodging costs, Joe and I stayed in the YMCA, which rented the two of us a room on the top floor, from which we could see the volcanoes Popocapétl and Iztaccíhuatl very clearly across the roof tops. The "Y" was beautifully clean and the breakfasts were excellent. In addition, the Mexicans were extremely friendly and helpful to the two young Americans, one white and one black (I especially remember one waitress who always greeted us with "*Qué quiren niños*"—"What do you want, babies?").

That trip was also my first experience with industrial strength American racism. When our bus passed through Texas—almost a full day of our four-day trip—Joe did not have to sit in a separate part of the bus, because the bus was an interstate one, but he did not leave the bus that whole day, because all the eating places were segregated, and I went out and bought us sandwiches and cokes to eat in the bus. Although Philadelphia was certainly not free of racism, Joe and I had never experienced "legal" racism before. And I could see Joe's enormous pleasure at experiencing life in (what at any rate seemed to us to be) a totally color-blind society. Together, Joe and I met writers and artists, including Magdalena Mondragon and Diego Rivera, and we even wrote a small volume of poetry together. When it was time to return to the States, I could feel Joe's deep sadness at leaving that oasis of equality.

In the course of those weeks, I suggested to Joe that he apply to the Linguistics program at Penn, which he did upon our return. In due course, he received the Ph.D., and went on to become America's leading expert on Berber and the professor of African studies at Howard University. Joseph Roy Applegate died in October, 2003. I still treasure the memories of that wonderful summer in Mexico.

V. PHILOSOPHY AT THE UNIVERSITY OF PENNSYLVANIA

I had remarkable philosophy teachers, beginning with C. West Churchman, and remarkable friends among the graduate students, who were, in a sense, also my "teachers," during those undergraduate years. Among the graduate teaching assistants (who were called "Instructors," a much more impressive title than "teaching assistant") who befriended me, were Sidney Morgenbesser, Richard Rudner, and the future anthropologist/sociologist Murray L. Wax, each of whom was to go on to make important contributions to philosophy or (in Wax's case) anthropology and sociology.

It was in Zellig Harris's courses that I met Murray Wax. And it was Wax who suggested taking Churchman's courses, and it was those courses that first interested me in philosophy of science. (I remember Murray saying, "I think Churchman would enjoy having a student who comes from Linguistics.")

Churchman later left philosophy to become a famous figure in operations research and systems theory. But in those years he was teaching an unusual course in philosophy of science. What made it exceptional was that he emphasized the fact that contemporary experimental design, to the extent it has been mathematized, is not based on determining the *probability that a hypothesis is true*, as Bayesian probability theory would have it. Instead, it is based on the notions of *likelihood*, and the related notions of "type one risk" (the risk of accepting a hypothesis even though it is false) and "type two risk" (the risk of rejecting a hypothesis even though it is true"). The important point here is that the notion of *likelihood*, unlike the classical notion of "the probability that a hypothesis is true," does not presuppose the knowledge of a *prior probability distribution* over hypotheses.

Twenty years later, Ian Hacking also tried to call the attention of the philosophy of science community to these matters in his book *The Logic of Statistical Inference*. Yet there is no mention of "likelihood" or twentieth-century theories of statistical inference, in any work by my future teacher, Hans Reichenbach, nor in any work by Rudolf Carnap, nor in the great majority of courses in "scientific method" to the present day.

What Churchman also pointed out was that no experimental design can simultaneously minimize both types of risk. The decision as to which type of risk to minimize involves a decision as to which type of error would have the graver consequences, and thus inevitably introduces values into the decision process. This argument was further developed and made famous by a 1953 paper by Churchman's student Richard Rudner, "The Scientist *qua* Scientist Makes Value Judgments." [12] Churchman's courses were the place where I first encountered the idea that judgments of fact and judgments of value are "entangled." Churchman did not take credit for originating this idea, however, although the use of the modern theory of experimental design to support it was his own (and Rudner's) contribution. Churchman often referred to his own teacher, E. A. Singer, Jr., by then a retired professor at Penn who had been a student of William James. I recall Churchman's writing on blackboard the following four principles which he attributed to Singer:

(1) Judgments of (particular) fact presuppose theories (i.e., general statements, which are themselves revisable).
(2) Judgments of theory presuppose judgments of fact.
(3) Judgments of fact presuppose judgments of value.
(4) Judgments of value presuppose judgments of fact.

The other professor at Penn who influenced me, and who (in my senior year) suggested to me the idea of applying to a graduate program in philosophy, was Morton White. [13] I did apply to the graduate program at Harvard, as he suggested, where I was admitted and stayed for one year. (I left because Harvard didn't offer me financial support, and went to UCLA.) Because White left Penn for Harvard exactly the year I went to Harvard, my conversations with him continued past my graduation.

VI. Morton White

During my undergraduate years (1944–1948), the basic logic course at Penn was still almost exclusively devoted to the Aristotelian syllogism, with perhaps a fortnight devoted to introducing the "novel" symbols of the modern propositional calculus, p · q, p ∨ q, ~p, p ⊃ q, p ≡ q. I do not think the quantifiers were mentioned; in any case, what we really learned in the course was the syllogism, including the traditional notations "SAP," "SIP," "SOP," "SEP" (for, respectively, "All S are P," "Some S are P," "Some S are not P," and "No S are P"), including the traditional ways of testing their validity and even the traditional Latin names, "Barbara," "Celerent," "Ferio," and so forth. Morton White breathed the fresh air of the new logic into this medieval atmosphere, with a course which not only taught what we now call logic, up to and including quantification theory, but even covered a major philosophical work on logic and semantics, Rudolf Carnap's then brand new (1947) *Meaning and Necessity*. White also offered a course on classical American thought, which covered John Dewey, Charles Beard, Oliver Wendell Holmes, James Harvey Robinson, and Thorstein Veblen. (Much of what we heard in that semester was included in the book White published the following year, *Social Thought in America: The Revolt Against Formalism*.)

In my one year as a graduate student at Harvard (1948-49), I was White's graduate assistant in his course in American Philosophy. What I especially recall from my conversations with him at that time is the idea that the analytic-synthetic distinction, especially as developed and used in philosophy from Leibniz's time on, was profoundly unsound.[14] Although the credit for this point often goes to Quine, it was, in fact, developed pretty much simultaneously (but not independently, since they were close friends) by White and Quine. What I mean by saying that the distinction is unsound is that as soon as philosophers try to go beyond trivial examples of "analytic statements," such as "All bachelors are unmarried," and claim that some metaphysically significant statements (e.g., "2 + 2 = 4," or "time travel is impossible," or "space is infinite") are "analytic," they are profoundly in error.

One important observation of White's, later to be incorporated in his *Towards Reunion in Philosophy*, ran as follows: the logical positivists take as basic the notion of an "observation sentence." Originally, an observation sentence was required (by them) to be about the observer's own private "sense data," but this was so out of keeping with the public nature of science that they revised their doctrine, and allowed sense date to be about "observable things" and "observable properties" of these things. Thus, "A ball hit a window," could now be counted as an "observation sentence." But ethical sentences were still regarded as "unverifiable," and therefore "meaningless." But why, White asked, is "steals" not an observation predicate? However, if, as Quine and White argued, there are no *pure* "statements of empirical fact,"[15] how can it be the case that the whole "cognitive meaning" of science is contained in and expressed by a privileged class of sentences, the so-called "observation sentences"? *Are there* any "observation sentences" that are not infected to one extent or another with theory, with "convention," and even (*shudder*) with valuation?

As White put it, "Incidentally, it would seem that stealing is a fairly clear notion by comparison to being an observable predicate."[16] In short, if the analytic/synthetic distinction is untenable and has to be given up, as Quine and White agreed it must, why is the evaluative/descriptive distinction not also untenable? Here White was unable to persuade Quine to follow him, but I believe that he was right.

VII. MATHEMATICS IN MY LIFE

Although I shall say more about my career as a mathematician later, I need to mention it now if I am to explain how I spent my one year as a graduate student at Harvard. I say "my career as a mathematician" because, in addition to my career as a philosopher, I have had a very satisfying second career as a mathematician. Over the years, I have published thirty papers in mathematical logic, recursion theory, and set theory (especially the "fine structure" of Gödel's hierarchy L of constructible sets) and related fields[17]: decision problems in number theory, including my contribution to the solution of Hilbert's Tenth Problem[18]; the Davis-Putnam (or, later, "DPLL") algorithm for satisfiability in propositional calculus; and the field of formal learning theory, which I helped to found. I was awarded tenure in the prestigious Princeton Department of Mathematics the same year (1960) that I received tenure in the Philosophy Department, and I taught advanced courses and directed Ph.D. theses in both the M.I.T. and the Harvard Mathematics Departments. But, strange to say, I did not take mathematics courses as an undergraduate apart from a required introductory course! The reason is that I was terrified of the idea of solving mathematics problems under time pressure, and hence of the idea of *taking examinations* in mathematics.

However, one of my best friends at Central High School, Norman Tyson Hamilton, was already planning to become a mathematician, as was my best friend at Penn, William Turanski (who is remembered as one of the pioneers of modern computer science), and over the years the two of them infected me with the mathematics "bug." In fact, "Tur" taught me group theory, and I went on to work through Courant's and Robbins's wonderful *What is Mathematics* on my own, with the result that when I went to Harvard in 1948 I already regretted not having taken mathematics courses. For that reason, two of the courses I took at Harvard that year were a course in Linear Algebra, taught by Garrett Birkhoff, and the only really advanced course in mathematics I have taken in my life, a course in Ideal Theory taught by Oscar Goldman. (At UCLA, where I was a graduate student in the two years 1949–1951, I took a Ph.D. in philosophy at high speed, and thus did not have time to take any more mathematics courses.)

VIII. My Undergraduate Years

I lived at home (3225 Powelton Avenue) my first three years at the University of Pennsylvania. In 1947, however, my parents decided to move to the country, and I roomed with Tur during my whole senior year. Not only did that give us even more of a chance to talk mathematics, it also infected me with a passion for bridge, albeit one that did not long outlive our graduation. (Tur and I came in second at a Duplicate Bridge tournament in Philadelphia, which earned us all of one tenth of a master point—or would have, had we registered it!) Tur was one of the most brilliant, witty, and also one of the sweetest human beings I have known in my life.

One day, being out of clean socks, I looked in Tur's drawer for a pair, and discovered, hidden under his underwear, a document which showed that he had been decorated for valor in the war. This makes it bitterly ironic that in 1959, while on the sidewalk preparing to enter Leary's famous bookstore in Philadelphia, he was struck and killed by a car whose driver lost control of the vehicle. After his death, I mentioned the decoration to his widow, Margaret—characteristically, Tur had never told her about it. I mourn Tur to this day.

IX. My One Year as a Graduate Student at Harvard

I arrived in Cambridge in the beginning of September 1948. Within a month I was followed by Erna Diesendruck, whom I had met and to whom I had become engaged over the summer, and we married on November 1. Erna had been working at the Jewish Publication Society in Philadelphia, and she helped support us in Cambridge by doing research for a Jewish scholar in Cincinnati whose name I do not recall.[19] I recall that we lived in a tiny apartment near the corner of Trowbridge Street and Massachusetts Avenue (in a building that no longer exists), and that we took most of our meals in the graduate dining hall together with Tur, who had also come to Harvard to do graduate work. Tur was the best man at our wedding. Our marriage fell apart in the late 1950s, and in 1962 we divorced, and I married Ruth Anna (née Jacobs), who has been my wife and my best friend ever since.

In addition to taking the two mathematics courses I described above, I took two semesters of mathematical logic in the Philosophy Department that year, one of them with W. V. Quine and one of them with Hao Wang. I no longer remember much about those courses, but I know we worked through Quine's book *Mathematical Logic*, and thus I learned Quine's rather idiosyncratic system of set theory a few years before properly learning standard (Zermelo-Fraenkel) set theory. In sum, nearly half of the courses I took that year were in mathematics or mathematical logic. I also took three remarkable courses in philosophy: C. I. Lewis's famous course in Theory of Knowledge, Harry Austryn Wolfson's course on Spinoza, and Morton White's course in American Philosophy.

If anything "happened" to me philosophically that year it was primarily due to my reading of Quine's "On What There Is," which introduced me to the idea that the very fact that mathematics says *there are* numbers with such-and-such properties shows that mathematics is *ipso facto* committed to the existence of numbers and other "abstract entities," and to my conversations with White about his and Quine's doubts concerning the analytic/synthetic distinction, doubts that I have already described. (I continue to reflect on and, in the end, reject, the former idea as late as my *Ethics without Ontology*, and I continue to reflect on, and in the end largely agree with, Quine and White's doubts about the analytic/synthetic distinction to this day.) One cloud hung over me that year, however. I had been admitted to Harvard, but not offered any financial aid (apart from a small sum I received for being White's assistant in the American Philosophy course), and my parents' resources had been strained to the limit by the expense of paying for my four years at Penn. In fact, my year of graduate study at Harvard was only made possible by the generosity of my uncle Peter Sampson. I obviously needed a scholarship, but when I asked about the possibility, the Harvard Department told me that I would have to pass the full set of "prelims," the written exams for Ph.D. candidates. Those exams were not to be given until the spring, and it seemed foolish to me to wait that long to find out if I would have any support the following year. So I applied for admission and financial assistance elsewhere. I don't know how many schools I applied to, but I do recall that I was offered teaching assistantships at Penn, where I had already spent four years, and UCLA, and I naturally chose to go to UCLA where I would meet a new set of philosophers.

Thus ended my one year as a "Harvard student." (If I had known, what I was later told by a senior member of the Harvard Department, that it was a fixed policy of the Department in the 1940s that sixty percent of the students who took the "prelims" should *fail* on their first attempt, I would certainly have been even more determined not to risk my future on those exams!)

X. UCLA 1949–1951

We arrived in Los Angeles in the fall of 1949. Erna continued to do research for the Jewish scholar in Cincinnati (communicating the results on 3x5 cards by mail), and although this paid very little, it was an indispensable supplement to the $100 a month that I received as a Teaching Assistant at UCLA. In spite of our poverty, we were very happy at UCLA, and delighted with the company of the friends we made there. Although I was on friendly terms with several graduate students in philosophy (I particularly remember Stanley Cavell, who had recently switched to philosophy from studying music, and who, many years later, was to become one of my dearest friends and one of my most important discussion partners, Martin Golding and his wife Naomi, Cynthia Schuster,[20] and Wesley Salmon, who was to continue the orthodox Reichenbachian approach to philosophy of science after Reichenbach's death), they were not our closest friends, nor were they the people with whom Erna and I usually spent the evenings. (I do, however, remember one evening at which Stanley read Auden's poem "On the Death of William Butler Yeats" to a group of us. That reading is still inseparable from that poem, for me.) Our three closest friends were two physics graduate students whom I met in Reichenbach's famous course on the Philosophy of Space and Time, Stephen Gasiorowicz[21] and Peter Kaus,[22] and Hans Meyerhoff, then an Assistant Professor in Philosophy, and already an outstanding humanistic scholar.[23] I met with Peter and Stephen almost every day, and many evenings as well, and we talked about every conceivable subject. During my second year at UCLA, 1950-51 we met once a week at Meyerhoff's apartment, where we spent a number of weeks hearing the great classical scholar Paul Friedlander demolish *everything* Karl Popper ever said about Plato, and another number of weeks reading through the second part of Goethe's *Faust* in German, and, of course, discussing all these things.

I also remember that C. G. Hempel (known to all his friends and acquaintances as "Peter" Hempel), who had been Reichenbach's student, came to visit Reichenbach while I was a graduate student, and that Reichenbach invited the graduate students to spend an evening with him in Reichenbach's living room. Hempel had been "won over" to the rejection of the analytic/synthetic dichotomy by Quine and White, and that was what we talked about all evening (Reichenbach stayed out of the conversation, so that it could be just a conversation between us and Hempel). One of the graduate students said, "I grant that one cannot draw a clear analytic/synthetic distinction in a natural language, but why can't one do it in a formalized language?" I have never forgotten Hempel's answer: "Every formalized language is ultimately interpreted in some natural language. The disease is hereditary![24]"

I completed my studies for the Ph.D. at UCLA in two years. Without a doubt, *the* great intellectual experience for me in that period was studying with Reichenbach, not only formally, by taking his classes and writing a Ph.D. dissertation under his direction, but also informally, in the course of conversations. In my dissertation, I proved a theorem about the frequency interpretation of probability that greatly impressed him. I also defended his claims that (1) although we cannot prove deductively that Reichenbach's "Rule of Induction" will lead to successful prediction, we *can* prove the weaker statement that the rule will lead to successful prediction in the long run *if* any method will do that, and (2) his rule of induction (and certain closely related rules) are the *only* rules for which such a proof is possible. However, I soon realized that Reichenbach's argument is fatally flawed. The problem was, in effect, pointed out by Nelson Goodman in lectures he gave in London in 1953,[25] although Goodman did not refer to the issue of "vindicating induction," but instead pointed out that there was a prior problem, the problem of *saying what induction is*. Goodman showed that straightforward traditional formulations of the rule of induction, including Reichenbach's, lead to inconsistent predictions. Reichenbach's celebrated conditional, "If successful prediction can be made by any method, it can be made by using the Rule of Induction," needs to be supplemented by a proof that the Rule of Induction is consistent. But, unfortunately, Reichenbach's rule is not consistent.[26] (Goodman later became a close friend, after he joined the Harvard Philosophy Department, and I still believe that his "demolition job" on the idea that we know what "inductive logic" *is* was a contribution of enormous importance.)

Reichenbach's warmth, the friendly and always helpful advice he gave to students, and the importance he attached to well prepared lectures were absolutely exemplary for me. He was unquestionably the best teacher I ever had, and the teacher who thought the hardest about *how* to present whatever topic he was lecturing on—how to present it to *that* audience. But it was his ideas and not just his fine character and wonderful teaching that had the lasting influence on me. I have also mentioned his vindicatory argument for induction. It is the other ideas, and my subsequent agreements and disagreements with them, to which I now turn. But first, let me try to clear up a widespread misunderstanding about Reichenbach. The misunderstanding is that Reichenbach, like his friend Rudolf Carnap, was a "logical positivist." Nothing could be farther from the truth. The fact is, as anyone who reads Reichenbach's great work on epistemology *Experience and Prediction* will know,[27] that although Reichenbach was the co-editor of the journal *Erkenntnis* with Carnap, and was quite willing to be called a "logical empiricist," "positivism" (which Reichenbach equated with the phenomenalism of Carnap's *Aufbau*[28]) was a position Reichenbach attacked.

XI. REICHENBACH ON PERCEPTION

In *Experience and Prediction*, Reichenbach objected to the traditional idea that knowledge of the external environment begins with the observation of one's own *sensations* ("impressions").[29] (Reichenbach believed that the need to appeal in epistemology to the phenomena of illusion and hallucination shows that we *infer* their existence—a fascinating and still neglected claim.) Our most primitive observations, he held, are observations of the things in our environment—an idea recently revived by many writers on the philosophy of perception, but not credited to Reichenbach.

Since this idea of Reichenbach's continues to influence my thinking about perception, I want to say more about its significance now. A skeptical problem that goes back to the days of Berkeley and Hume (it is often attributed to Descartes, but wrongly in my view), and that is presented with stunning effectiveness on the first few pages of Russell's *The Problems of Philosophy*,[30] runs as follows:

(1) When I look at an "external object," say a green fence, all I am directly aware of is my visual sense data (as of a green fence).

(2) So when I say "I see a green fence," I am not describing what I directly observe; rather, I am making an *inference*.

(3) But this inference is highly problematical, since the supposed connection between my inner observations and the external objects cannot itself be checked by inner observations of sense data.

This argument assumes that we *observe* our "experiences." In contemporary terminology, it assumes an "inner theater" conception, in which a mental faculty ("introspection") surveys mental objects ("sense data," "sensations," "experiences") on an internal stage.

What Reichenbach pointed out was that it is wrong to think of our experiences as objects we observe. What the argument from illusion really shows is that it is possible to be, in certain respects, in the same *state* (which Reichenbach, as a physicalist, took to be a neurological state), when I see, for example, a green picket fence and when I am caused to hallucinate a green picket fence, or dream of a green picket fence, or have a very good illusion of a green picket fence. But I don't *observe* that state (if I did, it would be a mystery that I never have an *illusion of a sense datum*—"How come introspection isn't subject to the errors that other perceptual faculties are?"[31]). I am *subject* to that state (that is, a sensation is a property, not a thing, a property that I have at a certain time, not a particular that I perceive). And it is the biological role of such states to enable me to register the presence of green things, the presence of things with certain shapes, and, when supplemented by the possession of a language, even to register the presence of a green picket fence. What I perceive are things; that perception is mediated by internal states, and the nature of those states, is something we have to discover, and that science is still in the process of elucidating. Our perceptual states are not a "veil" *between* us and the environment.

In *Experience and Prediction*, Reichenbach also argued against the idea that phenomenal reports are absolutely certain.[32] A much more detailed argument was presented in a symposium that I was fortunate enough to attend, entitled "The Experiential Element in Knowledge"[33] with Nelson Goodman[34] and C. I. Lewis,[35] and it was directed against the views of C. I. Lewis. Reichenbach describes a case in which I would accept an observation report in thing language even though it reported an event (my car speeding up when I pressed the brake pedal) which was highly improbable. And then he asks on Lewis's behalf, "Would we not be willing to defend in a similar way any individual phenomenal sentence against the totality of other sentences?"[36]

Against this rhetorical question, Reichenbach points out that my willingness to believe that my car really did speed up when I stepped on the brake pedal (in spite of the prior probability that it would not) is accompanied by a belief that further observational evidence will support the car speeding up.

In this example, to be sure, Reichenbach considered not phenomenal reports but sentences about a physical occurrence, but he says: "I do not see any reason why the procedure should be different in principle for phenomenal sentences. Retaining a phenomenal sentence against the indirect evidence derived from the total system of phenomenal sentences in which it is imbedded is equivalent to assuming that it will be extended so as to supply positive evidence for the sentence."[37] In this connection, Reichenbach introduced the notion of *inductive consistency*. Unlike deductive consistency, inductive consistency cannot always be achieved in the short run; but in a Peircean spirit, Reichenbach holds that we should strive to attain it in the long run. If I say that I have had a certain kind of sensation, but all the indirect evidence makes it more and more probable as time goes by that I did not have that kind of sensation, then inductive consistency requires that at some point I should give up the claim to have had that kind of sensation.

But what does it mean to give up the claim that one has had a sensation that one sincerely reported having? Must I plead a slip of the tongue? Here,

Reichenbach makes the extremely important point that to allow the notion of a "slip of the tongue" to become simply a wastebasket category, one into which we put *every* case in which we later realize that we made an incorrect phenomenal report, is to deprive that notion of all psychologically explanatory content. "It is true," he wrote, "that there are situations in which we say 'John' and mean 'Peter,' in which, therefore, at least subjectively the correct meaning can be said to exist. There are other situations, however, in which our attention is not fully focused on our words, and for which we cannot maintain that any distinct meaning was attached to our words. These transitional situations play a larger part than is usually recognized."[38] At this point, Reichenbach is at least touching the terrain that Wittgenstein touched in the Private Language Argument. The idea that whenever I make a false phenomenal report I must have had a determinate "meaning" in mind, a proposition in my head, and I merely failed to attach the correct words to the proposition, depends on the picture of meaning as (to use Wittgenstein's words) an "aura" surrounding our words. Once we realize that such a picture of meaning does not belong to empirical psychology, but to a metaphysical parody of psychology, a metaphysical mechanics of thought, we can see that Reichenbach's rejection of the idea that all misspeaking can be explained as "having the right meaning in mind, and failing to find the correct words to express it" was completely justified.

XII. REICHENBACH VERSUS CARNAP

As early as *Experience and Prediction*, Reichenbach also objected to the "methodological solipsism" of Carnap's *Aufbau*; that is, to the idea that the "cognitive content" of any meaningful assertion must always be to the effect that *my* sense data behave (or will behave, or have behaved) in certain ways. As Reichenbach wrote,

> The strictly positivistic language . . . has scarcely been seriously maintained; . . . its insufficiency is revealed as soon as we try to use it for the rational reconstruction of the thought-processes underlying actions concerning events after our death, such as [purchasing] life insurance policies . . . we find here that the decision for the strictly positivistic language would entail the renunciation of any reasonable justification of a great many human actions.[39]

It is not just that Reichenbach rejected phenomenalism—after all, Carnap also moved away from phenomenalism after the *Aufbau* (although he never exactly *repudiated* it). Although Reichenbach was extremely loath to criticize Carnap, the fact is that even after Carnap's phenomenalist period, the two of them had fundamentally different views of the task of philosophy. Carnap's position in *The Logical Syntax of Language* and thereafter was that philosophers of science should not do what had traditionally been called "philosophy" at all,[40] they should be engaged in studying the "logic of science." The centerpiece of Carnap's "logic of science" was the claim, put forward in a series of different formulations, that so-called "theoretical terms" in science, terms for such unobservable things and magnitudes as electrons and electromagnetism, are mere *constructs*, symbolic devices whose real function is to make it possible to describe regularities in the behavior of "observables." Reichenbach's view could not have been more different. First of all, he insisted that such entities as electrons and the electromagnetic force are *inferred entities* and not just symbolic constructs.[41] This is another of Reichenbach's ideas that continues to influence me to this day. Moreover, Reichenbach never attached great importance to the project of *formalizing* scientific theories, which is an essential part of what Carnap meant by "logic of science."

Reichenbach's conception of philosophy of science had another aspect. This aspect goes back to Locke's conception of philosophy as an "underlaborer" to the sciences, a conception to which Reichenbach sometimes referred in conversation. In Reichenbach's version of this underlaborer conception, the idea becomes that the *conceptual clarification* of scientific theories is a task to which both scientists and philosophers have important contributions to make. But Reichenbach's admiration for Leibniz and Kant led him to a somewhat more ambitious interpretation of the "underlaborer" idea than Locke's. For Reichenbach, physical theories attempt to say something about such traditional metaphysical issues as the nature of space, time, and causation, and the task for philosophers is to make clear just *what* they say. This idea also continues to influence me to this day, especially when I think about quantum mechanics.

Where I decidedly do not agree with *Experience and Prediction* is in its philosophy of language. Reichenbach mistakenly thought that the realist view of the entities spoken about by physical theories that he advocated was compatible with verificationism in semantics.[42] The view that I advocated in my 1962 "The Analytic and the Synthetic," on which *the reference of theoretical terms is preserved across most theory change*, although what counts as "verification" is frequently changed radically, is the beginning of what I now think of as a "realist semantics" for scientific theories, as opposed to the versions of verificationism advocated by Reichenbach and Carnap. But in 1951, when I received my Ph.D., I was still a committed Reichenbachian, and I didn't give up verificationism until I wrote the first draft of "The Analytic and the Synthetic" during the fall semester of 1957-58 that I spent at the Minnesota Center for the Philosophy of Science.

In spite of my criticisms, I continue to regard *Experience and Prediction* as one of the high water marks of analytic philosophy. But I also found Reichenbach's writing on the philosophy of space and time tremendously exciting. A few years later, I was to develop serious criticisms of those writings, it is true, but I would never have thought about those issues if Reichenbach had not convinced me, as he convinced all his students, that they were tremendously interesting issues, and that they lay at the cutting edge of both philosophy and twentieth-century physics.

XIII. My "Rockefeller Year"

I received a very prestigious Rockefeller Fellowship for the year after the completion of my studies at UCLA. In my application, I explained that I wanted to spend the year of this fellowship (1951-52) at Harvard, and to work with Quine. My proposal was to use the verifiability theory of meaning to clarify the notion of the "logical form" of sentences in natural language. Since I received the fellowship, I naturally assumed that the proposal had been accepted. But I was in for a surprise.

In the letter informing me that I had received the Rockefeller Fellowship, I was instructed to come to New York and talk to Chadbourne Gilpatric, an officer of the Foundation. Gilpatric told me that I was *not* to work with Quine, *not* to go to Harvard, but to work instead with Rulon Wells (a philosopher-linguist of whom I had never heard!) at Yale University, a University I had no particular interest in visiting at that time. But I was only twenty-five years old, and I was too timid to object. (In retrospect, I feel that this was utterly outrageous behavior on Gilpatric's part.) I settled in Manhattan, planning to travel to New Haven by train periodically for talks with Wells, but I never did talk to Wells, nor did the Foundation follow up on the progress of the fellowship in any way. (The checks did arrive on time, however.)

The project of writing a monograph on the logical form of sentences in ordinary language did not lead to anything that I regarded as worth publishing. In fact, the year would have been a total waste of time if I had not made two friends who are terribly dear to me: Ben-Ami Scharfstein and the young woman he was to marry a couple of years later, Ghela Efros (as she was then).

I met "Ben" at a talk on Jewish Philosophy at Columbia University. Like myself, he had done some graduate work at Harvard (in his case, an MA degree), and then gone on to receive the Ph.D. in only two years at Columbia University. Ghela, who had gone to Israel at age nineteen and had been wounded (not visibly, however) in the Israeli war of independence, was completing an undergraduate degree at Barnard College. They moved to Tel Aviv a few years after I met them, where Ben-Ami founded the Philosophy Department of Tel Aviv University, and where Ghela is a distinguished photographer. Since they are among my closest friends to this day, I shall pause to describe them, not simply as they were then, but as I know them today.

When Ben-Ami received the Israel Prize (Israel's most prestigious award) in 2006, the committee awarding the prize wrote, in part, "[Ben-Ami Scharfstein's] studies elucidate the deep structure of human thinking in all its facets, focusing on aesthetics, the study of mysticism, comparative philosophy, and philosophy in psychological and social contexts." This is, of course, a fancy way of saying that Ben-Ami's work exhibits both brilliance and a truly staggering breadth of knowledge. (Of his so far published books, my personal favorite is *Of Birds, Beasts and Other Artists*.)[43]

In addition to his knowledge of art, Ben-Ami has wide knowledge of Asian and African cultures—including the philosophy as well as the art of those cultures. His book, *Art without Borders: A Philosophical Exploration of Art and Humanity*, opens (and concludes) with a wonderfully cultivated meditation on the question of how we are to understand the notion of "art" in our present global village, and it draws on the best available relevant knowledge in psychology, anthropology, and art history. But it also enriches its discussion throughout with detailed examinations of the lives, accomplishments, reflections on art, and attitudes towards their work and their traditions of individual artists in a variety of cultures — Eastern as well as Western, "primitive" as well as "modern." Although Ben never tells an anecdote *just* for the sake of the anecdote, the richness of *human* detail is one of the great virtues of his way of explaining and illuminating the history of art. He can make a medieval Chinese or Japanese artist, or an aboriginal artist, or a French artist, academic or anti-academic, come completely alive as a human being, and in the process beautifully illustrate the points he is making about art and artists and viewers of art works. Of course, the Ben I knew in 1951-52 was not the ripened scholar I know today, but the interests listed by the Israel Prize Committee were already budding, if not yet blossoming.

We spent many evenings together. Sometimes we drew pictures, using crayons and India ink as our medium (I still have some of those pictures). Sometimes we wrote poems. For more than a quarter of a century, Ruth Anna and I have spent some time in Israel every year, always visiting the Scharfsteins. Since 2005 I have taught a seminar at Tel Aviv University every winter, and it is one of the great pleasures of my old age to be able to maintain the close bonds that I first formed with Ben and Ghela back in 1951.

In 1952, while still in New York, I also met a graduate student in Government at Columbia University called Raul Hilberg. Hilberg had served in the war, first in the infantry and then in the War Documentation Department, and his assignment to that department led him to examine archives all over Europe, and eventually to undertake the task of unraveling all the details of Hitler's "Final Solution," the extermination of six million Jews in Europe. But in 1952, neither gentiles nor Jews were inclined to support Hilberg's research into this topic! I recall one evening, in the apartment of our mutual friend, Eric Marder, when Hilberg expressed deep pessimism about his chances of either getting his work published, or finding an academic position when he completed his dissertation. (I can still hear his voice, saying, "I am the only expert on dead Jews, and no one has any interest in the subject.") Raul received his Ph.D. from Columbia three years later, and, although he had enormous difficulty in finding a publisher, his dissertation became the basis for his seminal work, *The Destruction of the European Jews*.[44]

XIV. NORTHWESTERN UNIVERSITY 1952-53

I was, of course, looking for an academic position during my year in Manhattan, and I obtained an Assistant Professorship at Northwestern University for the year, 1952-53. That turned out to be a very strange year, full of happy experiences and also full of anxiety about my future.

Although the philosophy department at Northwestern did not yet have a clear philosophical identity, it was dominated by a philosopher whom I have *never* heard mentioned since, an aesthetician named Eliseo Vivas, who had a profound antipathy to logical empiricism. A month after my arrival in Evanston, I gave a talk to the Department—I do not remember the title or the contents, but it would obviously have been philosophy of science or, perhaps, logical empiricist epistemology, since I was fresh from completing my Ph.D. with Reichenbach, and certainly not anything to do with ethics—and Professor Vivas said to me afterwards, "Your position is both false and immoral!" It was obvious that I would not be reappointed, and I spent most of the year 1952-53 looking for another job.

Apart from this distressing situation, and the anxiety it caused me, my year in Evanston was a lot of fun. The other department members, if they did not simply ignore me, were very friendly. I particularly remember William Earle and Robert W. Browning, both of whom were Assistant Professors at the time. And my students were very close to me in age—I was only twenty-six years old myself, and was treated by the graduate students and even the undergraduates as one of their age cohort rather than as one of their seniors. I somehow became friends with Bob Geary, the owner of

Great Expectations, the legendary bookstore under the El tracks in Evanston, and most nights my wife Erna and I used to stay there with a group of undergraduates until the store closed. Very soon, Bob Geary gave me a key to the store, which I kept until I left Evanston in June 1953. Geary told me that my group of undergraduates and Erna and I could stay as long as we liked! I would lock up at 11PM or later, and Erna and I would go to our apartment which was only a hundred feet or so away.

In those days, junior faculty were expected to teach three courses a quarter, and some of the courses were simply assigned to us. Thus, in addition to philosophy of science and a seminar on logical empiricist epistemology, which were considered "my" fields, I taught introduction to philosophy and an upper-level undergraduate course on the rationalists, and I do not know what else.

Of my students at Northwestern, I particularly recall Prescott Johnson, later written about by journalists as the professor who had widened Gary Hart's intellectual horizons in college, and the undergraduate students Andrew Oldenquist (the future author of *Alienation, Community and Work*) and Dean Miller (the future author of *The Epic Hero*).

Apart from these students, Erna's and my one close friend at Northwestern was a graduate student, R. Allen Gardner, who later because famous when he and his wife Beatrix taught the chimpanzee Washoe to communicate in ASL (American Sign Language). In 1952-53 Allen was still far from any interest in chimpanzees, but he had a wide range of interests and a gift for amusing comments on whatever was going on.

XV. Princeton

In the spring of 1953 I received an invitation to apply for a Visiting Assistant Professorship at Princeton. I recall that my Northwestern colleagues Bob Browning and Bill Earle coached me for my job interview. Evidently, their advice was good, because I got the job. But it was for one year, and since I was coming from a one-year teaching job at Northwestern preceded by a one-year post-doctoral fellowship, this was my third year in a row of being on the job market, and I recall thinking "If this happens one more time, I will have an ulcer." I was overjoyed to learn sometime in the second semester that I would be appointed as a tenure track Assistant Professor the following year. This was especially fortunate, because after my father's completely unexpected death (from a first heart attack) in January, 1950, my mother, after going back to the house she and my father still owned in Mirmande for a year to grieve in the place where they had enjoyed the last year of their stay in France, had found employment as secretary of the

Cosmic Ray Laboratory in Princeton. So I had a job in the same town as my mother, and when my first child, Erika, was born in 1955, she was in the immediate vicinity of her grandchild.

As had been the case at Northwestern, I had good relations with all but one of the members of the Philosophy Department at Princeton. The exception was James Ward Smith, and I have no idea why he took such a dislike to me, but evidently he never got over it, since I am conspicuous by my absence in his brief history of the Princeton Philosophy Department! Happily, I was unaware of his hostility for most of my years in Princeton, although I was eventually told of it by one of his colleagues, and even more happily, unlike Eliseo Vivas, James Ward Smith did not succeed in hindering my progress up the academic ladder. I was, however, informed by the Chairman in 1957 that I would probably not receive tenure at the end of my forthcoming reappointment (for three more years) as an Assistant Professor. This gloomy news led me to spend a couple of years looking for a position elsewhere. I eventually received an offer from George Nakhnikian to come to Wayne State University, where he was building a fine philosophy department, but by that time Princeton had changed its mind, and assured me that I would receive tenure. Perhaps the "bad news" I was given in 1957 was due to Smith's influence? I shall never know. It did cause me two years of insecurity and worry.

Although my formal philosophical education ended with the award of the Ph.D. by UCLA in June 1951, my development into a philosopher, as opposed to a student of philosophy, really took place at Princeton, between 1953, when I arrived, and 1960, when I left for a Sabbatical in Oxford and Paris, and did not return to Princeton. I arrived in Princeton knowing the philosophy of Hans Reichenbach in great detail, and, beyond that, knowing what a bright graduate student was expected to know of the various "fields" in which we were required to take written qualifying exams, but not yet having any original ideas of my own, or even a real program of research, and I left having written articles and lectures on philosophy of mind, philosophy of science, and philosophy of mathematics, some of which are still widely read, and having established a reputation as a mathematical logician as well, with nine articles, including one (with Martin Davis and Julia Robinson) which turned out to contain most of the solution to Hilbert's Tenth Problem. (The solution was completed in 1970 by a young Russian mathematician, Yuri Matiyasevich.) Thus my eight years on the Princeton faculty were the years of my real *Bildung*, both as a philosopher and as a mathematician. They were also the years when, apart from my absence on leave in Minnesota in the fall semester of 1957-58 and my sabbatical leave in the year 1960-61, I talked with Paul Benacerraf almost every day. That friendship has been one of the most important of my life both intellectually and personally.

XVI. Becoming a Mathematician

In 1953, when I arrived in Princeton, I had only taken one graduate-level course in mathematics in my life—Oscar Goldman's course in Ideal Theory at Harvard in 1948-49, and I had not proved any theorems or published any papers in mathematics.[45] Yet in 1960, my last year on the Princeton faculty, I became a tenured Associate Professor in the world famous Mathematics Department (as well as the Philosophy Department). A brief explanation of how this happened seems to be in order at this point.

Although I had taken Morton White's course in quantificational logic at Penn in 1947 or 1948 and courses from Hao Wang and Quine at Harvard in 1949-50 that covered Gödel's incompleteness theorems and Quine's eccentric system of set theory, my first acquaintance with mathematical logic beyond these courses came about by chance. In 1952 I came across—I no longer remember how—Paul Rosenbloom's remarkable *Elements of Mathematical Logic*.[46] That book, which deserves to be better known even today, vastly enlarged my view of what mathematical logic was about. Rosenbloom's algebraic approach to logic (which introduced me to the theory of the structure and representations of Boolean algebras) and the clear and concise exposition of the combinatory logics of Curry and Church interested me greatly. But what really fascinated me was the explanation of Post's Canonical Systems, and Rosenbloom's use of them to prove very simple versions of Church's Theorem and of the Gödel theorem. I incorporated that material into the logic class that I taught in Princeton the following years, thus making it the first logic class in the country that taught students how to write what amounted to a "computer program," at a time when computers and programming were still in their infancy.

The other big factor in my development as a logician was the presence in Princeton (on fellowships at the Institute for Advanced Studies) of Georg Kreisel and Martin Davis. In 1954 I said to Kreisel, whom I had just met, "I teach mathematical logic in the Philosophy Department here, and I would like to find out if I can prove an original theorem." Kreisel gave me generously of his time. He suggested problems, and taught me what I needed to know to work on them. The result was that in 1957 three different papers by me (one coauthored with Kreisel) appeared in logic journals.

Kreisel also got me interested in intuitionist mathematics. The "Intuitionists" were a school of mathematician-philosophers founded by L. E. J. Brouwer. This school rejects all "non-constructive" proofs in mathematics, including proofs of existence which proceed by assuming that the entity in question does not exist and deriving a contradiction. In order to ban such proofs, they (famously) rejected certain principles of classical propositional calculus, including the law of the excluded middle. For example, none of

the following theorems of classical propositional calculus: "p ∨ ~p" (excluded middle), ~~p ≡ p (double negation), and [~p ⊃ (q · ~q)] ⊃ p (proof
of an unnegated proposition by contradiction)—are theorems of intuitionist
propositional calculus.[47] My joint paper with Kreisel provided an "*Unable-
itsbarkeitmethode*" (a method of proving that a formula is not a theorem)
for intuitionist propositional calculus.

In 1954 I also met Martin Davis and his wife Virginia, who continue
to be dear friends. With Kreisel my relations were always somewhat more
formal, in part because something about his personality intimidated me and
in part because I became interested in Hilbert's Tenth Problem, and Kreisel
thought nothing would come of that interest and tried to discourage it. My
friendship with Martin Davis led to many conversations about matters other
than logic; in fact, there was (and is to this day) almost nothing under the
sun that Martin *was not* interested in! In addition, Martin was politically
radical, and reawakened my interest in radical economics and social theory,
although I did not become an activist until the period of the Vietnam war.
But for present purposes the important thing is that Martin aroused my
interest in one of the twenty-three famous problems set by David Hilbert
in his address to the International Congress of Mathematicians in Paris in
1900. In 1957 the Putnams and the Davises both spent the summer at the
Summer Institute in Symbolic Logic sponsored by the American Mathematical Society. I had read Martin's recently published "Arithmetical Problems
and Recursively Enumerable Predicates,"[48] and I suggested to him that the
techniques he used there could be used to make further progress towards an
attack on Hilbert's Tenth Problem, which was to find a decision method for
diophantine equations. A diophantine equation is an equation of the form
$P(x_1,x_2,\ldots,x_n) = 0$ to be solved in whole numbers, where $P(x_1,x_2,\ldots,x_n)$ is a
polynomial with integer coefficients. We began thinking about this project
then and there, and our first joint paper on Hilbert's Tenth Problem appeared
in June of the following year.

An incident at that Summer Institute not directly connected to my mathematical research that I recall vividly is recounted by Solomon Feferman.
As Feferman relates,

> After a lecture by George Dekker on the recursion-theoretic notion of isols, an
> interesting recursive analogue of Dedekind's definition of finiteness, Tarski rose
> to say that he did not find that direction of work at all worthwhile. He then went
> on at length to stress his own early work on Dedekind's and other notions of
> finiteness which require the axiom of choice for their equivalence, even though
> that was not directly relevant. Visibly annoyed, the then young logician and
> philosopher Hilary Putnam rose to say that he thought such critical remarks
> inappropriate and that they should be reserved for Tarski's autobiography. [49]

What Feferman does not mention is that several of Tarski's own graduate students were so pleased that someone had had the courage to "call" Tarski on his arrogance and bad manners that they took me out to lunch!

In 1957-58 Martin Davis was no longer in Princeton. He was teaching at the Hartford branch of Rensselaer Polytechnic Institute. In order to be able to continue our joint work on Hilbert's Tenth Problem, my wife and I rented a summer house on a lake not far from Hartford, and Martin and I worked together all summer. Our work resulted not only in our contribution to the "negative solution" of Hilbert's Tenth Problem—that is, to the proof that the decision method Hilbert wanted does not exist—but also in the Davis-Putnam algorithm for the satisfiability of formulas of propositional calculus in conjunctive normal form, an algorithm improved in 1962 to what is today known as the DPLL (Davis-Putnam-Logemann-Loveland) algorithm. As Martin generously describes our way of working in George Csicsery's film "Julia Robinson and Hilbert's Tenth Problem," I was a fountain of ideas, and Martin's role was to say, "That's ridiculous ... that's ridiculous ... that's ridiculous ..." until every so often one of my ideas wasn't ridiculous, and then we would both set to work on it. I know that my brain was on fire that summer. I often stayed up till three AM, continuing to think about what we had discussed during the day, but somehow I never felt tired the next morning. (This is the only time I have ever felt this much excitement about a mathematical problem, partly because the synergy between myself and Martin was so powerful.) At the end of the summer, what we had was still far from a proof that Hilbert's Tenth Problem was unsolvable, but we did have a proof that the decision problem for *exponential* diophantine equations (equations of the form, $P(x_1,x_2,...,x_n) = 0$ to be solved in whole numbers, where $P(x_1,x_2,...,x_n)$ is like a polynomial with integer coefficients except that the exponents in P are allowed to be variables) is unsolvable if the following conjecture PAP is true: *there are arbitrarily long arithmetic progressions consisting entirely of prime numbers*. If PAP had really been necessary to the proof, the complete proof of the unsolvability of the decision problem for exponential diophantine equations would have had to wait until 2004, when PAP was proved by Ben Green and Terence Tao. However, we sent our proof to Julia Robinson at the end of the summer of 1958, and she succeeded in simplifying the entire proof, and, in the process, eliminating the need to assume PAP. "The Decision Problem for Exponential Diophantine Equations" by Martin Davis, Hilary Putnam and Julia Robinson, was submitted to *Annals of Mathematics* two years later and appeared in November 1961.

Even before Martin and I began our joint work, Julia Robinson had shown that if even one diophantine equation had solutions with roughly exponential rate of growth, then the unsolvability of the decision problem for exponential diophantine equations would imply the unsolvability of Hilbert's Tenth Problem, and in 1970 an example of such an equation was provided by the then still young Yuri Matiyasevitch, completing the solution of the problem. Today the statement that the diophantine sets are exactly the recursively enumerable (a.k.a. "listable") sets is known as the DPRM theorem, after Davis, myself, Robinson, and Matiyasevitch. The unsolvability of Hilbert's Tenth Problem is an immediate corollary, since the nonexistence of a decision method for the listable sets is a well-known result in the theory of computable functions.

   Another by-product of my friendship with Martin Davis was that he interested me in the then abstruse subject of "hierarchy theory," a branch of recursion theory in which one asks such questions as "IF we had an 'oracle' that correctly answered questions of the form 'does such and such a number belong to S,' where S is a set which does not itself have a decision procedure (i.e., a 'nonrecursive' set), and IF our computer were allowed to ask this oracle any finite number of questions of that form, what sets would THEN be decidable by that computer?" For example, one can take S to be the set of indexes of Turing Machines that eventually halt, a classic example of a nonrecursive set, and then define a set, S-jump, of indexes of sets that would be 'decidable' IF our computer had available an 'oracle' for the set S. Using "computable ordinals" (ordinals of recursive well orderings of natural numbers), one can extend the sequence S, S-jump, S-jump-jump, through the constructive transfinite. I taught a little "noncredit" course on this subject in my apartment at 221D Halsey Street in Princeton for a small group of students—Paul Benacerraf and Peter Hempel among them!—in the late 1950s. Later my interest in hierarchy theory was to develop into the very first study of what came to be known as "the fine structure of L," where L is the "constructible universe"[50] defined by Gödel in the course of proving the consistency of the axiom of choice with the other axioms of Zermelo-Fraenkel set theory.[51]

XVII. Becoming a Philosopher: Carnap

Although I worked very hard at becoming a mathematician during my years at Princeton, I also needed to learn to be a philosopher. I have already said that when I arrived in Princeton in the fall of 1973 I did not yet have any original philosophical ideas, or even a program of research. As in the case of mathematics, it was the mentorship of someone who was at the Institute for Advanced Studies that got me started. The "someone," in this case, was Rudolf Carnap, who was still at the Institute in 1953-54, my first year in Princeton.

Carnap and Reichenbach had been close friends for many years (in fact, it was Reichenbach who introduced Carnap to Moritz Schlick, the doyen of what was to become the Vienna Circle, and Carnap and Reichenbach had been the coeditors of *Erkenntnis*, the publication of the logical empiricist movement). It was natural, therefore, for Reichenbach to provide me with introductions to Carnap and, his other old friend in Princeton, Albert Einstein. Although I only went to visit Einstein once, in the spring of 1954, I cannot resist digressing at this point to describe that visit.

I had tea with Einstein in his little house on Mercer Street. He was charming, warm, and unpretentious. Not unexpectedly, he talked about his dissatisfaction with quantum mechanics. On that occasion, Einstein did *not* say he could not accept a theory which is indeterministic (and we now know from work by Don Howard and other historians who have studied Einstein's unpublished correspondence, that the failure of determinism *was not* Einstein's real objection to quantum mechanics[52]). What he said on that occasion was something like the following: "Look, I do not believe that when I am not in my bedroom my bed spreads out all over the room, and whenever I open the door and come in it collapses into the corner."

In other words, Einstein could not believe Von Neumann's claim, then a part of standard quantum mechanics, that "observation" causes the wavefunction to "collapse." I left that meeting absolutely thrilled, needless to say, although I was only to start thinking seriously about quantum mechanics two or three years later.

Incidentally, my colleague and good friend at Princeton, Walter Kaufmann, also had a meeting with Einstein, to whom he was related. Einstein asked Walter what he taught, and Walter mentioned that he was teaching a course on Philosophy of Religion. [53] As Walter described it, Einstein chuckled, and said *"Ach, dass muss ein Eiertanz sein!"* ("That has to be a dance on eggs!")

Carnap, however, I visited every week. Like everyone else, including his wife Ina, I called him simply by his last name, "Carnap." The Carnaps were housed in a little bungalow on the campus of the Institute, and they had a German shepherd called "Marni" that I dreaded. Marni was ferocious, or so it seemed to me. In any case, whenever I came to visit "Carnap," I had to pass by Marni, who was chained to the side of the bungalow, close to the path on which I was walking. At the point of my closest approach Marni would leap, growling, and fail to reach me only because the chain stopped her with a very loud snap at the end of her powerful lunge. (I was always afraid the chain would break.) Once inside, I always had a wonderful time.

Carnap was world famous and I was a junior faculty member on a one-year appointment without a single publication in philosophy at that time, but I never detected the slightest sign of condescension on his part.

In fact, Carnap treated me as an equal, as I believe he treated everyone (or at least everyone whose mind he could respect), from our first meeting on. He often reminisced about the Vienna days, and I wish I had written down those stories. For example, one story that I remember is the following: at some point during the years that he was in Vienna, Carnap decided to grow a beard. His friends in the Vienna Circle did not like the way he looked with a beard, and so "They pushed me down to the floor, sat on me, and one of them shaved it off!" He told this story with obvious relish, and I have often reflected that he was the only German professor I have *ever* known who would not have been furious at such treatment. In truth, there was absolutely nothing corresponding to the "Herr Professor" stereotype about Carnap at all.

In one of our first conversations a puzzle about the theory of synonymy came up. The puzzle, first raised by Benson Mates, was this. If "Greek" and "Hellene" are synonyms (let us assume they are), then "All "All Greeks are Hellenes" is obtainable from the obvious tautology, "All Greeks are Greeks" by swapping the word "Hellenes" for the second occurrence of the synonymous word "Greeks." So, if swapping synonyms for synonyms preserves synonymy, as was implied by Carnap's theory in *Meaning and Necessity*, then "All Greeks are Hellenes" and "All Greeks are Greeks" are *synonymous*, which seems very counterintuitive, since someone might obviously believe that all Greeks are Greeks without believing that all Greeks are Hellenes.

I suggested that one might modify Carnap's theory by *counting differences in logical form as differences in meaning*. Carnap immediately told me to write up this suggestion, and submit it for publication, and I did. The result was my very first publication, "Synonymity, and the Analysis of Belief Sentences," which appeared in *Analysis* the next year. Although that was the only publication that grew *directly* out of a conversation with Carnap, the ten philosophy papers listed in my bibliography as published before 1959 all show Carnap's influence in one way or another. (Those papers were actually written prior to my leave at the University of Minnesota in the fall semester of 1957-58.) Although by the time I collected two volumes of my philosophy papers in 1975, I had moved away from the logical empiricist outlook to such an extent that I included only one of those papers in that collection,[54] it was certainly during the years 1953–1958 that I learned how to think and write like a philosopher, and it was Carnap's friendship and mentorship during the first of those four years that got me started.

Carnap hoped to recruit me to work on the project to which he devoted most of his formidable energy at that time, which was nothing less than a formalization of the scientific method, that is, of learning from experience, on the basis of his theory of "confirmation functions." I saw no future for that project, but he did succeed in impressing me with the importance of the question as to whether the project could succeed. A decade later, my negative answer to that question, in "Degree of Confirmation and Inductive Logic," and my more mathematical 1965 paper "Trial and Error Predicates and the Solution to a Problem of Mostowski's," together with related work by E. Mark Gold,[55] led to the now flourishing field of "recursive learning theory."

Carnap also introduced me to his old friend Paul Oppenheim and Paul's wonderful wife Gabrielle, whose Saturday lunches at their mansion in Princeton had some of the quality of classical *soirees*. One result of my friendship with Oppenheim was that we wrote a paper together, arguing that such "higher level" sciences as psychology, economics, and sociology are "reducible" to physics, albeit in a very liberal sense of "reducible." (Some years later, I criticized this view in a paper I published in a journal of cognitive psychology.[56]) Another result was that I got to know Kurt Gödel, who regularly attended the Oppenheims' Saturday lunches and with whom I occasionally discussed logical questions. (None of the signs of Gödel's reputed bipolar disorder manifested themselves on any of the occasions that we talked. I found him charming in an old-fashioned Viennese way, and, not surprisingly, the speed with which he could see to the bottom of a logical question was staggering.)

XVIII. A MEETING IN THE CARNAPS' LITTLE HOUSE

The most memorable event of my first year in Princeton was a small "conference" that Carnap arranged for a group of his close friends in the Carnaps' little house on the campus of the Institute for Advanced Study. The conference took place on Saturday and Sunday, January 2 and 3, 1954, and the invitees were Herbert Feigl, C.G. Hempel (who was still at Yale at that time), Ernest Nagel, Paul Oppenheim, Wilfrid Sellars, and two lads in their twenties: myself and Michael Scriven. (All of us had to pass the ferocious Marni to get in.) Each day began with a presentation of ideas that Carnap was thinking about (I still have his own outline of his presentation on January 2), which we discussed the rest of the day. The topic on Saturday was "laws, nomological statements, and causal modalities," and the topic on the second day was the nature of psychological concepts.

In his Saturday presentation Carnap accepted a view, defended by Reichenbach, that physical laws could be defined as "true nomological statements,"[57] but criticized Reichenbach's definition of "nomological statement." Carnap thought that an important unsolved problem was to give an account of what he called "the causal modalities," meaning the modal operators "it is physically necessary that" and "it is physically possible that."

I found the discussion of psychological concepts on Sunday much more interesting. Carnap put forward two ideas for discussion. The first (much later defended by Rorty, who may have heard it in Carnap's classes in Chicago[58]), was that one could imagine a language in which sensations and other mental states were referred to by naming the brain states with which they were (according to Carnap) identical. The speakers of this language would say, for example, "such-and-such a part of my brain is stimulated" rather than "I have a pain in my foot." In this culture, the closest one could come to asking "Is pain a brain state" is "Is stimulation of such-and-such a part of the brain a brain state," to which the answer would be, tautologically, "Yes." And (Carnap claimed) nothing would be lost.

The second part of the discussion, which went considerably deeper, proceeded to ask how we, who do not know which part of the brain or process in the brain pain is "identical with," can *now* refer to that part or process by the word "pain." There were two parts to Carnap's answer.

The first part of Carnap's answer was that "pain" is a "theoretical term," like "electric charge," and cannot be defined by an operational definition (in Carnap's jargon, a "reduction sentence" or set of "reduction sentences") of the form: "If x is in pain, then if such and such a test T is performed upon x, then reaction R will be observed," where both T and R are "observation terms."[59] Instead, Carnap suggested that (assuming we succeeded in analyzing the "causal modalities"), we could define pain as "That brain state that normally causes such and such reactions." This account is one that I defended in a paper titled "Psychological Concepts, Explication, and Ordinary Language." I regret that I did not mention that I had learned it from Carnap. I still defended that account in a paper written about 1962 titled "Brains and Behavior" that I thought well enough of to include in my 1975 collection, *Mind, Language and Reality* (volume 2 of my *Philosophical Papers*). Here is how I myself stated the view in that paper:

> We observe that, when a virus origin was discovered for polio, doctors said that certain cases in which all the symptoms of polio had been present, but in which the virus had been absent, had turned out not to be cases of polio at all. Similarly, if a virus should be discovered which normally (almost invariably) is the cause of what we presently call 'multiple sclerosis', the hypothesis that this virus is the cause of multiple sclerosis would not be falsified if, in some few exceptional circumstances, it was possible to have all the symptoms of multiple sclerosis for some other combination of reasons, or if this virus caused symptoms not presently recognized as symptoms of multiple sclerosis in some cases. These facts would certainly lead the lexicographer to *reject* the view that 'multiple sclerosis' means 'the simultaneous presence of such and such symptoms.' Rather he would say that 'multiple sclerosis' means 'that disease which is normally responsible for some or all of the following symptoms. . . .'[60]

Although this view of Carnap's was certainly an improvement on the view that psychological terms can be *defined* in terms of behavioral reactions, it assumes that pain is a "theoretical term," a view that I later rejected. As I wrote in "Logical Positivism and the Philosophy of Mind," a paper I wrote in the early 1970s, "The premise that 'pain', 'anger', etc. are theoretical terms in the positivistic sense. . . . is false because these terms have a reporting use, and thus would not be implicitly defined *merely* by a theory, even if it were true that theoretical terms are characteristically so defined."[61] If they *were* implicitly defined by a theory, the discovery that pain is not normally the cause of the sorts of behavior that we think it explains would show that pain does not really exist; so I could discover that I am not in pain by learning more about other people, regardless of what I feel! Since 1967, my view has been that, although the knowledge that pain typically causes certain sorts of behavior does help to *fix the reference* of the word "pain," the discovery that this is not the case would *not* show that pain does not really exist, as it would if the theory Carnap defended in the little conference in his bungalow on January 2–3, 1954 (and that I defended in the two papers I mentioned) were correct. In technical jargon, Carnap's theory was a *descriptivist* theory[62]: it held that "pain" and similar psychological concepts are *synonymous with descriptions*, though not with descriptions which use only observation terms (because they require that the "causal modalities" be available). I believe that such descriptions can be used to fix the reference of sensation terms (as can the acquisition of their reporting use, which I still regard as an essential part of our linguistic competence with those terms), but such terms are not synonymous with descriptions. But the distinction between a description's being used to fix the reference of a term and its being synonymous with the term—a distinction I had available after I wrote "The Meaning of 'Meaning'" (of which more later)—was not available to me in 1961 when I wrote "Brains and Behavior."

XIX. Leaving "Logical Empiricism" Behind

"The Analytic and the Synthetic" is the paper in which I found my own philosophical voice. A complete first draft of that paper was written at the Minnesota Center for the Philosophy of Science in the fall and winter of 1957-58. The philosophical outlook that informed that paper was very different from the Carnapian position that informed "Mathematics and the Existence of Abstract Entities," a paper I probably wrote in 1954 or 1955, as well as from the Reichenbachian view that informed "Three-Valued Logic." The change is announced from the first page of the "Analytic and the Synthetic," in which I speak of "errors in general philosophy which can have a far-reaching effect on philosophy of science,"[63] and give as my example "the confusion of meaning with evidence."[64] The Verifiability Theory of Meaning itself, the very hallmark of a logical empiricist doctrine, is now "a confusion.... whose effects are well known!"[65] And Reichenbach's view of geometry, that is the view he expressed in his *Philosophy of Space and Time* and in *The Rise of Scientific Philosophy*[66, 67] comes in for severe criticism: "Reichenbach suggested that 'straight line', properly analyzed, means 'path of a light ray', and with this 'analysis' accepted, it is clear that the principles of geometry are and always were synthetic. They are and always were subject to experiment.[68] Hume simply overlooked something which could *in principle* have been seen by the ancient Greeks. I think Reichenbach is almost totally wrong." I did not know at that time of Reichenbach's earlier and more plausible view, in his 1920 *Relativity Theory and Apriori Knowledge*, which Reichenbach had never mentioned in the class on the philosophy of space and time that I took at UCLA. On that earlier view, geometrical principles are "framework" principles, and that there is an epistemological problem of accounting for how framework principles can be revised is explicitly recognized. According to Michael Friedman, it was Carnap who talked Reichenbach into the more "conventionalist" position of the 1928 *Philosophy of Space and Time* that I criticized in "The Analytic and the Synthetic." The 1928 position is a more sophisticated version of an idea that goes back to Helmholz.[69]

This change in my philosophical outlook was not the product of any single influence. At least three factors contributed to bringing it about, among them (1) the effect of teaching philosophy of science every year; (2) the discussions that were taking place among the Princeton *junior* faculty in the early 1950s; and (3) the appearance of Stephen Toulmin's *The Philosophy of Science*,[70] which I discovered shortly after Carnap left Princeton in 1954.

XX. GETTING INTERESTED IN THE PHILOSOPHY OF MATHEMATICS

From my work with Kreisel on intuitionist propositional calculus I had acquired an interest in the epistemological views of the "intuitionist" school that Brouwer founded, and of the "formalist" school, founded by David Hilbert, that Brouwer opposed. From my years in graduate school at Harvard and UCLA I had, of course, learned about "logicism" (the view that "mathematics is logic in disguise," as the position of Frege and Russell is often described) and, of course, I was acquainted with Quine's views. In addition, as I mentioned, early in my Princeton years, while I was still strongly under the influence of Carnap, I wrote a paper ("Mathematics and the Existence of Abstract Entities") applying the idea that scientific theories are "partially interpreted calculi" to mathematics, but I soon became dissatisfied with that idea as I became dissatisfied with logical empiricism as a whole. But I was also dissatisfied with all the other philosophies of mathematics I knew of, including logicism, formalism, and intuitionism, and for that reason, my talks with my favorite discussion partner, Paul Benacerraf, more and more concerned these "schools," and, more broadly, the questions "What is the nature of mathematical existence?" and "What is the nature of mathematical truth?".

As a result, a few years later, probably about 1958, Paul and I decided to construct a "reader" that would bring together the papers a student needed to understand and think about those issues. The first edition of that reader appeared in 1964. A second edition, with a different publisher, appeared in 1983, and contained papers by myself and by Benacerraf as well as many of the papers from the first edition. (By that time we had each begun to work out positions of our own in the philosophy of mathematics.) Each edition had four parts. The titles of the first three parts were the same in both editions, although some of the readings in those parts had changed, largely in response to comments from users of the first edition. Those titles were: (Part I) "The Foundations of Mathematics," (Part II) "The Existence of Mathematical Objects," and (Part III), "Mathematical Truth—the very topics that Paul and I discussed in Princeton so many times. But Part IV was completely changed. Whereas in the first edition that part had been devoted to articles for and against the philosophy of mathematics of the later Wittgenstein—not because we endorsed it, but because it was not at that time well known to students of the philosophy of mathematics, and we felt it important to make it available—in the second edition we dropped it to make room for what had become of central importance after Paul Cohen proved in 1962 that neither the Axiom of Choice nor Cantor's famous Continuum Hypothesis could be proved from the standard axioms (the Zermelo-Fraenkel axioms) of set theory.[71] Since Gödel had published (in 1940) proofs that neither of these could be *disproved* either, the mathematical community now knew that "the structure of the universe of sets" is in important ways not determined by those axioms, and "what to make of this" has become one of the most hotly debated questions in philosophy of mathematics. For that reason, Paul and I felt it important to have a section of readings on the concept of set, including two essays by Gödel himself, one of which was a version of his "Cantor's Continuum Problem" updated to reflect his assessment of the most recent development, to wit, Paul Cohen's proof of the independence of the continuum hypothesis and of the axiom of choice. Dropping the Wittgenstein section was not an expression of disrespect on either of our parts; rather, as we explained, "In a number of cases (most notably the Wittgenstein material and "Two Dogmas of Empiricism") [which was also dropped in the second edition], the (present) availability of most of the material enabled us to omit it with less of a sense of loss."[72] However, when we had decided on the contents of the *first* edition, Cohen's work was still in the (near, as it turned out) future, and neither of us had yet made contributions of our own to the field that we were willing to include. What we did have was what turned out to be, for both of us, a life-long interest in the questions.

XXI. Teaching Philosophy of Science

During my first two years at Princeton I was the only one teaching philosophy of science (my predecessor was John Kemeny, who left Princeton in 1952). Although a much more famous philosopher of science than myself, namely, Hempel, joined the department as a full professor in 1955, I continued to teach the course titled "Philosophy of Science" every year. And because my favorite among the courses I had taken with Reichenbach had been his course on the philosophy of space and time, I naturally focused my lectures on this subject, and this too became a subject that I discussed constantly with Paul, who was my teaching assistant in that course. Although I was not aware that that was what was happening, my immersion in relativity theory had the effect of making the idea that great physical theories are nothing but devices for describing relations among "observables"—an idea that I still see as the very heart of Carnap's philosophy of science—ever less plausible. Here I was in agreement with Reichenbach, who, as already mentioned, saw theoretical entities as inferred entities ("illata," in his jargon) and not as "constructs."

But I also found myself dissatisfied with Reichenbach's view, according to which geometry, insofar as it is interpreted at all, is about *the paths of light rays* and *the behavior of rigid rods*. Reichenbach claimed that there were infinitely many possible alternative "coordinative definitions" of "straight line." But he contended that "a straight line is the path of a light ray" is the definition that "the sciences have implicitly employed all the time, though not always consciously," and I am sure he would have said the same thing about "congruent intervals are ones such that the same rigid rod will, if transported, coincide with first one and then the other."[73] It seemed obvious to me that, before the development of non-Euclidean geometry, people had as much of a right to think of "Two straight lines that are both perpendicular to the same straight line will never meet" as a necessary truth as *we* do to think of "A surface cannot be red (all over) and green (all over) at the same time" as a necessary truth. Yet, "two *light rays* cannot start out perpendicular to a third *light ray* and then later meet" was never regarded as a necessary truth, nor, of course, was "light travels in straight lines."

As I put it in "The Analytic and the Synthetic," "The principles of Euclidean geometry. . . . had the following status: no experiment that one could describe could possibly overthrow them by itself. Just plain experimental results without any new theory to integrate them would not have been accepted as sufficient grounds for rejecting Euclidean geometry by any rational scientist. After the development of non-Euclidean geometry, the situation was rather different, as physicists soon realized: give us a rival conceptual system, and some reason for accepting it, and we will consider abandoning the laws of Euclidean geometry."[74]

I meant the comparison with the statement that "A surface cannot be red (all over) and green (all over) at the same time" to show that the overthrow of Euclidean geometry was a *revolutionary event*, epistemologically speaking, and that Reichenbach's view in *The Philosophy of Space and Time* was a way of *minimizing the significance* of the fact that scientific revolutions can overthrow even statements *we have the right to* regard as necessary truths—a fact on which I have meditated ever since.[75]

In short, the more I immersed myself in relativity theory, the more obvious it became that "logical empiricist" philosophy of science falsified the nature and history of precisely the science that the logical empiricists respected the most: physics.

XXII. The Princeton Junior Faculty

When I joined the Princeton Department of Philosophy in 1953, there were only three full professors, one of whom retired at the end of the year. One of them I never got to know (and no one ever seemed to mention him), Robert Scoon. The other two were the chair, Ledger Wood, about whom more in a moment, and a charming and brilliant British philosopher, Walter Terrence Stace, whose *Philosophy of Hegel* was perhaps the first serious attempt to explain Hegel in terms intelligible to an analytic philosopher. Between 1910 and 1932, Stace had served in the Ceylon Civil Service, holding several positions in the Ceylonese government including that of Mayor of Colombo, and had gone on to have a distinguished career as Stuart Professor of Philosophy at Princeton. Although Stace was by no means hostile to religion, he had for some reason drawn the fire of the Roman Catholic chaplain at Princeton, who regularly thundered against the "atheist" philosophy department as a whole, and against Stace in particular. I recall asking Stace whether he was going to reply to these attacks. Stace smiled, and said, in his wonderful North-of-England accent, "If you kick a dung heap it just stinks the more."

Ledger Wood had been an active contributor to epistemology for a time, with eight published journal articles, many reviews, and a well-received book,[76] but after 1941 he apparently stopped publishing, apart from revising Thilly's history of philosophy.[77] His book, *The Analysis of Knowledge*, is hard to find today, but probably deserves more attention than it has received; it argued that the problems of epistemology properly belong to psychology (thus anticipating Quine's idea of "naturalizing" epistemology by "settling for psychology"[78]), but whereas Quine's favorite psychologist was the arch behaviorist Fred Skinner, Wood's was William James, and if the book was an explicit defense of "psychologism," it was a much richer psychologism than Quine's. However, in my view, Wood's great contribution was as chair of the department. When he became chair the department had no great distinction; Wood's way of rectifying the situation was, first, to look for the brightest recent Ph.D.'s or about-to-receive-their-Ph.D.'s he could find and hire them as assistant professors or "instructors" (if they didn't yet have a Ph.D.). Besides myself, Hugo Bedau, Sylvain Bromberger, and George Pitcher were all thus hired during his chairmanship. After that, he persuaded the department to hire C.G. Hempel and Gregory Vlastos (who succeeded him as chair). As a result, by 1955 Princeton was on the beginning of the way to becoming one of the world's leading philosophy departments.

The three junior faculty members I mentioned, Hugo Bedau, Sylvain Bromberger, and George Pitcher, were all enthusiastic about "ordinary language" philosophy at that time—something no one had mentioned at UCLA. At that time leading expositors of Wittgenstein—both disciples, like Norman Malcolm, and critics like David Pole[79]—read him as a verificationist, and many ordinary language philosophers either were or were suspected of being "logical behaviorists," that is, of holding that talk of mental states is either logically equivalent to talk of publicly observable behavior, or anyway possesses truth conditions that have to do with publicly observable behavior. Both this form of behaviorism and the form of verificationism that Malcolm defended seemed simplistic to me, in comparison even with the views of Carnap and Reichenbach (who at least took science seriously), and later in the 1950s and early 1960s I was to write several papers criticizing them. Although my initial reaction to ordinary language philosophy was to mock it, in the end I did not reject it entirely, in part because of Carnap.

XXIII. THE STORY OF CARNAP'S WIRE RECORDER

Carnap, as I discovered, was in the habit of dictating first drafts into a recorder. One of his many kindnesses to me in 1953-54 was to give me his old wire recorder when he bought his first tape recorder. I would not have known that there *was* such a thing, if Carnap had not given it to me—it literally recorded onto a metal wire. The quality might not have been good enough for music, but, as I recall, it was fine for recording dictation. When I turned it on the first time, I realized that I was hearing one of Carnap's drafts—a draft of a piece that I do not believe Carnap ever published, perhaps just remarks for his own use, although they were certainly polished enough to be published. Perhaps it was improper of me to do so, but I of course listened to the whole draft before erasing it. The subject was precisely what I was discussing with the other junior faculty members: the merits and demerits of "rational reconstruction" (a description that Reichenbach and Carnap used for their version of philosophy) and "ordinary language philosophy."

Although I was initially scornful of "ordinary language philosophy, that was not Carnap's attitude at all. Carnap began by describing Goethe's theory of color. The theory, *qua* theory, has long been rejected, but Goethe's *observations* of color phenomena continue to be admired. Goethe was, for example, the first to describe "edge" effects; that is, the phenomenon that the colors we see or appear to see in a scene frequently depend on what edges are visible in the scene—a phenomenon important for Edwin Land's research in the twentieth century. As Deane Judd, the author of the introduction to the 1970 MIT edition of Goethe's *Theory of Colors*, wrote:

> Most of Goethe's explanations of color have been thoroughly demolished, but no criticism has been leveled at his reports of the facts to be observed; nor should any be. This book can lead the reader through a demonstration course not only in subjectively produced colors (after images, light and dark adaptation, irradiation, colored shadows, and pressure phosphenes), but also in physical phenomena detectable qualitatively by observation of color (absorption, scattering, refraction, diffraction, polarization, and interference). A reader who attempts to follow the logic of Goethe's explanations and who attempts to compare them with the currently accepted views might, even with the advantage of 1970 sophistication, become convinced that Goethe's theory, or at least a part of it, has been dismissed too quickly.[80]

Carnap said something very similar, in that unpublished "piece" I listened to on the wire recorder! And after praising Goethe's work as a *description* and Newton's theory of color as a *theory*, he went on to make an astounding comparison (at least I found it astounding at the time, and, in a way, I am still astonished that Carnap made it). Carnap said that Newton's theory, like many theories, was an oversimplified description, and *needed* to be an oversimplified description in order to bring out the essential structure of the phenomena, but that it needed to be corrected by just the kind of detailed observation of those phenomena represented by Goethe's *Farbenlehre*. In Carnap's analogy, "rational reconstructionists" like himself were building the oversimplified but invaluable models, and "ordinary language philosophers" were supplying the needed corrective, by pointing out all the phenomena that the oversimplified models failed to capture. A truly generous attitude!

XXIV. Stephen Toulmin's *The Philosophy of Science*

As I mentioned, I read Toulmin's *The Philosophy of Science* shortly after it appeared, and it opened my eyes to a different way of thinking about scientific theories. Since this was intended as an introductory text, Toulmin chose a theory that could be more easily explained than relativity theory, namely the kinetic theory of gases. (In 1740 Bernoulli proposed that gases consist of great numbers of molecules moving in all directions, that their impact on a surface causes the gas pressure that we feel, and that what we experience as heat is simply the kinetic energy of their motion. These are still fundamental postulates of the theory.) Toulmin argued against the idea that the theory should be seen as just a set of postulates, of the sort that could be represented by a set of sentences in a formalized language. He pointed out that when we speak of "the kinetic theory of gases," we refer to a whole series of theories, each of which is a modification of earlier ones. Why do we consider these all versions of "the kinetic theory," rather than simply as different theories?

Here Toulmin introduced an idea later made famous by Patrick Suppes and today referred to as "the semantic view of theories." The idea is that a theory is associated with a "model," and that scientists evaluate models (and not only statements) for utility and fruitfulness. In the later history of the "semantic view," these models have often been associated with set-theoretic structures of the kind studied in the branch of mathematical logic known as model theory, but this actually loses Toulmin's insight. Toulmin had in mind visualizable structures, for example the "model" of the molecules of which a gas consists as little "billiard balls." Such a model is not "taken seriously" in the sense of being taken to be literally correct (one does not suppose the molecules of which a gas consists are shiny, for example), but they profoundly guide working with the theory, both mathematically and experimentally.

One virtue that such a model may possess is *extendibility*. When the laws suggested by the "colliding billiard ball model" turned out to be not exactly true, for example, one might consider the possibility that the "billiard balls" had "hooks" which sometimes "snagged." A good model is likely to have a whole series of natural extensions, which often lead to a whole series of theories.

Moreover, the scientist needs to know which elements of the "model" to take "seriously" and which to ignore as "artifacts" of the model. This means that an actual theory comes not only with a model, but with a *commentary* explaining how the model and the theory function together in practice; I still believe that Toulmin's ideas deserve more attention than they have received.

In sum, by the fall of 1957, the combined effects of teaching philosophy of science, thinking about the "metaphilosophical" issues posed by the confrontation of "ordinary language philosophy" and "rational reconstruction," and encountering Toulmin's book, were that (1) I moved away from "logical empiricism" to a much more independent position, and (2) in particular, I came to see philosophy of science (which was still all the philosophy I did) as concerned not just with formal theories and their supposed "coordinative definitions," but with physical theories as intellectual objects with complex histories and complicated links to a variety of practices which were themselves complex. It was in this new frame of mind, so different from my frame of mind when I received my Ph.D. in June 1951, that I took up my very first leave, a one-semester leave at the Minnesota Center for the Philosophy of Science in the fall semester of 1957-58.

XXV. Minnesota

The two leading figures at the Center were Herbert Feigl and Wilfrid Sellars, and their behavior towards me could not have been more different. The other people I saw a lot of at the Center were Paul Feyerabend, who paid the center a visit while I was there, and May Brodbeck, a member of both the Center and the Minnesota Philosophy Department, both of whom became friends—Feyerabend was not at that time the philosophical "anarchist" he subsequently became, by the way. Feigl was one of the most charming human beings I have ever known, warm, a fascinating conversationalist, and a philosopher who welcomed discussion and who, like Carnap, paid no attention to differences in academic status or in age; with me at least, Sellars was remote. In fact, I do not remember a single "one on one" discussion with Sellars during my whole semester in Minnesota. I frequently heard him speak in group discussions, however, and I soon realized that there were serious disagreements between my position and that of both Feigl and Sellars.

The two most serious of those disagreements concerned (1) the analytic/synthetic dichotomy (as it was understood by the logical empiricists, for whom all of mathematics was "analytic"); and (2) Adolf Grünbaum's views on physical geometry (which they liked, and I rejected).

1. My Disagreement with Sellars (and Feigl) about the Analytic/Synthetic Dichotomy

The notion of "analyticity" is often said to go back to Locke's talk of "trifling" propositions and to Hume's talk of propositions that are true because of the way our "ideas" are "related," and this talk (especially Hume's) helps to explain Kant's notion of an analytic judgment. Kant confined his definition to affirmative subject-predicate judgments (unlike Locke, for whom such negative propositions as "No hedgehog is a star" were examples of "trifling," that is, purely verbal, truths). An affirmative subject-predicate judgment is "analytic," by Kant's definition, just in case the predicate concept is "contained" in the subject concept; that is, the concept *bachelor* "contains" the concept *unmarried*. Unlike Quine, I always thought that there is something linguistically special about such "analytic sentences" as "All bachelors are unmarried" and "All vixens are foxes." [81] But, of course, that does not, at least on the surface (and, I would claim, not only on the surface) mean that the usual axioms of arithmetic, for instance "every number has a successor" and the instances of the schema of mathematical induction, are analytic, and looking at these mathematical sentences with the eye of a linguist, no one would suppose that they had the same character as "All bachelors are unmarried."

However, Leibniz already tried to solve the problem of the epistemological status of true mathematical propositions in the seventeenth century by claiming that they are all "identities," that is, simple analytic truths, a claim that Kant rightly rejected. The logical empiricists claimed that what was wrong with Leibniz's idea was that Leibniz had too simple a notion of what logic was, and that Russell and Whitehead had succeeded in showing that all mathematical propositions (not just subject-predicate ones, by the way) are "analytic" in a new sense, namely, in the sense of being *logical truths in disguise*, where "logic" meant the system of *Principia Mathematica*. (I call this new sense the "inflated" notion of analyticity). As Carnap put it in "The Old and the New Logic," "On the basis of the new logic, the essential character of logical sentences can be clearly recognized. This is of the greatest importance for the theory of mathematical knowledge..." [82]

And further:

> Mathematics as a branch of logic is also tautological. In the Kantian terminology: the sentences of mathematics are analytic. They are not synthetic a priori. Apriorism is thereby deprived of its strongest argument. Empiricism, the view that there is no synthetic apriori knowledge, has always found the greatest difficulty in interpreting mathematics, a difficulty which Mill did not succeed in overcoming. This difficulty is removed by the fact that mathematical sentences are neither empirical not synthetic apriori, but analytic. [83]

Against Carnap's claims, Quine made two telling objections, first in "Two Dogmas of Empiricism," and later in "Carnap on Logical Truth." [84] First of all, if we *define* an analytic sentence to be a theorem of *Principia Mathematica* or a sentence that follows from the theorems of *Principia* with the aid of such "Meaning Postulates" as "x is a bachelor if and only if x is an unmarried man," then to say that the theorems of *Principia* (including the Peano axioms, or their "translations" into *Principia* notation) are "analytic" just reduces to the statement that the theorems of *Principia* are theorems of *Principia*, and this, far from removing "a difficulty which Mill did not succeed in overcoming," say *nothing* about the epistemological status of those theorems. Secondly, if we say that the axioms of *Principia* are "Meaning Postulates"—are of just the same kind as "x is a bachelor if and only if x is an unmarried man,"—we stretch the notion of a "Meaning Postulate" to such a point that it is no longer clear what the content of that notion is.

I had been convinced by these arguments of Quine's (and related arguments of Morton White's) ever since 1948 (my first year of graduate work), but I had not encountered serious disagreement with them after that. (I have the impression that Reichenbach rather avoided the subject of the epistemology of mathematics; in any case, he had not spoken up when Hempel defended Quine's views in his living room in 1950.) So it was a shock to find that Quine's views had no weight at all in the eyes of Feigl and Sellars.

Here I must disagree with a claim that Rorty made in *Philosophy and the Mirror of Nature,* that Sellars, like Quine, rejected the analytic-synthetic dichotomy.[85] For Sellars in 1957-58 it was enough to say that "Meaning Postulate" meant "rule of the language," and, according to him, the notion of a "rule" is a rock-bottom notion that needs no further explanation.

The result of this direct clash between my views, which neither Sellars nor Feigl appeared to pay the slightest attention to, and theirs led me to write the first draft of "The Analytic and the Synthetic" while I was still at the Center. In that paper, in addition to the criticisms of the verifiability theory of meaning and of Reichenbach's views on geometry that I mentioned earlier, I argued that to conceive of definitions in science, e.g., "kinetic energy is one-half the product of the mass and the square of the velocity," as *analytic* would lead one to overlook the fact that relativity theory *forced* us to change this definition. The change was *not* a mere case of meaning-drift, as happened when the word *knave,* which originally meant "boy," came to mean "rascal." If "kinetic energy" is to refer to the magnitude we *intended* it to refer to, to a magnitude that obeys certain conservation laws, for example, and if the postulate of Special Relativity, that all physical laws are Lorentz-invariant is correct, then $e = \frac{1}{2}mv^2$ cannot be *exactly* correct, although it is very close to correct when v is small compared to c, the speed of light.

As I put it in "The Analytic and the Synthetic," even if we were to imagine that a congress of scientists had been convened in, say, 1780, and had legislated that the term "kinetic energy" was to be used for $\frac{1}{2}mv^2$, this would not have made the definition analytic:

The principle e = ½mv² may have been introduced, at least in our fable, by stipulation; the Newtonian law of gravity may have been introduced on the basis of induction from the behavior of the known satellite systems and of the solar system (as Newton claimed); but in subsequent developments these two famous formulas were to figure on a par. Both were used in innumerable physical experiments until they were challenged by Einstein, without being regarded as themselves subject to test in the particular experiment. If a physicist makes a calculation and gets an empirically wrong answer, he does not suspect that the mathematical principles used in the calculation may have been wrong (assuming that these principles are themselves theorems of mathematics) nor does he suspect that the law $f = ma$ may be wrong. Similarly, he did not frequently suspect before Einstein that the Newtonian gravitational law might be wrong. (Newton himself did, however, suspect the latter.) These statements, then, have a kind of preferred status. They can be overthrown, but not by an isolated experiment. They can be overthrown only if someone successfully incorporates principles incompatible with those statements in a successful conceptual system.[86]

These last two sentences represent the beginning of my subsequent account of conceptual "necessity." That account is one I have continued to refine ever since. It contrasts sharply with the Sellarsian (and Carnapian) view that logical and mathematical truths are just "rules of the language," as well as with Frege's view that they are "analytic" in a different sense (part of the very structure that makes thought thought) and the view of Kant that they are synthetic apriori.

2. My Disagreement with Feigl and Sellars about Grünbaum's Philosophy of Space and Time

In *The Philosophy of Space and Time*, Reichenbach held that the basic geometrical concepts of straight line and congruence required coordinating definitions. As I mentioned earlier, he further held (although as I shall explain shortly, there was a further "wrinkle" to his account) that the definition of a straight line as the path of a light ray corresponded to what scientists had meant by the term all along. However, logically speaking, he said, other coordinating definitions are possible—a concession to Poincaré's view that the laws of geometry are "conventions."

In several publications, Grünbaum, who was one of the leading philosophical interpreters of physical geometry (and a brilliant and friendly person, by the way), had emphasized this "conventionalist" dimension of Reichenbach's thought. According to Grünbaum, the reason different coordinating definitions of length and straightness are possible is that space is "intrinsically metrically amorphous" (language I never actually heard Reichenbach use). I was surprised that Feigl and Sellars accepted this Reichenbachian cum Grünbaumian account, and I argued against it at our conferences, to no avail. (A couple of years later, I wrote up my first criticism of these views for an internal publication of the Center. Since my "geometrical realist" view is now the standard one, it may be hard for younger philosophers of science to imagine the deafening silence with which my objections were met!)

In 1963 I published a full-length criticism of Grünbaum's views, in which I set out my realist view at length. Since that paper is an expansion of the views I just described, I shall describe that criticism at this point. The first part of my criticism was a statement of the realist view I mentioned, and the reasons one should accept it, and the second part was a criticism of Reichenbach's most sophisticated version of the "coordinating definition" story.

3. My Realism about Geometry

Reichenbach himself rejected operationalism in *Experience and Prediction* on the very solid grounds that statements about theoretical entities are not *exactly* equivalent to statements about measurement results; at best they are approximately and probabilistically equivalent. For example, it may have a very high probability that the needle of a voltmeter will be deflected if and only if electrons are flowing through a wire, but it is not physically impossible that electrons will flow even though the needle is not deflected, and not physically impossible that the needle is deflected for some other reason, even though no electrons are flowing.

To me it seemed obvious (and it still seems obvious) that the situation is the same with respect to what Einstein taught us to call the metrical field. If electrons are "illata" (inferred entities) and not constructs, as Reichenbach held, then the metrical field is also an "illatum" and not a construct. Moreover, a straight line is *not* exactly the path of a light ray, any more than an electric current is exactly a dispositional property of voltmeters. In fact photons do not have straight line trajectories according to any interpretation of quantum mechanics that I know of. And as for the definition of congruence in terms of transportation of rigid rods, if "rigid" means "does not change its length when transported," then the definition of "congruence" (equal length, in the case of line-intervals) in terms of "rigid" is simply circular, and if "rigid" is operationally defined, then, since no empirically constructible rod is in fact perfectly rigid according to the laws of general relativity, this definition will not be compatible with that theory. (In fact a famous textbook of general relativity makes just this point in its closing paragraphs,[87] although that textbook was published much later than my debate with Grünbaum.)

4. Reichenbach's More Sophisticated Story

Reichenbach was much too good a philosopher not to realize that the story about "straight line" meaning path of a light ray and congruence being "defined" by the transport of "rigid" rods was an idealization. He therefore supplemented it with what was supposed to be a more rigorous account.[88] On the idealized operationalist account we just criticized, the idea was that the world can be described by the combination of a system of physics cum geometry and a coordinating definition of distance and straightness. There are many such combinations that would "work," according to Reichenbach, and the trajectories they predict are the same, when we allow for the difference in the notions of distance in each case. They are, in Reichenbach's terminology, "equivalent descriptions." But, according to the familiar definitions of straight lines as light ray paths and congruence in terms of transport of rigid rods, such rods (or the rods that meet our operational tests for rigidity) will not change their length unless they are subjected to the action of "differential forces"—"real" forces with assignable sources. Suppose, for example, we live in a world whose geometry is Lobachevskian. We *could* in principle (Reichenbach points out) choose to describe that world in terms of a Euclidean geometry and explain the strange results of our measurements of angle and distance by saying that our measuring rods and protractors are being distorted by "universal forces"—forces postulated precisely to make Euclidean geometry come out true. But the Lobachevskian description allows us to choose a system of physics cum geometry which contains no universal forces, but only differential forces, and *this,* Reichenbach claims, will not be the case if we choose any other geometry. In sum, he claimed that there are infinitely many "equivalent" combinations of a system of physics cum geometry plus a set of coordinating definitions that fit our world, but *only one* of these combinations has the property that, according to the system of physics cum geometry it contains, there are no universal forces.

In terms of this way of telling Reichenbach's story (the way Reichenbach tells it in *The Rise of Scientific Philosophy*), the objection I stated above is that if the "coordinating definitions" are understood as *operational* definitions, then there is not even *one* combination consisting of a system of physics cum geometry and a set of coordinating definitions that fits our world. Certainly our actual physics is not compatible with any set of operational definitions being exactly right, as just explained.

To this Reichenbach's "sophisticated version" (as I called it) of his story consisted of the following reply: the *real* coordinating definition is simply the rule: *Choose that system of physics cum geometry such that when the measuring rods are "corrected" according to that very system then there is no need to postulate universal forces.* This works, according to Reichenbach, because if one system contains Euclidean geometry (for example) and another contains, say, Lobachevskian geometry, at least one of the two will have to invoke universal forces if they are both supposed to correctly predict the behavior of our measuring instruments.

Unfortunately, as I explained in "An Examination of Grünbaum's Philosophy of Geometry," it is *false* that there must be "universal forces" in any nonstandard metric. To see why it is false, let g_{ik} be the standard metric tensor,[89] and let P be the customary physics. It is possible, as Reichenbach recognized, to introduce an alternative metric tensor g'_{ik} leading to a quite different geometry and modify the physics from P to P' in such a way that the new world system g'_{ik} + P' is inter-translatable with g_{ik} + P. And Reichenbach is right that if the standard of congruence in the system g_{ik} + P is the solid rod corrected for differential forces, then upon going over to g'_{ik} + P' it will be necessary to postulate that the rod undergoes certain deformations. These "additional" deformations will be the same for all solid rods independently of their internal composition *relative to the original description g_{ik} + P*. Overlooking the fact that it is only *relative to the original description* that these additional forces affect all bodies in the same way, Reichenbach supposes that the new physics P' *must* be obtained by simply taking over the physics P and postulating an additional force U that affects all bodies in the same way. But, as I explained in the paper I mentioned, when we construct P', we don't have to simply take over the physics P and introduce an additional force U. This is not the only way of obtaining an "equivalent" world system based on the metric g'_{ik}. I proved that it can also happen that P' *changes the laws obeyed by the differential forces.* I showed that there can be two world systems, according to both of which there are no universal forces in Reichenbach's sense, and bodies change their lengths as they are moved about only at distances small compared to the nucleus of an atom, for example (so that operational tests of a macroscopic kind will not detect the changes), and the changes are only due to differential forces, including differential forces accounted for by their own atomic constitutions.

In sum, neither a "coordinating definition" of the kind first contemplated by Reichenbach (in terms of light rays and solid rods) nor a coordinating definition of the theoretical kind he also contemplated (namely, the "convention" of selecting the allegedly unique world system that fits the motions of the bodies and in which there are no universal forces) can be a *definition* of the fundamental metrical notions. Reichenbach should have extended his criticism of operationalism to a criticism of the (Helmholzian) view he espoused, and he should have recognized that the metrical field is a real physical entity. There are certainly equivalent descriptions in physics (more about this later!), but not for the reasons Reichenbach gave in his *Philosophy of Space and Time* and in *The Rise of Scientific Philosophy*.

I have stressed that I found no sympathy in Minnesota with either my criticisms of the analytic-synthetic dichotomy or my criticisms of Grünbaum's and Reichenbach's philosophies of geometry. Yet I was very happy that semester, and not simply because it was the first leave I had enjoyed since starting to teach in the fall of 1952. Feigl was a wonderful companion, and never upset by my disagreement with his views, Feyerabend was close to me in age and shared my interests, and I had marvelous working conditions. I even found time to do something I had never done before, which was to seriously study quantum mechanics (about which all I previously knew was Reichenbach's interpretation, which I defended in "Three-Valued Logic"). When I returned to Princeton in the Spring Semester of 1958, I was eager to share my experiences with Paul Benacerraf, and our discussions helped me greatly in turning the draft of "The Analytic and the Synthetic" that I brought back from Minnesota into a finished paper. I have recalled that semester in Minneapolis with a certain nostalgia many times since then.

XXVI. 1958-59

The two years that followed my semester in Minneapolis provided me with further stimulation and with opportunities for the development of new ideas and interests. But the most important event for me and for my students was the presence of Paul Ziff (whom I had not previously met) who was on leave from Harvard in 1958-59. Ziff was older than I, but seemed to me to be a fourteen-year-old in many ways, with the mixture of insight and occasionally poor judgment that I associate with brilliant adolescents. But in his seminar in Princeton, which became his book *Semantic Analysis*, Ziff was at his absolute best, and the fact that (in addition to Paul Benacerraf and myself) Jerry (Jerrold) Katz, and Jerry Fodor (the last two were both still graduate students) and two visiting graduate students from England (both future Oxford dons), David Wiggins and Christopher Kirwan, all attended every meeting of the seminar ensured sparkling discussions. Jerrold Katz later said of *Semantic Analysis* that it is "a pioneer work, in that it is the first to propose an empirically based theory of meaning to deal systematically with the various topics that are part of the subject of meaning, and to attempt to fit such a theory into the larger framework of structural linguistics." We all had the sense that what Ziff was doing was important and exciting for precisely the reasons that Katz gave, and Benacerraf, Katz, Fodor, and I discussed the issues that came up in Ziff's seminar virtually night and day. It was that seminar, combined with Chomsky's presence at the Institute for Advanced Study the following year, that turned my interests to philosophy of language. The first paper I wrote on the subject was "Some Issues in the Theory of Grammar." Further sources of stimulation were (1) a discussion I had with Brian McGuinness, who visited Princeton around that time (I do not recall exactly which year); (2) an invitation to give a talk at a conference on "Dimensions of Mind" at New York University May 15–16, 1959; (3) Austin's visit to the Princeton Department of Philosophy in 1958; and (4) the invitation to lecture at the International Congress in Logic, Methodology and Philosophy of Science in August, 1960. Here are some details on these stimulations.

1. The Conversation with McGuinness

In the conversation in question, McGuinness (whose writings on Wittgenstein's philosophy I very much admire, by the way[90]) claimed that time travel was a "conceptual impossibility." I replied that, in the light of Einstein's general relativity, we can now make perfect sense of the notion of the sort of "world lines" that would be involved in time travel.[91] In the paper that I wrote as a result of that conversation, in addition to presenting and spelling out that argument, I elaborated on the idea (which already figured in "The Analytic and the Synthetic"), that a statement can be *necessary relative to a body of knowledge, but* such "necessity" (which is the only sort of "conceptual necessity" I recognize) does not guarantee any sort of *absolute* immunity from future revision. That idea plays a central role in "Mathematical Necessity Reconsidered," as well as in "Rules, Attunement, and 'Applying Words to the World': The Struggle to Understand Wittgenstein's Vision of Language."

2. The Invitation to Talk at Sidney Hook's "Dimensions of Mind" Conference

In the late 1950s, an argument for dualism known as the "grain argument" was advanced in the philosophy of mind.[92] (The argument—that it is "unintelligible" to suppose that qualities whose "grains" are as different as those of neural properties and phenomenal properties are, in reality, identical—is an early ancestor of both Jackson's "knowledge argument" and Tom Nagel's "what it's like to be a bat" argument.[93, 94]) Although my lecture, published as "Minds and Machines," was later seen as important—by myself as well as by others—primarily because it suggested the functionalist account of mental states (of which more in a moment) the reason I wrote it was to argue that *if the grain argument is right, it is available to a robot as well*, and hence the form of "dualism" it is supposed to establish could not be any threat to materialism. What I argued was that the underlying "dualism" is the "dualism" of *knowing about a psychological property via a description* and *"knowing" about it by exemplifying it oneself*, and that this is an inevitable dualism, even for machines.[95]

I was a full-time mathematical logician as well as a philosopher and thus it is not surprising that the idea that the "mental states" of robots and possibly of people as well would be precisely their computational states should occur to me.[96] By 1959 that was an idea that I had been turning over in my mind for some time. In "Minds and Machines" it is only mentioned as a possibility, but in subsequent papers I defended it as an empirical hypothesis, and it is this hypothesis that became known as "functionalism."

In *Representations and Reality*, written some years later, I gave that hypothesis up, for a number of reasons. One reason is that, if we reflect on the very different ways in which propositional attitudes can be realized in an individual's beliefs and thought processes, we can easily see that it cannot be the case that there is a *one-to-one mapping* of such attitudes as *believing something*, *hoping for something*, *desiring something*, and the like, onto precise kinds of software as I had hoped. If such states are "realizable" in software at all, they are so in infinitely many different ways. One of the arguments I used against identifying mental states with *neurologically defined* brain states was that the propositional attitudes are "compositionally plastic"; a human, an extraterrestrial with a totally different sort of brain, and the famous android Commander Data (famous to viewers of *Star Trek: The Next Generation*) could all believe or fear or desire some of the same things, while having totally different brain states. A similar argument defeats my own functionalist hypothesis; *propositional attitudes are computationally plastic as well as compositionally plastic.*

Other reasons I had for giving up my 1960 version of functionalism ("computer-program functionalism," as we might call it) had to do with the *semantic externalism* that I began to defend in 1968.[97] For now, let me just say that although I have been a critic of my former functionalism since my 1985 *Representation and Reality*, it is wrong to think of that criticism as a total repudiation. I say not a *total* repudiation because I still believe that our so-called "mental states" are best thought of as *capacities to function*, though not in the strongly reductionist sense that that went with the model of those states as "the brain's software."

In any case, the question whether our minds or brains are best thought of as computers is important and exciting. Here, happily, is an area in which philosophers and scientists talk to each other and recognize the profit in doing so. Also, although the computer program functionalism I suggested in 1960 was too simple, it still seems to me an excellent entering wedge into the philosophy of mind in our computer age.

When Austin came to visit the Princeton Department, he read "Three Ways of Spilling Ink,"[98] and Paul Benacerraf reminds me that he and I cornered him afterwards and "persuaded him that these were empirical questions about which there was something to be learned from the linguists." The following term he and Grice had their Saturday morning seminar on Chomsky's *Syntactic Structures*.

3. The Invitation to Talk at the 1960 International Congress on Logic, Methodology and Philosophy of Science

My talk, titled "What Theories Are Not" was given on August 27, 1960, and I shall never forget it because it was the day on which I met Ruth Anna Mathers, as she was then, the love of my life, and, since August 11, 1962, my wife. We met at a reception in honor of Rudolf Carnap. But since this is an *intellectual* autobiography, I shall not divulge any details, except to say that we were madly in love before the conference ended. But back to philosophy!

The dominant account of scientific theories—I called it "the received view" in my talk—was that such theories are "partially interpreted calculi." This account had annoyed me for some time, because, as I put it in that paper:

> The notion of 'partial interpretation' has a rather strange history—the term certainly has a technical ring to it, and someone encountering it in Carnap's writings, or Hempel's, or mine[99] certainly would be justified in supposing that it was a term from mathematical logic whose definition was supposed to be too well known to need repetition. The sad fact is that this is not so! In fact, the term was introduced by Carnap in a section of his monograph[100] without definition (Carnap *asserted* that to interpret the observation terms of a calculus is automatically to 'partially interpret' the theoretical primitives, without explanation), and has been subsequently used by Carnap and other authors, including myself, with copious cross references but no further explanation.[101]

But it was not only the use of a technical term with no proper definition that annoyed me; I also criticized the idea that observation statements in science can be characterized simply in terms of their *vocabulary*. The vocabulary of science was supposed by Carnap to divide neatly into "observational terms," "theoretical terms," and "logical" (and mathematical) terms, and the "observation terms" were supposed to refer *only* to observable entities. I argued that while there is, to be sure, an important difference between *observation reports* and theories, the difference is not captured by the syntactic criterion just mentioned. In fact, typical observation terms (such as "smaller than") also apply to some things that are not "observable" in the positivists' sense, and some theories can be stated using only the observational vocabulary.

In addition, I listed three things that Carnap might have meant by "partial interpretation." The first was that to "partially interpret" a theory might mean to specify a nonempty class of intended models, and I commented that "it is necessary to use theoretical terms to specify even a *class* of intended models for the usual scientific theories."[102] The second was that to partially interpret a theory meant to specify a verification-refutation procedure which applies to some, but not to all possible, cases; a notion I mentioned only because it related to an earlier position of Carnap's, according to which the meanings of the theoretical terms had to be specified by a kind of operational definition Carnap called a "reduction sentence."[103] The third was that to partially interpret a calculus meant simply to *interpret part* of the language, for example "to provide translations into common language for some terms and leave the others mere dummy symbols." And I commented that this leads to the view "that theoretical terms have *no meaning at all*, that they are mere computing devices, and is thus unacceptable."[104]

Summing up these criticisms, I wrote that each of these notions of "partial interpretation" is "either unsuitable for Carnap's purposes.... *or incompatible with a rather minimal scientific realism* [emphasis added]; and in addition the second notion (the operationalist notion) depends on gross and misleading changes in our use of language.... in *none* of these senses is 'a partially interpreted calculus in which only the observation terms are directly interpreted' an acceptable model for a scientific theory."[105]

The words "incompatible with a rather minimal scientific realism" were seen (and I intended them to be seen) as raising a "realist banner" in the philosophy of science. Although the "received view" was being criticized by others on other grounds (e.g., for not being "historical" enough, or for thinking of theories as sets of sentences rather than classes of models), the idea that it was all right for a philosopher of science to actually say that physics is about real things, fields and particles, and that an interpretation which denies that physical theories are about those things is *ipso facto* unacceptable was unheard of. To my satisfaction, over the next twenty or so years a majority of philosophers of science joined the "realist" camp.

XXVII. CARNAP ON REALISM

In "What Theories Are Not," I pretended *not to know* what Carnap's response to my objections would be. But in fact, as I knew very well, from his earliest publications Carnap had always cited questions of the form "are such-and-suches *real*" as examples of *nonsense* questions. To take any form of "realism"—realism about *anything*—was, for Carnap, to be a "metaphysician" in the most pejorative possible sense of the term. The expression "a rather minimal scientific realism" would, to Carnap's ears, be as much of an oxymoron as "a rather minimal total nonsense." I want to expand on this point here.

Ever since Quine revived the word "ontology" in his celebrated essay "On What There Is" (a revival that Carnap regarded as a very bad idea, by the way), it has become customary to say things like this: "The ontology of Carnap's *Logischer Aufbau* is an ontology of elementary experiences [*Elementarerlebnisse*]." While this is true in the sense that the bound variables in the sentences of the *Aufbau* do range over *Elementarerlebnisse*, nevertheless, from Carnap's point of view—then, as well as later—it is profoundly misleading to put it in that "Quinean" way. For, while Carnap thought that there is a fact of the matter as to whether a certain experience (for example, of a red triangle on a purple background) is followed by a certain other experience (say of a blue square on a yellow background), it is meaningless to ask whether the "objects" involved in that sequence are "really" sensations, or "really" physical objects, or "really" brain events, or even really "entities." According to Carnap, I can say "the experience of a red triangle on a purple background was followed by an experience of a blue square on a yellow background," and regard that statement as "verified," but the question, "To what "ontology" does that statement commit me" was regarded by him as a *pseudoquestion*, early and late. Similarly, the idea that the acceptance of a theoretical language L_T in which terms like "charge density" or "mass density" appear "commits" scientists to recognizing the *reality* of charge and mass is utterly rejected by Carnap. In fact, in his last (1956) major paper on the interpretation of scientific theories, Carnap wrote:

> There is no independent interpretation for L_T [the "theoretical language"]. The system T [the scientific theory stated in L_T] is in itself an uninterpreted postulate system. The terms of V_T [the vocabulary of L_T] obtain only an indirect and incomplete interpretation by the fact that some of them are connected by the rules **C** with observational terms, and the remaining terms…are connected with the first ones by the postulates of **T**.[106]

To me this still sounds like the third of the three senses of "partial interpretation" that I described as "incompatible with a rather minimal scientific realism."

XXVIII. LEAVING PRINCETON

Although, upon my promotion to Associate Professor in both Philosophy and Mathematics, I automatically received tenure, 1960-61 turned out to be my last year on the Princeton University faculty, and I spent it abroad. It was at a reception in Carnap's honor, on August 27, 1960 (the day I delivered "What Theories are Not"), that I was introduced to Ruth Anna. A week later I flew to England to begin a year on a Guggenheim Fellowship, and Ruth Anna returned to the University of Oregon, where she was an Assistant Professor. (This meant that my continued courtship of Ruth Anna had to be via daily letters and weekly long distance calls for the next year. Although my marriage had already been a disaster scene for some time, I had great difficulty in reaching the decision to divorce Erna, which I finally did in 1962. I did not see Ruth Anna face to face, after our meeting in Stanford, until December 1961. We still celebrate August 27 every year as the anniversary of the day we met.)

Unlike the Rockefeller Fellowship I received in 1951-52, which had been somewhat messed up by the intervention of Chadbourne Gilpatric, my Guggenheim year went smoothly, although not in a way that was immediately productive. I divided the year thus: one semester at Oxford, where I made the valuable friendships of Elizabeth Anscombe, Paul Grice, and James Thomson, and one semester in Paris, where I attended Kreisel's seminar at the Mathematics Faculty of the Sorbonne. At Oxford, in addition to writing my daily letter to Ruth Anna, I talked a great deal with the three philosophers I just mentioned, and also with Jerry Fodor, who had been my student at Princeton, and who was in Oxford on a fellowship that same year. (I remember that Jerry and I both attended Elizabeth Anscombe's lectures on Wittgenstein's *Philosophical Investigations*, which Jerry described as "like attending lectures on the New Testament given by Mary.") The one philosophical lecture I gave at Oxford was "Do True Assertions Correspond to Reality," the most "metaphysically realist" piece I have ever written. But most of my research during the year was mathematical; I was engaged in what proved to be an unsuccessful attempt to prove a theorem that *was* proved two years later by Paul Cohen, namely that the Axiom of Choice (AC) cannot be *proved* in "ZF" [standard Zermelo-Fraenkel set theory]. Kurt Gödel had shown in 1933 that AC cannot be *disproved* in ZF. Thus the result that Paul Cohen obtained, and that I tried in vain to obtain in 1960-61, shows that AC is *independent* of the axioms of set theory used by the great majority of contemporary mathematicians. Paul Cohen received the highest award there is for mathematical research, the Field Medal, in 1966 for his proof.

In the summer of 1961, before returning to the United States, I revisited the little house in Mirmande where I had lived with my parents and where I had had my first two years of formal schooling. With Erna and with Jerry Fodor and his first wife, Iris Fodor, I also enjoyed the life of a tourist in Italy and in Denmark as well as France itself.

The big decision I had to make that year was whether to accept an offer to be the director of a proposed new program at MIT—in effect, to be the chairman of what amounted to a graduate department of philosophy,[107] although it was initially set up as an anonymous section of the Humanities Department. I would have the full support of the President, Julius A. Stratton, and of the Dean of Humanities, John Ely Burchard.

At that time John Rawls was still at MIT, but he informed me that he had already agreed to leave for Harvard in 1964. That left only the historian and scholar of religion, Huston Smith and the humanistic philosopher Irving Singer, as definite tenured colleagues; but Singer, Smith, and Rawls all assured me that it would be up to *me* to select a slate of philosophers for the new program. My title would be "Professor of the Philosophy of Science," and half of my teaching would be in the Mathematics Department. In short, at the age of 35, I would be able to create my own philosophy department!

On the one hand, I would be leaving my best friend—Paul Benacerraf—a friend with whom I had discussed every idea I had and every idea he suggested for the previous eight years (or seven, if we discount the year I spent in Europe). But the temptation was great, and in the fall of 1961 I moved to Cambridge, Massachusetts and to the Massachusetts Institute of Technology.

XXIX. My Developing Research Interests after Princeton and MIT

In the spring of 1963 I received an offer of a professorship from Harvard. By that time I was tired of the responsibilities that leading the "Graduate Program in Philosophy" at MIT had turned out to entail, and happy to take a position at a wonderful university where I would only be expected to teach and do research, and not to choose faculty members, argue for their promotion and tenure, and think about a million other administrative matters. In addition, I had become very close friends with members of the Harvard Department, especially Rogers Albritton, from whom I developed a lasting interest in Wittgenstein interpretation, and I already knew and admired Burton Dreben, Stanley Cavell, "Van" Quine, "Jack" Rawls, and Morton White. But I felt that I needed to stay another year at MIT to make sure the transition was smooth, and so I asked Harvard to delay the starting date of my appointment to July 1965, which it agreed to do. By that time, under my leadership, MIT had hired James Thomson from Oxford, Judith Thomson, Sylvan Bromberger, and Richard Cartwright, and had tenured Jerry Fodor and Jerrold Katz (who were instructors on one-year contracts when I came), and was quite able to get along without me.

Although I wrote a dozen papers in philosophy (and eight papers in mathematical logic) while I was at MIT, including "An Examination of

Grünbaum's Philosophy of Space and Time," "Brains and Behavior," "'Degree of Confirmation' and Inductive Logic," "Robots: Machines or Artificially Created Life?" and "A Philosopher Looks at Quantum Mechanics," it is only with hindsight that I can perceive in those papers what some of my future research interests would be. Moreover, one of those future interests, namely the theory of reference, had not yet developed at all, and my interest in the philosophy of mathematics had not yet resulted in any papers (unless one counts the introduction to *Philosophy of Mathematics: Selected Readings*, that Paul Benacerraf and I had edited together in Princeton and my early "Carnapian" paper on the "existence of abstract entities"). But two interests that were to grow in intensity in the coming years, were already present in a nascent form in those papers, namely, functionalism (in the sense of what I called "computer program functionalism" above), and my interest in the philosophy of physics, focusing originally on questions about space and time, but later to focus more and more on interpreting quantum mechanics. I want now to say something about how each of those four interests developed after I came to Harvard.

XXX. FUNCTIONALISM

As I explained earlier, the idea that a computer could be a model for the human mind is one that I had thought about some years before I delivered "Minds and Machines" at Sidney Hook's conference in New York in 1960, but even there I only mentioned computer program functionalism as a *possibility*, without actually advocating it. A paper I wrote while at MIT, "Robots: Machines or Artificially Created Life?" was also written to be delivered as a lecture, and it too was mainly devoted to arguing that the so-called "mind-body problem" would automatically arise for an intelligent robot (and that the "problem of other minds" would also arise, if the robot belonged to a community). But the references in that paper to "programming" the robot's mind/brain revealed that I was beginning to assume, and not merely consider, a functionalist conception of the mind. The move from suggesting functionalism as a possibility (and tacitly assuming it) to explaining and defending it explicitly was made in two papers I published in 1967.[108] The three-year gap between the publication of the former paper and that of the latter two is explained by my hesitation in moving from merely considering the possibility that two different concepts might refer to the same property even though the judgment that they do is not in any sense "analytic" or "conceptually necessary," an idea that was contrary to everything that Frege and Russell, the fathers of analytic philosophy, had taught, to accepting (and subsequently strongly advocating) that idea.

Thus in my 1960 "Minds and Machines," I was still quite tentative. I wrote, the criteria for identifying 'events' or 'states' or 'properties' are by no means so clear. An example.... is the following: Light passes through an aperture if and only if electromagnetic radiation (of such-and-such wavelengths) passes through the aperture. This law is clearly not an analytic statement. Yet it would be perfectly good scientific parlance to say that (i) light passing through an aperture and (ii) electromagnetic radiation (of such-and-such wavelengths) passing through an aperture are two descriptions of the same event .... It might be held, however, that *properties* (as opposed to events) cannot be described by different nonequivalent descriptions. In fact, Frege, [C.I.] Lewis, and Carnap all *identified* properties and 'meanings' ["intensions" or *Sinne*, in Frege's German], so that by *definition* if two expressions have different meanings, then they 'signify' different properties. This seemed to me very dubious.[109]

But it was only when I wrote "The Nature of Mental States" (published in 1967), that I had completed the move from regarding the idea that there cannot be such a thing as *empirically discoverable* property identities as "dubious" to strongly defending the idea that *there are* such property identities, and that is what cleared the way for me to state the functionalist hypothesis in that paper: ".... being capable of feeling pain *is* possessing an appropriate kind of Functional Organization."[110] [The capitals were used to indicate that the sense of "functional organization" in question was fixed by the model of a Turing Machine program.]

As I mentioned earlier, I eventually gave up that hypothesis both because it was incompatible with the "semantic externalism" that I defended from 1968 on, and because I came to realize that mental states were computationally plastic as well as compositionally plastic. In fact, the "functionalist hypothesis" of "The Nature of Mental States" (a paper originally titled "Psychological Predicates") was a clear example of reductionism. Not, to be sure, the very sort of reductionism that I attacked a few years later in "Reductionism and the Nature of Psychology," namely, reduction to elementary particle physics, but reductionism none the less. What I still believe is that *one useful level of description* of at least *some* brain processes is in computational terms, but *not* that the intentional level of description can be reduced to any of the various levels of description of the functioning of our neurons, including the computational level.

XXXI. A DIGRESSION ON PROPERTIES

The idea that there is such a thing as the empirical identity of properties seemed to me too important to leave to a few sentences in papers on the philosophy of mind, and so I published (1970) a full-length defense of it, titled "On Properties." I still agree with the main thrust of that paper, which was the idea of "synthetic identity of properties." As I argued in that paper, many of the "objects" of mathematical physics, particularly *fields*, have the character of properties (or the character of "magnitudes," which are like properties, except that instead of having only two values, "yes" and "no," magnitudes have a much more complex structure, which is why real and complex numbers, vectors, and tensors are needed to represent them mathematically). The idea that both Carnap and Quine (strangely, given his alleged "robust realism") favored, that space-time points are just quadruples of real numbers and fields are just mathematical functions on those quadruples seems completely "crazy" to me. It is not inconceivable that all the objects we encounter in daily life, and, for that matter, our own bodies, are fields, but that my body and the chair on which I sit, and house in which I am writing these words, and all the other things in my environment are nothing but mathematical functions is surely wrong!

I also think that "On Properties" was right in advocating the idea that we employ more than one standard of property identity. For example, if one says that being a female fox and being a vixen are the same property, one is employing the "Fregean" (or Carnapian) standard of property identity, namely that the predicates in question be analytically equivalent. But I had already argued in "The Analytic and the Synthetic" and "It Ain't Necessarily So" that analytic sentences in natural language are few and far between. Most of what we take to be "conceptually necessary" is at best necessary relative to one or another body of (putative) knowledge. Thus I should even then have seen that the standards of property identity exhibit considerable context sensitivity. There are not just *two* standards of property identity.

XXXII. Philosophy of Mathematics

The first two papers that I wrote on the philosophy of mathematics, "Mathematics and the Existence of Abstract Entities" and "The Thesis that Mathematics is Logic" now seem to me fatally flawed, albeit for different reasons.[111] But the views I expressed in (1967) "Mathematics Without Foundation," (1975) "What is Mathematical Truth," and subsequent papers (including two papers written in the twenty-first century, that will be included in my next collection of papers) are, with one unfortunate exception,[112] substantially the ones I hold today. Basically, I argued for three claims:

(1) *That the entanglement of physics and mathematics is such that one cannot consistently defend what I once called "a rather minimal scientific realism" and simultaneously accept an antirealist interpretation of mathematics.*

(2) *That mathematics need not be interpreted as asserting the existence of intangible entities, even by a scientific realist.*

(3) *That a full account of mathematical activity needs to recognize that mathematics involves not only proofs but what I call "quasi-empirical" arguments, arguments which resemble inferences to the best explanation in the natural sciences, except that the "evidence" is itself mathematical and not empirical.*

Now a word about each of these three claims:

Re (1): In "What is Mathematical Truth" the antirealist interpretation I considered was intuitionism. However, Hartry Field has recognized the seriousness of my objection to antirealism,[113] and has published a substantial body of work arguing that his "nominalist" position in the philosophy of mathematics can meet that objection. As I explain in my reply to his essay in the present volume, I believe that his work depends on a very narrow picture of physics and of the mathematics that is used in physics, and that in the end "nominalism" should be rejected. But I am delighted that he has been willing to explore the issue.

My argument against antirealism in the philosophy of mathematics has frequently been lumped together with an argument of Quine's (one to which I referred in *Philosophy of Logic*) under the name "the Quine-Putnam indispensability argument." For example, if one consults the *Stanford Encyclopedia of Philosophy* on the topic "Indispensability Arguments in the Philosophy of Mathematics,"[114] one finds the following paragraph:

> From the rather remarkable but seemingly uncontroversial fact that mathematics is indispensable to science, some philosophers have drawn serious metaphysical conclusions. In particular, Quine (1976; 1980a; 1980b; 1981a; 1981c)[115] and Putnam (1979a; 1979b)[116] have argued that the indispensability of mathematics to empirical science gives us good reason to believe in the existence of mathematical entities. According to this line of argument, reference to (or quantification over) mathematical entities such as sets, numbers, functions and such is indispensable to our best scientific theories, and so we ought to be committed to the existence of these mathematical entities. To do otherwise is to be guilty of what Putnam has called "intellectual dishonesty" (Putnam 1979b, p. 347). Moreover, mathematical entities are seen to be on an epistemic par with the other theoretical entities of science, since belief in the existence of the former is justified by the same evidence that confirms the theory as a whole (and hence belief in the latter). This argument is known as the Quine-Putnam indispensability argument for mathematical realism.

What I actually argued in "What is Mathematical Truth" was that *the internal success and coherence of mathematics* is evidence that it is true under *some* interpretation, and that its *indispensability for physics* is evidence that it is true under a *realist* interpretation. (Also, in both "What is

Mathematical Truth" and "Mathematics without Foundations" [the very papers the author of this article cites], I said that a realist interpretation of set theory did *not* have to assert the "existence of mathematical entities." This will be the subject of the next section.) And, unfortunately, there is a premise in the author's formalization of the supposed "Quine-Putnam indispensability argument" for "the existence of abstract entities" the "and only" part of which I have *never* subscribed to in my life, namely: "(P1) We ought to have ontological commitment to all *and only* the entities that are indispensable to our best scientific theories." (Taken according to the letter, this would preclude belief in the existence of *philosophical arguments*, for example, since our "best scientific theories" do not mention such entities.) In fact, my argument was, as I said, an argument for extending scientific realism to the domain of mathematics; it was *not* a claim that knowledge is exhausted by "our best scientific theories," a claim I explicitly repudiated in the introduction to *Mathematics, Matter and Method*.

Nevertheless, there was a common *premise* in my argument and Quine's, even if the *conclusions* of those arguments were not the same, since Quine's argument *was* an argument for the existence of abstract entities. That premise was "scientific realism," by which I meant the rejection of operationalism and kindred forms of "instrumentalism." I believed (and *in a sense*[117] Quine also believed) that fundamental physical theories are intended to tell the truth about physical reality, and not merely to imply true observation sentences.

However, where I most take issue with the account in *The Stanford Encyclopedia of Philosophy* is with the following analysis of my argument: According to that account, the supposed "Quine-Putnam indispensability argument" rests on (P1) above and "confirmational holism." Confirmational holism is explained thus:

> Confirmational holism is the view that theories are confirmed or disconfirmed as wholes (Quine 1980b, p. 41).[118] So, if a theory is *confirmed* by empirical findings, the *whole* theory is confirmed. In particular, whatever mathematics is made use of in the theory is also confirmed (Quine 1976, pp. 120–22). Furthermore, as Putnam (1979a) has stressed, it is the same evidence that is appealed to in justifying belief in the mathematical components of the theory that is appealed to in justifying the empirical portion of the theory.[119]

What can I say about all this? I have never claimed that mathematics is "confirmed" by its applications in physics (although I argued in "What is Mathematical Truth" that there is a sort of quasi-empirical confirmation of mathematical conjectures *within* mathematics itself). What I claimed in "What is Mathematical Truth" (and subsequently) is, I repeat, that a *prima facie* attractive position—realism with respect to the theoretical entities postulated by physics, combined with *antirealism* with respect to mathematical entities and/or modalities—does not work. But I do not think it at all plausible to think that numbers are "intangible objects"[120] whose existence we "confirm" in the same way that we confirm the existence of, say, mesons. My argument was never intended to be an "epistemology of mathematics." If anything, it was a *constraint* on epistemologies of mathematics from a scientific realist standpoint.[121] On that (the epistemology of mathematics), I agree with a view that John Burgess has expressed, that the best way to find out how mathematical knowledge is obtained is to look at what mathematicians do. I suspect that Burgess is also right in thinking that what we will find will not fit any epistemological picture so far proposed.

Re (2): ["That mathematic need not be interpreted as asserting the existence of intangible entities, even by a scientific realist."] In "Mathematics without Foundations," I proposed an interpretation of mathematics that I called "mathematics as modal logic." (In recent decades that interpretation has been developed in detail by Geoffrey Hellman.[122]) The point of that interpretation is that regarding statements of mathematical modality (statements of the form, "it is (mathematically) possible that . . . " and "it is (mathematically) necessary that . . .") as having a kind of truth and falsity that transcends decidability, as *true or false even when it is not possible to prove or disprove them*, does not commit one to asserting "the actual existence" of mathematical objects, possible worlds, or any other superphysical entities.

Nonetheless, I did not propose the modal-logical interpretation as a step to arguing that numbers do not really exist, as the title of Hellman's book "Mathematics without Numbers" might suggest. The idea that we are saying something *false* when we say "There is always a prime between n and $2n$" seems wrong to me. I prefer to say that what Hellman and I are doing is *explaining what mathematical "existence" comes to*.

In addition, the modal-logical interpretation provides a natural resolution to a problem raised in a famous paper by Paul Benacerraf.[123] The problem is that while the natural numbers can, as is well known, be identified with sets, they can be identified with sets in *infinitely many ways*. Shall we then say that quantification over natural numbers is a sort of deliberately *ambiguous* quantification over the successive elements of any infinite series of sets (any "ω-sequence") you like? But the same problem arises with quantification over sets! Sets can, after all, be identified with "characteristic functions" (functions whose range is $\{0,1\}$), as is standardly done in a good deal of recursion theory and hierarchy theory, for example. On the other hand, functions can be identified with ordered n-tuples. And ordered n-tuples can be identified with *sets*—in infinitely many different ways! Can there really be a "fact of the matter" as to whether *sets are a kind of function or functions are a kind of set* or as to what the "correct" definition of "ordered pair" is?

If, however, quantification over sets, functions, etc., is simply talk about possibilities and not quantification over actually existing entities, then the problem disappears in the sense that all of the different "translations" of number theory into set theory, and all of the different translations of set theory into function theory, and all of the different translations of function theory into set theory, are just different ways of showing what *sorts* of structures have to *possibly exist* in order for our mathematical assertions to be true. In my view, then, what the modal-logical "translation" of a mathematical statement gives us is a statement with the same mathematical content which does not have even the appearance of being about the actual existence of "intangible objects."

Re (3) ["That a full account of mathematical activity needs to recognize that mathematics involves not only proofs but what I call 'quasi-empirical' arguments, arguments which resemble inferences to the best explanation in the natural sciences, except that the 'evidence' is itself mathematical and not empirical."] Here I shall just remark that (3) is a point that every working mathematician knows very well to be true, but that the great majority of philosophers of mathematics continue to ignore to the present day.

XXXIII. Philosophy of Physics

I have described how, during my semester as a guest of the Minnesota Center for the Philosophy of Science in 1957-58, I first started to debate in writing with Adolf Grünbaum, by challenging his claim that space and time are "intrinsically metrically amorphous" as well as Reichenbach's position that the metric is determined by a "coordinative definition." I also mentioned how six years later, in 1963, I published a detailed criticism of Reichenbach's claim that we choose the (allegedly unique) physics + geometry according to which "universal forces vanish." Grünbaum in turn criticized my criticism of this claim of Reichenbach's,[124] and this led me to give a detailed proof of the following theorem in a paper I published in 1975:

THEOREM: Let P be a system of physics and E be a system of geometry compatible with P. Then the world described by E+P can be redescribed in terms of an arbitrarily chosen g_{ik} (compatible with the given topology) *without postulating universal forces.*

Philosophically, as I have already explained, the issue at stake in my disagreements with Reichenbach and Grünbaum had to do with the implications of scientific realism. My position was, and still is, that the metric field is identical with the gravitational field (as Einstein taught us) and that this field is a perfectly real physical entity; the Reichenbach-Grünbaum position is that we impose a geometry on space time by convention.

In addition, in 1967 I published a paper arguing for the reality of future events (and arguing, also, that statements asserting that future events will or will not take place have tenseless truth values) on the grounds that "presentism"—the view that only present events and objects are "real"—is incompatible with the special theory of relativity, which denies the existence of an observer-independent "now." Two important responses to my argument have appeared, one of which convinces me and one which does not.

The response that convinces me is due to Yuval Dolev,[125] who has argued that I should not have accepted the question "Is the future real," because it is not clear what the opposite of "being real" is supposed to be in this context. It can't be seriously thought that "time is imaginary," "time is fake," "time is make-believe," for example. Nor can "future events" be "unreal" in any of *those* ways. Nor can the question be: Are future events "real" in the sense of *being present events*?, since no one supposes that future events *could be* present events. But Dolev's argument, while it supports dismissing the question "Are future events real," does not disturb my argument that statements about future events have observer-independent truth values, truth values that are not relative to a time of utterance.

The objection that did not convince me was due to Howard Stein.[126] Stein's objection to my argument was that I overlooked the possibility of *relativizing the notion of reality* (or "having become," in his terminology). On his proposal, what "has become" relative to an observer at a time is what is in the "here-now" of that observer or else lies in the past light cone of that observer, and this is a relativistically invariant notion. In my view, Stein simply misses the issue I was addressing, which is whether future events are real *in the standard metaphysical understanding of "real,"* on which what is "real" is precisely supposed to be *mind-and-observer-independent*. At best, Stein's view, like Dolev's, rejects my question, but if one is going to reject the question, I prefer to be up front about that rejection, in the way Dolev is.

Since 1960, however, the area in the philosophy of physics that has most interested me is quantum mechanics, and the problem of extending scientific realism to that subject is one I have thought about and one that I have continued to discuss with friends ever since. Recently I have begun to be interested in the implications of the idea, believed by many of the physicists who work on quantum cosmology, that when space-time theory is properly reconciled with quantum mechanics (something we do not yet know how to do), we will have to extend the quantum mechanical idea of "superposition of states" to geometries; that is, accept the idea that *different space-time geometries* are superimposed, so that our space time itself has a geometry and even a topology which are quantum-mechanically indeterminate. In this way, my interest in quantum theory seems to be leading me back to an interest in space-time physics.

XXXIV. QUANTUM MECHANICS AND SCIENTIFIC REALISM

In 1965, I published a survey article on the philosophy of physics in a volume on contemporary American philosophy,[127] in which I began by explaining that the (maximally well defined) states of a physical system are represented mathematically in quantum mechanics as elements in a linear vector space. (These vectors can also be represented as complex-valued functions on the configuration space of the system. Thus we often find the terms "wave function," "psi-function," and "state function" used to describe the state vector.) I then went on to explain the famous problem of "Schrödinger's cat": letting X be the cat (who is supposed to be in "an isolated rocket ship") and A be a state in which X is alive and B one in which X is dead, then, what would ½A + ½B correspond to? It is incompatible with standard quantum mechanics (I pointed out) to hold that a system in a superposition is "really" in one of the components of the superposition, only we do not know which. Thus X cannot be alive. Neither can X be dead, or in any other thinkable macrocondition. However, it is one of the assumptions of orthodox (Copenhagen) quantum mechanics that ordinary macroscopic realism is tenable. [The Copenhagen interpretation *was* the "orthodox" one at the time I wrote.]

I went on to say that it seemed to me that this was self-contradictory. "On the one hand, we are told that states form a linear vector space, i.e., any two states can be superimposed. On the other hand, we are told that macro-conditions cannot be superimposed. Conclusion: something is wrong with the theory."[128]

Of course, the great figures of the founding generation of quantum mechanics were aware of the problem, and the solution favored by the fathers of the so-called "Copenhagen Interpretation," Born and Heisenberg, and incorporated into his axiomatization of quantum mechanics by von Neumann,[129] was to postulate that when a *measurement* is made on a quantum mechanical system, the wave function of the system "collapses." In vector language, what this means is that the original state vector is replaced by one of its projections onto a subspace determined by the particular measurement that is made—for example, the cat, in the case of Schrödinger's thought experiment, simply "jumps" into a live-cat state or into a dead-cat state when the measurement is made.

In 1965 I also published a longer paper on the topic, "A Philosopher Looks at Quantum Mechanics," with which I am still happy. And exactly forty years later I published a "sequel," titled "A Philosopher Looks at Quantum Mechanics (Again)." There, I began by explaining that I needed to return to the subject because "so much relevant theorizing was not known" forty years earlier, when I wrote the first paper. A section of this "sequel" was titled "Scientific Realism is the Premise of My Discussion," and there I explained that what I meant by "scientific realism" was the rejection of operationalism. And to emphasize that this was a point of agreement between the two papers, I quoted a long passage from the earlier one, including the following sentences:

> If the nonoperationalist view is generally right (that is to say, correct for physical theory in general—not just for Newtonian mechanics), then *the term 'measurement' plays no fundamental role in physical theory as such*. Measurements are a subclass of physical interactions—no more or less than that. They are an important subclass, to be sure, and it is important to study them, to prove theorems about them, etc.; but 'measurement' can never be an *undefined* term in a satisfactory physical theory, and measurements can never obey any 'ultimate' laws other than the laws 'ultimately' obeyed by *all* physical interactions. [130]

So, I have been thinking about how to interpret quantum mechanics in accordance with scientific realism for more than forty years. To describe in detail the various mathematical and physical problems that I had to think about, and the various ways I tried to deal with them in the course of my still unfinished struggle to understand quantum mechanics in a realist way, would not be appropriate in an "intellectual autobiography." I shall, however, try to describe the main issues as I see them now.

1. David Finkelstein and von Neumann's Quantum Logic

In August 1960 Martin Davis and I both attended an American Mathematical Society Summer Seminar on "Modern Physical Theories and Associated Mathematical Developments" in Boulder, Colorado. There I developed a friendship with the physicist David Finkelstein. [131] (Finkelstein and Davis were already friends, and had been so since their college days.) Finkelstein believes that the key to understanding quantum mechanics is *to give up the idea that the laws of classical logic hold in our world*. This is an idea he got from John von Neumann's classic text, *The Mathematical Foundations of Quantum Mechanics*, which proposed a new logic for quantum mechanics as early as 1932. Reichenbach too had proposed that we change our logic to interpret quantum mechanics, but there was an enormous difference between the two proposals. Reichenbach accepted the idea, central to Bohr's famous

"Copenhagen Interpretation" of quantum mechanics, that we must draw a sharp line between the properties of macroscopic objects dealt with in classical physics and the properties of elementary particles. Sometimes, to be sure, a "classical" property (e.g., a position) can be assigned to a particle, but, like Bohr, Reichenbach assumed this can only be done when a "measurement" is made, and, like Bohr, he believed that such measurements could always be described using *classical* physics. (Incidentally, today, very few physicists know or care about the details of the Copenhagen Interpretation. I once heard Murray Gell-Mann say in a lecture, "There is no Copenhagen Interpretation of quantum mechanics. Bohr brainwashed a generation of physicists."[132]) Statements about macroscopic phenomena, or about such "classical" magnitudes as the position, momentum, and energy of particles at times when a measurement is made, are, according to Reichenbach, true or false, and obey the laws of classical logic. At all other times, statements about the properties of micro-entities are neither true nor false. Reichenbach assigned them a third truth value "indeterminate," and his form of quantum logic accordingly used three-valued truth tables, instead of the usual two-valued ones. This was, of course, not claimed to be a "realist" interpretation of quantum mechanics. In fact, Reichenbach claimed to give a proof of what he called a "principle of anomaly"[133] according to which a realist interpretation is impossible.[134] By the time I participated in the Boulder seminar, Reichenbach's three-valued logic seemed to me a way of *avoiding* the problem of understanding quantum mechanics rather than a solution.

Von Neumann's idea, as developed and elaborated by Finkelstein,[135] was much more interesting. Analogously to intuitionist logic, which was based on the actual procedures of constructive mathematics, von Neumann's "modular" logic was based on the actual procedures of quantum physics. A further analogy is that neither of these logics is presented via truth tables. Instead, each logic sets out a "nonstandard" way of deciding what are and are not valid logic laws: by reinterpreting of the logical connectives, in the case of the logic proposed by Brouwer and Heyting, or by specifying that the valid laws of logic are to be fixed by the lattice of subspaces of the particular linear spaces ("Hilbert spaces") used in quantum mechanics, in the case of von Neumann's proposal. (This "non-truth table" character has led to many misunderstandings of both logics.)

The way in which this "fixing" of the logic by the Hilbert space used to represent the particular system is done, in the case of von Neumann's logic, is very simple. As already mentioned, the (maximally well defined) states of a physical system are represented mathematically in quantum mechanics as elements in a linear vector space. Think of each "vector," or rather, the one-dimensional subspace corresponding to that vector, as representing the proposition that the system is in the state in question.

Extending the correspondence between subspaces of the Hilbert space and propositions to propositions that are not maximally well defined is done as follows: the disjunction of two (or more) propositions is represented by the subspace of the Hilbert space spanned by the spaces corresponding to those propositions[136]; the conjunction is represented by the intersection of the subspaces in question, and the negation of a proposition is represented by the orthocomplement of the subspace corresponding to that proposition.[137] A quantum mechanical proposition S_1 *implies* a quantum mechanical proposition S_2 just in case the subspace that represents S_1 is included in the subspace that represents S_2. A *valid* law of quantum logic is simply a formula of propositional calculus each of whose substitution instances corresponds to the whole space.

Applying this form of quantum logic to "Schrödinger's cat," what do we have? According to von Neumann's axiomatization of quantum theory, *every* one-dimensional subspace of the appropriate "Hilbert Space" corresponds to a proposition about the system, a proposition that "says" that a quantum mechanical "observable" [technically: a magnitude corresponding to an idempotent operator on the Hilbert Space] has a definite value.

Well, if A is the vector representing the proposition that the cat is alive (at the relevant time), and B the vector representing the proposition that the cat is dead, then ½A + ½B is a vector whose corresponding one-dimensional subspace represents the proposition that a certain "observable" has a definite value r, which we will call proposition "C." And ½A + ½B obviously lies in the space spanned by A and B. Using the letters A, B, C to stand both for the one-dimensional subspaces and the corresponding propositions where it is clear which is meant, it follows from the description of von Neumann's logic just given that the proposition C (which says that the cat is in the superposition of being alive and being dead) implies the disjunction A ∨ B. And since C is a vector in the space spanned by A and B, the intersection of that C with that space is just C; that is, C implies C · (A ∨ B). So, if we take von Neumann's proposed logic "seriously"—which is what Finkelstein convinced me we should do—then we can say:

(a) The cat is in the particular superposition C *and* (the cat is alive *or* the cat is dead)—in propositional calculus notation: C · (A ∨ B).

Can we then draw the conclusion, which would certainly follow if the logic were "classical logic," that:

(b) [The cat is in the superposition C AND the cat is alive] OR [The cat is in the superposition C AND the cat is dead]—in propositional calculus notation: (C · A) ∨ (C · B)?

The answer is NO! For the two one-dimensional subspaces corresponding to C and A have the null space as their intersection, and likewise the two one dimensional subspaces corresponding to C and B likewise have the null space as their intersection, so (C · A) ∨ (C · B) corresponds to the null space; that means that the *negation* of (C · A) ∨ (C · B) is valid. Thus the distributive law, C · (A ∨ B) ≡ (C · A) ∨ (C · B) *fails* in quantum logic!

Of course, a host of objections arise, and in fact I am now chagrined that I was so quickly "won over" to this idea by Finkelstein, but (I reflected at the time), a host of objections arose when it was proposed that the geometry of the world might not be "classical" (that is, might not be Euclidean). When I wrote "Is Logic Empirical," the two proposals seemed completely analogous to me, that is, it seemed completely in the spirit of Quine's "Two Dogmas of Empiricism," as well as of my "The Analytic and the Synthetic" and "It Ain't Necessarily So," to argue that, in effect, "Non-Classical Logic is to Quantum Mechanics as Non-Euclidean Geometry is to Relativity Theory." And for a number of years I continued to defend precisely that idea.

The idea turned out, however, to be unworkable. (The interested reader may find the details in my "Reply to Michael Redhead" in *Reading Putnam*.)

2. Revising Logic?

Although the idea that the right way to understand quantum mechanics involves giving up the distributive laws of propositional calculus was a mistake on my part, the question as to whether anything survives of the traditional idea of a priori truth is one that I continue to think about. One period of intense concentration on it occurred during the 1970s; this can be seen from the fact that when I started to write "There is at Least One A Priori Truth" in the 1970s, I let the draft sit for some time while I argued with myself about what I had written. When I finally sent it to *Erkenntnis* to be published, it ended with a "Note" which read, "This is a first draft of a paper I never finished. I no longer agree with the conclusion for a number of reasons." [138] Even before the paper actually appeared, the editors of *Erkenntnis* allowed me to add a further note titled "Note to supersede (supplement?) the preceding note," [139] That note begins by saying "we philosophers are frequently torn between opposing considerations, but we rarely show it in print. What we do is let our selves be torn in private until we finally 'plonk' for one alternative or the other; then the published paper only shows what we plonked for, and not the being-torn. For once, the preceding paper-plus-potentially-infinite-series-of-notes *will* show the 'being torn'." [140]

The considerations between which I was "torn" were, on the one hand, the arguments of Quine's "Two Dogmas of Empiricism," and my own arguments in "The Analytic and the Synthetic" and "It Ain't Necessarily So," that obviously undermine the idea of an *absolute* category of a priori truth—arguments I still believe—and, on the other hand, the thought that, even if we grant for the sake of argument that we *might* someday revise our logic, even, perhaps, to the extent of allowing some statements of the form $\mathbf{p} \cdot \mathbf{\sim p}$ to be accepted (this has actually been proposed by the advocates of so-called "paraconsistent logic"[141]), still we could *never* accept "*every* statement is both true and false*,*" nor could we accept the rule, *from every set of premises, infer every p.*

As the title of the paper indicates, this led me to search for an example of absolutely a priori truth. My first candidate was what I called "the minimal principal of contradiction,"[142] namely "Not every statement is both true and false." But in the first of the "Notes" appended to the paper, I objected as follows:

> I think it is right to say that, within our present conceptual scheme, the minimal principle of contradiction is so basic that it cannot significantly be 'explained' at all. But that does not make it an 'absolutely *a priori* truth' in the sense of an absolutely unrevisable truth. Mathematical intuitionism, for example, represents one proposal for revising the minimal principle of contradiction: not by saying that it is *false*, but by denying the applicability of the classical concepts of truth and falsity at all. Of course, then there would be a new 'minimal principle of contradiction': for example, 'no statement is both proved and disproved' (where 'proof' is taken to be a concept which does not presuppose the classical notion of truth by the intuitionists); but this is not the minimal principle of contradiction. Every statement is subject to revision; but not in every way.[143]

To this, the second of my two notes objected by saying that "If it is true, as I argued in the preceding Note, that we can't give up the critical statement [i.e., the 'minimal principle of contradiction'] except by changing the meaning of 'true' and 'false' (i.e., 'giving up the concepts'), then the following hypothetical must be *absolutely* unrevisable: *If the classical notions of truth and falsity do not have to be given up, then not every statement is both true and false.* "[144]

Today, what I think is that we should simply abandon the notion of the "a priori" (and the related notion of "absolute unrevisability"). As I explain in "Rethinking Mathematical Necessity," that does not mean that we should agree with Quine that every statement is subject to revision; it rather means that the whole question is a mare's nest. (As for my "example" of an absolutely unrevisable truth, the very reference to "changing the meaning of 'true' and 'false'" in the sentence I quoted gives the show away; what I was claiming is that the minimal principle of contradiction is *analytic* of the "classical" concepts, *whether or not* those concepts have what Kant called "objective validity." I now think that "analyticity" (or "truth unless we change the meaning") is far too weak a reed to support any interesting notion of "a priori truth.")

But giving up talk of the a priori is not the same thing as abandoning the notion of conceptual truth. It means, rather, recognizing that even statements that we have a right to regard as conceptual truths might have to be given up, as the laws of Euclidean geometry had to be given up when we are talking about the space in which we are situated.

I referred a moment ago to Kant's notion of "objective validity." A large part of the project of *The Critique of Pure Reason* was to give a proof of the objective validity of our fundamental "categories." As Charles Travis has recently put it,[145] what I have been arguing ever since *The Analytic and the Synthetic* is that the search for a proof of objective validity of our fundamental concepts is misguided. There cannot be such a proof, and we have to live with the fact that our "categories" might turn out to need revision.

3. Quantum Mechanics Again

Living with the fact that we have no apodictic "proof of the objective validity of our categories" does not mean taking lightly the categories that we have, or moving quickly to change them (as I suggested we do in "Is Logic Empirical" (a.k.a. "The Logic of Quantum Mechanics"). I am not impressed by "paraconsistent logic," for example, because it does not do what the iterative conception of set (the conception of set embodied in Russell's theory of types and the corresponding hierarchy in Zermelo-type set theories) did, that is, provide a picture of the structure of the universe of sets, one that has proved immensely fruitful. (The stunning theorems of Gödel and Cohen could not have been proved without them.) All that paraconsistent logic does is apply a trick from relevance logic to "quarantine" contradictions, that is, to keep them from infecting the entire system with contradictions. (But this is by way of an aside.)

There are two ways to defeat the proposal that we give up what we take to be a conceptually necessary truth, namely, to show that the proposal runs into worse difficulties than the ones it purports to solve (this is what I did in the case of quantum logic in my "Reply to Michael Redhead"), or to show that the difficulties the proposal is meant to deal with can be plausibly overcome by less radical means. In the case of quantum mechanics, it is likely that this can be done. In fact, there at least two "live" approaches to doing this. But to explain what I have in mind, I need to describe the so far proposed "interpretations," ignoring the failed "quantum logical" one. Here is my list of the four kinds of possible interpretations:

(I) Interpretations in which there is a "collapse of the wave-function":

(Ia) *The Copenhagen interpretation.* The collapse is produced by something ("the observer") *external* to the physical system.

(Ib) *The Girardi-Rimini-Weber ("GRW") Interpretation.* The collapse is *spontaneous.* (An interesting modification suggested by Roger Penrose, but not yet worked out: the spontaneous collapse is produced by a cosmological constraint, thus connecting quantum mechanics and gravitational theory—IF it succeeds.)

(II) Interpretations in which there is *no* "collapse of the wave-function":

(IIa) *The "many-worlds" interpretation.*

(IIb) *The Bohm ("pilot wave") interpretation.*

A "collapse" interpretation is one according to which the state of the system abruptly changes in such a way as to became a state in which a quantity—say, the position of some macroscopic object—has a definite value (at least by macroscopic standards of "definiteness"). I mentioned the Copenhagen Interpretation in my list although, as already said, it is doubtful if it is an "interpretation" that a realist could accept, and it is objectionable on physical grounds as well, which is why it seems to be universally abandoned today. The physical grounds in question are (1) that the assumption that there has to be a "cut" between the measuring system and the quantum mechanical system assumes that quantum mechanics cannot be applied to the physical universe as a whole, but today there are many theorist who do contemplate superimposing whole space-times, as mentioned earlier. (2) The idea that measurement interactions must be described using classical physics and not quantum mechanics is simply false. Even if the "something external" mentioned in the table is not assumed to be a measuring instrument, these problems would not go away: if the whole space-time is the system, then there is literally nothing external, and if there is something external to the system, then it too must obey the laws of quantum mechanics, according to today's physics. (The idea that the "something external" is *consciousness* was mentioned by von Neumann and advocated by Eugene Wigner, but has been totally rejected by the physics community for decades. Unfortunately, it continues to be described as a part of quantum mechanics in the popular press, and by some scientifically uninformed theologians.)

The demise of the Copenhagen Interpretation does not, however, mean that the idea of a collapse can simply be discarded. In 1976, G.C. Ghirardi, A. Rimini, and T. Weber proposed that each particle has a *tiny* probability of *spontaneously* "collapsing" into a definite position state. For example, if the system consists of just one isolated hydrogen atom, one would have to wait, on the average, many thousands of years for it to "collapse" into a definite position state. *But*, as we all know, something like the table in front of me as I type these words consists of millions upon millions of particles. If there are many millions of particles, and they interact in an appropriate way, the object will, according to GRW theory, always have a definite position. (The "spontaneous collapse" idea has also been explored by Roger Penrose,[146] who believes that the collapses are connected with singularities in general relativistic space-time theory. In effect, the universe measures itself "from within" if a theory of this type is right.)

The "many-worlds" interpretation was originally proposed by Hugh Everett in 1957.[147] To explain the term "many-worlds," permit me to employ a more humane version of the Schrödinger's Cat thought experiment: in this version, a cat in an isolated laboratory (Sally's cat) is automatically fed if and only if a given atom in the laboratory has decayed. (Let the probability of this be ½.) On Everett's interpretation, this means that when Sally looks to see whether her cat has been fed or is hungry, the part of the wavefunction corresponding to the outcome "atom decayed/Sally's cat fed" corresponds to a physically real environment in which Sally observes a fed cat, and the part of the wavefunction corresponding to the outcome "atom didn't decay/Sally's cat hungry" corresponds to a physically real environment in which Sally observes a hungry cat.

The physical universe, in this ontology, does not "live" in $3 + 1$ dimensional spacetime, but in a Hilbert Space **H**. As the wave function y evolves according to the Schrödinger equation, it can happen that it takes the form of a superposition, say, ½ (Fed Cat & Sally seeing Fed Cat) + ½ (Hungry Cat & Sally seeing Hungry Cat); and this is the "ontological" reality corresponding to the fact that one Sally sees a fed cat and one Sally sees a hungry cat. Tim Maudlin rather scornfully describes this interpretation thus in a recent paper,[148] "What is the many-worlds theory but the claim that what we call 'observation' of a Schrödinger cat is not a process by which many people can come to agreement about the state of the cat, but rather a process by which many people all subdivide into many many people, largely unaware of each other's presence, with the illusion that everyone who looked 'saw the same thing'?"

An objection to the many-worlds theory that I develop in detail in "A Philosopher Looks at Quantum Mechanics (Again)" is that if all outcomes of all experiments are equally real, then assigning different probabilities to these outcomes is meaningless. (N.B.: *It is not normally the case, on the many-worlds interpretation, that the number of "equally real" branches or outcomes of a given quantum mechanical experiment in which a given event occurs is greater when the quantum mechanical "probability" of that outcome is larger.*[149])

People who hear my objection either agree at once, in which case they find the many-worlds interpretation incoherent (as I do), or they somehow think that it does not matter that all outcomes are equally real as long as we can assign real numbers to them that obey the axioms of probability theory, even if those numbers have lost all connection with *frequencies*.

Last but not least, there is the Bohm interpretation. The Bohm interpretation was first proposed in 1952, and rejected by me in "A Philosopher Looks at Quantum Mechanics" for reasons I retracted in "A Philosopher Looks at Quantum Mechanics (Again)."

It is certainly true that the Bohm theory implies certain "causal anomalies." But these are no reason for rejecting the theory, because we know that they really occur in nature. Bohm's theory implies nonlocality. Both Reichenbach and I worried about the question, "How come this Bohm "potential" (which we thought of as a force) does not get weaker with distance?" The answer, as we now know, is: "Because nonlocal correlations can appear over any distance." If we think of the "Bohm field" as *a mathematical description of nonlocality*, then we need no longer be bothered by the "causal anomaly."

Obviously, no one can claim that we have solved the problem of interpreting quantum mechanics in a "realist" way, but I still find reason to hope for an eventual solution, although much work needs to be done, especially in developing versions of the Bohm and GRW interpretations that will be compatible with relativity theory.

XXV. THE THEORY OF REFERENCE

On December 12, 1963, while I was still teaching at M.I.T., there was a meeting of the Boston Colloquium for the Philosophy of Science that turned out to be important in my philosophical life. The main speaker was J.J.C. Smart, who had become a close friend when he visited Harvard in (I believe) the spring of 1958. His paper was titled "Conflicting Views about Explanation,"[150] and the commentators were Wilfrid Sellars and myself. Sellars delivered an important paper, a major statement of his version of scientific realism,[151] and I delivered a short set of comments, with which I was soon very dissatisfied. My dissatisfaction with what I said in those comments, and my long reflections on that dissatisfaction, were what led me, about five years later, to propose the view that has become called "Semantic Externalism."

Smart's talk was not about his own philosophy, but about some new (at that time) ideas of Paul Feyerabend, and my comment was a criticism of those ideas (ideas which Sellars, more generously and more fairly than I, described as "impetuous, but challenging and illuminating"[152]). Feyerabend was present, and his reply to the comments is also published.[153]

My comment focused on what I described as Feyerabend's "identification of the *meaning* of a term with certain accepted *theory* containing the term," and I argued that we must reject that identification "if we are to talk about meaning, in the customary sense, at all." The meaning (in the customary sense) was supposed to be given, according to my comment, by "semantical rules." And it was my dissatisfaction with that claim that led me to "externalism."

I was dissatisfied because, try as I could, I could not come up with "semantical rules" that I was supposed to have implicit knowledge of *qua* speaker of English, and that fixed the meaning of the very word I had used as an example in the course of my remarks, the word "gold." I thought I recalled that Locke had claimed that "gold" is synonymous with "precious, incorruptible, yellow metal soluble in *aqua regia,*"[154] and I reflected that I had no idea what "*aqua regia*" *is*, and so that could not *possibly* be what I (or most other English speakers) *mean* by "gold." In "How Not to Talk about Meaning," I myself had remarked:

> Suppose, for example, that one asks a typical native speaker of English for the meaning of the word 'gold'. He is likely to give one a mass of empirical information about gold (that it is precious, normally yellow, incorruptible, etc.) in addition to the essential linguistic information that 'gold' is the name of a metal. Yet, if gold became 'cheap as dirt', or began to rust, or turned green, the meaning of the *word* 'gold' would not change. Only if we stopped using 'gold' as the name of a metal, or used it to name a different metal, would the primary meaning change. (I say "the primary meaning," because the *connotations* of 'gold' *do* depend on the facts that gold is normally yellow, precious, etc.).[155]

I even anticipated what I was to call "the linguistic division of labor" in "The Meaning of 'Meaning'" when I pointed out that

> One should notice, also, that one may know the meaning of the word 'gold' without knowing *how to tell* whether or not a given thing is gold. (Of course, someone must be able to *identify* gold; otherwise the word wouldn't be the name of a real metal; but it isn't true that only those people who are able to identify gold know the meaning of the word, or even that they know *more* of the meaning of the word. They simply know *more about gold*.)[156]

The problem I faced was this: if the meaning of the word *gold* is given by a battery of semantical rules, as I suggested in my comment on Smart's lecture, *what are those rules*? I had ruled out "'gold' is the name of a precious metal," "'gold' is the name of a yellow metal," indeed, everything except "'gold' is the name of a metal," in the passage I just quoted from

"How Not to Talk about Meaning," and clearly "'gold' is the name of a metal" is not sufficient as a description of the meaning of the word.

In 1967-68 (I believe in the spring semester) I taught "Philosophy of Language" at Harvard, and I discussed all this. But I did not only present the problem; I also presented a novel solution, the view that *the meaning of our words is not fixed by what is in our individual heads.* (I say a "new view" although I was later told that Saul Kripke had already entertained similar ideas when he was a member of Harvard's Society of Fellows [1963–1967]. I did not learn of Kripke's views until 1970, however, when news of his lectures at Princeton spread through the philosophical world.) On the view I proposed, the meaning of a "natural kind term" such as the word "gold" is partly fixed by the division of linguistic labor and partly by what I was later to call the shared "stereotype." The stereotype, that gold is yellow, precious, etc., is *not* analytic; it may well turn out to be wrong; but nevertheless the shared stereotype plays a role in stabilizing the use of "gold," and radical change in stereotype may be considered to be a "change of meaning," on the view that I proposed.

In the case of "gold," the linguistic division of labor is quite obvious, or, at least, obvious once pointed out; as I had said that evening in 1963 at the Boston Colloquium for the Philosophy of Science, "it isn't true that only those people who are able to identify gold know the meaning of the word, or even that they know *more* of the meaning of the word." Speakers who can identify gold—physicists, chemists, jewelers—rely on one another, and laymen rely on these experts. But what of the natural kind term "water"? We do not normally rely on experts to tell whether something is water (although in rare circumstances we may have to). I proposed that *the substance itself* helps fix the reference; that is to say, the agreement of the community on shared paradigms (any one of which *might* turn out "not to really be water") fixes the reference. (Something similar is also true in the case of the word "gold," but here it is not the average speaker who can reliably say which are the "paradigm" instances of the substance.) But the use of paradigms is not the whole story.

The other part of my story is the emergence of a tradition of scientific investigation, going back to ancient metallurgy (for which the question of telling how to tell whether a substance was really "pure" or not was of vital importance). We do not call any metal that superficially resembles gold "gold"—as the Greek ruler who asked Archimedes to determine whether his crown was "really gold" (or *chrysos*, in classical Greek) well knew. For that matter, we do not call any liquid that superficially resembles water "water" (it might, for example, be a mixture). What I said was that to be water, or gold, or some other natural kind, is to have *the same nature* as "this," where the "this" can be any one of the [majority of the] paradigms we point to, and "sameness of nature" is a scientific or protoscientific concept, not a metaphysical one. It is the world—the paradigms, and their natures, which it may take scientific research to discover—that ultimately fixes the reference of our natural kind terms.

I presented my account at the 1968 Summer Institute in Philosophy of Language in Seattle. (David Kaplan, who was present at those lectures, recently wrote me, "I remember your quickly disabusing me of the idea that the intension of a natural kind word (that which determines the extension in a possible world) is something we "grasp," as Carnap would have put it. It ain't in the head, as you put it. And almost as soon as you said it, it seemed right.") I also presented a single-lecture version of the theory at the University of Minnesota in 1969, and the first published version appeared in 1970, under the title "Is Semantics Possible."

At that time (1968–72), however, more and more of my time was committed to criticizing America's war in Vietnam. (I describe my political efforts and activities in that period in the next section.) In addition, I was still actively publishing papers and directing Ph.D. dissertations in mathematical logic. Also, I wrote and published a little book on philosophy of logic. I did publish "Is Semantics Possible" in 1970, but with all these other activities, I did not attempt to write a longer and more detailed account of my externalist theory of meaning until the end of 1972, when I wrote "The Meaning of 'Meaning.'" Although "The Meaning of 'Meaning'" is the version of my externalism that philosophers generally know best, my later paper "Meaning Holism" contains some improvements I regard as important, and I wish it were better known. But because "The Meaning of 'Meaning'" is so well known, I will not try to summarize it here. Instead, I will close the present section by mentioning some points that, it seems to me, are often misunderstood. Those are (1) the relation of "The Meaning of 'Meaning'" to my supposed metaphysical realism at the time. I say "supposed," because only one of the papers in the two volumes of my papers that I collected in 1975 actually defended industrial strength metaphysical realism, although all of them presupposed *scientific* realism. (The relation—and the *difference*—between these two will be the subject of a later section of this Intellectual Autobiography.) (2) The presuppositions of the "Twin Earth" thought experiment. (3) The supposed "scientism" in "The Meaning of 'Meaning.'"

1. The Relation of "The Meaning of 'Meaning'" to Metaphysical Realism

I have always been puzzled at the number of people who think of the "Meaning of 'Meaning'" as a metaphysically realist paper. In part this may be because I referred to Saul Kripke's notion of "metaphysical necessity" in that essay, although that is a notion that I never thought needed to be understood metaphysically, and which I later repudiated even under its non-metaphysical interpretation.[157] That is at least an intelligible reason. But a less sensible reason is that many people think that only metaphysical realists can be scientific realists, an error first committed, as far as I know, by Lenin in his attack on Machian positivism in *Materialism and Empirio-Criticism.* In any case, my own conception in 1968 (when I first taught externalism to my class in the Philosophy of Language), was that what I was proposing was what I called "a mild rational reconstruction" of just that "customary sense" of the notion of "meaning" that I had talked about in those comments at the Boston Colloquium for the Philosophy of Science in 1963. It may of course be that antirealist philosophers cannot give a satisfactory account of scientific talk, just as it may be the case that they cannot give a satisfactory account of talk about tables and chairs; but these are things that need to be *shown*, not simply assumed, by philosophers. In any case, I did not see "Is Semantics Possible" or "The Meaning of 'Meaning'" as presupposing any position on those difficult metaphysical questions.

2. The Presuppositions of the "Twin Earth" Thought Experiment

In the original "Twin Earth" story, Twin Earth "water" (the counterpart of our water—henceforth, "twater") is supposed to not be distinguishable from water by the chemical facts known in 1780 or thereabouts. *It was not supposed to behave identically with water in all possible chemical experiments*; it was simply not supposed to be distinguishable from Earth water by *typical* Twin Earth English ("Twinglish"?) speakers. Clearly, it would also not have been distinguishable from Earth water by typical Earth English speakers. But, as I pointed out in "Meaning Holism," *this last is not essential to my thought experiment.* Suppose, for example, that twater is actually a mixture of H_2O and forty percent grain alcohol, but that the taste buds of Twinglish speakers do not detect this (and their bodies "filter out" the alcohol before it reaches their brains). Suppose, in fact, twater tastes to Twinglish speakers just the way water tastes to us, the brain state of a Twinglish speaker who tastes twater, or talks or thinks about twater, is the same in relevant respects as that of an English speaker who tastes water, or talks or thinks about water. (Remember, that although there will be many differences in the behavior of water and of twater, we are considering only differences that are reasonably supposed to be known to every member of the linguistic community who counts as having mastered the linguistic item "water." Differences in normal *taste* are surely among these.) Then no

English speaker would feel the slightest temptation to say that "water" has the same meaning in English and in Twinglish, although the difference in meaning is not constituted by anything that is simply internal to the *brain state* of English/Twinglish speakers. The difference in meaning is not in the *brain*.

3. The Supposed "Scientism" in "The Meaning of 'Meaning'"

In "The Meaning of 'Meaning'," I did *not* claim that what is and is not water (for example) is simply decided by *science*. In fact, I wrote, "To be water....is to bear the relation same$_L$ [same liquid] to certain things. But what is the relation same$_L$? And I replied that "in one context, "water" may mean *chemically pure water*, while in another it may mean the stuff in Lake Michigan."

In "Meaning Holism" I went even further to distance myself from a "scientistic" reading of my externalism, when I wrote:

> In physics, 'water' means chemically pure water; in ordinary language, things are more complicated. On the one hand, 'water', in the ordinary sense, may have impurities; on the other hand, tea and coffee are not 'water'. What sort of or degree of departure from ideally "pure" taste, color, or odor disqualifies H_2O-cum-impurities from being 'water' in ordinary circumstances is interest-relative and context-sensitive. But this is not to say that 'water', in ordinary language, is an *operationally-defined* word, pure and simple.[158]

—And I ended the section by saying, "Ordinary language and scientific language are different but *interdependent*."

XXXVI. THE VIETNAM WAR

In his excellent essay (apart from one unfortunate inaccuracy concerning my philosophy of mathematics) in *American Philosophers, 1950–2000,* Lance Hickey writes,

> In the midst of this prodigious output of philosophical activity, Putnam was thrown into the controversy surrounding the Vietnam War. In 1963, while he was teaching at MIT, he organized one of the first faculty and student committees against the war. He was particularly outraged by David Halberstam's reporting, especially the claim that the U. S. was "defending" the peasants of South Vietnam from the Viet Cong by poisoning their rice crop. As the war

continued, Putnam's outrage intensified, and after moving to Harvard in 1965, he organized various campus protests, in conjunction with teaching courses on Marxism. He was the official faculty advisor to the Students for a Democratic Society, which was at that time the main anti-Vietnam War organization on campus, and eventually he became a member of the "Progressive Labor" faction, which espoused (in Putnam's words), an "idiosyncratic version of Marxism-Leninism." In time he became disillusioned with the group for what he perceived as the very same manipulative and exploitative measures that they were criticizing the U. S. for. While he broke with that line of thinking, he never abandoned the idea that philosophers have a social and political responsibility as well as an academic one. He has been outspoken on moral and political issues ever since, as some of his eloquent articles "How Not to Solve Ethical Questions" (1983) and "Education for Democracy" (1993) testify.[159]

Here I shall comment and expand upon what Hickey has written.

First, my outrage was *not* directed against David Halberstam, but against my government's action in poisoning the rice crop of the very peasants whose "hearts and minds" we were supposed to be trying to win over. For me and many others, David Halberstam was *the* journalist who opened our eyes to what was being done in our name. And there were more horrors to follow; the use of napalm bombs, the "free kill zones" which later covered much of the territory of South Vietnam, and which were designed to force the peasants to leave their plots and come to the cities, and much more. And while it is true that in 1963 I started a faculty/student committee at MIT to oppose America's actions in Vietnam, a more significant venture that I undertook, in concert with the microbiologist and Nobel laureate Salvador Luria, who was my colleague at MIT, as well as with faculty members at other universities in the Boston Area, was the creation of "BAFGOPI," the Boston Area Faculty Group on Public Issues, which raised money from professors all over the United States to put full page advertisements in the *New York Times* opposing the war. (Our first advertisement was headed "STOP THE BOMBING.")

In 1967, I also became involved with New England Resistance, the organization of young men who refused to be drafted for this unjust war. But as the war continued and intensified, I (and a number of the draft resisters as well), began to doubt the efficacy of "moral witness" against what we saw more and more as an "imperialist" war. By 1968 or 1969 my early Marxist upbringing had surfaced to the extent that, as Hickey describes, I joined "Progressive Labor," a step that was made easier for me by the fact that that faction did not pretend that any of the existing communist states, including the North Vietnamese, were really either socialist or democratic. The "Progressive Labor Party" did, however, hold that communism (and specifically Maoist communism) could be free of the faults of the so-called "actually existing socialist states." As Hickey says, I became completely disillusioned, and by the end of 1972 I had come to the conclusion that I would rather be governed by Nixon than by my own "comrades." I know that these are strong words, but my disgust and disappointment as I discovered that all of Progressive Labor's talk about being "democratic" was a complete sham still come back to me at times—they come back to me as I type these words, in fact. And the way the leaders of that faction talked about all of the leading liberals of the time and about rival socialist movements! "He should be shot," was a favorite expression, and I came to realize it was not just an "expression"—it was a symptom of a fixation, a fixation on the fantasy of a violent revolution in which all rival political leaders and intellectuals would indeed be killed. (And as I wrote in "How Not to Solve Ethical Problems," "What is wrong with the argument that 'it will take a revolution' to end injustice is that revolutions don't mean an end to injustice.") Marxism-Leninism, I came to realize, is not just an intellectual error, but a terrifying sickness of the soul.

XXXVII. "Internal Realism" and "Metaphysical Realism"

I resigned from the "Progressive Labor Party" in December 1972, after months of reflection and rethinking of my entire relation to Marxism and to communism. I decided to abandon political activism for the time being, apart from supporting Amnesty International, which Ruth Anna and I still do. The first fruit of that decision was "The Meaning of 'Meaning'" which I wrote that same month. I had been thinking about the issues for a long time, and evidently the text had been composing itself in my subconscious, because that paper flowed from my fingers via a new electric typewriter onto the paper as if it had been "there" waiting for a joyous release.

Although, as explained above, I did not think of "The Meaning of 'Meaning'" as presupposing any particular metaphysical position with regard to the question of the nature of the relation between linguistic representations and reality, in the years that followed I became more and more preoccupied with precisely that question, especially when I was writing *Meaning and the Moral Sciences*. That book ends with my presidential address to the Eastern Division of the American Philosophical Association in December, 1976, in which I defended a position I called "internal realism." (I expounded that position at greater length in my 1981 *Reason, Truth, and History*, the book that contains my thought experiment of imagining that we are all "brains in a vat," a thought experiment which was credited by Adam Gopnik in the May 19, 2003 issue of the *New Yorker* with inspiring the movie *The Matrix*.)

The central idea of internal realism was something I called "verificationist semantics." In my version,[160] truth was identified with verifiability under epistemically ideal conditions.[161] I conceded that, for a variety of reasons, we may be unable to *attain* epistemically ideal conditions with respect to some of our inquiries; thus, according to this theory, *truth may outrun what we can as a matter of fact verify*. (But as I later came to see, in admitting that philosophical realists are right about this, I reinstated just the problem of "access" to the real things that we refer to that "internal realism" was designed to block! If there is a problem as to how, without postulating "noetic rays," or something else magical, we can have access to external things, there is an equal problem as to how we can have referential access to "sufficiently good epistemic conditions.") On my "internal realist" picture, which differed in this respect from Dummett's "antirealist" one, the *world* was allowed to determine whether I am in a sufficiently good epistemic situation or only *seem* to myself to be in one—thus retaining an essential idea from commonsense realism—but the conception of our epistemic situation was the traditional "Cartesian" one, on which our sensations are an interface "between" us and the "external objects." By the time (14 years later!) of the Gifford Conference on my philosophy at the University of St. Andrews in 1990, I had decided that this just would not do.

The alternative was to return to the Cartesian predicament itself and see if it could be avoided. At that time I had begun to think that Austin's attack on the conception of our experiences as "sense-data" which somehow are directly perceived, while the "external objects" are only "indirectly perceived" was right. In addition, I had begun to read William James, and was impressed by his insistence that what he called "natural realism" could be defended. In sum, I began to think that the problem of "access" to external objects that I had elaborated in "Realism and Reason" and "Models and Reality" (with the aid of devices from model theory) was a replay of the older problem of epistemological dualism, even if the dualism was no longer a dualism of mental substance and physical substance, but one of brain states and everything outside the head. I came to believe, and still believe today, that "natural realism" with respect to perception can indeed be defended, and that with natural realism with respect to perception back in place the fear (or the bugaboo) that we may have no "access" to reality outside our heads can be dismissed as a bad dream.

In fact, on my "internal realist" picture it is not only our experiences (conceived of as "sense data") that are a screen *between* us and the world; our "conceptual schemes" were likewise conceived of as a screen. And the two screens were related: our ways of conceptualizing, our language games, were seen by me as controlled by "operational constraints" which ultimately reduce to our sense data. And to give up "internal realism" and return to "natural realism," or to a reasoned philosophical defense of natural realism, involves giving up of thinking of either experiences *or* concepts as "between" us and external realities. Or so I argued in my Dewey Lectures, and so I still believe.

For the benefit of readers who are familiar with John McDowell's great book *Mind and World,*[162] let me add that the problem with *Reason, Truth and History* was not that I failed to realize that experiences are *conceptualized.* On the contrary, even then, in 1981, I emphasized that they are conceptualized. However, unlike McDowell, I would limit this to what Kantians call "apperceptions," that is, experiences that are recognitions that something is the case. The problem was that I failed to see that one could think of both experiences and concepts as forms of *openness to the world,* to use McDowell's slang. In particular, I should not have seen us as "making up" the world, not even with the world's help. I should have seen us as interacting with the world in ways that permit aspects of it to reveal themselves to us. Of course we need to invent concepts to do that. There is plenty of constructive activity here. But we do not construct reality itself.

In "Realism and Reason" and subsequently I also used the term "metaphysical realism." I now think that the *way* I used it was unfortunate. It was unfortunate even though I carefully explained just how I was using the term, because there is a very natural understanding of the phrase "metaphysical realism" in which it refers to a broad family of positions, and not just to the *one* position I used it to refer to. Although I was usually impatient with critics who said "But you haven't refuted *my* form of metaphysical realism," when "their" form was not the one I was talking about, I now sympathize with them. In effect I *was* saying that by refuting the one philosophical view I called by that name I was *ipso facto* refuting anything that deserved to be called "metaphysical realism," and that was not something I had shown.

As I explained "metaphysical realism" in that period, what it came to was precisely the denial of the possibility of conceptual relativity. A "metaphysical realist" in my sense believed that a given thing or system of things can be described in exactly one way, if the description is supposed to be complete and correct, and that way is supposed to fix exactly one "ontology" and one "ideology" in Quine's sense of those words, that is, exactly one domain of individuals and one domain of predicates of those individuals. Thus it cannot be a matter of convention, as I argued that it is in *The Many Faces of Realism,* whether there are such individuals as mereological sums; either the "true" ontology includes mereological sums or it does not. And it cannot be a matter of convention, as I have also argued that it is, whether spacetime points are individuals or mere limits.

Today I would say that this is indeed *one* form, perhaps even the most common form that metaphysical realism can take. But if we understand "metaphysical realist" more broadly, as applying to any philosopher who rejects all forms of verificationism and all talk of our "making" the world, then I believe it is perfectly possible to be a metaphysical realist in *that* sense and to accept the phenomenon I am calling "conceptual relativity."

XXXVIII. CONCEPTUAL RELATIVITY

I am aware that the defense of "conceptual relativity" has been a controversial feature of my work. Indeed, this notion has often been seen as in itself an antirealist one, which is a reason that some commentators continue to describe me as an "internal realist," although I rejected the "verificationist semantics" which was the main idea of "internal realism" in 1990. For that reason, I want to briefly explain what conceptual relativity actually amounts to.

First, a story. I taught for a quarter at the University of Washington in 2002, and one day when I stopped for a cup of coffee at one of the little cafeterias on the campus I struck up a conversation with Matt Strassler, a physicist who was there to give a lecture. We started talking about quantum mechanics, and I became quite excited as I realized that he was describing a phenomenon I had written about for a long time under the name "conceptual relativity." Of course, he did not call it that (physicists call it "duality"), nor did he know of my writing, and I did not know the papers he referred to, although he was kind enough to send me a list. In brief, what he told me is that what an analytic philosopher would probably call the "ontology" of a conceptual scheme (specifically, a quantum mechanical theory of a particular system) is not regarded as, so to speak, the load-bearing aspect of the scheme, because such a scheme has many different "representations" (Strassler's term), which are regarded as perfectly equivalent. For example, these representations may differ in how many dimensions they treat space (or spacetime) as having and over whether the particles in the system are or are not bosons! My own notion of "conceptual relativity" (which I originally called "cognitive equivalence") is beautifully illustrated by the case Strassler described. The different "representations" are perfectly intertranslatable; it is just that the translations do not preserve "ontology."

What do they preserve? Well, they do not merely preserve macro-observables. They also preserve *explanations*. An explanation of a phenomenon goes over into another perfectly good explanation of the same phenomenon under these translations.

But who is to say what is a phenomenon? And who is to say what is a perfectly good explanation? My answer has always been: *physicists* are; not linguists and not philosophers.

Of course, in my writing I have sought for simple examples, and the simplest, one which is now well known, involves mereological sums. The question, "are there really mereological sums," is, in my view, a pseudo-question. Although it is obvious that we could not do with only particles (in, for example, classical physics), it does not follow that we have to accept all the axioms/theorems of mereology, including the statement that for every X and Y there is a smallest object having both X and Y as parts. We can perfectly well do classical physics using sets rather than mereological sums, and we need the axioms of set theory anyway. Given that *all* scientific and nonscientific discourse can be formulated perfectly successfully with and without the "assumption" of mereological sums, their "existence" is, in my view, best regarded as a matter of convention. The positivists got that one right (although for the wrong reasons). Similarly, I regard the question as to whether *points* (in space or in spacetime) are real "individuals" or simply logical constructs as a pseudoquestion.

I spoke of the existence of mereological sums as a matter of convention. To be more precise: saying that there are seven objects on a certain table, namely three billiard balls and four additional mereological sums of billiard balls, is a matter of fact *as opposed to saying* that there are three such objects [the second statement is true if there are two billiard balls on the table], while saying that there are seven mereological sums that can be formed of the objects on that table *as opposed to saying* that there are three individual objects on the table and eight *sets* of those objects [N.B. mereological sums are not sets, and there is an empty set but no empty object] is a matter of convention. The fact that we say X rather than Y may be a matter of convention, in whole or in part, while the fact that we say X rather than Z is not at all conventional.

XXXIX. The Compatibility of Conceptual Relativity with Realism

So how *should* realists who recognize the existence of cases of genuine conceptual relativity formulate their realism? Imagine a situation in which there are exactly three billiard balls on a certain table and no other objects (i.e. the atoms, etc., of which the billiard balls consist do not count as "objects" in that context). Consider the two descriptions, "There are only seven objects on that table: three billiard balls, and four mereological sums containing more than one billiard ball" and "There are only three objects on the table, but there are seven *sets* of individuals that can be formed of those objects." What it means to be a *realist who recognizes conceptual relativity* with respect to *this* case is to believe that there is an aspect of reality which is independent of what we think at the moment (although we could, of course, change it by adding or subtracting objects from the table), which is *correctly describable either way.*

The example is artificial because no one except philosophers, to my knowledge, *ever* talks about "mereological sums." But in mathematical physics conceptual relativity is a ubiquitous phenomenon, and there the correct attitude is the same (or so I maintain). To take an example from a paper with the title "Bosonization as Duality" that appeared in *Nuclear Physics* B some years ago, there are quantum mechanical schemes some of whose representations depict the particles in a system as bosons while others depict them as fermions. As their use of the term "representations" indicates, real live physicists—not philosophers with any particular philosophical axe to grind—do not regard this as a case of ignorance. In their view, the "bosons" and "fermions" are simply artifacts of the representation used. But the system is mind-independently real, for all that, and each of its states is a mind independently real condition, that can be represented in each of these different ways. And that is exactly the conclusion I advocate.

To accept that these descriptions are both answerable to the very same aspect of reality, that they are "equivalent descriptions" in that sense, is to be a metaphysical realist without capital letters, a realist in one's "metaphysics," but not a "metaphysical realist" in the technical sense I gave to that phrase in "Realism and Reason" and other publications. And if I have long repented of having once said that "the mind and the world make up the mind and the world," that is because what we actually make up is not the world, but language games, concepts, uses, conceptual schemes. To confuse making up the *notion* of a boson, which is something the scientific community did over time, with making up real quantum mechanical systems is to slide into idealism. And that is a bad thing to slide into.

XL. A Caution

It is important not to confuse conceptual relativity with the very different phenomenon of conceptual pluralism. The reader may have noticed that all my examples of conceptual relativity come from science, which is where the phenomenon seems to occur. At one time, I confused it with simple conceptual pluralism, and that led me to mistakenly give the fact that I can (depending on my interests) describe the contents of a room *either* by saying that the room contains a table and two chairs *or* by saying it contains such and such fields and particles, as an example of conceptual relativity. I do indeed deny that the world can be completely described in the language game of theoretical physics; not because there are regions in which physics is *false,* but because, to use Aristotelian language, the world has many levels of form, and there is no realistic possibility of reducing them all to the level of fundamental physics.[163] For example, a true description of one aspect of reality is to say that Immanuel Kant wrote some passages in *The Critique of Pure Reason* that are difficult to interpret, but that statement cannot be "translated" into the language of physics in any reasonable sense of "translated." And it is a true description of another aspect of reality to say that Andrew Wiles and Richard Taylor gave a correct proof of Fermat's Last Theorem, and that statement too cannot be translated into the language of *physics*. And it is a true description of a third aspect of reality to say that the reason I took a certain route to Harvard Square on a certain day was that I mistakenly believed that it would be quicker. And both of the above descriptions of the room could well be correct. *But* the fact that these descriptions do not belong to "schemes" which can be systematically translated into each other, means that they are *not* "equivalent" in the technical sense of mutually "relatively interpretable." For that reason they illustrate *conceptual pluralism* but not "conceptual relativity" in my technical sense.[164]

XLI. Discovering Judaism

Prior to 1975, my philosophical interests did not include religion. But 1975 was the year that the older of my two sons announced that he wanted to have a Bar Mitzvah! Although I had never belonged to a Jewish congregation, I *had* once given a Friday evening talk about the Vietnam war and my reasons for opposing it at the Harvard Hillel Foundation, and I had a powerful and favorable impression of the Rabbi who invited me to give it, and who participated in the discussion that followed. Rabbi Ben-Zion Gold was not only the director of the Harvard Hillel Foundation in those years, he was also the founder and spiritual advisor of one of the congregations that met for worship on the Jewish Sabbath. My memory is that there were three Hillel congregations in all, at that time (today there are more): an Orthodox congregation, a Reform congregation, and the one that Rabbi Gold had founded some decades previously, which called itself then and continues to call itself today simply "Worship and Study" (it uses the prayer book of the Conservative movement). So when I had to find a place for my son to have his Bar Mitzvah, I found it natural to go and talk to Rabbi Gold about the possibility of Samuel having the ceremony in the Worship and Study congregation. We agreed that my wife and I would come to services with Samuel for a year, and that he would study with Richard Claman, a philosophy major whom I knew, as it happened, to prepare for the ceremony. Long before the year was over, the Jewish service and Jewish prayers had become an essential part of our lives, and Rabbi Gold continues to be our teacher and friend to this day.

That there was and continues to be tension between the way I think when I "do philosophy" and the way I think when I view the world religiously is obvious, although, like Lessing,[165] I would not want it to be otherwise. In the course of the years, I have tried to connect my religious and my philosophical side by publishing a number of papers on religious themes, and my most recent book (as of this writing) is about (what I describe as) "3¼" Jewish philosophers (Buber, Rosenzweig, Levinas, and Wittgenstein). I can best describe the tension I speak of, and my present response to it, by quoting what I wrote in the introduction to that book:

> Wittgenstein wrote that "I am not a religious man: but I cannot help seeing every problem from a religious point of view."[166] For Wittgenstein, the problem was to combat simplistic ideas of what is to be religious, both on the part of anti-religious people and on the part of religious people, and (I believe) to get us to see the spiritual value that he thought was common to all religions. But he did not face my problem, which was to reflect on a religious commitment that I had made. *Renewing Philosophy* continued to defer addressing it. I had come to accept that I could have two different 'parts of myself,' a religious part and a purely philosophical part, but I had not truly reconciled them. Some may feel I still haven't reconciled them—in a conversation I recently had with an old friend, I described my current religious standpoint as "somewhere between John Dewey in *A Common Faith* and Martin Buber." I am still a religious person, and I am still a naturalistic philosopher (which, by the way, the three philosophers I describe in this little book were not). A naturalistic philosopher, but not a reductionist. Physics indeed describes the properties of matter in motion, but reductive naturalists forget that the world has many levels of form, including the level of morally significant human action, and the idea that all of these can be reduced to the level of physics I believe to be a fantasy. And, like the classic pragmatists, I do not see reality as morally indifferent: reality, as Dewey saw, *makes demands* on us. Values may be created by human beings and human cultures, but I see them as made in response to demands that we do not create. It is reality that determines whether our responses are adequate or inadequate. Similarly, my friend Gordon Kaufman may be right in saying that "the available God" is a human construct,[167] but I am sure he would agree that we construct our images of God in response to demands that we do not create, and that it is not up to us whether our responses are adequate or inadequate.

XLII. "Changing My Mind"

I revert now to my academic life.

A close friend recently told me that, in writing this autobiography, I should remember that "what people really want to know is how you view the accusation that "'you keep changing your mind.'" Well, Rudolf Carnap whose valuable influence on me at the beginning of my career I have described, often cited the fact that philosophical arguments are interminable as a reason for abandoning the subject, and turning to something he called "logic of science." Fortunately for us, he never did abandon the subject—he only thought he did. My own reaction to the history of philosophy is almost the opposite of Carnap's (official) reaction. If philosophical discussion is "interminable," that seems to me to be a good thing, not a bad one. After all, there are great questions in politics, in art, in spiritual life, and not only in academic philosophy, that by their very nature will always arise again and again, though in different forms (indeed, many of these can rightly be called "philosophical," even if they are marginalized or ignored in philosophy courses). The supposition that if philosophy cannot "become scientific" it must be "nonsense" is the bad legacy of positivism. To give up philosophy, or any part of it (including "metaphysics") would be like giving up serious political thinking or art or ethics or spiritual life. It would be a deep injury to the human spirit.

This is, in essence, my answer to the question about why I "change my mind" in philosophy. Reexamining questions, arguments, provisional conclusions, and sometimes whole world views is what philosophical life is all about. If there is something I hope will result from the effort of thinking about my philosophical life as a whole, and trying to describe what I found in these pages, it is that some young person will be inspired by them to devote her or his life to precisely those activities.

But I do not want the extent to which I "change my mind" to be exaggerated, as it often is, either. I want to point out that over the years I have only rejected the main ideas of *three* of the nineteen papers in *Mathematics, Matter and Method*, namely chapter 2, which defended a Russellian "if-thenist" position in philosophy of mathematics, and chapters 9 and 10, which dealt with quantum logic. Similarly, I only rejected the main idea of *four* of the twenty-two papers in *Mind, Language and Reality*, namely chapter 3, which is one of the few places in those two volumes where I defended just the sort of "metaphysical realism" that I later criticized, and chapters 18, 20, and 21, which proposed computer-program-functionalism in the philosophy of mind. Of course, there are individual arguments in all of my papers I would now like to improve, and formulations I now regard as needing qualification, but at no time did I repudiate them. And yet those volumes are often supposed to represent precisely a "metaphysical realist" period in my development that I repudiated! Although a confusion of this kind never seems to disappear from the literature, let me repeat and emphasize: I have *always* regarded myself as a scientific realist, though of course not *only* a scientific realist, as the introduction to the first of those volumes made clear. (However, in "Why Reason Can't Be Naturalized"—the essay I am truly unhappy about—I did in one place write "scientific realism" when what I meant to attack was "reductive physicalism"!)

My advocacy of "internal realism" in December 1976 (when I gave my lecture "Realism and Reason" to the American Philosophical Association") *did*, however, represent a sharp change in my philosophical outlook, and it was correctly perceived as such. The change back from "internal realism" to a more realist outlook, in contrast, took place more gradually, and is continuing to take place as I continue to work out just what I want to say about realism and the related questions of the proper account of truth and reference.

My interest in Dewey and in the later Wittgenstein did *not* mark a major change, or a "conversion," however, either to becoming a card-carrying pragmatist or to becoming a card-carrying "Wittgensteinian." I did, I admit, occasionally describe myself as a "pragmatist," but what makes me say I am not a "card-carrying" one is that I have *never* agreed with the several pragmatist "theories of truth" nor with the several grand metaphysical theories that James, Dewey, and Peirce proposed, although I certainly learned a great deal from reading them and from giving courses and seminars on their work. Similarly, I have learned a great deal from studying Wittgenstein's philosophy, but what makes me say that I am not a "card-carrying" Wittgensteinian is that, while I regard it as important to distinguish sense from nonsense in philosophy, I do not believe that that distinction is a "linguistic" or "grammatical" one. Thus, although I agree with Conant and the other "new Wittgensteinians" on the Interpretation of Wittgenstein's philosophy, that does not mean that I agree with a central aspect of that philosophy so interpreted. According to their interpretation, to say a philosophical view is nonsense is to say it is *literally* devoid of sense, or that the philosopher who advances that view is equivocating between incompatible senses without settling on either, or something of that kind. Like the "Baker & Hacker" view that the "New Wittgensteinians" oppose, this makes "nonsense" a term of *linguistic* criticism.

What does and what does not make sense in philosophy is a philosophical question, not a linguistic one. But in spite of these disagreements, I do feel a good deal of sympathy with the *impulses* the pragmatists and Wittgenstein represent in their different ways, as *Renewing Philosophy* and *Pragmatism: An Open Question* tried to make clear.

Although the 1980s were, as I recounted above, the last years of my "internal realist" period, not all the books and articles I published in those years actually presupposed "verificationist semantics," and in *Representation and Reality* and *The Many Faces of Realism* it is either not mentioned at all or played down. On the other hand, at least one of the articles I published in that decade, "Why Reason Can't Be Naturalized" is, in my present view, very badly marred by its presence. (That is an essay that makes me not just disagree but actually blush with embarrassment when I reread it.) As I explained, my purpose in it was to combat various attempts by materialists to reduce the fundamental notions of the theory of knowledge, for example, the notions of a belief's being *justified* or *rationally acceptable* to nonintentional and nonnormative notions. The attempts I examined included "evolutionary epistemology," "reliabilism," "cultural relativism" and "cultural imperialism" (both of which I attributed to Rorty), and "Quinian positivism," and my criticisms of those positions, while they include *some* arguments I would still use today, depended at a number of points on "verificationist semantics." But the main reason I blush at that essay is that in it I simply *gave* the word "naturalism" to reductive materialists instead of insisting that one can be a naturalist *sans phrase* without seeing any need to reduce the intentional to the nonintentional or the normative to the nonnormative.

XLIII. In the 1990s

The change from "internal realism" in both my self-conception and in the way I present myself when I write and lecture on philosophy came about very gradually, beginning with a visit to the University of St Andrews in the fall of 1990. I had been invited to give the Gifford Lectures, and those lectures were immediately followed by the "Gifford Conference" on my philosophy to which I referred earlier. In the Gifford Lectures themselves (published as *Renewing Philosophy*), I did not mention "verificationist semantics" or the realism/antirealism issue" (however, as already mentioned, in my reply to Simon Blackburn's paper at the Gifford Conference, I explicitly renounced it). What I did instead was to reflect on the current state of philosophy.

The first four lectures discussed currently influential attempts to reduce semantic notions not just to naturalistic notions, but explicitly to nonsemantic and nonnormative notions: the project of artificial intelligence, evolutionary accounts of representation, and Jerry Fodor's current (as of 1990) attempt to define reference using the notion "cause" plus counterfactuals. In the fifth lecture, I examined Bernard Williams's notion of an "absolute conception of the world" as the best attempt at a justification of the idea that the normative and intentional notions *must* be so reducible.

I also argued that relativism is an unsatisfactory alternative to the scientism that I saw as (unfortunately) fashionable among analytic metaphysicians. My examples of this alternative were the writings of Richard Rorty, Nelson Goodman, and Jacques Derrida, and I argued that there is a common idea underlying the errors of scientism and relativism, namely the denial of the *normative* element in cognition. Thus there was considerable overlap, as far as both my "targets" and my conclusions were concerned, with "Why Reason Can't Be Naturalized," but this time *none* of my arguments appealed to "verificationist semantics"!

In the last three Gifford lectures I presented almost wholly sympathetic interpretations of Wittgenstein (on religious belief) and Dewey (on the connections between the theory of inquiry and democratic theory). Although I take Wittgenstein at his word when he says he is not a believer, I see him as a naturalistic philosopher who appreciates religious forms of life in all their complexity. Throughout the 1990s, in fact, and especially in the series of lectures published as *Pragmatism: An Open Question,* I continued to publish lectures and essays about Wittgenstein, in which I praised his combination of nonreductive naturalism and antifoundationalism, and also stress the idea that, as he once put it, "Words only have meaning in the stream of life."[168] These aspects of his thought are valuable in themselves and also consonant with what I see as the best insights of the classical pragmatists, C. S. Peirce, William James, and John Dewey. I subsequently returned several times to interpreting Dewey's ideas (particularly on the connections between ethics, democratic theory, and what he called the "logic of inquiry"). The heart of my interpretation can be found in my 1994 "Pragmatism and Moral Objectivity." (Concerning that paper, Robert Westbrook has remarked that what I did was to put together pieces that are genuinely in Dewey in a way Dewey would have agreed with, but that the argument was never explicitly stated by Dewey himself in the way I gave it.[169] That is correct, and I am delighted that as fine a Dewey scholar as Westbrook says that Dewey would have agreed with what I wrote.) I also agree with Charles Travis's interpretation of Wittgenstein's later philosophy,[170] which employs Travis's own idea of "context-sensitive semantics," an idea which influenced much of what I wrote in *The Threefold Cord: Mind, Body, and World* and after.

Renewing Philosophy received fine responses in the form of reviews of the kind every philosopher hopes for (because they mingle praise with criticisms worth thinking about) from Alex Burri, Robert Brandom, and William Alston.[171] All three reviews, however, regretted that I chose to discuss the ways in which philosophy needed to change by indirection, by criticizing some philosophers and praising others, and did not go on to present a new philosophy of my own. The criticism is firmly stated by Alston in the last paragraph of his review:

> So the way to renew philosophy is to avoid naturalistic reconstructions of this or that, avoid fact-value dichotomies, steer clear of relativism and deconstructionism, and instead to emulate Wittgenstein and Dewey at their best. In

view of the fact that explicit philosophical manifestos from the seventeenth century to the present have been conspicuously unsuccessful in redirecting philosophical activity, one would be hard pressed to condemn Putnam for choosing to work for renewal by example rather than by pronouncement. But one may still wish that he had done a bit more to explicitly draw the morals from his case studies.[172]

To this my reply is that the morals *are* just about what Alston says they are, with one change: instead of "avoid naturalistic reconstructions of this and that," I would write "avoid scientistic attempts to 'reduce' this and that to the non-normative and non-intentional." But if I had gone on in those lectures to describe my own accounts of the right sort of realism or the right view of truth, the moral would inevitably have been taken to be that "the way to renew philosophy is to adopt Hilary Putnam's philosophy," and that is just the impression I wanted to avoid.

However, in the Dewey Lectures that I delivered at Columbia University in 1994 and in the Royce Lectures that I gave at Brown University in 1996 I did attempt to give my own solutions to those problems. The solutions I proposed, and would still [2014] in part defend, involved two main elements: (1) a return to "natural realism" in the philosophy of perception, and (2) a disquotationalist account of truth, which I also saw as a return to natural realism, natural realism with respect to the nature of truth. Some people call that a "deflationist" account, although I myself used the term "deflationist" for a view I *opposed* in *The Threefold Cord*. (Today I prefer to avoid the terms "disquotationalist" and "deflationist" because of the confusion as to just what views they denote, and to say that on my view "true" belongs to the family of words to which the logical constants belong, and not to the family of descriptive words.) I will now say something about each of these elements.

XLIV. "Natural Realism"

I have already related how, partly under the influence of John McDowell's *Mind and World*, I focused in the Dewey Lectures on the need to avoid thinking of either perceptual experiences or thoughts as a kind of interface (or a "screen") *between* us and the world. Today, part of the position I argued for has become almost an orthodoxy among philosophers of mind, namely that what we are aware of in normal veridical perception of the objects in our surroundings (say, of a bunch of red roses) is not mental objects or qualia but the external objects (the red roses) themselves. The picture of our minds as looking at an "inner movie screen" is decidedly out of favor.

Almost all philosophers of perception want to go back to "naïve realism" (the term that seems to be in favor at the moment, for what I called "natural realism") at least in part. But going back to natural realism is certainly more complicated than I made it seem in *The Threefold Cord*. One sign of the complexity of the issues involved is that in addition to the positions I discussed in the Dewey and Royce Lectures (the two series of lectures I collected in *The Threefold Cord*), namely the traditional sense data theory and "disjunctivism," there are today "phenomenists" and "representationalists" (aka "intentionalists"), and every one of these schools has subschools that differ on important issues. In addition, most (though not all) of these philosophers, including myself, are "wide functionalists," that is, they conceive of our successful perceptions as exercises of world-involving functional states, though not in general as *computational* states. (This last fact is connected, of course, with the abandonment of the picture of a perception as a matter of scanning an internal "movie screen," and with the fact that all [or, let us say for safety, almost all] of these philosophers claim to do justice to what was right in "naïve realism.")

So it is not surprising that when I reread *The Threefold Cord* now, I find myself pondering questions I did not face in 1994 and also raising problems with two of the arguments I gave in the lectures it contains. The questions I have in mind have to do with both the "what it feels like" aspect of perception (what is often referred to in the literature as the "phenomenal character" problem), and with the relation between phenomenal character and the representational character of perception. These are topics on which I am working at the present time.

The two arguments in *The Threefold Cord* that I now see problems with are both arguments against the possibility of identifying "appearances" with brain states or events. To explain the problems, I need to distinguish two senses of the word "appearance."

In one sense, an appearance is a property of what is perceived: we say the red roses "have a certain appearance," that is to say, they have the relational property of looking a particular way to a particular person when viewed under particular circumstances. In that sense of "appearance" it is trivial that appearances are not brain states; properties of roses, including properties that depend on a certain transaction between an organism and the roses, are not properties of brains, *period*. Some of what I wrote in *The Threefold Cord* was about appearances in that sense. But when I raised the question, whether appearances are identical with brain states, I was obviously thinking of "appearances" as identified simply by their phenomenal character, simply as "sensations," and not as relational properties of things. And I offered two arguments against the idea that appearances, in that "subjective" sense, could be identical with brain states.

One argument (128–32) was that "appearances," in that sense, are identified by subjective indistinguishability, and indistinguishability is not *transitive*. The problem I now see with that argument is that all it really shows is that there is no *precise* set of brain states with which a given sensation is identical, but if *that* fact were enough to rule out an identity theory, the theory that *light is electromagnetic radiation of certain wavelengths* would also be ruled out, because the boundary between "light" and other sorts of radiation is vague. There are what we might call "vague-boundary identities," and many of our best physical theories employ them, as the electromagnetic theory of light illustrates. The fact that the boundaries between one "appearance" and the next are vague does rule out the old idea that appearances have all and only the properties they *seem* to have (*esse est percipi*), as I argued in my Dewey Lectures, but if we are considering a psychophysical identity theory, we must have already discarded *that* principle anyway.

The other argument (30–38) was that we can only identify a phenomenon that belongs to one domain (say, the domain of optical phenomena) with a phenomenon that belongs to another domain, say, the domain of microphysical phenomena, if phenomena in the former domain obey *laws* that we are able to formulate, at least approximately, and to show that those laws (to the extent that they are accurate) are derivable from the laws of the putative reducing domain with the aid of the proposed "theoretical identifications." Although this picture of theoretical identification does fit the classic case of the reduction of optics to electromagnetic theory, and a very small number of similar cases in physics, it now seems to me that to insist that *all* theoretical identifications must satisfy such strong requirements is unreasonable. Very often, I believe, a scientist legitimately conjectures that one sort of phenomenon may be reducible to another without knowing precise laws that the phenomenon in question obeys. If such a proposed identification provides us with an attractive unification of our knowledge, it may well be accepted as an "inference to the best explanation."

In particular, I believe that some of the arguments that Ned Block has offered make it plausible that sensations may be identical with brain states/events.[173] That is one of the issues I am now thinking about. But, as Block himself observes, even if that is the case, it does not mean that we have to go back to the picture of our perceptual experiences as simply pictures on an "inner movie screen," because their phenomenal character is only part of the story; perceptual experiences also have representational aspects, and, as already mentioned, there is a deep question as to the relation between phenomenal character and representational character that I am now thinking about.

So, does all this mean that "I am changing my mind again"? If constantly rethinking one's philosophical arguments and commitments is "changing one's mind," then I hope I never stop "changing my mind." To my way of thinking, that is what philosophy at its best is all about. But if the question is do I anticipate that the outcome will be a radical change in my views of the kind represented by my turn to "internal realism" in 1976, then the answer has to be "no." What I hope for, as I think all serious philosophers of perception today hope, is a satisfactory synthesis of a philosophically satisfactory form of "naïve realism," psychological findings, and neurological findings.

XLV. Truth and "Disquotation"

I said above that the second element in the path to a philosophical defense of "natural realism" that I proposed in my Dewey Lectures was a "disquotational account of truth." To explain this, I shall briefly describe a family of (twentieth-century) theories of truth. This family is generally referred to by the term I just used, "disquotational" accounts of truth, but I argued in the Dewey Lectures that there are at least three very different versions of "disquotation": a Fregean version; a "deflationary" version, represented by Carnap[174]; and the version I defend (and attributed to the later Wittgenstein).

What these accounts share is the stress they lay on what Michael Dummett calls Frege's "Equivalence Principle" (an obvious anticipation of Tarski's "Convention T"),[175] namely that to state or judge that it is true that snow is white or that it is true that murder is wrong or that it is true that two is the only even prime (or whatever the example might be) is equivalent to judging, respectively, that snow is white or that murder is wrong or that two is the only even prime. If one assumes that judging that it is true that snow is white (etc.), is the same as judging that the *sentence* (in what Tarski called the "object language") "Snow is white" is true—this is one of the issues that distinguished Tarski from Frege—then one may express the Equivalence Principle by writing (with Tarski):

(T) "Snow is white" is true if and only if snow is white.

When I say that all versions of disquotationalism "lay stress" upon some version of the Equivalence Principle, what I mean is the following:

(1) Disquotationalists hold that when "true" is applied to a statement S that is explicitly given, the word is *eliminable*. In certain places, for example, Frege appears to hold that a metastatement like "It is true that snow is white" and the corresponding object statement "Snow is white" express one and the same judgment. If we used "true" only in sentences of the form: "S is true," where S is the quotation of a sentence, or in sentences of the form, "It is true that p," where p is a sentence, then the word would be *unnecessary*.

(2) The reason we need "true" and its synonyms in our languages is that we need to be able to use "true" in sentences of the form "x is true" where "x" is a *variable of quantification* and not, say, a sentence in quotation marks. For example, if I say, "At least one of the sentences John wrote on page 12 is true" [in Predicate Calculus notation: *(Ex)(x is written by John on page 12 & x is true)*], then I can "eliminate" the word "true" *if and only if* I know what sentences John wrote on page 12. That is, if I know that the only sentences John wrote on page 12 are "Snow is white," "Murder is wrong," and "Two is the only even prime," then I know that this statement has the same truth-value as: "John wrote 'Snow is white' on page 12, and snow is white, or John wrote 'Murder is wrong' on page 12, and murder is wrong, or John wrote 'Two is the only even prime' on page 12, and two is the only even prime, and these are the only sentences John wrote on page 12," and this longish sentence does not contain the word "true." But if I do not know *what* sentences John wrote, then I can not construct a materially equivalent sentence which does not contain the word "true."

In sum: a predicate with the logical property of *true* (the "disquotation property") is necessary for *logical* reasons, not for *descriptive* reasons.

The differences between the different versions of disquotation are very roughly as follows: For Frege, "true" is a predicate of "Thoughts" (*Gedanken*) and Thoughts do not consist of *words*. Whether they are Platonic objects or whether they defy the Platonic/non-Platonic dichotomy is a matter of controversy among Frege scholars; in any case, there is a metaphysics of "Thoughts" presupposed by Frege's version. Moreover, thoughts about empirical realities are *intrinsically* about those realities; for Frege, thoughts are not pictures painted with "mental paint" that somehow "correspond" to the world; they *assert* something about the world. For Tarski, at the opposite extreme, "true" is a predicate of sentences, and *sentences are mere sequences of marks on paper*. Tarski does say that he assumes that these marks have "concrete meanings," but this requirement is not part of the *definition* of truth, which makes truth simply a property of the marks, not a property that they have *when* they have those (undefined) "concrete meanings." Tarskian "truth definitions do not, contrary to what is often claimed, either presume or yield a "correspondence" notion of truth. For Carnap, who embraced Tarski's theory of truth, we understand a sentence, say, "Snow is white," by understanding its verification procedure, and we understand the corresponding metasentence "the sentence 'Snow is white' is true" by knowing that it has exactly the same verification procedure. (This is the "deflationary" account that I rejected in the Dewey Lectures.) For Wittgenstein (and myself) "true" is a predicate of *sentences used in certain ways*—that is, of objects, which are neither merely syntactic (like Tarksi's sentences) nor independent of the world-involving uses of syntactic objects in a particular language community. Like Frege's account, this entails that an assertion like "Snow is white" is not a picture in mental paint that somehow corresponds to snow's being white; the use of the sentence *involves* snow and whiteness. If there is a "correspondence relation" here, it is an internal relation, not an external or contingent one.

Many philosophers have professed to be puzzled about just what I meant by returning to "common-sense realism" in the Dewey Lectures. I do not know if what I have just written will satisfy them, but one can always hope! To sum up, "common-sense realism," in my sense, involves a negative element, the rejection of the idea that truth cannot outrun verifiability, and two positive elements: returning (as close as possible) to "naïve realism" with respect to perception, and a disquotational account of truth similar to the one I find in Wittgenstein. It differs from what I once *called* "metaphysical realism" in rejecting what I see as the fantasy of one final true and complete Ontology, but, of course, it is both metaphysical and realist in its own way.

XLVI. Fact and Value

I do not wish to give the impression that the only philosophical issues that I thought about in the closing decade of the twentieth century were (1) realism and (2) perception. The Royce Lectures, which I published together with my Dewey Lectures, took up many other issues in philosophy of mind and philosophy of language, and, as already mentioned, my interest in trying to "understand" quantum mechanics has been an ongoing one for more than forty years (as has, for that matter, my interest in philosophy of mathematics). And I have had the good fortune to be able to continue to pursue those interests into the first decade of the twenty-first century. In addition, I have been able to devote two books to an old interest of mine, the interest in criticizing the logical positivist idea that value judgments lack "cognitive meaning," an idea that has exerted a negative influence on many parts of our culture, and especially on the science of economics. My decision to devote more time to writing on these topics has been very much encouraged by my friendship with two wonderful economist-philosophers, Amartya Sen and Vivian Walsh.

I first criticized the fact/value dichotomy in 1976, in "Literature, Science, and Reflection," and I returned to the issue a number of times after that (particularly in "Pragmatism and Moral Objectivity"), but it was the invitation to give the Rosenthal Lectures at Northwestern University's School of Law that led to writing the first of the two books I just mentioned, *The Collapse of the Fact/Value Dichotomy*. I had been thinking for some time about the need to address the influence of logical positivism on economics, and particularly of the logical positivist claim that value judgments are "nonsense," and Vivian Walsh strongly urged me to focus on those issues in those lectures. He and I were and are strongly sympathetic to Amartya Sen's claim that economics, philosophy, and ethics need to relate to one another, and that judgments as to which human "capabilities" a just society needs to promote, while dependent on cultural, physical, and social context, and, of course, revisable, are both important and capable of being the subject of rational discussion, and, as I explained in that book, I wanted to provide a philosophy of language that supports his "capabilities approach" to welfare economics.

I will not even try to describe all the arguments that I gave in that book and subsequently for rejecting the positivist's fact/value dichotomy, but the following paragraph from a recent paper alludes to the principal ones:

> One may think of the logical positivists' fact/value dichotomy (and of the "emotivist" account of ethical language that goes with it) as the top of a three-legged stool. The three legs were (1) the postulation of theory-free "facts," leading to their dichotomy of observation and theory (as well a dichotomy of "experience" and "convention"); (2) the denial that fact ("science") and evaluation are entangled; and (3) the claim that science proceeds by a syntactically describable method (called "induction"). The fact that even theoretical physics presupposes *epistemic values* means that if value judgments were really "cognitively meaningless," all science would rest on judgments that are (to use Carnap's term), *nonsense*. That is why both Carnap and Reichenbach tried so hard to show that science proceeds by an *algorithm*, and the reason that Popper tried to show that science needs only deductive logic. Thus the failure of the third leg is also a failure of the second leg. But the second leg also broke because, as John McDowell, Iris Murdoch, Bernard Williams and others pointed out, facts and values—ethical values—are entangled even at the level of single predicates. And the first leg broke because the "two dogmas" on which it was based were refuted by Quine.[176]

Perhaps I should now explain what I mean by the failure of each of the three "legs," but if I did, that would mean doing what I just said I would not do, namely summarizing all my arguments. Instead, I will close with a word about my next-to-last book, *Ethics without Ontology*. What that book argues is that if we stand back from the details of the two subjects, we can see a remarkable similarity in the conundrums that perplex philosophers who work in foundations of ethics (often called "meta-ethics") and philosophers who work in foundations of mathematics. The conundrums arise, I argued there, because of a belief that all objectivity must be grounded in ontology. I believe that that is a mistake, and that seeing how it leads to the same difficulties in fields that one would expect to be very different gives us insight into why and how it is a mistake. But I will not try to summarize that book either, but just encourage you to read it.

So what will I work on now? Well, I am writing a book on perception with Hilla Jacobson, a young Israeli philosopher, and Ruth Anna and I plan to collect our papers on pragmatism. And after that....? Well, that remains to be seen.[177]

HILARY PUTNAM

CAMBRIDGE, MA
FEBRUARY 2009

NOTES

1. My parents decided at some point that my full name was "Hilary Whitehall Putnam." The "Whitehall" is in honor of Nicolas Whitehall, a favorite uncle of my father's and a freethinker, but this middle name does not appear on my birth certificate.
2. Toby Sampson b. 1865; d. Dec. 11, 1924; Michael Sampson b. 1856; d. Apr. 17, 1940.
3. Freely translated, "Listen old man, what the heck is going on?"
4. [François Rabelais:] Samuel Putnam, translator, *All the Extant Works of François Rabelais* (New York: Covici-Friede, 1929).
5. Peter J. King, *One Hundred Philosophers: The Life and Work of the World's Greatest Thinkers* (Hauppauge, NY: Barron's, 2004).
6. "Hilary Putnam," Wikipedia: The Free Encyclopedia, http://en.wikipedia.org/wiki/ Hilary Putnam (accessed December 4, 2009).
7. An excellent account of my father's communist period and his disillusionment can be found in Bertram D. Wolfe, *Strange Communists I Have Known* (New York: Stein and Day, 1965).
8. Friedrich Engels, *Socialism: Utopian and Scientific,* written in 1880 (New York: Progress Publishers, 1970).
9. Samuel Putnam, *Marvelous Journey: A Survey of Four Centuries of Brazilian Writing* (New York: A.A. Knopf, 1948). An excellent short account of my father's contribution to Brazilian studies is C. Harvey Gardiner, "Samuel Putnam, Brazilianist," *Luso-Brazilian Review* 8, no. 1 (Summer 1971): 103–14.
10. Quoted in Wolfe, *Strange Communists I Have Known*, 79.
11. My other best friend in high school was Sidney Halpern, who went on to become a professor of history at Temple University.
12. Richard Rudner, "The Scientist *qua* Scientist Makes Value Judgments," *Philosophy of Science* 20, no. 1 (1953): 1–6.
13. Nelson Goodman, who joined the Penn faculty in my senior year, did not teach any course open to undergraduates that year, and so I did not meet him until years later.
14. Leibniz was the first philosopher to argue that the truths of arithmetic are "analytic" truths, thus supposedly explaining how they could simultaneously be necessary and nonempirical.

15. Quine beautifully expressed this idea when he wrote in "Carnap and Logical Truth," collected in his *The Ways of Paradox and Other Essays* (New York: Random House, 1966), 125, "The lore of our fathers is a fabric of sentences. In our hands it develops and changes, through more or less arbitrary and deliberate revisions and additions of our own, more or less directly occasioned by the continuing stimulation of our sense organs. It is a pale gray lore, black with fact and white with convention. But I have found no substantial reasons for concluding that there are any quite black threads in it, or any white ones."

16. Morton White, *Towards Reunion in Philosophy* (Cambridge, MA: Harvard University. Press, 1956), 109.

17. See the bibliography.

18. For an account, see Ben H. Yandell, *The Honors Class: Hilbert's Problems and their Solvers* (Natick, MA: A.K. Peters Ltd., 2002). The story of the negative solution to Hilbert's Tenth Problem is told on pages 85–114.

19. Erna's father, Zvi Diesendruck, had been a philosophy professor at Hebrew Union College until his death, and Erna had taken courses towards a master's degree at that institution.

20. See "Cynthia Schuster 1910–1983," *Proceedings and Addresses of the American Philosophical Association* 58, no. 2 (Nov. 1984): 277, for a lovely memorial minute.

21. Stephen Gasiorowicz is now Professor of Physics emeritus at the University of Minnesota.

22. Peter Kaus is now Professor of Physics emeritus at the University of California, Riverside.

23. Hans Meyerhoff met his death in an automobile accident in 1964. He was only fifty years old when he died.

24. The "disease" being, of course, the lack of a precise analytic/synthetic distinction.

25. Reprinted as "Project 1953" in his *Fact, Fiction, and Forecast* (Cambridge, MA: Harvard University Press, 1955).

26. See my "Reichenbach and the Limits of Vindication," *Words and Life*, ed. James Conant (Cambridge, MA: Harvard University Press, 1944), 131–48.

27. Hans Reichenbach, *Experience and Prediction* (Chicago: University of Chicago Press, 1938).

28. Rudolf Carnap, *Der Logische Aufbau der Welt* (Leipzig: Felix Meiner Verlag, 1928); English translation by Rolf A. George, *The Logical Structure of the World and Pseudoproblems in Philosophy* (Berkeley: University of California Press, 1967).

29. Cf. Reichenbach, *Experience and Prediction*, 164.

30. Bertrand Russell, *The Problems of Philosophy* (London: Williams and Norgate, 1912).

31. This argument is not in *Experience and Prediction*, however.

32. Reichenbach, *Experience and Prediction*, 175–77.

33. Hans Reichenbach, "Are Phenomenal Reports Absolutely Certain?" *Philosophical Review* 671, no. 2 (April 1952): 147–59.

34. Nelson Goodman, "Sense and Certainty," *Philosophical Review* 671, no. 2 (April 1952): 160–67.

35. C. I. Lewis, "The Given Element in Empirical Knowledge," *Philosophical Review* 671, no. 2 (April 1952): 168–75.

36. Reichenbach, "Are Phenomenal Reports Absolutely Certain?" 154.

37. Ibid., 155.

38. Ibid., 156.

39. Reichenbach, *Experience and Prediction*, 150.

40. Rudolf Carnap, *The Logical Syntax of Language* (London: Routledge and Kegan Paul, 1937).

41. Cf. *Experience and Prediction*, 212ff.

42. See my "Hans Reichenbach: Realist and Verificationist," in *Future Pasts: The Analytic Tradition in Twentieth-Century Philosophy*, ed. Juliet Floyd and Sanford Shieh (Oxford: Oxford University Press, 2001).

43. Ben-Ami Scharfstein, *Of Birds, Beasts, and Other Artists: An Essay on the Universality of Art* (New York: New York University Press, 1988).

44. Raul Hilberg, *The Destruction of the European Jews* (Chicago: Quadrangle Press, 1961). The difficulties in finding a publisher are recounted in Hilberg's memoir, *The Politics of Memory: The Journey of a Holocaust Historian* (Chicago: Ivan R. Dee, 1996).

45. Actually, this is not quite true. In 1952 I succeeded in proving that the decision problem for satisfiability in a finite universe of formulas in first-order logic is unsolvable, only to discover that this result had been proved by Trachtenbrot in 1950. In March 2009, I gave a lecture to the Advanced Seminar in Logic and Formal Methods at Tel Aviv University at which Trachtenbrot was present. I told him what I have just written, and he chuckled and told me that *he* had later learned that what is to this day still known as "Trachtenbrot's Theorem" was actually earlier known to Kalmar!

46. Paul Rosenbloom, *Elements of Mathematical Logic* (Mineola, NY: Dover, 1951).

47. However, "~(p · ~p)" (absurdity of contradiction), "~~~p ≡ ~p" (triple negation), and "p ⊃ (q · ~q) . ⊃ . ~p" (proof of a *negative* by contradiction) are all intuitionistically valid!

48. Martin Davis, "Arithmetical Problems and Recursively Enumerable Predicates," *Journal of Symbolic Logic* 18 (1953): 33–41.

49. Solomon Feferman, "Alfred Tarski and a Watershed Meeting in Logic: Cornell, 1957," in *Philosophy and Logic: In Search of the Polish Tradition*, ed. Jaakko Hintikka et al. (Dordrecht: Kluwer, 2003): 151–62. (See page 157 for the anecdote about Tarski, Dekker, and myself.)

50. My first two papers on this topic were with George Boolos, "Degrees of Unsolvability of Constructible Sets of Integers," *Journal of Symbolic Logic* 33, no. 4 (Dec. 1968): 497–513 and with Stephen Leeds "An Intrinsic Characterization of the Hierarchy of Constructible Sets of Integers," *Logic Colloquium '69*, ed. R. O. Grandy and C. E. M. Yates (Amsterdam: North-Holland, 1971): 311–50. The term "fine structure" is due to Ronald Jensen, "The Fine Structure of the Constructible Hierarchy," *Annals of Mathematical Logic* 4 (1972): 229–308, whose work was of primary importance for the further development of the subject. Jensen told me that he was aware of my papers when he wrote this famous paper.

51. That my and my students's work was the first work on the "fine structure" of the hierarchy of constructible sets is pointed out by A. S. Kechris, in his review of George Boolos and Hilary Putnam, "Degrees of Unsolvability of Constructible Sets of Integers" (1969). Kechris's review appeared in *Journal of Symbolic Logic* 38, no. 3 (Dec., 1973): 527–28.

52. See Don Howard, "Einstein on Locality and Separability," *Studies in History and Philosophy of Science* 16 (1985): 171–201.

53. Both Kaufmann and Arthur Szathmary received promotion to Associate Professor at the end of my first year in Princeton. The two of them supported and encouraged me throughout my eight years on the faculty.

54. The "Reichenbachian" paper I did include in the first volume of my *Philosophical Papers* was "Three-Valued Logic," the first of a number of papers I was to write on the idea of using a nonstandard logic to interpret quantum mechanics.

55. E. Mark Gold, "Limiting Recursion," *Journal of Symbolic Logic* 30, no. 1 (1965): 28–48.

56. Hilary Putnam, "Reductionism and the Nature of Psychology," *Cognition* 2, no.1 (1973): 131–46. Reprinted in Putnam, *Words and Life*, 428–40.

57. Hans Reichenbach, *Nomological Statements and Admissible Operations* (Amsterdam: North Holland, 1954).

58. Richard Rorty defended this idea both in his "Eliminative Materialist" phase and later in his "Neopragmatist" period, notably in *Philosophy and the Mirror of Nature* (Princeton, NJ: Princeton University Press, 1979).

59. The idea of using reduction sentences to formalize operational definitions was proposed by Carnap in "Testability and Meaning," *Philosophy of Science* 3, no. 4 (Oct. 1936): 419–71 and 4, no. 1 (Jan. 1937): 1–40. Reprinted in part in *Readings in the Philosophy of Science*, ed. Herbert Feigl and May Brodbeck (New York: Appleton-Century and Crofts, 1953).

60. Hilary Putnam, "Brains and Behavior," in *Mind, Language, and Reality: Philosophical Papers*, vol. 2 (Cambridge, MA: Harvard Univiversity Press, 1975), 329.

61. Hilary Putnam, "Logical Positivism and the Philosophy of Mind," in *Mind, Language, and Reality*, 450.

62. The distinction between "descriptivist" theories of the meanings of certain terms and theories on which those terms are "rigid designators" was famously introduced by Saul Kripke in his path-breaking *Naming and Necessity* (Cambridge, MA: Harvard University Press, 1980); an earlier version was published in *Semantics of Natural Language*, ed. Donald Davidson and Gilbert Harman (Dordrecht: Reidel, 1972).

63. Hilary Putnam, "The Analytic and the Synthetic," in *Mind, Language and Reality: Philosophical Papers*, vol. 2, 33.

64. Ibid.

65. Ibid.

66. Hans Reichenbach, *Philosophy of Space and Time*, trans. Maria Reichenbach and John Freund (New York: Dover, 1958).

67. Hans Reichenbach, *The Rise of Scientific Philosophy* (Berkeley, CA: University of California Press, 1951).

68. In a footnote to this passage I qualified this statement as follows: "Reichenbach actually claimed that there were various possible alternative 'coordinative definitions' of 'straight line'. However he contended that this one (and the ones physically equivalent to it) 'have the advantage of logical simplicity and require the least change in the results of science'. Moreover: 'The sciences have implicitly employed such a coordinative definition all the time, though not always consciously'—i.e. it renders the customary meaning of the term 'straight line'." Putnam, "The Analytic and the Synthetic," 47.

69. For a description of Helmholz's view see Robert DiSalle, *Understanding Space-Time* (Cambridge: Cambridge University Press, 2006), 76ff.

70. Stephen Toulmin, *The Philosophy of Science: An Introduction* (London: Hutchinson's University Library, 1953).

71. The Continuum Hypothesis says that the cardinal number of the points on the real line—the "continuum"—is the smallest cardinal greater than "$\aleph_0$," the cardinal number of the natural numbers.

72. Paul Benacerraf and Hilary Putnam, eds., *Philosophy of Mathematics: Selected Readings*, 2nd ed. (Cambridge: Cambridge University Press, 1983), vii.

73. Hans Reichenbach, *Philosophy of Space and Time*, 19.

74. Putnam, "The Analytic and the Synthetic," 48.

75. Most recently in "Rethinking Mathematical Necessity" and in "Rules, Attunement, and 'Applying Words to the World': The Struggle to Understand Wittgenstein's Vision of Language."

76. Ledger Wood, *The Analysis of Knowledge* (Princeton: Princeton University Press, 1941).

77. Frank Thilly, *A History of Philosophy: Revised by Ledger Wood* (London: Allen and Unwin, 1955).

78. In "Epistemology Naturalized," Quine famously asked, "Why not settle for psychology? . . . scruples against circularity have little point . . . [i]f we are out simply to understand

the link between observation and science." Collected in W. V. Quine, *Ontological Relativity and Other Essays* (New York: Columbia University Press, 1969), 75–76.

79. David Pole's *The Later Philosophy of Wittgenstein* was devastatingly criticized by Stanley Cavell in his famous essay, "The Availability of Wittgenstein's Later Philosophy," collected in his *Must We Mean What We Say* (New York: Scribner's, 1969), 44–72.

80. Deane B. Judd, "Introduction," in Johann Wolfgang Von Goethe, *Theory of Colors*, trans. Charles Lock Eastlake (Cambridge, MA: MIT Press, 1970), XII–XIII.

81. Quine himself conceded that this is the case in *Word and Object* (Cambridge, MA: MIT Press, 1960), 57, saying that his account "fits with" mine in "The Analytic and the Synthetic." What Quine came to see is that what he was attacking was not the "synonymy intuition" itself, but the metaphysical use that philosophers make of it, for instance when Carnap made of it when he claimed that the sentences of mathematics are "analytic."

82. Rudolf Carnap, "The Old and the New Logic," in *Logical Positivism*, ed. A.J. Ayer (Glencoe, IL: Free Press, 1959), 141.

83. Ibid., 143.

84. W. V. Quine, "Two Dogmas of Empiricism," in *From a Logical Point of View* (Cambridge, MA: Harvard University Press, 1953); W. V. Quine, "Carnap on Logical Truth," in *The Philosophy of Rudolf Carnap*, ed. Paul Arthur Schilpp (LaSalle, IL: Open Court, 1963).

85. Rorty, *Philosophy and the Mirror of Nature*, 167. In chapter IV of that work Rorty equates Sellars and Quine as *both* having "raised the same sorts of questions about the possibility of apodictic truth which Hegel had raised about Kant." (A marvelous example of Rorty's intentionally wild way of doing the history of philosophy!)

86. Putnam, "The Analytic and the Synthetic," 45–46.

87. Charles W. Misner, Kip S. Thorne, John Archibald Wheeler, *Gravitation* (San Francisco: Freeman, 1970), 399.

88. Reichenbach, *The Rise of Scientific Philosophy*, 125–43.

89. The "g_{ik} tensor" is the mathematical object that determines the total spacetime distance between an arbitrary pair of "labeled" points (labeled by means of a suitable coordinate system).

90. I draw on McGuinness's *Approaches to Wittgenstein* (London: Routledge, 2002) in my "Wittgenstein and Realism," *International Journal of Philosophical Studies* 16, no. 1 (2008): 1–14.

91. This was shown in full mathematical detail by Kurt Gödel, "An Example of a New Type of Cosmological Solutions of Einstein's Field Equations of Gravitation," *Reviews of Modern Physics* 21 (1949): 447–50. Reprinted in *Kurt Gödel: Collected Works, Vol. II*, ed. Feferman et al. (Oxford: Oxford University Press, 1990).

92. A good (later) account is Michael Green, "The Grain Objection," *Philosophy of Science* 46 (1979): 559–89.

93. Frank Jackson, "Epiphenomenal Qualia," *Philosophical Quarterly* 32, no. 127 (1982): 127–36.

94. Thomas Nagel, "What Is It Like to Be a Bat?" *Philosophical Review* 83, no. 4 (1974): 435–50.

95. I devoted another paper to this argument shortly after my move to MIT in 1961. See my "The Mental Life of Some Machines."

96. I called these computational states "logical states" in "Minds and Machines."

97. I first explained and defended semantic externalism at my lectures in the 1968 Summer Institute in Philosophy of Language in Seattle. My first publication on the subject was "Is Semantics Possible?" in *Metaphilosophy* 1 (July 1970): 187–201; revised version in *Language, Belief, and Metaphysics: Contemporary Philosophic Thought: The International Philosophy Year Conferences at Brockport,* vol. 1, ed. Howard E. Kiefer and Milton K. Munitz (Albany: SUNY Press), 50–63. Reprinted in *Mind, Language, and Reality.*

98. John Langshaw Austin, "Three Ways of Spilling Ink," in his *Philosophical Papers* (Oxford: Clarendon Press, 1979).

99. I used the notion uncritically in "Mathematics and the Existence of Abstract Entities," *Philosophical Studies* 7 (1957): 81–87.

100. Rudolf Carnap, *The Foundations of Logic and Mathematics*, in *The International Encyclopedia of Unified Science* 1, no. 3 (Chicago: University of Chicago Press, 1939).

101. Hilary Putnam, "What Theories Are Not," in *Mathematics, Matter and Method: Philosophical Papers,* vol. 1 (Cambridge: Cambridge University Press, 1975), 220–21.

102. Ibid., 222.

103. Cf. Carnap's "Testability and Meaning."

104. Putnam, "What Theories are Not," *Mathematics, Matter and Method*, 224.

105. Ibid.

106. Rudolf Carnap, "The Methodological Character of Theoretical Concepts," in *Minnesota Studies in the Philosophy of Science,* vol. 1: *The Foundations of Science and the Concepts of Psychology and Psychoanalysis,* ed. Herbert Feigl and Michael Scriven (Minneapolis: University of Minnesota Press, 1956), 47. Note that Carnap is here guilty of using "incomplete interpretation" without giving that expression any precise sense, which is just what I accused him of in "What Theories are Not."

107. It was initially called "The Graduate Program in Philosophy in the Department of Humanities." Later, but after I had already left MIT for Harvard, it became the "Department of Philosophy," and still later the Department of Philosophy and the Department of Linguistics were merged into a single department.

108. "The Nature of Mental States" and "The Mental Life of Some Machines."

109. Hilary Putnam, "Minds and Machines," in *Mind, Language, and Reality: Philosophical Papers,* vol. 2 (Cambridge: Cambridge University Press, 1975), 376.

110. Hilary Putnam, "The Nature of Mental States" in *Mind, Language, and Reality: Philosophical Papers,* vol. 2 (Cambridge: Cambridge University Press, 1975), 434.

111. "Mathematics and the Existence of Abstract Entities" presupposed the Carnapian idea that scientific theories are "partially interpreted calculi," which I criticized in "What Theories Are Not." My disagreements with "The Thesis that Mathematics is Logic" subsequent to its original publication are explained in footnotes I added to the paper when I reprinted it in *Mathematics, Matter and Method*, specifically the footnotes on pp. 19, 31, and 33, especially the last.

112. The unfortunate exception is "Paradox Revisited II: Sets—A Case of All or None," in *Between Logic and Intuition: Essays in Honor of Charles Parsons,* ed. Gila Sher and Richard Tieszen (Cambridge: Cambridge University Press, 2000), 16–26, which showed the baneful influence of Wittgenstein's philosophy of mathematics. "Set Theory: Realism, Replacement, and Modality" (*Philosophy in an Age of Science*, 217–34) explains what I think was wrong with that lecture, and what I should have said instead.

113. Hartry Field, *Science without Numbers: A Defense of Nominalism* (Princeton, NJ: Princeton University Press, 1980).

114. Mark Colyvan, "Indispensability Arguments in the Philosophy of Mathematics," *The Stanford Encyclopedia of Philosophy* (Fall 2004 Edition), ed. Edward N. Zalta, <http://plato.stanford.edu/archives/fall2004/entries/mathphil-indis/>. Colyvan is also the author of *The Indispensability of Mathematics* (Oxford: Oxford University Press, 2001).

115. The author of this entry, Mark Colyvan, is referring to W. V. Quine, "Carnap and Logical Truth," *The Ways of Paradox and Other Essays,* rev. ed. (Cambridge, MA: Harvard University Press, 1976), 107–32, and in *Reading in the Philosophy of Mathematics,* ed. Benacerraf and Putnam (Cambridge: Cambridge University Press,1983), 355–76; W. V. Quine, "On What There Is," reprinted in *From a Logical Point of View,* 2nd ed. (Cambridge, MA: Harvard University Press,1980), 1–19; W. V. Quine, "Two Dogmas of Empiricism,"

reprinted in *From a Logical Point of View,* 2nd ed. (Cambridge, MA: Harvard University Press, 1980), 20–46; W. V. Quine, "Things and Their Place in Theories," in *Theories and Things* (Cambridge, MA: Harvard University Press, 1981), 1–23; W. V. Quine, "Success and Limits of Mathematization," in *Theories and Things* (Cambridge, MA: Harvard University Press, 1981), 148–55.

116. Colyvan is referring to "What is Mathematical Truth," in *Mathematics, Matter, and Method: Philosophical Papers,* vol. 1, 2nd ed. (Cambridge: Cambridge University Press, 1979), 60–78, and Hilary Putnam "Philosophy of Logic," in the same volume, 323–57.

117. For the reasons that I say "in a sense" see "The Greatest Logical Positivist" in my *Realism with a Human Face,* ed. James Conant (Cambridge, MA: Harvard University Press, 1990).

118. What Quine actually wrote is that "Our statements about the external world face the tribunal of sense experience not individually but only as a corporate body." This does not mention (1) "theories" or (2) "confirmation." When asked how exactly we go about judging statements about the external world in the light of experience, Quine's famous advice was to "settle for psychology." Quine was endorsing a Duhemian thesis in "Two Dogmas," not propounding a claim about the logic of "confirmation."

119. No such claim appears in "What is Mathematical Truth."

120. Quine wrote that numbers are "intangible objects . . . which are *sizes of* sets of apples and the like," *Theories and Things,* 149.

121. A common objection to arguments from indispensability for physics to realism with respect to mathematics is, of course, that we do not yet have, and may indeed never have, the "true" physical theory; my response is that, at least when it comes to the theories that scientists regard as most fundamental (today that would certainly include quantum field theories), we should regard all of the rival theories as candidates for truth or approximate truth, and that *any philosophy of mathematics that would be inconsistent with so regarding them should be rejected.*

122. Geoffrey Hellman, *Mathematics without Numbers* (Oxford: Oxford University Press, 1989).

123. Paul Benacerraf, "What Numbers Could Not Be," *Philosophical Review* 74, no. 1 (Jan. 1965): 47–73.

124. Adolf Grünbaum, *Geometry and Chronometry in Philosophical Perspective* (Minneapolis: University of Minnesota Press, 1968).

125. Yuval Dolev, *Time and Realism; Metaphysical and Antimetaphysical Perspectives* (Cambridge, MA: MIT Press, 2007).

126. Howard Stein, "On Einstein-Minkowski Space-Time," *Journal of Philosophy* 65, no. 1 (Jan. 11, 1968): 5–23.

127. Franklin H. Donnell, ed., *Aspects of Contemporary American Philosophy* (Würzburg: Physica-Verlag, Rudolf Liebing K.G., 1965). My paper is reprinted in *Mathematics, Matter, and Method,* 79–92.

128. Hilary Putnam, "Philosophy of Physics," in *Mathematics, Matter, and Method Philosophical Papers,* vol. 1 (Cambridge: Cambridge University Press, 1975), 80.

129. John von Neumann, *The Mathematical Foundations of Quantum Mechanics,* trans. Robert T. Beyer (Princeton: Princeton University Press, 1955).

130. "A Philosopher Looks at Quantum Mechanics" in *Mathematics, Matter, and Method: Philosophical Papers,* vol. 1 (Cambridge: Cambridge University Press, 1975), 132.

131. David Finkelstein is today an emeritus professor of physics at the Georgia Institute of Technology.

132. Gell-Mann's lecture is reprinted in *The Nature of the Physical Universe: 1976 Nobel Conference,* ed. Douglas Huff and Omer Prewitt (New York: John Wiley and Sons, 1979).

133. Hans Reichenbach, *Philosophical Foundations of Quantum Mechanics* (Berkeley: University of California Press, 1944). Reichenbach uses the term "principle of anomaly" on p. 129; the principle itself is stated on p. 34: *"We do not have one normal system for all interphenomena, but we do have a normal system of every [i.e. "each"-HP] interphenomenon."* [Italics in original]. By an "interphenomenon" Reichenbach means a micro-event on the quantum mechanical side of the cut between the quantum mechanical system being experimented upon and the measuring instruments which Reichenbach assumes, following Bohr and Heisenberg, can be treated as obeying the laws of classical physics. A normal system is a quantum mechanical system with no "causal anomalies." An example of an interphenomenon which can treated as a "normal system," according to Reichenbach (p. 35, n. 1) is a "swarm of particles which do not interact with each other such as electron swarms or light rays." Since nonlocality would count as a causal anomaly for Reichenbach, and we now know that nonlocality is a real phenomenon, and not just an artifact of, for example, the Bohm interpretation, Reichenbach is wrong about the possibility of eliminating "anomalies" even in the case of a system of two noninteracting electrons, but, by the same token, the admission of a "causal anomaly" in this sense is not the admission of something so repugnant to reason as to justify us in abandoning bivalence. Of course, Bell's Theorem establishing the impossibility of accounting for nonlocal correlations by means of any local hidden variable theory was proved long after Reichenbach wrote.

134. Reichenbach's term for what I am calling a "realist" interpretation was "exhaustive" interpretation. Reichenbach's view was that by showing that all exhaustive interpretations must involve "causal anomalies"—his "principle of anomaly"—he had removed any motive for seeking such an interpretation.

135. See David Finkelstein, "Matter, Space, and Logic," in *Boston Studies in the Philosophy of Science*, vol. V, ed. Robert S. Cohen and Max Wartofsky (Dordrecht, D. Reidel, 1969): 199–213.

136. The span of two subspaces of a vector space is the space of all vectors that can be represented as linear combinations of a vector in the one space and a vector in the other; this is the smallest subspace containing both of those spaces.

137. The orthocomplement of a subspace of a vector space is the subspace spanned by all the vectors orthogonal to that subspace.

138. Hilary Putnam, "There is at Least One *A Priori* Truth," in *Realism and Reason: Philosophical Papers*, vol. 3 (Cambridge: Cambridge University Press, 1983), 110.

139. Ibid., 111–14.

140. Ibid., 111–12.

141. See, for example, Graham Priest, et al., eds., *Paraconsistent Logic: Essays on the Inconsistent* (Munich: Philosophia Verlag, 1989).

142. Putnam, "There is at Least One *A Priori* Truth," 101.

143. Ibid., 111.

144. Ibid., 113.

145. Charles Travis, "The Shape of the Conceptual," in *Objectivity and the Parochial* (Oxford: Oxford University Press, 2011), 263–300.

146. See Stephen Hawking and Richard Penrose, *The Nature of Space and Time* (Princeton: Princeton University Press, 1996); Roger Penrose, *The Road to Reality* (London: Jonathan Cape, 2004).

147. Hugh Everett III, "Relative State Formulation of Quantum Mechanics," *Reviews of Modern Physics* 29 (1957): 454–62. Reprinted in John Archibald Wheeler and Wojciech Hubert Zurek, eds., *Quantum Theory and Measurement* (Princeton: Princeton University Press, 1983).

148. Tim W. E. Maudlin, "Completeness, Supervenience, and Ontology," *Journal of Physics A: Mathematical and Theoretical* 40, no. 12 (March 2007): 3151.

149. See Hilary Putnam, "A Philosopher Looks at Quantum Mechanics (Again)," *British Journal of the Philosophy of Science* 36 (2005): 615–34.

150. J. J. C. Smart, "Conflicting Views About Explanation," in *Boston Studies in the Philosophy of Science,* vol. 2, ed. Robert S. Cohen and Marx R. Wartofsky (New York: Humanities Press, 1965), 157–70.

151. Wilfrid Sellars, "Scientific Realism or Irenic Instrumentalism: Comments on J.J. Smart," in *Boston Studies in the Philosophy of Science,* vol. 2, ed. Robert S. Cohen and Marx R. Wartofsky (New York: Humanities Press, 1965), 171–204.

152. Ibid., 171.

153. Paul K. Feyerabend, "Reply to Criticism: Comments on Smart, Sellars and Putnam," in *Boston Studies in the Philosophy of Science,* vol. 2, 223–51.

154. But my recollection was in error. The nominal essence of the name "gold," Locke said, "is that complex Idea the word Gold stands for, let it be, for instance, a Body yellow, of a certain weight, malleable, fusible, and fixed." [*An Essay Concerning Human Understanding*, III.vi.2] But the same objection applies: I have no idea what the "certain weight" of gold is, and so, according to Locke, I do not know the "nominal essence," i.e., the meaning of the word. Locke did mention *aqua regia* in a different connection, when he said that an ideal knowledge of the microphysical constitution of gold would enable us to explain why gold dissolves in *aqua regia* and silver in *aqua fortis*, and not the other way around.

155. Hilary Putnam, "How Not to Talk about Meaning: Comments on J.J. Smart," *Boston Studies in the Philosophy of Science,* vol. 2, 217–18.

156. Ibid., 218.

157. See Hilary Putnam "Is Water Necessarily H2O?" in *Realism with a Human Face*, ed. James Conant (Cambridge, MA: Harvard University Press, 1990), 54–79. The non-metaphysical interpretation of Kripke's "metaphysical necessity" that I favored was one under which what is "metaphysically necessary" is what is necessary given a reasonable reconstruction of our use of counterfactual conditionals.

158. Putnam, "Meaning Holism," in *Realism with a Human Face*, 282.

159. Lance Hickey, "Hilary Putnam," in Philip B. Dematteis and Leemon B. McHenry, *American Philosophers, 1950–2000*, vol. 279 in The Library of Literary Biography (Detroit: Gale Group, 2003), 226–36.

160. Other versions have been proposed by Michael Dummett and Neil Tennant, among others.

161. However, I never, as some mistakenly took me to be doing, adopted the Peircean view that such conditions require infinitely prolonged scientific inquiry, or the corollary that truth about the past is determined by what we can or will find out in the future.

162. John McDowell, *Mind and World* (Cambridge, MA: Harvard University Press, 1994).

163. The Aristotelian language reflects the fact that Martha Nussbaum long ago instructed me in the importance of this insight of Aristotle's in present-day philosophy. One of the things I am proudest of, in connection with my service as Chairman of the Harvard philosophy department in the 1970s, was that I brought Nussbaum, who has just completed her time as the first woman member of Harvard's Society of Fellows, into the department as an Assistant Professor.

164. The mistake was first pointed out to me by Jennifer Case. See Jennifer Case, "The Heart of Putnam's Pluralistic Realism," *Revue Internationale de Philosophie* 55, no. 4 (December 2001): 430, and my *Ethics without Ontology* (Cambridge, MA: Harvard University Press, 2004).

165. Lessing [Gotthold Ephraim Lessing, 1729–1781] wrote that if God offered him the truth, with one hand, and "eternal striving" after the same with the other, he would choose eternal striving.

166. See Rush Rhees, ed., *Ludwig Wittgenstein: Personal Recollections* (Oxford: Oxford University Press, 1991), 94.

167. Gordon Kaufman, *In the Face of Mystery: A Constructive Theology* (Cambridge, MA: Harvard University Press, 1993).

168. Wittgenstein is quoted as saying this in Norman Malcolm, *Ludwig Wittgenstein: A Memoir* (Oxford: Oxford University Press, 1958), 75. See Ludwig Wittgenstein, *Last Writings on the Philosophy of Psychology,* vol. 1, ed. G.H von Wright and Heikki Nyman, trans. C. G. Luckhardt and Maximilian A. E. Aue (Oxford: Basil Blackwell, 1982), §913.

169. Robert Westbrook, "Pragmatism and Democracy: Reconstructing the Logic of Dewey's Faith," in *The Revival of Pragmatism: New Essays on Social Thought, Law and Culture*, ed. Morris Dickstein (Raleigh-Durham: Duke University Press, 1998).

170. Charles Travis, *The Uses of Sense* (Oxford: Oxford University Press, 1989).

171. William Alston's review was published in *Philosophical Review* 103, no. 3 (Jul., 1994): 533–35; Robert Brandom's review was published in *Journal of Philosophy* 91, no. 3 (March, 1994): 140–43; Alex Burri's review was published in *Erkenntnis* 42, no. 3 (May, 1995): 405–8.

172. Alston, "*Renewing Philosophy* by Hilary Putnam," 535.

173. Ned Block, "Wittgenstein and Qualia," *Philosophical Perspectives* 21, no.1 (2007): 73–115.

174. Rudolf Carnap, "Truth and Confirmation" in *Readings in Philosophical Analysis*, ed. Herbert Feigl and Wilfrid Sellars (New York: Appleton-Century-Crofts, 1949).

175. Michael Dummett, *Frege: Philosophy of Language* (London: Duckworth, 1973) and *The Interpretation of Frege's Philosophy* (Cambridge, MA: Harvard University Press, 1981); Alfred Tarski, "The Concept of Truth in Formalized Languages," in A. Tarski, *Logic, Semantics, Metamathematics; Papers from 1923 to 1938* (Oxford: Oxford University Press, 1958).

176. Hilary Putnam, "The Fact/Value Distinction and Its Critics," in *Stanley Cavell and the Education of Grownups*, ed. Naoko Saito and Paul Standish (New York: Fordham University Press, 2012), 50–51.

177. [*Added Dec. 5, 2014:*] What I wrote above, in 2009, about "disquotation," while not wrong, seems confusing to me now, primarily because I did not say anything about the relation between *reference* and *truth*. My most recent writing about truth is "Naturalism, Realism, and Normativity" which will appear in the first issue of the *Journal of the American Philosophical Association*. My present view is that if sentences are identified *inter alia* by *what their words refer to*, what I above called the "world-involving" character of syntactic objects in use becomes nonmysterious.

PART TWO

DESCRIPTIVE AND CRITICAL ESSAYS WITH REPLIES

1

Charles Parsons

PUTNAM ON REALISM AND "EMPIRICISM" IN MATHEMATICS

Hilary Putnam's considerable influence on the philosophy of mathematics rests largely on papers published between the mid-1960s and the early 1980s.[1] Some of these date from before his turn against "metaphysical realism" in the late 1970s, and the remainder are early expressions of that turn. Since then he has published relatively little on the subject, although his positions on more general issues are relevant. In the present essay I will single out some themes and issues from the earlier papers and follow their subsequent fate. This examination will lead to some questions about the evolution of his views and how they now stand. The specific foundational problems of set theory will be an issue throughout.

I

Putnam has for a long time been preoccupied with questions about realism. What is it? What versions of realism can one accept, in opposition to what alternatives? Some of his writings about mathematics reflect where this general meditation stood when they were written, and the most visible changes of view reflect his changes of view on the general issues. His much discussed "model-theoretic argument against metaphysical realism" is presented in most detail in "Models and Reality." Although its target is quite general, it is deployed in that paper against views about mathematics, some of which Putnam had himself defended in earlier writings.

Realism is at issue in a number of discussions in the philosophy of mathematics, many of them influenced by Putnam's earlier work but continuing without his active participation. For example, nominalism poses the question whether any form of mathematical realism could be true, since how could it be if there are no mathematical objects at all? Although it was Putnam's pupil Hartry Field who revived nominalism in 1980, Putnam himself has not shown much sympathy for nominalism or interest in the research program of reconstructing mathematics on a basis that could plausibly claim to be nominalistic. It was, however, his idea of "mathematics as modal logic" that suggested that the nominalist program could go farther than otherwise if modality were added to the nominalist's resources. I will say a little about this idea shortly. It remains the case that nominalist concerns are too distant from mathematical practice to enlist Putnam's engagement.[2]

Some form of realism about the objects of a discourse or theory can be distinguished from realism about the statements or claims of the theory. This distinction is particularly relevant to mathematics, because the question of the status of its objects has for so long been one of the most discussed philosophical questions. In mathematics, the "statement realism" would presumably survive the translation of mathematical language, or some relevant part of it, into a canonical form that is taken to avoid commitment to the mathematical objects at issue, but "objects realism" presumably would not.

Putnam does not put this distinction at center stage in his explicit discussions of realism. However, he has urged essentially the same distinction in some of his discussions of mathematics. In fact, early and late in his career he has tended to relegate questions of ontology in mathematics to a secondary role.[3] Thus in sketching his own view early in "Mathematics without Foundations" he writes, "In my view the chief characteristic of mathematical propositions is the very wide variety of equivalent formulations that they possess."[4] He refers briefly to the case of equivalent descriptions in physics. Then he singles out two ways of formulating mathematical statements that he regards as equivalent in roughly the same sense, "mathematics as modal logic" and "mathematics as set theory." The second is just the familiar framing of classical mathematics in axiomatic set theory, ZF (Zermelo-Fraenkel) or some extension by additional axioms. The first is illustrated by translating a number-theoretic statement such as (his example) the negation of Fermat's last theorem as "$\Box(AX \rightarrow\rightarrow \neg \ Fermat)$." In this essay, he proposes a more complicated method of translating statements of set theory into a modal language.[5] In both cases explicit statements of the existence of the mathematical objects are avoided, although this manner of presenting mathematics presupposes the *possible* existence of objects that stand in relations corresponding to the structure of the mathematical domain in question.

Putnam's way of looking at a construction of this kind is quite different from that of most of the writers influenced by it, who take it as a way of eliminating or at least greatly limiting reference to mathematical objects. Taken in that way it is subject to some criticisms.[6] Putnam, however, views the more conventional set-theoretic formulation of mathematics and the modal-logical formulation as equivalent descriptions, each corresponding to different pictures in something like Wittgenstein's sense. Each would shed light in its own way on the concepts involved. For example, the set-theoretic formulation serves to make clear at least the logic of the modalities, while the modal formulation brings out what is limited in the sense in which mathematics postulates objects.[7] Putnam does not say in so many words that the two formulations differ in their ontology, but this is clearly implied by some of his statements.[8] I think he wants to conclude that its ontological commitment, whether in the precise sense derived from Quine or some other, is not an essential or intrinsic feature of a mathematical theory. Rather than accepting or rejecting the "mathematical-objects picture" outright, his aim is to relativize it.

One of the features of the "metaphysical realism" that Putnam began to attack in the late 1970s is that according to it what objects there are and their individuation are fixed by "reality" independently of our theories and their formulation.[9] As regards mathematical objects, Putnam did not hold this view even in his early essays. To that extent, he was never a metaphysical realist about mathematics. However, he seems to have thought that some degree of "ontological relativity" was compatible with metaphysical realism.[10] But I do not believe he could have held such a compromise view about mathematics at the time of "Mathematics without Foundations," because there equivalent descriptions are advanced that differ in such a way that the objects of one do not arise at all within the other, even as constructions. However, he does not address the question of the compatibility of this aspect of the view of this essay with metaphysical realism.

What distinguishes most prominently the "internal realism" that Putnam espoused in the late 1970s and the early 1980s is not this ontological aspect but the embrace of an epistemically constrained notion of truth. What is common to a number of writings of this time is the rejection of the idea that what are according to all epistemological criteria our best theories could nonetheless be false because Reality does not correspond to them in the right way, for example if we are brains in a vat. Here Putnam seems clearly to have changed his view of the mathematical case between the time of "Mathematics without Foundations" and after the turn with which we are concerned.

In that essay, after mentioning the then recently established independence of the continuum hypothesis from ZFC (ZF with axiom of choice), he remarks, "It appears quite possible today that no decisive consideration will ever appear (such as a set-theoretic axiom we have 'overlooked') which will reveal that a system in which the continuum hypothesis is provable is the correct one, and that no consideration will ever appear which will reveal that a system in which the continuum hypothesis is refutable is the correct one."[11] He goes on to say that this implies that the truth value of the continuum hypothesis may be undiscoverable by rational beings, at least by any we have reason to think exist or will exist. Putnam considers some other propositions that we may have no reason to expect we can decide, in particular that there are infinitely many binary stars. Not only does he see no reason in either case for denying that the proposition has a truth value, he seems puzzled as to why philosophers should think otherwise. The view expressed here is a version of realism in the sense of Dummett, whose characterization Putnam echoes.[12] There he says explicitly that one can be a realist about mathematics without committing oneself to mathematical objects.

What is distinctive of his essay "What is Mathematical Truth?" is the claim that, as in the case of science, one can also for mathematics make a case for realism on the ground that it is the only philosophy that does not make the success of the subject a miracle. The argument he then sketches claims that mathematics and science are so intimately connected that one cannot be a realist about science (in particular physics) and a nominalist about mathematics. (The fuller version of the argument is in *Philosophy of Logic*; it is one of the principal versions of the "indispensability argument.") The revived nominalism that developed after these publications of Putnam either assumed geometrical objects as physical and so nominalistically admissible, or allowed modality.[13] So they are not standing on the same ground as what Putnam criticizes. Except for a brief comment about *Science without Numbers*,[14] Putnam has not discussed this later nominalism in print. As I have said, he would approve of the concern for the application of mathematics in science in evidence in the work of Field and others. But given his general tendency to relegate questions of ontology to a secondary role, he must find it hard to take seriously the ontological intuitions that drive nominalism.

It has frequently been pointed out that indispensability arguments have little force in justifying assumptions in set theory that are far removed from the application of mathematics in natural science.[15] That would have to be said already about the continuum hypothesis, the favored example in "Mathematics without Foundations." If such arguments are really arguments for *realism*, however, then it seems that, from Putnam's point of view of the time with which we are now concerned, they should at least justify the claim that propositions like the continuum hypothesis are either true or false, even if we have no way of knowing which and no prospect of obtaining one in the foreseeable future.

Here we confront a problem analogous to Quine's underdetermination of theory by evidence. Let us suppose we have two competing axioms $A1$ and $A2$, such that if $A1$ is added to our basic set theory ZFC, the continuum hypothesis CH follows, and if $A2$ is added, $\neg$CH follows. If we have some substantial reason, which is unlikely to be from application in science but which may be more mathematical, to prefer one axiom over the other, then CH is badly chosen as an example of a mathematical proposition that we have no way of deciding, since discovering and adequately motivating additional axioms that settle it *is* a possible way of deciding a mathematical problem. Putnam does not seem ever to deny that in general, although he is sometimes skeptical in particular cases. So let us suppose we have no such reason.[16] In particular, if we have reasons for thinking one consistent, we also have reasons for thinking the other consistent. In "Mathematics without Foundations," Putnam seems committed to holding that nevertheless at least one of the two proposed axioms must be false.

Now that is in a way a truism, since by propositional logic, from $A1 \rightarrow$ CH and $A2 \rightarrow \neg$CH each of which is by hypothesis provable in ZFC, $\neg(A1 \wedge A2)$ follows. So, one can well say, *of course* one must be false, assuming, as we can in this discussion, that we accept ZFC. But this reasoning assumes that there is no hidden ambiguity, that we are speaking fully in the same voice when reasoning from each of the axioms. That would in fact be an assumption on which many set theorists, at least the more realistically minded, would proceed. Speculations about a possible bifurcation of the concept of set, according to which incompatible extensions of ZFC would come to be equally acceptable, have been advanced a number of times. Even though many set theorists have been pessimistic about the possibility of settling CH in a really convincing way, the course of research in set theory has not so far given real substance to any speculation of that sort. But in section IV we shall consider the relation of Putnam's later views to such speculations.

In the absence of such a bifurcation, there is a kind of paradox in the development of set theory with regard to questions about realism. This is that the very developments that give general encouragement to realism in set theory tend to undermine proposed examples that would witness realism in Dummett's sense, namely examples of statements that have a definite truth value even though we have no way of knowing which. To illustrate the point, consider the somewhat crude reaction to the results of Gödel and Cohen concerning the continuum hypothesis, that the results show that the continuum problem is absolutely undecidable, and models of ZFC in which it is true and those in which it is false answer equally well to the concept of set. The realist will reply that the methods by which the known models were constructed does not encourage that way of looking at them. Following Gödel, he will observe that some statements independent of ZFC are extremely well motivated. The strong axioms of infinity that were already known before 1930, concerning inaccessible and Mahlo cardinals, are almost as well motivated as the axioms of ZFC themselves. But this means that statements that are undecidable in ZFC but decidable with the assumption of Mahlo cardinals cannot be offered as examples of statements that are true or false without our possibly knowing which.

So far the example shows little, because the assumption of Mahlo cardinals still leaves classical problems undecided, not only the continuum problem but other classical problems that, it has been shown, can be decided with much stronger axioms of infinity. Gödel hoped that the search for such axioms might be the right approach to the continuum problem. This hope was disappointed, but another program along the same lines offered a satisfying solution to the classical problems of descriptive set theory, the study of sets of real numbers that are in a generalized sense definable. Around 1970 it was shown that the axiom of Projective Determinacy (PD), to the effect that in certain infinite games one or the other player has a winning strategy, settled a raft of problems of descriptive set theory that had been open since the early days of the subject. Furthermore, the results derived from PD gave a picture of the projective sets of real numbers that made sense in a way that the picture that would have resulted from assuming $V = L$ did not.[17] In the 1980s it was shown that sufficiently strong axioms of infinity were sufficient to prove PD and generalizations of it. Thus although "Gödel's program" in its original form failed for CH, a program of the same kind succeeded for descriptive set theory. Although this solution is not universally accepted it is widely so, and it has been for some years now "the only game in town" as far as descriptive set theory is concerned. That is, what remains are doubts about whether it is totally convincing and more philosophical doubts about whether the problems are really well formulated rather than genuinely competing theories.[18]

But now the philosopher who insisted in 1965 that, say, the proposition that every projective set of reals is either countable or contains a perfect subset is either true or false, whether we can ever determine which, would by now be hard put to maintain that this proposition and others like it, from classical descriptive set theory, are appropriate examples of such "recognition-transcendent" statements. If he does not accept the solution given by PD (that it is true), then he surely has to offer an argument. Furthermore, general philosophical doubts about higher set theory suggest the wrong kind of argument, to the effect that the proposition itself is unclear or vague. Furthermore, at least some set theorists are now hopeful that by building on what has been done by means of PD, it should be possible to make progress with the continuum problem.[19] Thus CH as well is at least threatened as an example of a recognition-transcendent statement.

II

Another aspect of Putnam's earlier writing is his emphasis on the importance in mathematics of a kind of argument that is closer to empirical reasoning than to deductive proof, what Putnam calls quasi-empirical.[20] Putnam would have endorsed a frequently quoted statement of Kurt Gödel:

> There might exist axioms so abundant in their verifiable consequences, shedding so much light upon a whole field, and yielding such powerful methods for solving problems . . . that, no matter whether or not they are intrinsically necessary, they would have to be accepted at least in the same sense as any well-established physical theory.[21]

Gödel had most specifically in mind the sort of new axioms of set theory that might decide the kinds of questions mentioned in the previous section, especially CH. That is not what primarily interests Putnam. The first example that he gives is the assumption that there is a one-to-one correspondence between the points of a line and the real numbers.[22] When he does turn to set theory, he cites the introduction of the axiom of choice by Zermelo, and gives Zermelo's own justification as an example of this sort of justification.[23] He interprets Zermelo as holding that the axioms have some degree of "self-evidence,"[24] but that what is most objective in their justification is their being *necessary for science*, which means in the first instance mathematics. As he puts it, "Today it is not just the axiom of choice but the whole edifice of modern set theory whose entrenchment rests on great success in mathematical application—in other words, on 'necessity for science.' What argument, other than a quasi-empirical one, can we offer for the axiom of Replacement?"[25] Putnam also gives examples of quasi-empirical arguments for mathematical conjectures that mathematicians find convincing. But of course such conviction does not lead them to abandon the goal of obtaining a proof. It seems likely that it *would* lead them to regard the search for a counterexample as unpromising, and probably that is part of Putnam's idea.

Some writers, Gödel in particular, regard the existence of this sort of justification in mathematics as quite compatible with its a priori character. Putnam seems not to view the matter in this way. Sometimes he uses the term "a priori" so as to connote unrevisability. Then the incompatibility

seems obvious; it is hard to see how any proposition that is accepted in a
way where its consequences play an essential role could be unrevisable,
since new consequences will continue to come up, and some might lead to
revision of the assumptions from which they were obtained. But the kind
of justification Gödel has in mind is, or at least is thought by him to be,
quite nonempirical, on the ground that the consequences are not *empirical*
consequences. So far the difference seems merely terminological. But the
example in "What is Mathematical Truth?" of the correspondence between
the real line and the line in geometry shows that Putnam at this time did
not view quasi-empirical justification as uncontaminated by empirical considerations. Thus concerning the calculus he writes, "The point is that the
real justification of the calculus is its *success*—its success in mathematics, *and its success in physical science.*"[26] He clearly held the same view
about geometry, even though he insisted that in the early modern period
the geometry of physical space was regarded as part of mathematics. He
did use the term "necessity relative to a body of knowledge" to describe
cases such as the status of geometry in earlier times, but he did not, as far
as I know, apply this idea to a case like arithmetic, where it is not obvious
what the relevant body of knowledge would be.[27]

III

I now want to ask about the views of the later Putnam on these issues, in
particular to try to see how he might react to the line of thought presented in
section I and how his later views square with the observations about quasi-
empirical or actually empirical justification in mathematics. He commented
on the latter view in a paper of 1979.[28] Describing the view, he states as a
constraint on acceptance of mathematical theories "*agreement with mathematical 'intuitions,'* whatever their source."[29] "Intuitions" seem to be what,
in his earlier remarks about Zermelo, he called "self-evidence." This would
certainly have to be a defeasible constraint, because such intuitions can conflict. The problem Putnam raises apparently has to do with its compatibility
with realism: "The problem is that it is totally unclear what satisfying *this*
sort of non-experimental constraint—agreement with 'intuitions' whatever
their source—has to do with *truth*."[30] But Putnam seems to recognize that
the difficulty is not specific to a realistic view in any strong sense, such as
Dummett's or that of Putnam's own notion of metaphysical realism. The
question is roughly: how can intuitions regarding mathematical statements
have objective significance, particularly in the case of higher set theory
where one cannot rely in the end on an indispensability argument? Putnam
does not offer the reply that would be suggested by Gödel's remark, that

such intuitions might be borne out by the mathematical success of theories constructed on the basis of them. It is not clear from Putnam's later statements what he thinks about this reply.

"Models and Reality" is Putnam's principal statement in the philosophy of mathematics in this period.[31] Although it is not the only place where he presents a model-theoretic argument directed against metaphysical realism, it is where it seems specifically aimed at such a view of mathematics and the paper contains other remarks about issues about mathematics. I will not pursue issues about the strength of this argument itself but instead concentrate on questions about the evolution of Putnam's views. However, the reader should keep in mind that the change in Putnam's views during the late 1970s was driven largely by general reflections on the relation of language and mind to the world and not primarily by reflection on mathematics. It would be beyond the scope of this essay to explore the general reflection.

On pages 9–11 of "Models and Reality," Putnam seems to back away from the view of "Mathematics without Foundations," that a statement like the continuum hypothesis is true or false whether or not we can know which. This is not surprising since toward the end of the paper he regards adopting an epistemic notion of truth as part of the solution to the problem the model-theoretic arguments pose. However, Putnam's example seems not to turn on ignorance at all. He imagines an "extraterrestrial species of intelligent beings" who have developed sophisticated mathematics, including set theory, but who reject the axiom of choice (AC).[32] Possibly they accept the full axiom of determinacy, which has consequences incompatible with choice. AC is of course a statement that actual set theorists accept with much less hesitation than the proposed axioms going beyond ZFC that were discussed in section I, not to speak of any axioms that would decide CH. It is often regarded as at least as evident as the other axioms of ZFC, perhaps more so than at least Replacement.

Putnam says that although our mathematicians have excellent reasons for accepting AC, we are not entitled to say that the extraterrestrials are irrational; he does not think the reasons that mathematicians have are so strong as to warrant that conclusion. But he does not regard the case as one of ignorance either, where neither party *knows* that AC is true. He uses the language of conventionalism but is not quite satisfied with it and also proposes that statements like AC do not have a truth value independent of their "embedding theory."[33] This suggestion is along the lines of what Putnam elsewhere calls "conceptual relativity."[34]

This example seems to me underdescribed. We need to know quite a bit more about the mathematical practice of the extraterrestrials. From the point of view of actual set theorists, it would be tempting to suppose that the extraterrestrials have a perfectly consistent theory (even if they accept full determinacy, at least relative to large cardinal assumptions), where, however, their power sets fall short of being the full power set.[35] Then the extraterrestrials would be doing perfectly good mathematics, but they would be missing something. The set theorist would have good reason for holding that although they are right in what they affirm, they are wrong in what they deny. But Putnam has not told us enough to justify accepting or rejecting this analysis of the situation. If we just assume that it is right, then it follows that our own set theorists *will* find something irrational in the extraterrestrials' practice, in their refusal of what we think of as the full power set. But it is not quite as simple as their being *mistaken*, even though there are statements we accept, including AC itself, that they reject. The case is more like that of the more sophisticated classical mathematicians' reaction to intuitionism. Intuitionism also refuses a conception that seems to the classicist perfectly respectable, that of truth or falsity independent of provability. A developed mathematical practice is possible on this basis, but the failure of classical logical laws gives rise to many complications and restrictions, and concept formation seems to have a great deal less freedom than in classical mathematics. So the classicist has powerful reasons for not being an intuitionist, perhaps even for saying that it is irrational to do mathematics in the way the intuitionist does. But he cannot argue that intuitionist mathematics is mistaken or incoherent, as are for example, the attempts that are still made to refute well-established theorems.

The passage from "Models and Reality" that I have commented on is somewhat at right angles to the main argument of that paper, the well-known model-theoretic argument. That still seems aimed at the view that there is a fact of the matter about the truth value of statements that are left undecided by theories one has adopted, what he calls theoretical constraints. To give the argument greater generality, he also has a way of working in observational constraints. Mathematical axioms that are generally accepted presumably count as among the theoretical constraints, so that AC in particular would still be true in any of the models that are relevant to the argument. However, the manner in which Putnam addresses this issue in first drawing conclusions from a Skolem-Löwenheim argument raises questions.

Putnam seems to be arguing against Gödel's view that $V = L$ is false.[36] He argues that, given a real number that encodes all measurable physical quantities (in some idealized sense), there is an ω-model of ZF + $V = L$ that contains this number and thus satisfies all "empirical constraints."[37] Thus, on Gödel's view, this model could not be the intended model. "But why not? It satisfies all theoretical constraints, and we have gone to great length to make sure it satisfies all operational constraints as well."[38]

Putnam does not ignore the obvious suggestion that either $V \neq L$, or something that implies it, should be considered as a theoretical constraint.

"But, while this may be acceptable from a non-realist standpoint, it can hardly be acceptable from a realist standpoint. For the realist standpoint is that there is *a fact of the matter*—a fact independent of our legislation, as to whether $V = L$ or not."[39] Putnam seems to be saying that adopting $V \neq L$ as a theoretical constraint can only be a stipulation; a couple of sentences later he speaks of *deciding* to make $V = L$ true or to make it false.

I do not know quite what to make of what Putnam says here; what he wrote about mathematical "intuitions" (at the same time) does not square well with the idea that adopting $V \neq L$ has to be a decision. Furthermore, it is hard to see what turns on the question whether one's "theoretical constraints" in mathematics are limited to ZF or ZFC or include something further, unless that does mark the boundary between what is a matter of "decision" or "convention" and what is not. I do not think that squares with the manner in which Putnam develops his example of extraterrestrials who reject AC.

My suspicion is that Putnam has been a victim of just the problem raised at the end of section I above: he wants to argue against the realist claim that a statement in the language of set theory is true or false whether we know or can know which, but when he searches for an example it is at least a serious question whether it is genuinely recognition-transcendent. Apart from the purely mathematical difficulties of his argument,[40] if he did not choose $V = L$ or something that $V = L$ decides, he would not be able to apply his theorem 1.[41] It is quite possible that Putnam intended the argument based on that theorem to have merely illustrative force, since before presenting it he argues briefly that only a recursively enumerable set of axioms will be arrived at "in the limit of set-theoretic inquiry,"[42] and since only what is implied by those axioms could possibly count as theoretical constraints in set theory, what is independent of them will lack a truth value. However, this is an assertion of the absence of recognition-transcendent truth, not an argument for it.

We are left with some unclarity about what the target of the arguments of "Models and Reality" is meant to be, so far as they concern mathematics. The structure of the paper and its relation to some other writings of this period make this question difficult.[43] But it should be clear that Putnam intends that some version of realism should survive them, what he calls "internal realism" or "realism with a small r." Putnam misleads the reader of this essay by talking near the end of the paper of "non-realist semantics,"[44] even though he had already introduced the term "internal realism" in "Realism and Reason."

Both in "Models and Reality" itself and in other writings of the end of the 1970s and the early '80s, Putnam does appeal to some form or other of verificationism or an epistemically constrained notion of truth. He often speaks of truth as idealized rational acceptability. In spite of his own use of the term "internal realism," many would view that as nonrealist. However, since he has rather little writing about mathematics in this period other than "Models and Reality" itself, he does not make very clear what "idealized rational acceptability" will amount to in mathematics, specifically in set theory where the problems arise that we have been discussing. Clearly he holds that even in the limit of set-theoretic inquiry (assuming that to be well-defined), some statements will be left undecidable. It follows that, although for the reasons given above he will not be able to give a plausible example of such a statement, he is committed to their existence. And his view of truth implies that such statements will lack a truth value. But the view really leaves open the status of propositions like $V = L$ or CH, for which set-theoretic inquiry either offers or might offer an answer as to its truth value.

I am not sure that the verificationist view is essential to the point Putnam wants to make about models. First of all, although he says that some form of verificationism offers a solution to the problem that the Skolem-Löwenheim argument poses, he does not really argue that it is the only solution. But most important is that when Putnam talks about his internal realism, he seems to regard "internalism" as an independent dimension of it. For example, describing his alternative to metaphysical realism in *Reason, Truth, and History*, he calls it "the *internalist* perspective, because it is characteristic of this view to hold that *what objects does the world consist of?* is a question that it only makes sense to ask *within* a theory or description."[45] Although Putnam then attributes to this perspective viewing truth as idealized rational acceptability, it is not clear that that is what is most essential to the internalist perspective.

At the end of "Models and Reality," Putnam diagnoses how one could get into the predicament created by his model-theoretic argument.

> To adopt a theory of meaning according to which a language whose whole use is specified still lacks something—namely its "interpretation"—is to accept a problem which *can* only have crazy solutions. To speak as if *this* were my problem, "I know how to use my language, but now, how shall I single out an interpretation?" is to speak nonsense. Either the use *already* fixes the "interpretation," or *nothing* can.[46]

In such a statement, of course a lot turns on what counts as "specifying the use." At the time Putnam was evidently much influenced by, although not quite persuaded by, Michael Dummett's way of understanding this, which led toward verificationism and a case for intuitionism. But in the last paragraph of the paper, the underlying idea seems to me different. It is rather that we should allow ourselves to take our language, including such elementary semantical statements as "'cat' refers to cats" at face value. What we should not say is that in order to allow ourselves to use such language, on the presumption that we understand it, we have to specify an interpretation. Furthermore, regress to a metalanguage in order to specify the interpretation would not help, because we would have to understand *that*. I think that is the point of the closing remark, "Models are not lost noumenal waifs looking for someone to name them; they are constructions from within our theory itself."[47]

We might add that the point of the AC example seems to be different. The key remark is one already alluded to, that AC and CH might not have a truth value "independent of the theory in which they are embedded."[48] In many writings since 1980, Putnam has stressed a sort of pluralism about what he sometimes calls conceptual schemes. He seems in "Models and Reality" to be willing to credit actual set theorists with such a scheme within which AC does count as "rationally acceptable" and thus, provisionally as true; he does not raise doubts as to whether this acceptability will maintain itself in the limit of inquiry. Although he does not lay out clearly what it would be, he is prepared to credit the extraterrestrials with a scheme in which ¬AC has these attributes. Putnam's difficulty in laying it out is not surprising: what he is suggesting is a possible bifurcation of set theory or of the concept of set, a bifurcation at a more basic level than the speculations about that possibility have envisaged. He is almost by definition not able to give substance to the speculation by an appeal to the actual practice of set theory, as we pointed out above.

One might also ask how this view differs from a Carnapian one, according to which the question whether to adopt AC is an external question and the principle of tolerance implies that we are not entitled to say that the extraterrestrials are mistaken. Putnam addresses this question in another paper built around a simple example where the question is whether to admit mereological sums.[49] There he says there is no fact of the matter as to the correctness of a number of stances one might take toward the fact that one theory gives the existence of mereological sums and another does not. He does not quite explicitly reject the Carnapian view, but the claim that it does not help to move the issue to a metalinguistic level amounts to that.[50] He does not think that the concept of meaning and related concepts are so definite that they can yield clear results in a dispute as to whether the differences about whether to admit mereology are differences of meaning. However, this is a case where there is not much at stake, for in this particular example, the language admitting such sums is translatable into the language that does not admit such sums because both are built on only three atoms.

IV

I do not want to pursue further the verificationist understanding of internal realism, because Putnam no longer holds it and it offers only a partial answer to the questions we have been raising about his view of higher set theory. I want to comment on two papers from the 1990s, one that seems, at least at first sight, to back away from his emphasis on quasi-empirical justification, but with no comment on set theory, and another that does comment on set theory, but without making the connection to the issues about the relation of truth and justification.

In the first, "Rethinking Mathematical Necessity" (see note 27), Putnam is first of all focused on logic. In keeping with its origin in a conference on the philosophy of Quine,[51] it might be read as a commentary on Quine's view that no statement is immune from revision. Putnam begins with the idea that he finds in Kant and Frege, that thought that does not accord with the laws of logic is not properly thought at all, that a situation in which such a law is falsified is not just impossible but unthinkable. This leads him to argue to some extent against Quine, that for certain truths, of which basic logical truths are an example, we are not able to make sense of the idea that further inquiry might lead them to be revised. This is not quite to say that they cannot be revised; he explicitly qualifies the claim of an earlier essay that "[n]ot every proposition is both true and false" is unrevisable.[52] He offers as an example a riddle (which recurs in other late writings of his): A certain court lady fell into disfavor with the king. The king, trying to give her an order that would be impossible to obey, ordered her to appear at a ball neither naked nor dressed. She appeared wearing a fishnet. The point is that until we have the solution to the riddle, we have not really given sense to the possibility that she might appear neither naked nor dressed. Putnam claims that with respect to the idea that someone might discover a counterexample to a logical law, we are in the position of someone who has the riddle but not the solution. So we cannot say that we know that it will not happen, that some development in theoretical physics in the year 2020 will call into question "$7 + 5 = 12$," but we have as of now no conception of how that could be and would not have such a conception so long as the development of knowledge has not brought it about or brought about something close to it.

This example makes clear that the application of the view is not meant to be limited to logic in the strict sense; in particular it extends into mathematics. But Putnam does not say how far it extends. Do we have a conception of how it could be that Fermat's last theorem is false, or that someone might discover that it is false? For those of us who have little if any idea of the proof, it seems that we have as good a conception of that as of any other mathematical state of affairs where we do not have clearly in mind how it is proved. Presumably a conception of its falsity would have to include the idea that the known proof is mistaken, but in the case of such an intricate proof that seems available even to experts.

However things might be with that example, Putnam would have to jettison a lot of what he has previously said if he holds the same view about axioms of higher set theory, even generally accepted ones. I have not encountered any later commentary on the AC example of "Models and Reality." The view one derives from his earlier writings, still held with some worries in 1979, is that axioms of set theory get a certain plausibility as "intuitions" but get a stronger justification by being necessary for science, where science includes mathematics. "Rethinking Mathematical Necessity" is silent on these issues.[53]

Putnam addresses the question all too briefly in a somewhat later essay, the second of his two Tarski lectures delivered at Berkeley in 1995.[54] He pursues the idea of sets as pluralities, suggested by George Boolos's writings on plural quantification. On the basis of that he sees no problem about the power set axiom. But then he says he sees "no intuitive basis at all" for the axiom of replacement. He goes on to say that he "sees no basis at all at the present time for any of the proposed large cardinal axioms."[55]

The remark about Replacement could be seen in the light of his earlier remarks about mathematical intuitions as part of what one relies on in adopting axioms. Unless the essay just discussed meant to give up the whole idea of quasi-empirical justification in mathematics, his claim would be that the justification of Replacement rests purely on its consequences. Although I myself have argued that quasi-empirical considerations play a role in our accepting the axiom of Replacement (see the essay cited in note 25), I cannot accept the implication that "intuitive" considerations have no force. About his remarks on stronger axioms of infinity, as regards "small" large cardinals, one might still argue on intuitive grounds, building on the objections one might make to his remark about Replacement. Putnam himself stresses the inexhaustibility of the universe of sets and this is the source of conceptual considerations favoring Replacement and inaccessible and Mahlo cardinals. But even where that runs out, with stronger axioms, axioms that conflict with $V = L$, there are still very powerful arguments for them of a quasi-empirical nature.[56] It may be that the attitude Putnam expresses here does reflect a backing away from his previous view of that mode of argument. But he has not addressed either the arguments themselves or stated where he now stands about this kind of justification in mathematics. However, he does not seem to have abandoned the view implicit in the AC example from "Models and Reality," that it would not be irrational to conceive set theory differently and deny them.

Another recent paper, "Was Wittgenstein *Really* an Anti-realist about Mathematics?" (see note 14), indicates that with respect to realism, Putnam would distinguish between the mathematics that is applied in science and higher set theory. He aims to defend, both as an overall reading of Wittgenstein and as philosophy, "common-sense realism" about mathematics. He argues that a constructivist or verificationist view of mathematics founders when we consider the application of mathematics in physics. But he states explicitly that he is not discussing set theory and that it has special problems (note 37). He makes clear that he thinks the indispensability argument, as presented by Quine (and very likely in his own earlier writings), is bound up with views he no longer accepts.[57] But he clearly still holds to the view of the importance of application that underlies the indispensability argument, and he may think that applicability sets limits on a realistic view of mathematics that coincide roughly with those that an indispensability argument would set on what mathematics is justified.

The other issue that we have been pursuing in Putnam's development is how he views the idea that mathematical statements are true or false in a recognition-transcendent way. But I think his present view is that recognition-transcendent truth may arise within a theory because of its logical structure. This appears to go somewhat beyond what one would say about another kind of case that he has discussed, where there are matters about which we cannot know the truth, but where this is explained by rather specific cognitive limitations, including where we are in space and time. Thus, we may never know whether Lizzie Borden killed her parents, but of course we could have known if we had been at the right place at the right time.

In a discussion of Putnam's view of truth, Crispin Wright introduces the example "there are no intelligent extraterrestrials" as a "malign" example of recognition-transcendence.[58] Commenting on this example,[59] Putnam asks us to imagine a cosmological theory according to which there is a probability of .95 that the physical conditions for the emergence of life like what we know or can conceive to be possible exist somewhere other than on Earth. Thus, in some sense the theory makes it probable that there *are* intelligent extraterrestrials. But what is probable need not be true, and the lesson Putnam draws is that, according to the theory, it could *just happen* that there are none.

Now consider a mathematical example. Brouwer makes some of his counterexamples turn on whether there is a sequence of digits of the form 0123456789 in the decimal expansion of π. We all know how we could verify that there is such a sequence: the calculation of the expansion, nowadays by supercomputers, could just turn one up. Brouwer's point was probably that no one had the slightest idea how one might go about proving that there is no such sequence. I would be very surprised if the development of mathematics since Brouwer wrote (the 1920s) has changed that situation.[60] But of course by classical logic, it is either true or false that there is such a sequence. And for such a Σ_1 statement, no one will argue that there is some hidden ambiguity which might make the statement true in one way of understanding it and false in another. I think Putnam would view this case in the same way in which he viewed that of the existence of intelligent extraterrestrials.

I can only conjecture what Putnam might say about recognition-transcendence in set theory. The continuum hypothesis can be expressed in the second-order theory of real numbers or in third-order arithmetic. So once we allow ourselves to use this language, then we can formulate CH, and classical logic yields CH v ¬CH. That just puts us back where we were some time back. If we continue to see no way in which it might be decided, it does not seem to be what Wright calls a contingency of epistemic opportunity. And unlike in Brouwer's case, we cannot rule out that there is some conceptual obstacle. So I would rather suspect that Putnam's view is that it is only in a relatively trivial sense that CH is either true or false, which does not rule out either something unclear about the concepts involved or a bifurcation of the conception of set theory into conceptual bases for theories giving different answers to the continuum problem. I have pointed out that the development of set theory has not given any substance to speculations about such a bifurcation. Putnam might accept such a conclusion and rely on the fact that for all that, we do not have convincing grounds for ruling out bifurcation.[61]

CHARLES PARSONS

HARVARD UNIVERSITY
APRIL 2003

NOTES

1. In thinking about Putnam's influence, one should not forget the work of his pupils. It is remarkable how many of the figures in postwar American philosophy of mathematics have studied with Putnam. One might mention particularly Paul Benacerraf, the late George Boolos, Hartry Field, and Geoffrey Hellman. None could be described as an orthodox "Putnamian," if such exist at all. Three papers that will be prominent in the subsequent discussion are "Mathematics without Foundations," *Journal of Philosophy* 64, no. 1 (1967): 5–22, reprinted in *Mathematics, Matter and Method: Philosophical Papers,* vol. 1 (Cambridge: Cambridge University Press, 1975; 2nd ed. 1979), 43–59; "What is Mathematical Truth?" in *Mathematics, Matter and Method,* 60–78; and "Models and Reality," *Journal of Symbolic Logic* 45, no. 3 (1980): 464–82, reprinted in *Realism and Reason* (Cambridge: Cambridge University Press, 1983), 1–25. The first and third of these papers are cited according to the reprints.

2. Putnam does share with nominalism the stress on the fact that a philosophy of mathematics should make sense of the application of mathematics, particularly in science. Since

this stress, as part of the nominalist program, really begins with Hartry Field's *Science without Numbers* (Princeton: Princeton University Press, 1980), it probably owes something to Putnam's influence. In *Philosophy of Logic* (New York: Harper and Row, 1971), reprinted in the second edition of *Mathematics, Matter and Method*, 323–57, Putnam does give an extensive and highly critical discussion of nominalist views about *logic*.

3. That may not be true of the early essay "The Thesis that Mathematics is Logic," in *Bertrand Russell, Philosopher of the Century*, ed. R. Schoenman (London: Allen & Unwin Ltd, 1967) and reprinted in *Mathematics, Matter and Method*, 12–42, which develops an "if-thenist" program for eliminating reference to mathematical objects. He already hints there, however, that to be tenable it needs to be supplemented by modality, a step that he takes soon after in "Mathematics without Foundations." Then he has a quite different view of the significance of such an eliminative strategy; see the text below.

4. Putnam, "Mathematics without Foundations," 45.

5. Putnam never published the technical details of this translation, and his readers have had some difficulty working out his sketch. However, constructions serving the same end have been worked out by others, most extensively by Geoffrey Hellman in *Mathematics without Numbers* (Oxford: Clarendon Press, 1989).

6. Putnam deflates the claim made by some writers, that such a modal translation avoids the epistemological problem widely thought to exist for reference to mathematical objects. Whether, in the case of higher set theory, the possibility statements referred to above can be cashed in by objects that are, in any plausible sense, concrete or nominalistically admissible is questioned in §6 of my "The Structuralist View of Mathematical Objects," *Synthese* 84, no. 3 (1990): 303–46. That point affects remarks Putnam makes but, it seems to me, not the issues discussed in the text.

7. Putnam, "Mathematics without Foundations," 49.

8. E.g. ibid., 48.

9. See in particular "Realism and Reason," in *Meaning and the Moral Sciences* (London: Routledge and Kegan Paul, 1978), 123–38.

10. Ibid., 132.

11. Putnam, "Mathematics without Foundations," 52.

12. See Putnam, "What is Mathematical Truth?," 70.

13. For a general presentation see John P. Burgess and Gideon Rosen, *A Subject with no Object: Strategies for Nominalistic Interpretation of Mathematics* (Oxford: Clarendon Press, 1997). It surveys what has been achieved in the program of nominalistic reduction and judiciously assesses what might be achieved further.

14. "Was Wittgenstein *Really* an Anti-realist about Mathematics?" in *Wittgenstein in America*, ed. Timothy G.. McCarthy and Sean C. Stidd (Oxford: Clarendon Press, 2001), 140–94, n. 47.

15. One of the first to point this out was Putnam himself, *Philosophy of Logic*, 56.

16. It is natural to imagine that $A1$ is $V = L$, since it has been known since Gödel's work of the late 1930s that that implies CH. Since set theorists do have substantial reasons for rejecting $V = L$ as an axiom, the present supposition implies that $A1$ is not $V = L$.

17. Gödel had shown already in 1938 that $V = L$ solved some of these problems.

18. In particular, Solomon Feferman has for some years been advocating a skeptical view of higher set theory. See especially his "Does Mathematics Need New Axioms?" *American Mathematical Monthly* 106, no. 2 (1999): 99–111; also several of the essays in his *In the Light of Logic* (New York: Oxford University Press, 1998).

19. In particular, W. Hugh Woodin has developed an approach, although he does not maintain that it offers a solution; see "The Continuum Hypothesis," *Notices of the American Mathematical Society* 48, no. 6 & 7 (2001): 567–76, 681–90. In general see Kai

Hauser, "Is Cantor's Continuum Problem Inherently Vague?" *Philosophia Mathematica* 10, no. 3 (2002): 257–85.

20. See Putnam, "What is Mathematical Truth?," 62.

21. Kurt Gödel, "What is Cantor's Continuum Problem?," in *Collected Works, Volume II: Publications 1938–1974*, ed. Solomon Feferman et al. (New York: Oxford University Press, 1990), 261.

22. Putnam, "What is Mathematical Truth?", 64.

23. "Neuer Beweis der Möglichkeit einer Wohlordnung," *Mathematische Annalen* 65 (1908): 107–28. The argument Putnam quotes is on pp. 112–13, in English translation on pp. 187–88 of *From Frege to Gödel: A Source Book in Mathematical Logic, 1879–1931*, ed. Jean van Heijenoort (Cambridge, MA: Harvard University Press, 1967).

24. I would not use this term in that way, and so far as I know Putnam does only in this place. What he means is close to what I call "intrinsic plausibility" in "Reason and Intuition," *Synthese* 125, no. 3 (2000): 299–315.

25. Putnam, "What is Mathematical Truth?," in *Mathematics, Matter and Method*, 67. Although I put greater emphasis on intrinsic plausibility than Putnam does in this passage, the view I defend in "Reason and Intuition" is similar. That "quasi-empirical" considerations are needed to justify the axioms of Power Set and Replacement is argued in my "Structuralism and the Concept of Set," in *Modality, Morality, and Belief: Essays in Honor of Ruth Barcan Marcus*, ed. Walter Sinnott-Armstrong (in collaboration with Nicholas Asher and Diana Raffman) (Cambridge: Cambridge University Press, 1995), 74–92.

26. Putnam, "What is Mathematical Truth?" 66, second emphasis mine. In discussion, Michael Friedman questions how clearly Putnam at this time distinguished the "quasi-empirical and yet a priori" justification envisaged by Gödel and justification based on necessity for science where the latter includes *empirical* science. That sort of justification could have been called simply empirical. Gödel's conception seems to depend on the existence of a body of mathematical truth (elementary arithmetic and perhaps more) that would have a directly a priori justification. Putnam probably would not have accepted this assumption.

27. See Hilary Putnam, "It Ain't Necessarily So," *Journal of Philosophy* 59, no. 22 (1962): 658–71, reprinted in *Mathematics, Matter and Method*, 240 of reprint. Although he did not use the term "a priori" in describing the conception some years later he explained it by contrasting such statements with statements "empirical relative to a body of knowledge." See "Rethinking Mathematical Necessity," in *Words and Life*, ed. James Conant (Cambridge, MA: Harvard University Press, 1994), 245–63, term employed on 251.

28. "Philosophy of Mathematics: Why Nothing Works," in *Words and Life*, 499–512. Originally "Philosophy of Mathematics: A Report," in *Current Research in the Philosophy of Science: Proceedings of the P. S. A. Critical Research Problems Conference*, ed. Peter D. Asquith and Henry E. Kyburg, Jr. (East Lansing: Philosophy of Science Association, 1979), 386–98.

29. Ibid., 506. The emphasis is Putnam's.

30. Ibid., 507.

31. See Hilary Putnam, "Models and Reality," 1–25.

32. Ibid., 9.

33. Ibid., 10.

34. For example, see Hilary Putnam, *Representation and Reality* (Cambridge: MIT Press, 1988), 110ff.

35. Full determinacy holds in $L[R]$, the class of sets constructible from real numbers, if sufficiently strong large cardinal axioms hold. But the failure of AC would normally

be taken as a reason for thinking that already the sets of reals in $L[R]$ fall short of being *all* sets of reals.

36. Putnam, "Models of Reality," 7.

37. It seems to be presumed to satisfy the sentences that say that the measurements are as the number in question indicates.

38. Putnam, "Models of Reality," 7.

39. Ibid.

40. See Timothy Bays, "On Putnam and his Models," *Journal of Philosophy* 98, no. 7 (2001): 331–50.

41. Putnam, "Models of Reality," 6.

42. Ibid., 5.

43. Although "Models of Reality" is the locus classicus of the "model-theoretic argument against metaphysical realism," this argument is generally found by commentators in "Realism and Reason" (see note 9) and in *Reason, Truth, and History* (Cambridge: Cambridge University Press, 1981), 22–48. But the arguments of those texts are different and involve less logical machinery. Although I cannot argue this here, I do not believe either intends an argument against any form of realism about *set theory*, at least any form that is compatible with some version of structuralism.

44. Putnam, "Models of Reality," 24.

45. Hilary Putnam, *Reason, Truth, and History* (Cambridge: Cambridge University Press, 1981), 49.

46. Putnam, "Models of Reality," 24.

47. Ibid., 25.

48. Ibid., 10.

49. See Hilary Putnam, "Truth and Convention: On Davidson's Refutation of Conceptual Realitivism," *Dialectica* 41 (1987): 69–77, reprinted in *Realism with a Human Face*, ed. James Conant (Cambridge, MA: Harvard University Press, 1990), 96–104. Thanks to Øystein Linnebo for calling this paper to my attention.

50. Ibid., 103.

51. Presented at the conference "W.V.O. Quine's Contribution to Philosophy," held at the University of San Marino in 1990. The paper also appears as "Mathematical Necessity Reconsidered," in the proceedings of that conference, *On Quine: New Essays*, ed. Paolo Leonardi and Marco Santambrogio (Cambridge: Cambridge University Press, 1995), 267–82.

52. See Putnam's "There Is at Least One A Priori Truth," in *Realism and Reason*, 98–114.

53. Putnam does remark that there are "statements of mathematics whose truth value no human being may ever be able to decide." He responds that he is "not able to attach metaphysical weight to the principle of bivalence" but that a discussion of the issue would require another essay. See "Rethinking Mathematical Necessity," 259. Some idea of what he has in mind can be gleaned from the paper cited in note 14.

54. "Paradox Revisited II: Sets—A Case of All or None?" in *Between Logic and Intuition: Essays in Honor of Charles Parson*, ed. Gila Sher and Richard Tieszen (Cambridge: Cambridge University Press, 2000), 16–26.

55. Ibid., 24. In conversation, Putnam has said that his problem is with the available arguments motivating these axioms; he did not mean to object to them on more philosophical or otherwise fundamental grounds.

56. See for example Donald A. Martin, "Mathematical Evidence," in *Truth in Mathematics*, ed. H. G. Dales and Gianluigi Oliveri (Oxford: Clarendon Press, 1998), 215–31.

57. See "Was Wittgenstein *Really* an Anti-realist about Mathematics?," 149–53. The discussion mainly concerns the notion of object and how to take talk of objects in math-

ematics. Putnam's view of these matters requires separate treatment, which I hope to undertake elsewhere.

58. Crispin Wright, "Truth as Sort of Epistemic: Putnam's Peregrinations," *Journal of Philosophy* 97, no. 6 (2000): 353, 357.

59. Hilary Putnam, "When 'Evidence Transcendence' Is Not Malign: A Reply to Crispin Wright," *Journal of Philosophy* 98, no. 1 (2001): 597–98.

60. [*Note added October 2014.*] When I wrote this I was unaware that it had been discovered in 1997 that there *is* a sequence 0123456789 in the decimal expansion of π. See Jonathan M. Borwein, "Brouwer-Heyting Sequences Converge," *Mathematical Intelligencer* 20, no. 1 (1998): 14–15. (Thanks to Mark van Atten for this reference.) Brouwer's examples can be reinstated by choosing a more complicated sequence, say a sequence consisting of ten successive sequences of 0123456789. The remark that probably no one has any idea of how to prove that there is no such sequence probably still holds.

61. Earlier versions of this paper have been presented to the Indiana University Logic Colloquium, the UCLA Philosophy Colloquium, and the conference Sémantique et Épistémologie in Casablanca, Morocco. I am indebted to J. Michael Dunn, Solomon Feferman, Michael Friedman, Øystein Linnebo, and Hilary Putnam for helpful comments.

REPLY TO CHARLES PARSONS

Parsons is a philosopher whose work I have long held in extremely high regard. That work always examines fundamental issues, and it shows depth, originality, and impressive scholarship. My familiarity with it led me to expect that his essay for this volume would raise difficult and important questions, and it does—indeed, it raises a great many issues—so many that to comment on each of the points he raised would require making this reply tedious reading (not to mention, tedious writing). But I believe that if I state what my present position is on two central issues, it should be clear what I would say about all or most of the points he raises. The issues in question are:

(1) Realism and set theory
(2) The role and nature of "quasi-empirical" arguments in mathematics

In addition Parsons has a number of comments on a paper from my "internal realist" period, namely "Models and Reality." Since I repudiated the "internal realism" on which that paper is based in the 1990s (I give the details of this repudiation in my Intellectual Autobiography in the present volume), and I explain my reasons for repudiating it in some detail in *The Threefold Cord: Mind, Body and Word*, as well as in "Between Scylla and Charybdis: Does Dummett Have a Way Through?,"[1] and in my "Reply to Dummett" in the present volume, I shall "beg off" from responding to Parsons's comments on *that* paper, except to say that *nothing* in that paper corresponds to the way I think now.

REALISM AND MATHEMATICS

I do not believe and have in fact *never* believed that "indispensability arguments" *by themselves* suffice to justify the acceptance of the axioms of arithmetic or set theory, nor does Parsons claim that I do or did. What the indispensability of mathematics for physics shows, I claimed in "What is Mathematical Truth" (1975) was that "the internal success and coherence of mathematics is evidence that it is true under some interpretation," and that "its indispensability for physics is evidence that it is true under a realist interpretation" (the antirealist interpretation I considered there was intuitionism).

But I wish to comment on a worry of Parsons that I find strange. The worry has to do with *bivalence*. A realist about set theory believes that, unless there is good reason to believe that the notion of a *set* is ambiguous (for example, a good argument to show that there are two distinct notions of "set," both of which fit our mathematical practice and intuitions equally well, on one of which a statement of set theory, say, the Continuum Hypothesis—henceforth, "CH"—is true and on the other of which it is false), *one should regard that statement as having a truth value, even should it be the case that we can never know for sure what that truth value is.* In short, realists believe in "recognition transcendent truth," as Parsons puts it. Parsons and I agree that we do not know of such a good argument. But Parsons worries that I cannot give a definite *example* of a set theoretic statement whose truth value we can never find out. To this, I want to reply both "Of course" and "So what." "Of course," because, mathematics differs from physics in the following respect: physics itself can tell us that there are regions of spacetime from which we cannot receive information (for example, regions beyond our "event horizon"), and also tell us that it is possible that those regions contain X (where X is, for example, intelligent life) and possible that they do not.

Hence, we can give examples of statements about the physical universe such that *if they are true, we can never know that this is the case*—for example, the statement that those regions contain or fail to contain intelligent extraterrestrials (a statement that Parsons mentions).[2] However, there are no statements of pure mathematics that we can prove to be such that if they are true, we can never know that fact. The Gödel-Rosser Theorems show us how, given a formal system (say ZFC[3]), we can construct mathematical statements such that, if they are true, we cannot prove that they are in that formal system. But that we do not have and cannot have a formalizable notion of "proof" *überhaupt* (as opposed to proof-in-this-or-that-formal-system) is well known, and lacking that, the very notion of an absolutely unprovable mathematical statement has no mathematically precise sense. Moreover, Parsons is right that there may well be informal arguments that permit us to (tentatively) assign a truth value to CH. For example, there is a well-known argument by Chris Freiling that convinces many set theorists (including me) that CH is *false*.[4] So I can't use CH as an example of a statement which is such that if it is true (respectively, false) we can never know that it is.

That is why I say, "Of course." But I also say, "So what?" And I say this because it is hard to see the *relevance* of all this. Of course, if *every* statement expressible in the language of set theory (first order predicate calculus with the ε of set membership as the sole predicate) were "decidable" either by a formal proof or by a convincing informal argument, then both realists and antirealists could agree that set theoretic statements are bivalent, albeit for different philosophical reasons, and then the difference between the two positions (assuming there still were one) could not be characterized (as I did) by saying that realists believe that one should regard a set-theoretic statement as having a truth value, even should it be the case that we can never know for sure what that truth value is. But I cannot believe that Parsons thinks it is a serious possibility that *every* set-theoretic statement is "decidable" either by a formal proof or by a convincing informal argument. For one thing, since the number of such statements is infinite, the only way informal arguments could decide *all* of them would be if some finite subset, a finite set of statements each of which is short enough to contemplate and reason about, were a complete axiomatization of set theory *and* were such that each of those statements could be "verified" by an informal argument. But, then what about the statement that those statements are consistent? I repeat, I am quite unsure what Parsons is driving at here.

A more serious issue, and one that Parsons rightly raises, is whether one should regard *all* statements of set theory—even the much discussed "large cardinal axioms"—as "recognition transcendently" bivalent. Granting that so regarding them is the "realist" position, ought realism to extend so far? Let me briefly mention my reasons for rejecting the "No" answer I gave in 1980 and answering "Yes" today instead.

First (starting in the late 1950s when I wrote "The Analytic and the Synthetic"), I have long rejected instrumentalism and logical positivism as accounts of the meanings of the so-called "theoretical terms" of modern physical science. On those accounts, theoretical terms are just uninterpreted "machinery," machinery that is useful for predicting "observables." I believe that all or most successful physical theories are at least approximately true, and that their "theoretical terms" refer to real properties and relations. Indeed, I believe that by denying this, instrumentalism and logical positivism make the success of science an inexplicable miracle. Successful theories in a mature science (and not only physical theories) are usually successful because they are approximately true, and they are approximately true because some or all of their terms do have real referents, and because those referents behave approximately as the theory says they do.

Second, it is an uncontroversial fact that the theories of mathematical physics in particular use a great deal of mathematics (that is why it is called "mathematical physics"). In particular, the sentences that we take to express the fundamental principles of any one of those theories are in a "mixed" vocabulary: they contain both physical terms, such as *charge* or *mass*, and purely mathematical expressions, for example, expressions for integrals and partial derivatives. But from these two facts (assuming one accepts the first as well as the second as a fact) it follows that an interpretation of mathematics in isolation that does not extend to an interpretation of the mixed sentences under which the latter can be true or approximately true cannot be a correct interpretation of mathematics-in-use.

Strangely enough, this last point is widely ignored. Two examples of philosophies of mathematics that, in my opinion, suffer from ignoring it are predicativism[5] (for example, Feferman's *In the Light of Logic*) and the *intuitionism* of Brouwer and Heyting.

THE PROBLEM WITH PREDICATIVISM

One common objection to the idea that we should interpret the "mixed" statements of mathematical physics realistically is that we do not yet have the "true" physical theory. [6] My answer to that objection is that we should regard each of the rival theories as a candidate for truth or approximate truth, and that *any philosophy of mathematics that would be inconsistent with so regarding them should be rejected*. No doubt our present-day physics will turn out to be "idealized"; but to assume a priori that what succeeds it, or what should succeed it, had we enough wit and time to find it, would be a physics that never quantifies over an uncountable totality, is utterly unjustified.

With this in mind, let us turn to the claim that predicative set theory is adequate to the needs of physics. The statement "there is a point in spacetime corresponding to every quadruple of real numbers" is not, as far as I can see, *expressible* without quantifying over *all* quadruples of real numbers—which is something that predicative analysis forbids!

Of course one could (and many do) wax skeptical, not on physical but on supposedly "conceptual" grounds, about whether physics "really needs" to talk about every point in space or every region in space; but I have difficulty in seeing the difference between such skepticism and outright "instrumentalism." Indeed, if adequacy for "applications" just means adequacy for testable predictions, then the view that *that* is all that physics is after is precisely instrumentalism.

But what of the quantum theories of spacetime? It is true that in some of these we lose the notion of points and spheres as determinate objects in physical spacetime, but if anything it is even easier to show that the world view of quantum mechanics needs *all* the real numbers. The world view of quantum mechanics is that there is a definite totality of possible "time evolutions" of a physical system. And if it is physically possible that future time is infinite, then it is easy to show that there are as many distinct time evolutions of some very simple systems as there are real numbers.

THE PROBLEM WITH INTUITIONISM

Intuitionism, as is well known, gives the logical connectives a nonclassical interpretation; instead of stating truth conditions for sentences containing them (in terms of the classical notion of truth), it states conditions for *the constructive provability* of mathematical sentences, in an informal (and according to Brower *unformalizable*) sense of "constructive provability." But if we understand nonmathematical sentences about physical reality "realistically," and interpret the logical connectives they contain "classically" and mathematical sentences "intuitionistically," how are we supposed to understand the *mixed sentences* (including the fundamental laws of mathematical physics)?

Brouwer himself virtually ignored the problem of applying intuitionism in physics. Michael Dummett, the most sophisticated philosopher to defend intuitionism, proposes to interpret *all* statements, including empirical ones, in terms of "conclusive verification," and I explain my reasons for rejecting this idea in my reply to him in the present volume. In "Models and Reality" I too displayed an attraction to intuitionism, and proposed interpreting all statements in terms of verification under ideal conditions, an idea that I subsequently criticized in detail in a number of places.[7] But what all these defenses of intuitionism have in common is that they do not even try to show that scientific realism is compatible with intuitionism; instead they argue that one should reject scientific realism.

In sum, both predicativism and intuitionism should be rejected by scientific realists, because even if the predicativist or the intuitionist can derive the *theorems* of mathematics that are necessary for physics, they cannot provide an *interpretation* of those theorems that extends to an interpretation of the mixed statements that a realist can accept.

REALISM AND THE HIGHER REACHES OF SET THEORY

Realists in the philosophy of mathematics reject the idea that truth in mathematics can be equated with *provability*. They also hold that mathematical statements are *bivalent*. The second of these theses follows from the first, if we set aside as completely implausible the possibility that I said Parsons *may* be raising, that each statement of mathematics is either provable or disprovable from axioms that we would have good reason to accept if we thought about the matter in the right way, even though, by Gödel's and Rosser's theorems, there is no consistent formal system for all of mathematics *all* of whose axioms we have good reason to accept in which every statement is decidable. But why should we be realists about *all* of mathematics? Almost all philosophers of mathematics are realists about first-order arithmetic; but realism about the whole universe of sets seems counter-intuitive, to many thinkers. About the idea of "limiting" one's mathematical realism, I have three comments to make.

First, as Parsons explains, I do not believe that we have to think of the real numbers as "Platonic objects." On the ""modal-logical interpretation" of set theory that I pioneered in my "Mathematics without Foundations," quantification over sets, functions, etc., can perfectly well be regarded as talk about *possibility* and *impossibility* and not as quantification over actually existing entities.[8] I argued there, and I still believe, that all of the different "translations" of number theory into set theory, and all of the different translations of set theory into function theory, and all of the different translations of function theory into set theory, are just different ways of showing what structures have to *possibly exist* in order for our mathematical assertions to be true. In my view what the modal-logical "translation" of a mathematical statement gives us is a statement *with the same mathematical content* which does not have even the appearance of being about the actual existence of immaterial objects.

Second, for the reasons I just gave in connection with predicativism, realism about *only* first-order arithmetic is simply not realism enough. A realistic interpretation of the "mixed statements" of present-day physics (including all the proposed modifications or replacements or extensions of present-day quantum mechanics and cosmology) requires a realistic understanding of statements about real numbers, or, equivalently, second order number theory.

Third, the idea that we should be realists about first- and second-order number theory, but not, say, about third-order number theory (or about sets of rank greater than α for some α) requires both a good philosophical defense and a detailed technical spelling out, neither of which I have been able to find in the literature. Sometimes the fact that the axioms of set theory do not settle such questions as the truth or falsity of the axiom "V=L" (proposed, but later rejected, by Gödel) is offered as a reason to say that the notion of an arbitrary set is (partly) "indeterminate";[9] but the axioms of set theory also do not settle the truth value of the statement "all real numbers are constructible (in Gödel's sense)," and that statement is expressible in second-order arithmetic. If we are realists about second-order arithmetic, we will say, "Yes, there are statements about the real numbers (or, equivalently, about arbitrary sets of integers) that are independent of the axioms of present-day set theory; but we will not conclude that the notion "real number," or the notion "arbitrary set of integers" is *indeterminate* for that reason. Indeed it could be that the axioms of mathematics do not determine the truth value of the Twin Prime Conjecture, but we do not conclude that the notion *integer* is "indeterminate" on that account. And a technically satisfying way of justifying antirealism about ranks higher than α for some α would require explaining how the notion "set" can have two different interpretations, a realist one and an "antirealist" one (and how they fit together) and we certainly have not seen any such explanation. The possibility of a plausible combination of realism with respect to first- and second-order number theory and antirealism with respect to "higher" set theory is one that I certainly cannot rule out; but the "burden of proof" should lie on the side of those who believe in such a combination. My view is that realism with respect to set theory and, indeed, science as a whole, should be the default position, with exceptions being made only when they can be clearly explained and justified. This is my answer to Parsons's question as to my present attitude towards the existence of "recognition transcendent" truth in set theory.

The Role and Nature of "Quasi-Empirical" Arguments in Mathematics

Parsons has a number of comments on and questions about my claim that quasi-empirical arguments play a significant role in mathematical thought, and I shall try to respond to what I take to be the most important ones. Parsons is right that I "would have endorsed" what Gödel wrote in the passage he quotes, namely: "There might exist axioms so abundant in their verifiable consequences, shedding so much light on a whole field, and yielding such powerful methods of solving problems . . . that, no matter whether or not they are intrinsically necessary, they would have to be accepted at least in the same sense as any well-established physical theory." He states correctly that "Putnam also gives examples of quasi-empirical arguments for mathematical conjectures that mathematicians find convincing," and he adds, "But of course such conviction does not lead them to abandon the goal of obtaining a proof. It seems likely that it *would* lead them to regard the search for a counterexample as unpromising, and probably that is part of Putnam's idea."

That is indeed part of my idea. In addition, I wrote in the paper from which Parsons quotes, "Although it is rare that either mathematicians or philosophers discuss it in public, quasi-empirical methods are constantly used to discover truths or putative truths that one then tries to prove rigorously.

Moreover, some of the quasi-empirical arguments by which one discovers a mathematical proposition to be true in the first place are totally convincing to mathematicians."[10]

Parsons also writes, "Some writers, Gödel in particular, regard the existence of this sort of justification in mathematics as quite compatible with its a priori character. Putnam seems not to view the matter in this way." But of course I do not! In the very paper from which he quotes, I wrote: "In fact, I don't think there is any such thing as an a priori statement, unless 'a priori' just means unrevisable within a particular theoretical frame, characterized both by positive assumptions and a 'space' of theoretical alternatives."[11] I criticize the idea of absolutely necessary truth in the "Intellectual Autobiography" section of this volume, where I write that "such 'necessity' [necessity relative to a body of knowledge] ... is the only sort of 'conceptual necessity' I recognize."

Commenting on a paper of mine which stressed the difficulty of finding a satisfactory philosophy of mathematics ("Philosophy of Mathematics: Why Nothing Works"), Parsons points out that there I accept the idea that consonance with our mathematical intuitions has justificatory significance in set theory, but I worry about how this can be the case. He writes: "The question is roughly: how can intuitions regarding mathematical statements have objective significance, particularly in the case of higher set theory where one cannot rely in the end on an indispensability argument. Putnam does not offer the reply that would be suggested by Gödel's remark that such intuitions might be borne out by the mathematical success of theories constructed on the basis of them. It is not clear from Putnam's later statements what he thinks about this reply."

The answer is that I *agree* with Gödel here. In fact, I write in a recent paper, if one thinks, as most people do, that one should be a realist (in the sense I explained) about number theory, then one should note that set theory is indispensable to the proving of some of the most exciting results we have about the natural numbers. I am thinking of Wiles's proof of Fermat's so-called "Last Theorem," which employed techniques due to Grothendieck which themselves require set theory to formalize in a straightforward way in standard mathematical logic. Even if it proves possible to find "work-arounds" that enable us to code Wiles's proof into second-order or even first-order number theory, the result would not be the proof that mathematicians accepted and that convinced them that FLT is *true*. So, I would like to suggest a "bootstrapping" argument here: if the indispensability of mathematics (number theory and analysis) for physics is a good reason for interpreting at least number theory and analysis "realistically," *then why isn't the indispensability of set theory to number theory a reason for interpreting set theory realistically?*[12]

Parsons is right that "Rethinking Mathematical Necessity" is "silent on these issues," but they were not the topic of that paper. The issue that that paper was concerned with is discussed in my "Reply to Gary Ebbs" in this volume, and I will not repeat what I say in that reply at any length. But in brief, I hold that neither the notion of universal revisability ("every statement can be revised") nor the notion of absolute unrevisability has any clear sense. To the question Parsons asks, "Do we have a conception of how it could be that Fermat's last theorem is false, or that someone might discover that it is false?," my answer is that we have a *weak* conception of how this could be, even after Wiles's proof, based on a sort of extrapolation from other cases in which an error has been found in a very long proof, but that this *general* possibility of an error is no reason for skeptical worries about that proof. To what seems like an objection on Parsons's part to my notion of relative necessity, namely: "He did use the term 'necessary relative to a body of knowledge' to describe cases such as the status of geometry in earlier times, but he did not so far as I know apply this idea to a case like arithmetic, where it is not obvious what the relevant body of knowledge would be," my reply is as follows: first (a minor point), in that paper I had already changed "necessary relative to a body of knowledge" (the term I used in my much earlier "It Ain't Necessarily So") to "necessary relative to a conceptual scheme." Secondly, and substantively, since arithmetic is used in all areas of discourse, the relevant conceptual scheme is, of course, our existing body of (what we take to be) our knowledge as a whole.

H.P.

NOTES

1. "Between Scylla and Charybdis: Does Dummett Have a Way Through?" in *The Philosophy of Michael Dummett*, ed. Randall E. Auxier and Lewis Edwin Hahn (Chicago: Open Court, 2007), 155–67.

2. Suppose P is a physical theory according to which there is a high finite probability which is, however, less than one, that intelligent life exists in a certain region R, and also tells us that we can never receive signals from R to decide the matter. Then the conjunction of P with "There are no intelligent extraterrestrials in region R" will be a statement that (1) *could* be true (if the first conjunct is true, then the probability of the second conjunct is greater than zero) but which is *logically* impossible to verify if true.

3. "ZFC" is a common way of referring to Zermelo-Gödel-Fraenkel set theory plus the Axiom of Choice.

4. Chris Freiling, "Axioms of Symmetry: Throwing Darts at the Real Number Line" *Journal of Symbolic Logic* 51 (1986): 190–200.

5. According to this view, we are only allowed to quantify over sets and relations that are "definable" in a certain sense (the technical details make precise the idea that the definitions must in turn obey the same restriction on quantification over sets and relations).

A consequence is that in predicative mathematics no meaningful quantification can ever range over an uncontrolled totality.

6. The contents of this section are adapted from my "Indispensability Arguments in the Philosophy of Mathematics," in *Philosophy in an Age of Science* (Cambridge, MA: Harvard University Press, 2012).

7. For example, in my *The Threefold Cord: Mind, Body and World.* See also my "Reply to Michael Dummett" in the present volume.

8. This interpretation has been developed in detail in Geoffrey Hellman, *Mathematics without Numbers: Towards a Modal-structural Interpretation* (Oxford: Clarendon Press, 1989).

9. L is the proper class of all those sets that can be obtained by a certain transfinite "construction" process.

10. Hilary Putnam, "What is Mathematical Truth," in *Mathematic, Matter and Method: Philosophical Papers,* vol. 1 (Cambridge: Cambridge University Press, 1975; 2nd ed. 1979), 67.

11. Ibid, footnote to p. 63.

12. This is the closing paragraph of my "Set Theory: Realism, Replacement and Modality," in my *Philosophy in an Age of Science.*

2

Hartry Field

MATHEMATICAL UNDECIDABLES, METAPHYSICAL REALISM, AND EQUIVALENT DESCRIPTIONS

I. Metaphysical Irrealism in Mathematics

The term "metaphysical realism" admits a variety of interpretations; but as applied to mathematics, one natural interpretation is the doctrine that typical undecidable sentences in established branches of mathematics like set theory have determinate or objective truth value.

The reason for focusing on undecidable sentences is that decidable sentences could easily be held to get determinate truth values "cheaply": their being determinately true or determinately false could be held to just *consist in* (or *result from*) their being provable or refutable in some consistent axiom system, each of whose axioms and rules we are disposed to accept. For sentences not so decidable, there is no obvious means by which they could possess determinate truth values "cheaply," in other words, short of a thoroughgoing realist position about the nature of mathematics. Of course, they could *come to have* determinate truth values cheaply: we could conventionally decide to adopt new axioms that settle them. What takes a thoroughgoing realism is to hold that they have determinate truth value now, prior to and independent of any such decision.

Hilary Putnam's attitude towards this sort of metaphysical realism in mathematics has undergone a number of shifts through his long career of important articles on the subject. In 1967's "The Thesis that Mathematics is Logic," Putnam critically commented on the view that the continuum hypothesis has a determinate truth value that outruns our ability to decide it, and argued that this view depends on the dubious assumption that there is a determinate totality of all possible subsets of a given infinite set.[1] Soon afterward, in "Mathematics without Foundations," he changed his mind, and indeed scoffed at the earlier view.[2] But by "Models and Reality" he seems to have shifted back to something like his initial view, and he put forward a more explicit argument for it.[3] (He did not really endorse this argument, but he did think that reflecting on it undermined "metaphysical realism" in some sense of that phrase, and I *believe* he would have taken that to include the sense above.) The argument from "Models and Reality" is based on the idea that there seems to be nothing in our practice with the notions of "set" and "member of" that could single out "the standard model" of set theory as opposed to (typical) "nonstandard" ones.

This way of putting the matter is loose. For one thing, the naive way to understand set theory is to suppose that its quantifiers range over all sets (or all classes, if it admits proper classes); but since there is no set that contains all sets (or class that contains all classes), there is no such thing as "the standard model of set theory," at least not on any entirely obvious interpretation. So a better way to put Putnam's point is that there is nothing about our practice that determines that

(i) our restricted quantifier "all sets" ranges over *all sets*

and

(ii) our predicate "∈" applies to a pair <a,b> if and only if a is a member of b.

There are all sorts of possible alternatives to (i) and (ii). Of course, many of these alternatives can be ruled out as not according with our intentions: this is most obviously so for alternatives that would fail to validate the axioms for sets that we have laid down. But there are plenty of alternatives that validate all of the axioms we have laid down, and in some of these the continuum hypothesis has one truth value and in others another. Putnam seems at first blush to be arguing that there is no way that our practice with the terms "set" and "∈" could determine the semantics of these terms except by restricting the allowable interpretations to those that are consistent with the axioms we have laid down.

Actually, that is only a crude approximation to Putnam's argument. He does *not* argue that consistency with the axioms we have laid down is the only constraint on the interpretations of "set" and "∈"; on the contrary, he implicitly suggests a way in which the empirical applications of mathematics might restrict the range of acceptable interpretations. Although he himself does not argue that the empirical applications actually do rule out some interpretations that are consistent with the axioms, I think it is possible to argue persuasively that they do: in particular, they rule out interpretations whose number-theoretic fragments are nonstandard (in other words, in which the quantifier "only finitely many" comes out nonstandard). If so, all undecidable sentences of number theory (and certain "atypical" undecidable sentences of set theory) do get determinate truth value even assuming Putnam's argument. I have argued this elsewhere[4]; and a careful reading of Putnam's "Models and Reality" makes it pretty clear that the point was not news to him. What Putnam argues there (in contrast to the crude approximation in the last sentence of the previous paragraph) is that even making an allowance for how the empirical applications of mathematics can constrain the allowable interpretations, there is no way that they could constrain them *enough* to determine truth values for typical undecidable sentences of set theory, such as the continuum hypothesis. His argument that the empirical applications can only do so much seems to me thoroughly convincing, but I have discussed this in the papers cited and do not want to go into it again.

For my purposes here, the difference between the cruder argument and the more sophisticated argument will not matter. A key claim of both is that there is no way our practices could determine the extensions of "set" and/ or "∈'" sufficiently to give the continuum hypothesis objective truth value.

But as Paul Horwich has noted, there is an ambiguity in the notion of determination.[5] In a weak sense of the term, all that is required for our practices to "determine" the extension of a term is that its having that extension supervene on those practices. So one could maintain that reference is determined by our practices (for example, by our accepting axioms X involving "set" and "∈") simply by maintaining that anyone who accepted those axioms would inevitably be using the word "set" for all and only the sets and "∈" for all and only the membership pairs. But it is natural to expect more than this: an explanation of why those practices suffice for that extension. If we are happy with a bare supervenience claim, there is no obvious reason why the axioms X need be true or even approximately true for sets and membership. For all that has been said, the acceptance of axioms that intuitively seem wholly inappropriate to sets but appropriate instead to kangaroos or harmonic oscillators could "determine" that our words are about sets and membership. Also, the weak determination claim allows that while our acceptance of axioms X "determines" that our words are about sets and membership, someone else could accept completely analogous axioms that differed only in having different words in place of "set" and "∈," and his words would have different extensions: there is no obvious reason why the orthography of our words could not be part of the supervenience base.

What Putnam clearly wanted was an illuminating account of *why* using words in the way we use "set" and "∈" makes them words for all and only the sets and all and only the membership pairs. And there is a very natural stronger sense of "determines" in which only such an account would be an account of how our practice determines the semantics of these predicates. His point was that while our acceptance of certain axioms involving "set" and "∈" can (if the axioms are consistent) plausibly be held to determine in the strong sense that the extensions of these predicates are such as to obey these axioms, it is not in the least clear how accepting those axioms, or anything else about our practice, can (in the strong sense) determine the extension finely enough to settle typical undecidable sentences.

Prima facie, the desire for an account of how semantic notions are determined in the strong sense is completely reasonable. It is, after all, what we expect for most nonsemantic notions (outside of basic physics, which is what we take to be the source of determination). For instance, it is one thing to know that the property of having a gene for hemophilia is weakly determined by (supervenes on) having DNA with a certain feature, and another to know exactly why that feature leads to hemophilia; in other words, to have an account of how, in the strong sense, that feature of the DNA determines the possession of the gene. Lacking such an account of how DNA strongly determines phenotype would be intellectually unsatisfying, and a persuasive argument that there could be no such account would put us in a major intellectual crisis. Why should we not be in a comparable intellectual crisis if we thought that there were objective facts about reference but that they were not strongly determined? If the strong determination of reference cannot be maintained, it would seem better to give up the objectivity of reference.

It is natural, then, to assume the following principle:

(P) If no account is possible of how our practice with a term determines (in the strong sense) whether it is true of x, then it cannot be objectively (determinately) true of x or objectively (determinately) false of x.

This principle or something like it is assumed in Putnam's argument. I do not say he *believed* the principle: at the very end of the article he renounces the argument he developed in the early sections, and as I understand him, it is Principle (P) that he is renouncing. I will come back to this. But whatever his ultimate judgment, Principle (P) has considerable initial plausibility, and putting it together with the argument that nothing in our practice can strongly determine the extensions of "set" and "∈" finely enough to fix the size of the continuum, we get the conclusion that there can be no objectively correct answer as to what the size of the continuum is.

There is an obvious point in common between Putnam's "The Thesis That Mathematics Is Logic" argument and his "Models and Reality" argument. The former was centered on a claimed unclarity in the notion of 'all sets,' and in the latter argument we get a "semanticized" version of the same thing: there is nothing to determine the semantics of "all sets" uniquely, so it is indeterminate. Recently Vann McGee has argued that what makes our quantifiers determinately range over everything is simply their obeying the ordinary rules; to make them range over less than everything, one would need to do something special to restrict them, and the fact that we have not done that means that our quantifiers determinately range over everything.[6] I am not fully persuaded, but let us suppose he is right. It still does not follow that "all sets" is determinate, for that is a restricted quantifier whose determinacy is affected by that of "set."

Moreover, even if one were to grant that "all sets" was completely determinate, Putnam's argument would be little affected: the indeterminacy in "∈" is all he needs. The intuitive idea behind his argument, after all, is this: suppose, with the mathematical realist, that somewhere outside of space-time there resides a vast array of hunks of platoplasm. Then even if it is somehow determinate which hunks our word "set" applies to, there is still the question of which pairs of such hunks are in the extension of our symbol "∈." What is there about our use of this term that could settle the matter? The acceptance of axioms of pure set theory could partially constrain it by ruling out extensions that would make the axioms come out false. The acceptance of impure set theory could add additional constraints, alluded to seven paragraphs back (paragraph beginning "Actually ..."), which serve to rule out the *arithmetically* nonstandard interpretations. But there do not seem to be any *other* constraints, and if not, then there is nothing to give determinate truth value to the continuum hypothesis. *Even without questioning the determinacy of "all sets,"* we have an argument against there being a determinate truth value for typical undecidable sentences of set theory.

Afficionados of second-order set theory often argue that Putnam's whole line of reasoning is invalidated by his insistence on using only first-order set theory; second-order set theory is supposed to avoid the problem, because the standard semantics for it does not recognize something as an "interpretation" if the predicate variables do not range over all the subclasses of the domain. But it is a complete illusion to think that you can avoid the problem in this way, as Weston noted long ago[7]: one might as well "avoid the problem" by using first-order set theory but with a stipulation that by "interpretation" one will mean "standard interpretation." I am not objecting to second-order reasoning, any more than to first-order set-theoretic reasoning; but it begs all the questions at issue to suppose that second-order assertions are all semantically determinate, just as it would beg all the questions at issue to suppose that first-order set-theoretic sentences are all semantically determinate.[8]

An interesting recent variant of the use of second-order set theory to respond to Putnam's argument is the use of "schematic first-order set theory": first-order set theory in which the schematic letters (in the replacement and separation schemas) are taken to be extendible as the language evolves. Interesting arguments that this view of schemas is enough to evade Putnam-like problems can be found in McGee's "How We Learn Mathematical Language," Lavine's *Understanding the Infinite* and "Skolem Was Wrong," and with a bit more qualification, in Shapiro's *Foundations without Foundationalism*.[9] I have examined these arguments elsewhere, and will here simply report my conclusion, which is that they do not get off the ground.[10]

I think, then, that Putnam's argument survives the sort of attacks so far considered: the sort of attacks that do not challenge the basic assumption (P). But is (P) itself a reasonable principle?

II. "Non-realist Semantics"

Putnam himself challenged (P) at the end of "Models and Reality." The challenge was based on a view he called "non-realist semantics."

I should say at the start that Putnam had put himself in a corner where he had little choice but to challenge (P): he had argued earlier in the paper that (P) leads almost inevitably not merely to such conclusions as that there is no determinate fact as to the size of the continuum, but to somewhat analogous "antirealist" conclusions about theoretical entities of science, about macroscopic material objects, and about sensations. In my opinion these extensions of the original model-theoretic argument are quite uncompelling.[11] But I do not want to discuss that matter here; I mention it only to make clear why Putnam had so strong a motivation for challenging (P).

How does he challenge it? (P) could easily be restated as a principle about what makes an interpretation of an expression or mental state "the intended one." What Putnam says in response is that what makes an interpretation in which "cat" refers to cats intended and one in which "cat" refers to dogs unintended is simply that we intend "cat" to refer to cats and not to dogs. Similarly, we intend "is a member of" to refer to the membership relation; so any argument based on interpretations in which it refers to a relation membership* which need not be the membership relation is irrelevant.

One's first reaction to this idea may well be that it ascribes to us mysterious mental powers. To suppose that we can "intend" cats but not dogs, or membership but not membership*, while also supposing that there is no way of physically grounding that intention, seems to be tantamount to supposing that when one uses the word "cat" (or the word "∈"), Brentanian rays emanate from one's mind and latch onto all and only the cats (or all and only the pairs in which the second is a set and the first is a member of the second), and that these rays ground the intended semantics of the word. But of course Putnam rejects any such view; he calls it an "occult" theory of reference. (And as noted by Lewis,[12] it is in any case hard to see how such a view would really help in escaping the destructive impact that Putnam alleges in his extended model-theoretic argument.)

If Putnam is not advocating an occult theory of reference, what is he advocating? Obviously the idea is to somehow trivialize the fact that "cat" in our language refers to cats and "is a member of" to the membership relation. There is at least one way of doing this: the disquotational theory of reference. The disquotational view trivializes reference for our own language, and reduces reference for other languages to reference for our own language plus translation; it also severely limits the explanatory role of reference, and of related semantic notions such as truth conditions. These things together can be used to explain why weak determination of reference by the physical facts is all we should expect. However, Putnam himself quite explicitly rejects disquotational semantics in many places, so it is clear that that is not what he has in mind.[13] Then what *does* he have in mind?

Putnam begins his presentation of his positive view by saying,

> The predicament [i.e., the inability to explain from a naturalistic viewpoint how 'cat' can be true of all and only the cats and how 'is a member of' can be true of all and only the pairs whose second element is a set and whose first element is a member of it] only *is* a predicament because we did two things: first, we gave an account of understanding the language in terms of programs and procedures for *using* the language (what else?); and then, secondly, we asked what the possible "models" for the language were, thinking of the models as existing "out there" *independent of any description*.[14]

As the "what else?" indicates, Putnam has no problem with the first of these two steps. Putnam himself had given a persuasive articulation and defense of the procedural account of understanding a couple of years before; his judgment there "that the account according to which understanding a language [either a natural language or Mentalese] *consists* in being able to use it (or to translate it into a language one *can* use) is the only account now in the field"[15] (italics his) is evidently one that he still adhered to.

The step he found problematic, then, was the second, according to which models are "out there independent of any description." But it is not really the models that are relevant, it is the entities in the domains of the models, and the relations that the models postulate. Is the "problem" with the model-theoretic argument supposed to lie in the assumption that cats and the like exist independent of our descriptions of them?

It is *possible*, if not very charitable, to interpret Putnam as holding that the existence of cats depends on the use of the word "cat"; and that this dependence gives the referential connection between the word "cat" and cats. Reference is trivial (for our own words anyway—or for others' words too if their use of language has a part in sustaining the existence of cats and dogs). It is trivial, for instance, that "cat" applies to all and only the cats and that "set" applies to all and only the sets. And the reason it is trivial (according to this construal of Putnam) is that cats and sets are shadows of our language-using activity. This constructionist view seems to me to have quite a bit more plausibility for sets than for dogs and cats, and one might consider trying to confine it to that realm. But Putnam is insistent that the model-theoretic argument applies just as much to cats and dogs as to sets, so if we really are to construe him as adhering to constructionism for his way out, we must construe him as a constructionist even about cats.

I am loath to attribute such an implausible doctrine to Putnam (though I must admit that some of his other writings from the period strongly suggest it).[16] And much of the end of "Models and Reality" seems thoroughly sensible. For instance: "To speak as if *this* were my problem, 'I know how to use my language, but, now, how shall I single out an interpretation?' is to speak nonsense. Either the use *already* fixes the 'interpretation' or *nothing* can."[17] This certainly seems right; indeed, it could be expanded to say that *to the extent that* the use does not already fix an interpretation, nothing can. Unfortunately, this sensible remark is no solution to the problem: the problem was that it is unclear how the use can completely fix the interpretation, and so, by the principle just enunciated, the interpretation is not completely fixed. That is, we have indeterminacy; and arguably, an unacceptably high degree of indeterminacy. To point out that the argument for indeterminacy leads to indeterminacy is not to give us a means for escaping the argument.

Another thoroughly sensible remark at the end of "Models and Reality," this one more to the point, is that (in accordance with the use theory of understanding) we do have a perfectly good understanding of "cat," "set," "member of," and "refers"; and

> so we can *say and understand* "'cat' refers to cats." Even though the [nonstandard] model referred to satisfies the theory, etc., it is "unintended"; and we recognize that it is unintended *from the description through which it is given*.[18]

This seems exactly right to me; and it is just the diagnosis given by the disquotationalist, which leads one to wonder how exactly Putnam's view is different from disquotationalism.

I am not saying that Putnam is best understood as a disquotationalist: his repeated negative remarks about disquotationalism suggest otherwise. But I suspect that any coherent interpretation of his remarks that avoids ascribing a grossly implausible constructionism must be in terms of a position *not so far from* disquotationalism. At the very least, it must, like disquotationalism, give some kind of explanation of why semantic terms are unlike typical terms of special sciences, in that for semantic terms weak determination by the physical facts is all we need.

In one respect I share with Putnam a worry about disquotationalism. Disquotationalism not only undercuts the sort of argument for indeterminacy considered in the opening section, it *appears* to undercut the very coherence of indeterminacy; if the appearance is correct, that strikes me as a reductio of the position. I will consider this matter in the next section, and in the following three sections will consider three possible ways for resuscitating the possibility of indeterminacy. (The first attempt at resuscitating it probably presupposes some kind of disquotationalism; the two subsequent ones are compatible with disquotationalism, but very likely are also compatible with whatever alternative way around the argument of section 1 Putnam might prefer.) And in section 8 I will suggest that some of the ideas involved in these defenses of indeterminacy shed some light on one of the most interesting aspects of Putnam's opposition to "metaphysical realism" (not just in mathematics but more generally): his doctrine of equivalent descriptions.

III. Militant Disquotationalism

Let us begin with a militant version of disquotationalism, according to which the very idea of indeterminacy is nonsensical. The militant disquotationalist agrees with Putnam's point that we obviously understand terms like "cat," "set," "member of," "mass," and "bald" perfectly well, in that we know how to use them; we also understand "refers," "true of," and "true" perfectly well, and understand them to be governed by the schemas

1) "t" refers to t and nothing else, if t exists, and otherwise refers to nothing,
2) "F" is true of all and only those things that are F (for 1-place predicates); "R" is true of all and only those pairs $\langle x,y \rangle$ such that xRy (for 2-place predicates); etc.,
and
3) "p" is true if and only if p.

She then claims both (A) that this removes the motivation for positing indeterminacy, and (B) that it shows the idea of indeterminacy to be incoherent.

The point is not merely that disquotationalism makes it incoherent to give up these schemas and undermines the motivations for doing so. Any sophisticated advocate of indeterminacy can agree that the schemas are sacrosanct, that is, that their instances must be regarded as determinately true. How? By supposing that words like "refers," "true of," and "true" are themselves indeterminate, and their indeterminacy is "correlative to" that of each indeterminate object level term. There are legitimate interpretations in which the extension of "bald" is B_1 and in which $<\text{'bald'},x>$ is in the extension of "true of" iff x is in B_1, and other legitimate interpretations in which the corresponding things hold for a set B_2 distinct from B_1; but there is none for which the extension of "bald" is B_1 and in which $<\text{'bald'},x>$ is in the extension of "true of" iff x is in B_2 (or the analog with B_1 and B_2 reversed). So the determinate truth of (the instances of) the schema "'F' is true of all and only the Fs" does not imply the determinacy of whether the instances of 'F' are true, and does not imply the schema "'F' is determinately true of all and only the Fs." Similarly, the determinate truth of the schema "'p' is true if and only if p" does not imply the schema "'p' is determinately true if and only if p."

If the issue is not about the schemas, what is it? Let us begin with point (A). The motivation for indeterminacy was that it is hard to see how any theory of reference for "set" and "$\in$" (in terms of which "$2^{\aleph_0}$" and "$\aleph_1$" are defined) could determine the reference sufficiently to make one rather than the other of "$2^{\aleph_0} = \aleph_1$" and "$\neg(2^{\aleph_0} = \aleph_1)$" determinately true (given, for example, that no combinations of the axioms we are disposed to accept decide the matter). Similarly, it is hard to see how any theory of reference for "rich" or "bald" could determine of each person, no matter how apparently borderline, whether he is rich and whether he is bald. But a disquotationalist insists that we do not need theories of reference in the sense required, that is, theories of *in virtue of what* names refer to what they refer to, or *in virtue of what* atomic predicates are true of what they are true of. But then it is hard to see how lack of such theories—or even arguments for the impossibility of such theories—should give us reason to believe in indeterminacy.

I think point (A) is largely correct: more specifically, I agree that disquotationalism undermines any motivation for indeterminacy *based on the theory of reference*. The basic idea of the disquotationalist doctrine is that theories of reference do not serve the philosophical purpose that they have been assumed to serve, and in particular are not needed to ground claims of determinateness of reference. So I am inclined to agree with the disquotationalist that arguments for indeterminacy based on the theory of reference need to be either recast or abandoned. (The issue of how exactly to recast them, or what arguments might be used in their place, is a pressing one, but beyond the scope of this essay.)

The more dramatic claim of militant disquotationalism—the part that makes it militant—is (B). The argument for (B) is as follows: Consider any purported example of indeterminacy, for example, of truth value: say the continuum hypothesis, $2^{\aleph_0} = \aleph_1$. The truth schema implies both that "$2^{\aleph_0} = \aleph_1$" is true iff $2^{\aleph_0} = \aleph_1$ and that "$\neg(2^{\aleph_0} = \aleph_1)$" is true iff $\neg(2^{\aleph_0} = \aleph_1)$. By classical logic it follows that either "$2^{\aleph_0} = \aleph_1$" is true or "$\neg(2^{\aleph_0} = \aleph_1)$" is true (and not both). But this seems to eliminate indeterminacy in any interesting sense. Admittedly, we can stipulate *senses* of indeterminacy that are not ruled out: for example, unknowability. But the *intended* sense of indeterminacy of truth value is something like: there is no fact of the matter. And it would seem that if "$2^{\aleph_0} = \aleph_1$" is true (and "$\neg(2^{\aleph_0} = \aleph_1)$" is not), then there is a fact of the matter as to which is true, namely that it is "$2^{\aleph_0} = \aleph_1$"; similarly, if "$\neg(2^{\aleph_0} = \aleph_1)$" is true (and "$2^{\aleph_0} = \aleph_1$" is not), then there is a fact of the matter as to which is true, viz. that it is "$\neg(2^{\aleph_0} = \aleph_1)$"; so either way, there is a fact of the matter. By similar reasoning, there is a fact of the matter as to whether Joe is rich, or bald, or whatever, no matter what the state of his finances or his scalp may be.

It is, I think, extraordinarily difficult to accept the conclusion of this argument. It is, nonetheless, not at all easy to find a convincing reply.

IV. Leeds's Way Out

I will now consider three ways to modify militant disquotationalism to make it more believable. The first is due to Stephen Leeds.[19] Begin by noticing that the schemas for reference, truth, and so on, apply in the first instance to our own language; so if the determinacy of reference and truth is to be grounded in these schemas, then all we directly get is that it is determinate what *our own terms* refer to and whether *our own sentences* are true. The usual disquotationalist treatment of foreign terms and sentences is via translation; so as long as translation can be indeterminate, we are at least able to recognize an indeterminacy in foreign terms and sentences. And Leeds does so: he says, for instance, that it is indeterminate how to translate certain terms from past theories into our own language, and so it is indeterminate what they refer to. This is the first of his two steps to weakening the militant disquotationalist view. The second step is to suppose that we can make a contextually relative distinction between *serious* language and *nonserious* language.[20] In our serious moods, we accept the disquotation schema only for serious language; if it is indeterminate how to translate nonserious language into serious, then reference is indeterminate even for nonserious parts of our own language.

A worry that might be raised about step 1 of this proposal is whether Leeds can allow the appeal to indeterminacy of translation. "Synonymous," after all, is a term of our language; but Leeds apparently accepts the disquotationalist view that positing indeterminacy *in our own language* makes no sense, so it follows that we must regard our term "synonymous," as perfectly determinate. So how can there be indeterminacy of translation?

Although Leeds does not consider this objection, I think it is clear what his reply ought to be: that we should insist that the concept of synonymy (in its interlinguistic applications) is not to be included in serious language. By doing so, we avoid serious commitment to the claim that either the foreign term w is synonymous with our term w* or it is not, so we avoid the conclusion that it is determinately synonymous or determinately nonsynonymous with a given term of ours. If the concept of interlinguistic synonymy is so disavowed, what is translation? In translating a term we are not making any claim about its synonymy to one of our terms, we are simply correlating it with one of our terms for various purposes. Indeterminacy of translation simply means that there is no best policy for translating w; or better, it simply means that given any policy that translates it as w*, there is another policy, neither better nor worse, that gives it an incompatible translation w**. Indeterminacy of translation so understood seems to raise no problems for the disquotationalist.[21]

Another objection to step 1 is that we do not need to translate foreign terms into our language; we can incorporate them. Suppose we are trying to understand an earlier theory involving a term that seems to have no best translation into modern language: say *"Kraft"* as used in eighteenth-century German physics. (This is Leeds's own example; "Kraft" is sometimes translated as 'energy' and sometimes as 'force'.) Rather than translating it, we may simply adopt it into our language for purposes of evaluating or commenting on the theory. But then when we do so (the objection goes), we have lost any means for regarding the term as indeterminate. But this objection too is handled by step 2 of the proposal: although we incorporate "Kraft" into our language, we do not take it fully seriously, so there is no problem in saying that it is indeterminate what it stands for.

Not only does step 2 handle the objections above, it also provides a way for recognizing ordinary vagueness in our own language. It is true that insofar as we regard "bald" as part of serious language we must say that there are no borderline cases: everyone is either determinately bald or determinately not bald, in any but an irrelevant sense of "determinately," for in the only sense that is relevant, "determinately" is redundant as applied to our serious language. But we do not in all contexts regard "bald" as part of our serious language, and insofar as we do not we can recognize indeterminacy as resulting from an indeterminacy as to how to translate it into serious terms.

I am fairly sympathetic to Leeds's view of indeterminacy (which is not to say that I am sure it is ultimately defensible). Supposing for the sake of argument that it is right, what consequences does it have for indeterminacy about sentences like the continuum hypothesis? In my view, it allows for their indeterminacy. Of course, insofar as we regard the standard language of set theory as part of our serious language, we cannot make sense of the idea that the continuum hypothesis is indeterminate, any more than we can regard Joe as a borderline case of baldness insofar as we regard "bald" as in our serious language. But there are plenty of alternatives to regarding the language of set theory as part of serious language. For instance, we can take the language in some sort of fictionalist spirit. And even if we are platonists in the sense of believing (in the fullest and most serious sense) that there are infinitely many nonphysical eternally existing objects and that set theory is best understood as having them (or some of them) as its subject matter, we need not understand the language of set theory as meeting the most demanding standards of seriousness. Maybe when being *really* serious, we just say, without set-theoretic vocabulary, (i) that there are infinitely many nonphysical eternally existing objects (which can be said without the term "infinitely" by using infinitely many axioms), and (ii) that standard set theory is consistent.[22] We then translate the language of set theory into the theory consisting of (i) and (ii), by taking "set" to be true of some or all of the nonphysical eternally existing objects and by interpreting "member of" in any way that makes the usual axioms come out true. There are multiple ways of doing this, and different ones make different sentences about the size of the continuum come out true. So we get a multiplicity of translations between the language of set theory and the fundamental platonistic theory, and the continuum hypothesis comes out lacking in determinate truth value.[23]

I think then that even Leeds's close relative of militant disquotationalism leaves room for the idea that we should not be "metaphysically realist" about mathematical undecidables.

V. Abandoning Excluded Middle

Leeds's view is only one of several responses to the militant disquotationalist argument against indeterminacy. Another more obvious one is to reject the supposition in the argument that the law of excluded middle holds for indeterminate language. Putnam once recommended the use of intuitionist logic for handling one form of indeterminacy, namely, vagueness.[24] Much more promising, I think, is the use of the logic associated with the strong Kleene 3-valued "truth tables," with only the top value "designated."

What I want to focus on is not the Kleene semantics, but the logic associated with it: more specifically, the logic in which an inference is valid iff in any model in which the premises have the designated value, so does the conclusion. The semantics is a heuristic for the logic, and shows that the logic is consistent and weaker than classical logic, and gives a useful tool for determining what is and especially what is not a consequence of what; but the logic stands on its own, and needs no justification from the semantics. This is exactly the same as the role of 2-valued semantics in classical logic. Classical logic is *prior to* classical 2-valued semantics: you need logic in developing 2-valued semantics, and it is well known that any purported justification of classical logic in terms of the notion of truth is circular. The same holds for Kleene logic. This logic can easily be codified, say in a natural deduction system; the proposal under investigation is simply that that is the logic that we ought to use as our all-purpose logic (though in contexts where we accept appropriate instances of excluded middle we get the effect of classical logic). The logic needs no justification in terms of the Kleene truth tables or the three semantic values that appear in them, and any such purported justification would be circular.

Incidentally, it is important to realize that if we adopt the Kleene logic as our basic logic, then that is the logic that we should use in our semantic discussion: in particular, we should be prepared for the possibility that for certain A we will not accept such instances of excluded middle as:

Either the semantic value of A is 1 or the semantic value of A is not 1.

To assume such instances of excluded middle, in the context of this approach to indeterminacy, would be to assume that "the semantic value of A is 1" is determinate: it would be to rule out a certain kind of higher order vagueness. I do not mean to suggest that it is of no value to develop the consequences of the semantics on the assumption that such instances of excluded middle hold: that is useful in giving certain kinds of consistency proofs and for illustrating the general flavor of the theory in cases where higher order vagueness can be ignored. But it can give a misleading picture of the overall approach (as the frequent objections to the approach on the grounds that it "rules out higher order vagueness" amply illustrate).

A final preliminary: It is common to think of the three semantic values that appear in the Kleene tables as "true," "false," and "neither true nor false." For reasons that will become clear, I regard these usual readings as unacceptable.[25] I prefer to simply use the labels 1, 0, and ½. If one insists on giving them a more colorful reading, one can use "determinately true," "determinately false," and "neither determinately true nor determinately false." But one should not assume that in providing these labels one has really provided any explanation: any genuine meaning that any of the labels has must come from the theory in which it figures. It is in order to prevent a false sense of explanatoriness that I think the colorless labels better, at least initially.

Getting back to indeterminacy, it is clear that with excluded middle rejected, argument (B) for the incoherence of indeterminacy (given at the end of section 3) collapses. The argument was that by the truth schema, it is both the case that "$2^{\aleph_0} = \aleph_1$" is true iff $2^{\aleph_0} = \aleph_1$ and that "$\neg(2^{\aleph_0} = \aleph_1)$" is true iff $\neg(2^{\aleph_0} = \aleph_1)$; so by excluded middle (and noncontradiction), either "$2^{\aleph_0} = \aleph_1$" is true or "$\neg(2^{\aleph_0} = \aleph_1)$" is true (and not both). But by eliminating excluded middle (and/or noncontradiction), the conclusion is avoided.

But is avoiding the conclusion enough to make positive sense out of indeterminacy? Intuitively, a sentence A is indeterminate if and only if there is no fact of the matter as to whether it is true. That is, iff it is not a fact that it is true, and it is not a fact that it is not true. That is, assuming that "true" and "it is a fact that" are the trivial operators the disquotationalist takes them to be, iff $\neg A \wedge \neg\neg A$. But an advocate of the Kleene logic will not count $\neg A \wedge \neg\neg A$ (or its equivalent $A \wedge \neg A$) acceptable, so we have not made it acceptable to assert that there is no fact of the matter as to whether A is true. Nor can we achieve the effect by denying excluded middle: for that is equivalent to asserting $A \wedge \neg A$ in the logic.

One possible response ("para-consistency") is to modify the logic so as to make it acceptable to assert certain instances of $A \wedge \neg A$. One well-known way to do that is to continue to base the logic on the Kleene semantics, but now with ½ as well as 1 taken as "designated."[26] An alternative and perhaps preferable way is to demote the idea of designatedness from the logic to the pragmatics: an inference is logically valid iff in any model the value of the conclusion is at least as high as the greatest lower bound of the values of the premises; but in different contexts we can set different standards of which values are designated (good enough for correct assertion). On either of these views (and also on certain other views that broaden the semantic framework slightly),[27] we could hold that to say that there is no fact of the matter as to whether A is to say that $\neg(A \vee \neg A)$ (hence $A \wedge \neg A$).

While I believe that it is perfectly coherent to allow instances of $A \wedge \neg A$ to be accepted in some contexts, I will not press this point; from here on out I will grant the assumption that instances of excluded middle are never to be denied.

Given this, we are back to our problem; we are in no position to accept of any sentence that there is no fact of the matter as to its truth. But perhaps, though we cannot *accept* the claim that there is *no* fact of the matter, we can *reject* the claim that there *is* a fact of the matter? This of course would require a notion of rejection that does not amount to acceptance of the negation. Can a suitable such notion be found?

There is an obvious *unsuitable* notion: refusal to accept. It does have one virtue: It does seem fairly natural to suppose that if we are convinced that a certain claim is indeterminate (for example, the continuum hypothesis, or the claim that Joe is bald), then we should refuse to accept excluded middle for it. The problem is that we want to allow for uncertainty as to whether Joe is an indeterminate case of baldness, say when we have seen him only from a distance. Similarly, we want to allow for uncertainty as to whether the continuum hypothesis is indeterminate. (Maybe we do not know of the independence proof, or do not know of Putnam's argument that there is no way of giving sense to the idea of an "intended" model, or do not know whether there is a good reply to it.) And if we do not accept excluded middle for sentences we are convinced are indeterminate, we presumably should not accept it for sentences we think are *very likely* indeterminate either; or even, for sentences for which we think there is about a 50 percent epistemic probability that they are indeterminate. But if the latter, then *unwillingness to accept* excluded middle is too weak to serve as a test of belief in indeterminacy.

What we need, then, is a sense of rejecting excluded middle that is stronger than refusing to accept it, but weaker than accepting its negation. Is there such a notion? I once thought it would be difficult to find one,[28] but now think I was missing the obvious. Let us think of the matter in terms of degrees of belief. Accepting a sentence is intimately connected with having a high degree of belief in it: say, higher than a certain threshold T, where $T > \frac{1}{2}$. Similarly, I suggest, rejecting it seems connected with having a correspondingly low degree of belief in it: lower than the *co-threshold* $1 - T$, which is less than T. So rejecting it is certainly stronger than not accepting it: it requires that the degree of belief be lower. Is rejecting weaker than accepting the negation? *Given the assumption that degrees of belief obey the classical probability law $P(\neg B)=1 - P(B)$*, rejecting A in the sense defined is precisely equivalent to accepting its negation. But it seems intuitively clear that if we abandon excluded middle we ought to modify the probability calculus to allow that $P(B) + P(\neg B) < 1$, and this makes it possible to reject B while also rejecting $\neg B$.

In particular, we can do this when B is of the form $A \vee \neg A$. It might have seemed impossible to make sense of assigning a degree of belief less than 1 to $A \vee \neg A$: how could that have probability 1 without its negation having probability greater than 0? And yet its negation is equivalent to $A \wedge \neg A$, so presumably *cannot* have probability greater than 0 (given that we are ruling the para-consistency line out of consideration). But on the nonclassical probability option, one can maintain that the probability of $\neg(A \vee \neg A)$ is always 0, while holding that $P(A \vee \neg A)$ can nonetheless be less than 1.

One might try to avoid introducing nonstandard degrees of belief, and instead invoke the notion of truth. One often hears it said that although the proponent of a logic without excluded middle should not deny any instances of excluded middle, she should deny of certain instances *that they are true*. (Take denial to mean simply, acceptance of negation.) If this proposal were acceptable, then rejection of an instance of excluded middle could simply be explained as denial *of its truth*. Similarly, we could coherently have a degree of belief of 0.5 in the claim that A ∨ ¬A is true and a degree of belief of 0.5 in the claim that it is not true, without any nonstandardness in our degrees of belief. Unfortunately, this proposal is *not* acceptable with any notion of truth that obeys the standard equivalence between Tr(<B>) and B: that equivalence precludes denying the truth of A ∨ ¬A without denying A ∨ ¬A itself, and we are conceding here that instances of excluded middle are never to be denied. If we are going to make sense of the idea of rejecting there being a fact of the matter in terms of a logic that gives up excluded middle, I think we have no alternative but to invoke nonstandard degrees of belief.

The proposal for making sense of the rejection of factuality, then, involves both a nonclassical logic in which excluded middle does not hold in general, and a corresponding nonclassical probability theory for our degrees of belief, in which $P(A) + P(\neg A)$ can be less than 1.[29] One believes a sentence A determinate to the degree that one believes A ∨ ¬A. To be convinced that Joe is determinately bald or determinately not bald (even if one does not know which) is to believe "Joe is bald or not bald" to a degree close to 1; to be convinced that Joe is a borderline case is to believe it to a degree close to 0; to be unsure is to have a degree of belief more in the middle; similarly for beliefs about the determinacy of the continuum hypothesis.

As stated so far, the proposal does not literally allow that there be a proposition about which people disputing the determinacy of the continuum hypothesis (or of Joe's baldness) disagree; rather, the disagreement is in attitude about what degrees of belief to have. But there is a natural extension of the proposal, on which we can interpret discussions of determinateness and indeterminateness at face value. The extension is to introduce a new determinateness operator G, governed by certain constraints on the nonclassical degrees of belief in sentences containing it. Actually it is simpler to take as basic an operator D, where DA means that it is determinately the case that A. The claim GA that A is determinate (i.e., that it is determinate *whether* A) is the claim that DA ∨ D¬A.

One constraint I propose for the application of D to atomic sentences (or atomic formulas under an assignment to the variables) is

$$P(X \wedge DA) = P(X \wedge A),$$

where X is any sentence at all. This implies that $P(X \wedge DA_1 \wedge ... \wedge DA_n) = P(X \wedge A_1 \wedge ... \wedge A_n)$. I propose also that

$P(\neg DA) \in [P(\neg A), 1 - P(A)]$,

and more generally that $P(X \wedge \neg DA_1 \wedge \ldots \wedge \neg DA_n)$ is in the interval $[P(X \wedge \neg A_1 \wedge \ldots \wedge \neg A_n), P(X) - \Sigma_i P(X \wedge A_i) + \Sigma_{i,j \text{ distinct}} P(X \wedge A_i \wedge A_j) \ldots + (-1)^n P(X \wedge A_1 \wedge \ldots \wedge A_n)]$. (This more general conclusion does not follow from the more specific version.) The reason I specify only a range for $P(\neg DA)$ (and more generally, $P(X \wedge \neg DA_1 \wedge \ldots \wedge \neg DA_n)$) is to allow for higher order indeterminacy. But when there is no higher order indeterminacy, $P(\neg DA)$ will simply be $1 - P(A)$; and in typical cases, where the amount of higher order indeterminacy is small relative to the amount of first-order indeterminacy, $P(\neg DA)$ will be much closer to $1 - P(A)$ than to $P(\neg A)$. Finally, I propose that to obtain the probability of any other sentence (or formula under an assignment) in the language with D, we drive the D inward, by successively replacing

$D(A \wedge B)$ by $DA \wedge DB$; $D[\neg(A \wedge B)]$ by $D(\neg A) \vee D(\neg B)$
$D(A \vee B)$ by $DA \vee DB$; $D[\neg(A \vee B)]$ by $D(\neg A) \wedge D(\neg B)$
$D[\forall x A(x)]$ by $\forall x DA(x)$; $D[\neg \forall x A(x)]$ by $\exists x D(\neg A(x))$
$D[\exists x A(x)]$ by $\exists x DA(x)$; $D[\neg \exists x A(x)]$ by $\forall x D(\neg A(x))$
$D(\neg \neg A)$ by $D(A)$.[30]

These rules allow a high degree of belief to claims of form $\neg D(A \vee \neg A)$ when the degree of belief in $A \vee \neg A$ is low: indeed when there is no higher order indeterminacy, $P(\neg D(A \vee \neg A))$ will be $1 - P(A \vee \neg A)$.

Now that we have the D operator, we can use it to explain a "stronger than disquotational" notion of truth: A is strongly true iff DA is true in the ordinary disquotational sense; or equivalently, iff A is disquotationally true and GA. We met the notion of strong truth four paragraphs back (paragraph beginning "One might try to avoid . . ."): it is what is involved when, while refusing to assert $\neg(A \vee \neg A)$, one asserts that neither A nor $\neg A$ is true. That paragraph may have seemed to suggest that the disquotationalist would have a problem accepting such a notion of truth. But what I really meant was (i) that she cannot accept it as her basic notion of truth; (ii) that she cannot accept it at all without some kind of explanation; (iii) that she cannot use the strong notion of truth in explaining indeterminacy unless she can explain the strong notion of truth without relying on the notion of indeterminacy. The present discussion by no means takes this back: rather, what I am now proposing is

(a) that we clarify the notion of determinateness in the way we clarify most logical notions, in terms of its conceptual role;
(b) that the relevant conceptual role is specified not just by the logical laws governing the notion—these do not take us very far—but by more general constraints on the degrees of belief in sentences that involve the notion;

(c) that once we have the notion of determinateness, we get the strong notion of truth as a byproduct, defined from D or G and disquotational truth.

The order of explanation is the opposite of the one rejected in the earlier paragraph.

I conclude this section with the observation that the disquotationalist has special reason to take seriously the use of a nonclassical logic of something like the sort discussed here: in classical logic or even intuitionistic logic one cannot consistently accept the intersubstitutability of T(<B>) and B, for all B, because of the Liar paradox and the Curry paradox. That equivalence can however be maintained in the logics here considered.[31]

VI. A Classical Variant

In section 3 I considered the militant disquotationalist's rejoinder to the model-theoretic argument against the determinacy of typical undecidable sentences of set theory (a rejoinder which, you will recall, seems not so different in spirit from Putnam's own rejoinder). But I noted that militant disquotationalism seemed grossly implausible because it disallows *all* indeterminacy, even in the case of vagueness. So I promised three ways to make disquotationalism less implausible. The first was the one developed by Stephen Leeds. The second was the one just considered, involving nonclassical logic. (Actually the second one subdivided, into a simple version without a determinateness operator and another version, more satisfactory I think, that uses the simple version to introduce a determinateness operator.) Now for the third.

Despite the significant reason given at the very end of the last section for favoring a nonclassical logic over classical—namely, the semantic paradoxes—classical logic has obvious virtues of its own. Is it possible to adopt the core idea of the nonclassical logician's response to the militant disquotationalist, but within classical logic? It is indeed. I will be sketchy about this, because I have developed the details elsewhere.[32]

We have seen that a main component of the solution involving nonclassical logic is not the nonclassical logic itself, but the associated theory of epistemic probabilities (degrees of belief). Might it not be possible to respond to the militant disquotationalist by adopting a nonstandard probability theory even in the context of classical logic?

The probability theory will not be quite the same as the one for the nonclassical logic, because any decent probability theory for classical logic must give all theorems of classical logic probability 1, and so in particular $P(A \lor \neg A)$ must always be 1. But we can still get that $P(A) +$

$P(\neg A) < 1$ for certain A, if we give up the law (accepted in the nonclassical case: see note 29) that $P(A \lor B) + P(A \land B) = P(A) + P(B)$. A neat probability-like theory based on an alteration of this law was developed by Shafer in his *A Mathematical Theory of Evidence*, [33] and it turns out that reflections rather like those in the previous section, but in a classical logic context, lead to it.

Recall that the solution in the last section had two stages. In the first stage, it was not literally possible to believe that any claims are indeterminate: no notion of determinacy was introduced. What I did in the first stage was to give intelligible laws governing degrees of belief that permit instances of excluded middle to have degree of belief less than 1. This allowed us to do two things: (I) to capture the attitude one has when one "believes to a certain degree that a given claim is determinate," without actually using the notion of determinacy; (II) to defuse the argument that indeterminacy is unintelligible since there is always a fact of the matter. Now (II) is trickier in the classical logic case: we cannot simply point out that the argument relied crucially on excluded middle. We will come back to this. But part (I) works very much as it does for nonclassical logic: by altering the laws for degrees of belief, we can use $P(A) + P(\neg A)$ as a measure of the extent to which one believes A determinate.

The second stage in the nonclassical case was to use the nonstandard degrees of belief to literally introduce a notion of determinateness into the language: the degrees of belief allowed us to give a conceptual role account of a determinateness operator G. This can be done, too, in the classical case. As in the nonclassical, we take as basic a simpler operator D, where DA means that it is determinately the case that A; GA, meaning that it is determinate whether A, is defined as $DA \lor D\neg A$. The laws governing D make it a necessity-like operator; degrees of belief in DA and $\neg$DA for atomic A are governed by the same rules as in the nonclassical case, though now they must be supplemented by the rule that $P(DA \lor DB)$ is $P(A) + P(B) - P(A \land B)$. Again we get the nice result that $P(GA)$ is $P(A) + P(\neg A)$. And here too the approach allows for higher order indeterminacy.

I think that this provides a very natural account of the conceptual role of our beliefs about determinacy and indeterminacy in a classical logic setting. But we have yet to deal with question (II) above: how exactly are we to defuse the argument against the coherence of indeterminacy (argument [B] of section 3)? After all, the reply to that in the case of nonclassical logic turned on the rejection of excluded middle.

One way of trying to reply to that argument is to use the idea of strong truth, according to which for A to be strongly true is for DA to be (weakly, or disquotationally) true; equivalently, for A and GA both to be (weakly) true. The idea would be that what we mean when we say "there is no fact of the matter as to whether A" is simply that neither A nor $\neg$A is strongly true, i.e., that neither DA nor D¬A is true in the ordinary sense. This would of course be a totally cheap and unilluminating reply if we had not given a conceptual role account of the operator D, and thus of strong truth, in terms of our degrees of belief. But we have.

Even so, I do not think that this is by itself an adequate reply to argument (B). The challenge that argument (B) poses is to explain why it is reasonable to say "there is no fact of the matter as to whether A," in situations where A holds but DA does not or where ¬A holds but D¬A does not. It may well be that what we mean when we say that there is no fact of the matter as to whether A is that neither A nor ¬A is strongly true; still, that does not answer the question of why by "no fact of the matter" we *should* mean lack of strong truth as opposed to lack of weak truth. To put the matter more pointedly, the functional import of the notion of "no fact of the matter" is supposed to include this: for anyone who believes that there is no fact of the matter as to whether A, it would be pointless and misguided to wonder whether A, or to hope that A, or anything like that. But given just the above account of the conceptual role of D and the explanation of "no fact of the matter" in terms of it, it is not at all clear why there being no fact of the matter as to whether A *should* have that functional role. Why is it incoherent to say: I know that ¬DA ∧ ¬D¬A, but nonetheless I wonder whether A, and I very much hope that ¬A? Given that by classical logic A ∨ ¬A, the reason for the incoherence of this is far from obvious.

There are two ways one might try to answer this question.

(I) The most obvious approach is to expand the account of the conceptual role of the D operator; or better, to provide a fuller account of the role of the nonstandard degrees of belief in terms of which it was explained. In the crudest version of this, we might simply build into the functional role of degrees of belief that only to the extent that the degrees of belief in A and ¬A add to a reasonably high value (in other words, only to the extent that P(GA) is high) is it rational to wonder or hope whether A. Is this *ad hoc*? I do not think it is. The intuitive idea we are trying to capture is that only to the extent that P(A) + P(¬A) is high is one regarding A as factual; ¬GA asserts in effect that A is to be treated in a rather instrumentalist spirit, merely a useful component of genuinely significant claims (which include A ∨ ¬A). The idea that we should not wonder about or have hopes about a claim A for which P(A) + P(¬A) is low is simply part of the intuitive idea that we were trying to explicate by introducing nonstandard degrees of belief, not an *ad hoc* addition to it.

(II) I am reasonably happy with the above response, but it is worth mentioning an alternative, which locates the instrumentalism differently. The alternative is to say that even if we adhere to classical logic when dealing with indeterminate language, we should regard it as simply a convenient device that does not get us into trouble if we use it in a certain limited way;

the ultimately more basic logic is the sort of nonclassical logic discussed in the previous section, for which excluded middle fails. (So this response differs from the previous in taking the claims we are instrumentalist about to include certain instances of A ∨ ¬A.)

I think that there is a way to make sense of this in terms of the non-standard degrees of belief that I have advocated for both the classical logic and nonclassical logic cases; the basic idea would be that a degree of belief function for vague language based on classical logic really just serves as a useful device for reaching conclusions about an associated degree of belief function based on nonclassical logic. Here is how the idea would work for a propositional language L (in other words, one without quantifiers or the new conditional suggested in note 31). Let an *elementary sentence* be a conjunction of atomic sentences and their negations. I have pointed out elsewhere that for each (nonstandard, that is, Shafer) degree of belief function Q for classical logic there is a unique degree of belief function R_Q for Kleene logic *that gives exactly the same degrees of belief for elementary sentences.*[34] This suggests that one might take a classical logic degree of belief function seriously only as regards its pronouncements about elementary sentences: it is easier to think in terms of classical logic, and provided we use nonstandard degree of belief functions there, we will not be led to error about the appropriate degrees of belief for elementary sentences. I do not know that this is really such an appealing approach, but it is one that is worth considering.

VII. SUMMARY

It is worth noting that there is a connection between the views considered in the last two sections and the Leeds view considered earlier. Leeds's view involved a distinction between serious and nonserious language, *with the distinction made on the basis of vocabulary*: in certain contexts, we take a predicate like "bald" nonseriously, and that means in effect that we take *all assertions involving it* nonseriously. Precisely what it is to take an assertion nonseriously, according to Leeds, is a matter I did not consider. Presumably it means in part that we do not have normal degrees of belief in such sentences; but that is not to say that we must have nonstandard degrees of belief of the sort I have considered in sections 5 and 6. But one way to look at the point of introducing these nonstandard degrees of belief is that it allows us to make a more refined distinction between serious and nonserious language, one not made simply on the basis of vocabulary. For instance, plenty of assertions involving "bald" will be perfectly "serious," in the sense that my degrees of belief in them will be normal: this will include my degrees of belief in the baldness of anyone I think not to be borderline (even if I have no idea which side of the border they are on), and on my preferred version of the classical logic view (version [I]), it will include all instances of classical logic involving the term.[35] This means, for instance, that we can regard the question of the size of the continuum as "nonserious," that is, indeterminate, while not regarding the predicates "set" and "$\in$" in terms of which it is framed as nonserious.[36] I regard this as a considerable improvement in detail over Leeds's view, but perhaps it does not alter its fundamental spirit.

VIII. Equivalent Descriptions

As I said at the start, it is natural to interpret the term "metaphysical realism" in such a way that one is abandoning metaphysical realism in mathematics if one holds that typical undecidable questions are indeterminate in truth value. I have sketched several ways in which the idea of such indeterminacy might be filled out. But the question arises whether the picture of indeterminacy that emerges from these sketches has much to do with metaphysical irrealism as Putnam understood it.

I am inclined to think that the answer is yes. In my view, the most suggestive aspect of Putnam's discussion of metaphysical irrealism has been his doctrine of "equivalent descriptions," according to which prima facie incompatible theories often amount to the same thing. What I would like to do in this final section is suggest that the kind of machinery suggested for making sense of indeterminacy can also be used to shed light on the phenomenon of equivalent descriptions.

Let us consider a very simple example of the sort of thing Putnam had in mind: not a very exciting example, but one that avoids some distracting issues that may arise with more interesting examples. The example involves two trivial theories.[37] T_1 says that the universe contains n point particles and nothing else, and says something about their properties and locations. T_2 says that the universe contains $2^n - 1$ objects: namely, the mereological sums of n point particles, in other words, the n point particles together with the $2^n - n - 1$ mereological sums of two or more such objects. And it agrees with T_1 about the locations and properties of the n particles. (There is also a third theory T_3, that says that the universe contains 2^n objects, viz., those of T_2 plus an additional "null object.") Putnam's view—and it is hard not to sympathize with it—is that any debate between these theories is empty: there is no fact of the matter as to which is right.

Putnam argues, though, that it is not easy to make sense of the emptiness of the debate without giving up "metaphysical realism." And I think that even without being very precise about what "metaphysical realism" comes to, we can get a feel for what is bothering him.

The problem is *not* that advocates of one of these theories cannot recognize a dispute with advocates of other of these theories as verbal. Certainly an advocate of T_2 can do this: she merely says that the advocate of T_1 is employing restricted quantifiers. She says, "Although the advocate of T_1 appears to be saying that the only things that exist are the point particles, he does not really mean *exist* when he says 'exist', he means 'exists and is not a sum of two or more objects.' Once this is recognized, we see that the advocate of T_1 is not disagreeing with me." The advocate of T_1 may be able to do something similar by interpreting the quantifiers of the advocate of T_2 as expressing some sort of "pretend existence." Or alternatively, maybe he interprets the T_2-theorists sentences at other than face-value; their real content is simply that part of their apparent content that concerns point particles. (There may be some difficulty making literal sense of one or both of these lines within T_1; let us not go into that.)

But even if advocates of either doctrine can recognize the distinction as verbal, this does not seem to do full justice to the emptiness of the dispute. For as Putnam indicates, either way of regarding the distinction as verbal is a *partisan* one, it assumes one of the two views and argues that anyone apparently advocating the opposing view can be interpreted as not really doing so. What Putnam wants is a way of making sense of the idleness of the dispute that is not, in this sense, partisan.

Is there a way of avoiding partisanship? At one point Putnam seems to suggest that the key is to give up the erroneous supposition that "exists" is univocal. But that does not really help. For the partisan of the broader ontology can grant that "exists" is not univocal: it could mean unrestricted existence, or it could mean the more restricted ("exists and is not a nontrivial mereological sum"). Similarly, if the partisan of the narrower ontology can interpret the partisan of the broader ontology in terms of pretend existence, he can regard that as an alternative possible meaning of "exists." The partisanship comes out not in the insistence that "exists" is univocal, but in the biased way of explaining alternative existence concepts.[38]

Can partisanship be avoided? It certainly can in one way: simply refusing to take a stand between the ontologies, in other words, being agnostic. But that does not give us what Putnam wants either. He wants that there is simply no matter of fact to take a stand about. And this of course brings us to a familiar problem: how can there fail to be a fact of the matter? For, putting aside both genuinely distinct theories and additional theories like T_3 that raise the same problem, we have that either T_1 is true or T_2 is true but not both. But then, which is it?

The problem, actually, is in some ways worse than for vagueness and indeterminacy. One familiar approach to making sense of vagueness and indeterminacy is in terms of the theory of reference: nothing in our use of "rich" could have settled whether we are taking those with such and such assets and liabilities to be included in the extension. That is basically the approach to indeterminacy that is assumed in the Putnamian argument I considered in section 1. Putnam rejects that approach, as we saw in section 2, and I think he is right to do so, but it is an approach that makes a certain amount of initial sense. But the approach seems to require a commonality of underlying ontology: the apparent issue as to whether Jones is rich is an issue about the application of "rich" to entities that exist whichever stand we take on the breadth of "rich." It is quite unclear how to adapt this approach to disputes over the breadth of application of "exist": at least, how to do so without taking a partisan approach in favor of the broader ontology.

Do any of the models for understanding indeterminacy developed in sections 4–6 help? It does not seem that the Leeds model does. For it is hard to see how there can be any reasonable interpretation of "serious language" on which existential quantification will not be part of such language; so unlike apparently empty questions about richness, which simply cannot be stated in "serious language" under some reasonable interpretations of that, apparently empty questions about ontology will surely be expressible.

But the models involving nonstandard degrees of belief seem more promising. The attitude of thinking that either T_1 or T_2 is correct, but that there is no fact of the matter as to which, does seem to be fairly well captured in accordance with the model of section 6: we attach a high degree of belief to their disjunction but a degree of belief 0 to each disjunct. And this combination of degrees of belief does not require that we in any way privilege one of the theories over the other. The attitude is captured even better, perhaps, on the alternative model in section 5, in which classical logic is rejected. Here we assign a degree of belief 0 to the disjunction of T_1 and T_2, as well as to T_1 and T_2 themselves, so there is no case to be made that we regard one of the two as correct; at the same time, we assign a low degree of belief to the negations of these theories, and a high degree of belief to the negation of the disjunction of the alternatives to them, making clear the sense in which T_1 and T_2 unlike the alternatives to them are acceptable. I know of no better way to capture the attitude of believing that there is no fact of the matter as to which of T_1 and T_2 is correct.[39]

HARTRY FIELD

NEW YORK UNIVERSITY
JULY 2002

NOTES

1. In a footnote added when the paper was republished he says: "I no longer (1974) agree that the notion of 'set' presupposes the notion of *definability*" (Hilary Putnam, "The Thesis That Mathematics Is Logic," in *Mathematics, Matter and Method: Philosophical Papers*, vol. 1 [Cambridge: Cambridge University Press, 1975], 19). This is puzzling, because the paragraph of the original paper to which the footnote was attached argued that the totality of definable subsets is perfectly clear, it is the totality of *undefinable* subsets of an infinite set that is unclear.

2. After putting into the mouths of the metaphysical antirealist a verificationist argument, he writes:

> This "argument" is sometimes taken to show that the notion of a set is unclear. For since the argument "shows" (sic!) that the continuum hypothesis has no truth value and the continuum hypothesis involves the concept of a set, the only plausible explanation of the truth-value failure is some unclarity in the notion of a set. (It would be an interesting exercise to find *all* the faults in this particular bit of reasoning. It is horrible, isn't it?) [Putnam, "Mathematics without Foundations," in *Mathematics, Matter and Method* , 52; italics and 'sic' are his.]

Later paragraphs make clear that his opposition is not just to the verificationist argument (which was not the argument of the earlier "The Thesis That Mathematics Is Logic"), but to the position of that earlier paper.

3. See Hilary Putnam, "Models and Reality," *Journal of Symbolic Logic* 43 (1980): 464–82.

4. See Hartry Field, "Are Our Logical and Mathematical Concepts Highly Indeterminate?," *Midwest Studies in Philosophy* 19 (1994): 391–429. And "Which Undecidable Sentences Have Determinate Truth Values?," in *Truth in Mathematics*, ed. H. Garth Dales and Gianluigi Oliveri (Oxford: Oxford University Press, 1998), 291–310; reprinted with new Postscript in Field, *Truth and the Absence of Fact* (Oxford: Oxford University Press, 2001).

5. Paul Horwich, *Meaning* (Oxford: Oxford University Press, 1998.)

6. Vann McGee, "Everything," in *Between Logic and Intuition: Essays in Honor of Charles Parsons*, ed. G. Sher and R. Tieszen (Cambridge: Cambridge University, 2000).

7. Thomas Weston, "Kreisel, the Continuum Hypothesis, and Second Order Set Theory," *Journal of Philosophical Logic* 5 (1976): 281–98.

8. Just as there is an issue as to whether second-order quantification is determinate, there is an issue as to whether even first-order quantification is completely determinate. (The most obvious possibility here is an indeterminacy as to whether the quantifier is restricted; this was alluded to above in connection with McGee.) There is even an issue as to whether truth-functional operators are completely determinate. In taking the notion of model and the usual valuation procedure for models for granted, Putnam's model-theoretic arguments might be thought to *under*state the possibilities for indeterminacy. I will not pursue this worry here.

9. Vann McGee, "How We Learn Mathematical Language," *Philosophical Review* 106 (1997): 35–68, Shaughan Lavine, *Understanding the Infinite* (Cambridge, MA: Harvard University Press, 1997), Lavine, "Skolem Was Wrong (unpublished), and Stewart Shapiro, *Foundations without Foundationalism* (Oxford: Oxford University Press, 1991).

10. Parsons gives analogous arguments in the case of number theory. See Charles Parsons, "The Uniqueness of the Natural Numbers," *Iyyun, A Jerusalem Philosophical Quarterly* 39 (1990): 13–44. In my critique of Lavine, McGee, and Shapiro I asserted that the same critique applied in the number theory case, but I recently heard a lecture by Parsons in which he plausibly differentiates the cases.

11. See David Lewis, "Putnam's Paradox," *Australasian Journal of Philosophy* 62 (1984): 221–36. Michael Devitt, "Realism and the Renegade Putnam," *Nous* 17 (1983): 291–301. Clark Glymour, "Conceptual Scheming, or Confessions of a Metaphysical Realist," *Synthese* 51 (1982): 169–80.

12. Lewis, "Putnam's Paradox."

13. For example, Hilary Putnam, "Vagueness and Alternative Logic," in *Realism and Reason: Philosophical Papers*, vol. 3 (Cambridge: Cambridge University Press, 1983).

14. "Models and Reality," 23–24. Italics his.

15. Hilary Putnam "Reference and Understanding," in *Meaning and the Moral Sciences* (London: Routledge, 1978), 97.

16. Hilary Putnam, *Reason Truth and History* (Cambridge: Cambridge University Press, 1981).

17. "Models and Reality," 24. Italics his.

18. Ibid., 25.

19. Stephen Leeds, "Incommensurability and Vagueness," *Nous* 31 (1997): 385–407.

20. Leeds is not explicit that the distinction between serious and nonserious is to be context-relative, but it seems to me that that is required if the proposal is to have a chance.

21. To say that the translations are incompatible may involve saying that w** is not synonymous with w*; but w* and w** are both in our language, so this would not require the *interlinguistic* notion of synonymy here at issue.

22. In, say, the modal sense of consistency discussed in Hartry Field, "Metalogic and Modality," *Philosophical Studies* 62 (1991): 1–22, which does not presuppose set theory.

23. There is a complication: to handle the applications of mathematics to nonmathematical domains like physics and psychology, we need that these set theories are not merely consistent but jointly consistent with our consistent nonmathematical theories. And we must also suppose that each theory T of physics or psychology or whatever formulated in our ordinary set theory could be reformulated using the alternative platonistic theory. One way to do so would be to replace it by a nominalistic theory. Another would be to replace it by the claim that all of the nominalistic consequences of T-plus-some-chosen-set-theory are true. This second route may seem like a cheap trick. Note though that on the second route, the chosen set theory need not be one that decides the size of the continuum, though it could if that turned out to be useful in the particular physical or psychological theory in question. Also, the set theory chosen for one physical or psychological theory need not be compatible with the one chosen for another: this makes clear that the truth of the set theory is not being assumed in the superior conceptual framework, only its instrumental utility in a particular application.

24. See Putnam, "Vagueness and Alternative Logic," in *Realism and Reason*, 271–86.

25. See also, Field, *Truth and the Absence of Fact*, 145–46.

26. Graham Priest, "The Logic of Paradox," *Journal of Philosophical Logic* 8 (1979): 219–41.

27. For example, supposing merely that the set of semantic values forms a deMorgan lattice, not necessarily linearly ordered.

28. Hartry Field, "Disquotational Truth and Factually Defective Discourse," *Philosophical Review* 103 (1994): 405–52. Reprinted in Field, *Truth and the Absence of Fact*.

29. Probabilities are to be real numbers in the interval [0,1]; if A implies B in the logic, $P(A) \leq P(B)$; $P(A \lor B) + P(A \land B) = P(A) + P(B)$; and $P(A \land \neg A) = 0$. It follows that $P(A) + P(\neg A) \leq 1$.

30. These rules for D have a somewhat unappealing consequence, noted in Kit Fine, "Vagueness, Truth and Logic," *Synthese* 30 (1975): 265–300: they prohibit "penumbral connections" among predicates, so that to call something determinately either green or blue commits us to its being either determinately green or determinately blue. Note though

that the advocate of this approach can always introduce a new primitive predicate "blue-to-green" not equivalent to the disjunction but related to it by such laws as that blue-to-green and not-blue entail green. Even without this, there may be a way to represent penumbral connections in an expanded logic based on the Kleene logic, but with an additional operator ⇒ of the sort mentioned below in note 31: the penumbral connection might, for instance, consist in the assertion ∀x[Blue(x) ⇒ ¬Green(x)]. However, the addition of such an operator to the language would require a considerable complication in the theory of probability for the language; this goes well beyond the scope of this paper.

31. To get a satisfactory solution to the paradoxes, one needs to expand the logic to include a new conditional ⇒ that is arbitrarily embeddable, and for which A⇔A and (A⇔B)⇒(Θ$_A$⇔ Θ$_B$) are logical truths (where ⇔ is defined from ⇒ in the usual way and where Θ$_B$ results from Θ$_A$ by substituting B for one or more occurrences of A). Then the intersubstitutability of T(<B>) and B implies T(<B>) ⇔ B, and conversely, and we need that these equivalent adequacy conditions on truth hold. For a proof that one can avoid all semantic paradoxes in such an expansion of the logic, see Hartry Field, "Saving the Truth Schema from Paradox," *Journal of Philosophical Logic* 32, no. 1 (2002): 1–27.

32. Field, *Truth and the Absence of Fact*, ch. 10 and the Postscript to it. The treatment there was for the classical case directly, rather than the idea here of basing it on the nonclassical case.

33. Glen Shafer, *A Mathematical Theory of Evidence* (Princeton: Princeton University Press, 1976)

34. To get the value R$_Q$(A), first put A into a Kleene-equivalent disjunctive normal form (being careful not to use excluded middle to simplify); take R$_Q$(A) to be the sum of the Q-values of the disjuncts, minus the sum of Q-values of conjuncts of two distinct disjuncts, plus the sum of the Q-values of conjunctions of triples of distinct disjuncts, and so on.

35. On view (II), the degree of belief given by my Q-function is itself not taken seriously in some cases: my real degrees of belief are given by R$_Q$, and it is that that determines "seriousness."

36. Indeed, in the classical logic development of the idea (or version [I] of it anyway), one can continue to reason with these predicates in a fully classical way.

37. From chapter 1 of Putnam, *The Many Faces of Realism* (La Salle, IL: Open Court, 1987).

38. How about simply adopting two existence concepts, without saying how they relate? That seems like taking a partisan stand for the broader ontology: unless one does something to make clear that one has in mind a fictionalist or non-face-value reading of the broader quantifier, it is hard to see why one is not advocating the ontology of one's broadest quantifier (or the union of the ontologies of one's quantifiers, if there is no inclusion).

39. Thanks to Kit Fine and Stephen Schiffer for helpful comments on an earlier draft.

REPLY TO HARTRY FIELD

Hartry Field correctly observes that during my "internal realist" period (1976–1990),[1] I gave up the scientific realist view of mathematics that I had defended in "What is Mathematical Truth?" (1975) (and that I believe was correct). And in "Models and Reality" (1980),[2] I defended the view that some sentences of pure mathematics are "indeterminate" (in Field's terminology), that is, are not determinately either true or false. He then explores the difficult question of how to give a precise and plausible account of the notion of "indeterminacy," and he again shows the remarkable combination of philosophical and logical sophistication and originality for which he is justly admired. I shall not, however, comment on the details of his proposal, although I like it and hope to make use of it in the future in contexts in which I believe there is genuine indeterminacy (e.g., cases of vagueness). Instead, I shall explain why I no longer share the view that many sentences of set theory are "indeterminate," and hence I do not now feel the need to worry about how to make precise the assertion that they are.

What Field believes is that at least some set-theoretic propositions ("such as the continuum hypothesis"[3]) that are "undecidable in all candidates for our fullest [mathematical-] theory"[4] do not have determinate truth values. He does, however, think that the quantifier "there are finitely many x such that" *does* express a "determinate" notion, provided certain "cosmological hypotheses" are true, and hence that the propositions of first-order arithmetic may well have determinate truth values. Although these beliefs are not defended in Field's present essay, they obviously constitute its *raison d'être*, and so I shall devote this reply to discussing *them*.

The beliefs that I just mentioned are explained and defended by Field in a paper titled "Which Undecidable Mathematical Sentences Have Determinate Truth Values?"[5] Although I do not think that truth in either number theory or set theory *is* indeterminate, one of my disagreements with the paper just mentioned is that I do not believe that Field has given a good reason (that is, one which is good from his own premises) for holding that the situation in number theory is more "determinate" than the situation in set theory. The first section of this reply explains why I say this. The second section discusses Field's view on the indeterminacy of set theory under the scenario in which the cosmological hypotheses that are supposed to make arithmetic notions determinate are true. The remainder of my reply explains why I believe a scientific realist (which I am, and I believe Field also is) ought to be just as realistic about mathematics as about physics, regardless of whether they are true.

I. FIELD ON OMEGA SEQUENCES

Field's basic idea is that if there is a specifiable omega sequence in (physical) nature, then the determinacy of the mathematical concept of finiteness is secured through the determinacy of the relevant physical concepts. He argues that there are such sequences with the aid of two "cosmological assumptions."[6] The two assumptions can be combined into one, namely:

> (Infinity in nature): There are arbitrarily long *finite* sequences, but no *infinite* sequences of events with a first and a last member (in time) and a separation in time between any two of their members (if there are at least two) of at least one second.

The problem with this, as Otávio Bueno has pointed out, is that "the notion of *finiteness* occurs" in the cosmological assumptions thus summed up.[7] As Bueno points out, this means that standard model theoretic arguments can be used to generate a nonstandard interpretation of "finite" (in fact, a nonstandard "spacetime") in which the cosmological assumptions hold, but in which "finite" is satisfied by nonstandard sequences that are (externally) infinite. Field tries to block this by requiring that spacetime have an "allowable" model, but I agree with Bueno that this too begs the question.[8] For Field's notion of an "allowable" notion of an "event" simply builds in the assumption that there cannot *be* nonstandard sequences of events. "Allowable" too presupposes that the interpretation of "finite" has been fixed; it cannot be used to fix it.

II. WHAT IF FIELD'S COSMOLOGICAL ASSUMPTIONS ARE TRUE?

Now I want to consider what happens, on Field's view, if his cosmological assumptions are true. Field assumes (as I did in "Models and Reality") that empirical predicates are allowed to occur in the comprehension axioms (the axioms of set existence) of set theory[9]; otherwise we could not even prove the existence of a set of all carbon molecules, or a set of all planets, and, as a result, mathematics (as formalized within set theory) would have no use in physical science. But the presence of those axioms, plus the assumed truth of the cosmological assumptions summarized above as "*infinity in nature*" has as a consequence that the "allowable" models of the whole theory (set theory plus the scientific theories from which the empirical predicates are drawn) are required to be models in which the sequences that are omega sequences from the "internal point of view" (the sequences that satisfy the predicate "is an omega-sequence" *in the model*) are *really* omega sequences. The sentences of arithmetic have the same (standard) truth values in every "allowable" model. Moreover, any statement which follows from the set theory (with the empirical predicates given their—assumed determinate—physical interpretations[10]) plus the totality of physical truths has a determinate truth value, on this assumption, although the truth value of certain statements of set theory, the continuum hypothesis, for example, will probably still be "indeterminate." As said above, all this depends on the claim that the cosmological assumptions *do* fix the notion *finite*, and I do not believe that they do. And if this objection is right, *infinity in nature itself* lacks a determinate truth value (unless "finite" is made clear in some way that Field has failed to provide).

III. IF "FINITE" IS INDETERMINATE . . .

Now I want to consider what happens if we are unable to help ourselves to the idea that "cosmological" facts bestow a determinate extension upon the predicate "finite." If (we should know that) this is the case, then, Field reassures us, mathematical reasoning (as opposed to philosophical commentaries on that reasoning) will be totally unaffected:

> When I say that certain mathematical sentences might lack determinate truth value, I do not intend to suggest that we must abandon classical reasoning in connection with those sentences. In my view a great many concepts involves some sort of indeterminacy—for instance, vagueness—and as a result many sentences involving them lack determinate truth value. It would cripple our ability to reason if we were prevented from using classical logic whenever indeterminacy might arise. Fortunately, it is not necessary to do so. . . . What is crucial to the logic of vagueness is not that we give up classical logic but that we add to it a new "determinately" operator—in effect, the notion of a sentence being determinately true. The same holds in the case of other sorts of indeterminacy. Consequently standard mathematical reasoning can go unchanged when indeterminacy in mathematics is recognized: *all that is changed is philosophical*

commentaries on mathematics, commentaries such as 'either the continuum hypothesis is determinately true or its negation is determinately true.'[11]

What Field writes here reminds me of the often heard claim that it makes no difference to scientific practice whether *scientific realism* is accepted or rejected. In that case, the claim seems to me a half-truth; it indeed makes no *inevitable* or *necessary* difference to her practice if a particular scientist is an antirealist or a realist, but historically it does often make a difference. In fact, Mach's antirealism about atoms stood in the way of taking atom theories seriously for several decades. If antirealism about the "large cardinal axioms" that Hugh Woodin hopes may help us decide the continuum hypothesis prevails, will the following assurance really have no effect on that kind of research?

> I think it is pretty clear that the sort of considerations just given in the case of the theory of natural numbers do not extend to typical undecidable statements such as the continuum hypothesis. This does not seem to me in the least disturbing: I do not see any pretheoretic reason why such statements should be assumed to have determinate truth value. Their lack of determinate truth value seems to me to be fully compatible with accepted methodology in mathematics. I have already pointed out that the recognition of indeterminacy in no way forces us to give up classical reasoning. Also, we can still advance aesthetic criteria for preferring certain values of the continuum over others; we must now view these not as *evidence that* the continuum has a certain value, but rather as *reason for refining our concepts so as to give* the continuum that value, but I do not see this as in violation of any uncontroversial methodological demand.[12]

It is clear to anyone who knows the work of Hugh Woodin and his co-workers that they do *not* conceive of what they are doing as "advancing aesthetic criteria for preferring certain values of the continuum over others," and I doubt that their investigations would ever have been undertaken if that *were* their attitude to the continuum hypothesis. No doubt some philosophers (though I hope not Hartry Field) will dismiss this last remark as mere "psychology"; but I cannot see why the beliefs that scientists have about what they are doing should be so dismissed, while the beliefs that *philosophers* have about what scientists are doing are taken seriously (especially when renamed "intuitions").

At any rate, I do not think that Hartry Field thinks that *all* those sentences of set theory that are "undecidable in all candidates for our fullest theory" are undecidable; I assume that he is aware that some of the "undecidable statements of set theory," including certain large cardinal axioms, have been shown by Harvey Friedman to imply (undecidable) *number theoretic statements.* Since Field believes that all number theoretic statements have "determinate" truth values, any statement of set theory that implies a *false* number theoretic statement must be determinately false (on his view), even if it is not *provable* that the number theoretic statement in question is false; and this means that some of the "typical undecidable statements of set theory" may well be "determinately" false, even if Field's views are correct.

However, as explained above, I believe that Field's grounds for believing in the determinacy of number-theoretic truth are faulty, and I have argued that what Field *ought* to say is that undecidable statements of number theory also have indeterminate truth value. Field recognizes that he may have to say this (for example, if his cosmological hypotheses are false), and he is clear on just how far reaching the consequences would be. Since a "formula" is defined to be a *finite sequence* of symbols with certain properties, and a "proof" is defined to be a *finite* tree of formulas with certain properties, if "finite" is indeterminate, then so are "formula" and "proof." Hence, as Field writes, "If we do not have a determinate notion of finitude, then we do not have a determinate conception of *formula of a given language*, or *theorem of a given system*, or *consistency of a given system*."[13] If I am right, then Field ought to accept all of this indeterminacy as a consequence of his antirealism. If that antirealism cannot account for the existence of "a conception of finitude" without "cosmological hypotheses," then it cannot do so with their help either.

IV. FIELD AND WITTGENSTEIN

Some years ago I criticized Wittgenstein for writing:

> Suppose that people go on and on calculating the expansion of π. So God, who knows everything, knows whether they will have reached "777" by the end of the world. But can his *omniscience* decide whether they *would* have reached it after the end of the world? It cannot. I want to say: Even God can determine something mathematical only by mathematics. Even for him the rule of expansion cannot decide anything that it does not decide for us.[14]

It seems to me that the most plausible interpretation of this remark is that (when he wrote it) Wittgenstein thought that a mathematical proposition cannot be determinately true unless it is "humanly" possible to prove it. And it likewise seems to me that, on Field's view, if "proof" turns out to be as indeterminate as his view would imply (even if he resists the implication!), then something like this must also be true. My objection to Wittgenstein's view would then apply to Field's view as well. The objection in question is the following: If the statement is that the equations of motion of a system S have a solution (say "P(t) is in the interval between 3.2598 and 3.2599") where P is a mathematical function whose values are asserted by our best physical theory to be those of some physical parameter and t is the time, then *if it is not physically possible for human beings to compute P(t), or to prove by some deduction from acceptable axioms that P(t) is or is not in the interval between 3.2598 and 3.2599*, then there is no fact of the matter (no "determinate truth") as to whether P(t) is in that interval or not. But to accept this is very close to being a verificationist in one's physics. It is to give up a claim which we assumed to be part of our best physical theory of the world, the claim that the equations of that theory describe the behavior of certain systems accurately and completely, in the sense that those equations have *solutions* for each real value of the time parameter t, and those solutions give the value of the physical parameter P in question regardless of whether it is humanly possible to verify that they do in any particular case.[15] Systems of equations are, on a verificationist view, just prediction devices, and when it is not possible to derive a prediction from them (even if we are allowed to go on calculating until "the end of the world"), then there is nothing that they say about the case in question. I will not review the arguments *against* verificationism and *for* scientific realism here; but I believe that Field is not a verificationist, and if he is not, then I think he needs to reconsider his philosophy of mathematics.

H.P.

NOTES

1. As I explain in my Intellectual Autobiography in the present volume, my first "internal realist" lecture/publication was my Presidential Address to the Eastern Division of the American Philosophical Association in December 1976; the first lecture/publication in which I repudiated the "verificationist semantics" which was the core of "internal realism" was my "Comment on the paper of Simon Blackburn" at the Gifford Conference held in my honor at St. Andrews University in November 1990, published in *Reading Putnam*, ed. Peter Clark and Robert Hale (Oxford: Oxford University Press, 1994).

2. "What is Mathematical Truth?" in *Mathematics, Matter and Method: Philosophical Papers*, vol. 1 (Cambridge, MA: Cambridge University Press, 1975). "Models and Reality," *Journal of Symbolic Logic* 45, no.3 (Sept. 1980): 464–82; reprinted in *Realism and Reason: Philosophical Papers*, vol. 3 (Cambridge: Cambridge University Press, 1983).

3. Hartry Field, "Which Undecidable Mathematical Sentences Have Determinate Truth Values?" in *Truth in Mathematics*, ed. H. Garth Dales and Gianluigi Oliveri (Oxford: Oxford University Press, 1998), 300.

4. Ibid., 305–6.

5. See ibid., 306n2; this paper is also collected in Hartry Field, *Truth and the Absence of Fact* (Oxford: Oxford University Press, 2001).

6. Ibid., 298.

7. Otávio Bueno, "On the Referential Indeterminacy of Logical and Mathematical Concepts," *Journal of Philosophical Logic* 34, no. 1 (Feb. 2005): 65–79, see 75.

8. Ibid., 76–77.

9. An example of such an axiom could be $(\exists x)(y)(y \varepsilon x \Leftrightarrow \text{Higgs-boson}(x))$, which asserts that there is a set of all Higgs bosons.

10. The assumption that physics can be formalized using just predicates, rather than functions from physical systems to mathematical objects (real numbers, complex numbers, tensors, subspaces of Hilbert space, etc.) may be a remnant of Field's earlier nominalism.

11. Field, "Which Undecidable Mathematical Sentences Have Determinate Truth Values?," 295 emphasis added.

12. Ibid., 300.

13. Ibid.

14. Ludwig Wittgenstein, *Remarks on the Foundations of Mathematics*, Part IV, §34 (Oxford: B. Blackwell, 1956). I criticized this view in the Appendix to "Was Wittgenstein *Really* an Antirealist about Mathematics?" in *Wittgenstein in America*, ed. T. McCarthy and S. C. Stidd (Oxford: Oxford University Press, 2001).

15. A common objection to arguments from indispensability for physics to realism with respect to mathematics is, of course, that we do not yet have, and may indeed never have, the "true" physical theory; my response is that, at least when it comes to the theories that scientists regard as most fundamental we should regard all of the rival theories as candidates for determinate truth, and that *any philosophy of mathematics that would be inconsistent with so regarding them should be rejected.*

3

Felix Mühlhölzer

PUTNAM, WITTGENSTEIN, AND THE OBJECTIVITY OF MATHEMATICS

Not empiricism and yet realism in philosophy, that is the hardest thing.
—LUDWIG WITTGENSTEIN, *REMARKS ON THE FOUNDATIONS OF MATHEMATICS*, VI § 23

Talk of what an ideal machine could do is talk within mathematics; it cannot fix the interpretation of mathematics.
—HILARY PUTNAM, "ANALYTICITY AND APRIORITY: BEYOND WITTGENSTEIN AND QUINE," 119

The philosophy of mathematics has played a major part in Hilary Putnam's philosophical career, and from very early on the philosophy of mathematics of the later Wittgenstein[1] has served as one of Putnam's sources of inspiration and, at the same time, as a target for his critical reflections. At the beginning of Putnam's paper "Truth and Necessity in Mathematics," the German version of which was presented in 1964, Wittgenstein's spirit can be felt in a statement like the following: "I hope to indicate just how complex are the facts of mathematical life, in contrast to the stereotypes that we have so often been given by philosophers as well as by mathematicians pontificating on the nature of their subject."[2] However, later on in the paper, Putnam is extremely critical of the Wittgensteinian view that mathematical propositions are merely "rules of description," commenting as follows: "[Wittgenstein's] picture is misleading in that it suggests that once a mathematical assertion has been accepted by me, I will not allow anything to *count* against this assertion. This is an *obviously* silly suggestion."[3]

It is, above all, the *objectivity* of mathematics which Putnam sees threatened by a Wittgensteinian view. Instigated by interpretations of Stroud and Dummett, he once described this view as "claiming that mathematical truth and necessity arise *in us*, that it is human nature and forms of life that *explain* mathematical truth and necessity," and he instantaneously rejected it by the exclamation: "If this is right, then it is the greatest philosophical discovery of all time. Even if it is wrong, it is an astounding philosophical claim."[4] It is true that since 1964 Putnam has come gradually closer to Wittgenstein's position, but if I am not mistaken, he still has severe qualms about the anthropocentric outlook of Wittgenstein's philosophy of mathematics, and he still cannot accept what in 1964 he called "the linguistic account of mathematical truths," which regards mathematical propositions as "grammatical propositions" that serve as "rules of description." However, there can be no doubt that exactly this is the central message of Wittgenstein's philosophy of mathematics, and Wittgenstein expressed it in many passages, as, for example: "Let us remember that in mathematics we are convinced of *grammatical* propositions; so the expression, the result, of our being convinced [of the truth of a mathematical proposition] is that we *accept a rule*."[5] Thus, Putnam's approximation to Wittgenstein stops halfway. In fact, Putnam's Wittgenstein, as presented, for example, in *The Threefold Cord* and "Was Wittgenstein *Really* an Anti-Realist about Mathematics," appears as a sort of commonsense philosopher who, compared to the real Wittgenstein, has had several teeth extracted.

In this essay, I shall contrast the philosophy of mathematics of the real Wittgenstein with that of Putnam's Wittgenstein, and I want to defend the former as far as I can. To this end, I shall discuss several objections Putnam raises against the real Wittgenstein—or certain tendencies of the real Wittgenstein that Putnam cannot accept—objections he has upheld for a long time, possibly until the present day, though I am not sure about this.

I. Putnam's First Objection: Revisability

Putnam's harsh critique—"an *obviously* silly suggestion"—just cited was directed at a view he characterized as follows: "that once a mathematical assertion has been accepted by me, I will not allow anything to *count* against this assertion."[6] Formulated in this way, however, it is an extremely crude position that should not be laid at the door of a philosopher like Wittgenstein, who was obsessed by doing justice to the complications of our actual practices. When characterizing Wittgenstein's "linguistic account of mathematical truths" (to adopt Putnam's term), it cannot be enough to speak of the "acceptance" of a mathematical assertion without specifying the *ways* of acceptance that should be deemed appropriate here. In fact, this account should be applied only to mathematical assertions that are accepted either as *axioms* or as having been *proved*; i.e., it should be applied only to mathematical assertions that are accepted as *theorems*.[7] The status of sentences formulated in mathematical language that are not accepted as theorems is an open question in Wittgenstein's approach, and Wittgenstein himself has not said very much to it. So let us restrict his account to theorems and let us call it, accordingly, "linguistic account of mathematical *theorems*." Furthermore, as far as I know, Wittgenstein himself never claimed that we do not allow anything to count against propositions accepted as mathematical theorems, and in any case, such a claim would be ridiculous because of the sorts of obvious contrary reasons presented on p. 9ff. of Putnam's "Truth and Necessity in Mathematics" (1964): We may (a) find a mistake in the proof of an alleged theorem *p*; or (b) find, in the presence of a theorem *p*, also a proof of ¬p, without being able to detect a mistake in any of the proofs (a situation which certainly cannot be ruled out a priori). In case (a), of course, we will withdraw *p* as a theorem, and if we additionally find a proof of ¬p, we will revise *p*; and in case (b) we will revise *p* if there are good reasons to prefer ¬p, or we may withdraw both *p* and ¬p as theorems if we do not want this alternative to be decided.[8]

Despite his crude initial formulations of a Wittgensteinian account of mathematical theorems, Putnam actually knows, and knew, very well that Wittgenstein was not blind to the complications just mentioned, and at the very end of his 1964 paper, Putnam hints at a Wittgensteinian position that may be formulated as follows:

> Once a mathematical assertion *p* has been accepted by me as a mathematical theorem, I will not treat it as a description, i.e. as a statement which can 'conflict with the facts,' no matter whether these are platonic facts or empirical ones. On the contrary, I will not allow anything to count as a 'fact which conflicts with *p*,' because *p* is used only as a 'rule which determines the meanings' of the mathematical terms occurring in it.

Of course, this formulation, too, can only be a first approximation to Wittgenstein's actual view, and the expressions put in quotation marks have to be fleshed out. In fact, exactly this, to flesh them out, is one of the main tasks of Wittgenstein's philosophy of mathematics in its entirety. Still, this formulation, coarse as it may be, already has two plain philosophical merits. First, it allows the *revision* of a proposition *p* that has been initially accepted by us as a mathematical theorem, when this proposition is confronted with the discovery of a mistake in its proof or with a contradiction to other theorems, as described above. It allows such a revision *because* revisions for just those reasons should not be described as induced by newly discovered "facts conflicting with p"—at least not if we take as our paradigms of such revisions those typical of the empirical sciences. Second, this formulation tries to capture the characteristic *necessity* which we bestow on mathematical theorems by diagnosing this necessity as being of a linguistic nature: it is the necessity of a "rule of language."

To Putnam, however, who grew up philosophically with "Two Dogmas" and who, in his important papers "It Ain't Necessarily So" and "The Analytic and the Synthetic" of 1962, launched his own attacks on philosophical positions that make essential use of the distinction between revising a description and revising a *rule* of description, [9] this Wittgensteinian view must be anathema. Therefore, in "Truth and Necessity in Mathematics," it is turned down flat with the following brief comment: "But this trick [namely: to make use of said distinction] succeeds *too* well: for *any* statement can be regarded as a 'rule of language' if we are willing to say 'well, they changed their rule' if speakers ever give it up. Why should we not abandon this line once and for all?"[10] This retort obviously is a reverberation of Quine's notorious "Any statement can be held true come what may" from "Two Dogmas,"[11] and with it Putnam proceeds in familiar Quinean lines.

But these lines stand in marked contrast to the Wittgensteinian reminiscences with which Putnam begins his paper of 1964, where he says that he hopes "to indicate just how complex are the facts of mathematical life, in contrast to the stereotypes that we have so often been given by philosophers as well as by mathematicians pontificating on the nature of their subject."[12] Is it really true that the facts of our mathematical life, together with the facts of our scientific life in general, allow us to regard *any* statement as a "rule of language," as Putnam suggests at the end of his paper? Does not Putnam here simply replace the stereotypes of the logical positivists with the stereotypes of Quinean holism? It seems to me that a truly Wittgensteinian approach, with its sense for the multifarious differences in our use of language, should show us that Putnam's Quinean criticism of Wittgenstein's "linguistic account of mathematical theorems" is not convincing. Let me indicate some of the points a Wittgensteinian can make against this criticism.

A first noticeable trait of Putnam's procedure is how quickly the question of mathematical *necessity* is replaced by the question of mathematical *truth*. Although necessity is explicitly mentioned in the title of Putnam's 1964 "Truth and Necessity in Mathematics," in his very characterization of Wittgenstein's view—"linguistic account of mathematical truth"—it has already been supplanted by "truth." But Wittgenstein himself does not seek any account of mathematical truth. As already stated, it would be better to call his view a "linguistic account of mathematical theorems"—or perhaps even better: "linguistic account of mathematical *necessity.*" One can plausibly argue that *the* central complex of problems dealt with in Wittgenstein's philosophy of mathematics concerns mathematical necessity. In *Remarks on the Foundations of Mathematics* I, after some preparatory reflections about rule-following, he starts his investigation of *mathematics* proper by raising the question: "But then what does the peculiar inexorability of mathematics consist in?"[13] This question haunts him throughout the whole book. On the other hand, there is not the slightest indication that he is concerned with mathematical *truth.* On the contrary, he regularly dismisses questions about truth, as in the notorious deflationary remarks in *Remarks on the Foundations of Mathematics* and *Philosophical Investigations* (which I need not recapitulate here).[14] How far-reaching Wittgenstein's deflationary attitude toward truth actually was is a difficult and presumably unanswerable question, but there can be no doubt that "truth," including "mathematical truth," is not a subject he was interested in. When at the very end of "Truth and Necessity in Mathematics," Putnam writes: "in my opinion, the investigation of mathematics must *presuppose* and not seek to *account for* the truth of mathematics,"[15] supposing that Wittgenstein had intended to give just such an account, he misunderstands Wittgenstein's aim. What Wittgenstein seeks is not an account of the *truth* of mathematics, but an account of its *necessity* not in the sense of giving a philosophical theory of mathematical necessity, but in the sense of opening our eyes for the specific function of mathematical propositions and the specific use we make of them, which is responsible for our talking of "mathematical necessity."

In contrast to this, Putnam, in "Truth and Necessity in Mathematics" (1964), and again in "Analyticity and Apriority: Beyond Wittgenstein and Quine" (1979), shows the disrespect for mathematical necessity that is so characteristic of somebody who is deeply molded by the philosophy of Quine. It is therefore important to examine Putnam's development in "Rethinking Mathematical Necessity" of 1990, where already the title promises a reorientation and where in fact a dissociation of the Quinean heritage is explicitly announced at the very beginning.[16] Before discussing this paper, however, I want to look more closely at a Wittgensteinian account of possible revisions of mathematics and at its resources to withstand Putnam's criticism of 1964. If, as Wittgenstein suggests, mathematical theorems function like rules, then their revisions should resemble the revisions typical of rules, at which we therefore must look.

In the case of rules, I think, there are typically the following two sorts of revisions: (i) revisions on the basis of purely *pragmatic* considerations; and (ii) revisions concerning a whole *system* of rules—where different rules are depending on each other or some rules are "derived" from others[17]—which may be necessary because of *tensions* or outright *contradictions* within the system or because one discovers *mistakes* in the derivations that one had performed. It is characteristic of rules, however, that they are *not* revised on the basis of "tensions with or contradictions to experience" in the way that is typical of statements of empirical science.

Let us now examine these points, which are characteristic of rules, with regard to mathematical theorems. As for (i), there is in mathematics the obvious pragmatic aspect that one chooses a certain axiomatic system within which one wants to move: the axioms of group theory, of topology, of the theory of vector spaces, of different geometries, and so on. Such choices are not "aimed at the truth"—the question as to whether such a system is true does not make any sense at all—rather they are motivated by pragmatic values concerning the structural richness of the system, its mathematical fruitfulness, and similar ones. Accordingly, the possible revisions of these systems, too, only concern such pragmatic aspects.

Of course, in this easy way, substantive questions about mathematical truth and mathematical factuality cannot be really avoided, for is it not a hard mathematical fact that *this* sentence *is*, or is *not* a *theorem in* axiomatic system so-and-so? One of Putnam's favorite argumentations against Wittgenstein's anthropocentric outlook on mathematics actually proceeds, or proceeded, along just these lines, and it certainly must be taken seriously.[18] However, I want to postpone its discussion until the next section, because this argumentation is not immediately relevant to our present topic: the possible *revisability* of mathematical statements. The sort of revisability of axiomatic systems just mentioned certainly *is* a purely pragmatic matter, and it is in harmony with Wittgenstein's view.

What cannot be postponed, though, is the exceptional status of the axioms of *arithmetic* and *set theory*, for which it is not at all senseless to raise questions concerning their "truth." In their case, the revisability issue has a different character. Pragmatic considerations are relevant as well, but they are of a very different nature than the ones just mentioned. They belong in the context of Quinean epistemic holism, which Putnam always has in mind when arguing against Wittgenstein. In Quine's holistic picture, as outlined in "Two Dogmas," mathematics in its entirety is considered as reconstructed within set theory (and arithmetic reconstructed within set theory); that is, it is simply identified with the theory of sets (or "classes," depending on the specific set theory chosen); and it is regarded as an integral part of our total theory of the world, alongside all the empirical theories properly so called that belong to physics, chemistry, biology, and so on.[19] And since, according to this picture, not only these empirical theories but also set theory is essentially involved in drawing empirical consequences from our total theory, even set theory, in all its abstractness, is not put beyond the reach of the "tribunal of experience" and may also be revised if recalcitrant experience makes it seem advisable. Viewed like that, it would simply be bad scientific methodology to restrict our theoretical possibilities in such a way as to immunize set theory against empirically motivated revisions. Furthermore, such revisions of set theory should not (as proposed, for example, by Carnap) be described as motivated by "purely pragmatic" considerations, making them fundamentally different from revisions of empirical theories. For in the case of empirical theories, pragmatic considerations are also essential, in such a way, in fact, that a principled difference between the pragmatic components in our acceptance or nonacceptance of set theory on the one hand and empirical theories on the other cannot be detected.

However, this Quinean view, which seems to have had considerable influence on Putnam until today, misrepresents the actual status of set theory and its relation to empirical theories. Of course, set theory *can* be seen in the Quinean way, but this way is merely the product of a philosophical fantasy that does not have very much to do with scientific practice, especially the practice of mathematicians, not to mention set theorists. In *real* science and *real* mathematics, set theory is viewed not as the most abstract part of our total theory of the world, susceptible to empirical findings, analogous to all other parts, but in quite different functions. One is *foundational*: to provide a foundation of mathematics.[20] Another function is to provide a conceptual framework that *unifies* mathematics. A further function is to enhance the *precision*, the *rigor*, of mathematical concepts and proofs. A paradigmatic example for this is the concept of the continuum, which was settled by the set-theoretic definitions of Cantor and Dedekind. All this is not in the least geared to any empirical findings. The set-theoretical assertions about the continuum, for example, are of course *used* in the empirical sciences, but no empirical theory about the continuous or discontinuous structure of space-time, of fields, of matter, or of other real world affairs will have any *retroactive effect* on what set theory says or should say about the continuum.

What, then, *is* the relation of set theory to the empirical sciences? I think there is a simple and plausible answer: Set theory provides us with all the mathematical, structural concepts of which we can consistently think and that *might* be useful in science. Seen in that way, it is bad methodology to constrain set theory by empirically oriented considerations or Quinean sentiments of ontological parsimony since the history of science gives us ample evidence of how often abstract mathematical concepts that once seemed to be far away from anything empirical suddenly proved to be useful or even necessary to our theorizing about the empirical world.[21] This is a reasonable and realistic view of set theory and of mathematics quite generally which lays stress not on the adaptation of mathematics to our empirical needs here and now, but on its *flexibility* with respect to any conceptual needs that may arise. The consequences of this view for possible *revisions* of set theory are then straightforward: We must reject the Quinean claim that the pragmatic motives that may suggest such revisions are importantly similar to the motives we meet in, say, theoretical physics. The latter ones are geared to our empirical findings, and their goal is to devise the best total theory of the world; but in set theory one tries to provide a universal and flexible conceptual repertoire, which should not be constrained by empirical findings.

What has all this to do with Wittgenstein? It shows that the Quinean assimilation of mathematics to the empirical sciences, which may be presented as the scientifically minded opposition to Wittgenstein's view, is an unconvincing philosophical fantasy, and it directs our attention to the *actual* use and function of mathematics, which is Wittgenstein's most important concern.[22] Our conclusion that set theory should be considered as a universal provider of structural concepts resulting in manifold applicability is in fact quite in tune with what Wittgenstein thinks about mathematics in general: "I should like to say: mathematics is a MOTLEY of techniques of proof.—And upon this is based its manifold applicability and its importance."[23] This perspective allows Wittgenstein to give "foundational" systems like set theory a perfectly good place, as is shown in the passage immediately following the one just cited: "But that comes to the same thing as saying: if you had a system like that of Russell [or like, say, ZFC (F.M.)] and produced systems like the differential calculus out of it by means of suitable definitions, you would be producing a new bit of mathematics."[24] In this way Wittgenstein, or the Wittgensteinian, can very well acknowledge the value of set theory: its foundational value, appropriately understood; its unifying power that increases the connections between different mathematical propositions; and the increase in rigor it brings about.

Let us turn now to the two other cases of possible revisions of mathematical theorems that I mentioned above: revisions because of the discovery of (a) contradictions in our system of mathematics or of (b) mistakes in calculations and proofs. Are these cases sufficiently similar to corresponding revisions of typical systems of *rules* such that Wittgenstein's assimilation of mathematical theorems to rules appears adequate? This question, of course, demands thorough investigations that I cannot even begin here. One should discuss Wittgenstein's notoriously nonchalant attitude toward contradictions in general and what he has to say to the scenario presented in Putnam, where both, a mathematical proposition p and its negation $\neg p$, have been proved and no mistakes in the proofs can be discovered.[25] To a Wittgensteinian it is simply a fundamental fact of the empirical world that we only very rarely meet such a situation, a fact, however, which is extremely important to the spirit and the functioning of our mathematical practice.[26] Likewise, it is a fundamental fact of our mathematical practice that mistakes in our calculations and proofs are relatively rare and that, when discovered, they can normally be identified, at least by the experts, with relative ease and without dispute. This, again, is an important topic that I cannot really go into here and which, unfortunately, also Wittgenstein himself avoided like a hot potato.[27]

One point, however, should be evident from the outset: revisions of mathematical theorems by way of the discovery of mistakes in proofs and calculations are of a completely different kind than the typical revisions in the empirical sciences. There we ponder, often on the basis of far-reaching considerations, whether to regard a given proposition as true or false, and very often this involves protracted disputes among the scientists. Not so in the case of a mathematical proposition for which a proof has been found.[28] Normally, such a proof is accepted without much dispute, and if a mistake in the proof is discovered, again this normally does not cause much dispute since the mistake normally can be exactly localized and identified, at least by the experts in the field.[29] All this, obviously, is typical of mathematics and it is *very* different from what we typically encounter in the empirical sciences. And I expect that detailed investigations in a Wittgensteinian descriptive spirit about the subject "mistakes in calculations and proofs" would only deepen the contrast between mathematics and the empirical sciences.

The upshot of all this is that there is sufficient reason not to be pessimistic about Wittgensteinian resources to counter Putnam's Quinean critique of 1964. One may suspect, however, that Putnam himself has retracted this critique since then, especially in "Rethinking Mathematical Necessity" of 1990, where he explicitly distances himself from Quine's view on mathematical necessity and announces an approximation to Wittgenstein.[30] Was the defense of Wittgenstein which I just tried to give superfluous in view of what Putnam thinks today?

In "Rethinking Mathematical Necessity" Putnam in fact takes important steps towards a Wittgensteinian position, but it seems to me that he still remains at a considerable distance to Wittgenstein's actual philosophy of mathematics. Putnam gives the following account of mathematical truths: "as a matter of descriptive fact about our present cognitive situation, we *do not know* of any possible situation in which the truths of mathematics (as we take them to be) would be disconfirmed, save for situations in which the meanings of terms are (by our present lights) altered."[31] With this move, he tries to dissociate himself from Quine, who insists that all these mathematical statements *must* be considered falsifiable (in the liberal Quinean sense of this term), a sense that, according to Putnam, goes too far. At the same time he tries to remain dissociated from Carnap, who insists that we *stipulate* the mathematical truths—Putnam explicitly mentions arithmetic truths like "$5 + 7 = 12$" and set-theoretic truths—to be unrevisable, in the sense that they simply belong to our "linguistic framework": a position that, according to Putnam, is as open to the criticism of "It ain't necessarily so" as ever.

Putnam's 1990 idea of steering between Carnap and Quine is certainly important, but I doubt that it is really an idea of *mathematical necessity*, an idea that adequately captures what we mean when we say that 5 plus 7 *must* be equal to 12, that in the decimal expansion 0.333... of ⅓ the figure 3 *must* be repeated infinitely often, that in Euclidean geometry the sum of the angles of any triangle *must* be equal to two right angles, and so on. It seems to me that what we mean by "mathematical necessity" does not have very much to do with our inability to conceive of possible situations in which the truths of mathematics would be disconfirmed, that is, with our inability to *imagine* finding out this or that.[32] This is especially clear in the case of geometry. It is a necessary truth, for example, that the sum of the angles of any plane triangle equals two right angles—in the framework of Euclidean geometry. But, of course, we can imagine it to be otherwise—in the framework of non-Euclidean geometry. Here, clearly, mathematical necessity turns out to be a framework-relative notion, quite as Carnap understood it—and as Wittgenstein understood it. Despite their deep differences, both Carnap and Wittgenstein agree that mathematical necessities have to be regarded as *rules* of description that are to be strictly distinguished from the descriptions themselves.

This view is suited not only to geometric necessities but to other necessities as well. Within the framework of Brouwerian intuitionism, for example, any function from real numbers to real numbers is necessarily continuous; but in Putnam's sense of the term "imagine" Brouwer can very well "imagine" it to be otherwise: of course, he is aware of the way of thinking within classical mathematics where discontinuous functions from real numbers to real numbers abound. He can "imagine" the classical way of thinking, but he does not accept it, and the mathematical necessities he considers depend on what he accepts and not on what he is able to imagine. The same is true, it seems to me, also in the case of elementary arithmetic (think of Putnam's "5 + 7 = 12"), where it is not that easy, and may currently even be impossible, to imagine acceptable alternatives. But this appears to be irrelevant to the way we understand arithmetical *necessity*. For example: In order to treat "5 + 7 = 12" as necessary, it is enough that—irrespective of what we can *imagine*—when we *actually* count from 1 to 5 and then add further seven steps of counting, we normally get 12; and that we normally get 12 when we unite 5 and 7 objects (in reality or in thought). These familiar experiences are then "hardened [by us] into a rule," as Wittgenstein says, and it is exactly this process of transforming them into a rule that brings about the necessity of the statement "5 + 7 = 12."[33]

In the context of just this philosophical observation, Wittgenstein makes his notorious remark: "Not empiricism and yet realism in philosophy, that is the hardest thing. (Against Ramsey.),"[34] which refers back to an earlier section, where he writes: "It is as if we had hardened the empirical proposition into a rule. And now we have, not an hypothesis that gets tested by experience, but a paradigm with which experience is compared and judged. And so a new kind of judgment."[35] It is exactly this use as a "paradigm with which experience is compared and judged," that is, this use as a *rule*,[36] that empiricists like Ramsey (whom Wittgenstein explicitly mentions) or Quine (whom Wittgenstein *would* have mentioned) disregard. To an empiricist like Quine, all statements are essentially on a par: they are fact-stating assertions, located in our web of belief, with the only epistemologically relevant difference that their "distance" from the web's periphery (which is directly connected with experience) can be greater or smaller. But Quine is insensitive to the very different *functions* in which these sentences are used in scientific practice. And it seems to me that Putnam, too, still underestimates the deep functional difference between mathematical theorems and the propositions of empirical science. To say that the necessity of the former ones resides simply in our inability to imagine things otherwise does not throw any light on their specific *function*, and, if my foregoing considerations are correct, it does not capture what we really mean by "mathematical necessity."

Actually, at first glance, it does not seem to be *mathematical* necessity at all that is the focus of Putnam's "Rethinking Mathematical Necessity," but rather *logical* necessity, and the paradigmatic example with which Putnam motivates his considerations is a logical necessity of a particularly fundamental kind, namely the proposition "For all statements p, '$\neg(p \wedge \neg p)$' is true." Putnam's central idea, then, is that it *does not make sense* to negate necessities of this sort, that we simply do not *understand* such negations:

> My suggestion is not, of course, that we retain [an] idea of a nature of thought (or judgment, or the ideal language) which metaphysically guarantees the unrevisability of logic. But what I *am* inclined to keep from this story [which is told, in one way or another, by Kant, Frege and the Wittgenstein of the *Tractatus*] is the idea that logical truths do not have negations that we (presently) understand. It is not, on this less metaphysically inflated story, that we can say that the theorems of classical logic are "unrevisable"; it is that the question "Are they revisable?" is one which we have not yet succeeded in giving a sense.[37]

Accepting this, at least provisionally, as an adequate analysis of a certain variety of logical necessity, the question arises: What, then, about *mathematical* necessity, which the title of Putnam's paper refers to?

Let us consider Putnam's own example, the mathematical proposition "5 + 7 = 12." As already said before, it seems to me that the necessity of "5 + 7 = 12" does *not* rest on our inability to make sense of "5 + 7 ≠ 12." Even *if* we could imagine practices in which "5 + 7 ≠ 12" would make sense, these practices would not be ours, and our imagining them would not affect *our* practice in which we treat "5 + 7 = 12" as necessary. When Wittgenstein states his own view of mathematical necessity, he only refers to just these practices, without any pondering of what we might be able to imagine.[38] This is obvious, for example, when he writes, "'It must be so' [e.g., that 5 plus 7 must be 12] means that this outcome has been defined to be essential to this process [namely: the outcome 12 to the process of adding 5 and 7]."[39] Wittgenstein's thought is that another outcome than 12 would show that we would not have *added 5 and 7*; and that this is quite different in the case of an experiment: There we set up an apparatus, and it is *this* apparatus—an ammeter, say—independently of the result it produces. In a certain situation it may produce this or that result and nevertheless remains *this* apparatus which we have identified as an ammeter (at least when the results lie within reasonable bounds). But the process of *adding*, when applied to 5 and 7, cannot produce this or that result and remain *this* process: It is the process of *adding* only if it produces the result 12. That is the way we use the word "add" and the corresponding symbol "+," and in precisely this use lies the mathematical necessity of "5 + 7 = 12."[40] Of course, we sometimes make *mistakes* when adding, and the Wittgensteinian analysis has to cope with this fact. But, as already noted before, we should be optimistic about Wittgenstein's resources in this respect.

That Wittgenstein's analysis of mathematical necessity has nothing to do with the existence or nonexistence of certain alternatives of which it would make sense for us to conceive is very clearly displayed in the way Wittgenstein himself discusses alternatives to our actual practice. Take the famous example from *Philosophical Investigations*: By means of the usual explanations a pupil has learned ("judged by our usual criteria," as Wittgenstein says) to develop the sequence of even numbers such that, e.g., he understands the order "+2" to develop this sequence. But beyond the number 1000 he finds it obvious to go on not with 1002, 1004, 1006, but with 1004, 1008, 1012, in such a way that "we might say, perhaps: It comes natural to this person to understand our order with our explanation as *we* should understand the order: 'Add 2 up to 1000, 4 up to 2000, 6 up to 3000 and so on.'"[41] Of course, the necessity to say "1002" after "1000" in developing the sequence of even numbers is a paradigmatic example of mathematical necessity, but Wittgenstein, in contrast to Putnam, is *not at all* tying it to the inconceivability of alternatives. Neither here nor anywhere else does he say that a behavior like the one shown by the deviant pupil above cannot be consistently or coherently understood by us. In "Remarks on the Foundations of Mathematics" he writes, "somebody may reply like a rational person and yet not be playing our game [like the deviant pupil above],"[42] and the point here is not at all that this person's alternative way of conceptualizing and thinking *cannot* be given a sense by us; the point is which sense we *actually give* our words. This sense depends on what we actually find natural and what appears to us as a matter of course and has nothing to do with what we are able or unable to *imagine*.[43]

To this, Putnam will presumably reply that the deviant pupil of PI § 185 has given the term "even number," or the sign "+2," a different *meaning* and that his, Putnam's, analysis of mathematical necessity only refers to cases where the meanings of terms are *not* altered. Remember Putnam's explanation already given: "As a matter of descriptive fact about our present cognitive situation, we *do not know* of any possible situation in which the truths of mathematics (as we take them to be) would be disconfirmed, save for situations in which the meanings of terms are (by our present lights) altered."[44] In this passage, Putnam makes essential, albeit only implicit, use of a distinction between "meaning" and "sense," where sense is constituted by such use-oriented things as our actual practice of disconfirmation, etc., and he wants to say that the necessity of a mathematical truth *p* should be seen in the fact that, *under the presupposition* that the meanings of the terms in *p* are not altered, the negation of *p* does not possess any sense. And so the necessity to step from "1000" to "1002" when obeying the order "+2" consists in the fact that any other step would only make sense when one alters the meaning of the term "+2."

If I understand it correctly, *meaning*, as Putnam uses this notion here, is essentially conceived as an invariant under translation. To take an example that figures prominently in his work: According to our actual translation practice, the term "momentum,"[45] as used by Newton, did *not* alter its meaning when used by Einstein, despite the fact that Einstein negated Newton's assertion

(1) Momentum is the product of mass and velocity;

a negation that Newton himself could not give any sense.[46] What Putnam means by *sense* in this case is essentially the same as what Wittgenstein means by "use," where "use" is understood in a pragmatically respectable way that includes, for example, methods of confirmation and disconfirmation, and similar things.

I think that the distinction between "meaning" and "sense," which Putnam presents in "Rethinking Mathematical Necessity," is a very important one, and Wittgensteinians, who tend to be strongly concerned with "sense" alone at the expense of "meaning," should come to grips with it.[47] At the same time, however, it seems to me that this distinction has got substance only in the case of empirical science and not in the case of mathematics. Let us consider one of the mathematical examples that Putnam himself discusses in this context[48]:

(2) A plane triangle has at most one angle that is a right angle.

Putnam says that the negation of (2) would not be *intelligible* to someone who has not yet conceived a coherent alternative to Euclidean geometry, and that only with the advent of non-Euclidean geometry did mathematicians *give sense* to this negation.[49] This certainly is a fair description, but Putnam then immediately adds: "[this] doesn't mean that we are *stipulating a new meaning* for one or more of the words in the sentence in question." I think that this stronger claim cannot be maintained when (2) is read as a statement of mathematics and not as a statement of physical geometry. In the latter case one can in fact sensibly say that the words occurring in (2) do have an *invariant meaning* from Euclid's time to ours, for the simple reason that we can point to concrete constellations of, say, mountaintops or stars, generating plane triangles, that remained the same from Euclid to us, and to methods of measurement directed at such constellations, which were not overthrown in the course of time but only refined. All this may give us very good reasons to translate "plane triangle" and "angle of a plane triangle" homophonically from Euclid to our time. But we do *not* have such reasons in the purely mathematical case! There, we can only refer to the mathematical practices in the periods in question, which only involve certain symbolic manipulations (constructing figures, proving theorems) without any anchor in time-invariant things that we could point to and in measuring procedures directed at these things.

Thus, to say that one should "translate the term 'plane triangle' homophonically" when comparing Euclidean geometry with one of the non-Euclidean geometries is inappropriate. Mathematicians attribute great importance to keeping apart the individual mathematical theories, and the question as to whether the term "plane triangle" as used in Euclidean geometry "has the same meaning" as that used in a non-Euclidean geometry is totally foreign to mathematical practice.[50] Consequently, in mathematics there remains only "sense," or we may simply let "sense" and "meaning" coincide. But then Putnam's talk of "giving a sense" coincides with "giving a meaning," and how does this differ from a Carnapian, or a Wittgensteinian, "*stipulating* a meaning," which Putnam rejects? Of course, neither in Carnap's view nor in Wittgenstein's is a conceptual "stipulation" of this sort something *arbitrary*. Many of the acts of giving sense that Putnam has in mind, appear very natural to us, even to be forced upon us, and many can be warranted; but the same is true of Carnapian and Wittgensteinian stipulations, and this does not alter the fact that they *are* stipulations. Hence, Putnam's view, when applied to mathematics, actually coincides with a Carnapian view or, for that matter, a Wittgensteinian one.

The upshot of this lengthy discussion about the subject "revisability" then, is that Wittgenstein's "linguistic account of mathematical theorems" can be very well defended against the arguments put forth in Putnam's "Truth and Necessity in Mathematics," and that Putnam's own reflections in "Rethinking Mathematical Necessity" should actually lead to just such an account when important peculiarities of mathematics, which distinguish mathematics from the empirical sciences, are taken into consideration.

II. Putnam's Second Objection: Mathematical Facts

Let us come back now to an issue that was postponed in the previous section: the fact that it does not make sense to ask whether, say, the axioms of group theory are "true;" whereas it does make sense to ask whether it is true that sentence p, formulated in the language of group theory, is a *theorem of* group theory. And if p is a theorem of group theory, is this not, then, a hard mathematical *fact*? And does this not immediately show the inadequacy of Wittgenstein's "rule of language" account of mathematical theorems? For when we prove that p is a theorem of group theory, this—*that p* is a theorem of group theory—is a mathematical theorem too, albeit a theorem of *meta*mathematics. But metamathematics *is* a part of mathematics because it deals with combinatorial facts concerning finite strings of symbols, which can be viewed as a relatively simple, calculatory part of arithmetic. To say that this part of mathematics deals with genuine *mathematical facts* sounds extremely plausible, and that this refutes the Wittgensteinian view of mathematics has been claimed by Putnam many times.

In his paper "Analyticity and Apriority: Beyond Wittgenstein and Quine" of 1979, Putnam discusses in detail one particular example of such a combinatorial fact, expressed by the statement

(F) Peano arithmetic is 10^{20}-consistent.

"10^{20}-consistent" means that in the formal system of Peano arithmetic there is no proof with fewer than 10^{20} symbols that proves the formula "$0 = 1$." Thus, the truth or falsity of (F) can be effectively decided by simply checking all proofs with fewer than 10^{20} symbols; i.e., it is effectively *determined* whether (F) is true or false. Now, let us assume that (F) is true (which we all, in fact, take for granted, of course). Putnam, then, gives the follow-ing philosophical analysis of this truth: "the fact that Peano arithmetic is 10^{20}-consistent depends on our nature [namely: on our dispositions to a specific verbal behavior that determines what we *mean* by our words], but also on more than our nature; it . . . is not a truth that is *explained* by facts about human nature; it . . . does not *arise from us*."[51] According to Putnam, this contradicts the following two theses which he attributes to Wittgenstein: "(1) mathematical statements do not express objective facts; and (2) their truth and necessity (or appearance of necessity) arise from and are explained by *our* nature."[52] Consequently, Wittgenstein is refuted. Putnam backs up this argument with the following consideration: To say that the 10^{20}-consistency of Peano arithmetic *arises from us* and is *explained by our nature* would only make sense if we had, whenever we would come across a proof that shows a 10^{20}-*in*consistency, the habit to forcibly reinterpret our rules of proof in such a way that this inconsistency is circumvented, i.e., if we had the habit to avoid any 10^{20}-inconsistency in a purely *ad hoc* way. But this scenario—it is Putnam's *Scenario 2*[53]—has nothing to do, of course, with our actual practice, in which we reject such high-handed maneuvers. Consequently, the truth of (F) does not "arise from us," and Wittgenstein's view is wrong.

I think, however, that Wittgenstein would have no problems defending his position against this sort of objection. He could, (a), point out that Putnam has misrepresented his actual view, and he could, (b), actively argue in favor of the view that (F), in its actual function, is much more similar to a rule than to a typical description of facts. As for (a), I would like to mention, first, what has already been at the focus of the foregoing section: that Putnam is concerned with (F)'s *truth* at the expense of (F)'s *necessity*, whereas Wittgenstein's concern is the opposite. Second, when Putnam says things like the following: "Our nature, our forms of life, etc., may explain why we *accept* the Peano axioms *as opposed to some other consistent set*; but our nature cannot possibly make an *inconsistent* set of axioms true,"[54] assuming that it is Wittgenstein who strives for such "explanations," he misunderstands Wittgenstein. Nothing could be further from Wittgenstein's intentions than to use concepts like "form of life" in an explanatory function. Wittgensteinian terms like "form of life," "practice," or "language game" are not fit for explanations, and Wittgenstein never used them in such a way, which could only be a mystifying one in view of the obvious vagueness of these terms. It is *not* that our form of life explains "why we *accept* the Peano axioms," etc.; rather, *that* we accept the Peano axioms, etc., is a fact that is *characteristic* of our form of life. Wittgenstein uses the term "form of life" merely to direct our attention to facts of this sort, because he regards them as philosophically important. Thirdly, Putnam's "arise from us" talk is much too placard-style. It is a metaphysically charged manner of speaking that any Wittgensteinian would try to avoid, or, alternatively, that any Wittgensteinian would counter by the question as to which *sense* the expression "a fact so-and-so arises from us" has been given here. Putnam actually *has* given it a sense, the sense exemplified in his *Scenario 2* mentioned above, but this *obviously* cannot be what Wittgenstein had in mind when he emphasized the anthropocentric traits of mathematics. In this way, Wittgenstein is turned into a straw man.

Note that Wittgenstein does not prohibit the talk about "mathematical facts" *per se*, which can be quite harmless talk within mathematics (in contrast to philosophy).[55] The important point to Wittgenstein is not whether we talk about "mathematical facts," but rather that the mathematical *propositions* expressing such facts are *used* in a way that is more similar to the way we use typical propositions expressing rules than to the way we use typical empirical propositions (like propositions of botany or zoology) that we take to be paradigms of "descriptions of facts." And exactly this should now be shown in the specific case of the proposition (F) presented by Putnam.

Of course, I cannot really do that here. But, at least, I would like to briefly point out one important strand of such an investigation that shows these similarities and dissimilarities particularly clearly.[56] This strand concerns the question of how the truth of (F) is *determined*, and what the word "determined" can actually *mean* in this context. Putnam seems to rely on the following model for this determination: He admits that the *interpretation* of the terms figuring in (F), and in the proof of (F), is fixed by our dispositions alone, but according to him this is not enough to determine the *truth* of (F). Something more is required: "*the 10^{20}-consistency of Peano arithmetic is still not an artifact of this dispositionally fixed interpretation. . . .* the fact that Peano arithmetic is 10^{20}-consistent depends on our nature, but also on more than our nature."[57] However, Putnam does not tell us what this "more" could be. In the case of empirical propositions, this could be easily said: the "more" consists of the factual course of natural events and processes that normally do not belong to "our nature." But in the case of mathematical propositions, only the staunchest empiricist would be tempted to give such an answer, and Putnam is not such an empiricist. Thus, he seems to have a *Platonist* answer in mind: the truth of (F) is determined not only by our nature but also by something nonempirical that lies beyond our nature.

We are now amidst the problem of following a rule that, according to my reading of Wittgenstein, is precisely the problem of *how*, when we understand a rule or a system of rules, the applications of these rules are *determined*, as well as which *sense* the word "determined" can have in this context. As everyone knows, Wittgenstein's solution, or dissolution, of this problem rejects any mentalistic or Platonist models of rule-following and directs our attention to our actual practices. And Putnam himself has expressed his inclination to accept this philosophical stance.[58] So nowadays, it seems to me, Putnam should be bound to a wide-reaching abandonment of his anti-Wittgensteinian arguments of 1979 as just presented, and the way should be open to reconsider statements like (F) and to appreciate the similarities they have with rules and their dissimilarities with descriptions as these are typically used in the empirical sciences.

III. Putnam's Third Objection: Mathematical Understanding

Again and again, and at quite different places in his later philosophy, Wittgenstein discusses the Brouwerian question of whether a certain finite sequence φ of digits occurs in the decimal expansion of π, where it is presupposed that we—at present or maybe until the end of the world—do not have any means to decide it.[59] Wittgenstein investigates what this question might *mean* because he thinks that we have a tendency to misunderstand it, especially when we insist on the law of excluded middle ("in the decimal expansion of π either the group '7777' occurs, or it does not—there is no third possibility"[60]), which may be associated with philosophically misleading pictures. In "Remarks on the Foundation of Mathematics," Wittgenstein calls the Brouwerian question "queer" ("how queer the question is whether . . . a particular arrangement of digits, e.g., '770' . . . will occur in the infinite expansion of π"[61]), and it is this attitude against which Putnam lodges a vigorous protest in his article "Was Wittgenstein *Really* an Anti-realist about Mathematics?" There he says:

> Contrary to what Wittgenstein writes about the question (he calls it "queer"), I think we should regard the question whether 770 . . . ever occurs in the expansion of π as a perfectly sensible mathematical question. For example, if mathematicians were to make the conjecture that this is the case, try to prove this conjecture in various ways, and so on, they would be doing something that makes perfect sense. What Wittgenstein should have said is that the mathematicians do understand the question whether 770 ever occurs in the decimal expansion of π, and that they have learned to understand such questions by learning to do number theory; and that something that they have also learned by learning to do number theory is that either 770 will occur in the expansion or 770 will never occur in the expansion. (Indeed, this seems to be what Wittgenstein *does* say in *Philosophical Investigations*, §516—the paragraph I chose as the epigraph to this paper.)[62]

This protest, however, is rather puzzling because it contradicts Putnam's impressive sensibility concerning the many different degrees and the strong context-dependence of our understanding, which he shows at other places in his more recent writings.[63] In his "Rethinking Mathematical Necessity" of 1990, "understanding" is intimately tied to "use" and Putnam there states that he is no longer "able to attach metaphysical weight to the principle of bivalence [and thus (I infer) to the law of excluded middle as well]."[64] And in *The Threefold Cord* he distinguishes between "intelligibility" and "*full* intelligibility" and shows in a particularly beautiful way why a certain philosophical hypothesis—the hypothesis SOULLESS, considered by Jaegwon Kim—is "lacking *full* intelligibility."[65] I think that in view of his own insights, as expressed from 1990 to 1999, Putnam should withdraw his protest against §5 *of Remarks on the Foundation of Mathematics* V.

In the passage just quoted, Putnam distances himself from Wittgenstein's claim that the Brouwerian question is "queer" by arguing (a) that we "have learned to understand such questions by learning to do number theory," (b) that we thereby "have also learned . . . that either 770 will occur . . . or 770 will never occur in the expansion [of π]," and (c) that it makes perfect sense to conjecture that, say, 770 will occur in the expansion and to try to prove this conjecture.[66] But this certainly is not sufficient to show that the Brouwerian question is *not* queer. As for (a), it is evident that the simple fact that we have learned to do number theory is not enough to make the Brouwerian question "perfectly sensible," as Putnam says, because Brouwer himself and his followers—mostly people who certainly had learned a lot of number theory—felt it to be queer. Its queerness seems to be quite similar to the queerness of the question of somebody who has learned only Euclidean geometry in the style of Euclid's *Elements* and who asks whether the regular heptagon is constructible. He presumably thinks that this construction, if possible, should be analogous to, say, the construction of the regular pentagon, but this, of course, is completely off the mark in view of the fundamental difference between regular 5- and 7-gon that is revealed by analytic geometry. And if he conjectures that this construction is not possible, he does not have any respectable mathematical idea of what it could mean to claim this impossibility. This claim gets *mathematical* content only with the advent of analytic geometry, which provides the necessary conceptual apparatus to prove it. This certainly is a rather good case in which, by projecting ourselves into the position of the Euclidean geometer just described, we might say, as Wittgenstein does, that we could "be mistaken in thinking that we understand [the] question."[67] And who knows whether the *Brouwerian* question, too, is a case of just this sort? We cannot rule this out at present.[68] Therefore, I think, Wittgenstein has very good reasons to call the Brouwerian question "queer."

As for (b), concerning the law of excluded middle, applied to the alternative which is the subject of the Brouwerian question, Wittgenstein sees only two possibilities of maintaining it: (i) to simply postulate it as a rule,[69] or (ii) to consider it as the expression of a full-blooded Platonism, where the alternative is regarded as already decided (by the Platonic world itself, so to speak), although we humans at present do not know how to decide it in a mathematically respectable way. Both choices, however, are not based on *mathematical* ideas or techniques, such that we can say, as Wittgenstein does, that they do not, strictly speaking, bestow on the law of excluded middle a validity "*inside* mathematics."[70] This is obvious for case (ii), but it is also clear in case (i), because the simple *postulation* of the universal validity of the law of excluded middle can only be supported by *pragmatic* considerations aiming at a system of mathematics that is maximally rich in proofs and results, and this, in turn, may be justified by the usefulness of such a system in physics, etc. *This*, then, may be the ultimate reason to accept the law of excluded middle without restriction.[71] So we are confronted here with the queer fact that, strictly speaking, the acceptance of the law of excluded middle in case of the Brouwerian question leads us *outside* mathematics.

One might object—as Putnam does according to (c)—that this cannot be true because it is an important part of our normal mathematical practice to make *conjectures* about the correct answer to the Brouwerian question and try to prove such conjectures. Must it not, therefore, be the case that this question "makes perfect sense," as Putnam says? But this is not necessarily so. Does it make perfect sense to say, from the point of view of Euclid's *Elements*, that the regular heptagon is constructible or that it is not constructible? I think this *remains* doubtful in view of the reasons mentioned above, notwithstanding the fact that people within the Euclidean tradition of course *made* conjectures about it and tried to prove them. But the philosophical task here is to better understand the nature of these "conjectures" in order not to fall prey to philosophical naivetés.[72] And exactly the same might be our task in case of the Brouwerian question.

Thus, Putnam's insistence that this question is "a perfectly sensible" one is not philosophically helpful. This is especially true when we take Putnam's term "perfectly" seriously.[73] As I understand Wittgenstein's remarks in *Remarks on the Foundations of Mathematics*, one of his main points is to *reject* all ideas and notions of *perfect intelligibility*—or *full intelligibility*, as Putnam calls it in *The Threefold Cord*—and accompanying ideas and notions of a *perfect* or *full understanding*.[74] When Wittgenstein writes: "'Understanding a mathematical proposition'—that is a very vague concept,"[75] this is not a *complaint*, but an important philosophical insight concerning our mathematical practice that implies that all positions in the philosophy of mathematics that make such ideas and notions of perfect intelligibility conceivable must be inadequate. Within *Remarks on the Foundations of*

Mathematics his main targets are positions that regard mathematics as an activity practiced in accordance with precisely specified rules and that contain the idea of a "complete analysis" of the mathematical propositions—as in logicism (Fregean or otherwise) or in set-theoretic reductionism—such that the full understanding of a proposition can be reached by recognizing its fully analyzed form ("logical form," "set-theoretic form," etc.). *All* these positions can be rejected in one fell swoop by gaining Wittgenstein's insight that "'Understanding a mathematical proposition' is a very vague concept"![76]

Of course, I do not suggest that Putnam holds views of *this* kind (e.g. logicist or set-theoretic reductionist ones), nor do I want to suggest that by using expressions like "perfectly sensible" or "full intelligibility," he intended any emphatic notion of "perfect understanding,"[77] not to mention any notion that is precise or theoretically underpinned. But the way in which he couples his own use of "sensible," "understanding," etc., with an emphatic rejection of Wittgenstein's sensitive reflections in *Remarks on the Foundations of Mathematics* suggests a philosophical position that is much coarser than the position he displays on other occasions. I think it is philosophically fruitful to take the "vagueness" of the concept of understanding seriously and to examine, from case to case, how far our understanding of a given question or proposition actually reaches. In the case of the Brouwerian question, it does not reach as far as we are prone to think, and that is what Wittgenstein suggests in §516 of *Philosophical Investigations*.

IV. Putnam's Fourth Objection: Truth and Proof

Perhaps I have not yet stated the proper reason why Putnam disapproves of Wittgenstein's calling the Brouwerian question "queer." This question cannot (so it is supposed) at present be mathematically decided. Maybe it will even *never* be mathematically decided, and Putnam thinks that "Wittgenstein *was*, I believe, attracted to the idea that mathematical propositions which are not humanly decidable *lack* a truth value."[78] Perhaps he thinks that Wittgenstein's queerness claim is intimately tied to *this* idea, an idea that Putnam finds "deeply problematic."[79] After having interpreted Wittgenstein as some kind of commonsense philosopher, Putnam asks, "how Wittgenstein can have been led to the extremely *un*commonsensical view that provability . . . is a necessary condition for mathematical truth"[80]—or even a view "which identifies mathematical truth with provability"[81]—and he argues that this view is not compatible with Wittgenstein's commonsense realism about rule-following. So it must be rejected.

I think, however, that this criticism is not justified, for the simple reason that the later Wittgenstein never regarded provability as a necessary condition for the truth of a mathematical proposition, not to mention an outright identification of mathematical truth with provability. Wittgenstein, notoriously, had a tendency to identify "p is true" with p. But to identify, in the mathematical case, "p is true" with "p is provable," would then mean to identify "p is provable" with p, and this would amount to an extremely forcible philosophical move that I cannot find in Wittgenstein's texts. When Wittgenstein writes: "'p' is true = p,"[82] he simply declares the topic "truth" to be a red herring that tends to distract us from what is really important. What is really important is not the question about p's truth, but the question about p's *use*. In a sense, Putnam is perfectly right when, in the context of a discussion of Wittgenstein's supposed deflationism, he writes, "Our understanding of what truth comes to, in any particular case (and it comes to very different things), is given by our understanding of the proposition, and that is dependent on our mastery of the 'language game.'"[83] But Wittgenstein would simply reply that then we should concentrate on the language games and put "truth" aside.

Not only is there clear textual evidence for neither a Wittgensteinian identification of mathematical truth with provability nor for his regarding provability as a necessary condition for mathematical truth, there is rather clear evidence to the contrary.

> Professor Hardy says, "Goldbach's theorem is either true or false."—We simply say the road hasn't been built yet. At present you have the right to say either; you have a right to *postulate* that it's true or that it's false.—If you look at it this way, the whole idea of mathematics as the physics of the mathematical entities breaks down. For which road you build is not determined by the physics of mathematical entities but by totally different considerations.[84]

This is certainly not the voice of someone who regards provability as a necessary condition for mathematical truth! I interpret this passage to say that Wittgenstein here warns against associating the wrong pictures with mathematical propositions: when they are regarded in analogy to propositions of physics, or, worse, when one hypothesizes certain mechanisms operating behind the scenes that "make" them true or false. Against this, Wittgenstein suggests, as a sort of antidote, that we simply *could postulate* that, say, Goldbach's conjecture is true. Of course, he cannot be unaware of the fact that our *actual* mathematical practice does not allow such postulations. In our actual mathematical practice, normally, the ultimate criterion for the truth of a mathematical proposition p is the presence of a proof of p, and we refrain from claiming "p is true" when we do not possess such a proof.[85] This practice, however, is far away from making mathematical propositions similar to propositions of physics, etc., and it is *nearer* to

Wittgenstein's suggested practice (in which we simply postulate the truth of Goldbach's conjecture) than to the practice of making *empirical* claims as in physics. At least, that is the way I interpret the passage just quoted.

To say that (a) provability is a *criterion* for truth, as just explained, is, of course, not at all the same as to say that (b) provability is a *necessary condition* for truth. I think Wittgenstein accepts (a) and rejects (b). With this view, he is justified in calling the Brouwerian question "queer"—because our *understanding* of it leaves a lot to be desired—without being thereby committed to the uncommonsensical claim that provability is a necessary condition for mathematical truth, against which Putnam rightly objects.

But is what Wittgenstein says in the following notorious passage not a clear indication that he regards provability as a necessary condition for mathematical truth?:

> Suppose that people go on and on calculating the expansion of π. So God, who knows everything, knows whether they will have reached '777' by the end of the world. But can his *omniscience* decide whether they *would* have reached it after the end of the world? It cannot. I want to say: Even God can determine something mathematical only by mathematics. Even for him the mere rule of expansion cannot decide anything that it does not decide for us.

> We might put it like this: if the rule for the expansion has been given us, a *calculation* can tell us that there is a '2' at the fifth place. Could God have known this, without the calculation, purely from the rule of expansion? I want to say: No.[86]

This passage even seems to suggest something much stronger, namely, that for Wittgenstein *actually being proved until the end of the world* is a necessary condition for mathematical truth. Wittgenstein has been interpreted in such a way by Michael Dummett, to whom *Remarks on the Foundations of Mathematics* in its entirety expresses a particularly radical and unacceptable form of "anti-realism."

Putnam, at the end of his essay "Was Wittgenstein *Really* an Anti-realist about Mathematics?" stands up for Wittgenstein against *this* charge, by claiming that Wittgenstein, in the passage just quoted, only wants to say that "not even God can decide whether the pattern ['777'] does or does not occur in the expansion of π except by a calculation which is *actually*—not just 'mathematically'—possible [and not, as Dummett insinuates, which is actually done until the end of the world]."[87] In a footnote Putnam suggests that the notion of "actual possibility" that he uses here is some theoretical notion of "physical possibility," and in this footnote, he even speculates whether Wittgenstein might be "willing to allow us to idealize human abilities to calculate to the uttermost limits of physical possibility."[88] But this *cannot* be the view of the later Wittgenstein, who held that philosophy should refrain from imitating science (for which it is characteristic to put forth theoretical constructions like "idealized human abilities" etc.), and who even said that philosophy should do without theses that anyone would dispute!

In his beautiful statement, which I used as one of the epigraphs of the present essay, ("Talk of what an ideal machine could do is talk *within* mathematics; it cannot fix the interpretation *of* mathematics"), Putnam expressed Wittgenstein's central anti-Platonist insight in his philosophy of mathematics in an unsurpassably pithy way, but now it seems as if Putnam wishes to replace the *ideal* possibilities of *ideal* machines, which are not able to fix the interpretation of mathematics, by the *physical* possibilities of real machines or organisms; as if *these* possibilities—as they are manifested not only in factual, but also in contrafactual situations before and after the end of the world—would be of more help for the interpretation of mathematics. This, however, is a questionable philosophical move, and a move that certainly would be foreign to Wittgenstein. Why should the physical possibilities, in the ambitious sense intended by Putnam, be important for the way we understand our mathematical practice? This understanding is reached not by any speculations about the physical possibilities of the practitioners but by observing what these practitioners *actually do*. And it is precisely this that Wittgenstein looks after in his philosophy of mathematics. So a Wittgensteinian would formulate the following statement as an important addition to Putnam's statement about ideal machines: Talk of the physical *possibilities* of real machines and organisms (in contrast to what the real machines and organisms *actually do*) is talk that is irrelevant to mathematics and cannot fix the interpretation of mathematics.

How, then, is Wittgenstein to be understood? The most important point is to see that the *subject* of the quoted passage is *not* "Mathematical Truth" (with the message that mathematical truth must coincide with provability, or even with being proved until the end of the world), but rather: "Mathematical Theorems as Rules." Here, Wittgenstein fathoms the central insight of his philosophy of mathematics, the insight that mathematical theorems function like rules, and he wants to know what this insight precisely involves. Therefore, in the first section, he asks about the *purposes* which these rules might serve. He then states that a philosophy of mathematics that clings to the *form* of mathematical propositions instead of their *use*—or that even *projects* certain forms into mathematics, as it is done by "Russell's prose"—puts us on the wrong track. And the same is true, he then suggests, of a philosophy of mathematics that (explicitly or implicitly) fancies a God who, for example, knows all the irrational numbers, who can survey the entire decimal expansion of π, and so on. All these ways of thinking about mathematics miss the important insight expressed in the paragraph that immediately follows: "the expression of the rule and its sense is only part of the language game: following the rule." In an earlier paragraph he expresses it thus: "Following according to the rule is FUNDAMENTAL to our language-game."[89] This means that there is nothing *more* fundamental: *neither* "ideal machines," which our rule-following behavior might be responsive to, *nor* the "physical possibilities" of mathematicians.

In view of this insight, the notorious passage quoted above should be interpreted as follows: When Wittgenstein talks about "mathematics" there, he refers to *our* mathematical practice with *our* language-games of following rules. This practice has an end with the end of the world (at the latest), and therefore it makes no sense even for God to go beyond it. God's omniscience may be able to achieve much, but when God deals with our mathematics, he must take into account the limitations characteristic of it, and when he goes beyond them, he deals with something else but no longer with our mathematics.

But suppose that, until the end of the world, we were not able to decide whether a certain pattern φ occurs in the decimal expansion of π. Should we not say, then, that it is *not determined* whether φ does or does not occur in it? According to Michael Dummett's interpretation, Wittgenstein would answer: In fact, it is *not* determined. But Wittgenstein's actual answer in the *Philosophical Investigations* is: "The question contains a mistake"![90] The mistake lies in the pretension that it is clear what "determined" means here. This is certainly wrong, and Wittgenstein therefore goes on as follows: "We use the expression: 'The steps are determined by the formula. . . .' [for example, a formula for the expansion of π]. *How* is it used?"[91] And when we face up to this question,[92] we certainly find uses such that the occurrence of φ has to be regarded as *not* determined (for example, when "determined" is understood in the sense of "actually decided until the end of the world") and uses where the occurrence *has* to be regarded as determined. Within classical mathematics, for example, it *is* regarded as determined, in the plain sense that one *accepts the law of excluded middle*; that is, it is the use of this law that gives sense to the term "determined" (whereby one has in the background all the techniques that classical mathematics provides). As I said in section III, the adoption of classical mathematics, with its universal acceptance of the law of excluded middle, may be strongly motivated by our wish to have at our disposal a powerful instrument for empirical applications, and we might say, therefore, that it is ultimately this motivation that lets us say that the occurrence of φ in the decimal expansion of π *is determined*. However, we should not forget what *this* use of "determined" involves and what it does not involve. What it does *not* involve, of course, is a Platonist metaphysics.

At the same time, when interpreted in such a relaxed way, the notorious passage quoted above also does not express any "antirealism" about mathematics because one has left behind the obsession with the subject "Truth" that is so characteristic of the realism/antirealism issue. But then, neither does it make much sense to call Wittgenstein a "realist," in whatever sense of this term (when meant as a technical term of philosophy). The philosophy of the later Wittgenstein is at cross-purposes with the realism/antirealism debate and should be approached with other philosophical categories.[93]

FELIX MÜHLHÖLZER

DECEMBER 2002

NOTES

1. In what follows, by "Wittgenstein" I will always mean the later Wittgenstein.
2. Hilary Putnam, "Truth and Necessity in Mathematics," in *Mathematics, Matter and Method: Philosophical Papers*, vol. 1 (Cambridge: Cambridge University Press, 1975), 1.
3. Ibid., 8.
4. Hilary Putnam, "Analyticity and Apriority: Beyond Wittgenstein and Quine," in *Realism and Reason: Philosophical Papers*, vol. 3 (Cambridge: Cambridge University Press, 1983), 117.
5. Ludwig Wittgenstein, *Remarks on the Foundations of Mathematics*, rev. ed., ed. G. H. Rhees and G. E. M. Anscombe, trans. G. E. M. Anscombe (Cambridge, MA: MIT Press, 1978), III §26.
6. Putnam, "Truth and Necessity in Mathematics," 8.
7. I use "theorem" as synonymous with "proved proposition," with axioms regarded as limiting cases, whereby the term "proof" is not to be exclusively understood in a formalistically constricted way, but also in the ways that are customary in the usual mathematical practice. — What, then, about propositions like "5 + 7 = 12"? Are they theorems in my sense? I will treat them as such, because there exist respectable technical proofs for them, for example, in Peano arithmetic; and also because even the nontechnical warrants given for them in primary school *can* be considered as proofs.
8. Putnam, "Truth and Necessity in Mathematics," 9ff.
9. Reiterated over and over again since 1962, until 2001: see Putnam's "Rules, Attunement, and 'Applying Words to the World': The Struggle to Understand Wittgenstein's Vision of Language," in *The Legacy of Wittgenstein: Pragmatism or Deconstruction*, ed. Ludwig Nagl and Chantal Mouffe (New York: Peter Lang, 2001), 18.
10. Putnam, "Truth and Necessity in Mathematics," 11.
11. W. V. O. Quine, "Two Dogmas of Empiricism," in *From a Logical Point of View: Nine Logico-Philosophical Essays*, 2nd ed. (New York: Harper and Row, 1961), 20–46.
12. Putnam, "Truth and Necessity in Mathematics," 1.
13. Wittgenstein, *Remarks on the Foundations of Mathematics*, I §4.
14. See Wittgenstein's *Remarks on the Foundations of Mathematics*, Appendix III §6, and *Philosophical Investigations*, 2nd ed., ed. G. E. M. Anscombe and R. Rhees, trans. G. E. M. Anscombe (Oxford: Blackwell, 1958), § 136.
15. Putnam, "Truth and Necessity in Mathematics," 11.

16. "These views of Quine's [concerning apriority and necessity, especially with respect to mathematics] are views that I shared ever since I was a student (for a year) at Harvard in 1948-49, but, I must confess, they are views that I now want to criticize." See Putnam's "Rethinking Mathematical Necessity," in *Words and Life*, ed. James Conant (Cambridge, MA: Harvard University Press, 1994), 246.

17. In chess, for example, the fundamental rules of the game imply that a bishop always remains on squares of the same color—a proposition which can be regarded, then, as a "derived rule."

18. See Putnam's "Truth and Necessity in Mathematics," 11; "Analyticity and Apriority,"119–24; "Philosophy of Mathematics: Why Nothing Works," in *Words and Life*, 500ff.

19. "The abstract entities which are the substance of mathematics—ultimately [!] classes and classes of classes and so on up—are another posit in the same spirit. Epistemologically these are myths on the same footing with physical objects and gods, neither better nor worse except for differences in the degree to which they expedite our dealings with sense experiences." See *From a Logical Point of View*, 45. This Quinean identification of mathematics with the theory of sets can be criticized in many different ways, especially from a Wittgensteinian point of view. Here, however, I will not criticize the identification *per se*, but the *conformation* of mathematics to the empirical sciences to which it gives rise in Quine's thinking.

20. See Penelope Maddy's *Naturalism in Mathematics* (Oxford: Clarendon Press, 1997), chapter I.2 and "Some Naturalistic Reflections on Set Theoretic Method," *Topoi* 20: 17–27. These two texts provide very illuminating discussions of how "foundation" should, and should not, be understood here. I am very much in agreement with Maddy's view of set theory, expressed within her "mathematical naturalism," which supports what I argue for in the present context.

21. See Maddy, "Some Naturalistic Reflections on Set Theoretic Method," 22–26 for convincing examples.

22. It is true, of course, that Wittgenstein seems to betray this very concern by his notorious, obstinate hostility toward set theory. But this hostility was simply a mistake, caused by a severe lack of mathematical knowledge on his part, and it does not in the least impugn the value of his philosophical approach. Wittgensteinians with more mathematical competence should feel invited to correct him here.

23. Wittgenstein, *Remarks on the Foundations of Mathematics*, III §46.

24. Ibid.

25. Putnam, "Truth and Necessity in Mathematics," 9.

26. See Felix Mühlhölzer, "Wittgenstein and the Regular Heptagon," *Grazer Philosophische Studien* 62 (2001): 215–47. Here, I offer a discussion of this point in the specific case of an alleged Euclidean construction of the regular 7-gon in the face of the well-known proof that such a construction is impossible.

27. This is evident from the way he deals with it in *Lectures on the Foundations of Mathematics*, ed. Cora Diamond (Ithaca, NY: Cornell University Press, 1976), 110 and at the very end of part III of *Remarks on the Foundations of Mathematics*.

28. Of course, this is quite different in the case of mathematical *conjectures* for which a proof is missing. With respect to them, a "quasi-empiricist" approach, as envisaged by Putnam may be appropriate. See his "What is Mathematical Truth?" in *Mathematics, Matter and Method*, 60–78. But I am concerned here with *proved* propositions only, which have quite a different status.

29. I ignore anomalous cases like Zermelo's proof of the theorem that every set can be well ordered, which was hotly debated. It seems to me, however, that such cases cannot take away the deep differences between mathematics and the empirical sciences with

which I am dealing here. In any case, they demand a totally different treatment which is beyond the scope of the present paper.

30. "My strategy in this essay will be to suggest that there is a different way [a way different from Carnap's way] of stripping away the transcendental baggage [to be found in Kant and Frege]; a way which has features in common with the philosophy of the later Wittgenstein." Putnam, "Rethinking Mathematical Necessity," 246.

31. Ibid., 258.

32. Putnam himself expresses his ideas by talking about "imagining" so and so; see his "Rethinking Mathematical Necessity," 250.

33. Wittgenstein, *Remarks on the Foundations of Mathematics*, VI §§22–23.

34. Ibid., VI §23. Much of the significance of this remark, and especially its relation to Ramsey, is explained in chapter 1 of Cora Diamond's *The Realistic Spirit: Wittgenstein, Philosophy, and the Mind* (Cambridge, MA: MIT Press, 1991).

35. Wittgenstein, *Remarks on the Foundations of Mathematics*, VI §22.

36. Or as *measure*, as Wittgenstein writes in *Remarks on the Foundations of Mathematics*, III § 75: "What I want to say is: mathematics is always measure, not thing measured."

37. Putnam, "Rethinking Mathematic Necessity," 255–56.

38. In quite another context, the context of "privacy" as investigated in *Philosophical Investigations* §§243–315, Wittgenstein briefly discusses exclamations like "I can't imagine the opposite of this [e.g., that only I myself can know whether I am feeling pain]," but he treats them as indicators of grammatical propositions: "These words are a defence against something whose form makes it look like an empirical proposition, but which is really a grammatical one," Ibid., §251. This philosophical move is quite the reverse of the one proposed by Putnam.

39. Wittgenstein, *Remarks on the Foundations of Mathematics*, VI §7.

40. See Felix Mühlhölzer, "*Regelfolgen und die Identität von Begriffen*," in *Institutionen und Regelfolgen*, ed. Ulrich Baltzer and Gerhard Schönrich (Paderborn: Mentis, 2002), 147–56.

41. Wittgenstein, *Philosophical Investigations*, §185.

42. Wittgenstein, *Remarks on the Foundations of Mathematics*, I §115. Part I of *Remarks on the Foundations of Mathematics* was written in 1937–38, but this last sentence of § 115 is an exception: It was added in 1944, as the editors inform us in a footnote. Thus, it was certainly important to Wittgenstein to make just this point. Of course, it is not an easy point and it is one that invites controversial discussion, the more so when one takes a look at the German original, which reads as follows: "*er kann antworten wie ein verständiger Mensch und doch das Spiel nicht mit uns spielen.*" The German word "*verständig*" does not exactly mean the same as "*vernünftig*," that is, "rational," as the English translation wants to have it. It is much more vague. To my mind, it here means that the person in question *may* behave in a way that appears extremely alien to us, but that we nonetheless should not judge him to be someone who has *not understood* what he has been taught, but who understands it *differently* than we do. This does not exclude the fact that we might manage to understand him, alien as he may be, and that his linguistic behavior may even be more successful than ours.

43. See Wittgenstein's *Philosophical Investigations* §238: "The rule can only seem to me to produce all its consequences in advance if I draw them as a *matter of course* . . . (Criteria for the fact that something is 'a matter of course' for me)."

44. Putnam, "Rethinking Mathematical Necessity," 258.

45. Ibid., 257. The example of "momentum" is completely analogous to the example of "kinetic energy" discussed already in Putnam's "The Analytic and the Synthetic" and in many other texts since then.

46. Thus (1) is, as Putnam calls it, *necessary relative* to Newton's body of knowledge, but it is no more necessary relative to Einstein's, since there it is even rejected.

47. For an instructive attempt in this direction, see Cora Diamond's "How Old are These Bones? Putnam, Wittgenstein and Verification," *Supplement to the Proceedings of the Aristotelian Society* 73: 99–134.

48. See Putnam's "Reply to James Conant," *Philosophical Topics* 20: 374–77 and his "Rules, Attunement, and 'Applying Words to the World,'" 13–23.

49. Putnam, "Reply to James Conant," 375.

50. The same point, but in much more detail, is made in Mühlhölzer, "Wittgenstein and the Regular Heptagon," for the case of Euclidean geometry as presented in Euclid's *Elements* versus Cartesian analytic geometry.

51. Putnam, "Analyticity and Apriority," 121.

52. Ibid., 126.

53. Ibid., 120.

54. Ibid., 118.

55. See, for example, Wittgenstein's *Lectures on the Foundations of Mathematics*, 147ff.

56. [*Note added in 2014.*] Another strand of this issue, concentrating on the *objects* of metamathematics, is discussed in Felix Mühlhölzer, "Wittgenstein and Mathematics," in *Wittgenstein: Zu Philosophie und Wissenschaften,* ed. Pirmin Stekeler-Weithofer (Hamburg: Felix Meiner, 2012), 102–28.

57. Putnam, "Analyticity and Apriority," 120–21.

58. See, for example, Hilary Putnam, "Was Wittgenstein *Really* an Anti-realist about Mathematics?" in *Wittgenstein in America*, ed. Timothy McCarthy and Sean C. Stidd (Oxford: Oxford University Press, 2001), 140–94.

59. The specific patterns φ that Brouwer and Wittgenstein actually gave as examples (for example "0123456789," "7777," or "770") have become obsolete because modern computers actually *found* them, but they can be replaced by other patterns such that the question remains open. In what follows, I will retain Wittgenstein's examples in order not to complicate the presentation of his thoughts.

60. See Wittgenstein's *Philosophical Investigations*, §352.

61. Wittgenstein, *Remarks on the Foundations of Mathematics*, V §9.

62. Putnam, "Was Wittgenstein *Really* an Anti-realist about Mathematics?" 178f.

63. Another reason to be puzzled is Putnam's reading of *Philosophical Investigations* §516. In this paragraph, Wittgenstein actually wants to say just the opposite of what Putnam ascribes to him. Wittgenstein points out here that our understanding of the Brouwerian question does not extend very far and that our tendency to see it otherwise is based on a delusion. The context of §516 makes this abundantly clear. In §513 Wittgenstein gives an example that shows "how it is that something can look like a sentence which we understand, and yet yield no sense." In §517 he suggests that we can very well "be mistaken in thinking that we understand a question," which he substantiates as follows: "For many mathematical proofs do lead us to say that we *cannot* imagine something which we believed we could imagine. (E.g., the [Euclidean] construction of the heptagon.) They lead us to revise what counts as the domain of the imaginable." —The pertinent commentaries on *Philosophical Investigations* are very clear about Wittgenstein's intent in §516: See Peter Hacker, *Wittgenstein: Mind and Will (An analytical commentary on the* Philosophical Investigations, *Volume 4)* (Oxford: Blackwell, 1996), 308f, and Eike von Savigny, *Wittgensteins "Philosophische Untersuchungen: Ein Kommentar für Leser, Band II, Abschnitte 316–693,* 2nd ed. (Frankfurt am Main: Vittorio Klostermann, 1994), 203. Note that *Philosophical Investigations* §516 goes back to Wittgenstein's MS 163, which was written in 1941; that is, it was written earlier than *Remarks on the Foundations of*

Mathematics V (where Wittgenstein talks about the "queerness" of Brouwer's question), which was not begun before 1942.

64. Putnam, "Rethinking Mathematical Necessity," 259.

65. Hilary Putnam, *The Threefold Cord: Mind, Body, and the World* (New York: Columbia University Press, 1999), 15 (*"Understanding is having the abilities that one exercises when and in using language."*). See also 89–91 and 98–100.

66. Most mathematicians are convinced that *any* finite block of digits occurs in the decimal expansion of π, but one seems to be far away from a proof of this conjecture. See Ivars Petersen, "Pi à la Mode," *Science News* 160 (2001): 136–37.

67. Wittgenstein, *Philosophical Investigations*, §517.

68. The regular heptagon is explicitly mentioned in *Philosophical Investigations* §517. And in *Remarks on the Foundations of Mathematics* V, shortly after having claimed, in §9, the queerness of the Brouwerian question, Wittgenstein asks in §12 with respect to *this* question too: "may I not believe I understand it, and be wrong?"

69. Wittgenstein, *Remarks on the Foundations of Mathematics*, V §9.

70. Ibid., §18.

71. A sentiment like this is expressed by Hermann Weyl in his *"Wissenschaft als symbolische Konstruktion des Menschen," Eranos-Jahrbuch 1948*, 375–431.

72. See Mühlhölzer, "Wittgenstein and the Regular Heptagon," for an attempt to clarify the nature of such conjectures.

73. More seriously, I presume, than he himself wanted to take it.

74. See Putnam, *The Threefold Cord*, 56, 60, 83, and 98f.

75. Wittgenstein, *Remarks on the Foundations of Mathematics*, V §46.

76. See also *Remarks on the Foundations of Mathematics*, VI §13, where Wittgenstein discusses our understanding of Fermat's Last Theorem and where he asks (in 1943/44 when the mathematicians were far away from a proof of it): "Don't [the mathematicians] *understand* it just as completely as one can possibly understand it?" He then rejects this naïve question by noting: "'Understanding' is a vague concept." This is the same philosophical move as in *Remarks on the Foundations of Mathematics, V* §46.

77. As Wittgenstein calls it in *Remarks on the Foundations of Mathematics, VI* §13.

78. Putnam, "Was Wittgenstein *Really* an Anti-realist about Mathematics?" 140–41.

79. Ibid., 141.

80. Ibid., 192.

81. Ibid., 187.

82. See Wittgenstein *Remarks on the Foundations of Mathematics*, I, Appendix III, §6, or *Philosophical Investigations* §136.

83. Putnam, *The Threefold Cord*, 67.

84. Wittgenstein, *Lectures on the Foundations of Mathematics*, 138f.

85. This is different, of course, in the case of axioms, but axioms are not my topic now. For a discussion of this, see William W. Tait, "Beyond the Axioms: The Question of Objectivity in Mathematics," *Philosophia Mathematica* 9, no. 1 (2001): 21–36.

86. Wittgenstein, *Remarks on the Foundations of Mathematics*, VII, §41. Also see V §34 in the *original* edition, which Putnam exclusively refers to in his essay, "Was Wittgenstein *Really* an Anti-realist about Mathematics?"

87. Putnam, "Was Wittgenstein *Really* an Anti-realist about Mathematics?" 193.

88. Ibid., n93.

89. *Remarks on the Foundation of Mathematics, VI*, §28.

90. Wittgenstein, *Philosophical Investigations*, §189.

91. Ibid., §189.

92. As Wittgenstein himself does in the remainder of *Philosophical Investigations* §189. But, of course, it is not difficult to do that for oneself, without necessarily following his lead.

93. I am grateful to Olaf Müller for his comments on an earlier version of this paper and to Marianne Mühlhölzer and the participants of my *Oberseminar "Philosophisch denken"* for the many discussions I was able to have with them about Wittgenstein's philosophy of mathematics. Part of the work on this essay has been supported by the *Deutsche Forschungsgemeinschaft* (grants Mu 687/3–1, 3–2, and 4–1).

REPLY TO FELIX MÜHLHÖLZER

Felix Mühlhölzer and I have enjoyed arguing about questions of Wittgenstein interpretation for decades, and it is a great pleasure to be able to continue our argument in this place. He is clear and forthright about his disagreement with my views, and I am sure he expects me to be equally clear and forthright about my disagreements with his, and I shall be, to the best of my ability.

Like Parsons's essay, Mühlhölzer's raises a great many issues, and I will follow the strategy of saying what my position is on two central ones, in the hope that it will be clear what I would say about all or most of the points he raises. The two issues I will discuss in detail are the particular "rule of language" account of mathematics that Mühlhölzer defends, and the account of physical geometry that accompanies that account. First, however, I need to say something about his interpretations of Wittgenstein, myself, and Quine.

Mühlhölzer notes that he and I interpret Wittgenstein's philosophy of mathematics differently. In my view, Mühlhölzer's interpretation puts Wittgenstein's philosophy of mathematics much too close to Carnap's, whereas my own interpretation agrees on some key issues with Cora Diamond's.[1] However, here I will criticize Wittgenstein's view *as interpreted by Mühlhölzer*, setting aside, for the most part, my own interpretation.[2]

In my opinion, Felix Mühlhölzer's essay gets both Quine and me wrong while also getting wrong the nature of my divergences from Quine.[3] Part of what I refer to is this: the innocent reader of Mühlhölzer's essay might well get the impression that neither Quine nor I are/were aware that one does not perform experiments to test mathematical theorems! But the question *is not* whether it is the case that (with rare exceptions[4]) one does not perform experiments to test mathematical statements; the question is whether this fact shows that mathematical theorems should be assimilated to "rules of language" as Mühlhölzer's Wittgenstein (henceforth: "Wittgenstein^M") claims they should. In fact, the idea that one can account for the isolation of theorems of pure mathematics from experiment *without* accepting a "rule of language" account (either that of Wittgenstein[M] or of the real Wittgenstein) has been at the heart of my own writing on philosophy of mathematics (including geometry) from "It Ain't Necessarily So" and "The Analytic and the Synthetic" to the present time. Mühlhölzer does mention "It Ain't Necessarily So," as well as the more recent "Rethinking Mathematical Necessity," but he apparently takes my remarks to the effect that before the discovery of non-Euclidean geometry scientists could not *imagine* the falsity of certain statements (for example, the statement that two straight lines that intersect cannot both be perpendicular to a third straight line) as the *definition* of my term "necessary relative to a body of knowledge," and thus accuses me of putting too much weight on the problematic concept of imagining something.[5] What I in fact wrote (in the later paper, but describing what I already said in the earlier paper) was:

> call a statement empirical *relative to a body of knowledge B* if possible observations (including observations of experiments people with that body of knowledge could perform) would be *known* to disconfirm the statement (without drawing on anything outside that body of knowledge). It seemed to me that this captures pretty well the traditional notion of an empirical statement. Statements which belong to that body of knowledge but which are not empirical relative to that body of knowledge I called "necessary relative to the body of knowledge." The putative truths of Euclidean geometry were, prior to their overthrow, synthetic and necessary (in this relativized sense). The point of this new distinction was to emphasize that there are at any given time some accepted statements which cannot be overthrown merely by observation, but can only be overthrown by thinking of a whole body of alternative theory as well. And I insisted (and still insist) that this is a distinction of methodological significance.[6]

Here I gave an account, in purely logical/methodological terms, of how certain statements (including, obviously, the statements of pure mathematics that have been accepted as proved at a given time) could be such that one cannot perform experiments to test them, *without* assuming that they could not be revised if "a whole body of alternative theory" were someday invented, and without its being the case that if they *were* revised, then the meanings of some words would necessarily have changed. And it is not just that my account is *preferable* to the "rules of language" account of mathematical and geometrical statements favored by Wittgenstein[M]; I believe that the latter account is vulnerable to well known arguments against verificationist accounts of the meanings of scientific terms, as I shall explain below.

I. Further Word on Mühlhölzer's Quine/Putnam Interpretation

One respect in which Mühlhölzer gets both Quine and myself wrong is in portraying Quine (and myself when my views were closer to Quine's) as holding that mathematics is *empirical*. But "empirical," in the traditional terminology, means "synthetic and a posteriori," and Quine thought the traditional analytic/synthetic distinction and the a priori/a posteriori distinction both rest on false assumptions. Here he had a truly important idea, which he somewhat muddled up by connecting the idea that the analytic/synthetic (and a priori/a posteriori) dichotomies are problematic with the bad idea that there is nothing to the notion of synonymy.

Nevertheless, as I pointed out above, holding that all our scientific claims (including logical and mathematical ones) are revisable is not the same as holding that they are all "empirical." And if I have moved away from Quine (by questioning the idea that there is any clear sense to saying that, for example, "2 + 2 = 4" is "revisable"), that does not mean that I now believe that "2 + 2 = 4" is "unrevisable." What I say is that we cannot have a guarantee that even "2 + 2 = 4" will not someday be revised (or that the "meanings of the words" will have undergone a change if it is revised)—this is the truth in fallibilism—and that is why the *unrelativized* notion of an "a priori" truth (as opposed to the notion of a statement that functions as a "framework principle" in our conceptual scheme at a given time) is one we should reject. The important thing is that Quine and I are both fallibilists, but being a fallibilist does not mean thinking that mathematical "theorems" are "empirical." (Since this is the subject of my exchange with Gary Ebbs in the present volume, I will say no more about this here, but refer the reader to Ebbs's essay and my reply.)

II. Verificationism and the "Rule of Language" Account

As Mühlhölzer explains it, Wittgenstein[M]'s view has two principal features: (1) theorems of mathematics are said to be "rules of language" (Mühlhölzer also calls them "rules of description"—this does seem to be correct as a description of the real Wittgenstein, apart from the claim that the rules we accept completely fix the meanings of the mathematical expressions); and (2) theorems of mathematics are statements that belong to "systems" (the "rules" being the rules of those systems) for which the question of truth or falsity does not even arise. What arises is the question whether a given statement is a theorem of a given system.

Let us suppose, for the sake of argument, that Wittgenstein[M] is right, and the "theorems" of mathematics are rules that fix the meanings of the mathematical expressions. The question, central for both Quine and myself, at once arises: how do these "rules" fix the meanings of those mathematical expressions *when they occur in empirical statements*? For example, Maxwell's equations in their customary form contain symbols for the divergence and curl of two vector fields, the electric field and the magnetic field. As mentioned, Wittgenstein^M thinks that the notion of truth is not useful in mathematics; he thinks that what is important is that the theorems are necessary, where this amounts to the claim that changing the system is ipso facto changing the meaning of the mathematical expressions.[7] Cora Diamond contests this as a description of Wittgenstein's view, as already mentioned.[8] But the Maxwell equations are not necessary truths; they are *empirical statements that contain mathematical symbols*. If they are true, or approximately true, how can that be the case? What do those symbols mean when they occur *outside of the "system" to which they belong*, on Wittgenstein^M's account? Given what Mühlhölzer has to say about physical geometry, it seems that understanding the symbols contained in the Maxwell equations can only mean knowing how the theorems of vector calculus, etc., allow us to derive predictions from, for example, the Maxwell equations plus given boundary conditions. But if that is what Wittgenstein^M thinks, then Wittgenstein^M must regard Maxwell's theory and other physical theories as no more than prediction devices, and that is positivism pure and simple!

In "Was Wittgenstein *Really* an Anti-realist about Mathematics," a paper Mühlhölzer discusses at length, I suggested that Wittgenstein was at one time attracted to the view that a mathematical calculation has a reasonably well-defined outcome (that is, there are rational numbers such that it is correct to say "the value of the function being calculated is between r_1 and r_2, where r and r are rational numbers) only if the calculation is feasible for human beings to carry out by "the end of the world."[9] So, suppose that the temperature of the gas in a certain small region in the sun cannot be measured directly or indirectly. To say in that case that the notion of the temperature of the gas in the region lacks intelligibility would be one form of classical logical positivism. Now, suppose instead that although the temperature of the gas cannot be measured directly, there is an equation whose solution, *according to a physical theory we accept*, is the temperature in question (to a given accuracy). To say that whether the notion of the temperature of the gas in the region is intelligible or not depends on whether such a calculation is possible for human beings to carry out would be just as verificationist; in fact, it would probably be more verificationist than the later Carnap. If, on the other hand, Wittgenstein^M agrees that the statement that a certain calculation yields a certain value can be *true* (pardon me, "necessary"—see Mühlhölzer's essay) *even if the proof is not one that human beings could write down "before the end of the world,"* just how is that supposed to fit with the "rule of language" story? When he discusses this issue, Mühlhölzer's response is to say that Wittgenstein would not want us to talk about "physical possibility" in philosophy, where what that comes to seems to be that we cannot even raise the question as to whether a mathematical statement that cannot be proved by humans could nonetheless have a truth value![10] I do not see any reason to believe this, and frankly, I do not see how Mühlhölzer's account of "application" can be understood in any but a verificationist way.[11] Mühlhölzer is right that in "Rethinking Mathematical Necessity" I said that I was unable "to attach metaphysical weight to the principle of bivalence." I think that was a serious error on my part.[12]

Of course, my own scientific realism goes beyond believing that statements about the values of recursive functions that our constitution may make it impossible for us to prove do, nonetheless, possess definite truth values. As I say in my "Reply to Charles Parsons," I also believe that we should regard fundamental physical theories such as Newton's or Einstein's or present theories of quantum gravity as candidates for *truth* (or approximate truth), and that any philosophy of mathematics that would be inconsistent with so regarding them should be rejected. As we presently understand them, all the theories just mentioned describe entities we cannot directly observe in a purely mathematical language. (This is particularly true of quantum mechanical entities.) If Wittgenstein[M] thinks those mathematical descriptions are merely tools for deriving predictions (or for other so-called "applications"), then Wittgenstein[M] is just a positivist, whether or not he accepts the label. If Wittgenstein[M] agrees, however, that those descriptions are capable of being true or false, and not merely useful in making predictions, building bridges, and so on, then he owes an account (which he has not even begun to sketch) of how his view of mathematics as, in effect, just a collection of different "systems" that are not susceptible to judgments of truth and falsity, is compatible with this much realism.

III. WITTGENSTEIN[M] AND REICHENBACH ON PHYSICAL GEOMETRY

In *The Philosophy of Space and Time* and in *The Rise of Scientific Philosophy*, Reichenbach gave an account of geometry that has two principal features: (i) theorems of Euclidean, Riemannian, or Lobachevskian geometry (or of a geometry of variable curvature) are statements that belong to "systems" (the axioms being the rules of those systems) for which the question of truth or falsity does not even arise. What arises is the question whether a given statement is a theorem of a given system. (ii) Statements about the geometry of physical space are really statements about light-ray paths (or other physical phenomena) which we obtain by, for example, pretending that those light rays are ideal straight lines in the sense of obeying the laws of one or another mathematical geometry. As far back as "The Analytic and the Synthetic," I objected to this logical positivist account,[13] writing: "Reichenbach suggested that 'straight line,' properly analyzed, means 'path of a light ray,' and with this 'analysis' accepted, it is clear that the principles of geometry are and always were synthetic. They are and always were subject to experiment. Hume simply overlooked something which could in principle have been seen by the ancient Greeks. I think Reichenbach is almost totally wrong."[14] (The reader who is interested in seeing a very detailed argument that Reichenbach's views—and Adolf Grünbaum's similar ones—are wrong may find it in my "An Examination of Grünbaum's Philosophy of Geometry," chapter 6 of *Mathematics, Matter and Method*.)

Now, what of Wittgenstein[M]'s views on geometry? As described by his creator,[15] Felix Mühlhölzer, those views have, again, two principal features: (i) theorems of Euclidean, Riemannian, or Lobachevskian geometry (or of a geometry of variable curvature) are statements that belong to "systems" (the axioms [or perhaps all the theorems we have accepted as proved?] being the rules of those systems) for which the question of truth or falsity does not even arise. What arises is the question whether a given statement is a theorem of a given system. (ii) With respect to physical geometry, what Mühlhölzer considers is the statement

(2) A plane triangle has at most one angle that is a right angle.

and he writes in his essay above:

> Putnam says that the negation of (2) would not be *intelligible* to someone who has not yet conceived a coherent alternative to Euclidean geometry, and that only with the advent of non-Euclidean geometry did mathematicians *give sense* to this negation. This certainly is a fair description, but Putnam then immediately adds: "[this] doesn't mean that we are *stipulating a new meaning* for one or more of the words in the sentence in question." I think that this stronger claim cannot be maintained when (2) is read as a statement of mathematics and not as a statement of physical geometry.[16] In the latter case one can in fact sensibly say that the words occurring in (2) do have an *invariant meaning* from Euclid's time to ours, for the simple reason that we can point to concrete constellations of, say, mountaintops or stars, generating plane triangles, that remained the same from Euclid to us, and to methods of measurement directed at such constellations, which were not overthrown in the course of time but only refined.

This is identical with Reichenbach's positivist view!

IV. A Concluding Remark

At certain points Mühlhölzer raises the spectre of "Platonism." For example,

> Thus, [Putnam] seems to have a *Platonist* answer in mind: the truth of (F) is determined not only by our nature but also by something nonempirical that lies beyond our nature. [(F) is the mathematical statement that "Peano Arithmetic is 10^{20} consistent"].

> However, Putnam does not tell us what this "more" could be. In the case of empirical propositions, this could be easily said: the "more" consists of the factual course of natural events and processes that normally do not belong to "our nature." But in the case of mathematical propositions, only the staunchest empiricist would be tempted to give such an answer, and Putnam is not such an empiricist. Thus, he seems to have a *Platonist* answer in mind: the truth of (F) is determined not only by our nature but also by something nonempirical that lies beyond our nature.

My response is that the truth of (F) is determined by the objective fact that it is not mathematically possible to construct a contradiction from the axioms of Peano Arithmetic, and *a fortiori* it is not possible to construct a contradiction with fewer than 10^{20} symbols.[17] Of course that is not an *empirical* fact; that mathematical facts are not "empirical" is something Mühlhölzer himself stresses. And I do believe in objective (and in some cases recognition-transcendent) mathematical facts. But that does not mean that I subscribe to Platonic metaphysics, although I grant that realism is a position in metaphysics. Where I break with Wittgenstein (and not only with Wittgenstein[M]) is in thinking that the idea that metaphysics should be abandoned was a twentieth-century mistake that we should outgrow. (On this, see my "Reply to Maudlin.") Calling realism with respect to arithmetic (and even set-theoretic) truth "Platonism" does not refute it. Indeed, what I have been arguing all these years is that if you want to be a realist about modern *physics*, then you had *better* believe that there is such a thing as mathematical truth, and that it outruns human provability. Of course, some philosophers will reply that realism about physics is also a form of nonsense requiring Wittgensteinian therapy. But, and this is the question I have been pressing throughout this reply, how does rejecting scientific realism differ from regarding our best theories of the physical universe as mere prediction devices?

H.P.

NOTES

1. See my "Reply to Cora Diamond" in the present volume. An important point of disagreement between Mühlhölzer's interpretation of Wittgenstein[M] and my own is that, while I do agree that our uses of words are *subject* to rules, I deny that those uses can be completely described by describing those rules, or that Wittgenstein believes that "nonsense" always results when we depart from or change those rules.

2. See, for example, my "Rules, Attunement, and 'Applying Words to the World': The Struggle to Understand Wittgenstein's Vision of Language," in *The Legacy of Wittgenstein: Pragmatism or Deconstruction*, ed. Chantal Mouffe and Ludwig Nagl (New York: Peter Lang, 2001): 9–23, and Cora Diamond's essay in the present volume.

3. One of my differences with Quine is described in "Indispensability Arguments in the Philosophy of Mathematics," in my *Philosophy in an Age of Science* (Cambridge, MA: Harvard University Press, 2012).

4. I say, "with rare exceptions," because if we ascertain that a number is overwhelmingly probably prime using the Rabin-Miller primality test (choosing numbers at random and checking to see whether they are "strong witnesses" to the compositeness of p or not), we do run a real world experiment to determine if a mathematical conjecture—p is prime—is *probably* true or not!

5. Mühlhölzer does not, in fact, really address the question as to whether we can conceive "Two straight lines that intersect cannot both be perpendicular to a third straight line" to be *false of the space we inhabit*. What he addresses instead is the question whether we can imagine "Two straight lines that intersect cannot both be perpendicular to a third straight line" *not to be a theorem of Euclidean geometry*. What goes missing in his entire discussion is the idea that there is such a question as *is space Euclidean?*

6. See "Rethinking Mathematical Necessity," in *Words and Life*, ed. James Conant (Cambridge, MA: Harvard University Press, 1994), 251.

7. According to Mühlhölzer, when Wittgenstein writes "'p' is true = p," "he simply declares the topic 'truth' to be a red herring." I find this interpretation decidedly odd. For my explanation of what Wittgenstein meant, see *The Threefold Cord: Mind, Body and World* (New York: Columbia University Press, 1999), 66–69.

8. Cora Diamond, "The Face of Necessity," collected in her *The Realistic Spirit* (Cambridge, MA: MIT Press, 1991).

9. In *Remarks on the Foundations of Mathematics*, Wittgenstein writes, "Suppose people go on and on calculating the expansion of p. So God, who knows everything, knows whether they will have reached '777' by the end of the world. But can his omniscience decide whether they would have reached it after the end of the world? It cannot. I want to say: even God can determine something mathematical only by mathematics. Even for him the mere rule of expansion cannot decide anything that it does not decide for us" (part V, §34). To say that omniscience cannot decide a question is, I believe, Wittgenstein's way of saying that there is no answer to be known, i.e. it is an illusion that there must be a right answer.

10. The notion of "a proof that human beings could not find" is imprecise, but it is not *so* unclear that the question of whether a statement that does not have such a proof lacks sense. On *any* view of human capabilities, the number of theorems in a given system we could prove must have a finite upper bound, whereas the number of theorems is infinite.

11. Although Mühlhölzer urges us to look at the "application" of mathematics, there is not a *single example* of an application of mathematics *in* physics in his essay. (And none in Wittgenstein's RFM either.) For my disagreements with Wittgenstein's views of what he calls "set theory" see my "Wittgenstein and the Real Numbers," in *Wittgenstein and the*

Moral Life, ed. Alice Crary (Cambridge, MA: MIT Press, 2007), 235–50. Note that my criticisms do not depend on reading Wittgenstein as Mühlhölzer does.

12. What is unfortunate about that sentence is that the view I have held at least since I wrote "What is Mathematical Truth" (published in 1975), and that I have not given up, is that *the internal success and coherence of mathematics* is evidence that it is true under *some* interpretation, and that its *indispensability for physics* is evidence that it is true under a *realist* interpretation (the antirealist interpretation I considered there was Intuitionism); pooh-poohing the question as to whether statements of mathematics are bivalent can hardly be described as understanding mathematics realistically. See my "Reply to Charles Parsons" in the present volume.

13. See "The Analytic and the Synthetic" in *Mind, Language and Reality: Philosophical Papers*, vol. 2 (Cambridge, MA: Cambridge University Press), 47.

14. As I mention in my Intellectual Autobiography, Reichenbach claimed (*Philosophy of Space and Time*, 19) that "a straight line is the path of a light ray" is the definition that "the sciences have implicitly employed all the time, though not always consciously."

15. I call Mühlhölzer Witttgenstein[M]'s "creator" because I see no adequate evidence for identifying many of Witttgenstein[M]'s views with the real Wittgenstein's.

16. Mühlhölzer appears to think that "straight line" has *different meanings* in Euclidean and non-Euclidean geometries *when those are not given a physical interpretation*. I believe that the terms have *no* meaning when they occur in *uninterpreted* formal systems, and that the philosophically relevant interpretation of those systems is the one in which "straight line" refers to *geodesics in space-time or in 2- or 3-dimensional foliations of space-time* ("space"). As Quine put it (but I do not recall where), physical geometry is "about form and void" (not, for example, light rays). —And if "straight line" has no meaning in uninterpreted geometries, a fortiori it does not have a different meaning in those different "mathematical geometries."

17. A constructive proof of this statement was given in G. Gentzen, "*Die Widerspruchfreiheit der reinen Zahlentheorie,*" *Mathematische Annalen* 112 (1936): 493–565. Translated as "The Consistency of Arithmetic," in *The Collected Works of Gerhard Gentzen*, ed. M. E. Szabo (Amsterdam: North Holland, 1969).

4

Steven J. Wagner

MODAL AND OBJECTUAL

I. INTRODUCTION

In his "Mathematics without Foundations" (1967) and "What is Mathematical Truth?" (1975), Hilary Putnam proposed to formulate mathematics through sentences expressing possibility and necessity, rather than, for example, through sentences asserting the existence of sets and numbers and relations among them.[1] Part of what was original in Putnam's proposal was advancing this idea in the context of full, classical mathematics, not in a constructivist program. The possibilities in question were in no way dependent on mental operations. Another key feature was to affirm the modal side in its own right, when most philosophers were going in the opposite direction by explicating modal notions through possible worlds—taken either as set-theoretic structures or as concrete individuals. Putnam's idea has come to be called "modalism," and has provided much of the subsequent agenda for the philosophy of mathematics.

These papers, however, adumbrated not one position but three markedly distinct ones. Two of these have received much attention; together with work by Paul Benacerraf they inspired structuralism in the philosophy of mathematics.[2] Modalism is sometimes seen as a version of this. The third, although stated just as clearly in the original papers, never seems to have been taken seriously by anyone. I think it is easily the strongest. On the occasion of a landmark volume celebrating Hilary Putnam, this idea of his own is what I will recommend to him. From our starting point in the philosophy of mathematics we will work toward the most general questions about existence, modality, and truth. In this we align ourselves with

Putnam, whose body of work demonstrates for our own time that there is no such thing as a specialized philosophical question.

I will call the first two positions *semantic* modalism. They share the idea of a systematic mapping from the sentences of set theory (thus of mathematics generally) to modal sentences, sentences asserting the possibility of abstract or concrete objects in certain relations. The modal side is regarded as a full expression of our mathematics, standing independently of any set theory. There are two versions of semantic modalism: eliminationist and translational. The former holds that the mapping lets us drop the set theory, except as a convenient fiction, thus avoiding mathematical objects. The latter holds that the set theory is nonetheless also true and adequate; its sentences are correct and mathematically equivalent to the corresponding modal ones. The third position, which I will call the *heuristic* reading (and for which "modalism" is not felicitous at all), is not ontologically revisionary and requires no comprehensive or systematic mapping. It regards the description of objects and of possibilities as two distinct mathematical viewpoints either of which might take priority in a given context of discovery, although not necessarily (and perhaps necessarily not) to the exclusion of the other.

Logically either of the semantic positions could admit the heuristic one. We could take the metaphysics of mathematics to be given by a purely modal formulation, and on the translational view by a Platonistic formulation also, while at the pragmatic level welcoming different balances of modal and objectual thinking in different contexts. For eliminationists the objectual thinking is make-believe, but that is no pragmatic objection. Yet I will contend that both semantic positions exhibit serious weaknesses—it is telling that Putnam's present view is an unstable compromise between them. Dropping both and developing the heuristic interpretation is more promising—and it turns out to have metaphysical depth of its own. I will begin by cataloguing problems for semantic modalism, then move to a constructive development of Putnam's original intuitions.

II. MODALISM: ELIMINATIVE AND TRANSLATIONAL

Eliminationism is the more straightforward semantic position. While it, like translational modalism, requires mapping from set theory to a modalized mathematics, the eliminationist takes the mapping to show only that the modal side is adequate to all mathematical purposes. Since one is not claiming any translation, one need not explain in what the equivalence of set-theoretic and modal sentences might consist, or how they "say the same thing mathematically." It is far from clear how that might be done. A semantic equivalence claim requires a semantic theory. All forms of semantics with any currency, however, whether extensional or intensional, are set-theoretic. Using such a framework to argue for modal theory and set theory as equivalent, fundamental forms of mathematical expression would appear question-begging. If instead the set theory is held to be false or anyway untrue, one needs no formal theory of its content. The eliminationist just asserts the modal mathematics.

Admittedly the modalist must explain wherein the "adequacy" of modal set theory consists. We accept set theory in part for its role in unifying various problems, clarifying key mathematical concepts (such as function and order), and allowing new theorems even in elementary domains. If set theory answers to the rest of mathematics in this way, under modalism that mathematics too receives a modal formulation. The question what *it* is adequate to arises in turn. But this is just the general problem of the point of mathematics, which the Platonist had to answer as well. The point seems to break down into (A) empirical application, and (B) the idea of mathematics as making precise and generalizing certain intuitions, concerning, for example, counting and collecting, patterns and symmetries, which are fundamental to thought. So under (A) one must show how modal mathematics works for physical and social science. Under an equivalence claim the modalism could just avail itself of the Platonist answers, but the eliminationist must show the applications directly. This is the subject of intricate arguments which lead Hartry Field and Geoffrey Hellman, for example, to opposed conclusions within not readily commensurable frameworks.[3] Since we cannot take this up, we shall follow Putnam in provisionally assuming that the modalist can apply mathematics without, on the face of it, commitment to such Platonic entities as real-numbered measurement values. (B) is a matter of finding direct modal expression for our intuitions; and far from being a problem for the modalist, this is a strength. Countless writers have remarked that mathematics arises naturally from thinking about possible operations. So while there is much more to be said under both headings, we will let the eliminationist claim a genuine advantage. While needing to spell out how to mimic Platonist applications without trading on Platonist assumptions, the eliminationist need not assert an equivalence which the present state of semantic theory forces us to leave completely vague. Let us move to another eliminationist advantage, which brings its selling points to the fore. This is the emphasis on structure as opposed to objects.

If the modal element in modalism/structuralism is Putnam's contribution, Benacerraf did the most to inspire both the emphasis on structure and the search for nonformalist alternatives to Platonism. Via the phenomenon of arbitrary construction, Benacerraf's "What Numbers Could Not Be" made it hard to see how mathematics could be about any particular objects. His "Mathematical Truth" convinced many people that Platonic objects obstruct any reasonable mathematical epistemology. So the idea of avoiding the objects through a modal formulation became attractive.

It is worth noting that Field's position, which employs modality differently, stems from the same motives. For Field, mathematics is fiction, to be replaced in principle by a relatively weak second-order theory of space-time regions. That theory is held to be nominalistic and simply true; its metatheory however requires a primitive notion of logical possibility. Here the ontology of actual space-time regions is intended to avoid epistemic access problems. The fictionalism defuses the arbitrariness, since mathematical (re)constructions are now just a special case of the freedom to redescribe our fictional characters as we please.[4] Field, then, is putting modal elements together somewhat differently for much the same reasons; having criticized Putnam he concludes, "Putnam and I are trying to get to essentially the same place, even if we disagree about the best route for getting there."[5] The attempt to avoid the Benacerraf problems has been at the heart of recent philosophy of mathematics.

This viewpoint distinctly favors the eliminationist. If either arbitrary construction or epistemic access is a problem for objectual mathematics, and if that side is taken also to be true, it is hard to see how objectual-modal equivalence could cancel it. Assuming the objectual side is true, we still have to know the Platonic objects, even if we know modal sentences too. If the latter are somehow epistemically prior, still we have to know them to be equivalent to sentences asserting the existence of abstract, mind-independent things. Similarly for arbitrariness. If the problem is that we find ourselves with sufficient grounds to take both of "$2 = \{\{\emptyset\}\}$" and "$2 = \{\emptyset, \{\emptyset\}\}$" to be true, translating them into a consistent pair of modal sentences leaves that untouched. Perhaps one could argue that a problem-free modal side, plus equivalence, clears up the interpretation and epistemology of set theory, but it looks more sensible just to eliminate the side where the problems are. To the extent that familiarity and naturalness might nonetheless continue to recommend the set theory, a fictional treatment plus a mapping into the preferred modal language can do justice to that. So it is unsurprising that elimination is preferred by both Hellman and Field (in his variant but overlapping framework). It is also, with qualifications to be noted, Putnam's preference. Let us consider its merits more closely.

In addressing Putnam we may take an argumentative shortcut. In "What is Mathematical Truth?" he did consider an epistemic advantage for modalism, but did not pursue the suggestion and has conspicuously avoided it since. And I agree. Despite the intuitive power of Benacerraf's 1973 challenge, finding a perspicuous and analytically compelling formulation is quite another matter. Perhaps there is a special problem about abstract objects, but Benacerraf's route would appear to turn on very delicate, tendentious formulations regarding causation and its role in justification. Nothing like this has been worked out at all. I also see no comparative advantage on the modal side. Neither Hellman's nor Field's position includes any serious epistemology, and can therefore support no claim to have made epistemic progress. And if what was supposed to generate the Platonist's problem was causal theories of knowledge—will anyone claim that mathematical modality comes off well by that standard? It appears rather that, regarding how mathematics is known, only a double standard will favor modalism. So I will join Putnam in setting epistemic arguments for modalism aside.

Putnam does, however, maintain that modalism helps with arbitrariness. This is critical, since Benacerraf's 1965 problem is a real threat to standard conceptions of mathematical objects. And here the eliminationist's first step is easy. If no objects exist, there is no arbitrary construction of them. If mathematics can, at least in principle, all take place on the purely modal side, we need not even pass through the seemingly incompatible construction statements, so the issue does not even come up. The broader question, though, is whether our representation of mathematics avoids all arbitrary choices and does so without significant philosophical cost. There matters are not so clear.

To see this, consider that modalism must assert the existence of some *type* of possibility, for which there are two options, which we may call modal-nominalist, as in Putnam's 1967 article, and modal-structuralist, as in Hellman. Putnam defined mathematical truth with reference to possible concrete objects: pencil dots connected by arrows, in layers extended into the transfinite. In contrast Hellman's arithmetic is, in effect, a modalized Ramsification of the conjunction $\&PA^2$ of the second-order axioms. We relativize $\&PA^2$ to a domain X (the "numbers"), replace "successor" by "f," and assert:

Hellman's (*) $\Diamond \, \exists X \, \exists f \, (\&PA^2)^X$

The theorems of arithmetic are then what hold "wherever" this possibility obtains. An analogous construction, with second-order Replacement and Selection, extends the idea to set theory. We use second-order logic (SOL) to interpret mathematics in terms of pure relational structures ("pure" in the sense of being free from any informally meaningful mathematical terms, say, *successor, collecting,* or *graph*). So one option, Putnams's, involves the possibility of a specific object, concrete albeit not found in experience, while Hellman applies a modal operator to a completely general form.

It is hard to see why the modal-nominalist has not just traded one kind of arbitrary choice for another. If what is possible are directed pencil graphs—how large are the dots, how soft the graphite, how dark the arrows? One may object that we need not specify such details in order to give truth conditions for mathematics; that we accept statements of possibility as clear and sufficient without asking for irrelevant detail. If I say you ought to button your shirt because *it is possible someone will come to the door*, you may find that fully specific and adequate, rather than asking, say, what color their eyes would be. It is not at all clear whether this reply would do in Putnam's mathematical context, but if so—why mention pencil graphs at all? The structure could as easily—as possibly—be meringues connected by spider's silk, with directionality indicated by a thickening of the strand. Or why a graph at all? Perhaps mathematics is to be understood in terms of mermaids, singing to each other selectively, as required by the structure of the membership relation, ever northward across transfinite seas? That would serve just as well. The modal-nominalist faces a dilemma. If the concrete possibilities are at all specified, one way is as good as countless others. If one claims that any of several ways will do, that each is as good as the next for interpreting the mathematics in question, there is no improvement over the Platonist's Benacerraf problem. Should one deny the need to specify, holding rather that the mathematics is true due to *any* possibility of a certain kind, or to *all* such possibilities, then one must surely use something like Hellman's formulas to express this. Now the position does not differ interestingly from modal-structuralism. True, one has specified something Hellman himself leaves open, namely that the possibilities are "concrete." But that looks like an empty gesture. So if either modalist option is to help with arbitrariness, it will have to be the structuralist form.

Here the modal-structuralist looks to be in excellent shape. Hellman's axioms involve no choice of actual or possible objects, and he avoids a problem that plagues other structuralist approaches. Much literature bears out the suspicion that "structures" end up looking like just one more species of mathematical objects (indeed the term is set/class/ordinal-theoretic on its face); or that "positions" and such invite the same permutation-type challenges that numbers did. Commendably, Hellman does not fall into these difficulties. Because his notion of possibility is primitive, the question over which domain to interpret it (thus perhaps some class-like field of possibilia) does not arise. There certainly are open questions. For example, which rules govern the modality. But these are just normal tasks for theory. Not even a loose analog for the Benacerraf problem appears. However, in the larger perspective that does not make a full case for the position. We will encounter new difficulties below; meanwhile the Platonist has her own resources. Still, avoiding any form arbitrariness is a substantial plus. Before moving on, however, I do wish to note a price that comes with the success.

The price is that the purely formal character of such an axiom as Hellman's * leaves it unclear why anyone should accept it. This is not the broad challenge to any nontrivial knowledge of modal sentences. That would be Hume's (and Quine's) skepticism about modality, the counterpart to Benacerraf's (and, perhaps Aristotle's) doubts concerning the knowability of purely abstract things. One might have to face this at some point, but the present question is more specific. We are asked to accept that some objects might stand in some relation, while not being able to name, or allowed to suggest, any relation, or objects, that could satisfy this. We could not say, "this is possible because, for example, the successor relation behaves like this," because on the doctrine of *Mathematics without Numbers* there is no successor relation. We are in the odd position of affirming completely unspecified possibilities. Now if this is offered as an objection the modalist might find it question-begging. If someone believes in the successor relation, and can therefore offer it as exemplifying the possibility *, then they already believe the objectual mathematics that * was supposed to replace. The modalist's very point was to show how we could accept mathematical, mathematically adequate, sentences independently of belief in *successor*, *subset*, and the rest of the usual furniture. But our question does not concern the dialectic with the objectualist. Rather, we are asking: how well does the modal-structuralist position stand on its own? Let us sketch a problem in very rough terms.

Normally, instances are in some way our guides to possibility. It is possible for clever solvers to finish this crossword in an hour, because Marie did. Pandora should be able to climb this tree, because Circe climbed that one (and pairwise they are similar enough). Dana can run ten miles, because he did run nine and there was no reason for him to stop there. Such remarks are no more than informal data, barely scratching the surface of an extremely complex, variegated epistemological situation. Nonetheless, they exemplify actual modal reasoning. If we reject direct a priori modal insight (as Putnam did long ago) then any account of knowing possibilities would seem to involve forms of drawing on instances via generalization, extrapolation, transposition, and the like. What else? And this observation, analytically unsatisfactory as it is, poses a question for modal knowledge within a position whose exact point is to purge instances. We have learned that insisting that possibilities are possibilities about some specific type of instances invites arbitrariness problems. By starting with complete generality the modal-structuralist avoids arbitrariness. But one wonders whether this generality will turn out to be just the other side of Benacerraf's skeptical coin.[6]

So far we have assumed that the modal mathematics can be warranted without recourse to sets. This is crucial to any semantic modalism: while the translational interpretation may have no objection to sets, the point is to get an equivalent, set-free view by adding modality. Now one sort of question is whether the relevant possibilities do not already trade on our objectual doctrines. For example, Parsons notes the iterated transfinite size of Putnam's possible graphs and asks where all those ranks come from,[7] Mc-Carthy asks why we should accept size limitation for the concrete models.[8] Analogous questions arise for the relatively strong logical possibilities in Field's conservativeness arguments. These are real worries. Here though I shall consider another issue, due to the infinity of any mathematical theory. To present such a body of doctrine, finite beings must employ logic. To genuinely excise Platonism from our mathematics, we need to make sure we are not hiding it in our logic. Here the modalist's difficulties appear to have been widely underestimated.

Both Hellman and Field couch their alternative mathematics in a nonelementary logic. Apparently the attempt to avoid Platonist set theory requires this. We have some latitude in choice of logic: SOL can trade off against plural quantification; Field arranges to get by with a monadic second-order quantifier. But the options share the lack of a complete and sound proof procedure. Lindstrom's theorem shows that a finitary notion of proof is a highly distinguishing feature of first-order logic (FOL). Also familiar is the inability of first-order axiomatizations to definitely (categorically) characterize significant mathematical structures, beginning with the natural numbers. Hence an extensive literature explores higher-order expressions of mathematical concepts.[9] Mathematically this is uncontroversial, as the felicity of the Dedekind formulation of arithmetic already shows. But that does not answer whether nonelementary logic can serve a purely modal mathematics. Maybe the felicitous expressions work just by trading on our understood set-theoretic background. That was Quine's charge of "set theory in sheep's clothing," and I believe his instinct was correct.[10] Although we must be rather brief, I have previously developed much of the story.[11]

The first critical point is to recall what asserting a theory T involves. This is conventionally done through asserting some set of axioms Ax, but that is straightforward only when T is first-order. For of course we mean to be asserting not just Ax but Ax *and every sentence which follows from this by logic*; Ax plus its consequences. In the first-order case this elaboration adds no commitments of interest. Ax is a finite list of sentences (or schemata). A consequence is anything obtained from some finite subset of these through finitely many steps, each of which is decidable and, given the meanings of the connectives, self-evident. Making this explicit shows that in asserting T we are committed to *finite sequence*, thus to elementary arithmetic, and to a notion of logical form. But—as Poincaré reminded the logicists—these notions are irreducibly essential to thought, and as clear as anything mathematical gets. So for first-order T the elaboration can go without saying. In other cases though we need to ask what more the notion of consequence might bring in.

Suppose then that my proposed substitute for ordinary set theory is a set of axioms *A2* in second-order logic. Take *A2* to be something like the modalized ZF^2 of Hellman, where all quantification is governed by the modal operators; our discussion will carry over to such variants as Field's theory or options using plural quantification. What I assert as my mathematics is: *A2*, and all its ("standard") consequences. How well, then, do we understand this? Boolos famously insisted that there is nothing particularly unclear about second-order implication: it is a mathematically natural extension of first-order implication, with a lot of overlap in the model theory.[12] Nonetheless second-order implication is mathematics. I explain it by reference to all models of a certain kind, whereas for first-order *Ax* all I need is elementary syntax and an understanding of the connectives.

One could object that SOL, for example, deserves the title *logic* for its role in the natural presentation of mathematical concepts. The first-order advocate assumes that we can work in FOL while owing no further gloss on what we mean by implication; but if SOL instead merits the title of logic, then second-order implication deserves the same treatment. As it stands this is hardly an argument, since the first-order side can say that FOL is logic in part for being a fundamental medium for reasoning, in which *ø follows from the set* $\sum$ is paradigmatically clear. If SOL has a different claim, then one cannot assume that its notion similarly requires no explication. It matters not just what we call logic—there may be diverse credible honorees—but on what grounds the title is awarded. This somewhat question-begging objection does, however, focus attention on the relative clarity of first- versus second-order implication. Grant that the former is exemplary. If Boolos is right, then the latter is roughly as well understood, so that *A2* can be considered a clear, adequate expression of our mathematical beliefs.

It is not fruitful to ask whether second-order implication somehow seems clear enough to the mind. While conceptual clarity is very hard to define (and a graveyard of philosophical theories), no one doubts that our ability to tell, in relevant circumstances, whether something *a* falls under the concept *C* has something to do with it. In this respect first-order implication is the best we can ask for. We have, up to computational limits, a decisive positive test for consequences of our first-order *Ax*, plus systematic ways to build counterexamples in some cases. In the case of *A2* our recourse is only to do model theory for the axioms—work which takes place inside set theory. By the same token, that set theory is in practice first order. If we wish we can "define the set universe" in second-order language, but when we start reasoning about what holds in all models of *A2*, we carry out first-order arguments.

There is no need to disparage second-order formulations. It is better to say that something like *A2* constitutes an elliptical presentation. It omits the mathematics that one will need in order to reason from it. One can quibble over whether SOL—or Boolos's plural logic—is "really set theory," or over what "commitments" may show up, or be implicit, in one formalization or another, but Quine was addressing a substantive issue. A theorist who asserts *A2* can be asked to clarify her understanding of consequence, since it compares unfavorably with first-order implication. Her reply will show that she is using sets as well. Should she decline to clarify—aiming to evade further ontology—the sets will nonetheless appear when she uses *A2* in actually doing mathematics. Quine was asking what you commit yourself to believing in through asserting the theory *T*. By this standard *A2* commits one to sets. In effect, ontology is hidden in the consequence relation. On this ground Quine recommends elementary logic, which precludes that, as a clear medium for ontological communication. At the end of this essay we will with Putnam's help amend this view, but not revise it.[13]

To summarize, starting with eliminative modalism: We have, with Putnam, set aside the notion of any global epistemological advantage; seen that it is beset by its own arbitrariness problems in one version, while avoiding them at obscure cost in the other; and found that its nonelementary logics leave the claim to have dispensed with sets unsupported and unexplained at best. Translational modalism buys all the same problems and perhaps additional ones specific to Platonism as well. So far we have not examined Putnam's own interpretation of semantic modalism. We will do so and then move to a positive reconstruction of the modal idea from Putnam's own materials.

III. PUTNAM'S SEMANTIC MODALISM

Putnam holds both that there are no such objects as sets and that the theorems of objectual set theory are true. By the first conjunct, this can be taken as an eliminationist position. The modal theorems are affirmed without qualification, while sets disappear. By the second, it can be read as a mutant translational position: for any modal theorem a corresponding objectual theorem is affirmed, and held in some sense to say the same thing mathematically; yet the objectual content is cancelled. The two parts have distinct sorts of motives. Putnam calls the theorems true in order to respect the ordinary existential assertions of mathematical practice. Here the reason is clear. While denying truth is an option in the philosophy of mathematics, it requires explanation. Because the apparent truth of the usual theorems is very hard to deny, a revisionist philosopher must show how it can be only *apparent*. Just assigning the usual truth values avoids a serious complication. But to do so, and then to deny objects of reference anyway, is rather more curious.

Putnam's motive is a view of Platonic objects that, indeed, goes beyond philosophical critique to outright repugnance and offense.[14] But that must surely be reconsidered, for Putnam's modalism sits between two chairs. His combination of views would be permissible under formalism or some other nonstandard account of mathematical truth, but Putnam has always flatly rejected that. If the theorems are read at face value, and we do not just have an unexplained philosophical distinction, then the only visible options are (1) a throwback metaphysical distinction between, say, real and existent objects; (2) fictionalism. Despite its charm (1) is out of the question. (2) in contrast offers a completely natural reading: the familiar truth of the theorems becomes fictional truth, and stepping out of the fictional context we deny the ontology (as Field and I have). But this too is just not Putnam's view. So we need to sort out the issues about Platonic objects more carefully.

Ethics without Ontology makes clear Putnam's concern with objectivity for both mathematics and ethics, and rejects objects of reference for both on the grounds of constituting pseudosolutions to objectivity problems. His motto is "objectivity without objects."[15] There is something odd about this. Objectivity worries in a given domain concern whether our discourse admits genuine argument and is responsive to something other than our own (individual or collective) opinions and states. If it seems so, we may posit a subject matter as part of a world outside of ourselves, and suppose that our discourse so far has achieved at least some fraction of truth. Anyone can see that this characterization is shot through with circularity and question-begging; even so we recognize in it the actual worries that have beset various domains and styles of thinking, including philosophy. For mathematics, where the argumentation tends to be impressive, the concern has nearly always been what sort of "world outside ourselves" could be in play and how it relates to the one we move in. Ethics brings both this concern and grave doubts about the force of reason. Now, claiming that we have objects cannot be the response to objectivity doubts. Anyone questioning the value of our arguments in a given domain wants to be shown that those arguments are better than they seem or can be improved. No one asking whether anything "outside of our opinions" is at stake—whatever that exactly means—will be impressed by a *claim* that we successfully refer. In ways appropriate to the topic at hand, we need to examine the discourse with regard to how beliefs seem to arise, how disagreement is handled— regarding how, perhaps, opinion and evidence, perception and logic seem to enter into it. All this is clear (and perhaps the most one can say at this level of generality). Yet it is another matter to suggest that objects would *impede* an account of objectivity.[16] Moreover, one wonders about Putnam's polemical target. Given how philosophy goes, there are sources, no doubt, but it is not easy to find a philosopher of any credibility meeting objectivity worries with such a jejune mix of *ignoratio* and question-begging. (That would just be a travesty of Plato, whom Putnam does mention.) Possibly there is objectivity in mathematics, or ethics, while objects somehow do not enter into the story—that can be investigated. But leaving this hypothesis open does not explain the preemptive attack on objects; nor does it explain how to conjoin that with taking sentences to be true at face value.

There is a view of truth theory which, while not Putnam's own, has important points of contact with views he does hold and would undo the quandary. Start with the idea of truth as a genuine property of sentences in use—not one to be "deflated" or otherwise denied. Take Tarskian semantics as contributing to the explanation of truth values. Part of why a given token of "snow is white" is true is that snow is white, but Tarski provides the semantic component of the explanation. While the Tarskian format is set-theoretic, using intensions or properties as the semantic values will not change the point. In any format this manner of explanation requires abstract denotata for open sentences. To call the enterprise Tarskian is a kind of shorthand, however, since it originated with Frege, and was seen by Tarski neither as applying to natural languages nor as providing explanations. The term is nonetheless apt as well as familiar; yet the matter of explanation is crucial. We shall understand "explanation" not as some loose sort of label but as having theoretical force. That means, first, giving truth values standing as phenomena, as questions that have a claim on our intellect. The systematic patterns in the truth values of sentences are puzzles that demand resolution. Second, we take explanatory success as grounds for unqualified belief. If the truth of a token of "He apologized for the inconvenience" seems at least somewhat, passably, explained along Tarskian lines, and no roughly equal alternative suggests itself, then we infer this explanation. Third, the inference here has the same ontological force as an inference in natural science. If it introduces new objects, sets for example, then we believe in these as we would in a new sort of star system or chemical bond. Each of these three points involves a rejection of Quinian empiricism and physicalism. They are Aristotelian and specifically pragmatist: we construe the task of sense-making broadly and follow where it leads. So they exemplify Putnam's project of renewing philosophy; and if accepted justify Platonism on pragmatic and rational grounds.[17]

On this view, where there are truths there are abstract denotata. Do these offer a spurious objectivity? The objects as such must be blameless, since they arise wherever we speak truly, regardless of topic. Putnam's question would be whether giving the Platonistic semantics means offering the appearance of objectivity without the substance. Not on my account, since the semantics comes in at a different level, posterior to objectivity concerns.[18] To be explaining the truth values of sentences in a certain (sub)language L, I must believe they have them, thus that in a fundamental sense objectivity already obtains. Legitimate objectivity disputes are addressed by looking at questions of usage and evidence as they pertain to L. We do topic-specific epistemology. There is no danger of an illegitimate conferral of objectivity. Putnam's objection could arise from overlooking an ambiguity in "explaining why sentences are true or false": in one sense the semantics does this, in another not at all. He certainly did not make this mistake, yet emphasizing the distinction may remove the worry.

So Putnam's hybrid of eliminative and translational modalism is unjustified. I have also suggested that the drive to avoid abstract mathematical objects may be frustrated in two ways: they are implicit in the modalist's nonelementary logics; and they come in by another route anyway, when we do semantics. Looking back over our critique, much needs to be elaborated and connected. But, to borrow a figure of Putnam's, the critique is sufficient to show that the stool on which semantic modalism has rested is poorly engineered, with brittle legs.

IV. HEURISTIC PERSPECTIVES: THOUGHT AND THE WORLD

All the trouble, I think, has come from seeing modal and objectual formalizations as strict alternatives, and yoking the former to an anti-Platonist agenda. When Putnam in his papers of 1967 and 1975 characterized the two as heuristic perspectives in mathematics, he expressed a very different view. He rightly described modal-versus-objectual as an ancient dualism in mathematics, but it is not a dichotomy. We can work from either side or combine them; each partakes of the other anyway. This is not to say you can move from either side to the other in response to quandaries over abstract objects or modalities. Philosophical difficulties in principle will still be there when you move back; this is the flaw in Putnam's view.[19] But this opportunism is exactly apt for trying to get new ideas.

Pluralism about heuristics goes without saying, of course. There is also no purity law; I may emphasize mathematics as objectual, yet in certain ways consider possibilities which apply to the objects; or turn this around. Once the heuristic interpretation of a modal viewpoint is separated from an ontological agenda, Putnam can readily accept this amendment.

Although the heuristic view has no semantic or reductive commitments, it is not metaphysically neutral. Objects and possibilities both provide on their face legitimate ways of expressing the content, or representing the subject matter, of mathematics. The option of arguing that inquiry in some finished form can omit one of the elements remains open, but to the extent that the use of both seems natural and illuminating, the burden is on the philosophical critic. Quine and Putnam have both accepted this burden, taking opposite sides. Let us reconsider their dispute.

An oddity shows up in Putnam's judgment of an exchange between Quine and Parsons. Where Quine writes that modal formulations can hide ontology, Putnam responds sharply: this "shows just how deep the Platonist bug had bitten Quine."[20] But in Putnam's translational modalism, *hiding ontology* is just what the modal versions do. The same bug would have bitten Putnam just as hard; so what is Quine's mistake supposed to be?

The two disagree, but it is over the legitimacy of modal operators at the basic level. Where they agree—on one interpretation of Putnam—is in treating the modal and objectual perspectives as opposed to and excluding each other. This is Hume's legacy. Were we speaking not in the mathematical but in the material (and moral) domain, Putnam would surely favor a different option, one we know from Aristotle and Kant: that objectual and modal thought inform each other and are inextricable.[21] We do not understand what a tree is apart from the possibilities (or necessities) into which trees enter. Nor do we understand possibilities, say that of space travel, apart from a grasp of the objects they mention. Ordinary language supports no division of terms into modal and nonmodal, except on superficial grounds (such as the presence of the suffix "_ble") or relative to some passing purpose. Apart from any such purpose, which of, say, *skull, next to, river, stock market, dilemma, betray, subduction, dragon, epidemic, gambit, fatigue, push, scarlet,* and *feast of St. Stephen* are modal?

I am sure Putnam would agree, yet when he turns to mathematics he writes, "Sets, to parody John Stuart Mill, are permanent possibilities of selection."[22] The delightful parody declares a mistaken allegiance. This is the language of phenomenalism, a position which got things half right. Holding a perceptual belief does mean being disposed to accept all sorts of beliefs about possible sense experiences. The error was in trying to deploy this idea to reduce away talk of material objects. On the contrary, material objects always show up in the possibilities.[23] Similarly, in accord with one of the authors of "Mathematics without Foundations," I propose the following: understanding the role of modality in talking about mathematics requires getting away from the idea that it could replace talk of material objects.

While Aristotle showed the interplay of modal and objectual thinking in the sublunary realm very well, the extension to mathematics is not straightforward. Putnam has aired the idea that within (pure) mathematics too there are possible yet not true sentences, thus mathematical contingencies. This would facilitate the analogy with the material realm, but I doubt that it can work. Assume rather the standard view of mathematical truth as being necessary. Then the task is to see how objectual and modal ways of representing mathematics both grow out of how we think of ordinary objects as entering into necessities and possibilities. In light of how mathematics aids us in describing structures found in science, and in formulating laws for them, there should be ample ground for both viewpoints. We want to see how solving scientific problems naturally leads us sometimes to formulate an explicitly modal thesis somewhat abstracted from physical constraints, sometimes what we regard as a necessary statement about abstract things.

Here, though, the task becomes less purely analytical, and more a matter of philosophical interpretation of the historical record. If the viewpoints really are heuristic, and not theorems of metaphysics, then we need to be investigating their role in actual discovery. Note how welcome this should be to Putnam. Blurring the justification/discovery line is one of the great insights of pragmatism: thus the investigation will concern not "just heuristics" but what mathematical reason is, at least for such creatures as ourselves. The record from Greek geometry on will offer any number of cases for study, surely linked less by clear principles than by family resemblance. One could begin with two recent developments that Putnam knows intimately, the creations of computation theory and set theory. Turing's work had its impact partly for constituting a compelling analysis of *function which can be computed purely mechanically.* As for hierarchies of sets, the literature shows how we continue to lean on modal language in our struggle to understand them. Parsons has emphasized that the constraining intuitions here seem to be connected not just to mathematical combination and iteration, but more directly to predication, to what we will consider as the extension of a possible predicate. The notion of *Aussonderung* may go beyond what we think can be "selected" through an act of the mind, but that is where it starts. There is presumably rich study material for the heuristic interpretation here. Since all this is work for other occasions, I shall end on a very general note.

To call a way of thinking heuristic is not to take its philosophical commitments less seriously. In some cases the heuristic may just be a passing aid to inspiration, but that is true for beliefs and theories in general. Some ways of trying to know may be written deeply into our conception of inquiry, in which case we accept whatever comes with them. The record in no way suggests that conceiving mathematics modally is somehow dispensable, in the long run or at least in principle. Even if there should be reason to prefer purely objectual language when giving bodies of mathematics their mature formulation, the modal viewpoint would, as far as we can now tell, remain part of our quest for mathematical understanding at any point short of omniscience. I myself have defended a somewhat Quinian distinction between grade B and serious doctrines. We see acceptance of the former as a function partly of our contingent limitations; the latter appear as candidates for membership in the idealized comprehensive theories ("systems of the world") Quine envisions in *Word & Object.*[24] But even by this standard there is no reason to suspect that modal views of mathematics fall short.

Consider then such idealized theories. For Quine they quantify over sets, so the ontology is Platonistic. As for modality, "avoidance of modality is as strong a reason for an abstract ontology as I can well imagine;"[25]

quotidian uses of "necessary" and "possible" are theoretically dispensable. Putnam in his anti-Platonist program has insisted on the great difference between asserting possibilities and asserting objects. This is in full accord with Quine—indeed Putnam's is exactly the sentiment just quoted with the terms exchanged. I believe each side is half right. While reserving judgment over sets I have defended the Platonism, thus also upholding Quine's posing of the ontological question. But from Putnam we should take a broader conception: not of ontology, a term which retains Quine's meaning, but of the content of a scheme. Holding a total view means affirming possibilities as well as actual objects and relations. If this carries over to Quinian idealized systems, then modality is ineradicable even out towards the limits of inquiry. To put this in terms of systems of the world, *the world* is necessities and possibilities as well as things—even just in its mathematical aspect. We side decisively with Putnam against Quine and Hume.

It is for the most part meaning which occupies Carnap in *Meaning and Necessity*. He leaves the question what modal system we shall accept for the end, at which point he can simply explicate necessity as the already established notion of L-truth.[26] This is a definite interpretation relative to semantics; the rules fall out as S5. The stance is reductive regarding modality; Quine took the step to elimination by abandoning meaning as Carnap required it. Putnam in turn has followed Quine's critique of the Carnap semantics, yet reversed both judgments on modality: *possible* is required, while allowing no more explication, no more fixing through analysis, than do *object* and *true*. Regarding these notions I disagree with Putnam on the admittedly elusive matter of whether they are unitary—as Quine maintained—or plural, and partly amenable to convention, as in Putnam's doctrine of conceptual relativity.[27] But we agree that they are irreducible, and modality joins them as an element of thought at the most general level. So I would answer Frege's question regarding the natural medium of rational thought by saying, after Quine, that the logic must be first-order, with a finitary, conceptually transparent concept of proof, and, after Putnam, that it is modal as well.

In various specific domains different sets of rules are likely to govern our modal inferences. To suggest any definite formalism, or way of systemizing the fundamental, framing, modality, would be premature. After all we have only now even conjectured it. *Contra* Carnap, however, it might be rather weak, just enough modal logic to reflect the fact that the possibilities are alethic and may apply to anything which exists.[28]

STEVEN J. WAGNER

UNIVERSITY OF ILLINOIS, URBANA-CHAMPAIGN
SEPTEMBER 2011

NOTES

1. "Mathematics without Foundations" and "What is Mathematical Truth?" both reprinted in *Mathematics, Matter, and Method: Philosophical Papers,* vol. 1 (Cambridge: Cambridge University Press, 1975).

2. Paul Benacerraf, "What Numbers Could Not Be," *Philosophical Review* 74, no. 1 (1965): 47–73, and "Mathematical Truth," *Journal of Philosophy* 70, no. 19 (1973): 661–79.

3. Hartry Field, *Realism, Mathematics, and Modality* (Oxford: Blackwell, 1989); Geoffrey Hellman, *Mathematics without Numbers: Towards a Modal-Structural Interpretation* (Oxford: Oxford University Press, 1989). On the technical situation see Timothy McCarthy's "Book Reviews: Geoffrey Hellman. *Mathematics without Numbers,*" *Notre Dame Journal of Formal Logic* 38, no. 1 (1997): 136–61.

4. As was also my view in "Arithmetical Fiction," *Pacific Philosophical Quarterly* 63 (1982): 255–69.

5. Field, *Realism, Mathematics, and Modality*, 281.

6. One possible move is to generate a certain supply of instances "in intuition," then offer the stronger modal axioms as extrapolating (in some sense) from these. That would address the problem. However, it is definitely not Hellman's or Putnam's view. Parsons explores this idea in *Mathematical Thought and Its Objects* (Cambridge: Cambridge University Press, 2008). He arrives at a structuralism quite his own; I am however unsure how well it escapes the difficulties sketched here. Insofar as it involves arguing away the informal content of set theory as being mathematically irrelevant (124 ff.), it faces the formalist's problem of what motivates the mathematics at all. Field's situation (*Realism, Mathematics, and Modality*, 88–94) is analogous, because he needs to be able to assert ◊NBG, in the absence, of course, of support from instances of any kind. No straightforward comparison of Field and Parsons is possible though, because (i) Field's notion of possibility is intended to be "purely logical"; (ii) the alternative position on modal knowledge which he opposes is quite different from either Parsons's or what I adumbrate here (and I agree that it is untenable). We can however pose one clear difficulty. For Field, our core ground for believing NBG formally consistent, hence "possible," is that we have not been able to derive any contradiction from it. I doubt this. I suggest that failure to derive contradictions can be good reason to believe in the consistency of a theory we *understand*. But the purely modal view of mathematics needs to explain and justify itself without resorting to Platonic entities. This seems to leave Field a choice. (A) View NBG formalistically (as is indeed the thrust of his whole position). In my view then the confidence in its consistency drops away. (B) Make genuine understanding of NBG essential to rational acceptance of the rewritten mathematics, even though the theory discards NBG as fiction. As it were, a ladder one cannot kick away. This cannot be ruled out but would appear to require serious discussion. Anyway neither option aids Hellman or Putnam, who do need the modal mathematics to be understood independently of the set theory.

7. Parsons, *Mathematical Thought and Its Objects*, 99ff.

8. McCarthy, "Review of Geoffrey Hellman's *Mathematics without Numbers*."

9. For example, Jon Barwise, "Model-Theoretic Logics: Background and Aims," in *Model-Theoretic Logics*, ed. J. Barwise, et al. (New York: Springer, 1985); Stuart Shapiro, *Foundations without Foundationalism: A Case for Second-Order Logic* (Oxford: Oxford University Press, 1991).

10. W. V. Quine, *Philosophy of Logic*, 2nd ed. (Cambridge, MA: Harvard University Press, 1986).

11. "The Rationalist Conception of Logic," *Notre Dame Journal of Formal Logic* 28 (1987): 3–35. Congenial in a far more mathematical setting are Jouko Väänänen, "Second-

Order Logic and Foundations of Mathematics," *Bulletin of Symbolic Logic* 7, no. 4 (2001): 504–20, and Peter Koellner, "Strong Logics of First and Second Order," *Bulletin of Symbolic Logic* 16, no. 1 (2010): 1–36. I thank Charles Parsons for bringing these to my attention via his "Quine's Nominalism," *American Philosophical Quarterly* 48, no. 3 (2011). Indeed, it will be clear that the present essay is in no small measure a tribute to Parsons as well as to Putnam.

12. George S. Boolos, "On Second-Order Logic," *Journal of Philosophy* 72, no. 16 (1975): 509–27.

13. As I explained in 1987 (see "The Rationalist Conception of Logic"), the first-order presentation of set theory does mean taking "set" to be understood in a standard way that axiomatization does not capture. However, this does not make the first-order formalization inferior, nor, *pace* Shapiro and others, does it acquiesce in relativism about "set." It may well mean that our "standard" grasp of the notion has a provisional or experimental character—an outcome congenial to the larger argument of this paper.

14. Deconstructionists will savor the figurative language of his envoi at *Ethics without Ontology* (Cambridge, MA: Harvard University Press, 2004), 84–85.

15. Ibid., 51ff.

16. Field noticed this oddity (see his *Realism, Mathematics, and Modality*, 272). Related and illuminating is Charles Parsons, "Putnam on Existence and Ontology," in *Reading Putnam*, ed. Maria Baghramian (New York: Routledge, 2012).

17. This is my argument from "Prospects for Platonism" in *Benacerraf and His Critics*, ed. Adam Morton and Stephen Stich (Cambridge: Blackwell, 1996), indebted to Field's "Tarski's Theory of Truth," *Journal of Philosophy* 69, no. 13 (1972): 347–75, and Benacerraf's "Mathematical Truth." Compare Charles Parsons's long-standing studies of the dialectic of semantic ascent and descent in our attempt to express logical principles (see his *Mathematical Thought and Its Objects* and "Quine's Nominalism"): If one interprets this as a task of explanation, as I would conjecture, our viewpoints converge. "Prospects for Platonism" also argues that starting from semantics may offer a principled way of avoiding Benacerraf-style arbitrariness.

18. Thus my "Consistent, Integrated Systems of the World: Pragmatism, Relativity, and Ideals of Reason" to be published by Oxford University Press in the volume of a 2011 conference celebrating Hilary Putnam's 85th birthday.

19. Putnam, "Mathematics without Foundations," 49.

20. Putnam, *Ethics without Ontology*, 82. For Quine's view see "Reply to Charles D. Parsons" in *The Philosophy of W. V. Quine*, ed. Lewis E. Hahn and Paul A. Schilpp (La Salle, IL: Open Court, 1986), 397.

21. In view of Aristotle and Kant elaboration is hardly necessary, nor could one easily improve on them. Yet Hume's spell led Stuart Hampshire to restate the idea, effectively, in *Innocence and Experience* (Cambridge, MA: Harvard University Press, 1989), ch. 3, "Hume's Ghost." An analogous effort on behalf of "metaphysical modality" misfires in Williamson, *The Philosophy of Philosophy* (Oxford: Wiley-Blackwell, 2008), ch. 5, but in many points harmonizes with Hampshire.

22. Putnam, "What is Mathematical Truth?" 71.

23. Roderick Chisholm, "The Problem of Empiricism," *Journal of Philosophy* 45, no. 19 (1948): 512–17.

24. On this see my "Truth, Physicalism, and Ultimate Theory" in *Objections to Physicalism*, ed. Howard Robinson (Oxford: Blackwell, 1993) and "Searching for Pragmatism in the Philosophy of Mathematics," *Philosophia Mathematica* 9, no. 3 (2001): 355–76.

25. Quine, "Reply to Charles D. Parsons," 397.

26. Rudolf Carnap, *Meaning and Necessity: A Study in Semantics and Modal Logic*, 2nd ed. (Chicago: University of Chicago Press, 1956), 173ff.

27. This question is the focus of my "Consistent, Integrated Systems of the World."

28. It is not enough to thank Richard Warner for his exemplary editorial and philosophical judgment. Without his unfailing support in all ways I would quite literally have been unable to complete this essay in time for inclusion in the present volume.

REPLY TO STEVEN J. WAGNER

S teve Wagner is a very good friend and a philosopher I admire as well; in fact, he was the one person with whom I discussed all the preliminary drafts of my Prometheus Lecture to the American Philosophical Association.[1] Although we are obviously not in agreement on the philosophy of mathematics, I take his objections/queries/suggestions concerning my modal-logical interpretation very seriously (as the length of this reply will testify), and I am happy to have the opportunity to respond to them.

I. "WHY MENTION PENCIL GRAPHS AT ALL?"

When I was a child I learned to count *un, deux, trois, quatre,. . .*[2] I learned that *deux et deux font quatre,* that *deux fois trois font six*, and many similar facts. When my parents moved back to the United States, I learned, of course, that *two and two are four*, that *two times three is six*, and many similar facts. Moreover, I knew that *deux et deux font quatre* and *two and two are four* are two ways of saying the same thing. I did not learn that two is not identical with Julius Caesar[3]; that question simply did not arise. Nor did I trouble my head with the question, whether "deux" and "two" are or are not the same "object"; it never occurred to me to ask if numbers are objects at all. As even Frege realized, for the purposes of *doing and using arithmetic*, answers to such questions are not needed.[4]

I am not sure when I learned that "one can always add one more to any number"—certainly before I was 10 years old. But what sort of a "can" is this "can"? I believe that it is the "can" of *mathematical possibility*. It is not just the "can" of logical possibility, understood (as it often is) as mere freedom from contradiction; and it certainly had nothing to do with physical possibility. (I think I would have already understood the question: "Could one build a machine that went on forever, starting with 1, and 'adding one' time after time, to produce 1, 2, 3, 4, 5, 6, 7, 8, 9, 10, 11. . . . *forever,*" and

I think I would have laughed at the idea.) "One can always add one to a number" is not a statement about empirical, or technical, or physical possibility. And yet it is perfectly intelligible, even to most children.

In one place, Wagner writes, "If we reject direct a priori modal insight (as Putnam did long ago) then any account of knowing possibilities would seem to involve forms of drawing on instances via generalization, extrapolation, transposition, and the like. What else?" But this is not right (except for the words "a priori"). We do have modal insight. For we do understand the "and so on" in "one, two, three, *and so on*," that is, the idea of an ordinary infinite sequence.[5] Doubting that we understand this "and so on" realistically is the primrose path to nominalism—a position that, as both Quine and I saw long ago, does not fit the way science actually works. Even a child can grasp the amazing fact that "one can always go on" (with the series 1, 2, 3. . .). Do I have an account of how this is possible? No. I do not have an "epistemology" of mathematics (other than to say that one should look at the way mathematicians and physicists actually *do* mathematics). Apparently Wagner thinks that "mathematically possible" is unclear, even when the possibility in question is the possibility of an ordinary infinite sequence (an "omega sequence," in the jargon of set theorists). Unlike Wagner, I find "omega sequence" perfectly clear as it stands.

But—possibilities have to be possibilities *of* some state of affairs obtaining. There cannot be an omega sequence consisting of *nothing*. Nor can there be a well-founded model of Zermelo set theory (up to a certain rank) consisting of *nothing*. There could be an omega sequence consisting of, for example, *lampposts*—that is to say, *it is mathematically possible* (though probably not physically possible) that such a sequence could exist. I chose pencil points and lines, but I could have chosen just about anything else. But I could not have just *mere* possibilities, possibilities that are not possibilities of *something*. That is part of my answer to the following objection of Wagner's:

> why mention pencil graphs at all? The structure could as easily—as possibly—be meringues connected by spider's silk, with directionality indicated by a thickening of the strand. Or why a graph at all? Perhaps mathematics is to be understood in terms of mermaids, singing to each other selectively, as required by the structure of the membership relation, ever northward across transfinite seas? That would serve just as well. The modal-nominalist faces a dilemma. If the concrete possibilities are at all specified, one way is as good as countless others. If one claims that any of several ways will do, that each is as good as the next for interpreting the mathematics in question, there is no improvement over the Platonist's Benacerraf problem.[6]

Of course I *agree* that "The structure could as easily—as possibly—be meringues connected by spider's silk, with directionality indicated by a thickening of the strand. Or . . . mermaids, singing to each other selectively, as required by the structure of the membership relation, ever northward across transfinite seas." Yes, all of these possible structures are equally good for mathematical purposes. The fact that mathematics is indifferent to which possible structures we choose to interpret arithmetic, set theory, etc., as long as they are isomorphic, does not constitute a *dilemma* for my position; it is essential to the position.

II. A SUPPOSED DIFFERENCE BETWEEN MY VIEW AND HELLMAN'S

Wagner sees my position as significantly different from Geoffrey Hellman's, and I do not. He writes,

> Putnam defined mathematical truth with reference to possible concrete objects: pencil dots connected by arrows, in layers extended into the transfinite. In contrast Hellman's arithmetic is, in effect, a modalized Ramsification of the conjunction $\&PA^2$ of the second-order axioms. We relativize $\&PA^2$ to a domain X (the "numbers"), replace "successor" by "f," and assert:
>
> Hellman's (*) $\Diamond\ \exists X\ \exists f\ (\&PA^2)^X$
>
> The theorems of arithmetic are then what hold "wherever" this possibility obtains. An analogous construction, with second-order Replacement and Selection, extends the idea to set theory. We use second-order logic (SOL) to interpret mathematics in terms of pure relational structures ("pure" in the sense of being free from any informally meaningful mathematical terms, say, *successor*, *collecting*, or *graph*). So one option, Putnam's, involves the possibility of a specific object, concrete albeit not found in experience, while Hellman applies a modal operator to a completely general form.

My response is that the possibility of "a specific object, concrete albeit not found in experience" *implies* the truth of Hellman's (*) by one use of Existential Generalization applied to the appropriate "concrete object," and, conversely the truth of (*) together with the modal fact that the existence of such a "concrete object" (say, an omega-sequence of lampposts) is *possible* (and any such object is trivially isomorphic to any other "witness" to the truth of (*)) implies the truth of the instance of (*) in which an infinite series of "lampposts" (or whatever) replace the variable domain "X" and the existential quantifier is deleted.

But what of the second-order quantifiers in PA^2 itself? Here, it is important to notice that since any model of PA (any "concrete object" that makes PA true) trivially allows the definition of a pairing function (for example, the function 2^x3^y), formalizing PA^2 requires only *monadic* second order logic,[7] and monadic second order logic is equivalent to "plural quantification," as Boolos pointed out long ago.[8] Hellman's (*) and the points I made in the preceding section are simply two ways of saying that the modal-logical interpretation of PA is that there are *possible* structures that satisfy the matrix of (*); in the two papers Wagner discusses, I concentrated on mentioning *examples* of such structures, and Hellman's book *formalized* the fact that the position does not depend on *choosing a particular example*. I see no disagreement here.

III. Wagner on SOL

Wagner writes,

> Boolos famously insisted that there is nothing particularly unclear about second-order implication: it is a mathematically natural extension of first-order implication, with a lot of overlap in the model theory. Nonetheless second-order implication is mathematics. I explain it by reference to all models of a certain kind, whereas for first-order *Ax* all I need is elementary syntax and an understanding of the connectives.

However (1) Wagner's claim that second-order consequence (or equivalently, second-order validity) is explainable using quantification over models is a mathematical error; (2) far from it being the case that the interpretation of SOL presupposes set theory, it is the standard interpretation of set theory that presupposed SOL; (3) the claim about first-order logic is correct only when and because "elementary syntax" presupposes SOL.

Let me now explain these points:

(1) "Models," in model theory, are sequences of *sets*, the domain of objects the quantifiers of a theory range over in a given model is one of the elements (usually the first) of the sequence. When I say that it is an error to say (at least I take this to be what Wagner means by saying that second-order consequence is explainable by reference to models) that a second-order inference is valid just in case the conclusion is true in all models in which the premises are true, I do not mean that this claim is *false*; I mean that it is unproven, and, in fact, unprovable from the axioms of presently accepted set-theory. Wagner's claim, if I interpret it correctly (and I cannot think of any other plausible interpretation), presupposes that if a formula

is satisfied under *any* interpretation of its quantifiers, then it is satisfied in some universe that is a *set*; if so, any *second-order* formula that is satisfied over an interpretation in which its *first-order* quantifiers range over *all sets* is already satisfied in some model that is a set; and this is at least as powerful as Bernays's reflection principle, which implies the existence of an inaccessible cardinal. I fear that Wagner does not realize this.

Incidentally, Kreisel pointed out that the identification of even *first-order* validity with truth in all models is a substantive mathematical claim and not a piece of conceptual analysis, for a similar reason.[9] In the case of first-order logic, however, the mathematical claim follows from the method of proof of the Gödel Completeness Theorem, which shows us how, given a formula that is satisfiable under some interpretation (not necessarily in a *model*—that is, not necessarily over a universe that is a *set*), to construct an interpretation that satisfies the same formula over the natural numbers (in fact, by a theorem I proved long ago,[10] an interpretation in which the predicates are truth functions of recursively enumerable predicates).

(2) A standard model for set theory is a well-founded model such that the "the set of all subsets *in the model*" of a set x in the model is the set of all subsets of x "in reality." This requires a second-order quantifier to express.

(3) "Elementary syntax" had *better* be able to say that a proof is a finite sequence of formulas (or, if a Gentzen-style formalism is preferred, that a proof tree has a finite number of nodes). But the quantifier "there are finitely many" expresses a second-order notion (which is why Frege was forced to use second-order logic). Of course one can also use set theory to express this, but only provided one assumes a standard model for set theory itself; if the purpose is to restrict syntax (or first-order arithmetic) to standard interpretations, then using set theory and assuming a standard model for the latter is using more SOL than is actually needed. I refer the reader to my "Reply to Hartry Field" in the present volume for a discussion of the connection between the "there are finitely many" quantifier and SOL: Field, indeed, sees the problem, but tries to avoid SOL with the aid of physical assumptions. As I say in that Reply, "Field's basic idea is that if there is a specifiable omega-sequence in (physical) nature, then the determinacy of the mathematical concept of finiteness is secured through the determinacy of the relevant physical concepts. He argues that there are such sequences with the aid of two 'cosmological assumptions.'" But the problem is that those assumptions themselves employ the notion of *finiteness*, so a second-order logical notion is not avoided.

That neither first- nor second-order validity can be defined without using a second-order notion, does not mean, on my view, that we do not *understand* these concepts; it means that the second-order notion of an "interpretation" (in "validity is truth under all interpretations") cannot be eliminated in favor of a set-theoretic or syntax-theoretic substitute. If Hellman's (*) presupposes a second-order notion, so do set theory, syntax, and, for that matter, first-order arithmetic. For the "there are finitely many" quantifier is indispensable in these subjects. Wagner believes that modal logic "hides" commitment to sets ("ontology is hidden in the consequence relation"), because he thinks second-order validity must be explained set theoretically; but it does not have to be explained that way, and moreover (as far as we know) it *cannot* be explained that way.

IV. A NICE OBSERVATION OF BOOLOS'S

Consider the following inference:

(1) $(x) (fx0 = s0)$
(2) $(x) (f0sx = ssf0x)$
(3) $(x)(y) (fsysx = fyfsyx)$
(4) $D0$
(5) $(x) Dx \supset Dsx)$
∴ (6) $Dfssss0ssss0$

["D" is a unary predicate, "0" a name constant, "s" a unary and "f" a binary function.]

This is a valid first-order inference, and hence has a proof in first-order logic, but Boolos showed[11] that the length of the shortest such proof is greater than present estimates of the number of particles in the universe! At the same time, a proof using SOL can be written on one page.

Wagner writes,

> It is not fruitful to ask whether second-order implication somehow seems clear enough to the mind. While conceptual clarity is very hard to define (and a graveyard of philosophical theories), no one doubts that our ability to tell, in relevant circumstances, whether something *a* falls under the concept *C* has something to do with it. In this respect first-order implication is the best we can ask for. We have, up to computational limits, a decisive positive test for consequences of our first-order *Ax*, plus systematic ways to build counterexamples in some cases.

—but Steve, it cannot be that we understand the notion of first-order validity only "up to computational limits"! Perhaps Wittgenstein thought something like this,[12] but if so he was mistaken. As I have argued elsewhere,[13] realism about what is and is not a *consequence* of given assumptions had *better* extend beyond what humans can actually compute (with or without the aid of computers) if we are to interpret physical science realistically at all—and I continue to maintain that we should.[14] Moreover, even *our understanding of the programs we ourselves write for the computers* presupposes that we understand the notion of a "finite number of steps" to be determinate; it is not a straightforward empirical notion (as Field realizes, although Wagner ignores the issue). Boolos remarked that the "there is" in the statement that "there is a proof of (6) from premises (1), (2), (3), (4), (5)" is a mathematical "there is"; we cannot check the existence of any proof by using a "decisive positive test" with the aid of computers. Nevertheless, in the mathematical sense (which Hellman and I argue should be understood modal-logically), "there is" such a proof, and we know that it *exists via the second-order proof* (plus the proof of the completeness of first-order logic that Gödel provided).

V. THE SUPPOSED SEMANTIC DILEMMA

Wagner sees my position as an unstable compromise between two versions of "semantic modalism." Here is his description:

> There are two versions of semantic modalism, eliminationist and translational. The former holds that the mapping ["from the sentences of set theory (thus of mathematics generally) to modal sentences"] lets us drop the set theory, except as a convenient fiction, thus avoiding mathematical objects. The latter holds that the set theory is nonetheless also true and adequate; its sentences are correct and mathematically equivalent to the corresponding modal ones.

I see two problems with this description: Problem (1) What is the word "semantical" doing here? and Problem (2) Why "convenient *fiction?*" Before I describe these, however, let me quote Wagner's description of the alternative he will go on to recommend:

> The third position, which I will call the *heuristic* reading (and for which "modalism" is not felicitous at all), is not ontologically revisionary and requires no comprehensive or systematic mapping. It regards the description of objects and of possibilities as two distinct mathematical viewpoints either of which might take priority given a context of discovery, although not necessarily (and perhaps necessarily not) to the exclusion of the other.

I will discuss this alternative in the last two sections of this Reply.

Turning now to my Problem (1), Wagner uses the term "semantical" although none of these positions, as he states them here, refers to *Sinne* (intensions), *Bedeutungen* (extensions), translations, or other obviously semantic entities.[15] Presumably the term "convenient fiction" is meant to convey that the first position includes the claim that the sentences of arithmetic and set theory are *false* (a position I have never entertained), and "true" and "false" are certainly among the semantic notions that Frege used, and Tarski did call his famous idea "the semantic conception of truth." But if these facts make the first position "semantic," then every time anyone says that something is false, she makes a "semantic" claim, which seems to me to swell the realm of "semantics" to an alarming extent. And the second position, as stated here, uses the term "mathematical equivalence," which, as I understand it, is not a semantic term at all. Indeed, it seems obvious to me that constructing the modal-logical "mapping" that I sketched (that Hellman constructed in detail) is doing mathematics. Moreover, it is perfectly correct *as a mathematical claim* to say that each sentence on the modal-logical side of the mapping is equivalent to its image on the set-theoretic side of the mapping. *Of course, they are mathematically equivalent!* The question is: does that fact have any *philosophical* significance?

Postponing discussion of Wagner's expression "convenient fiction" for the moment, the answer to my Problem (2) becomes clear when we see Wagner shifting smoothly from talking of mathematical equivalence to talk of "semantic equivalence," for instance *here*:

> Eliminationism is the more straightforward semantic position. While, like translational modalism, it requires a mapping from set theory to a modalized mathematics, the eliminationist takes the mapping to show only that the modal side is adequate to all mathematical purposes. Since one is not claiming any translation, one need not explain in what the equivalence of set-theoretic and modal sentences might consist, or how they "say the same thing mathematically." It is far from clear how that might be done. *A semantic equivalence claim requires a semantic theory. All forms of semantics with any currency however, whether extensional or intensional, are set-theoretic. Using such a framework to argue for modal theory and set theory as equivalent, fundamental forms of mathematical expression would appear question-begging.* [emphasis added—HP]

So, it turns out, what I am really charged with is having held that the modal-logical sentences and their set-theoretic images *have the same meaning* (since that is what "semantic equivalence" means). But I have long rejected *that* view (just as I have denied holding that arithmetic and set theory are *fiction*). So I do not face this particular "dilemma." Nevertheless, I am grateful to Wagner for raising this question, because in the process of thinking about why "semantic equivalence" is not what I have ever claimed (between modal-logical mathematics and set theory, arithmetic, etc.), I *have* discovered a dilemma in the neighborhood of the one Wagner poses for me, and thinking through what I want to say about that dilemma is something I found extremely valuable.

VI. The Real Dilemma

First, the reason I say that semantic equivalence is *not* what I have ever claimed, is that I have long written papers[16] defending the idea that two theories that have incompatible ontologies or make incompatible claims *if* we take them at "face value," are nevertheless sometimes "equivalent descriptions," and I have frequently said that this is *not* a claim about "translation practice," that is, about semantics.

An example I have used for many years is the following: imagine a situation in which there are exactly three billiard balls on a certain table and no other objects (for example, the atoms, etc., of which the billiard balls consist do not count as "objects" in that context). Consider the two descriptions, "There are only seven objects on that table: three billiard balls, and four mereological sums containing more than one billiard ball" and "There are only three objects on the table, but there are seven *sets* of individuals that can be formed of those objects." What it means to be a *realist who recognizes conceptual relativity* with respect to *this* case is to believe that there is an aspect of reality which is independent of what we think at the moment (although we could, of course, change it by adding or subtracting objects from the table), which is *correctly describable either way.*

I do not think that the two sentences I just used as examples *have the same meaning* by any reasonable and nontendentious standards of sameness of meaning. For one thing, the first sentence implies the existence of mereological sums, and the second implies the existence of sets, and I do not see that someone who accepts the first sentence is committed to the ontology of sets at all, or that someone who accepts the second is committed to the ontology of mereological sums at all. These are not synonymous sentences. They are not "semantically equivalent." And similarly, an arithmetic sentence, or a sentence of set theory, is not synonymous with its image under the sort of mapping of mathematical sentences onto modal logical sentences I sketched in the two papers Wagner discusses. These pairs of sentences are not semantically equivalent. But, I claimed, they are "equivalent descriptions." But what is the criterion?

The example of the three balls was an artificial one. In my closing lecture to the conference in honor of my eightieth birthday in Dublin, I said the following about a genuine scientific example (a case of quantum-mechanical "duality"):

> My own notion of "conceptual relativity" (which I originally called "cognitive equivalence") is beautifully illustrated by [the duality example]. The different "representations" are perfectly intertranslatable; it is just that the translations don't preserve "ontology."
>
> What do they preserve? Well, they don't merely preserve macro-observables. They also preserve *explanations*. An explanation of a phenomenon goes over into another perfectly good explanation of the same phenomenon under these translations.
>
> But who *is* to say what is a phenomenon? And who is to say what is a perfectly good explanation? My answer has always been: *physicists* are; not linguists and not philosophers.[17]

—And I gave a similar explanation in my *first* paper on this sort of equivalence in 1978.

But now, I admit, a problem like Wagner's "dilemma" does arise. Of course, if we are to apply this criterion to mathematics, we shall have to say that it is *mathematicians* and not physicists who should be the ones to say. But now a number of problems arise, problems that make me think I should not have tried to "export" the notion of "equivalent descriptions" from empirical science to the present case at all. Mathematics, after all, is not about "phenomena," but about proofs, ways of conceiving of mathematical problems, mathematical approaches, and much more. And it does not seem reasonable to think that the mapping Hellman and I proposed of mathematical assertions onto modal-logical assertions *preserves* these. It is not just that a proof and its formalization in modal logical terms are not "semantically" equivalent; if the criterion is supposed to be that the *mathematician* would regard them as the same, the objection immediately arises that the modal-logical version, unlike the quantum-mechanical representations I mentioned in Dublin, is not one mathematicians are even aware of. (And if they were, I doubt very much that they would regard them as equivalent, except in the sense of deducible from each other, which is clearly insufficient.) The pragmatic criterion of equivalence I proposed for physics has no obvious analogue here. So, though not for Wagner's reasons, I do see a real difficulty with "translational semantic modalism."

At the same time, I am not willing to accept "eliminationist semantic modalism," at least not as Wagner describes it. This is connected to what I called Problem (2) [Why "convenient *fiction?*"]. But there is a third possibility that I am surprised Wagner fails to consider: the interpretation of arithmetic and set theory as modal statements is neither a piece of straightforward semantics nor a substitute for something we have come to reject as false (which is what "fiction" implies). Our interpretation is a *rational reconstruction.*

VII. The Modal-Logical Interpretation as Rational Reconstruction

Although Rudolf Carnap introduced the idea of rational reconstruction in his great work on epistemology,[18] for our purposes it can be better illustrated with the story of "imaginary" numbers. As Menachem Fisch has described, British algebraists were tormented for nearly a century by the question of the "reality" of what we now call the "complex numbers."[19] Yet, in the end, even introductory textbooks in analysis often tell us that we can stipulate that a complex number is simply an ordered pair of members of R, the field of real numbers. And real numbers can be identified with Dedekind cuts on the field Q of rational numbers, that is, with pairs of disjoint nonempty sets {A,B} of rationals such that A ∪ B is the whole set of rationals and every member of A is less than each member of B. And rationals themselves can be identified with ordered pairs of members of Z, the ring of the positive and negative integers together with zero, or rather with equivalence classes of such ordered pairs.[20] And what are the "integers" of which Z is composed? We can stipulate, for example, that they are ordered pairs consisting of a natural number and one of three objects (say, the null set Ø, its singleton {Ø}, and zero) thus [in the present sentence only, I will use numerals in regular font for the natural numbers and the italics for the members of Z]: *1, 2, 3* . . . are stipulated to be <Ø,1>, <Ø,2>, <Ø,3>, . . .; *0* is stipulated to be <0,0>; *-1, -2, -3* . . . are stipulated to be <{Ø},1>, <{Ø},2>, <{Ø},3>,. . . .; and multiplication and addition are defined in accordance with the rules that the product of two numbers of unlike sign (i.e. of a positive number and a negative number) is negative, and the product of two numbers of like sign is positive (for example, <Ø,2> × <{Ø},3> = <{Ø},6>). *And what are the natural numbers?* Well, von Neumann taught us that we can *stipulate* that they are Ø, {Ø}, {Ø,{Ø}},{Ø, {Ø,{Ø}}}, . . .[21] And just as we stipulate definitions for multiplication and addition of members of Z (that is, for addition and multiplication of the ordered pairs with which they were identified) so that the usual rules for multiplication and addition of "arbitrary integers" hold, so we stipulate definitions for addition and multiplication of complex numbers (that is, for addition and multiplication of the ordered pairs with which they were identified) so that the usual rules for the multiplication and addition of "complex numbers" hold. Of course, it is necessary to prove that all these stipulations are consistent, and that the distributive, commutative, associative, etc., laws are all forthcoming, but that is straightforward mathematical work. And *voila!* a century of worry by some of the greatest algebraists in the world over the "reality" of, for example, the square root of minus one is *passé*: $i =_{df} <0,1>$, 1(the complex number) = $<1,0>$ [the ordered pair of two real numbers], and "$i \times i = -1$" becomes "$<0,1> \times <0,1> = <-1,0>$" — and we *define* "multiplication" of these particular ordered pairs so that this follows immediately from the definition. I repeat: an ontological worry about the "existence" of the complex numbers (and particularly about the existence of such a strange thing as a "square root of minus one") is replaced by a mathematical problem—and not that difficult a one—of establishing the consistency and the logical consequences of a set of *stipulations*.

Of course, these stipulations have the strange consequence that there are now *five* "ones": one the "natural number" (for example, {Ø} if we adopt von Neumann's system); one the member of "the ring of integers" Z; one the rational number (the equivalence class to which 1/1, 2/2, . . .and -1/-1, -2/-2,. . . all belong); one the real number (the Dedekind cut whose left member A is the set of rational numbers less that the "one" of Z); and one the complex number! And what do mathematicians do about that? Why they simply ignore it!

Note that Benacerraf's problem *could* have been raised here, but was not. One *could* have said that these definitions have many alternatives which would work just as well (which is of course true), so how can it be that any one of them is "really right"? What the complex numbers really are has not been answered. But no one supposed, after the century of torment that Fisch describes so well, that there was such a thing as "what the complex numbers really are." Dedekind did suppose that there was such a thing as what the integers really are, namely "a free creation of the human mind" and Kronecker famously said that "God made the natural numbers. Everything else is the work of man,"[22] but basically there was no problem—or not until Frege, and the "Julius Caesar problem" mentioned above. But once the idea of treating complex numbers as appropriate logical constructions had taken hold—together with the idea that this could be done in different ways— and once Whitehead and Russell had used the same technique to build up, successively, the ring Z, the field Q, the field R, and the field of complex numbers C, starting with their own construction of the natural numbers (of each type from the second up) as sets of sets, nothing but sets was left as a basis.[23] Reference to the natural numbers too dissolves into reference to any infinite sequence of sets you choose. But why did Benacerraf worry about that fact, whereas Quine, for example, did not?

Perhaps for the simple reason that Quine, who felt forced, as a self-described reluctant Platonist to simply "acquiesce" in the existence of sets,[24] was simultaneously (if strangely) a complete skeptic about reference, and thus could never take seriously the problem of how we can *refer* to sets if sets are causally inert entities. In contrast, Benacerraf was a realist about reference. This is what Wagner refers to when he writes, "but Bena-cerraf's route would appear to turn on very delicate, tendentious formulations regarding causation and its role in justification." While this may be right as a description of the paper to which Wagner refers, I suspect that there was much more behind Benacceraf's raising the problem of reference to mathematical entities in the way he did. I will come back to this suspicion of mine in a moment. But right now I want to note the following: *if*, for the time being, we are willing to take reference to sets for granted, then the example of what has become the standard way of introducing the natural numbers (for example, von Neumann), the ring of integers Z, the rationals Q, the reals R, and the complex numbers C, shows how a rational reconstruction can "defuse" a metaphysical problem, *not* by showing that there is one right way to think about the issue, but by showing a number of ways we *could have decided to think and talk that would work equally well*. And this applies not only to ontological issues, although such are our concern here, but to rational reconstruction in general; it is not important that the theory of truth can be formalized à la Tarski or à la Kripke;[25] what is important is that our concept of truth *can* be rendered noncontradictory.

Bringing this back to Wagner: one could have asked the mathematicians who decided to "identify" complex numbers with ordered pairs of reals, "Are you making the *semantic* claim that, for example, "3 + 5i" *means* <3,5>?" What possible semantic theory can support that? Why do you not say that the square root of minus one is a *fiction*, and we can now live without it? One could have asked Frege, are you saying that, for example, "two" *means* the property of being an extension (that is, a set) that can be put in one-to-one correspondence with the integers zero, one? What possible semantic theory can support that? Why do you not say that arithmetic is a fiction, and we can now live without one, two, three, . . . etc.? One could have asked Tarski, are you not saying that the idea that there is such a thing as "truth" was a *fiction* and we can now live without it? In sum, that a concept needs to be replaced by a less problematic one, and that this can be done in more than one way, does not mean that the original concept was a *fiction*. I am not an eliminationist with respect to arithmetic, and I am not a semantic-modalist either; I am proposing a *rational reconstruction*.

But, granted that some rational reconstruction is called for here (and a great deal of it has taken place in mathematics itself since the nineteenth century), why can we not stop with Quine? Why not just take sets as basic, and accept it that the work I described above of providing satisfactory definitions of Z, Q, R, and C has done the "housecleaning" work that was sorely needed? The answer is that a rational reconstruction is meant to defuse a paradox. Defining a problematic concept in terms of *equally problematic* concepts is not rational reconstruction. The work of rational reconstruction done by the nineteenth-century mathematicians and their twentieth-century successors was not designed to resolve Benacerraf's problem. It put the theory of real and complex variables on a firm footing, and that was a great achievement. But that is not our task here.

I said above that "I suspect that there was much more behind Benacerraf's raising the problem of reference to mathematical entities in the way he did." What I have in mind is this: Benacerraf is a Frege scholar, and he knows that the notion of "set" was quite unclear as late as the beginning of the twentieth century. I do not have in mind simply the Russell paradox; I have in mind that the question of whether sets are simply the extensions of (possible) predicates haunted the whole late nineteenth- early twentieth-century discussion. Today that idea has been rejected (in part because possible predicates, or "properties" seems more problematic than sets, and in part because another notion, the so-called notion of a "random" set, or an "arbitrary" collection" has come to seem more suitable for mathematics). But if the natural numbers seemed to be "the work of God,"[26] set theory seems too recent (and too recently problematic) an invention to have such a sanctified metaphysical status. And aside from the fact that "set" is somewhat of a neologism, the fact is that sets too can be identified with other mathematical entities; in fact *functions* would seem to be a natural choice. Should we just say that here too there are simply "alternative rational reconstructions"? It is true that Benacerraf himself only speaks of the problem of the arbitrariness involved in identifying numbers with the members of any particular omega-sequence; I hope he will not mind if, when his problem is extended to *all* mathematical entities, as illustrated by the fact that sets themselves can be identified with functions and vice versa, I henceforth speak of *Benacerraf's Paradox*.

If, as I believe, Benacerraf's Paradox shows that the notion of sets as *objects* and arbitrary functions as *objects* are less than fully clear; if we do not, in fact, know what it *means* to be a "Platonist about *sets* or functions" (especially if, as Wagner explicitly does, we reject the idea of equivalent descriptions or "conceptual relativity"!), how can showing that one could take *either* as basic and treat the other as a construction help? Granted, that I could think of functions as "real" and sets as different sorts of functions (and say, truly, that this can be done in more than one way, as far as mathematics is concerned), and granted that I could think of sets as "real" and functions as different sorts of sets (and say, truly, that this can be done in more than one way, as far as mathematics is concerned), how can that satisfy my desire to be clear about what I am doing when I do one or the other? Quine tells me to be a "sectarian," and choose one and reject the other, but perhaps change my choice from time to time for some sort of enlightenment[27] and Wittgensteinians will say that my worry is "metaphysical"—but of course it is! What I am seeking is the *right* metaphysics.

VIII. Wagner's "Positive Reconstruction of the Modal Idea"

The last part of Wagner's essay (beginning with the sentence, "So far we have not examined Putnam's own interpretation of semantic modalism. We will do so and then move to a positive reconstruction of the modal idea from Putnam's own materials") looks to me as if it were written by a different Steve Wagner. Some elements of the preceding are still there, to be sure, particularly the mistaken claim that second-order logic is just set theory, and the bad idea that the first-order consequence relation is totally clear but second-order consequence is not are still there, but the idea that the only clarity that set theory possesses consists in the possibility of proving theorems from the axioms via first-order logic goes missing now. And Benacerraf's Paradox, which was earlier recognized as my reason (and not only *my* reason) for advocating a form of structuralism is conspicuous by its absence when my supposedly unaccountable resistance to positing mathematical objects is described by Wagner. Indeed, what the "third position that [Wagner] will call the *heuristic* reading (and for which 'modalism' is not felicitous at all)" turns out to be is simply to accept *both* objectual mathematics, including its ontology of sets, *and* modal mathematics, including unreduced modalities, as equally parts of total science without assigning metaphysical priority to either. What puzzles me is how this Wagner (the Steve Wagner who produced the "third position") thinks one can be a full-blown realist about sets if one still thinks, as the Steve Wagner who wrote the rest of this paper does, that our understanding of set theory is just our ability to use a bunch of axioms formulated in first order logic (with the latter's "clear" consequence relation), which would seem to be a variant of Formalism. But rather than try to reconcile the two Steves, I will simply reply to the Realist one now.

    This Steve Wagner offers two reasons for realism with respect to sets. The first, that the supposed modal alternative "hides" sets anyway depends, I have argued, on a mathematical error. The second, and new (new to me, and also new up to this point as far as Wagner's essay is concerned) is that an ontology of sets is supposedly needed for Tarskian semantics. I close by examining this reason.

IX. TARSKIAN SEMANTICS IN A MODAL SETTING

Wagner's assumption that Tarski's technique *does not work* if the mathematical language is modal logical rather than set theoretic is quite mistaken. To see why it is mistaken, let us recall that Tarski defines "true in L" in terms of *satisfaction*, and recall further that Tarskian "satisfaction" is defined inductively (I would write, "recursively," except that term has been preempted by computer science), and note that the inductive definition is extendable to modal operators. The clause for existential quantification (simplifying greatly for expository purposes) tells us, for example, that an object a satisfies a monadic formula $(\exists y)F(x,y)$ just in case $(\exists y)F(a,y)$, the clause for negation tells us that a satisfies $-F(x)$ just in case a does not satisfy $F(x)$, and the clause for disjunction tells us that a satisfies $(F \vee G)$ just in case a satisfies F or a satisfies G. If a modal primitive is added to the language, say the symbol $\Diamond$ (for possibility) then the appropriate clause will read: a satisfies $\Diamond F$ just in case $\Diamond(a$ satisfies F). Here is a word example: take $(F(x)$ to be $(\exists y)(x$ loves y). Interpret $\Diamond$ as psychological possibility, and take a to be Alice. Then "a satisfies $\Diamond F$" says that Alice satisfies "it is possible x loves somebody," "$\Diamond(a$ satisfies F)" says that it is possible that Alice satisfies "x loves somebody" and these two formulas have the same truth condition, namely that in some possible world there is a person whom Alice loves. In mathematical jargon, "satisfies" commutes with $\Diamond$.

Wagner quite rightly points out that a Tarskian truth definition for a nonmodal language shows how truth and falsity depend on the extensions of the predicates of the language; but it is equally true that a Tarskian truth definition for a modal language shows how truth and falsity depend (in the case of the modal formulas) on the *possible* extensions of the predicates, which is what one would expect. If the first sort of truth definition counts as "explaining the distribution of truth values over the formulas of the language," so should the second.

In the case of languages for a part of mathematics that does not require quantification over sets of unbounded rank, inductive (or "recursive") definition of truth via "satisfaction" can be replaced by an explicit definition in a metalanguage that quantifies over sets of still higher rank by a familiar technique due to Frege, and this metalanguage can, in turn be given a modal-logical equivalent. When the original language formalizes all of extant mathematics, including set theory, then the inductive definition has to suffice. But, unless one's purpose requires coding inductive definitions into set theory, there is no reason to require the explicit definition; inductive definitions are perfectly mathematically kosher. And, in any case, the impossibility of an *explicit* Tarski-style truth definition for the whole language of mathematics applies to *both* the "objectual" form of the language and the "modal" form; neither scores a point against the other here.

H.P.

NOTES

1. This Prometheus Lecture is collected as "Corresponding with Reality," in my *Philosophy in an Age of Science*, ed. Mario de Caro and David Macarthur (Cambridge, MA: Harvard University Press, 2012).

2. As explained above in my Intellectual Autobiography, my parents took me to France when I was six months old, and I spoke only French until 1933.

3. The question as to whether any of the natural numbers is identical with Julius Caesar (and if not, why not) was famously raised by Frege. The best discussion I know of on this topic is in Richard Heck, *Frege's Theorem* (Oxford: Oxford University Press, 2011).

4. They were, however, needed, if numbers and ordinary objects such as Julius Caesar were to be "objects" of the same type, as Frege wanted for formal reasons (and not just for the sake of his post-1891 semantic theories). See the book by Heck cited in the preceding note for an account of those reasons. Contrary to what is often taken for granted, Frege did *not* claim that numbers (e.g., 2) are in fact identical with the extensions of concepts; *stipulating* that they are was, for him, a convention. (In *Grundlagen der Arithmetik*, §107, he wrote that "This way of getting over the difficulty [that such identity statements as "2=Julius Caesar" have not been assigned a truth value] cannot be expected to meet with universal approval, and many will prefer other methods of removing the doubt in question. *I attach no decisive importance even to bringing in the extensions of concepts at all.*" (Gottlob Frege, *The Foundations of Arithmetic*, trans. J. L. Austin [Evanston, IL: Northwestern University Press, 1980], 117 [emphasis added—HP].)

5. As Dedekind famously put it, "I regard the whole of arithmetic as a necessary, or at least natural, consequence of the simplest arithmetic act, that of counting, and itself as nothing else than the successive creation of the infinite series of positive integers in which each individual is defined by the one immediately preceding." (Richard Dedekind, "Preface" to "Continuity and Irrational Numbers," in *Essays on the Theory of Numbers*, trans. W. W. Beman [Mineola, NY: Dover, 1963], 4.)

6. The "Benacerraf Problem" is that, since the natural numbers can be identified with the elements of infinite series as far as mathematics is concerned, it is hard to see how there can be a fact of the matter as to *which* infinite series is *the* series of natural numbers. But if there is no such fact of the matter, then the natural numbers are not determinate objects!

7. For those unfamiliar with the point: quantification over *dyadic* predicates is equivalent to monadic quantification over *ordered pairs*. (Ordered triples, quadruples, etc., can be defined in terms of ordered pairs in well-known ways.)

8. George Boolos, "To Be is to Be the Value of a Variable (or Some Values of Some Variables)," *Journal of Philosophy* 81, no. 8 (1984): 430–50.

9. George Boolos, *Logic, Logic, and Logic*, ed. Richard Jeffrey and John Burgess (Cambridge, MA: Harvard University Press, 1998), 10: "an old observation of Georg Kreisel" that "the standard definition of validity considers only interpretations in which the quantifiers range over some *set* of things."

10. See my "Trial and Error Predicates and the Solution to a Problem of Mostowski, *Journal of Symbolic Logic* 30, no. 1 (1965): 49–57.

11. Boolos, *Logic, Logic, and Logic*, 377. I learned about this from Marcus Rossberg.

12. In *Remarks on the Foundations of Mathematics* Wittgenstein wrote, "Suppose that people go on and on calculating the expansion of p. So God, who knows everything, knows whether they will have reached '777' by the end of the world. But can his *omniscience* decide whether they *would* have reached it after the end of the world? It cannot. I want to say: Even God can determine something mathematical only by mathematics. Even for him the rule of expansion cannot decide anything that it does not decide for us." (*Remarks on the Foundations of Mathematics*, ed. G. H. von Wright, R. Rhees, G. E. M. Anscombe, trans. G. E. M. Anscombe [Cambridge, MA: MIT Press, 1967], V, §34.)

13. See "Wittgenstein, Realism and Mathematics," in my *Philosophy in an Age of Science*, 421–40.

14. For my reasons, see "On Not Writing Off Scientific Realism," 91–108 and "Indispensability Arguments in the Philosophy of Mathematics," 181–201, in my *Philosophy in an Age of Science*.

15. *Sinn* and *Bedeutung* are, famously, Frege's terms for the connotation and denotation (or intension and extension) of the terms of a language and of its sentences as wholes.

16. My first paper about cognitive equivalence of theories which are incompatible if simply conjoined was "Equivalenza," trans. P. Odifreddi, *Enciclopedia*, vol. 5 (Torino, Italy: Giulio Einaudi Editore, 1978), 547–64; English version published as "Equivalence" in *Realism and Reason*, 26–45. After that came my 1987 Carus Lectures, *The Many Faces of Realism*, in which I used the mereological sums example for the first time; "Reply to Jennifer Case," *Revue Internationale de Philosophie* 55, no. 4 (Dec. 2001): 431–38; Lecture 2 in *Ethics without Ontology*; "Sosa on Internal Realism and Conceptual Relativity" in *Sosa and His Critics*, ed. J. Greco (Oxford: Blackwell, 2008); and probably others I have forgotten.

17. "From Quantum Mechanics to Ethics and Back Again," in my *Philosophy in an Age of Science*, 57.

18. Rudolf Carnap, *Logische Aufbau der Welt* (Berlin-Schlachtensee: Weltkreis Verlag, 1928), 138 ff. Carnap wrote "*rationale Nachkonstruktion*"; in the English translation, *The Logical Structure of the World* (Berkeley: University of California Press, 1967), 220, this is translated as "rational reconstruction." "Rational reconstruction" was also used by Hans Reichenbach, who attributed the term to Carnap in *Experience and Prediction* (Chicago: University of Chicago Press, 1938), 5 fn. 1.

19. Menachem Fisch, "'The Emergency Which Has Arrived': The Problematic History of Nineteenth Century British Algebra—A Programmatic Outline," *British Journal for the History of Science* 27 (1994): 247–76.

20. One chooses equivalence classes and not simply ordered pairs consisting of the numerator and the denominator so that 3/7 and 6/14 will turn out to be the same rational number.

21. That is, $0 = \emptyset$, $1 = \{0\}$, $2 = \{0,1\}$, $3 = \{0,1,2\}$ ... each natural number, starting with zero, is the set of all smaller natural numbers!

22. Both quotations are taken from Stanley Burris, "What are numbers, and what is their meaning?: Dedekind," available online at (http://www.math.uwaterloo.ca/~snburris/htdocs/scav/dedek/dedek.html). Accessed May 2012.

23. I am describing the theory of types as Ramsey simplified it here, not as Whitehead and Russell presented it.

24. In *Theories and Things* (Cambridge, MA: Harvard University Press, 1990), 100, Quine famously described himself as a reluctant Platonist ("I have felt that if I must come to terms with Platonism, the least I can do is keep it extensional").

25. Saul Kripke, "Outline of a Theory of Truth," *Journal of Philosophy* 72, no. 6 (1975): 690–716.

26. Leopold Kronecker famously said that *"Die ganzen Zahlen hat der liebe Gott gemacht, alles andere ist Menschenwerk."* Quoted in H. Weber, "Leopold Kronecker," *Mathematische Annalen* 43 (1893): 1–25.

27. Quine wrote "[The sectarian] is as free as the ecumenist to oscillate between [empirically equivalent but incompatible] theories for the sake of added perspective [*sic*] from which to triangulate on problems. In his sectarian way he does deem the one theory true and the alien terms of the other theory meaningless, but only so long as he is entertaining the one theory rather than the other. He can readily shift the shoe to the other foot." *Pursuit of Truth* (Cambridge, MA: Harvard University Press, 1990), 100.

5

Geoffrey Hellman

INFINITE POSSIBILITIES AND POSSIBILITIES OF INFINITY

In the first part of this essay, the origins of modal-structuralism are traced from Hilary Putnam's seminal article, "Mathematics without Founda-tions" to its transformation and development into the author's modal-struc-tural approach.[1] The addition of a logic of plurals is highlighted for its recov-ery (in combination with the resources of mereology) of full, second-order logic, essential for articulating a good theory of mathematical structures. The second part concentrates on the motivation of large transfinite cardinal numbers, arising naturally from the second-order machinery combined with an *extendability principle* on structures for set theories due independently to Zermelo and Putnam. The power of this is enhanced by a novel *modal reflection principle* recently introduced by the author. This is illustrated in detail with the first axiom of infinity: After reviewing some of the trouble this basic classical axiom has caused for previous foundational programs, we show how it is derived easily using the reflection principle and a weak form of extendability for finite structures. We conclude with some compara-tive remarks on how this improves on the closest set-theoretic analogue to the present proposal.

I. Origins of Modal-Structural Foundations

The creative and leading role of Hilary Putnam's thought is perhaps no-where better illustrated than in the philosophy of mathematics. Especially in, "Mathematics without Foundations," he boldly broke new ground by sketching a substantial alternative to the received view of mathematics as fundamentally part of set theory. The alternative he sketched recast mathematics in a framework of modal logic, making explicit a conception of mathematical existence as a unique kind of logico-mathematical possibility, leading naturally to a new resolution of the set-theoretic paradoxes associated with putatively maximal totalities (containing *all* sets, *all* ordinals, etc.). Notably, however, Putnam presented his ideas, not as a rival to set-theoretic foundations, but rather as a *mathematically equivalent* alternative picture that could be helpful in connection with the paradoxes or with problems associated with abstract ontology. Far from *replacing* set-theoretic foundations, the modal framework could call upon it to help illuminate the notion of "mathematical possibility" through its notion of "satisfaction in a model." As implied in his title, after all, mathematics can survive perfectly well without *any* particular *foundation*, set-theoretic, modal, or otherwise.

The key idea of "mathematics as modal logic" was to construe a sentence S of ordinary mathematics (concerning, for example, integers or real or complex numbers and functions thereof, etc.) as elliptical for expressing "what would necessarily hold in any model of the appropriate theory involved," where this would take the form of a conditional whose antecedent would contain relevant axioms of the ordinary mathematical theory, with the relation and operation constants replaced with schematic variables, and whose consequent would be the original sentence in question similarly modified. Putnam also explicitly recognized that a key background assumption would state that *some* model of the relevant theory is *possible*. Thus, although the translation of ordinary mathematical sentences is hypothetical in form, this was not simply a modal version of "*if-then*-ism," which Russell had (notoriously) resorted to in the attempt to "reduce mathematics to logic." (To prevent the hypotheticals from being vacuously true in case no model exists [mathematically], the modal framework needs to assert categorically [either as a postulate or derived somehow as a theorem] that relevant models are possible.) Furthermore, Putnam took initial steps in illustrating how modal translation would proceed without falling back on set-theoretic language normally associated with "models." To this end, he introduced models of Zermelo set theory as "concrete graphs" consisting of "points" and "arrows" indicating the membership relation, so that, except for the modal operators, the modal logical translation required only nominalistically acceptable language. Finally (in this brief summary), Putnam proposed an intriguing translation pattern for set-theoretic sentences of unbounded rank (standardly understood as quantifying over arbitrary sets of the whole cumulative hierarchy or set-theoretic universe) in which all quantifiers are restricted to items of a (concrete, standard[2]) model but the effect of "unbounded rank" is got by modally quantifying over[3] arbitrary possible extensions of models. The significance of this innovation is still unfolding and will be emphasized below.

Now as interesting as all this seemed to me, already when I was a graduate student of Putnam's in the late 60s, it was only in the middle of the 1980s, after absorbing a lot more mathematics, logic, and philosophy, that I felt capable of undertaking a full-scale development of the program informally sketched in "Mathematics without Foundations." By then, Hartry Field's important contribution, *Science without Numbers* (*SWON*), had appeared and was stimulating a lot of discussion about the scope of nominalist methods in philosophy of mathematics and challenges to claims of indispensability of mathematical *abstracta* (numbers, sets, functions, etc.) for applications of mathematics in the sciences.[4] While Field's work succeeded in demonstrating the adequacy of a certain kind of nominalism for an account of mathematical applications in some areas of physics (namely, classical field theories), I was not satisfied with the approach on two principal related counts: first, it does not even attempt to respect mathematical truth, even of elementary mathematics, but treats mathematics as merely a useful but ultimately dispensable tool for encoding information about physical systems. This seemed to me far too narrow a view of mathematics and one that gave unjustifiable weight to a philosophical view of ontology bordering on what Stewart Shapiro has aptly dubbed a "Philosophy first" stance, whereas a more appropriate one—especially in relation to so successful a subject as mathematics—would be "Philosophy last, if at all"! Secondly, a detailed examination of Field's methods revealed that his approach needed to take seriously statements to the effect that certain portions of mathematics (including a good deal of analysis, applied in, for example, Newtonian gravitation theory, which Field showed how to nominalize) are *consistent*. To express this, either one would fall back on arithmetic itself (in which one can formalize consistency claims of mathematical theories), which is, of course, not nominalistically acceptable as it stands; or one would have recourse to modal notions in a theory of comparable number-theoretic strength, to express, for example, that "it is impossible to derive a contradiction from such and such starting points," etc. But if one is prepared to work with modal operators suitable for capturing number theory, why not try to respect purely mathematical truth along the lines Putnam had sketched in "Mathematics without Foundations" (which, recall, appealed only to nominalistically acceptable notions aside from the modal ones)? And then one could save a lot of effort in accounting for applications of mathematics in the sciences, as one would have available in effect the resources of a fair amount of set theory (whose applicability to material systems is fairly well understood). Field's representation theorems, highlighted in

SWON, would still be worth having, but they would be seen as illuminating certain resemblances between mathematical and physical structures rather than as enabling a proof of logical conservativeness of mathematics over a nominalized physics. (This should have been welcome also in part because of various technical difficulties Field's program encountered with proofs of conservativeness.[5]) In sum, it appeared that Field's background language would have to include a modality of the very sort Putnam's program employed, and that, with that extra machinery, it should be possible to achieve much more, that is, a full-fledged account, not just of *science* without numbers, but indeed of *mathematics* without numbers!

Having thus "derived" what would become the *title* of my project, the task then became the far weightier one of actually carrying it out, which kept me well-occupied over the next few years.

At the outset, I wanted the modal approach to apply directly to theories encountered in everyday mathematics, that is, to arithmetic, analysis, algebra, geometry, etc., without relying on a detour through set theory, which contains strong axioms not needed for the development of the vast bulk of mathematics as practiced. Since the approach requires claims of possible existence of structures investigated in ordinary mathematics, it appeared advantageous to assume only what was needed for the branch of mathematics involved. In particular, a (modal) nominalist framework would encounter problems with transfinite iteration of the power set axiom, excessive (fortunately) for the needs of most mathematics, where the countably infinite often suffices (even for a lot of analysis, including a good theory of continuous or piece-wise continuous functions, etc.) or where the power of the continuum suffices. The task was then to devise methods of describing a wide variety of mathematical structures forming the subject matter of the various branches of mathematics. Set theory (and its cousin, model theory) of course embodies a general theory of mathematical structures, but we were pursuing an autonomous alternative. Thus, modal mathematics suitably tailored to mathematical needs would become modal-*structural* mathematics.

But without set theory, how was one to describe mathematical structures, essential in articulating the translation of ordinary mathematics into a modal-structural language? Furthermore, how was a sentence's "holding in a structure" to be expressed, without employing the set-theoretic machinery of "satisfaction" (à la Tarski)? Some of Putnam's examples suggested appealing to axioms of the theory in question. For arithmetic, one would naturally use the "Peano axioms" (really due to Dedekind, as Peano himself noted). But Peano Arithmetic ("PA") is normally presented nowadays as a first-order theory, and this raises two serious problems: first, nonstandard models arise, so that translating an ordinary arithmetical sentence as one saying what would hold in *any* model of those axioms would fail to assign a truth value to any arithmetical truth not provable in PA. Furthermore, PA has infinitely many axioms (including all first-order instances of the scheme of mathematical induction), so one would have a large task on one's hands just to write down such a translate! Furthermore, in order to describe "structures of the appropriate type" for a mathematical theory, one needs to be able to speak of (and quantify over) relations, functions, and operations on a domain, but without set theory it was not obvious how that could be done.

All of these problems could be solved at once if we could employ the resources of *second-order logic*. It is well known that second-order axiom systems for the various number systems of arithmetic and analysis are finite (for example, for arithmetic, a single axiom of mathematical induction covers far more than the first-order scheme with its merely countable many instances; similarly, for real analysis, a single axiom of continuity (least-upper-bound principle) covers far more than the first-order scheme); moreover, they are categorical, that is, all models are isomorphic to one another, so the modal translation scheme would be bivalent; and, of course, second-order logic embodies a full theory of relations, hence functions and operations. Furthermore, by simply relativizing (first- and second-order) quantifiers of a given sentence to a given domain, one directly expresses that the sentence "holds over the domain," and one achieves this without semantic ascent, that is, without transforming mathematics into *meta*mathematics. Now mereology with an axiom of atomicity (stipulating that all individuals are composed entirely of atoms, that is, individuals lacking proper parts) already mimics *monadic* second-order logic, as mereological sums (wholes or fusions of atoms) correspond exactly to (nonempty) sets or classes of atoms. If then we could speak of ordered pairs, triples, etc. of atoms as themselves atoms, wholes of these could serve as relations, etc. This was the route originally taken in *Mathematics without Numbers* (*MWON*).[6] It was a rather "brute force" method, positing just enough extra atoms coding ordered pairs and triples as needed to carry out the analysis of the classical number systems and segments of a cumulative hierarchy of sets as well. While I regarded this as somewhat *ad hoc*, a better alternative was not yet available, and it did do the job. Then, within a couple of years of the publication of *MWON*, more general methods of incorporating second-order machinery were discovered: combining Boolos's ideas about plural quantifiers[7] (quite common in ordinary English and many other languages, but hitherto neglected by logicians) with mereology, Burgess, Hazen, and Lewis discovered various (essentially equivalent) ways of introducing (iterable) ordered pairing of arbitrary individuals without positing extra atoms beyond a given infinitude of them, needed anyway, at least as *possible*, for the modal-structural analysis of classical number systems and analysis.[8]

This then became the preferred method of incorporating second-order logic within modal-structural mathematics (reflected in "Structuralism Without Structures").[9] In any case, including resources of second-order logic enabled modal-structural translations to be finitely formulated, fully truth preserving (as proved in *MWON*, ch. 1), and yielded a general theory of structure true to mathematical intentions and practice, yet without falling back on set theory, but rather in effect recovering much of its expressive power by quite different means. This supported an insight of Putnam's announced at the opening of "Mathematics without Foundations," that essentially equivalent mathematical content can be arrived at in a surprising variety of distinct ways, and that this sheds considerable light on the whole subject.

With the basic machinery in place, some of the more challenging issues in set theory itself could then be addressed. Once again, the incorporation of second-order resources proved surprisingly consequential, now affording a method of motivating stronger and stronger axioms of infinity "from below," helping make the case that the study of "large cardinals" in set theory—cardinal numbers so large that they cannot be proved to exist even in ZFC—is a very natural outgrowth of methods already used or available within standard systems of set theory.

As it turned out, this could be modeled on the approach to the small, large cardinals pioneered by Zermelo's then underappreciated 1930 paper, "*Über Grenzzahlen und Mengenbereiche.*"[10] Indeed, Zermelo introduced the first large cardinals, strongly inaccessibles, and proved them to be the "boundary numbers" associated with standard models of his axioms of set theory (which now included the second-order statement of Replacement, proposed by Fraenkel as an addition to Zermelo's original list from 1908). Due to the second-order Replacement axiom, a universe for such a model must contain many ordinally indexed levels beyond what can possibly be "measured" by any set, no matter how large that set is. Equally significantly, Zermelo had introduced an extendability principle which was nearly identical to the one Putnam had formulated in "Mathematics without Foundations," except that it omitted modal operators and was applied to standard models of ZFC rather than Z. The beauty of this was that, from the assumption of the mere logico-mathematical possibility of a (standard) model of ZFC, it followed directly from extendability that there would occur a strongly inaccessible cardinal as a "set" in any proper extension of the hypothesized model, that is, Putnam's translation of the unbounded set-theoretic sentence, $\forall \alpha \exists \beta [\beta > \alpha \ \& \ \beta \text{ inaccessible}]$ (α and β ordinals)—known as the axiom of inaccessibles (AI)—would follow directly from the extendability principle (EP) for such models. This strongly motivated adopting AI as a new axiom, and postulating the possibility of a full, well-founded model of *it*. And then, applying the EP to ZFC +

AI, we would verify the Putnam translate of the axiom of *hyperinaccessibles*: The height (Zermelo's "boundary number") of any such model is a strongly inaccessible cardinal κ with κ-many strongly inaccessibles below it (which defines "*hyperinaccessible*"). Obviously this can be iterated to higher and higher levels of inaccessibility (generalized nicely by Mahlo's work on inaccessible fixed-point cardinals). In effect, Putnam's work (specified to incorporate second-order formulations, essential for all these constructions) had provided Zermelo's original work with a proper modal framework in which his insights could be realized without any commitment to a fixed, maximal background universe of "all possible models" or "all possible large cardinals." Indeed, if one simply cast Zermelo's work in standard, second-order logical form, one would immediately derive the existence of such monstrous totalities from logical comprehension. But with modality, there came new freedom, namely, to restrict comprehension so as to generate "classes" only within a "world" or "model," not across or "throughout" them. The net effect was a framework that respected the unrestricted force of extendability principles, exploited the expressive strengths of second-order logical machinery, but quite naturally blocked any reemergence of "proper classes" or an absolutely infinite universe (for example, of "possible models," etc.). In short, we could claim to have arrived at a new and fruitful resolution of the set-theoretic paradoxes.

Apart from the incorporation of the logic of plurals, mentioned above, no substantial alterations were made to the systems developed in *MWON* until around the summer of 2009, when I received a paper by Hilary Putnam, written in honor of Paul Benacerraf, in which Putnam explained his current thinking about the Axiom of Replacement.[11] Harking back to "Mathematics without Foundations," he pointed out that what we have called the "Putnam translate" of that axiom (or its instances in the case of the first-order scheme) is quite clearly correct, given the possibility of standard models of Zermelo set theory along with the extendability principle applied to them; and that this was grounds for accepting the axiom, despite earlier doubts regarding the difficulty of basing it on an "iterative conception of sets." While I basically agreed with this (never having been persuaded, for example, by Boolos's skepticism regarding Replacement), it seemed that a crucial further step needed to be taken if the axiom is to have its full mathematical effect. That step was to move from the truth of the Putnam translate of Replacement to its satisfiability in some possible model of ZC (Zermelo set theory with the Axiom of Choice), that is, a model of ZFC (in second-order form). This could be viewed as an instance of a "*reflection principle*" which could be well motivated in a manner appropriate to the modal-structural framework, something I had not seen how to provide when working on *MWON*. It then became evident that other instances of such reflection would generate all the large cardinals reached in *MWON* and substantially larger ones as well, and it would do this in a uniform, well-motivated way, significantly improving on the original form of the MS program. Moreover, evidently a similar application would yield a new derivation of the very first axiom of infinity, that is, that a (possibly only countable) infinitude of objects are simultaneously possible, something that had had simply to be postulated in the original presentation, and that had been the source of an early objection (raised by Bob Hale).[12] It seems appropriate, then, that the rest of this paper elucidate this basic, but critical step, *arriving at the infinite from the finite*, one that has proved deeply challenging to the philosophy and foundations of mathematics since the work of Frege.

II. The Axiom of Infinity: A Brief History of Failures

What foundational scheme or philosophical approach to mathematics has not experienced trouble over the axiom of infinity? Let us begin by recalling what befell Frege's logicism in connection with the mathematical existence of infinite totalities. Once he had defined the primitive predicates and operations of arithmetic, including "natural number," it was an immediate consequence of Basic Law V that there exists the class of natural numbers (more properly, the concept and its extension), appealing to the complex predicate "natural number" itself, as it had been defined. Obviously, this extension could not be in one-to-one correspondence with any finite extension (say of concepts of the form, "preceding *n* in the natural number series," for any particular numeral in place of *n*. It appeared that the existence of an infinite totality was provably a logical necessity. But, as we all know, this complacency was short-lived: for Frege himself, the discovery of Russell's paradox eventually brought on despair, for Frege rightly came to see that, without Basic Law V, it would be necessary in effect to postulate separately the axiom of infinity or something equally strong, and that this would undermine the logicist claim that the principles needed for classical analysis are reducible to logic. Surely enough, this shows up in the modern neologicist program: although a consistent system of "Frege arithmetic" (relative to PA^2) gets by with essentially "Hume's Principle" (or the equivalent principle Boolos formulated and dubbed "Numbers") together with second-order logical comprehension, this combination immediately yields the coexistence of an infinitude of numbers and then, in one more step, concepts with infinite extensions. This approach will be implicated in the *finale* below.

Russell, of course, fared no better, although he began where Frege left off, recognizing that restrictions on concept- and class-comprehension

principles are essential to avoiding inconsistency, and that, once such restrictions were in place, the existence of infinite totalities would have to be
taken as an axiom. Moreover, he recognized this for the embarrassment to
logicism that it was. For how could the existence of infinitely many things
be regarded as a purely logical truth? The trick of recasting all theorems
of mathematics requiring the axiom of infinity in conditional form with
(essentially) the axiom as antecedent and desired theorem as consequent
surely *should* have been cause for further embarrassment, if indeed it was
not. As Quine noted many years later, such "reduction to logic" could be
applied to any subject whatever and is not worthy of the name. (For Russell,
it must have offered all the advantages of theft over honest toil, which he
had famously decried in another context.)

Contemporaneously with Frege, Dedekind, in his great essay, "*Was Sind
und Was Sollen die Zahlen?*" recognized the need for a proof that infinite
sets (what he called "systems") exist, and he offered one in his notorious
section 66 based on the assumptions (1) that all those things that "could
be objects of [his] thought" form a system, (2) that some such object is not
itself a thought and (3) that, given any such object, a (new) thought arises
that *that* object can be an object of [his] thought (whence this can in turn
become an object of a further thought, etc.). In addition to the curious
appeal to psychological predicates of a vague character quite foreign to
pure logic or mathematics, however, there is the problem that assumption
(1) has nowhere been established and, moreover, is suspect for harboring
paradox, for example, along the lines of Cantor's involving "the set of all
sets," since it would seem that any set "*can* be an object of [his] thought."
Not surprisingly, Dedekind's "proof" survives mainly as a *curiosum* and
has all but been forgotten in foundations of mathematics.

Contemporaneously with Russell and type theories was Zermelo's set
theory, which, with the addition of Fraenkel's Axiom of Replacement, became the favored system of modern set theory as a branch of higher mathematics. Zermelo's system, based on iterating the power set operation along
ordinally indexed cumulative levels (collecting all earlier levels at limits),
proved fruitful indeed for mathematics and at the same time turned out to
provide a comprehensive, unified framework in which virtually all known
mathematics could in principle be translated and derived. But it did not purport to rest on or consist in logic alone, and so it caused no embarrassment
in simply taking the existence of a set of, for instance, all finite ordinals (à
la Zermelo or von Neumann, say) as a separate axiom. For the purposes
of working set theory, this, of course, is no failure; but for the purpose of
deriving, or at least independently motivating, the infinite from anything
more fundamental, it simply refuses to engage in the quest.

The story with category theory is more complex but has an essentially similar upshot. The complexity derives from the dual nature of category theory, both as an abstract algebraic framework of functional and functorial relations shedding light on aspects of algebraic topology and geometry, etc., on the one hand—in which the assertion of existence axioms is unnecessary—and as a foundational approach to mathematics generally, purportedly providing an interesting alternative to set-theoretic foundations, on the other—for which the assertion of existence axioms is essential. In its latter role, the austere language of objects and arrows is used to define what it is to be a "natural-numbers object" (that is, structure), with arrows having this object as domain and codomain representing the natural numbers, and it is then stipulated that such a category occurs as part of a large category (for example, a topos), either of sets or of categories. Thus the *description* of the infinite is new, but, as with set theory, there is no attempt to *derive* this form of axiom of infinity from anything more fundamental.

What about constructive alternatives to classical mathematics, such as intuitionism, Bishop constructivism, etc.? We need not dwell on these for present purposes, since the classical notion of a "completed" ("objective") infinite totality is one of the main things to which these programs object and which they seek to live without. This too is, of course, not a failure except in the sense of "a failure to take seriously." Really what we have is a *change of subject* leading to a thorough reworking of analysis and other areas based on ideas of "the potentially infinite," framed in terms of rules of construction, paradigmatically of indefinitely many items of a sequence, for example, serving as natural numbers, values of constructive functions, etc.

Finally, the semiconstructive approach of *predicativism* retains classical logic (including the laws of excluded middle, double negation elimination, proof of existence by *reductio*, etc.) but restricts set-existence principles to sets that can be explicitly defined using formulas quantifying only over "already recognized or accepted" objects (made precise in various axiomatic systems developed by Feferman et al.).[13] When it comes to infinite sets, the usual procedure is just to start by taking the set of natural numbers for granted. This may seem justified on practical grounds if one's main interest is in reconstructing analysis. But it seems unfortunate as a matter of principle when we recall that the logicist reconstructions of arithmetic (of both Frege and Dedekind) resorted to *paradigmatically impredicative definitions* (essentially the method of introducing the minimal closure of a set under a unary operation). As an improvement, alternatively, one can start with a weak theory of finite sets and classes, but even here, axioms on individuals immediately imply a countable infinitude of objects forming a class.[14] No uncountable infinities are recognized, but again, the countably infinite is in effect simply postulated at the outset, not derived from anything else.

Let us now proceed to the new modal-structural approach via a form of modal reflection together with extendability principles.[15]

III. Reflections on Reflection

Let us begin by reviewing the first-order reflection scheme of ZF(C). Let $\phi(x_1,...,x_n)$ be a first-order formula (without abstraction terms) with just the x_i free, let V_β be a term for the βth rank, and let $\phi^{V_\beta}(x_1,...,x_n)$ be the result of restricting all quantifiers in ϕ to V_β:

$$\forall \alpha \exists \beta > \alpha \forall x_1,...,x_n \in V_\beta \, [\phi(x_1,...,x_n) \leftrightarrow \qquad (RF_0)$$
$$\phi^{V_\beta}(x_1,...,x_n)]$$

This can be read: "The true situation (in the universe of sets) is reflected in arbitrarily high levels of the cumulative hierarchy." In any case, all instances of this scheme are provable in ZF, which we may summarize as:

Theorem 1 (*ZF*): All instances of the scheme (RF_0).

Interestingly, there is a converse, although some care must be taken in specifying the system in which it is proved. Drake suggests Scott's axioms for ZF based on cumulative levels.[16] This is summarized as:

Theorem 2 (*Scott's Axioms of Extensionality, Separation, Accumulation, and Restriction*): (Suitable instances of) (RF_0) → Replacement Scheme & Infinity.

The modal-structural approach, however, does not like the usual reading of (RF_0), even less such a reading of second- or higher-order reflection principles, as such readings make reference, at least implicitly, to a single fixed universe of sets, at odds with unrestricted extendability, (EP). Is there an alternative way to read reflection principles more in harmony with the structuralist spirit of Replacement as a largeness condition on structures of interest? Yes, quite simply, as follows:

We are interested in structures so large that certain attempts to describe them fail to distinguish them from various proper initial segments—hence small fragments—of them.

In the first-order case, ZF already implies that no finite information about the items succeeds in marking such a distinction. (NB: (RF_0) has no generalization to countably infinite sets of sentences, due to Gödel's Second Incompleteness Theorem; and its ZF^1-provability shows that ZF^1 is not finitely axiomatizable.)

Treating Reflection, like Replacement, as a largeness condition helping characterize structures of interest is a first step in bringing reflection principles within the purview of the modal-structural program. But more is required if we are to transcend the limits of (ZF-demonstrable) first-order reflection. For instance, once we introduce a second-order principle, we risk commitment to "the universe of sets" as is evident from the form of a second-order reflection scheme (investigated by Tait[17]):

$$\forall X[\Phi(X) \rightarrow \exists \beta (\Phi^\beta(X \cap V_\beta)], \qquad (RF_1 X)$$

in which $\Phi(X)$ is a set-theoretic condition with free second-order variable, X, and Φ^β designates the formula with quantifiers restricted to sets of rank $< \beta$. The problem is that, here, there is no relativization of the second-order quantifier, $\forall X$, to a domain, and this invites an absolutist interpretation involving the class of "all sets," the class of "all ordinals," etc., alien to the modal structural approach. The challenge, then, is somehow to bring principles like $(RF)_{1X}$ within the *relativized*, modal second-order framework.

The strategy which we now propose utilizes the Putnam translation scheme for unbounded set-theoretic sentences, extended to include second-order sentences, as deployed in *MWON*, ch. 2. The basic idea is to treat unbounded universal (respectively, existential) set quantifiers not as ranging over elements of a fixed, maximal universe, but as ranging over any items of any (respectively, some) model of the set-theory we are considering that there might be. More precisely, we relativize such quantifiers to the domain of any (respectively, some) possible extension of any model "already assumed" as illustrated by, say, the Axiom of Inaccessibles:

$$\forall \alpha \exists \beta > \alpha[Inac(\beta)]. \qquad (AI)$$

The Putnam translate of this, call it AI_{PT} is

$$AI_{PT} = \Box \forall M, \alpha \in |M| \; \Diamond \exists M', \beta \in |M'|[M' > M \; \& \qquad (AI_P T)$$
$$\beta > \alpha \; \& \; Inac(\beta)].$$

In this manner, all unbounded quantifiers of the original sentence become relativized to models in the modal translate, as desired. Only the modal quantifiers over models are unrelativized, which is as it should be. It is straightforward to generalize this pattern to sentences with any finite number of unbounded quantifiers,[18] and to allow unbounded second-order quantifiers as well.[19]

Now we can utilize the Putnam translation scheme to formulate an appropriate MS reflection scheme as follows: Given a first- or second-order set-theoretic sentence S with unbounded quantifiers, take its Putnam translate, S_{PT}, to express the antecedent of an instance of MS reflection on S, that is, S_{PT} replaces, by a kind of approximation to "absolute infinity," the condition in ordinary reflection principles that expresses that S "holds in the set-theoretic universe." It does this in a manner appropriate to MS in that it considers what holds in arbitrary extensions of set-theoretic models (as possibilities). The conclusion, then, of such a reflection principle simply asserts that it is possible that S itself holds in some set-theoretic model, that is, that, with respect to what S says about sets, it fails to discriminate between arbitrary extensions of models and some fixed model. Summarizing, then, the form of MS reflection is this:

$$S_{PT} \rightarrow \Diamond \exists M[\text{``}M \text{ models } T \& S\text{''}], \qquad (MSR)$$

where T stands for a set theory (or a precursor) already "secured" (that is, such that the possible existence of a model is already accepted), and where "models $T \& S$" abbreviates the result of writing out the axioms of $T \& S$ with quantifiers relativized to the domain $|M|$ of M (officially treated with a plural variable), replacing occurrences of $\in$ with a term referring to the binary relation playing the role of $\in$ in M.

Thus, we can supplement the motivation for reflection principles framed above in terms of our interest in studying "large structures" as follows:

The mathematical possibilities of ever larger structures (of appropriate type) are so vast as to be "indescribable": whatever condition we attempt to lay down to characterize that vastness fails in the following sense: if indeed it is accurate regarding the possibilities of mathematical structures, it is also accurate regarding a mere segment of them, where such a segment can be taken as a single structure (of the relevant type).

This is the intuitive idea that MSR attempts to capture formally.

Applying this to our example, the axiom of inaccessibles, AI, we see that AI_{PT} holds for $T = ZF^2C$, as it follows from the quasicategoricity of second-order models of ZF^2C that the height of any is a strongly inaccessible cardinal, and by extendability, (EP), that cardinal appears as a "set" in any proper extension satisfying the definition of such a cardinal. Thus, this instance of MSR yields the possibility of AI's holding in a single possible model. The height of such will then be a fixed point in the enumeration of strongly inaccessibles, that is, a strongly inaccessible κ with κ-many strongly inaccessibles beneath it, that is, a *hyperinaccessible*. Evidently the combination of *MSR* and EP has climbing potential.

As it stands, however, we cannot lay down *all* instances of *MSR* on pain of contradiction. This is because there are cases of set-theoretic sentences *refutable* in standard systems of set theory whose Putnam translates nevertheless are true (given basic principles of MS, for example, EP). For an instructive example,[20] consider the sentence expressing that every class is coextensive with some set, that is, $\forall X \exists y \forall z[X(z) \leftrightarrow z \in y]$. Obviously this leads to contradiction via Russell's paradox, or Cantor's, that is, instantiate on X with the class of all z such that $z \notin z$ to obtain Russell's paradox, with the class of all z such that $z = z$ to obtain Cantor's, etc. However, the Putnam translate of this sentence looks like this:

$$\Box \forall M, X \subseteq |M| \, \Diamond \exists M' \succ M \exists y \in |M'| \Box \forall M'', z \in |M''| \, [X(z) \leftrightarrow z \in y],$$

which follows easily from the fact that in any extension M' of M, say of height κ, the κth rank exists and has the domain $|M|$ of M occurring as a set. Thus, this instance of *MSR* would have it that possibly there is a set-theoretic model of the original S, which is impossible. One obvious solution, adopted here, is to restrict *MSR* explicitly to sentences S that are consistent with the accepted set theory, T.[21]

Proceeding a bit further with the example of AI, we arrived at

$$\Diamond \exists M[\text{``}M \text{ models} \wedge \text{ZF}^2\text{C \& AI''}].$$

As already noted, such M would itself have inaccessible height κ with κ-many inaccessibles below it, that is, κ hyperinaccessible. Now this process can be iterated, for example, by applying *MSR* to $T = \text{ZF}^2\text{C} + \text{AI}$, and $S =$ the axiom of hyperinaccessibles, namely:

$$\forall \alpha \exists \beta \succ \alpha[Hyperinac(\beta)], \hspace{2cm} \text{(AHyperI)}$$

observing that EP yields the antecedent, AHyperI_{PT}, whence we have $\Diamond \exists M[\text{``}M \text{ models ZF}^2\text{C \& AHyperI''}]$, and so on. Stronger extendability principles can be devised that, with *MSR,* imply the possibility of α-hyperinaccessibles, arbitrary ordinal α from a given model of, say, $T = \text{ZF}^2\text{C} + \text{AHypI}$.

Such methods allow us to climb much further,[22] but let us look back down and see how we could have obtained *the very first* strongly inaccessible cardinal, the countably infinite, using a suitable instance of MSR together with a variant of EP. Let T be the theory, I, with just the nonlogical axiom $\exists x(x = x)$. Now let us adopt a special case of extendability principle restricted to models of I with finite domains of atomic individuals:

$$\Box\forall M[\text{"the } |M| \text{ are finitely many"} \rightarrow \qquad\qquad \text{(FEP)}$$
$$\Diamond\exists M'(\text{"the } |M'| \text{ are finitely many"} \;\&\; |M'| \supsetneqq |M|)],$$

where "the atoms X are finitely many" can be spelled out in terms of the principle of "finite-set induction," applied to mereological fusions of atoms. (That is, the atoms X are *finitely many* if their fusion is one among every plurality among which occurs an atom and among which occurs the adjunction (fusion) of any of them with one new atom.") Now let us define "*X is infinite*" to mean: $\exists M[|M|$ is finite $\&\ |M| \subsetneqq X] \;\&\; \forall M[|M| \subsetneqq X \;\&\; |M|$ is finite $\rightarrow \exists M'(|M'| \subsetneqq X \;\&\; |M'| \supsetneqq |M| \;\&\; |M'|$ is finite$)]$.[23] (We can then define "the X are countably infinite" as "the X are infinite $\&\ \forall Y[$the Y are infinite $\rightarrow \exists f(f$ maps X 1-1 into $Y)]$".) Now consider the instance of MSR for the formula S: $\forall M[|M|$ finite $\rightarrow \exists M'(|M'|$ finite $\&\ |M'| \supsetneqq |M|)]$. Then S_{PT} is equivalent to FEP! Then the conclusion of this instance of MSR is

$$\Diamond\exists L[L \text{ models I } \&\ S],[24]$$

which implies that possibly there is an infinite totality (or plurality) L, which is an appropriate modal-structural (first) axiom of infinity.[25]

Let us conclude this section by considering two important extensions of this form of argument. First, let us show how it leads from the countably infinite to the *un*countably infinite. Let S' be the sentence: "Any countably infinitely many X's have a proper extension X' which are countably infinite," that is:

$$\forall X[\text{"the } X \text{ are countably infinite"} \rightarrow \exists X'(X' \supsetneqq X \;\&\; \text{"the } X' \text{ are countably infinite"})].$$

Then the Putnam translate of this, S'_{PT}, follows from a (clearly acceptable) extendability principle, that every possible countable infinity of objects can be properly extended to another. Now from the previous result on the possibility of an infinitude of objects, it follows easily that it is possible that there is a *countable* infinitude of objects. Applying a suitable instance of MSR, that is, to the conjunction of S and S', then yields

$$\Diamond\exists Y[\exists X \subsetneqq Y \;\&\; \text{"the } X \text{ are countably infinite"} \;\&\; \text{"the } Y \text{ model } S'\text{"}].$$

It follows that such Y cannot be countably infinite (otherwise they would have to include a proper extension of themselves, as relativization to them as domain satisfying S' requires).

Clearly this pattern of argument can be repeated indefinitely to obtain larger and larger transfinite cardinalities. (With the addition of a form of axiom of choice, it will be laborious but routine to generate Cantor's alephs.) Much more efficiently, however, one obtains all the (accessible) transfinite cardinals of ZF^2C by Replacement[2], the possibility of which is itself easily derived from MSR along with EP applied to models of Z^2C. Let S be the second-order statement of Replacement namely:

$$\forall F \forall x \exists y[\text{``}F \text{ a function defined on } x\text{''} \rightarrow y = F[x]],$$

where the consequent says that y is the forward image of F on x, that is, contains exactly all $F(b)$ for $b \in x$. The Putnam translate, R^2_{PT}, of this is clearly correct according to EP (as, for any F relative to any standard Z^2C model, M, its forward image on any "set" of M is either already a "set" of M or is certainly a subset, in which case it occurs as a "set" in any proper extension of M). Applying MSR to R^2 then directly yields

$$\Diamond \exists M[\text{``}M \text{ models } Z^2C \ \& \ R^2\text{''} \text{ (i.e. } M \text{ models } ZF^2C)].$$

This brings us "full circle,"[26] and so appropriately concludes this section.

IV. COMPARISON WITH SET THEORY

The closest analogue in set theory of the derivation of the Axiom of Infinity just presented is probably what we called Theorem 2 above, the derivation from Scott's axioms of the Axiom of Infinity (along with the Replacement scheme) from the first-order Reflection scheme, RF_0. Obviously that is much weaker, however, as it uses only first-order Reflection and cannot get us beyond ZF^1C. But even with regard to the Axiom of Infinity *per se*, that theorem is weaker in a significant way than the MS result above. For it builds upon the "actual infinity" of hereditarily finite sets, forming a model of the basic Scott system (and of ZC minus Infinity), that is, one has to embrace infinitely many finite sets "all together" in a single structure as input to the theorem, which then delivers the missing set of all of them. In contrast, the hypothesis of the MS derivation merely uses the possibility of ever extending a given hypothetical finite structure by a finite increment, *something any constructivist accepts*. Only in the conclusion of the theorem does a "completed infinity" appear in a single structure. From the MS standpoint, it is only slightly exaggerating to say that the first-order proof engages in circular reasoning, beginning as it does with infinitely many finite things within a single structure. The conclusion then only adds what the language of plurals takes as already evident, the legitimacy of introducing a term referring to "all of them" at once, but of course in singularist fashion by reifying "all of them" as "the set of them."[27] In the MS proof, getting infinitely many things together in a common structure is the heart of the matter, and that's the conclusion of the argument, expressed with a monadic plural variable. It is of course possible to step up one level (invoking EP again) so that one can speak of an individual functioning as a "set" of all the finite domains (already taken as "sets" in all proper extensions of their respective original models). This last step is, in comparison with the main task, a modest addendum. The conclusion to be drawn is that MSR is indeed far more powerful than RF_0, and it helps earn its keep by enabling a genuine derivation of the infinite out of the finite.

In conclusion, let us say something about our view of the modal-structural framework as "foundational" vis-à-vis Putnam's announced "anti-foundationalist" stance in his "Mathematics without Foundations." Here my sense is that there is less difference in substantive views than in our rhetoric. As other writings of mine make clear, I do have a pluralistic view of mathematical foundations, and I have cited with approval Feferman's remark from a famous paper of 1977 dealing with category theory and foundations, that to understand mathematics as a whole, given its complex nature, we may need several approaches, that perhaps no single one that we can devise will be fully adequate for all recognized purposes.[28] Feferman suggested this might be the case regarding constructive foundations vs. classical. But perhaps it also is true of set-theoretic, category-theoretic, and modal-structural foundations. Each has valuable insights to contribute not readily seen in the others, but then none can claim exclusive superiority on all relevant counts. In the cases of set theory versus modal-structural mathematics, the former contributes a uniform explication of "mathematical possibility" via a rigorous definition of "satisfaction in a structured set"; but as we have seen, it pays a price with its fixed, maximal universe of sets and ordinals, whereas MS reaps significant advantages from abandoning this in favor of unrestricted extendability and its modal reflection axioms, including strong motivation of the infinite from below, including even generating the infinite out of the finite, as we have just seen. For different purposes, each approach is valuable; and it says something significant about our subject that, so far, no single framework has been devised which reaps all the advantages and none of the disadvantages at once. An analogy with the pro's and con's of first- and second-order axiom systems suggests itself: the former benefit from logically complete proof procedures, but they suffer from expressive weakness; whereas second-order systems (in well-known key cases) are categorical, fully characterizing their intended structures, but the logic cannot be recursively axiomatized. As Gödel's work tells us, this reflects the nature of our subject and cannot be avoided. Thus we need both sorts of axiom systems, but for different purposes. My guess is that Putnam would endorse all of this, suggesting that any difference between us in this area is really rhetorical: whereas he wrote "Mathematics without Foundatons," I might have written instead "Mathematics with Multiple Foundations." But clearly more work needs to be done to sustain such pluralism while at the same time showing how to avoid "double-think" ("multi-think"?) and even outright inconsistencies (on the metamathematical level).[29] But philosophy thrives when papers end by indicating more work to be done.

GEOFFREY HELLMAN

UNIVERSITY OF MINNESOTA
JULY 2010

NOTES

1. Hilary Putnam, "Mathematics without Foundations," *Mathematics, Matter, and Method: Philosophical Papers*, vol. 1 (Cambridge: Cambridge University Press 1967), 43–59.

2. A model of Zermelo (or Zermelo-Fraenkel) set theory is standard in Putnam's sense just in case (1) it is well-founded (no infinite descending membership chains), and (2) power sets are maximal.

3. As Putnam intended, this is to be understood formally, not as introducing a new category of objects called "possible worlds" or "possible models."

4. Hartry Field, *Science without Numbers* (Princeton: Princeton University Press, 1980).

5. See, for example, Stewart Shapiro, "Conservativeness and Incompleteness," *Journal of Philosophy* 80, no. 9 (1983): 521–31.

6. Geoffrey Hellman, *Mathematics without Numbers: Towards a Modal-Structural Interpretation* (Oxford: Oxford University Press 1989).

7. George Boolos, "Nominalist Platonism," *Philosophical Review* 94 (1985): 327–44.

8. John Burgess, A. P. Hazen, and Daniel Lewis, "Appendix on Pairing" in Daniel Lewis, *Parts of Classes* (Oxford: Blackwell, 1991).

9. Geoffrey Hellman, "Structuralism without Structures," *Philosophia Mathematica* 4, no. 2 (1996): 100–123.

10. Ernst Zermelo, "Über Grenzzahlen und Mengenbereiche: Neue Untersuchungen über die Grundlagen der Mengenlehre," *Fundamenta Mathematicae* 16 (1930): 29–47.

11. Hilary Putnam, "Set Theory: Realism, Replacement, and Modality," in *Philosophy in an Age of Science*, ed. Maria De Caro and David Macarthur (Cambridge, MA: Harvard University Press, 2012).

12. Bob Hale, "Structuralism's Unpaid Epistemological Debts," *Philosophia Mathematica* 4, no. 2 (1996): 124–47.

13. See Soloman Feferman, *In the Light of Logic* (Oxford: Oxford University Press 1998) for examples and further references.

14. See Soloman Feferman and Geoffrey Hellman, "Predicative Foundations of Arithmetic," *Journal of Philosophical Logic* 24 (1995): 1–17.

15. As indicated above, extendability is a key principle of Zermelo's "Über Grenzzahlen und Mengenbereiche" and Putnam's "Mathematics without Foundations," that any model of, say, second-order Zermelo set theory with Choice, Z^2C, can be properly extended, which we formalize as

$$\Box \forall M \Diamond \exists M'[M' \succ_e M],$$

where the variables range over standard models of Z^2C and where $\succ_e$ means "is a proper end-extension of." Analogous principles can be invoked for models of any set theory (or suitable precursor theories) that one likes.

16. F. R. Drake, *Set Theory: An Introduction to Large Cardinals* (Amsterdam: North Holland, 1977).

17. W. W. Tait, "Constructing Cardinals from Below," in *The Provenence of Pure Reason* (Oxford: Oxford University Press, 2005), ch. 6

18. One first transforms the sentence to prenex form and then proceeds from left to right, as illustrated in the example.

19. Relativizing a universal second-order monadic quantifier, $\forall X[...]$ to a domain D means writing $\forall X[X \subseteq D \rightarrow ...]$; a second-order monadic existential, $\exists X[...]$, goes over to $\exists X[X \subseteq D \ \& \ [...]$. ($\subseteq$ is defined in the obvious way via second-order or plural predication.) Generalization to polyadic second-order quantifiers is straightforward.

20. Pointed out to me by Øystein Linnebo in correspondence.

21. As this volume was in the final stages of preparation for printing, it emerged that MSR, even with the restriction to sentences consistent with the underlying set theory, has instances leading to contradiction. Now it may be that a further restriction could be found that is well-motivated and (demonstrably) restores consistency. There is, however, at least one alternative means of introducing second-order reflection (say of form (RF$_1$), above) into the modal-structural framework, one that is clearly consistent relative to relevant standard set-theoretic axioms. Just as MS postulates the possibility of models of ZF^2C and extensions thereof, it can postulate the possibility of a structure, S, so vast as to be "indescribable," as formalized by (RF$_1$) itself. (Here the initial universal quantifier on X is relativized to the domain of S, despite standard set theory's unrelativized formulation, acknowledged above.) If the other axioms are taken, e.g. as those of Z^2C less the Axiom of Infinity, then the latter along with Replacement[2] and small large-cardinal extensions through the indescribables will demonstrably hold of the postulated structure (following from standard set-theoretic results). In contrast to standard set theory, however, where reflection principles generally are postulated of "all sets" or "the universe, V," S has a proper extension, i.e. EP remains exceptionless, as desired. While the informal motivation for this procedure is indeed somewhat different from that given above for MSR, in that no reference need be made to "(all) the possibilities [of structures]," that is in one way a virtue in not encouraging the idea of "ultimate totalities," even if plurally and modally described, anathema to the MS program.

A more detailed presentation of this option will appear in my contribution to *Logic, Philosophy of Mathematics, and Their History: Essays in Honor of W.W. Tait*, ed. Erich H. Reck.

22. See the forthcoming paper cited in the previous note.

23. Of course, we already have available the notion "the atoms X are not finitely many," which would serve, but this second definition is convenient in relation to the notion of extendability of domains.

Note also that the restriction to finite subpluralities in this definition is necessary: were it simply dropped (and not replaced by any other restriction), the result would fail to define anything, as the domain X less a single atom would lack any proper extension as a proper subplurality of the X. And, of course, if the requirement "proper subplurality of the X" were replaced with mere "subplurality of the X," then the X themselves would violate the resulting condition, lacking any proper extension $X \subseteq X$!

24. "L models S" means $\forall M [|M| \subset L$ & $|M|$ finite $\rightarrow \exists M' (|M'| \subset L$ & $|M'|$ finite & $M' \succ M)]$.

25. Note the role of MSR in enabling us to pass from the mere possibility of proceeding to ever larger finite multiplicities to (the possibility of) a single "world" or model in which all such multiplicities are represented (that is, up to one-to-one correspondence).

26. Recall that it was Putnam's inference that the correctness of his modal translation of Replacement justifies our taking it as an axiom that led to these developments.

27. As suggested in the introduction, these remarks apply also—*mutatis mutandis*—to the neologicist derivation of the axiom infinity from "Hume's principle" together with second-order logical comprehension.

28. Soloman Feferman, "Categorical Foundations and Foundations of Category Theory," in *Foundations of Mathematics and Computability Theory*, ed. R. E. Butts and Jaakko Hintikka (Dordrecht: Reidel, 1977), 149–69.

29. Geoffrey Hellman and J. L. Bell, "Pluralism and the Foundations of Mathematics," in *Scientific Pluralism*, Minnesota Studies in Philosophy of Science XIX, ed. C. K. Waters, H. Longino, and S. Kellert (Minneapolis: University of Minnesota Press, 2006).

REPLY TO GEOFFREY HELLMAN

With exemplary clarity, Hellman describes the sketch of a "modal logical interpretation of mathematics" in my 1967 article, "Mathematics without Foundations" and his own impressive contribution in turning that sketch into a detailed proposal for understanding the whole of classical (pure and applied) mathematics. That contribution was much more than just a "working out of the details" of what I had suggested. It had long been recognized that "objectualist" interpretations[1] of second-order logic are problematic, because they require a domain of "all properties" (or, for Frege, "all concepts") which cannot be the same as the "all sets" of Zermelo set theory and its successors (problematic as that totality already is from a structuralist point of view). It cannot be the totality of all sets, because one of the applications we want to be able to make of second-order logic is to express the fact that a formula of logic (first-order logic, logic with branching quantifiers, or what have you) is true under *all* interpretations, including ones in which the relevant domain of things is too *big* to be a set (for example, interpretations of a formula over the "universe" of "all sets"). And to say that the "properties" quantified over in second-order logic are all the sets *plus* all the "proper classes" just pushes the problem "upstairs." (What are "proper classes" anyway, but more *sets* under another name?) However, Boolos realized that monadic second-order logic can be interpreted as *plural quantification* over individuals, and a fortiori as not introducing any additional ontology. Hellman saw that as the aim of modal-structuralism: to show a way to be fully realistic (as opposed to intuitionist, finitist, constructivist, predicativist, etc.), *but not objectualist* in one's interpretation of classical mathematics, and Boolos's aim of showing a way to be fully realistic but not objectualist in one's interpretation of an important part of second-order logic, complement each other beautifully. He also brought in other resources from mereology that are equally free of "abstract entities." And he used these resources to great effect in his *Mathematics without Numbers.*[2]

Of course, critics have raised many objections to this whole program. I have replied at such length to Steven J. Wagner's searching paper in the present volume to make clear how I respond to the objectors, and to present my view of the *rationale* for modal structuralism, and rather than repeat all that here, I refer the reader to that reply. Let me just say this much: the Benacerraf problem, in particular, seems to me to be the Achilles's heel which in the end proves fatal to objectualist pictures of mathematics. But it is not the *only* fatal or near fatal problem for objectualism; a second problem, which I did not take the occasion to mention in my "Reply to Wagner," is that if there is a totality of objects (say, "all sets") that mathematics is *about* then it needs to be an *extendable* totality. Modal structuralism has the resources to make sense of the notion of an extendable totality; I have not seen any objectualist account of this crucial notion.

Turning from the philosophical virtues of modal structuralism to its mathematical virtues, Hellman has recently joined the idea of "extendable totalities" as *possible totalities which themselves have possible extensions*, proposed in my 1967 paper (Hellman calls it my "extendability principle," and he also found it in "Zermelo's then underappreciated 1930 paper") with a powerful modal structuralist reflection principle ("MSR") of his own, thus opening a whole new approach to the subject of large cardinal axioms. I am thrilled by the possibilities here.

Of course, caution is in order. Reflection principles have in the past sometimes proved inconsistent! I will disclose (with Hellman's permission) some recent correspondence between us on this topic.

I. A TECHNICAL QUESTION

The question I put to Hellman is this: "if you accept all instances of MSR with S consistent with the accepted set theory T, what happens if two of the instances are not consistent with (the conjunction of T with) each other? Or if S is omega-inconsistent?"

To the first part of my disjunctive question, Hellman's response was (as I in fact expected) to write:[3]

> Suppose that S and S' are inconsistent with one another but each separately is consistent with the accepted set theory. Suppose further that one could prove (in our modal logic plus extendability principles, etc.) the Putnam translates of S and of S'. Then what follows? Merely that possibly a model of the set theory satisfies S and that a model satisfies S'. Nothing requires that those two models have a common extension. Instead, we would have a branching structure of possibilities. E.g., let T be ZFC + Axiom of Inaccessibles (or Mahlo's, or other small large cardinals) and let S be that there exists an Erdös

cardinal, and S' that there does not. Then one branch of models would include one with an Erdös cardinal, and another would not. No inconsistency there.

And to the second half of my disjunctive question (about which I am more concerned) the response[4] was:

> It all depends on how strictly we want to construe "mathematical possibility" (say in connection with set theory). Given our second-order resources, we can express the "standard model" of, e.g., Z, ZF, ZFC + Axiom of Inaccessibles, etc., and, if we wish, we can stipulate that all models be standard (well founded, with full power sets). That's the way I've been thinking about models of ZF^2C (+ various small, large cardinal axioms) all along. But then, you make a good point that, in applying MSR, we had better also require omega-consistency with the set theory to avoid the unwelcome conclusion that such things as non-standard numbers are possible. (It would be nice to see an example where the Putnam translate of an omega-inconsistent statement is derivable in our 2d-order logic cum possibility axioms. I haven't thought one up yet, but there may well be such.) In effect, on this option, we don't want to be forced to recognize non-standard models as genuinely possible.

On the other hand, we could, more liberally, allow nonstandard models as genuine possibilities (conceding this much to Quine and the first-orderists). Then my guess is that omega-inconsistent sentences with true Putnam translates will simply force us to recognize certain nonstandard models, much as Gödel's incompleteness theorems did. (I have a mild preference for this latter option. It has the expected virtues of liberalism, while still allowing us to use our second-order resources to restrict attention to standard models, e.g. in considering whether CH is determinate, etc.)

With this amendment to Hellman's paper, I am in agreement. Hellman's closing paragraph begins: "In conclusion, let us say something about our view of the modal-structural framework as "foundational" vis-à-vis Putnam's announced 'anti-foundationalist' stance in his "Mathematics without Foundations." I note that since my lecture "Set Theory: Realism, Replacement, and Modality" that Hellman recalls receiving a copy of in 2009,[5] I have become, not indeed more "foundationalist" in an epistemological sense, but less ecumenical with respect to objectualism. My reasons have been described above and in the reply to Wagner. As for constructivism, and predicativism, I do not believe that either is compatible with a scientific realist attitude to physical science, as I have argued elsewhere.[6] But I do agree with Hellman that "to understand mathematics as a whole, given its complex nature, we may need several approaches, that perhaps no single one that we can devise will be fully adequate for all recognized purposes."

H.P.

NOTES

1. I take the term "objectualist" from Steve Wagner's paper in the present volume.

2. The resources of plural quantification were brought into the modal-structuralist program in Hellman's paper, "Structuralism without Structures," *Philosophia Mathematica* 4 (1996): 100–123.

3. Personal communication.

4. Personal communication.

5. The lecture was actually given in Princeton, at a conference in May 2007, in honor of Paul Benacerraf. It is collected in *Philosophy in an Age of Science*, 217–34.

6. See the Appendix to "Indispensability Arguments in the Philosophy of Mathematics" in *Philosophy in an Age of Science*, 181–201.

6

Charles Travis

ENGAGING

How do we engage with the world in thought? Putnam's answer to that question changes, among other things, the way we need to engage with philosophy itself. But its import, particularly in that respect, is often missed. One reason, perhaps, is that Putnam's answer is often confused with, or assimilated to, another—one running in a diametrically opposed direction. This is an attempt to set the record straight.

Quine published "Two Dogmas of Empiricism" in 1951. In 1962, Putnam published "The Analytic and the Synthetic." By 1962, Quine was widely held to have demolished that distinction. Why, then, did Putnam bother with what *seems* to be just a second proof? A superficial answer is that Putnam in fact defended an attenuated analytic/synthetic distinction. That does show that Quine and Putnam had very different points to make. Quine's claim was that the very idea of analyticity is senseless. That cannot be Putnam's. In fact, though, most of Putnam's essay was an attack on analyticity, or at least on what philosophers had supposed that notion to be. There are two reasons why it was well worthwhile. First, Putnam's points are very different from and run much deeper than Quine's. Putnam showed something fundamental about the form of human thought—about, as one might put it, our cognitive economies. More specifically, he showed in what way our thought is, and thus how it could be, under the control of the world—responsive to the way things are. Putnam's point matters crucially to how nearly any philosophical problem may be fruitfully discussed, whereas Quine, as I will try to show, was just expressing empiricist prejudice. Second, Quine's arguments are not cogent. Putnam's are. Seeing Putnam and Quine together as jointly having made something called "the case against analyticity" loses sight of what Putnam had to say. Recent philosophy not infrequently goes astray in just that way.

In this essay, I will first identify some main features of Quine's case. I will then, in condensed form, say what Putnam's point is—in one way among many that this might be said. Finally, I will consider one example of a philosopher who, though he thinks (perhaps rightly) that he accepts Quine's case against analyticity, is the worse off for missing Putnam's point. The example I choose is Christopher Peacocke. I choose him because, first, he is very clear about what he is up to, and, second, he is a particularly clear case of missing the point.

I. INTRODUCTION

Writing of "Two Dogmas," Putnam once said,

> At a superficial level, what is going on in "Two Dogmas of Empiricism" looks quite simple. . . . Quine is going to show us that there is no sense to be made of the notion of analyticity by showing that all of the suggested definitions lead in circles. But . . . it is puzzling why this is supposed to be a good argument. . . . a mere demonstration of definitional circularity would hardly seem to be enough to overthrow as widely accepted and used a notion as the notion of analyticity.[1]

He went on to suggest that Quine's real argument against analyticity (or a priority) lies elsewhere, in what Putnam describes as a normative history of science. I will take up that other argument in the next section. But Quine took the argument Putnam dismisses very seriously. In its several variants, it occupies at least three quarters of "Two Dogmas." Seeing, in general outline, why the argument would impress Quine will help identify what is left to his case when it is removed.

Arguing in the way Putnam dismisses merely reflects, I think, Quine's very traditional form of empiricism, which, takes in broad outline the following shape. Quine supposes that there is a class of privileged facts. Quine is prepared to tell us what these facts are. Roughly, they are what is "really" observable as to how things are. There may then be, he allows, other nonprivileged or not obviously privileged facts only insofar as these are analyzable in terms of privileged facts. At the very least, "analyzable" means that we can specify what would be a proof of the obtaining of such a fact, where the proof appealed only to privileged facts, and we can do so in such a way that there would be such proofs (in favorable enough circumstances). (Quine supposes a notion of proof such that the obtaining of what proves a nonprivileged fact leaves no logical possibility of that fact's nonobtaining. So in effect, what is demanded is that, for any nonprivileged fact, there be some set of privileged ones that are logically equivalent to it.) Ultimately, for Quine, the privileged facts are facts about our own sensations. For working purposes, though, when it is facts about language that are the nonprivileged facts that concern us, we may suppose privileged facts to be facts about behavior of speakers of a language, where "behavior" is used in a familiar proprietary sense—roughly, mere bodily movements.[2]

In "Two Dogmas," Quine sets out to pass various supposed linguistic phenomena through this framework, to see whether, by these standards, there could really be facts of the supposed sorts at all. The key notions are analyticity, synonymy, and meaning. We can see how that attempt plays out by looking at Quine's treatment of Carnap. Carnap proposes that for an artificial language one might just have a rule that recursively specified a set of sentences that, by the rule, were to be true. Those sentences, true no matter what, would be the analytic ones. Abstracting from the notion of a rule, Carnap's idea was this: If one creates an artificial language, one is free to stipulate what the language is going to be (as long as one does so coherently). One of the things one may stipulate is that certain sentences of the language are to be true. What stipulation does is this: one will be speaking the language in question, or something is a given instance of speaking it, just in case the stipulations in question hold of the language one speaks. So one would be speaking Carnap's artificial language and a given sentence one produced would be a sentence of that language only if the rule that such-and-such sentences were to be true held of the language one was speaking, or of that sentence produced.

Carnap's idea can be extended to natural language. His proposed rule stipulates that certain sentences are to have a certain role. That role is to be true no matter what. Expressions of a natural language do not, as a rule, have properties by stipulation. But one might hypothesize that there are sentences, for example, of English that do play the role just specified: their role, or an essential part of it, is to be true no matter what. That, of course, would leave it open which English sentences these were. I will return to that presently. First, though, consider Quine's reaction to all this. Quine allows that Carnap's rule might be clear enough. It might be clear enough, that is, which sentences of his artificial language are the ones whose function is to be true (no matter what). And, unlike Putnam, Quine does not question our powers of stipulation. But, he thinks, Carnap's proposal is no help in allowing us to understand what it is for a sentence to be analytic. Why not? Here is what Quine says:

> Still, there is really no progress. Instead of appealing to an unexplained word "analytic," we are now appealing to an unexplained phrase "semantical rule."

Not every true statement which says that the statements of some class are true can count as a semantical rule—otherwise *all* truths would be "analytic" in the sense of being true according to semantical rules. Semantical rules are distinguishable, apparently, only by the fact of appearing on a page under the heading "Semantical Rules"; and the heading is itself then meaningless.[3]

But this is manifestly unfair to Carnap. We already know something about semantical rules. They are stipulations that fix what it is for something to be the language in question. Call the language L. Then a given bit of discourse is, in fact, in L—*inter alia*, it consists of L-ish sentences—only if those stipulations hold of it. So if it is stipulated that such-and-such sentence of L is true no matter what, then any given bit of the discourse is an instance of that sentence only if it is true no matter what. That seems clear enough. And since I really have not specified any particular artificial language in saying all this, it seems that we have at least one clear way that an artificial language may contain analytic sentences and distinguish them from others. What more do you want?

Carnap has specified the role that an analytic sentence is to play: its role is to be true (no matter how things are). In the case of an artificial language, he has said how it is that a sentence comes by that role: by stipulation as to what it is for something to be *that* sentence of that language. If one finds all that in order—as Quine does—it is unfair then to complain that "semantical rule" is an empty term. Insofar as it is empty, we can dispense with that. Of course, to get to a notion of analyticity in a natural language we separated those two things that Carnap did. We abstracted the role he assigned an analytic sentence from his account of the way a sentence in an artificial language came by that role. For in natural language (unenriched by technical terms), sentences do not come by roles by stipulation. We might reasonably see that as Quine's real worry: we have not made sense of the notion of analyticity in the general case—specifically not in its application to natural language—because we have not explained how a natural language sentence might come by that role— in that sense, what it would be for a natural language to have it. We might frame this in terms of a conceit due to Michael Dummett. We might think of the word "analytic" as governed by an introduction rule and an elimination rule. In the case of natural language, Carnap has given us an introduction rule. We know what follows if a sentence is analytic. But he has not given us an elimination rule. So, Quine insists, the term remains without a (definite) sense. In his account of synonymy, Quine makes it clear what an adequate introduction rule would be. In effect, he demands a discovery procedure for analytic sentences in an arbitrary language, a specifiable and failure-proof way of recognizing, in terms of the "linguistic behavior" of speakers of the language when a sentence has the role Carnap describes. (Thus "Two Dogmas" contains the same demands on facts about meaning as does the later "Indeterminacy of Translation Again."[4]) So the complaint turns out to rest on a familiar idea: there are facts about analyticity only if such facts are analyzable, in a suitable sense, in terms of a different class of relatively privileged facts—facts about behavior, in the familiar proprietary sense.

Quine is rightly pessimistic about there being such analyses. But then, as Putnam notes, if not, that should leave us unimpressed. Suppose we had reason to believe that some sentences in English had the role Carnap identifies. We might begin to investigate that hypothesis by asking which sentences these would most reasonably be taken to be, given that the hypothesis is true. To answer that, we might rely on all that we know or are prepared to recognize as competent English speakers. The upshot might be that we fail to identify any such sentences. In that case, we would say that analyticity is not a property any English sentence has. Or it might be that there was a set of sentences that were those most reasonably taken to have the relevant role if any sentences do and reasonably enough taken to have it. In that case, the behavior of those sentences might lead us to revise somewhat our initial conception of the role. But we would rightly regard a Quinean claim that the very coherence of the notion is hostage to its analyzability in terms of "behavior" as mere empiricist prejudice.

II. EXPERIENCE

I turn now to the argument Putnam views as a "normative history of science." It is, perhaps, more a vision of Duhemian paradise. As such, it is initially appealing. On inspection, though, it invokes a dubious notion of experience and of the relation between experience and thought. Moreover, its upshot is roughly the opposite of Putnam's point about cognitive economy, and undermines it.

Quine's vision is apparent in the following bits of "Two Dogmas":

> The dogma of reductionism survives in the supposition that each statement, taken in isolation from its fellows, can admit of confirmation or infirmation at all.

> My countersuggestion . . . is that our statements about the external world face the tribunal of sense experiences not individually but only as a corporate body.

> The statement, rather than the term, came with Russell to be recognized as the unit accountable to an empiricist critique. But what I am now urging is

that even in taking the statement as unit we have drawn our grid too finely. The unit of empirical significance is the whole of science.

> . . . it is misleading to speak of the empirical content of an individual statement. . . . Any statement can be held true come what may, if we make drastic enough adjustments elsewhere in the system. Even a statement very close to the periphery can be held true in the face of recalcitrant experience by pleading hallucination or by amending certain statements of the kind called logical laws.[5]

Quine's suggestion is thus that for anything we may think (any statement we hold true) and any conceivable experience we might have, we might, for all of that experience, consistently continue to believe that thing. The experience itself, and our having it, are, strictly speaking, consistent both with our belief being true and with it being false. What we should believe given that experience can only be relative to the adjustments we are prepared to make to the rest of our beliefs. For all that, an experience may be recalcitrant. That is, it may call for change of belief *somewhere*, though at no particular point. It may be inconsistent with the total way we think the world to be. There are four points to make about this vision. First, this notion of experience is not ours. In fact, Quine is committed to viewing our ordinary notion of experience as badly mistaken. Second, the notion Quine needs here is doubtfully coherent. Third, Quine creates an illusion of the availability of the notion he wants by construing experience as a matter of sensations, thus eliminating perception from the picture. Fourth, there are familiar enough philosopher's notions of experience that capture the noncommittal feature Quine wants here, but they threaten the notion of belief (or thinking so).

First, then, Quine's is not our ordinary notion of experience. As we ordinarily think of things, our experience is *of* our surroundings, and what is in them, and of those things being particular ways (which they are). Or it typically, or often, is that. (There is such a thing as inner experience.) Moreover, experience normally involves at least some degree of awareness of what it is that is experienced. This morning, leaning on a fence post, I watched a pig wallowing in the mud in the damp field on the other side. The pig splattered me. That was my experience. Moreover, I was aware of what I saw. It was plainly, unmistakably, what I just said it was. That, too, was part of my experience. In two ways, that experience is very specific as to point at which change in belief may be mandated, or inescapable. First, if that was my experience, then the fact of my having it is just plain inconsistent with there having been no pig in that field, or no pig wallowing, and with propositions such as that pigs just do not wallow. So if I had thought any of those things, then the fact of my experience entails that those things are false. If I did continue to believe such falsehoods, I would simply be failing to take on board the lessons experience had to teach. I would not be believing what was compatible with my experience. Second, in these respects, I was aware of what I experienced. In point of logic, that rules out my believing these particular falsehoods. To be thus aware of how things are is, ipso facto, not to think otherwise. The general moral: we (normally) cannot say what an experience was, and certainly do not try to, in a way that leaves it open such that, change in (so preservation of) belief may come *anywhere*. Our only ways of saying what an experience is dictate *some* specific places where change must come or preservation is called for.

Sometimes we do not know what we are experiencing, or do not know what to make of our experience. Sometimes we are mistaken as to what it is we experience. I cannot tell in this light whether those are real flowers or silk. I cannot quite hear whether the gas is on or water is running in distant pipes. I think it is a pig wallowing before me, but it is a tapir. Such possibilities do not help Quine's case. First, ignorance or error as to what I experience is just that: I do not *know* what (or all) my experience shows as to which of my beliefs are correct. That is not to say that, for each of them, my experience is compatible both with its correctness and its incorrectness, so that it is left open where revision may *correctly* come. Second, if experience is some form of awareness of surroundings, then ignorance and error are never (or seldom) complete. I cannot tell whether those items in the vase are real flowers or silk. That is a situation in which I am aware of there being a vase at a certain place containing what are either real flowers or silk. What I am aware of is not, in point of logic, compatible with continuing to believe (or ceasing to believe) just anything.

If I do not know whether the flowers are real or silk, I can try to find out. Meanwhile, not knowing, I simply do not think either that they are real or that they are silk. (I can, of course, speculate.) If I do find out—say, that they are silk—I can then think no other than that. I cannot, not knowing what they are, just *decide* to believe one thing or another (or to make "compensating changes elsewhere"). If I do not know, I do not know. Nor can I decide what to believe after I have found out. We do not, and cannot rationally, decide what to believe in such cases. That is not a psychological shortcoming.

Quine's vision demands a notion of experience in which, as opposed to our ordinary notion, experiences are noncommittal as to how things are—though not too noncommittal: they must still be able to be recalcitrant, that is, incompatible with our total body of belief. An experience, for Quine, must be *locally* everywhere noncommittal: for anything we think, for all of that experience, things may or may not be that way. But it must be *globally* committal: it may be consistent or inconsistent with our total body of belief. Moreover, Quine needs us to be wrong in supposing that we ever have experiences, on our ordinary conception of what an experience is, for if we did, our beliefs would not, in any such case, face the tribunal of experience *merely* as a corporate body. Given experiences would make specific ones, per se, true or false. The notion with which Quine would replace our ordinary notion, though, is doubtfully coherent. At least insofar as a body of belief consists in a body of beliefs, it is hard to see how experience, no matter how conceived, could be locally noncommittal, globally committal. Perhaps, though, there is the illusion of that possibility in this way of thinking of experience:

> Certain statements, though *about* physical objects and not sense experience, seem peculiarly germane to sense experience—and in a selective way. . . .

> As an empiricist I continue to think of the conceptual scheme of science as a tool, ultimately, for predicting future experience in the light of past experience. Physical objects are conceptually imported into the situation as convenient intermediaries. . . . The myth of physical objects is epistemologically superior to most in that it has proved more efficacious than other myths as a device for working a manageable structure into the flux of experience.[6]

Statements about physical objects do not, for Quine, report (sense) experience. So if I say, "A pig is wallowing before me," or "I see a pig wallowing before me," I do not say what my experience was. That makes perception drop out of Quine's picture entirely. What is left over for the role of what is experienced is sensations, including (supposed) visual ones, and including, if there be such, sense data. An experience would consist in having such things. There is, say, a certain porcine quality to the appearances that appear to be before me. Now, with one important class of (possible) exceptions, sensations do seem to be noncommittal in a way that perception never is. The fact of having had a certain sensation is noncommittal, in the presently relevant sense, as to how, otherwise, things are. If I feel myself falling over backwards, then I am falling over backwards. But if I merely have the sensation of falling over backwards, I could, for all that, be floating on my back in a tepid pool. (The possible exceptions are cases of bodily sensations, such as feeling your toes itch. To my ear, at least, it takes toes to do that—though philosophers have denied that. But I cannot think of cases where the fact of a sensation has entailments for extradermal states of affairs.[7]) Now if we set sensation reports aside, we may, following Quine's suggestion, think of the remaining statements we hold true at a time as a mechanism for generating predictions of future sensations on the basis of past ones. And then, when the mechanism fails, generating false prediction, of course, for all that, revision may come anywhere.

This conceit depends on the idea of predictions that may prove false. What those predictions predict is future sensations. So sensations, at least, or their having, are not quite *everywhere* locally noncommittal. For any future sensation or its absence, there is a specific belief that, if we held it, would thereby be shown false. And for Quine, sensations, or their having, are just what experiences are. So experiences are not really, as he makes out, everywhere locally noncommittal. We have not seen how experience can be everywhere locally noncommittal while globally committal (recalcitrant). Nor, I think, is that something one could see. There is, though, a familiar family of philosophical conceptions of experience that make it perhaps even more thoroughly locally noncommittal than Quine does. The genre is one in which an experience consists in things appearing, or seeming, to its subject a certain way. Within it, one might, with the Pyrrhonians, deny that things appearing thus and so says anything at all about how things are. That would be local noncommitment everywhere. A variant within this genre has it that experience consists in the world being *represented* to the subject as being thus and so. If pigs are represented to me as eating the tulips in my garden, then, for all that, they may be, and they may not be. In a suitable sense, I may choose to believe that representation or not—to trust the representer or not. (*Caveat*: I am not always free to trust people or not according to my wishes, any more than I am, in general, free to decide what to think. For all that, experience itself, on this account, is noncommittal.) In the nature of the case, what goes for pigs and tulips goes for any representation whatsoever. No matter how the world is represented to me as being, I may always continue to think it otherwise, making due adjustments in my other beliefs. (I will, for example, need to think that some misrepresentation has taken place.) So here, perhaps, we have a rare example of philosophic progress. A currently widespread view of experience makes it even more thoroughly neutral as to how things are than Quine does.

What is now threatened, though, is the very idea of thinking things (or at least sublunary things) so. Suppose I think that pig is eating tulips. Part of taking the attitude I thus do is supposing that there is a definite way for things to be, which is a way things determinately either are or are not. If they are that way, then what I think is true. And no view on which that pig is not eating tulips can be made true by adjustments in other parts of it. If they are not, then what I think is false, and would not be true no matter what else I also believed. Since I take it that the pig is eating tulips, I take myself to think the only thing there is to think truly on that question, full stop. That can also be said this way: in thinking that that pig is eating tulips, I take myself to be, thus far, properly responsive to how things are—either just seeing them to be that way, or at least seeing what is indicated. Leaving pure speculation to one side, all this just elaborates what an attitude of thinking something so is. A view of experience as thoroughly noncommittal undoes all that. Part of that view is that I can *never*, in the nature of the case, *experience* that things are (or are not) the way I think (that that pig is [is not] eating tulips). So my thinking so cannot be seeing how things are. But then neither can it be seeing what is indicated. For that involves seeing something (to be so) which indicates that that is how things are. But, on that view, my ability to see that things are thus and so is *everywhere* absent. My thinking so thus cannot be the responsiveness to how things are that I take it for. This much makes room for a Duhemian vision: in any sense in which I can think correctly, there is something for me to think, part of which is that that pig is eating tulips, and something for me to think, part of which is that it is not, where it is equally correct for me to think either of these, and equally correct to think either as to think anything else on the topic. Or, if there is some sense in which only the one thing, and not the other, is the correct thing to think, then whether I think correctly in that sense is a matter of pure chance. For me to think of my thinking as relating to experience in that way is for me to be simply unable to take the attitude that thinking (so) is. And if this is the correct view of that relation, then I can only take the attitude of thinking something so incorrectly. As Pyrrho said (but not necessarily for his reasons), it is always an error to think anything.[8]

What matters most at present, though, is that this view of experience (and any Duhemian vision that depends on it) is the very opposite of what Putnam needs and argues. Putnam's point is that experience has, or may have, certain sorts of lessons for us. It may show that we are wrong on some of the points we thought *most* secure. It may even show that, in cases where we were certain there was something we did think, there is really nothing for us to have thought at all. The view is that experience may *show* such things. It is not as if we may escape the lessons by making revisions elsewhere in our beliefs. It is not as if, for example, we could just designate certain propositions as true no matter what, or, with Carnap, stipulate that that is part of their being the ones they are, and then, with mere ingenuity, make good on that. (Whereas, on Quine's vision, that course should be as available as any other.) What Putnam needs—and goes some distance to establish—is just our ordinary conception of experience as contact with—and, to a sufficient extent, awareness of—that in the world to which we rightly take our thinking to be properly responsive.

III. Presumption

The discussion so far identifies two features by which Putnam contrasts with Quine. First, the conclusion of Quine's first argument is that there is (or we have) no coherent notion of analyticity. It is an idea one cannot make sense of. Whereas for Putnam it is clear enough what status philosophers typically ascribe to propositions in holding them analytic. It is just that (with some possible trivial exceptions) that is not a status enjoyed by propositions we assert or entertain. A mistake about the structure of our thought wrongly suggests that such a status is available where it is not.

Second, the message of Quine's second "argument" (the Duhemian vision), I have argued, is that the world holds *no* real lessons for us, or none experience might teach us. At most, our sensations might create the uneasy feeling that it would be better not to suppose the world to be, in every respect, *precisely* as we suppose. (Nor, I have suggested, does Quine's picture leave room for such a feeling to be genuinely well founded.) Putnam's point runs radically in an opposite direction. It is conventional wisdom that for a wide range of the questions we pose, or that might interest us, the world decides their answers. We want to know whether things are thus and so— whether there is petrol in the tank, whether our train has left the station. The world speaks as to whether these things are so. Whether they are is a matter of how things are. Putnam's point, though, is that the world also has a say as to what it would be for these things—or for anything—to be so; not just whether they are, but when they would be. On a traditional view, what it would be for petrol to be in the tank, or for a car to be blue, is decided by the concepts involved, or by "what we mean" by these things; and decided in a way independent, in principle, of how the world is. Putnam rejects that view. So rather than holding that the world holds no lessons, Putnam holds that its lessons—ones experience *may* teach us—are unbounded, and more profound than philosophy had supposed.

A third feature, which will emerge here, is that that point, while it certainly bears on issues of analyticity, as it does on a priority, necessity, conceivability, and a host of other notions, is not specifically confined to any of these, nor exhausted by any set of them. Perhaps you could consistently accept Quine's claims about analyticity while continuing to think of traditional approaches to the a priori as unproblematic. Many have tried that. There is no chance of localizing Putnam's point in that way.

For all that, and for all that Quine's empiricist prejudices confuse issues, there may well be something Putnam and Quine do have in common. Certainly Putnam, and probably Quine, belonged to a small group of philosophers, around midcentury, who realized that changes in physics around the beginning of the century had revolutionized, not just the ways we need to think about space, time, motion, and related notions but also the ways we need to think about (our own) thought. That realization was also shared by, for example, Reichenbach and Feyerabend. But different philosophers reacted to it in different ways. The present brief is that it is

Putnam's particular, unique, reaction that, more than anything, makes him the important philosopher that he is; and that that reaction is absolutely different from Quine's.

The shared reaction, in perhaps its most neutral form, is found in Reichenbach (as related to me by Putnam, with my own abstraction from the example). The general point might be put this way. Let an empirical concept be a concept of a way things, or some things, might, or might not, be. Then for many, or perhaps all, empirical concepts we employ, any way of deciding what fits a given such concept and what does not—any notion of what it would be for something, or things, to fit that concept—on which there are, often enough, facts as to what fits the concept and what does not will rely on, or conform to, some principles which are at least not obviously necessary. Any account of when something would fit the concept, or what it would be for something to do so, which has the consequence (the world being as it is) that such-and-such is what fits, and such-and-such is not, will rely on some nonnecessary, or at least not obviously necessary, principles. To take Reichenbach's example, we have (or at least in a certain position we had) no idea of what it would be for some things to be six feet long and others not to be that does not rely on the principle that things do not change length merely in changing spatial position. Yet that does not seem to be a necessary truth. It seems to be the sort of thing physics might disconfirm.

This nearly neutral point does little more than capture what needs reacting to. To see how Putnam differs from the traditional picture of thought which Reichenbach's point challenges, and thus how he differs from other reactions to that point, I begin with what I think a respectable intuition. The core of the intuition is the idea that there is no intelligible question as to whether things are *thus* unless there is something—and enough—to be understood as to what it would be for things to be that way—for any concept deployed in posing the question, enough to be understood as to what fitting that concept would be. What question was posed is fixed in part by what there is thus to be understood. No investigation could settle a question for which not enough was to be understood in this respect. Nor, without such an understanding, could anything so much as count as genuinely investigating it. As one might put it, the intelligibility of a question rests on a sufficiently determinate conception of what it would be for things to be the way asked about. Having a proper conception of this is part of taking the question for the question that it is. Suppose, for example, that the question is whether your car is blue. I look at your car and see how it is colored. Then that *that* color (pointing at the *carrosserie*) is (or is not) the color asked about (blue, on the understanding of that on which it is blue that was asked about) may well be just part of what the question was to be understood to be. But your upholstery, dashboard, etc., are not blue. Again, it is part of what the question was to be understood to be that such is not required for a car to count, on the relevant understanding, as being colored blue. Such is a guide to where investigation may end, where its outcome would be positive, where negative, and thus to the form an investigation might take. The intuition is that something like this is needed for there to be an intelligible question at all.

There is a subsidiary intuition. It is that something which functions, in the above way, as fixing what it is for a thing, or things, to be some relevant way, cannot *while so functioning* itself admit of empirical investigation. For that would mean that there was some other way of fixing what being the relevant way was. So, for example, while there may be an intelligible question as to whether that color (pointing) is what is meant, for purposes of the question at hand, by blue, there is no intelligible question as to whether nature is so arranged as to make that color (a shade of) blue. Though there may be an intelligible question as to whether, in the relevant sense of being colored blue, grey upholstery is compatible with a car's being colored blue, there is no intelligible question as to whether nature has contrived to make it so that what has grey upholstery may, or cannot, exhibit this further phenomenon. Whether a car with grey upholstery may, for all that, be colored blue is not a matter of natural law. We do not turn to scientists to settle such questions. We cannot understand anything as so much as being an empirical investigation of them.

In general, then, where we take a question for the one it is, we ipso facto take, or are prepared to take, certain things as so, and as part of what it would be for things to be those ways the question asks after, and, in the ways noted, to treat those things accordingly. Taking a question for what it is means conceiving in certain ways of the ways it asks about. The relevant conceptions need not admit of being made exhaustively explicit. Considerable reflection may be needed to make anything about them properly explicit. But in specific cases there are specific things to be said correctly as to what the right conceptions are—as illustrated in the case of the question whether a certain car is blue.

I have labored to express these intuitions as ones I think unobjectionable. Labor is needed. For they lie close to others much less innocuous. There is, for example, a familiar take on them, which I will call the *constitution model*. On this model, for any concept, there is a conception which is intrinsic to it. This means that, no matter what, what fits the concept (what the concept is true of) is only, and can only be, what the conception is true of. The conception decides what it would be for something to fit the concept; and that it does does not, and is not liable to, depend on anything else. That conception could not be other than a correct conception of fitting that concept, no matter what. So if the question is, say, whether a certain car is blue, then a conception might *ever* be correctly taken as fixing what it would be to be the way in question, and might *ever* be correctly taken as not open to empirical investigation, only if it would *always* have that status. This intrinsic conception would thus be part of what there was to be understood about any deployment of the concept, thus as to what any question was which was expressed, *inter alia*, in terms of that concept. Full mastery of that concept, and of any bit of language which expressed it, would thus entail full grasp of that conception (which is to say that, on the constitution model, there is an intelligible notion of full mastery).

The original intuition was that an intelligible question as to whether things are thus and so requires a determinate enough conception of what it would be for things to be thus and so. Questions are posed, examined, considered, investigated, on particular occasions; and there are particular occasions for doing such things. The core intuition is that whenever we do such a thing, a determinate enough conception must be part of what is to be understood as to what we are then doing. Otherwise we cannot be regarded as posing, investigating, etc., a genuine question at all. Nothing in that idea requires per se that for any question that can ever be posed, there must be some conception such that *that* is part of what is to be understood wherever it is that that question is raised. Familiar ways of thinking of individuating thoughts, or propositions, or questions, may make such an idea seem plausible. If Putnam is right, though, such ways are themselves in need of scrutiny. In any case, the constitution model, with its notion of conceptions intrinsic to a concept, endorses the idea that the conception that is part of what is to be understood where a given concept is in question depends only on what concept that is, and not on the occasion on which deploying that concept is part of posing, investigating, answering, and so on, some question. That is certainly a point at which the model is open to challenge.

If we combine the constitution model with Reichenbach's point, the result is that our (empirical) concepts are always liable to fail to have any application to the world. We conceive of the color of a car, say, as a visible feature of it. This means that it is a feature one (a human being) can see if the human is suitably equipped, and looking under suitable conditions. But suppose there were no constancy at all in what people were prepared to say about the color of cars: anything like consistency was simply unattainable by any reasonable restrictions on viewing conditions, condition of the viewer, and so forth. It seems not a matter of *necessity* that such is not the case. Then we could not correctly take there to be any *visible* feature of a car for its color to be. Since it is intrinsic to the concept of being colored that being colored a certain color *is* a visible feature, we would have to conclude that there is no such thing as an object, or anyway a car, being colored. Our concepts of objects being colored, we would need to conclude, simply have no application to the phenomena of the world we confront. Combining the Reichenbach point with the constitution model in this way is the reaction to it of such philosophers as Paul Feyerabend and Paul Churchland. On their views, if the conception intrinsic to a given concept is not (entirely) true of anything, then the concept has (as Feyerabend would put it) no application to reality. Such outcomes are always among the possibilities we must reckon with.

Putnam's departure from the constitution model can be seen as, in the first instance, a question of attitude. On the constitution model, if we understand what there is to be understood about a given question, posed on an occasion, and thus grasp that a certain conception of the way for things to be that is asked about is to be taken as operative, then our attitude towards that conception (or anyway, the proper attitude) will be: "That just is (if anything is) what it is for things to be the way in question, *fertig.*" For Putnam, understanding what someone is doing in raising a given question may mean taking a certain conception as fixing the way for things to be in question; as what one would (then) suppose as to what that way is. But the right attitude towards that conception is roughly this: "That is what, in this posing of the question, the way in question was represented as being; it is, *ceteris paribus*, what the way in question is to be *presumed* to be as things stand." It is because of that difference in attitude that I label Putnam's picture of things the *presumption* model. That model leaves room for honoring what I termed the harmless intuition. It may well be that we can have no adequate grasp of what it is that is in question on a particular occasion unless we have (and there is available) a rich enough grasp of what is to be presumed as to what it is that is in question. To have an intelligible question as to the color of a car, we must have a rich enough set of presumptions as to what it is for a car to be colored a certain color. But to treat all this as presumption is to say this: we acknowledge that there is, or for all that such is to be presumed, may be, such a thing as these presumptions being false; and there is such a thing as particular considerations showing them false. For any such presumption, we are prepared to recognize, should there be occasion for it (should there be such a thing to recognize) *proofs* (as proof) that it is false. Nothing in what we understand, or what is to be understood, as to what it is that is in question rules out such outcomes. This is not to say that we can say in advance what such a proof would, or must, or even might, look like. It is not to say that we have any adequate conception of a situation such that, should *that* obtain, then the presumption would be false. There are, though, a few general things to say about the structure of such proofs. These emerge when we look at what there is in favor of the presumption model.

Putnam points to two general considerations in favor of the presumption model—both in favor of adopting it, and in favor of thinking it correct of our thought. The first of these is what I will call *diversity*. The point is that if we choose some familiar way for things to be and reflect on what we do understand as to what it is for things to be that way, we will see that there are a variety of things we thus suppose, where these things are independent of each other: nothing about the suppositions themselves rules out a situation in which one of these is true only of what another is not; otherwise put, the suppositions are not jointly true of anything. For example, if (in a familiar way) I describe my car as blue, then one thing to be supposed is that I am speaking of a way for my car visibly to be. Another may be that I am speaking of a stable feature of the car—a feature which the car could only lose (if it has it) in a range of familiar ways (acid, fire, abrasives, new paint). What the suppositions as such do not rule out is that nothing visible is stable: competent observers agree on when to say my car is a certain color, but if they are thus recognizing a feature of the car, it is not one that goes along with stability in any reasonable sense. Variety plus independence equals diversity in my sense. This point as it stands may seem not overly impressive, especially if the question is whether the presumption model or Feyerabend's view is the right reaction to Reichenbach's point. It will become more impressive presently, though, when we add a further observation.

The second consideration is that there are limits to our knowledge of what we mean. Where the world thoroughly enough exceeds those limits, it may turn out that there is nothing we mean (or at least if we thought we meant some way for things to be, no way which is what we did, in fact, mean). That limits to our knowledge of what we mean, and, correlatively, to the understandings our words bear, are sometimes exceeded is a familiar phenomenon. Elsewhere I have referred to it as "natural *isostheneia*."[9] One can see the general phenomenon in a case of Austin's. Pia wants to phone Max to invite him to the pub. She wonders whether he is at home or in the office. Sid, having spoken with Max earlier, says, helpfully, "Max is at home." Shockingly, though, Max has just expired in his armchair. Is Max the way Sid said he was? There is an understanding of being at home on which the recently expired, their earthly remains still in their armchairs, are there. But there is another on which they are not: to have expired is to be no more, or at least to be no more spatially locatable, or at least not by the location of one's body. Knowing that Max is dead, one might speak in either way of his location. For Pia and Sid, though, his death will be a shock. That eventuality was not foreseen. As a result, Sid's words, in speaking of Max's location, bear neither the one understanding nor the other. There is an equal balance of reasons for taking them the one way and for taking them in the other. That is what I mean by natural *isostheneia*. There is nothing to know either about what those words said, or about what Sid meant, that would settle whether the way things are is the way Sid said, or meant, they were. There lies a limit to our knowledge of what we mean.

One point Putnam emphasizes is that limits to our knowledge of what we mean (or say) may sometimes be exceeded systematically and pervasively. To mention one of his examples, we think (or at one time thought) that we know what we mean by a straight line. On the conception we think, or thought, to be in force, part of what it is to be a straight line is (speaking intuitively) to look straight. (Straightness is, very roughly, a visible feature of lines.) But there is something we did not anticipate. When paths in space are long enough, whether they look straight, in this intuitive sense (insofar as that sense applies at all to such things) depends on the position from which they are being observed. So in a case where someone might plausibly claim that a pair of paths were parallel straight lines that met, there would be equally good reason for and against saying that those lines looked straight. Our knowledge of what we mean by looking straight will have been exceeded. That problem transfers automatically to our knowledge of what we mean by something's being a straight line *if* we hold onto the idea that looking straight is part of what being straight is.

If we accept the presumption model, then the two phenomena just described—conflict between diverse parts of a conception and exceeding the limits of knowing what we mean—point to what, in very abstract form, a proof might look like that a conception which was to be presumed correct was, in fact, wrong. If one held to the constitution model, though, one might rather be inclined to say this: a conception which turned out to have the above defects would, for all that, be intrinsic to the concept we took it to identify; it is just that that concept would turn out to lack application to the world—if the concept was of being F, then, it would turn out, there is no such thing as being F. On that view, for example, what we learn in learning that we do not know what we mean by being straight is that there is no such thing as a straight line in space. But, Putnam points out, in a great many cases this is not a way to save the constitution model. For in a great many cases it is part of our conception of a given way for things to be—an ineliminable part of what fixes, for the questions we pose and investigate, what would, and what would not, count as things being that way—that the way in question is a *familiar* way, a way many things are, and others, by contrast, are not.[10] The point is obvious for such things as being water, or gold, or a pig. In that case, to say that there is no such thing as something's being that way (that the relevant concept lacks application to the world) is to abandon the conception, not preserve it.

For Putnam, though, the most important argument in favor of the presumption model, and against the constitution model, deployed as just described, is an argument from what we are prepared to recognize. Given the presumption model, the question we ought to ask where we confront phenomena of the sorts described—de facto conflict between diverse parts of a conception, exceeded limits of knowing what we mean—is why we would have presumed what we did as to what it would be for something to be the way (to fit the concept) in question. Often the answer will be that we suffered certain specifiable misunderstandings, or ignorance, as to how things were. Often it will be possible to say what it would have been reasonable to presume had we not so suffered. In many cases what it will thus have been reasonable to presume is that such-and-such else is what it would be for something to be the way in question. With the usual idealizations built into "prepared to recognize," these are results that normal, intelligent human beings are prepares to recognize as correct. Which is to say that the presumption model, and not the constitution model, is what corresponds to what human thinkers are prepared to recognize.

In particular (to mention one more point Putnam emphasizes), often, where, for a given putative way for things to be, there are the above sorts of troubles with what was to be presumed as to what it would be for things to be that way, there is a way of drawing a genuine distinction, which distinguishes, roughly, what we would have been prepared to recognize as being that putative way from what we would have been prepared to take as not that way. In many cases, though not in all, that will be reason enough for taking that putative way to be a genuine way some things are and others are not (so the concept of it to be one with genuine application to the world), and to take the right way of drawing this distinction to exhibit the right way of conceiving of that way for things to be. That is, the fact that there is a distinction to be drawn that divides up cases in much the way one would have presumed the distinction we thought we were drawing did is good reason for saying that we really were drawing a distinction that, in fact, divides up cases in pretty much that way. That is to endorse the presumption model, as against, the constitution model. What backs that endorsement is just what we are prepared to recognize in, and of, particular cases. There are, of course, exceptions to the rule. It may be that roughly the women who would have been supposed witches would in fact turn out to be witches if we took the right conception of being a witch to be simply having a wart on one's nose. But there is too much mischief in the notion of being a witch for us to take that to mean that there is really such a thing as being one after all. Such exceptions, though, do no damage to the general case in favor of the presumption model.

The presumption model, with the above defense, captures something special and important in Putnam's reaction to a problem about how our concepts can apply to things. I will mention four ways that reaction is significant. First, Putnam's defense relies heavily on facts about what we (that is, we human beings) are prepared to recognize. In specific cases where diversity yields conflict, *we* would recognize particular new conceptions as reasonable, and as correct of that way for things to be which the old, troubled conception aimed to capture. We do not, in fact, think of things in the way Feyerabend says we should. In his style of argument, Putnam thus allies himself with such philosophers as Austin, and, earlier, Moore. He does not erect an impenetrable wall between the object of his inquiry and psychology, but rather avows an interest in the form of a human competence—an interest to which psychological fact *may* be relevant. Putnam's result is thus one about the form of *human* thought; not one about the necessary form of thought of any (empirical) thinker whatsoever. Moreover, the result itself makes that sort of modesty of ambition in order. If presumption is the right attitude towards our conceptions of the objects of our concepts, that result cannot be stopped short of our conceptions of the forms thought itself might take. It is not just some of our concepts for which conceptual truth can have at most presumptive status. That leaves little sensible, and much less interesting and true, to say about what the form of any possible thought *must* be.

The second point concerns the nature of our conceptual capacities, and the way they relate to ordinary recognition capacities. To begin with recognition, most of us can, normally, recognize a pig when we see one. Presumably we are sensitive to certain features of porcine physiognomy (fairly abstract ones, perhaps). Psychologists might reasonably hope to say, some day, what these are. He might then tell us, roughly, that when we registered such features in a beast before us, we would, all else equal, take it for a pig (or at worst be unable to see how it was not one).[11] Moreover, the features by which we distinguish pigs from other beasts, we hope, actually do distinguish pigs from other beasts. After all, we have a *competence*; we can tell. So, when the psychologist is done, we might build a machine which would, say, flash a light when, and only when, confronted with a pig. Ordinary recognition capacities, though, are environmentally sensitive. In some environments, pigs cannot be told from other beasts in the way we (or our subdoxastic mechanisms) do it. In those environments, perhaps, we simply could not tell pigs from other beasts. Or, perhaps, we could learn to do it in some other way.

The general point is this. There may be perfectly definite features we rely on in a perfectly definite way, at least on certain occasions, in telling pigs from other beasts. But no one would suppose that to be a pig just is to have those features. A recognition competence is not responsible for relying on features with such a status. If we think of any specifiable recognition capacity as operating with some conception of its object, then we can say that our concept of a pig is not, or need not be, exhausted by whatever conception a recognition capacity of the kind just described might work with. We are prepared to count, or recognize, something as being a pig (or as not) despite its lacking (or possessing) those features such a conception requires. What, then, fixes, in the general case, what *would* count as a pig—as that very thing our concept of a pig is of? On the constitution model, what fixes this is something in principle no different from a recognition capacity of the kind just described, though, in most cases, much more complex (in fact, so complex, that we do not know how to say what it is). What fixes it is a conception of a pig which is intrinsic to the concept of being a pig. What answers to that conception is a pig, what fails to answer to it is not, no matter how the world may be, or what lessons it might hold for us. Though we are in no position to spell out such a conception, it is the way one would conceive being a pig in fully grasping what the concept of a pig was.

On the presumption model, no such superconception is called for. To have the concept of a pig (know what a pig is) one need have no more of a conception of a pig than would confer recognition capacities of the kind we ordinarily possess, or know, or suppose, no more about what being a pig is than those of us who manifestly do know what a pig is do know. What fixes, in the general case, what it is to be a pig is just, on the one hand, the way the world is, and, on the other, our capacity to recognize when the conceptions we do have ought, or ought not, to be acknowledged as wrong. Nor need that capacity consist in a sensitivity to some specifiable set of features of the world, of a sort corresponding to principles by which one might calculate, from values of those features, what it is we are thus prepared to see. For Putnam, then, a genuine conceptual capacity is more powerful than—not exhausted by—any recognition capacity on the above model. But having it does not require extrapotent conceptions—or anything beyond our ordinary conceptions—of that our concepts are concepts of. That is a view to keep in mind when one considers for what achievements, and when, our conceptual capacities (as opposed to simple recognition capacities) are genuinely needed.

Third, Putnam suggests a way of putting a certain Kantian problem to rest, and (in case we needed that) an account of why we should want to. Kant thought there was some kind of problem about justifying the employment of concepts (showing their "right" to be employed), or showing "how they can relate to objects," or proving their "objective reality"—showing how they can have any application to the way things are. Or at least he thought that for a certain class of concepts—ones "marked out for pure *a priori* employment."[12] As for the contrasting class, "empirical concepts," Kant remarks that, in many cases, "Since experience is always available for the proof of their objective reality, we believe ourselves, even without a deduction, to be justified in appropriating to them a meaning, an ascribed significance."[13] In the case of a priori concepts, Kant emphasizes, a proof that they have a genuine employment—that there is, indeed, a definite way they relate to objects—must be a purely a priori proof, relying in no way on the deliverances of experience.

I will not try to say what Kant understood by a concept's having a genuine employment, or "right to be employed." One would think, innocuously, that for a concept to have a genuine employment, or application to the way things are, is for there to be a determinate enough way (relevant) things sort out as fitting the concept or not. If one followed Leibniz, one would take it that there are, for a given concept, certain principles which are intrinsic to it: wherever the concept applies to something, those principles are true (of it); for it to apply to something is (*inter alia*) for them to be true. For example, one might hold that it is part of what identity is that the standard laws of identity (Leibniz's law, etc.) hold (of it); and part of what being an object is that objects are terms in this relation, so subject to these laws. So for the concept of identity, or the concept of an object, to apply to anything is for these laws to be true. Generalizing, for a concept to have a genuine employment is for such-and-such laws, or propositions, to be true, where the identity of the concept tells us which laws these are. Showing a concept to have a genuine employment would then mean showing these laws true.

Seeing Kant as one with Leibniz here invites a comparison with Feyerabend. On the resultant conception of what justifying the employment of a concept would be, Feyerabend holds such justifications to be needed even in the case of what Kant would regard as empirical concepts: that they have genuine employment is not something just obvious from experience; scientific investigation may show it false even where it seemed to be true. In such cases, a justification would be "empirical," in the sense that it would be the task of science to supply it. Nor, contrary to Kant, does Feyerabend seem to recognize a line, or at least a fixed line, between "empirical" concepts and concepts of some other sort—ones either in need of, or admitting, justification of some other sort. If one remains within the Leibnizian framework to the extent that Feyerabend does, then all that is part of a natural move away from Kant in the light of Reichenbach's point.

For Kant there are two major problems about the sort of justification he sought, in the cases that really matter to him. First, Kant was one with Leibniz before him, and Frege after, in thinking that the concepts of central concern to him—what he calls "categories"—are ones without which we cannot think at all. So, taking a Leibnizian view of the relation between concepts and laws (as Frege certainly does), one cannot have a thinker who does not acknowledge, or at least respect, the laws by which those concepts are, in part, identified. So, while Kant allows that we may, occasionally, uncover a bogus empirical concept, which we would then abandon (he suggests *fortune* and *fate* as examples), there is no question in the cases that matter to him, of our discovering that there is no justification for the employment of these concepts and then (as the empirical case would suggest, and as Feyerabend would insist) abandoning them. Whatever the reason for our needing a justification, *our* employment of those concepts cannot be hostage to it. Second, there is no neutral standpoint from which, suspending belief in the relevant laws, we can somehow examine the question whether they are true. We can only examine any question by subscribing to them. That casts doubt on the possibility of a non-question-begging justification (and even on the intelligibility of such an idea). There is a parallel problem for Feyerabend if there is a genuine question as to how we know that *any* of our empirical concepts has any genuine employment. We can take a neutral stance towards any one of these, perhaps, by employing others. But it is unclear what we should do if all of them came into question at once. Perhaps Feyerabend owes us some account of why that cannot happen.

Putnam's contribution to this particular discussion is to change the nature of the questions there are intelligibly to ask. On occasion, the world, in turning out other than expected, in fact confronts us with specific, determinate questions: there has proven to be conflict between diverse presumed aspects of a given concept, or way for things to be, where each aspect seemed central to a thing's being that way. Or there turns out to be systematic and intolerable *isostheneia*. The question, then, is how the conflict there in fact is is to be resolved, or how our conception of the way in question is to be elaborated so as to make the *isostheneia* vanish. Such questions, where determinate enough to admit of answers, are ordinary, not in the sense of everyday (which they usually are not), but in the sense that they are nonphilosophical. Answering them requires nothing like a "sideways-on," or transcendental, perspective. Nor does it require suspending (entirely) the use of any concept. If the question (as it might once have been posed) is whether part of being water is being H_2O, then part of what may contribute to an answer is the fact that such-and-such is, in any case, water. Nothing excludes in principle that the answer to such a determinate question, in a particular case, may be: "Jettison the concept!" But, given the presumption model, that would be an exceptional result (a sort of last resort). Ordinary questions, in this sense, are questions as to *how* a concept would properly apply. Such a question does not automatically raise any question as to whether the concept applies at all.

We might begin to try to get a philosophical question in view by asking, in advance of the world's raising any actual question about it, whether there might not, anyway, be some sort of conflict between two aspects of a concept, or *isostheneia* in some unexpected place. We can then ask how we can know, or with what right we suppose, that no such thing is the case. (We might try to ask Kant's "Quid juris?") But, as Putnam has emphasized, such questions are not automatically determinate questions at all, at least if a determinate question is one for which there may be such a thing as a correct answer.[14] For genuinely to conceive, for example, of conflict at a given place is to fix, determinately enough, the form that conflict would take. ("Suppose it is discovered tomorrow that some things we had every reason to suppose were water are not H_2O." Given our present state of knowledge, just how is this supposed to have been discovered, and just how is it supposed to be so? Without more detail, it is indeterminate just what conflict needs to be resolved, or what resolution might be.) Similarly, without a determinate enough conception of what a conflict might be, we do not have a determinate question how we know there are none. The point can be seen as a general point of epistemology. "How do you know you have ten fingers?" is not a determinate question at all, except in circumstances where it is determinate enough just how things might be otherwise.

So if we try for philosophy by asking a hypothetical question about conflict or *isostheneia*, the result is either an ordinary question (in the present sense) or no question at all. Now, the question Kant tried to ask (of some concepts), put in Putnamian terms, would look something like this: "How do we know, or what ensures (or such-and-such concept) that it cannot turn out to suffer from conflict or systematic *isostheneia*?" But we are now left with no idea of how that could be an intelligible question at all (for any concept). The unintelligibility of that question could be put by saying that we cannot have what Kant would recognize as a justification for the employment of our concepts (or the ones of concern to him). But where there is nothing justification might be—where there is no coherent idea of what justification might be—having none is not falling short of some ideal to which we might intelligibly aspire. Nor if, in that sense, we lack justification for the employment we in fact make of our concepts, need there, for all that, be any doubt as to whether they in fact have those employments. (And, again, where there *is* an intelligible doubt, it will not be a philosophical one.) That, I think, is the way a Kantian problem should be put to rest if it is going to be put to rest at all.

Finally, a brief comment on Putnam's relation to Frege. Frege famously inveighed against mistaking the psychological for the logical. In perhaps the most central case his brief was that a law of logic may, perhaps, be explained in terms of other logical laws; but where that is not possible, it admits of no explanation at all; *a fortiori* no psychological one. This insistence on such an end to explanation should alert us that Frege's case invokes the constitution model. The model of that invocation would be this. One may sensibly ask why (or whether) the English "and" is governed by the rule of conjunction introduction.[15] For the fact one states in saying so might have failed to be so had English been otherwise. An answer might appeal to facts about English and its speakers—*inter alia* psychological ones. But one cannot sensibly ask why a word that expresses (the concept of) conjunction is governed by the rule of conjunction introduction: that is just part of what it is to express conjunction. Or so one might hold. But holding that is applying the constitution model, at least in the case of logical concepts—something Putnam scrupulously avoids doing. If Putnam has shown that that model is the wrong model of the form our thinking takes, then that is occasion for thinking Frege's position through again. If the sins to be committed in mixing logic with psychology are, for all that, precisely what Frege thought they were, that must be for reasons independent of that model. It would then be nice to know just what those reasons are. But I will not pursue that project here.

IV. POSSESSION

Putnam and Quine each find something wrong with some notion of analyticity. But they part ways at that point. For Quine the central point is that the notion of analyticity (or any in the cards), fails to meet empiricist standards for making sense. It (and they) are thus just disguised nonsense. For Quine that makes analyticity no different than our usual notion of (linguistic) meaning. For Putnam, the problem is not that the notion is nonsensical, but rather that it embodies a false conception of the way in which our thoughts identify that in the world in virtue of which they are true, or, *casu quo*, false; one which Putnam replaces with what is thus a new view of the harmony, or harmonizing, of thought and reality. Quine's point thus admits of accommodation, or resistance, in ways that Putnam's does not. It is for that reason that it is of the greatest importance to keep the points distinct.

Christopher Peacocke is a clear example of a philosopher who misses Putnam's point, while accommodating much of Quine's. That contrast shows up clearly in Peacocke's notion of a concept. In brief, on it, concepts are to be elements in thoughts. Thoughts are to mark "all the distinctions there are to be drawn" between thinking one thing and thinking another. Conventional ideas as to what those distinctions are mean that we must thus leave open the possibility of different thoughts of the same things as being the same ways. Correspondingly, there may be different concepts of being some given way. At the same time, we are to suppose that a thought's identity fixes when it would be true. That is read as meaning that for any given thought, that it is about such-and-such things (or just things) being such-and-such way (or ways) fixes (all that is fixed) as to when it would be true. Correspondingly, that a concept is of such-and-such fixes what it would be true *of.* Peacocke speaks of such things as what a concept is of as at "the level of reference."

A concept is thus not (fully) individuated by its referent (what it is of). Instead, Peacocke postulates, for each concept, a condition which is *the* condition for possessing it, and takes concepts to be individuated by these conditions. As he puts it, "Concept F is that unique concept C to possess which a thinker must meet condition $\mathcal{A}(C)$."[16] A possession condition requires, for a start, that one take certain propositions to be true (and/or certain inferences to be valid). (One must, moreover, take these to be "primitively compelling," but the further content of that idea need not detain us here.)

Possession conditions are to link to referents as follows: the referent of a concept will be that which makes the things one must take true in order to have the concept in fact true.[17] So if we think in terms of (what we call) cabbages and kings, or sheep and goats, or position and momentum, and we thereby think genuine thoughts at all, then there are things one must take true to have the concepts in terms of which we thus think. Since we do think in those terms we do take those things to be true. Our so taking them (and so taking them in the way we do) is what identifies them as the concepts in terms of which we think. The referents of those concepts will be just whatever it is that make those things true. In thinking in terms of cabbages and kings, the idea is, we take certain things to be true; and do so in a way such that those things identify the concepts in terms of which we thus think—those concepts, namely, possession of which requires one to take just those things to be true in just those ways. And then what we thus think of is just whatever it is that makes those things true. So it follows from there being those concepts in terms of which to think that those things are true. Here we have a clear version of the constitution model: for any concept, its existence, or availability, entails that certain propositions are true (or inferences valid). And that is just what Putnam says there cannot be.

Peacocke does not reach this position on concepts by argument. As said already, he simply cannot see Putnam's position as within the space of positions at all. Of course, Peacocke reaches his notion of a concept by stipulation: this is just what a concept is to be for his purposes. But Putnam's position, famously, sets limits to our powers of stipulation. Peacocke postulates elements in thought which, if Putnam is right, simply are not there, at least in human thought. For any proposition that might identify (in part) what we mean (or are talking about) in talking about cabbages, we are prepared to recognize, if circumstances should so dictate, that that proposition is false of *cabbages*.

But if Peacocke does not have Putnam in sight, he certainly applauds Quine. Writing with Paul Boghossian, he says, "Quine decisively refuted the idea that anything could be true purely in virtue of meaning."[18] How can someone who thinks that also find room for a notion of a concept that links it with possession conditions as Peacocke does? If truth always involves more than meaning, why should having a given concept require anyone, regardless of his situation in the world, to find precisely such-and-such things true (or valid)—which, moreover, must in fact, *be* that? Why that departure from Putnam?

Part of an answer may be that Quine's thesis is very specifically about *meaning*, that is, about language. Taking a Fregean view, we might see meaning, like grammar, as a peculiar mixture of the psychological and the logical. Suppose someone says, "Mary had a little lamb." Whether he spoke of pets or dinner may well be a psychological matter. *If* he spoke of pets, then, on this view, what it would take to make his statement true is a logical, and not a psychological, matter. Now, a sentence, or statement, has a definite truth condition—and thus is even in the market for being analytic—only if there is enough determinacy in the psychological side of this cooperative enterprise; only if it is determinate enough which option for a thing to say the words in question latched onto. Quine's point is just that such is never determinate enough for that. As he sometimes puts it himself, many (mutually incompatible) translation manuals are equally good. What that leaves intact is the idea that there is plenty of determinacy in the logical side of things, that is, in the options to be chosen among. The intended role for Peacockian concepts is just to be elements in those options. From the indeterminacy of the psychological (if Quine were right about this), nothing would follow about *their* structure.

To think of concepts in this way is not yet to find any determinacy as to which concepts (if any) we in fact have. Here, though, Peacocke seems much more optimistic than Quine would be (optimistic enough to make one wonder whether he really does take Quine on board). For, Peacocke thinks, "a possession condition for a concept states a requirement which a subpersonal algorithm or mechanism must meet if it is to realize a subject's possession of the concept,"[19] where the role of such a mechanism is to effect transitions between "propositional attitude states," and, perhaps, between those and action. I suspect that Peacocke thinks that future psychology, in revealing what our "subpersonal mechanisms" in fact are, will show what such requirements they satisfy, thus identifying which concepts we in fact possess. (Though if there is that much determinacy in human psychology, it is hard to see why Quine is right about meaning.)

But there is a still more important way in which Quine's view leaves room for Peacocke's. The key here is Quine's Duhemian vision, which Peacocke applauds, and from which he draws the following moral: "The celebrated arguments of Duhem and Quine . . . establish that a possession condition which mentions a role in a theory cannot be reduced to one which assigns observational significance to contents containing the concept in a one-to-one manner."[20] Part of the vision is that any experience, so any observation, is compatible with the rejection, or retention, of *any* bit of theory. So if a concept plays a role in theoretical statements, that role had better not be to make the verifiable, or falsifiable, by any possible experience. So such a concept had better not have "observational significance" of that sort. Quite so. But that is a superficial reading of the point. As we saw, Quine makes experience always neutral, or noncommittal as to how things are (that is, as to whether they are any way we take them to be)—noncommittal in the sense that, for all that we have actually experienced in any given experience, anything we take to be so might either be so or not. That opens the following possibility. Imagine a thinker who just happens to be so designed that, no matter what happens, he will never give up (or find a need to give up) thinking certain things—nothing he could experience would count for him as refuting those things. That is, imagine a perfectly un-Putnamian thinker. If Quine is right about experience, then such a thinker will never fly in its face; what he thinks will never be at odds with, or contradicted by, experience; it will never be flatly inconsistent with the way things have been shown to be. In that sense, there is, if Quine is right, nothing wrong with being such a thinker. Thinking these things true could then plausibly be taken as just part of what it is to be thinking about what this thinker does think about. Now, I think, Peacocke's suggestion is that such a thinker is us. That Quine leaves such a position open, while Putnam does not, makes the difference between the two manifest.

V. Concluding

Putnam changed the framework in which to think about thinking. It is not as if he merely made a point about analyticity, or a priority, or necessity, or conceivability, though his more fundamental point has important consequences for all those notions. Though he has done much to point to these consequences, many of them remain to be worked out, and to be digested so that they take their proper place in the practice of philosophy. What we can see is that the change of framework, once digested, changes profoundly the practice, and the look, of philosophy itself.

CHARLES TRAVIS

KING'S COLLEGE LONDON
MAY 2002

NOTES

1. Hilary Putnam, "'Two Dogmas' Revisited," in *Contemporary Aspects of Philosophy*, ed. G. Ryle (Boston: Oriel Press, 1976), 202–13. Reprinted in *Realism and Reason: Philosophical Papers*, vol. 3 (Cambridge: Cambridge University Press, 1978), 87–97, quote from 88.

2. It certainly seems odd that Quine should wield such a framework in light of his Duhemian vision, to be set out in the next section. It would be interesting to detail why it is that he may feel no tension there. Nonetheless, when it comes to phenomena of language, this is the framework Quine deploys. That is plain enough in "Two Dogmas." But see, notably, "Indeterminacy of Translation Again," *Journal of Philosophy* 84, no. 1 (Jan. 1987): 5–10.

3. W. V. O. Quine, "Two Dogmas of Empiricism," *Philosophical Review* 60 (1951): 33.

4. See note 2.

5. Quine, "Two Dogmas," 38–40.

6. Ibid., 40–41.

7. Feeling the barbell press against your chest is a case of perception.

8. I recognize that Quine puts his point, not in terms of beliefs, but in terms of statements, and holding them true. One might urge here that one can always hold a *statement* true no matter what by, in effect, tampering with its content. That, though, is a cheat. It invokes a notion of a statement (as identified by some mere concatenation of empty signs) that makes the resultant "Duhemian vision" totally uninteresting. (Quine should then be convicted of false advertising.) In fact, I think, it is viewing Quine's point as about statements in this very attenuated sense that allows some to think that they can *agree* with Quine and go on to postulate various sorts of conceptual truth. What is crucial for present purposes is that this is certainly, and explicitly, not what Putnam has in mind if he says that any statement is susceptible to revision.

9. See my "Sublunary Intuitionism," *Grazer Philosophische Studien* 55 (1998): 169–94.

10. It may also be that a phenomenon (straightness of a line, say) is inextricable from other familiar ones (phenomena of motion, say), or at least inextricable without abandoning physics, or something else it would be crazy to jettison. In that more complicated case the same point holds.

11. In the long run, this is likely to be an overly simple model of a recognition competence. It will do, though, for the contrast I am trying to draw.

12. Immanuel Kant, *Critique of Pure Reason*, A85 and B117.

13. Ibid., A84 and B116–117.

14. For example, see Putnam's "Rethinking Mathematical Necessity," in *Words and Life*, ed. James Conant (Cambridge, MA: Harvard University Press, 1994), 245–63.

15. As it doubtfully is.

16. Christopher Peacocke, *A Study of Concepts* (Cambridge, MA: MIT Press, 1995), 6.

17. Ibid., 19.

18. Christopher Peacocke and Paul Boghossian, introduction to *New Essays on the A Priori*, ed. P. Boghossian and C. Peacocke (Oxford: Oxford University Press, 2004), 4.

19. C. Peacocke, "A Moderate Mentalism," *Philosophy and Phenomenological Research* 52 (1992): 427.

20. Ibid., 426.

REPLY TO CHARLES TRAVIS

C harles Travis is a creative philosopher whose insights have been of great importance for my own work.[1] I could reply to his beautiful essay in one word: "Right!" But I want to say a little more about an essay which shows so deep an understanding of what I tried to do in the papers he discusses, and so deep an appreciation of why it matters. Since I agree totally with what he says, this response will not be a "reply to a critic," but rather a response to a wonderful interpreter.

What Travis points out is that, as I say in my Intellectual Autobiography:

> What I have been arguing ever since "The Analytic and the Synthetic" is that the search for a proof of objective validity of our fundamental concepts is misguided. There cannot be such a proof, and we have to live with the fact that our categories might turn out to need revision.

In brief, all our ideas of what is required in order for a concept to apply to something always rest on a huge background of tacit assumptions; and it is a mistake to argue, as some philosophers unfortunately have, that the model of our concepts as having "analytic" (or anyway unrevisable) "possession conditions" is not fatally injured by that fact. That model, which Travis calls "the constitution model," could, indeed, be immunized from refutation by saying "Well, if the world turns out to be such that the possession conditions for a concept C can never be met, then that just means that there are not any instances of C in the world," but that immunization strategy is a great mistake. It is a great mistake because that is not the way that we actually proceed, nor is it the way we ought to proceed if we want to understand our world.

In "The Analytic and the Synthetic," an example I used was that of the concept of *kinetic energy*. One of the things Einstein taught us was that the whole group of accepted possession conditions for that concept was not fully satisfiable in our world, because of the demands of Lorenz invariance. It turns out, for example, that one half the product of the mass of an object and the square of its velocity (the Newtonian "definition" of kinetic energy) is not conserved in elastic collisions. But no one ever seriously considered concluding that "kinetic energy does not exist" or "kinetic energy is not conserved in elastic collisions." Rather, just as we gave up certain obviously "synthetic" statements because of their conflict with Relativity (for example, the statement that "an object does not change its length simply because it moves with a uniform velocity"), so, *in an exactly similar fashion*, "Einstein, as we all know, changed the definition of kinetic energy. That is to say, he replaced the law 'e=1/2mv^2' by a more complicated law."[2]

I. The Case of Logic

In "Is Logic Empirical?," I argued that something similar needs to be done to bring propositional calculus into agreement with quantum mechanics. Eventually I came to the conclusion that my proposal did not work,[3] and, moreover, that it is not necessary to change our logic to achieve an interpretation of quantum mechanics that we can understand.[4] Many philosophers would say I need not have spent all those years trying to make it work; we know "a priori" that logic cannot be revised, or that any "revision" would amount to merely "changing the meaning" of the logical words. The question comes to this: can a proposal like mine, or like John von Neumann's in his *Mathematical Foundations of Quantum Mechanics*,[5] be ruled out without examining the *details* of the proposal or the *reasons* advanced for accepting it? My position is that although we cannot presently conceive of good reasons for revising propositional calculus, neither can we dogmatically say that there could not be such reasons. (The exchange between myself and Gary Ebbs in the present volume concerns related issues.) In the "quantum logic" that von Neumann proposed the rule of conjunction introduction *fails*[6]; thus if that proposal had turned out to be one we should accept, we would have had to revise our conception of what a conjunction is, *pace* Peacocke. I do not believe that this can be ruled out once and for all.

II. Analyticity

I have to admit that I see Travis's criticisms of "Two Dogmas" as extremely uncharitable. I say this, not because those criticisms are inaccurate, but because they are one-sided. When "Two Dogmas" was published, many of us had read "Truth by Convention," and we knew that Quine had devastating arguments against Carnapian conventionalism, arguments that do *not* depend on extreme empiricism. So readers like myself naturally, and, I believe, not incorrectly, saw "Two Dogmas" as a continuation of the earlier paper, that is, a continuation of an attack on a notion of "analyticity" that had been overblown to the point of becoming a philosophical monster. Moreover, Quine and Morton White were both discussing the problematic character of analyticity (as that notion was used by philosophers) for many years before "Two Dogmas" was published. I knew of those conversations because Morton White was my teacher (see my Intellectual Autobiography), and, in fact, White published *his* attack *before* Quine did.[7] And White was no "extreme empiricist," and he never attacked the notion of "meaning" in the way Quine did in "Two Dogmas" and in *Word and Object*. Last but not least, both Quine and White were led to their positions (in considerable part) by Tarski, who was also neither an extreme empiricist nor inclined to give up talk of meanings entirely.[8] So I believe the radical empiricism, and the criticism of "synonymy talk" were *additions* by Quine to a sound suspicion of an inflated notion of analyticity, but those unfortunate additions should not deprive us of the ability to see that the appearance of "Two Dogmas" marked a much needed beginning of the demise of an unfortunate way of philosophizing. And a host of other philosophers, I believe, see it the same way; they learned from "Two Dogmas" to distrust appeals to "analyticity" in philosophy, without following Quine into the doctrines Travis criticizes.

In "The Analytic and the Synthetic," I do, by the way, defend the idea that there is a limited use for the notion of analyticity in connection with such sentences as "All bachelors are unmarried," "All vixens are female," and so on, and Quine later seems to concede this to me,[9] but that limited use does not require us to think of even *these* truisms as immune from revision. (An example due to Charles Travis, in conversation: suppose we discover that foxes do not actually reproduce sexually, but we are right to think there are two kinds [which we mistake for genders], and one kind ["the cute ones"] raise the cubs. We might well keep up calling the cute ones "vixens" and give up "all vixens are female.")

III. GEOMETRY

It has turned out that our spacetime has curvature that is variable, and at least locally positive in the vicinity of a star—a fact mentioned by Travis. One reason that the constitution model fails to accommodate the resulting non-Euclidean behavior of straight lines deserves mention: even if we were willing to say "it has turned out that there are no straight lines" (because the alleged "possession conditions" for that concept are never fulfilled in our world), the fact is that as long as non-Euclidean geometry was inconceivable, it was also inconceivable that a three-dimensional space should be such that *no path in that space is straight.* If anything, it is *more* inconceivable that there are no straight paths than that straight paths should obey the axioms of Riemannian or Lobachevskian geometry rather than Euclidean! So no insight is afforded into what happens in such a scientific revolution by such a move. In addition, as Travis points out, saying that whenever anyone called anything straight she was *wrong* is hardly in accordance with accepted (or good) linguistic practice. Using an image that Cora Diamond once used,[10] I would say that we "see the face" of our original notion of straightness in the geodesics of our not exactly Euclidean world, and that is why we can continue to speak of "going straight from A to B," "taking the shortest path," and so forth.

In closing, let me say that Travis's essay, especially when read together with Gary Ebbs's essay, and with my exchange with Mühlhölzer (which also touches on geometry and on the issue of the necessity of mathematics), would make wonderful material for a seminar on the subject of necessity. Travis's essay is also rich in its historical references, particularly to Kant and to Frege. I agree with Travis that the implications of giving up the "constitution model" are enormous, and cannot be confined to any one field (or even two or three fields) of philosophy.

H.P.

NOTES

1. I am thinking particularly of Travis's idea of "context-sensitive semantics" and his insights into the way in which context-sensitivity bears on issues in a number of areas of philosophy, including philosophy of mind and epistemology.

2. "The Analytic and the Synthetic," collected in *Mind, Language, and Reality: Philosophical Papers*, vol. 2 (Cambridge: Cambridge University Press, 1975), 44.

3. I explained the reasons it does not work in my "Reply to Michael Redhead" in *Reading Putnam*, ed. Peter Clark and Bob Hale (New York: Wiley-Blackwell, 1996), 242–54.

4. See "A Philosopher Looks at Quantum Mechanics (Again)," *British Journal for the Philosophy of Science* 56, no. 4 (Dec. 2005): 615–34.

5. John von Neumann, *Mathematical Foundations of Quantum Mechanics*, trans. R. T. Beyer (Princeton: Princeton University Press, 1955).

6. Specifically, quantum mechanically "incompatible" propositions do not have a *false* conjunction in von Neumann logic; they have no "conjunction" at all.

7. Morton White, "The Analytic and the Synthetic: An Untenable Dualism," in *John Dewey, Philosopher of Science and Freedom*, ed. Sidney Hook (New York: Dial Press, 1950).

8. See Morton White, "A Philosophical Letter of Alfred Tarski," *Journal of Philosophy* 84, no. 1 (Jan. 1987): 28–32.

9. W. V. Quine, *Word and Object* (Cambridge, MA: MIT Press, 1960), 54–57.

10. Cora Diamond, "The Face of Necessity," in *The Realistic Spirit* (Cambridge, MA: MIT Press, 1991).

7

Alan Berger

WHAT DOES IT MEAN TO SAY "WATER IS *NECESSARILY* H_2O"?

I. INTRODUCTION: THE ASSUMED BACKGROUND

In his article, "Meaning and Reference," and his seminal work, "The Meaning of 'Meaning,'"[1] Hilary Putnam sums up the traditional received view of meaning and its relation to reference by stating two important assumptions made by the traditional view. He states,

1. That knowing the meaning of a term is just a matter of being in a certain psychological state (in the sense of 'psychological state,' in which states of memory and psychological dispositions are 'psychological states'; no one thought that knowing the meaning of a word was a continuous state of consciousness, of course).
2. That the meaning of a term (in the sense of 'intension') determines its extension (in the sense that sameness of intension entails sameness of extension, or of its referent).

These two assumptions, Putnam maintains, entail a view that cannot be held. It is the view captured by the slogan that "'meanings' are in the head." This slogan is supposed to mean that since according to (1) one knows the meaning of a term if you are in a certain psychological state, and according to (2) the meaning of the term determines its reference or extension, then it would follow that if you are in a certain psychological state, then you can determine the term's referent merely from being in that state alone, that is, from the fact that metaphorically speaking the "meaning of the term is in your head." Putnam, with his typical ingenious science fiction thought experiment, has us consider somewhere in the galaxy a planet that we shall call Twin Earth. Twin Earth is very much like Earth; there is a part of Twin Earth called the U.S., and most people there speak English. We all have doppelgangers, and there are corresponding rivers, lakes, etc., with the same phonetic name that we have in the U.S., and so on. Twin Earthians have a few dialectical differences in their English from that of us Earthlings.

One central difference is that the liquid called "water" on Twin Earth, that fills their lakes, oceans that they use to bathe in and quench their thirst, etc., is not H_2O but a different liquid whose chemical formula is very long, but which we shall abbreviate as XYZ. Putnam has us supposing that XYZ is indistinguishable from water at normal temperatures and pressures.

Hence, if a spaceship from Earth ever visits Twin Earth, then the supposition at first will be that the word "water" has the same meaning on Earth and on Twin Earth. This supposition will be corrected when it is discovered that "water" on Twin Earth is XYZ, and the Earthian spaceship will report the following: "On Twin Earth the word 'water' means (or refers to, or has the extension) XYZ."

Symmetrically, if a Twin Earthian spaceship visits Earth, their supposition that the word "water" has the same meaning on Earth and Twin Earth would be corrected when it is discovered that "water" on Earth is H_2O. The Twin Earthian spaceship would then report: "On Earth the word 'water' means (refers to) H_2O."

In short, anything that we may temporarily call "water" we would reject once we discover its underlying structure to be different. On Putnam's view, XYZ is not what we would consider the same liquid as H_2O. So, anything that we would call "water" would have to be (that is, would necessarily be) H_2O.[2]

When some of these metaphysical ramifications of the new theory of reference came to light and began to be challenged, Putnam wrote a classic essay, "Is Water Necessarily H_2O?"[3] where he emphasizes some of his differences with Saul Kripke, who also defends the new theory of reference. This essay can be viewed as a commentary on Putnam's classic essay mentioned above. I will concentrate on the different notions of necessity (and possibility), such as physical, metaphysical, and logical necessity, and I will avoid the metaphysical issue of absolute versus relative (or sortal) identity. More specifically, I will maintain the following:

1. The relation between conceivability and possibility is obscure at best. In any event, one notion is epistemic, whereas the other is metaphysical, and I for one believe that these notions are distinct and not to be confused.

2. Some (or most) metaphysical principles are discovered empirically, that is, they are not a priori.

3. There does not seem to be any criteria for picking out a class of metaphysical principles that uniquely specify a class of metaphysically possible worlds. My primary aim is to argue that a view I call "modified actualism," which I tend to endorse, and that Kripke hints at endorsing as well, entails physical necessity. If I am right that modified actualism entails physical necessity, then, as I hope to show, there is no need for a separate notion of metaphysical necessity.

II. CONCEIVABILITY AND POSSIBILITY

In his article, "Is Water Necessarily H$_2$O?" Putnam says that:

> Kripke does advance the view that it is "epistemically possible" that water is not H$_2$O in the sense that we can imagine a world in which an "epistemic counterpart" of water—something which looks like water, plays the role of water, and about which (up to the present time) we have all the same well-confirmed information that we have in the actual world about water—turns out in the future (as a result of new information which we get in that world) not to be H$_2$O. But does this example show that *it is conceivable that water is not H$_2$O*, or only that *it is conceivable that stuff that resembles water*[from an epistemic point of view] *should turn out not to be H$_2$O*? If only the latter, then Kripke, at least, may hold the view that . . . *it isn't conceivable* that water isn't H$_2$O.[4]

Putnam is suggesting that for Kripke the illusion of the conceivability that water is not H$_2$O occurs when someone could in a sense be in the same epistemic situation, that is, be under the appropriate *qualitatively* identical evidential situation that the person was under originally when the person took this evidence as evidence for the claim that water *is* identical to H$_2$O. But when we are in this same epistemic situation, our evidence is really evidence for a statement, not about water, but for some counterpart of water not being the same as H$_2$O.

If this is Kripke's view, and I believe it is, then of course Kripke is committed to the view that conceivability entails possibility. Putnam, on the other hand, maintains that his own view is and always was that it is, indeed, conceivable that water is not H$_2$O. What Putnam, Kripke, and I deny is that it is possible that water is not H$_2$O, given the fact that water *actually is* H$_2$O. Alternatively stated, what we would all assert is that if water *actually does equal* H$_2$O, then necessarily water equals H$_2$O. This agreement among the three of us masks an important difference that we may have regarding what we mean by "necessarily." We will turn to that in the next section. For now, however, it is important to see that Putnam disagrees with Kripke that conceivability entails possibility. Although I disagree with Kripke, I do not quite agree with Putnam either. My position is that I fail to understand what "conceivability" means in any nontrivial or nonvacuous sense.

Quite frankly, I have no idea what I am supposed to conceive of in order to conceive that water is (or is not) H_2O. I certainly do not envisage a water drop as consisting of a particular molecular structure that is different than a molecular structure of, say, H_2O, or different from any other molecular structure for that matter. If the word "conceivability" is to have any significance in arguments that require guiding us to what is objectively possible, then the word must mean something different than "objective possibility." Clearly, "conceivability" cannot mean "possibility" in the sense that something, a state, or "hypothetical situation" say, can or could have been realized independently of our knowledge of this state or hypothetical situation. For, if it did, then it would be vacuously true that conceivability entails possibility. There would then be no need to introduce the notion of conceivability as a guide to determining possibility. Perhaps this is why I cannot find anything in Kripke's writings where he uses the word "conceivability." Further, how would this sense of possibility clarify what I am supposed to conceive of when I am "conceiving" that water $= H_2O$, that is, the specific water structure of H_2O?

I agree with Putnam that the notion of conceivability is an epistemic, not a metaphysical notion. Nevertheless, "conceivability" must also mean something different than being in the same epistemic situation that I am in when I have evidence that water is H_2O, if it is to be a guide to what is possible regarding water. For, in the case of some necessary a posteriori statements, we can say that under appropriate qualitatively identical evidence, an appropriate corresponding qualitative statement, not about water, but about its counterpart, might have been false. In short, this very same evidence might turn out to be evidence, not for water failing to be H_2O, but instead for water's counterpart failing to be H_2O. This problem arises since there is a sharp distinction between epistemic and metaphysical notions, and one does not entail the other.

III. METAPHYSICAL NECESSITY: SOME PROBLEMS

I have said above that what Putnam, Kripke, and I would all assert is that if, in fact, water does equal H_2O, then necessarily water equals H_2O. Kripke would say that this follows from the law of substitutivity of identity: for any objects x and y, if x is identical to y, then if x has a certain property φ, so does y:

 1. $(x)(y)[(x = y) \rightarrow (\varphi(x) \rightarrow \varphi(y))]$,

where, φ may instantiate modal properties.
and from 2: Every object is necessarily self-identical:

 2. $(x)\square(x = x)$

3 is a substitution instance of 1, the substitutivity law.

 3. $(x)(y)(x = y) \rightarrow [\square(x = x) \rightarrow \square(x = y)]$

Last, from 2 and 3, we can conclude that, for every x and y, if x equals y, then, necessarily x equals y:

 4. $(x)(y)[(x = y) \rightarrow \square(x = y)]$

I presume that Putnam agrees with the above argument, or at the very least with its conclusion. Although Kripke (and I) maintain that the argument is a priori, we all agree that when 4 is instantiated by a necessary a posteriori truth, we can empirically discover that the antecedent to 4 is false. In fact Putnam says that "the claim that it is necessary that water is H$_2$O is a *defeasible* claim . . . and discovering that water is not H$_2$O in the *actual* world is what it takes to defeat it."[5]

   But so far, nothing said commits any of us to any specific notion of necessity, (except, perhaps, the epistemic notion whose possible worlds may be represented by a maximally consistent class of sentences).

   In his article, "Is Water Necessarily H$_2$O?" Putnam says some very interesting things about necessity and possibility. He points out that according to common sense, there are objective facts about what is *possible and impossible in the world*. It is clear that what Putnam believes is that the discovery of scientific laws is the discovery of what is or is not possible. He says, "We discovered that perpetual motion machines are a physical impossibility by discovering the First and Second Laws of Thermodynamics; but it would have been a physical impossibility even if these laws had never been discovered." He goes on to state that this is the picture of the working scientist, and therefore it is simply obvious that the "conceivability" of a perpetual motion machine has nothing to do with its possibility. I agree completely. He goes on to say that "what Kripke claimed to do in *Naming and Necessity* . . . was to generate another, stronger notion of *objective* (nonepistemic) necessity, a notion of objective necessity stronger than physical necessity."[6]

Putnam, in effect, goes on to say that there are two serious problems with Kripke's new notion of necessity, which is called "metaphysical necessity." The first problem that Putnam presents for interpreting the necessity operator in the sentence "Water is necessarily H_2O" as "metaphysical necessity" is based on what ultimately determines whether we are talking about *the same liquid as what we call "water."* It is not, Putnam rightly maintains, whether we think that there are laws regarding observational characteristics in a prescientific period that govern a certain liquid, but rather, whether, in fact, *it is possessed by the same underlying chemical composition or not* and *whether it obeys these*-[same]-*laws—whether we know it or not*—that the stuff we call "water" on Earth possesses and obeys. As Putnam says, it is sufficient to take "has the same physicochemical composition and obeys the same laws" to be the criterion of "substance-identity."[7] In my view, we picture all substances as possessing a subvisible underlying structure. And as Putnam rightly says, part of what that subvisible structure explains is why different substances obey different laws, and that is what makes *microscopic composition* important. Thus "has the same composition and (therefore) obeys the same laws" becomes the criterion of substance-identity. What Putnam believes Kripke left out of this picture is that he only talks about the composition, not the laws, and without the laws, he misses the need to talk about only physical possibility, that is, only possible states in which the laws of physics are true.

Now the second, and central, objection that I see Putnam as having against metaphysical possibility is the following. Suppose that in the actual world, water is H_2O and composition does determine behavior, but there is a (metaphysically) *possible* world in which composition does not determine behavior and some H_2O does not fall as rain, allay thirst, quench fires, and so forth. Would that hypothetical stuff still be water? Putnam says that "this seems to me to be a case in which the answer is utterly arbitrary."[8] Putnam's central objection, his second objection to notions of "objective" possibility beyond physical possibility, ties in with his first. If you omit the metaphysical principle that the same laws necessarily govern the same substance, you will end up with a possible world described above, and then it is not so clear whether to include the possible world in which H_2O does not fall as rain, allay thirst, quench fires, and so forth, as a possible world in which water fails to have those properties, that is, as a possible world in which water does not equal H_2O. This problem does not arise if we restrict the class of possible worlds to only physically possible worlds. Let us look at how physical possibility deals with this case.

As we have said above, what Putnam believes is that the discovery of scientific laws is the discovery of what is or is not possible. This is his point about perpetual motion machines not being possible due to the first and second laws of thermodynamics.

Now, if the same physicochemical composition obeys the same laws in the actual world, then it is physically impossible for there to be a physically possible world in which this physicochemical composition obeys different laws than what governs them in the actual world. For, what it means to be a physically possible world is that it represents a state the world could have been in, since in that state (and hence in that possible world) the actual laws of physics are true. But if there were really such a case as described in Putnam's central objection to metaphysical possibility I believe that Putnam would say that we were wrong to think that the internal composition of water is an essential property of it. As he says in a footnote to "Is Water Necessarily H$_2$O?": "what would [we] say if we *actually* discovered that composition is not what determines behavior?" He responds to his own query by saying that he would say that *"my view was wrong*—I never claimed that it was *a priori!"*[9] And I think that is the exact right response; the statement that water is necessarily H$_2$O is not a metaphysical statement that is a priori. It is an a posteriori question whether water $=$ H$_2$O.

In my book, *Terms and Truth*, I claimed that part of what motivates the new theory of reference picture is what I called, for lack of a better word, a Leading Principle or a Working Research Hypothesis (to guide future research projects in science). Once the Periodic Table in chemistry was developed, chemists took what I am calling a Working Research Hypothesis to be that each substance is determined by its micro or submolecular structure. Hence for each substance, they tried to discover which microstructure that substance consists in. They discovered that Gold $=$ AU$_{79}$, not to be deceived by iron pyrite, or "Fool's Gold." They discovered that Water $=$ H$_2$O, and so on. In biology, the germ theory of diseases was formed. Each disease was not to be identified with its symptoms.

We learned this from Putnam back in 1962, in his seminal paper, "Dreaming and 'Depth Grammar,'"[10] where he raises the question of whether someone can have all the external symptoms of multiple sclerosis and not have this disease. Rather, biologists formed as a Working Research Hypothesis for future scientific research that every disease is identical with a specific germ, and the scientific goal is to discover for each disease which germ it is identical with. Future Working Research Hypotheses in biology may already be established with the genome project. Perhaps the Working Research Hypotheses for future research based on this project is the following: each species will be identified with a specific genotype.

Now, we as philosophers (and many scientists, perhaps less consciously) are motivated by these Working Research Hypotheses, and we form meta-physical principles from them. For example, we may form the metaphysical principle that if something is a substance, then necessarily it is identical with a certain microstructure. If something is a disease, then it is necessarily identical with a specific germ, and so on. These metaphysical principles are of course not a priori. As noted above, Putnam says "the claim that it is necessary that water is H$_2$O is a *defeasible* claim . . . and discovering that water is not H$_2$O in the *actual* world is what it takes to defeat it."

Formulated slightly differently, many of these Working Research Hypotheses give rise to instances of the form:

$$(x)(y)[(x = y) \rightarrow \Box(x = y)],$$

that is, same substance, necessarily the same micro or submolecular struc-ture; same disease, necessarily the same germ, etc.

Putnam has rightly moved one step further in this move. As I have at-tributed to him above, in the case of substance terms, these principles are based on the fact that the underlying composition of substances is *governed by the same laws*. In other words, if necessarily the same microstructure, then necessarily the same laws govern them. Similarly for the germ theory of diseases and so on. It is the same germ or microstructure that determines and justifies the same laws governing them. And Putnam's further insight is to maintain that if the above is the case, then why do we need any kind of possible worlds other than ones in which the natural laws hold in order to account for what is or is not possible in the natural world?

IV. METAPHYSICAL PRINCIPLES IN PHYSICS AND HYPOTHESIZING NEW ENTITIES CLAIMED TO EXIST OR CLAIMED COULD HAVE EXISTED

I have maintained that what I have been calling "Working Research Prin-ciples" are metaphysical principles that guide scientific research. The sci-entist need not be conscious of using these principles nor of their status as metaphysical principles. To be sure, these working research principles are not a priori. Scientific evidence to the contrary will make the scien-tist give up these metaphysical principles. Success in these principles will encourage the scientist to believe the principle is true, and try to discover other confirming instances. I would now like to present a brief history of a metaphysical principle that motivated scientific theorizing in physics but was dropped when evidence to the contrary was given.

Let us consider the metaphysical principle of mechanism. In a mechanis-tic universe one physical entity has a causal efficacy on another by being in immediate physical contact with it. There are no other mutual actions that can take place in a mechanistic universe. This assumption was challenged when Sir Isaac Newton developed classical mechanics. There he introduced the notion of "action at a distance" in order to account for the force due to gravity in determining weight. But many scientists insisted that there can only be one kind of force in nature, and that therefore, Newton must be wrong in attributing two kinds to nature. They insisted that mechanism still holds and "action at a distance" must be some sort of illusion. What is really going on, they insisted, is that there is a medium permeating space, either by very tiny movements or by some sort of elastic deformation of this medium.

In order to defend the metaphysical principle of mechanism in light of classical mechanics making use of the notion of "action at a distance," and thus to also have a unified view of the nature of all forces, many scientists insisted that the notion of ether be introduced. H. A. Lorentz came a long way in destroying the notion of ether, but he left one mechanistic spoke in the notion—immobility. Einstein took this last mechanistic spoke out of ether with his special theory of relativity.

This brief history of science shows how one metaphysical principle—mechanism—is refuted by empirical science. I mention this brief history of science not only to illustrate that at least some metaphysical principles are not a priori, but also to ask the question of whether ether *could have existed*. And if so, in what sense? I reject the *possibility* of ether's existence. There is no possible state of the actual world in which ether exists. But one might question this by saying, "clearly any concept clear enough to be refuted by science is clear enough to be talked about, and if that is so, are scientists not referring to ether when they use the word 'ether'?" Further, if that is so, can we truly say that we are merely referring to nothing when we use the word "ether"? But then how do we explain why "ether" plays one role in science and the planet "Vulcan," which allegedly also refers to nothing, plays a very different role?

The received views of Russell and Frege can easily account for this. Russell's theory of descriptions takes any sentence containing the name "Vulcan" or "ether" and assumes that these terms contain descriptive content. It then takes its descriptive content and places it in predicative position and then reinterprets any sentence in which these terms appear as an existential sentence (or the negation of one).[11] But the whole point of the new theory of reference of Putnam and Kripke is to refute this traditional Russell/Frege view of reference, and I endorse the new theory of reference.

My answer to these questions is first, that both "ether" and "Vulcan" do, indeed, fail to refer (except in the sense of a mythological object introduced by scientists). But when scientists introduce hypotheses containing new terms, we do not presuppose that they are referring to something that does or even could have existed. Such scientific hypotheses are introduced by means of *nonsubjunctive, ordinary, truth-functional conditionals*. Accordingly, any model that makes use of possible worlds in order to capture an alleged modality of necessity of such "entities" introduced by, say, "Vulcan" or "ether" (or anything else whose existence about which a scientist may speculate), cannot be representing objective possibility, or what is often called—metaphysical, or genuine—possibility. Metaphysical, or genuine, possibility consists in states that could obtain, whether we know it or not. Not so, for merely capturing what might exist according to a scientist's speculative hypothesis. So, I, along with Putnam, maintain that not only do Vulcan and ether not exist, it is also not possible for them to exist.

When the scientist introduces a new hypothesis containing new terms, prior to testing the hypothesis the scientist does not yet know whether the hypothesis is true or not, and accordingly, whether the terms in this hypothesis do or do not refer. For this reason any model that introduces possible worlds in order to capture whether the scientist's hypothesis containing new terms refers to something that does or could have existed, is merely an *epistemic* notion. All that would be required of such possible worlds is that they are consistent, and they might even be represented by a class of maximally consistent sentences. So, this epistemic notion has nothing to do with genuine possibility, and has nothing to do with representing metaphysical principles.

V. Metaphysical Principles, Metaphysical Possibility, and Actualism

Now, one of the things that I have learned from my readings and other remarks of Kripke is that he suggests adopting as a metaphysical principle, the slogan, "Same substance, necessarily the same laws."[12] So, it seems to me that, in many ways, he too is motivated by the view that discovering certain laws is discovering what is and is not "objectively possible." And since it appears that the underlying composition of substances is governed by the same laws, that fact gives rise to the view held by Putnam and Kripke in their new theory of reference regarding substance terms. Accordingly, they both accept as a metaphysical principle:

> If substance A is identical with substance B, then necessarily the substance is governed by the same laws that actually govern it.

Since Kripke suggests that he accepts this metaphysical principle (and considers it a metaphysical principle), all his metaphysically possible worlds would require this principle to be true.

I call this notion of metaphysical possibility *modified actualism*. On this view, possible worlds may have as members of their domain entities that, in fact, do not exist (that is, not all domains of possible worlds are subsets of the actual world) but they cannot have as members of their domain entities that could not have existed, given the actual laws of science. So, for example, according to this view, there cannot be a possible world in which there are flying pink elephants (assuming that such an animal would violate scientific laws of biology and/or evolution) or anything else that is a violation of the laws of science. Modified actualism has a very different view of what is to count as an acceptable possible world than that of *possiblism*.

Possiblism allows such entities that are properly called "possibilia," a name that allegedly refers to unactualized possible objects. As such, it is subject to Quine's classic problem posed by his questions of "how many possible fat men are there in that doorway? Are there more thin ones than fat ones? How do we decide?" Quine overgeneralized his objection to possible worlds and thought that his criticism shows all notions of possible worlds are nonsense.

It is important to note that modified actualism, as does physical possibility, avoids Putnam's powerful central objection to metaphysical possibility. That objection, recall, is how do we restrict the class of metaphysically possible worlds so that there are no metaphysically possible worlds in which, say, composition of a substance does not determine its behavior, for instance, H$_2$O does not fall as rain, allay thirst, quench fires, and so forth, contrary to what occurs in the actual world. But there is a price Kripke must pay for being a modified actualist. If all the laws of nature are required to hold in each possible world (at least with regard to substances, diseases, species, and many other natural kind terms), the class of metaphysically possible worlds constituting modified actualism collapses into the class of physically (or naturalistic) possible worlds. Modified actualism requires that the class of possible worlds all have the relevant laws of physics (or of any science) be true. Further, as we have seen in the previous two sections, many of these metaphysical principles can only be known a posteriori.

VI. IS THERE ANY NEED FOR METAPHYSICAL NECESSITY?

Thus far, I have been arguing that we really do not need to interpret the word "necessarily" in the sentence "Water is necessarily H$_2$O" as metaphysical necessity. We can accomplish all we would want to claim, and should claim, by interpreting the word as "physical necessity." So, is there any reason why we would need the notion of metaphysical necessity, and what would determine the class of metaphysically possible worlds if it is to have any interest beyond what is physically possible?

As to the former question, I believe that there is a basis for some notion of possibility that is not just physical possibility, but I am dubious as to whether it would be reasonable to call this possibility "metaphysical" or whether this is what Kripke has in mind when he speaks of "metaphysical possibility." Let us consider as an example: a game of chess. We can talk both about possible continuations of a given position in a game of chess, as well as possible continuations of an earlier position that could have led us to a different given position. We can in effect talk about different ways the game might have gone. Although chess games are realized with physical objects in the actual world, it should be obvious that corresponding to each possible state of the chess game are several physical states that can realize them. Further, the problem is worse when we talk about the realization of abstract mathematical objects, such as finite automata, Turing machines, and various primitive abstract mathematical notions such as dimensionless points and solely one-dimensional lines, where nothing can literally realize them. Perhaps this is why Hilary Putnam, Charles Parsons, and Geoff Hellman defend a modal interpretation of set theory and mathematics in general. Another example of a use for this notion of necessity would be to prove the principle of the necessity of identity (which we proved above in the section, Metaphysical Necessity: Some Problems).

So, there might be a need for more than physical (or natural law) necessity, but is it reasonable to call this notion, metaphysical necessity? Since this additional notion of necessity includes possible states of a game of chess, the necessity of identity and other things of that ilk, we shall call it *abstract object necessity*, rather than simply mathematical necessity. It applies to various abstract objects, such as rules governing games and language, as well as various notions in mathematics and logic. But the crucial point for us is that this notion of necessity clearly cannot include various metaphysical principles that Kripke endorses, such as the principle that the same substance necessarily is governed by the same laws, that the same substance necessarily has the same microstructure, and consequently, for Kripke, these metaphysical principles that cannot be accounted for solely in abstract object necessity nevertheless must hold in all metaphysically possible worlds. There are other metaphysical principles that Kripke may or may not endorse, which also cannot be included in this notion of abstract object necessity.

At this point someone might object, "But are there not other examples that Kripke presents in *Naming and Necessity* that require more than just physical possibility and/or abstract object possibility in order to account for our intuitions of the necessity of principles suggested by these examples?"

Although a full-blown discussion of these important examples will have to wait for a further discussion elsewhere, it seems that the following can be said that I hope will shed some light on why I do not think we need a special notion of metaphysical necessity in order to account for our intuitions regarding these examples.

Let us consider, first, Kripke's famous Queen of England example. Suppose that the Queen really did come from those parents that we assume she came from, that is, the original king and queen. Suppose, further, that by "parents" we mean the people whose body tissues are sources of the biological sperm and egg that form a given person. Can we imagine a situation in which it would have happened that *this very woman* (whom we believe to be the Queen of England) was the child of Mr. and Mrs. Truman? Kripke argues that such a case strikes him as impossible, and I agree. The question is, can we account for this impossibility by means of natural necessity and abstract object necessity alone, or do we need to assume some other "metaphysical" necessity as well in order to account for this impossibility.

Regarding this first example, the Queen of England case, I consider this case consisting primarily of biological necessity (natural necessity) once we have defined what we mean by a "parent." Indeed, Kripke in a footnote states that "[his] view . . . that a person could not have come from a different sperm and egg from the ones from which he actually originated implicitly suggests a rejection of the Cartesian picture. If we had a clear idea of the soul or the mind as an independent, subsistent, spiritual entity, why should it have to have any necessary connection with particular material objects such as a particular sperm or particular egg?"[13]

The above remark seems to come from the following metaphysical principle:

> If sperm A unites with egg B to form person C and either sperm D is not identical with sperm A or egg E is not identical with egg B, then necessarily person C cannot be formed by the uniting of sperm D with egg E.

I take this metaphysical principle to rely on two assumptions:

1. The laws of biology;
2. The metaphysical principles that give rise to Kripke's view of the necessity of origin.

Since our first example seems to depend upon the status of Kripke's famous thesis known as "the Necessity of Origin," we shall presently turn to this thesis, which is illustrated by his next example. We consider a particular table (that we shall assume is being pointed at). Let us further assume that this table is made from some hunk of wood, regardless of whether we know which hunk of wood the table came from. Kripke then has us asking, "Now could *this table* have been made from a completely *different* block of wood, or even of water cleverly hardened into ice—water taken from the Thames River?"[14] Kripke's intuition is that although we can imagine making a table out of a different block of wood or even from ice, no matter how much the table formed from either of them is identical in appearance with *this one* (the original one), this is *not* to imagine *this* table as made of a different block of wood or ice, but rather to imagine another table, *resembling* this one.

The thesis suggested by our intuitions of this example can be stated as follows:

> If a material object has its origin from a certain hunk of matter, it could not have had its origin in any other matter.

Here, too, I am in agreement with Kripke's intuitions on this case. But do we need a special notion of metaphysical necessity in order to account for these intuitions?

Regarding this thesis, Kripke says in a footnote that in a large class of cases the principle is perhaps susceptible of something like a proof, using the principle of the necessity of identity for particulars. Later, in the same footnote, he corrects himself and points out that strictly speaking, the "proof" uses the necessity of distinctness, not of identity. He rightly points out that nevertheless, "the same types of considerations that can be used to establish the latter can be used to establish the former. (Suppose $X \neq Y$; if X and Y were both identical to some object Z in another possible world, then $X = Z$, $Y = Z$, hence $X = Y$.)" Kripke also acknowledges that the vagueness of the notion of hunk of matter leads to some problems.

If for now we ignore the vagueness of the notion of hunk of matter, Kripke's "proof" of his thesis of "the Necessity of the Origin" is an argument that involves only logical consequences of the notion of distinctness. The proof holds because of similar reasoning to our game of chess, where we talked both about possible continuations of a given position in a game of chess, as well as possible continuations of an earlier position that could have led us to a different position. In that sense, we can in effect talk about different ways the game might have gone.

In short, we only consider different possible states from a given fixed history of the world. Change that point in history, and we might change various properties of an object. For example, if the wooden table would have been nicked five minutes ago, necessarily it would have been nicked five minutes ago because we are only considering how the table can change now (five minutes after the wooden table was nicked) and still be the same table. It might not involve anything having to do with necessary properties of material objects, and it can be proved to hold of necessity within our notion of abstract object necessity together with the laws of science holding true in all possible states. Thus it might be only a notion of temporal change, "what properties must an object retain if it is not to cease to exist," which is a temporal question that Kripke has warned us to not confuse with the question "what (timeless) properties could the object not have failed to have." It would be quite an irony if Kripke, himself, confused his intuitions regarding these two different sorts of questions.

Neither in Kripke's footnote, nor any place else of which I am aware, does Kripke prove his thesis of the necessity of origin. There is no proof of the necessity of origin once we eliminate notions, such as vagueness, the principle of the distinctness of necessity or assume the necessity of identity plus the "Brouwersche" axiom, or equivalently, symmetry of the accessibility relation between possible worlds, views that I believe to which Kripke does not hold.[15]

But what about the necessity of the origin principle for material objects? After all, the thesis is not merely a logical thesis about abstract objects. Abstract objects do not have a principle of origin. Rather, it is supposed to be a thesis regarding material objects, and this is what gives the principle its special appeal as a metaphysical thesis. In my opinion, the closest Kripke comes to demonstrating this principle is where he talks about his notion of fixing the reference of an object. We must also look at how we apply mathematical and other abstract objects to the material world as viewed by Hans Reichenbach. He was Putnam's teacher, and he introduced the notion of a coordinative definition. We apply an abstract concept to the material world by finding some observable property or properties and stipulating that whatever has these properties satisfies what we are referring to by this concept. In this way we can interpret primitive vocabulary in a formal system in the physical world. The most common examples of coordinative definitions are those used in setting up measurement. By using this type of definition, we can apply abstract notions and objects to the physical world. But in practice, we often do not do this. We may simply use ostension to illustrate what we have in mind as instantiating some abstract notion. This is especially true when it comes to individuation of material objects. Such objects may be vague as long as they meet various practical, social, and other considerations.

This is where Kripke's remarks about the vagueness of the notion of hunk of matter enters. I agree that the notion of hunk of matter is vague. Consequently, the thesis of the necessity of origin for material objects is vague. Would a given table be the same table if it were originally made from the hunk of wood that it was actually made from, but with one less molecule of wood in that hunk? And what about possible worlds that are identical with the possible world we just described but for the fact that the wooden table's origin consists of still one less molecule of wood than the possible world that already contains one less molecule for the origin of the table than the actual world? And so on. And how do we decide this and similar cases? Likely, these problems lead to paradox. The metaphysical principle of the necessity of origin applied to material objects is, indeed, vague, and as such is not strictly correct. It is correct when we apply it to abstract objects whose identity conditions are sharp. That is all that we can prove to hold of necessity within abstract object necessity. But to go beyond that might imply a notion of necessity whose principles and how they arise are far from clear.

ALAN BERGER

BRANDEIS UNIVERSITY
AUGUST 2012

NOTES

1. Hilary Putnam, "The Meaning of 'Meaning,'" in *Language, Mind and Knowledge*, Minnesota Studies in the Philosophy of Science, vol. II, ed. Keith Gunderson (Minneapolis: University of Minnesota Press, 1975). Hilary Putnam, "Meaning and Reference," *Journal of Philosophy* 70, no. 19, Seventieth Annual Meeting of the American Philosophical Association Eastern Division. (Nov. 1973): 699–711.

2. In my book, *Terms and Truth* I stressed counterexamples to this last claim (*Terms and Truth* [Cambridge, MA: MIT Press, 2002], 199). For current purposes, we shall ignore these counterexamples, as I believe that this insight of Putnam's is essentially correct.

3. Hilary Putnam, "Is Water Necessarily H_2O?" in *Realism with a Human Face* (Cambridge, MA: Harvard University Press, 1990).

4. Ibid., 55.

5. Ibid., 62.

6. Ibid., 56, 57.

7. Ibid., 60.

8. Ibid., 326n8.

9. Ibid., 326–27n8. (Emphasis added on "actually.")

10. Hilary Putnam, "Dreaming and 'Depth Grammar,'" in *Analytical Philosophy: First Series*, ed. R. Butler (Oxford: Oxford University Press, 1962).

11. For present purposes, we need not discuss how Frege's notions of sense and reference gives a somewhat different account of how to handle such sentences.

12. As we shall see later on in this section, this statement commits Kripke to physical necessity as all that is required of any metaphysical necessity. See also Kripke's remark in *Naming and Necessity*, where he says, "Physical necessity *might* turn out to be necessity

in the highest degree" (Saul Kripke, *Naming and Necessity* [Cambridge, MA: Harvard University Press, 1980], 99).

13. Ibid., 155n77.

14. Ibid., 113.

15. Ibid., 114n56. Kripke points out in this footnote that one can prove the metaphysical principle of the necessity of the origin from the necessity of identity plus the "Brouwersche" axiom, or, equivalently, symmetry of the accessibility relation between possible worlds.

REPLY TO ALAN BERGER

Alan Berger and I are largely "on the same wavelength," particularly concerning the otioseness of the notion of "metaphysical possibility," and, *if* his reading of Kripke is right,[1] both of us largely agree with Kripke. But there is a clarification I wish to make, and there are some disagreements and/or possible disagreements, which is a good thing because it will give Alan and myself occasion for a discussion that I very much look forward to when next we meet!

The three issues I shall discuss are the following:

(1) I shall clarify my position on the identity of natural kinds, which is more nuanced than Berger describes, although the nuances do not affect the issues about conceivability and about kinds of possibility that are the concern of his paper (which is probably why he did not mention them).
(2) Berger says, "[His] position is that I fail to understand what 'conceivability' means in any nontrivial or nonvacuous sense." I believe that there is a nontrivial, very important, notion of conceivability, but that conceivability in the sense I have in mind does not entail (physical or 'metaphysical') possibility.
(3) I shall explain why I disagree with Kripke on "the Necessity of Origin."

I. On Identity Conditions for Natural Kinds

Since *Representation and Reality* and "Meaning Holism," I have not made the mistake of supposing that biological species are characterizable in terms of genotype alone. Ernst Mayr, Richard Lewontin, and others have taught us that what it takes to be a dog is to belong to a certain *population*; dogs do not all have the same genotypes, and the very first dogs had genotypes that, had history been different, would have been the genotypes of wolves (they would have been members of a different population). In sum, biological natural kinds have very different identity conditions than do substances. I talk about this in my "Reply to Ian Hacking" in the present volume, to which the reader is referred, and in more detail, in "Meaning Holism" and *Representation and Reality*.[2] In addition, in "The Meaning of 'Meaning,'" I pointed out that natural kind words have a range of senses, and that while there *is* a sense of "water" such that something has to be H_2O in order to be in the extension of "water" *in that* sense, and that sense is certainly important scientifically and metaphysically, there are a number of other senses.

II. AN EPISTEMIC NOTION OF CONCEIVABILITY

Berger writes, "'conceivability' must also mean something different than being in the same epistemic situation that I am in when I have evidence that water is H_2O, if it is to be a guide to what is possible regarding water." As I will now explain, being "a guide to what is possible" is not exactly the function of conceivability in the sense that interests me. Once we know that something is actually the case (that water is actually H_2O), we of course know that it is possible $[p \rightarrow \Diamond p]$, and also that it is conceivable (because one cannot "know" what one cannot conceive), and indeed none of this is an instance of "conceivability" "in any nontrivial or nonvacuous sense." But consider the situation that obtained when there was good evidence for the existence of the ether (yes, there was such a time, and detailed mathematical work went into showing how ether mechanics could play explain various phenomena[3]; "ether" theory was not *mythology*). The existence of the ether was conceivable *at that time* in the following sense: *we knew of a possible epistemic situation in which one would be justified given currently available background theory in accepting the* [ether] *hypothesis*. This is an important sense of "conceivability," not because conceivability in that sense is a good guide to possibility (it very often turns out that the hypotheses whose truth is "conceivable" at a time, do not describe possible states of affairs), but because conceivability in this sense is a *prerequisite* for empirical testability. Note that conceivability in this sense is also something that can be *lost*; it was once conceivable that the ether really exists, but it is not any longer. [I am not sure which of us Kripke agrees with, because this account of conceivability is something that was suggested to me by reading Kripke's *Naming and Necessity*, although he does not mention the role of currently available background theory.]

III. WHY I AM SKEPTICAL ABOUT "NECESSITY OF ORIGIN"

Kripke's thesis is (to quote Berger's essay): "If a material object has its origin from a certain hunk of matter, it could not have had its origin in any other matter." And Berger immediately adds that he is "in agreement with

Kripke's intuitions on this case." However, at the end of the essay he also says that, when we take into account the vagueness of the identity conditions for being a particular hunk of matter,

> The metaphysical principle of the necessity of origin applied to material objects is, indeed, vague, and as such is not strictly correct. It is correct when we apply it to abstract objects whose identity conditions are sharp. That is all that we can prove to hold of necessity within abstract object necessity. But to go beyond that might imply a notion of necessity whose principles and how they arise are far from clear.

So this is very qualified agreement indeed! However, I do not agree that the principle is correct as stated even if we prescind from the vagueness of the identity conditions for material objects.

Here is the problem that I see with the supposed "principle." Let us stick to Berger's example of a table, but instead of imagining the table made from a single block of wood (a highly unlikely event), let us imagine it as consisting of several table leaves plus several legs, all manufactured separately. We now imagine an alternative world—obviously a physically possible one, one represented by a different trajectory in configuration space—in which the atoms that, in the actual world, ended up forming the table in question, ended up in the leaves and legs of a number of different tables,[4] and the purchaser of the table we are speaking of—call him "Theseus"—purchased a different (but qualitatively indistinguishable) table from the same factory. Suppose that over time Theseus replaces the legs of the table he purchased with legs and leaves that are, atom for atom, identical with the leaves of the table that he purchased in the actual world. After the replacement, the Theseus in our world and the Theseus in the merely possible world own tables that are atom for atom identical. Are those tables not, then, *the same table*? Why should identity of constitution *at origin* matter more than identity of constitution *now*?

I am undecided between the following two views on this: (1) they are now the same table, and difference of constitution at the origin does not necessarily mean nonidentity *later*. (2) *It is not clear* whether they are the same table now or not. In either case, "The metaphysical principle of the necessity of origin" is either false or unclear.

Now for the case of Queen Elizabeth II. Of course, she could not have been the child of President Truman and his wife, for we can safely assume that they do not have the right genotypes. But there could have been [physical possibility again!] a world in which the very atoms that made up the zygote from which Queen Elizabeth II grew (or, if you prefer, the very atoms that made up the newborn baby that became Queen Elizabeth II) ended up forming the zygote produced by a different mating than the mating that produced Elizabeth in the actual world (respectively, an atom for atom identical newborn baby). Of course, the parents would have had to have genotypes that contain the appropriate genes, but there is nothing physically impossible about any of this—we are just imagining different trajectories in configuration space. In this case, even assuming Kripke's "principle of necessity of origin," the resulting human being would have been Elizabeth, although she might have been American rather than British, and her name might have been "Jocelyn Ginsburg" and not "Elizabeth"! Kripke's argument assumes that a zygote of a particular material constitution could have originated from only one pair of human beings, but I have no idea why he thinks he is entitled to this premise. We can combine the two arguments: Most cells in the body are replaced over time (though most, if not all, neurons are not). If (the merely possible) Jocelyn Ginsburg was born with the same neurons as (the actual) Queen Elizabeth, indeed atom for atom the same brain, but the rest of their bodies consisted of different cells, would Jocelyn be identical with Elizabeth? If not, what if after seven years the two were to consist of the same atoms? Could a *different* (possible) seven-year-old be atom for atom identical with Elizabeth? Surely this is a total mess!

IV. A Diagnosis of the Problem

Here is a diagnosis of the origin of the difficulty: natural science deals with *kinds*, not with individuals. That is why the question, "What is the nature of water?" makes scientific sense, but "What is the nature of Queen Elizabeth" (or "What is the nature of *this very table*") does not.

The Important Thing

As I explained at the beginning of this Reply, I raise these points because I look forward to discussing them with Alan. But if I have focused on disagreements and possible disagreements in our views, I want to close by emphasizing that we agree on the most important points in his essay, in particular on the two following points:

   (1) There is no need for, and no clarity in, a notion of "metaphysical possibility" that is supposed to transcend physical possibility.
   (2) However, there are kinds of possibility over and above physical possibility, particularly mathematical and logical possibility.[5]

H.P.

NOTES

1. I had been inclined to think that, for Kripke, metaphysical possibility was supposed to be an independently clear notion, and that its coextensiveness with physical possibility was an undecided metaphysical hypothesis. I explain my view on *conceivability* later in this essay.

2. "Meaning Holism," in *The Philosophy of W. V. Quine*, ed. Lewis E. Hahn and Paul A. Schilpp (La Salle, IL: Open Court, 1986). *Representation and Reality* (Cambridge, MA: MIT Press, 1988).

3. See, for example, John Worrall, "How to Remain (Reasonably) Optimistic: Scientific Realism and the 'Luminiferous Ether,'" *PSA: Proceedings of the Biennial Meeting of the Philosophy of Science Association* (1994): 334–42.

4. Almost all the atoms in a table (or a human body) are highly stable, and have extremely long lifetimes. Thus if we start with a world that was identical to ours many thousands or even millions of years ago, and imagine that quantum mechanical uncertainty resulted in those same atoms arriving in different places and forming part of different objects, we can "stipulate" the identities of the relevant atoms at the start of the divergence of the history from that of our actual world in just the way Kripke does when considering nonactual possible worlds.

5. On which, see my replies to Wagner and to Hellman in the present volume.

8

Ian Hacking

NATURAL KINDS, HIDDEN STRUCTURES, AND PRAGMATIC INSTINCTS

This essay examines Hilary Putnam's work on natural kinds, and not his indexical theory about the common nouns that name them. His approach is splendidly pragmatic, in the spirit of Charles Sanders Peirce. It is the most viable analysis of the concept of a natural kind. It is altogether different from Saul Kripke's vision of natural kinds, and Putnam's theory of names overlaps only in part with Kripke's semantics. There is no such thing as the Kripke-Putnam or the Putnam-Kripke theory of natural kinds.[1] The brilliant series of publications by Kripke and Putnam appearing during the 1970s were the high noon of natural kinds. To admire Putnam's work, and to say that he differed in motivation, method, aims, and results from Kripke, is not to disparage Kripke's contributions. They are extraordinary, but here I shall say nothing about them at all.

After that wonderful decade, the seventies, the philosophy of natural kinds slowly degenerated into a multitude of incompatible sects, to the extent that there is no well-defined or definable class whose members are all and only natural kinds. In brief, although of course some classifications are more natural than others, there is no such thing as a natural kind.[2]

I. KINDS

To query the idea of a distinct class of natural kinds is not to query classification, kinds, sameness of kind, or nature. All these notions and practices are central to human thought and action. As Putnam's favorite pragmatist, William James, said with characteristic exuberance:

> Kinds, and sameness of kind—what colossally useful *denkmittel* for finding our way among the many! The manyness might conceivably have been absolute. Experiences might have all been singulars, no one of them occurring twice. In such a world logic would have had no application; for kind and sameness of kind are logic's only instruments. Once we know that whatever is of a kind is also of that kind's kind, we can travel through the universe as if with seven-league boots.[3]

How right he was! It is not "kinds" or sameness of kind that concern us here, however, but the idea that there is a designated class of kinds, the natural kinds.

Note that although the expression "natural kind" was in philosophical use at the time James wrote, he said "kind," not "natural kind." Another notable pragmatist, namely Quine, dropped the adjective "natural" three pages into his famous "Natural Kinds."[4] That paper, published in 1969, paved the way for the semantics of natural kinds that surged forth within a couple of years. No one noticed that he had forayed into the discourse of natural kinds and sashayed out again, back, as it were, to William James. He concluded with scientific triumphalism that went far beyond James: "In general we can take it as a very special mark of the maturity of a branch of science that it no longer needs an irreducible notion of similarity and kind. It is that final stage where the animal vestige is wholly absorbed into the theory . . . a paradigm of the evolution of unreason into science."[5]

II. PUTNAM'S WORK

"The Meaning of 'Meaning'," first published in 1975, must be Putnam's most memorable single contribution to the philosophy of language. It is also a sort of plateau in his reflections about natural kinds and their names. That is, earlier papers built up to it, and subsequent papers tapered off, commenting, modifying, and clarifying the work. Work leading up to and including the plateau is conveniently published in the second volume of his *Philosophical Papers*, titled *Mind, Language and Reality*.[6] I shall not offer a historical exegesis of Putnam's intellectual journey, but it is a good idea to remember the order in which these pieces were published. Here is a list with shorthand labels:

DDG: Dreaming and 'Depth Grammar' (1962)
A&S: The Analytic and the Synthetic (1962)

B&B: Brains and Behavior (1963)
HNT: How Not to Talk about Meaning (1965)
ISP? : Is Semantics Possible? (1970)
E&R: Explanation and Reference (1973)
L&R: Language and Reality (1975)
MoM: The Meaning of 'Meaning' (1975)[7]

All page references in the text (as opposed to footnotes) below are to the 1975 volume, in which these papers are collected.

III. REFERENCE-CONSTANCY

"Dreaming and 'Depth Grammar'," the first item above, is about dreaming. What has that to do with natural kinds? Soon after Rapid Eye Movement had been publicized, popular science held that REM was a sure sign that someone was dreaming. Some said that a person dreamt only when his eyes were rapidly moving.[8] Starting from his understanding of Wittgenstein, Norman Malcolm argued in 1959 that at best REM was a new criterion for dreaming, and that the very meaning of the statements about dreams would be altered if we were to adopt this criterion.[9] Putnam protested in 1962 that sleep research had merely found out more about dreaming, not that any meanings had changed.

The implications went far beyond dreams, for those were the years in which incommensurability, so vividly presented by Feyerabend and Kuhn, held sway. That was combined with the old Carnapian notion that the meanings of theoretical terms in science, terms that denote unobservable entities such as "electron," were given by the theories in which they occur. Hence if a theory changed, the meaning of a term such as "electron" or even "acid" had to change too. Putnam protested that it would be absurd to say that, given the (false or inadequate) content of Niels Bohr's 1911 theory of the electron, there were "*no* particles 'in Bohr's sense.' (And no 'electrons' in Bohr's sense of 'electron,' etc.)" (E&R, 197).

Putnam's account of the reference of natural-kind terms made most philosophers abandon the idea that theories determine meanings, and hence to grant that meanings persist even when theories change. Bohr was talking about electrons, the very same electrons that play a theoretical role in quantum electrodynamics, and a practical one in an old-fashioned TV (cathode ray) screen. There is no question what "Explanation and Reference" is about: "The main technical contribution of this paper will be a sketch of a theory of meaning which supports" such insights (E&R, 197).

Putnam always held fast to the doctrine of "meaning constancy," with its maxim that meanings should not be multiplied beyond necessity. Referential semantics became a lynchpin of this doctrine: common stereotypes of dreaming, chemical acids, or electrons might change as we found out more and more about dreams, acids, and electrons, but the reference of the nouns "dream," "acid," and "electron" did not.

IV. The Inner Constitution of Things

Although he insisted from the start that the reference of a common name typically persists as scientific knowledge grows, Putnam did not dabble in essences. The closest he got may have been in a remark about gold. When Archimedes said in Greek that something was gold, "he was not just saying that it had the superficial characteristics of gold . . . ; he was saying that it had the same general *hidden structure* (the same 'essence', so to speak) as any normal piece of local gold" (MoM, 235). Essence is an aside. This is "essence" in scare quotes, "so-to-speak-essence." Putnam never intended that a resuscitated idea of essence could do any work. He did write earlier that the presence of characteristics found in a lemon "is likely to be accounted for by some "essential nature' which the thing shares with other members of the natural kind" (ISP?, 140). Once again, "essential nature" is in scare quotes, or perhaps quotation marks indicating amusement or irony. Up to and including Quine's paper of 1969, the tradition of writing about natural kinds was wholly nominalist, utterly skeptical about the idea of essence, and rather pragmatic. Mill, Venn, Russell, Broad, Quine: Putnam is a proud member of that company.

Hidden structure, as my title announces, is at the core of Putnam's understanding of natural kinds. In this respect he is curiously reminiscent of Locke. Thanks to an influential paper by John Mackie, philosophers started using Locke's strange expressions, "real essence" and "nominal essence."[10] These phrases were seldom used in English-language philosophizing after Locke, and before Mackie. The casual new readers whom Mackie introduced to Locke did not notice that Locke was a supreme ironist, from the generation of English writers that was to be followed by great satirists such as John Arbuthnot and Jonathan Swift. "If therefore any one will think, that a *Man*, and a *Horse*, and an Animal, and a Plant, *etc*. are distinguished by real Essences made by Nature, he must think Nature to be very liberal of these real Essences, making one for Body, another for an Animal, and another for a Horse; and all these Essences liberally bestowed upon *Bucephalus*."[11]

We should be cautious in reading Locke out of context. He was still fighting scholastic demons that we no longer even understand. Nevertheless, we may say without too much anachronism that Locke trashed essence.

Leibniz knew that, and rightly feared what Locke was up to.[12] John Stuart Mill, perennial nominalist that he was, delighted in Locke's "immortal Third Book," precisely because it demolished essence.[13]

Locke did say that the "real internal, but generally in Substances, unknown Constitution of Things, whereon their discoverable Qualities depend, may be called their *Essence*."[14] Locke, self-styled underlaborer to the Royal Society, was at one with "those, who look on all natural Things to have a real, but unknown Constitution of their insensible Parts, from which flow those sensible Qualities, which serve us to distinguish them one from another, according as we have Occasion to rank them into sorts, under common Denominations."[15] That is as close to a late seventeenth-century explanation of Putnam's "hidden structure" as could be. Locke's subsequent use of the expression "real essence" can be read as no more than Putnam's so-to-speak-essence. To treat seriously of essences is only to invite hapless ghosts to haunt your Putnamian (or Lockeite) house.[16]

Like most empiricists after him, up to and including Bas van Fraassen, Locke doubted that we would ever know the internal Constitution of Things, but he understood the idea perfectly. Perhaps only early in the twentieth century could we honestly be said to know a great deal about hidden structures of substances, which is, of course, the point from which Putnam starts. Note that Locke spoke of substances, such as gold. He did not put kinds of substances together with kinds of living things, as two sorts of "natural kinds." That happened later, thanks to John Stuart Mill.

V. Natural Kinds as Part of a Theory of the World

Perhaps only in the 1990s did Putnam make clear that natural kinds not only lack essences, in any interesting sense of that word, but also lack necessary and sufficient conditions (unless we define them into being). "Natural kinds, when we examine them, almost always turn out to have boundaries which are to some degree arbitrary, even if the degree of arbitrariness is much less than in the case of a completely conventional kind like 'constellation.'"[17] And speaking of his own reading of Aristotle, he wrote that "the greatest difficulty facing someone who wishes to hold an Aristotelian view is that the central intuition behind that view, that is, the intuition that a natural kind *has* a single determinate form (or 'nature' or 'essence') has become problematical."[18]

Putnam made clear from the start that there is no clear and unequivocal sense to the term "natural kind." We cannot give a good definition of this expression from the philosophy of logic and natural science. It is "in the same boat as the more familiar meta-scientific terms 'theory' and 'explanation,' as far as resisting a speedy and definitive analysis is concerned" (ISP?,

141). But at least "explanation" is a common word of ordinary English, so there are centuries of understanding upon which it is grounded. Few people who are not philosophers use "natural kind." Putnam did venture a definition sketch of the term—with an immediate retraction:

> Even if we *could* define 'natural kind'—say, 'a natural kind is a class which is the extension of a term *P* which plays such-and-such a methodological role in some well-confirmed theory'—the definition would obviously embody a theory of the world, at least in part. It is not *analytic* that natural kinds are classes which play certain kinds of roles in theories; what *really* distinguishes the classes we count as natural kinds is itself a matter of (high level and very abstract) scientific investigation and not just meaning analysis. (ISP?, 141)

VI. IMPORTANCE AND SPEAKER'S INTEREST

Although my concern is natural kinds and not their names, Putnam's analyses of the 1970s tend to explain each in terms of the other. So let us briefly recall his "theory that natural-kind words like 'water' are indexical" (MoM, 234).[19] Much of his classic paper was dedicated to overcoming the idea that meanings and reference are private, "in the head." Many of us had already learned that from Wittgenstein. But Putnam urged a far stronger claim with his famous Twin Earth example. Not only is the meaning of a word such as "water" not determined by what we have in mind when we use it, but also it is partly determined by what water is, namely H_2O.

Putnam wrote that his "theory can be summarized as saying that words like 'water' have an unnoticed indexical component: 'water' is stuff that bears a certain similarity relation to the water *around here*" (MoM, 234). This idea is distinct from the baptismal model of names for natural kinds. In that picture, some stuff was named a long time ago, and the name, by a historical tradition, continues as the name of that very stuff. Doubtless the mention of "local gold" in the quotation about Archimedes suggests the historical tradition: "gold" refers to stuff that is the same stuff as the gold around Archimedes, which I take to be the same stuff as the small amount of gold about my person right now.

But first, what is "the same stuff"? In the case of water, Putnam says that water is anything that is the same liquid as the water around here. But what, he asks, is this relation, "same$_L$" (namely, "being the same liquid as")? (MoM, 238). Putnam's response is typically pragmatic. First of all, "natural-kind words typically possess a number of senses." He attributes to Paul Ziff the idea that they may even possess a continuum of senses (MoM,

238). It is not often noticed that Ziff's *Semantic Analysis* and *Understanding Understanding* cast quite a long (and in my opinion desirable) shadow on Putnam's earlier work.[20] Or perhaps it was discussions with Ziff himself that had the influence, as acknowledged in the first footnote to ISP?. (In the 1975 collection, *Mind, Language and Reality,* only Quine, among living philosophers, is cited more often than Ziff.) Putnam says that one thing bears the "same liquid" relation to something else if they are both liquids, and the two "agree in important physical properties."

> Importance is an interest-relative notion. Normally the 'important' properties of a liquid or solid, etc., are the ones that are *structurally* important: the ones that specify what the liquid or solid, etc., is ultimately made out of— elementary particles, or hydrogen and oxygen, or earth, air, fire, water, or whatever—and how they are arranged or combined to produce the superficial characteristics. (MoM, 239)

The point is that structural similarities are what are "normally" important for "us," educated persons in a scientific culture, especially when we profess to be discussing logic or the philosophy of the sciences.

VII. WATER

In more ordinary life, when we are not playing the role of scientific persons, it may or may not be important whether the water is pure. How pragmatic can you get? "Interest-relative": we are not far from Goodman's "relevant kinds."[21] There is a splendid lack of dogmatism in Putnam's discussions. There is a core use of the word "water" in which water is HOH, or, as we usually but less informatively write the formula, H_2O. Then there is a whole range, perhaps a continuum, of uses of the word "water," which do not primarily involve hidden structure. Water from the tap is water. I filter it before making tea. It is now water with fewer impurities. I then make tea. The resulting liquid is not water, it is tea, even though it still has fewer "impurities" than unfiltered water from the tap. The sameness relation depends upon what you are interested in. The example has occurred to many people. Malt estimates that her tea bag tea is 91 percent H_2O, water more pure than much that we call water.[22] Chomsky also used tea, in part to criticize Putnam.[23] And yet it is as if he were quoting Putnam with approval rather than opposing him, when he writes that "whether something is water depends on special human interests and concerns." In 1990, before these papers by Malt and Chomsky were published, Putnam had already made clear that even when our interests are chemistry, water is not H_2O:

Water, for example, is not really just H_2O: real water always contains H_4O_2, H_6O_3 . . . as well as D_2O, D_4O_2 D_6O_3 . . . as well as superpositions (in the quantum mechanical sense) of all of the foregoing. Suppose one had a bowl full of H_4O_2; would it be a bowl of *water*?[24]

VIII. KINDS OF LIVING THINGS

Hidden structure needs no explanation when we think of water or gold or similar "stuff": the hidden structure is what we are taught in elementary chemistry. During the 1970s heyday of natural kinds, popular science expected that every species would have a unique DNA, which was necessary and sufficient for being of that species. Hence Putnam's optimistic remark about lemons. Things have not turned out that way. Each species is at best characterized by a cluster of "hidden" DNA structures. That leads essentialists to maintain that species are not natural kinds.[25]

Putnam prudently stayed away from biological species, which are not his forte. Recall his confession about leaving the difference between beech and elms to the experts (MoM, 226), or his assertion that "gorse" and "heather" are "exact synonyms" (MoM, 261).[26] Nevertheless the problems about what were called natural groups in eighteenth-century natural history—species, genera, and families—motivated the natural kinds discourse that began in the nineteenth. Species are paradigmatic natural kinds if anything is. But if "Natural kinds, when we examine them, almost always turn out to have boundaries which are to some degree arbitrary" the fact that species are more like clusters than chemical compounds, might leave Putnam unmoved. The lemon tree, *citrus limon*, will count as a cluster style natural kind. Presumably the fruit, lemons—which were Putnam's usual example in this domain—will too. But maybe hidden structure is not the way to go. A more dynamic story may be better suited to species. Putnam's former student Richard Boyd has presented one such story, his theory of homeostatic property cluster kinds.[27]

According to Putnam, natural kinds are relative to interest. Students of organisms have various interests, and hence they could have different species concepts, for each of which there is a class of natural kinds. There could be kinds for evolutionary theorists, kinds for ecologists, kinds for the fisheries. Kinds for old-fashioned students of natural history, bird watchers, butterfly collectors, where morphology is king. Exactly such a doctrine was long urged by John Dupré under the heading of promiscuous realism, and by Philip Kitcher as pluralism.[28] The extent to which hidden structure is the appropriate ground for a natural kind depends upon the field of interest. "To sum up: if there is a hidden structure, then generally it determines what it is to be a member of the natural kind, not only in the actual world, but in all possible worlds" (MoM, 241). *Generally.* Not always. Curiously, the very word that Locke used, "generally, in Substances."

IX. The Contingencies of Naming: Diseases

Putnam summed up with that word "generally" on a page that discusses jade and diseases. Each deserves mention, not so much to clarify hidden structures as to show that our practices of naming are through and through contingent. Contrary to the way in which many philosophers write, there is no such thing in general as "what we would say *if*" some state of affairs came to pass. "We" have said a lot of different things, *when.* Putnam's Twin Earth story relies heavily on what "we" would say in a certain eventuality. I have no quarrel with the moral of the story, that meanings are not in the head, but I think the argument is defective. We have no idea what we would say if the events Putnam imagined were to come to pass. There are no sound rules or valid intuitions about "what we would say *if.*" I shall first tell the histories of a few words in more detail than is customary among analytic philosophers, and then pass to a general conclusion based on these cautionary tales.

Since Putnam included diseases among his examples, it is convenient to consider the contingencies of names of diseases. Here are some examples to show that (a) Names of diseases often incorporate a theory on the cause of the disease; (b) When a cause of a disease or disorder is discovered, so that the old causal understanding of the disease is modified or eliminated, the disease can be renamed in one European language by the name for the cause, and in another as a syndrome; (c) When a disease is reclassified as two distinct diseases with different clinical profiles, and there were two names for the undifferentiated disease, one European language can choose one name for one disease and the other name for the other disease, while another European language can keep both names for one disease and invent another name for the other disease. We are not talking recherché languages and diseases, but French and English, multiple sclerosis, polio, gout, Down's syndrome, and measles. No one could have predicted what "we" would come to say in any of these actual cases. Part of the proof of that is the French "we" did one thing and the English language "we" did another.

Putnam first addressed "names of diseases" (his expression) in 1963, in "Brains and Behavior" (329, line 4). Polio and multiple sclerosis were the examples. In those days the leading conjecture about MS was that it was caused by a virus. He said that, "when a virus origin was discovered for polio, doctors said that certain cases in which all the symptoms of polio had been present, but in which the virus had been absent, had turned out not to be cases of polio at all." Likewise, if a virus for MS were found, then without change in meaning the lexicographer "would say that 'multiple sclerosis' means 'that disease which is normally responsible for some or all of the following symptoms . . .'" (B&B, 329). The criteria for being MS would change: laboratory tests would become definitive. That would not imply that the meaning of "multiple sclerosis" had changed, only that we had found out more about it, *and* that clinical diagnosis had been trumped by laboratory analysis. The laboratification of a disease is a fundamental change in practice, diagnosis, treatment, doctor-patient relations, and research direction, but it is not a change in meaning.

In 1975 Putnam returned to multiple sclerosis:

> There are, in fact, almost continuously many cases [in connection with diseases]. Some diseases, for example, have turned out to have no hidden structure (the only thing the paradigm cases have in common is a cluster of symptoms), while others have turned out to have a common hidden structure in the sense of an etiology (e.g. tuberculosis). Sometimes we still don't know; there is a controversy still raging about the case of multiple sclerosis. (MoM, 241)

A tremendous amount has been learned about MS since 1975—autoimmune diseases, T-cells, and much else. MRI for diagnosis, interferon for treatment, genetic research—but the root cause or causes are still unknown, as is any effective cure.

"A common hidden structure in the sense of an etiology": an etiology is defined as the cause or origin of a disease or disorder. Thus for diseases, hidden structures are causes or origins. Hidden structure becomes more and more metaphorical. Rickets is caused by a vitamin deficiency. Only by a stretch of metaphor can one call a deficiency a "structure."

Putnam spoke as if we knew only the clinical symptoms of multiple sclerosis. In fact the very name of this disease refers to at least an intermediate cause. Jean-Martin Charcot is better known for his studies of hysteria than for his work in histology, but he and his assistant first identified MS as patches (plaques) of sclerosis (hardening) on the myelin sheathes in the spinal cord. So in 1865–68 they named it *sclérose en plaques*; this became associated with a wide range of neurological degeneration. The French name emphasizes the patches, the English name emphasizes the way in which the hardening of the myelin sheathes occurs in multiple sites. Thus the names are redolent with connotations: a French scientist might ask, "Why patches?" An English one might ask, "Why are the patches distributed in this haphazard way?"

The clinical symptoms of MS were never the final arbiter of whether one had MS. Only autopsy was definitive. This does not call in question any philosophical thesis advanced by Putnam, but it is useful to notice that a name such as "multiple sclerosis" is no mere label. It connotes those multiple plaques. The same goes for Putnam's very first example, polio: Poliomyelitis was named in the 1930s, adapted from Greek meaning "gray marrow," a phrase that points at histological pathology rather than clinical symptoms. When a causal explanation dies, the connotations may become extinct. Gout was once loaded with theory, for it comes from the Latin word for "drop" and the theory that gout was caused by drops of morbid humors. (In French, the disease "gout" = *goutte* = 'drop,' as in drops of water.)

Down's syndrome illustrates another contingency of naming. It was identified by Langdon Down in 1866. He drew attention to the developmental difficulties, and also to the unusual physiognomy of afflicted children: their faces seemed to him to look Mongolian, and he thought the children might be a kind of throwback to an earlier stage of human evolution. "Mongolian idiocy" it was called.

The name lasted for almost a century, until in 1959 Jérôme Lejeune established that the syndrome is produced by an extra chromosome 21. In 1961 a group of genetic experts wrote to the *Lancet* suggesting four alternatives for renaming the syndrome, thereby dismantling its stigma. The editor chose the name "Down's syndrome" from among the four, and this is now the official name in English, although in the U.S. people often say Down syndrome. In French, where "mongolisme" had been the common name, the name "trisomy" became official. (Official in the sense that these are the World Health Organization names and those approved by various national bodies.)

In French the disability became named by its cause, while in English it is named as a syndrome. There is a significant difference between the two names. Much the same syndrome can be produced by other anomalies on chromosome 21, rather than by a supernumerary chromosome. It is also believed that some fetuses with an extra chromosome 21 do not develop into a significant expression of Down's syndrome. Thus if we take the names literally, Down's syndrome and *trisomie 21* overlap, but there may be cases of the syndrome without *trisomie*, and cases of *trisomie* without Down's. In practice, however, the two names are intertranslatable.

Down's syndrome has one cause, a genetic one. What if two causes are discovered? Putnam once called the form of words, "that disease which is normally responsible for some or all of the following symptoms . . ." a *definition* of a disease. "This kind of definition leaves open the question whether there is a single cause or several" (B&B, 329). There are different ways in which a disease can have several causes. There may be, to use an old fashioned language, predisposing and occasioning causes—an impaired immune system and an opportunistic infection. The causes may be multifactorial, as one now conjectures for many diseases and disorders, including multiple sclerosis. But Putnam also said we might come to speak of "discovering a single origin for polio (or two or three or four)" (B&B, 329). What happens when we find two distinct and independent causes for what had been thought of as a single disease? There is no a priori thing that "we would say." Here is what physicians did say in the case of measles.

"Measles" is an old English word. In 1830 two names were synonyms for a highly infectious disease of early childhood, "measles" and the pseudo Latin "rubeola." In midcentury, German epidemiologists clinically distinguished two diseases, one more benign but with a longer incubation period. That came to be called German measles, now rubella, no longer thought of as a kind of measles at all. "Measles" and "rubeola" were both kept for the more common, quicker incubating disease. Only in 1942 was it established that rubella is far from benign for a pregnant mother: it kills or maims her fetus. Only in the 1950s were the distinct viral causes of the two diseases identified.

In French there were also two common names, "rougeole" and the Latinate "rubéole." The latter is of course the same word as our "rubeola." French took the common name, "rougeole," just as English took the common name "measles," to be the name for what we now call measles. But whereas we kept "rubeola' as the name for measles too, the French more sensibly took the existence of two current names as an opportunity. In French, "rubéole" names rubella. So great was the confusion in the English medical world that by 1900 authorities were advising, without success, that the English name "rubeola" should be dropped altogether. *In French an existing name was adopted for one disease, while in English the same existing name was adopted for the other disease.*

X. THE CONTINGENCIES OF NAMING: JADE

Putnam drew attention to a gemstone with two distinct hidden structures but a common name, jade.

> Although the Chinese do not recognize a difference, the term 'jade' applies to two minerals: jadeite and nephrite. Chemically, there is a marked difference. Jadeite is a combination of sodium and aluminum. Nephrite is made of calcium, magnesium, and iron. These two quite different microstructures produce the same unique textural qualities! (MoM, 241)

Joseph LaPorte looked into the history of jade and found that the story is more complex.[29] Here are some elements from my version of the story.[30] The first bears on the baptism account of names of natural kinds. "Jade" comes from the Spanish, and the Spanish word was in effect used to name the substance the invaders encountered in the Americas. There it was valued far more than gold. What the Spaniards encountered was jadeite. So if "jade" were the name of *that* stuff, it would be the name of jadeite.

Since Europeans destroyed Mesoamerican civilization, we do not know much about its conception of jade, but we know a vast amount about the Chinese conception. The character *yu* denoting jade—parts of three interlocking bracelets—is one of the oldest signs in the Chinese language. It connotes, roughly speaking, all things truly excellent. Throughout Chinese history there have been more names for kinds of jade than was once alleged for kinds of snow among the Inuit. There still are.

Nearly all the jade in China was nephrite, although small bits of jadeite were in circulation, some of which in admiration were called kingfisher jade. Then in 1784, after the conquest of Burma, jadeite mines were established. Jadeite of the purest kingfisher feather green became the fashion at court, and no one questioned that it was the most superb *yu*.

Putnam was wrong to say the Chinese do not recognize a difference between the two minerals: skilled persons can tell them apart by feel. Their texture is *not* the same. Jadeite is also heavier and harder, but both can be worked by abrasion (not by carving) into exquisite shapes. *That* is the property of interest that leads to *yu* being used as the name of both minerals. (Contrast measles, where prognosis, treatment, and, in the end, vaccination are the aspects of interest, so that two different names are introduced for the two different hidden structures, namely measles and rubella.)

Meanwhile in the barbarian West, a standard classification of minerals current in Germany around 1780 called Chinese jade "nephrite." Remind you of nephritis? I said the Spanish named jadeite "jade." They also learned from the Americans that jadeite applied to the small of the back was good for what the Spaniards called kidney disease. If the Americans were right, and jadeite (but only jadeite) is good for kidney disease, the Germans (or more probably Swedes) named the wrong stuff nephrite.

And so on. Nephrite, under the name of "white jade," was chemically analyzed in France in 1848. After the sacking of the Summer Palace in Peking, a lot of stolen jadeite jewelry came to Europe, and the same French chemist analyzed it under the name of "green jade" in 1863, and proposed it be called *jadéite*, which became English "jadeite." In English there was a real question as to whether to use the old name "jade" for both nephrite and jadeite. LaPorte cites the *Encyclopedia Britannica* insisting that only nephrite be called jade. In the end, English followed Chinese practice, with "jade" and "yu" denoting gemstones of either mineral. No surprise: by the turn of the century the British controlled the world jade market out of their new colony in Hong Kong, but their principal customers were rich Chinese, so English followed Chinese.

Incidentally, the history of the relevant words in German is largely different, with the name *Jade* for the gemstone coming into common use only after the two minerals were shown to be chemically distinct. I have only sampled the history but have already said more than enough. For the record, Mother Earth also had a joker up her sleeve, or rather in northern British Columbia. No longer is nephrite rare. A single shop in Vancouver has enough nephrite to supply the world market for 300 years, at present rates of consumption. It comes from nephrite mountains from which twenty-ton jade boulders are routinely extracted with dynamite.

XI. Cautionary Tales

These are cautionary tales that suggest philosophers be prudent with their philosophical fictions. Directly after the jade example, Putnam wrote that "if H_2O and XYZ had both been plentiful on Earth," the situation would be like that for jade. "And instead of saying that 'the stuff on Twin Earth turned out not to really be water', we would have to say 'it turned out to be the *XYZ kind of water*'" (MoM, 241). But we do not say that the mountains in British Columbia turn out to be the nephrite kind of jade, we say they turn out to be nephrite. And measles reminds us that there is nothing predetermined that "we would have to say." For a moment, in English, some doctor may have said, "Your child turns out to have the German kind of measles." But rubella is not a kind of measles *at all*. Moreover, the temptation to speak of *rubéole* as a kind of (German) *rougeole* never existed in French.

These remarks do not pertain to the possible worlds version of the Twin Earth story, because what philosophers choose to say about a logically possible world is largely a matter of stipulation. But in the real world version, where Putnam considers what "one should say, if such a planet is ever discovered,"[31] there is no such thing as "what one should say" in advance of the local contingencies. Note that the analogy to jade is curiously exact. Although *XYZ* and water are not both "plentiful" on any one planet, there are regions of the imagined universe (namely, Earth and Twin Earth) where one or the other is plentiful. Likewise jade is not plentiful on Earth, although there are regions where it is (namely, northern Burma where jadeite is easily found, and northern British Columbia where nephrite is truly plentiful).

Most philosophers became fascinated by Putnam's writing about natural kinds because of its elegant contribution to referential semantics. I have no intention of pursuing that interest. A glance at what speakers of this or that actual language have actually come to say in historical situations may, however, dispel some of the seeming luster of that a priori discipline. What remains correct is the core insight that the meaning of a natural kind term is not to be given solely by a definite description of the natural kind.

XII. REALITY

Evidently I am cautious about the language part of the papers collected in 1975 in *Mind, Language and Reality*. What about the reality part? The parts were of course closely connected. Putnam said that the meaning of a natural kind term (and many others terms) should be given in "normal form" by a vector, "(1) syntactic markers; (2) semantic markers; (3) a description of the additional features of the stereotype; (4) a description of the extension" (MoM, 269). Putnam's vector is almost exactly equivalent to an entry in a desktop dictionary, although the dictionary parses things a little differently. Putnam includes "natural kind" as a semantic marker, while dictionaries wisely do not. Otherwise what Putnam gives for "water" (MoM, 269) is equivalent to what one finds in a dictionary. Indeed where Putnam wrote "H_2O (*give or take impurities*)" under EXTENSION on that page, and only later acknowledged that "real water always contains H_4O_2," etc., *Webster's Third New International Dictionary* was there already: water "when pure consists of an oxide of hydrogen H_2O or $(H_2O)_x$."

But there is a slide. Putnam's normal form has "(4) a description of the extension." A few lines lower, in an example, we have a display, where in the fourth column we see "EXTENSION." It is as if Putnam would like to actually put in a sample of the extension for us to look at or point to. Dictionaries do the next best thing when they can. When I look up "emu" in *Webster's*, I see an emu, or rather an excellent drawing of an emu. Putnam is candid. He continues at the top of the next page: "although we have to use a *description* of the extension to *give* the extension, we think of the component in question as being the *extension* (the *set*), not the description of the extension."

Sorry, I can only take that as *legerdemain*, the old magician's hand has waved once too often. Putnam wanted his normal form vector to hook up with the world. On page 269 the fourth component is "(4) a description of the extension." But on page 270 we are told to think of this component as being *water*, as being H_2O *itself*, the italicized *set* of all water. No amount of italics and "thinking of" can effect this sleight of mind. As I once unkindly put it, it is "as if some mighty referential skyhook could enable our language to embed within it a bit of the very stuff to which it refers."[32] In my opinion, Putnam's semantic version of the Skolem paradox, and his subsequent internal realism, all result from the fact that skyhooks do not exist. On realism I prefer to wait for a more pragmatic Putnam, who repudiated the "common philosophical error of supposing that the term 'reality' must refer to a single super thing, instead of looking at the ways in which we endlessly renegotiate—and are *forced* to renegotiate—our notion of reality as our language and our life develops."[33]

XIII. PRAGMATICISM

I have suggested that Putnam's use of qualifiers such as "generally," and "normally" betoken a thoroughly pragmatic attitude—in the nonphilosophical sense of that word. But it is also pragmatic in the philosophical sense of pragmatism, or more specifically, in the sense of Charles Sanders Peirce's pragmaticism. Not only Peirce, of course. Philip Kitcher has put the point well.

> There is a line of thought that runs from Kant through Peirce to recent writers such as Sellars and Putnam that can usefully be adapted here. Consider science as a sequence of practices that attempt to incorporate true statements (insofar as is possible) and to articulate the best unification of them (insofar as is possible). As this sequence proceeds, certain features of the organization of beliefs may stabilize: predicates of particular types may be used in explanatory schemata and employed in inductive generalization; particular schemata may endure (possibly embedded in more powerful schemata). The "joints of nature" and the "objective dependencies" are the reflections of these stable elements. The natural kinds would be the extensions of the predicates that figured in our explanatory schemata and were counted as projectible in the limit, as our practices developed to embrace more and more phenomena.[34]

Note the mention of "in the limit" so reminiscent of Peirce. Kitcher's account, though excellent, might be supplemented. Science is not just a sequence of practices that attempt to incorporate true statements in a unificatory structure. Insofar as science can be thought of as a single "it," it is also a sequence of practices that interfere in the world, create new phenomena, purify substances, generate technologies and render both substances and laws of nature visible in an artificial but pure and isolated state. Most of the more cosmic natural kinds, the substances, and the particles of fundamental physics, about which we believe we have almost certain and exact truths, seldom exist in isolation. Even pure gold, pure water, are hard to come by in the universe outside of human cultivation, and phosphorus occurs naturally only in compounds. We might even continue the metaphor of the limit: a great many natural kinds come to exist in the limit of perfected and retained laboratory practice, namely off-the-shelf instruments from the scientific equipment manufacturers. Or the practice turns into a family of techniques embodied in a host of processes and buildings full of equipment. But let us take all that as read, or as incorporated into Kitcher's paragraph, and attend to two of the philosophers he mentioned, Peirce and Putnam.

In a trenchant article for Baldwin's *Dictionary*, Peirce recalled that "J. S. Mill, . . . in his *System of Logic*, Bk. I. chap. vii. § 4, erected the word ['Kind'] into a technical term of logic, at the same time introducing the term 'real kind'."[35] After a succinct demonstration of what was wrong with Mill's account, Peirce concluded his article with the words:

> The following definition might be proposed: Any class which, in addition to its defining character, has another that is of permanent interest and is common and peculiar to its members, is destined to be conserved in that ultimate conception of the universe at which we aim, and is accordingly to be called 'real'.

Here we have, in a phrase, a central ingredient of Peirce's pragmaticism: "destined to be conserved in that ultimate conception of the universe at which we aim." Peirce did not say that he knew for sure that there is an ultimate conception of nature. He did not say that the real kinds are the ones that are of permanent interest in an ultimate conception of nature that we *know* to exist. He said only that in science we aim at such a conception. Water, for example, is a real kind, *if* it is destined to be of permanent interest in such a conception.

Two "ifs": *if* an ultimate conception were to come to pass, and, *if* the class "water" were conserved there. Putnam, in an only slightly different context, regards the first "if" not as a conditional but as an idealization. He uses the frictionless surface to illustrate the idea. Elementary mechanics treats of inclined planes and pulleys. It states laws for frictionless pulleys and planes. Such laws do not state that *if* there were a frictionless inclined plane down which a frictionless body was sliding, *then* such and such will follow. They state what would happen to an ideal body on an ideal plane. That may be regarded as the unattainable limit of a sequence of increasingly friction free planes. Likewise, we, or rather somewhat idealized scientific communities, aim at ultimate conceptions of nature.

Putnam's analogy seems strained. We have a concept, the coefficient of friction (the ratio between two forces), of which the least value is zero. This coefficient is measured on a linear scale. We can imagine a monotone decrease in friction. Each improvement in our technology decreases the coefficient of friction, that is, takes us closer to zero. The difference of the actual from the ideal has an exact measure, and decreases monotonically.

But idealized progress towards an ultimate conception of the universe is not linear, it is not monotonic, and it is not measurable. Hence Putnam's analogy should be regarded as suggestive, but not exact.

The idea, of an ultimate conception of the universe at which we aim, is central to Peirce's pragmaticism. In a related context Peirce made a remarkable statement about logic. He was discussing the frequency idea of probability. He thought that the probability of an event is the frequency in the limit with which that event would occur, if an unending sequence of trials were to be made. Here the analogy to a frictionless plane is more attractive: the limit of an actual sequence of improved planes is a definite number, 0, while the limiting relative frequency of an actual sequence of trials on a chance set-up is supposed to be a definite number, the frequency type probability of an event on trials of some kind.

But how do we know that there is such a limit? And even if there is such a limit, why should what happens in an endless long run be a practical guide in life, *now*? Peirce answered his own question with something no previous logician had ever thought. His famous "Three Sentiments" correspond roughly to Paul's trio in his *Epistle* (1 Cor. xiii, 9–13), namely, faith, hope, and charity (or love, *caritas*). Hardly anyone has ever taken Peirce seriously. Putnam did: "the problem Peirce raised is so deep."[36] Kitcher's paragraph is strictly conditional, "consider". . . "may" . . . "would be." If we are prepared to go beyond these, to Peirce's faith in, hope for, and love of scientific destiny, we may be led to a position akin to Peirce's.

Peirce spoke of kinds that were destined to be of permanent interest—permanently relevant kinds, one might say, paraphrasing Nelson Goodman. What interests might those kinds serve? The interests of Peirce, "the man of science" (a phrase that occurs in the dictionary article). That is, the interests of understanding, predicting, and explaining, in virtue of the laws of nature in which those kinds are embedded, usually making use of underlying hidden structure. And so we may produce a characterization of a natural kind, in the spirit of both Peirce and Putnam:

> A *natural kind* is a class that is related to others in a network of scientific laws, typically having an underlying causally important microstructure, and that will prove of permanent interest because of the value of those laws for understanding, making predictions, and providing explanations; and it is that class which will be retained in ideal theories of the universe at which we aim and towards which the sciences are tending.

This may be *the most viable account* of natural kinds.[37] It does not provide a precisely well-defined class whose members are all and only natural kinds. That is a good thing, for Putnam, as we have seen, did not think that the class was a precise one. Instead it is a loosely specified class that makes sense of the idea of a natural kind. It makes natural kinds out to be an important subset of Goodman's relevant kinds, namely the kinds that are relevant to Peirce's somewhat optimistic "man of science." It is not to be read, or is no longer to be read, as assuming that science needs to aim at exactly one true theory of everything, one ultimate conception, or a "complete" description of the universe, notions against which Putnam has inveighed. It is, in short, ecumenical and pluralistic.

This definition does embed the concept of a natural kind in a scientistic world view, with a faith in scientific methodology and nineteenth-century progress. Even for those of us who are skeptical of scientistic dogma, this is an account of natural kinds that is faithful to the roots of the idea, an idea that emerged in the glory days of the industrial revolution. But it does demand, as Peirce and, I think, Putnam knew well, faith, hope, and charity as regards scientific enterprises. This should present no problem for natural kind theorists, who are not inclined to reflect on their scientism.

IAN HACKING

UNIVERSITY OF TORONTO
DECEMBER 2009

NOTES

1. I explain this in "Putnam's Theory of Natural Kinds and Their Names is not the Same as Kripke's," *Principia: Revista Internacional de Epistemologica* 11, no.1 (2007): 1–24. Putnam mentioned a few central differences in "Is it Necessary that Water is H_2O?" for a previous volume in The Library of Living Philosophers, *The Philosophy of A. J. Ayer*, ed. L. E. Hahn (La Salle, IL: Open Court, 1992). This was first published as "Is Water Necessarily H_2O?" in *Realism with a Human Face*, ed. James Conant (Cambridge, MA: Harvard University Press, 1992), 54–79.

2. Ian Hacking, "Natural Kinds: Rosy Dawn, Scholastic Twilight," in *The Philosophy of Science*, ed. A. O'Hear (Cambridge: Cambridge University Press, 2007), 203–39.

3. William James, *Pragmatism: A New Name for Some Old Ways of Thinking* (New York: Longmans Green, 1907), 179.

4. W. V. Quine, "Natural Kinds," in *Ontological Relativity and Other Essays* (New York: Columbia University Press, 1969), 138.

5. Ibid., 138.

6. Hilary Putnam, *Mind, Language and Reality: Philosophical Papers*, vol. 2 (Cambridge: Cambridge University Press, 1975).

7. A short version, which included the Twin Earth argument, was published earlier, "Meaning and Reference," *Journal of Philosophy* 70 (1973): 699–711.

8. I put it in this way because (a) the basic phenomenon was quite easily observable without all the apparatus of the sleep laboratory. The sleep labs did not so much discover the phenomenon as publicize it. (b) REM is not the sure fire criterion everyone once thought

it was. Indeed, popular science still vastly overrates REM. For the past and present, see Kenton Kroker, *The Sleep of Others and the Transformations of Sleep Research* (Toronto: University of Toronto Press, 2007).

9. Norman Malcolm, *Dreaming* (London: Routledge & Kegan Paul, 1959).

10. J. L. Mackie, "Locke's Anticipation of Kripke," *Analysis* 34 (1974): 177–80; cf. Mackie, *Problems from Locke* (Oxford: Oxford University Press, 1976).

11. John Locke, *An Essay Concerning Human Understanding*, ed. P. H. Nidditch (Oxford: Clarendon Press, 1975), 460 (III.vi.32).

12. G. W. Leibniz, *New Essays on Human Understanding*, trans. and ed. Peter Remnant and Jonathan Bennett (Cambridge: Cambridge University Press, 1981), 293 (III.iii.15).

13. John Stuart Mill, *A System of Logic, Ratiocinative and Inductive. Being a Connected View of the Principles of Evidence and the Methods of Scientific Investigation*, in *Collected Works of John Stuart Mill*, ed. J. M Robson, vols. VII–VIII (Toronto: University of Toronto Press, 1973), vol. VII, 115. (Bk. I, ch. vi, § 3).

14. Locke, *Essay*, 417 (III.iii.15).

15. Ibid., 418 (III.iii.17).

16. Curiously it took some time before anyone urged in print that Locke goes very well with Putnam, and very poorly with Kripke: D. Galperin, "Locke as an anticipator of Putnam rather than Kripke on Natural Kinds," *History of Philosophy Quarterly* 12 (1995): 367–85. Most philosophers seem to have ignored the clear demonstration that Locke was no essentialist: W. L. Uzgalis, "The Anti-essential Locke and Natural Kinds," *Philosophical Quarterly* 38 (1988): 330–38.

17. Hilary Putnam, *Renewing Philosophy* (Cambridge, MA: Harvard University Press, 1992), 112. The use of star constellations, as an extreme example of an arbitrary or conventional class, goes back at least to Cournot, who wrote that Orion, Cassiopeia, etc. "are obviously artificial groups, where the individual objects are associated, not because of true relationships between their sizes, distances, or physical magnitudes, but because fortuitously, the angles that separate the rays of light they cast on earth are smaller than those between other stars." A. A. Cournot, *Essai sur les fondements de nos connaissances et sur les caractères de la critique philosophique* (Paris: Hachette, 1851), 201.

18. Hilary Putnam, "Aristotle after Wittgenstein," in *Modern Thinkers and Ancient Thinkers*, ed. R. W. Sharples (London: University College of London Press, 1993), 117–37. Reprinted in *Words and Life*, ed. James Conant (Cambridge, MA: Harvard University Press, 1994), 62–81, see 74.

19. This is commonly called the causal theory of reference. Putnam called his theory indexical. In an earlier paper he attributed the causal part of his theory to what he had gleaned from reports of Kripke's lectures: "Kripke's work has come to me second hand; even so, I owe him a large debt for suggesting the idea of causal chains as the mechanism of reference" ("Explanation and Reference," in Putnam, *Mind, Language and Reality*, 198).

20. Paul Ziff, *Semantic Analysis* (Ithaca, NY: Cornell University Press, 1960). Cf. his *Understanding Understanding* (Ithaca, NY: Cornell University Press, 1972).

21. "I say 'relevant' rather than 'natural' for two reasons: first, 'natural' is an inapt term." Nelson Goodman, *Ways of Worldmaking* (Indianapolis: Hackett, 1978), 10. For connections between Goodman and natural kinds, see Putnam's *Renewing Philosophy*, ch. 6.

22. Barbara C. Malt, "Water is Not H_2O," *Cognitive Psychology* 27 (1994): 41–70, 47.

23. Noam Chomsky, "Language and Nature," *Mind* 104 (1995): 1–61, 22.

24. Putnam, *Renewing Philosophy*, 216n8.

25. This includes modest essentialists such as T. E. Wilkerson (*Natural Kinds* [Aldershot: Avebury, 1995]), and hardline essentialists such as Brian Ellis (*Scientific Essentialism* [Cambridge: Cambridge University Press, 2001]). The essentialist reason for denying that

species are natural kinds is entirely different from the evolutionary reason that Michael Ghiselin has been arguing for over forty years. He summed up his grand argument in his *Metaphysics and the Origin of Species* (Albany, NY: State University of New York, 1997).

26. They are the names of radically different plants. Heather is a low lying gentle shrub whose flowers are usually a shade of reddish purple. Gorse is a shrub the reaches six feet and has cruel thorns and yellow flowers. Both flourish on Scottish moors and in Scottish novels.

27. Richard Boyd, "What Realism Implies and What it Does Not," *Dialectica* 43 (1989): 5–29. "Homeostasis, Species and Higher Taxa," in *Species: New Interdisciplinary Essays*, ed. Robert A.Wilson (Cambridge, MA: MIT Press, 1999), 141–86. Boyd's idea, that natural kinds of living things are characterized by causally connected clusters of properties, was anticipated by A. A. Cournot, op. cit. note. 17.

28. John Dupré, "Natural Kinds and Biological Taxa," *Philosophical Review* 90 (1981): 66–90. Philip Kitcher, "Species," *Philosophy of Science* 51 (1984): 308–33. Dupré, *The Disorder of Things: Metaphysical Foundations of the Disunity of Science* (Cambridge, MA: Harvard University Press, 1993).

29. Joseph LaPorte, *Natural Kinds and Conceptual Change* (Cambridge: Cambridge University Press, 2004), 94–100.

30. More information and full references are provided in Ian Hacking, "The Contingencies of Ambiguity," *Analysis* 67 (2007): 269–77. Significant differences between my amateur fact hunting and LaPorte's are immaterial to the philosophy, although my tale offers even more semantic contingencies than his.

31. Hilary Putnam, *Reason, Truth and History* (Cambridge: Cambridge University Press, 1981), 23.

32. Ian Hacking, *Representing and Intervening* (Cambridge: Cambridge University Press, 1983), 130, referring back to the transition from chapter 6, about Putnam's theory of reference, to chapter 7, Putnam's theory of internal realism. I have found that although the noun "skyhook" is still in use in the Canadian construction and logging industries, it is unknown to more intellectual readers. It seems to have emerged in print in ironic WWI stories, in which juniors were asked to do the impossible. The *OED* defines the word as meaning, "an imaginary contrivance for attachment to the sky," *Webster's* as "a hook conceived as being suspended from the sky."

33. Hilary Putnam, "Sense, Nonsense and the Senses: An Inquiry into the Powers of the Human Mind," *Journal of Philosophy* 91 (1994): 445–517, 452. Incidentally, to approve of these pragmatic instincts is not to be a pragmatist in any strict philosophical sense of the word. See I. Hacking, "On Not Being a Pragmatist: Eight Reasons and a Cause," in *New Pragmatists*, ed. C. Misak (Oxford: Oxford University Press, 2007), 32–49.

34. Philip Kitcher, *The Advancement of Science: Science without Legend, Objectivity without Illusions* (New York: Oxford University Press, 1993), 172.

35. C. S. Peirce, "Kind," in *Dictionary of Philosophy and Psychology*, ed. J. M. Baldwin (New York: Macmillan 1903), vol. I, 600–601. Peirce was faithful to Mill's own words, for only in 1866 was Mill's technical term "real Kind" changed, by John Venn, into "natural kind."

36. Hilary Putnam, "Pragmatism and Moral Objectivity," in *Words and Life*, ed. James Conant (Cambridge, MA: Harvard University Press, 1994), 151–81, 164. I also take Peirce's trio to be profound; see I. Hacking, *Logic of Statistical Inference* (Cambridge: Cambridge University Press, 1965), 47 and *Introduction to Probability and Inductive Logic* (Cambridge: Cambridge University Press, 2001), 265f.

37. Or, at any rate, of natural kinds of stuff. The Cournot-Boyd account of natural kinds of organisms, in terms of causally connected clusters of properties, may be the most viable account in that domain. Cf. note 27 above.

REPLY TO IAN HACKING

Ian Hacking is both a brilliant philosopher and a true polymath, and both traits are very much in evidence in the present essay. Ever since I read his *The Logic of Statistical Inference*[1] in the year it was published (1965), I have been an admirer of his originality and his breadth of knowledge, and I have followed with interest his many references to the topic of natural kinds in the course of the years. Yet I confess that I was unsure what to expect on the present occasion. In fact, before reading his essay, I formulated the following question for myself:

> I believe that given the interests that structure the various natural sciences, some classifications are objectively more natural than others. This does not mean that all the natural sciences must use the same classification: a molecular biologist may legitimately classify organisms differently than an evolutionary biologist. And, the 'joints' may have boundaries that are more indeterminate in some fields than in others. What are nature's 'joints' certainly depends on why we are asking the question and what we intend to do with the answer. But the idea of 'cutting nature at the joints' is neither fictitious nor hallucinatory. Does Hacking disagree?

Have I now received the answer to my question? Not surprisingly (given the nature of philosophers) the answer seems to be *yes and no*. It seems that Hacking agrees that the idea of "cutting nature at the joints" is neither fictitious nor hallucinatory, but that he regards it as at best the expression of a Peircean hope for the progress of future science. So we are obviously still in some disagreement. But I will describe our disagreement (from my side of the debate, of course) only at the end of this reply. I want first to spend some time commenting on a number of the points he makes, many of which I agree with, and that I wish were more widely appreciated.

(1) I agree with Hacking that "[Putnam's account] is altogether different from Saul Kripke's vision of natural kinds, and it overlaps only in part with

Kripke's semantics of names of natural kinds. (There is no such thing as the Kripke-Putnam or the Putnam-Kripke theory)." I did not appreciate how different Kripke's and my visions are until I heard Kripke's lecture to the Seventeenth World Congress of Philosophy in Montreal,[2] a lecture almost entirely devoted to criticizing my account for being insufficiently metaphysical! In my Intellectual Autobiography to the present volume I point out that "part of my story is the emergence of a tradition of scientific investigation, going back to ancient metallurgy (for which the question of telling how to tell whether a substance was really 'pure' or not was of vital importance). We do not call any metal that superficially resembles gold 'gold'—as the Greek ruler who asked Archimedes to determine whether his crown was really 'gold' (or *chrysos*, in classical Greek) well knew. For that matter, we do not call any liquid that superficially resembles water 'water' (it might, for example, be a mixture). What I said was that to be water, or gold, or some other natural kind, is to have *the same nature* as 'this', where the 'this' can be any one of the [majority of the] paradigms we point to, *and 'sameness of nature' is a scientific or protoscientific concept, not a metaphysical one*" (emphasis added). It is precisely the idea that the relevant notion of natural kind depends on "a tradition of scientific investigation" that Kripke *criticized* in Montreal. And as for Kripke's famous notion of "metaphysical necessity," when I first encountered that notion, I assumed that it could be given a nonmetaphysical interpretation along the following lines: take Kripkean worlds to be something like Carnapian "state-descriptions" (take them to be *stories*, in other words), and take the notion of metaphysical possibility to be this: a state-description corresponds to a metaphysically possible world just in case it is allowed as the antecedent of a counterfactual in a reasonable, rational reconstruction of our linguistic practice with counterfactuals). When it became clear to me that Kripke would never be satisfied with such a linguistified version of his notion, I started to examine it more closely and came to the conclusion that "metaphysical possibility" is a notion that has never received any clear explanation at all. I am amazed that it is regarded as respectable notion by so many philosophers.

(2) I am slightly puzzled, however, when Hacking writes, "In brief, although of course some classifications are more natural than others, there is no such thing as a natural kind. Kinds of things, and sameness of kind, yes: natural kinds, perhaps no." I would have thought that if there are kinds, and some of them are unified by the explanatory principles sought for by a given science or a different subdiscipline of a science, then from the point of that science or subdiscipline those kinds are the "natural kinds." But perhaps it is the idea that which are the natural kinds is not relative to the interests of a science or subdiscipline that Hacking is attacking. If so, we are together on this.

(3) I am also slightly puzzled that Hacking seems to approve of Quine's saying, "In general we can take it as a very special mark of the maturity of a branch of science that it no longer needs an irreducible notion of similarity and kind. It is that final state where the animal vestige is wholly absorbed into theory . . . a paradigm of the evolution of unreason into science." What Quine does not mention is that the "final state" when science no longer needs what I once called "broad spectrum" concepts such as kind and similarity,[3] is a completely *idealized* "final state." That concepts still indispensable in our nonangelic "vestige" are going to be unnecessary *in the wholly indescribable state of finished science* seems to me no reason to scorn them, and given Hacking's obvious distaste for what he himself describes as "scientific triumphalism" I would have expected him to agree with me.

(4) Hacking's "list with shorthand labels" of my publications on reference to natural kinds stops with "The Meaning of 'Meaning.'" But there are important restatements of and modifications to the theory in three publications after "The Meaning of 'Meaning.'" They are "Meaning Holism" (1986) (my favorite version of the theory, in many ways), *Representation and Reality* (1988), and "Aristotle after Wittgenstein" (1994). The latter two, by the way, point out that, contrary to what I assumed in "The Meaning of 'Meaning,'" the nature (or "essence" in shudder quotes) of a biological species is *not* given by its molecular constitution. Of this more shortly.

(5) Hacking's discussion of "reference-constancy" again stresses the nonmetaphysical nature of my concept of a natural kind. This is much appreciated! And I agree with him that since "according to Putnam, natural kinds are relative to interest," he could allow that students of life, who have various interests, "could have different species concepts, for each of which there is a class of natural kinds. . . . kinds for evolutionary theorists, kinds for ecologists, kinds for the fisheries. Kinds for old-fashioned students of natural history, bird watchers, butterfly collectors, where morphology is king." But the phrasing is a little strange. For it is not just that I "could allow" this; it was what I *said* in the post–"Meaning of Meaning" publications that I mentioned above. My view of biological "species" has for many years been taken from Ernst Mayr.[4] With him I believe that the "lines" between species are somewhat indeterminate and have to be legislated by us. And I agree with him that this is not an imperfection in population biology but a consequence of the antiessentialist nature of Darwinian evolutionary theory. I have hardly kept these views a secret: in the very paper that Hacking quotes, "Aristotle after Wittgenstein" (1993; collected 1994), I wrote, "Suppose someone asked the question, 'Is it part of the essence of dogs that they are descended from wolves?' The answer seems to be 'yes' from an evolutionary biologist's point of view and 'no' from a molecular

biologist's point of view."[5] And again, "As Mayr has said, the evolutionary biologist's notion of a species is more or less the lay notion of a species, and it is not a defect of the notion of a species that some species do not have sharp boundaries."[6] Indeed, much the same view already appears in my *Representation and Reality*.[7]

(6) In the first sentence of his essay, Hacking writes that his essay will be about natural kinds and not about my account of "the common nouns that name them." Yet the section of Hacking's essay entitled "The Contingencies of Naming: Diseases" is entirely about the historical behavior of the common nouns that name such diseases as multiple sclerosis, measles, and German measles (to use the contemporary lay English terms). My view is that, given that the interest of medical scientists is in determining not merely what the symptoms of these diseases are, but in determining their etiology, then, for example, measles and "German measles" are two distinct natural kinds, and *were* two distinct natural kinds, even when this was not known, and even when, as a result of that ignorance, the behavior of these names "fluctuated." I hope that Hacking's purpose in shifting attention from the natural kinds to the common nouns that name them was not to cast doubt on the notion of a natural kind itself! (As I said at the beginning of this reply, I am still uncertain as to whether Hacking is not, at bottom, a natural kind skeptic.)

(7) Hacking emphasizes that, "there is no such thing as 'what one should say' in advance of the local contingencies." Again, I wish he had looked at my *post*–"Meaning of Meaning" writings, for example at "Meaning Holism," where I recognized that the use of ordinary language terms differs significantly from the scientific use, but, in agreement with my realism about natural kinds, I wrote:

> Ordinary language philosophers . . . tend to compartmentalize the language; the presence of water in a physical theory ('Water is H_2O') is held to involve a different use (i.e., a different sense) from the 'ordinary use'. (This compartmentalization is often ascribed to Wittgenstein; incorrectly, in my opinion.) This compartmentalization theory seems to me to be simply wrong. Our language is a cooperative venture; and it would be a foolish layman who would be unwilling to ever accept correction from an expert on what was or was not water, or gold, or a mosquito, or whatever. Even if I drink a glass of "water" with no ill effects, I am prepared to learn that it was not really water (as I am prepared to learn that a ring that seems to be gold is really counterfeit); we do not and should not treat scientists' criteria as governing a word which has different application-conditions from the "ordinary" word water, in the sense of having unrelated (or only weakly related) application-conditions. A thought-experiment may be of assistance here. Let us suppose there exists a

liquid which is colorless, tasteless, odorless, harmless, but does not satisfy the need for water. (For all I know, there may actually be such liquids.) Call this liquid "grook." Let us suppose that a mixture of 50% grook and 50% water will pass all the lay tests for being water, excluding "sophisticated" tests (such as distilling the liquid, or measuring its exact boiling point or freezing point with a thermometer). On the theory that "water" means "odorless, transparent, tasteless, liquid which quenches thirst and is not harmful to drink,"grook plus water just is water, "in the ordinary sense." But this is plainly wrong; even a layman, on being told by a scientist that what he is drinking is a mixture of a liquid which is indistinguishable in composition from paradigm examples of "water" and a liquid which does not occur as a part of typical water, will say that what he is drinking is not water (although it is 50% water). Ordinary language and scientific language are different but interdependent. [8]

I could have used "jade" just as well as "water" as my example. That there are, from a chemist's point of view, two different natural kinds that are both referred to as "jade" in ordinary language is perfectly consistent with my account of natural kind terms and natural kinds.

(8) At one point, Hacking engages in somewhat inflamed rhetoric: ("Sorry, I can only take that as *legerdemain*, the old magician's hand has waved once too often. Putnam wanted his normal form vector to hook up with the world. On page 269 the fourth component is '(4) a description of the extension.' But on page 270 we are told to think of this component as being *water*, as being H_2O *itself*, the italicized *set* of all water. No amount of italics and 'thinking of' can effect this sleight of mind."). Technically Hacking is right, but what I meant to say has never eluded any previous reader that I know of, namely that the first three components of my "meaning vector" describe matters of which competent speakers are supposed to have tacit knowledge, while the fourth, the description of the extension of the natural kind term, is not necessarily known to speakers (not even tacitly), although it is what they would discover to be the nature of the natural kind if they inquired successfully. (And in a section of "The Meaning of 'Meaning'" titled "Other Senses"[9] I emphasized that in ordinary language this "scientific realist" sense is only *one* of a range of senses available to speakers. But it *is* available; the question "is my jewelry really gold" normally presupposes it.)

(9) Hacking closes by proposing "a characterization of a natural kind, in the spirit of both Peirce and Putnam," namely;

A *natural kind* is a class that is related to others in a network of scientific laws, typically having an underlying causally important microstructure, and that will prove of permanent interest because of the value of those laws for understanding, making predictions, and providing explanations; and it is that class which will be retained in ideal theories of the universe at which we aim and towards which the sciences are tending.

Sorry, Ian, but I do not want any part of this! Not only because, as already said, I have long been aware that biological species do not have a *single* "causally important microstructure"; although that is part of my problem, and I doubt (with Hacking) that diseases have a single causally important microstructure (that Hacking himself is aware of this suggests this proposal is not exactly a friendly suggestion). The real disagreement between us is that, for Ian Hacking, scientific realism is at best a "hope." I am not a skeptic about natural kinds. True, we may never have more than the approximate truth about the structure of water, but I believe we *do* have an approximately true theory about the structure of water (and about the evolutionary history of animal populations, and about the etiology of a great many diseases), and to be skeptical about that because we are sometimes wrong is as misguided as being skeptical about whether there are positrons (to use an example Hacking himself once used of something he is *not* skeptical about). If I am skeptical about anything, it is about Peircean counterfactuals about what science would converge to if inquiry went on forever. Knowing the nature of water—something we know an *enormous* amount about—is knowing about *water*, it is not knowing about what will be "retained in ideal theories of the universe at which we aim and towards which the sciences are tending."

I close as I began by expressing my genuine admiration for Ian Hacking's virtuosity and his enormous knowledge, and for his careful study of so much of my writing (even if he missed a few things). I only wish I could convince him that the realism he once professed about positrons should be extended to explanatory properties (and hence to *kinds*) as well.

H.P.

NOTES

1. Ian Hacking, *The Logic of Statistical Inference* (Cambridge: Cambridge University Press, 1965).

2. Saul Kripke, "A Problem in the Theory of Reference: The Linguistic Division of Labor and the Social Character of Naming," in *Philosophy and Culture: Proceedings of the XVIIth World Congress of Philosophy* (Montreal: Editions Montmorency, 1986), 241–47.

3. In my "What Theories Are Not," in *Mathematics, Matter and Method: Philosophical Papers*, vol. I (Cambridge, MA: Harvard University Press, 1975).

4. For example, Ernst Mayr, *Populations, Species, and Evolution* (Cambridge, MA: Harvard University Press, 1970).

5. "Aristotle after Wittgenstein" in *Words and Life*, ed. J. Conant (Cambridge, MA: Harvard University Press, 1994), 75.

6. Ibid. See the whole of pp. 75–76 for more on Mayr and on the evolutionist's conception of a species.

7. In *Representation and Reality*, I wrote, "We do not expect any two members of a biological species to exhibit the same behavior or to have exactly the same appearance (Siamese cats do not have exactly the same appearance as European cats); but we do have the expectation that (with occasional exceptions) two members of a species who are of opposite sex and who are biologically fertile will be able to mate and to have fertile offspring. If Twin Earth "cats" were never able to mate with Earth cats (and produce fertile offspring), then not only biologists but laymen would say that Twin Earth cats are another species. They might, of course, say that they were another species of cat; but if it turned out that Twin Earth cats evolved from, say, pandas rather than felines, then in the end we would say that they were not really cats at all, and Twin Earthers would similarly say that Earth cats were not really cats at all." The only point at which there is a reference to physical constitution in that discussion was in the remark that if Twin Earth cats turned out to be *robots* we would say that they are not really cats. (*Representation and Reality* [Cambridge, MA: MIT Press, 1991], 35.)

8. "Meaning Holism," in *The Philosophy of W. V. Quine*, ed. Lewis E. Hahn and Paul A. Schilpp (La Salle, IL: Open Court, 1986), 408.

9. "Other Senses" can be found in *Mind, Language and Reality: Philosophical Papers*, vol. II (Cambridge, MA: Harvard University Press, 1975), 238–41.

9

Robert K. Shope

THE STATE OF AFFAIRS
REGARDING TRUE ASSERTIONS

In some of the more recent of his extraordinarily numerous writings, Hilary Putnam has urged philosophers to recognize the respectability of employing a nonreduced concept of intentionality ("aboutness") as well as a concept of states of affairs.[1] He has also proposed that we should develop an account of representing that does not tie thought and language too closely to processes involving entities of the sort that cognitive scientists and some materialists call representations.[2]

I have previously sought to follow those paths when analyzing representing in *The Nature of Meaningfulness*.[3] I propose here to explore the application of that analysis to Putnam's views about correspondence truth and about the plausibility of a thesis that he shares with a deflationary view of truth. Let us call it the Minimal Assertion Thesis, the claim, roughly, that to assert that *h* is true is to assert no more than that *h*. I shall defend the thesis by means of the account of representing from *The Nature of Meaningfulness* so as to develop and apply an analysis of assertion. A linked result will be to show that truth involves a certain type of correspondence, which is nonetheless distinct from what is spoken of in a classical correspondence "theory" of truth and correctly rejected by Putnam.

I. CONTEXT SENSITIVITY

It will be important to adopt the perspective that Putnam and Charles Travis trace to Wittgenstein and John L. Austin,[4] which treats the context in which one utters a declarative sentence in our language as almost always part of what determines what one succeeds thereby in asserting. Putnam illustrates such sensitivity to context by considering how the assertion made in uttering the sentence S1: "There is a lot of coffee on the table," can vary in what he technically calls its "truth-evaluative content" depending on the context of utterance, even though the meaning of the words do not vary.[5] The truth-evaluative content can be imagined to vary as we shift, for instance, from thinking of a context where, briefly put, the speaker is about to add, "Help yourself to a cup if you like," to a context where the speaker is about to say, "I hope the weight of the cartons won't collapse the table," to a context involving the supplement, "Get a towel to mop it up." Let us consider in our example the latter context, calling it the spill context. In a context, the truth-evaluable content of a given sentence is treated by Putnam as another sentence whose truth value in the context determines the same truth value for the given sentence, for example, the truth-evaluable content of S1 in the spill context is S2: "a lot of liquid coffee is spread over the surface of the table." (Of course this is roughly put, since, for one thing, what counts as a lot is sensitive to context.)

II. An Analysis of Representing

My previous analysis of representing in *The Nature of Meaningfulness* spoke of a state of affairs so as to distinguish it from the obtaining of the state of affairs, allowing that some states of affairs (for example, an Illinois governor's being corrupt; the car's being brought home very low on gas) can obtain more than once (in these cases, regrettably often) although others can obtain at most once. Although we often refer to a state of affairs by a gerundive, this is not always grammatically possible, and in previous work I employed for general purposes phrases of the form, "the state of affairs that *h*," for example, "the state of affairs that the car was brought home very low on gas," and spoke of the obtaining (and in some cases the occurrence) of the state of affairs that *h*. Although I shall continue to employ such terminology, I promise to consider later whether some other forms are preferable as canonical ways of referring to state of affairs. With the help of that terminology, an application of my earlier analysis of representing will be able to provide us with some starting points. A few caveats: First, it will not reduce the usefulness of the analysis in the present discussion if we consider it in a slightly simplified form. Secondly, the wording of the analysandum takes the form, "*x* represents *y*," and the analysis is not seeking to cover representing something *as* something, nor does it concern an event of representing or a representation as some sort of structural analogue. Thirdly, although I have argued in *The Nature of*

Meaningfulness that numerous cases that we commonly regard as examples of representing fit the analysis so that it is plausible to regard the analysis as a counterfactual-sustaining biconditional, nonetheless, when we use it in order to develop another topic, for example, to articulate an account of meaning or of knowing, it is possible to regard the analysis merely as an implicit definition of technical expressions of the form, "*x* represents *y*," which are useful in abbreviating complex points about the further topic. I shall here employ the analysis of representing in that spirit, so as to avoid reviewing the numerous ordinary examples of representing dealt with in *The Nature of Meaningfulness*. Finally, I shall also avoid reviewing the explanation provided in that book of the distinction appealed to in the analysis between deviant causal chains and nondeviant ones.

In a simplified form, the analysis of "*x* represents *y*" presented in *The Nature of Meaningfulness* runs as follows:

> (R) *x* represent(s) *y* [relative to a what-question, *Q*, concerning *y*] if and only if for some occurrence, *Sy*, of a state of affairs involving *y*, and some occurrence, *Sx*, of an affect upon *x* or upon the manner in which *x* is present, when *Sy* is non-deviantly the cause of *Sx*, that to at least some degree justifies a specific answer to *Q* (provided certain other statements are justified).[6]

Applying the analysis involves thinking of what I technically called a "sketch of a background." For brief practice we can utilize the following sketch of a background in order to show that the rings in the cross section of a given tree represent the age of the tree: (*x*) the number of rings in the tree's cross section; (*y*) the tree's age; (*Sy*) the tree's actually having reached whatever age it has; (*Sx*) the ring's number's actually being *n*; (*Q*) What is the age of the tree? (*A*) The age is *n* years. Here, *Sx* is an effect on the manner in which the number of rings is present, namely, their being present in the number *n* rather than some other number. The additional justified propositions that are relevant in this example will concern, among other things, there having been normal climatological and biological conditions for the tree's growth.[7]

III. A Type of Correspondence Involved in Truth

As an initial step toward uncovering a type of correspondence, we can apply analysis (R) in order to show the following concerning the coffee example:

> (c) In the spill context, sentence S1, "there is a lot of coffee on the table," represents the state of affairs that *H*: a lot of liquid coffee is spread over the surface of the table.

Claim (c), which remains noncommittal concerning the truth of S1, is supported by the following sketch of a background: (x) the sentence S1, "there is a lot of coffee on the table"; (y) the state of affairs that H: a lot of liquid coffee is spread over the surface of the table; (Sy) the speaker's actually intending that when uttered by the speaker in the context, S1 is to be about the state of affairs that H; (Sx) the speaker's actually uttering S1 in the context; (Q) What in the context is something about the state of affairs that H? (A) Sentence S1 is about the state of affairs that H. Here, Sx involves an effect upon the way that x is present, that is, by being used in a complete utterance to make a statement rather than in some other fashion, such as to illustrate correct English grammar.

We can utilize (c) in order to derive a conclusion about what might be called a type of correspondence concerning truth. From the perspective on states of affairs to be defended later, it is reasonable to begin that derivation from the following claim:

(1) H only if the state of affairs that H obtains.

Inasmuch as we commonly grant that, at least in nonparadoxical contexts, truth is factive, we have as a further premise:

(2) In the spill context S2: "a lot of liquid coffee is spread over the surface of the table" is true only if H.

It follows (from 1 and 2) that

(3) S2 is true in the spill context only if the state of affairs that H obtains.

The following holds for the present example:

(4) The truth-evaluable content of S1 in the spill context is S2.

At this point we can appeal to claim (c) and argue that it follows (from that claim, 3 and 4) that

(5) the truth-evaluable content of S1 is true in the spill context only if the state of affairs represented by S1 obtains.

So, as a final result, it follows (from 5 and the use of the technical expression, "truth-evaluable content") that

(6) S1 is true in the spill context only if the state of affairs represented by sentence S1 obtains.

The upshot of this line of argument is that when S1 is true in the spill context then there is in the context a mapping of the sentence onto the state of affairs it represents and thereby onto an obtaining of that state of affairs. This illustrates what might be called some kind of correspondence of a true sentence to the obtaining of something, yet without committing us to any of the controversial aspects of a classical correspondence "theory."[8]

IV. REPRESENTING THE OBTAINING OF A STATE OF AFFAIRS

Since a sentence, even a true one, can be employed without making an assertion, for instance, in order merely to express a guess, we made little advance toward an analysis of asserting when we applied (R) in defense of claim (c). However, its applicability to sentence S1 may encourage us to consider applying it to the speaker's action of uttering that sentence. We may do so in order to defend the following claim concerning Putnam's example:

> (c*) In the context, the speaker's uttering S1 represents the obtaining of the state of affairs that H (that is, represents a lot of liquid coffee actually being spread over the surface of the table).

The defense of this claim takes advantage of the fact that discussion in *The Nature of Meaningfulness* showed analysis (R) to fit examples such as an architect's sketch representing the future Civic Auditorium, whether or not the building ever gets constructed.[9] An analogous application supports claim (c*), which is a claim that is neutral as to whether the state of affairs that H does indeed obtain. The following is a sketch of a relevant background: (x) the speaker's uttering S1; (y) the occurrence of the state of affairs that H; (Sy) the speaker's actually intending that an utterance of S1 in the context by the speaker is (exactly) about the occurrence of the state of affairs that H; (Sx) the speaker's actually uttering S1 in the context; (Q) What in the context is something about the occurrence of the state of affairs that H? (A) The speaker's uttering S1 is about the occurrence of the state of affairs that H. Here again, Sx involves an affect upon the way that x is present, that is, by constituting the making of a statement rather than in some other fashion, such as constituting the illustrating of correct grammar.

V. ANALYZING ASSERTION

I suggest that we should take account of both (c) and (c*) in formulating as a necessary condition of a speaker's asserting that h in uttering sentence S

in a context such as the following: in the context the speaker's uttering S represents the obtaining of the state of affairs represented by S. However, the condition alone is not sufficient since even the psychological states involved in the aforementioned sketches of backgrounds for (c) and (c*) can be present in examples where the utterance is only a guess, a conjecture, or a speculation, all of which, as the entry on assertion in the *Stanford Encyclopedia of Philosophy* puts it, are "allowed to be wrong."[10] We shall need to seek an additional condition specifying some other psychological or personal feature required of the speaker.

When discussing possible psychological or social aspects of the speech act of asserting, some philosophers, for example, Robert Brandom,[11] have not sought results adaptable to the form of an analysis of the type sought here, viz. a counterfactual-sustaining biconditional. Others, sometimes aspiring even to a meaning or conceptual analysis, have encountered a variety of objections.[12] A novel path to explore toward a workable analysis begins with the following approximation:

> (A) One asserts that h in the context in uttering/inscribing sentence S if and only if in the context (i) S represents the state of affairs that h; (ii) one's uttering/inscribing S represents the obtaining of that state of affairs; and (iii) one's uttering/inscribing S expresses an intention to challenge any statement entailing that the state of affairs does not obtain.

It would, of course, be circular to speak instead in (iii) of challenging any *assertion* that the state of affairs in question does not obtain. Indeed, even the present wording may appear circular, since philosophers tend to interchange the phrases "making a statement" and "making an assertion." Yet there are reasons to regard such interchange as mistaken. One reason arises from the point made by Roger J. Stainton that we can sometimes properly use a subsentential phrase, for example, "John's father," (pointing at a man), or "very fast," (staring at a car) so as to make an assertion, even though the phrase is not an elliptical sentence.[13] Since it is plausible to suppose that making a statement requires that the words one utters constitute a sentence, the existence of Stainton-type cases are examples of assertions that are not statements.[14]

Although these considerations spare formulation (A) from a charge of circularity, they also reveal that the formulation is too narrow. Roughly, one concern is that in making an assertion a person is in some way opposed not only to statements with the entailments mentioned in (iii) but even to Stainton-type cases that make contrary assertions. For example, if I assert that Archie's jalopy is slow and someone disagrees by uttering "very fast," we are in disagreement. Indeed, the very wording of the analysandum in

(A) is undesirably narrow by failing to cover Stainton-type cases. The following is an improvement:

> (A*) One asserts that h in the context in uttering linguistic expression W if and only if in the context (i) W represents the state of affairs that h;[15] (ii) one's uttering/inscribing W represents the obtaining of that state of affairs; and (iii*) one's uttering/inscribing W expresses an intention to challenge any utterance/inscription in the context made by using linguistic expressions whose utterance/inscription in the context represents the obtaining of something inconsistent with or contrary to the obtaining of that state of affairs.

Even though this reformulation avoids the previous shortcomings, it requires a further tweak, since the idea of challenging is not what is needed. Roughly, the problem is that we challenge a person or challenge the making of a statement, whereas the analysans should focus on an attitude regarding what might be stated, not the stating of it.[16] Asserting need not express an intention to seek out and confront persons or their speech acts, but instead a readiness to deny certain things. Perhaps the following employs a non-circular, Stainton-compatible way to characterize those things:

> (A**) One asserts that h in the context in uttering linguistic expression W if and only if in the context (i) W represents the state of affairs that h; (ii) one's uttering/inscribing W represents the obtaining of that state of affairs; and (iii**) one's uttering/inscribing W expresses a readiness to state the denial of what one takes to be stated in statements inconsistent with or contrary to the obtaining of that state of affairs.

The wording of (iii*) in the earlier formulation spoke of an intention, and so should have provided a psychologically plausible way of specifying the content of the earlier intention so as to extend even to opposing relevant Stainton-type cases. Yet there was no obvious way to achieve this since there are no statements made in such cases, and merely to say that the intention in question is to challenge what is asserted in those cases introduces circularity. In contrast, the reformulation in (iii**) speaks not of an intention but of a readiness and so has more flexibility because the type of analysis sought here is a counterfactual-sustaining biconditional. Although (iii**) focuses on statements and so does not refer to Stainton-type cases, I see no reason to think it really possible to have the readiness specified in (iii**) and yet not to have a readiness to state the denial of what one takes to be asserted in Stainton-type cases when what is asserted is inconsistent with or contrary to the obtaining of the state of affairs that h.[17]

VI. The Minimal Assertion Thesis

We shall soon be able to apply (A**) in support of a version of the Minimal Assertion Thesis. At one point, Putnam touches upon this thesis when he writes, "My own view of truth, ever since my Dewey lectures has been what I described as [a] 'disquotational one' in a sense of that term I connected with Frege. *To make a statement is to assert something, and to say that that something is true is to assert the same thing.*"[18] Yet this formulation is not broad enough to cover speaking of true assertions regarding Stainton-type cases, where no statement is made. Moreover, the entry on asserting in the *Stanford Encyclopedia* at one point treats the sentence, "Asserting a proposition is asserting that it is true," as saying that asserting that *h* is the same as asserting that it is true that *h*.[19] Admittedly, in his Dewey lectures Putnam writes, "to call a proposition true is equivalent to asserting the proposition,"[20] yet I shall avoid construing the Minimal Assertion Thesis as implying such equivalence, so as not to rule out the possibility that some language lacks a truth predicate.

Putnam comes closer to expressing the thesis elsewhere in those lectures. For instance, he rejects the position of the metaphysical realist, describing him as a philosopher who wants "a property that he can ascribe to all and only true sentences . . . that corresponds to the assertoric force of a sentence" and who "needs to argue that there is something we are saying when we say of a particular claim that it is true over and above what we are saying when we simply assert the claim."[21] Again, Putnam writes, "What is right in deflationism is that if I assert that 'it is true that *p*,' then I assert the same thing as if I simply assert *p*."[22] These remarks are a bit limited in scope to provide a general formulation of the thesis, which should speak not just of true sentences but also of true assertions. Nor is it obvious that the form, "it is true that *h*," is tantamount to some form about a sentence or assertion. Moreover, as Putnam's coffee example illustrates, what one asserts in uttering the sentence, "It is true there is a lot of coffee on the table," is not satisfactorily revealed merely by the phrase, "that there is a lot of coffee on the table."

I suggest that a sufficiently general formulation of the relevant thesis is the following:

> *The Minimal Assertion Thesis (MAT)*: In asserting a specific thing to be true, one makes in the context no assertion beyond an assertion that someone might make in the context involving exactly that thing.[23]

For instance, in asserting in the spill context, "Sentence S1 is true," the speaker makes no assertion beyond the assertion (namely, the assertion that

H: a lot of liquid coffee is spread over the table) that someone might make in the context involving—as the sentence uttered—exactly S1. In asserting in the spill context, "The assertion that *H* is true," one makes no assertion beyond the assertion one might make in the context involving—as the assertion made—exactly that assertion. In asserting in the spill context, "That *H* is true," one makes no assertion beyond the assertion someone might make in the context involving—as what is asserted—exactly that *H*.[24]

We can defend (MAT) by applying analysis (R) of representing and analysis (A**) of asserting. Sticking with the coffee example, we can begin by applying (R) so as to support

> (I) In the context, sentence S3: "It is true that there is a lot of coffee on the table," represents the state of affairs that H.

The sketch of a supporting background runs as follows: (x) sentence S3; (y) the state of affairs that *H*; (Sy) the speaker's actually intending that when uttered by the speaker in the context, S3 is to be about the obtaining of state of affairs that *H*; (Sx) the speaker's actually uttering S3 in the context; (Q) What in the context is something about the state of affairs that *H*? (A) S3 is about the state of affairs that *H*. Here, Sx involves an effect upon the way that x is present, namely, it is present by being used in a complete utterance to make a statement rather than in some other fashion, such as to illustrate correct grammar.

Similarly, we can apply (R) so as to support

> (II) In the context, making a statement in uttering S3 represents the obtaining of the state of affairs that H.

The sketch of a supporting background runs as follows: (x) making a statement in uttering S3; (y) the obtaining of the state of affairs that *H*; (Sy) the speaker's actually intending to make a statement in the context about the obtaining of state of affairs that *H*; (Sx) the speaker's actually making a statement in uttering S3 in the context; (Q) What in the context is something about the obtaining of the state of affairs that *H*? (A) The speaker's statement in uttering S3 is about the obtaining of the state of affairs that *H*. Here, Sx involves an affect upon the way that x is present since Sy makes a difference as to which person makes the statement.

The conjunction of (I) and (II) implies that in the context the speaker's making a statement in uttering S3 represents the obtaining of the state of affairs represented by S3, and so implies the satisfaction of requirements (i) and (ii) in (A**) for asserting that *H*. I see no reason to doubt that (iii**) is satisfied in the type of situation in question, provided that we remember that (iii**) concerns expressing a readiness, and we recognize that such readiness can be present even when one is insincere, for instance, when one makes a lying statement.[25]

While my defense of (MAT) in this example has shown that if one asserts in the spill context that S3 is true, then one asserts what one might assert in that context in uttering exactly S3. This does not prove that one actually asserts nothing beyond that. Since it is difficult to prove a negative, I can do no more than confess puzzlement as to how to sketch any plausible backgrounds for the application of (R) in relation to any additional assertions. For instance, in view of Putnam's exposure of the muddle constituted by a classical correspondence "theory" of truth,[26] it is pointless to construe *Sy* as the speaker's actually intending a sentence or statement to be about a classical correspondence "relationship."

Putnam might be construed as expressing discomfort with wide-ranging talk of states of affairs when he writes,

> But, although there is a sense in which a true description "corresponds" to an aspect of reality, or to an actual state of affairs, or a way things actually happen to be (take your pick!), not all true sentences are *descriptions*. My own view of truth, ever since my Dewey lectures has been what I described as [a] "disquotational" one. . . . But that does not commit me to inventing states of affairs to correspond to all the things that can be correctly asserted. And if one does invent such "states of affairs," then nothing is thereby added to the account of truth.[27]

Yet I have not spoken of states of affairs in order to add to an account of truth but in order to develop a useful analysis of representing, one applicable to many examples in light of sketches of background that characterize statements, thoughts or intentions as being about various things. Moreover, the type of correspondence I advocated above concerning true assertions is not the one Putnam rejects here, and allows unlimited range concerning the complexity of what the assertion is about.

VII. DISTINGUISHING STATES OF AFFAIRS

When an assertion has a low degree of complexity in its content, for example the assertion that the cat is black, we can employ a gerundive to say what the assertion is (exactly) about, for example, "the cat's being black." Yet we need not go very far in the direction of increasing complexity of assertive content before gerundives fail us. For example, suppose that it is vital during a repair of an important piece of equipment to keep it from starting up, and that it can be started in either of two ways, by throwing switch S or by pressing button B. We might ordinarily say that the state of affairs in which S is thrown or B is pressed is to be kept from occurring at all costs. Yet the phrase, "S's being thrown or B's being pushed," is not a gerundive but a disjunction of gerundives.

In response it might be proposed that states of affairs are what can be referred to by either gerundives or at least logical constructions out of gerundives. It is not clear that any account is available of how such construction can proceed. The possibility of such an account is doubtful if one supposes, as I do, that it is appropriate to speak of states of affairs in relation to statements of unlimited complexity.

Such latitude might grate with philosophers who approach the topic of states of affairs from an ontological starting point and who wish to avoid extravagance when listing the things that exist. Yet I am instead approaching the topic from the side of intentionality and a concern with what we think about and talk about. As Putnam observes,[28] we need not reify or hypostasize something merely because it is a type of thing we think about and talk about.

How, then, might we characterize the state of affairs that h so as to distinguish it from what is not a state of affairs? A different question, for later concern, is what constitutes a canonical form for speaking about a specific state of affairs; is it "the state of affairs that h," or instead, "its being the case that h," or "things being such that h," or yet another form?

In dealing with the first question, I shall take account of the distinction between one's thought, statement, sentence, or assertion being about a thing (in the widest sense of "thing") and its being exactly about it. For instance, the statement that the cat is black is about the cat, about blackness, about exemplification and about the cat's being black, but only the latter is what it is exactly about. Although I cannot define a state of affairs, perhaps the following considerations are a reasonable response to the first question.

Suppose that in uttering an indicative sentence (e.g., S1) in a context (e.g., the spill context) under an understanding (e.g., the understanding under which the truth-evaluable content of S1 is S2), the speaker makes a statement (e.g., the statement that there is a lot of coffee on the table); what the statement and the sentence are each exactly about (something in this example that does have a gerundive label, namely, "a lot of liquid coffee being spread over the surface of the table") is an illustration of a state of affairs—whether or not the statement is true. This is not to imply that every state of affairs has been or can ever be (canonically) labeled in a human language.

Although Christopher Hill has speculated that states of affairs may just be what we commonly call possibilities,[29] we do ordinarily distinguish possible states of affairs and impossible states of affairs without implying that the latter are not states of affairs (in the way a toy duck is not a duck). Putnam writes that a certain proposal "isn't describing a possible state of affairs," perhaps meaning that it describes an impossible one.[30] There is no obvious reason to rule out examples of making a statement in uttering an indicative sentence under some understanding where what the statement and sentence are exactly about is physically, even logically, impossible.

When we think that a statement is true, we are prepared to accept a further statement about that which it is exactly about, namely, the statement that the latter obtains (and in some illustrations, occurs). This point regarding statements and states of affairs is quite general. I have admitted that Putnam may resist its generality. He does maintain, "We should be willing to say that empirical statements do correspond to states of affairs that obtain, and that this has explanatory value, for example it enables us to see how there can be what I call 'equivalent descriptions' with startlingly different 'ontologies' in physics,"[31] yet he speaks only of correspondence with "facts about possibility and impossibility" with regard to mathematical statements.[32] He explains his reluctance to speak of states of affairs regarding the latter as follows: "I think of mathematical truths as corresponding to, precisely, *possibilities and impossibilities*, and relations between them, and not to 'entities' or to 'reality' (because so-called 'entities' easily get confused with *objects*, and possibility—and its absence, impossibility—is very different from reality)."[33] Putnam continues:

> there are truths (e.g., "it's wrong to covet your neighbor's property" whose function isn't to describe a state of affairs in the natural world (to describe "reality"), and also isn't to describe a mathematical possibility or impossibility. Couldn't we say they "correspond to obligations"? Why should we? . . . There is no philosophical point that I *need* that jargon to make.[34]

I have suggested a general perspective on states of affairs that has been useful in *The Nature of Meaningfulness* when explaining my treatments of representing and meaningfulness, and that is useful in the present discussion when dealing with assertion and a kind of correspondence which is not limited to the contexts where Putnam acknowledges a type of correspondence concerning descriptions and yet which is free of the ontological concerns permeating discussions of the classical correspondence "theory" of truth. This perspective places no special limitations on a true sentence, statement, or assertion, in particular, none on whether or not it is about objects, entities, or a reality. This is not to deny that for a subclass of states of affairs, for example, the cat's having been born black, the obtaining of the state of affairs, for example, the cat's actually having been born black, is identical with an occurrence in reality that involves actual objects or actual "things" (in the broadest sense). We may wish to speak of true statements (exactly) about such occurrences as reporting events but we do not always speak that way concerning a true empirical statements about the obtaining of a state of affairs, for example, a statement that a specific subject matter is governed by a specific law of nature. This perspective does not introduce states of affairs as ghostly counterparts of sentences, and does not rule out Putnam's thesis that sometimes contingent identities hold between (the obtaining of) states of affairs.

VIII. Canonical Labels for States of Affairs

With respect to a canonical form for denoting states of affairs, I admit that I may miss some candidates. One complication is that some philosophers regard "state of affairs" as a technical expression while others, such as Christopher Hill, have noted its employment in ordinary discourse in a manner that connects importantly with practical and theoretical reasoning. My concern is linked with the latter perspective and with a respect for ordinary language which takes account of John Austin's observation that in a mature natural language it is unlikely that two terms or short phrases will have the same use.[35]

Even if we prefer to employ the phrase, "state of affairs," in keeping with ordinary language when we seek to articulate a canonical form for referring to what I have been calling a state of affairs, finishing that task requires facing the variety of ways in which the phrase can appear in fuller expressions, for example, of the forms, "state of affairs in which h," "state of affairs where h," "state of affairs such that h," and, of course, "state of affairs that h." Before dealing with that variety, let us consider some other options.

Can we find helpful hints in Putnam's suggestion that we should take our pick among different ways of saying what it is that a true empirical description in a sense corresponds to, including "an actual state of affairs," or "a way things actually happen to be." The latter expression may not be helpful for present purposes. Consider a context where the cat actually is black. The phrase, "being black," labels the way (or part of the way) the cat actually happens to be. Yet that phrase is about blackness, not about the cat's exemplifying it.[36] Perhaps we might treat the phrase, "the way things (actually) happen to be," as labeling the collection of all instances of the obtaining of any empirical states of affairs and regard speaking of a way things happen to be as in keeping with Charles Travis's remark that sometimes we factor out a particular way things are from the way things are.[37] Yet does such a manner of speaking hint at a canonical form for labeling a particular way things happen to be?[38]

One might reply that it does invite us to regard the sought for canonical form as w: "things being in such a way that h." (I take it that my regarding an expression of the form "things being such that h" as elliptical for one of form w does not violate the spirit of the Austinian observation.) Consider how we understand statements of form f: "Xs are in such a way that h." We do not regard them as tantamount to a statement of the form, "something about Xs entails that h," at least, not if we allow that necessary truths are entailed by anything that does entail something. The equivalence in question would underwrite the statement that cats are in such a way that $2 + 2 = 4$. To avoid such oddity we should analyze statements of form f as stating that because of something about X, h. Yet this shows that the statement, "my car is such that it will soon break down" does not merely imply the obtaining of the state of affairs that my car will soon break down, but also implies that there is a reason involving the car.

Although philosophers often treat "it is the case that h" as tantamount to "it is true that h," the Austinian observation prompts us to seek separate roles for locutions of those two forms and for pairs of closely related forms. Consider Hill's inclination to accept as our sought for canonical label one of form c: "its being the case that h," where this form is not to be regarded as tantamount to "its being true that h."[39] This option offers us differing labels for differing examples of states of affairs, where the example varies along with variations in what is instantiated for h. The procedure is in line with our ordinarily speaking of examples as cases. Many ordinary locutions utilizing "case" do speak somehow of examples, for example, "consider the case of a dodo," "in case you leave," "the detective is on the case," "I'm on your case, Mister," "getting down to cases," and "as the case may be."[40]

However, several objections arise: (1) Hill says that he prefers to avoid relying on form c because to his ear "its being the case that h" suggests factuality. Yet one might reply that such a suggestion rests on an ambiguity, namely, that a phrase of that form sometimes functions not as a nominative but as tantamount to a "since" clause. For instance, we may say, "Its being the case that you refused my last offer, I am prepared to increase the amount." (2) To some ears, "it is the case that h" is linguistically inappropriate when what is instantiated for h is a necessary truth[41] and this impression may yield discomfort with respect to such instantiations in "its being the case that h." (Similar concerns might arise with respect to "the situation/circumstance/occasion that h.") Yet it is not obvious that such linguistic intuitions are widely shared. (3) A greater difficulty may arise when we reflect upon the list of locutions given above involving the term "case." Contexts in which such locutions are used typically allow us to ask, "A case of what?" and to answer by mentioning a type of thing of which there can be examples, such as: "an extinct creature," "your coming behavior," "a reported crime," "a person to be carefully watched or investigated," respectively. It may seem strained to do so regarding the locutions, "getting down to cases" and "as the case may be," yet perhaps these involve speaking of examples of contextually relevant matters. Nonetheless, it is indeed difficult to answer the question, "A case of what?" in regard to "its being the case that h," except by resorting to the answer, "a state of affairs" or "the obtaining/occurrence of a state of affairs." To respond that we are speaking in an ordinary sense of circumstances or a situation or an occurrence isn't broad enough to cover, for example, instantiations for h that articulate a law of nature. (4) The form, "its being the case that h," does not provide a hint concerning a satisfactory nominative for general purposes, in contrast to the manner in which "the state of affairs that h" hints at the noun phrase, "state of affairs." The plural noun, "cases," is awkward for such a purpose, partly because its use invites the question, "Cases of what?" Furthermore, although we can speak of a contingent, necessary or impossible state of affairs, it may be odd to speak of a necessary case. And what could "a case in which h" concern except an example of a state of affairs in which h? Furthermore, when we are able to refer to a state of affairs by a gerundive, we can speak of that state of affairs as being the case. (Thomas Wetzel offers the example, "Gato's weighing ten pounds is the case.")[42] It is obfuscating to say that this involves speaking of a case as being the case.

These objections may not be conclusive, but they motivate continuing to rely upon explicit inclusion of the phrase, "state of affairs," in the wording of a canonical form. In order to proceed, however, we should note two matters, first, an ambiguity concerning the phrase, and secondly, the variety of longer linguistic forms, noted earlier, in which the phrase is embedded.

Philosophically important expressions may be ambiguous. For example, various philosophers, including Putnam, have noted that the term, "sentence," is ambiguous, in one sense concerning something within a language and not susceptible of being true or false, and in another sense meaning a token of the former sort of thing as uttered or inscribed on an occasion. Similarly, we should recognize that there is not only a meaning of "state of affairs" that I have been drawing upon, but another ordinary sense that concerns an obtaining of such a thing. Perhaps the phrase is ordinarily used (and occurs in Putnam's writings) most frequently in the latter sense, as when we say, "That state of affairs caused us much difficulty/surprised us." Yet there is also the former meaning, which is involved when we say, "The occurrence of that state of affairs would cause us much difficulty/surprise us," or, "We must check to see/to ensure that that state of affairs does obtain."[43] Putnam employs this manner of speaking when, for example, he writes that "we should be willing to say that [true] empirical statements do correspond to states of affairs that obtain."[44]

A canonical label in ordinary language for a specific state of affairs does not take either of the forms, "state of affairs in which h" or "state of affairs where h," since instances of each can refer to a state of affairs wider than what I have been calling the state of affairs that h. For example, the state of affairs that $g \& h$ is a state of affairs in which h and is also a state of affairs where h.[45] Another form that may be too broad is "state of affairs such that h." My car's being about to run out of gas is a state of affairs such that I regularly seek to avoid its occurrence, yet the canonical label for that state of affairs is not "state of affairs such that I regularly seek to avoid its occurrence." So we are (unsurprisingly) left with the form that I have been relying upon all along as canonical, namely, "state of affairs that h."[46]

Just as we may think and speak indirectly about a statement without being able to make the statement, for example, think or speak of the fifth statement on a secret list in someone else's pocket, so we may think or speak indirectly about a state of affairs. This possibility is illustrated by Putnam's view that we might suspect that a presently unknown property explains a number of known phenomena even if humans lack—and may be unable to conceive—a canonical name for that property.[47] Since something's possessing a property is one type of state of affairs, Putnam's proposal implies that we suspect that the range of phenomena in question is explained by the occurrence of such a state of affairs for which we nonetheless lack a canonical label and about which we are thinking indirectly.

IX. CONCLUSION

The perspective that I have been advocating is not subject to Putnam's prior objections to various views on correspondence truth. I have not implied that there is a single, fixed relation that somehow underlies each true statement's being true, nor have I taken any stand on whether for each true statement there is something that makes it true.[48] Indeed, I have not tried to discuss whether, and if so how, various sorts of true statements have "truth-makers." In speaking of the obtaining of a state of affairs, the account remains sufficiently general to cover as instantiations for h indicative sentences uttered when making statements that are not purported descriptions, and there is no reason to suppose that statements of the form, "the state of affairs that h obtains," imply the existence of any objects, entities, or "things" beyond what are already implied to exist by the statement that h. Nor have I treated the obtaining of a state of affairs as the existence of a sentence-shaped thing in the world. Finally, the account leaves room for Putnam's important proposal that there can be contingent identity of the obtaining/occurrence of states of affairs.

Granted, Putnam may judge that I have been extending the family of uses of the broad-spectrum locution, "state of affairs," rather than resonating to prior linguistic employment of it. That is a distinction whose correct application to my own state of affairs I may not be in an ideal position to perceive.

ROBERT K. SHOPE

UNIVERSITY OF MASSACHUSETTS AT BOSTON
SEPTEMBER 2011

NOTES

1. Hilary Putnam, *The Threefold Cord: Mind, Body and World* (New York: Columbia University Press, 1999), and "From Quantum Mechanics to Physics and Back Again," in *Reading Putnam*, ed. Maria Baghramian (London: Routledge, 2013), 72; reprinted in Hilary Putnam, *Philosophy in an Age of Science* (Cambridge, MA: Harvard University Press, 2012), 55–76.

2. Hilary Putnam, "Corresponding with Reality," in *Philosophy in an Age of Science* (Cambridge, MA: Harvard University Press, 2012), 77–94.

3. Robert K. Shope, *The Nature of Meaningfulness: Representing, Powers, and Meaning* (Lanham, MD: Rowman & Littlefield, 1999).

4. Charles Travis, *The True and the False* (Amsterdam: J. Benjamins, 1981), *The Uses of Sense* (Oxford: Clarendon Press, 1989), and *Unshadowed Thought: Representation in Thought and Language* (Cambridge, MA: Harvard University Press, 2000).

5. Hilary Putnam, "Skepticism" in *Philosophie in Synthetischer Absicht*, ed. Marcelo Stamm (Stuttgart: Klett-Cotta, 1998), 239–68; reprinted with the title "Skepticism and Occasion-Sensitive Semantics" in *Philosophy in an Age of Science*, 486–503, *The Threefold Cord*, and "Skepticism, Stroud and the Contextuality of Knowledge," *Philosophical Explorations* 4 (2001): 2–16; reprinted in *Philosophy in an Age of Science*, 465–85.

6. Shope, *The Nature of Meaningfulness*, 39

7. Henceforth, I shall suppress mention of such additional statements when speaking of a sketch of a background.

8. Restricting himself to states of affairs designated by a gerundive concerning an object's being in a certain way, Putnam suggests that "the way I think the object is is in fact the way it is (when I judge correctly, of course). "Comment on John Haldane's Paper," in *Hilary Putnam: Pragmatism and Realism*, ed. James Conant and Ursuk M. Zeglen (London: Routledge, 2002), 107. The perspective advanced below widens the correspondence I am suggesting to cover sentences with truth-evaluable content about states of affairs too complex for gerundive designation.

9. Such examples of representing are pointed out by Dennis Stampe, "Show and Tell," In *Forms of Representation*, ed. Bruce Freed, Ausonio Marras, and Patrick Maynard (Amsterdam: North Holland, 1975), 221–45.

10. Peter Pagin, "Assertion," *The Stanford Encyclopedia of Philosophy* (Summer 2011 Edition), ed. Edward N. Zalta, http://plato.stanford.edu/archives/sum2011/entries/assertion.

11. Robert Brandom, "Asserting," *Nous* 17: 637–50.

12. For a survey see Pagin, "Assertion."

13. Roger J. Stainton, "What Assertion Is Not," *Philosophical Studies* 85 (1996): 57–73.

14. There may be further reasons for distinguishing statements from assertions: in making an ironic or sarcastic statement that h one may succeed in asserting that not-h; some malapropisms involve a person's making an amusing statement even though the assertion made is neither amusing nor articulable by a sentence whose utterance would be amusing.

15. Some past philosophers have spoken of sentences or statements as representing states of affairs, but may have meant that they are *about* states of affairs. Those philosophers did not analyze the type of representing of concern in (R), and did not deal with Stainton-type cases, where, for instance, "very fast" represents the car's being very fast, although the phrase retains its ordinary meanings of being (exactly) about a range of speed or ability to attain a range of speed rather than being about the car's traveling or being able to travel within that range.

16. I owe this concern to Lynne Tirrell.

17. The following sketch of a background allows us to apply analysis (R) in support of the claim that in the preceding Stainton-type example, the objector's uttering "very fast" represents the obtaining of a state of affairs that the jalopy is very fast (something inconsistent with the obtaining of the state of affairs that the jalopy is very slow): (x) the speaker's uttering "very fast"; (y) the occurrence/obtaining of the state of affairs of the jalopy's being very fast; (Sy) the speaker's actually intending that an utterance of "very fast" in the context by the speaker is about [although not exactly about] the state of affairs of the jalopy's being very fast; (Sx) the speaker's actually uttering "very fast"; (Q) What in the context is something about the occurrence/obtaining of the state of affairs of the jalopy's being very fast? (A) The speaker's uttering "very fast" is about the occurrence/obtaining of the state of affairs of the jalopy's being very fast.

18. Putnam, "From Quantum Mechanics to Physics and Back Again," 72. Reprinted in *Philosophy in an Age of Science,* 55–76.

19. See Pagin, "Assertion."

20. Putnam, *The Threefold Cord,* 68

21. Ibid., 55.

22. Ibid., 56.

23. The thesis is a tool against what Putnam calls metaphysical realism and is not intended as a conceptual or meaning analysis of being true. So it is not intended to clarify anaphoric contexts such as a situation where, not having any idea what John said in his court testimony, my trust prompts me to assert that whatever assertions he made were true.

24. The modifier, "exactly," is needed since without it (MAT) could not, for example, count asserting that H as an assertion one might make in the context where one has asserted that S1 is true. Someone might in the context make an assertion by uttering exactly a conditional sentence in which S1 is involved only as antecedent or consequent. So to make no assertion beyond that would require not making the assertion that H.

I suspect that Putnam regards saying something of the form, "that h is true," or of the form, "it is true that h," as just another way of saying something of the form, "sentence 'h' is true," but I have worded (MAT) so as to be neutral on the issue.

25. I do not share the view of some philosophers that a necessary condition of assertion is for one's remark to be directed toward an actual or potential audience. I sometimes assert premises during solitary reasoning aloud when seeking to develop a proof but do not aim those comments (as opposed to inscription of the premises in later manuscripts) toward even a potential audience. Again, *some* mentally disturbed people walk the street asserting strange things without *always* aiming their remarks toward an actual, possible, or imagined audience. (I owe the latter illustration to Lawrence Kaye.) Yet if an audience-concerning condition is indeed necessary to include within the analysans of (A**), I see

no reason to anticipate any conflict with the conditions that I have proposed, nor with the remainder of the present discussion.

26. Hilary Putnam, "Truth, Activation Vectors and Possession Conditions for Concepts," *Philosophy and Phenomenological Research* 52 (1992): 431–47, *The Threefold Cord*, and "From Quantum Mechanics to Physics and Back Again."

27. Putnam, "From Quantum Mechanics to Physics and Back Again," 72–73.

28. Putnam, "From Quantum Mechanics to Physics and Back Again."

29. Christopher Hill, "The Marriage of Heaven and Hell: Reconciling Deflationary Semantics with Correspondence Intuitions," *Philosophical Studies* 104 (2001): 291–321.

30. Putnam, *The Threefold Cord*, 100.

31. At one point Putnam says that the description that there is a green sofa in front of me corresponds on an occasion to the ordinary object which is a green sofa. "Was Wittgenstein *Really* an Antirealist about Mathematics" in *Wittgenstein in America*, ed. Timothy McCarthy and Sean Stidd (Oxford: Oxford University Press, 2001), 140–94. Reprinted in *Philosophy in an Age of Science*, 341–88; 364. Cf. Putnam, "Truth, Activation Vectors and Possession Conditions for Concepts," 433, regarding a blue chair. Yet most often he speaks of empirical descriptions as corresponding to external states of affairs rather than objects.

32. The comment appears in a new footnote (668n54) to the reprinting in *Philosophy in an Age of Science*.

33. Putnam, "Reply to Frederick Stoutland" in this volume.

34. Ibid. Thus, Putnam may protest the breadth of premise (1) in my earlier argument for a different type of correspondence relationship. He appears to count being a description as a necessary condition for what he calls correspondence, yet not as a sufficient condition, since he allows that the evaluation, "Hitler was a monster," is indeed a true description. "From Quantum Mechanics to Physics and Back Again," 56.

35. Putnam once expressed sympathy with a common philosophical view that saying that it is a fact that *h* is just a syntactic and semantic variant of saying that it is true that *h*. See "Was Wittgenstein *Really* an Antirealist about Mathematics," 364. Yet his present position regarding facts about possibilities and impossibilities in mathematics is more in keeping with the Austinian observation.

36. Putnam employs similar wording that is problematic for present purposes when he goes on to say that when we describe things we are answerable to them and "when we describe them correctly there is an aspect of reality that is as we assert it to be" ("From Quantum Mechanics to Physics and Back Again," 73) . When we assert truly that the cat is black, it is the cat that is as we assert it to be (cf. Putnam, "Comment on John Haldane's Paper," 106–7). Putnam comes closer to the present focus when saying of an empirical conjecture transcending ideal verifiability that it may "correspond to a reality; but one can only say what reality corresponds to it, if it is true, by using the words themselves" (*The Threefold Cord*, 58).

37. Travis, *Unshadowed Thought: Representation in Thought and Language,* 134–43.

38. Granted, "*x*'s state of affairs" and "the state of affairs regarding *x*" can sometimes mean the way things are for *x* or concerning *x* (cf. the title of the present essay).

39. Hill, "The Marriage of Heaven and Hell: Reconciling Deflationary Semantics with Correspondence Intuitions."

40. In an extended sense, making a case for a verdict or statement is providing an example of reasoning that functions to support acceptance of that verdict or statement regarding further reasoning or proceedings, where its acceptance is, roughly, readiness to use it by "premising it." Cf. Jonathan L. Cohen, *An Essay on Belief and Acceptance* (Oxford: Oxford University Press, 1992). In a more extended sense, a carrying case for something functions to provide physical support for keeping the item ready at hand for further use.

41. I owe this concern to Nelson Lande.

42. Thomas Wetzel, "States of Affairs," *The Stanford Encyclopedia of Philosophy* (Summer 2011 Edition), ed. Edward N. Zalta, http://plato.stanford.edu/archives/sum2011/entires/states-of-affairs.

43. A similar ambiguity occurs with respect to property labels. We may say of the center line on a road, "That whiteness extends for miles, until it turns to three colors in the Italian area of town," or say of the lighting in a cave, "That inky blackness extends for miles." Here the expressions "whiteness" and "inky blackness" are used to label not properties but their exemplification.

44. See note 32. Putnam also speaks of true empirical descriptions as corresponding to "real states of affairs" ("Reply to Fredrick Stoutland" in this volume).

45. Even prefixing "the" does not rule out an example where, during a discussion focusing on two states of affairs, one that $g\&h$ and the other that $g\&k$, I might indicate an intention to say something about the former rather than the latter by calling it the state of affairs in which h.

46. Perhaps we could refer to the state of affairs that h by the form, "the way for things to be where h." We do indeed speak of a necessary/possible/impossible way for things to be. Yet it is awkward to employ this terminology when speaking of occurrences, for example, awkward to speak of a causal situation by beginning, "The occurrence of the way for things to be where h caused . . . ."

47. Hilary Putnam, "On Properties" in *Essays in Honor of Carl G. Hempel: A Tribute on his Sixty-Fifth Birthday*, ed. Nicholas Rescher et al. (Dordrecht: Reidel, 1970), reprinted in Hilary Putnam, *Mathematics, Matter and Method: Philosophical Papers*, vol. 1 (Cambridge, MA: Cambridge University Press, 1975), 305–22, and "On Not Writing Off Scientific Realism," in *Philosophy in an Age of Science*, 95–111.

48. However, the obtaining of the state of affairs that h may be what constitutes or at least is in some way involved in its being true that h. I suspect that it is involved as the "goal"—as distinct from the aim—of inquiry whether or not h, but that is a topic for discussion elsewhere.

REPLY TO ROBERT K. SHOPE

If I prescind from things I wrote on the subject between 1976 and 1990 (that is, the "internal realist" stuff that I have long regarded as mistaken), then my publications on truth probably do not come to more than twenty pages—which does not mean that I have not thought long and hard about the issues. But the lack of a long essay by me on the subject does reflect the fact that I am still groping for a formulation that will completely satisfy me. In the meantime, Robert Shope's essay comes as close to filling the lacuna as I can possibly imagine. That essay is, moreover, not simply a work of exegesis, although the exegesis by itself is remarkable for its combination of accuracy and clarity; it is nothing less than a rational reconstruction of the view of truth I have been developing in various publications starting with *The Threefold Cord: Mind, Body and World*. It is also an application of the powerful theory that Shope developed in *The Nature of Meaningfulness*; an application which is an excellent introduction to that theory. I am pretty much in total agreement with what Shope writes. This "pretty much" reflects worries of mine, ones that Shope himself reports, concerning the applicability of the "correspondence" picture to "ought" statements, and to mathematics and pure logic, which I shall say a little about below.

To begin, however, with what I think Shope's reconstruction of my view clearly accomplishes: if we confine ourselves to descriptive statements about the empirical world, then it shows what is importantly right about the idea of truth as correspondence. It shows with great clarity that the picture of truth as correspondence does not require any objectionable hypostatizations or reifications. And it shows how what is right in "the deflationary view of truth" is consistent with, rather than incompatible with, what is right in the idea of truth as correspondence. I shall make a few further remarks about these matters now.

I. How Bad Is "Hypostatization" Anyway?

Although Quine, Davidson, and Goodman all regarded talk of "states of affairs" as unintelligible, I believe that they were seriously mistaken. Although (as Shope points out) I do not agree with these philosophers that to quantify over *anything* (or "anythings") is ipso facto to reify the anything-or-things, I also want to say that if they were right in this case, then by gum we *ought* to "reify" properties and states of affairs. But I need to explain.

In "On What There Is,"[1] Quine rejects the inference from Px—for example, "This table has mass"—to (Ex)Px—"This table has a property" (namely, mass). In addition, he argues, or rather assumes, that if properties exist, the criterion for identity of properties must be synonymy, a criterion he famously rejects as meaningless. But, as I pointed out in "On Properties,"[2] this short way with the realist arguments for the existence of properties ("universals," in traditional terminology) is too short by a good deal. It is too short because the criterion for the identity of properties in physical science (which Quine himself regards as authoritative in metaphysical matters) is not synonymy at all. A chemist will tell you, for example, that being "soaking wet" and being "saturated with H_2O" are the same property, and he is not talking about the linguistic meanings of those expressions at all. Although Frege and Russell may have led logicians to identify properties with *concepts*, that identification has nothing "scientific" about it. Secondly, the idea that we arrive at properties by starting with a predicate P and existentially quantifying it ignores the fact that we often discover the existence of properties we *do not yet have a name for*. A physicist may say, "I think these atoms have a property in common that causes them to behave in such and such a way," and he is stating a perfectly meaningful hypothesis that *requires* quantification over properties that we may not have a "predicate" for. Quine's loyalties as a philosopher were hopelessly divided between physics worship and worship of first-order logic, but when they conflicted, the loyalty to first-order logic always won. First-order logic is a wonderful beginning, but to take it as the ultimate tool for the analysis of all discourse is a serious error. Science, I claim, including physics, is deeply committed to quantification over universals, and if that be "hypostatization," then all the better for hypostatization.[3]

II. The Applicability of the "Correspondence" Picture to "Ought" Statements, and to Mathematics and Pure Logic

I wrote above that I have "worries" about this picture. Specifically, I find it odd to describe the fact that a state of affairs is "possible" as a further state of affairs. But I also recognize that, as the late Robert Richman once put it, "sometimes our intuitions of oddity only show the oddity of our intuitions." A further consideration is that my indispensability arguments for quantification over empirical states of affairs do not obviously carry over to modal and normative contexts. [4] But perhaps having accepted such quantification in empirical contexts, one should accept it "across the board"? I remain undecided.

H.P.

NOTES

1. "On What There Is" was published in *Review of Metaphysics* 5, no. 8 (1948): 21–38. Reprinted in W. V. Quine, *From a Logical Point of View* (Cambridge, MA: Harvard University Press, 1953).

2. "On Properties," in *Essays in Honor of Carl G. Hempel: A Tribute on the Occasion of his Sixty-Fifth Birthday*, ed. Nicholas Rescher et al. (Dordrecht: D. Reidel, 1970), 235–54. Reprinted in *Mathematics, Matter and Method*, 305–22.

3. For my reasons for (also) regarding quantification over "states of affairs" as perfectly legitimate see "From Quantum Mechanics to Ethics and Back Again," collected in *Philosophy in an Age of Science*.

4. See the paper cited in the previous note.

10

Gary Ebbs

PUTNAM AND THE
CONTEXTUALLY A PRIORI

From its seeming to me—or to everyone—to be so, it doesn't follow that it is so. What we can ask is whether it can make sense to doubt it.

—LUDWIG WITTGENSTEIN, *ON CERTAINTY*, §2

When is it reasonable for us to accept a statement without evidence and hold it immune from disconfirmation? This question lies at the heart of Hilary Putnam's philosophy.[1] He emphasizes that our beliefs and theories sometimes prevent us from being able to specify how a statement may actually be false, in a sense of "specify" that goes beyond just writing or uttering "~," "Not," or "It is not the case that" immediately before one writes or utters the statement. (To save words, from here on I will assume that to specify how a statement *S* may actually be false, one must do more than write or utter words that ordinarily express negation—words such as "~," "Not," or "It is not the case that"—immediately before one writes or utters *S*.) In the eighteenth century, for instance, scientists did not have the theoretical understanding necessary to specify how the statement that physical space is Euclidean could be false.[2] Today, however, after Lobachevsky and Riemann discovered non-Euclidean geometries, and Einstein developed his general theory of relativity, scientists believe that physical space is non-Euclidean, and they can specify in rich detail why the statement that physical space is Euclidean is false. Generalizing from this example, we may conclude that our *current* inability to specify how a statement may actually be false does not guarantee that we will never be able to do so. Nevertheless, when we cannot specify how a statement may actually be false it has a special methodological status for us, according to Putnam—it is *contextually a priori*.[3] In these circumstances, he suggests, it is *epistemically reasonable* for us to accept the statement without evidence and hold it immune from disconfirmation.[4]

Against this, many philosophers are inclined to reason as follows. "It is epistemically reasonable for a person to accept a particular statement only if she has epistemic grounds for accepting it. But a person's inability to specify a way in which a statement may actually be false gives her no epistemic grounds for accepting it. Therefore, if the epistemic role of the statement for her is exhausted by her inability to specify a way in which the statement may actually be false, it is not epistemically reasonable for her to accept it." Those who find this reasoning compelling typically conclude that if we want to show that it is epistemically reasonable to accept some statements without evidence, we must to try to explain how it is possible for a person to have *grounds* for accepting those statements without evidence.

In my view, however, it is more illuminating to question the idea that it is epistemically unreasonable for a person to accept *any* statement—even one that she cannot make sense of doubting—unless she has epistemic grounds for accepting it. To question this idea, I will first clarify my use of some key terminology (§I), present a more detailed version of the skeptical reasoning sketched in the previous paragraph (§II), summarize my misgivings about standard responses to it (§III), and explain my strategy for disarming it (§IV). I will then examine some of Putnam's remarks about the contextually a priori (§§V–IX), and argue that if a person is unable to specify any way which a statement may actually be false, she cannot make sense of the skeptic's requirement that she provide grounds for accepting it (§§X–XII).

I. Three Constraints

I assume that the phrase "contextually a priori" contrasts with "contextually a posteriori." These are terms of art that can be used in different ways; one must place constraints on their use before one can raise any interesting questions about how to apply them. As I see it, ideas we associate with the words "a priori," "a posteriori," and "contextually" may guide, but do not determine, the proper use of "contextually a priori" and "contextually a posteriori": these grammatically complex terms are *logically* simple. In addition, I place three preliminary constraints on my of "contextually a priori," "contextually a posteriori," and related epistemic terms.

The *first constraint* is that the terms "contextually a priori" and "contextually a posteriori" apply to a person's *reasons* for believing that S or her *entitlement* to believe that S, where "S" is replaced by a particular use in a given context of a declarative sentence.[5] (I will often use "accepting that S" in place of "believing that S," and "accept that S" in place of "believe that S." I will also assume that a particular use in a given context of a declarative sentence S expresses a *statement*, and that "S" stands in for such a statement.)

The *second constraint* is that a person has a *reason* for believing that S only if she can say *why* she believes that S *without presupposing that S*. (Although we sometimes say that a person has a reason for believing that S even if all her best attempts to explain why she believes S presuppose that S,[6] I will not use "reason" in this way.)

The *third constraint* is that a person has an *entitlement* (or is *entitled*) to believe that S if and only if she has no reason for believing that S—she cannot say *why* she believes that S without presupposing S—but it is (epistemically) *reasonable*, in a sense yet to be clarified, for her to believe that S.

To highlight by contrast familiar examples of contextually a priori entitlements, I will now briefly describe examples of contextually a posteriori reasons and entitlements, and contextually a priori reasons.

Suppose you and I are watching a bird perched in a nearby tree; I say "That's a robin," and you ask, "How do you know?" I reply, "It has a red breast." I thereby offer you a *reason* why I believe that the bird is a robin.[7] This reason does not presuppose that the bird is a robin, but provides grounds for accepting that it is a robin. Suppose I *see* that the bird has a red breast, and would not otherwise believe that it does. In this context, my reason—"It has a red breast"—is contextually a posteriori.

Now suppose that you and I both see that the bird has a red breast, I also *claim* to see that the bird has a red breast, and you challenge me to say how I know that I see that the bird has a red breast. Although it is completely obvious to me that I see that the bird has a red breast, I find I am unable to say anything persuasive or informative about why I believe this. Nevertheless, relative to the ordinary standards in that context, it seems I am *entitled* to believe that I see that the bird has a red breast even if I cannot give a reason for this belief. This entitlement is contextually a posteriori.

Well-constructed proofs of logical or mathematical theorems—proofs that may presuppose special axioms and rules of inference, but do not presuppose that the theorems in question are true—are examples of contextually a priori reasons for believing the theorems.

Unlike a theorem that I can prove, however, some statements are such that I cannot say why I accept them without presupposing that they are true. For instance, I cannot say why I believe that no statement is both true and false without presupposing that no statement is both true and false. Nevertheless, in ordinary contexts it seems *reasonable* for me to believe this. Thus, it seems I have a contextually a priori entitlement to believe that no statement is both true and false. Similarly, as Putnam has emphasized, the belief that physical space is Euclidean was so basic for scientists in the eighteenth century that they could not say why they accepted it without presupposing it. (I will discuss this claim in more detail below.) Yet it seems that relative to the scientific standards at the time, it was *reasonable* for them to believe this. Thus, it seems that scientists in the eighteenth century had a contextually a priori entitlement to believe that physical space is Euclidean.[8]

II. A SKEPTICAL CHALLENGE

Beliefs that we ordinarily take for granted in giving reasons for our claims—beliefs to which we seem to be *entitled* by ordinary practice—seem especially vulnerable to skeptical challenge. Consider our confidence that we have contextually a priori entitlements to accept certain statements. I am unable to give any reasons that support my belief that no statement is both true and false, for instance, but I nevertheless take it to be reasonable to accept it. Ordinarily no one would challenge me to say why it is reasonable to accept it. But suppose someone *does* challenge me to say why.[9] I might reply that I cannot *make sense* of doubting that no statement is both true and false. But on further reflection I would realize that my inability to doubt the statement is not a reason for thinking the statement is true. At best it explains why I *take* it to be true. Why then do I think it is *reasonable* to accept the statement? I feel at a loss to answer this question, and so I begin to doubt that I have any contextually a priori entitlements, despite my initial confidence that I do.[10]

This skeptical reasoning implicitly depends on the assumption that our practices of making and evaluating statements commit us to four generalizations. The first is that:

(1) Belief does not logically imply truth.

Our commitment to this generalization is reflected in our response to the skeptical question of why we think it is reasonable to accept our belief that no statement is both true and false. We realize that we cannot adequately respond to this challenge by citing our *conviction* that no statement is both true and false, since our conviction does not show that our acceptance of the statement is reasonable. We also realize that what counts as reasonable is intersubjective, in the sense that other participants in our search for knowledge should in principle be able to agree with us about whether it is reasonable to accept a given statement. Thus, we seem committed to a second generalization about our epistemic practices:

(2) Epistemic reasons and entitlements are intersubjective.

The skeptical reasoning implicitly combines these two generalizations to suggest that

(3) It is epistemically reasonable for a person to accept a statement only if she has grounds for thinking that the statement is true.

The progression from (1) and (2) to (3) seems almost inevitable. Given (1) and (2), we cannot respond to a skeptical challenge by citing our conviction that the statement in question is true. We therefore feel we must try to explain to the skeptic why it is reasonable for us to accept the statement. But it seems that any such explanation would in effect be a reason for accepting it. In other words:

(4) A person has grounds for thinking that a statement is true only if she has reasons for accepting it.

But if we have a reason for accepting a given statement, then according to the second and third constraints of §1, it is not a statement that we have an *entitlement* to accept. We therefore seem forced to the conclusion that we have no contextually a priori entitlements.

III. Can We Accept (1)–(3) but Reject (4)?

Many philosophers are inclined to accept generalizations (1)–(3) but reject (4). Some would argue that even if we have no reasons for accepting a given statement, we can have grounds for taking it to be contextually a priori if the psychological processes that led us to accept it reliably yield true beliefs.[11] Others would argue that we have a capacity for "rational insight" that enables us to know directly, without reasons, that a given statement that we take to be contextually a priori is likely to be true.[12] Yet, others argue that we are entitled to accept some statements without providing any reasons for accepting them, because our acceptance of them is "constitutive" of the meanings of the words we use to express them.[13]

One problem with all of these approaches is that the skeptic of §II takes (4) to be a *consequence* of (2), the generalization that reasons and entitlements are intersubjective. Standard ways of trying to reject (4) are not designed to convince such a skeptic,[14] from whose perspective they amount to rejections of (2), on its most natural interpretation. Yet (2) is part of the reasoning that apparently supports (3), the crucial premise in the argument that leads to the skeptical problem that these theories are supposed to solve.

Another problem is that the standard rejections of (4) tend to conflate contextually a priori entitlements with a priori entitlements. Such rejections are at best vindications of traditional examples of a priori entitlements, such as our entitlements to accept basic logical inferences or "conceptual" truths, not of Putnam's paradigm example of a contextually a priori entitlement—the entitlement of scientists in the eighteenth century to believe that physical space is Euclidean. According to the implicit meanings strategy, for instance, scientists in the eighteenth century were entitled to accept the statement that physical space is Euclidean without providing any reasons for accepting it *only if* their acceptance of the statement was "constitutive" of the meanings of the words they used to express it. We now know that the statement that physical space is Euclidean does *not* follow from the implicit meanings of the words that scientists in the eighteenth century used to express it: in the sense of meaning that is relevant to truth, we did not change the meanings of these words when we discovered that physical space is non-Euclidean. Hence the implicit meanings strategy cannot help us to avoid skepticism about such contextually a priori entitlements. Some philosophers try to make a virtue of such limitations of their epistemological theories by arguing that Putnam should not have used the word "a priori" (even qualified by "contextually") to describe the eighteenth-century scientists' attitude toward the statement that physical space is Euclidean.[15] But the important question is how we are to understand the methodological status of such statements, not whether we call them a priori.

IV. My Strategy

In contrast with these standard ways of reacting to skepticism about contextually a priori entitlements, I recommend that we question whether (3) applies to all statements, including those that we take ourselves to have contextually a priori entitlements to accept. I take for granted that (3) applies to *many* statements that we accept. But the skeptic's implicit argument for (3) is entirely general: according to the skeptic, (3) follows inevitably from (1) and (2), and, like them, applies to all statements. Perhaps (3) does *not* follow in this way from (1) and (2). It may be that (1) and (2) hold for all statements, but (3) does not. In particular, perhaps (3) does not apply to statements that we take ourselves to have contextually a priori entitlements to accept. If (3) does not apply to these statements, then the skeptical reasoning of §II depends on an overgeneralization, and the standard responses to the skeptical argument are confused and irrelevant.

My strategy is guided by the idea that a person who regards a statement *S* as contextually a priori cannot specify any way in which *S* could be false, and therefore cannot *make sense* of applying (3) to *S*, or of the skeptic's demand that she provide grounds for accepting *S*. To develop this idea I will explore some of Putnam's remarks about the contextually a priori. These remarks suggest an instructive but ultimately unsatisfactory reason for thinking (3) does not hold for all statements. I will explain why the reason is unsatisfactory, and then propose a better way of understanding why (3) does not hold for statements that we take ourselves to have a contextually a priori entitlement to accept.

V. Conceptual Schemes and Contextually A Priori Entitlements

To explain why inquirers have contextually a priori entitlements to accept certain statements, Putnam once suggested that a statement can be "necessary relative to the appropriate body of knowledge":

> when we say that a statement is necessary relative to a body of knowledge, we imply that it is included in that body of knowledge and that it enjoys a special role in that body of knowledge. For example, one is not expected to give much of a reason for that kind of statement. But we do not imply that the statement is necessarily *true*, although, of course, it is thought to be true by someone whose knowledge that body of knowledge is.[16]

Strictly speaking, Putnam should not have spoken of necessity relative to a body of knowledge, since to say that a statement is necessary or that a belief is knowledge is normally to imply that it is true. Acknowledging this point, he now recommends that we speak of "*quasi*-necessity" relative to a "conceptual scheme."[17] We must therefore ask,

(a) In what sense was the belief that physical space is Euclidean *quasi*-necessary relative to the eighteenth-century scientists' conceptual scheme?

and

(b) How does this show that it was reasonable for them to accept this statement without evidence?

I will address (a) in this section and (b) in the next.

Putnam's answer to question (a) is that scientists in the eighteenth century could not have revised their belief that physical space is Euclidean without developing a new theory of physical space. Contextually a priori statements

> can only be overthrown by a new theory—sometimes by a revolutionary new theory—and not by observation alone . . . Euclidean geometry was always revisable in the sense that no justifiable canon of scientific inquiry *forbade* the construction of an alternative geometry; but it was not always 'empirical' in the sense of having an alternative that good scientists could actually conceive.[18]

To understand this passage, one must know a little about the history of scientific theorizing about the shape of physical space from the eighteenth century until Einstein's development of the general theory of relativity.

Scientists in the eighteenth century did not distinguish between applied, or physical, geometry and pure, mathematical geometry.[19] It was only in the nineteenth century, after Lobachevsky, Riemann, and others discovered that they could consistently describe mathematical "spaces" in which Euclid's parallel postulate did not hold, that it became possible to draw this distinction. The mathematical discovery of non-Euclidean geometries might have suggested to some that physical space may be non-Euclidean. Nevertheless, around 1830, when he first published his results, Lobachevsky called his new topic "imaginary geometry."[20] Even in the late nineteenth century, after Riemann had developed non-Euclidean geometries of curved surfaces, few philosophers or mathematicians took seriously the idea that physical space is non-Euclidean. They might have regarded it as in some sense an empirical question. But the sense in which the question is empirical only became clear after Einstein changed the way we think about light and gravity. Einstein's general theory of relativity both showed how to make questions about the shape of physical space empirical, and convinced many physicists and philosophers that physical space is non-Euclidean.[21]

In the eighteenth century, scientists lacked many of the conceptual resources necessary to grasp this possibility. Their failure to see any alternative to their belief that physical space is Euclidean was not based in simple oversight or ignorance. Perhaps it took longer than it might have for mathematicians and physicists to come to see how physical space could be non-Euclidean. But the eighteenth-century scientists' belief that physical space is Euclidean was not epistemically irresponsible. Their understanding of geometry and physical space prevented them from seeing alternatives to Euclidean geometry, and it was no simple matter for them to overcome this obstacle. A great deal of mathematical and physical theorizing was required.

Putnam thinks there are important methodological lessons to be learned from the history of our gradual realization that questions about the shape of space are empirical. In particular, he stresses that

> Before the development of general relativity theory, most people, even most scientists, could not imagine any experiences that would lead them to give up, or that would make it rational to give up, Euclidean geometry as a theory of actual space; and this is what led to the illusion that Euclidean geometry was *a priori*.[22]

By describing the methodological roles of such sentences in our rational inquiries, Putnam tries to show that some statements are so basic for us at a given time that it would not be reasonable to give them up at that time, even if we have no guarantee that they are true. He tries to convince us that if a person cannot specify any way in which a statement *S* may be false, then she has a contextually a priori entitlement to accept *S*, even if someone else, or she herself at some later time, can specify a way in which *S* may be false.

In short, Putnam's answer to question (a)—"In what sense was the belief that physical space is Euclidean *quasi*-necessary relative to the eighteenth-century scientists' conceptual scheme?"—is that scientists in the eighteenth century had not yet developed the mathematical and physical theories that would later make it possible to specify a way in which their belief that physical space is Euclidean may actually be false. The idea is that this limitation of their "conceptual scheme" *explains* why they were unable to specify any way in which their belief that physical space is Euclidean may actually be false.

VI. THE CONCEPTUAL SCHEME EXPLANATION

Let us now consider question (b)—"How does this show that it was reasonable for them to accept this statement without evidence?" Note first that Putnam's explanation of why the scientists were unable to specify any way in which their belief that physical space is Euclidean may actually be false does *not* show that they had any epistemic grounds for accepting it, or that it was likely to be true. If one accepts that (3) applies to the statement that physical space is Euclidean, then one will conclude that it is epistemically irresponsible to accept the statement unless one has grounds for accepting it. Since Putnam's explanation of why the eighteenth-century scientists accepted the statement strongly suggests that they had no grounds for accepting it, his explanation seems relevant only to psychology, not methodology (epistemology). Yet Putnam insists that

> the difference between statements that can be overthrown by merely conceiving of suitable experiments and statements that can be overthrown only by conceiving of whole new theoretical structures—sometimes structures, like Relativity and Quantum Mechanics, that change our whole way of reasoning about nature—is of logical and methodological significance, and not just of psychological interest.[23]

How can we make sense of this?

Consider the following explanation. "Suppose we regard a statement as contextually a priori in Putnam's sense. Then, our present system of beliefs—our conceptual scheme—*prevents* us from specifying any ways in which that statement may actually be false. To make sense of doubting such statements we would need to develop a new way of thinking, one that goes beyond our current understanding. But if we cannot specify any alternatives to a given statement, and no one else shows us how to do so, then we cannot see how the statement could be false, and so we cannot make sense of applying (3) to it. For the same reason, we cannot understand the skeptic's demand that we give grounds for accepting it. Hence, Putnam's description of the role of contextually a priori statements is of methodological (epistemological) interest: it dissolves the skeptical challenge of II."

This is what I will call *the conceptual scheme explanation*. I will raise three problems for it (in §§VII–IX), and then suggest (in §§X–XII) a better way of understanding why (3) does not apply to statements we treat as contextually a priori.

VII. Two Preliminary Problems for the Conceptual Scheme Explanation

The first problem is that there are statements that count as contextually a priori according to the constraints in §I that are not contextually a priori according to the conceptual scheme explanation. For instance, Frege had no difficulty understanding Russell's explanation of the contradiction that arises in Frege's logic. Frege's assumption that his logic was consistent was therefore not contextually a priori according to the conceptual scheme explanation. Yet prior to Russell's letter, Frege could not specify any way in which his logic was inconsistent. He could not offer any *reasons* to back up his assumption that his logic was consistent, either. He was exacting and precise about all his assumptions, however, and in this sense his belief was reasonable. It therefore seems that according to the constraints in §I, Frege had a contextually a priori entitlement to believe that his logic was consistent. Yet, according to the conceptual scheme explanation his belief was not contextually a priori, since it did not lie deep in his system of beliefs—he could immediately see that Russell's paradox undermined his belief that his logical system was consistent.[24]

A natural reply to this objection is that the conceptual scheme explanation concerns a slightly different topic from the topic that is implicitly defined by the constraints in §I. Suppose this is so. Still, the conceptual scheme explanation does not show why it was reasonable for Frege to accept that his logic was consistent. It also suggests that since there is no deep explanation of why Frege did not see that his logic was inconsistent, (3) applies to Frege's belief that his logic was consistent, so, given (4), it was *not* reasonable for him to accept it without providing reasons for it.

This suggests a second, more serious objection to the conceptual scheme explanation: we have no criterion for determining whether or not our current failure to specify a way in which a particular statement may actually be false shows that the statement is contextually a priori in the proposed sense, or whether we are just overlooking something that we would immediately recognize as a way of specifying how the statement may actually be false. Let us say that a statement is *deep* for a person if and only if she would have to develop a fundamentally new way of thinking even to conceive of how that statement may actually be false. Suppose that you are unable to specify a way in which a given statement S may actually be false. The difficulty for the conceptual scheme's explanation is that you cannot tell whether or not S is deep for you. Tomorrow you might discover that you overlooked something, just as Frege was surprised when he read Russell's letter. But if S is not deep for you, then the conceptual schemes explanation gives us no grounds for claiming that (3) does not apply to it. And if (3) does apply to it, then you are vulnerable to the skeptical reasoning presented above, because you are unable to provide any grounds for accepting the statement.

VIII. Two Arguments by Analogy

The most serious problem with the conceptual scheme explanation is that the imagined methodological perspective from which our statements are classified as deep or not deep for us apparently licenses an argument by analogy that would enable us to make sense of applying (3) even to statements that *are* deep for us. To understand this argument by analogy, it helps to consider first a simpler argument by analogy that is easier to disarm.

First Argument by Analogy

The simpler argument may be stated as follows. "Suppose we cannot presently specify a way in which a given statement S may actually be false. We nevertheless know that some statements that once seemed beyond doubt in this sense are now regarded as false. Based in our experience with such statements, we feel we understand how statements that we once regarded as beyond doubt can come to seem doubtful, and even false. By analogy with such statements, it seems that we can make sense of the possibility that S is false, even though we cannot now specify any way in which S may be false."

According to this simple argument by analogy, we understand the skeptic's suggestion that S is possibly false, so (3) applies to S and it is therefore unreasonable to accept S unless we have some reason to think it is true. In this way, the argument by analogy suggests that (3) applies to *all* our statements. Once again, however, if (3) applies to all our statements, we are vulnerable to the skeptical challenge presented above: unless we can provide some reason for thinking that a given statement S is true, it is unreasonable for us to accept it; we therefore have no contextually a priori entitlements.

But the argument is too simple. The natural response to it is that the analogy fails. There is a crucial difference between statements that once we could not doubt but now we can doubt and statements that we cannot now doubt. The fact that once we could not doubt but now we can doubt a particular statement only establishes that we are fallible, and that our failure to be able to doubt a particular statement in no way guarantees it is true. This does not go beyond (1), so it does not establish that (3) applies to statements that we now regard as contextually a priori. Our fallibility does not by itself give any meaning to the claim that a particular statement may actually be false. If we cannot specify a way in which it is false, then merely mentioning our fallibility will not help us to specify a way in which it may actually be false.

Second Argument by Analogy

A more challenging argument by analogy results when we supplement the first with a description of the methodological roles of our statements. As we saw in §VII, Putnam says that contextually a priori statements are "quasi-necessary" relative to a "conceptual scheme." This suggests that we can describe the methodological roles of such statements, and thereby explain *why* investigators regard them as "quasi-necessary" relative to their "conceptual scheme."

The appeal of this kind of explanation can be explained as follows. We now see that scientists in the eighteenth century did not simply fail to consider ways in which their statement that physical space is Euclidean may actually be false; their beliefs and theories *prevented* them from doing so. But we do not have this retrospective understanding of the centrality of any of our *current* beliefs. Tomorrow we might find that we overlooked something that we could easily have seen today. This suggests that to take ourselves to have a contextually a priori entitlement to accept a given statement S, we must assume that S is deep for us, so our failure to specify ways in which S may actually be false is not due to a simple oversight on our part. To classify statement S as contextually a priori for us now is therefore to take a certain methodological perspective on our own current beliefs—to assert that our acceptance of S is deeply imbedded in our "system" of beliefs, and that is *why* we find ourselves unable to specify a way in which it may actually be false.

Supplemented with this methodological perspective, the first argument by analogy is transformed into a second argument by analogy that can seem more persuasive (though I will question it below). As before, the argument begins with the observation that we are now able to doubt some statements we were previously unable to doubt. Thus, a contextually a priori statement may end up being doubtful, even false. The argument then continues as follows. "Statements that we currently regard as contextually a priori are from a methodological point of view no better off than those that we regarded as contextually a priori in the past. By *methodological analogy* with cases in which statements actually became doubtful, we can make sense of the possibility that a statement we now treat as contextually a priori is false, even though we cannot now specify any way in which it could be false."

Like the first argument by analogy, this argument suggests that we understand the skeptic's claim that a statement we now treat as contextually a priori may actually be false, and that it is therefore unreasonable to accept the statement unless we have some reason to think it is true. In this way, the second argument by analogy suggests that (3) applies to statements that we take to be a contextually a priori, and so the strategy of answering the skeptic by denying that (3) applies to statements we regard as contextually a priori fails.

IX. Limits of the Second Argument by Analogy

Sometimes Putnam characterizes contextually a priori statements in a way that leaves our acceptance of them vulnerable to this second argument by analogy. In "There is at Least One A Priori Truth," for instance, Putnam contrasts contextually a priori statements with "absolutely" a priori statements—statements that "it could never be rational to revise," and thereby suggests that to call a statement contextually a priori is to say that it could someday be rational to revise it.[25] This conception of contextually a priori statements suggests that we understand how some contextually a priori statements may actually be false, even if we cannot now *specify* a way in which they are false.[26]

Even if it is successful in some cases, however, there are limits on the application of the second argument by analogy. As Putnam emphasizes in "There is at Least One A Priori Truth," we can make no sense of the suggestion that it may be reasonable some day to give up the minimal principle of contradiction, according to which not every statement is both true and false. This limits the argument by analogy by emphasizing that we do not have even the *vaguest*, purely methodological idea of how we could end up accepting that every statement is both true and false.[27] Hence, it shows that (3) does not apply to the minimal principle of contradiction.

By blocking the argument from analogy for the minimal principle of contradiction, this reasoning suggests that we can discredit the skeptical challenge in this case. Nevertheless, the second argument by analogy suggests that many of the statements that we now take ourselves to have a contextually a priori entitlement to accept may actually be false. In this way, the second argument by analogy suggests that (3) applies to these statements. This leaves us vulnerable again to the skeptical reasoning of §II. To accept this reasoning is to think that almost all cases in which we take ourselves to have contextually a priori entitlements are of psychological interest only, and tell us nothing about which statements it is epistemically reasonable to accept. In this way, the methodological perspective that lies behind the conceptual scheme explanation and the second argument by analogy apparently undermines the assumption that contextually a priori statements are of methodological and not only psychological interest.

X. The Second Argument by Analogy Disarmed

Despite its initial appeal, the second argument by analogy is really no better than the first one. The first one fails because the fact that we have been wrong in the past is not a reason for thinking that we are wrong now; at most it shows that we are fallible. The second analogy aims to provide an *additional* reason for thinking we understand how a statement that we now regard as contextually a priori may actually be false. The additional reason is suggested by the conceptual scheme explanation of why we are entitled to accept some statements as contextually a priori. According to that explanation, we are entitled to treat a statement as contextually a priori only if it is deep for us. But to make sense of the claim that a statement we now accept is deep for us, we must imagine that we can describe the "methodological role" of this statement in our current "system" of beliefs. The problem is that from our current perspective, the most we can do to clarify the methodological role of a statement that we currently accept without evidence is to search for ways of specifying how it may actually be false and report on the results of our search. Looking back on our previous beliefs, we can distance ourselves from them enough to see that in some cases we were prevented from entertaining alternatives. But we cannot take this kind of perspective on any belief that we *now* regard as contextually a priori. To imagine that we can is to imagine that we accept the belief *because* our current "conceptual scheme" prevents us from seeing any alternatives to it. But that is not a *reason* for accepting a belief. Someone *else* might be able to explain our acceptance of the belief in this way, and perhaps we will be able to explain it in that way at some future time, but right now we cannot take this perspective on it. To take this perspective on it is to undermine it. And this explains what is wrong with the second argument by analogy: the fact that we can look back on our previous beliefs and see that in some cases we were prevented from understanding alternatives to them does not show that we can make sense of the claim that our *current* beliefs prevent us from understanding alternatives to the beliefs that we now regard as beyond doubt.

The imagined methodological perspective that the second argument by analogy tries to apply to our current beliefs is an imagined third person perspective. We are tempted to think that we can take up this third person perspective on our own current beliefs by the conceptual scheme explanation, which suggests that we cannot trust the beliefs that we now treat as contextually a priori unless we assume that they are deep for us. But the most we can coherently claim about the methodological status of beliefs we now regard as contextually a priori is that we cannot specify any ways in which they may actually be false. If we were convinced that our failure to see ways in which the statement may actually be false is due to some kind of limitation of our "conceptual scheme," we would no longer take ourselves to be entitled to accept the statement. To take ourselves to be entitled to accept the statement, however, is not to take ourselves to have some kind of guarantee that we will not find out that we are mistaken. There is a crucial distinction between admitting we are fallible, even about whether it is possible to make sense of doubting a particular statement, on the one hand, and concluding that we *understand* how the statement could actually be false, on the other. Both arguments by analogy elide this distinction.

In short, what the argument from analogy overlooks is that *to make sense of doubting a given belief one must be able to specify a particular way in which the belief may actually be false*. A corollary is that human fallibility is not by itself a reason for doubting any of our beliefs.[28] For this reason, (3) does not apply to a statement if we cannot specify any way in which it may actually be false.

At any given time we accept some statements that we cannot doubt, in the sense that we are unable to specify any ways in which they may be false. When we accept such statements, we cannot coherently distinguish between those that are revisable and those that we could never reasonably reject. Hence we cannot make sense of Putnam's suggestion (discussed in §IX above) that some statements are "absolutely a priori." If we cannot now specify any way in which a particular statement we accept may actually be false, we cannot be sure that we will *never* be able to make sense of giving it up without changing the topic. Nor can we be sure that we *will* someday be able to make sense of giving it up without changing the topic. The most we say is that given our current understanding of the topic, *we see no way* to give up those statements without changing the topic. Since we see no way to give up those statements without changing the topic, we cannot make sense of applying (3) to them. Hence the skeptic's demand that we give grounds for these statements has no content for us.

I conclude that if a person accepts a statement S and she cannot specify a particular way in which S may actually be false, her acceptance of S is epistemic bedrock for her, for the moment, at least, and she cannot *make sense* of the skeptic's "demand" that she give grounds for accepting S. In these circumstances, she has what I call a contextually a priori entitlement to accept S.

XI. INTERSUBJECTIVITY

Suppose Alice can specify a way in which a given statement S may actually be false but Bob cannot. In these circumstances, Bob has a contextually a priori entitlement to accept S, but Alice does not. In effect, Alice and Bob have arrived at different conclusions about whether it is reasonable to treat S as contextually a priori. This seems to conflict with (2), according to which epistemic entitlements are intersubjective.

As I understand (2), however, it requires only that two inquirers should always be able to discuss and, in principle, to agree about whether a given person can specify a way in which a given statement may actually be false. When the two inquirers are discussing the beliefs of a third person, without including her in the conversation, they should be able to agree about whether she can specify a way in which a given statement may actually be false. Things become more complicated if two inquirers together discuss the question whether one of them can specify a way in which a given statement may actually be false. Inquirers often share the background beliefs that are relevant to determining whether or not they can specify a way in which a given statement may actually be false, and so they often agree about which statements to treat as contextually a priori. But there could be two inquirers, the first of whom can specify a way in which a given statement may actually be false, the second of whom cannot. The complication is that if they communicate about this, the second person may learn from the first one how to specify a way in which the statement may be false.

This can happen, for instance, in a case where one of the inquirers knows very little about a topic, and the other is a respected authority on it. Most students first learning about the shape of space are unable to doubt that it is

Euclidean because that is the only notion of physical space that they have.[29] Once they learn more geometry and physics, or read popular explanations of discoveries in these areas, they learn that it is possible to doubt that physical space is Euclidean. Before such a student learns enough to make sense of doubting that physical space is Euclidean, she has a contextually a priori entitlement to accept it. Her entitlement is intersubjective in the sense that anyone who properly understands how she thinks about physical space will see that she cannot specify any way in which that statement may actually be false.

But one might think that if she cannot specify any way in which that statement may actually be false, then she cannot *learn* from someone else that this statement is true: if she hears someone utter the words "Physical space is not Euclidean," she should not take these words at face value; she should instead try to reinterpret them in a way that fits with what she already believes.[30]

This reasoning overlooks the fact that we typically take each other's words at face value unless we have good reason in a given context not to do so. What counts as a good reason of this kind is something that we can only discover by looking carefully at what we *actually* count as a good reason of this kind. For instance, we know that the British-English word "football" is translated by the American-English word "soccer"; if a British person says "Brazil has an excellent football team," we (American-English speakers) have good reason not to take his term "football" at face value. We all know, however, that a student first learning about physics typically has no good reason not to take the words of her teachers at face value, even if prior to her studies, she cannot make sense of doubting that space is Euclidean. Similarly, scientists who discover radically new theories typically take themselves to be talking about the same topics into which they were inquiring before they came up with their new theories. In practical terms, this means that scientists often take themselves to use the same words with the same denotations, both at a given time and over time. Speakers of the same language typically take each other's words at face value in this way. Sometimes, as in the "football" example, there is good reason not to do so. But a person's present inability to make sense of doubting a given statement S is not by itself a good reason for her to refuse to take at face value a fellow speaker's utterance of the negation of S.[31] She will naturally want an explanation of how S could be false. Once she hears the explanation, however, she may begin to see how S could be false, and she may even be convinced that S *is* false.[32]

This observation should also dispel the worry that if a speaker has a contextually a priori entitlement to accept a statement S, then her acceptance of S cannot be challenged or criticized. One might think that by *relativizing* our understanding of when a person has a contextually a priori entitlement to accept a statement S to our understanding of whether she can specify a way in which S may actually be false, we commit ourselves to an *epistemological relativism* according to which some statements are so basic to a person's way of looking at the world that no one who does not accept those statements can challenge or criticize her acceptance of them. As the example of the student who learns about non-Euclidean geometry and the general theory of relativity shows, however, a person may *lose* her contextually a priori entitlement to accept a statement S by learning how to specify ways in which S may actually be false. In this case, we see that at one time she had a contextually a priori entitlement to accept that physical space is Euclidean, because at that time she could not specify any way in which the statement could be false. Now that she has learned more, however, she no longer has a contextually a priori entitlement to accept that physical space is Euclidean. Whether or not she has a contextually a priori entitlement at a given time to accept a statement S depends on whether at that time she can specify a way in which S may be false. The relativity about whether or not a given speaker has a contextually a priori entitlements to accept a sentence S does not insulate her acceptance of S from all challenges or criticisms, since she may have a contextually a priori entitlement at one time to accept a given statement S, and later lose that entitlement, because she has learned how to specify a way in which S may be false.

This sketch of the sense in which our practice of attributing entitlements is intersubjective partly elucidates (2), according to which reasons and entitlements are intersubjective. It also partly elucidates (1), by reminding us that we are fallible, and that our acceptance of a belief does not make it true. At the same time, however, we have concluded that if a speaker cannot specify a way in which a given statement may actually be false, then she cannot apply (3) to it, and she cannot make sense of the skeptic's demand that she provide grounds for accepting it. We can therefore accept (4)—the observation that one has grounds for accepting a given statement S if and only if one has reasons for accepting it—without committing ourselves to skepticism about contextually a priori entitlements.

XII. Conclusion

The conceptual scheme explanation creates the confused impression that we can *explain* why it is reasonable for us to accept some statements by saying that they are deep for us—that we would not be able even to make sense of giving up the statements unless we developed a new way of thinking about them. The trouble is that we cannot make sense of the claim that a sentence we *now* accept is deep for us. We might be able to make sense of this at some point in the future. But to say that a sentence is deep for us is to say that our failure to be able to specify a way in which it is false is explained by a *limitation* of our current conceptual scheme. And if we were convinced that our current acceptance of the statement is explained by a conceptual limitation of this kind, we would no longer accept it.

Our discovery of our own previous conceptual limitations shows us that our estimations of whether it is possible to specify a way in which a given statement may actually be false are fallible. But this fallibility by itself does not give any content to the claim that a given statement that we now accept is deep for us. Without any understanding of this explanatory claim, we cannot make sense of the analogy that is supposed to give content to the conceptual scheme explanation. We cannot make sense of the imagined perspective from which our current beliefs, taken together, constitute a "conceptual scheme" with built-in limitations on our ability to specify ways in which some of our statements may actually be false. For the same reason, we cannot make sense of the idea (discussed in §IX above) that among the statements we now accept there are some that we could *never* reasonably reject. This idea has content only if we can contrast such statements with other statements that are deep for us, but revisable. Since we cannot make sense of the idea that some statements we now accept are deep for us, we cannot make sense of the idea that some statements we now accept are "absolutely a priori," in the sense that we could never reasonably reject them.

The moral is that we cannot *explain* or *justify* our current contextually a priori entitlements. To have such entitlements is just to rely on statements that we find ourselves unable to doubt. In many cases this reliance is unreflective, yet reasonable: if challenged, we would not be able to make any sense of the possibility that the statement is false. In other cases, we persistently search for ways of specifying how a statement that we accept may be false, and fail to find any. Since we fail to find any, we cannot make sense of applying (3) to the statement, and we cannot make sense of the skeptic's demand that we provide grounds for accepting it. In both kinds of cases, if we have not irresponsibly ignored clues or hints about how to specify a way in which the statement may be false, we are epistemically entitled to accept it.[33]

GARY EBBS

INDIANA UNIVERSITY
JANUARY 2003

NOTES

1. I present some of my reasons for this claim (though not the claim itself) in my paper "Realism and Rational Inquiry" (in *Philosophical Topics* 20, no. 1 [1992]: 1–33), and in chapters 6, 7, and 9 of my book *Rule-Following and Realism* (Cambridge, MA: Harvard University Press, 1997). Putnam himself once wrote: "I think that appreciating the diverse natures of logical truths, of physically necessary truths in the natural sciences, and of what I have for the moment lumped together under the title of framework principles—that clarifying the nature of these diverse kinds of statements is the most important work that a philosopher can do. Not because philosophy is necessarily about language, but because we must become clear about the roles played in our conceptual systems by these diverse kinds of truths before we can get an adequate global view of the world, of thought, of language, or of anything" (in "The Analytic and the Synthetic," reprinted in *Mind, Language, and Reality: Philosophical Papers,* vol. 2 [Cambridge: Cambridge University Press, 1975], 41).

2. Probably no scientist in the eighteenth century would have said, "Physical space is Euclidean." We may summarize the eighteenth-century scientist's views of space in this way only if we keep in mind that in fact their acceptance of Euclidean geometry was expressed by their commitment to such principles as that straight lines cannot form a triangle the sum of whose angles is more than 180 degrees. We now know that this principle conflicts with the view that a straight line is a path of a light ray, and that in some regions of space-time, paths of light rays form triangles the sum of whose angles is more than 180 degrees (see Hilary Putnam, "The Analytic and the Synthetic," 46–50). To save words, in the rest of this paper I use "the statement that physical space is Euclidean" as shorthand for a family of related principles that we would now call Euclidean.

3. In "'Two Dogmas' Revisited," reprinted in *Realism and Reason: Philosophical Papers,* vol. 3 (Cambridge: Cambridge University Press, 1983), 87–97, Putnam writes: "there are statements in science which can only be overthrown by a new theory—sometimes by a revolutionary new theory—and not by observation alone. Such statements *have* a sort of 'apriority' prior to the invention of the new theory which challenges or replaces them: they are *contextually a priori*" (95).

4. As far as I know, Putnam has not used the phrase "epistemically reasonable" in this way. But his remarks about the methodological significance of contextually a priori statements suggest that he could endorse this way of expressing his view.

5. We can define further applications of these phrases by using these primary ones. For instance, we can stipulate that a person's belief that *S* is contextually a priori (or a posteriori) for her if and only if she has a contextually a priori (or a posteriori) reason for believing or an entitlement to believe that *S*, and that *S* is contextually a priori (or a posteriori) for her if and only if she believes that *S* and her belief that *S* is contextually a priori (or a posteriori) for her.

6. For instance, some philosophers believe that by appealing to semantical rules for using our logical connectives, we can give good *reasons* for accepting the inference rule modus ponens, even though we must rely on modus ponens to give those reasons. This use of "reason" is suggested by what Michael Dummett says about the justification of deductive inferences in his paper "The Justification of Deduction" (in Michael Dummett, *Truth and Other Enigmas* [Cambridge: MA: Harvard University Press, 1978], 290–318).

7. This example is modeled on J. L. Austin's goldfinch example, from his paper "Other Minds" (reprinted in his *Philosophical Papers*, third edition, ed. James O. Urmson and Geoffrey J. Warnock [Oxford: Oxford University Press, 1979], 76–116; the goldfinch example is discussed on pages 77–86).

8. Recall that I use "the statement that physical space is Euclidean" as shorthand for a family of related principles that we would now call Euclidean. See note 2.

9. Many statements we accept are so basic to our way of thinking that we can see no point in asserting them or questioning them. It is only in the context of a skeptical challenge that we would become aware that we accept them at all. Are they genuine statements before we are aware of accepting them? The answer depends on what is meant by "statement." I use this word in a way that covers both acknowledged and unacknowledged commitments, where the commitments themselves are understood partly in terms of the inferences a person draws from sentences she explicitly asserts.

10. The skeptical reasoning presented in this section resembles the "Agrippan" skepticism that Michael Williams describes on pages 61–63 in his book *Problems of Knowledge* (Oxford: Oxford University Press, 2001). It applies to contextually a posteriori entitlements too. But the skeptical challenge to contextually a posteriori entitlements must be treated differently from the skeptical challenge to contextually a priori entitlements, so I will not address it in this paper.

11. Georges Rey, "A Naturalistic A Priori," *Philosophical Studies* 92 (1998): 25–43.

12. Laurence Bonjour, *In Defense of Pure Reason* (Cambridge: Cambridge University Press, 1998), and Jerrold Katz, *Realistic Rationalism* (Cambridge, MA: MIT Press, 1998).

13. Paul Boghossian, "How Are Objective Reasons Possible?" in *Philosophical Studies* 106 (2001): 1–40, and "Knowledge of Logic," in *New Essays on the A Priori*, ed. Paul Boghossian and Christopher Peacocke (Oxford: Oxford University Press, 2000), 229–54. See also Christopher Peacocke, "Explaining the A Priori: The Programme of Moderate Rationalism," in *New Essays on the A Priori*, 255–85.

14. For instance, speaking about a skeptic who would challenge his explanation of why it is warranted for us to accept modus ponens, Paul Boghossian writes: "We cannot accept the claim that we have no warrant whatsoever for the core logical principles. We cannot conceive what such a warrant could consist in . . . if not in some sort of inference using those very core logical principles. So, there must be genuine warrants that will not carry any sway with a skeptic" ("How Are Objective Reasons Possible?" 36.) By "warrant" Boghossian means what I call "grounds." This passage therefore expresses Boghossian's choice to reject (4).

15. See Jerrold Katz, *Realistic Rationalism*, 49. For a similar objection, but without explicit reference to Putnam, see Georges Rey, "A Naturalistic A Priori," 28–29.

16. Hilary Putnam, "It Ain't Necessarily So," in Hilary Putnam, *Mathematics, Matter and Method: Philosophical Papers*, vol. 1 (Cambridge: Cambridge University Press, 1975), 240.

17. Hilary Putnam, "Rethinking Mathematical Necessity," in Hilary Putnam, *Words and Life*, ed. James Conant (Cambridge, MA: Harvard University Press, 1994), 245–63; the new formulation is presented on 251.

18. Hilary Putnam, "'Two Dogmas' Revisited," 95.

19. Hans Reichenbach, *The Philosophy of Space and Time*, trans. Maria Reichenbach and John Freund (New York: Dover, 1958), ch. 1.

20. Carl B. Boyer, *A History of Mathematics* (Princeton: Princeton University Press, 1968), 587.

21. Laurence Sklar, *Space, Time, and Spacetime* (Berkeley: University of California Press, 1974), chs. II and III.

22. Hilary Putnam, "There is at Least One A Priori Truth," in Hilary Putnam, *Realism and Reason: Philosophical Papers*, vol. 3 (Cambridge: Cambridge University Press, 1983), 98–114; quotation from 99.

23. Hilary Putnam, "It Ain't Necessarily So," 249. Putnam still endorses this passage from "It Ain't Necessarily So," which was published in 1962. In "Rethinking Mathematical

Necessity," Putnam writes "there are at any given time some accepted statements which cannot be overthrown merely by *observations*, but can only be overthrown by thinking of a whole body of alternative theory as well. . . . I insisted (and still insist) is that this is a distinction of methodological significance" (251).

24. Frege's reaction to Russell's letter was more complicated than this brief characterization suggests. In the appendix to his *Grundgesetze der Arithmetik*, vol. II, Frege shows how to derive Russell's contradiction within Frege's own *Begriffsschrift*. But, as Michael Kremer pointed out to me, Frege also suggests that the derivation shows that some expressions of his *Begriffsschrift* have not been given any *Bedeutung*. Since Frege rejected the idea that deduction can be understood purely formally, he might have thought that his "derivations" of Russell's contradiction were not genuine derivations at all. Nevertheless, Frege found these "derivations" compelling enough to give up his basic law (V) (*The Frege Reader,* 279). In his letter to Russell dated June 22, 1902, six days after Russell sent Frege his famous letter about the contradiction, Frege wrote, "Your discovery of the contradiction has surprised me beyond words and, I should almost like to say, left me thunderstruck, because it has rocked the ground on which I meant to build arithmetic. It seems . . . that my law V ([*Grundgesetze*] §20, 36) is false" (*The Frege Reader*, ed. Michael Beaney [Oxford: Blackwell, 1997], 254). In the appendix to *Grundgesetze*, vol. II, where Frege shows how to "derive" the contradiction within his *Begriffsschrift*, he concludes at one point that "law (V) itself has collapsed" (*The Frege Reader*, 284). The change in Frege's attitude toward law (V) came about very swiftly, without the development of a fundamentally new theory of logic; in this respect it was unlike the change in attitude toward Euclidean geometry that Putnam highlights in his accounts of the contextually a priori.

25. Hilary Putnam, "There is at Least One A Priori Truth," 99.

26. Putnam doesn't always describe contextually a priori statements in this way. In "Rethinking Mathematical Necessity," he writes that "if we cannot *describe* circumstances under which a belief would be falsified, circumstances under which we would be prepared to say that –B had been confirmed, then we are not presently able to attach a clear *sense* to "B can be revised." In such a case we cannot, I grant, say that B is "unrevisable," but neither can we intelligibly say "B can be revised" (Hilary Putnam, "Rethinking Mathematical Necessity," 253–54).

27. We must keep in mind, however, that our current inability to doubt the minimal principle of contradiction is not a reason for thinking that it is true. To make sense of asking for or providing such a reason, we must be able to make sense of the "possibility" that the statement is not true. If we can not make sense of the "possibility" that every statement is both true and false, we cannot make sense of raising any substantive question about whether the minimal principle of contradiction is true, and therefore it is a confusion to suggest that we have some reason to think it is true. For this reason, it is misleading to say that the minimal principle of contradiction is a priori. It is better to emphasize that we can make no sense of the "possibility" that every statement is both true and false.

28. This point is well expressed by J. L. Austin in "Other Minds." He writes that "being aware that you may be mistaken doesn't mean merely being aware that you are a fallible human being: it means that you have some concrete reason to suppose that you may be mistaken in this case" (98).

29. One might think that a speaker could accept the statement that physical space is Euclidean, for instance, without having any idea of what physical space is or of what it is for physical space to be Euclidean, hence without being able to specify any way in which physical space may actually be Euclidean. Similarly, one might think, such a speaker can also make sense of the negation of the statement that physical space is Euclidean even though she is unable to specify a way in which the statement may actually be false. This

objection overlooks the crucial point that to count as expressing the thought that physical space is Euclidean by using the sentence "Physical space is Euclidean," a speaker must be at least *minimally* competent in the use of the words that occur in the sentence, and this involves having some idea of what thought is expressed by using that sentence. I explain this point about minimal competence in chapter seven of my book *Rule-Following and Realism*, and in my paper "A Puzzle about Doubt," in *New Essays on Semantic Externalism and Self-Knowledge*, ed. Susana Nuccetelli (Cambridge, MA: MIT Press, 2003), 143–68. The same observations about minimal competence can also be used to correct a misunderstanding of "understanding." It might seem that to understand a statement that *p* one must be able to distinguish circumstances in which *p* is true from circumstances in which *p* is false. But this would imply that to understand the statement that *p* one must be able to specify a way in which *p* may be false, and therefore that no one understands any statements that I call contextually a priori. This overlooks our ordinary criteria for taking a person to be competent in the use of a sentence, hence to have at least a minimal understanding of the thoughts she expresses by using it.

30. Donald Davidson's principle of charity leads inevitably to this unacceptable conclusion (despite his occasional claims to the contrary), for reasons I explain in my paper "Learning From Others," *Noûs* 36, no. 4 (Dec 2002): 525–49.

31. The relationship between what we can make sense of doubting, and what we can understand another person to have said is subtle and context-sensitive. I know of no easy generalizations about this relationship. To understand it better, one would need to look carefully at what we would say in practice to a wide range of cases in which the limits of what a person can make sense of doubting are apparently challenged or extended by what another person writes or says.

32. Similarly, a mathematics student who is unable to see how a certain solution to a mathematical problem she is trying to solve could possibly be correct is not thereby entitled to believe that the proposed solution is incorrect. If the proposed solution comes from a trusted and authoritative source, such as an accomplished mathematician or a respected textbook, she should suspend her belief until she understands it better.

33. In October 2001 I presented an early draft of this paper at a philosophy colloquium at Northwestern University, and discussed it with Derrick Darby, Peter Hylton, Richard Kraut, Cristina Lafont, Tom McCarthy, Axel Mueller, and Charles Travis, among others. A month later with Hilary Putnam I briefly discussed the question of whether we can make sense of the claim that a belief we now accept is contextually a priori. He mentioned that he now thinks we cannot make sense of this claim, and I briefly explained how I think we *can* make sense of it, if we reject some of his earlier characterizations of the contextually a priori. Prompted by these discussions and by my own dissatisfaction with the paper, I rewrote it from beginning to end. Putnam's comments on the new draft led to further refinements. Paul Horwich later alerted me to a possible misunderstanding of my view. Finally, in January 2003 I presented the penultimate draft to the Wittgenstein Workshop at the University of Chicago, where I received many probing and insightful comments from Jim Conant, Michael Kremer, and David Finkelstein, among others. Thanks to all. Warm thanks especially to Hilary Putnam, whose fertile writings have shaped my thinking on almost every philosophical topic, and whose curiosity, insight, and brilliance, punctuated by the sheer delight he takes in doing philosophy, are a continuing source of inspiration to me.

REPLY TO GARY EBBS

I have long been an admirer of Gary Ebbs's work, and in particular of his *Realism and Rule Following*, a book that contains the best discussion of my Brains in a Vat argument that I have seen to date, as well as brilliant interpretations and original criticisms of important philosophical views, including those of Carnap, Kripke, and Quine— as well as of mine. In that book and in the disquotational account of truth that he presents in his recent *Truth and Words,* Ebbs has made major contributions to the philosophy of language. I was thus eager to see what he would write for the present volume. Although, as will be seen, I do not accept a criticism that he makes of my view of contextually necessary truth, that disagreement is not important in my eyes (although he may, naturally, think differently about its importance), and I am in substantial agreement with the other points that he makes. I also found many of his formulations to express precisely the direction in which I have been moving in recent years. Indeed, his formulations are possibly clearer than those at which I have been able to arrive. Let me accordingly begin with the points on which he and I are in agreement.

1. We both see the sense in which, prior to the working out of an alternative geometry (and an idea of how it might be concretely applied in physics) the falsity of the propositions of Euclidean geometry was inconceivable as of profound methodological significance. To dismiss that sort of "inconceivability" as of merely "psychological" significance is wrong, because the kind of inconceivability in question—which is what I tried to explain in the papers Ebbs discusses, and what he tries to clarify with his formulations—determines what can and cannot be investigated, undermined or defended, supported or called into question, in a given scientific context. On the other hand, to claim (as Stephen Mulhall did in a discussion he and I had a few years ago) that those propositions *were* genuinely necessary, and that non-Euclidean geometry merely "changed the meaning" of the term "straight line" is equally untenable, as one can see by asking: "then which paths in space, pray tell, are the 'straight lines' *in the old sense*"?

The propositions of Euclidean geometry were not true, and a fortiori not a priori, but they were, to use Ebbs's terminology, *contextually a priori*. On this we are in complete agreement.

2. I agree with Ebbs that "if a person is unable to specify any way which a statement may actually be false, she cannot make sense of the skeptic's requirement that she provide grounds for accepting it." This is a nice trenchant way of explaining why, as I just said, what is contextually inconceivable determines what can and cannot be investigated, undermined or defended, supported or called into question.

3. Ebbs quotes with approval my saying (in "Rethinking Mathematical Necessity") that "if we cannot *describe* circumstances under which a belief would be falsified, circumstances under which we would be prepared to say that –B had been confirmed, then we are not presently able to attach a clear *sense* to 'B can be revised'. In such a case we cannot, I grant, say that B is 'unrevisable', but neither can we intelligibly say 'B can be revised.'" He is quite right that this is an example of convergence in our views.

4. He criticizes my having (more than thirty years ago) entertained the view that there is at least one absolutely a priori truth. (But he does not mention that the published paper ends with a "Note" which reads, "This is a first draft of a paper I never finished. I no longer agree with the conclusion for a number of reasons.") In addition to having said at the time of its publication that I do not agree with the conclusion of that paper, I also criticize the idea of absolutely necessary truth in the Intellectual Autobiography section of this volume, where I write that such "necessity" (necessity relative to a body of knowledge) . . . is the only sort of "conceptual necessity" I recognize. Here, however, Ebbs and I are not in complete agreement because he thinks that it makes no sense to say that a statement is necessary relative to our *present* body of knowledge, and I do not accept his argument for this claim. But on the rejection of the notion of the "absolutely a priori" we *are* in agreement.

5. Obviously the overthrow of Euclidean geometry (and the overthrow, by quantum mechanics, of the principle that every event has a cause, and different events must have different causes) is "behind" our loss of confidence in the idea of the absolutely a priori. But to "argue by analogy" that *anything* we believe may, for all we know, be false, and hence that the skeptic is right, is a mistake. Where such an "argument by analogy" goes wrong is well explained by Ebbs when he writes, "There is a crucial distinction between admitting we are fallible, even about whether it is possible to make sense of doubting a particular statement, on the one hand, and concluding that we understand how the statement could actually be false, on the other . . . arguments by analogy elide this distinction."

I now come to the point at which we have a disagreement. As Ebbs writes,

In short, Putnam's answer to question (a)—"In what sense was the belief that physical space is Euclidean *quasi*-necessary relative to the eighteenth-century scientists' conceptual scheme?"—is that scientists in the eighteenth century had not yet developed the mathematical and physical theories that would later make it possible to specify a way in which their belief that physical space is Euclidean may actually be false. The idea is that this limitation of their "conceptual scheme" *explains* why they were unable to specify any way in which their belief that physical space is Euclidean may actually be false.

So far so good.

Ebbs has three objections to this. I will discuss the second one first, because he regards it as "the more serious objection." It is as follows:

> we have no criterion for determining whether or not our current failure to specify a way in which a particular statement may actually be false shows that the statement is contextually a priori in the proposed sense, or whether we are just overlooking something that we would immediately recognize as a way of specifying how the statement may actually be false. Let us say that a statement is *deep* for a person if and only if she would have to develop a fundamentally new way of thinking even to conceive of how that statement may actually be false. Suppose that you are unable to specify a way in which a given statement S may actually be false. The difficulty for the conceptual scheme's explanation is that you cannot tell whether S is deep for you. Tomorrow you might discover that you overlooked something, just as Frege was surprised when he read Russell's letter. But if S is not deep for you, then . . . you are vulnerable to the skeptical reasoning presented above, because you are unable to provide any grounds for accepting the statement.

Let me henceforth write "framework principle" for Ebbs's "contextually a priori," because I think it captures better the idea we have in mind. In this terminology, Ebbs's claim is that "you cannot tell" whether a statement is or is not a framework principle. But now two problems arise.

The first problem is that Ebbs thinks of "contextually a priori" as a status that *entitlements* have, whereas I think of being quasi-necessary relative to a conceptual scheme (being a "framework principle," in short) as a status that statements have at a given time. Although he rejects the skeptical demand that one must be able to provide a *justification* for every statement one accepts, he does seem to accept the question "what *entitles* one to accept it," where the "one" is an *individual*. Here, strangely, he resembles the traditional epistemologist. But I am not a traditional epistemologist, and that is not the question I was addressing. The second, more serious problem, is that, in my view, it *is* possible to tell what the framework principles of a science at a given time are. This is something that historians of science and philosophers of science do all the time. I grant that if they are formalizers they probably disagree about what to take as "axioms" and what to treat as "theorems," and just exactly how to formalize the science in question, but I do not think that disagreements in how to formalize, say, Euclidean geometry or Newtonian mechanics would affect the conclusion that the parallels postulate, for example, was part of the "framework" of classical geometry and of Newtonian mechanics-plus-geometry. And historians of science are also able to tell us whether alternatives to the framework principles of a given science have or have not been proposed at a given time. Ebbs's worry that "tomorrow you might discover that you overlooked something, just as Frege was surprised when he read Russell's letter" is a classical skeptical worry. If the possibility that one might have "overlooked something" really shows that one cannot know that the parallels postulate was a framework principle with no alternatives in sight in seventeenth- and eighteenth-century physics, then it equally "shows" that one "can't know" that one has correctly formalized elementary number theory ("Tomorrow you might discover that you overlooked something"). Indeed, the skeptical argument would "show" that one cannot know that one has washed all the dishes, when one has ("Tomorrow you might find a saucer you overlooked"). Ebbs's worry about a "criterion" for being deep is, again, reminiscent of the skeptical side of traditional epistemology. As Cavell taught us in the *Claim of Reason*, there is not a "criterion" for being a real object (imagine a skeptic asking "is it real?" about a *tomato*), but it does not follow that "you cannot tell" when you are seeing a real tomato. And there is not a criterion for not having overlooked anything, but there are circumstances under which one can say "I am sure I washed them all." A good historian/philosopher of science *can*, I believe, tell what at least some of the framework principles of Newtonian mechanics are, or what at least some of the framework principles of present-day quantum mechanics are, and whether alternatives have been proposed.

Now I will consider Ebbs's example of Frege's letter to Russell ("The first problem is that there are statements that count as contextually a priori according to the constraints in §I that are not contextually a priori according to the conceptual scheme explanation. For instance, Frege had no difficulty understanding Russell's explanation of the contradiction that arises in Frege's logic.") All right, but there is a sense in which *any* significant group of beliefs could be overthrown by showing them to be *logically* inconsistent. The task would then arise of finding a way of repairing the breach in our scientific system. If you like, instead of saying, as I did, that a framework principle can be refuted "only by conceiving of whole new theoretical structures," I could have written (had I worried about the problem of hidden logical inconsistencies): "only by conceiving of whole new theoretical structures, or by showing it to be inconsistent, in which case the scientific community will be forced to conceive of a whole new theoretical structure." And "conceive of a whole new theoretic structure" is precisely what Russell did with his theory of types. A logical contradiction can, indeed, sometimes be overlooked; but the possibility of non-Euclidean geometry (or, in the case of the principle of determinism, the possibility of indeterministic quantum mechanics) is not something one simply "overlooks."

Ebbs's third objection to what he calls my "conceptual scheme explanation" is that it leaves us vulnerable to the following "argument by analogy":

> Statements that we currently regard as contextually a priori are from a methodological point of view no better off than those that we regarded as contextually a priori in the past. By *methodological analogy* with cases in which statements actually became doubtful, we can make sense of the possibility that a statement we now treat as contextually a priori is false, even though we cannot now specify any way in which it could be false.

Ebbs also explains in more detail why he supposes this to be a problem for "conceptual scheme explanation":

> According to that explanation, we are entitled to treat a statement as contextually a priori only if it is deep for us. But to make sense of the claim that a statement we now accept is deep for us, we must imagine that we can describe the "methodological role" of this statement in our current "system" of beliefs. The problem is that from our current perspective, the most we can do to clarify the methodological role of a statement that we currently accept without evidence is to search for ways of specifying how it may actually be false and report on the results of our search. Looking back on our previous beliefs, we can distance ourselves from them enough to see that in some cases we were prevented from entertaining alternatives. But we cannot take this kind of perspective on any belief that we *now* regard as contextually a priori. To imagine that we can is to imagine that we accept the belief *because* our current "conceptual scheme" prevents us from seeing any alternatives to it. But that is not a *reason* for accepting a belief. Someone *else* might be able to explain our acceptance of the belief in this way, and perhaps we will be able to explain it in that way at some future time, but right now we cannot take this perspective on it. To take this perspective on it is to undermine it.

This argument of Ebbs's resembles Kant's first antinomy: one cannot meaningfully suppose that space is finite (so goes one half of the antinomy), because if one could conceive of a limit to space one would automatically be able to conceive of something beyond the limit, which would then be space outside of space.[1] Similarly, Ebbs claims that to say that something is a framework principle is to posit a "limit"; it is to posit that we only accept it because $((\exists x)(x$ is a way it could be false & we are unable to conceive of x). So to say that something is (still) a framework principle is already to say that we have passed *beyond* the stage at which it is a framework principle, and thus contradictory in exactly the way that passing beyond the limits of space is a contradiction. But that is not at all what is involved in describing the framework principles of a particular science in the present tense. If someone in the eighteenth century had said that if Euclidean geometry could be false, it would have to be in a way we cannot presently conceive, he would have been saying something quite reasonable. (It is not unimaginable that a nineteenth-century thinker could have said such a thing, regardless of the skeptical worry that he might have "overlooked" something.) Ebbs reiterates his "limit" talk: "The trouble is that we cannot make sense of the claim that a sentence we *now* accept is deep for us. We might be able to make sense of this at some point in the future. But to say that a sentence is deep for us is to say that our failure to be able to specify a way in which it is false is explained by a *limitation* of our current conceptual scheme." This is simply false. It is to say our failure to be able to specify such a way is explained by the *structure* of our present conceptual scheme, without prejudice to the question whether that structure is a *limitation* (a defect) or not.

I fear that this disagreement between us is important in Gary Ebbs's eyes because of the number of times he repeats the claim that we cannot now be entitled to say that a statement (not, by the way, a "sentence"!) is deep for us (that is, a framework principle) until it has been superseded; but I am happy to say that it is unimportant in my eyes because I can totally agree with Ebbs's reply to the skeptic without in any way committing myself to that claim. When Ebbs writes that, "There is a crucial distinction between admitting we are fallible, even about whether it is possible to make sense of doubting a particular statement, on the one hand, and concluding that we understand how the statement could actually be false, on the other. Both arguments by analogy elide this distinction" he is, in my view, absolutely right. I have already described this as a notable point of convergence in our views.

H.P.

NOTE

1. Needless to say, Kant did not envisage the possibility of space being finite but unbounded!

11

Michael Dummett

WHAT DO PERMUTATION ARGUMENTS PROVE?

Hilary Putnam is well known for having used model-theoretic arguments against what he called "metaphysical realism." I deprecate the use of this last term, if it is intended, as Putnam intended it, to designate a particular variety of realism. *Every* form of realism is a metaphysical doctrine, one that rests on a particular type of theory of meaning (or theory of the content of thoughts). Let us use the term "hard realism" for what Hilary Putnam called "metaphysical realism," leaving it open whether there is such a form of realism as "soft realism" to contrast it with.

Among the model-theoretic results Putnam has deployed against hard realism are the downwards and upwards Löwenheim-Skolem theorems, which concern the cardinality of the domains of models. But he also deploys the simple permutation argument, which relies on the obvious fact that any model is isomorphic to one that results from the first by a permutation on the elements of the domain; that is, if M is a model of a given theory, and j is a permutation of its elements, then M* is also a model, where the denotation of an individual constant **c** in M* is $\phi(a)$ if a denotes **c** in M, an element a satisfies a primitive one-place predicate **F** in M* if and only if $\phi^{-1}(a)$ satisfies **F** in M, and so on. This permutation case may be taken as representative of the model-theoretic arguments used by Putnam against hard realism. What does such an argument prove?

In section 10 of *Grundgesetze der Arithmetik*, vol. I, Frege employs a permutation argument to convince his readers that he has not yet fixed the references (*Bedeutungen*) of the value-range terms in his formal language.[1]

The axiom governing value-range terms is the notorious Axiom V, which says that the value range of a function Φ coincides with that of a function Ψ if and only if $\Phi(x) = \Psi(x)$ for every x (Frege of course did not know at this time that the axiom was inconsistent). Frege's permutation argument runs as follows. Let X be any one-one function (permutation of the domain.) Then X (the value range of Φ) will still coincide with X (the value range of Ψ) if and only if $\Phi(x) = \Psi(x)$ for every x. This shows, Frege says, that the references of value-range terms have not yet been fixed.

What is the remedy? It is, Frege says, to ensure that every function representable in the formal language has a determinate value for any value range as argument; we must here remember that Frege is taking not only truth functions, the *Bedeutungen* of sentential operators, but also concepts and relations, the *Bedeutungen* of one- and two-place predicates, as functions whose values are truth values. It is necessary to ensure this only for primitive functions. In section 10 Frege runs through the primitive functions so far introduced, and decides that it is only for the equality function = that the condition has not been met. The defect arises when one argument of the binary identity function is a value range and the other an object that has not been overtly given as a value range. This is the analogue of the "Julius Caesar problem" that had arisen in Frege's *Die Grundlagen der Arithmetik*, concerning identity statements in which a numerical term stands on one side of the sign of identity and a term of another sort on the other side: how are we to specify what the truth value of such a sentence as "The number of planets = Julius Caesar" should be?[2] The only objects that are the references of terms in the formal language of *Grundgesetze* and have not hitherto been identified as value ranges are, Frege says, the two truth values: so we may solve the problem by equating each of them with its own unit class, classes being the value ranges of concepts considered as functions. Now truth values have been identified with particular value ranges. Hence the stipulation corresponding to Axiom V will determine the value of the identity function for every pair of objects that are the references of terms of the formal language, including all those pairs of which one member is explicitly given as a value range: in other words, the truth value of every identity-statement involving a value range.

In section 29 Frege asks the question, "When does a name refer to (*bedeuten*) something?"[3]; here by a "name" Frege understands any semantically significant expression, whether including an argument place or not, and so uses it to cover function names. But he immediately goes on to equate the expression "to refer to something" (*bedeuten etwas*) with "to have a reference" (*haben eine Bedeutung*) and with "to be referential" (*sein bedeutungsvoll*), and, for each category of expression, to lay down the condition for it to have a reference or to be referential. That is, he does not treat "*be-*

deuten" as a transitive verb by laying down the condition for an expression of a given category to refer to such and such a particular thing; he treats "refers to something" as a unitary predicate, equivalent, as he has said, to "is referential." In the stipulations governing the primitive vocabulary of his formal language Frege had specified what object an expression referred to whenever it referred to a truth value, and also when it was formed by means of the description operator, but in no other cases. He uses "proper name" to mean what we call a "singular term" (which, for him, includes complete sentences without the judgment stroke or assertion sign). The condition he states in section 29 for a "proper name" to have a reference is that every term that results from putting it in the argument place of a referential name of a function with one argument has a reference (including a name of a function of two arguments of which one argument place has been filled). This is the principle to which Frege was appealing in claiming in section 10 to have secured references to value-range terms. It is also the *Grundgesetze* version of the context principle of *Grundlagen*, that it is only in the context of a sentence that a word has a *Bedeutung*. In the *Grundgesetze* version sentences (what in that book Frege calls "names of truth values") play no distinguished role: a singular term has a reference if every more complex term of which it is part has a reference. Let us call this the "generalized context principle for singular terms," or "GCP." I do not propose here to examine how far these stipulations incur the defect of circularity.

It can surely not be supposed that Frege's *Grundgesetze* had many readers in his lifetime. But, of those, there can have been few who failed to observe that Frege's solution to the problem of securing a reference for value-range terms in no way answered the permutation argument which raised the problem. I do not suppose that Frege was muddleheaded; so I do not imagine that he was unaware of this point. The enunciation of the GCP is a declaration that the permutation argument is irrelevant.

For whom is it relevant? It is plain that for us to specify a permutation of the value ranges, or, let us say, just of classes, we must refer to value ranges or classes and specify their images under the permutation. We cannot by these means prove that it is indeterminate what our value-range terms or class names refer to, since, in so specifying the permutation, we are assuming that we already know what they refer to. To be worried by the permutation argument, someone unaware of the inconsistency of Frege's Axiom V would have to think that in mathematical space there were objects which, in and of themselves, *independently of anything we might or can say*, are value ranges of particular functions. To assign a reference to a value-range term would be, for him, to effect a link between that linguistic (or symbolic) term and some particular one of these abstract objects. The question would then arise whether we had assigned the *right* references to our terms: when, for example, we use the term "the class of prime numbers" are we really speaking about that object which, in and of itself, is the value range of the function which maps prime numbers on to the value *true* and everything else on to the value *false*? The permutation argument shows that we cannot be sure of this, given only the stipulations that Frege has made, in particular that embodied in Axiom V. It challenges us to hit on further stipulations which will avoid this calamity, but will guarantee that in speaking of the class of prime numbers we are really speaking of that abstract object which is in truth—in the eyes of God—the genuine class of prime numbers.

This is hard realism with a vengeance. Hilary Putnam is quite right that a permutation argument shows it to be quite untenable. More exactly, it is the *failure* of the permutation argument that shows hard realism to be untenable. If hard realism were correct, the permutation argument *would* show that we may well not be referring to what we think we are referring to. But it is quite clear what we are referring to. Therefore hard realism is not correct, and the permutation argument has no force against our confidence that we mean what we think we mean.

But permutation arguments, and their cousins, are everywhere: are we to think that philosophy faculties are manned by hard realists? Fairly recently, it has been argued that the fact that the complex numbers have a nontrivial automorphism, namely one that maps every complex number $x + yi$ on to its conjugate $x - yi$, poses a difficulty for Frege. What is the problem? Well, may it not be that what you refer to as the number i is what I refer to as $-i$? Nothing that either of us can say can dispel this disquieting possibility: there is an isomorphism between our models of the complex numbers. What makes it a possibility? The thought that there are in mathematical space objects which are, in and of themselves, i and $-i$. You, happily, are perhaps using the mathematical terms to refer to the right ones; I, unhappily, am referring to the wrong ones, and neither of us can discover this fact. But there is no such problem: we both use the symbolism in the same way, and so no question can arise about whether we are referring to the same things. We can postulate that there is a square root of -1; if we do, we are bound to recognize that there will be another, distinct but not distinguishable from it, whose square is also -1; they are distinct because each is distinguishable by reference to the other. In Winchester College there is in the dining hall a two-sided brazier which is lit on the feast of Sts. Simon and Jude, and whose sides are called "Simon" and "Jude." The only answer to the question, "Which is Simon?" admitted as correct is "The one that is not Jude," and likewise for the question, "Which is Jude?" It is so for the two square roots of -1, and none the worse for that. Armed with the GCP, Frege would have made short work of any cavils about it. Of course, it could be laid down which side of the brazier was which, because we possess other means of distinguishing each side than by reference to the other. Likewise, if we spurn postulation as theft, we may construct the complex numbers, say by identifying them with ordered pairs of real numbers; we shall then be able to say which is i and which is $-i$, and the automorphism will leave us untroubled. The critics believe that the automorphism would have been an embarrassment for Frege, because they suppose him to have been a hard realist. He was a realist, certainly; but a hard realist he was not.

Another example is the kind of argument used by Paul Benacerraf to show that numbers are not objects. Frege characterized both the natural numbers and the real numbers by appeal to their uses, as cardinal numbers and as measurement numbers respectively. But suppose we characterize the natural numbers as Dedekind did, namely by characterizing the abstract structure of the sequence of natural numbers under the successor relation. It may then be objected that if we map each even number on to its successor and each odd number on to its predecessor, we shall still have an ω-sequence, with a deviant successor relation, and there will be no saying *which* ω-sequence we were referring to as the sequence of natural numbers. We do not need even to consider a permutation of the natural numbers: we can consider the ω-sequence consisting of just the even numbers, with the successor operation replaced by that of adding 2. The situation is the same as with Frege's permutation of the value ranges. To specify any such deviant ω-sequence, we have to assume the natural numbers as already known and identifiable; so there is no problem about deviant ω-sequences as specified by us in our language. The problem arises only for hard realists, who think that objects having determinate positions in the sequence of natural numbers exist in mathematical space; in mathematical space, they suppose, there are also ω-sequences derived by permutations of or selections from the natural numbers—permutations and selections effected in mathematical space, not by us. There will indeed be a problem for them: which ω-sequence we are referring to—the real one or an *ersatz* one—when we speak of the sequence of natural numbers. For anyone not a hard realist there is no such problem.

If we take a first-order formal system as attempting to characterize a mathematical structure, the hard realist does not need to invoke isomorphism but the weaker notion of elementary equivalence to generate similar problems. For instance, if we try to characterize the natural numbers by a first-order system of Peano arithmetic, Gödel's incompleteness theorem shows that the system will have nonstandard models as well as that which we intend to characterize by it. How do I know that when you speak of the natural numbers as characterized by that system, you are not referring to one of the nonstandard models, and how do you know that I am not? If we regard mathematical structures as given only by the descriptions of them we formulate, and as existing only in virtue of being capable of being so described, then the problem does not arise; for any description by means of which we may refer to a specific nonstandard model must make use of the notion of the sequence of natural numbers as already understood. The problem appears baffling only if we think of the structures which constitute models of Peano arithmetic as subsisting in mathematical space, independently of our thought or our means of describing them, and of our grasp of a model of a formal system as consisting in some nonsensory intellectual apprehension of such a structure. On the contrary, mathematical objects and mathematical structures exist only as describable by us in terms that allow us to communicate with each other. The only intellectual acts that are necessary are to frame and to understand such descriptions.

So far all our examples have been drawn from logic and mathematics. How is it with reference to objects in the physical world? In section 26 of his *Grundlagen*, Frege gives a bold example. He begins by drawing a distinction between the subjective and the objective.

> Space, according to Kant, belongs to the phenomenal (*Erscheinung*). It would be possible that to other rational beings it appeared quite otherwise than to us. Indeed, we cannot even know whether it appears to one person as it does to another; for we cannot lay the intuition of space that one has beside that of the other, in order to compare them. Yet it contains something objective nevertheless; all recognise the same geometrical axioms, if only by their actions, and they must do so in order to find their way in the world. What is objective in it is what is subject to laws, what can be conceived, what can be judged, what can be expressed in words. What is purely intuitable is incommunicable.[4]

He then gave an example, a fantasy in relation to which he offered a startling permutation argument.

> Let us suppose two rational beings for whom only projective properties and relations are intuitable: the lying of three points on a straight line, of four points on a plane, etc.; and let what to one perceives (*anschaut*) as a point appear to the other as a plane and conversely. What for one is the line connecting certain points will be for the other the line of intersection of certain planes, and so on, always in dual correspondence. They would then be well able to understand one another, and would never become aware of the difference in their perceptions (*ihres Anschauens*), since in projective geometry there corresponds to every theorem another dual to it; for the divergence in an aesthetic evaluation would be no certain sign. In respect of all geometrical theorems they would be in full agreement; it is only that they would translate the words differently into their intuitions. With the word "point" one would

connect this intuition, the other would connect that one. Thus one can always say that this word means (*bedeutet*) something objective; it is just that one ought not to understand by this meaning (*Bedeutung*) what is special to their intuitions. In this sense the axis of the Earth is likewise objective.[5]

We are tempted to say that one of the individuals in Frege's fantasy may use the word "point" to refer to points, while the other uses it to refer to planes, although neither can become aware of this discrepancy. But that is like saying that one mathematician may use the symbol "*i*" to refer to *i*, while another uses it to refer to its (additive and multiplicative) inverse, although neither can know of the difference between them; it is not the moral Frege intends to draw from his example. For him what is objective is what is communicable. Meaning is objective, being what is communicated by words; the senses of our words are objective, and, since sense determines reference, their references are objective too. We can say only that both speakers use the word "point" to refer to point/planes, objects which can be taken under one geometrical systematization to be points and under another to be planes; they use the word "plane" to refer to plane/points. When Frege says, in introducing the example, that what one of the two perceives as a point, the other perceives as a plane, he is using words of *our* language: the moral of the example is precisely that in *their* language the words "point" and "plane" differ in meaning just as do the mathematical terms "*i*" and "-*i*."

Frege treats the sense of a symbol, word, or expression as a feature of the common language. This is admittedly an idealization. Speakers of the same language may attach different senses to the same word. It would, however, be wrong to infer that the understanding of words, and the way we mean them in speaking to others (or to ourselves), are purely private matters. Communication depends upon the hearer's grasping the senses which the speaker attaches to the words he uses. It is for this reason that the senses of words in general are common to all speakers of a language, and why there is a question what sense a word has in that language. A speaker can succeed in communicating his thoughts to another only when he attaches to most of the words he uses the senses that his hearer attaches to them. The hearer will understand him (at least understand him fully) only if he apprehends in what senses the speaker is using those words by which he means something different from what the hearer would mean by them. The hearer may do so by guessing, from the likelihood of the speaker's saying one thing rather than another, or by the similarity between certain words and others, what the speaker means. Or he may ask the speaker what he means, and receive an explanation that suffices to inform him. Again, he may, perhaps at the time, perhaps not until sometime later, derive from the speaker's use of those words—his reactions to the use of them by others or his own utterances and actions—what senses he attaches to them. Sense is communicable: we have means to convey to others what senses our words bear. That is why the idealization according to which all speakers of a language similarly understand all of its words which they use does not distort the nature of language.

The thesis that sense determines reference is not one Frege advanced at the time of writing *Grundlagen*; at that time he conflated what later became the two notions of sense and reference (*Bedeutung*). A theory of the *Bedeutungen* of the words and expressions of a language—a theory such as that which Frege supplied in his *Grundgesetze* for his formal language—is a semantic theory, since the *Bedeutung* of a sentence is its truth value; Frege's notion of *Bedeutung*, as applied to expressions of all categories, is best rendered "semantic value." The semantic value of an expression is that whereby it contributes to the determination of a sentence in which it occurs as true or false. It is better to say that the sense of an expression determines the *condition* for it to have a particular semantic value than that it determines its semantic value, since, in holding that sense determines *Bedeutung*, Frege meant to allow that it does so in light of how things are in the world: the reference of "the population of Tokyo on New Year's Day 2004" depends on how many people were living in Tokyo on that day. The thought expressed by a sentence does not determine its truth value regardless of anything else: it determines only its truth condition.

What is hard realism, and does it have a soft counterpart? Realism of any kind is linked to a truth-conditional theory of meaning. Such a theory is one according to which the meaning of a declarative sentence consists in the condition for it, considered as uttered on any particular actual or hypothetical occasion, to make a true statement. Hard realism regards the truth conditions of a statement as obtaining independently of our linguistic practice. There are two versions of its account of sense or understanding. According to one, we understand a language, and so grasp the senses of its sentences, if we have a mastery of the conventional practice of using the language; we must therefore know what is conventionally accepted as justifying an assertion, and what are the conventional consequences of making it or of accepting it as correct. But these features of linguistic practice do not, according to the hard realist, determine what the truth conditions of our assertions really are, nor can those truth conditions be derived from the facts of linguistic practice. According to the other version, our understanding of a statement consists in our grasp of the condition for it to be true; but our conventional practice in judging whether or not we are entitled to take it as true does not determine that condition.

It is evident that hard realism, in either version, is vulnerable to a generalized form of skepticism. Since the truth condition of a statement is not given in terms of what we take as establishing that statement as true or of what we take as justifying us in making it or accepting it, then, however strong we may take our grounds for believing it to be, it may nevertheless not be true. Hence the possibility will always be left open that, however fully the conventional requirements for rating it as true may be met, it may nevertheless not accord with reality: it may be false.

This is a classic—indeed, it is the generic—instance of the illusion that Hilary Putnam calls that of an interface, and I should prefer to call that of a veil. We are inescapably imprisoned behind the veil: the reality about which we speak and think is, for the most part, located beyond the veil. We can never know for certain what lies in the transvelar region.

A truth-conditional theory of meaning, conceived in this way, stultifies the entire purpose of a theory of meaning. We can know, of someone else, what he means by what he says only by attending to what else he says and how he responds to what others say to him—in short, by how he uses the language he speaks. A theory of meaning for that language ought therefore to explain the link between its characterization of the meanings of the words and sentences of the language and the uses its speakers make of them. A salient feature of those uses is what the users of the language take as being required for each statement in the language to be recognized as correct, or for a speaker to be entitled to assert it.

For a proponent of the first of the two versions of hard realism, a theory of meaning for a language admits no connection between the sense attached to its sentences and the conditions for utterances of them to be true. It therefore leaves unexplained the need for the notion of truth conditions in the first place, since they have no bearing on our judgment of assertions made in the language as correct or incorrect. The second version of hard realism severs the link between the senses of sentences of the language, as it characterizes them, and the uses which speakers make of sentences. It therefore leaves open two possibilities. First, that someone might master the practice of speaking the language without understanding it, that is, without associating with its sentences the senses that the theory ascribed to them. To all appearance, such a speaker would behave as if he understood the language: nothing he said or did in response to what was said to him would betray any failure of understanding on his part. And yet, according to that theory of meaning, he would not really understand the language, because he would not attach to its sentences the senses which the theory declared them to express. The reverse possibility would also be open. This is that someone might by some means have contrived to associate with the sentences of the language the senses that the theory attributed to them, without succeeding in grasping how those sentences were to be used in actual linguistic interchange between speakers. For those senses are supposed to be explained by the theory in a manner that does not display how they are to be used: so it must be possible in principle for someone to grasp those senses without understanding the use of the sentences in discourse.

Obviously these imagined states of affairs are senseless fantasies: a theory that makes either of them a genuine possibility thereby reveals itself as failing to carry out the task it purported to undertake. Ideally, a theory of meaning for a language ought to give a comprehensive description of how the language functions in the use we make of it, stated without presupposing an understanding of how any other language functions. The salient features of the use of a declarative sentence are what we take as warranting its assertion, and what we treat as the consequences of accepting such an assertion. To satisfy the criterion for being a satisfactory theory, it ought at least to indicate how the salient features of the use of the language—of the practice of speaking it—can be derived from the senses of its sentences as characterized by the theory. It must also explain the connection between the notion of truth, as the theory applies it to statements made in the language, and the uses of those statements.

Putnam is right to repudiate all notions of an interface or veil: such a notion is symptomatic of the hard version of realism. He identifies as one such notion that which is invoked in the causal theory of perception, in that version of the causal theory which takes our beliefs in propositions concerning material reality that are grounded upon observation as *inferences* from our sense impressions to their causes (of which we can know nothing directly). We should, I believe, take a generous view of the scope of a theory of meaning; I do not believe that a theory of meaning is a mere engine for generating propositions of the form "'I can see a tree 50 meters ahead of me,' said by a speaker *s* at a time *t*, is true if and only if *s* can, at the time *t*, see a tree 50 meters ahead of him." If we take such a generous view, we shall rate the causal theory of perception as that part of the theory of meaning that treats of statements that can serve as reports of observation. In its classic form, it belongs to a hard realist theory that divorces the condition for the truth of such statements from what we treat as warranting our making them.

I think, nevertheless, that more caution is needed than Hilary Putnam exercises in repudiating the causal theory of perception, since causal notions are genuinely bound up with our concepts of sense perception. Indeed, when, by looking out of my window, I come to know that there is an ash tree a few meters in front of my house, I am not making an inference. My seeing it, my wife's seeing it too, perhaps my touching it, my neighbor's concurring when I make remarks about it to him, together constitute an indefeasible warrant for saying that there is a tree there; that they do so is intrinsic to the meaning of "There's a tree there." But from some advocates of the thesis of "direct" perceptual apprehension—though not from Putnam himself—there emanates a conception of a quasi-mystical rapport between the perceiver and the perceived object that is little short of superstitious. As Kant said, every object is given to us in a particular way. When I see a tree, I am indeed in "cognitive contact" with the tree; that is, I apprehend that there is a tree there. But I apprehend its presence in a particular way.

Our understanding of the particular way in which, by seeing it, I apprehend its presence, is, I believe, informed by certain rudimentary causal notions. I think that we have to explain what it means to say that I can now see a tree outside the window as involving that light from the tree is entering my eyes. That we see with our eyes, and not, say, with the backs of our hands, is intrinsic to the concept of sight; analogously for the other senses. That there are sources of light, but not sources of darkness, that we cannot see an object that is not there, or with our eyes shut, or in the dark, that is, in the absence of a source of light, or when there is an opaque object in the line of sight, that is, between it and our eyes: all this belongs to the concept of sight. It is not part of some protoscientific *theory*: it belongs to the *concept*.

Likewise, it does not seem to me that the distinction between primary and secondary qualities is inextricably entangled with the theory that we infer the existence of material objects from our sense impressions. It makes sense to ask what color is in itself. We cannot fully answer the question until we can say just what light is (an electromagnetic wave? a stream of photons? both at once? one on some occasions and the other on others?); but we can get part of the way. By contrast, it does not make sense in the same way to ask what shape is. As Putnam says, when I look at an object from some given standpoint, I perceive how it looks from that standpoint; perhaps how it looks from that standpoint to someone wearing a particular kind of spectacles, or to someone with a particular defect of vision. But, more generally, I perceive how it looks to a human being or to one with the visual equipment and perhaps conceptual repertoire of a human being, not how it looks to a fox, a pigeon, or a butterfly. The question what physical reality is like in itself is not senseless. It may be one to which we cannot in principle give an ultimate answer: but it is one which we are impelled to try to answer. As Putnam himself has remarked, there is such a thing as excessive recoil.

Permutation arguments relate directly to the notion of reference, specifically that of the reference of singular terms: characteristically, they are to the effect that under some given permutation of their referents, and consequential modification of the semantic values of the predicates, the truth values of the sentences will be invariant. A fully fledged realist theory of meaning not only rests on a bivalent notion of truth for statements of the language and a truth-conditional semantics for them, but on a classical semantics for subsentential expressions as well, taking sentences of natural language at face value. Taking them at face value involves treating whatever behaves like a singular term as genuinely a singular term. If we press this criterion, Russell's theory of descriptions constitutes a mild derogation of realism, and Frege's view of sentences containing empty terms, as opposed to that of Meinong (with his realism about nonexistent objects), an even milder one. I do not think that these consequences show the criterion to be incorrect, only that we are usually more interested in more robust departures from realism.

Now hard realism, with its repudiation either of the thesis that sense determines reference, or of the principle that sense is exhibited by use, treats the reference conditions of terms as it treats the truth conditions of statements: they are independent of the use made of those terms, as the truth conditions are of the use made of sentences. The reference of a term, as uttered in a given context, is determined by a suitable causal connection between an object and that utterance, or some analogous relation. But the truth conditions of sentences are determined by the semantic values of the words and phrases that make them up, including, of course, the singular terms occurring in them, as displayed in a classical two-valued semantic theory. So if the truth conditions of sentences are to be determinate, the references of singular terms must be determinate. But the permutation arguments show that the references of the singular terms cannot be determinate, even if the truth values of all particular statements are held fixed. Hence the permutation arguments refute hard realism.

The late great philosopher of language, Donald Davidson, welcomed permutation arguments as showing that the notion of reference is idle in the theory of meaning: all that matters are the truth conditions of sentences. This looks strange from one who has long been preaching that the correct form of a theory of meaning is a theory of truth, embodying a classical semantic theory adapted for natural language; for the notions of reference and satisfaction are essential to such a theory. Davidson's point, however, is that a different theory of truth, obtained by a permutation of the referents of the singular terms, and an adjustment of the conditions of satisfaction of the predicates, will determine just the same truth values for all the statements. This seems like an argument, not that the notion of reference can be dispensed with, but that it makes no difference whether or not we assign the *right* references to our terms. The notion of getting it right that is here invoked may give a first impression that Davidson, like Putnam, is attacking a hard realist position, according to which objects in the world are, say, in and of themselves, Paris or Florence, just as there are for the hard realist objects in mathematical space that are, in and of themselves, i and $-i$. This is, however, not so. One is tempted to ask whether Davidson thought it for some reason illicit, or merely unnecessary, to inquire of a subsentential expression how it contributes to determining a statement in which it occurs as true or as false, that is, to ask for its real semantic value. That is of importance in characterizing the means we employ to find out or establish whether a sentence is true. To determine the truth value of "Oxford is more populous than Reading," we count up or estimate the number of people living *in Oxford* and the number living *in Reading*. Suppose we consider a permutation that maps the denotations of all (terrestrial) place names on to an area of the same shape fifty miles to the west. To preserve truth values, we must reinterpret "is more populous than" so that "*a* is more populous than *b*" is true just in case an area fifty miles to the east of *a* is more populous than an area fifty miles to the east of *b*. The result will be that, in order to determine the truth value of "Oxford is more populous than Reading" under this interpretation, we shall still need to verify the population figures for *Oxford* and *Reading*. The notion of the *right* denotations for "Oxford" and "Reading" is not a mythological one like that of "*i*" and "*-i*." It relates, rather, to the objects we have to examine in determining the truth value of a sentence containing those names. Davidson's argument is, rather, based on the assumption that all that matters to a theory of meaning is that it get the truth conditions of the sentences right: such a theory must be seen as no more than an engine for generating T-sentences. But the argument does not vindicate this assumption: the assumption was made at the outset. The assumption is false. In constructing a theory of meaning, we must inquire into the true meanings of all words of the language, since it is by understanding the words that we understand the sentences of which they are composed. A sound theory of meaning must enable us to give a good account of linguistic understanding as well as of linguistic meaning.

Hilary Putnam at one time attacked the thesis that sense determines reference by means of fantasies such as that of Twin Earth. I do not think that such fantasies are necessary to the argument, nor that the argument touches the essence of the thesis. The argument concerns terms that may be called indexical in a wide sense: their reference depends, not on the individual speaker's identity or location, or on the time of his utterance, but on the position of the human race as a whole in the cosmos. To illustrate this, we need not choose a term like "water," and resort to far-fetched tales; a term such as "the Sun" will do. In a great many cases, the sense of an expression, as Frege conceived it, may be identified with its meaning in the language, as we ordinarily think of this; but in others not. It is natural to say that a word within indirect speech retains the meaning that it has in direct speech; but, since Frege's theory of indirect speech assigned to such a word a different reference from that it has in direct speech, he was forced by the thesis that sense determines reference to attribute a different sense to it also. Indexical expressions most obviously exemplify the distinction between our customary notion of meaning and Fregean sense. We ordinarily think of the word "here" as having the same meaning wherever it is uttered; but, since the whole point of such a word is to have a different reference according to where it is uttered, Frege was bound to maintain that its sense varies. He did so, rather awkwardly, by making the place of utterance contribute to the sense. This maneuver is far from ideal; but it shows that the thesis that sense determines reference was not so intended as to be refutable by the case of indexical expressions. By parity, it is not to be refuted by expressions that are indexical in the wide sense. The Sun is that star around which *our* planet orbits, and that gives *us* light and warmth. Intelligent beings on a planet with a time of rotation on its axis comparable with twenty-four hours, in orbit around a single star comparable to our Sun, would refer to that star by a name having the same meaning, in the ordinary sense, as "the Sun" or "die Sonne." The fact is of interest as requiring the notion of indexicality in the wide sense; it does not refute the thesis that sense determines reference, as Frege meant that thesis to be understood.

Is there a soft realism to be contrasted with the hard realism that Putnam has so successfully attacked? Hilary Putnam's announcement of his reconversion to realism suggests that there must be; and the example of Frege confirms it. Such a soft realism must allow a notion of sense as based upon the semantic theory it adopts, and one that determines the use of the language in practice: sense, semantic value, and use must be connected. To be a form of realism, it will have to embrace as its semantic theory classical two-valued semantics. A position of this form is readily conceivable, is instantiated by Frege's philosophy, and is presumably that to which Putnam has now returned.

The two most important notions in the theory of meaning are, naturally, those of truth and of meaning or sense. The notion of truth has its home in the theory of meaning: meaning and truth must be explained together. In his writings concerning realism, Hilary Putnam has concerned himself much more with the notion of truth than with that of meaning. Since intuitionists explain the meanings of mathematical statements in terms, not of what is needed for them to be true, but of what will count as a proof of them, it appears at first sight that the notion of truth is dispensable for them. Similarly, if meaning is explained generally in terms of what justifies us in accepting statements or in asserting them, the notion of truth appears to become redundant. If this were so, a theory of meaning of such a kind would lose its metaphysical resonance: for it is truth that is the hinge on the door that leads from the theory of meaning to metaphysics. Reality is constituted, not just by what objects there are, but by what facts obtain, as is stated at the outset of the *Tractatus*, and facts are true propositions.

Hence, if metaphysics is concerned with the general character of reality, it must inquire into the correct conception of truth.

Putnam is right to hold that the notion of truth *cannot* be dispensed with, even if our interests are purely meaning-theoretical rather than metaphysical. It may not be needed for the direct characterization of meaning, but it is needed for important purposes that relate to the use of language. Truth is whatever must be preserved from premises to conclusion in a valid deductive argument. The condition for a statement to be true is the condition that a hearer takes to obtain if he accepts that statement to have been correctly asserted. What anyone primarily wants to know about an argument is whether it guarantees that, if he is entitled to assert the premises, he is entitled to assert the conclusion.

With different theories of meaning go different conceptions of truth. But there is no simple path from meaning to truth. A theory of meaning must incorporate a conception of truth that is suitably connected with that in terms of which it specifies the meanings of sentences; just what form the connection will take is by no means given by any general schema. What is the conception of truth implicit in Hilary Putnam's present version of realism, and what is the conception of meaning on which it rests?

We learn from *The Threefold Cord* that, in Putnam's view, the hard realist is wrong to call truth a "substantive property" and to characterize this property as that of corresponding to a reality. He wants, Putnam says, a property that corresponds to the assertoric force of a sentence—"a very funny property," Putnam comments.[6] Putnam is here, consciously or unconsciously, echoing a remarkable passage from a fragment in Frege's *Nachlass*. "The word 'true,'" Frege says, "seems to make the impossible possible: it allows what corresponds to the assertoric force to assume the form of a contribution to the thought."[7] His idea here is this. We may merely express or entertain a proposition (a thought, in his terminology). If we move from this to asserting it or judging it to be true, we are advancing from the thought to the truth value: we are saying or thinking *that it is true*. So it seems that what we then do is to ascribe a certain property to it, that of being true. But this is *not* what we are doing. Suppose that we regard a sentence, say "Seawater is salty," simply as expressing a thought, not yet as being used to assert that thought to be true. We may indicate this by rendering it as a clause "that seawater is salty." We shall not transform this into a form of words that serves to assert that the thought is true by adding "It is true": "It is true that seawater is salty" still only expresses a thought. We need to attach assertoric force to the sentence: and this is not the attribution of a *property* to the thought.

It does not follow that truth is not a property of propositions, but rather the semantic value of some sentences expressing them. Some propositions are expressed by sentences having the value *true*, others are not, and this is sufficient to make truth a property of propositions. What Putnam urges is that truth is not a *uniform* property. "Our understanding of what truth comes to, in any particular case (and it can come to very different things)" he says, "is given by our understanding of the proposition"; again, "To regard an assertion or a belief or a thought as true or false *is* to regard it as being right or wrong . . . [but] just what sort of rightness or wrongness is in question varies enormously with the *sort* of discourse."[8] That is certainly a sound objection to explaining truth as a uniform relation of correspond-ing to reality. Indeed, it is an objection to classical theories of truth, the coherence theory as well as the correspondence theory, that has been in vogue for several decades. Those theories presume that we can first know what propositions our statements express, that is, can first understand those statements, and then go on to ask what it is for any such proposition to be true, whereas the condition for a statement to be true varies according to the proposition it expresses. Truth and meaning must be explained together.

It is the same with winning a game. You cannot give a general condition for winning: what constitutes winning a game depends on what the game is. It does not follow that the word "win" is equivocal: winning plays the same role in every game that can be won or lost. If we read, in the rules of some game, "The winner is the player who has obtained all the points, or otherwise has the lowest total of points," we understand the rule because we know the role of winning in a game of this kind. Likewise, "true" is not equivocal. We know its role in the practice of using language. To explain the word "win" is to explain the role of winning in games in which it has a place; and to explain the word "true" is to explain the role of saying some-thing true in the practice of using language. Unquestionably it is integral to the practice of making assertions—of saying that something is so—that a speaker can be right or wrong, and this notion is obviously the source from which the concepts of truth and falsity take their origin. A philosophical account of truth must explain their roles in linguistic practice. But we can no more question the equivocity of the notion of truth than we can question that of being right—or that of winning a game.

Soft realism does not, like hard realism, provide an entry for skepticism. Instead, it encourages its opposite, credulity. Examples of this are all about us: in philosophy, modal realism, according to which possible worlds have as much reality as the actual one, which differs from the others only in that it is the one we happen to inhabit; in cosmology, the multiverse, comprising many universes besides our own; in physics, the Everettian interpretation of quantum mechanics, according to which reality is constantly splitting, say into a half in which Schrödinger's cat is alive and a half in which it is dead. We have no direct knowledge of these parallel realms, and *could* not have; but the soft realist believes that we can intelligibly postulate their existence. We understand what it is for them to exist; he thinks, since their existence, like the truth of propositions in general, is quite independent of our knowledge or our capacity to know. Realism is an essential foundation for these fantasies; it is not itself a superstition, but it is the mother of superstitions.

A soft-realist conception of truth rests on a truth-conditional theory of meaning. On such a theory, there is no uniform condition for the truth of our statements to be applied after their meanings have been fixed; rather, meaning and truth are connected by the fact that the meaning of a statement is constituted by the condition for it to be true. The principle of bivalence holds good: every statement that is a genuine candidate for being either true or false is determinately one or the other, independently of our knowledge. Truth is not to be equated with verifiability.

But what entitles Putnam to embrace soft realism? To vindicate a truth-conditional theory of meaning, two things are necessary. First, it must be possible to show how the two salient features of the use of sentences of the language can be determined from the conditions for their truth when uttered in one or another situation. Secondly, it must be possible to show that an account of the practice of speaking the language *requires* attributing to the speakers a grasp of the conditions for the truth of statements made in it: that is, that a mastery of the use of sentences of the language involves an implicit conception of those conditions. The language may not, of course, contain a word for "true." But, if a truth-conditional theory of meaning is to be capable of yielding an account of speakers' understanding of the language, it is essential to it to be able to maintain that, in order to be able to operate with the language, a speaker must have a tacit grasp of the concept of a statement's *being* true, independently of whether it is taken as true.

It is in its correlative account of understanding that a truth-conditional theory of meaning is at its shakiest. Putnam is insistent, throughout *The Threefold Cord*, that to talk of the mind is to talk of a complex of abilities that we possess. I agree that this is often so, but doubt if it always is. If a would-be hypnotist says, "Make your mind a blank," he does not mean, "Divest yourself of those abilities." In any case, the thesis wars with a truth-conditional account of linguistic understanding. For, on such an account, a speaker's understanding of a statement does not consist in his ability to accept or assert a statement on the basis of observation or of a cogent argument, or to draw practical or theoretical consequences from his acceptance of it: it consists of his inner *conception* of what it is for it to be true. The understanding of the verbal expression of thought goes, on such an account, beyond our abilities to handle such expressions in the course of linguistic exchange: it explains that understanding in terms of our associating with our sentences unverbalized thoughts of great complexity. Insofar as language is the vehicle of thought, the account is irredeemably circular.

If he is to justify his reconversion to realism, Hilary Putnam has a good deal of justifying to do.

MICHAEL DUMMETT

NEW COLLEGE, OXFORD
JUNE 2004

NOTES

1. Gottlob Frege, *Grundgesetze der Arithmetik*, vol. 1 (Jena: Verlag Hermann Pohle, 1893). (Reprinted at Hildesheim: Georg Olms Verlagsbuchandlung, 1962). In English translation as *The Basic Laws of Arithmetic*, trans. and ed. Montgomery Furth (Berkeley: University of California Press, 1967), §10, 45–49.

2. Gottlob Frege, *Die Grundlagen der Arithmetik* (Breslau: Verlag Wilhelm Koebner, 1884). (Reprinted at Breslau: Verlag M. & H. Marcus, 1934, and at Hildesheim: Georg Olms Verlagsbuchandlung, 1961.) In English translation, with German text on facing pages, as *The Foundations of Arithmetic*, trans. J. L. Austin (Oxford: Basil Blackwell, 1953).

3. Frege, *Grundgesetze der Arithmetik*, §29. Furth's translation renders the phrase: "When does a name denote something?" *The Basic Laws of Arithmetic*, 84.

4. Frege, *Die Grundlagen der Arithmetik*, §26 [translation is Dummett's]. For Austin's translation, see *The Foundations of Arithmetic*, 35e.

5. Ibid. [translation is Dummett's]. For Austin's rendering, see *The Foundations of Arithmetic*, 35e–36e.

6. Hilary Putnam, *The Threefold Cord: Mind, Body, and World* (New York: Columbia University Press, 1999), 53, 55.

7. Gottlob Frege, *Posthumous Writings*, ed. H. Hermes, F. Kambartel, and F. Kaulbach, trans. P. Long and R. White (Oxford: Basil Blackwell, 1979), 252.

8. Putnam, *The Threefold Cord*, 67, 69.

REPLY TO MICHAEL DUMMETT

My debt to Dummett's writings through the years is enormous. Even though we disagree on almost every issue he discusses in the present essay (and disagreed on them even in my "internal realist" period, as I shall explain), I have *never* come away from an exchange with Dummett without a deeper feeling of both the seriousness and the difficulty of the realism issue. He is a great philosopher, and I am honored, not just because he agreed to write for the present volume, but because he has used his essay to make a major statement of his position, indeed to make what amounts to an extended transcendental argument for verificationism, an argument that will be studied for many years to come.

I. The Very Idea of a "Meaning Theory"

My response to Dummett's transcendental argument: A "meaning theory," in Dummett's sense, is supposed to specify "how the salient features of the use of the language—of the practice of speaking it—can be derived from the senses of its sentences as characterized by the theory." Unfortunately, in many places in this essay Dummett appears to identify knowing the "salient features of the use of a sentence" with knowing how to verify it plus knowing "the conventional consequences of making it or of accepting it as correct." I shall henceforth assume that this identification is *not* essential to Dummett's argument (otherwise, every opponent of verificationism is declared guilty before trial of supposing that we can understand a sentence without knowing how to use it!]). But even if we restrict ourselves to the question: Could there be a "meaning theory that derives the ways in which the sentences of the language are verified from the senses of those sentences as specified by the theory?" and leave out the identification of those ways with "the salient features of the use" of the sentence, such a theory seems to me utterly impossible.

The reasons it does not seem so to Dummett are twofold: first, he still holds to the idea that there are "indefeasible" warrants for making statements ("My seeing [the tree], my wife's seeing it too, perhaps my touching it, my neighbor's concurring when I make remarks about it to him, together constitute an indefeasible warrant for saying that there is a tree there; *that they do so is intrinsic to the meaning of* 'There's a tree there.'") (emphasis added); and second, he believes that the warrants that are "intrinsic to the meaning" of our sentences are associated with them *conventionally* (the term "conventional" occurs five times in two paragraphs of Dummett's essay). Both Quinian holism and Quine's demolition job on the analytic/ synthetic dichotomy are completely rejected by Dummett. My philosophical commitments are quite different: "My seeing it, my wife's seeing it too, perhaps my touching it, my neighbor's concurring when I make remarks about it to him" are not, in my view, "an indefeasible warrant for saying that there is a tree there"; what we see there might be a tree statue (perhaps one made of wood, with real bark glued on to the outside), or even an extraterrestrial disguised as a tree. There are *countless* possibilities; to say this is not to deny that one can be quite certain (in a perfectly legitimate sense of "certain") that none of these fantastic possibilities obtains here and now, but that sort of certainty is a matter of what Kant called "motherwit," and not of applying a "meaning theory."

When I was an "internal realist" I agreed with Dummett that we need to interpret the notion of "truth" in a verificationist way, but my reasons were *never* that I believed in "indefeasible" warrants for our statements, or in analytic connections between our warrants and the truth of the statements they warrant. (My reasons were, of course, the "model-theoretic arguments," which I repudiated in my 1994 Dewey Lectures.) Moreover, I did not at any time believe and I do not now believe that what warrants our statements is just a matter of "conventional" practices. As I wrote in "Meaning Holism":

> Let us suppose there exists a liquid which is colorless, tasteless, odorless, harmless, but does not satisfy the need for water. (For all I know, there may actually be such liquids.) Call this liquid "grook." Let us suppose that a mixture of 50% grook and 50% water will pass all the lay tests for being water, excluding "sophisticated" tests (such as distilling the liquid, or measuring its exact boiling point or freezing point with a thermometer). On the theory that "water" means "odorless, transparent, tasteless, liquid which quenches thirst and is not harmful to drink," grook plus water just is water, "in the ordinary sense." But this is plainly wrong; even a layman, on being told by a scientist that what he is drinking is a mixture of a liquid which is indistinguishable in composition from paradigm examples of water and a liquid which does not occur as a part of typical water, will say that what he is drinking is not

water (although it is 50% water). Ordinary language and scientific language are different but *interdependent*.[2]

Since the rise of modern science, it is not just "conventional practices" that determine the extensions of our terms; *science* plays a huge role as well, in the way illustrated by this example. And long before the rise of science, many forms of practical expertise, for example metallurgy,[3] played that role. If the "tree" were really a *robot* or an intelligent animal, it would doubtless be scientific tests cum theories that revealed this, and not "conventional" practices. There is no possibility of surveying all the different things that might warrant a speaker in saying (or denying) "that is a tree" in a "meaning theory," and none of those different things is an "indefeasible warrant." There are no indefeasible warrants.

II. DUMMETT'S TWO DESCRIPTIONS OF "HARD REALISM"

The fourth sentence of Dummett's essay begins "Let us use the term 'hard realism' for what Hilary Putnam called 'metaphysical realism'." Later in the essay, however, we find:

> What is hard realism, and does it have a soft counterpart? Realism of any kind is linked to a truth-conditional theory of meaning. Such a theory is one according to which the meaning of a declarative sentence consists in the condition for it, considered as uttered on any particular actual or hypothetical occasion, to make a true statement.

I find it difficult to reconcile these two descriptions of "hard realism." My own description of "metaphysical realism," which according to the first description is what Dummett means by "hard realism," was as the conjunction of the following three theses (Putnam 1981,[4] 1983[5]) none of which contains the word "meaning":

(1) THE WORLD consists of a fixed totality of mind-independent objects.[6]
(2) There is exactly one true and complete description of THE WORLD.
(3) There is a determinate relation of reference between terms [in any language L] and pieces (or sets of pieces) of THE WORLD in terms of which "true in L" is to be defined.

Item (3) does mention "true in L," but not "meaning." That "true in L" can be defined in terms of the relation "refers to" between terms in L and objects in the universe of discourse (and ordered pairs, triples, etc., of those objects), for any formalizable language L, is something that follows trivially from what Tarski showed in his famous paper on the concept of truth,[7] and this is what (3) presupposed. But a definition of truth *in terms of refers-to-in-L* is not even a *candidate* for a "theory of meaning" for L, unless it is supplemented with a *definition* of "reference-in-L," and the idea that *that* combination of things is what a *theory of meaning* should look like is unique to Davidsonians. But Davidson was certainly no friend of metaphysical realism, and metaphysical realists are usually not Davidsonians. Thus I see nothing in my definition of "metaphysical realism" that supports the claim that metaphysical realism is "linked to a truth-conditional theory of meaning."

The point is not a "nitpicking" one. As I explain in my reply to Ben-Menahem, my present position is that it is perfectly possible to be a realist in one's metaphysics and to accept the existence of pairs of descriptions that correspond to the same state of affairs but describe those states of affairs in terms of different "ontologies." In short, one can completely reject the conception of ontology that is presupposed by (1), (2), and (3), because that conception rejects the entire idea of radically different but intertranslatable descriptions which describe the world equally well, while still believing that truth outruns what humans can verify, and further believing that reality is not (with the obvious exception of human material and intellectual products) "mind-dependent." And not only do I believe that this is a *possible* position; it is my present position.

As for "meaning" my view is the one I presented in the "Meaning of 'Meaning'" (and subsequently modified in certain details in the ways I describe in my reply to Ian Hacking in the present volume). On my view, the meaning of (for example) the words in the sentence "the stuff in that glass is water" is given by "meaning vectors" with a number of components. For present purposes, the upshot is that the truth condition for that sentence (in the majority of the contexts in which it is used) is that the stuff in the relevant glass is H_2O plus or minus a certain number of allowable "impurities," where what counts as disqualifying the stuff as being water (and causes us to call it "tea" or "coffee" or something else instead) and what counts as a mere impurity, or as too high a proportion of "impurities," is highly interest relative and context sensitive. For present purposes, the key point is that *knowledge of the fact that water is H_2O may not be possessed by the speakers of the language.* In such case *the truth condition for such a sentence is something that science can discover, but not something "in the head" of any individual speaker, and possibly something not yet known to anyone.*

Perhaps Dummett might object that it is part of the concept of a "competent speaker" that a competent speaker knows the truth conditions of sentences she understands, but an "externalist" like myself will, of course, respond that the appropriate sense of "know the meaning" here is not the sense of knowing propositions, but the sense of knowing how to do something.[8] Being a competent speaker is, for an externalist, possessing a set of *world-involving abilities*. Users of the word "water" are in touch with H_2O, whether they know that that is what they are in touch with or not.

III. DUMMETT ON "INDEXICALITY"

Needless to say, I do not accuse Dummett of having failed to read the "The Meaning of 'Meaning.'" He even refers to it in the present essay. But what he discusses is what he describes as the "indexical" nature of natural-kind terms, while ignoring the elements of the theory which, it seems to me, pose a problem for his view.

Here is what he writes:

> The argument concerns terms that may be called indexical in a wide sense: their reference depends, not on the individual speaker's identity or location, or on the time of his utterance, but on the position of the human race as a whole in the cosmos. To illustrate this, we need not choose a term like "water," and resort to farfetched tales; a term such as "the Sun" will do. In a great many cases, the sense of an expression, as Frege conceived it, may be identified with its meaning in the language, as we ordinarily think of this; but in others not. It is natural to say that a word within indirect speech retains the meaning that it has in direct speech; but, since Frege's theory of indirect speech assigned to such a word a different reference from that it has in direct speech, he was forced by the thesis that sense determines reference to attribute a different sense to it also. Indexical expressions most obviously exemplify the distinction between our customary notion of meaning and Fregean sense.

—But the subject of "The Meaning of 'Meaning'" was natural kinds like water, and not "the Fregean notion of meaning." If what speakers intend the term "water" (respectively, the term "tree") to refer to is, as I claimed in that essay, whatever has the same *nature* as *this liquid* (respectively, "as *this* bit of plant life"—where "this" can be any example that does not turn out to differ radically from other paradigm examples of water (respectively a tree)—then, to repeat, the judgment that something I perceive is water (or, to use Dummett's own example, a *tree*) must be essentially revisable in the way all scientific judgments are. I am disappointed that Dummett, so to speak, walks right past this issue.

IV. Skepticism

Dummett writes:

> It is evident that hard realism, in either version, is vulnerable to a generalized form of skepticism. Since the truth condition of a statement is not given in terms of what we take as establishing that statement as true or of what we take as justifying us in making it or accepting it, then, however strong we may take our grounds for believing it to be, it may nevertheless not be true. Hence the possibility will always be left open that, however fully the conventional requirements for rating it as true may be met, it may nevertheless not accord with reality: it may be false.

I agree, but what Dummett calls "skepticism" ("however fully the conventional requirements for rating [a statement] as true may be met, it may nevertheless not accord with reality: it may be false") seems to me better called *fallibilism*, a thesis that I accept.[9] If Dummett believes that fallibilism implies the conclusion that we do not know, for instance, what city we live in, then I, of course, disagree. To justify the claim that I know I live in Arlington, Massachusetts I do not have to rule out such possibilities as the possibility that my memories have been altered by aliens from Arcturus, or even the possibility that I now have senile dementia (not yet, anyway). If Dummett believes that we have "indefeasible warrants" that such things did *not* happen, then we simply disagree. That fact that we do not possess a "refutation" of skepticism does not mean that we have to withdraw our ordinary knowledge claims.[10]

V. Mathematics

If I understand Dummett aright, he maintains that the way to avoid model theoretic arguments for the indeterminacy of reference in the mathematical case is to accept a view I claim that Wittgenstein once flirted with[11]: the view that mathematical truth does not outrun what it is possible for human beings to prove. I give my reasons for rejecting that view (reasons that admittedly depend on my "scientific realism" with respect to physics) in my reply to Hartry Field, and I will not repeat them here.

Dummett refers to Benacerraf's Problem, which is that while the natural numbers can be identified with sets—for instance, with the von Neumann ordinals, $\varnothing, \{\varnothing\}, \{\varnothing, \{\varnothing\}\}, \{\varnothing, \{\varnothing\}, \{\varnothing, \{\varnothing\}\}\}, \ldots$—they can be identified with sets in *infinitely many ways*. (For example they could also be identified with the Hao Wang ordinals, $\varnothing, \{\varnothing\}, \{\{\varnothing\}\}, \{\{\{\varnothing\}\}\}, \ldots$.) And to stamp one's feet and insist that "the natural numbers are not identical with sets at all" would be arbitrary—in set theory we do often identify them with progressions of sets after all, and have from the first days of modern mathematical logic.

My preferred solution to Benacerraf's problem is that all of the different "translations" of number theory into set theory, and all of the different translations of set theory into function theory, and all of the different translations of function theory into set theory, are just different ways of showing what sorts of structures have to *possibly exist* in order for our mathematical assertions to be true. In my view, then, what the modal-logical "translation" of a mathematical statement—the sort of translation I proposed in "Mathematics without Foundations," and that Geoffrey Hellman has worked out in detail[12]—gives us is a statement with the same mathematical content as the original statement that does not have even the appearance of being about the actual existence of "Platonic objects." Unlike Dummett, I think permutation arguments do raise a significant puzzle about the meaning of quantification over so-called "mathematical entities," but I do not think the solution to the puzzle is the verificationism that Dummett defends.

VI. My Alleged "Soft Realism": (1) Perception

Dummett believes that I am offering a "soft realism" as alternative to what he calls "hard realism." I have already said that I do not understand the latter term (because his two descriptions of "hard realism" do not seem equivalent to me), but I am indeed offering an alternative to what I once called "metaphysical realism." So let us take it that I am, in that sense, offering an alternative to "hard realism." But is my alternative the same as Dummett's "soft realism"? Again, I have trouble answering that question because I am not clear on what "soft realism" is supposed to be. Much of Dummett's criticism is directed at the paragraphs in my Dewey Lectures in which I offered a version of a deflationary account of truth that I claimed to be close to (or at least suggested by) both certain remarks of Frege's and certain remarks of Wittgenstein's. That account was supposed to be compatible with realism, but I did not say that only a realist could accept it; I would have thought deflation was neutral on the realism/antirealism issue.[13] In fact, I find two very different explanations of what is supposed to be my "soft realism" in this essay. One occurs at the very end, and has no relation whatsoever to anything I believe:

> on such an account [mine!—HP], a speaker's understanding of a statement does not consist in his ability to accept or assert a statement on the basis of observation or of a cogent argument, or to draw practical or theoretical consequences

from his acceptance of it: it consists of his inner *conception* of what it is for it to be true. The understanding of the verbal expression of thought goes, on such an account, beyond our abilities to handle such expressions in the course of linguistic exchange: it explains that understanding in terms of our associating with our sentences unverbalized thoughts of great complexity.

But perhaps the following is supposed to be the explanation of "soft realism"?

A soft realist conception of truth rests on a truth-conditional theory of meaning. On such a theory, there is no uniform condition for the truth of our statements to be applied after their meanings have been fixed; rather, meaning and truth are connected by the fact that the meaning of a statement is constituted by the condition for it to be true. The principle of bivalence holds good: every statement that is a genuine candidate for being either true or false is determinately one or the other, independently of our knowledge. Truth is not to be equated with verifiability.

—If this *is* the explanation, however, it too is not a description of my present position (or my position in the Dewey Lectures), because, I do not and did not accept the idea of a "truth-conditional theory of meaning," or, indeed, of a "theory of meaning" in Dummett's sense, truth-conditional or not, nor have I ever accepted the idea that "the meaning of a statement is constituted by the condition for it to be true."

But something that I did see as an essential part of my return to realism was what I wrote about *perception* in the Dewey Lectures. Today I am working on a book on the topic of perception together with Hilla Jacobson, and I will not try to describe here the ways in which the two of us are trying to go beyond what I wrote in the Dewey Lectures.[14] But I will discuss the remarks Dummett makes on perception, although to a certain extent I have to guess at their motivation. I can, however, say what *my* motivation in writing about perception was. Although Dummett does say this:

Hilary Putnam is quite right that a permutation argument shows [hard realism] to be quite untenable. More exactly, it is the *failure* of the permutation argument that shows hard realism to be untenable. If hard realism were correct, the permutation argument *would* show that we may well not be referring to what we think we are referring to. But it is quite clear what we are referring to. Therefore hard realism is not correct . . .

that short way with metaphysical realism is too quick by half in my view. When we move from the two square roots of -1 to ships and shoes and sealing wax, the reason that the permutation argument has no force, or so I argued in the Dewey Lectures, is that we *do* have access, perceptual access, to shoes and ships and sealing wax (and, with the aid of instruments plus theory, to atoms and subatomic particles and viruses, etc., as well). What was wrong with the permutation argument of "Realism and Reason," in my present view, was that it accepted a late logical-positivist picture of our access to reality as limited to constructing theories and applying "observational constraints" and "theoretical constraints" to them, where the observational constraints were, fundamentally, just internal perceptual states. That this was a mistake is something that, I take it, Dummett and I agree on. But then why does Dummett write,

> I think, nevertheless, that more caution is needed than Hilary Putnam exer-cises in repudiating the causal theory of perception, since causal notions are genuinely bound up with our concepts of sense perception. Indeed, when, by looking out of my window, I come to know that there is an ash tree a few meters in front of my house, I am not making an inference. My seeing it, my wife's seeing it too, perhaps my touching it, my neighbor's concurring when I make remarks about it to him, together constitute an indefeasible warrant for saying that there is a tree there; that they do so is intrinsic to the meaning of "There's a tree there." But from some advocates of the thesis of "direct" perceptual apprehension—though not from Putnam himself—there emanates a conception of a quasi-mystical rapport between the perceiver and the per-ceived object that is little short of superstitious.

My best guess is that this is meant as an attack on "disjunctivism," and Hilla Jacobson and I now (in the twenty-first century) agree with Dummett that some versions of disjunctivism[15] go too far in the direction of "naïve realism."[16] (And although I called myself a "disjunctivist" in the Dewey Lectures, it was McDowell's version that I had in mind.) So I cannot agree either with the disjunctivists in question *or* with Dummett's verificationist way of giving us access to, for instance, *trees*. What I think is that what is involved in accessing facts about trees, perceptually or otherwise, is a complex set of world-involving abilities, perceptual, social, technological, and so on, that both science (though not primarily the reductionist kind of scientific investigation[17]) and philosophical reflection (though not primarily "conceptual analysis") can enable us to better understand and describe.

That Dummett thinks such a reply underplays the role of pure conceptual analysis is shown by the following words in his essay:

> we have to explain what it means to say that I can now see a tree outside the window as involving that light from the tree is entering my eyes. That we see with our eyes, and not, say, with the backs of our hands, is intrinsic to the concept of sight; analogously for the other senses. That there are sources

of light, but not sources of darkness, that we cannot see an object that is not there, or with our eyes shut, or in the dark, that is, in the absence of a source of light, or when there is an opaque object in the line of sight, that is, between it and our eyes: all this belongs to the concept of sight. It is not part of some protoscientific *theory*: it belongs to the *concept*.

The last words virtually wave an anti-Quinian flag. ("So much for skepticism about analyticity!") But that light travels from the tree to our eyes is not something that the ancient Greeks knew, although they did have a word that means "see." (Yesterday's scientific discovery became today's "conceptual truth"!) And could it not turn out that some people can see in the dark? Is it true that *nothing* would count as showing that? (In the ordinary language sense of "see in the dark," bats and cats and owls and opossums and certain fish can see in the dark![18]) If it is now a "conceptual truth" that we cannot see in the dark, it is so by virtue of having become necessary relative to our body of knowledge,[19] not by virtue of being a "conceptual truth" in Dummett's sense.

VII. My Alleged "Soft Realism": (2) Conception Outruns Verification

Where I expected Dummett to take issue with what I wrote in my Dewey Lectures, however, was principally with the claim that we can *conceive of* situations that we are unable to verify, and know that we are conceiving of a state of affairs that either does or does not obtain, whether or not it can be verified that it does. Perhaps Dummett passes by this issue because one of my main examples was a claim about the past,[20] and what to say about the past is an issue on which Dummett himself seems to be coming closer to realism. On his most recent view,[21] one can understand a statement about the past even if no present warrant exists for asserting or denying it, provided that *past* observers (who may now be dead) verified it or falsified it, and regardless of whether they transmitted the information that they did so to us. The new view includes the ideas that (1) the semantically crucial verification of a statement about the past is not the present "indirect" verification, via a memory, or, in the case of the distant past, via a historical trace, that the statement is true, but the verification by a witness at the time ("Dying does not deprive anyone of the status either of an observer or of an informant"[22]); and (2) that while that "direct" verification may be transmitted to us via a trace, it counts as a verification whether it is transmitted or not ("For all the messages that have been lost, it remains that statements about the past must count as having been directly established, and therefore as true, if someone observed them to be true at the, or an, appropriate time"[23]).

In *Truth and the Past*, Dummett speaks of a child's "treating the utterances of others as extending his range of observations," where this treating is supposed to account for the child's grasp of the fact that a statement about the past may be true even though *no* testimony is any longer available. (Dummett also speaks of the child's forming a mental "grid" that shows the relations of other places and times to one another and to the child's present location.) I agree that we have these abilities, of course. But once one grants that we do, I see no reason to balk at the idea that we grasp the fact that a statement about the past ("A meteorite struck the earth at such and such a place and time") may be true even if it was not observed at all. If I can form a mental "grid" that shows the relation of other places and times to my present location, why does the knowledge that certain events either did or did not happen at those places and times have to depend on whether observers were there *then*? Can *meteorites* not occupy positions in a mental grid? Originally the rationale of verificationism was the idea that my understanding of such sentences about the past *consists* in *my* ability, the *speaker's* ability, to verify them or falsify them. Once one says, "it does not have to be the speaker herself; it can be some other speaker, even someone who never communicated with the speaker," then it seems to me that she has made a huge concession to realism without appreciating just how huge it is. But small or large, once Dummett has made such a concession, it seems to me that he has done two things, either of which would be fatal to his case for verificationism, namely, (1) he has admitted that the arguments for verificationism are, at best, not conclusive, for if they were they would show the concession to be a mistake; and (2) he has at least tacitly admitted that a "pure" verificationism, verificationism with no taint of realism, degenerates into *solipsism*.[24]

VIII. Dummett on "Credulity"

Dummett writes,

> Soft realism does not, like hard realism, provide an entry for skepticism. Instead, it encourages its opposite, credulity. Examples of this are all about us: in philosophy, modal realism, according to which possible worlds have as much reality as the actual one, which differs from the others only in that it is the one we happen to inhabit; in cosmology, the multiverse, comprising many universes besides our own; in physics, the Everettian interpretation of quantum mechanics, according to which reality is constantly splitting, say into a half in which Schrödinger's cat is alive and a half in which it is dead. We have no direct knowledge of these parallel realms, and *could* not have; but

the soft realist believes that we can intelligibly postulate their existence. We understand what it is for them to exist; he thinks, since their existence, like the truth of propositions in general, is quite independent of our knowledge or our capacity to know. Realism is an essential foundation for these fantasies; it is not itself a superstition, but it is the mother of superstitions.

Dummett is of course right to point out that once one repudiates verificationism, as I have, one can no longer appeal to a "theory of meaning" to reject all of the scenarios he mentions in this paragraph as "meaningless." Nor do I want to. But here I have a confession to make: as late as my Royce Lectures (collected with the Dewey Lectures as *The Threefold Cord: Mind, Body and World*), I tried to defend the idea that various metaphysical scenarios lack "full intelligibility." My reasons were not verificationist but broadly "Wittgensteinian"; however, my present view is that—while the New Wittgensteinians are right to deny that Wittgenstein was a verificationist,[25] and right to say that Wittgenstein (in the *Tractatus* and later) thought that metaphysics is nonsense of "the garden variety kind," that is, that he thought that the *language* of the metaphysician literally fails to make sense—I was right in my younger days when I argued that there is no kind of "failure to make sense" that only (Wittgensteinian) philosophers can spot and linguists and ordinary speakers cannot.[26] In sum, the New Wittgensteinians have Wittgenstein right, but Wittgenstein was wrong. (Wittgenstein thought metaphysics was nonsense already as a young student of Russell's circa 1912, possibly under the influence of Boltzmann, whom Brian McGuinness describes as Wittgenstein's "first idol,"[27] and he seems to have retained that prejudice—for it is a prejudice—against metaphysics throughout his life, e.g. as evinced by the deservedly little discussed sneers at Plato in his work.) This is not to deny that Wittgenstein was a great philosopher of language; but it is to deny that he was a great metaphilosopher. I hope to expand on these remarks elsewhere, on a suitable occasion.

But, returning to Dummett's remarks, the fact that I would not say of any of the scenarios he cites in the above passage that they are (literally) "meaningless" does not mean that none of them can be *rejected* on rational grounds. It does mean that there is no *one* objection that counts against all of them at one fell swoop. This is not "credulity," it seems to me, but sophistication. For example, David Lewis's idea that "possible worlds" are not simply stories, but actual worlds, as real as the one we (parochially) call "the actual world," does seem crazy to me. I do not see a shred of a reason to believe it, but do see a host of problems with supposing it to be true. On the other hand, "multiverse cosmology" cannot, in my view, be ruled out at the present time. But it can be said that it is not worked out as a detailed physical theory; it depends (speculatively, at that) on string theory, and string theory itself is an incomplete and empirically unconfirmed theory. Finally, the Everett Interpretation was put forward to avoid the need for a "collapse postulate" in quantum mechanics; I have argued that it fails to make the required sense of quantum mechanical probabilities.[28]

The nonreductive naturalist picture of our relations to our language and our world does, indeed, leave both scientists and philosophers with a great deal of work to do. But it is not incoherent, as I have claimed antirealism is,[29] at the end of the day.

H.P.

NOTES

1. Consider, for example, the unverifiable sentence "There are no intelligent extraterrestrials." Even if this sentence cannot nondeviantly be used to make an assertion (itself a debatable claim) its possible truth can be *discussed*, it can be used to make a *conjecture*, one can have an attitude towards its truth (hoping, fearing, etc.), one can ever make estimates of its *probability*. It has *lots* of "uses." (See my "When 'Evidence Transcendence' is Not Malign," *Journal of Philosophy* 98, no. 11 [Nov. 2001]: 594–600.)

2. Hilary Putnam, "Meaning Holism," in *The Philosophy of W. V. Quine*, expanded edition, ed. L. E. Hahn and P. A. Schilpp (La Salle, IL: Open Court, 1998), 408–9.

3. On this, see Cyril Stanley Smith, *A History of Metallurgy: The Development of Ideas on the Structure of Metals before 1890* (Cambridge, MA: MIT Press, 1960).

4. Hilary Putnam, *Reason, Truth, and History* (Cambridge: Cambridge University Press, 1981).

5. Hilary Putnam, *Realism and Reason: Philosophical Papers*, vol. 3 (Cambridge: Cambridge University Press, 1983).

6. "THE WORLD" (in small capitals) was my notation for the metaphysical realist's supposed mind-independent world in my (1976) Presidential Address to the Eastern Division of the APA, "Realism and Reason."

7. Alfred Tarksi, *"Der Wahrheitsbegriff in den formalisierten Sprachen,"* *Studia Philosophica* 1 (1936): 261–405 (offprints dated 1935). "The Concept of Truth in Formalized Languages," translation of the preceding by J. H. Woodger in Alfred Tarksi, *Logic, Semantics, Metamathematics*, second edition (Indianapolis: Hackett, 1983).

8. For Dummett, knowing the meaning of a sentence is a mental act: "grasping a sense." Thus he writes, "For those senses are supposed to be explained by the theory in a manner that does not display how they are to be used: so it must be possible in principle for someone to grasp those senses without understanding the use of the sentences in discourse."

9. More precisely, I accept it subject to certain qualifications in the case of "framework propositions" whose negations may not be conceivable relative to a particular body of (putative) knowledge. On this subject see my "Reply to Gary Ebbs" in the present volume.

10. See my "Skepticism, Stroud and the Contextuality of Knowledge," *Philosophical Explorations* 4, no.1 (2001): 2–16.

11. I discuss Wittgenstein's "flirtation" with this idea in the Appendix to my "Was Wittgenstein *Really* an Anti-Realist about Mathematics" in *Wittgenstein in America*, ed. T. McCarthy and S. C. Stidd (Oxford: Oxford University Press, 2001).

12. Geoffrey Hellman, *Mathematics without Numbers; Towards a Modal-Structural Interpretation* (Oxford: Clarendon Press, 1993).

13. I would also have thought that accounting for the normative force of ascriptions of truth is not hard for a deflationist: why cannot both deflationists and nondeflationists alike say that a principal norm governing assertion is that one should do one's best to avoid asserting any *p* that is not true? It is true that it is that norm that gives truth the significance it has in our lives, and if you want to say that therefore it is part of the "concept" of truth, then, fine, provided you do not think conceptual analyses are a priori correct. That deflation does not *completely* describe the notion of truth is, indeed, very plausible.

14. One can get an idea of my current thinking from my chapter (titled "Hilary Putnam") in *Mind and Consciousness: Five Questions*, ed. Patrick Grim (Copenhagen: Automatic Press/Vince Press, 2009).

15. I am thinking of the writings of Michael Martin and J. M. Hinton here.

16. On this, see "Hilary Putnam" in *Mind and Consciousness: Five Questions*.

17. In particular, the use of the sort of psychology that itself employs intentional notions to better describe intentionally is not, in my view, viciously circular, when the search is for nonreductive understanding.

18. It is true that there is some light in these cases, but in the case of light that is in the infrared or the ultraviolet, that "light" was discovered by scientific instruments, and the discovery that "light is electromagnetic radiation" is also involved. Did the "concept" of seeing" really require that this be the case?

19. See the discussion of this notion in my "Reply to Gary Ebbs."

20. The example was "Lizzie Borden killed her parents with an axe."

21. Michael Dummett, *Truth and the Past* (New York: Columbia University Press, 2004).

22. Ibid., 68.

23. Ibid.

24. I argued this in "Between Scylla and Charybdis: Does Dummett Have a Way Through?" in *The Philosophy of Michael Dummett*, ed. R. Auxier and L. E. Hahn (La Salle, IL: Open Court, 2007).

25. The best statement I know of the New Wittgensteinian interpretation is "On Reading the *Tractatus* Resolutely," in *The Lasting Significance of Wittgenstein's Philosophy*, ed. M. Kölbel and B. Weiss (London: Routledge, 2004).

26. I argued this in "Dreaming and Depth Grammar" and "Brains and Behavior," both of which are collected in my *Mind, Language and Reality: Philosophical Papers*, vol. 2 (Cambridge: Cambridge University Press, 1979).

27. McGuinness writes, "If Boltzmann was his first idol, how does Wittgenstein still contrive to value the thinker [Schopenhauer] who seemed to Boltzmann to represent philosophy at its most sterile and ridiculous? Once again the answer lies in Wittgenstein's wish to transcend the old philosophy. He uses Schopenhauer's terms, or ones like them, to make philosophical moves that confirm Boltzmann's hostility to philosophy." (McGuinness, *Approaches to Wittgenstein* [London: Routledge, 2002], 133.)

28. I argue this in "A Philosopher Looks at Quantum Mechanics (Again)?," *British Journal for the Philosophy of Science* 56, no. 4 (Dec. 2005): 615–34.

29. See my "Between Scylla and Charybdis: Does Dummett Have a Way Through," and "Between Dolev and Dummett: Some Comments on 'Antirealism, Presentism and Bivalence,'" *International Journal of Philosophical Studies* 18, no. 1 (2010): 91–96.

12

Yemima Ben-Menahem

REVISITING THE REFUTATION OF CONVENTIONALISM

Putnam's influential critique of conventionalism has played a significant role in the demise of this once powerful position. Rather than focusing on the impact of Putnam's critique on the history of conventionalism, however, this paper focuses on the impact of conventionalism on the development of Putnam's philosophy. It seeks to show, first, that Putnam's engagement with conventionalism was a catalyst for several of his best-known philosophical contributions, and, second, that despite his critical stance vis-à-vis conventionalism, he is, in no small measure, as much an ally of conventionalism as a critic.

The transformation of Putnam's thought on conventionalism can be discerned in the titles of his papers on the subject: the transition from "The Refutation of Conventionalism" to "Convention: A Theme in Philosophy" suggests a conciliatory move, a relinquishing of outright opposition in favor of friendly respect. Indeed, the argument shifts from a sweeping critique of the conventionalist position to critique of the truth/convention dichotomy, underscoring the entanglement of these categories. Throughout, however, Putnam is more sympathetic to some conventionalist theses than to others. Rejection of the thesis that we can make our theories true by adopting truth-generating *definitions* (I will argue below, though, that this is a misleading characterization of conventionalism) is an enduring theme in Putnam's writings, remaining constant through changing conceptions of realism. At the same time, Putnam emphasizes the significance of another conventionalist thesis, namely, that seemingly incompatible theories may nonetheless be equivalent or interchangeable. The existence of these different strands in

Putnam's response to conventionalism reflects differences between versions of conventionalism that have generated considerable disagreement and ambiguity over what, precisely, the conventionalist position is. As it is impossible to do justice to Putnam's position without clarifying these ambiguities, I begin with a discussion of conventionalism. I proceed to examine Putnam's earlier responses to conventionalism, highlighting the impact of conventionalism on his philosophy. Finally, I conclude with comments and questions on the relation between conventionalism and Putnam's more recent ideas on conceptual relativity.

I. CONVENTIONALISM

Let me first note, and then elaborate on, two misunderstandings of conventionalism.

1. Several distinct—indeed, potentially conflicting—conventionalist positions have been conflated in the literature. The two most salient such positions are the underdetermination of scientific theory and the linguistic account of necessary truth, both of which have their origins in Poincaré's conventionalism.[1] A third conventionalist argument, inspired by both of the above, has been advanced in the context of the debate over the foundations of the theory of relativity. Here, the conventionalist maintains that the definition of the metric, the centerpiece of the general theory of relativity, is a convention. Putnam's critique of conventionalism was originally directed at this position (Grünbaum's argument, in particular), but has led him to a more wide-ranging repudiation of conventionalism.

2. A widely prevalent misconception of conventionalism construes it as advocating *truth* by convention. Generally (though not exclusively), it is the critics of conventionalism who think of it in this misleading way. Putnam's critique is no exception; it is the notion of truth by convention, or truth by definition, that is its primary target. Whereas a position that sanctions the stipulation of truth clearly offends against realist intuitions about truth, a more accurate understanding of conventionalism makes it plain that conventionalism does in fact accommodate a realist notion of truth by distinguishing truths properly so called from conventions masquerading as truths. Naturally, the realist may still disagree with the conventionalist over the status of a particular set of statements—questioning whether they are truths or conventions—but, unlike the verificationist, the coherence theorist, or the postmodern relativist, the conventionalist need not dispute the realist understanding of truth.

To elaborate: the first version of conventionalism, based on the underdetermination of scientific theory, must be distinguished from the second—

the doctrine that truths traditionally conceived as necessary are actually conventions.[2] Thus formulated, these are obviously distinct ideas, and the warning against their conflation would be misplaced, were it not a matter of historical fact that the term "conventionalism" has been inadvertently applied to both. In the context of the philosophy of science, the term "conventionalism" has been used to refer to the underdetermination associated with Duhem's philosophy. In this context it denotes the freedom to choose from among empirically equivalent scientific theories. Such choices are said to be guided by convention, for they are not uniquely determined by logic or observation. In other areas of analytic philosophy, "conventionalism" generally denotes the idea that so-called necessary truths, as distinct from ordinary contingent truths, function as definitions or rules of grammar and are, therefore, anchored in convention rather than fact. The origin of this daring idea is in the Hilbert-Poincaré conception of the axioms of geometry as *implicit definitions* of the primitive geometrical terms. Typically, such implicitly defined terms receive a plurality of interpretations and thus fail to point to a unique set of objects as their extension. This conception of axioms as definitions is sometimes summed up, quite misleadingly, as I noted, by the adage that the axioms are "true by convention."[3]

Both versions of conventionalism highlight the role of human decision, but the two are independent of each other. Quine clearly espoused the underdetermination of theory while repudiating the conventionalist account of the truths of logic and mathematics, invoking the former thesis as one of his arguments against the latter. Let me enumerate some of the key differences between these two versions of conventionalism.

1. Whereas the focus of underdetermination is *scientific theory*, that is, empirical, contingent truth, the second form of conventionalism is first and foremost an account of *necessary truth*.[4] One version of conventionalism thus addresses the problem of scientific method, while the other seeks to provide a novel answer to the age-old question of the epistemic basis of logical and mathematical knowledge. Furthermore, espousal of the latter version of conventionalism is typically accompanied by endorsement of a sharp dichotomy between contingent truth, grounded, it is claimed, in fact and experience and so-called necessary truth, claimed to be grounded in convention and altogether lacking the status of truth.

2. Underdetermination is generally characterized as an ongoing methodological problem: at any given moment in the scientific process, the scientist faces real choices between real alternatives. Even where the scientist is unaware of any actual alternative to the particular theory she subscribes to, the existence of such alternatives is envisaged by the scientific community, and is taken into account by its members. By contrast, the conventionalist account of logical and mathematical truth does not always affirm the

existence of concrete alternatives to logic or arithmetic. Rather, it is a response to philosophical concerns about the nature of necessity. Admittedly, grounding necessary truth in definitions, rules or commitments we have made suggests that our definitions, rules and commitments could have been otherwise. However, the conventionalist account does not draw its force from acquaintance with such alternatives. On the contrary, the entrenchment of habit and commitment is sometimes thought to explain the *absence* of alternatives, or their awkwardness when they do come to mind. Discretion, the principal message of underdetermination, is not a central issue here; to the extent that it is invoked, it is generally construed as *de jure* rather than *de facto* discretion.[5]

3. The term "convention" has a different meaning in each of the two versions of conventionalism. The first regards the need for convention as akin to the need for judgment and good reason, which we must call upon when more rigid standards fail to single out a unique theory. Flexible and not fully articulated, such conventions are not explicitly part of the theory in question. The second version of conventionalism, however, regards conventions as the stipulated basis of logic and mathematics. They comprise a small number of fixed rules or schema, the axioms and inference rules of a formal system, from which all other necessary truths then follow.

These two versions of conventionalism differ in the problems they address, the solutions they offer, and the notion of convention on which they rest, so much so that from the perspective adopted here, use of the same name for both seems like pure equivocation. Poincaré's writings, however, reveal subtle connections between the two.

Like several of his predecessors, Poincaré was intrigued by the logical and conceptual problems raised by the emergence of non-Euclidean geometries. The consistency of non-Euclidean geometries, or rather their consistency relative to Euclidean geometry, had by then been demonstrated by constructing models for non-Euclidean geometries within Euclidean geometry. Such modeling, to which Poincaré himself contributed some beautiful constructions, involves what Poincaré calls a "dictionary"; terms such as "straight line" or "distance" receive different meanings in different models. As the different geometries are interpreted *within* Euclidean geometry, they are consistent to the degree Euclidean geometry is consistent. Nonetheless, different geometries are *incompatible* with each other and with Euclidean geometry; one and the same model, that is, one particular interpretation of the geometrical primitives, will not satisfy different geometries.

Once relative consistency has been demonstrated, the question of truth arises: are the axioms of the different geometries true? Indeed, are they, like other mathematical truths, necessarily true? But can there be incompatible necessary truths? Can the negation of a necessary truth, supposedly true in all possible worlds, also be true? Poincaré framed the question in Kantian terms: given the multitude of alternative geometries, how can the axioms of geometry be synthetic a priori, as Kant believed?

In response to this dilemma, Poincaré, who otherwise approved the Kantian scheme, reconsidered the status of geometry. His celebrated solution was that the axioms of geometry (and the theorems that follow from them) are *disguised definitions* of the primitive geometrical terms appearing in them. Since different geometries are characterized by different sets of axioms, and since these sets of axioms are satisfied by different kinds of entities, definition by axioms can confer different meanings/interpretations on the same terms. The mystery surrounding the incompatibility of different geometries vanishes once we realize that the seemingly incompatible axioms and theorems refer to different sets of entities. Since Poincaré maintains that different geometries vary in usefulness from context to context and their endorsement in any particular case is a matter of convenience, he also refers to the axioms as conventions.

Though, from this perspective, the question of which geometry is true no longer arises, it might still make sense to raise the question of which geometry is true of "our" space, the space of experience. Poincaré maintained, as did Riemann and Helmholtz, that as spatial relations are in principle inaccessible to measurement, the question is undecidable, and, indeed, senseless. Helmholtz, however, claimed that this indeterminacy does not carry over into physics.[6] Once we take the laws of physics into account, he argued, the question becomes empirical: some physical laws valid in Euclidean space, for instance, the principle of inertia, will no longer hold in non-Euclidean space.

Poincaré disagrees: physics does not provide any means for distinguishing between the alternative geometries, for we can tailor the laws of physics to fit either one. He brings the aforementioned logical relations between the different pure geometries to bear on the geometric description of physical space, arguing for the *underdetermination of geometry by experience*. Using the technique of modeling one geometry within the other to devise compensating physical effects, he generates examples of empirically equivalent physical geometries, and concludes that the adequacy, not only of pure geometry, but of physical geometry as well, is a matter of convenience rather than truth.[7] Poincaré's argument goes beyond Duhem's methodological argument from the holistic nature of confirmation: he is asserting not merely that it is in principle possible to come up with empirically equivalent scientific theories, but the much stronger claim that there is a *constructive method* for actually producing such equivalent descriptions. The argument applies to geometry, however, and not to science in general.[8]

Poincaré's conventionalism has two focuses: the idea that the axioms of geometry should be viewed as definitions in disguise rather than necessary truths and the argument for the empirical equivalence of different geometries under all possible observations. Here we find the roots of the two versions of conventionalism that I distinguished. In the context of the philosophy of logic and mathematics, the thesis that axioms are definitions has been the more influential of the two. It remained at the forefront of the debate on the foundations of mathematics from the time of the Frege-Hilbert correspondence on Hilbert's *Foundations of Geometry* well into the twentieth century. In the philosophy and methodology of science, by contrast, the more influential thesis has been the argument that any conceivable experience is amenable to incompatible geometric interpretations, undermining the possibility of a uniquely correct geometry of experience. It is the latter aspect of Poincaré's conventionalism that is emphasized, for example, in Einstein's 1921 "Geometry and Experience."

Poincaré's followers developed his conventionalism in two different directions. Some argued that the axioms of geometry are not unique in lacking empirical underpinnings: science in general is *underdetermined* by experience. When a choice is made in favor of a particular alternative, it is a conventional choice rather than a truth forced on us by either logic or experiment. This extrapolation of Poincaré's insight converges with Duhem's conception of science. Others, taking Poincaré to have shown that a number of so-called necessary truths—the axioms of geometry—are in fact conventions, sought to extrapolate to the more radical view that *all* so-called necessary truths must likewise be seen as conventions. Poincaré explicitly distanced himself from both these more radical forms of conventionalism. Moreover, he held fast to a fairly Kantian view with respect to the foundations of arithmetic, regarding the principle of mathematical induction as synthetic a priori. Nevertheless, in the years that followed, these extrapolations of Poincaré's modest conventionalism brought about its bifurcation into the two versions of conventionalism we find in later thinkers.

Turning, now, to the second misunderstanding about conventionalism, that is, its identification with the misguided idea that truths can be stipulated, I want to stress that for Poincaré—and this is the main thrust of his position—conventions are not truths: not empirical truths, a priori truths, contingent truths, or necessary truths. They are, he claimed, analogous to systems of measurement, which can only be more or less useful. This was perhaps a misfortunate analogy, for unlike systems of measurement, the axioms of geometry are seen by Poincaré as *conditions* satisfied by some entities and dissatisfied by others (true under some interpretations and false under others). Still, the point of the analogy was that despite appearances, the axioms of geometry are not ordinary assertions and would not fit the exhaustive dichotomy between necessary and empirical truths. Rather than truths (be it necessary or empirical) about well-specified entities, we should conceive of axioms as unspecified formulas, open to various interpretations, that cannot, as they stand, be considered true or false. We are thus free to lay down axioms, but not free to *make* them true of a particular set of entities. According to Poincaré, our freedom to lay down such axioms/definitions is constrained only by the demand for consistency. Here Hilbert, who does not refer to his own view as conventionalism, agrees with Poincaré—hence the crucial importance he ascribes to consistency proofs. Critics of this construal of axioms, Frege and Russell in particular, maintain that definitions must fit specific (intuited) entities, disallowing any freedom in their choice (except for the insignificant freedom as to which formulas may be regarded as axioms and which as theorems). Consequently, they see no need for consistency proofs—the consistency of adequate definitions is ensured by their being *true*! Again, to make sense of the conventionalist position, we must keep the notion of truth distinct from that of convention. Axioms can be seen as conventions precisely because they should be construed as conditions, not as truths. Far from trumpeting the idea that truth can be arbitrarily legislated into being, conventionalism sought to alert us to the tendency to *mistake conventions for truths*.

The conventionalist position had an enormous impact on the next generation of philosophers, who went on to challenge traditional conceptions of necessary truth. As is well known, Wittgenstein, though certainly not a self-proclaimed conventionalist, rejected the notion of logical *truth* already in the *Tractatus*, and continued to ridicule it, later dubbing it "a kind of ultra physics."[9] Deeply influenced by Wittgenstein's formal account of logic, but contesting some of its central consequences,[10] Carnap put forward a thoroughly conventionalist alternative. He distinguished sharply between the truths expressible in a language and the conventions constituting its structure (formation rules and transformation rules). In general, empiricists were disposed to accept the conventionalist account of (so-called) necessary truth, for it enabled them to render all truths true by virtue of experience and completely renounce the nonempirical notion of "truth across possible worlds." Whatever falls outside the scope of the empirical, they could now assert, is not really truth at all. Even the positivists, then, did not subscribe to a stipulative conception of truth; the widespread belief that conventionalism sanctions the legislation of truth is no more than a caricature made popular by the misleading idiom "truth by convention."[11]

In the wake of the formulation of the theory of relativity, conventionalism took yet another turn, focusing, eventually, on whether there is a unique definition of the space-time metric. Among the protagonists of conventionalism were Schlick, Reichenbach, and Grünbaum, all of whom employed Poincaré-type thought experiments to argue that the metric of Einstein's general theory of relativity is not the only one compatible with experience.

Here, conventionalism is neither a general claim about the status of necessary truths, nor a general assertion that science is underdetermined. In this
respect it is close to Poincaré's geometric conventionalism. At the same
time, the focus on the definition of one particular entity, the metric, suggests
that this type of conventionalism takes something more akin to an *explicit*
definition to be the seat of convention. Not quite, though. Schlick and
Reichenbach referred to this kind of definition as "coordinating definition,"
the idea being that the theoretical terms of science must be *coordinated*
with the concrete objects of experience and their relations. To the extent
that different (and incompatible) coordinations are possible, coordinating
definitions are conventional. For example, it might be argued that to define
the notion of a time interval we must coordinate it with a concrete way of
measuring time; the conventionalist claim will then be that it is one stipulation among many possible ones that clocks tick at the same pace at different
positions in space. We will see that the emphasis on freedom pertaining to
a single definition, be it explicit or coordinative, is the target of Putnam's
critique. Since the debate on the theory of relativity stimulated Putnam's
engagement with conventionalism, I will briefly review its basic points.

The general theory of relativity (from here on, GR) completely transformed the question of the conventionality of geometry.[12] Despite Poincaré's
influence on twentieth-century epistemology in general, and on the emergence and interpretation of the theory of relativity in particular, the details
of his analysis do not apply in the new context. For one thing, departure
from Euclidean geometry, which Poincaré had deemed merely a theoretical
possibility, was declared inevitable by Einstein. For another, the geometry
adopted by Einstein is a Riemannian geometry of *variable* curvature, a geometry Poincaré had claimed was not applicable to physical space, even in
theory. More importantly, in the equations of GR, the mathematical entities
representing geometrical features of space-time are determined by the mathematical entities representing the distribution of masses and fields. Indeed,
the uniqueness of the mathematical terms expressing the metric leaves no
room for discretion. Finally, according to GR, the metric tensor has a dual
meaning, representing gravity as well as geometry. Integrated into the network of physical laws, geometrical properties turn out to be as empirical and
nonconventional as any other physical magnitude. There is thus a clear sense
in which, in GR, geometric conventionalism has been overtaken by geometric
empiricism. This was certainly Einstein's understanding of the matter and has
remained the majority view among physicists up to the present. Conventionalists such Schlick, Reichenbach, and Grünbaum failed to acknowledge these
implications of Einstein's theory. It was Putnam's critique of conventionalism
in the 1970s that signaled the change of the tides, highlighting Einstein's
dynamical conception of space-time on which geometry and physics are

mutually dependent and thus equally empirical. Within a decade, the anti-conventionalist position, further elaborated for example by Friedman (1983) and Torretti (1983), became the orthodoxy in the philosophy of science.

To complicate matters further, however, it should be noted that Einstein's understanding did not remain completely unchallenged. Motivated by the need to integrate gravity into the framework of other forces so as to unify the theory of relativity and quantum mechanics, a number of physicists, Richard Feynman and Steven Weinberg, in particular, have considered the possibility of deriving Einstein's equations from field theoretic considerations. Precisely because the metric tensor has a dual meaning, proponents of this approach were able to focus on its gravitational rather than its geometrical meaning. On their understanding, then, GR is a theory of gravity, uncommitted to Einstein's geometrical interpretation and the dynamical space-time it implies. Is this yet another example of empirically equivalent theories that indicates the underdetermination of geometry by experience? Is conventionalism still a viable option? Surprisingly, the question has been generally ignored by philosophers (not by physicists, though, even if they couch it in different terms) and I will not attempt to address it here.[13] Instead, let me turn to Putnam's arguments against conventionalism and their place in his philosophy.

II. Putnam's Response to Conventionalism

In his response to Grünbaum's claim regarding the conventionality of the metric, Putnam makes an observation that becomes exceedingly important as his conception of meaning evolves: the basic terms of science, he contends, do not acquire their meaning through explicit definition. Even when new definitions are introduced, they do not exhaust the conceptual innovations that characterize scientific revolutions. Specifically, the conventionalist errs in reducing the novelty of GR to changes in the definition of the metric. This rather modest claim turns out to have far-reaching implications for the progress of Putnam's philosophy. Here are some examples.

A. Holism and Conceptual Change

As a rule, definitions are contrasted with empirical propositions. Construing the transition from Newtonian mechanics to the theory of relativity as a change of definition places the entire explanatory burden on a change in terminology rather than on a new set of laws. The question of why a mere terminological change should have any empirical or explanatory import does not receive a satisfactory answer from the conventionalist. Putnam argues for a holistic conception on which concepts and definitions prove their worth through the theories that incorporate them, and are therefore sensitive to the same factors that impact the adequacy of theories themselves—empirical confirmation, explanatory import, simplicity, and so on. In cases of dramatic conceptual change, our creation of new concepts and our coming to accept new laws and theories go hand in hand. Redefining terms such as "simultaneity," "straight line," or "metric" leads, ipso facto, to revision of beliefs previously taken for granted. For example, GR predicts and explains the bending of light in a gravitational field. What is involved, therefore, is the empirical adequacy of a new set of beliefs—a new scientific theory, rather than the convenience of arbitrary definitions that cannot be put to the test. This conception is in line with Quine's critique of the analytic/synthetic dichotomy, which is likewise rooted in holism.

The conclusions Quine draws from holism, however, are unacceptable to Putnam. Whereas Quine employs holism to supplement underdetermination so as to make room for freedom and discretion, Putnam reverses the argument! In his view, an *illusion* of freedom is indeed fostered by the conventionalist portrayal of scientific revolutions as hinging on definitions as arbitrary stipulations. But the same illusion is encouraged by Quine's emphasis on underdetermination. By contrast, Putnam's holism highlights the role of *constraints* on the overall coherence of the theory; constraints in the light of which many allegedly feasible "definitions," or allegedly feasible alternative "theories," become highly unreasonable. Poincaré would be the last to underestimate the role of Putnam's constraints. His point was not that scientists are unable to decide between alternatives, but that their decisions involve cognitive values such as simplicity. Thus, much like Putnam, he was arguing against the view that there is an *algorithm* for confirmation, not against the rationality of science. Poincaré differs from Putnam, however, in distinguishing matters of fact from matters of methodological norm, not considering the latter to be indicators of *truth*, as Putnam does. The constraints that, according to Putnam, serve to single out the true theory, Poincaré sees as simply singling out a convenient theory. It is only on the pragmatic view according to which fact and (cognitive) value have parity as indicators of truth that the need to comply with desiderata such as simplicity can serve as an argument *against* discretion.

B. Conventionalism and the Indeterminacy of Translation

A similar argument highlighting the role of methodological constraints leads Putnam to reject the indeterminacy of translation. As is well known, Quine considers science as a whole to be interconnected and strongly underdetermined by experience.[14] He argues that holism tells against the traditional division into analytic and synthetic truths, and further, that an analogous underdetermination deflates the traditional concept of meaning. Hence the indeterminacy of translation. In "The Refutation of Conventionalism," Putnam turns his argument against the conventionality of the metric into a parallel argument against Quine's indeterminacy of translation. Ironically, Quine is accused of having made a conventionalist move that betrays his own holistic insights.

According to Putnam, in both cases—Grünbaum's metric and Quine's indeterminacy of translation—the root of the problem is an overly narrow notion of definition. Both Grünbaum and Quine pick a set of conditions supposedly necessary and sufficient for the term in question ("metric" and "translation," respectively), and proceed to show that this set of conditions does not uniquely determine the entity satisfying the definition. The conventionalist thesis regarding the underdetermination of the metric by experience, and of translation by speakers's dispositions, rests on the assumption that the definition is adequate, that it captures the meaning of the term in question. Putnam considers this assumption a disguised form of essentialism. His own position is that no such narrow set of conditions exhausts the meaning of either "metric" or "translation." An adequate metric or translation mandates satisfaction of a broader set of desiderata, narrowing down the number of feasible alternatives. A "metric" that unduly complicates the theory of which it is part will not do as a metric even if it satisfies Grünbaum's definition. Likewise, a "translation" that preserves only truth, but not explanatory and inferential links, will be unacceptable. The freedom posited by the conventionalist is again severely curtailed by Putnam.

C. From Coherence to "The Meaning of 'Meaning'"

Grünbaum's conventionalism, we saw, made no general claim as to the conventional status of necessary truth or the underdetermination of science. Instead, it limited conventionality to the definition of the metric. Clearly, restricting the scope of convention in this way has the advantage of enabling us to treat the rest of science as factual. This advantage, however, also generates an intractable problem for conventionalism. Definitions, it would seem, only fix the meanings of terms; how can they possibly carry the entire weight of the argument for freedom with respect to theory construction? Should we not be entitled to use language as we please, without thereby compromising a theory's merits relative to other theories? Moreover, if convention only fixes the meaning of terms, is conventionalism not reduced to an utterly trivial thesis? Indeed, the threat of "trivial semantic conventionality" (from here on, TSC), as it has been aptly termed by Grünbaum, is the most pressing problem confronting conventionalism.

The problem was first raised by Eddington in the prologue to *Space, Time and Gravitation*, where he responds to Poincaré's conventionalism: "I admit that space is conventional—for that matter, the meaning of every word in the language is conventional."[15] Eddington notes, further, that altering the meaning of the term "space" mandates redefinition of the magnitudes "length" and "distance," "quantities which the physicist has been accustomed to measure with great accuracy; and enter fundamentally into the whole of our experimental knowledge of the world."[16] He illustrates his point with another example. We could save Boyle's law (which we know to be only approximately correct) by changing the meaning of the term "pressure." "But it would be high-handed to appropriate the word 'pressure' in this way, unless it had been ascertained that the physicist has no use for it in its original meaning."[17] Bearing this critique in mind, Grünbaum insists that the alternative "metrics" satisfying his definition preserve the core meaning of the original term. The *extension* of the term has changed, not its intension. To Putnam, this seems like a desperate attempt to have it both ways—to both change the meaning of the term "metric," and preserve it.[18] In any case, this attempt does not alleviate the danger of triviality. Putnam remarks bluntly: "The question is just this: *can* the conventionalist successfully defend the thesis that the choice of a metric or the choice of a translation manual is a matter of convention, and not have this thesis be either false or truistic, that is, be either false or an instance of TSC? In my opinion he cannot."[19] The problem runs deeper, however, for Putnam realizes he has no ready answer to the question of what, precisely, constitutes a change in meaning. This is the question that comes to the fore in Putnam's seminal papers on meaning—"Explanation and Reference" and "The Meaning of 'Meaning.'" The connection between the puzzle about trivial conventionality and the need for a new conception of meaning is made explicit in the sentence that follows the remark just quoted:

> The conventionalist fails precisely because of an insight of Quine's. That is the insight that *meaning* in the sense of reference is a function of theory, and that the enterprise of trying to list the statements containing a term which are true by virtue of meaning, let alone give a list of statements which *exhausts* its meaning, is a futile one. . . . Reichenbach convincingly shows that reference is not, so to speak, an act of God. . . . But . . . reference need not be fixed by convention. It can be fixed by *coherence*.[20]

Putnam's objective is clearly set out in this passage—formulation of a theory of reference that depends neither on convention alone, nor on a magical bond between words and reality. This remains a central goal of Putnam's later arguments in support of realism and against brains-in-a-vat skepticism. The quotation suggests, however, that Putnam was entertaining the idea that reference is fixed by coherence, a move that amounts to viewing theories as implicit definitions. This is the conclusion reached in the debate with Grünbaum: "What appears . . . to be the case is that the metric is implicitly specified by the whole system of physical and geometrical laws. No very small subset by itself fully determines the metric."[21] But Putnam senses that this route may lead him to relativism rather than realism: If scientific theories serve as implicit definitions of their terms, *theory change will result in meaning change*—the very observation underlying the Kuhn-Feyerabend argument for incommensurability and the radical relativism it engenders. Aware of this complication, and apparently not fully satisfied with his suggestion that "*meaning* in the sense of reference is a function of theory," Putnam adds a long footnote that opens with the warning: "This insight must not be confused with Feyerabend's position, that a term cannot have the same reference in substantially different theories ('incommensurability')."[22] Putnam clearly faces a dilemma: to counter conventionalism, he must avoid the excessively narrow confines of explicit definition, but construing entire theories as implicit definitions lands him squarely in the relativist camp, a position he finds equally unattractive. Putnam's response to this dilemma introduces ideas that have come to epitomize his philosophical outlook, first and foremost his externalism. It is thus the encounter with the conundrum of conventionalism, more than encounter with Frege's legacy, that leads Putnam to "The Meaning of 'Meaning.'" The rest is Twin Earth history.[23]

The dilemma described above was not unprecedented. Putnam, we saw, was apprehensive that in allowing reference to be fixed by theory, its moorings in the real world were being compromised, precipitating the slide toward relativism. Poincaré had experienced the same apprehension: his geometrical conventionalism inspired more radical conventionalist positions that advocated the conventionality of arithmetic, on the one hand, and the conventionality of empirical science, on the other. Strongly committed to the synthetic a priori (rather than conventional) character of the principle of complete induction fundamental to arithmetic, and taking science to be anchored in experience in ways that preclude it from being wholly conventional, Poincaré did not go along with either of these developments. He declares:

> Here are three truths: (1) the principle of complete induction; (2) Euclid's postulate; (3) the physical law according to which phosphorus melts at 44 degrees. . . . These are said to be three disguised definitions: the first that of the whole number, the second that of the straight line, the third that of phosphorus. . . . I grant the second. I do not admit it for the other two.[24]

The intricacies of Poincaré's argument against the conventionality of arithmetic will not concern us here, but his objection to the proposed definition of phosphorus calls to mind Putnam's position. Reference to physical objects cannot be completely accomplished through theory, but must involve practices and causal connections. Dismissing the above "definition" of phosphorus, Poincaré anticipates externalism: "The true definition," he suggests, is "phosphorus is the bit of matter I see in that flask."[25]

D. Trivial Semantic Conventionality

The problem raised by Eddington—whether there is a nontrivial role for convention—intrigued Wittgenstein, who widened its scope. How are we to understand the special status of necessary truth in general? A conventionalist answer to this question yields the second version of conventionalism identified above, namely, the view that necessary truths are akin to definitions, and anchored in convention rather than fact. Wittgenstein wavered somewhat in his response to conventionalism. On the one hand, he affirms the triviality of convention: "The steps which are not brought in question are logical inferences. But the reason why they are not brought in question is not that they 'certainly correspond to the truth'—or something of that sort —no, it is just this that is called 'thinking,' 'speaking,' 'inferring,' 'arguing'."[26]

This seems as trivial as conventionality can get. But, on the other hand, Wittgenstein also allows for a connection between our concepts and certain basic facts. Citing measurement, the conventionalist's preferred analogy, he notes: "It is one thing to describe methods of measurement, and another to obtain and state results of measurement. But what we call 'measuring' is partly determined by a certain constancy in results of measurement."[27] A similar sentiment was voiced by Poincaré—the world itself makes some conventions more convenient than others. In a well-known passage, Wittgenstein invokes "the deep need for the convention" as though he seeks to forestall the charge of triviality, but given his suspicion of the depth metaphor, we should perhaps read this passage cautiously, if not ironically.[28] It seems to me that Wittgenstein never solved the problems surrounding the notion of convention to his own satisfaction. Perhaps this is fitting, for the question of how to distinguish trivial from nontrivial conventions is too close to that of why language is the way it is—surely a dead end from Wittgenstein's point of view.

And yet, some progress has been made. The distinction between trivial and nontrivial conventionality seems reasonable enough as long as we take nontrivial conventions to generate truth, and trivial ones to merely assign meanings to linguistic expressions. But if I am correct in claiming that conventionalism does not advocate truth by convention, then perhaps its proponents need not be apprehensive in the face of triviality. The conventions it points to may indeed be trivial, but this does not trivialize the conventionalist position. On the contrary, recognition of the trivial nature of what we usually take to be fundamental and profound constitutes a weighty philosophical insight.

Wittgenstein, though generally sympathetic to such iconoclasm, would not be happy with this response to the charge of triviality. For one thing, he is almost as wary of allegations of triviality as he is of traditional accounts of necessity. As he repeatedly reminds us, we are unable to abstract from the language we actually use and the meanings we assign, trivially or nontrivially, to its expressions. Both the traditional concept of necessity and its conventionalist counterpart invoke the same vexing element of modality—what is or is not possible, conceivable, and so on. Committing ourselves to the view that we could have reasoned differently is just as unintelligible as committing ourselves to the view that we could not have done so. In "The Refutation of Conventionalism," Putnam is confident in the distinction between trivial and nontrivial conventionality and the ensuing trivialization of conventionalism. Under the growing influence of Wittgenstein's writings, this confidence may have waned somewhat. It would be interesting to have Putnam revisit this question today.

E. Relative Necessary

In the face of non-Euclidean geometries and their potential use in physics, Poincaré concluded that we had been wrong about the *status* of our beliefs—what we took to be necessary truths were in fact conventions. Putnam draws a simpler conclusion: we were wrong about the beliefs themselves—what was once considered necessarily true turned out to be false. Recall that it was the attempt to avoid this very conclusion that motivated conventionalism. But what, precisely, is so objectionable about it? Can we not be in error about necessary truth the same way we are so often in error about empirical truth? And if we can, do we thereby erase the difference between the necessary and the empirical? Seeing the axioms of geometry as conventions, Poincaré does not believe any empirical test can refute them; in this respect they are different from empirical propositions.[29] Putnam reasons differently. It is not that experience has no impact whatsoever on the axioms of geometry, but rather, the point is that within the boundaries set by the conceptual horizons of Euclidean geometry and classical mechanics, it was extremely unlikely any experience would have been declared recalcitrant. For there to be any likelihood of this occurring, a new conceptual framework had to emerge. And while Poincaré and Putnam are divided on the issue of convention, both assume that potential counterexamples to the received geometry cum physics would be explained away by tinkering with physics, not geometry.

From Putnam's point of view, it is a mistake to take later developments to imply that the axioms of Euclidean geometry were either conventions all along, or ordinary empirical conjectures up for refutation. Their status can only be assessed relative to a specific conceptual horizon. As long as replacing them was not a "live option" (to use James's term) within the boundaries of that horizon, they had to be seen as necessities; albeit (from our point of view) *relative* necessities. Now Putnam has never settled for a relative notion of truth. When later discoveries refute beliefs once taken to be true, we must conclude they had not, in fact, been true prior to those discoveries. But a belief can be false and still enjoy the status of relative necessary. That we have indeed experienced conceptual revolutions in the past should tell us something about the status of beliefs we currently hold necessary. As we can think of no intelligible alternatives, we take them to be necessarily true, but, applying the lessons of history, we cannot exclude the possibility that they too will prove to have been false all along when new conceptual vistas open up. Somewhat paradoxically, then, "necessary truths" need not be true, though they are still (relatively) necessary.[30] Divorcing the notion of necessity from the notion of truth in this way, Putnam is making a concession to historicism, for necessity is judged by what seems intelligible in a particular historical context. It is significant, therefore, that Putnam, unlike the garden variety historicist, does not make an analogous concession about truth.

The notion of relative necessity has an interesting genealogy. Reichenbach distinguished between two aspects of Kant's notion of synthetic a priori, the necessity of the truths in question, and their constitutive role with regard to empirical knowledge.[31] The lesson of the theory of relativity, he argued, is that these two aspects do not always converge; the axioms of Euclidean geometry may not be necessary truths, but they do play a constitutive role within the framework of Newtonian physics. Reichenbach seeks to retain the notion of the constitutive a priori, but, liberating it from the Kantian demand for necessity, he construes it as relative to the theory constituted. As Friedman has shown, Reichenbach, influenced by Schlick, revised this view, so that in his later book on the subject, convention takes the place of the relative a priori.[32] The theory Putnam proposes as an alternative to the conventionalism of Grünbaum and (the later) Reichenbach thus revives some of Reichenbach's earlier insights.

I started this paper with a distinction between conventionalism as promoting the underdetermination of theory by experience, and conventionalism as an account of necessary truth. Putnam, we have seen, is particularly critical of the conventionalist construal of GR, but is also averse to the two more general forms of conventionalism. I have tried to show how the struggle against conventionalism is related to two of Putnam's most celebrated doctrines—semantic externalism and relative necessity. It is thus not solely a refutation of conventionalism that Putnam was undertaking, but also the creation of elaborate alternatives to the conventionalist understanding of both empirical and necessary truth. And yet, as these alternatives were taking shape, Putnam became intrigued by the question of *equivalent and intertranslatable descriptions*—the very core of Poincaré's conventionalism. In the case of demonstrated equivalence, Putnam comes to concede that the conventionalist picture of an interest-driven choice between alternatives has an important application. Moreover, he maintains that such equivalence is a profound characteristic of modern science![33] This conventionalist insight has been integrated into Putnam's thinking, as we shall see in the next section.

III. Conceptual Relativity: Fact and Convention in Putnam's Later Philosophy

By 1985, when Putnam gave the lectures published as *The Many Faces of Realism*, the debate on conventionalism seemed to have cooled down. Putnam's major concern was now to articulate his new internal (pragmatic) realism, distinguishing it from the naïve conception he calls metaphysical realism. What makes it naïve, he argued, is its obliviousness to the role of language, its pre-Kantian aspiration to represent reality "in itself" independent of our modes of description. It should come as no surprise that the ripening of internal realism has made Putnam more suspicious of ontology insofar as it purports to make claims that are absolute and language independent. Identifying examples of *conceptual relativity* that illustrate the relativity of ontology to schemes of representation thus becomes exceedingly important for him. In this endeavor, however, the conventionalist is no longer an opponent, but rather a source of inspiration. I will try to distinguish between different cases that Putnam discusses in this context.

A. Equivalence

Putnam uses a simple example to underscore the problematics of the notion of an object. A world taken to consist of three objects could also be considered to consist of seven objects if mereological sums are regarded as objects.[34] From the perspective of internal realism, the question of the "real" number of its objects makes no sense. Its dismissal is not grounded in a general antimetaphysical or verificationist sentiment—how would we put such ontological assertions to the test?—but in the observation that the two frameworks in question, though seemingly incompatible, are nonetheless equivalent in the following sense. Sentences in each have parallels in the other, so that whatever can be said in one language can also be expressed in the other. For example, there can be exactly one green object and one red one in the first framework if and only if there is exactly one object in the second that is partly green and partly red. Putnam cites other examples of competing ontologies that are equivalent in the same way: different definitions of numbers, different definitions of geometrical points. An analogous situation occurs in science when equivalent (or empirically equivalent) theories postulate different entities as the basic constituents of reality, but are equivalent in terms of their predictions and theoretical apparatus.

In all these cases we can interpret each theory within the language of the other theory, that is, construct a "translation" converting every true sentence of one theory into a true sentence of the other. It is intertranslatability that establishes equivalence and justifies the claim that there is no fact of the matter as to which of the alternatives provides the true description of reality. Such "translations" differ from what we would ordinarily consider to be a translation in that they preserve truth but not meaning. This is precisely the sense of translation invoked by Quine to derive the indeterminacy of translation. Putnam's point against Quine was, it will be recalled, that this notion of translation is too weak to sustain Quine's negative conclusions about meaning; additional constraints help pick out translations that capture meaning more adequately. In the present context, however, the question is whether any of the equivalent alternative "translations" has a stronger claim to *truth*. Truth-preserving but non-meaning-preserving "translations," therefore, are acceptable.

Putnam's paradigmatic cases of equivalence call to mind Poincaré's original argument for the conventionality of geometry, which likewise pivoted on the mutual interpretability of the two languages. If every theorem, fact, or prediction following from one geometry has its counterpart in another, Poincaré argued, what basis can there be, other than convenience, for choosing between them? While later forms of conventionalism have been discredited by Putnam, he now embraces Poincaré's affirmation of the role of convention in cases of demonstrated equivalence.[35] Note that neither Putnam nor Poincaré maintain that every scientific theory or ontology will have equivalents that support conventionalism. Neither argues for the radical underdetermination of science or ontology. Their argument is restricted to those cases in which equivalence can be established via a "translation," that is, cases in which the equivalence itself comes to be seen as reflecting structural features of the domain in question.[36]

B. Conceptual Relativity

Eddington opens *The Nature of the Physical World* with a puzzle about his two desks—the familiar desk of everyday life, and the desk of science, a swarm of invisible molecules in constant motion. He wonders which one is the real desk, implying that only one of the two can be real; the other must be in some sense fictional, or reducible to the first. Refusing to be pressured into choosing between the desks, Putnam challenges the assumption that there is a uniquely correct description of reality. Pluralism about modes of description, which he refers to as conceptual relativity (and more recently, simply "pluralism"), is a theme that gains prominence in the essays collected in *Realism with a Human Face*.

As Putnam is well aware, there has been some confusion between conceptual relativity and equivalence.[37] Although both concepts have been used apropos the attempt to accommodate alternative descriptions, it is important not to confuse them. There are at least three ways in which they differ. The first relates to translatability. Whereas equivalence consists in intertranslatability, the possibility of reformulating each of the competing descriptions in the terminology of the other, the ordinary and the scientific descriptions of Eddington's desk are not mutually interpretable in this way. Indeed, even the weaker relation of reduction—unidirectional translation—does not obtain here. Evidently, many properties of the ordinary desk are explained by properties of the scientific desk, but the former cannot be completely reduced to the latter. More generally, science often aims at, and sometimes succeeds in, reducing a certain class of phenomena to a more basic explanatory level.[38] Conceptual relativity, though acknowledging the role of scientific reduction, denies that such reduction justifies the allegation that only the scientific desk is real. We may want to know how much the desk costs, whether it fits into a certain corner, whether it matches other pieces of furniture in the room, whether it reminded Eddington of his grandfather's desk, and so on. None of these questions can be completely reduced to questions about the atomic world, certainly not in a manner that makes the reduction necessary, or even useful, for producing better answers than those already available at the ordinary level. From the pragmatic point of view, therefore, the reality of the ordinary desk is as secure as reference to physical entities can be. At the same time, there is no reason to regard only the ordinary desk as real, and dismiss the swarm of molecules as a fiction. Given the role of atoms and molecules in scientific explanation, their reality is also as secure as reference and reality can be within the bounds of human fallibility. What we must give up, on Putnam's view of conceptual relativism, is neither the reality of ordinary physical objects nor the reality of nonobservable entities discovered by science, but the dream of a fundamental ontology to which all other ontologies can be neatly reduced.

Another difference is that in the case of equivalent descriptions, each of the alternatives is optional: since every theorem or prediction formulated in one language has its equivalent in the other, we could, in principle, restrict ourselves to the use of one only. By contrast, precisely because of the failure of equivalence, we cannot forgo reference to either the ordinary or the scientific desk; both are indispensable. The same is true of other contexts where we have multiple modes of description, for instance, where we have mental and physical descriptions of the same events.

Finally, whereas, in cases of equivalence, the alternatives, though ultimately consistent with each other, are incompatible if taken at face value, Putnam maintains that the descriptions sanctioned by pluralism are not even prima facie incompatible. I will return to this claim shortly.

The relativity of truth to context that is associated with conceptual relativity (pluralism) diverges from relativism as commonly conceived. When the garden variety relativist asserts that, given the dependence of truth on "context"—a set of assumptions or norms—there is no fact of the matter, she usually affirms, in addition, that there is no fact of the matter as to *which context is the right context.* Unless this assumption is made, the relativist's conclusion that different verdicts on a specific question are equally sound does not follow. The conceptual relativist's orientation is quite different. He believes that there *is* a fact of the matter as to whether this desk fits into that corner, and further, he believes that the context is dictated by the question, and is not a matter of arbitrary choice. The same goes for harder questions, such as "do you love me?" Even when the addressee is not sure about the answer, she or he can identify the relevant context and the conditions it imposes on acceptable replies. It is not merely that we are unable to answer such a question by citing neurological activity or physical/mathematical calculations; a scientific response (I am not sure, wait a minute, let me measure the level of neural activity in my amygdala) would be abusive even were science to come up with a theoretical account of mental states. Moreover, denying the objectivity of truth, the garden variety relativist might feel compelled to deny the objectivity of truth-relative-to-a-context.[39] Putnam's conceptual relativist will not be pulled in this direction.

Donald Davidson has subjected the thesis of conceptual relativity to a thoroughgoing critique. In "On the Very Idea of a Conceptual Scheme," he notes that though "conceptual relativism" is "a heady and exotic doctrine," it is "hard to improve intelligibility while retaining the excitement." Where precisely does conceptual relativism lapse into incoherence? Some of Davidson's arguments target metaphors he associates with the thesis: "The dominant metaphor of conceptual relativism, that of differing points of view, seems to betray an underlying paradox. Different points of view make sense, but only if there is a common co-ordinate system on which to plot them; yet the existence of a common system belies the claim of dramatic incomparability."[40] The metaphor of different types of organization is likewise found untenable: "We cannot attach a clear meaning to the notion of organizing a single object (the world, nature etc.) unless that object is understood to contain or consist in other objects. Someone who sets out to organize a closet arranges the things in it. If you are told not to organize the shoes and shirts, but the closet itself, you would be bewildered."[41] But the inadequacy of these metaphors, which, admittedly, are widely used, would be harmless if conceptual relativity could be formulated in less metaphorical language. And indeed, this seems to be the case. Conceptual relativity, we saw, espouses pluralism rather than reductionism. The metaphor of different perspectives on the same thing, or different ways of organizing the same thing, is not only unnecessary for conveying this idea, but in fact quite misleading here, for it is precisely the idea of an underlying ontology that is being called into question. Putnam explicitly denies that the debate is over different ways of organizing some yet to be organized "thing."[42] Certainly, the idea of an amorphous substrate, an unconceptualized "thing," is anathema to Putnam, as it is to Davidson.

Metaphors aside, the main issue of contention between Davidson and the conceptual relativist he has in mind is relativism per se. The concluding passage leaves no doubt about what Davidson sees as the thrust of his paper:

> In giving up dependence on the concept of an uninterpreted reality, something outside all schemes and science, we do not relinquish the notion of objective truth—quite the contrary. Given the dogma of dualism of scheme and reality, we get conceptual relativity, and truth relative to a scheme. Without the dogma, this kind of relativity goes by the board. . . . In giving up the dualism of scheme and world we do not give up the world, but re-establish unmediated touch with the familiar objects whose antics make our sentences and opinions true or false.[43]

Davidson implies that scheme/content dualism provides the relativist with tools enabling her to construe substantive conflicts as resting on incommensurable schemes and hence as undecidable. I have already noted that conceptual relativity as such does not entail garden variety relativism. Let me note, further, that the converse is also false: relativism, as generally understood, does not entail conceptual relativity. Consider polygamy. Different societies have different moral attitudes to this social arrangement. The moral relativist who maintains that there is no objective moral truth about polygamy need not argue from incommensurability or take differences in "content" to be differences in "scheme." She maintains that the parties use precisely the same language, but, nonetheless, differ in their values, values she herself sees as a subjective matter of taste or culture. Giving up scheme/content dualism will in no way eliminate this type of relativism.

The conceptual relativist Davidson is out to refute, however, does argue from incommensurability. The question is, therefore, whether conceptual relativity, as understood by Putnam, implies this particular kind of relativism after all. If not, perhaps Davidson and Putnam are using the term differently. To add to our puzzlement, recall that at least in one much discussed case, that of the mental and the physical, Davidson himself has stressed irreducibility. While accepting the identity thesis, namely, that every mental event is a physical event, he rejects reductionism, denying the existence of type-type regularities such as "all mental states of type M are physical states of type P." Absent such regularities, we are unable to predict or explain the mental on the basis of the physical. Although the mental is not to be conceived of as constituting a distinct "entity," mental discourse remains both irreducible and indispensable. Given that this appears to be an instance of conceptual relativity as the notion is understood by Putnam, it is unlikely that Putnam's notion is the target of Davidson's attack. The thesis of incommensurability, on the other hand, is directly affected.

C. Incommensurability

How does incommensurability differ from the two other variants of relativity we have examined, namely, equivalence and conceptual relativity? Equivalent descriptions, we saw, raise two problems, consistency and communication, that are resolved when mutual translatability is established. Conceptual relativity is altogether innocent of these difficulties. Speakers can be fluent in a number of irreducible but peacefully coexistent languages. As long as speakers know which language is to be used in a given context, the languages are never in competition with each other, so to speak. Now incommensurability, like equivalence, arises from an apparent conflict that is resolved by postulating meaning variance. In contrast to equivalent descriptions, however, incommensurable theories are claimed *not* to be intertranslatable. Furthermore, each, it is claimed, is *true* in its own particular sphere, that is, *relatively* true. Davidson takes issue with the former claim, but it seems to me that the latter is at least as problematic, and that it is only the conjunction of the two that offends against the realist concept of truth. For instance, it is not the claim that Aristotelian physics is incommensurable with Newtonian physics that is troubling, but the intimation that there is no fact of the matter as to which of the two is the true, or even the more reliable, theory. If they are incommensurable, so the argument goes, they cannot be compared to or tested against each other; from which we are somehow to infer that they are equally respectable descriptions of reality. But as it stands, the conclusion does not follow. "There are five apples on the table" may be "incommensurable" (and thus consistent) with "there are three oranges in the fridge," but there is no reason why both sentences, or either one of them, must be true (unless, of course, we have already made some further relativist assumptions necessitating that conclusion). Note that in genuine instances of equivalence, we can demonstrate, via translation (that is, "translation"), that insofar as one description is correct, the others are too. But since intertranslatability is denied in cases of (alleged) incommensurability, no such argument is forthcoming here.

Relativism based on incommensurability, we see, is in trouble even before we get to the metaphors Davidson associates with it, or the question of scheme/content dualism. As a relativist, the incommensurability theorist is attracted to the idea that different theories (paradigms, schemes), though incompatible, provide equally valid answers to the *same* questions. To avoid the charge that these different theories are inconsistent, this relativist then reverts to meaning change and incommensurability. The claim that observation terms are also theory laden leads to the further assertion that, indeed, not only theoretical terms, but the entire vocabularies of the rival theories, are at variance. This strategy blocks the charge of inconsistency, but at a very high cost—the motivating idea, namely, that of the same problem receiving equally reliable solutions in competing theories, can no longer be expressed. Unless this idea is recovered, there is little motivation for the meaning-variance strategy. The position associated with Kuhn and Feyerabend implies that Newtonians were merely deluding themselves when they had supposed that they had surpassed the Aristotelian solutions to problems such as the trajectory of projectiles; "in fact" (if we can use the phrase at all), the Aristotelians had done just as well on their own terms. If this bold idea cannot be expressed, incommensurability loses much of its appeal. Be that as it may, the thrust of Putnam's conceptual relativity (and Davidson's anomalous monism) is different. The various languages sanctioned do not really compete, and the descriptions couched in these languages are assumed from the outset to be consistent.

But are they? Is Putnam not overly confident in the compatibility of the descriptions permitted by his pluralism? Davidson provides for consistency in his own example of an irreducible language by means of the identity thesis, but Putnam appears to have a wider range of examples in mind, and some of them may cast doubt on the compatibility assumption. Although the following have not been mentioned by Putnam as examples of conceptual relativity, we may stop to inquire as to whether he would be willing to consider them as such. The ordinary concept of time does appear incompatible with its relativistic counterpart, and the exercise of free will in decision making has yet to be reconciled with our scientific picture of the world, whether it is based on underlying determinism or underlying chance. Two responses to examples of this kind are plausible. A restricted pluralism will approve of alternative descriptions only when they are known to be compatible. If ordinary time is indeed incompatible with relativistic time, one of these concepts must go. Similarly, if the discourse of freedom is to be tolerated, it must be shown to be compatible with our best scientific theory. More radical pluralism that makes room for autonomous discourses that cannot be harmonized will forgo the demand for consistency in such cases. Radical pluralism can still distance itself from popular forms of relativism, since it does not challenge the notions of scientific truth, objective moral values and so on. In a way, it seeks to defend these notions (though the criteria for their application may vary from context to context) by anchoring them in what it takes to be indispensable autonomous discourses, but the renunciation of overall consistency may seem too dear a price. Nevertheless, I find this position attractive, even if only because I do not know what it would mean for the ordinary concept of time or the ordinary concept of freedom to lapse until someone came up with a way of harmonizing them with our best scientific theory. Radical pluralism can, I believe, be traced to two philosophers Putnam holds in high respect, James and Wittgenstein. Apropos the issue of freedom, James urged that we make a decision, and Wittgenstein maintained that scientific confirmation of determinism will not necessarily force upon us a change in our notion of freedom.[44] As far as I can tell, Putnam has not crossed the line from restricted to radical pluralism; I wonder whether this is an option he would consider.

YEMIMA BEN-MENAHEM

THE HEBREW UNIVERSITY OF JERUSALEM
FEBRUARY 2003

NOTES

1. However, later versions of both these ideas diverge from Poincaré's original arguments; see below. Popper clearly has the underdetermination thesis in mind when he critiques conventionalism in his *The Logic of Scientific Discovery* (London: Hutchinson, 1959) and "Science: Conjectures and Refutations" in *Conjectures and Refutations* (London: Routledge and Kegan Paul, 1962). See also L. Sklar's characterization of conventionalism in *Space, Time, and Spacetime* (Berkeley: University of California Press, 1974), 128 and M. Friedman, *Foundations of Space-Time Theories* (Princeton: Princeton University Press, 1983), ch. 7. On the other hand, Quine uses the term "conventionalism" only with

reference to a linguistic account of logical and mathematical truth, never apropos underdetermination. The linguistic understanding of conventionalism is also the subject of Ayer's *Language Truth and Logic* and the symposium on "Truth by Convention" in *Analysis* 4 (1936): 28–32.

2. I use the term "necessary truth" broadly. The doctrine has been variously construed: as accounting for the a priori, for the analytic, the synthetic a priori, logic and logic plus mathematics. For the moment, we can ignore these finer distinctions.

3. The term "implicit definition" originates in Gergonn's 1818 treatise on definitions, which contrasts implicit and explicit definitions and anticipates some of the ideas that were raised around 1900 (Gergonne, J. D. "Essai sur la théorie des définitions," *Annales de Mathématiques* 9 [1818]: 1–35). Although neither Poincaré nor Hilbert used the term to introduce their conception of axioms as definitions, it soon became the accepted term designating this conception.

4. Quine sees underdetermination as extending to logical truth.

5. Wittgenstein often warns against the construing of habit as metaphysical necessity. Carnap's *Logical Syntax of Language*, advocating *de facto* discretion in logic, constitutes an exception.

6. H. von Helmholtz, "The Origin and Meaning of Geometrical Axioms," *Mind* 1 (1976): 301–21. Reprinted in *From Kant to Hilbert: A Sourcebook in the Foundations of Mathematics*, vol. II, ed. William Ewald (Oxford: Clarendon Press, 1999), 663–85.

7. Poincaré's best-known example: a world enclosed in a large sphere of radius R with a temperature gradient such that the temperature at point r is proportional to $R^2 - r^2$. Consequently, the dimensions of material objects are affected by changes in temperature, so that lengths vary in accordance with the same law. Further, light is refracted in this world according to an analogous law: its index of refraction is inversely proportional to $R^2 - r^2$. In this world, sentient beings are more likely to see themselves as living in a Lobaschewskian space, where light travels in (Lobaschewskian) straight lines, but can also see themselves as described by Poincaré, namely, as living in a Euclidean sphere in which bodies contract as they travel away from the center, and light is refracted in accordance with the said law. The physical laws required for the Euclidean description are closely related to, and follow naturally from, the "dictionary" correlating the different geometries. Were it not for the modeling of Lobaschewsky's geometry within Euclidean geometry, it is extremely unlikely that we would have 'discovered' such a peculiar law of refraction, but given the modeling, its discovery was straightforward.

8. According to Poincaré, although conventions can be found throughout the physical sciences, they are weaker cases of conventionality. See H. Poincaré, *Science and Hypothesis* (New York: Dover, 1952), 136–37. For an analysis of Poincaré's conventionalism, see my *Conventionalism* (New York: Cambridge University Press, 2006). (Note that this book was written later than the present paper.)

9. Ludwig Wittgenstein, *Remarks on the Foundations of Mathematics*, ed. G. H. von Wright and G. E. M. Anscombe, trans. G. E. M. Anscombe, rev. ed. (Oxford: Basil Blackwell, 1978), I, § 8.

10. Carnap particularly objected to the idea that language cannot express its own structure, and thus to Wittgenstein's say-show distinction, and the ensuing concepts of sense and nonsense.

11. Quine's famous 1936 title "Truth by Convention" is probably partly responsible for the popularity of the caricature. Misconception of conventionalism is very common even among leading philosophers of science. Sklar, for instance, put forward in all seriousness the following argument: "Suppose our choice of a Euclidean as opposed to non-Euclidean world really is merely a decision to be made on our part. If our decision really is arbitrary,

what useful purpose is served by calling the theory of our choice true?" (*Space, Time, and Spacetime*, 128). As I have shown, the conventionalist does not maintain that convention establishes truth. In addition, conventionalists explicitly deny that the decision is arbitrary: "Conventions, yes; arbitrary, no" (Poincaré, *Science and Hypothesis*, 110).

12. The question of whether there are conventional assumptions in the special theory of relativity is less relevant to Putnam's work. Pertaining to the definition of simultaneity, it has already been raised by Einstein and is still being debated. See R. Anderson, I. Vetharaniam, and G. E. Stedman, "Conventionality of Synchronization, Gauge Dependence and Test Theories of Relativity," *Physics Reports* 295 (1998): 93–180 for a comprehensive review of work on this problem.

13. The Putnam-Grünbaum debate took place before the alternative interpretation of the general theory of relativity was proposed. See R. P Feynman, *Lectures on Gravitation*, ed. F. B. Morinigo and W. G. Wagner (Pasadena: California Institute of Technology, 1971) and S. Weinberg, *Gravitation and Cosmology: Principles and Applications of the General Theory of Relativity* (New York: John Wiley and Sons, 1972) for the gravitational approach. An opposite interpretation, on which GR explains away gravity in favor of geometry was put forward by J. L. Synge, *Relativity: The General Theory* (Amsterdam: North Holland, 1960). Recent critique of Weinberg's view can be found in L. Smolin, *Three Roads to Quantum Gravity* (New York: Basic Books, 2001).

14. By "strongly underdetermined," I mean that science is said to be underdetermined by the entire body of observable facts, so that further observation will not decide between alternatives, in contrast to ordinary cases of inductive uncertainty.

15. A. S. Eddington, *Space, Time and Gravitation* (Cambridge: Cambridge University Press, 1920), 9.

16. Ibid., 10.

17. Ibid.

18. In "The Meaning of 'Meaning,'" Putnam construes his opponent as making two assumptions: that intension determines extension—it is impossible for two terms to have the same intension but differ in extension; and, that meanings are determined by psychological states. The first of these assumptions is renounced by Grünbaum when he asserts, contra Eddington, that the various definitions retain the meaning (intension) of "metric," though not its extension. Putnam is unwilling to pursue this tack and prefers to let go of the second assumption.

19. Hilary Putnam, *Mind, Language and Reality: Philosophical Papers*, vol. II (Cambridge: Cambridge University Press, 1975), 164.

20. Ibid., 164–65.

21. Hilary Putnam, *Mathematics, Matter and Method: Philosophical Papers*, vol. I (Cambridge: Cambridge University Press, 1975), 83. Although written about ten years before the above quoted passage on coherence, the line of thought is quite similar. Apprehensiveness over the dangers of relativism is, however, only voiced in the later paper.

22. Putnam, *Mind, Language and Reality*, 164–65 and notes.

23. In "The Meaning of 'Meaning,'" Putnam's point of departure is Frege's theory of meaning, which is also the backdrop for Kripke's *Naming and Necessity*. But whereas in Kripke's case the Fregean context is indeed indispensable, I have tried to show that Putnam's work grew out of his debate with conventionalism.

24. J. H. Poincaré, "Mathematics and Logic" in Ewald, *From Kant to Hilbert*, 1049.

25. Ibid., 1051.

26. Wittgenstein, *Remarks on the Foundations of Mathematics*, 156, 96.

27. Ludwig Wittgenstein, *Philosophical Investigations*, trans. G. E. M. Anscombe (New York: Macmillan Company, 1970), 242, 88

28. Wittgenstein, *Remarks on the Foundations of Mathematics*, I 74:

> It is as if this expressed the essence of form.—I say, however, if you talk about *essence* —, you are merely noting a convention. But here one would like to retort: there is no greater difference than that between a proposition about the depth of the essence and one about—a mere convention. But what if I reply: to the *depth* that we see in the essence there corresponds the *deep* need for the convention.
>
> Thus, if I say: "It's as if this proposition expressed the *essence* of form"—I mean: it is as if this proposition expressed a property of the entity *form!*—and one can say "the entity of which it asserts a property, and which I here call the entity 'form,' is the picture which I cannot help having when I hear the word 'form.'"

29. Clearly, the discovery of non-Euclidean geometries per se does not constitute a refutation of the axioms of Euclidean geometry, but both Putnam and Poincaré stress that it does imply that beliefs formerly held to be necessary (Putnam's example is the impossibility of returning to the same place when following a straight line in the same direction) have been falsified.

30. Putnam, *Mathematics, Matter and Method*, 93. Putnam does not sanction the locution "necessary falsehood." He uses the term "quasi a priori" for truths once thought to be a priori and now deemed false, but it is significant that he does not qualify the term "truth" itself in a similar way.

31. H. Reichenbach, *The Theory of Relativity and A Priori Knowledge*, trans. M. Reichenbach (Los Angeles: University of California Press, 1920).

32. M. Friedman, *Reconsidering Logical Positivism* (Cambridge: Cambridge University Press, 1999). H. Reichenbach, *The Philosophy of Space and Time*, trans. M. Reichenbach and J. Freud (New York: Dover 1928).

33. See "Equivalence" in Hilary Putnam, *Realism and Reason: Philosophical Papers*, vol. III (Cambridge: Cambridge University, 1983), 26–45 and Hilary Putnam "Truth and Convention: On Davidson's Refutation of Conceptual Relativism," *Dialectica* 41 (1987): 69–77.

34. If we count the null object, there would be eight objects.

35. Putnam seems to be unaware of the similarity between his account of equivalence and Poincaré's original argument.

36. Putnam entertains the idea that "the nature of the world itself explains why it admits of these different interpretations," but ultimately rejects it (*Realism and Reason*, 44).

37. See J. Case, "On the Right Idea of a Conceptual Scheme," *Southern Journal of Philosophy* 35 (1997): 1–18, for an analysis of Putnam's notion of conceptual relativity. I go along with Case in distinguishing conceptual relativity from equivalence, but differ in my characterization of the former.

38. Typically, the reduction works in a few paradigmatic cases, but cannot be carried out in detail across the board. Thus, although physicists believe that in principle, chemistry is reducible to quantum mechanics, they are unable to solve the Schrödinger equation for most atoms, let alone complex molecules. Moreover, even the model case of successful reduction, the reduction of thermodynamics to classical mechanics, is known to raise fundamental problems that are as yet unresolved.

39. This happens, in particular, when the relativist denies the objectivity of logical inference.

40. D. Davidson, *Inquiries into Truth and Interruption* (Oxford: Clarendon Press, 2001), 184.

41. Ibid., 192.

42. See H. Putnam, *The Many Faces of Realism* (LaSalle, IL: Open Court, 1987), 32ff on the metaphor of the dough and the cookie cutter.

43. Ibid., 198.

44. William James "The Dilemma of Determinism," in: *The Will to Believe* (New York: Dover, 1956), 145–83; Ludwig Wittgenstein "Lectures on Freedom of the Will" in: *Philosophical Occasions,* ed. J. C. Klagge and A. Norman (Indianapolis: Hackett, 1993), 429–44. On the view usually referred to as compatibilism (James dubbed it "soft determinism") a free action is simply an action according with our will and there is thus no conflict between determinism and freedom. However, neither James nor Wittgenstein argue from a compatibilist point of view.

REPLY TO YEMIMA BEN-MENAHEM

I was introduced to Yemima Ben-Menahem by Joseph Raz in 1976 when I was in Oxford giving the John Locke Lectures, and we talked philosophy (and she taught me Hebrew, in preparation for my upcoming trip to Jerusalem later that spring) almost every day during that "Hilary Term." Starting in the same year, the year of a memorable conference in honor of the recently deceased Yehoshua Bar-Hillel, I have visited Israel almost every year for at least two weeks, and often for several months, and most of those years also included at least one philosophical conversation with Yemima Ben-Menahem. She has always been a probing, constructively critical, and imaginative interlocutor. As she passed from being a graduate student to becoming a member of the distinguished faculty of the Hebrew University of Jerusalem, these qualities were augmented by increasingly broad and deep scholarship. All of these traits are on display in her brilliant book *Conventionalism*, some of whose themes she briefly recapitulates in the present paper. She shows in that book (and this is something that she briefly summarizes here) that quite incompatible doctrines have been repeatedly lumped together under that rubric. Disentangling the issues enables Ben-Menahem to deal with the fundamental debates about the conventionality or nonconventionality of the metric of space-time, from Poincaré and Reichenbach to Adolf Grünbaum and myself as well as with the (perhaps even more fundamental) debates about whether the rules and axioms of mathematics and logic are or are not "conventional," from Carnap and Quine to the earlier and later Wittgenstein. I agree with virtually everything she says on these topics.

As is appropriate to an essay on my philosophy, she goes into detail here on my own relations to conventionalism, in both senses. In this reply, I will first remind the reader of the two different meanings of "conventionalism" that are in play in her book and in her contribution to this volume (both of which she traces back to Poincaré). Then I will say what my *present* position on the issues she discusses is, and then I will close with some short comments about her paper, focusing on points at which I wish either to correct or to amplify something that she writes about my views.

I. Two Senses of "Conventionalism"

Here are the two senses that Ben-Menahem distinguishes: the first, for ease of reference let us call it "conventionalism₁," "denotes the freedom to choose from among empirically equivalent scientific theories. Such choices are said to be guided by convention, for they are not uniquely determined by logic or observation." The second, let us call it "conventionalism₂," "generally denotes the idea that so called necessary truths, as distinct from ordinary contingent truths, function as definitions or rules of grammar, and are therefore anchored in convention rather than fact." According to Ben-Menahem, "The origin of this daring idea is in the Hilbert-Poincaré conception of the axioms of geometry as *implicit definitions* of the primitive geometrical terms." (For Poincaré, as she emphasizes, the truths of *arithmetic* were, however, *not* conventions in any sense.) She also emphasizes that calling the axioms of geometry "conventions" did not mean that they were asserted to be *true* by convention; for Poincaré and Hilbert implicit definitions are not true or false at all. (It is also worth noting that although Carnap took a strongly conventionalist view of logic in his 1932 piece "The Elimination of Metaphysics Through Logical Analysis of Language,"[1] he too would not have said that theorems of logic were *true*; in fact, prior to the 1930s, when Carnap enthusiastically embraced Tarski's semantical conception of truth, Carnap avoided the concept of truth.[2]) As Ben-Menahem points out, Poincaré was, however, prepared to use the concept of truth for both correct empirical statements and correct mathematical statements (apart from geometrical theorems). These technicalities aside, however, she is right to distinguish two different notions of "conventionalism" here, and this is a very important contribution to clarifying the history of philosophy of science and philosophy of mathematics.

II. My Present Position(s)

1. With Respect to Conventionalism

At the beginning of my "internal realist" period,[3] I used the existence of pairs of equivalent descriptions that have (by Quine's well-known criterion[4]), different "ontologies" as an argument against realism and for "verificationist semantics." My present view is that, on the contrary, it is perfectly possible to be a metaphysical realist (in the sense of rejecting all forms of verificationism, including my "internal realist" version, and all talk of our "making" the world), and to accept the existence of such pairs of descriptions. In present day quantum field theories the existence of such pairs is known as "duality"; one startling example concerns representations of the same system (or at least of what are regarded as correct representations of the same system) that differ in how many dimensions they treat space (or spacetime) as having, and even over whether the particles in the system are or are not bosons.[5] (Of course there are much simpler examples of "equivalent descriptions" with different ontologies, for example my well-known example involving mereological sums that Ben-Menahem mentions.)

Obviously, one can *define* a metaphysical realist as someone who denies the existence of such pairs of equivalent descriptions, and that is what I did in "Realism and Reason."[6] But that now seems to me a bad idea. As I explained in the lecture I gave at a conference in celebration of my eightieth birthday,[7] even if "bosons" and "fermions" are sometimes artifacts of the representation of a quantum mechanical system that we choose, as many physicists contend, the system is mind-independently real, for all that, and each of its states is a mind-independently real condition, albeit one that can be represented in each of these different ways. To accept that these descriptions are both answerable to the very same aspect of reality, that they are "equivalent descriptions" in that sense, is to be a metaphysical realist without capital letters, a realist in one's "metaphysics" (but not a "metaphysical realist" in the technical sense I gave to that phrase in "Realism and Reason" and related publications). And if I have long repented of having once said that "the mind and the world make up the mind and the world," that is because what we actually make up is not the world, but language games, concepts, uses, conceptual schemes. To confuse making up the *notion* of a boson, which is something the scientific community did over time, with making up real quantum mechanical systems is a serious metaphysical error. And of course the point generalizes to all the other cases of "equivalent descriptions"; this is not just a point about recherché examples from quantum mechanics.

One further remark about conventionalism$_1$: "intertranslatability" (mutual relative interpretability) (or, more precisely, intertranslatability preserving observation sentences) is *not* a sufficient condition for equivalence in my sense. (In fact, it is not hard to give examples of pairs of theories that are mutually relatively interpretable that no realistically minded scientist would regard as having the same content. I believe Poincaré's own examples have this character.) In the case of the different pairs of quantum mechanical representations I referred to, the "translations" from the language of one representation into the language of the other do not merely preserve so-called "observation sentences." They also preserve *explanations*. An explanation of a phenomenon goes over into another perfectly good explanation of the same phenomenon under these translations. In my Dublin lecture I said, "But who is to say what is a phenomenon? And who is to say what is a perfectly good explanation? My answer has always been: *physicists* are; not linguists and not philosophers." I do not find any of this in Poincaré.

As I mentioned, "duality" is a controversial phenomenon. It is, of course, conceivable that physicists will someday find reasons to prefer one particular "ontology" to all others (Sheldon Goldstein calls such an ontology a "fundamental ontology"). Of course, physics is not all of human knowledge and even if physics finds a fundamental ontology, examples like the mereological sums example will still persist. And, as I remarked to Goldstein in a recent conversation, "Our problem now is not that we have more than one satisfactory candidate for a 'fundamental ontology,' but that we do not yet have even one."

2. With Respect to Conventionalism

As I make clear in my reply to Hartry Field in the present volume, I believe that the sentences of competently formalized pure mathematics have determinate truth values, regardless of whether it is possible in any particular case for human beings to determine those truth values. But I also believe that the phenomenon of "conceptual relativity" (equivalent descriptions) also appears in pure mathematics. One can formalize mathematics taking sets as primitive, and identify functions with certain sets (there is more than one way of doing that!), or one can take functions as primitive and identify sets with certain functions (again, in more than one way!). And one can even take *modality* (mathematical possibility) as primitive, rather than assume any "abstract objects" at all. There is a role for convention here, but it is a modest one. Whether the Riemann Hypothesis is true or not, and whether the Continuum Hypothesis is true or not, does not and cannot call for a "convention." Whether the integers are to be identified with the von Neumann integers or with some other set theoretic constructs (of the right order type) does call for one.

III. Closing Comments on Ben-Menahem's Essay

(a) Ben-Menahem writes: "Whereas a position that sanctions the stipulation of truth clearly offends against realist intuitions about truth, a more accurate understanding of conventionalism makes it plain that conventionalism does in fact accommodate a realist notion of truth by distinguishing truths properly so called from conventions masquerading as truths." This is correct as far as Poincaré's conventionalism was concerned. Very few American philosophers, regrettably, have read Poincaré with any care (if at all), and no doubt Ben-Menahem's claim is that an important position therefore goes missing in the discussion. But it does go missing. For most American philosophers, "truth by convention" is something that they identify with Carnap as interpreted by Quine. And while Quine is not always the fairest interpreter of Carnap, I do not think that Poincaré's version of conventionalism was defended by Carnap at the time Quine met Carnap, or subsequently. For the 1933 Carnap, "true" was still a term to be avoided in scientific philosophy, and as for a "realist notion of truth," I have noticed that Carnap's favorite examples of "metaphysical" questions (which he regarded as nonsensical) tend to be questions of the form "are so-and-sos (or "is such and such") *real.*" After Carnap's conversion by Tarski, to which I alluded earlier, Carnap held a deflationist conception of truth, and for a deflationist, mathematical sentences and even garden variety "analytic" sentences can still be called "true." (Is "All bachelors are unmarried" true? Well, it is true if and only if all bachelors are unmarried. QED) Ben-Menahem does write, "Carnap put forward a thoroughly conventionalist alternative. He distinguished sharply between the truths expressible in a language and the conventions constituting its structure (formation rules and transformation rules)," but the theorems of logic and mathematics are not "formation rules and transformation rules." After he accepted Tarskian semantics, Carnap did call some of them "meaning postulates"; but meaning postulates are within the scope of the truth predicate; they are true analytic sentences, in Carnap's view.

That a deflationist cannot be a "realist" is also far from obvious. In brief, I am not sure I know what Ben-Menahem means by "a realist conception of truth." And I do not know whether Carnap's post-Tarski position counts as "conventionalism" in her sense, although it obviously has conventionalist aspects. I think that Ben-Menahem needs to say more about what "conventionalism" comes to after Tarski enters the picture.

(b) Ben-Menahem raises the interesting question as to whether Weinberg's "flat space time" quantum field theory and General Relativity (GR) are equivalent descriptions. The answer is that in their present form, they certainly are not, and not just because Weinberg's theory includes quantum mechanics and GR does not. A deeper reason is that Weinberg's theory, by excluding spatial curvature thereby excludes black holes. That GR allows for black holes (and even predicts them, under certain circumstances) was shown by Schwarzschild in 1916—one year after Einstein produced GR.

(c) Ben-Menahem writes, "It is only on the pragmatic view according to which fact and (cognitive) value have parity as indicators of truth that the need to comply with desiderata such as simplicity can serve as an argument *against* discretion." I agree completely, but this aspect of pragmatism, I wish to emphasize, does not appeal to or depend on the several "pragmatist theories of truth," all of which I find unacceptable. It depends on the pragmatist rejection of noncognitivism with respect to values plus the equally pragmatist insight that facts and values (including cognitive values) are entangled.

(d) Ben-Menahem is absolutely right that I was dissatisfied with my claim (that I made in a paper contesting Grünbaum's views) that "reference is fixed by coherence." This section of her essay is truly rewarding reading!

(e) Ben-Menahem portrays me as coming closer and closer to conventionalism as my philosophy "ripens," and this is not a picture I can accept. (This is my one real disagreement with her essay.) Thus whereas she claims that "It should come as no surprise that the ripening of internal realism has made Putnam more suspicious of ontology insofar as it purports to make claims that are absolute and language independent. Identifying examples of conceptual relativity that illustrate the relativity of ontology to schemes of representation thus becomes exceedingly important for him. In this endeavor, however, the conventionalist is no longer an opponent, but rather a source of inspiration." The problem with this goes beyond the fact that my interest in "identifying examples of conceptual relativity" grew precisely as I was *returning* to metaphysical realism (even if I called it "common sense realism," or sometimes even "pragmatic realism," but not all my readers were fooled!), and not when my "internal realism was ripening." What "the relativity of ontology to schemes of representation" shows, in my present view, is not that conventionalism is right, but that, at least in fundamental physics, it is states of affairs that are fundamental and not objects. (Brian Skyrms long ago called this "Tractarian Nominalism."[8])

(f) Ben-Menahem closes by asking my attitude towards what she calls "radical pluralism" and explains thus: "A restricted pluralism will approve of alternative descriptions only when they are known to be compatible. If ordinary time is indeed incompatible with relativistic time, one of these concepts must go. Similarly, if the discourse of freedom is to be tolerated, it must be shown to be compatible with our best scientific theory. More radical pluralism that makes room for autonomous discourses that cannot be harmonized will forgo the demand for consistency in such cases." My answer is that I am definitely a "restricted pluralist." She worries that the relativistic picture of spacetime may be incompatible with our ordinary conceptions and with our conception of our freedom, but I do not share those worries. Relativistic physics does not imply that our ordinary statements about before and after lack sense, and it does not imply that statements about future events are "already true." (As Quine saw, what it implies is that the truth value of statements about events, past present and future, is *tenseless*, although Einstein himself seems not to have grasped the difference in some of his popular utterances.) In sum, I have no use for the idea of genuinely incompatible "truths."

H.P.

NOTES

1. "The Elimination of Metaphysics Through Logical Analysis of Language" in A. J. Ayer, *Logical Positivism* (Glencoe, IL: The Free Press, 1959), 61–81.

2. Ruth Anna Putnam's and my conversations with Carnap lead me to believe that prior to this point Carnap regarded the notion of truth as "metaphysical"; Thomas Ricketts has a different view, however. See his "Carnap: From Logical Syntax to Semantics" in *Origins of Logical Empiricism*, ed. Ronald N. Giere and Alan W. Richardson (Minneapolis: University of Minnesota Press, 1996), 231–50. Ricketts, however, did not have the benefit of hearing Carnap reminisce, as Ruth Anna and I did.

3. *I* date my "internal realist" period as starting with my giving "Realism and Reason" as an Address to the Eastern Division of the American Philosophical Association in December 1976 and ending with my reply to Simon Blackburn at the Gifford Conference in St. Andrews in 1990 (reprinted in Peter Clark and Robert Hale, *Reading Putnam* [Oxford: Blackwell, 1994]), in which I described the idea that true statements are those that we would "converge" to were conditions to become more and more ideal as an unfortunate "concession to verificationism." I explained my reasons for giving it up in detail in my 1994 Dewey Lectures.

4. Quine's famous criterion for ascertaining a theory's "ontological commitments" was first stated by him in "On What There Is," *Review of Metaphysics* 2 (1948/1949): 21–38; collected in his *From a Logical Point of View* (Cambridge, MA: Harvard University Press, 1953).

5. Cliff P. Burgess and Fernando Quevedo, "Bosonization as Duality," *Nuclear Physics* B421 (1994): 373–90.

6. For example, in "Realism and Reason."

7. Conference in honor of the 80th Birthday of Hilary Putnam at University College Dublin, March 11–14, 2007. The lecture was titled "From Quantum Mechanics to Ethics and Back Again."

8. Brian Skyrms, "Tractarian Nominalism," *Philosophical Studies* 40, no. 2 (Sept. 1981): 199–206.

13

Tim Maudlin

CONFESSIONS OF A HARDCORE, UNSOPHISTICATED METAPHYSICAL REALIST

I. In Defense of Metaphysical Realism

It goes without saying—although there is a point in repeating it here—that one cannot write an essay simply about "Hilary Putnam's view on x" for any significant x. Putnam has wrestled with the deepest problems in philosophy for many years, and in that struggle has been wise enough and honest enough to change his views, so my topic must perforce be Putnam's view during some delimited period. I have chosen the latter part of the 1970s for purely autobiographical reasons: I read the essay, "Realism and Reason," in graduate school during a formative stage of my philosophical career, and it left an indelible impression. I hope it might be useful to go back to that essay and reflect on the issues it raises.

"Realism and Reason" appears to mark a critical change in Putnam's views. In "The John Locke Lectures" at Oxford in early 1976, Putnam used the unadorned term "realism" as shorthand for what "is often called 'scientific realism' by its proponents,"[1] and the lectures are largely a defense of this form of realism. But by the time of the Paul Carus Lectures in 1985 (published under the title, *The Many Faces of Realism*), the "Scientific Realist" has become cast as the evil "Seducer" in a nineteenth-century melodrama, tempting the "Innocent Maiden," Common Sense, but leaving her at last bereft of her world of pink ice cubes and chairs.[2] "Realism and Reason," written in the fall of 1976, appears to mark the decisive shift. In one dramatic paragraph of that paper, Putnam declares that he has "given to Dummett all he needs to demolish metaphysical realism—a picture I was wedded to!"[3] Putnam's response is to let metaphysical realism go, retaining only internal realism: "*Internal realism is all the realism we want or need.*"[4] At this point we need a program to keep track of the players: metaphysical realism is definitely out, internal realism definitely in, and scientific realism (the hero of the Locke Lectures and villain of the Carus Lectures) has gone missing altogether. So it is a worthwhile project to begin by sorting out these various forms of realism in order to assess the virtues ascribed to them and the charges against them.

It would be helpful to begin by characterizing the sort of philosophical theory realism (of any stripe) is supposed to be, but even here matters are murky. Is realism a *semantic* thesis or an *epistemic* claim? And what does one even mean by "semantics"? In one sense, any theory of how sentences in a language acquire truth values qualifies as "semantics." But Putnam often uses the term also when discussing theories of *understanding*: under what conditions can a language user properly be said to understand a sentence? At the beginning of "Realism and Reason," Putnam characterizes the "canonical versions" of metaphysical realism as postulating the necessary conditions for understanding a term as "knowing what piece of THE WORLD it refers to (or in knowing a necessary and sufficient condition for it to refer to a piece of THE WORLD, in some versions)."[5] But he also immediately goes on to exclude this account of understanding from his characterization of metaphysical realism: "I shall not assume this account of understanding to be part of the picture in what follows, although it certainly was assumed by metaphysical realists in the past."[6] This abandonment of any truth-conditional account of understanding comports well with the conclusions of "The Meaning of 'Meaning.'" There we are taught that the conditions required to be accepted as a competent user of terms such as "tiger" and "elm" in English have nothing at all to do with the conditions which determine the referents of those terms. Indeed, what is required to "know the meaning" of a term is a highly variable and context-dependent affair, which no general theory can articulate.

Unfortunately, "Realism and Reason" does not really set the theory of understanding aside. Indeed, the argumentation in the critical paragraph cited above appears to rest crucially on a particular theory of understanding:

> The point is that Dummett and I *agree* that you can't treat understanding a sentence (in general) as knowing its truth conditions; because it then becomes unintelligible what *that* knowledge *in turn* consists in. We both *agree* that the theory of understanding has to be done in a verificationist way. . . . But now it looks as if in conceding that *some* sort of verificationist semantics must be given as our account of understanding (or 'linguistic competence',

in Chomsky's sense), I have given Dummett all he needs to demolish meta-physical realism.[7]

The most sympathetic reader may encounter some cognitive dissonance at this point. If metaphysical realism is *not* characterized as committed to any particular theory of understanding, how could the acceptance of a verifica-tionist theory of understanding undermine it? And were not the verification-ists exactly the same philosophers who insisted that understanding a term consisted in knowing the conditions under which the term could be truly as-cribed to an object, conditions spelled out in terms of observable conditions? So is not a verificationist semantics exactly the semantics ascribed to the metaphysical realist? (It does not help matters much that a page earlier Put-nam says that he is using "verificationist semantics" in the place of "nonreal-ist semantics.") We need a place to get a firm foothold amidst the terminology.

Let us start again. Instead of focusing on what metaphysical realism is not, we should examine what it is. Putnam characterizes the position as committed to two theses:

> Minimally, however, there has to *be* a determinate relation of *reference* between terms in L and pieces (or sets of pieces) of THE WORLD, on the metaphysical realist model, whether *understanding* L is taken to consist in 'knowing' that relation or not. What makes this picture different from *internal* realism (which employs a similar picture *within* a theory) is that (1) the picture is supposed to apply to *all* correct theories at once (so that it can only be stated with 'typical ambiguity'—i.e. it transcends complete formalization in any one theory); and (2) THE WORLD is supposed to be *independent* of any particular representation we have of it—indeed, it is held that we might be *unable* to represent THE WORLD correctly at all (e.g. we might all be 'brains in a vat', the metaphysical realist tells us).

> The most important consequence of metaphysical realism is that *truth* is sup-posed to be *radically non-epistemic*—we might be 'brains in a vat' and so the theory that is 'ideal' from the point of view of operational utility, inner beauty and elegance, 'plausibility', simplicity, 'conservatism', etc., *might be false*. 'Verified' (in any operational sense) does not imply 'true', on the meta-physical realist picture, even in the ideal limit.

> It is this feature that distinguishes metaphysical realism, as I am using the term, from the mere belief that there *is* an ideal theory (Peircean realism), or, more weakly, that an ideal theory is a regulative ideal presupposed by the notions 'true' and 'objective' as they have classically been understood. And it is this feature that I shall attack![8]

We now have something quite concrete to discuss. The metaphysical realist thinks that an *operationally* ideal theory, a theory ideal *as far as we can tell*, might actually be false. This is a thesis that appears to be clear and concise. It is also a thesis that I take to be true, and took to be true as a graduate student. So the most enduring impact "Realism and Reason" had on me, despite its intent, was to make me a confirmed metaphysical realist.

What I would like to do is articulate the reasons why I take metaphysical realism to be correct, but first it will be best to distinguish some preliminary issues. For this purpose, I propose to define several kinds of realism. These definitions are my own, and do not purport to exactly follow Putnam's usage.

(1) *Internal Realism* is the thesis that any acceptable account of the world should explain how language use helps people to prosper in their interactions with the world.

(2) *Metaphysical Realism* is the thesis that at least some significant parts of language have definite truth conditions such that it is possible for an operationally ideal theory, stated in this part of the language, to be false.

(3) *Mild Scientific Realism* is the thesis that most scientific theories that meet a certain standard of evidential support (there is debate over how to characterize this) are true or approximately true (there is debate over "approximately true").

(4) *Optimistic Scientific Realism* is Mild Scientific Realism plus the claim that for every interesting fundamental question about the world, unfettered rational inquiry would eventually yield a unique scientific theory that settles the question and obtains the level of evidential support constitutive of Mild Scientific Realism.

(5) *Peircean Realism* is Optimistic Scientific Realism together with the thesis that the true theory *is nothing but* the theory that would eventually be accepted by unfettered rational inquiry.

Peircean Realism contradicts Metaphysical Realism, but Metaphysical Realism is compatible both with Mild and Optimistic Scientific Realism and with their denials. I take Scientific Realism to be primarily an epistemic claim, about the reliability of theories that meet a certain evidential threshold. A radical skeptic is a metaphysical realist who denies even the mildest form of Scientific Realism: no amount of "evidential support" gives us good reason to accept a theory as true, or approximately true. This comports with Putnam's remarks about brain-in-a-vat scenarios. But the brain-in-a-vat is not the most powerful weapon in the metaphysical realist's arsenal. As Putnam notes, articulating a semantic theory, i.e. a theory of truth conditions, for the brain is nontrivial: "Suppose we (and all other sentient beings) are and always were 'brains in a vat'. Then how does it come about that *our* word 'vat' refers to *noumenal* vats and not to vats in the image?"[9]

The metaphysical realist can sidestep this difficulty by using another familiar skeptical scenario. Suppose the universe as a whole began just six thousand years ago in exactly the physical state that actually obtained six thousand years ago. All that the metaphysical realist needs to have granted is that this is, in an appropriate sense, a possibility. If that is how the universe began, then unfettered rational scientific inquiry into the universe will still lead to the very same conclusions as it does in the actual world: reasonable people would conclude that the universe is much, much older than six thousand years. The theory that the universe is at least billions of years old has as much operational utility (no matter how that is understood) as, and more elegance, plausibility, simplicity, etc., than the alternative "young universe" theory. So if the "young universe" theory *could* be true, then the more operationally ideal theory *could* be false, as the metaphysical realist maintains.

The "young universe" theory does not face the same problem with semantics as the brain-in-a-vat scenario: the terms "rock," "star," and "planet" refer to exactly the same sorts of the things irrespective of the age of the universe. The relevant linguistic practices would have developed in identical physical circumstances. But the sentence, "There were many stars in existence six million years ago," is true if the universe is as the best confirmed theory says it is, and false if the "young universe" theory is correct. It would be false in such circumstances even though any reasonable researcher would accept it.

How could Putnam come to deny such a possibility? The line of argument seems to be the following. Begin with an operationally ideal theory, that is, a theory upon which reasonable researchers would eventually agree. The metaphysical realist insists, as we have seen, that such a theory could nonetheless be false. But Putnam points out that so long as the cardinality of elements of "THE WORLD" is consistent with the ideal theory, there are model-theoretic interpretations of the language that use elements of "THE WORLD" as the domain of the interpretation and make the operationally ideal theory come out true. He wonders how one could possibly reject such an interpretation as a *correct* interpretation of the language:

> So, the interpretation of 'reference' in L as SAT [one of the interpretation functions that makes the operationally ideal theory true] certainly meets all *operational* constraints on reference. But the interpretation of 'reference' as SAT certainly meets all *theoretical* constraints on reference—it makes the *ideal* theory, T_1, come out *true*.
>
> So what *further* constraints on reference are there that could single out some other interpretation as (uniquely) 'intended', and SAT as an 'unintended'

interpretation (in the model-theoretic sense of 'interpretation')? The supposition that even an 'ideal' theory (from a pragmatic point of view) might
really be false appears to collapse into *unintelligibility*.[10]

The problem with this argument is that it begs the central question. The
metaphysical realist certainly does not admit as a theoretical constraint on
intended interpretations that they make a *pragmatically* ideal theory come
out true; it is the metaphysical realist's central contention that such an ideal
theory need not be true! As to the relevant further constraints on intended
interpretations, we have just mentioned an extremely plausible candidate:
supervenience on the relevant local physical situation of the language users. Since the language users in the "young universe" and "old universe"
scenarios live in locally identical circumstances, it is plausible that the
intended referents of terms such as "star," "year," and "ago" would be the
same. So the truth conditions of "There were stars six million years ago"
should be the same. And since nothing existed six million years ago in the
"young universe" scenario, that sentence is false, even though it passes all
pragmatic verifications.

From this perspective, the brain-in-a-vat scenario attempts to establish
the same conclusion, but with a much narrower supervenience base: the
physical state of a single language user's brain. The considerations brought
forward in "The Meaning of 'Meaning'" have undercut the plausibility of
such a narrow supervenience base. But nothing in that essay would similarly
rule out the much wider supervenience base employed here. Speakers in
the "young universe" and "old universe" scenarios mean the same thing by
"There were stars six million years ago," and given what they mean, this
perfectly reasonable belief is false in the "young universe" setting.

If we accept this conclusion, then Peircean Realism is also refuted.
Rational inquirers can suffer epistemic bad luck: doing the best they can,
accepting the most reasonable and best confirmed hypotheses, they still
may settle on false beliefs. This conclusion is, however, compatible with
both Mild and Optimistic Scientific Realism, since these theses only assert the general reliability of well-confirmed theories, not some necessary
guarantee of their truth.

What then is the status of the supposed theoretical constraint on reference, that is, that the intended interpretation of a pragmatically ideal theory
make the theory come out true? It is a close cousin of the so-called "principle
of charity" that is sometimes postulated as a regulative principle for translation: translate a language in such a way as to maximize the number of the
speaker's beliefs that come out true. Stated baldly this way, the principle
has nothing evident to recommend it. Take the following example: Aristotle
believed something expressed by Greek equivalent of the sentence "water

is homoiomerous." If we understand "homoiomerous" in the obvious way, given its etymology, Aristotle's belief was false; water is not divisible into arbitrarily small parts all of which are water. Aristotle's belief, on this understanding, is incompatible with both the atomic theory of matter and the molecular structure of water. Now it would no doubt be possible to translate "homoiomerous" in some other way so as to make the belief come out true, for example, as "effectively homogeneous at mesoscopic scale." But I contend that making this belief come out true carries *zero* weight when evaluating possible translations. Aristotle was not in a position to have any reliable access to the microscopic structure of water. Since there is no particular reason to think he would have gotten the theory of microscopic structure right, there is no pressure at all to translate his pronouncements on that topic in such a way that they come out true.

Similarly, the ancients believed that the sun moved through the sky. That belief, as Copernicus argued, was false. But a clever translator could contend that "moves" (or the correlative term in the original language) ought to be translated "is in relative motion with respect to observers on Earth." Under such a translation the belief is made true, but the history of science is made hash.

I do not pretend to have a general account of translation, but only observe that the "principle of charity" as I have formulated it has no plausibility. And I see no reason why things change if the theory being translated (or interpreted) is pragmatically ideal. If we live in a young universe, then the pragmatically ideal theory is still the old universe theory: it is the simplest and most elegant, and exactly as empirically adequate as the young universe theory. The model-theoretic considerations Putnam mentions do show that the old universe theory would have many models whose domain is the young universe. But for all that, those models do not provide the intended interpretation of the old universe theory, exactly because the old universe theory *ought to* come out false.

The normative prescription behind the "principle of charity"—try to make the beliefs held by the speaker come out true—also seems to motivate the position Putnam calls "sophisticated realism." In "Realism and Reason," he considers two theories of the fundamental geometrical structure of a world that is a single line. Story 1 contends that there are spatial points in this world, and that the whole world (the line) is the mereological sum of those points. Some collections of points constitute extended segments (that is, intervals) of the line, but there are single points of measure zero as well. The points themselves are mereologically atomic elements of the world according to Story 1. Story 2 contends that there are no points; there are only counterparts of what Story 1 would call intervals and collections of intervals. There are no atomic parts of the geometry according to Story 2, since every interval contains proper subintervals. Every geometrical part of the world has a measurable extension.[11]

Putnam comments:

> A 'hard-core' realist might claim that there is a 'fact of the matter' as to which is true—Story 1 or Story 2. But 'sophisticated realists', as I have called them, concede that Story 1 and Story 2 are 'equivalent descriptions'. In effect, this concedes that line segments are a suitable set of 'invariants'—a description of THE WORLD which says what is going on in every line segment is a *complete* description. In the past, I argued that this is no problem for the realist—it's just like the fact that the earth can be mapped by different 'projections', I said (Mercator, Polar, etc.).[12]

The passage goes on to renounce this conciliatory move: the price of allowing both Story 1 and Story 2 to be true, despite their apparent incompatibility, is to make THE WORLD as-it-is-in-itself ineffable. Every feature we can (truly) ascribe to it would be only theory-relative.

But the question is why one would be tempted to adopt "sophisticated realism" in the first place. Story 1, which asserts the existence of geometrical parts with zero measure, flatly contradicts Story 2, which denies the existence of such parts. Our initial reaction is that the truth of Story 1 precludes that of Story 2 and vice versa. This immediate reaction is blunted by Putnam's decision to make the narrator of Story 2 a sophisticated realist:

> 'Of course,' the teller of this story says, 'I'm not saying Story 1 is *false*. You just have to understand that *points* are logical constructions out of line segments. Point talk is highly derived talk about convergent sets of line segments.'[13]

But according to the hardcore, unsophisticated realist, this is incorrect. Indeed, contemporary defenders of Story 2 (which goes under the moniker "gunk") argue for its superiority exactly because it endorses *fewer* geometrical facts and possibilities than Story 1. For example, if Story 1 is true, then there are four distinct geometrical possibilities for the one-dimensional world: an endpoint in both directions, in neither direction, or in only one of the two directions. But Story 2 cannot acknowledge these as distinct possibilities, since they differ only on a set of measure zero. The sophisticated realist wants to dismiss these as real differences—but on what grounds? Since Putnam does not say, we must cast about for a motivation.

One possible motivation is epistemic. Let us suppose that there is a real, factual question about whether the actual world has point-like spatial (or spatiotemporal) parts. It is plausible that no empirical test will be able to uncontroversially settle this question. The postulation (or denial) of such points may make the physical theory simpler or more elegant, but it seems unlikely that any observable phenomenon either requires or is incompatible with them. So if one takes the difference between the stories to be factual, one is less likely to be an optimistic scientific realist. Conversely, if one can argue that Story 1 and Story 2 do not really contradict each other, then ongoing scientific research need not decide between them. The Peircean ideal of eventual convergence on all *real factual* disputes becomes commensurately more plausible.

The hardcore, unsophisticated realist is not moved by these considerations. The attempt to *define* truth by reference to convergence on the ideal limit is a nonstarter for this troglodyte, and the likelihood of such convergence (as the optimistic scientific realist expects) seems dim. It is a plain fact that physicists are *not* converging on a fundamental physical ontology, as any survey of opinions about quantum theory reveals. Furthermore, the existence of incompatible physical theories that are either fundamentally or practically indistinguishable by experiment is real and widespread. For example, theories about the spatiotemporal location of an electron radically diverge: according to some particle ontologies, an electron is a point particle, whose world line is one-dimensional; according to a more field-like ontology (the "matter density ontology"), an electron is "smeared out" in space; according to the so-called "flash" ontology, an electron is only spatially located at a series of discrete point events; and one could fatten up a point particle or a flash to give it a three-dimensional volume without affecting the observable predictions.[14] The hardcore, unsophisticated realist thinks that it is remarkable that we are able to confidently discover *anything* about the universe, and sees no reason at all to expect we will eventually discover *everything*.

The wildly optimistic view that even ideal rational inquiry would eventually settle all questions about the structure of the world, and furthermore settle them *correctly*, seems to be a vestigial remnant of logical empiricism. If the cognitive meaning of any contingent sentence must be equivalent to some set of claims made in an "observation language," then a sufficient amount of observation would settle all meaningful contingent questions. But once the empiricist theory of meaning has been abandoned, the epistemic situation swings back in favor of the skeptic. All actual empirical evidence is compatible with alternative, incompatible theories. It is doubtful that any extraempirical virtues (such as simplicity or elegance, etc.) will anoint exactly one among these empirically adequate competitors, and even if by chance that happens, it is not analytic that the anointed champion will be true.

The hardcore, unsophisticated metaphysical realist is therefore a fallibilist through and through. He (or she) is never a Peircean realist, and most unlikely to be an optimistic scientific realist. The only epistemological options left are

Mild Scientific Realism and outright skepticism concerning the prospects for eventual scientific consensus and the reliability of whatever theories such consensus might endorse.

This particular hardcore, unsophisticated metaphysical realist (for this is, after all, a confession) is a mild scientific realist. Even in the absence of any complete, uncontroversial confirmation theory, and bereft of crystal balls, I believe that certain scientific conclusions are here to stay, and that they are correct. For example, no matter the vicissitudes of fundamental physics, the atomic theory of matter, including the claim that water has a molecular structure made up of two hydrogen atoms and one oxygen, will never be overturned. This claim will be accounted as true no matter what the fine structure of electrons, protons, and neutrons happen to be. And I think this claim *is* true. I do not believe this on account of some principle of charity in interpretation, but because of the central role of the atomic theory in explaining such a huge variety of observable phenomena. Similar remarks apply to the structure of DNA, the attendant account of cellular reproduction, the basic outline of evolutionary theory, and so on. These theories represent permanent and accurate triumphs of scientific theorizing, and our inability to confidently discover the structure of the universe at all scales of time and space does not detract from them.

The Putnam of "Reason and Realism" rejects the idea that "THE WORLD" has some objective, mind-independent structure that scientific inquiry can aim to discover. The hardcore, unsophisticated metaphysical realist believes in exactly such a structure, which includes the atomic structure of matter and the double-helix form of DNA. (The hardcore, unsophisticated metaphysical realist is also puzzled about the significance of capitalizing the letters in "THE WORLD.") It seems to him that a scientific realist of any stripe makes a mistake by becoming "sophisticated," that is, by insisting that *prima facie* incompatible ontological accounts must be really somehow compatible if they are equally able to save the phenomena. Geometrical theories that assert and deny the existence of points fall in this category: the sophisticate, in trying to maintain that somehow they could both be true, is left having to concede that "THE WORLD," in itself, neither has nor fails to have points. Our unwashed, belch-at-the-table metaphysical realist has none of this: the universe either has fundamental space-time points or it does not, and if we cannot tell which, we should just suck it up and admit uncertainty.

It is curious that Putnam chose the example of Mercator and Polar projections to illustrate the variety of theories that the sophisticate is willing to countenance. These projections present no difficulty at all: given the different representational conventions involved, the various maps can all represent the earth as having exactly the same geography. These projections do not even *appear* to present alternative, incompatible accounts of, say, the relative surface areas of the various continents. Story 1 and Story 2, in contrast, are presented as flatly contradictory: Story 1 asserts and Story 2 denies that there are points. The unsophisticated, hardcore metaphysical realist takes these claims at face value, and cannot regard both stories as true. Perhaps the preponderance of evidence will favor one account over the other, in which case our realist may endorse it. But as befits the metaphysical realist, no matter how extensive the evidence there will always be room for doubt.

II. How the Scientific Realist Became the Villain

I have tried to defend hardcore, unsophisticated Metaphysical Realism against the arguments brought forward in "Realism and Reason." But the term "scientific realism" does not appear in that paper, so the status of scientific realism (however one might construe it) would still be an open question. However, as noted above, by the time *The Many Faces of Realism* is written, the scientific realist is cast as the Snidely Whiplash of philosophy, seducing and then abandoning poor commonsense. What can we make of these charges?

The Many Faces of Realism begins with Arthur Eddington's famous pair of tables: the table of the man on the street, who envisages it as "*mostly* solid matter," and the table of physics, which is described as "mostly empty space."[15] Putnam describes Wilfrid Sellars's view of the situation as similar to Eddington's: there is a death struggle between these two tables which only one can survive. According to Sellars, writes Putnam, we should "deny that there are tables at all as we ordinarily conceive them."[16] And Putnam goes on to attribute this understanding of the situation to the scientific realist:

> But when they have travelled together for a little while the 'Scientific Realist' breaks the news that what the Maiden is going to get *isn't* her ice cubes and tables and chairs. In fact, all there *really* is—the Scientific Realist tells her over breakfast—is what 'finished science' will say there is—whatever that may be. She is left with a promissory note for She Knows Not What, and the assurance that even if there *aren't* tables and chairs, still there are some *Dinge an sich* that her 'manifest image' (or her 'folk physics', as some Scientific Realists put it) 'picture'. Some will say that the lady has been had.[17]

Putnam immediately assures us that not all forms of realism act so caddishly towards common sense: some forms of realism maintain that there *really are* tables and pink ice cubes. But the term, "scientific realist," has been affixed to the position that somehow wants to deny the very existence of middle-sized furniture. Since I want to defend a form of Mild Scientific Realism, I am interested in refuting this particular charge.

The problem originates with Eddington. He begins: "I have settled down to the task of writing these lectures and have drawn up my chairs to my two tables."[18] But of course there are not two tables. From this beginning, it would appear that acceptance of the "scientific table" must perforce entail the *nonexistence* of the "commonsense table," lest the world become over-populated. And indeed, Eddington states directly that "modern physics has by delicate test and remorseless logic assured me that my second scientific table is the only one which is really there."[19]

But Eddington also has the good sense to take this back:

> "You speak paradoxically of two worlds. Are they not really two aspects or two interpretations of one and the same world?"
>
> Yes, no doubt they are ultimately to be identified after some fashion. But the process by which the external world of physics is transformed into a world of familiar acquaintance in human consciousness is outside the scope of physics.[20]

Even Eddington does not mean to deprive common sense of ice cubes and tables. Rather, he simply finds a striking way to illustrate how unexpected the microscopic structure of tables has turned out to be.

And common sense, being sensible, will not feel bereft. If common sense conceptualizes tables as solid through and through, she also recognizes this belief as idle speculation. After all, common sense knows that she cannot see, or otherwise directly perceive, the microscopic structure of things. The microscopic structure of tables is not, in Sellars's terminology, part of the manifest image of the world, which is how the world seems before we begin to postulate unobservable entities. So no theoretical account of that microscopic structure could possibly conflict with the manifest image, or require its renunciation.

The opening passages of *The Many Faces of Realism* suggest an apparently irreconcilable conflict between science and common sense by means of a dangerously ambiguous locution.

> One reaction to this state of affairs [i.e. Eddington's two tables], the reaction of Wilfrid Sellars, is to deny that there are tables at all as we ordinarily conceive them . . . The commonsense conception of ordinary middle-sized material objects such as tables and ice cubes (the 'manifest image') is simply *false* in Sellars's view (although not without at least some cognitive value—there are real objects that the 'tables' and 'ice cubes' of the manifest image 'picture',

according to Sellars, even if these real objects are not the layman's tables and ice cubes). I don't agree with this view of Sellars's.[21]

To "deny that there are tables at all as we ordinarily conceive them" can be read in two ways. On one reading, it is to say that tables, that is, the things you conceive of under the term or concept, "table," do not exist. This seems to be a reading ascribed to the scientific realist, by which he deprives common sense of her ontology. But the more pedestrian reading is just to deny that tables are *as one conceives them to be*, that is to assert that one has some false beliefs about tables. And if common sense thinks that tables are homogeneously solid through and through and at all spatial scales, then she is indeed misinformed about tables. To repeat: such a belief about tables is not part of the manifest image of the world—tables do not present themselves to perception as having *any* particular microscopic structure. But if Maiden Common Sense has fallen into such a misapprehension, she should be grateful to have the mistake corrected, and not get the vapors upon being so informed.

Of course, if the "commonsense conception" of tables is that they are homogenously solid at microscopic scale, then the commonsense conception *is* simply *false*, and I cannot imagine that Putnam really wants to disagree. The disagreement seems to be about whether there are tables *at all*, and it is hard to imagine any participant in the melodrama wanting to deny this. The scientific realist, after all, claims that we have discovered some interesting and surprising facts about the microstructure *of tables*. There is no scientific classification of the Loch Ness Monster, and there would be no scientific account of the structure of tables if there were no such things.

Let me, then, rewrite the script of the melodrama as I think it should go. The scientific realist does not leave common sense only with a promissory note for It Knows Not What, and certainly does not say that the world is "what finished science will say it is." The scientific realist does not recognize such a state as "finished science," or refer to any "ideal limit." Even theories that are established beyond reasonable doubt—such as the atomic theory of matter—are never beyond further test. And a theory that has passed all possible tests *could still be wrong*, as the metaphysical realist insists.

The scientific realist will not, then, deprive common sense of her tables. The scientific realist will offer the best account we have at present about the structure of tables, and encourage commonsense to keep an open mind and to follow current thinking about the physical structure of the world. As time goes on, one hopes, better data will become available, more discriminating experiments possible, and more theoretical possibilities carefully mapped. All of this work might lead to more consensus or it might not. The scientific realist merely believes that this is the best that can be done given our situation, and the mildly optimist scientific realist believes that it is good enough to uncover at least some interesting facts about what there is. That, I confess, is the position I find myself in today.

Perhaps all of this discussion of Metaphysical Realism has a slightly musty odor about it. Perhaps everything I have confessed to and tried to defend in this essay seems mild, and even uncontroversial, today. If so, let the essay stand as a reminder of another time in philosophy. When I first read "Realism and Reason," the great debate in philosophy of science was between realism and antirealism, and the antirealists, at that time, seemed to have the upper hand. Indeed, realism was portrayed as both reactionary and naïve; science was widely regarded as a series of ideologically driven Kuhnian revolutions leading nowhere in particular. At that time, it was not popular to be a metaphysical realist, or a scientific realist of any stripe. And it pained me personally to be (or at least to seem to be) on opposite sides in this debate from Putnam, whose work I ardently admired.

I am under no illusion that I have provided a complete and coherent account of either Metaphysical or Scientific Realism here. I have assumed that there is such a thing as an intended interpretation of terms like "star," "year," and "ago" that is precise enough to render "There were stars six million years ago" false in the young universe scenario, but I have not even attempted to provide an account of how such an interpretation is fixed. I have adverted to empirical support for scientific theories, but have not provided an explicit theory of confirmation. And I have focused exclusively on questions of physical ontology, leaving aside the problems of values and norms that greatly concerned Putnam.

But physical ontology is a wide and fascinating field. I cannot, myself, see how to work in that field without being a metaphysical realist and a mild scientific realist to boot. If I took to heart the rejection of Metaphysical Realism found in "Realism and Reason," I would have to abandon the philosophical projects I have embarked upon. Like most confessions, this one is also an attempt at self-justification. I leave it in the hands of the reader to render judgment on that score.

TIM MAUDLIN

NEW YORK UNIVERSITY
SEPTEMBER 2010

NOTES

1. Hilary Putnam, *Meaning and the Moral Sciences* (London: Routledge & Kegan Paul, 1978), 19.

2. See Hilary Putnam, *The Many Faces of Realism: The Paul Carus Lectures* (LaSalle: Open Court, 1987), 4.

3. Putnam, *Meaning and the Moral Sciences*, 129.

4. Ibid., 130.

5. Ibid., 124.

6. Ibid., 124.

7. Ibid., 129.

8. Ibid., 125.

9. Ibid., 127.

10. Ibid., 126.

11. See ibid., 130–31.

12. Ibid., 131–32.

13. Ibid., 131.

14. See Valia Allori, Sheldon Goldstein, Roderich Tumulka, and Nino Zanghi, "On the Common Structure of Bohmian Mechanics and the Ghirardi-Rimini-Weber Theory," *British Journal for the Philosophy of Science* 59, no. 3 (2008): 353–89.

15. Putnam, *The Many Faces of Realism*, 3.

16. Ibid., 3.

17. Ibid., 4.

18. Arthur Stanley Eddington, *The Nature of the Physical World: The Gifford Lectures* (New York: The Macmillan Company, 1929), ix.

19. Ibid., xii.

20. Ibid.

21. Putnam, *The Many Faces of Realism*, 3.

REPLY TO TIM MAUDLIN

I remember reading Tim Maudlin's *Quantum Non-Locality and Relativity*[1] about the time it was published (1994), and being, as they say, "bowled over." The power of the thought, the clarity of the writing, and the courageous willingness to swim against the stream of received opinion[2] that were evident in every chapter evoked, and continue to evoke, my highest admiration. My "A Philosopher Looks at Quantum Mechanics (Again)"[3] and "Quantum Mechanics and Ontology"[4] acknowledge the importance of Maudlin's work for my own reflections on the philosophy of physics. The same traits are fully evident in Maudlin's more recent book, *The Metaphysics within Physics*,[5] a book that inspired me to send him a message (with the subject line "Best summer reading since *The Girl with the Dragon Tattoo*") saying that I loved the book, was stunned by the conclusions, but was sympathetic to them, and wanted to think them over. (I continue to be sympathetic to them, by the way.)

The clarity and power that I have been speaking of are fully evident in the present essay. If I were still an "antirealist," I would be very disturbed by Maudlin's conclusions, but, as I wrote in my Reply to Yemima Ben-Menahem and explain in my Intellectual Autobiography, I gave up "antirealism" in 1990,[6] and my present position is actually quite close to his. I do have one disagreement, a disagreement which makes me a "sophisticated" (rather than a "Hardcore Unsophisticated") metaphysical realist, but I hope that disagreement will not cause the reader (or Maudlin himself) to miss the large areas of agreement that remain.

Since Maudlin's terminology is a little different from the terminology I myself used—not always consistently—in the years he writes about (the seventies and eighties), I shall begin by classifying my present position in *his* terminology. Then, I will explain how I was led to the views that Maudlin rightly criticizes, and lastly I will discuss the remaining disagreement between us.

I. Maudlin's Terminology and My Comments Thereupon

(1) *"Internal Realism* is the thesis that any acceptable account of the world should explain how language use helps people to prosper in their interactions with the world."

This is more or less how I myself explained "internal realism" *in the opening sentences* of "Realism and Reason."[7] Unfortunately, *later* in that essay, in a section titled "Why all this doesn't refute internal realism," I identified "internal realism" with the view that whether a theory has a unique intended interpretation "has no absolute sense." And from that moment on, I used "internal realism" as a name for the antirealist position that Maudlin criticizes,[8] a position that included a defense of something I came to call "verificationist semantics."[9] So I prefer to say that I am *no longer* an internal realist, meaning, that I am not an *antirealist*. When I do use the term "internal realism" in what follows, I will be referring to the form of antirealism that I defended in the late 1970s and '80s.

(2) *"Metaphysical Realism* is the thesis that at least some significant parts of language have definite truth conditions such that it is possible for an operationally ideal theory, stated in this part of the language, to be false."

I agree, and I would add: "and furthermore possible for at least some statements to be determinately true even though there is no possibility of ever verifying them." (On this, see my Reply to Michael Dummett.) I feel sure Maudlin would not object to this addition. In Maudlin's sense, I *am* (since 1990) a "metaphysical realist."

(3) *"Mild Scientific Realism* is the thesis that most scientific theories that meet a certain standard of evidential support (there is debate over how to characterize this) are true or approximately true (there is debate over 'approximately true')."

By this definition I am and have always been *at least* a "Mild Scientific Realist."[10] It is true, as Maudlin says, that in *The Many Faces of Realism* I attacked something I called "Scientific Realism," but I did *not* mean by that term either "Mild Scientific Realism" (which I endorsed, though not of course using that terminology, in the very volume in which "Realism and Reason" was published) or "Optimistic Scientific Realism." What I had in mind as the position to be refuted was Wilfrid Sellars's "Philosophy and the Scientific Image of Man."[11] I used "manifest image" in *The Many Faces of*

Realism as Sellars used it, and the claim that the solidity of pink ice cubes is contradicted by the (better) "scientific image" was Sellars's own claim. I agree with Maudlin, that, contrary to Sellars, the commonsense conception of ice cubes (or tables, to use Eddington's example) is not contradicted by the fact that ice cubes (and tables) have an atomic microstructure. I regret having identified the Sellarsian position with "Scientific Realism," for precisely the reasons Maudlin gives.

> (4) "*Optimistic Scientific Realism* is Mild Scientific Realism plus the claim that for every interesting fundamental question about the world, unfettered rational inquiry would eventually yield a unique scientific theory that settles the question and obtains the level of evidential support mentioned in Mild Scientific Realism."

I thoroughly share Maudlin's doubts about "Optimistic Scientific Realism." (Of course, it would be nice if it were right.)

> (5) "*Peircean Realism* is Optimistic Scientific Realism together with the thesis that the truth of a theory *is nothing but* it being the theory that would eventually be accepted by unfettered rational inquiry."

Like Maudlin, I reject Peircean Realism. Even in my antirealist days, I never employed the counterfactual that this definition of truth uses,[12] and I fully share Maudlin's doubts about it.

II. How I Was Led to the Positions Maudlin Rightly Attacks

Maudlin admits, "I have assumed that there is such a thing as an intended interpretation of terms like 'star' and 'year' and 'ago' that is precise enough to render 'There were stars six million years ago' false in the young universe scenario, but I have not even attempted to provide an account of how such an interpretation is fixed." It was not a failure to see the *attractiveness* of a view like Maudlin's that led me to the antirealism of "Realism and Reason" and *Reason, Truth, and History*, but precisely a set of worries about how [a unique] interpretation could possibly be "fixed." Hence, although I share Maudlin's love of "physical ontology" as a subject for reflection, in order to explain how I worked my way into (and subsequently worked my way back out of) antirealism, I need to say something about areas of philosophy very different from physical ontology, the areas called "philosophy of language" and "philosophy of mind."

III. "Functionalism" Pushed Me towards Antirealism

As I explain in my Intellectual Autobiography, in the 1960s and '70s, I was wedded to a philosophical position in the philosophy of mind that I called "functionalism." Today I prefer to understand "functionalism" in a very wide sense, as the view that our minds are not *objects* but systems of (environment involving) *abilities*, or functional capacities, rather than in the narrow sense which identifies those capacities with computer programs, but the narrow sense was, unfortunately, the sense I gave to the term in that period, and the assumption that this sort of functionalism—call it "computational state functionalism"—was the correct philosophy of mind was the assumption that led me to find what I thought were insuperable difficulties with "metaphysical realism." (A fine critical discussion of my views in that period is Louise Antony's "Semantic Anorexia: On the Notion of Content in Cognitive Science."[13] By the time it was published I had already seen the error of my ways, but had it appeared earlier, it might well have helped me see the light sooner.)

Most versions of antirealism (including the version I espoused in "Realism and Reason," *Reason, Truth and History*, "Models and Reality," etc.) are simply versions of verificationism; thus what I am saying is that functionalism pushed me in the direction of verificationism. The place in which this is most evident is "Computational Psychology and Interpretation Theory," (published the same year as *Reason, Truth and History*), and there I wrote that "The brain's 'understanding' of its own 'medium of computation and representation' consists in its possession of a *verificationist semantics* for the medium, i.e. of a computable predicate which can represent acceptability, or warranted assertibility or credibility."[14] This is the "functionalist" picture of what I called "the mind/brain" that I had at the time. As I put it in that essay: "verificationist semantics is the natural semantics for functionalist (or 'cognitive') psychology. Such a semantics has a notion of 'belief' (or 'degrees of belief') which makes it *cognitive*; at the same time it is a *computable* semantics, which is what makes it functionalist."[15]

IV. The Connection between "Verificationist" Semantics and the Model-Theoretic Argument

Because I did not spend many pages on my underlying picture of the mind in *Reason, Truth, and History*, or its precursor, the lecture "Realism and Reason," but rather made "the model-theoretic argument" the center of attention, it is not surprising that almost all the discussions of my "internal realism" of the late 1970s and the '80s discussed only the model-theoretic argument. That argument, however, assumed that the verificationist picture of what I called "the mind/brain" was itself coherent. In addition, because the only version of functionalism I considered was "internalist" (that is, mental states were thought of as literally "inside" the brain) and highly reductionist, the possibility of a nonreductive and externalist conception of mental states was completely missed (as I explain in my Reply to John McDowell in the present volume). Once it was missed, the idea that our words correspond to things and properties outside the brain looked to me as if it required "noetic rays"—some sort of magic!

Today I see the situation very differently: "verificationist" semantics seems to me to imply the solipsistic conclusion that the truth makers for all our sentences must lie inside our own heads, and plausibly to the further conclusion that we cannot think of anything outside our "psychological present" (solipsism of the present moment), a view which is certainly incoherent; while a liberalized and nonreductive functionalism does not lead to or fit with the sort of "semantics" that I advocated in my "internal realist" period.[16]

V. "Sophisticated Metaphysical Realism"

By "sophisticated realism" what I meant was a realism that accepts the idea that the same state of affairs can sometimes admit of descriptions that have, taken at face value, incompatible "ontologies," in the familiar Quinian sense of "ontology." I still advocated sophisticated realism, in that sense, and I devoted a whole chapter (titled "A Defense of Conceptual Relativity") to it in *Ethics without Ontology*. I shall not repeat that whole defense here, but just make a few remarks.

Up to now, I have indicated that I am in large agreement with Maudlin on a host of issues. I am happy to call myself a realist in my metaphysics. So I do not regard my disagreement with Maudlin on this one issue as a fundamental one, although I regret that I have not yet managed to get him to see the light here. Here are a few words that I hope might cause him to reconsider (one can always hope).

First, when I say that the two "stories" about the "ontology" of the one-dimensional Euclidean world (or the two corresponding stories about a 4+1-dimensional Einsteinian spacetime), are "equivalent descriptions," I do not pretend that this equivalence claim is a *conceptual* truth. It could turn out that particles really have zero diameter, for example, and that would mean that regions of space with zero diameter ("points") can be the locus of real mass energies. That would certainly justify "point realism." What is and what is not a question of convention can, in my view, be itself a partly empirical question. But in a classical Newtonian world, or an Einsteinian world without point particles, it seems to me that the idea that "points" are optional elements of the ontology is well justified.

What I mean by an optional element of one's ontology is something I have long illustrated with the case of mereological sums. As a former David Lewis student, it may well be that Tim Maudlin is also a "Hardcore Unsophisticated Metaphysical Realist" about mereological sums, but I have to admit that that seems crazy to me. That there is an individual material thing which has both Canada and my wife as parts, and no parts that are wholly disjoint from both Canada and my wife, seems, at first absurd. Then one learns "how to talk that way," and then one knows how to use the phrase "the mereological sum of Canada and Ruth Anna Putnam." Has one thereby *discovered* that such a thing really exists? Or has one merely learned a different way of talking? To me it seems that the latter alternative is far more plausible.

In mathematics, cases of conceptual equivalence that do not respect "ontology" are even more rife. We all know that functions can be identified with certain sets. Usually one identifies them with sets of ordered n-tuples, for the appropriate n, and "n-tuples" are something we have long identified with sets; but there are different ways of doing that, and that means there is no fact of the matter as to *which* sets are "really" the functions, does it not? Moreover, it is just as easy to identify sets with certain functions as to identify functions with certain sets; Tim, would you advocate "Hardcore Unsophisticated Metaphysical Realism" with respect to whether sets are a sort of function or functions are a sort of set? Last but not least, quantification over mathematical objects can be reinterpreted as talk of *possible* existence, as in my "Mathematics without Foundations" or Geoffrey Hellman's *Mathematics without Numbers: Towards a Modal-Structural Interpretation*. In fact, I myself believe that the modal-structuralist interpretation makes better sense of the phenomenon I just pointed out, the conventionality (as I would describe it) of the aforementioned identifications in mathematics. If I were a "Hardcore Unsophisticated Metaphysical Realist" in philosophy of mathematics, I would express this by saying that I think the modal-structuralist interpretation is "the right one," and that it is false that "there are such objects" as numbers. But then I would have to say that, when we say "there are perfect numbers greater than 6," we are uttering a falsehood (notwithstanding the fact that 28 and 8128 are perfect), because (I would have to say) "there are no numbers; a fortiori no perfect numbers" (and likewise, no prime numbers, no odd numbers, etc.). But that too seems crazy to me! It seems more reasonable to say, instead, that the modal-structuralist interpretation represents one of several ways of expressing mathematical facts (namely, translating them into possibility locutions), but those same facts admit of other formulations. If "ontology" is not invariant under conceptual equivalence, let us just say so much the worst for "ontology."

H.P.

NOTES

1. Tim Maudlin, *Quantum Non-Locality and Relativity* (Oxford: Blackwell, 1994).

2. In the case of *Quantum Non-Locality and Relativity*, the swimming against the stream consists in the suggestion that quantum mechanics may simply not be metaphysically compatible with what is usually taken to be the "lesson" of Special and General Relativity, namely that there is no such thing as a preferred foliation of space-time (that is, an objective "simultaneity").

3. "A Philosopher Looks at Quantum Mechanics (Again)," *British Journal for the Philosophy of Science* 56, no. 4 (Dec. 2005): 615–34.

4. "Quantum Mechanics and Ontology," in Hilary Putnam, *Philosophy in an Age of Science*, ed. David Macarthur and Mario De Caro (Cambridge, MA: Harvard University Press, 2012).

5. Tim Maudlin, *The Metaphysics within Physics* (Oxford: Oxford University Press, 2007).

6. I publicly renounced the thesis that true statements are those that we would accept were conditions to become sufficiently "ideal," which was the form of antirealism I defended in the late 1970s and '80s, as a mistaken "concession to verificationism," in my reply to Simon Blackburn at the conference on my philosophy at the University of St. Andrews in November, 1990. The "written-up" version of that reply is published in *Reading Putnam*, ed. Peter Clark and Bob Hale (Oxford: Blackwell, 1994). The reasons I gave up antirealism are stated in the first three of my replies in "The Philosophy of Hilary Putnam," an issue of the journal *Philosophical Topics* 20, no. 1, Spring 1992), where I give a history of my use(s) of the unfortunate term "internal realism," and, at more length, in my *Dewey Lectures* (collected in Hilary Putnam, *The Threefold Cord: Mind, Body and World*). See also my exchange with Crispin Wright: Crispin Wright, "Truth as Sort of Epistemic: Putnam's Peregrinations," *Journal of Philosophy* 97, no. 6 (June 2000): 335–64; Hilary Putnam, "When 'Evidence Transcendence' is Not Malign: A Reply to Crispin Wright," *Journal of Philosophy* 98, no. 11 (Nov. 2001): 594–600.

7. Hilary Putnam, "Realism and Reason," in *Meaning and the Moral Sciences* (London: Routledge and Kegan Paul, 1978), 123–38. What I actually wrote was "The realist explanation [of the contribution of language-using to getting our goals], in a nutshell, is not that language mirrors the world but that *speakers* mirror the world—i.e. their environment—in the sense of *constructing a symbolic representation* of environment. . . . let me refer to realism in this sense—acceptance of this sort of scientific picture of the relation of speakers to their environment, and of the role of language—as *internal* realism." Ibid., 123.

8. For an explanation of how I came to slide from the earlier to the later sense of "internal realism" in one and the same essay, see "From Quantum Mechanics to Ethics and Back Again," in my *Philosophy in an Age of Science*.

9. For "verificationist semantics" see Hilary Putnam, "Computational Psychology and Interpretation Theory," in my *Realism and Reason: Philosophical Papers*, vol. 3 (Cambridge: Cambridge University Press, 1983), 143.

10. See, for example, *Meaning and the Moral Sciences*, 20, where I endorse Richard Boyd's view that "the laws of a theory belonging to a mature science are typically approximately *true*." This is a little stronger than Maudlin's "Mild Scientific Realism"; hence the "at least."

11. "Philosophy and the Scientific Image of Man" is the first essay in Wilfrid Sellars, *Science, Perception and Reality* (New York: Humanities Press, 1963).

12. I did, however, employ a different counterfactual, namely I identified truth with what would be verified *if conditions were sufficiently close to ideal*. This too seems problematic to me (now), but it is very different from the Peircean "if enquiry were indefinitely prolonged." See Hilary Putnam, *Reason, Truth and History* (Cambridge: Cambridge University Press, 1981), 54–56; and for a criticism of my former view, see Hilary Putnam, "Between Scylla and Charybdis: Does Dummett Have a Way Through?" in *The Philosophy of Michael Dummett*, ed. Randall E. Auxier and Lewis Edwin Hahn (Chicago: Open Court, 2007), 155–67.

13. Louise Antony, "Semantic Anorexia: On the Notion of Content in Cognitive Science" in *Meaning and Method: Essays in Honor of Hilary Putnam*, ed. George Boolos (Cambridge: Cambridge University Press, 1990). Here I shall talk about only one of the many issues she discusses in that essay; I do not agree with her suggestion that postulating "innate Mentalese" is something cognitive science needs to do, for instance.

14. See Putnam, "Computational Psychology and Interpretation Theory," 142.

15. Ibid., 143.

16. See my Reply to Michael Dummett in the present volume for further discussion of this point.

14

Frederick Stoutland

PUTNAM AND WITTGENSTEIN

Putnam has written about most of the central topics of philosophy and hence even a paper confined to his debt to Wittgenstein must be very selective. There is one topic, however, that is relevant to most of his work, namely, *realism*: What is it to be a realist? How can it be defended? What are its implications? What is an adequate realist conception of truth and reference? Putnam gave different answers to these questions depending on his conception of realism, and as that changed, so did his views on other philosophical topics, the amount of attention he gives to each varying with the view of realism he held. Getting clear about his conception of realism, therefore, is a way to understand his overall philosophical views, and getting clear about how Wittgenstein influenced his later conception of realism is a way to understand Wittgenstein's influence on Putnam's later philosophical work. To keep this paper at a reasonable length, therefore, I will omit any sustained discussion of topics like philosophy of mind, of science, of logic and mathematics, even though his current views on those topics are decisively shaped by what he learned from Wittgenstein.

Putnam's philosophical work can be divided into three phases, each of which involves a version of realism. The first is *metaphysical realism*, the second *internal realism*, and the third is *commonsense realism*, his present view. These are versions of a genus that Putnam characterized in a number of informal ways. "The great question of realism," he wrote, is "How does mind or language hook on to the world?"[1] His main concern was to undermine skeptical answers to this question—answers that doubt our capacity to represent in thought and language things in the world that are not part of our thought and language.[2] He therefore rejected the positivist idea that we are restricted to representing relations between sense impressions or to predicting our own experiences, as well as the Rortian claim that thought and language do not aim to represent the world but to cope with it.

I will begin with a brief discussion of metaphysical and internal realism and then turn to commonsense realism, which is grounded in Putnam's understanding and use of major themes in Wittgenstein's work. The focus of my discussion is Putnam's rejection of the "interface notion" of perception and conception, and I will consider how that rejection is worked out in his account of language, perception, intentionality, and truth. I will then discuss his Wittgensteinian conception of philosophy and conclude with some critical remarks. There will be few of the latter because I largely agree with Putnam's Wittgensteinian views. My main concern is to give a charitable reading of those views, and I hope Putnam will comment on how well I understand them.

I

Putnam began his career as an advocate of scientific realism, and his version continues to have many defenders in spite of his rejecting it. His main aim was to defend the reality of the forces and particles posited by current physical theories against positivist restrictions of truth and reference to the observable. He later called this view "metaphysical realism" because he came to think that it rested on assumptions that did not belong to science but were part of a metaphysical theory. He articulated four such assumptions: (1) a fixed totality of all objects; (2) a fixed totality of all properties; (3) a sharp line between properties we "discover" in the world and properties we "project"; (4) a fixed relation of "correspondence" in terms of which truth is supposed to be defined.[3]

The last is fundamental: a statement is true in virtue of corresponding to the fact that makes it true, which is construed nonepistemically so that truth transcends warrant. Correspondence is a fixed relation between a statement and a fact that does not vary with the kind of statement, its subject matter, or its role in the life and discourse of the subject.[4] Reference is also conceived as a fixed relation that obtains between a predicate and the objects that have the property denoted by the predicate. Two things are distinctive of this. One is Putnam's claim that understanding a statement is not a matter of knowing its truth conditions, but of knowing how to use it in accordance with the degree of warrant speakers of the language would assign its assertion under various conditions. This is also a theory of what *constitutes* sounds and marks as meaningful expressions: they become so *as a result of* being used in that way.

The second is Putnam's claim that, although one need not know the correspondence between statements and facts in order to use one's language, there is such a correspondence nonetheless.[5] The argument is, first, that our discourse is largely successful in predicting and explaining phenomena in everyday life and science, and, second, that the best explanation of this success is that most of the statements we accept correspond to the facts and most of our predicates denote objects that have the corresponding property.[6] He took the explanation to be empirical, claiming that it is a question of science (mainly of physics) what facts explain the truth of our scientific statements (indeed, given physicalism, what facts make *any* statements true) or what objects our terms refer to. Early scientists, for example, thought that 'heat' refers to caloric fluid, but contemporary science tells us that it refers to kinetic energy, and hence the statement that a substance is getting hot is made true by an increase, not in caloric fluid, but in kinetic energy.

It was, nevertheless, "the most important consequence of metaphysical realism . . . that *truth* is supposed to be *radically non-epistemic*—we might be 'brains in a vat' and so the theory that is 'ideal' from the point of view of operational utility, inner beauty and elegance, 'plausibility,' simplicity, 'conservatism,' etc., might be false. 'Verified' (in any operational sense) does not imply 'true' . . . even in the ideal limit."[7] The fundamental reason for this is the dichotomy between understanding statements and knowing their truth conditions, which means we can be competent speakers of a language even if radically mistaken about the truth or falsity of its statements.

The other assumptions of metaphysical realism are intertwined with its account of truth and reference. The assumption that there is a sharp line between properties we "discover" and properties we "project," corresponds to a distinction between statements that are true only because they correspond to the facts and those whose truth depends on our conceptual schemes and experience, and to a distinction between facts that are independent of our thought and experience and those that are not thus independent. Metaphysical realists contend that inquiry is successful only if it formulates truths that depend entirely on the facts.

The other assumptions follow: that there is a fixed totality of all objects and a fixed totality of all properties. These are best understood in the context of Putnam's physicalist construal of metaphysical realism, according to which the world consists of the particles and forces of an ideal physics, and hence that any true description describes those physicalist elements. While it does not follow that all true descriptions are physicalist—they may be computational, everyday, and so on—*what* are described are those physical elements. Those are the world's *basic* objects and properties—a "fixed totality of mind-independent objects and properties"—on which all objects and properties are supervenient. Any true description of the world is ultimately a description of those basic elements, and any true and complete description of them is equivalent to any other true and complete description of them. "In short, the picture is that what an 'object' of reference is, is fixed once and for all at the start and that the totality of objects in some scientific theory or other will turn out to coincide with the totality of All the Objects There Are." [8]

II

Putnam characterized metaphysical realism as presupposing an *externalist* perspective (a "God's Eye point of view") from which we could view the relation between the world and our language, thought, and experience. Around the end of the 1970s he concluded that we cannot occupy such a perspective and that "*everything* we say about an object is of the form: it is such as to affect *us* in such-and-such a way." The world "as it is 'in itself' independently of its effect on us" is Kant's noumenal world, which we cannot even describe because "we can form no clear conception [of it]." [9] We can occupy only an *internalist* perspective, so called because "it is characteristic of this view to hold that *what objects does the world consist of?* is a question that it only makes sense to ask *within* a theory or description," [10] hence the term *internal realism*. [11]

Putnam replaced the correspondence theory of truth with an epistemic theory that identifies truth with warranted assertibility—not with what we *are* warranted to assert but what we *would* be warranted in asserting in ideal epistemic circumstances. [12] A main motivation for this was his objection to the metaphysical realist theory of *reference*, according to which to understand a predicate is to know how to use it, which we can do without knowing what objects are in its extension, even though predicates generally do refer to such objects.

This theory, Putnam held, assumes the model-theoretic distinction between a language, understood in terms of use, and its interpretation, understood in terms of a fixed notion of correspondence truth and reference. But results from model theory show that, given that distinction, use cannot determine reference. No matter how successful our use of expressions, even if our theories are ideal, there are many ways to assign objects as the reference of terms, no one of which is any more correct (or incorrect) than any other, because any consistent reference assignment preserves the truth conditions of our statements. The point is not that we do not know which (basic) objects terms refer to, but that there is no such thing as referring to one specific object rather than any other. Given metaphysical realism, reference is relative (or indeterminate), which Putnam took to be a *reductio* of the view. "Ontological relativity [is] a refutation of any philosophical position that leads to it."[13] It cannot be avoided by taking reference to be causally determined, for what is needed is causal *explanation*, which is interest-relative and irreducibly intentional, and hence no more capable of fixing reference than language itself.

If metaphysical realism is wrong about reference, it is also wrong about truth. If referents can be shifted arbitrarily while preserving truth conditions, then the facts that statements correspond to can be shifted in the same way, so that any number of different facts would make the same statement true, which evacuates any intelligible content from the correspondence theory of truth.

It was to insure determinacy of reference and the intelligibility of truth as a substantial property that Putnam adopted an epistemic theory of truth. Doing so eliminated the dichotomy between a language and its interpretation that led to the indeterminacy of reference. It eliminated it because, if to understand a statement is to know the conditions that warrant its assertion, and if for a statement to be true is for its assertion to be warranted under ideal conditions, then to understand a statement *is* to know the conditions that, if idealized, would make it true. There is, therefore, no metaphysical dichotomy between truth and warrant, and the threat of "brain in a vat" skepticism is eliminated.

A similar point holds for reference: to understand a (referring) term is to use it to refer to the kind of objects it is taken to refer to in one's linguistic community. But there is no fixed totality of objects that terms must refer to, because how objects are individuated depends on the language or conceptual scheme to which the term belongs.

> A sign that is actually employed in a particular way by a particular community of users can correspond to particular objects within the conceptual scheme of those users. . . . We cut the world into objects when we introduce one or another conceptual scheme of description. Since the objects and the signs are alike internal to the scheme of description, it is possible to say what matches what.[14]

On this view, although it is relative to a language or a conceptual scheme which objects our terms refer to, we can refer determinately to any of them from within a language or scheme.[15] Reference is determinate and not relative just because there is no language independent fact of the matter about how objects are individuated or which are basic.

The view is realist in admitting that the *existence* of objects is independent of language or conceptual scheme, but it denies that their *nature* is thus independent. Central to internal realism is *conceptual relativism*, the view that "the notions of object and existence have a multitude of different uses rather than one absolute 'meaning.' . . . 'Which are the real objects?' is a question that makes [no] sense independently of our choice of concepts."[16] While this admits the reality of the objects of physical science, it rejects the physicalist view that they are the *basic* objects on which all others are supervenient. For internal realists, truth consists in its "fitting the world as the world presents itself to some observer or observers,"[17] a view Putnam ascribed to Kant. The only world that can explain the truth or falsity of our statements is the joint product of our sense awareness and categorical scheme, whose formal structure, therefore, is not independent of our thought and language.

Internal realism presumes the intelligibility of a metaphysical distinction between what is mind-independent and what is mind-dependent, between facts that do not depend on our linguistic and conceptual perspectives and facts that do. That distinction is also fundamental to the metaphysical realist claim that the facts that make statements true and the objects to which terms refer must be mind independent. If metaphysical realism is the view that we can think and talk about things whose structure is independent of our thought and language, internal realism is the view that this is something we cannot do because we can think and talk only about things as conceptualized by us.[18] But if this dichotomy between mind-dependent and mind-independent reality is itself rejected, then we need not choose between metaphysical realism and internal realism, and the way is open for a third alternative.

III

This third alternative was a turn to Wittgenstein, whose work Putnam came to understand more deeply and appreciate more fully, which led him to a new way of dealing with the issues that had long concerned him.[19] The result was his *commonsense realism*, which he put forward, not as any kind of theory, but motivated, as Wittgenstein put it, by the aim of bringing words "back from their metaphysical to their everyday use."[20] He took both metaphysical and internal realism to be the kind of metaphysical theories whose explanatory pretensions Wittgenstein aimed to undermine.

Putnam's references to Wittgenstein were not new. There are also references in his metaphysical realism phase, although they are infrequent and largely critical. He spoke disparagingly, for example, of the influence on philosophy of science of "the linguistic philosophy of Wittgenstein"[21] and wrote that the premises of logical behaviorism (which he opposed) are "suggested in Wittgenstein's *Philosophical Investigations*." Best known is his criticism of Norman Malcolm for asserting "certain general doctrines having to do with language . . . [that] can be read as simple versions of some famous arguments of Wittgenstein . . . [which are] bad arguments and prove nothing."[22] Although he prefaced that criticism with the cautionary remark, "if this interpretation is faithful to what Wittgenstein had in mind" (an interpretation Putnam later rejected), many of his readers assumed that Malcolm got Wittgenstein right and that Putnam's criticism of Malcolm was a fair criticism of Wittgenstein.

There are considerably more references to Wittgenstein in Putnam's internal-realist phase, and they are largely favorable. That reflects both a more sympathetic way of reading Wittgenstein and changes in Putnam's own views, which are in some respects closer to Wittgenstein's. But in a number of ways they are not, as Putnam came to recognize. For instance, Putnam took his internal realism to draw on Michael Dummett's "antirealism," which both thought to be inspired by Wittgenstein. But he later argued that Dummett's antirealism was a metaphysical view that Wittgenstein neither held nor encouraged.[23]

Moreover, Putnam continued to treat Wittgenstein's writing as a source of theses that were to be used selectively in one's own theories. In the introduction to volume 2 of his *Collected Papers*,[24] he wrote of the conception of philosophy he then held:

> I see philosophy as a field which has certain central questions, for example, the relation between thought and reality. . . . It seems obvious in dealing with these questions philosophers have formulated rival research programs, that they have put forward general hypotheses and that philosophers within each major research program have modified their hypotheses by trial and error. . . . To that extent Philosophy is a 'science.'

This conception of philosophy dominates contemporary analytical philosophy, especially so-called "analytic metaphysics," and Putnam's early work played no small part in making it dominant. But it differs profoundly from Wittgenstein's conception, and in rejecting metaphysical and internal realism, Putnam abandoned the conception of philosophy at work in their development in favor of one similar to Wittgenstein's, who had written in *Philosophical Investigations*:

> It was correct that our considerations must not be scientific ones. . . . We may not advance any kind of theory. There must not be anything hypothetical in our considerations. All *explanation* must disappear, and description alone must take its place. And this description gets its light—that is to say its purpose—from the

philosophical problems. . . . The problems are solved, not by coming up with new discoveries, but by assembling what we have long been familiar with.[25]

Shifting to such a view was crucial in shaping Putnam's later work, not least in enabling him to get a more perceptive and illuminating understanding of the range of Wittgenstein's work. (In what follows, when I refer to "Putnam's view," I mean his current view—his turn to Wittgenstein.)

IV

Putnam did not deny that we can make a distinction between facts or truths that are dependent on our linguistic and conceptual perspectives and those that are not. What he denied was that there is a metaphysical dichotomy between them such that we can separate the one from the other and characterize in particular cases what the world contributes from what is contributed by our thought and language. On his view, true statements state the facts, but what is true and what is fact depends on both the world and our minds, and the notion of sorting out the contribution of each is unintelligible. The claim is not merely that the contribution each makes is something we cannot know, but that the notion of a separable contribution cannot be made intelligible.

To appreciate the force of Putnam's claim (to which I return in section X), we must consider his numerous objections to what he calls the "interface" notion of perception and conception. This is the notion that "our cognitive powers cannot reach all the way to the objects themselves"[26] because there is a gap between our minds and the world that must be bridged if we are to refer to, describe, or know the world. Wittgenstein held the contrary in writing that "When we say, *mean*, that such-and-such is the case, then, with what we mean, we do not stop anywhere short of the fact, but mean: *such-and-such—is—thus-and-so*."[27] Putnam's later work aimed to undermine opposition to this Wittgensteinian claim by philosophers who denied it or, more often, simply took its falsity for granted.

The most common way philosophers have dealt with the gap is by positing intermediaries between mind and world—inner representations that mediate between ourselves and what we think about, describe, or perceive. Perceptual intermediaries are sense impressions, sense data, stimulations of nerve endings, and so on, which we have in virtue of objects in the world causally affecting our senses. Nonperceptual representations are thoughts, beliefs, or other mental states, together with words, statements, or other linguistic items, whose contents are taken to be representations of objects in the world that are not currently affecting our senses. The assumption in both cases is that we are in direct cognitive contact only with inner representations and not with objects in the world external to them.

Philosophers who accept what Sellars called the "myth of the given" think that sense impressions are *both* causal and cognitive intermediaries between the external world and our perceptual beliefs: they not only cause the latter but are reasons for them. Philosophers who reject the myth contend that sense impressions are *only* causal intermediaries between the world and our perceptual beliefs: sense impressions are not *reasons* for beliefs because only other beliefs can be such reasons. Although the latter is not a foundationalist view of perceptual knowledge, it is, nevertheless, an interface view insofar as it includes the claim that our only cognitive contact with the world is by way of beliefs, which, since they are justified only by other beliefs, are intermediaries between mind and world.

Putnam thought that modern philosophy had been dominated by the view that representations are necessary to bridge the gap between mind and world created by the interface notion. He also thought that view was crucial to both metaphysical and internal realism, in the first instance in their use theory of language, which yielded the model-theoretic distinction between a language and its interpretation, a distinction that is a linguistic version of the interface notion. As a metaphysical realist, Putnam attempted to bridge the gap by claiming that the predicates we use to refer can be interpreted as denoting objects with the corresponding properties, because that is the best explanation of the success of our discourse. As an internal realist, he attempted to bridge it by an epistemic theory that claimed that a language connects with objects of reference only as the objects are conceptualized by us.[28] Both attempts to bridge the gap also assumed a parallel theory of truth.

Putnam argues that we would see there is no need for such theories if we recognized that the gap depends on the language/interpretation dichotomy that results from the use theory of understanding held by both metaphysical and internal realists. That theory contends that what we use are mere sounds and marks that become meaningful words only *after* being used in accordance with community standards of warrant. The claim is usually defended on the ground that, since we have the knowledge of what speakers mean that is required for communication, such knowledge must be accessible to speakers regardless of their language. Because mere marks and sounds are accessible to anyone with normal sense organs, it is knowledge of them that makes possible communication between speakers.

Putnam's view is that it is not possible to attach conditions of warranted assertibility to mere marks or sounds, because only already meaningful statements can have degrees of warrant. While he agrees that an account of understanding must permit public knowledge of what speakers mean, he thinks it is a mistake to require that such knowledge be accessible to persons regardless of their language. "The use of words in a language game," he wrote (referring to Wittgenstein), "cannot, in most cases, be described without employing the vocabulary of that game or a vocabulary internally related to the vocabulary of that game."[29] This means that language is public, not in the sense that speakers who do not know the language can recognize what is going on, but in the sense that anyone who understands the language (and is not deaf) can *hear* it as meaningful. It also means a rejection of the metaphysical and internal realist use theory of language, which Putnam called "scientistic," in favor of a Wittgensteinian account that is quite different. "The difference between the scientistic and the Wittgensteinian purport of the slogan 'meaning is use' is stark," Putnam wrote. The former involves a utopian notion of scientific psychology, which at its worst "lowers the level of philosophical discussion to that of popular 'scientific journalism'." The latter simply says that "understanding is having the abilities that one exercises when and in using language."[30]

V

The interface view is also implicit in Putnam's functionalism, which is the mentalist equivalent of the use theory of language he rejected. Just as understanding a language is using sounds and marks in accordance with community standards, so having thoughts is manipulating brain states in accordance with a computer program. Putnam did not regard functionalism as an account of the meaning of mental terms or as a conceptual analysis of mental concepts: he did not take the assertion that S believes p to *mean* that S has certain brain states. He put it forward as a scientific hypothesis that beliefs and other psychological states are in fact identical with neural states characterized not as physical states, but in terms of their functional, causal explanatory roles in perception and behavior.

   Although functionalism became a widely held view in the philosophy of mind, Putnam came to reject it for a number of reasons, including its commitment to the problematic interface notion of the relation of mind and world. A functionalist account of perceptual belief, for instance, posits perceptual inputs to the brain, which processes them to yield behavioral outputs. But the perceptual inputs, Putnam wrote, "are the outer limits of our cognitive processing; everything that lies beyond those inputs is con-nected to our mental processes only causally, not cognitively. . . . Every-thing outside our skins is outside our cognitive processing."[31] The account assumes the dichotomy between language and interpretation and hence "Interpretations of our language . . . can agree on what those inputs are while disagreeing wildly on what our terms actually refer to. . . . Everything that happens within the sphere of cognition leaves the objective reference of our terms, for the most part, almost wholly undetermined."[32]

Putnam's externalism about meaning and content (developed most famously in his "The Meaning of 'Meaning'"[33]) is consistent with this critical point. He did not hold that use can be *exhaustively* described by computer programs in the brain, because "one would not only have to talk about the functional organization of the language user's brain but one would also have to specify the sort of environment in which the language user was embedded."[34] He never succeeded, however, in bringing these together satisfactorily. "There was the computer program in the brain and there was the description of the external causes of the language user's words,"[35] two matters that he was unable to integrate. In particular, the functionalist view that meaning and content are in the head requires that they not be individuated by external factors, while the fact that use is dependent on the language user's environment means that they should be so individuated. Because these two views were not reconciled, a functionalist view of the mental retained the interface view and ruled out the possibility of perception and cognition reaching the things themselves.

VI

Putnam contended that the interface view "has no sound arguments to support it" and is objectionable in making it "impossible to see how persons can be in genuine contact with a world at all."[36] Given the view,

> One is left—if one does not wish to think of "intentionality" as a magical power—with the task of trying to show that the referential directedness of our thinking at the objects we think about can be constituted out of or in some way "reduced to" the *causal* impacts of those objects upon us; a task so hopeless that philosophers have been repeatedly led to recoil to one or another version of idealism. . . . Since the seventeenth century, philosophy has oscillated between equally unworkable realisms and idealisms.[37]

What, then, is the alternative? We can divide the question in two: what notion of perception does not assume the interface view, and what conception of intentionality in general does not assume it?

Putnam's account of perception was that "'external' things, cabbages and kings, can be *experienced*. (And not just in the Pickwickian sense of *causing* "experiences," conceived as affectations of our subjectivity.)"[38] The account was not meant as a theory of perception but as an alternative to theories in general. It was what William James called "the natural realism of the common man, . . . a denial of the necessity for and the explanatory value of positing 'internal representations' in thought and perception."[39] While sense impressions or sense data may play a causal role in perception, they have no role as representations that cognitively mediate our experience of objects in the world, because perception is "acquaintance with genuine properties of objects."[40]

The main argument for positing sense impressions as cognitive intermediaries is that perception is not infallible: we may be convinced that we perceive something that does not exist, or that we perceive it as such and such when it is not so. Sense impressions account for such error, it is argued, because we have direct experience of them, which are as they seem, whereas we know external things only by fallible inference from the sense impressions.

Putnam rejects the argument that "perception is not infallible, therefore it cannot be direct"[41] and criticizes the appeal to perceptual intermediaries in a number of ways, of which I will discuss two. One is to argue that the difference between veridical and nonveridical perception is not that in the first case we *infer* correctly from how things seem to us to how they really are, whereas in the other case we *infer* incorrectly. That view assumes that perception begins with how things merely seem to us—with an awareness of sense impressions—that is common to both veridical and nonveridical perception. He rejects that view in favor of a *disjunctive* view: in a perceptual situation we either have a veridical perception of what is in the world or we do not have such a veridical perception. We may, on an occasion, confuse the two situations, thinking, for instance, that we see a cow when we merely seem to see one. But there is no relevant common factor that the two situations share; we do not in both cases merely seem to see a cow (and then *infer*, correctly in the first case, wrongly in the second), nor are there sense impressions that we are aware of in both situations. In the first case, it is true that I see a cow; in the second case, it is false that I see a cow. I may in the latter case be aware of something, but there is no reason to think I am then aware of the same thing I am aware of when I see a cow.

The other criticism concerns the way our perceptual experience depends on the perceptual situation in a way the objects of perception do not. White things appear green under a green light, things that are straight appear bent when immersed in water, sweet things taste sour when one is ill. These facts lead to the claim that since the properties of the objects themselves do not depend on our experience, what is experienced must be sense impressions, which do depend on our awareness of them. Putnam replies that the properties we perceive, colors, for instance, have *looks*, which are "irreducible (though relational) aspects of reality that depend upon the way those things reflect light, the conditions under which they are viewed, etc."[42] Similar things hold for other properties—shape, smell, sounds, and so on. In all such cases it is, Putnam writes, a mistake to think "that perspectival properties are subjective, not really properties of 'external things.'"[43]

Putnam intends his complex treatment of the problem of perception to restore what he calls "a second naïveté," which he attributes, not only to William James, but to Husserl and Austin, and also to Wittgenstein. This is often missed because Wittgenstein's "private language argument" has been widely misunderstood, either as a defense of behaviorism or as the denial that knowledge claims are responsible only to communal agreement. Putnam thinks the "argument" is not a theory of the nature of language or the mental but a subtle undermining of false or unintelligible construals of both language and the mental. That is also his stance toward theories of perception: the philosopher's task is not to develop a theory of perception but to convince us that "Since everything lies open to view, there is nothing to explain."[44] There are, of course, things to elucidate or clarify, just as there are misunderstandings to be dealt with and, above all, problems to be resolved. But "The problems are solved," Wittgenstein wrote, "not by coming up with new discoveries, but by assembling what we have long been familiar with."[45]

VII

Intentionality or conception is broader than perception, for we have the capacity to refer to, think about, and describe objects that we do not perceive because they are distant from us in space or time. What is fundamental is not knowledge of such objects, but the capacity to think about or describe them whether truly or falsely, which Putnam called "Kant's Problem,"[46] although it was also a problem Wittgenstein came to terms with in similar ways. Putnam thinks that capacity presumes the capacity to perceive—we learn to refer to distant objects by our perceiving nearby ones—while going beyond it. Like Wittgenstein, he is not skeptical about the capacity but about various philosophical attempts to give it a theoretical explanation.

Putnam approached intentionality much as Wittgenstein approached the so-called "rule-following considerations" involved in our capacity to understand a rule and then apply it to continue a series indefinitely: for example, the series "1, 5, 11, 19, 29, . . ."[47] Philosophers have argued that there must be an underlying connection between the rule and the series, which explains how our understanding of the rule enables us to continue the series correctly. Some have suggested that understanding the rule is having an immediate grasp of the whole series it requires, others that getting the series right is explained by a brain/mind mechanism that guides our application of the rule. Others have thought in terms of a Platonic vision of how grasping a rule logically necessitates following it in the correct way.

Wittgenstein argued that if we consider exactly what these attempts at explanation amount to, we will see that they are empty or unintelligible and that, in any case, our ordinary practice needs no such explanation. Nothing *compels* us to continue the series in one way rather than another, and there is no *guarantee* that we will get it right. But we do continue it as our ordinary understanding of the rule requires because so doing is a practice in which people generally get such things right. If they do not, they can be corrected by appealing to features implicit in the practice without which there would be no such thing as applying a rule, even incorrectly. Getting the series right is not necessitated, but it does not follow that it is merely accidental.

Putnam thought that the "referential directedness of our thinking," like our correctly following a rule, does not stand in need of explanation. The belief that it does assumes the interface notion that reference is by way of inner representations. He rejected "magical theories of reference" that explain it by holding that representations somehow reach out to objects like light rays or have a logically necessary connection with what they represent. "Thought words and mental pictures do not *intrinsically* represent what they are about."[48] The objection was the Wittgensteinian one that reference is not to be explained in a Platonic way as a "freestanding activity, unsupported by many other activities, linguistic and nonlinguistic."[49]

Nor is reference to be explained, as Fodor put it, as "a matter of [a word's] causal attachments to the world."[50] That view aims to explain intentionality by reducing it to nonintentional relations between sounds or marks and objects in the world, but Putnam objects that the notion of causation in play here is irreducibly intentional, and hence the reduction fails. Moreover, reference requires not mere marks or sounds but *words* that speakers use to refer to objects.

While Putnam's externalism about meaning and content implies that reference partly depends on a speaker's causal connections with her physical and social environment, he denies that causation constitutes reference. "A certain referring use of some words would be impossible if we were not causally connected to the kinds of things referred to; . . . But that is to say there are causal constraints on reference, not that the referring is the causal connection."[51] Causation determines in part what a speaker's use of a meaningful word refers to in a given physical or social environment. What the word "water" means, for example, depends on the language in which it occurs, but what it is used to refer to (hence the content of the concept) depends in part on the environment in which speakers use it. This is something we normally take for granted but do not notice, which Putnam intended his thought experiments about twin earth to call to our attention. They were not moves in a theoretical explanation of what it is to refer because he thought that his externalism neither is nor assumes a theory of reference.[52]

Like following a rule, referring is not a freestanding activity but one embedded in our practice. It is rooted in the cognitive abilities we share with other animals.

> A wolf could expect to find deer on a meadow, and its ability to expect that is a primitive form of our ability to expect to find deer on a meadow. Our highly developed and highly discriminating abilities to think about situations we are not observing are developments of powers that we share with other animals. . . . Our power of imagining, remembering, expecting what is not the case here and now is a part of our nature.[53]

Because we have natural powers other animals do not have, we acquire abilities beyond what they are capable of. These have made it possible for us to develop specifically human practices into which we are inducted as we mature and that support activities like following a rule or referring. This is not a scientific explanation that appeals to the brain processes on which our powers depend, nor an explanation of why any particular act of referring succeeds or what any act of referring consists in. But it dispels any mystery of why referring succeeds in general. Like Wittgenstein's language game, referring is a "whole, consisting of language and the actions into which it is woven."[54] "Our ability to refer," Putnam writes, "is not one ability but a whole complex of abilities, including our perceptual abilities."[55] Language and perception are interwoven and, because both involve contact with the objects themselves, there is no place for the permutation and switches that undermine the determinacy of reference. Reference is not indeterminate in Quine's sense, Putnam wrote, because "When we use the word, 'Tabitha,' we can refer to Tabitha and not to the whole cosmos minus Tabitha (that is, to a permutation of the reference scheme), because after all we can see the cat, and pet her, and many other things, and we can hardly see or pet the whole cosmos minus Tabitha."[56]

VIII

If intentionality is the capacity to think and talk about objects both near and far, success in exercising that capacity is truth. Making true statements is, like referring, not a freestanding activity but embedded in a practice that is rooted in our animal nature and developed by our participation in increasingly complex language games. I will take this for granted and focus here on Putnam's view of what it is for this activity to be successful—what it is for a statement to be true.

In rejecting metaphysical and internal realism, Putnam rejected the theory of truth each held in favor of "commonsense realism." It was, he said, a return to realism after a detour through internal realism, but it was not a return to metaphysical realism. Commonsense realism is not a theory of truth at all. Of course it aims to clarify the concept of truth, to relate it to other concepts, to resolve the problems we confront in reflecting on truth; but achieving those aims would not be furthered by a philosophical theory about the essence of truth. To construct such a theory would be, once again, to be in the grip of the interface view of the relation of mind and world.

Putnam defends the commonsense claim that truth transcends warrant by arguing that the belief that it cannot do so is a consequence of the use theory of language held by antirealists. If to make a statement is to utter mere sounds in accordance with the standards of warrant in one's linguistic community, it is natural to assume that the truth value of one's statements cannot transcend what is in principle thus warranted. Metaphysical realists, who also held that use theory, tried to avoid its antirealist consequence by an "elaborate metaphysical fantasy."[57] Putnam avoids it by rejecting the conception of use that is its main support, a conception often attributed to Wittgenstein but that he explicitly rejected.

Consider Putnam's example of whether Lizzie Borden killed her parents with an axe, a famous case that is beyond our knowing the truth of the matter. Antirealists maintain that we cannot understand what it would be for the statement "Lizzie Borden killed her parents with an axe" to be true or false, since that would require that either it or its negation is warranted by community standards, neither of which is here the case. To understand the statement, we have to take it to be neither true nor false, and hence to be indeterminate whether or not Lizzie did the evil deed, which is at best an extravagant (if intriguing) claim. But if we drop that use theory, nothing hinders the commonsense notion that we understand what it is for the claim to be true (or false). "What makes it true, if it is, is simply that Lizzie Borden killed her parents with an axe. The recognition transcendence of truth comes, in this case, to no more than the 'recognition transcendence' of some killings. And did we ever think that all killers can be recognized as such?"[58]

One feature of internal realism that commonsense realism includes is conceptual relativism: "there are many usable extensions of the notion of an object and many alternative ways of describing objects," and hence "we should not think of the world as consisting of objects and properties in some one, philosophically preferred sense of 'object' and 'property.'"[59] The point applies also to *events*, to *states of affairs*, even to *exist*, which are to be "conceived in terms of an open and ever extendable family of uses."[60] This was not a feature of metaphysical realism, which regarded truth as correspondence to a fixed totality of basic objects and spoke "of 'all propositions' as a determinate and surveyable totality."[61] On this view a statement has the property of being true in virtue of corresponding to a particular fact or a particular complex of facts.

As a commonsense realist, Putnam also thinks that a statement that is true corresponds to reality, but his view of correspondence differs from the metaphysical realist's in a number of fundamental ways. One is that correspondence does not obtain between a statement and a particular fact but between a statement and reality or the world. The truth of a negative statement ("there is not a fireplace in the house") does not, therefore, require either a negative state of affairs or a reformulation of the statement.

Whereas metaphysical realists take correspondence to be an ordinary nonnormative relation between a statement and a fact, commonsense realists take correspondence, and hence truth, to be inescapably normative. "Truth is a normative property [because] calling statements true and false is evaluating them."[62] True statements make claims about reality that are correct, false statements claims that are incorrect. "Correct" here does not mean "warranted" or "verified"; it means what it is right to claim about reality, whatever our reasons for making the claim.

Whether a statement is true or false depends on—is responsible to—the world in that as the world changes, so does the truth value of relevant statements. Which changes in the world result in which changes in the truth value of our statements is a complex matter, and the more complex the statements, the more complex the changes in the world that alter their truth value. Philosophers of a holist persuasion may think that the truth of every statement depends on the world as a whole. Putnam thinks that such dependence varies with the kind of statement. We cannot "speak once and for all of 'all propositions' as if these constituted a determinate and surveyable totality, and of one single 'truth predicate,' whose meaning is fixed once and for all."[63]

Putnam denies that what it is for a statement to be correct or right in the sense of being true can be characterized in any general way.

> If Wittgenstein was right, how should his reflections affect our view of the concept of truth? On the one hand, to regard an assertion or a belief or a thought as true or false *is* to regard it as being right or wrong; on the other hand, just what sort of rightness or wrongness is in question varies enormously with the sort of discourse. *Statement, true, refers,* indeed, *belief, assertion, thought, language*—all the terms we use when we think about logic (or "grammar") in the wide sense in which Wittgenstein understands that notion—have a

plurality of uses, and new uses are constantly added as new forms of discourse come into existence.[64]

There are no fixed and unique standards for getting things right because such standards are internal to the kind of discourse to which a statement belongs. They depend on the statement, on the kind of description, on the circumstances under which we assert it, on the sort of rightness required. "Whether a sentence is true or not typically depends on whether certain things or events satisfy the conditions for being described by that sentence—conditions which depend on the ongoing activity of using and reforming language."[65]

This point involves conceptual relativism's claim that there is no such thing as *the* right way of using the notions of *object, property, event, state of affairs,* or *exist.* We must simply choose a scheme for using them but, having made that choice, there is such a thing as a right way to use them in describing the world. "Accepting the ubiquity of conceptual relativity does not require us to deny that truth genuinely depends on the behavior of things distant from the speaker, but the nature of the dependence changes as the kinds of language games we invent change."[66] The distinction between a statement's being warranted and its being right is also dependent on such factors. There is no absolute distinction between the two, and what is only warrant in one situation may be truth or correctness in another (and vice versa).

The point also involves what Putnam calls *conceptual pluralism*: "We employ many different kinds of discourses . . . subject to different standards and possessing different sorts of applications, with different logical and grammatical features—different 'language games' in Wittgenstein's sense."[67] This means both that the same situation can be described in different ways without inconsistency and that there is never one philosophically correct description. For example "the contents of a room may be partly described in the terminology of fields and particles and . . . partly described by saying that there is a chair in front of a desk." The two descriptions, one from physics, one from everyday, are not cognitively equivalent but are, nevertheless, compatible, and we need not "reduce one or both of them to some single fundamental and universal ontology."[68]

IX

Commonsense realism can be said to be a deflationist version of metaphysical realism, as Putnam suggested in writing that metaphysical realism is an inflation of commonsense realism "with the aid of a great deal of supposedly explanatory machinery."[69] But since he also thought that deflationism is the worst of all the accounts of truth, we should consider the sense in which he is or is not a deflationist. The central issue is the status and role of the so-called disquotational (or equivalence) principle—"p" is true if and only if p—which I shall abbreviate as "DQ." Tarski made the principle famous, but Frege had earlier made it explicit, claiming that the concept *true* does not change the content of statements to which it is attached: to assert *that p is true* does not alter the content of asserting *that p.*

The metaphysical realist claim that a statement is true in virtue of corresponding to a particular fact, can be seen as an explanatory use of DQ: what explains its being true that p is (corresponding to the fact) that p. It is true (if it is) that Lizzie Borden killed her parents with an axe *in virtue of* the fact that she did kill them with an axe. The claim is often taken to be a necessary truth—the *truth-maker* of "p" necessarily is p—which may be complicated by the contention that to get at the *real* truth-maker, "the fact that p" has to be construed in the light of the best scientific results. Although the latter are not necessary truths, truth-maker theory begins with DQ as a necessary truth.

Putnam accepts DQ and consequently the claim that to assert that "p" is true is just to assert that p (and vice versa), but (like Wittgenstein) he denies that the principle is either explanatory or necessarily true. It is a contingent bi-conditional that is much too thin to be explanatory. It is no explanation of why it is true (if it is) that Lizzie Borden killed her parents with an axe that she killed her parents with an axe, because to assert that it is true that she did the killing just *is* to assert that she did the killing.

Putnam takes "true" to denote the property of being true but he denies that the property is *substantive* because that invokes the kind of metaphysical theory he rejects,[70] and he hence holds that the property neither has nor provides a substantive explanation. There is an unobjectionable sense of "making true" that is yielded by DQ: since to assert that p is true is to assert that p, what makes it true that p is just what makes it so that p. Thus what explains why it is true that Putnam is so cheerful is just what explains why Putnam is so cheerful: his genes, his good wife, his good health, etc. But this is not the explanation of why a statement is true that defenders of a substantive property of truth have in mind. Nor does Putnam think his claim that a statement is true if it corresponds to reality provides such an explanation; it is not an account of what makes it true but of what it is to be true.

A similar point applies to truth as itself being explanatory. Given DQ, the claim, "'*p*' *is true* explains such and such" has the same content as "'*p* explains such and such." While the latter applies to many instances of *p*, reformulating the claim as "'*p*' *is true*" adds no explanatory force.

The denial that "true" denotes a substantive or explanatory property is central to deflationism. It regards DQ as the fundamental fact about truth, although it does not regard the truth predicate as redundant.[71] "Everything that follows from a true statement is true," for instance, is a claim whose sense cannot be expressed without using "true." The crucial role of the truth predicate is precisely to permit such generalizations, which are particularly prominent in philosophy, where we make such statements as "Skeptics claim that most of our beliefs might be false," or "Most of our beliefs are true," statements we could not make without a truth predicate.

So why is commonsense realism not just a version of deflationism? Putnam's first objection is that deflationism is itself a metaphysical view in that it assumes that, because truth has no metaphysical content, it is a pointless concept we should drop. This is Putnam's formulation of his differences with Rorty in the face of Rorty's puzzlement over where they disagree,[72] and I think Rorty did show signs of disillusion stemming from an unsatisfied yearning for metaphysics. But deflationism need not be rooted in such disillusion, and if "what we are destroying are only houses of cards,"[73] it is not nihilistic either. Moreover, deflationism does not drop the concept of truth; the question is whether it has a larger role to play than deflationists admit.

Putnam's second objection is that deflationism assumes a use theory that is not only "the most disastrous feature of the antirealist view that brings about the loss of the world (and the past)"[74] but is also responsible for many of the defects of metaphysical realism.

This objection might be met by adopting a different account of use, in particular, the Wittgensteinian one. On that account, what a speaker knows how to use are not mere marks or sounds, but words or statements that already have a meaning in her language. Her knowing how to use them is simply her knowing what they can be used to assert, but, given DQ, knowing that would also be knowing the conditions under which what is asserted is true. On this view, neither assertibility conditions nor truth conditions are construed as antirealists or metaphysical realists construe them. For example, to understand "neutrinos have mass" is to know that it can be used to assert that neutrinos have mass, and hence to know that it can be used to assert that it is true that neutrinos have mass. To understand what is being asserted requires knowing some physics, but that is sufficient to understand the conditions under which what is being asserted is true.

Consider another example: to understand "There is a lot of coffee on the table" is to know that *if* it is used to assert that there are a lot of coffee bags stacked on the table, then it is true if and only if there are a lot of coffee bags stacked on the table. It is also to know that if, in a different context, it is used to assert that there is a lot of coffee spilled on the table, then it is true if and only if there is a lot of coffee spilled on the table, and so on for other uses of the statement. In these cases, one has to know a great deal to know what assertion is being made in the context, but what one knows are the conditions under which the statement, as asserted in that context, is true.[75]

Putnam's third objection is that deflationism excludes the possibility of any normative account of truth. This is correct if the only essential function of DQ is to permit the kind of generalizations noted above. The objection to that is that if truth is not a normative property, neither are assertion or judgment (belief), but any account that leaves out their normative dimension—their being correct or incorrect—is surely mistaken.

One response (which I have made elsewhere[76]) is to distinguish between truth as contrasted with error and truth as contrasted with falsity. The contrast between truth and error applies to assertion or judgment *as* asserting or judging, not to *what* is asserted or judged considered in abstraction from its being asserted or judged. What is asserted or judged is true or false; asserting and judging are truthful or erroneous, correct or incorrect.[77] Normativity is relevant only when statements are asserted or denied, because there would be nothing wrong with false statements if we never asserted (or accepted) them, just as there would be nothing right with true sentences if we always denied (or rejected) them. This is to agree with Putnam that "truth is a *normative* property," if 'truth' refers to the truth (correctness) of an asserting or judging, while agreeing with deflationism that the truth of *what* is asserted or judged is not normative.

What then of the *ground* of the normativity we ascribe to assertions or judgments in evaluating them as correct or incorrect? Metaphysical realists maintain that it must be that *what* is asserted is true in the substantive sense of corresponding to a fact that makes it true. That account is not open to Putnam and faces the difficulty that since metaphysical realists do not think the correspondence relation is normative, it is problematic if it can ground the normativity of assertion or judgment. Epistemic theories of truth do better because they ground the true/false contrast in the truth/error contrast rather than the other way around: what is asserted is true if the asserting of it is warranted. This yields a normative conception of truth, but Putnam rightly rejects such antirealist theories for reducing what is true to what is warranted.

The alternative is to give an account of what it is for an assertion or judgment to be true (rather than erroneous) without grounding it in what is true rather than false, namely, to ground it in the reasons we have for what we assert or believe. These reasons are both extraordinarily diverse and dependent on the variety of contexts in which assertions and judgments are made and beliefs formed and changed, and hence they have no underlying essence. We may be able to formulate generalizations about our reasons for assertion, judgment, or belief but those generalizations will often be imprecise and apt to mislead, and they will in any case depend for their explanatory force on the instances they generalize over.

It does not follow that the true/false contrast plays no role in the truth/error contrast. It plays a crucial *expressive* role in this sense: it is correct to assert that p only if "p" is true.[78] That does not mean that it is *because* "p" is true that an assertion of p is correct, but rather that "true" enables important generalizations, which, as we have noted, is precisely its indispensible role. The general claim that it is correct to assert that p only if "p" is true, cannot be formulated without "true," but we can formulate *instances* of it without it. For example, the claim, "it is correct to assert that neutrinos have mass only if it is true that neutrinos have mass," can be reformulated without loss as "It is correct to assert that neutrinos have mass only if neutrinos have mass." To generalize that requires "true," but it does not follow that the generalization refers to some property that makes its instances correct; on the contrary, the content of the generalization is derived wholly from its instances.

This response to Putnam's third objection to deflationism rests on making a sharp distinction between the true/false contrast and the truth/error contrast, which means abstracting the content from an assertion or judgment and ascribing *true* (or *false*) to the content alone. This yields an abstract notion of *true*, the *true* of formal logic, which is not normative and does not come in different kinds, unlike the *true* of assertion or judgment, which is normative, complex, and comes in diverse kinds. Putnam rejects this sharp distinction, and I am no longer convinced that it can save a deflationist account of "true."[79] The latter is useful for certain purposes, in formal logic, for instance, or to clarify the Frege-Geach point that the antecedent of a conditional is not asserted. But the distinction does not have the general significance needed if the true/false contrast is to be neither normative nor diverse.

The distinction corresponds roughly to the distinction between the sense of a statement and its force, the true/false contrast applying to the sense, and the truth/error contrast applying to the force. But the sense/force distinction is neither unproblematic nor simple. There are no conventions or rules determining the force of a statement, and hence the distinction between sense and force has to be made by discerning many, often complex, facts about the speaker and the context of her statement. Assertion itself is a complex kind of speech act, which comes in diverse forms, and therefore evaluation of it is complex and multifaceted. It is simplistic to think that we can invariably and cleanly separate out from a statement that aspect (its sense) to which the true/false contrast applies from that aspect (the asserting) to which the truth/error distinction applies, and hence simplistic to characterize the former as too thin to be normative and the latter as fully normative.

Because of Putnam's rejection of deflationism, differentiating commonsense realism from metaphysical realism is subtle. Commonsense realism is like metaphysical realism in holding that truth transcends knowledge. Both views deny that truth is unobtainable, that it is merely a projection of what individuals or societies accept, that there is no such thing as objective truth.

Given the fundamental role of DQ, commonsense realism will resemble metaphysical realism's correspondence theory and may be mistaken for it. If we deflate that correspondence theory in the right way, we get commonsense realism; if we inflate the latter, we may get the correspondence theory. But this does not mean that the contrast is insignificant. There is a great difference between aiming at a metaphysical theory of a substantive property and trying to understand the role of the concept in our lives. As Putnam put it, "Giving up on the funny metaphysical somethings does not require us to give up on concepts that, whatever our philosophical convictions, we employ and must employ when we live our lives."[80]

X

I return now to Putnam's claim that the notion of a separable contribution of the world and of our minds to what is true and what is a fact is unintelligible. "To ask which facts are mind independent in the sense that nothing about them reflects our conceptual choices and which facts are 'contributed' by us is to commit a 'fallacy of division.'"[81] The division is a fallacy because if we think through what it involves, Putnam thinks we will see that it cannot be made intelligible. It appears intelligible only if we accept the interface notion and the representations that are posited to bridge the gap it creates. If to refer to or describe an object in the world requires having a representation of it, we can always ask to what degree the representation corresponds to the object or to what degree it reflects our conceptual choices and interests. Or we can ask the extent to which the representation is guided by the world or by our perspectival experience and conceptual scheme. Or we can ask which features of the representation accurately represent the world and which features are merely perspectival. These are taken to be questions that have intelligible answers, whether or not we know what they are.

Putnam urges that we "distinguish carefully between the activity of 'representation' (as something in which we engage) and the idea of a 'representation' as an interface between ourselves and what we think about."[82] He does not follow Rorty in rejecting altogether the notion of our representing the world in favor of our coping with it. He rather rejects representations as objects that mediate our cognitive relations to the world, contending that we directly represent the world that we describe or perceive. We, of course, represent it as the knowers and agents that we are, with the conceptual and perceptual powers that we have, and the idea of representing it from no particular perspective is merely an empty abstraction from particular representations. But the notion that we could separate *how* we represent from *what* we represent is not intelligible. We cannot represent the world itself with one part of our representing, while another part only reflects our conceptual and experiential perspective. Putnam's externalism—"the content of our thoughts is individuated in part by the sort of environments we inhabit"[83]—entails that representing the world cannot be done in abstraction from the peculiarities of our environments as knowers and agents. But it also helps us understand how representing often succeeds.

Some philosophers seem to think of the world as "having its very own language which is waiting for us to discover and use."[84] But that picture makes sense only if nature is seen as a divine book, a conception that theists and nontheists have long thought irrelevant to this philosophical problem. Others argue that there is one uniquely privileged way of representing the world that yields the one true description of the way the world is. But it is, in Putnam's view, wrong to think there is such a thing as either *the* true description of the world or *the* way the world is. "There are many ways of describing things, some better and some worse and some equally good but simply different, but none which is Nature's own way. . . . [None] describes it 'in itself,' not because the 'in itself' is an unreachable limit but because the 'in itself' does not make sense."[85]

Those influenced by Kant emphasize that representing is a conceptual activity, and hence that conceptual structure is the fundamental contribution of the mind to our representing. What we represent when we represent truly is what is the case (what is a fact), a state that is conceptually structured because of the nature and role of human thought. But, again, the idea of separating out the contribution of conceptual thought to what is the case from the world with which we interact is not intelligible. The truth (or falsity) of our judgments and statements about the world depends on what the world is like, but only because the world shows up in perception, thought, and action as conceptually structured. A thought of what the world would be like without conceptual structure—the world as it is in itself—is no thought at all because all thought is of what is conceptually structured as what is the case.

A parallel point holds for the world as it was before human beings existed or as it would be had human beings never existed. What we think or know about such a world requires that we represent and describe it as the kind of thinkers and experimenters that we are. That means that we describe it from the perspective of our language and conceptual scheme (that regardless of origin becomes ours in use) and that when we describe it truly, we describe what is the case. Again, the thought of what the world was like or would be like in abstraction from our perspective and conceptualizing activity is no thought. The world as it is in itself is not beyond us; the very notion is unintelligible. While Putnam insists that "what is the case" is used in diverse ways, all thought is of what is the case in one of these ways.

We should not, therefore, distinguish realism about existence from realism about the nature of what exists—as though we could posit the existence of things independent of our minds, and then consider whether our representing of them depends on what they are like in themselves or on our perspectival view of them. We simply represent the world and attempt to articulate true statements about it that depend on the world *and* reflect the perspective from which we articulate them. Although there would have been no true statements (and hence no truth) had there been no human beings,[86] we can nevertheless say what would have been the case. But our saying that presumes that we take what we say to be true, which reflects an indivisible mix of mind and world.

Putnam has a similar view of the fact/value distinction. His main concern is to reject the widely held view that statements of fact are objectively warranted and true, whereas statements of value are not. He traces the dichotomy back to Hume, "who assumed a metaphysical dichotomy between 'matters of fact' and 'relations of ideas'"[87] and hence between facts and values. Putnam does not deny that we can make a fact/value distinction that is useful in various contexts and for various purposes. What he denies is a dichotomy between fact and value so that it is always possible to separate the value component from the fact component. This, he argues, is "not a distinction but a *thesis*, namely the thesis that 'ethics' is not about 'matters of fact.'"[88] The objection to that is the dogmatic and narrow notion of "matter of fact" held by Hume and developed by positivists like Carnap. On Putnam's view, there is no "notion of *fact* that contrasts neatly and absolutely with the notion 'value'... invoked in talk of the nature of all 'value judgments'."[89]

Putnam argues for the "entanglement of fact and value." He contends that the Quinean critique of the positivist picture of the language of science as neatly divided into a factual and an analytic part shows that "the whole argument for the classical fact/value dichotomy [is] in ruins."[90] He first makes the point that science itself presupposes values, namely epistemic values, and that those are essential to the kind of objectivity that characterizes science's pursuit of a "right description of the world," which means that fact and value are entangled in science itself.

He then argues that the objectivity implicit in the notion of a "right description of the world," which is something like "correspondence to objects," cannot be the only kind of objectivity we recognize and pursue because mathematical and logical truth are examples of "objectivity without objects."[91] "The attempt to provide an Ontological explanation of the objectivity of mathematics," he writes, is, "in effect, an attempt to provide *reasons which are not part of mathematics for the truth of mathematical statements*."[92] This can help us recognize the Wittgensteinian point that there are many kinds of statements that are neither descriptions nor simply projections of our attitudes, but "are under rational control and governed by standards appropriate to their particular functions and contexts."[93] These include many kinds of value statements, in particular, ethical statements, which are like mathematical and logical statements, both as instances of "objectivity without objects" (hence the title of his book, *Ethics without Ontology*) and as having reasons for their truth that are part of ethics itself. The latter point means that in order to use ethical terms "with any discrimination one has to be able to identify imaginatively with an *evaluative point of view*."[94]

Ethical statements exhibit the entanglement of fact and value most obviously in the "thick" concepts of ethics. These are not thin, abstract concepts like *good, bad, right, wrong, ought*, but concepts like *cruel, generous, suffering, courageous*, which cannot be factored into a factual and an ethical component. The attempt "to split ethical concepts into a 'descriptive meaning component' and a 'prescriptive meaning component' founders on the impossibility of saying what the 'descriptive meaning' of, say 'cruel' is without using the word 'cruel' or a synonym."[95] The same point applies to other kinds of value concepts, the attempt to factor them into a descriptive and a normative concept leading to difficulties similar to those that result from the attempt to factor out the contributions of mind and world to truth and fact.

XI

Putnam's acceptance of a Wittgensteinian conception of philosophy is crucial to his later work, playing a major role in his criticism of other views and in shaping his own. It is also the most controversial feature of his turn to Wittgenstein. The divide between philosophers who are sympathetic to Wittgensteinian avoidance of metaphysical theories, and those who regard theory construction as the soul of serious philosophy is very deep. Whereas the divisions between the analytic tradition and the continental tradition are fading, controversy over the role of theories in philosophy is increasingly fierce, even hostile, and there appear to be no neutral grounds for adjudicating the issue.

Some of the hostility may rest on misconstruing Putnam's view on this matter. His rejection of explanatory theories is not a rejection of theory in all senses. Some philosophers who characterize their work as "theoretical" simply mean they are engaged in reflection rather than political activity or consciousness raising, or that they intend to be rigorous or methodical, and Putnam is theoretical in that sense. His skepticism about theoretical explanation does not rule out explanation in the sense of clarification or elucidation, untangling intricate arguments and reformulating positions. He does not avoid making claims and giving extended arguments for them, or engaging seriously with views he rejects, and he certainly does not think the Wittgensteinian view aims to put philosophy at an end. Although he uses "metaphysical" as a pejorative term, he rejects any positivist criterion of meaning, and his central focus is on the philosophical topics traditionally called "metaphysical": the relation of the mental and the physical, the nature of truth and the mind, what it is to be an event, a property, a fact, a value, what it is to intend, to act, to know, to have a reason, and so on. His aim is not to avoid the philosophical problems raised by reflection on such metaphysical topics but to give a nonmetaphysical resolution of them.

What is a nonmetaphysical resolution of a philosophical problem? The crucial factor is taking seriously Wittgenstein's remark that "Philosophy just puts everything before us, and neither explains nor deduces anything.— Since everything lies open to view, there is nothing to explain. For whatever is hidden is of no interest to us."[96] Timothy Williamson claims that this remark expresses the Cartesian view of self-knowledge "enlarged . . . to everything that is of interest to philosophy," Descartes and Wittgenstein agreeing "on our possession of a cognitive home in which everything lies open to view." The contrary, Williamson contends, is that "Much of our thinking—for example, in the physical sciences—must operate outside this home."[97]

The view Williamson criticizes is, of course, silly, but it is also silly to ascribe it to Wittgenstein or Putnam, both of whom reject a Cartesian view of self-knowledge and, moreover, believe that many things, especially in the physical sciences, do not lie open to our cognitive view. The issue is whether genuine philosophical problems are resolved "by coming up with new discoveries [rather than] by assembling what we have long been familiar with."[98] Wittgenstein urges the latter, even while noting that it may not be easy to discern because "The aspects of things that are most important for us are hidden because of their simplicity and familiarity."[99]

They are hidden, therefore, not because they lie behind or beneath the phenomena to be uncovered by empirical research or posited by theory construction, but because we fail to notice them, reflect on them with care, understand their connections, or get an undistorted view of what they are. Philosophical problems are of the form "I don't know my way about"[100] and hence are not resolved by uncovering hidden mechanisms or positing new entities and deep structures to explain the phenomena. Such theoretical moves simply assume that we do know our way about—that we are clear about the working of our concepts of mind, truth, fact, action, intention, and so on. The real philosophical work, on this view, is not to get a clear overview of how our concepts work but to construct theories that explain their working in terms of hidden mechanisms and structures.

The quest for such theoretical explanation is a legitimate task of the physical sciences, but when it is undertaken in philosophy the result, in Putnam's view, is objectionable metaphysics. Metaphysics aims to give substantive explanations that are modeled on those of physical science, but are not supported by empirical data or linked with accepted theories. The result is what are purported to be explanatory claims that have no substantive force and that waver between being empirical and being conceptual claims. Putnam put it this way: "There is no analogy at all between a serious scientific theory and a typical construction in 'analytic metaphysics.' Most constructions in analytic metaphysics do not extend the range of scientific knowledge, not even speculatively. They merely attempt to rationalize the ways we think and talk in the light of a scientistic 'ideology'."[101]

Such rationalization does not explain the phenomena but takes them for granted in the form of philosophers' intuitions, which are reformulated in technical philosophical terms and then incorporated in a system of hypotheses constituting a theory of the phenomena. The theory is tested by its ability to solve problems that do not arise from reflection on the phenomena but are generated by the theory itself, which is confirmed if it resolves more such problems than alternative theories. It thereby deflects reflection on how our concepts—of truth, intention, the mental, the self—work in our life and thought to reflection on how a technical concept fits into a theoretical construction and how the latter deals with the problems it generates.[102]

Putnam contends not only that these metaphysical constructions of what is hidden fail to explain the phenomena as they intend, but that an adequate understanding of the phenomena will show that there is nothing to explain in this quasiscientific, metaphysical sense. We do not need, he writes, "mysterious and supersensible objects *behind* our language games; the truth can be told in language games that we actually play when our language is working, and the inflations that philosophers have added to those language games are examples, as Wittgenstein said . . . of 'the engine idling'."[103]

The philosophical task is not to reformulate our concepts in technical philosophical terms in order to fit them in an established vocabulary, received distinctions, or the theoretical constructions of a research program. We should rather ask, "Is the word ever actually used in this way in the language game in which it is at home?" and then "bring words back from their metaphysical to their everyday use."[104] This is objectionable "quietism" if one thinks the phenomena stand in need of such explanation, but it is not if one thinks an adequate understanding of the phenomena shows it needs no such explanation. This view leaves many tasks for philosophy and is neither quietism nor the end of philosophy but a new way of formulating its essential task.

XII

In discussing Putnam's critique of metaphysics, I did not mention his contention that its (purported) claims are often unintelligible rather than false, extravagant, or based on bad arguments. Putnam's conception of *unintelligibility* (and numerous related notions like *senseless, incoherent, inconceivable*), which he uses so often in criticizing the views of others, deserves a section (or a paper) of its own, but I shall only make some critical remarks on the topic before expressing brief criticisms of a couple of related points.

A Wittgensteinian conception of philosophy would make unintelligibility central to philosophical criticism. Wittgenstein wrote in 1929 that his "new way of philosophizing . . . consists essentially in leaving the question of *truth* and asking about *sense* instead,"[105] a way of philosophizing that Putnam takes seriously. I noted that in discussing his criticism of the interface notion, in particular, his claim that a dichotomy between mind-independent and mind-dependent truths and facts is unintelligible. This line of criticism is especially prominent in his critical discussion of issues in the philosophy of mind.

Although it also figures in his critique of metaphysics, I have not noted that. One reason is that I do not think that this aspect of Putnam's criticism is very successful. Showing that philosophical "statements" are unintelligible requires considerable argument. It is not sufficient simply to say that metaphysical constructions are flights of fantasy, that they make no sense, or cannot be understood, since the metaphysician can reply that such criticism rests on an uncharitable construal of what is said. Presumably almost any sentence can be construed so as to make sense, and so as not to make sense, and the critic must show why it must be construed in the latter way and why, construed in that way, it makes no sense.

This point applies particularly to metaphysics, for no sentence is metaphysical in itself but only in the way it is used in a given context. While Putnam does undertake to show that certain sentences that are intelligible in some contexts—everyday contexts or religious contexts—fail to be intelligible in the context in which philosophers use them, this is infrequent and often casual and will not satisfy metaphysicians. The latter, moreover, will be offended by the claim that their writings often fail even to reach the level of being implausible or false because they are unintelligible and senseless.

Putnam's critique often functions like an unfocussed shotgun. His opponents' views are, inter alia, unintelligible, not fully intelligible, inconceivable, senseless, without clear sense, incoherent, confused, not understandable, chimerical, absurd, vague. Do these terms have different critical import, and if so, how do they differ? Do some apply to language—words and sentences—and others to concepts and views, and is this a significant distinction? Is a "view" or "statement" with any of these features incapable of being false, implausible, underargued, more or less explanatory, a consequence or having consequences—characteristics that presume intelligibility or sense? A general account of all this is too much to ask, but if the criticism is to carry much weight, it needs to be set out more carefully.

When Putnam does discuss this issue explicitly, he makes a number of compelling points. He rejects any philosophical theory that yields "a general method for assessing the meaningfulness of arbitrary statements."[106] He claims that the notion of *senseless* has no timeless application because "there are some 'statements' to which we are presently unable to attach any sense," but which might come to have sense "as a result of new knowledge of one kind or another"—something which is "a description of our lives with our language, rather than a piece of metaphysics." At the same time, we must realize that "from the fact that . . . words may in the *future* come to have sense we will understand, it [does not follow] that they *now* express anything we can understand."[107]

His discussion of the point that the sense words have (if any) depends on the context in which they are used, is stimulating and intriguing, particularly the way he applies it to religious language. He asserts that the Cartesian idea of "the mind as an immaterial object 'interacting' with the body is an excellent example of an unintelligible position in the philosophy of mind,"[108] which would imply that the Platonic notion of the soul as immaterial that "under St. Augustine's influence . . . became dominant Christian doctrine for several centuries"[109] is also unintelligible. But he distinguishes a religious use of *soul* from a philosophical use:

> The role that may be played by talk of the soul in a particular religious form of life is so different from the role played by talk of the soul in a philosophical argument that the use of the word in the latter context simply cannot be projected in any reliable way from the former. . . . Purely *religious* uses of the word *soul* (even in the context of talk of an 'afterlife,' 'Resurrection', etc.) leave one completely free to accept or reject *philosophical* talk of the soul as 'completely immaterial.'[110]

Augustine, he argues, did not *base* his religious views of the soul on philosophical views. Rather the time in which he lived "created a climate in which Augustine (under the influence of Neo-Platonism) could introduce the philosophical doctrine [of an immaterial soul] as an *exegesis* of the religious doctrines and hopes." The "semblance of intelligibility that philosophical hypotheses [like Cartesian dualism] possess may, in part, be inherited from the intelligibility of the religious myths, but those myths do not depend for their *religious* functioning" on any philosophical hypothesis. In Putnam's view, the intelligibility of religious discourse is not based on the intelligibility of philosophical doctrines like dualism, and "religious ways of think-ing . . . do not support the intelligibility of the philosophical hypotheses," though the latter may seem to be intelligible because of their connection with religious ways of thinking.[111]

These points may be a fruitful use of Wittgensteinian themes, but I am not sanguine about the general use of his way of criticizing philosophical doc-trines. Wittgenstein was a master at critique that asked about sense rather than truth, and I think he often showed the unintelligibility of certain metaphysical notions and philosophical assumptions. But his criticisms were directed at relatively few notions and assumptions (although they were so fundamental that undermining them undermined much else), and for that reason he was able to focus on them and develop the kind of intricate critical case neces-sary to show that their purported claims, if construed as philosophers seem to, are unintelligible. Because Putnam has used this kind of critique on so many scattered targets, he has failed to make the kind of detailed critique of particular claims that would persuade those not already convinced.

Following Wittgenstein in this respect requires the kind of dialectic he practiced in all his work, something it is very difficult to practice in a fruitful and convincing way and that too often results in just the kind of dogmatism he set himself against. I think a better strategy is the one I suggested above, namely to argue that metaphysics attempts to solve philosophical problems by constructing explanatory theories of the phe-nomena that aim to uncover what is hidden. This attempt fails because its purported explanations lack explanatory force and because what they purport to explain does not stand in need of such explanation. While it may be possible to show that the purported explanations are unintelligible, that is not necessary to undercut the pretensions of metaphysics. Indeed the argument might be that the claims are intelligible enough to show why their purported explanations fail to explain.

A related point holds for criticism of metaphysical realism, a view Put-nam encapsulated in terms of four assumptions that I listed at the outset. Putnam rejected those assumptions "not as false assumptions but as, ulti-mately, unintelligible"; indeed, he claims that "each and every one of those assumptions [is] unintelligible."[112] But there is little argument for that claim, and I do not think it is true. I sketched out earlier a way of understanding the assumptions in terms of the physicalism Putnam held at the time that, I think, makes them intelligible (on the plausible assumption that physical-ism is intelligible) and suggests why physicists accept them. It also makes them, in my view, very implausible—as implausible as physicalism, but that is another matter—which presumes they are intelligible.

I will conclude with a couple of other questions about Putnam's work. One result of Wittgenstein's leaving truth for sense is his remark that "If someone were to advance *theses* in philosophy, it would never be possible to debate them because everyone would agree to them."[113] This appears to imply that, insofar as philosophers make philosophical claims, they should avoid controversial claims in favor of those agreeable to everyone; that is at least the ideal. It might seem that commonsense realism, or other commonsense claims, would fit this ideal. The difficulty, of course, is that many philosophers would reject commonsense realism or Putnam's other commonsense views, for instance, his account of perception

The question is why commonsense realism is not a theory that competes with the theories of metaphysical and internal realism—a better theory perhaps, but still a theory. Is a disjunctivist account of perception a theory, and if not, why not? Should semantic externalism not be seen as a component of a theory of language, methodologically on a par with the numerous other theories of language on offer? How do we tell the difference between "metaphysical excessive baggage that should be jettisoned"[114] and bold and intricate accounts? How, to put the point generally, do we distinguish between philosophical accounts that amount to a metaphysical theory and accounts that are ordinary commonsense and use concepts "we employ and must employ when we live our lives."[115]

One final query concerns the concept of "responsible to reality" that is central to Putnam's commonsense realism about truth. I agree that reality, by being present in our experience, may directly yield reasons for judgment or assertion, and I agree that "responsible to reality" may amount to different things depending on the discourse. As Putnam notes, "We constantly add to the ways in which language can be responsible to reality . . . [and] we endlessly renegotiate . . . our notion of reality as our language and our life develop."[116] I also accept Putnam's idea that the distinction between truth and justification should not be construed as a metaphysical dichotomy. But Putnam's rejection of the antirealist notion that truth *is* sufficient justification means that reasons for a judgment or assertion do not entail that either is true. The issue is how to distinguish "responsible to reality" in the sense of justification from "responsible to reality" in the sense of truth. Given the diversity of the concept, there will be no *general* way of knowing when "responsibility to reality" means justification and when it means truth, but there should be a way of characterizing the difference in an informative way—of characterizing the kind of responsibility to reality that *is* truth.[117]

FREDERICK STOUTLAND

ST. OLAF COLLEGE
UPPSALA UNIVERSITY
JANUARY 2011

NOTES

1. Hilary Putnam, *Words and Life*, ed. James Conant (Cambridge, MA: Harvard University Press, 1994), 28.

2. Cf. Ibid., 299.

3. Hilary Putnam, *The Threefold Cord: Mind, Body, and World* (New York: Columbia University Press, 1999), 183n41.

4. I will use "statement" throughout this essay as the default term for what is said to be true (or false), which means that the term will vary in sense depending on the context. The context will usually make it clear whether the term is used to refer to a declarative sentence (which may or may not be meaningful), to an assertable sentence (which may not be declarative), or to what is (or would be) stated by the assertive utterance of a sentence in a particular context (which is my own view of what is properly said to be true or false). My use of "statement" resembles Wittgenstein's "Satz," which can have the sense of either "proposition" or "sentence."

5. This can be seen as an application of what Putnam at the time called Wittgenstein's "two theories of meaning": a use theory of understanding statements and a picture theory of what makes them true. He has since given up that reading of Wittgenstein.

6. "Reference and truth are so construed that [given ordinary circumstances] sentences will tend to be accepted in the long run if and only if they are *true*, and predicates will be applied to things if and only if those things have the properties corresponding to those predicates." Hilary Putnam, *Mind, Language and Reality: Philosophical Papers*, vol. 2 (Cambridge: Cambridge University Press, 1975), 289.

7. Hilary Putnam, *Meaning and the Moral Sciences* (London: Routledge and Kegan Paul, 1978), 125.

8. The first quotation is from Hilary Putnam, *Reason, Truth, and History* (Cambridge: Cambridge University Press, 1981), 49; the second from Putnam, *Meaning and the Moral Sciences*, 120.

9. Putnam, *Reason, Truth, and History*, 61.

10. Ibid., 49.

11. For an account of how this term came to be used, cf. Putnam, *The Threefold Cord*, 182 n36.

12. The reference to ideal epistemic circumstances was meant to distinguish the theory from Dummett's.

13. Putnam, *Words and Life*, 280.

14. Putnam, *Reason, Truth, and History*, 52.

15. John Searle simply misses the point with his often repeated criticism of Putnam for ignoring the fact that we can always speak of a definite number of objects provided that we fix the sense of "object." Putnam does not ignore that fact; he agrees with it: "We can think of our words and thoughts as having determinate reference to objects (when it is clear what sort of 'objects' we are talking about and what vocabulary we are using)" (Putnam, *Words and Life*, 309). His point is that we have no conception at all of what it would be for objects or properties to exist in the world as it is in itself. The concepts apply only to the phenomenal world, and since the structure of that world depends on our language and conceptual schemes, so does the object-property structure. But from within a language or conceptual structure we can refer determinately to both objects and properties.

16. Hilary Putnam, *The Many Faces of Realism* (La Salle, IL: Open Court, 1987), 17, 19, 20.

17. Putnam, *Reason, Truth, and History*, 50.

18. He wrote, "I regret having myself spoken of 'mind-dependence' in connection with these issues in *Reason, Truth, and History*" (Putnam, *The Threefold Cord*, 178n8).

19. Putnam's turn to Wittgenstein is best seen in *The Threefold Cord*. An early version of the turn can be seen in Hilary Putnam, *Renewing Philosophy* (Cambridge, MA: Harvard University Press, 1992), his Gifford Lectures from 1989. His *The Collapse of the Fact/ Value Dichotomy and Other Essays* (Cambridge, MA: Harvard University Press, 2002) is a Wittgensteinian work, as is his *Ethics without Ontology* (Cambridge, MA: Harvard University Press, 2004). The two volumes of his essays edited by James Conant (*Realism with a Human Face* [Cambridge, MA: Harvard University Press, 1990] and *Words and Life*) contain many papers that are Wittgensteinian, along with others that are not. Conant's long introductions to both works articulate features of the turn. Putnam's "A Half Century of Philosophy, Viewed from Within" (in *Daedalus*: Proceedings of the American Academy of Arts and Sciences 126, no. 1 [1997]: 175–208) is an informative and charming autobiography that discusses some of the persons who influenced him in his turn to Wittgenstein.

20. Ludwig Wittgenstein, *Philosophical Investigations*, rev. 4th ed., trans. G. E. M Anscombe, P. M. S. Hacker, and Joachim Schulte (Oxford: Wiley-Blackwell, 2009), §116.

21. Putnam, *Mind, Language and Reality*, 33.

22. See "Dreaming and Depth Grammar" in Putnam, *Mind, Language and Reality*.

23. Putnam, *The Threefold Cord*, 44.

24. Putnam, *Mind, Language and Reality*, xvii.

25. Wittgenstein, *Philosophical Investigations*, §109.

26. Putnam, *The Threefold Cord*, 10.

27. Wittgenstein, *Philosophical Investigations*, §95.

28. "My own model-theoretic argument against realism . . . was, at bottom, a form of 'Berkeleyan skepticism,' and I believe that there is no way to defeat those doubts if the interface conception of perceptual experience is left standing." Putnam, *The Threefold Cord*, 169.

29. Ibid., 14.

30. Ibid.

31. Ibid., 16.

32. Ibid.

33. In Putnam, *Mind, Language and Reality*.

34. Putnam, *The Threefold Cord*, 14.

35. Ibid.

36. Ibid., 11.

37. Ibid., 43–44.

38. Ibid., 20.

39. Ibid.

40. Ibid., 169.

41. Ibid., 25.

42. Ibid., 39.

43. Ibid., 159.

44. Wittgenstein, *Philosophical Investigations*, §126.

45. Ibid., §109.

46. Putnam, *Renewing Philosophy*, 35.

47. See Wittgenstein, *Philosophical Investigations*, §143, §185.

48. Putnam, *Reason, Truth, and History*, 5.

49. Putnam, *The Threefold Cord*, 47.

50. Cited in Putnam, *Renewing Philosophy*, 37.

51. Ibid., 165.

52. That may not have been Putnam's view when he wrote "The Meaning of 'Meaning,'" but it is what he has come to think about the claims made in that paper.

53. Putnam, *The Threefold Cord*, 48.

54. Wittgenstein, *Philosophical Investigations*, §7.

55. Putnam, *Words and Life*, 289.

56. Ibid., 283f.

57. Putnam, *The Threefold Cord*, 68n56.

58. Ibid., 65.

59. Putnam, *Words and Life*, 305; Putnam, *Renewing Philosophy*, 122.

60. Putnam, *Words and Life*, 301.

61. Putnam, *The Threefold Cord*, 68.

62. Hilary Putnam, "Truth, Activation Vectors and Possession Conditions for Concepts," in *Philosophy and Phenomenological Research* 52, no. 2 (June 1992): 431–47, 436.

63. Putnam, *The Threefold Cord*, 68.

64. Ibid., 69.

65. Putnam, "Truth, Activation Vectors and Possession Conditions for Concepts," 432.

66. Putnam, *Words and Life*, 309.

67. Putnam, *Ethics without Ontology*, 21–22.

68. Ibid., 48, 49.

69. Putnam, *Words and Life*, 303.

70. Putnam, *The Threefold Cord*, 54.

71. Thus Paul Horwich writes that "It is a mistake to think that truth is a substantive property with some unified underlying nature awaiting philosophical articulation. Rather, our truth predicate is merely a logical device enabling simple formulations of certain kinds of generalizations. . . . And the concept of truth is entirely captured by the equivalence scheme." (Quoted in Putnam, *The Threefold Cord*, 193n26.)

72. Cf. Putnam, *Words and Life*, 300, or Conant's "Introduction," *Words and Life*, xxiv.

73. Wittgenstein, *Philosophical Investigations*, §118.

74. Putnam, *The Threefold Cord*, 55.

75. For discussion cf. Frederick Stoutland, "Wittgenstein on Certainty and Truth," in *Philosophical Investigations* (July 1998): 203–21. The point of view is defended at length in Charles Travis's *The Use of Sense* (Oxford: Oxford University Press, 1989), a book to which Putnam often refers.

76. I gave that response in "Putnam on Truth" (in *The Practice of Language*, ed. M. Gustafsson and L. Hertzberg [Dordecht: Kluwer Academic Publishers, 2002], 147–76), which contains a much more detailed account of the response, as well as further discussion of Putnam's metaphysical and internal realisms.

77. On this see Josiah Royce's article "Error and Truth" in the *Encyclopedia of Religion and Ethics*—interestingly, the only article on truth in this famous old encyclopedia. For some of the complications about what the true-false contrast applies to, see my "Putnam on Truth."

78. It is not a sufficient condition because someone may assert "p" and "p" may be true, but he may assert it for reasons that are very bad or irrelevant so that his asserting the truth was sheer accident. *What* was asserted was true, but his asserting it did not meet norms of correctness.

79. This paragraph was inspired by criticism pressed by Martin Gustafsson.

80. Putnam, *The Threefold Cord*, 70.

81. Putnam, *Renewing Philosophy*, 58.

82. Putnam, *The Threefold Cord*, 59.

83. Putnam, *Words and Life*, 306.

84. Ibid., 302.

85. Ibid., 303.

86. Ibid., 302.

87. Putnam, *The Collapse of the Fact/Value Dichotomy*, 14.

88. Ibid., 19.

89. Ibid., 26.

90. Ibid., 30.

91. Ibid., 33.

92. Putnam, *Ethics without Ontology*, 3.

93. Putnam, *The Collapse of the Fact/Value Dichotomy*, 33.

94. Ibid., 39.

95. Ibid., 38.

96. Wittgenstein, *Philosophical Investigations*, §126

97. Timothy Williamson, *Knowledge and Its Limits* (Oxford: Oxford University. Press, 2000), 93.

98. Wittgenstein, *Philosophical Investigations*, §109.

99. Ibid., §129.

100. Ibid., §173.

101. Putnam, *Renewing Philosophy*, 141.

102. See Ibid., 135f and Stoutland, "Analytic Philosophy and Metaphysics," in *Wittgenstein and the Method of Philosophy*, ed. Sami Pihlström (*Acta Philosophica Fennica* 80, 2006).

103. Putnam, *Ethics without Ontology*, 22.

104. Wittgenstein, *Philosophical Investigations*, §116.

105. Ludwig Wittgenstein, *Culture and Value*, rev. ed., trans. Peter Winch (Oxford: Wiley-Blackwell, 1998), 3.

106. Putnam, *The Threefold Cord*, 84.

107. Putnam, *Words and Life*, 259; Putnam, *The Threefold Cord*, 172.

108. Putnam, *The Threefold Cord*, 78.

109. Ibid., 97.

110. Ibid.

111. All quotations here are from ibid., 96f.

112. Ibid., 183n41.

113. Wittgenstein, *Philosophical Investigations*, §128.

114. Putnam, *Words and Life*, 254.

115. Putnam, *The Threefold Cord*, 70.

116. Putnam, *The Threefold Cord*, 9.

117. Thanks to Lilli Alanen for a critical reading of my paper and for her support in my writing it.

REPLY TO FREDERICK STOUTLAND

I realize that when one receives a warm invitation to stay in someone's house it is bad manners to say "No, I don't want to," and Frederick Stoutland has indeed issued a warm welcome to consider myself a Wittgensteinian. My long engagement (and at times struggle) with Wittgenstein's difficult and deep philosophical texts has indeed deepened my conviction that we need the sort of philosophical vision that is capable of recognizing the plurality of what Wittgenstein calls our "language games" and of the "forms of life" with which they are interwoven: the sort that is thoroughly antiessentialist and free both of fantasies of reducing all the kinds of truth and objectivity there are to the kind of truth and objectivity characteristic of the exact sciences and of metaphysical fantasies with no connection either to real life or to real science. Stoutland is right to point to a number of places where this influence is perceptible in my writings; nevertheless, as I shall explain, I am not a "Wittgensteinian." So, while I am grateful for the friendly spirit in which the invitation is issued, I do have to decline.

I. On "Unintelligibility"

Stoutland's essay is long and complex, and, if this reply is not to be excessively long, I will have to focus on a few issues. Perhaps I can get more quickly to the most essential issues if I begin by discussing two passages. Here is the first, from Stoutland's section XII:

> Wittgenstein was a master at critique that asked about sense rather than truth, and I think he often showed the unintelligibility of certain metaphysical notions and philosophical assumptions. But his criticisms were directed at relatively few notions and assumptions (although they were so fundamental that undermining them undermined much else), and for that reason he was able to focus on them and develop the kind of intricate critical case necessary to show that their purported claims, if construed as philosophers seem to, are

unintelligible. Because Putnam has used this kind of critique on so many scattered targets, he has failed to make the kind of detailed critique of particular claims that would persuade those not already convinced.

By speaking of "unintelligibility," Stoutland touches on what has proved a *minefield*. Wittgensteinians have divided themselves into many camps, the two most famous in the last decade of the twentieth century being the "Baker & Hacker"[1] camp (sometimes referred to as "orthodox" Wittgensteinians) and the second camp being the "New Wittgensteinians," for example, James Conant and Cora Diamond.[2] The two camps agree that a Wittgensteinian critique of metaphysics involves showing the metaphysician's sentences to be *nonsense*.[3] Where they differed is on the abstruse issue of what "nonsense" means here.[4] I disagree totally with the "Baker & Hacker" position, but I also have to say that I find the "New Wittgenstein" camp too extreme.

Briefly, I now believe that the New Wittgenstein camp is right on the question of what Wittgenstein *meant*, but both camps are wrong (and Wittgenstein was wrong) in thinking that the sentences that typical metaphysicians (as well as skeptics, and other philosophers allegedly in need of "therapy") utter are *totally* nonsensical—nonsensical because they violate rules that are constitutive of sense, according to the "Baker & Hacker" interpretation, and nonsensical simply because they lack any determinate sense (no matter what the reason might be that leads the philosopher to *think* she is saying something meaningful), according to the "New Wittgenstein" interpretation. I have explained elsewhere[5] why I reject the Baker & Hacker view. And to proponents of both views I want to say that while of course there is a perfectly good use of the epithets "nonsense" (and in my writing, which Stoutland cites, "unintelligible") to describe what one finds either extremely unreasonable or significantly lacking in clarity, that the epithet is justified in any particular case is something that needs to be argued *philosophically*, not linguistically. (On that, I believe, Stoutland and I are in complete agreement.) But I would emphasize (and I wonder if Stoutland would agree?) that unreasonable statements and unclear concepts are not *literally* devoid of sense—and I have never thought that philosophers of language have a *better* notion of "sense" than linguists or ordinary speakers, by the way.[6] For example, if someone argues (as several students did in a seminar on skepticism that I once gave at the University of Tel Aviv) that the statement "Two plus two may turn out not to be four" is true, on the ground that we have been wrong in the past even about statements that seemed at the time to be necessary truths, my reply would *not* be that this sentence is literally "devoid of meaning," but I *would* say that it lacks full intelligibility because the students who said this were totally unable to say *how* it could "turn out" that two plus two is not four.[7]

Similarly, I cannot understand such alleged "metaphysical possibilities" as the possibility that some human beings are zombies, because I cannot say *how* something could have the same physical makeup as a normal human being (and the same behavior, with the same physical causes) and lack consciousness. To think that zombies are a possibility I would have to assume that our entire view of the world is wrong in a way I am utterly unable to make cohere with anything I believe. Indeed, when it came *to religious* (as opposed to metaphysical) utterances, Wittgenstein himself said (about certain sentences about the Last Judgment, presumably about separating the saved from the damned) that he is unable to say he "understands" them because "I haven't got these thoughts or anything that hangs together with them,"[8] while refusing to say that those utterances are nonsense, lack meaning, or anything of the kind.

Although I myself was not clear on this when I wrote *The Threefold Cord: Mind, Body and World,* The problem with understanding "some individuals are actually zombies," like the problem with understanding "there will be a Last Judgment, and the saved will be separated from the damned," is not a *linguistic* one; it is not that the words literally do not have a meaning in that sentence.

To sum up: one can appreciate what I described as Wittgenstein's pluralistic vision of life and language without sharing with him, or with today's "Wittgensteinians," the idea that *metaphysical sentences are literally devoid of meaning.* Plato's writings are not nonsense, nor are Spinoza's, nor are Leibniz's, nor are Hegel's. I cannot inhabit the intellectual world of these philosophers, but to suggest that what they wrote was "nonsense" is a hangover from the mistaken idea that metaphysics is *passé* that Wittgenstein, the Logical Positivists, and Heidegger all shared. (Nor do I agree with Wittgenstein's famous remark about Socrates.[9])

I also believe that we need to rescue Wittgenstein's genuine insights from that moment in his thought which is characterized by the use of the term "grammar." The idea that in *some* sense (which no one has ever succeeded in making clear) philosophical problems are "grammatical" was, I believe, a *picture* of what has (allegedly) gone wrong in a philosophy whose grip Wittgenstein unfortunately never managed to shake off. To say this is not to deny that there are points at which all the metaphysicians I listed fail to say things that we *today* can find fully intelligible. But that is not because they made "grammatical" mistakes; we (or, more precisely, I) cannot find classical "ontotheology" intelligible because I have a whole world view shaped by science and by the Enlightenment. If someone rejects that whole world view, then I can only say (quoting a moment in Wittgenstein that I very much admire), "this is where my spade is turned."[10] But we can still read the great metaphysicians with pleasure and frequently with instruction.

II. Must Philosophy Eschew Explanation?

Stoutland, I think, is also in the grip of the idea I mentioned that traditional metaphysics was a *mistake*. I suspect this, because he advocates a profoundly *limiting* idea of what is left for philosophy. In witness to this, here is the second passage that I wish to quote:

> In rejecting metaphysical and internal realism, Putnam abandoned the conception of philosophy at work in their development in favor of one similar to Wittgenstein's, who had written in *Philosophical Investigations*:
>
> *It was correct that our considerations must not be scientific ones. . . . We may not advance any kind of theory. There must not be anything hypothetical in our considerations. All explanation must disappear, and description alone must take its place. And this description gets its light—that is to say its purpose—from the philosophical problems. . . . The problems are solved, not by coming up with new discoveries, but by assembling what we have long been familiar with.*[11]
>
> Shifting to such a view was crucial in shaping Putnam's later work, not least in enabling him to get a more perceptive and illuminating understanding of the range of Wittgenstein's work. (In what follows, when I refer to "Putnam's view," I mean his current view—his turn to Wittgenstein.)

In fact, the idea that philosophy should eschew *explanation* once and for all is, and has always been, foreign to my thought. Since this is something that, lamentably, Stoutland gets wrong, let me first say a word about my "internal realist" period (1976–1990).[12] Stoutland equates scientific realism with what I called "metaphysical realism" (which he also misdescribes).[13] I defined the terms "internal realism" and "metaphysical realism" in my Presidential Lecture to the Eastern Division of the American Philosophical Association in December 1976, titled "Realism and Reason."[14] In the very first sentences of that lecture, I explained the term "internal realism" as *synonymous* with "scientific realism" (which I opposed to "metaphysical realism"):

> In one way of conceiving it, realism is an empirical theory. One of the facts that this theory explains is that scientific theories tend to 'converge' in the sense that earlier theories are, very often, limiting cases of later theories (which is why it is possible to regard theoretical terms as preserving their reference across most changes of theory) . . . Let me refer to realism in this sense—acceptance of this sort of scientific picture of the relation of speakers to their environment—as *internal* realism.

Confusingly, later in that same lecture, in a section titled "Why all this doesn't refute internal realism," I identified "internal realism" with the view that whether a theory has a unique intended interpretation "has no absolute sense."[15] But I did not suggest or think that this was in any way inconsistent with the opening sentences of the lecture; I was simply adding a further element to the position, namely the claim that *accepting scientific realism in no way commits one to accepting metaphysical realism*; on the contrary, I argued, an internal realist in my sense could be a verificationist and still be a card carrying "scientific realist." So scientific realism was not the same thing as "metaphysical realism," and, in fact, I have never given up scientific realism (but more of that in the next section).

Nor can I agree with what Stoutland writes about me in the following passage:

> Putnam thought that modern philosophy had been dominated by the view that representations are necessary to bridge the gap between mind and world created by the interface notion. He also thought that view was crucial to both metaphysical and internal realism, in the first instance in their use theory of language, which yielded the model-theoretic distinction [sic] between a language and its interpretation, a distinction that is a linguistic version of the interface notion.[[16]] As a metaphysical realist, Putnam attempted to bridge the gap by claiming that the predicates we use to refer can be interpreted as denoting objects with the corresponding properties, because that is the best explanation of the success of our discourse. As an internal realist, he attempted to bridge it by an epistemic theory that claimed that a language connects with objects of reference only as the objects are conceptualized by us. Both attempts to bridge the gap also assumed a parallel theory of truth.

Unfortunately, Stoutland's remarks are inaccurate as an account of my philosophical development, because, as I just pointed out, my claim that the hypothesis that (most of) our theoretical predicates succeed in referring to real objects and properties, even if we often have a conception of those objects and properties that is destined to be eventually superceded, is "the best explanation of the success of our discourse" was a claim of *internal realism* (and not necessarily of metaphysical realism). And I do not agree that internal realism and metaphysical realism assume "a parallel theory of truth" (not if "parallel" means "similar," anyway). But I am not sure what this last claim means.

However, I have not been an "internal realist" for more than twenty years, so let me turn to my *present* reasons for not agreeing with Wittgenstein's recommendation that "All explanation must disappear, and description alone must take its place." To explain why I reject it, I find it easiest to proceed by simply giving three examples of problems concerning which I believe (and also believed before and after my "internal realist" period) that the philosophical task does involve explanation, even if it be only partial explanation, and not just description. The three problems are (1) the role of reference to real entities, states, and processes in empirical science; (2) the objectivity of mathematics; and (3) the problem of perception. I shall discuss them in turn.

III. My "No Miracles" Argument

In the fortuitously named Hilary Term of 1976, in the second of my Locke Lectures at Oxford University,[17] I said that

> The modern positivist has to leave it without explanation . . . that 'electron calculi' and 'space-time calculi' and 'DNA calculi' correctly predict observable phenomena if, in reality, there are no electrons, no curved space-time, and no molecules. If there are such things, then a natural explanation of the success of these theories is that they are *partially true accounts* of how they behave. And a natural account of the way in which scientific theories succeed each other—say, the way in which Einstein's Relativity succeeded Newton's Universal Gravitation—is that a partially correct/partially incorrect account of a theoretical object—say, the gravitational field or the metric structure of space-time, or both—is replaced by a *better* account of the same object or objects. But if these objects don't really exist at all, then it is a *miracle* that a theory which speaks of gravitational action at a distance correctly predicts phenomena; it is a *miracle* that a theory that speaks of curved space-time correctly predicts phenomena; and the fact that the laws of the former theory are derivable 'in the limit' from the laws of the latter theory has no methodological significance.[18]

Approximately thirty years later, Yemima Ben-Menahem published a list of the principal criticisms of my "no miracles" argument to that date,[19] to which I responded in a lecture to the Boston Colloquium for the Philosophy of Science.[20] In my response, I point out that the "no miracles" argument was not intended as an argument against skepticism about the existence of the external world. As I just pointed out, an antirealist about *truth* could quite well accept the "no miracles" argument. A lecture in which I made just that point was collected in the very same volume as my Locke Lectures, and in that lecture ("Realism and Reason") I advocated such an antirealism, whereas I now find it (and a related form of antirealism defended by Michael Dummett) to be incoherent. (Because I explain why in my Reply to Michael Dummett in the present volume, I will not go into details about why I find those versions of "antirealism" incoherent in *this* reply.) However, I do not believe that refuting *antirealism about truth* makes it *unnecessary* to refute *instrumentalism*, and the arguments against instrumentalism necessarily depend upon looking at actual science, as I argued in those Locke Lectures, and upon asking for the best *diachronic* explanation of the success of science. After all, instrumentalists about theoretical entities can perfectly well be "commonsense realists" about ordinary middle-sized objects. They do not have to defend any antirealist theory of truth; they can just say that while realist truth may be fine in its place, it has no application to, say, quantum reality. There are both scientists (for example, Niels Bohr) and philosophers who have been perfectly happy to be realists about macro-observables, such as ships and shoes and sealing wax, while denying that the particles and fields spoken of in theoretical physics are real. (Niels Bohr: "There is no quantum world. There is only an abstract quantum mechanical description.")[21] And the instrumentalist position has had real world consequences. It was precisely because influential scientists (and logical empiricist philosophers as well) were content to say that quantum mechanics could only be understood as an algorithm for predicting the behavior of "observables" that serious investigation of the possibility of a realist interpretation of the theory was seriously neglected for decades. Fortunately, one great physicist philosopher, J. S. Bell, fought against the current, and because of his efforts investigation into the possibility of a realist interpretation compatible with Relativity is now alive and well.[22] When one reads Bell's papers,[23] it becomes obvious that Bell was led to his proof of his famous theorem establishing the essentially nonlocal nature of quantum mechanics by his stand against the "antirealist" consensus about quantum mechanics. The sharp separation between physics and metaphysics that both Wittgenstein and the positivists believed in was a mistake; both subjects are more likely to flourish when they interact.

I just said that the arguments against instrumentalism necessarily depend on looking at actual science. The reason is, as I said in my Locke Lectures, that it is, after all, contingent that, to take an example, "present day theory does assert the existence of entities which fill many of the *roles* that Bohr's 'electrons' [in the Bohr-Rutherford model] were supposed to fill, even if these entities have other, very strange, properties that Bohr-Rutherford 'electrons' were not supposed to have."[24]

I continued, "But what if we accept a theory from the standpoint of which electrons are like *phlogiston*?" And I answered:

Then we will have to say electrons don't really exist. What if this keeps happening? What if *all* the theoretical entities postulated by one generation (molecules, genes, etc., as well as electrons) invariably 'don't exist' from the standpoint of later science? This is, of course, a form of the old skeptical 'argument from error'—how do you know you aren't in error *now*? But it is the form in which the argument from error is a *serious* worry for many people today, and not just a 'philosophical doubt'.[25]

The question is serious because, in the scenario I just described, eventually the following pessimistic metainduction would become completely warranted: *just as no theoretical term used in the science of fifty years ago referred to anything that actually exists, so it will turn out that no term used in present-day science refers to anything that actually exists.*[26] But, I argued, on a proper theory of reference for theoretical terms (the sort of account that I defended in "The Analytic and the Synthetic," "The Meaning of Meaning," and "Explanation and Reference," it is *not* the case that "no theoretical term used in the science of fifty years ago referred to anything that actually exists."

All of this I still believe. Thus I still see conceptual arguments (arguments about the nature of reference to theoretical entities) and empirical considerations—the argument that the hypothesis that theoretical terms mostly refer is part of the only available *explanation* of the sort of "convergence" that we see in scientific theories, and of the success of the science of the last few centuries—as supporting one another. Philosophy, as I conceive it, is not just "description." I do not agree that *"*All explanation must disappear, and description alone must take its place."

IV. The Objectivity of Mathematics

Because my philosophy of mathematics is often misdescribed,[27] I shall begin with a brief description that I do find acceptable. Such a description is given by Mario De Caro and David Macarthur in their introduction to a collection of my papers that they edited. As they write,

> Early in his career Putnam presented an argument for the thesis that mathematics should be taken as true under some interpretation (against, above all, the formalist), which was dependent on considerations internal to mathematics, e.g. its coherence, fertility, and success. He then developed an argument based on considerations external to mathematics, to the conclusion that mathematics is true on a realist interpretation (against intuitionists, operationalists, if-then-ists, and the like).[28] The latter argument is his famous indispensability argument.
>
> This argument's first premise is that physics is true in a realist sense; its second premise is that mathematics is indispensable to physics; its third premise is that

the only way of accounting for the indispensable applications of mathematics to physics requires that mathematics is interpreted as true in a realist sense; and it thus concludes that mathematics is true in a realist sense. 'Realism,' throughout, is to be understood as implying that the statements of physics and mathematical statements are either true or false where these notions are not to be understood in antirealist terms, that is, in terms of, say, verifiability or provability. Contra Mark Colyvan,[29] the argument is not an ontological one and, in particular, it does not imply any form of Platonism in the philosophy of mathematics. Consequently, many theoretical issues that are currently debated in connection with Colyvan's formulation of the argument miss their intended target.[30]

Given that De Caro and Macarthur get me right, where does this place my view in terms of Stoutland's "explanation/description" dichotomy? And, for that matter, where does it place Wittgenstein's views on the same issues?

My answer was given in the Locke Lectures referred to earlier, when I wrote: "Philosophy is (in part) *normative* description of our institutions: theory of knowledge seeks to explain and describe our practice that contributes to the success of inquiry."[31] In sum, philosophy does involve description, but description that has a normative purpose, and that is related to explanation.

What about Wittgenstein? Here it makes sense to distinguish between what Wittgenstein says in the passage Stoutland quotes, and what he actually *does* when he turns to precisely the issue of the objectivity of mathematics in a realist sense, as explained by De Caro and Macarthur. In the passage in question, Wittgenstein says that "All explanation must disappear, and description alone must take its place. And this description gets its light—that is to say its purpose—from the philosophical problems . . . . The problems are solved, not by coming up with new discoveries, but by assembling what we have long been familiar with."[32] If there is a normative purpose here, it is "solving" (by which Wittgenstein means *dissolving*) "philosophical problems." This sort of description only teaches us how to avoid certain confusions; it does not lead to a deeper understanding of our practices or how those practices contribute to the aims of inquiry.

In contrast to my conception of the task, in Wittgenstein's copious writing on what he was pleased to call "foundations of mathematics," Wittgenstein repeatedly suggests that mathematics is *not* objective in a realist sense[33] (without so much as addressing the question of the relation between mathematics and mathematical physics!), and that, moreover, enormous parts of nineteenth-, twentieth-, and now twenty-first-century mathematics are themselves just "language idling." For example, he goes so far as to deny that there is such a thing as a "set of all irrational numbers."[34] It seems that Wittgenstein simply gave what I regard as a profoundly untenable "solution" to the problem of the objectivity of mathematics. (I explain why I say "profoundly untenable" in "Wittgenstein and the Real Numbers,"[35] and I will not repeat the arguments here, beyond saying that rejecting the very idea of a set of all real numbers is rejecting an enormous amount of perfectly standard mathematics, and not just some bad philosophy). Stoutland is quite wrong to suggest that I have become a "Wittgensteinian" in my philosophy of mathematics.

V. The Problem of Perception

Not surprisingly, even though the topic is very different, some of the same methodological issues will be visible when we turn our attention to the topic of *perception*. I do not see the role of the philosopher as simply one of *dissolving* problems caused by false pictures that have us in their grip any more here than in philosophy of science or philosophy of mathematics. As I write in my Reply to John McDowell in the present volume,

> According to McDowell . . . the right way . . . [to view it] is "to see perceptual experience as actualization of conceptual capacities in sensory receptivity." And . . . I find this "unbelievable." For example, there is nothing in current neurological or psychological studies of vision to support in any way the idea that the conceptual capacities involved in conceptual thought are necessary for the mere having of visual experience. I fear that McDowell may reply that experiences, including color experiences, are outside the sphere of brain science altogether, but if that is what he thinks, then I do not agree. I think that neurology and brain science and phenomenology and reflection on the grammar of our psychological terms are *all* relevant to discussions of the nature and etiology of color experiences. Here too, and not only in moral philosophy, I think we should seek for what John Rawls called a "reflective equilibrium," in this case one which will best enable us to accommodate, to interpret, and, to be sure, sometimes to revise, the various things we are inclined to say about perception. And I see no serious reason to think, either *pre* or *post* such reflection, that *conceptualization* is necessary to the having of, say, color experiences. Indeed, if we follow McDowell and see color experiences as "actualizations" of cognitive capacities that we have and animals (and prelinguistic infants) lack, then the color experiences of those animals and those infants must indeed be "ineffable" for us. But there is no good reason to think that they are.

As another example of the way in which neurological and experimental studies in perception can impact philosophical conclusions, I will just describe the recent development of those views.[36] Stoutland gives an excellent account of my views as of when I wrote *The Threefold Cord: Mind, Body and World.* And he is right that in that book I accepted much of McDowell's disjunctivism. But it is relevant to mention that a paper by Ned Block criticizing one of my arguments has caused Hilla Jacobson and me to abandon that position.[37] And Block's paper draws heavily on empirical data, as well as providing sound philosophical arguments for the *relevance* of such data. Of course, giving up disjunctivism does not mean giving up the idea that we need to move closer to naïve realism. But there are many ways in which one might do that. I know that for some (perhaps most) Wittgensteinians, the idea that philosophy of mind, brain science, and experimental psychology need to "talk to" one another and condition one another is anathema (although Wittgenstein did make impressive use of the "duck-rabbit" phenomenon that he learned of from reading Jastrow);[38] for me, the idea of a fence between philosophical and empirical questions is wholly untenable (as is the idea of an absolute dichotomy between a "realm of reasons" and a "space of [natural] law"). My aim in philosophy of perception, as in philosophy of science and philosophy of mathematics, is, once again, *normative description of our practice.*

VI. STOUTLAND'S CLOSING QUESTIONS

Stoutland poses a number of questions at the very end of his paper to which I shall very briefly reply.

(1) *The question is why commonsense realism is not a theory that competes with the theories of metaphysical and internal realism—a better theory perhaps, but still a theory.* Is a disjunctivist account of perception a theory, and if not, why not? **Answer**: I am no longer a "disjunctivist" (I call my most recent position "transactionalism,"[39] because it emphasizes that perceptual experience is conditioned by both the nature and history of the subject and the features of the environment being attended to. So, is "transactionalism" a theory? Yes. I have no trouble with the idea that there should be theories in philosophy.

(2) *Is a disjunctivist account of perception a theory, and if not, why not?* **Answer:** It is a theory, but one that does not account for all the phenomena. The reader will have to wait for Hilla Jacobson and me to finish our book to find out why I say this; I will not try to spell out our arguments here.

(3) *Should semantic externalism not be seen as a component of a theory of language, methodologically on a par with the numerous other theories of language on offer? How do we tell the difference between "metaphysical excessive baggage that should be jettisoned" and bold and intricate*

accounts? How, to put the point generally, do we distinguish between phil-
osophical accounts that amount to a metaphysical theory and accounts
that are ordinary commonsense and use concepts "we employ and must
employ when we live our lives." **Answer:** I see my semantic externalism
(for example, "The Meaning of 'Meaning'") as what I like to call a "mild
rational reconstruction" of our ordinary notion of meaning, in the sense of
"meaning" appropriate to such areas as linguistics and lexicography. That
there is such a sense, and that it does work in our lives seems to me obvious. Even Quine admitted that these notions (which he regarded as part
of a second class conceptual system) are indispensable in practice. What I
objected to in *Ethics without Ontology* was not rational reconstruction, but
the sort of pseudoexplanation that postulates "entities" unknown to either
ordinary language or science (I called this "inflationary" metaphysics), as
well as pie-in-the-sky fantasies of reducing our intentional concepts, our
normative concepts, and so forth, to the concepts of the exact sciences. Do
I have a criterion for being a "pseudoexplanation" to offer? Of course not.
Do I have a criterion for when a reduction program is "pie in the sky"? (or
for when a proposal to simply "eliminate" part of our conceptual vocabulary
is unreasonable?) Of course not. It is in each case a matter of good judgment
and informed discussion.

(4) *One final query concerns the concept of "responsible to reality"*
that is central to Putnam's commonsense realism about truth. I agree that
reality, by being present in our experience, may directly yield reasons
for judgment or assertion, and I agree that "responsible to reality" may
amount to different things depending on the discourse. . . . The issue is
how to distinguish "responsible to reality" in the sense of justification
from "responsible to reality" in the sense of truth. Given the diversity of
the concept, there will be no general *way of knowing when "responsibility*
to reality" means justification and when it means truth, but there should
be a way of characterizing the difference in an informative way—of char-
acterizing the kind of responsibility to reality that is truth. **Answer:** I do
not agree that "there should be a way of characterizing the difference in an
informative way" that applies to all the different sorts of statements that we
describe as true or false, justified or unjustified. In the case of statements
about the natural world, the reader who has followed me this far will not be
surprised to learn that I think it is "informative" to say that true empirical
descriptions do correspond to real states of affairs,[40] and that there is all
the difference in the world between, say, the state of affairs "Lizzie Borden
being guilty of murder" and the state of affairs "Our having good reason
to believe that she is guilty of murder." One sort of responsibility is getting
the facts right, and the other is having good reason for what one says. But I
do not find it informative to say that (logical or physical) possibility state-

ments, for example, "It is possible that Lizzie Borden is guilty of murder" correspond to "states of affairs" or anything like that. I would see that as just talk, if someone proposed it. If we need to quantify over such things, there is a perfectly good sortal available: we could speak of "possibilities," for example. But, in the case of empirical descriptions, we do not have any simple alternative to "state of affairs," although, of course, one could "cook up" one. The point, as I say in my Reply to Charles Parsons and my Reply to Geoffrey Hellman, is that I think of mathematical truths as corresponding precisely to *possibilities and impossibilities* and relations between them, and not to "entities" or to "reality" (because so called "entities" easily get confused with objects, and possibility—and its absence, impossibility—is very different from reality), and distinguishing between sentences which correspond to possibilities and impossibilities (and their relatives) and sentences which correspond to states of affairs fits well with both my account of empirical science and my modal-structuralist account of mathematics. And in the mathematical case, the difference that Stoutland asks about is the difference between correctly saying that certain structures are possible or impossible, and having a proof (or, sometimes, a sound mathematical reason short of proof) for what one says.

Do I have a "correspondence theory of truth" then? No, because there are truths (for example, "it is wrong to covet your neighbor's property") whose function is not to describe a state of affairs in the natural world (to describe "reality"), and also is not to describe a mathematical possibility or impossibility. Could we not say they "correspond to obligations"? Why should we? I have said that empirical statements correspond to states of affairs[41] because, for one thing, that enables me to explain why we should not be surprised if statements of very different "logical form" sometimes turn out to be "equivalent descriptions." I am willing to say that mathematical statements correspond to *possibilities and to their absence* (in a sense of "possibilities" peculiar to mathematics), because that makes it easier to explain what I just called the "modal-structuralist" position. But saying that moral statements "correspond to obligations" would be (a) misleading (not all moral statements are about obligations) and (b) unnecessary. There is no philosophical point that I *need* that jargon to make.

In sum, there are various ways of "characterizing the kind of responsibility to reality [sic] that is truth" in the case of particular areas of discourse, but no way I know of characterizing it for all kinds of discourse at once, as Stoutland (surprisingly) seems to be asking.

Why then do we use "true" and "false" in all these cases? Because, when we extend the truth concept to a new area of discourse, we always take care to preserve the logical properties, in particular disquotation, that appertain to "true." In that respect "true" belongs to the family of the logical words (for example, the connectives and quantifiers), which also are used in every area of discourse. But the importance of disquotation does not mean that one should be a "deflationist," in the sense of saying that "true" is *merely* a device for disquotation, that is, that "true" does not correspond to a genuine property. Similarly, the fact that "refers" has the disquotational property[42] does not mean that, when we say that a predicate of "ordinary" objects (tables and chairs and trees and the like) or of scientific objects (bosons and fermions and like) refers to such and suches, "refers to" does not correspond to a genuine relation between linguistic items and extralinguistic objects. To do justice simultaneously to the plurality of our uses of "true" and to the logical unity of the concept of truth is difficult; in my third Dewey Lecture,[43] I argued that Wittgenstein did recognize both, but the demand for characterization of the difference between truth and justification in *all* areas at once is not one that he tried to meet, nor one I tried to meet.

H.P.

NOTES

1. I take the expression "Baker & Hacker," including the ampersand, from Stephen Mulhall, "The Givenness of Grammar: A Reply to Steven Affeldt," *European Journal of Philosophy* 6, no. 1 (April 1998): 32–44. This is a fine example of an "orthodox" Wittgensteinian replying to a "new Wittgensteinian." Gordon Baker defected from the "Baker & Hacker" camp late in his life (see his "Wittgenstein on Metaphysical/Everyday Use," *Philosophical Quarterly* 52, no. 208 [2002]: 289–302).

2. See *The New Wittgenstein*, ed. Rupert Read and Alice Crary (London: Routledge & Kegan Paul, 2000).

3. What they differ about is whether Wittgenstein thought that this sort of nonsense should be ascribed to violations of "criteria" (the "orthodox" interpretation), or, following Cavell in *The Claim of Reason* (Oxford: Oxford University Press, 1979), they deny that criteria are meant to determine what is and is not nonsense. James Conant has emphasized the idea that there is only one sort of nonsense: metaphysical sentences are nonsense *tout court*, they are sentences with no determinate meaning. See his "Mild-Mono-Wittgensteinianism," in *Wittgenstein and the Moral Life: Essays in Honor of Cora Diamond*, ed. Alice Crary (Cambridge, MA: MIT Press, 2007). He suggests in "On Wittgenstein's Philosophy of Mathematics" *Proceedings of the Aristotelian Society* 70 (1996): 243–65, that what leads the metaphysician to utter such sentences is that he hovers between incompatible meanings without seeing that they are incompatible.

4. "Mild-Mono-Wittgensteinianism" (see previous note) is a charming account of the debate from the "New Wittgenstein" side.

5. Cf. my "Rules, Attunement, and 'Applying Words to the World': The Struggle to Understand Wittgenstein's Vision of Language," in *The Legacy of Wittgenstein: Pragmatism or Deconstruction*, ed. Chantal Mouffe and Ludwig Nagl (New York: Peter Lang, 2001), 9–23.

6. For example, I rejected the idea of a "depth grammar" accessible to philosophers but not to linguists and anthropologists in "Dreaming and Depth Grammar," *Analytical Philosophy, First Series*, ed. R. J. Butler (Oxford: Basil Blackwell, 1962), 211–35. Collected in *Mind, Language and Reality*, 304–24.

7. See Gary Ebbs's paper in this volume and my reply.

8. Ludwig Wittgenstein, *Lectures and Conversations on Aesthetics, Psychology and Religious Belief* ed. Cyril Barrett (Berkeley, CA: University of California Press, 1966), 55.

9. "Reading the Socratic dialogues one has the feeling: what a frightful waste of time! What's the point of these arguments that prove nothing and clarify nothing?" Wittgenstein, *Culture and Value*, 14e.

10. "If I have exhausted the justifications, I have reached bedrock and my spade is turned. Then I am inclined to say: 'This is simply what I do.'" Wittgenstein, *Philosophical Investigations,* 3rd ed. (Oxford: Blackwell, 1958), §217.

11. Wittgenstein, *Philosophical Investigations*, §109. (Emphasis added.)

12. As I point out in my reply to Tim Maudlin, I renounced internal realism in a reply to Simon Blackburn in the volume *Reading Putnam* (Blackwell, 1994) (the reply was delivered orally at a conference in St. Andrews in 1990). The reasons I gave it up are stated in the first three of my replies in "The Philosophy of Hilary Putnam," the 1992 issue of the journal *Philosophical Topics*, where I give a history of my use(s) of the term "internal realism," and, at more length, in *The Threefold Cord: Mind, Body and World.*

13. For example, I did not characterize metaphysical realism as holding that "a statement is true in virtue of corresponding to the fact that makes it true." I did not attribute talk of "facts" to the metaphysical realist at all.

14. That lecture is collected in *Meaning and the Moral Sciences*, 123–38. The quotation is from 123.

15. According to Stoutland, it was also part of my internal realism that "*everything* we say about an object is of the form: it is such as to affect *us* in such-and-such a way." But this was my description of *Kant's* position, not mine. (Kant uses virtually these words in his *Metaphysical Foundations of Natural Science*.) When I said, "we can form no clear conception [of Kant's noumenal world]" I meant that the notion of a noumenal world is senseless, not that there is an *etwas* of which we can form no clear conception. Although I saw Kant as a forerunner of "internal realism," I was not *equating* internal realism with these views of Kant's.

16. There are three serious errors in this sentence of Stoutland's: (1) I did not include the interface conception in my list of principles that constitute metaphysical realism (in my sense of the term; indeed, I did not include any epistemological views at all, apart from the view that truth is completely nonepistemic); (2) I did not include a use theory of language in my list of principles that constitute metaphysical realism—indeed, I did not include any theory of language understanding at all (see for example, *Meaning and the Moral Sciences,* 125, "whether *understanding* is taken to consist in knowing that relation or not" [emphasis in the original]); and (3) model theory is a branch of pure mathematics whose distinction between a formal system (not a "language") and its interpretation is purely set theoretic, and has nothing to do with a "use theory of meaning."

17. My Locke Lectures titled "Meaning and Knowledge" were published as Part I of my *Meaning and the Moral Sciences* (London: Routledge and Kegan Paul, 1978 [reissued 2009 by Routledge Revivals]).

18. Ibid., 18–19.

19. Y. Ben-Menahem, "Putnam on Skepticism" in *Hilary Putnam*, ed. Yemima Ben-Menahem (Cambridge: Cambridge University Press, 2005), 125–55; the quotation is from 127–28.

20. The lecture, titled "On Not Writing Off Scientific Realism," was delivered on April 15, 2010. It is collected in my *Philosophy in an Age of Science* (Cambridge, MA: Harvard University Press, 2012).

21. M. Jammer, *The Philosophy of Quantum Mechanics* (New York: John Wiley, 1974), 204; quoting A. Petersen, *Bulletin of the Atomic Scientist* 19, 12 (1963).

22. For an account of some of those investigations, see Tim Maudlin, *Quantum Non-Locality and Relativity* 3rd ed. (Oxford: Blackwell, 1994, 2011).

23. Collected as *Speakable and Unspeakable in Quantum Mechanics*, rev. ed. (Cambridge: Cambridge University Press, 2004),

24. *Meaning and the Moral Sciences*, 24. The sentence "But what if we accept a theory from the standpoint of which electrons are like *phlogiston?*" follows immediately on the same page.

25. Ibid., 24–25.

26. Ibid., 25. The precise form in which I stated the "meta-induction" there was "*just as no theoretical term used in the science of more than fifty* (or whatever) *years ago referred, so it will turn out that no term used* (except maybe observation terms, if there are such) *now refers.*" The suggestion that even our observation terms might turn out not to refer now seems to me crazy.

27. For an explanation of why I say "misdescribed" see my "Indispensability Arguments in the Philosophy of Mathematics," in Hilary Putnam, *Philosophy in an Age of Science* (Cambridge, MA: Harvard University Press, 2012). The reader can also find a description of my philosophy of mathematics in my Reply to Charles Parsons.

28. In "What is Mathematical Truth?" collected in my *Mathematics, Matter, and Method*, I summed this up (on 74) as follows: "In a little book I published not long ago (*Philosophy of Logic*, 1971), I argued in detail that methematics and physics are integrated in such a way that it is not possible to be a realist with respect to physical theory and a nominalist with respect to physical theory. . . . Mathematical experience says that mathematics is true under some interpretation; physical experience says that that interpretation is a realist one."

29. See Mark Colyvan, "Indispensability Arguments in the Philosophy of Mathematics," *The Stanford Encyclopedia of Philosophy*, ed. E. N. Zalta (Fall 2004 Edition), URL = <http://Plato.stanford.edu/archives/fall2004/entries/mathphil-indis/>.

30. I wrote this in 2009 from a draft of the Introduction, the final version of this quotation can be found in: Putnam, *Philosophy in an Age of Science: Physics, Mathematics, and Skepticism*, ed. Mario de Caro and David MacArthur (Cambridge: Harvard University Press, 2012), 27–28.

31. *Meaning and the Moral Sciences*, 47. Emphasis in the original.

32. Wittgenstein, *Philosophical Investigations*, §109

33. For a discussion of one place where he does this, see my "*Wittgenstein, le réalisme et les mathematiques,*" in *Wittgenstein, dernières pensées*, ed. Jacques Bouveresse, Sandra Laugier and Jean-Jacques Rosat (Maseilles: Agone, 2002), 289–313. My original English text ("Wittgenstein, Realism, and Mathematics") is collected as chapter 24 of *Philosophy in an Age of Science*.

34. Wittgenstein wrote, "It might be said, besides the rational points there are diverse systems of irrational points to be found in the number line. There is no system of irrational numbers, but also no super-system, no 'set of irrational numbers' of higher-order infinity," Ludwig Wittgenstein, *Remarks on the Foundations of Mathematics*, ed. G. H. von Wright, R. Rhees and G. E. M. Anscombe (Cambridge, MA: MIT Press, 1991), §33.

35. "Wittgenstein and the Real Numbers," in *Wittgenstein and the Moral Life*, ed. Alice Crary (Cambridge, MA: MIT Press, 2007), 235–50. This is collected as chapter 25 in *Philosophy in an Age of Science*.

36. Those views are in the process of being worked out together with Hilla Jacobson, with whom I am writing a book on perception. A preliminary account of our views is available in chapter 15 (titled simply "Hilary Putnam") in *Mind and Consciousness: 5 Questions*, ed. Patrick Grim (Copenhagen: Automatic Press, an imprint of Vince Inc., 2009).

37. Ned Block, "Wittgenstein and Qualia," *Philosophical Perspectives* 21, no. 1 (2007): 73–115.

38. Joseph Jastrow, "The Mind's Eye," *Popular Science Monthly* 54 (1889): 299–312.

39. In Grim, *Mind and Consciousness: 5 Questions*.

40. To Davidson et al. I say, "Yes, there are no precise identity conditions for *states of affairs*. But there are no precise identity conditions for *properties*, either, and I have long argued that such concepts as property and state of affairs are indispensable in science." See my "On Properties" and "From Quantum Mechanics to Ethics and Back Again," in *Philosophy in an Age of Science*.

41. In "From Quantum Mechanics to Ethics and Back Again."

42. The "disquotational property of reference" is that, given the same idealizations that we make when we say that all the instances of the Tarski T-schema are true, all instances of the following schema are also true (where P is a monadic predicate): "'P' refers to Ps." Using Tarski's notion of "satisfaction" instead of reference this generalizes to formulas with an arbitrary number of free variables; for example (in the case of a formula with two free variable, x_1 and x_2: "The sequence $(a_1, a_2 \ldots)$ satisfies $F(x_1, x_2)$ if and only if $F(a_1, a_2)$."

43. "The Face of Cognition," reprinted in *The Threefold Cord: Mind, Body, and World*, 41–70.

15

Carl Posy

REALISM, REFERENCE, AND REASON: REMARKS ON PUTNAM AND KANT

> *The transcendental idealist is, therefore, an empirical realist, and allows to matter, as appearance, a reality which does not permit of being inferred, but is immediately perceived. Transcendental realism, on the other hand, inevitably falls into difficulties, and finds itself obliged to give way to empirical idealism, in that it regards the objects of outer sense as something distinct from the senses themselves, treating mere appearances as self-subsistent beings, existing outside us.*
>
> —KANT, *CRITIQUE OF PURE REASON* A371
> ("FOURTH PARALOGISM")

Separated though they are by two centuries of science and philosophy, Putnam and Kant nevertheless share a common large-scale vision: "realism with a human face." The human side is that our science, our minds (and for Putnam, our language) manage to describe reality truly. The realist side is that we do not make that reality; the world, for the most part, would be as it is even if we humans had never evolved.[1] Putnam started his philosophical path as a stark "metaphysical realist," to use his term. His first attempt to add a "human face" to his realism was the "internal realism" that he held from the 1970s until about 1990. He now rejects that in favor of the "naïve realism" spelled out in *The Threefold Cord* and subsequent essays. Kant's transcendental idealism expresses the human side of his philosophy. He designed it to show that human science does indeed manage to describe reality. And Kant combines this with his empirical realism, which aims to support the nonmental objectivity of that reality.

The two thinkers are also united by a polemical temperament—Kant stands against transcendental realism, Putnam opposes first metaphysical realism and then his own internal realism—together with a respect for their rivals.[2]

But most of all, these are two careful philosophers. Their global visions and their polemics stand on local doctrines and on precise arguments. For Kant, a host of principles and distinctions together with a score of famous arguments all buttress Kant's mature (critical) philosophy. There are distinctions between intuitions and concepts and doctrines about space, time, and empirical objects. And the arguments include four antinomies, three paralogisms and the notorious "transcendental deduction," to name but a few. Putnam, for his part, based his internal realism on his then functionalist view of mind, on his conception of an ideal scientific theory, and on some of his most famous arguments (brains in a vat, twin earth, and the model-theoretic argument). And, having jettisoned the internal realism, he now rejects the model theoretic argument and underwrites his new naïve realism with his notion of "direct perception" and the liberal functionalism that he is currently developing.

In what follows I want to use the precision of Kant's and Putnam's arguments and local doctrines to give a more nuanced picture of their systematic kinship. In section I, I will show you that they agree on the broad foundation of realism. Specifically, they agree that the notion of reference is central in their respective realisms, and they agree on three main properties of that notion. But, in section II, I will point out that they differ on the underlying theory of truth and its attendant logic. As I interpret him,[3] Kant combines reference with what I call assertablism—the view that ties truth to knowledge—and consequently adopts a nonclassical logic. Putnam does neither.

Now it may seem that they disagree further: The Kantian picture that I will sketch in section I and II seems to run afoul of Putnam's new theory of perception and his naïve realism. But section III argues that when we look at Kant's ideas about scientific and philosophical discourse—the ideas that ultimately define his transcendental idealism and realism—we will find that these ideas provide a natural framework to express Putnam's more recent views.

Given these strong affinities, we must ask whether Putnam should or can accept the Kantian amalgam of reference and assertability. More pointedly, can he buy the assertability component? So section IV examines Putnam's objections to assertablism. There are strictly *philosophical* assaults. I will show that the Kantian amalgam withstands these; and if these were the only quibbles, then a Putnamian might do well to adopt the Kantian amalgam.

But there are also objections that rest on contemporary mathematics and empirical science. Here, Kant alone will fall down. However, at that point I will make some extrapolations from Kant's thought and suggest some Kant-inspired doctrines of contemporary significance. Though speculative, this updated Kantianism might well be worthy of Putnam's consideration.

I. PUTNAM AND KANT AGREE ABOUT REFERENCE

Kant and Putnam both define realism in terms of the way our language or thought hook up with the world; what we today call "reference." I will show you that they agree not only on the centrality of reference, but also on three deep properties of the reference relation.

1. Realism and Reference

My first point is that both Putnam and Kant rest their respective scientific realisms on the relation of reference; or "correspondence with reality." Traditionally this relation holds between our representations on the one hand—be they thoughts or judgments, propositions or sentences—and the "world" and its parts, on the other.

A) Putnam

The link between scientific realism and reference appears explicitly in Putnam's work, and, I might add, it is a nontrivial matter. Here is one characteristic account of metaphysical realism that shows the point:

> The metaphysical realist pictures the world as a totality of language-independent things, a totality which is fixed once and for all; and, at least in the case of an ideal language, one (and only one) reference relation connecting our words with that totality is supposed to be singled out by the very way we understand our language. This description is meant to capture . . . traditional metaphysical realism: its insistence on a unique *correspondence* (to a fixed, mind-independent Reality) as the basis of truth and falsity.[4]

The *internal realism* that replaced this metaphysical realism had its own theory of reference. Here is Putnam's description in *Reason, Truth, and History*:

> In an internalist view . . . signs do not intrinsically correspond to objects, independently of how those signs are employed and by whom. But a sign that is actually employed in a particular way by a particular community of

users can correspond to particular objects *within the conceptual scheme of those users.* 'Objects' do not exist independently of conceptual schemes. *We* cut up the world into objects when we introduce one or another scheme of description. Since the object *and* the signs are alike *internal* to the scheme of description, it is possible to say what matches what.[5]

During this period, Putnam viewed assertablism—the conception which links truth to warranted assertability—as the only semantics geared to accommodate this sort of reference fixing by conceptual schemes. All of this was still realism, as he now says, because the assertability was to be assertion in the best possible scientific theory, taken under "epistemically ideal" conditions. These superlatives "bestowed a realist aspect on internal realism."[6] Indeed, he now rejects this internalism as insufficiently realist, precisely because he now finds it insufficiently referential. And, his recent *natural realism* rests on a robust, "unreduced" reference relation. "We have no idea," he says, "how to reduce the predicate 'refers to' to non-intentional predicates."[7]

Let me say that this linkage of realism with reference is not at all trivial. Michael Dummett, for instance, defines linguistic realism as the claim that truth may be recognition transcendent; that is, there may be true sentences that we humans cannot come to recognize as true. This and the attendant bivalence rather than correspondence or reference are the benchmarks of realism for him.[8] And so, Putnam's connection of realist truth with reference is a substantive philosophical doctrine.

B) Kant

Kant's focus on how our thoughts hook up with the world motivated his turn in the 1770s to the "critical" philosophy, and this issue ("reference" in modern parlance) lay at the heart of his mature, critical thought.

Look at this passage from a letter of Kant's to his student Marcus Herz. The letter was written about a year after Kant's Inaugural Dissertation, the last of his precritical works. Here Kant is saying that the "Dissertation" did not properly account for the correspondence of our "intellectual" representations to reality, nor did it allow for our knowledge of that correspondence.

The sensible representations represent things as they appear; the intellectual representations represent them as they are. But . . . if such intellectual representations rest on our inner activity, whence comes the agreement which they [the intellectual representations] are supposed to have with objects, the objects not being originated by this activity; and whence is it that the axioms of pure reason concerning these objects agree with them, without this agreement being permitted to derive assistance from experience.[9]

Kant's "critical philosophy" turns certain of those "intellectual representations" into his famous "categories"—theoretical concepts like "cause," "quantity," "substance"—and it is fair to say that one of the main aims of the "Transcendental Deduction" in the *Critique of Pure Reason* is just to show that those categories are applicable to reality, or in his terms, "relate to the objects of experience."
Thus at A85/B117:

> Now among the manifold concepts which form the highly complicated web of human knowledge, there are some which are marked out for pure *a priori* employment, in complete independence of all experience; and their right to be so employed always demands a deduction. For since empirical proofs do not suffice to justify this kind of employment, we are faced by the problem how these concepts can relate to objects which they yet do not obtain from any experience.[10]

And, of course, the categories are not alone. In the "Aesthetic" of the *Critique of Pure Reason* Kant does the same for the intuitions of space (for him, Euclidean space) and time:
Thus at A27-8/B44:

> Our expositions accordingly teach the *reality* (i.e., objective validity) of space in regard to everything that can come before us externally as an object.

at A34/B51:

> If I can say *a priori*: all outer appearances are in space and determined *a priori* according to the relations of space, so from the principle of inner sense I can say entirely generally: all appearances in general, i.e., all objects of the senses, are in time, and necessarily stand in relations of time.

and at A35/B52:

> Our assertions accordingly teach the *empirical reality* of time, i.e., objective validity in regard to all objects that may ever be given to our senses.

So, yes, Kant, no less than Putnam, rests his scientific realism on the correspondence of our representations to reality. But now, as I said, I want to take this confluence a level deeper. If we look at Putnam's three famous arguments about reference—twin-earth, brain-in-a-vat, and the model-theoretic argument[11]—we will find that each highlights a distinct property of the reference relation. I call these externality, bipolarity, and homomorphism. We will discover that Kant's notion of reference presupposes these very same properties.

2. *Putnam on the Properties of Reference*

Now I want to show that Putnam's arguments presuppose externalism, bipolarity, and homomorphism.

A) Externalism

The famous twin-earth examples aim to show that our real world interaction with things takes part in determining our referential relation to those things. Famously, when twin-earth Oscar thinks about or uses the term "water" he is thinking or speaking about the stuff (whose chemical composition is XYZ and not H_2O) that runs in the rivers and lakes of twin earth; his physical relation to that twin-earth water is what makes this so. He may not know its constitution, or he might have it wrong, still it is XYZ to which he is referring.

Similarly, we can be wrong, individually or collectively, about the properties of gold. As Putnam points out in "The Meaning of 'Meaning'," though "[t]he stereotype of gold . . . contains the feature *yellow* even though chemically pure gold is nearly white"[12]; still it is gold about which we speak.

One practical upshot of this way of thinking is the incompleteness of our descriptions. We cannot give a full characterization of a substance, for there will always be other details to learn. Another result is the corrigibility of knowledge; no description alone and no subjective state of mind can guarantee the reference of our terms. In a moment I will show you that we will find externality with these very same signs in Kant's notion of reference as well.

B) Bipolarity

The brain-in-the-vat argument goes like this: Putnam tells me to imagine that I am no more than a brain in a vat and to consider the possibility that my impressions of the world are all illusory: firings of my "receptor" neurons without any independent stimulus. Putnam goes on to point out, that, were this scenario to be the case, I could never say so (or know so). For, were this to be the case, I could have no terms to refer to the vat or to my neurons. That is because I have no perceptual contact with these things at all.[13] Putnam is appealing to his externalist notion of reference and using it here to support the connection between reference and existence. Strictly speaking, this argument works to support my right to assume that that there is always something "out there," outside my mind, to which my thought or word refers; in this case to the existence of an "external" stimulus of my receptor neurons. At stake here is the robust "two sidedness" of the reference relation, which I called "bipolarity." This too will be in Kant.

C) Homomorphism

Here we are concerned with the reference of predicates. I do not mean the traditional question of universals, but rather I have in mind the question of application: whether a given predicate actually applies to anything at all. That is the job of what I call homomorphism; and it is supported by the "model-theoretic argument" that targeted metaphysical realism and underwrote (the then favored) "internal realism."

Putnam's model-theoretic argument starts by asking us to consider humankind's "best possible scientific theory." This will be a theory which meets all conceivable epistemic criteria. Such a theory, like any nontrivial theory, has many different models: its language is subject to many different interpretations. Now, Putnam notes, the metaphysical realist will say that exactly one of these interpretations is the correct one; and even if that interpretation satisfies all the observation sentences in our perfect theory, nevertheless there may be sentences in the theory that are not satisfied. That theory might be false. Thus, in Putnam's example, the word "cow" might refer to some class of entities other than the things that we see as cows, and it might turn out to be false that there are cows with the properties we attribute to them. To be sure, because of our misuse of the term "cow," we will never come to learn of this falsity.

But if our best theory could be false, if it could just be "spinning its wheels," then, says Putnam, we could have no *a priori* knowledge unless it came from some special sort of intuition. We could not even have analytic knowledge. Were there no truth-giving contact with the world, then to hold a proposition like "all bachelors are male" as unrevisable, would just be stubbornness.[14] So clinging to her belief that humankind's best possible theory might be wrong leads the realist to unacceptable conclusions.

To say that our best theory cannot be wrong about cows is to say that there are things in the world whose parts are arranged in exactly the way that theory describes cows. The same holds for other kinds of things of which the theory speaks. I call this fit between theory and world "homomorphism," because it says that the things to which the term cow applies must really be arranged in the way our theory spells out for cows.[15] Of course we do not have this ideal theory in hand, but I find it helpful to say that Putnam's argument for bipolarity of reference attributes existence to at least some of our singular terms; and the thrust of homomorphism is that at least some of our general terms apply to the world.

3. Kant's Notion of Reference

Now to Kant: The Kantian equivalent of bipolarity is his notion of the referential strength of empirical intuitions (perceptions); homomorphism amounts to the applicability of concepts[16]; and externalism goes with Kant's treatment of empirical definability. I want to show you that each of these participates in its own special Kantian argument.

A) Perception and Bipolarity

Bipolarity stands behind the role of perception in justifying existential claims. An excellent example is Kant's argument about our knowledge of the extent of the physical universe. The argument aims to show that we can know neither that matter extends finitely into space nor that it extends infinitely. His reasoning goes like this:

Suppose that we have so far found a sequence of n inhabited spatial regions (each farther from the earth than its predecessor by at least a fixed minimal distance); and suppose we want to know whether or not there is a yet farther inhabited region (call it the $n+1$st region). So we commission a space explorer to report on the first of each month as to whether or not she has found an $n+1$st region containing some matter. On the first day of each month we will get one of two possible reports: *yes* (the $n+1$st region has been found) or *no* (she has not yet succeeded in finding such a region). Should our explorer ever report an $n+1$st inhabited region then we would extend the mandate to find an $n+2$nd region, and so on.

Now when we get a positive report, the explorer and we have no way of knowing whether this is the last such occupied region and the search for the next region will go on forever (in which case the universe would be finite). For, our explorer cannot get outside of herself to look at the whole and see whether the exploration has reached an end or whether it will go on forever. The same reason shows that neither she nor we can know whether there will be a next such state and always a next one after that (in which case the universe would be infinite).

For Kant, this ignorance stems from the fact that our perceptions are *receptive* and receptivity, in my present terminology, *presupposes bipolarity*: The explorer is reporting the existence of something outside herself, indeed independent of all of us. There is the source on the one hand, and there is the intuition on the other. She and we must wait to receive intuitive information; neither she nor we can just conjure it up. Indeed, Kant takes this further and says that because of this receptivity our empirical science will always be uncertain and incomplete. For, as he says:

> In natural science . . . there is an infinity of conjectures in regard to which certainty can never be expected. For, natural appearances are objects that are given to us independently of our concepts. Therefore the key to them lies not in us, and our pure thinking but outside us, and precisely because of this, in many cases this key cannot be found and hence no secure information can be expected.[17]

B) Concept Homomorphism and Kant

"Objective validity" is Kant's terminology for saying that a concept applies to reality. A concept is objectively valid if there are things in the world whose parts are arranged in the way that this concept describes. This is "homomorphism," the idea that there is an arrangement preserving map between the representation and the things represented.

The quotations about space and time alluded to this notion of reference, but Kant's "transcendental deduction" of the categories is the most powerful argument for objective validity and homomorphism. In this case it is not particular objects but the world itself that is to be arranged in the way dictated by the concepts in question.

Here are the three main steps, as they apply to the category of "quantity":

(1) Concepts codify regularities. "Cow," for instance, codifies (at least) the regular association of certain parts arranged in a cow-like shape. So applying a concept in an ordinary perceptual judgment (say, "here is a cow") involves predictions that future experience of that object will confirm that shape. Seeing the cow *qua* cow involves predicting that I will continue to see its cow-like shape.

(2) The cow related predictions could only be justified if we are justified in assuming that things maintain their shapes. And it is the concept *quantity*'s applicability that guarantees that things maintain their shapes. (Preservation of shape is preservation of lengths, angles, etc.)

(3) Finally, the very possibility of experience presupposes that such perceptual judgments are (at least sometimes) justified. For, only the conceptual regularity codified in perceptual judgments can bind separate representations into a coherent experience.[18]

In a nutshell: If the category of quantity were a mere wheel spinning then ordinary concepts, like "cow," would not apply. There would then be no regularity in our impressions, and without regularity—says Kant—there could be no experience. If we are justified in our belief that there is experience, then we are no less justified in our belief in the objective validity of the category of quantity.

This form of argument works for "causality" too: When I see a boat move, I predict that the order of positions will remain constant under different reports; and that prediction could only be justified if I were able to find a causal explanation of the motion, which in turn dictates the order of the boat's positions. Similar arguments serve the other categories, and indeed, for the objective validity of the notion of space itself: You cannot distinguish one thing from another—for example, an asteroid in region $n + 1$ from a similar object in region $n + 2$—unless geometric concepts, and hence, for Kant, the notion of space, applies to reality.

As with bipolarity, the argument is epistemic; it is about justification. But the belief being justified is simply my belief that that my concepts—empirical concepts and ultimately categories—map onto a mind-independent reality. He says so explicitly in the summation that he gives in §19 in the B-Deduction. The things combined by the concept, he says, are combined "not merely . . . in perception . . . *but . . . in the object, i.e., combined independently of what the subject's state is.*"[19] We are talking here, Kant says, about "objective validity"; and this relation, I repeat, is what, in Putnam's case, I called homomorphism.

C) Externalism

Finally, let me point out that when Kant considers ordinary empirical concepts, like "gold" and "water," his notion of correspondence is no less "externalist" than Putnam's. Regarding "gold" he says:

> Thus in the concept of *gold* one man may think, in addition to its weight, colour, malleability, also its property of resisting rust, while another will perhaps know nothing of this quality. We make use of certain characteristics only so long as they are adequate for the purpose of making distinctions; new observations remove some properties and add others; and thus the limits of the concept are never assured.[20]

And, speaking of water he asks: "What useful purpose could be served by defining an empirical concept, such, for instance, as that of water?" And he answers,

> When we speak of water and its properties, we do not stop short at what is thought in the word, water, but proceed to experiments. The word, with the few characteristics which we attach to it, is more properly to be regarded as merely a designation than as a concept of the thing, the so-called definition is nothing more than a determining of the word.[21]

So, for Kant, as for Putnam, no internal state and no formal definition can fix the reference of such empirical concepts. We again have incompleteness and corrigibility.

To sum up, Kant and Putnam each bases his own brand of scientific realism on a notion of reference; and for each the reference relation is bipolar, homomorphic, and externalist.

II. PUTNAM AND KANT DIFFER ABOUT TRUTH

So far basic representations have been the focus—terms, for Putnam; intuitions and concepts, for Kant—but the realist cares even more about representations with propositional content: *judgments*. Realism says that the world is what makes our judgments *true*; and Kant and Putnam part ways on the issue of truth. Both have a referential theory of truth; but I will show you that Kant, unlike Putnam, combines this with what I called the assertability account of truth. This is a conception of truth Putnam once accepted and now rejects.[22] I will also show that Kant, again unlike Putnam, uses assertablism to revise our logic.

4. Reference and Assertability

Nowadays, we view reference-based truth as the irreconcilable rival of assertablism. After all, the two conceptions differ philosophically about predication and technically about the truth conditions for the logical particles.

> *Predication*: The referentialist says that "the house is white" is true in virtue of properties of the house itself. For the assertablist the truth of that judgment amounts to my (or someone's) coming to know that fact.
>
> *Recursive truth conditions*: The conditions for conjunction and disjunction read the same in both cases; the other particles diverge. A negation, $\sim p$, is referentially true if p is not true; while assertablistically, $\sim p$ is true if we have evidence that p can never be proved. A referential universal statement, $\forall x R x$ is true if R holds for every element, of the domain; but the assertablist allows that $\forall x R x$ is true only if we have a method showing that sufficient evidence that s is in the domain will lead to sufficient evidence that R holds of s. Finally, an existential $\exists x R x$ can be referentially true if $\sim \forall x \sim R x$ is true; while, assertablistically $\exists x R x$ is true only if we have a means of actually showing an element of the domain which satisfies R, or we know that we can eventually provide such an element.

Let me add that this assertablist condition for existential quantification defines what I call "mild assertabilism." A stricter assertability condition would require that the witness element is already in hand.

Kripke captured all of this formally in the difference between ordinary model theory and the multi-node formal semantics he developed for intuitionism.[23] In that semantics the nodes represent "epistemic situations," and truth at a node may well depend on what will or can happen at subsequent nodes.

Given all of this, it is no surprise that Putnam, along with many others, believes that if you adopt the one of these conceptions of truth you must reject the other. When he was an internal realist, he accepted an assertablist notion of truth in which warranted assertability was defined as assertability in that "best possible theory." He thought then that he could get the effect of reference, without appealing to actual reference, from the perfection of that ideal scientific theory. But, he could not. So now he has abandoned internal realism—and assertablism—precisely because he thinks that these have no room for reference.

5. Kantian Semantics

Yet Kant does cling to both conceptions of truth simultaneously. He is a referentialist about truth—he says so outright. "If truth consists in the agreement of knowledge with its object, that object must thereby be distinguished from other objects; for knowledge is false, if it does not agree with the object to which it is related, even though it contains something which may be valid of other objects."[24] Agreement *with the object*, Kant says—not with any condition of the subject—is what makes a judgment true.

However, he simultaneously holds an unmistakable assertability theory of truth. Thus, for instance, because we cannot know whether the physical universe is finite or infinite, Kant concludes that the universe is *not finite* and that it is *not infinite*! Only an assertablist will find this a valid inference, concluding $\sim\varphi$ from the fact that φ can never be asserted.

Indeed, when we go formal, we see that Kant's strong conclusions from the space explorer story play on the assertablist reading of the negation and the quantifiers.

(i) $\sim(\exists x)(\forall y_{\neq x})\, Fxy$

formalizes the claim that the world is not finite; and

(ii) $\sim(\forall y)(\exists x)Fxy$;

captures the claim that it is not infinite. Now read negation and the quantifiers in the assertablist fashion, and you can see that then the space explorer argument is exactly the way that an assertablist will argue for these claims.

Indeed, we can depict the space explorer's situation graphically. Recall that right now (when there are *n*-known occupied regions, and when our explorer is searching for the *n*+1st region) we do not know whether n is the outermost region or whether there may be a further region. (Because, recall, neither she nor we can get out of the search itself.) So the situation is described by the long, thin flowchart in figure 1.[25]

Recall that whenever our explorer reports having found a populated region we extend the mandate to find yet another region, and so on. Graphically this means that we append a version of figure 1 to each node that reports a new region. So in fact we currently envisage a flowchart which

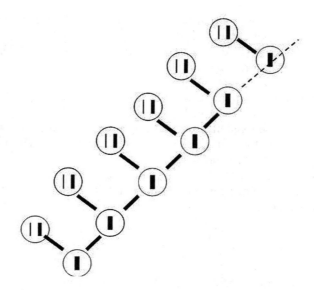

Figure 1

looks schematically like this (figure 2):

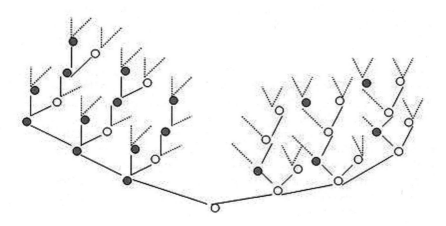

Figure 2

White circles denote a situation in which no further region has been found since the last report. Each solid circle denotes a situation in which we have found a new region and thus embark upon a fresh search. The branching represents our ignorance at any given time. Figure 2 gives a Kripke model that verifies formulas (i) and (ii).

So there is certainly assertablism here. It is, in fact, what I above called a "mild assertablism"; delayed existentials count as true. Here's Kant: "We can . . . know the existence of the thing prior to its perception . . . if only it be bound up with certain perceptions, in accordance with the principles of their empirical connection."[26]

This, then, is one point of difference: Kant combines assertablism with reference; Putnam most pointedly does not. The logic of assertablism is a second difference.

6. Logic

Michael Dummett has argued powerfully that adopting an assertablist theory of truth must lead one to reject classical logic and replace it with a logic—like intuitionistic logic—that rejects the law of excluded middle (p ∨ ~p) and with it many standard classical logical principles.

Though the change in logic is profound, the reason for it is quite easy to see. There are propositions which are not established to be true, but about which we cannot claim that they will never come to be established. For such a proposition, p, neither p nor ~p is assertable; the semantics are not bivalent. Moreover, we see that the disjunction (p ∨ ~p) is not assertable either.

A) Putnam

Following the Dummett line would have required Putnam to abandon classical logic and adopt intuitionistic logic during his internal realist period. However, Putnam did not follow this line. Instead in "Models and Realty" and *Meaning and the Moral Sciences* he invoked a metatheorem proved by Gödel in 1931.[27] This theorem defines a rewriting of the connectives in such a way that the classical tautologies come out as valid. Thus, for instance, "p ∨ q" is rewritten as "~(~p & ~q) ." So, even though the underlying semantics might not be bivalent, still (p ∨ ~p)—which is now to be written as ~(~p & ~~p)—comes out valid. Thus, Putnam preferred to have an assertablist semantic theory without changing his logic.[28]

B) Kant

Kant on the other hand does link his human assertablism with a change in logic, a rejection of classical logic. This is clear in his famous antinomy argument, which effectively says that if you accept assertablism about the spatial extent of the universe then you must also reject a classical logic on pain of contradiction.[29] For accepting classical logic would lead you to say that the world must be either finite or infinite. *That is because classical logic validates:*

$$(iii) \; (\exists x)(\forall y_{\neq x}) \; Fxy \lor (\forall y)(\exists x)Fxy$$

as a logical truth.[30] Assertablism tells us that formulas (i) and (ii) above still hold. These, together with (iii) are an *inconsistent set.*

But Kant's "empirical logic" is not quite the standard intuitionistic logic. At A571–2/B599–600 Kant says: "But every *thing* is, with regard to its possibility, subject also to the principle of *thoroughgoing determination*, whereby of *all possible* predicates of *things*, insofar as these predicates are compared with their opposites, one must belong to the thing."

Here is where the referential component comes into play: If I see a cow, or have sufficient cow-reporting evidence, then there is, in fact, a cow there. And it is there to supply whatever information I may want to squeeze from it. Unlike the world as a whole, there will be no hint of unanswerable basic questions about the cow. In a formal semantics this means that we would have standard clauses for atomic predications and their negations on referring terms, and then assertability clauses for the remaining statements. Because of this full determination, the Kantian semantics will validate the locally classical schema:[31]

$$(iv) \; (\exists x)(x = t) \rightarrow Pt \lor \sim Pt$$

Classical logic is "locally valid."

This then is Kant's amalgam: Assertablism-like semantics with its nonstandard logic together with the full threefold Putnamian notion of reference

III. REMOVING THE REPRESENTATIONAL LADDER

7. A Worry about Perception

This Kantian amalgam quite apparently sets perceptions as conscious inner states opposite the things perceived as outside, so to speak. This smacks of what Putnam calls old fashioned "representationalism," a picture he dubs as dangerous and misleading.

Representationalism is dangerous because its separation of representations (perceptions, concepts, judgments, any intentional mental state at all)

from nonmental perceived things leads some philosophers to say that the objects of our intentional mental states are themselves mental things. You can think of qualia, or Russellian sense data, or Husserlian noemata here.

Putnam gives a nice example of a subject, he calls her Helen, who dreams that she is seeing the Taj Mahal, and then subsequently does travel to India and actually does see the Taj Mahal. Since clearly in the first instance she perceives only mental material, some philosophers will claim that she perceives only mental material in the second instance as well.

Alternatively, philosophers who resist bloating the ontology with such ghostly things will simply deny the outer side and head for some sort of skepticism or idealism. Putnam faults Rorty for this in one place and Berkeley in another.

Putnam says that his own earlier work suffered from this picture. The Kantian picture I have painted so far also seems steeped in this world-independent representationalism. How else are we to understand the Kantian story about intuitions, concepts and the like?

By contrast, Putnam's new picture of direct perception is simply this: the Taj Mahal itself is as much a part of Helen's seeing the Taj Mahal as is her internal configuration, or sense of seeing. Following William James, Putnam calls this "natural realism" about our perception. Sometimes he simply calls this view "naïve realism."

But a deeper look at Kant's critical philosophy gives a context that in fact underwrites Putnam's ideas about direct perception. Putnam's naïve realist notion of perception will be an instance of what I call beneficial mixing of two Kantian inquiries, the empirical inquiry and the transcendental inquiry.

8. Two Inquiries and Their Norms

A) Empirical Inquiry

Our space explorer is engaged in an empirical investigation, as are microphysicists, botanists, and historians. Each of these investigations has its own objects: asteroids, atoms, electrons and quarks, cabbages, and kings. We can group these investigations together into a grand empirical inquiry, all of whose objects are perceivable (in principle) or have perceivable traces and are predicatively complete. The concepts at work in the inquiry include all of our sortal and descriptive empirical concepts, abstract and concrete alike.

More than ontology and "conceptology" mark this inquiry; it rests on a system of norms: methodological, epistemic, semantic, and logical. Methodologically, we must position ourselves to receive perceptions, wait for the outcome and only assert claims that can be thus perceptually based, and we must always be ready to revise. Epistemologically, we know that knowledge (and hence justification) rests on perception. In Kant's terms that is the work of the "Faculty of Understanding." Semantically we have reference with assertability. And the logic is, as we have seen, locally classical and globally intuitionistic.

B) Transcendental Inquiry

Space exploration is part of the empirical inquiry, but *examining the norms* of that empirical inquiry is a separate inquiry, with its own collection of specific investigations. They include theoretical ontology, methodology, epistemology, semantics, and logic. For historical reasons Kant will speak of this as the *transcendental* inquiry. Kant will put mathematics here as well; for Kant, mathematics studies not empirical objects, but the forms of our intuition of those objects.[32]

This inquiry—and not the empirical inquiry—is the place where we note that the concepts and logic of the empirical enquiry are human centered. It is here in this inquiry that Kant will call the collection of empirical norms "transcendental idealism": "idealism," because it is human centered, and "transcendental" because the observation about this human centeredness is part of the transcendental inquiry.

The transcendental inquiry has its own objects—intuitions and judgments, truth and inference, scientific theories themselves—and its own special concepts. And once again, it has its own underlying system of norms, uniting the various investigations that comprise it.

Methodologically, reasoning in all of these transcendental investigations is a priori and has apodictic force. This reasoning belongs to what Kant calls the "Faculty of Reason." Unlike the "understanding," we are now studying our own faculties; and thus there is no external receptivity, and thus no "wait and see." Epistemologically, this means that we can optimistically expect that there will be no unanswerable questions in this enquiry about our own abilities. Says Kant: "It is not so extraordinary as at first seems the case, that a science should be in a position to demand and expect none but assured answers to all the questions within its domain (*quaestiones domesticae*), although up to the present they have perhaps not been found. In addition to transcendental philosophy, there are two pure rational sciences, namely, pure mathematics and pure ethics."[33]

As for the semantics and logic of the transcendental inquiry: Optimism in the context of assertability yields nonbranching models and a classical logic.[34] And this means that, from the transcendental perspective, we would turn figure 2 into figure 3, a crisp set of possible models of how our knowledge will proceed.

When doing semantics we assume that one of these models will be the actual path of our knowledge, and thus is a mirror of the complete world-whole.

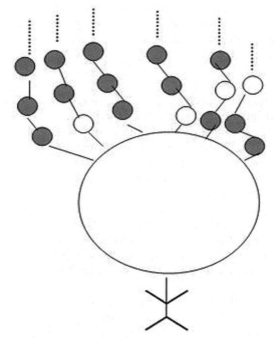

Figure 3

The thin models of figure 3 have no empirical standing. We can think about those thin paths and speak of them, but from the empirical point of view, we cannot point to them, denote them, or even claim that they exist. They are important notions—they provide the model of receptivity and the image of the world that goads our research. But they are not empirical objects. Ditto for mathematical objects; they too have no empirical existence.[35] The same goes for the notion of intuition itself. It belongs to epistemology and derivatively to semantics, but not to any part of the empirical inquiry.

9. Mixing the Inquiries

Now in the dynamics of day-to-day life we blithely jump back and forth between the two inquiries. Thus, for instance, you might ask whether next month's report about an $n+1$st region will be positive; and I would answer "I do not know." Empirical question, transcendental answer, just fine. This is a benign mixing. Applied mathematics is also a benign—indeed a beneficial—mixing. Mathematics, recall, is purely rational, it belongs to "reason"; but we use its concepts and its objects daily in our empirical work. A third instance is Kant's famous notion of "regulative force": The image of figure 3—the idea that there is a complete model of our knowledge of the world—this idea goads us on continually to "extend the mission," and always to keep on searching. This is the idea that led us to create in the first place the mindset reflected in figure 2.

Kant goes on to warn, however, that these successful mixings tempt us to step too far: to assume that there is only one inquiry, and thus inevitably to substitute the norms of one sort of inquiry into the practice of the other. *This amalgam of the two enquiries is what Kant calls "transcendental realism."* It results in error and inconsistency, says Kant; it inevitably leads to a clash of norms.

Thus, for instance, we may take epistemology to be an empirical investigation, and import empirical (sensory) standards of knowledge to this investigation. Skepticism results from this; transcendental questions are not amenable to sensory solutions. This is the point of the "Paralogism" passage that I quoted in the epigraph: transcendental realism leads to empirical idealism.

Or we might apply the classical logic of transcendental enquiry to empirical investigations. This leads to Kant's "Antinomy": The transcendental realist imports the machinery of Reason's transcendental inquiry—the models of the world-whole, the attendant classical logic—to the empirical enterprise. And that in turn is what commits him to that inconsistent set of claims: The empirical assertability commits him to (i) and (ii) the classical logic commits him to (iii).[36]

Kant's methodological advice: Mix yes, but with discipline. Never mix in a way that causes the norms of Reason and Understanding to clash. He sometimes expresses this ontologically: do not take the world-whole as if it were an empirical object; and sometimes epistemologically: do not treat our conceptual grasp of the world as if it were an intuition. The practical effect is expressed in the nonclassical logic of empirical discourse.

10. Back to Perception

Now let us return to the theory of perception and natural realism. Putnam tells us that we always individuate mental things for a purpose, and the purpose will tell us what to look for as we pick out a perception: "our psychological characteristics are, as a rule, individuated in ways that are context sensitive and extremely complex, involving external factors (the nature of the objects we perceive, think about, and act on), social factors, and the projections we find it natural and unnatural to make."[37]

Why do we care about perceptions and their parts? What philosophical task is this notion of perception intended to play? If our answer is that we want to know about perception to satisfy our scientific curiosity, to complete our picture of the world; then what we want is a physical or neurological theory. Putnam's theory has no such aim. Our aim might be purely phenomenological. Then we would want a fully internalist conception of perception: think of Husserl's theory, for instance, with its suspension of the "natural attitude." Once again, that is not Putnam's aim.

But what if Putnam's notion of perception belongs to what I called the transcendental inquiry? Suppose, perhaps, that he wants to explore the part that perceptual experience plays in justifying scientific theories. In this context Putnam's natural realism about perception—the Taj Mahal participates in the perception of the Taj Mahal—mixes the transcendental and empirical inquiries. Why is Putnam's description of Helen's perception a mixing? Simply put, Helen's perception belongs to the transcendental landscape. Perceptions, intuitions as posited in semantics and epistemology, have no empirical standing; but, the Taj Mahal, on the other hand, is an empirical object.

Putnam's individuation criterion actually works nicely here to draw the difference between the Taj Mahal and the perception. Buildings are physical objects, ultimately individuated by their physical parts and locations. To use Kant's image, their parts are combined in the object and not in our heads. Helen, on the other hand, might have singled out her *perception* of the Taj Mahal in order to justify a claim about its size, or its color, or just its existence. Or she might have used her Taj Mahal experience to justify a claim about the weather at the moment she saw it, or a claim about the tourist traffic around it. This is the right level of looseness in the transcendental project. So indeed, including the building as a component of perception is a mixing of inquiries. It is a beneficial mixing, telling us about the nature of perception and the origin of knowledge, that does not, by itself, mix norms.

Indeed, Putnam is criticizing the rival theories of perception for assuming that there is but a single enquiry and thus consequently mixing the norms. Consider those who posit some mental intermediary between the perception and the perceived, for example, Russell, Husserl, et al. These "interfacers" are simply generalizing the mechanical causal order that might characterize the empirical world, and saying any that connection—mental or physical or something else—is a mechanical connection, a connection between connectable things. Of course, no such connection exists within the transcendental project and there is none between the projects. This is the invalid mixing that leads to a bloated ontology.

And now the skeptics: What they do is twofold. On the one hand they set up a rather idealized conception of the "external." It is, as Putnam sometimes puts it, a complete set of objects and properties. From the Kantian perspective, it assumes the sort of totality and completeness—as depicted, for instance, in figure 3—that only Reason (or the transcendental project) permits. Yet together with that, they impose the empirical epistemic norm: no knowledge of ideal totalities. The result: no knowledge of the external. Here invalid mixing yields skepticism. This is precisely Kant's reasoning in the paralogism: transcendental realism combined with empirical epistemic norms yields a skeptical idealism.

And so we see that Kant has a full-blooded, three-faceted, Putnamian reference together with an assertablist notion of truth. And this amalgam—with its underlying theory of empirical and transcendental enterprises—provides a setting for Putnam's new naïve realism.

We must thus ask, as I said at the outset, how much of this underlying assertablism could Putnam now accept?

IV. Kantian Assertablism Today

So let us examine Putnam's antiassertablist complaints. I see two sorts: strictly philosophical complaints and those generated by modern mathematics and science. First I will briefly take up the philosophical complaints, and I will say that the Kantian amalgam, in Kant's own terms, withstands the assault. But then I will turn to three thrusts stemming from modern mathematics and science. Kant—smart as he was—could not field these alone. So, as I said, I will go speculative: I will extrapolate an extended Kantian position that does comport with the modern point of view. The final result will be an updated Kantianism which may well be worthy of Putnam's consideration.

11. Philosophical Objections to Assertablism

There are two strictly philosophical complaints. One says that assertablism is too strong, the other that it is too weak.

A) Assertability Conditions Are Too Strong

Assertability conditions cannot, it is claimed, properly accommodate non-normative, empirical generalizations like "all crows are black." These generalizations abjure any necessary connection between crows and blackness, and they are corrigible. Assertablism, it is alleged, simply pushes too hard on both of these issues. It requires necessary connections and presumes incorrigibility.

The worry about necessary connection really stems from too strong a reading of the assertability condition for universal generalizations. In mathematical contexts—the place where assertablism came into the late twentieth-century spotlight—the condition is often stated as:

(x) Fx is assertable at an epistemic situation s, only if s contains a method for converting any proof that t is in the domain into a proof of F(t);

and mathematical proofs establish necessary connections. But, in fact, the more general version of this condition is, as we saw:

(x) Fx is assertable at an epistemic situation s, only if at s we have evidence to the effect that any evidence that t is in the domain will yield evidence supporting the claim that F(t).

In empirical discourse, empirically acceptable inductive evidence supporting "all crows are black" is evidence supporting the claim that any sighting of a crow will be a sighting of a black thing. It says no less than that, but no more either. No special theory of sighting is needed here.

I will return to this issue in §11C below, when I take up cases in which no crow sighting is possible. But, for now, my point is that empirical evidence does not ordinarily support a claim of necessary connection, and empirical assertability does not require it.

As for corrigibility: This is the worry that assertablism demands that a claim be settled forever before it can be asserted. The formalism of Kripke models reinforces this impression. And once again, this seems much too strong a requirement for contingent claims like "all crows are black."

Kant in fact gives the response to this. For him assertability and non-revisability are—indeed have to be—two separate modalities. §3B mentioned the stable order of boat-positions that is presumed when I claim that the boat moved. But on further evidence I might revise my claim that the boat moved; the semantics should catch that possibility.[38] So these local projections are different from the "global" ones—recurrence of the initial conditions yields recurrence of the objective effect—that attend a causal law. This is a more solid regularity, but we may err about empirical laws as well. That too will be reflected in the semantics. Kant's point is that we do not err in our assumption that some causal law does hold. The projections entailed by that assumption are not up for revision and will have semantic expression. Kant argues, to be sure, that one sort of regularity is justified by another here. Nonetheless, it is very important for Kant to separate different sorts of projections.[39]

B) Assertablism Is Too Weak

The thrust of Putnam's recent attacks on the old model-theoretic argument is that it has too wan a grasp of reality. For this reason, he says, an assertablist semantic theory must inevitably come up solipsistic; and following Dummett,[40] he says, such a theory leads to skepticism about the past. Solipsistic: because, after all, everything comes down to *my* having or not having particular sense experiences. Skeptical about the past: again, only currently present experiences can serve as evidence for the existence of particular past events.

Kant need not be weak on the past. The very same principles that guide his picture of how we know about occupied space—principles of receptivity and reference—will secure our knowledge of the past. Objects have histories no less than they have futures; and the physical existence of the objects guarantees that the facts about its history are there to be learned. Empirically established existence is real existence whether for past events or for spatial regions.

As for solipsism: Kant cannot allow solipsism. His justification of causality only works if we assume that there are other observers in the world. Recall, I invoke causality to justify my predictions about my future experiences of a particular event, but that event will no longer be there for me to experience again. The only thing I can predict is reports that other observers experienced what I did.

Similar gripes based on assertablism's anemic grip on the world will similarly be answered. Perhaps Putnam's critiques would apply to a pure assertablism that is ungrounded in real reference. Kant's is not such a theory.

12. The Modern Challenge

The main challenge to the Kantian picture comes not from pure philosophy. Rather, some things we have learned since Kant's time about mathematics and science sour assertablism for Putnam. Issues from pure mathematics, applied mathematics, and empirical science itself raise Putnam's hackles. I will look at these assertability unfriendly issues in that order.

A) Pure Mathematics

Mathematics for Kant is bivalent. That is because he combines his mild assertablism with the optimistic belief that all mathematical problems are solvable in principle. The optimism in turn comes from cancelling receptivity in mathematics. Mathematics, recall, belongs to Reason's transcendental inquiry.

Now this view of mathematics raises some points of agreement. There is logical agreement: Like Putnam, Kant advocates classical logic for the practice of pure mathematics.[41] There is ontological agreement too: Kant, as we saw, denies actual existence to mathematical objects, and Putnam is like-minded. In *Ethics without Ontology*, he chastises those who advocate a special logical and mathematical ontology. Ethics has no ontology of its own, says Putnam, and neither does mathematics. And there is also a subtle agreement about the nonuniformity of truth. Both thinkers allow that some discourse is bivalent, and some is not. Ethics—unlike mathematics and empirical discourse, is not bivalent for Putnam. And we have seen that Kant's amalgam of assertability and reference plays out differently in different areas of discourse.[42]

There is, however, a point of deep disagreement: Putnam is not a mathematical optimist![43] He announces this in *Ethics without Ontology*. His detailed reasoning is spelled out in "The Gödel Theorem and Human Nature,"[44] but his bottom line: there may well be mathematical truths that we cannot come to know. So, were Putnam to be an assertablist, this pessimism would close off mathematical bivalence to him.

One cannot require Kant, smart as he may have been, to have anticipated formalized arithmetic and the Gödel theorems, nor the discussions of Hilbert, Brouwer, Gödel himself, Fefferman, and others about the existence of absolutely unsolvable mathematical problems. Whatever else they may show, modern developments do cast water on Kant's idea that cancelling receptivity is enough to support optimism, but I want to show you that the Kantian source of that optimism does presage a modern theme. I call this aspect of Kant's thought "equilibrium," and the idea is this: on the one hand, empirical thought embodies a certain imbalance (disequilibrium) between the things whose existence we can prove and those whose existence we naturally (even necessarily) contemplate but cannot prove or assert. The larger and larger chunks of the universe that our space explorer reveals fall into the former camp, the universe as a whole into the latter. We cannot help thinking about the universe and its extent (that is what goads us to renew our space explorer's mandate); but on pain of antinomy we cannot assert its existence. This gap between Reason's ontological reach (towards things we want—even need—to exist) on the one hand and Understanding's epistemic grasp on the other on the other (of things whose existence we can assert), this gap is an indelible part of empirical knowledge.[45] It is the source of nonbivalence and global intuitionism-like logic.

But on the other hand, when we move to the transcendental enterprise (mathematics included) the gap dissolves. Here we are using our cognitive power to reflect upon those same cognitive powers. The ontology and epistemology match; there is equilibrium. In this case, Kant says, we are optimistic. With that optimism come bivalence and classical logic.

Now maybe—because, perhaps, of the factors revealed in Gödel's theorem—Kant is wrong here about optimism. But the idea that epistemic ontological equilibrium yields a "classical point of view" has a powerful modern expression in Gödel's proof of the consistency of the axiom of choice and the continuum hypothesis with the axioms of set theory. These principles smell nonconstructive. The first asserts the existence of choice functions some of which have no algorithmic expression; the second asserts the existence of subset of the reals which cannot be constructively generated. But Gödel showed that a model whose domain is restricted to the "constructive universe" will make these principles come out true. Gödel describes this restriction as V = L (the full and the constructive domains are equal, what can be constructively grasped is what there is), but in my terms it is straightforward equilibrium.[46] Gödel's constructive universe is far from Kantian perception; but, still, the generalized Kantian point is quite powerful: that balance of grasp and reach gives the mathematical effect of Reason and in this case (not classical logic, that is already there, but) classical mathematics.

B) Mathematics and Its Applications
Once again, we start with agreement. Putnam—citing Wittgenstein—insists that mathematics must be applied. He says:"If mathematics were not applied outside mathematics, that is, if there were not "mixed" statements—empirical statements that contain mathematical terms—then there would be no reason to view it as more than a game."[47] And this is exactly Kant's view. At A239/B298 he says that without the "data for possible experience" a priori principles would "have no objective validity whatever, but [would be] mere play, whether by the imagination or by the understanding, with their respective presentations." The context makes it clear that mathematics would be "a mere play of the imagination" without empirical applicability.[48] This is the beneficial "mixing" of mathematics and empirical discourse of which I spoke above.

But, once again, the paths diverge: Kant's assertablism extends to applied mathematics; Putnam says that we cannot be assertablists here. His reason is that modern mathematical physics uses noncomputable functions. Citing a paper by Pour-El and Richards, he gives the example of a wave equation whose solution cannot be calculated even to the first decimal place.[49] An assertablist should say that if it is not feasible to compute a solution to a problem then there is not a solution. But, Putnam insists, we must not say that values of those physically applied noncomputable functions do not exist.[50]

Once again, we cannot fault Kant for his ignorance of modern physics and computability. But I think we can extrapolate an "updated" Kantian view that does have room for noncomputable applications of mathematics. Specifically, I think the best interpretation of Kant's ideas about applied mathematics is a position that, when translated into contemporary terms, remains assertablist while still allowing noncomputable applications of mathematics to be empirically true. I think this because (a) I interpret some famous Kantian texts as showing that he took Leonhard Euler's side in a dispute (both scientific and philosophical) between Euler and Jean le Rond D'Alembert; and (b) I believe that the best contemporary embodiment of that dispute puts D'Alembert on the side of restricting mathematical applications to computable ones, and puts Euler (and with him Kant) on the side that allows the existence of true but noncomputable solutions.

The Kantian passages I have in mind are those expressing Kant's view that our grasp of space involves a grasp of physical motion. They are B154, where Kant says that we "cannot think a line without *drawing* it in thought, or a circle without *describing [i.e., tracing]* it"; and A169–71/B211 where he rests the continuity of space upon a notion of succession which itself rests on the possibility of motion.

The scientific debate between Euler and D'Alembert concerns the famous vibrating string problem. In 1747 D'Alembert published a differential equation designed to describe the positions over time of a vibrating string. Euler rejected this solution because it required that the initial shape of the string had to be given by a single equation taken from a then restricted class of expressible equations. In order to have a mathematically adequate theory, Euler claimed, we must allow ourselves to consider initial shapes corresponding to functions that cannot be calculated by analytically described procedures. There are more curves than can be so defined, and thus more ways of individuating points in space. These additional unrepresented functions are given, he says, by "description" in the geometric sense, and he speaks of the various possible free motions of a hand. If we think of the value of a function as the individuation of a spatial point, then Euler is saying that the class of (then) explicitly definable functions is not sufficient to individuate all the points in space.[51]

A larger dispute about the application of abstract science to experience lies behind this mathematical debate. D'Alembert says we proceed from the abstract mathematics and science and fit the cases to it. That is precisely his view in the vibrating spring problem. Euler holds exactly the opposite view: physical intuition is the arbiter, and our physical intuition gives us more than the abstract description of a single equation.

The Kantian passages I cited above show that Kant sides with (indeed almost explicitly quotes) Euler regarding the grasp of space. Kant is saying that we need to take the notion of free motion as basic in order to individuate the points in space. I take Kant to be siding with Euler in the larger debate as well.

We have here an origin for one of Kant's most important distinctions: Kant generalizes D'Alembert's notion of the formally describable to his own notion of the conceptually describable. He looks upon D'Alembert's view as an eighteenth-century avatar of a Leibnizian monadism that reduced the description of reality to the combination of infinite complete concepts. And Kant took Euler's insistence on the primacy of physical intuition as a source for his own view that empirical intuition outruns abstract conception. Kant's larger point—like Euler's—is that conceptual description alone cannot suffice to give us a scientific grasp of reality.

On the other hand, we have here the path to our modern issues. The real debate between Euler and D'Alembert is about whether applicable mathematics must be restricted to some basic concepts together with their combination according to a pre-set collection of patterns. D'Alembert favored this restriction—he thought it crucial to being able to apply mathematics in practice[52]—and Euler rejected it. In a famous piece of 1748 Euler argued against the hegemony of his sort of abstract combinatorial thought. The idea he champions is that physical intuition (in all its hurly burly) is the touchstone of scientific truth. Metaphysics and mathematics must answer to physical reality, and not vice versa.[53]

On this reading of the debate D'Alembert is the forerunner of combinatorial (recursive) constructivism. Euler gives the nonrecursive foil: physical science (including applied mathematics) can establish existence without providing recursive definability. This is the modern updated Kantian view to which I alluded. It is the view that full mathematics applies to reality without restriction to calculability. Assertability goes with what is given in a scientific theory and not with algorithmic calculability. Science can establish the existence of some objects and the truth of some claims in ways that do not provide a recursively calculable specification. This point about nonrecursive grasp (using the machinery of physical intuition) fits with the applications that Putnam cites. Physics is an extension of physical intuition and not of conceptual calculation; the wave equation whose solution cannot be calculated still gives us a legitimate physical magnitude.[54]

This view takes science as an extension of our perceptual faculty, and takes mathematics as the idealization of that faculty. Science, then, defines what I above called our epistemic grasp. That is the spirit in which I want to approach the third issue, the issue of assertablism and empirical science.

C) Assertablism and Empirical Science

Assertablism seems hard pressed today to accommodate all that is scientifically acceptable. Today we may well speak of the temperature on stars too far to measure, or of particles that are in principle too small or too short-lived to be perceived. Putnam himself speaks of events and things outside our light-cone, which thus in principle will never be observed. He believes that the strict assertablist must thus abstain from judgments about these and similar things. But science does no such thing.

The stellar example, of course, is the question of the physical universe's extent. Kant denied that the "entire physical universe" is a legitimate empirical object; and he did so on assertablist grounds. We do admit this object; and, unlike Kant, we entertain as legitimate empirical hypotheses the possibility that the universe is infinite in extent and the possibility that it is finite.

But it is important to see that the reason for this change is that cosmology has evolved in a way that now makes these questions amenable to empirical research and not merely a priori speculation. Measurements of red shifts and the like bear on determining the physical universe's magnitude. So, I believe, the updated Kantian will now embrace these hypotheses. Indeed, the modern Kantian should even extend the range of what I called locally classical logic to this research. For we now have grounds to take the physical universe as an object within our epistemic grasp.

Interestingly, in a remarkable passage Kant says something that shows sympathy to this possibility:

> It is a matter of indifference whether I say that in the empirical advance in space I can meet with stars a hundred times farther removed than the outermost now perceptible to me, or whether I say that they are perhaps to be met with in cosmical space even though no human being has ever perceived or ever will perceive them. . . . Only in another sort of relation, when these appearances would be used for the cosmological idea of an absolute whole, and when, therefore, we are dealing with a question which oversteps the limits of possible experience, does distinction of the mode in which we view the reality of those objects of the senses become of importance, as serving to guard us against a deceptive error which is bound to arise if we misinterpret our empirical concepts.[55]

What has happened since Kant is that the limit of possible experience has evolved with science. The notion "possible experience" is no longer limited by the limit of actual perception, and even not by length of calculations. It is limited by what empirical science can get at. So I believe an updated Kantian would extend the same liberal attitude to distant stars and to minute particles (banned by Kant himself). If physics says there must be a temperature on a distant star, then there is one, even if we cannot calculate it. If there is scientific reason to consider regions beyond our light cone, then consider we will. We will apply the locally classical logic as well. If there is such a region then either there are crows there or there are not, and if there are crows there then either they are all black or not, though we may never come to know which.[56]

It follows from these sorts of examples that our knowledge may well be gappy even about parts of reality that are not gappy themselves. (The unseen stars are still there, the humanly-unperceivable objects do have their proper properties.) Once again, I think this is a place where the strong theory of reference does its work, especially what I called the "bipolar" (existence related) part: having established the existence of something—once the term for that thing legitimately refers—then we will assume that there is material there to support the determinations of parts and locations, even if those determinations are not ever made.[57]

13. Updated Kantianism

This Kant-inspired position that I have sketched has a built-in ontological thesis and a semantic one as well. The ontological side is that the objects in the world are exactly the things that science can deal with. Science (with its mathematics) describes reality. The semantic point is, as I have been saying, that reference and (scientific) assertability coincide. Our terms refer—in the rich conception of reference I sketched—to empirical objects. Since these objects are scientifically knowable, scientific assertability indeed establishes the truth about them. That, if you like, is the transcendentally ideal part of the picture. In Kantian terms, however, we can say that the empirical realism that goes along with this antirealism is a strong realism indeed: knowledge is gappy; there are things about reality which we may never be able to calculate.

Given this liberal attitude, given the rather broad applicability of classical logic (both inside and outside mathematics) and the gap between knowledge and reality what's left to distinguish the antirealist from a full-blooded realist? In Kantian terms: what is there to distinguish this strong empirical realism from full-fledged transcendental realism?

That passage from A496–7/B524–5 gives the clue. The Kantian realist gets stuck because he mixes empirical and philosophical reasoning in considering the extent of the physical universe. The modern equivalent of Kant's transcendental realist is someone who would blindly attempt to extend our current cosmological theory beyond the extent of the physical universe and stretch Kant's notion of an "absolute whole" in a contemporary way.

This realist might place the physical universe in an even larger setting, one that includes consideration of what lies beyond the physical universe, and might then ask questions about what goes on outside the physical universe. These are the questions that go beyond "the limits of possible experience." (If the universe is finite, the realist will ask, and even if it is not, what else is there beside it, or outside it?) Now, I did not say "apply physics" or "apply cosmology" here; that is what in principle we cannot do. If we are to think about this question, it will only be in a priori speculation and importing ideas and methods, perhaps from one of our Reason's nonempirical pursuits, that exceed the reach of scientific inquiry. That would be the equivalent of extending Reason's reach beyond Understanding's grasp. But the question about what lies beyond the physical universe is not grammatically ill formed. So this would be the place where the contemporary Kantian might well go for nonclassical logic.

Yes, the Kant-style antirealism does seem liberal, but it still does come with a Kant-style demand for discipline; and it does not collapse into outright metaphysical realism. This is the position that I said is worth considering.[58]

CARL POSY

THE HEBREW UNIVERSITY OF JERUSALEM
OCTOBER 2011

NOTES

1. This formulation comes from Hilary Putnam, *Words and Life*, ed. James Conant (Cambridge: Harvard University Press, 1994), 430.

2. See Putnam's "Wittgenstein: A Reappraisal" for a discussion of respect for one's philosophical rivals.

3. Much of what I say about Kant derives from an interpretation using modern logical and semantic techniques that I have been developing for some time.

4. Putnam, *Words and Life*, 352.

5. Hilary Putnam, *Reason, Truth, and History* (Cambridge: Harvard University Press, 1981), 52.

6. Hilary Putnam, "Corresponding with Reality," in *Philosophy in an Age of Science* (Cambridge: Harvard University Press, 2012), 82.

7. Ibid.

8. Michael Dummett, *The Logical Basis of Metaphysics* (Cambridge: Harvard University Press, 1991), 182–83.

9. Immanuel Kant to Marcus Herz, 21 Feb. 1772, in *Kant: Selected Pre-Critical Writings and Correspondence with Beck*, trans. G. B. Kerferd and D. E. Walford (Manchester: Manchester University Press, 1968), 113.

10. Immanuel Kant, *Critique of Pure Reason*, trans. Norman Kemp Smith (Hampshire: Palgrave Macmillan, 2007), A85/B117.

11. For twin earth see Hilary Putnam, "The Meaning of 'Meaning,'" in *Minnesota Studies in the Philosophy of Science vol. VII: Language, Mind, and Knowledge*, ed. Keith Gunderson (Minneapolis: University of Minnesota Press, 1975). Brains in a vat occurs in *Reason, Truth, and History,* the model-theoretic argument is in "Models and Reality" in *Journal of Symbolic Logic*, no. 3 (1980): 464–82 and "Realism and Reason" in *Meaning and the Moral Sciences* (London: Routledge and Kegan Paul, 1978).

12. Putnam, "Meaning of 'Meaning,'" 170.

13. Nor, for that matter, do I have the requisite contact with a scientist who might be manipulating my neurons or with a Cartesian evil demon playing the same role.

14, Putnam, *Meaning and the Moral Sciences,* 137.

15. Tyler Burge (in his Review Essay of Donald Davidson, *Truth and Predication*, in the *Journal of Philosophy* 104, no. 11 [Nov. 2007]:580–608) lists Putnam among those who are insensitive to the special semantics of predication. It seems to me that, though Putnam eventually comes to reject the model theoretic argument, the structure of that argument shows that he is indeed sensitive to how predication works.

16. Kant's distinction between intuitions and concepts roughly parallels our modern distinction between singular and general terms: "an objective perception is *knowledge* (*cognitio*). This is either *intuition* or *concept* (*intuitus vel conceptus*). The former relates immediately to the object and is single, the latter refers to it mediately by means of a feature which several things may have in common." [A320/B376]. The parallel is not complete, however: concepts are components of judgments for Kant; intuitions are evidence for singular judgments but are not parts of the judgments.

17. Immanuel Kant, *Critique of Pure Reason*, trans. Werner S. Pluhar (Indianapolis: Hackett, 1996), A480/B508. For more detail on Kant's reasoning here see my "Intuition and Infinity: A Kantian Theme with Echoes in the Foundations of Mathematics," in *Kant and Philosophy of Science Today: Volume 63 (Royal Institute of Philosophy Supplements)*, ed. M. Massimi (Cambridge: Cambridge University Press, 2008), 165–93.

18. Kant's full reasoning here uses his notion of the self. His point is that *sans* self there could be no experience; and, like Hume, he admits no self beyond the experienced representations. So the coherence of separate experiences is tantamount to their belonging to a single self.

19. Kant, *Critique of Pure Reason*, trans. Pluhar, B142. (italics added)

20. Kant, *Critique of Pure Reason*, trans. Kemp Smith, A728/B756.

21. Ibid.

22. In most of his writings Putnam speaks of this as verificationism. Since, I will not here discuss Putnam's ideas about degrees of verification, I will stick with the term assertability (or warranted assertability, as Dewey first phrased it). I prefer this term because of its natural connection with justification.

23. S. A. Kripke, "Semantical analysis of intuitionistic logic," in *Formal Systems and Recursive Functions*, ed. J. N. Crossley and M. A. E. Dummett (Amsterdam: North-Holland Publishing, 1965), 92–130.

24. Kant, *Critique of Pure Reason*, trans. Kemp Smith, A58/B83.

25. I speak of "flowcharts" rather than mathematical "trees" to emphasize that we are depicting rules for proceeding in the empirical search. This corresponds to Kant's way of speaking at A519/B547.

26. Kant, *Critique of Pure Reason*, trans. Kemp Smith, A225/B273.

27. Kurt Gödel, "*Zur intuitionistischen Arithmetik und Zahlentheorie*," *Ergebnisee eines. mathematischen. Kolloquiums, Heft 4* (1933), 34–38.

28. In Hilary Putnam, *The Threefold Cord: Mind, Body, and World* (New York: Columbia University Press, 1999), 54–59, Putnam speaks sympathetically of Dummett's logical revisionism. But, interestingly, he ties this revisionism to the theory of understanding and not to the assertabilist theory of truth. It appears that he *still* of the view that assertablism *per se* need not entail a change of logic.

29. See my "Dancing to the Antinomy: A Proposal for Transcendental Idealism," *American Philosophical Quarterly*, no. 20 (Jan. 1983): 81–94 and also my "Intuition and Infinity: A Kantian Theme with Echoes in the Foundations of Mathematics" for details. See also §8 below.

30. We need of course to add the axioms saying that F is a linear order.

31. See A573/B601 where Kant explicitly restricts this complete determination to "existing" things. So in fact, in general this will be a "free" intuitionistic logic. My "The

Language of Appearances and Things in Themselves" (in *Synthese: An International Journal for Epistemology, Methodology, and Philosophy of Science*, no. 47 [May 1981]: 313–52]) gives some details, and my "A Free IPC is a Natural Logic: Strong Completeness for some Intuitionistic Free Logics" (in *Philosophical Applications of Free Logic*, ed. Karel Lambert [Oxford: Oxford University Press, 1991], 49–81) provides a completeness theorem.

32. See my "Mathematics as a Transcendental Science," in *Phenomenology and the Formal Sciences*, ed. T. Seebohm (Dordrecht: Kluwer, 1991), 107–31.

33. Kant, *Critique of Pure Reason*, trans. Kemp Smith, A480/B508.

34. Actually we need to use the fact that it is "mild assertability." See my "Kant's Mathematical Realism," in *Kant's Philosophy of Mathematics: Modern Essays*, ed. C. J. Posy (Dordrecht: Kluwer, 1992), 293–313.

35. See Kant, *Critique of Pure Reason*, A719/B747.

36. See my "Dancing to the Antinomy" and "Intuition and Infinity" for more detail on this argument.

37. Putnam, *The Threefold Cord*, 132.

38. See my "The Language of Appearances and Things in Themselves," where I proposed a formal semantics that captures this distinction by allowing "inaccessible galaxies" as parts of model structures: The assumption that p will remain verified is expressed "vertically," in the standard way, by projections of p's stability into accessible nodes. The fact that p might be refuted is expressed "horizontally" by the presence of another (presumably, nonactual) situation together with its own "vertical" projections of ~p).

39. Strawson (in *The Bounds of Sense: An Essay on Kant's Critique of Pure Reason* [London: Methuen, 1966], 137) claims that Kant's move from the irreversibility of the sequence of perceptions to the irreversibility of the boat's positions is "a non-sequitur of numbing grossness." Lovejoy, in "On Kant's Reply to Hume" (in *Archiv für Geschwulstforschung* 19, no. 3 [1906]: 380–407) raises a similar objection. These both stem from failing to note the distinction between the two sorts of projections and failing to see the relation of dependence between them. See my "Transcendental Idealism and Causality," in *Kant on Causality, Freedom and Objectivity*, ed. W. Harper and R. Meerbote (Minneapolis: University of Minnesota Press, 1984), 20–41.

40. See Michael Dummett, "The Reality of the Past" in *Truth and Other Enigmas* (Cambridge: Harvard University Press, 1978), 358–74. It is worth noting that Dummett, himself, has retreated from his denials of the reality of the past. See "Statements about the Past" in *Truth and the Past* (New York: Columbia University Press, 2004).

41. At A792/B820 Kant says that mathematics admits indirect proofs.

42. At A58/B82 Kant asks "What is truth? The nominal definition of truth, that it is the agreement of knowledge with its object, is assumed as granted; the question asked is as to what is the general and sure criterion of the truth of any and every knowledge." And then he goes on to say: "Now a general criterion of truth must be such as would be valid in each and every instance of knowledge, however their objects may vary. It is obvious however that such a criterion [being general] cannot take account of the [varying] content of knowledge (relation to its [specific] object). But since truth concerns just this very content, it is quite impossible, and indeed absurd, to ask for a general test of the truth of such content." (A58–59/B83, trans. Kemp Smith.) Of course, as we saw above, for Kant, pure ethics will be bivalent, but that is not the point here.

43. Putnam's argument rests on a clever generalization of Gödel's theorem to the notions of competent human reasoning and justified assertion, together with reflection about the possibility of codifying human mathematical competence. His variation on Gödel's proof shows that if the human mind can be modeled as a Turing machine, then it would not be able to know (justifiably to assert) which Turing machine it is.

44. Putnam, *Ethics without Ontology*, 65; Hilary Putnam, "The Gödel Theorem and Human Nature," in *Kurt Gödel and the Foundations of Mathematics: Horizons of Truth*, ed. M. Baaz, C. H. Papadimitriou, H. Putnam, D. S. Scott, C. L. Harper Jr. (Cambridge: Cambridge University Press, 2011), 325–37.

45. In the opening passage of the *Critique of Pure Reason* Kant says: "Human reason has a peculiar fate in one kind of its cognitions: it is troubled by questions that it cannot dismiss, because they are posed to it by the nature of reason itself, but that it also cannot answer, because they surpass human reason's every ability" (Avii, trans. Pluhar).

46. See my "Epistemology, Ontology, and the Continuum" (in *The Growth of Mathematics Knowledge*, ed. E. Grosholz and H. Breger [Dordrecht: Kluwer, 2001], 199–219) where I apply this idea to notions of continuity. Interestingly, Cohen's proof of the consistency of the negation of the continuum hypothesis relies on a method (forcing), which generalizes disequilibrium.

47. Hilary Putnam, "Wittgenstein, Realism, and Mathematics," in *Philosophy in an Age of Science*, ed. M. DeCaro and D. Macarthur (Cambridge: Harvard University Press, 2012), 423.

48. It is transcendental philosophy itself that would be the "mere play of the understanding" without such application.

49. Marian Boykan Pour-El and Ian Richards, "The Wave Equation with Computable Initial Data Such That Its Unique Solution Is Not Computable," *Advances in Mathematics* 39, no. 3 (1981): 215–39.

50. In this case Wittgenstein is a culprit. At Part V, §34 of the *Remarks on the Foundations of Mathematics* Wittgenstein says: "Suppose that people go on and on calculating the expansion of π. So God, who knows everything, knows whether they will have reached '777' by the end of the world. But can his *omniscience* decide whether they *would* have reached it after the end of the world? It cannot. I want to say: Even God can determine something mathematical only by mathematics. Even for him the mere rule of expansion cannot decide anything that it does not decide for us." (Ludwig Wittgenstein, *Remarks on the Foundations of Mathematics* [Cambridge: M.I.T. Press, 1964], 185e.)

Putnam interprets that as saying that if it is unfeasible to compute the value of a function at a point then there isn't a solution. He suggests that Wittgenstein went astray because he contemplated only tamer applications of mathematics.

51. D'Alembert: "But under this supposition one can only find the solution of the problem for the case where the different forms of the vibrating string can be written in a single equation. In all other cases it seems to me impossible to give a more general form" (J. B. le R. D'Alembert, *Addition au mémoire sur la courbe que forme une corde tendüe mise en vibration* [Paris, 1752], 358, as quoted in Umberto Bottazzini, *The Higher Calculus: A History of Real and Complex Analysis from Euler to Weierstrass*, trans. Warren Van Egmond [New York: Springer-Verlag, 1986], 24).

Euler: "The various similar parts of the curve are therefore not connected with each other by any law of continuity, and it is only by the description that they are joined together. For this reason it is impossible that all of this curve should be included in any equation" (L. Euler, "Remarques sur les memoires precedens de M. Bernoulli," in *Opera Omnia* 2, no. 10 [1755]: 233–54, as quoted in Bottazzini, *The Higher Calculus*, 26).

52. "Most physico-mathematical questions are so complicated that it is necessary to consider them first in a general and abstract manner, and to climb by degrees from simple cases to more composite ones. If any progress has been done up to now in the study on nature, it is due to the constant application of this method." (J. B. le R. D'Alembert, *Réflexions sur la cause générale des vents* [Berlin: Haude & Spener, 1747], viii, as quoted in François de Gandt, "The Limits of Intelligibility: The Status of Physical Science in

D'Alembert's Philosophy," in *Between Leibniz, Newton, and Kant*, ed. Wolfgang Lefèvre [Dordrecht: Kluwer, 2001], 50.)

53. "The principles of mechanics are already so solidly established that it would be a great error to continue to doubt their truth. Even though we would not be in condition to prove them through the general principles of metaphysics, the marvelous accord of all the conclusions that one obtains through calculation, with all the motion of bodies on earth both solid and fluid, and even with the motion of celestial bodies, shall be sufficient to put their truth beyond doubt. It is therefore an indisputable truth that a body once at rest will remain perpetually at rest, unless its state is disturbed by some outside force. It is equally certain that a body put into motion will continue to be in motion with the same speed following the same direction, provided that it does not meet any obstacles contrary to the conservation of this state.

"As so indubitably established, these two truths must be absolutely grounded upon the nature of bodies; and as it is metaphysics which is concerned with the study of the nature and properties of bodies, the awareness of these truths will be able to serve as a guide in these thorny investigations. For we shall be right to reject in this science all reasoning and all ideas that lead to conclusions contrary to these truths, however justified they may be elsewhere; and we shall be authorized to admit only principles that are consistent with these same truths" (L. Euler, "Reflexions sur l'espace et le tems," *Memoires de l'academie des sciences de Berlin*, 4 [1750]: 324–33, trans. M. P. Saclolo and P. Wake as "Reflections on Space and Time." The Euler Archive: http://eulerarchive.maa.org/docs/translations/ E149tr.pdf [accessed October 4, 2013]).

54. The underlying formal semantics for this view would have to take functional application as giving primitive singular terms.

55. Kant, *Critique of Pure Reason*, trans. Kemp Smith, A496–97/B524–25.

56. Actually in the "Postulates of Empirical Thought" Kant does adopt this liberal view. (See in particular A225-6/B272-3)

57. I find, by the way, an analogy to Kant's treatment of infinite divisibility versus the infinite extent of the world (A524–27/B552–55): In the case of the extent of the universe we have a series that (for Kant) proceeds *in indefinitum*. But when it comes to the division of matter, we speak of a sequence that proceeds *in infinitum*. The difference is that in the latter case, the matter is known to be already there.

58. I thank David Kashtan and Hilary Putnam for comments and correspondence, which helped me write these remarks. This essay was written with the support of the Israel Science Foundation Grant 172/06. I am grateful for that support.

REPLY TO CARL POSY

Carl Posy belongs to the handful of the world's best Kant scholars, but he is by no means only a "Kant scholar." As a Kant scholar, he combines a mastery of Kant's whole corpus (one that I would call "awesome," if that word was not so cheapened by the young nowadays), with a powerful interpretation of that corpus and a remarkable ability to explain the ways in which Kant is relevant to issues that philosophers like myself discuss today.[1] But Carl also has a mastery of mathematical logic and other branches of mathematics, and a mastery of the difficult program of mathematical intuitionism proposed by L. E. J. Brouwer in both its mathematical and philosophical aspects—and much more besides. The exposition of Kant's ideas in the present paper is one from which I have learned much, and so are the suggestions as to how Kant can be interpreted in the light of modern versions of what he calls "assertablism" (an offshoot, as far as logic is concerned, of the Brouwerian intuitionism just mentioned). Posy even suggests how a Kantian might want to correct some of Kant's doctrines in the light of twentieth- and twenty-first-century science. For all this I have nothing but admiration.

However Posy also wants to know (1) whether I could agree that Kant avoids or evades the criticisms I have made of assertablism in the past,[2] and (2) what I would say about the "Kant-style antirealism" that he speculatively proposes in the last sections of his paper. I shall respond to these questions in turn.

I. Did Kant Avoid My Criticisms of "Assertablism"?

Posy is right that there is in Kant a way of combining elements of assertablism and elements of realism that I had not seen, and that way does avoid *some* of my criticisms, but not all. Nor is it clear that its failure to avoid all of them is explained by developments in modern science that Kant cannot be blamed for not foreseeing. But this last remark may reflect a failure to fully understand what Posy has in mind; if so, I look forward to learning that in future conversations with him. But let me begin my restating Posy's interpretation in my own words.

There are three parts to that interpretation, namely a part that deals with singular statements that report, or could be used to report, an observation, such as "That is a cow," a part that deals with the logical connectives, and a part that deals with "the transcendental inquiry." I shall comment mainly on the first two; my comment on the third will be confined to a brief explanation of why I am unsympathetic to the whole idea of the "transcendental inquiry."

A) The Interpretation of Singular Statement

Posy's interpretation of singular statements is *simultaneously* "assertablist" and "realist." What makes this possible is that the interpretation is not tied to Dummett's "manifestation argument." Instead, it is tied to an account of perception that is realist, like John McDowell's, but still has Kantian features that McDowell thinks we must discard. As a naïve realist *cum* "disjunctivist," McDowell sees intuitions as making available to us how things really are *punkt*. If I have an intuition of a cow in front of me, I simply take in the fact that there is a cow in front of me. And since that is the sort of thing a normal human is equipped to perceive, that means that "There is a cow in front of me" is, if true, also assertible if conditions are good enough. But it is assertible by *anyone* under suitable conditions; thus the threat of solipsism does not even arise (at least it does not arise if we prescind from questions about the assertability of judgments about past events). But McDowell explicitly rejects the idea that intuitions do not extend to things as they are *an sich*, and Posy does not reject that idea. That is why (or so I venture to conjecture) Posy's interpretation posits that our intuitions are *homomorphic* to the things they concern, rather than, as McDowell does, that they are in themselves, *revelatory* of how those things are (and not just of how "their parts are arranged"). Posy's interpretation thus conforms to a statement that I recall reading in Kant's *Metaphysical Foundations of Natural Science* that we know only "relational" properties of things. That we do not know a single property that a thing has *an sich* (something Kant also says in the same work) is incompatible with McDowell's detranscendentalized Kantianism, but not with Posy's Kantianism.

B) The Interpretation of the Logical Connectives

Following a way of formalizing Brouwer's ideas that goes back to Gödel[3] and Heyting[4], Posy presents an "assertablist" interpretation of the logical connectives. According to that formalization, as Posy explains,

(x) Fx is assertable at an epistemic situation s, only if s contains a method for converting any proof that t is in the domain into a proof of F(t);

—and this clearly will not work for empirical generalizations such as "All crows are black." For this reason, Posy replaces the foregoing with:

(x) Fx is assertable at an epistemic situation s, only if at s we have evidence to the effect that any evidence that t is in the domain will yield evidence supporting the claim that F(t).

—But this, coupled with the proposal to understand "true" as "assertible," makes "true" relative to an epistemic situation, which I believe is simply wrong.[5] (And to identify truth with "assertability under sufficiently good epistemic circumstances requires that we may able to say what "sufficiently good" means without using *classical* logic. "Assertability in the Peircean limit" also does not work, for many reasons.)

C) My Lack of Sympathy with the Idea of "the Transcendental Inquiry"

The idea of "the transcendental inquiry" presupposes the Kantian belief that methodology should be a priori. Rejecting a similar idea in McDowell, the idea of sharp line between a space of reasons and a realm of law, I wrote[6]:

That line is, indeed, sharp when "justification" has the sense of *deductive* justification; questions of what follows from what deductively are not decidable by experiment. But the whole history of science suggests to me that, when it comes to *nondeductive justification*, the line between "fact" and "method," is blurry: we are often led by the success of novel sorts of theories to reconsider our canons of justification themselves. (The whole history of science since the Enlightenment could be described as a sequence of such reconsiderations.) We did not perform *experiments* to decide that, e.g., it is not a principle required by reason itself that every event must have a cause, and that a difference in the effects must be traceable to some difference in the causes, but neither did we discover that independently of being impressed by the success of quantum mechanical theories which denied this ancient principle. The dichotomy of a "space of reasons" and a "realm of law" is a last gasp of the analytic/synthetic and a priori/a posteriori dichotomies. And it is not only when questions of fundamental physical theory are involved that we are forced to reconsider "what justifies what": at one time, people thought they knew very well that certain experiences confirm judgments that so-and-so is a witch, to cite a familiar example, but that "knowledge" had to be revised, and much more was involved in revising it than confronting judgments with sense impressions.

—And that is still my view. (I also reject the Kantian idea that mathematics is about human reason, which, it seems to me, Posy comes close to endorsing. My own view is explained in my replies to Parsons and to Mühlholzer in the present volume.)

H.P.

NOTES

1. A fine example of this is his "Immediacy and the Birth of Reference in Kant: The Case for Space" in *Between Logic and Intuition: Essays in Honor of Charles Parsons*, ed. Gila Sher and Richard Tieszen (Cambridge: Cambridge University Press, 2000). Another, of course, is his present paper.

2. See my "Between Scylla and Charybdis; Does Dummett Have a Way Through," in *The Philosophy of Michael Dummett,* and "Between Dolev and Dummett: Some Comments on 'Antirealism, Presentism and Bivalence,'" *International Journal of Philosophical Studies* 18, no. 1 (2010): 91–96 (and, of course, my Reply to Michael Dummett in the present volume).

3. Kurt Gödel, *"Eine Interpretation des intuitionistischen Aussagenkalküls,"* *Ergebnisse eines mathematischen Kolloquiums* 4 (1933): 39–40. Reprinted with an English translation in Kurt Gödel, *Collected Works*, vol. I (Oxford: Oxford University Press, 1986).

4. Arend Heyting, *Intuitionism: An Introduction* (Amsterdam: North-Holland Publishing Co., 1956).

5. To identify truth with "assertibility under sufficiently good epistemic circumstances," as I did in my "internal realist" period, requires that we be able to say what "sufficiently good" means without using *classical* quantifiers. "Assertibility in the Peircean limit" also does not work, for many reasons.

6. In "Corresponding with Reality," collected in my *Philosophy in an Age of Science*, ed. Mario De Caro and David Macarthur (Cambridge, MA: Harvard University Press, 2012).

16

Cora Diamond

PUTNAM AND WITTGENSTEINIAN BABY-THROWING: VARIATIONS ON A THEME

I. The Theme: Wittgensteinian Baby-Throwing

Putnam began his Dewey Lectures by saying, "The besetting sin of philosophers seems to be throwing the baby out with the bathwater."[1] He drew attention to the pattern of "recoil" in philosophy,[2] in which philosophers who "recoil from the excesses of various versions of metaphysical realism" take up peculiar views instead—forms of antirealism, idealism, or relativism—while those who recoil from what they take to be a giving up on the whole idea of an objective world, come up with attempts to rescue objectivity by such mysterious notions as that of cross-world identity or an "absolute" conception of the world.

In an earlier essay, "Does the Disquotational Theory of Truth Solve All Philosophical Problems?"[3] Putnam examined two accounts of truth influenced by readings of Wittgenstein, those of Michael Williams and Paul Horwich. Putnam criticized their appeal to assertibility conditions in their accounts of truth, and argued that their attempts to show that the philosophical problems concerned with truth are pseudoproblems serve as an illustration of how philosophical attempts to reject metaphysics may lead philosophers into a kind of disguised metaphysics, in this case a kind of empiricist metaphysics. In his critical account of these approaches to truth, Putnam also questioned whether they really do reflect Wittgenstein's ideas.

Putnam has had a long-term interest in throwings out of the baby with the bathwater by philosophers who take themselves to be getting rid of objectionable forms of metaphysics, and to be making use of Wittgenstein's later philosophy in doing so. The three such baby-throwers most important for Putnam's writings are (I should say) Norman Malcolm, Michael Dummett, and Richard Rorty. Putnam's objections to the antirealism and verificationism that have been drawn from Wittgenstein's later writings go back to the earliest years of his career, when, as he says, much of his activity "was devoted to refuting Malcolm's version of Wittgensteinianism,"[4] and he adds that Stanley Cavell was at that time devoting much of his time to showing that the view that Putnam was criticizing was not indeed Wittgenstein's. In his 1992 lectures on pragmatism, Putnam notes that Rorty's interpretation of Wittgenstein is in some ways close to Malcolm's, and (as he takes it) equally misleading as a reading of Wittgenstein.[5] Section II of this chapter is about the dispute between Putnam and Rorty. Sections III through V look at Putnam's ideas in relation to those of İlham Dilman, a Wittgensteinian philosopher who resembles Rorty in taking his own views to be far closer to Putnam's than they are. The appendix to section V is about Peter Winch's treatment of magic, and his attempt to rule out certain kinds of criticism of forms of thought distant from our own. In section VI, I look at what makes baby-throwing attractive, and I draw some conclusions about Putnam and commonsense realism.

II. THE RELATIVIST MENACE?

A striking feature of the dispute between Putnam and Rorty is their disagreement about how far apart their views are from each other. This has been an issue in the dispute since its beginnings in the early 1980s. The most important statement by Rorty of how he sees the dispute, his essay "Hilary Putnam and the Relativist Menace,"[6] takes its title from the disagreement about what the disagreement is about. By speaking of Putnam's view of him as a "Relativist Menace," Rorty distances himself from relativism (or at any rate intends to do so), and suggests that Putnam has been attacking a straw man. Rorty was responding to Putnam's remark, in lectures which Putnam gave in 1981, that "cultural relativists usually *deny* that they are cultural relativists"[7]—a remark that Putnam had explained by pointing to Rorty's views, which combine an attack on relativism with a view of truth that is, so Putnam suggests, plainly committed to relativism. Rorty's first response to the accusation was in "Solidarity or Objectivity?," his Howison lecture, in early 1983. "Relativism," he said, "is the traditional epithet applied to pragmatism by realists."[8] He distinguished three views which may get labeled "relativism," the first of which is self-refuting and the second eccentric, neither of which he holds. The third view is Rorty's version of pragmatism, which he describes as a kind of ethnocentrism about truth and rationality. He adds that there is really no good reason for calling it "relativist," since it does not involve holding of anything that it is relative to something else. The view might appear to be self-refuting if one took it to involve a theory of truth, identifying truth with the opinions of some group. But that, Rorty says, is a misinterpretation, which underlies the way realists respond to this sort of pragmatism. He adds that his view is in fact quite close to Putnam's 1981 "internalism," since Putnam rejects a God's-eye view of things. The criticisms that Putnam had directed against "relativists," Rorty says, do not apply to him. In particular, he does not hold the kind of "incommensurability" view for which Putnam had criticized Kuhn and Feyerabend; and there does not appear to be any other matter on which Putnam could take himself to be in disagreement with Rorty, or so Rorty says.[9]

Putnam was not convinced. In his Kant lectures, in 1987, he took Rorty's formulations of his own views about truth and rationality to be deeply different from his own, and he argued that Rorty, though not a typical Relativist, is indeed a Relativist. Putnam expressed his own commitment to what, in Rorty's terms, is a form of ethnocentrism: our norms and standards are *our* norms and standards and reflect *our* interests, but Putnam insisted on not drawing the kinds of conclusions that Rorty had taken to follow. According to Putnam's principles, there usually is, in ordinary circumstances, a fact of the matter whether the statements people make are warranted or not; further, the possibility that our norms and standards may improve is not the same as saying that they will come to seem better to us, or come to be accepted by our cultural peers. "From within *our* picture of the world . . . *we* say that 'better' isn't the same as '*we* think it's better'."[10]

"Hilary Putnam and the Relativist Menace" was Rorty's considered response. He objected strongly to being confused with his evil twin, "the Relativist,"[11] while reiterating the sorts of view that had made Putnam call him a relativist in the first place. For example, he committed himself to the view that all that can be meant by talk of "a fact of the matter about whether *p* is a warranted assertion" is "a fact of the matter about our ability to feel solidarity with a community that views *p* as warranted."[12] From Rorty's point of view, the situation was extremely puzzling, since Putnam appeared to him to accept the same pragmatist principles which Rorty himself did. To bring out the extensive agreement between his own views and Putnam's, Rorty listed five passages from Putnam's writings, expressing principles that he himself wholeheartedly shared. In these passages, Putnam repudiates metaphysical realism and insists on the importance of our situatedness as thinkers, and on the inseparability of our interests and our values from any view we may have of the world. And that, for Rorty,

was the source of his puzzlement: what is it that Putnam thinks really differentiates Rorty's thought from Putnam's own? Without falling back into
metaphysical realism, he asked, what sort of content can be given to any of
the notions which Putnam uses in expressing his criticisms of Rorty?[13]—It
is possible to explain why Rorty thought that there was no room for a view
between metaphysical realism on the one hand and on the other his own
version of pragmatism. But here what I want to note is simply that Rorty
took his philosophical commitments to be virtually the same as Putnam's,
but Putnam understood—and understands—those commitments very differently from Rorty. Putnam's picture of Rorty's views repeatedly elicited
from Rorty a "Who, me?" response. Rorty's "Who, me?" responses to
criticisms are highly characteristic of his style of controversy, and I want
to end this section by a brief look at this sort of response.

Suppose that there are indeed two philosophers, Rorty and his evil twin
the Relativist. There is then a question why so many philosophers confuse
them, and ascribe to Rorty the views of his evil twin. A part of the answer
to the question is that, although Rorty regularly takes a stance of metaphilosophical purity in which he disowns philosophical positions, he combines it
with down-and-dirty philosophical argumentation which appears (to many
readers) to commit him to the views of his evil twin. He gives arguments
that disallow certain sorts of possibility, but shifts from the arguments
over to the metaphilosophical purity line, and says that he is not arguing
for views like those of his evil twin, but is merely recommending shifts in
how we talk. Here is an example of how the metaphilosophical purity line
seems to be used by Rorty to provide a kind of plausible deniability for
the philosophical views which his arguments seem to express. Putnam had
criticized Rorty for his account of what it would be for our standards of
warrant to become better, after Rorty had explained "betterness" in terms
of what seems better to our cultural peers. Such an account of "better,"
Putnam said, cannot be justified by an appeal to what we accept, since we
have a very different picture of what it would be for our standards to be
better; and so it looks as if Rorty is implicitly working with the idea that,
from a God's-eye view, there is nothing else for "betterness of warrant" to
amount to.[14] Rorty, in response, went metaphilosophical, and claimed that
all he was doing was recommending that we replace our way of talking
of "better" with what he thinks that we will find to be more convenient.[15]
But I have quoted above a passage which seems entirely inconsistent with
such a description of what Rorty was doing, the passage in which he claims
that all that can be meant by talk of "a fact of the matter about whether p
is a warranted assertion" is a fact about what sort of community we can
feel solidarity with. The idea is that there is no alternative to that sort of
Rortian pragmatism; apparent alternatives will involve appeals to the way

God sees things, or to some other metaphysically fishy idea.[16] Rorty says that he is only making recommendations, not analyzing meanings; but he in fact makes claims about what we *can mean*. He plainly appears to be arguing that there is no space for meaning anything by "better" but: what "will come to seem better to *us*."[17] That is, there is no room for Putnam's "commonsense realism"—a view that does not take "betterness" to be a matter of "what will come to seem better to us." It is hardly surprising that Putnam suggested that, underneath all the wrappings, Rorty is still trying to say what, from a God's-eye view, there *is not*. In Rorty's approach to the issue there is visible a feature of much Wittgensteinian baby-throwing philosophy: the insistence that there are, in connection with some issue, only two alternatives: a metaphysically fishy one and the baby-throwing one. Commonsense realism is not seen at all, and the baby-throwing argument implicitly relies on a God's-eye view of what there is not.

The difficulty of keeping Rorty's views distinct from those of his evil twin can be seen also from what we might call the dinosaur angle. It is supposedly his evil twin, and not Rorty himself, who holds that there were no dinosaurs until, as our science progressed, they were "invented."[18] But Rorty does rather encourage one to confuse him with his evil twin when he says that, in a suitably broad sense, dinosaurs are "social constructions," and when he tells us that neither giraffes nor dinosaurs are "out there" apart from human needs and interests.[19] I shall return to the dinosaur line in section III.

III. With Friends Like These . . .

Putnam said that cultural relativists usually deny being cultural relativists. Wittgensteinian idealists characteristically deny being idealists of any sort. A very good example is Derek Bolton, who defended a view that he took to be Wittgenstein's, and that he took to exclude every form of idealism. But on this view, a method of inquiry makes possible the empirical facts that it brings to light.[20] Bolton might well have been using "makes possible" in a blurry sort of way. That is, he might not have distinguished between a method of inquiry making it possible for us to take in something as an empirical fact, and a method of inquiry making certain sorts of empirical facts possible simpliciter. His words do suggest that he meant the latter. As a response to the accusation by Bernard Williams that Wittgenstein's later thinking is a form of idealism, Bolton's response amounts to describing it so that it is indeed a form of idealism, and then denying that it is idealism. I shall look in more detail at a different view of this sort, that of İlham Dilman.[21] He, like Bolton, expounds a view that he takes to be Wittgenstein's, and that he denies is a kind of idealism. Dilman also takes himself to be in agreement with Putnam's views about truth and realism, and with Putnam's criticisms of Rorty. He puts forward a kind of idealism of exactly the sort Putnam ascribes to Rorty: "a doctrine of the dependence of the way things are on the way we talk." Dilman, indeed, insists far more unequivocally than Rorty on such dependence. Putnam had said that Rorty's retention of this "dependence" way of speaking "betrays his deep linguistic idealism."[22] Dilman also takes a view far from Putnam's on the incommensurability of what may be said in different languages. Thus, like Rorty, Dilman is someone who sees the distance between himself and Putnam to be far less than what it looks like from Putnam's angle of vision. In this section and the two that follow, I try to bring out some of the ways in which Dilman, while taking himself to agree with Putnam, argues for views of which Putnam has been an acute critic.

It is very difficult, when one first formulates an approach to a topic, to see what kinds of misunderstandings of what one is saying are likely. It is indeed the responses of other philosophers to what one has said, responses that one may come to see as misunderstandings, that help one to better understand one's own views and one's commitments. This certainly is what happened with Putnam's ideas about the "dependence" of the way things are on the way we talk. Putnam had in fact begun the passage that I just quoted, about Rorty's "linguistic idealism," by referring to Rorty's claim that we are not in a position to formulate any kind of distinctively realist view if indeed "there are no objects which are what they are independent of our ways of talking."[23] Putnam said that such talk of independence, which is not meant to be either ordinary causal or ordinary logical independence, makes little sense. He added that, for the reasons he was giving, he had recently been trying "*not* to state my own doctrine as a doctrine of the dependence of the way things are on the way we talk."[24] The suggestion is that his earlier way of talking, invoking a kind of dependence, was far less clear. He did not specify the earlier formulations that he had in mind, but one can see in *Reason, Truth and History* exactly the kind of talk he was now (in 1993) trying to avoid. What he had claimed was that "objects" do not exist independently of conceptual schemes, and that the kinds of objects that the world does indeed consist of are not mind-independent. That this way of talking could be taken to express a kind of metaphysics became clear; and that was one reason Putnam gave it up. But it was exactly that view, which Dilman thought he could see in Putnam's writings of the 1980s, that underlay his sense that Putnam's approach and his own were very close.

Dilman is less philosophically subtle than Rorty, and his response to Putnam's 1993 remarks about independence reveals, without wrappings, the views that Putnam had taken Rorty to have held underneath wrappings and despite disclaimers.[25] Dilman wants to grant that the truth of what we say about dinosaurs is independent of our saying those things; but he wants to insist as well that what *can* be the case about dinosaurs is dependent on our having a language in which we establish what is so and what is not so about dinosaurs.[26] This is in fact very close to the view that Rorty had put by saying that, in a suitably broad sense, dinosaurs were "social constructions."[27]

We can see the difficulties in Dilman's view if we consider its application to a culture discussed by Dilman, that of thirteenth- and fourteenth-century Europe. He says that the skies of Dante's *Divine Comedy* and the sky and stars of modern astronomy belong to two different "universes of discourse."[28] (He does not use the word "astronomy" except to speak of modern astronomy, and it is not clear whether there is anything that he would call "medieval astronomy." His discussion of medieval thought reflects a very strong conception of incommensurability between their modes of thought and ours, and an apparent denial of continuities between medieval thought and Greek and Islamic scientific traditions.) We might, Dilman says, take it to be an unfortunate thing that the people of the Middle Ages had lost interest in scientific investigation; and he adds that someone might say that their religious beliefs had prevented the development of scientific modes of inquiry, of the sort begun by the Greeks. But, he says, we cannot actually fault their conception of the universe on the basis of our astronomical knowledge; we cannot use our own criteria in criticism of their understanding of the universe. Their sky and their stars are not ours.[29]

In Dilman's discussion of the world view of the thirteenth and fourteenth centuries, we can see him throwing out the baby of the world with the bathwater of metaphysical realism. Some ideas of Robert Brandom's can help bring this out. Brandom has argued that we have a "perspectival grip on a nonperspectival world."[30] He has an example which, almost exactly as it stands, is applicable to Dilman on the Middle Ages. Brandom's example is: "Ptolemy claimed *of* the orbital trajectories of the planets that they were the result of the motion of crystalline spheres."[31] With a small change to make it fit the period discussed by Dilman, it becomes "Albertus Magnus claimed *of* the orbital trajectories of the planets that they were the result of the motion of crystalline spheres."[32] Brandom's idea, then, is that we can use this *de re* way of speaking in giving the views of Ptolemy, or (if we like) those of Albertus Magnus. Here we take ourselves to have a different grip from that of Ptolemy or Albertus on the "nonperspectival" world, on what Putnam refers to as "*the world*." One of the ways in which Dilman has given up on any idea of *the* world, on which we and others have this or that perspectival grip, is in refusing to countenance such *de re* talk, from our perspective, of things which were conceived by Albertus Magnus and his contemporaries in totally different terms, not (indeed) as planets in our sense at all. It is not metaphysical realism to think of the planets as there to be thought about, in an admittedly very different way, by people very distant from ourselves in their conception of the world. What then is it that makes such an understanding of our relation to medieval thought—that we think about the same world, albeit in very different ways—unacceptable to Dilman? That is the question to which I turn in sections IV and V.

IV. THROWING OUT THE BABY

What rules out, for Dilman, the idea that we and the people of the thirteenth and fourteenth centuries may think in very different ways about the same world and about such things in it as planets and their motion, is his understanding of *objects of thought*. He takes *objects of thought* to be available to us within our "universe of discourse." Within the "universe of discourse," there is a grammar through which such things can be thought about, a grammar which enables us to refer to them, and to make true or false statements about them. The things we talk about *can* be objects of thought through lying within our "universe of discourse." What we can take to be possible, what we can look into the truth of, wonder about the truth of, take to be or not to be the case—these are possibilities within the "universe of discourse"; they are dependent on our language. The world that we can think about, the only world that makes sense to us, "does not exist independently of our language."[33] Here it looks as if we have reached the conclusion that nothing that we think about could be thought about except within our "universe of discourse." It has its possibilities only there, only within "our world."

There are two sources of philosophical confusion in the views of Dilman's that I have just summarized. One of them is a conception of grammatical rules and of the dependence upon such rules of the sensefulness of what we say. This conception is criticized by Putnam in "Rules, Attunement, and 'Applying Words to the World': The Struggle to Understand Wittgenstein's Vision of Language."[34] I shall discuss Putnam's view and its relation to Dilman's ideas in section V. In the rest of section IV, I shall be concerned with the other source of confusion: Dilman's view of *objects of thought*. To see what is problematic in his view, we should remind ourselves of the grammar of our language: the grammar of our talk of objects of thought. Dilman has (as I shall try to show) missed out what that grammar allows us to do.

I take my account of this grammar from Anscombe, from "The Intentionality of Sensation,"[35] which begins with an account of *intentional objects*. She uses the vocabulary of "intentional object" and "material object" to lay out how we talk about such cases as that in which a man "aims at a stag;

but the thing he took for a stag was his father, and he shoots his father."[36]
In this context, to say that he "aimed at his father" would be ambiguous.
There is a sense in which it is true: he aimed at a dark patch in the foliage;
that dark patch was his father's hat, and his father's head was in it. To say
that what he aimed at was his father is to give *the material object* of aiming;
it gives what, materially speaking, he aimed at. (This use of "material" is
not the same as that in which we speak of things like tables or lumps of
butter as "material objects." Such things as a promise, or debt, or the sky, or
a scandal might be the material object of someone's thought, for example.)
But "he aimed at his father" is false if it is meant to give the *intentional
object* of aiming. In that sense, what he aimed at is given by the phrase
"a stag." The phrase "dark patch in the foliage" also gives the intentional
object of aiming, and (in this example) that phrase also gives the material
object. In some cases, questions about the identity of an intentional object
are a matter of the identity of a material object. That is part of the grammar of intentionality, in cases in which there is a material object. If one is
talking to a child about the planet Venus, one may pick it out for the child
as "that bright thing in the sky." This phrase gives what is both the material object and the intentional object of the child's thought, as she looks at
what you have pointed out. What you have drawn to the child's attention
is the planet Venus. The fact that we might say that "*planets* are not yet in
the child's thought-world" is not relevant to the question whether what the
child has had her attention drawn to is a planet, since that bright thing in
the sky is the planet Venus. "The planet Venus" gives the material object
of the child's thought; and this has nothing to do with whether the child is
capable of thinking about planets as planets. People in the thirteenth and
fourteenth centuries could talk of the planet Venus as "that bright thing
in the sky," as we do when we pick out such things. They could also talk
about it, as we can, as one of the things of which it is true both that it can
be seen in the night sky and that it appears in different positions relative to
other luminous bodies in the night sky whose positions relative to each other
appear fixed.[37] Since they also thought of that bright thing in the sky as a
luminous ethereal globe affixed to an ethereal sphere, we can say that they
believed *of* the planet Venus that it was a luminous ethereal globe affixed to
an ethereal sphere. The planet Venus is the material object of their thought,
since that bright thing over there that they are talking about, one of the ones
that appear in different positions relative to other luminous bodies in the
sky, is the planet Venus. The intentional object of their thought is one of
the "wandering stars" or *planete*, not a planet in our sense, for they do not
have our conception of a planet—and the *planete* included the sun and the
moon. It would have been utterly puzzling to have said that the Earth was a
planeta, since it plainly was not a luminous celestial body. We can say that

planets, conceived as we conceive them, do not exist in their "universe of discourse"; but that does not imply that the planet Venus is not the material object of some of their thoughts. The grammar of intentionality allows us to speak of there being different ways of thinking about the things in the sky. It allows us to think about the difference between what people long ago believed *of* the motion of Venus and its distance from the Earth and what we believe about such things; it allows us to think about the development over time of very different ways of thinking and speaking about things in *the world*, like the planet Venus and its motion. This is not metaphysical realism; it is simply a matter of an application which our grammar allows of the distinction between material and intentional objects.

Dilman would not deny that we can give the material object (in Anscombe's sense) of someone's thought. But his view puts narrow limits on the language within which the material object can be given. If people do not have available within their "universe of discourse" some way of speaking, that way of speaking cannot be used in giving the material object of some thought of theirs. He says that the objects, events, and situations that they meet up with, or that they are thinking about, cannot be identified in any way that is independent of how they think of these things.[38] Here are five points about this central moment of Dilman's thought, the moment at which the baby of the world is going right down the drain.

A. It is by no means part of the grammar through which we speak of the identity of various sorts of things that we cannot identify what some people are talking about unless we use a way of speaking which is available within their "universe of discourse." On the contrary, grammar does allow us to identify what they are speaking about, using our ways of speaking, even where these ways of speaking depart significantly from what would be available to the people themselves whose thought we are describing. This was Brandom's point: that one main use of *de re* constructions is precisely to give what people are speaking about in terms which are different from theirs and which they themselves would not necessarily be able to take in.

B. The view which Dilman puts forward he takes to be Wittgenstein's, but it is not. Wittgenstein is perfectly happy to speak of people whom he imagines, whose view of the moon is quite weird, as having views about *the moon*. They have no knowledge of physics; what they think the moon *is*, what they understand by *where it is*, or by *what it would be to fly there*, would be totally different from what we understand. But Wittgenstein uses our words, "the moon," to give the material object of their thinking.

C. I mentioned Putnam's argument that Rorty is engaged in a self-refuting attempt to have and at the same time to deny an "absolute perspective." The same issues arise once again here. We do not actually take ourselves to be limited in our description of other cultures in the ways laid out by

Dilman. His account is wrong if taken as an account of *what we do*. But, if Dilman wants to hold that what we do is wrong or confused, such a line of argument might appear to require a perspective outside our own mode of thought from which philosophical criticism could be leveled at that mode of thought. But Dilman does not want to argue from a perspective outside all "universes of discourse." But he does nevertheless want to generalize about them, and about the ways in which objects of thought can be spoken of, *in any "universe of discourse."*

D. Underlying Dilman's argument is the view that we cannot criticize a mode of thought from outside it. He has built up a metaphysical structure which rules out our saying such things as that our astronomy has got a much better account of the movements of Mercury, Venus, Mars, Jupiter, and Saturn, as well as of their distances from the Earth and of what sorts of thing they are, than does the astronomy of Albertus Magnus. If, as Dilman says, the objects that our astronomy is concerned with were not in the "universe of discourse" of the Middle Ages, and if they therefore could not have been seen[39] or thought about by Albertus, then he cannot have had any views of *their* motion, and therefore cannot have had less adequate views of their motion than ours. I shall have more to say about this, because the desire to insulate modes of thought from criticism is a very strong motive for Wittgensteinian baby-throwing. But here I want only to lay out the connection to issues raised by Putnam in his criticism of Rorty on betterness of warrant. What most strikingly revealed to Putnam how far he and Rorty were from each other was Rorty's view of what it is for our standards of warrant to become better. All that this can amount to, Rorty had said, was for new standards to seem better to our cultural peers. But, said Putnam, we have a very different picture of what it would be for our standards to become better. Rorty, Putnam argued, is ruling out judgments we do want to make. Here again, with Dilman's insulation of "universes of discourse" from any judgments of "better" or "worse" apart from those available within the "universe of discourse," we come up against the philosophical insistence that there is no room for the kind of judgment of betterness that we do want to make, and that our picture of the world does leave room for. Our picture of the world and our situation in it is of our coming in some cases to have much better knowledge of some objects than people had at some earlier time, where the people in question (about whom we say that our knowledge of these objects is better than theirs) had profoundly different modes of thought from ours. (This is an issue on which Dilman criticizes Elizabeth Anscombe, and I come back to it in section VI. For Putnam's view, see, for example, *Pragmatism*, p. 38.)

E. Putnam gave up speaking of his own view as "internal realism" when he became aware of how open that way of speaking was to misunderstanding.

Dilman writes about Putnam's worries here, and takes them to be inappli-
cable to the kind of view he is putting forward.[40] He notes that a language
and the modes of thought belonging to it can develop; and he allows that it
is possible to think one's way into the modes of thought of an alien culture.
But these considerations are limited, and do not reach to the issue that I am
labeling baby-throwing: getting rid of the world while seeking to avoid metaphysical realism. One sees only the two contrasting types of alternatives:
of some version of metaphysical realism on the one hand, and on the other
a conception of *what we are thinking about* which does not allow Albertus
Magnus and ourselves to have different takes on *the world*, and which puts
him and ourselves into different worlds. This is an equally metaphysical
alternative, and it depends (as Putnam notes) on a deeply problematic idea
of the *dependence* of the things we think about on our language.

V. WHAT WE CAN TALK ABOUT

On Dilman's view, what we can talk about depends upon our "universe
of discourse." The rules of grammar of our language provide the logical
space within which this or that can be the case or not the case, within which
there are such-and-such sorts of objects, events, and situations. Through
this grammar there is for us a world which we can speak about. What
can sensefully be said is determined by this grammar; the grammar fixes
the criteria for things being as we say they are. Some of Putnam's most
important criticisms of this view are developed in "Rules, Attunement,
and 'Applying Words to the World'." He gives numerous examples of how
words may be used in entirely new ways, and of how we *pick up on* such
uses, although we have never come across them before, and although the
grammatical rules of the language do not anticipate such uses. The sensefulness of what we say is not dependent upon rules already in place in the
language. New metaphors are one sort of example; as Putnam points out,
we do not need a structure of rules in order to recognize an entirely new
metaphor as strikingly appropriate. Think of Wittgenstein's: "The rose
has teeth in the mouth of a beast"—which might appear to go against the
grammatical rules which allow talk of teeth in the case of animals, various tools and machines, and the margins of leaves, but not in the case of
flowers like the rose.

Putnam has in various contexts mentioned another kind of example: that
of speculation. People can speculate about how things might be, whether
or not they have any way of establishing that such things indeed are the
case. He has taken as one kind of example *things too small to be seen with
the naked eye*. That phrase does not depend for its intelligibility, he says,

on "the invention of an instrument that allows us to see things smaller than . . . the naked eye can see."[41] But this already shows the problematic character of Dilman's idea that the people of the thirteenth and fourteenth centuries had a "universe of discourse" which did not include the objects of our astronomy. That would mean that their "universe of discourse" did not include celestial objects *too far away and too small to be seen with the naked eye.* But it is hardly the case that talk of such objects would have been senseless. Anyone who speculated about such objects might well have been asked why God would have made such objects, since the celestial objects were intended (according to the Bible) to be used by us as signs, to mark day and night, and the different seasons. But the possibility of such an objection would not mean that the speculation itself would have been unintelligible. There are in any case various replies that might be made to the objection, including the obvious point that our knowledge of God's purposes is limited. The possibility of such speculation about things we do not yet have any way of establishing to be the case goes with another idea of Putnam's, that we are "endlessly . . . *forced* to renegotiate . . . our notion of reality as our language and our life develop."[42] Speculation about what might lie too far off for us to see with the naked eye reflects the possibility that we might indeed have to renegotiate our notion of reality to take in things that have had no place in our "universe of discourse." Here it is misleading to speak as Dilman does of the reality of the physical world as "internal to language," for this appears to rule out the idea that our thinking and our language will have to accommodate "the reality of the physical world" in as yet unforeseen ways.

Dilman's ideas about the dependence of what we can talk about on our "universe of discourse" are very close to those of Peter Winch and were influenced by Winch's discussion of Azande rituals.[43] Winch makes a contrast, which Dilman picks up, between magical practices within our culture and the practices of the Azande. What both Winch and Dilman say is that, within our culture, shaped by Christian ideas, we can reject as *irrational* magic and witchcraft as practiced within the culture; such a judgment rests on criteria available within our "universe of discourse." In contrast, the system of magical beliefs and practices of the Azande is part of a very different "universe of discourse," within which there are no criteria by which the practices could be judged to be irrational. If there is, within their "universe of discourse," a conception of reality and clear ways of establishing which beliefs are and which are not in agreement with that reality, then individual Zande beliefs about (for example) whether a witch has caused some harm may, by their criteria, be rational or not so, but the practice itself cannot be judged to be irrational. The two halves of this philosophical conception are equally problematic.

(A) There is the general privileging of criteria available within a "universe of discourse" when those criteria are used to criticize practices that depart from mainstream practices and ways of establishing what is the case, or what is rational, and which make use of concepts taken from the mainstream discourse. The example, used by both Winch and Dilman, of black magic within our culture may make the general principle look better than it has any business looking. Because the example is important for both of them, and because the example itself, Winch's argument about it, and the principle on which it rests are problematic, I have discussed it further in an appendix to this section. The principle has been the basis for criticism of Wittgensteinian ideas as socially conservative.[44] Winch himself wanted to allow for critical thinking within a society about the concepts and practices of that society,[45] but his own discussion of the case of black magic in our society suggests a tension within his views, and leaves it very unclear whether his views can accommodate genuinely revolutionary innovations if the innovations involve radical shifts in the ways old concepts are employed. The point to be made here, against both Winch and Dilman, is that, if some application of the concepts available within a culture deliberately departs from what is taken to be appropriate or allowable or sensible or rational in the established grammar of those concepts, the question of irrationality has to be examined in the particular case, and cannot be settled merely by noting that the the established grammar apparently provides a basis for concluding that the application is irrational or unintelligible. There is no general philosophical argument for privileging criticism from the point of view of the established use of the concepts.

(B) Winch's and Dilman's approach also involves ruling out the possibility of criticism of a mode of thought or practice by standards which are not part of the "universe of discourse" within which the mode of thinking lies. I shall discuss this issue in the appendix to section V and in section VI, but here I want to focus on the particular issue raised by Putnam, of the impossibility of deciding what is or is not "intelligible" by reference to grammatical rules that determine what sorts of things can be established to be the case and in what ways. Such a principle makes problematic the sensefulness of many things that we take ourselves to understand perfectly well, as comes out in the examples of metaphor and speculation. It also makes problematic what one might call the ordinary skepticism that people have about many things that are taken to be unquestionable within some "universe of discourse." Thus, for example, whatever the grammatical rules were about the reality of the resurrection of the dead, say in fourteenth-century France, it was entirely intelligible there, as in any culture where the resurrection of the dead is part of the established system of thought, to say, "You know, I don't believe that. I think we rot after we are dead, and that's all."[46]

How might Dilman have replied to the kinds of consideration I have been urging? He says that it is indeed possible, on his view, for someone to lack any apprehension of some of the realities which lie within the "universe of discourse" within which he lives.[47] Such a person might express the kind of skepticism that I have just described. On Dilman's view, then, such skepticism might evince a failure of sensitivity to the realities present in the skeptic's "universe of discourse." But this would not be an adequate response, as comes out if we note that the kind of skepticism that I mentioned, among ordinary people in fourteenth-century France, included skepticism about the Mass, calling into question the reality of the sacrifice and the reality of Christ's presence, which were part of the system of thought taught to Catholics and accepted by most of them.[48] Such skepticism is part of a continuing history, within which lie the Protestant criticisms of the Catholic understanding of the reality present in the Mass, from Wycliffe onwards. Dilman's view seems to leave room for two alternative accounts of those criticisms: either the early reformers were oblivious to realities which were there to be apprehended within the world of their language and culture, or they were criticizing the Catholic world from the outside, and not genuinely speaking of the reality of the Mass, as it was apprehended within the "universe of discourse" of Western Christendom at the time. But the problem with Dilman's view, then, is that in neither case can the critics be understood in *their* terms. Here we see sharply the objection to dismissing the fourteenth-century rural skeptics as blind to a reality present within their "universe of discourse." In both cases—the fourteenth-century skeptics and the early Protestant critics—we have a form of thinking that calls into question, quite radically, fundamental ideas of a "universe of discourse"; and an important objection to a view like Dilman's is that it does not allow for the real force of any criticism that might be taken to be a form of "skepticism."[49] While such accounts allow that there can indeed be such skepticism, they do not allow the reality internal to a "universe of discourse" to be *genuinely challenged* by skeptics. In "Rules, Attunement, and 'Applying Words to the World'," Putnam argues that skeptical claims, although they may involve the use of words "outside or apart from" their criteria, cannot be rejected a priori on the basis of some kind of general argument. Putnam's argument can be applied also to the case mentioned above, of criticism of the Zande magical beliefs as *irrational*. The Putnamian argument would be that we cannot rule out such criticisms a priori on the basis of general philosophical argument, and in particular that we cannot rule out such criticisms on the basis of a general philosophical argument about the criteria on which such criticisms would supposedly depend. The rest of this chapter is about this disagreement between Putnam and Wittgensteinians like Winch and Dilman. I discuss the issues in relation to Winch's treatment of magic in the appendix to section V, and in relation to Wittgensteinian baby-throwing more generally in section VI. A good example to keep in mind throughout this discussion is that of the medieval Karaite challenge to the rabbinic understanding of the authority of tradition. Dilman's approach leads to the conclusion that the validity of the tradition is internal to the "universe of discourse," and that the Karaites showed a failure to appreciate a reality present in that "universe of discourse." They lose, by an a priori argument; on Putnam's sort of view, the case cannot be settled in that way.

APPENDIX TO SECTION V: WINCH ON MAGIC AMONG US

Winch lays out his account of magic within "our own culture" in connection with his argument that a "primitive" system of magic, like that of the Azande, can be taken to constitute a "coherent universe of discourse like science," within which there is an intelligible conception of reality and clear ways of deciding which beliefs are and which are not "in agreement with this reality."[50] There is, he argues, a contrast between that sort of case and the case of magical beliefs and magical rituals in our culture. He makes the general claim that the concepts of witchcraft and magic in our culture have been "at least since the advent of Christianity . . . parasitic on, and a perversion of other orthodox concepts, both religious and, increasingly, scientific."[51] He then gives the case of the Black Mass as an "obvious example." He says that "you could not understand what was involved in conducting a Black Mass, unless you were familiar with the conduct of a proper Mass and, therefore, with the whole complex of religious ideas from which the Mass draws its sense."[52] You could not understand the relation between the Black practices and the religious ideas from which those practices draw their sense, and on which they are parasitic, without taking account of the fact that, by the standards available within the system of religious ideas, the Black practices count as *irrational*. The Black practices have an "essential reference" to a system of ideas outside themselves; and it is that parasitic character that makes possible a demonstration of their irrationality. Hence, criticism of such practices as "superstitious" or "irrational" or "illusory" is not, Winch says, simply a matter of "being on the side of the big battalions"[53]; his basic argument is that the beliefs and practices derive such sense "as they seem to have" from their relation to other practices within our culture, and the standards available within those other practices enable us to criticize the magical practices and beliefs in "culturally relevant" terms. I am going to examine Winch's argument as he put it forward originally in 1964. Much of his argument depends on principles that he had laid out more fully in 1958, in *The Idea of a Social Science and Its Relation to*

Philosophy. In 1990, in his preface to the second edition of that book, he criticized some of the ideas in it, including in particular his conception of the "self-contained" character of such "modes of social life" as science or religion.[54] This idea comes into his 1964 discussion of magic, but I do not think that his later criticisms of the book affect the fundamental line that he wanted to take in "Understanding a Primitive Society." Although the detail of the argument would have been altered if he had reformulated it later on, the problems with the argument would remain. They are connected directly to the idea that the relation between reality and what is said or thought in some culture is internal to the language spoken by the people whose culture it is. What underlay Winch's critique of Evans-Pritchard on the Azande was that Evans-Pritchard took Azande thought about the use of oracles not to accord with reality; he criticized the Azande by appeal to our system of thought. Winch held that you cannot do *that.*

Winch's account of magic in our culture has two parts: (1) a general and very strong claim about what magic and witchcraft in our culture have been like since the advent of Christianity, including the claim that the character of these practices is well exemplified by the Black Mass, and (2) an argument that we have a "culturally relevant" basis for condemning the Black Mass, using standards belonging to the system of thought on which it is parasitic. The first claim, about the general character of concepts of magic and witchcraft within our culture, is not given any backing by Winch. It is indeed odd that, while Winch depends for his account of Zande magic on a classic anthropological study, he gives no source at all for anything he says about magic within our culture. I shall discuss the Black Mass below, but it is important that it is in various ways not an "obvious example" of what magic is like in our culture, but quite an odd case, since it is apparently a myth. Ordinary magical practices in our culture may have no connections with Christianity, for example the use of love potions, or of lodestones to attract business customers. It is certainly true that magical practices among us frequently do have Christian elements, in some cases added on to what were older pagan practices or imported practices from other cultures. Such practices as that of burying a statue of St. Joseph upside down to help sell a house, or that of saying a spell to get rid of the ants in your house, invoking this or that saint, have a Christian element, but they are merely somewhat superficially Christianized versions of the kinds of practices that people in all sorts of cultures go in for. There are problems with Winch's argument based on the supposed "parasitism" of magical practices in our culture, but even supposing that the argument could go through in cases like that of the Black Mass, it requires a much stronger dependence of the magical practice on some other system of thought than is evident in many typical magical practices among us, like the practices I have mentioned. It is in fact noteworthy that Catholic discussion of whether the practice of burying a statue of St. Joseph to help sell one's house is superstitious does not treat as relevant the question whether the practice is "parasitic" on other Catholic practices. The issue, as discussed in many Catholic websites, is the simpler one of whether, in the carrying out of the practice, one takes oneself to be doing something which is itself efficacious or itself brings "good luck." In both those cases, the practice as one engages in it would be superstitious.[55] A Protestant condemnation of the practice would be unlikely to use a distinction like that drawn by Catholics between superstitious and nonsuperstitious versions of the practice, but would involve an understanding, similar to that in Catholic discussions, of why the practice as normally carried out is superstitious. Again the issue of "parasitism" is not the point; what is crucial to taking the practice to be superstitious is belief by those who carry out the practice that it is efficacious or brings "good luck." This would also be a central point for many non-Christians in our culture who would regard the practice as superstitious.[56] If one wanted to provide an example of a superstitious practice, one could hardly come up with anything much better than the sale and use of "real estate spell kits." The trouble, from Winch's point of view, though, is that the simple condemnation of this practice as superstitious, on the sorts of grounds that I have mentioned, does not appeal to any standard internal to some system of beliefs on which the practice itself is dependent for its sense, and Winch is concerned to contain the force of any criticism of magic so that it does not reach to self-contained systems of magic like that of the Azande. That is why he gives an argument that is meant to apply only within our culture, and that depends upon the supposedly "parasitic" character of the magical practices in question. It is further plain that the Catholic and Protestant condemnation of the practices that I have mentioned is the same sort of condemnation that would be given of similar practices in other cultures. The Catholic understanding of what constitutes superstition developed in relation to pagan practices (a development that altered older notions of superstition), and the Protestant understanding developed partly in relation to Catholic practices, but neither understanding of what constitutes superstition depends on the practice in question making a kind of parasitic use of concepts internal to Christianity. Winch is concerned to head off anthropological and philosophical criticisms of magical practices in other cultures, but it is important that the cultural construction, within our own culture, of "magic" is historically tied to Christian condemnation of pagan practices. The criticism of what goes on in "alien" cultures, using our standards, is not a matter of recent anthropology and philosophy; it has been part of "our" form of life for a very long time.

It is worth emphasizing here how various the forms of magic and witchcraft and necromancy and fortunetelling (and so on) have been in our culture in the period covered by Winch's claim (the centuries "since the advent of Christianity"), how many strata of society have been involved in different ways and with different understandings of what they were doing, how many influences from the ancient world and from Jewish and Muslim thought have played a role, and how various, even within a single cultural context, may be the understandings that different individuals have of the same practice. Wittgenstein warned against a too thin diet of examples in philosophy, and Winch's argument is un-Wittgensteinian in ignoring the significance of the variety in what we have taken, or may take, to be magical practices or beliefs in our culture. His argument about the grounds for criticizing magic and witchcraft in our culture depends entirely on the supposed parasitic character of these practices, and he provides no evidence that the practices do in general have such a character.

I turn now to Winch's discussion of the Black Mass. He says that "you could not understand what was involved in conducting a Black Mass unless you were familiar with the conduct of a proper Mass, and with the whole complex of religious ideas from which the Mass draws its sense."[57] His idea that the concepts involved in the Black Mass depend on the Mass has a grounding somewhat different from what he takes it to be. The "Black Mass" is to a considerable degree a myth, constructed (indeed) from ideas about the Mass.[58] The writings of Christian demonologists and witchcraft experts from the fifteenth century on contain accounts of the witches' supposed Sabbats or Sabbaths, sometimes including desecration of the Host. The idea that witches perform inversions of Christian rituals played a role in Christian demonology, and descriptions of such rituals were frequently elicited under torture from those accused of witchcraft. The accounts of the witches' supposed rituals were also frequently read out loud when witches were executed, and thus ideas about the Sabbats had wide currency. Winch's argument about the practice of carrying out the Black Mass is based on the idea that it was not a self-contained practice. Interestingly, the Catholic and Protestant demonological theories, integrated into the respective religions and legal systems, and taken together with the practices of accusing witches, torturing them, and executing them or punishing them in other ways—all this seen together with the background of folk beliefs about witches, and the presence within early modern Europe of numerous healers, "cunning folk," and so on—do appear to constitute self-contained systems of belief and practice.[59] At any rate, they do not appear to be any less self-contained than the Zande system of thought and practice.[60] Further, it does look as if Winch's idea that the Zande system of magic constitutes a coherent universe of discourse, in terms of which there are an intelligible conception of reality and clear ways of deciding which beliefs are or are not in agreement with this reality applies (if it really does apply to the Zande) equally to the system of witch-hunting beliefs and practices of Christian Europe. That culture too certainly had methods of determining which beliefs were or were not in agreement with their intelligible conception of reality—of determining, that is, which accusations that someone had made a pact with the devil and had used the powers she had thus acquired to harm her neighbors were true. As I have mentioned, ideas supposedly derived from Wittgenstein about realities as internal to a "universe of discourse" provide a kind of immunity to skepticism about such realities and a general argument about the position of skeptics. Someone within a culture may lack an awareness of one of the realities that is supposedly there to be apprehended within the "universe of discourse"; so anyone who doubted the whole witch-hunt business could (in accordance with these "Wittgensteinian" ideas) be said to be unaware of the relevant reality. This (it seems to me) is a perfectly appalling conclusion. The conclusion is equally appalling if put in a somewhat different form: we cannot coherently hold, of a self-contained system of thought, that it involves a collective delusion.[61] But the idea that Europe had numerous men and women who had made pacts with the Devil, and who engaged in magical activities with the cooperation of demonic powers, activities which profoundly endangered the social world, together with the idea that the truth about these activities could be revealed through torture, was a collective delusion.

I have argued that the Black Mass is not a model for what magic in our culture is generally like, but there is in any case a further problem about Winch's argument. It depends on a general principle which is hardly self-evident. Concepts and practices may well develop from and in response to some other set of concepts and practices, and (so far as this relationship is important in understanding the later set of concepts and practices) might be said to be "parasitic" upon those earlier concepts. Those who accept the original concepts and practices may appeal to them in condemning the new concepts and practices. But Winch is not arguing (what would be obvious) that those who accept the original concepts and practices may take themselves to have grounds for condemning the practice. His point about the Black Mass is not merely that Christians have grounds to condemn it as irrational, using their standards. He is trying to reach a stronger conclusion than that. His argument is aimed at showing that the condemnation on the basis of Christian concepts is a condemnation available to "us." Given that the Black Mass is parasitic on Christian concepts, and given that, by the standards internal to the Christian "universe of discourse" *on which it is dependent*, the Black Mass counts as irrational, we can show it to be irrational. The Black Mass derives what sense it appears to have from the Christian concepts on which it is dependent; and its sense can be shown to be merely apparent by reference to those concepts. If we speak of the Black Mass as irrational or superstitious or illusory, we "have the weight of our culture behind us."[62] I said in section V that Winch's principle derives what appearance it has of plausibility from the particular example to which it is applied, of a practice which we are not eager to regard as having anything to be said for it. But even in relation to the Black Mass, the principle has problems. For suppose that, in the eighteenth century, a group of libertines performs some version of a Black Mass with the aim of doing something blasphemous and transgressive; the performance might have political meaning as well. Winch's argument is essentially that what sense, if any, a performance of a Black Mass has is determined by the Christian concepts on which it depends, and that its sense can be shown thereby to be merely apparent. But the sense of the activity of the libertines is not determined by the Christian concepts. They live in a culture in which a blasphemous performance of a religious ceremony has a point; the Christian culture does not "own" the sensefulness of what is done when its concepts are taken over and deliberately misused. If we consider Winch's principle in relation to cases other than the Black Mass, its problematic character comes out even more sharply. What if we think about Winch's principle in relation to Judaism and Christianity? If the Black Mass, as Winch sees it, involves a perversion of Christian concepts,[63] is Christianity vulnerable to the charge of involving a perversion of Jewish concepts? For it is certainly the case that central concepts of Christianity are dependent in complex ways on the concepts and practices of Judaism; and from the point of view of a Jew, why should Christian concepts and practices not appear to be a perversion of Jewish ones? What account might Winch have been able to give of the difference between a Christian criticism of the Black Mass as a perversion of Christian concepts and a Jewish criticism of Christianity as a perversion of Jewish concepts? Christians have, indeed, interpretations of the situation according to which the Jews fail fully to grasp what is internal to their own concepts, and so (from their point of view) the dependence of Christian concepts on the Jewish concepts cannot ground the kind of condemnation that Winch describes, but this defense depends upon specifically theological views, and is not the sort of argument that Winch could use to distinguish the cases. The conclusion I should want to reach here is that there is no general philosophical principle by which any such matter can be adjudicated. When concepts from one "thought world" are taken over and given a new use that remains partially dependent on the old use, and when those who hold to the old mode of thought and practice can use it as a basis for attacking the new as senseless or irrational or superstitious, philosophy can provide no general principle by which "we" can show that adherents to the older system are right in their criticisms.

Winch's argument does not work. He has not shown that magical beliefs and practices in our culture are subject to criticism because of their "parasitic" character, and hence has not been able to make out the kind of difference he wants to make out between Zande magical practices, which we supposedly cannot criticize as irrational, and magic in our own culture, which we supposedly can criticize as irrational, on the basis of the general considerations he has adduced. His argument was meant to be an application of Wittgenstein's philosophical ideas, but how much support does Wittgenstein provide? Winch takes from Wittgenstein the idea that there is not one single form of intelligibility, and there is not one "norm for intelligibility in general."[64] He rejects as incoherent any idea that we can criticize a system of beliefs and practices through criteria which are "a direct gift of God."[65] But there is no obvious justification in Wittgenstein for Winch's *further* idea that the criticism of a practice or belief must be based on criteria which are "culturally relevant" in that they belong to the "universe of discourse" to which the practice or belief itself belongs. Winch is using a form of the argument we have seen in Rorty and Dilman, in which a pair of alternatives is set up, a fishy metaphysical one on the one hand and a strong "Wittgensteinian" one on the other. The ruling out of the fishy metaphysical alternative is treated as if it left us with no alternative but the strong Wittgensteinian one—in this case, the conclusion that it is conceptually confused to think that a practice can be judged irrational by standards that do not belong to the "universe of discourse" of which the practice is part.

Winch's "Wittgensteinian" argument is that it is not possible for there to be something against which the use, in language, of a conception of reality can be appraised; and he accuses Evans-Pritchard of "trying to work with a conception of reality which is *not* determined by its actual use in language."[66] But there is something odd in Winch's argument, since it does appear to be Winch, more than Evans-Pritchard, who fails to attend to the actual use in language of conceptions of reality. In our culture, we have historically constructed a number of contrasts, various versions of which have been used in criticizing whole systems of belief and practice. The terms of these contrasts include (on the one hand) superstition and false religion, or superstition and irrationality, and (on the other hand) ordinary rationality, or what is in keeping with how things genuinely are—including, in some conceptions, a true understanding of God. These contrasts are highly contested in the particular forms they may be given. This sort of contrast is historically ancient, with a variety of roots in Christian, Jewish and Greek ideas, and should not be treated as if the use of such a contrast simply privileged scientific rationality. In some versions, what this sort of contrast very strongly unprivileges, as one might say, is certain forms of pagan thought and practice, as for example in the case of ancient Hebrew beliefs about neighboring tribes, and Jewish and Christian condemnations of forms of divination. One of the most characteristic uses of such a contrast has been in Protestant criticisms of

Catholicism. Some such contrasts are extremely crude; some have a simple scientist character. But their existence is not a reason for thinking we ought to do without any such contrast, or to replace them with a philosophically purified version.[67] An important feature of these contrasts, in many of their forms, is their connection with what we take to be real. Whole systems of thought have been, in our history, taken to be out of touch with reality, or to provide only a highly devious or distorted understanding of reality. This is one main use of the notion of reality among us. In the history of the use of our language, criticisms of magic and of idol-worship have frequently been tied to ideas that these systems of thought and practice involve a false and superstitious conception of reality. It is for this reason, then, that I am suggesting that Winch fails to attend to the use of the conception of reality in *our* language. I do not see how it can be argued that Wittgenstein, who asks us to attend to the ways we do use our language, provides a justification for thinking that such criticisms of whole systems of thought are fundamentally wrong. He provides impressive examples of misunderstandings of what goes on within systems of thought which we may think of as primitive. We should learn from him how difficult it is not to misconstrue what people in some other culture are doing.[68] But that hardly shows that there can be no basis ever for concluding that some system of interwoven beliefs and practices constitutes a kind of collective delusion, or that it is false and idolatrous, or superstitious and irrational. Winch says that it is not possible for there to be something against which the use "in language" of a conception of reality can be appraised. But so far as the Azande have in their language a "conception of reality," there is no impossibility of appraising it, any more than there is any impossibility of appraising other conceptions of reality. *Our* language has, in use, modes of appraisal of conceptions of reality; highly contested modes of appraisal, modes of appraisal which one might hope may be bettered as we continue to think about how people think and what they do, and as we continue to think about how we have with more or less confusion and self-deception thought about how people think and about what they do. If, following Wittgenstein, we attend to the ways we do use language, what can be seen is that there is no closing off of the *questions* here. I take this point, that there is no closing off of these questions, to belong also to Putnam's thought about realism and his criticisms of Wittgensteinian baby-throwing. I shall return to this connection with Putnam in section VI.

VI. What's the Point of Getting Rid of the World?

Putnam has criticized "orthodox" Wittgensteinian philosophy for attempting to refute traditional philosophy, and in particular for trying to find a general refutation of skeptical arguments.[69] In this section, I shall consider the connection between that Wittgensteinian aim and Wittgensteinian baby-throwing, as well as the connection between baby-throwing and the desire for a general argument against "external" criticism of forms of thought. These connections are particularly clear in Dilman's writings. Baby-throwing attracts philosophers for many different reasons, and I can discuss here only some of the things that make it attractive.

Consider a case described by Elizabeth Anscombe, of a man who is totally hallucinated, and shoots at something that he has hallucinated.[70] His shot hits his father, but his father is not, in this case, the material object of his aiming. There is in this case no description of the intentional object which describes anything actual, and so there is no material object of aiming. Anscombe then gives an application of the point that there may be an intentional object but no material object. People may worship something, but if no intentional description of what they worship is also a description of something actual, then, "materially speaking, [they] worship a nothing, something that does not exist."[71] In such a case, there are sentences of the form "They worship such and such" which are true, as for example, "They worship Baal," but this is compatible with giving the material object this way: "What they worship is nothing."

There is an important contrast from the point of view of Dilman, between the shooting case and the worshiping case. His account leaves room for material descriptions of an intentional object, but only in terms which are available within the language of the people whose thought is being described. He can allow for the description of the shooter as having shot, materially speaking, at nothing, since this is a case imagined as within our own culture, and our language allows for a case in which someone is hallucinated and shoots at nothing real. But the case of the Baal-worshipers is different. On Dilman's view, their language has internal to it what constitutes the reality of the things spoken of in the language. Since their understanding of the reality of what they are speaking about is determinative, there is no position from which *we* can say that *what they worship is nothing.* The reality that Baal has can be seen in the ways the beliefs and practices of Baal-religion enter their lives. So the kind of criticism that Anscombe evidently has in mind (of tribes who worship such gods as Baal) cannot be made, on the view taken by Dilman.

It should be evident that this sort of philosophical move, that treats all questions about material objects of thought as determined entirely by the standards of what counts as being the case, what counts as real, within a particular "universe of discourse," provides (or seems to provide) a quick way with skepticism. General questions about the reality of physical objects (for example) cannot arise, since the reality of physical objects is internal to the "universe of discourse."[72] (This is consistent with holding that particular questions about particular intentional objects can arise, questions whether someone was hallucinated, for example, and aimed at nothing real.)

That there is something the matter with this quick way with skepticism might be suggested by its being too quick with the claim that Baal is a nothing. Here we run up against the same problem that Putnam drew attention to in Rorty's thought: it rules out a way of thinking that is characteristic of a culture, or was characteristic of a culture, and it seems to require an "absolute perspective." For it certainly was an important part of the thinking of Jews and Christians that there are tribes that worship false gods. This was taken to be entirely consistent with the tribes in question having an understanding of the reality of their gods according to which the gods were as real as anything. The idea that that sort of external criticism of a religion can be ruled out a priori appears to clash with what was for a very long time the grammar of false-god-criticism within the Judaeo-Christian tradition. The issue of false-god-criticism is quite closely related to that of philosophical skepticism, and is an important kind of case for an understanding of Putnam's commonsense realism and its relation to baby-throwing.

In discussing the problems here, we need to distinguish between a philosophical criticism of false-god-criticism and a kind of general attitude of tolerance towards the gods of other tribes. Such an attitude was prevalent in the ancient world, and is described by Anscombe in "Paganism, Superstition and Philosophy."[73] Similar attitudes have wide prevalence today. In the ancient world, the tolerant attitude of the pagans went with a condemnation of Jews and Christians for their intolerance, for their disdain for all the pagan gods, and their insistence on the importance of the contrast between the true God and false gods. Within contemporary Jewish and Christian thinking, one can find various views about other religions and their gods, including on the one hand an acceptance of "religious pluralism," and on the other, a rejection of false gods and false religions, continuous with the older Judaeo-Christian view. While the attitude of tolerance for the gods is distinct from the philosophical view that rules out external criticism of a tribe's or a culture's religious views, someone who rejects the older Judaeo-Christian attitude to religions and gods may also hold some version of the philosophical view.

It is worth clearing up two possible confusions here. (1) A form of religious thinking that condemns some other religions as false and idolatrous, or as superstitious, may *also* regard idolatry and superstition as temptations even within the religion taken to be true. The Catholic catechism (for example), which condemns polytheism, also expresses as clearly as anything in *The Concluding Unscientific Postscript* the point that worshiping an idol can go on anywhere, including within a Catholic church. The idea of a religion as true and of other religions as false is entirely compatible with such a conception of idolatry. (2) The philosophical view that rules out external criticism of a religion may involve an assumption that taking a religion to be true, or taking other religions to be false, must involve an understanding of religious belief as like scientific beliefs. I shall return to this issue, but it should be mentioned here as an unobvious assumption. In what follows I defend what I take to be a Putnamian view that there is no general a priori way of disposing of skepticism and false-god-criticism, while Wittgensteinian baby-throwing, in contrast, appears to offer just such a general way of disposing of these questions.

Wittgenstein's discussion of language games has been used as the basis for arguments against external criticisms of religious belief. An extremely well-known example of such a Wittgensteinian approach is Norman Malcolm's defense of an argument that he thinks can be found in Anselm. He argues that what is said within the "language games" of Jewish and Christian religion settles the coherence of the conception of necessary existence within those language games, and that therefore "There is no God" is not something that can be meaningfully said or thought,[74] since it is not compatible with the necessity of God's existence, as spoken of within the language games. Dilman takes a view like Malcolm's, but it is couched in more general terms and has a consequence that goes beyond anything in Malcolm's account. Dilman invites us to imagine someone who is able imaginatively to understand the thought and the practices of an alien culture. He comes to see how people in this culture conceive of the reality of the things they speak about, and how their conceptions are applied in their lives. If he does achieve this, he will have, Dilman says, an enlarged conception of how one may think about reality. The person who has achieved this imaginative "internal" understanding will have got beyond the stage at which he might have been inclined to think that there was some error or illusion involved in their beliefs and practices.[75] The inclination to think that the other people were in some way *deluded* in their beliefs or practices is, on this philosophical account, an indication only of failure to comprehend the realities internal to their language. What is the matter with the story Dilman gives us, of what goes on when one comes to a deeper understanding, is that he excludes the case in which the result of the deepened understanding is that one sees more clearly that their practices are (for example) idolatrous rubbish, that the "realities" they believe in are illusions. The idea that, if you were really to grasp how the practices are understood, you would *lose* the basis of your radical criticism of the practices involves a judgment that the kind of criticism that has been central in Judaism, Christianity, and Islam has invariably been based on failure of understanding or some sort of confusion. Dilman takes himself to be in disagreement with Anscombe, not only about the situation of someone wanting to criticize another culture, but also about Wittgenstein's view of the relation between people who have incompatible world pictures.

How then does Anscombe see the situation? She says that it may seem as if Wittgenstein's arguments (in *On Certainty*) imply that, where world pictures are incompatible, we cannot speak of one of them being right and the other wrong. But she thinks that there are questions here. What Wittgenstein had spoken of as a world picture "partly lies behind a knowledge system."[76] We indeed have a richly developed knowledge system. Here then are two questions that she raises about Wittgenstein's view: "But when, speaking with *this* knowledge system behind one, one calls something error which *counts as knowledge* in another system, the question arises: has one the right to do that? Or has one to be "moving within the system" to call anything error?"[77]

Her discussion of these questions is not complete, but it seems clear that her answer to the first one is that Wittgenstein did not hold that one would have no right to do so, and her answer to the second is that Wittgenstein did not hold that one would have to be "moving within the system" to call something error. One can call something error, even though within their system and by their standards, it is correct. She takes the answers which she thinks Wittgenstein gives to these questions (answers which she herself would also give) to mean that he avoids cultural relativism. The point about whether we can call something in "their system" error, even though we are not "moving within the system" would seem to apply not only to the kind of case which Anscombe was discussing—knowledge of such things as the character of the earth and moon, and of what would be involved in a human being getting to the moon—but also to the ethical views of some alien tribe, or to the (as it might be) evil nature of their god, as he is portrayed in their culture. There is no good philosophical argument that we cannot judge to be evil what the people in some tribe count as good, what counts by all their criteria as good. Some such judgments, and the inclinations to make them, are stupid and ill-judged, based on misunderstandings or complacent pride; such judgments may be profoundly ideological. But they need not be. Thus, for example, it may be that the British in India constructed the threat of the supposed religious sect of thugs and that it was a myth which served their purposes. But there is no good philosophical argument that, had there been a religious system of thuggee, part of a system of thought in which the ritualized killings of travelers constituted praiseworthy service of the god Kali, it could not have been condemned from an external point of view.[78]

Anscombe's point applies also to what we, with our knowledge system, take to be knowledge. It may at some time rightly be judged from an external point of view. We ourselves, or people of subsequent generations, or people from some quite different culture, may some time rightly judge that we were wrong, by criteria of which we have no conception.

Wittgenstein's authority is sometimes invoked for the philosophical view that I have been questioning. The first of his "Lectures on Religious Belief" has been taken to provide an argument that only within a language game can someone contradict what is said within the language game.[79] This would apparently then provide support for the answer "Yes" to the question asked by Anscombe about Wittgenstein, whether (on his view) one has to be "moving within their system" to call something "they" say error. Such a reading of Wittgenstein's Lecture is questionable, but since I have discussed it in detail elsewhere,[80] I shall focus instead here on a striking passage in Wittgenstein's Remarks on Frazer's *Golden Bough*.

> Frazer's account of the magical and religious views of mankind is unsatisfactory: it makes these views look like *errors*.

> Was Augustine in error, then, when he called upon God on every page of the *Confessions*?

> But—one might say—if he was not in error, surely the Buddhist holy man was—or anyone else—whose religion gives expression to completely different views. But *none* of them was in error, except when he set forth a theory.[81]

The crucial ideas in this passage are those of "being in error" (*im Irrtum*) and of "setting forth a theory" (*aufstellen eine Theorie*). Thus, for example, someone engaged in practical efforts to arrest global warming might be said to be "in error" if her actions rested on a theory about the causes of temperature change, and if that theory was wrong. But it is not easy to see how to apply this sort of idea of *error* and *theory* in thinking about religion and about Augustine in particular. Augustine's *Confessions* do not contain just invocations of God, but also an account of a false understanding of God, which had left Augustine mired in sin. As he tells the story of his becoming a servant of God, it is inseparable from the story of his coming to a true understanding of God. It is plain that he takes heresy to be a profound danger to the soul. There is no reason to think that he had not called on God frequently during the period that he later describes as involving his own being mired in sin through his inability to see what he later took to be the truth.

There seem to be two possible ways in which we can try to connect these earlier invocations of God to Wittgenstein's remarks about error and theory, but neither way is satisfactory. (1) Wittgenstein's view might be that, when Augustine called on God, in the early days, he was not in error merely because he was a Manichean; he was no more in error through being a Manichean than is Wittgenstein's Buddhist holy man in being a Buddhist. Augustine (on this reading) could be taken to be in error only when setting forth his theoretical (Manichean) account of God's nature, the nature of evil and of Jesus, and so on. On this view, his actual invocations of God are not somehow turned all wrong because of his erroneous theological understanding. But this picture of Augustine is dramatically at variance with Augustine's own narrative, in which (for example) his misunderstanding of the death of Jesus's body is inseparable from the real death of his own soul, the real distance between himself and God. (2) The alternative account would be that Wittgenstein gave to the word "theory" a narrower sense than I was assuming there, and that the Manichean views that Augustine accepted were not a "theory" in Wittgenstein's sense. So although Augustine describes himself as having been in error, we might try to read his views as not theoretical in the sense Wittgenstein means; we might say that what Augustine speaks of as error is not error in Wittgenstein's sense. But this approach is no better than the first at enabling us to connect Wittgenstein's remarks with Augustine's own self-understanding. We can use the words "theory" and "error" in such a way that it will be correct to assert that Augustine's Manicheanism is not a theory, and that his Manichean religious life is not a case of being in error; but then what are we to say about the pernicious errors from which Augustine took himself to have suffered? If these are errors in some other sense, they are nevertheless of central significance to Augustine's religious understanding. Wittgenstein says that Frazer's account of the religious views of mankind is unsatisfactory in making them look like errors; but it is not as if the only alternative to Frazer's view is that the only errors in the religious realm occur in the setting forth of theories. Wittgenstein stresses that, of those who call on God, of those who accept some religion, "*none* of them" is in error, except when setting forth a theory; this seems simply to contradict the view of anyone like Augustine who takes heresy to involve a kind of fatal illness of the soul. The Manichees *are* deeply lost in their confusion, no matter how deep their religious feelings as they call on God; that, at any rate, was Augustine's view. Wittgenstein once said to Drury that "all genuine expressions of religion are wonderful, even those of the most savage peoples."[82] That is a conception of religion profoundly at odds with Augustine's; Augustine's picture of the soul and of the needs of the soul is also at odds with that of Wittgenstein.

Augustine's view, that heresy is akin to death of the soul, underlay the crusade against the Albigensians (among other things). But an idea like Augustine's of the significance of religious truth does not have to exclude recognition of religious liberty. I am interested in a different issue here: the kind of conflict there is between Wittgenstein's view of the relation between religion and falsity and that of Augustine. I am suggesting that we see both views within a history of appraisals of whole systems of thought and practice and of contestation of such appraisals, in which terms like *rational, irrational, superstition, idolatry, reality, truth, heresy,* and *magic* have been taken up or rejected, appropriated or disowned, shaped and reshaped. Anscombe's discussion of paganism (mentioned above) is helpful here, and in particular her remarks about the strand in contemporary philosophy influenced by Wittgenstein, in which there is a rejection of the idea of a religion's being true, and in which it is taken to be "contemptible to be scornful" of any of the religions of different peoples. This way of thinking is related, she says, to the ancient pagan hatred of the exclusivity of the Jews, and her essay was an attempt to bring out the connection. She refrained from actually ascribing this sort of view to Wittgenstein himself, though she gives remarks of his that suggest that it was a view to which he was strongly attracted, and the remark I have quoted, from conversation with Drury, also suggests his strong attraction to the "pagan" view. But she also mentions remarks that suggest at least a degree of attraction to the opposite view, in at least some contexts. The context of thought about Frazer's *Golden Bough* was one in which Wittgenstein's inclination towards the "pagan" view of religions came out strongly. He hated Frazer's treatment of magical and religious views, and takes up in response a view which (as I have argued) is profoundly opposed to Augustine's. But if this is the expression of an inclination towards the kind of paganism that Anscombe describes, what philosophical significance do his remarks have, beyond showing that this is one kind of responsiveness to religion? As Anscombe mentions, philosophers who are attracted to this sort of paganism sometimes put the point that there is no such thing as a religion's being true by saying that religious propositions are not like propositions of natural science. But this would hardly indicate that there is no such thing as a religion's being true, unless the only possible way of understanding such truth was on the model of some or other kind of natural scientific truth. The remarks of Wittgenstein's about Frazer that I have quoted, while they evince an attitude towards religion, provide no argument that the opposite view is in some way philosophically confused. The fact that Wittgenstein was strongly attracted to the view opposed to Augustine's is deeply interesting; but it leaves us just where we were.

I should like to put the issue here another way. On the view taken by Wittgensteinian philosophers of religion, a religious doctrine cannot be understood apart from the role of the doctrine in people's lives; if it is so separated, it is treated as a kind of "theory," and this is conceptual confusion. Typically, then (on this view) criticism of a religion as false is based on such a treatment of its doctrines as theories, and involves a confused failure to appreciate what is genuinely meant. Supposedly, then, the realities spoken of by the believers are not seen; the critics are not then really criticizing the doctrines, which they have not genuinely understood. On the opposite view, though, there is room for the idea that Jews and Christians (for example) might have had a particularly *adequate* view of the realities spoken of by the pagans, a particularly adequate view of the emptiness and soul-killingness of those realities. This is a matter not of ignoring the life within which lie the beliefs and practices they are criticizing, and not of ignoring the role of the beliefs *within* that life, but of seeing that life, as they think, more truly than do those whose life it is.[83] Anscombe once said, "I would rather a man were like Bertrand Russell than that he were a worshipper of Dourga," expressing her sense of the spiritual dangers of Dourga-worship; Rhees said that worship of Dourga "should have the respect due to a form of *worship*."[84] I believe that it is a mistake to try to settle this sort of dispute, as some Wittgensteinian philosophers have tried to do, by general a priori arguments about what is conceptually confused. I think Putnam would agree. This would in no way be incompatible with his expressed sympathy for the view that Wittgenstein takes, or with his rejection of Franz Rosenzweig's "exclusivist" response to religions other than Judaism and Christianity.[85]

Putnam's essay "Rules, Attunement and 'Applying Words to the World'" engages with the "orthodox" reading of Wittgenstein, according to which what makes sense is fixed by a framework of rules, and according to which there is therefore available a criticism of uses of language that do not remain "within" the framework, or that violate the rules—a criticism of such uses as unintelligible, nonsensical or conceptually confused. What is or is not intelligible, Putnam argues, is not determined by the rules of language, by criteria which settle for us what makes sense. That refusal of Putnam's to allow sensefulness to be confined within a structure of rules and criteria is inseparable from his realism, from the conception he has of our being "*forced* to renegotiate . . . our notion of reality as our language and our life develop."[86] Renegotiating means that what one might call the structure of old negotiations, embodied in existing rules and criteria, does not constrain what we can go on to do with words. These renegotiations, not constrained by existing rules, are essential to our being open to *the* world. The *practice* of thought-being-in-relation-to-the-world involves this: that there is no general philosophical story about "confusion" that will enable one to rule out in advance any and all appraisals of systems of thought, as for example that of the Azande, or that will enable one to rule out a priori all philosophical skepticism, or all traditional metaphysical realism. All that one can do (in the commonsense realism *style* of thought) is take things one at a time. When the demand for justification makes sense, Putnam says, it "is met in *particular* ways, depending on the particular claim that is called into question."[87] He says also that "the philosopher's claim to be justified in using [words] outside or apart from their (Wittgensteinian) criteria *cannot* be rejected *a priori*."[88] One has to listen, he says, to the story the philosopher tells; if indeed what she says is incoherent, one has to show why and how it is, in the particular case. The commonsense realism style of thought, just described, applies also to nonphilosophical skeptics, critics, and speculators who say things apparently not allowed for by established rules and criteria. Wittgensteinianism should be stripped of the appearance, Putnam says, of being a machine for refuting traditional philosophy. Such a machine works by enforcing a conception of the boundaries of sense; it puts what "can be spoken of" into an "inside"—whether of our "form of life," our "universe of discourse," our "language games," "what our grammar allows." When Putnam is read, as by Rorty and Dilman, as taking a view close to their own, this reflects the invisibility to them of the style of thought that commonsense realism is, its style of openness to the world. *"Language,"* Putnam says, *"opens to us different kinds of form that the world already has."*[89] In many of his writings Putnam has described himself as a pragmatist; and I have tried here to bring out, not "that he is a pragmatist" (as if there were one thing that that was, and we were already clear what that one thing is), but rather that he shows us a philosophical practice of openness to the world, and extends in that way what we can understand "pragmatism" to be.[90]

CORA DIAMOND

UNIVERSITY OF VIRGINIA
APRIL 2010

NOTES

1. Hilary Putnam, "Sense, Nonsense, and the Senses: An Inquiry into the Powers of the Human Mind," *Journal of Philosophy* 91, no. 9 (Sep. 1994): 445.

2. Ibid., 446. Putnam picks up this use of "recoil" from John McDowell's *Mind and World*.

3. In Hilary Putnam, *Words and Life* (Cambridge: Harvard University Press, 1995), 264–78.

4. See Hilary Putnam, *Pragmatism: An Open Question* (Oxford: Blackwell, 1995), 33.

5. Ibid.

6. Originally published in *Journal of Philosophy* 90 (1993), 443–61, reprinted in Richard Rorty, *Truth and Progress* (Cambridge: Cambridge University Press, 1998), 43–62.

7. Hilary Putnam, "Why Reason Can't Be Naturalized," in *Realism and Reason: Philosophical Papers*, vol 3 (Cambridge: Cambridge University Press, 1983), 235.

8. In Richard Rorty, *Objectivity, Relativism, and Truth* (Cambridge: Cambridge University Press, 1991), 23. Two versions of the essay had been published earlier.

9. Ibid., 24–25.

10. Hilary Putnam, "Realism with a Human Face," in *Realism with a Human Face* (Cambridge: Harvard University Press, 1990), 26. See also R. L. Goodstein, "Language

and Reality," in *Essays in the Philosophy of Mathematics* (Leicester: Leicester University Press, 1965), 23–41. Goodstein's view is in some ways very like Rorty's, and involves a similar mix of pragmatism with ideas derived from Wittgenstein. See especially Goodstein's discussion of different norms for deciding whether it is true that objects of different weights, placed in a vacuum, fall with the same speed. One norm is that of looking in a book to see what Aristotle said about the matter. If that is the criterion of truth, Goodstein says, and if Aristotle said that large objects fall more swiftly, then Galileo was deluded. We can choose a different language; but there is here no question of betterness of norms apart from the norms in question being part of a language that we have decided to use.

11. Richard Rorty, "Hilary Putnam and the Relativist Menace," in *Truth and Progress: Philosophical Papers*, vol. 3 (Cambridge: Cambridge University Press, 1998), 51.

12. Ibid., 53.

13. Ibid., 60.

14. Putnam, "Realism with a Human Face," 24–25.

15. Rorty,"Hilary Putnam and the Relativist Menace," 55, 57.

16. Ibid., 55.

17. See also Cora Diamond, "Between Realism and Rortianism: Conant, Rorty and the Disappearance of Options," *Harvard Review of Philosophy* 21 (2014): 56–57.

18. Rorty, "Hilary Putnam and the Relativist Menace," 57.

19. Richard Rorty, "Charles Taylor on Truth," in *Truth and Progress*, 83.

20. Derek Bolton, "Life Form and Idealism," in *Idealism, Past and Present*, ed. Godfrey Vesey (Cambridge: Cambridge University Press, 1982), 279.

21. İlham Dilman, *Wittgenstein's Copernican Revolution: The Question of Linguistic Idealism* (Basingstoke: Palgrave, 2002).

22. Putnam, "The Question of Realism," in *Words and Life*, 301; also Putnam, "Truth, Activation Vectors and Possession Conditions for Concepts," *Philosophy and Phenomenological Research* 52 (1992): 443.

23. Putnam was quoting Rorty's "Putnam on Truth," in *Philosophy and Phenomenological Research* 52 (1992), 416.

24. Putnam, *Words and Life*, 301.

25. Putnam, "Realism with a Human Face," 25.

26. See especially Dilman, *Wittgenstein's Copernican Revolution*, 168–69. There is a criticism of this feature of Dilman's thought in the review in *Notre Dame Philosophical Reviews* by Eric Loomis, who says that the obvious problem with a view like Dilman's, which tries to treat facts as independent of language but their possibility as dependent on language, is that a fact cannot exist independently of its possibility.

27. See also Dilman's refusal to make a distinction between the kind of dependence the reality of promises has on our practices and modes of talk and the supposed dependence of the reality of dinosaurs on our practices and modes of talk. Ibid., 118.

28. Ibid., 48–49.

29. See especially p. 49. I am not sure how extreme Dilman's view is intended to be. I think he does want to deny that we could say such things as that medieval calculations of the distance to Saturn (as less than a hundred million miles) were wrong. I think he would want to deny that the planet Saturn about which we think and speak is the Saturn of which they spoke and thought. This would be a consequence of his view that the reality of what we are speaking of, and hence its identity, is internal to the "universe of discourse." I discuss Dilman's view in Diamond, "The Skies of Dante and Our Skies: A Response to Ilham Dilman," *Philosophical Investigations* 35 (2012): 187–204. Sections 3 and 4 of that essay draw on some material from this chapter.

30. Robert Brandom, *Making It Explicit* (Cambridge: Harvard University Press, 1994), 594.

31. Robert Brandom, "Replies," *Philosophy and Phenomenological Research* 57, no. 1 (1997): 198.

32. Dilman speaks both of Dante's skies and of the universe of the "Middle Ages." Albertus's views are relevant here as one of the sources of Dante's conception. My sentence about Albertus as it stands leaves unclear what was meant by "crystalline" in this context. For what the celestial spheres were thought to be made of, see Edward Grant, *Planets, Stars, and Orbs: the Medieval Cosmos 1200–1657* (Cambridge: Cambridge University Press, 1996).

33. Dilman, *Wittgenstein's Copernican Revolution*, 151.

34. In Chantal Mouffe and Ludwig Nagl, eds., *The Legacy of Wittgenstein: Pragmatism or Deconstruction* (Frankfurt: Pter Lang, 2001), 9–23.

35. In Anscombe, *Metaphysics and Philosophy of Mind* (Oxford: Blackwell, 1981), 3–20, reprinted from *Analytical Philosophy* (second series), ed. R. J. Butler (Oxford, 1965).

36. Ibid., 9–11.

37. Dante and his contemporaries were aware that what Aristotle had counted as the "fixed stars" themselves exhibited some shift, a degree every century. The shift had been discovered by Hipparchus, and was described by Ptolemy.

38. Dilman, *Wittgenstein's Copernican Revolution*, 82.

39. This is indeed what Dilman says: our language gives us our world; it gives us the objects we see. Ibid., 81–82.

40. Unfortunately Dilman does not consider a very important point here, which is that even in the early stages of Putnam's "internal realism," he clearly rejected ideas of the incommensurability between different modes of thought. See especially Putnam, *Reason, Truth and History* (Cambridge: Cambridge University Press, 1981), 113–19. Dilman's distance from Putnam on this matter is indeed considerably greater than is Rorty's.

41. Putnam, "Sense, Nonsense, and the Senses," 502

42. Ibid., 452.

43. "Understanding a Primitive Society," in Peter Winch, *Ethics and Action* (London: Routledge, 1972), 8–49, reprinted from *American Philosophical Quarterly* 1 (1964): 307–24.

44. For a discussion of the questions whether Wittgenstein's own arguments rule out criticism of a language game or form of life or system of thought, and whether his philosophy is therefore politically or socially conservative, see Alice Crary, "Wittgenstein's Philosophy in Relation to Political Thought," in *The New Wittgenstein*, ed. A. Crary and R. Read (London: Routledge, 2000), 118–45.

45. Peter Winch, "Comment," in *Explanation in the Behavioural Sciences*, ed. R. Borger and F. Cioffi (Cambridge: Cambridge University Press, 1970), 249–59.

46. See Emmanuel Le Roy Ladurie, *Montaillou* (New York: Braziller, 1978) for a number of cases of such skepticism. Ladurie notes that such skepticism is in no way unusual. The context from which his evidence comes (evidence from inquisitorial investigations in Occitania) has some unusual features, in that there was not one single religion practiced there, but two quite distinct ones, so that many people within the culture had some familiarity with the central ideas of both. But skepticism about what happens to us after we are dead was not dependent upon that particular feature of the culture, and did not involve accepting the views of either the Catholics or the Cathars. We should not regard it as problematic that people can take up, in relation to some set of practices and beliefs, a critical stance not supported by any principles internal to the ways people establish such things within the culture. See also Naomi Scheman, "Forms of Life: Mapping the Rough Ground," in *Cambridge Companion to Wittgenstein*, ed. H. Sluga and D. G. Stern (Cambridge: Cambridge University Press, 1996), 383–410, especially 398–99. See also section VI on these issues.

47. See pp. 50–51 for Dilman's discussion of this sort of case.

48. On skepticism about transubstantiation, and more generally about the Mass, see Le Roy Ladurie, *Montaillou*, 266; see 311 for widespread knowledge by peasants of the notion of transubstantiation; also 304.

49. For a discussion of the corresponding issues in relation to Wittgenstein's thought, see Crary, "Wittgenstein's Philosophy in Relation to Political Thought."

50. Winch, "Understanding a Primitive Society," 14.

51. Ibid., 15.

52. Ibid.

53. Ibid., 16.

54. Peter Winch, *The Idea of a Social Science and Its Relation to Philosophy* (London: Routledge, 1990), Preface to the Second Edition, xiv–xvi.

55. The Catholic discussions in general treat the practice as not invariably superstitious, since it need not be carried out with the idea that it is itself efficacious. There is a difference in the style of advertisements for the St. Joseph real estate kits, depending on whether they are offered on Catholic websites or sites for magical products. The former never use the word "spell." Even so, some Catholic religious goods shops will not handle the kits, as they are all too plainly likely to be used in a superstitious way.

56. There are significant differences between religious and nonreligious understandings of superstition, as involved in practices thought of as bringing good luck or avoiding bad luck, but I cannot here discuss this complex issue.

57. Winch, "Understanding a Primitive Society," 15.

58. See Michael D. Bailey, *Historical Dictionary of Witchcraft* (Lanham, MD: Scarecrow Press, 2003), 18. The Black Mass "has no historical reality, and certainly no association with witchcraft, either historical or modern." It was apparently thought up in the eighteenth century, and "projected back into earlier periods."

59. The demonological theories made clear the need for judicial torture, in the face of the Devil's efforts to prevent the accused witch from telling the truth about the rituals; and the confessions of accused witches, arrived at through torture, often provided extremely detailed corroboration of demonological theories of what witches did. An important part of demonological theory was the idea that a witch had no supernatural powers independent of the cooperation of demons or of the Devil. Hence the importance in the theory of the idea of the witch as making a pact with the Devil; hence the importance in the narratives produced by accused witches, of accounts of such commitments and of ritual occasions when the relation with the Devil was cemented, and the Devil gave instruction in magical operations. When interrogated, witches were pressed to provide the names of other witches, present on the supposed ritual occasions. The idea of a widespread conspiracy was thus supported by the testimony of accused witches. Another important part of this system of thought and practice in some parts of Europe was that those who expressed doubts of the reality of witchcraft could be charged with heresy, and the voicing of such doubts might even be taken to suggest that the doubters were witches. See Wolfgang Behringer, *Witches and Witch-hunts* (Cambridge: Polity Press, 2004), 173.

60. Winch mentions the point made by Evans-Pritchard that there were in Zande society people who were skeptical about some of the witchcraft beliefs; there were certainly in European society during the witch-persecutions skeptics about the system of beliefs involved in witch-hunting. As Winch himself points out, the presence of such skepticism does not imply that the conception of reality internal to the system of thought and practice is problematic. Winch, "Understanding a Primitive Society," 23.

61. See also H. O. Mounce, "Understanding a Primitive Society," *Philosophy* 48 (1973), 349. In letters to Mounce, published in *Rush Rhees on Religion and Philosophy* (Cambridge:

Cambridge University Press, 1997), 110, Rhees questioned Mounce's reading of Winch, and in particular questioned the importance of the notion of "parasitism" for Winch's discussion of magic. But Mounce's reading appears to be straightforwardly correct; Winch's account of how a practice can be parasitic on another is intended as an explanation of what is involved in a "culturally relevant" criticism of a practice.

62. Winch, "Understanding a Primitive Society," 16.

63. Winch's use of the notion of "perversion" in connection with the relation between the Black Mass and the Christian Mass involves other questions which I shall just mention here. Many people would be quite unwilling to speak of anything, in propria persona, as a "perversion of the Mass." Winch seems to be suggesting that the use of the word "perversion" can be justified purely on the basis of a philosophical account of the relation between the Black Mass and the Christian Mass. But for those who do not see a Mass at all as something which there is a right way to perform, the idea of a "perverted" performance of the Mass or a "perverted" concept of the Mass involves taking up a form of speech which they reject. This seems to me to be connected with some unclarity in Winch's argument about what makes a description "culturally relevant." The problem arises also in connection with Dilman's description of the case.

64. Winch, *Idea of a Social Science*, 102.

65. Ibid., 100, See also p. xv.

66. Winch, "Understanding a Primitive Society," 13.

67. For an account of a particular use of the word "superstition" as supposedly unconfused, all other ways of using it being "conceptually confused," see D. Z. Phillips, "Just Say the Word," in *Religion and Wittgenstein's Legacy*, ed. D. Z. Phillips and M. von der Ruhr (Aldershot: Ashgate, 2005), 177–78.

68. See also Alasdair MacIntyre, "Is Understanding Religion Compatible with Believing?," in *Rationality*, ed. B. R. Wilson (New York: Harper, 1970), 71; also the very valuable account of Western and Indian descriptions of sati in *Sati: the Blessing and the Curse*, ed. J. S. Hawley (New York: Oxford University Press, 1994). Rhees ascribes to Wittgenstein the view that we cannot understand what the practice of child sacrifice meant to those who engaged in it, or even to the children themselves ("Letter to Drury," in *Rush Rhees on Religion and Philosophy*, 308). But the Hawley volume on sati shows that, whether or not this was indeed Wittgenstein's view, if it was meant to apply to all practices involving sacrificial deaths of human beings, it is questionable. The complex and paradoxical character of sati certainly has made it difficult to understand, and not just for those outside Indian culture, but there are better and worse understandings of its meanings; and there is no reason to throw up our hands and say "we cannot understand what it means for those involved."

69. See Putnam, "Rules, Attunement, and 'Applying Words to the World.'"

70. Anscombe, "Intentionality of Sensation," in *Metaphysics and the Philosophy of Mind,* 10.

71. Ibid.

72. Dilman, *Wittgenstein's Copernican Revolution* , 34.

73. In Anscombe, *Faith in a Hard Ground* (Exeter: Imprint Academic, 2008), 49–60.

74. Norman Malcolm, "Anselm's Ontological Arguments," *Philosophical Review* 69, no. 1 (Jan. 1960): 56, 61.

75. Dilman, *Wittgenstein's Copernican Revolution* , 126–27; see also 91–95.

76. "The Question of Linguistic Idealism," in Elizabeth Anscombe, *From Parmenides to Wittgenstein* (Oxford: Blackwell, 1981), 131.

77. Ibid.

78. See Rhees, letters reprinted in *Rush Rhees on Religion and Philosophy*, 100–102 and Phillips, "Just Say the Word," 182, for philosophical arguments that it is confused to

criticize ritual practices like human sacrifice as atrocities, or in any other way to judge such actions by the standards we use in judging actions in our own society.

79. For a wide-ranging discussion of Wittgenstein's views on this topic, see Crary, "Wittgenstein's Philosophy in Relation to Political Thought."

80. See "Wittgenstein on Religious Belief," in *Religion and Wittgenstein's Legacy*, 99–137, especially 103–4.

81. Ludwig Wittgenstein, *Philosophical Occasions 1912–1951* (Indianapolis: Hackett, 1993), 119.

82. M. O.'C Drury, "Some Notes on Conversations with Wittgenstein," in *Recollections of Wittgenstein*, ed. Rush Rhees (Oxford: Oxford University Press, 1984), 93; cf. also 102.

83. The claim to have a particularly adequate view of the realities in some form of religious life may be based, as in the case of Augustine, on experience, or it may be taken to be based on revelation; cf. for example, Ezekiel 6, on which see Anscombe, 53. See also Karl Barth, *Church Dogmatics*, vol. 3, part I (Edinburgh: T & T Clark, 1958), 166, on what is lost within human life when heavenly bodies are divinized. The dispute between the "pagan" view of religions and the older Judaeo-Christian view is internal to contemporary Judaism and Christianity, and involves questions about the role and nature of revelation, questions which I cannot discuss here.

84. Rhees, *Rush Rhees on Religion and Philosophy*, 309.

85. Putnam, *Jewish Philosophy as a Guide to Life: Rosenzweig, Buber, Levinas, Wittgenstein*, ch. 1; see also Putnam, "Wittgenstein on Religious Belief," *On Community*, 56–75.

86. Putnam, "Sense, Nonsense, and the Senses," 452.

87. Putnam, "Rules, Attunement, and 'Applying Words to the World'," 20–21.

88. Ibid., 23.

89. Putnam, in Putnam and Boros, "Philosophy Should Not Be Just an Academic Discipline," in *Common Knowledge* 11, no. 1 (2005): 132. See the statement of a closely related view about the relation between form and language in Anscombe, "The Question of Linguistic Idealism," 112–16. Dilman (110–18) argues against Anscombe's view; this is another point at which it comes out that Dilman's distance from Putnam's views is far greater than he recognizes. Dilman plainly rejects the idea that "the world already has" different kinds of form, which are opened to us by language.

90. I am very grateful to Alice Crary for comments and suggestions.

REPLY TO CORA DIAMOND

Some years ago I described a collection of Cora Diamond's essays as "showing the full range and power of one of the best philosophical minds I know."[1] The same power and wide range are visible in her present essay. In it she describes and interprets a good many of my own writings about Wittgenstein, and approves of my claims that (1) Wittgenstein should not be read as *any* sort of a verificationist; not as a verificationist of the strong Dummettian variety (on which variety see my Reply to Dummett in the present volume), nor as a verificationist of the subtler variety that one gets when one conjoins the "orthodox" Wittgensteinian reading of Wittgenstein's philosophy as claiming that the meaning of a sentence is given by a set of "rules" for its "use" (so that every change in those rules would ipso facto have to be a change in the meaning of the sentence) with the idea that "use" means "assertibility conditions"[2]; nor as a "linguistic idealist" like Winch or Dilman; and certainly not as a Rortian *avant la lettre*. (Diamond's account of my debates with Rorty is the best I have seen anywhere.) And I am glad that she approves of all these claims, for it was reading her essay "The Face of Necessity" that suggested to me the possibility of reading Wittgenstein in a way that did not impute to him any of these metaphysical errors. (I vividly remember reading that essay for the first time: it happened when I was spending a semester in Tel Aviv in 1985; and I still recall the stunning impact that reading had upon me.)

In recent years I have taken to avoiding the term "commonsense realism,"[3] not because I have changed my mind about the correctness of that position, but because the term turned out to be a sort of "Rorschach test"; each of my critics read a different meaning into it! But Cora Diamond does understand what I meant very well, and she sums it up beautifully in this essay. And she is right that an essential aspect of what I meant by the term is that language does not create the world, but rather it opens to us different kinds of form that the world already has.[4] Diamond tries to reconcile my self-description as a commonsense realist with the fact that I sometimes identify myself as a "pragmatist," writing, "In many of his writings Putnam has described himself as a pragmatist; and I have tried here to bring out not 'that he is a pragmatist,' as if there were one thing that that was, and we were already clear what that one thing is, but rather that he shows us a philosophical practice of openness to the world, and extends in that way what we can understand 'pragmatism' to be." But ever since I completely abandoned "internal realism" as an account of *truth*,[5] I have tried to point out in my writings on pragmatism that my admiration for the classical pragmatists does *not* imply acceptance of their several theories of truth.[6] So it is not ultimately important to me whether we change "what we can understand 'pragmatism' to be," as Cora Diamond suggests, or simply say that we can learn from pragmatism without being ourselves "pragmatists."[7]

H.P.

NOTES

1. See my words on the back cover of her book *The Realistic Spirit* (Cambridge, MA: MIT Press, 1995).

2. Needless to say, it is *both* conjuncts that I object to in the essays Diamond discusses.

3. I used that term to describe the view that replaced my (misguided, as I now see it) "internal realism" in *The Threefold Cord: Mind, Body and World*.

4. In *The Threefold Cord*, the other essential aspects of commonsense realism had to do with the rejection of what I called "interface conceptions" of both perception and conception.

5. The precise point at which I first abandoned the internal realist picture of "what truth comes to" *in public* was in my "Reply to Simon Blackburn" delivered at the Gifford Conference on me at the University of St. Andrews, in November 1990 (printed in Peter Clark and Bob Hale, *Reading Putnam* [Oxford: Blackwell, 1995], 242–43). In that reply I stated that "I no longer accept that picture [internal realism]" and "The point of the picture was to combine realism with a concession to moderate verificationism (*a concession I would no longer make, by the way*): the concession being the idea that truth could never be totally recognition-transcendent." [Emphasis added]

6. For example, in my *Pragmatism* (1995), I wrote "Unlike the pragmatists, I do not believe that truth can be *defined* in terms of verification." And my paper, "Pragmatism" (in *Proceedings of the Aristotelian Society* 95, no. 3 [March 1995]: 291–306), was almost entirely devoted to a rebuttal of the pragmatist theories of truth.

7. And likewise it goes without saying that one can learn from Wittgenstein without being a "Wittgensteinian," with or without shudder quotes.

17

John McDowell

PUTNAM ON NATURAL REALISM

I

In his 1994 Dewey Lectures, Hilary Putnam recommends what William James called "the natural realism of the common man" as a refuge from an oscillation between fantasy and irresponsibility.[1]

Of course, these labels for the alternatives are controversial. Philosophers who think they can find peace on one side or the other of what Putnam sees as an uncomfortable oscillation will not accept that they are falling into fantasy or irresponsibility. But Putnam argues that natural realism affords the only genuine escape from the pendulum's swing.

With natural realism not in view as an option, it seems that, to reassure ourselves that we are responsible to our subject matter in our thinking, we need to embrace some substantial metaphysical theory. When we honestly assess philosophy of this kind in its own right, abstracting from the thought that we need it to protect a bit of common sense, we find it incredible. That makes it seem that the supposed bit of common sense cannot after all be common sense; we recoil to the other side, and give up trying to conceive our thinking as answerable to reality. But this looks like acquiescing in irresponsibility. So we are under pressure to recoil back into extravagant philosophical construction, now again seeming necessary to protect the idea that our thinking can be responsible to how things are. But nothing has happened to make the resulting philosophy look any more credible than it did; we have been here before, and there is nothing to prevent the pendulum from continuing to swing. Putnam's claim for natural realism is that it enables us to sustain the idea that we are responsible to reality without seeming to be committed to extravagant philosophy, so it brings this oscillation to a satisfying stop.

I have every sympathy with this aim of bringing peace to philosophy, but I am going to raise questions about some of the details of what Putnam does in executing the aim.

II

I shall begin with a couple of preliminaries.

First, what is it that needs to be defended? In his opening remarks, Putnam expresses the thought he wants to defend like this: "there is a way to do justice to our sense that knowledge claims are responsible to reality without recoiling into metaphysical fantasy."[2]

But why focus on *knowledge* claims as that whose responsibility to reality philosophy brings into question? Not that it is wrong to say we see knowledge claims as responsible to reality. That idea is indeed at risk in the sort of philosophy from which Putnam aims to rescue us. But surely this is just one case of the point. In making a claim at all, whether or not one explicitly represents oneself as knowledgeable, one makes oneself answerable to reality. If one claims that things are thus and so, the question whether one's claim is true is the question whether things are thus and so. And for one's activity to be intelligible as claim making at all, its correctness in the dimension of truth must depend on how things are. It is the possibility of making claims in general, not knowledge claims in particular, that is threatened by Putnam's oscillation.

As he goes on, Putnam himself describes the "realism issue" without special reference to knowledge, for instance as the "how does language hook on to the world" issue.[3] So it may seem captious to object to his opening formulation. But in noting the unwarranted narrowness of the epistemological way he introduces his topic, I am anticipating a more significant question about how the "realism issue" arises for modern philosophy.

III

First, one more preliminary point.

Putnam places Michael Dummett's "antirealism" as one variety of the recoil from the extravagance of metaphysical realism.[4] The label "antirealism" might seem to require this placement. Natural realism is a less metaphysically demanding realism than metaphysical realism, so one might expect it to be intermediate between metaphysical realism and antirealisms of whatever sort, including that of Dummett.

But the recoil from metaphysical excess is supposed to be a recoil into giving up responsibility, and that makes this map of the landscape unsatisfactory. Dummettian antirealism is not a version of the thought that on pain of fantasy we must give up trying to see ourselves as answerable to reality. Dummett argues that for languages whose expressive resources enable claims that are not effectively decidable, we cannot understand the semantics of sentences suitable for claim making in terms of conditions for their truth. Instead we need to consider conditions for assertibility, evidentially relevant conditions of sorts whose members, unlike truth conditions, are recognizable as obtaining whenever they obtain. This is not a *substitute* for seeing ourselves as responsible to reality in our claim making. What Dummett offers, rather, is an account of how we should conceive the responsibility to reality that continues, in this way of thinking, to be a condition for the very possibility of claim making. According to Dummett, lack of effective decidability prevents us from cashing out the idea directly, in terms of truth conditions, and he offers assertibility conditions as an alternative, indirect resource for saying what our responsibility to reality comes to.

So Putnam's placing of Dummett is wrong. Natural realism is to enable us to keep responsibility as an aspiration without falling into philosophical excess, and if we conceive the pitfalls on either side of natural realism in these terms, Dummett's antirealism belongs with the kind of realism Putnam rejects as fantastic, not with renouncing responsibility.

In urging the credentials of natural realism, Putnam has opponents in two directions. Confronting people—for instance, perhaps, Richard Rorty—who are willing to settle for what he stigmatizes as irresponsibility, he has behind him, joining in his attack on these opponents, Dummettian antirealists no less than metaphysical realists. When he turns to confront these erstwhile allies, the situation is symmetrical; now the renouncers of responsibility are behind him, and join him in accusing the others of philosophical extravagance. It is that accusation, rather than a reproach of irresponsibility, that Putnam ought to direct against Dummett. The trouble with Dummett, by what ought to be Putnam's lights, is not that he abandons responsibility to reality, but that he thinks the idea is problematic, and needs its tenability demonstrated by an elaborate philosophical construction.

Of course, in other ways, Dummett's proposal is radically unlike metaphysical realism. This belongs with the fact that it is not straightforward to line up the supposed difficulty it responds to—the fact that truth conditions are not recognizable whenever they obtain—with any felt difficulty to which metaphysical realism could seem to be a response. I shall come back to this.

IV

In a way I applaud, Putnam thinks the main thing he needs to do in order to reinstate natural realism is to explain its tendency to be forgotten. How has it become so easy to suppose the idea of responsibility to reality must be either propped up with abstruse philosophy or abandoned? Putnam's answer points to the emergence, in the early modern period, of the idea that perceptual access to the "external" world can only be indirect, mediated by "impressions" understood as effects of impacts made by bits of the world on our subjectivity. He thinks the way to bring natural realism back into view, as a metaphysically undemanding frame for reflection about how intellectual activity relates to the world, is to discard this view of perception. According to Putnam, the reason many contemporary philosophers find realism problematic is that they neglect perception. In spite of the efforts of James, Husserl, J. L. Austin, and Wittgenstein, a version of the idea that perception makes contact with the world only at an "interface" constituted by impressions is widely taken for granted. "[I]s it any wonder," he asks, "if, after thirty years of virtually ignoring the task taken up by my handful of philosophical heroes—the task of challenging the view of perception that has been received since the seventeenth century—the very idea that thought and language do connect with reality has come to seem more and more problematical? Is it any wonder that one cannot see how thought and language hook on to the world if one never mentions perception?"[5]

In the first of several generous acknowledgments of my work,[6] Putnam credits this diagnosis to my *Mind and World.*[7] I appreciate his generosity, but the diagnosis is not the one I meant to offer. Let me try to explain, and thereby to embark on raising a question about Putnam's diagnosis.

Consider how C. I. Lewis argues that we must acknowledge a given element in perceptual experience.[8] Lewis starts from the thought that conceptual activity, in, say, thinking aimed at the formation of empirical beliefs, is *activity*, freely undertaken. According to Lewis, this requires us to recognize a given element in experience, constraining the freedom of conceptual activity. If we do not acknowledge this external constraint, our picture of conceptual activity loses its intended subject. We must see the freedom of conceptual activity as constrained from outside its own sphere, on pain of losing our hold on thought's possession of content. "If there be no datum given to the mind," Lewis writes, "then knowledge must be contentless and arbitrary; there would be nothing which it must be true to."[9] To paraphrase: if we do not acknowledge a given element in experience in our attempt to characterize the acquisition and possession of an empirical world view, then we depict the so-called world view as a wholly unconstrained construction on the part of its possessor. There is nothing to distinguish the activity involved in acquiring and maintaining a world view from mere caprice. But in that case, our picture cannot contain anything recognizable as a world view.

Lewis is in a transcendental bind here, in a way he comes close to recognizing. On the one hand, he needs to conceive the given element in experience as *warranting* cases of conceptual activity. On the other hand, the very point of the given is to constrain conceptual activity *from outside its sphere.* The bind is that these two requirements on the given are not obviously satisfiable together. As Lewis recognizes, the fact that the given is to do its constraining from outside the sphere of the conceptual implies that "in a sense the given is ineffable, always."[10] Or again: "we cannot describe any particular given *as such*."[11] Or again: "for any mind whatever, [an item of experience] will be more than what is merely given if it be noted at all."[12] If something is noted, it is noted as instantiating this or that concept, and as soon as a concept is in play, both of Lewis's two elements, conceptual activity and reception of the given, are on the scene; we have failed to isolate the element of givenness. By Lewis's own lights, it is impossible to *state* the supposed ultimate warrant for a bit of empirical thinking. We might be reminded of Wittgenstein's remark, in a related context: "So in the end when one is doing philosophy one gets to the point where one would like just to emit an inarticulate sound."[13] How can we credit something we are committed to seeing as inexpressible with the sort of justificatory function Lewis wants to attribute to getting a bit of the given?

Lewis strains to make out a way the given can serve its warranting function even though it cannot be conceptually articulated. The given is "a colligation of sense-qualities,"[14] and he wants to exploit the implication of universality, repeatability, in "qualities." His basic picture is that in order to isolate the given, we must strip away in thought, as "brought to this experience by the mind," the "meaning" or "value" that is also contained in any actual experience.[15] Any actual experience involves both the given and the "value" that is the mind's contribution, and we can focus on the given only by abstracting away the mind's contribution; the given is not simply found in experience. But Lewis makes an exception for "immediate value or the specificity of sense-quality," which he takes to be in the given itself, not brought to experience by the mind. This conception shows up in a distinction he draws between qualia and universals.[16] The sense-qualities that constitute the given are like universals in that they have instances; they are repeatable. But universals are the contents of concepts, and Lewis cannot equate what it is for something to be an instance of a sense-quality—the kind of thing colligations of which make up the given itself—with what it is for something to satisfy a concept. As before, that would involve a contribution from the mind. The presence of a sense-quality on an occasion of experience is not to be such that, in order to isolate the given element, we would need to strip away something brought to the experience by the mind. Sense-qualities are to be repeatable qualities, but present to experiencing minds independently of any actualization of conceptual capacities. On these lines, Lewis contrives to give an appearance of making it intelligible that a case of pure givenness can be conceived as the presence to a mind of a sense-quality. And that looks like the kind of thing that might warrant an exercise of a concept.

But it is clearer why he wants to be entitled to talk like this than that we can really make sense of it. By his own showing, a patch of some color, say, cannot be present to a perceiver's mind *as* a patch of that color; that would once again bring in the other element in the duality. Of course, there is no problem about seeing how the presence to a perceiving subject of a case of redness as such might warrant, say, a judgment in which the concept of red is exercised. What is peculiar about Lewis is that he hopes to keep the intelligibility of a structure on these lines even though he is clear that he cannot keep "as such," and this looks like wishful thinking.[17]

That the given must constrain conceptual activity figures, in the line of reflection Lewis pursues, as a condition that must be met for thinking to be contentful (as of course it must be if it is to be thinking)—for conceptual activity to be answerable to something outside its own twists and turns. Against this background, the doubt I have been pressing, about whether the condition can be met, has the effect of putting in question the very possibility of contentful conceptual activity—activity in which subjects make themselves answerable to objective reality. That is why I described Lewis's bind as transcendental; Lewis's supposed requirements confront us with an apparent difficulty about the very possibility of activity on the part of subjects that is *of objects*, in the way that inquiry and claim making are. The difficulty is transcendental in something like the sense Kant confers on the term when he says: "I entitle *transcendental* all knowledge which is occupied not so much with objects as with the mode of our knowledge of objects in so far as this mode of knowledge is to be possible *a priori*."[18]

But another way of putting this point is to say that Lewis's bind suggests a possible answer to Putnam's diagnostic question: why do philosophers suppose there is a problem about conceiving thought and language as responsible to reality? We would have an answer to that question, with respect to at least some philosophers, if we could say that they feel—at least inchoately—the force of the condition Lewis places on the very possibility of content, and that they are—at least inchoately—aware of the problem I have been pressing about whether the condition can be met. This is the diagnosis that figures in my *Mind and World*, though I do not there formulate it in terms of Lewis.

Note that Lewis's bind does not have its source in the *indirectness* of perceptual contact with the "external" world, in what Putnam calls the "received" view of perception. Lewis is not urging a version of the "received" view. Getting the given, in Lewis, does not correspond to access to the immediate objects of perception, as the "received" view conceives that. What figures in the philosophy Putnam focuses on as immediate access to "internal" objects, which are supposed to intervene between minds and "external" things, would, by Lewis's lights, still require us to abstract away a contribution from the active mind before we could claim to have isolated the given element. Lewis does not cast his givens as objects for the perceiving mind at all, whether "internal" or not. (They are objects only for the mind of the philosopher who performs the transcendentally required abstraction.) As soon as there are objects for the perceiving mind, Lewis might say, there is more than the given. The trouble about Lewis's given is not that it is "internal," intervening between perceivers and "external" reality, but that it is supposed to do its constraining from outside the sphere of conceptual activity. That is why it is ineffable, and that is why there is a problem about its capacity to warrant cases of conceptual activity, as it must if it is to serve the transcendental function for which Lewis thinks we need to invoke it.

The immediate objects of perception that figure in the "received" view are not supposed to be ineffable, like Lewis's given. Now, perhaps this is self-deception on the part of adherents of the "received" view. Perhaps inwardly-directed content is intelligible only in a context that includes outwardly-directed content, understood as involving cognitive powers that the "received" view cannot countenance, powers of direct cognition that, as Putnam puts it, "reach all the way to the objects themselves."[19] But this does not undermine the difference I am urging between Lewis's conception and the "received" view. If the "received" view involves a self-deception in this area, it is one that the very point of Lewis's postulation immunizes him against. His givens must not be objects, not even "internal" objects, for the minds to which they are given, on pain of turning out after all not to be pure givens.[20]

When Putnam explains the "received" view's "interiorization" of the immediate objects of perception, one of the forces he points to is a "mathematized" conception of nature that has become hard to resist in the modern era. "Color and warmth seemed to have no place in such a conception of nature, and were banished to the status of mere subjective affectations of the mind."[21] It can be tempting to generalize this "interiorization" to include any putative aspects of reality that are available to the senses. No doubt this is at least part of why it can seem indubitable that the immediate objects of perception are "internal."[22]

Now when Lewis tries to characterize the given, he focuses on qualities that are available to the senses. But we should not conclude that Lewis's thinking is a case of the mathematically inspired "interiorization" that Putnam describes. Lewis focuses on sensory qualities not because he sees them as "internal," but because the only possible answer to the question "What is the given given to?" is "The senses." Heidegger remarks that Kant's concept of sensibility is "ontological rather than sensualistic."[23] Just so, Lewis's concept of sensibility is not sensualistic but transcendental. The supposed need to recognize the givenness of sense qualities is generated by the need to accommodate the contentfulness of conceptual activity. It has no necessary connection with the supposed need to find a home, elsewhere than in the objective world, for qualities that are not susceptible of mathematical treatment.

V

The "mathematized" conception of nature is only one part of an admirably complex picture Putnam gives in explaining how the "received" view of perception has become compelling in modern philosophy. But there is one factor Putnam does not mention, which makes it possible to effect a sort of connection between the "received" view of perception and the transcendental difficulty that is almost explicit in Lewis. "Interiorizing" the objects of perceptual experience can seem to supply perceptually based knowledge with firm foundations. This reflects a hope that we can resist being unnerved by the fallibility of our capacities to acquire knowledge about "external" things, reassuring ourselves by taking it that such knowledge is based on infallible knowledge about immediate objects of perception that are "internal."

It is a good question whether this picture can supply a genuinely satisfying reassurance. If we take this line, we persuade ourselves that we are secure in the supposed foundations of our knowledge of the world, but only at the cost of making vivid the size of the gap between these foundations and what is supposed to be based on them. But, though on closer inspection the hope of reassurance looks faint, the wish for secure foundations is surely a familiar motivation for the idea that the immediate objects of perception are "internal."

Now it is possible to see the craving for epistemic security that figures in this motivation for "interiorizing" the immediate objects of perceptual experience as an intelligible, though inept, response to an inchoate form of the anxiety Lewis almost formulates. Lewis's difficulty makes it look as if there is an urgent question about how content is possible. One might feel the force of what is in fact that question, but without getting it into focus. The sense of a difficulty that results might take shape as a thought to this effect: our hold on the world is coming into question. And if a difficulty presents itself in that unspecific guise, it could easily be misconstrued as epistemological—as threatening our capacity to achieve knowledge of the "external" world, rather than threatening the very idea that our thinking relates to the world at all, whether knowledgeably or not. Once we are in this frame of mind, the idea of secure foundations can seem to promise reassurance. So philosophers who are incipiently vulnerable to what is in fact Lewis's transcendental difficulty might find that familiar illusory comfort in "interiorizing" the immediate objects of perception.

VI

Of course we should not let Lewis's bind persuade us that the possibility of content is mysterious. An inkling of Lewis's bind might explain why someone finds content mysterious. But if we leave everything in place, what follows is that content is impossible; a condition for its possibility cannot be met. We cannot leave everything in place and take ourselves to have a *problem* about content—as if we could keep all the assumptions but, perhaps with difficulty, force content into the picture. We need to identify a misstep in the reasoning that leads to the conclusion that Lewis's assumptions make content impossible.

Clearly there are various points at which the reasoning could be questioned. One could claim that there is nothing right about the thought that experience must supply an external constraint on conceptual activity. Or one could defend the idea that qualities that are given in experience independently of concepts, and hence are in themselves ineffable, can warrant exercises of concepts. But we need not go in either of these directions. The problem vanishes if we can contrive to see perceptual experience as actualization of conceptual capacities in sensory receptivity. This invocation of receptivity accommodates what led Lewis to think there must be a purely given element in experience. But the sensory receiving that this conception makes room for is not what figures in Lewis as getting the purely given. So there is no need to keep concepts out of the picture in isolating it, and we are not subject to Lewis's difficulties in making out how sensory receiving can warrant conceptual activity. In *Mind and World*, I urge this conception of experience on essentially these grounds.

Avoiding Lewis's transcendental difficulty on these lines does not require more than the bare idea that conceptual capacities can be actualized in receptivity. There is no need to be specific about the conceptual capacities in question. But minimal reflection suggests that there is no basis for restricting the relevant concepts to concepts of "internal" objects and their properties. The notion of actualizations of conceptual capacities in sensory receptivity fits experiences in which subjects *take in* "external" states of affairs. This allows us to say our sensory receptivity reaches all the way to "external" objects. No one could accept this conception of experience, with this refusal to place a restriction on the relevant concepts, and stick to the "received" view of perception. So there is a convergence with Putnam's agenda.

But it is not the primary point of the conception, arrived at like this, to undermine the "received" view. Its point lies in its power to liberate us from Lewis's bind. In doing that, it undercuts the possible motivation for the "received" view I described in the last section, an anxiety that is actually transcendental, but misconstrued as relating to our capacity to acquire knowledge in particular. But the "received" view is not itself the primary target of this bit of philosophical therapy.

VII

This has a bearing on the one critical note Putnam sounds about me. He says: "McDowell mars an otherwise fine defense of a direct-realist view of perception by suggesting that animals do not have *experiences* in the same sense that humans do."[24] It is true that I exclude nonhuman animals from the scope of the conception of experience I recommend. By assimilating my primary concerns to his, Putnam makes it look as if this is a dispensable quirk in a diagnostic move that could perfectly well be made without it. But it is the whole point of my move—which, as I have indicated, impinges only indirectly on the "received" view of perception—that it is *conceptual* capacities, in a sense that connects with the freedom implicit in the idea of responding to reasons as such, that we can see as actualized in sensory receptivity. Only so can we find something right in Lewis's intuition about the need for external constraint without running into his troubles about how getting the given can intelligibly be a subject's reason for, say, a judgment. Talking, as Putnam thinks I should have, about actualizations in sensory receptivity of "protoconceptual" capacities—the sort of "discriminatory abilities" that are possessed by, say, dogs—would not have the same power to free us from Lewis's bind. In seeing or smelling things, dogs do not acquire reasons for bits of intellectual activity aimed at the fixation of belief; that is not something it makes sense to think of dogs as going in for at all.

I can insist on this while acknowledging what Putnam thinks I must "fail to see": "that the discriminatory abilities of animals and human concepts lie on a continuum." Putnam writes as if the only possible meaning for "experience" is something that applies at all points on such a continuum. I agree that there are perception-related concepts that apply both to us and to dogs: for instance the concept of being, as we say, on to things in the environment.[25] And one can use the word "experience" for a concept of that sort if one likes. But I can still urge that we instantiate such concepts by having *conceptual* capacities actualized in our sensory receptivity, and that that is not true of dogs. It should not seem that anything substantive turns on my appropriating the *word* "experience" to characterize this distinctive way of instantiating the general concept of perceptual awareness.

I have taken Putnam's "continuum" talk to affirm commonalities in what can be truly said about human and nonhuman perceivers. It could be taken more strongly, as rejecting any discontinuity. But I think on this reading the "continuum" claim would be wrong. Without denying the commonalities, we can insist on distinguishing animals that can be in responsible control of their cognitive and practical lives, as we can, from animals that cannot. There is an intelligible idea of doing things for reasons, in either intellectual or practical activity, that belongs in the context of this capacity to take charge—to step back from what would otherwise be mere incentives and assess their cogency as reasons. And in the intuition that drives Lewis's thinking, the requirement of constraint from outside conceptual activity—which I have suggested is all right, as long as it is not understood as a requirement of constraint from outside the sphere of the conceptual—acquires its urgency precisely because the activity in question exemplifies the freedom that goes with responsiveness to reasons as such. This context defines the restricted application I give to the idea of conceptual abilities. And the context dictates that it is conceptual abilities, in that restricted application of the idea, that I need to appeal to in my proposal about how to see through the apparent problem about content generated by Lewis's intuitions. In order to free ourselves from the apparent problem while respecting the intuitions that generate it, we need to organize what we say around a discontinuity between animals that can step back from what inclines them in this or that direction and animals that cannot, and so do not do things for reasons in the relevant sense at all.

VIII

We are not yet in a position to stage a comparison of two competing diagnoses. Suppose I am right that some philosophers are at least inchoately troubled by a puzzlement, about the very possibility of content, that can be spelled out in terms of Lewis's intuitions. Suppose, further, that the way to avoid the puzzlement is to realize that the constraint from receptivity that Lewis rightly takes to be needed can be supplied by a receptivity that is already conceptually shaped. So far, this just raises another diagnostic question: what makes that realization difficult?

I think the answer is that the idea of sensory receptivity is, on the face of it, the idea of something natural. And in an intellectual climate shaped by modern science, it can easily seem impossible, or at least problematic, to find room in nature for instantiations of concepts that characterize subjects who are in rational control of their lives. The transcendental bind that almost comes to expression in Lewis thus emerges as a case of a genre of philosophical difficulty we can easily feel when we try to find room in nature for responsiveness to reasons as such. Lewis's reflections are one way into difficulties about finding room for rational freedom, and so mindedness, in the natural world, conceived in a way that threatens to be coercive as a result of bedazzlement by science.

I have deliberately expressed this in Putnam-like terms. When Putnam sets out to dislodge the idea that the "received" view of perception is intellectually compulsory, much of his effort is devoted to undermining the appearance that, on pain of a return to prescientific superstition, we must suppose everything true can be said in terms suitable for incorporation into a discipline that functions as the paradigmatic natural sciences do. Putnam's diagnosis, like mine, traces the philosophical trouble he considers ultimately to scientism. This convergence might suggest that it is only a question of taste whether to approach scientism, as the ultimate source of the trouble, through Lewis's bind or through the "received" view of perception. On this view, there would be no real competition between the diagnoses.

I am not sure if Putnam would be willing to place the "received" view of perception like this, as just one way the philosophically unhealthy effects of scientism show up. It seems, rather, that he wants to trace philosophical forgetfulness of natural realism to the "received" view, and only then to blame scientism for the "received" view. But if that is how he thinks, it seems a pity. I shall end by making two points in this connection.

First, consider Dummett again. Dummett thinks the understanding of a language must make contact with reality, so to speak, at conditions recognizable whenever they obtain. This rules out truth conditions, at least for sentences that are not effectively decidable, and requires that we focus on assertibility conditions instead. My point earlier was that this "antirealism" is a *defense* of realism, in the sense of the idea that thought and speech are responsible to reality, though of course not a defense of *natural* realism; from the standpoint of natural realism, Dummettian antirealism belongs with metaphysical realism, in holding that responsibility to reality needs elaborate philosophical underpinning. The different point I want to make now is that it would be wrong to blame the "received" view of perception for the difficulty Dummett finds in cashing out the idea of responsibility to reality in terms of truth conditions, a felt problem that can be framed as a form of failure to appreciate the availability of natural realism. Dummett's idea that assertibility conditions, rather than truth conditions, are the point of contact between understanding and reality has no affinity with the "received" view. Assertibility conditions are not pushed inside the mind by the requirement that they be recognizable whenever they obtain.

No doubt it would be equally wrong to go quickly to scientism, in attempting to diagnose where Dummett goes wrong, by the lights of natural realism, when he supposes we need elaborate philosophy about how thought and language are connected with reality. But consider Dummett's conviction that there *must* be substantive answers to such questions as "What does it consist in that someone understands such-and-such a sentence?" (Not just answers on the lines of "It consists in her knowing that the sentence is true if and only if ...", with the sentence itself inserted in the gap.)[26] Dummett thinks it must be possible to specify what it is to understand a language otherwise than from a perspective on reality constituted by possession of that very understanding. Now why should this seem compelling? Obviously, I cannot deal properly with Dummett's thinking at this stage of this essay. But a diagnosis in terms of an intellectual climate shaped by scientism might be at least on the right track to explain why Dummett finds it obvious that what it is to understand a language should be capturable without dependence on a particular point of view, that constituted by understanding the language in question.

The second point is this: even if it is placed less ambitiously, as just one way into an ultimate diagnosis in terms of scientism, I am not convinced that the "received" view of perception deserves as much attention as Putnam gives it. (Of course this is not to defend the "received" view.)

The attempt to fit everything real into the mold of the natural sciences generates difficulties about mindedness. Central to how this happens is a conception of the mind as an organ—or, in a primitive version of the conception, a para-organ. (Putnam himself makes this a target.)[27] On such a conception, the mind is internal to its owner, literally or (in the primitive version) quasi-literally. A good way to bring out how this makes mindedness problematic is to invoke an image of Daniel Dennett's: mindedness involves content, but an organ, say the brain, could be at most a syntactic engine, not a semantic engine.[28] The pseudoconception of a para-organ merely pretends to escape this impasse, through an appeal to something like magic; one might say, again echoing Dennett, that one pretends to understand a para-organ as a semantic engine, but only by conceiving it as made of wonder tissue.[29] (Again, this is a way of gesturing at a point that Putnam himself makes.) So this interiorizing of the mind makes it a mystery how states or episodes "in" the mind can have content at all. And now we seem to need elaborate philosophy to regain entitlement to the idea that thought is answerable to the world.

This mystery does not come into focus in the "received" view of perception, which just helps itself to contentful states or episodes "in" the mind. The mystery reflects the fact that interiorizing the mind makes the mind out to be a syntactic engine, and so obliterates content altogether. This is merely obscured by a picture of perception that purports to find content as such unproblematic, but brings the immediate objects of perceptual states or episodes inside the mind. The real trouble is a supposed interiority on the part of the mind itself, which makes a mystery of how the mind can have objects at all. This trouble is not addressed by attacking a picture according to which the mind's possession of objects is unproblematic so long as the objects are internal to the mind.

Perhaps the "received" view owes its attractions in part to the idea that it enables us to see how a syntactic engine could, after all, be in touch with its world. But such an idea would be merely confused; a syntactic engine could not be in touch with its world. Our primary target should be the framework conceptions that make it seem that the mind would have to be a syntactic engine, not the "received" view, which figures in this context only as a self-deceptive attempt to mitigate the bad effects of such a conclusion. Of course, it is a fine thing to join Putnam's heroes in undermining the "received" view of perception. But if our concern is with the harmful effects of scientism in modern philosophy of mind, and in particular with the way scientism leads to finding a problem in thought's answerability to its subject matter, the "received" view of perception warrants no more than a marginal place in the picture.

John McDowell

University of Pittsburgh
December 2004

NOTES

1. Hilary Putnam, "Sense, Nonsense, and the Senses: An Inquiry into the Powers of the Human Mind," *Journal of Philosophy* 91 (1994): 454, 446–47.

2. Ibid., 446.

3. Ibid., 456.

4. See ibid., 446, where he groups Dummett's antirealism with deconstruction and Nelson Goodman's "irrealism."

5. Ibid., 456.

6. Ibid., 453.

7. John McDowell, *Mind and World* (Cambridge, MA: Harvard University Press, 1994); reissued with a new introduction in 1996.

8. See C. I. Lewis, *Mind and the World Order* (New York: Scribner's, 1929), ch. II.

9. Ibid., 38–39.

10. Ibid., 53.

11. Ibid., 53.

12. Ibid., 50.

13. Ludwig Wittgenstein, *Philosophical Investigations*, trans. G.E.M. Anscombe (Oxford: Blackwell, 1953), §261.

14. Lewis, *Mind and the World Order*, 49.

15. Ibid., 50–51.

16. Ibid., 60–61.

17. It is a curiosity that Lewis is not mentioned in Wilfrid Sellars's attack on the Myth of the Given, in "Empiricism and the Philosophy of Mind" (in *Minnesota Studies in the Philosophy of Science*, vol. 1, ed. Herbert Feigl and Michael Scriven [Minneapolis: Minnesota University Press, 1956], 253–329; reprinted with some added footnotes in Sellars, *Science, Perception and Reality* [London: Routledge and Kegan Paul, 1963], 127–96; reprinted, without the 1963 footnotes, as a monograph by Harvard University Press [Cambridge, MA: 1997].) Sellars looks further back in the history of philosophy for his announced targets, but the way he frames his attack makes it easy, at several points, to suppose he has Lewis in mind.

18. Kant, *Critique of Pure Reason*, trans. Norman Kemp Smith (London: Macmillan, 1929), A11–12/B25.

19. Putnam, "Sense, Nonsense, and the Senses," 453.

20. Putnam obscures this point to some extent, when he introduces the "received" view (453) as *including* the thought that "impressions" (or their counterpart in the contemporary materialized version of the view) are "linked to 'external objects' only causally, and not cognitively." Perhaps it is self-deceptive to suppose that impressions, conceived as the "received" view conceives them, could be cognitively linked to the objects that we are supposed to perceive through their mediation. But that is an objection to the view. It would defeat the very purpose of the view to make it part of the view's content, as Putnam does.

21. Ibid., 468.

22. However, one might want to devote more attention than Putnam does to the question how the "received" view obliterates the thought that qualities of things that *are* mathematically capturable, such as their shapes and sizes, are directly available to the senses.

23. Martin Heidegger, *Kant and the Problem of Metaphysics*, trans. Richard Taft (Bloomington: Indiana University Press, 1990), 18.

24. Putnam, "Sense, Nonsense, and the Senses," 493.

25. This is not a matter of just any discriminatory response to such features—so that rusting iron filings would have to count as being on to the presence of moisture in the sense in which animals can be on to the presence of food. The reaction must fit in a suitable way into the purposive shape of an animal's life. We cannot understand a cat's stalking a bird without supposing that it is, in the relevant sense, on to the bird's presence. But a contraction of the pupils does not require us to suppose that a creature is on to an increase in the level of illumination. I make these remarks, which merely scratch the surface of a large topic, in order to emphasize my distance from the fanatics who are the appropriate target of the reproaches Putnam wrongly directs at me.

26. See Putnam, "Sense, Nonsense, and the Senses," 495–96.

27. See "Sense, Nonsense, and the Senses," 452–53. I mean this to be understood on the model of Gilbert Ryle's accusation that the Cartesian picture of the mental is para-mechanical. See *The Concept of Mind* (London: Hutchinson, 1949).

28. See Dennett's "Beyond Belief," in *Thought and Object: Essays on Intentionality,* ed. Andrew Woodfield (Oxford: Clarendon, 1982), 26.

29. About wonder tissue, see Dennett's "Cognitive Wheels," in *Minds, Machines and Evolution: Philosophical Studies*, ed. Christopher Hookway (Cambridge: Cambridge University Press, 1984), 149–50.

REPLY TO JOHN MCDOWELL

Reading McDowell's great book, *Mind and World*, and discussing it with successive academic generations of students was the beginning of a continuing engagement on my part with the topic of perception, and I remain lastingly grateful to John McDowell for his influence on me, even if it did not extend quite as far as he clearly would wish it had.

James Conant has distinguished between two kinds of skepticism, which he calls "Cartesian skepticism" and "Kantian skepticism."[1] "Cartesian skepticism," in Conant's sense, is skepticism about the possibility of *knowing* anything about an "external world"; "Kantian skepticism" is a worry about *how it is possible that* our thoughts, whether supposedly about an external world or even about our own sense impressions, really have *content* at all. (Note that this is not supposed to be an *epistemological* question.) Through the years, both Conant and McDowell have taken me to task,[2,3] because, as they see it, in my Dewey Lectures I mistook the target of *Mind and World* to be the "Cartesian" variety of skepticism,[4] whereas it was actually the "Kantian" variety that McDowell was concerned to exorcise. In fact, I was not wholly wrong: McDowell *does* explicitly reject the "interface conception" of our sensations as something "between" us and the external world in *Mind and World*[5], and that rejection is what influenced me; but in an important sense they are right. The main target of *Mind and World* was not epistemological skepticism, but "Kantian" skepticism, and that fact eluded me when I praised *Mind and World* so highly in my Dewey Lectures. In that respect, I misread *Mind and World*, and much of McDowell's present essay is a careful attempt to explain in detail why and how that is a misreading. (McDowell's way of raising the Kantian problem in *Mind and World* is via the premise that our thoughts can only have content if they are capable of being *justified* by sensory experiences.)

In the present essay, McDowell, instead of appealing to Kant to explain the kind of nonepistemological skepticism that concerns him, chooses to appeal to C. I. Lewis. McDowell explains what he calls Lewis's "transcendental bind" thus:

On the one hand, [Lewis] needs to conceive the given element in experience as *warranting* cases of conceptual activity. On the other hand, the very point of the given is to constrain conceptual activity *from outside its sphere*. The bind is that these two requirements on the given are not obviously satisfiable together. As Lewis recognizes, the fact that the given is to do its constraining from outside the sphere of the conceptual implies that "in a sense the given is ineffable, always." Or again: "we cannot describe any particular given *as such*." Or again: "for any mind whatever, [an item of experience] will be more than what is merely given if it be noted at all." If something is noted, it is noted as instantiating this or that concept, and as soon as a concept is in play, both of Lewis's two elements, conceptual activity and reception of the given, are on the scene; we have failed to isolate the element of givenness. By Lewis's own lights, it is impossible to *state* the supposed ultimate warrant for a bit of empirical thinking.

As McDowell explains in the next paragraph, for Lewis the given is "a colligation of sense qualities." And McDowell claims that the right way to avoid landing oneself in Lewis's bind is to see that:

The problem vanishes if we can contrive to see perceptual experience as actualization of conceptual capacities in sensory receptivity. This invocation of receptivity accommodates what led Lewis to think there must be a purely given element in experience. But the sensory receiving that this conception makes room for is not what figures in Lewis as getting the purely given. So there is no need to keep concepts out of the picture in isolating it, and we are not subject to Lewis's difficulties in making out how sensory receiving can warrant conceptual activity. In *Mind and World* I urge this conception of experience on essentially these grounds.

I find this "bind" spurious and the proposed way of making the problem "vanish" unbelievable. Let me explain why I say this.

I. Why I Find Lewis's "Bind" Spurious

William James once asserted that in the case of a "presented and recognized material object . . . Sensations and apperceptive ideas fuse . . . so intimately that you can no more tell where one begins and the other ends, than you can tell, in those cunning circular panoramas that have lately been exhibited, where the real foreground and the painted canvas join together."[6] In one of the *Afterwords* in my book *The Threefold Cord: Mind, Body, and World*,[7] I used James's notion of "fusion" as a way of trying to take the appearance of metaphysical strangeness out of McDowell's notion that perceptual experiences are conceptualized (while also restricting that point to apperceptions—experiences in which something is "presented and recognized"—which McDowell obviously does not do). For Lewis, what is given in experience was "sense qualities" (in his lectures at Harvard that I heard in 1949, he also used the term *qualia*). And the alleged problem is that while I know what an *apperceived* quale feels like, I cannot know what a quale that I do not apperceive, that is, do not conceptualize as the quale that it is, is like. The "bare" quale, the quale "in itself," becomes "ineffable."

To be specific, let us take the quale to be my sense impression of a particular red patch on a particular occasion. Lewis was sure that I cannot know what that particular red "quality" is like when I do not conceptualize it.[8] But I have vivid eidetic memories of past scenes, including the colors of various objects that I am sure I was not recognizing (apperceiving, conceptualizing) at the times in question. For example, I can call up many details of a scene which is engraved in my memory because my mother had just burned her hand and was shouting with pain; if I was conceptualizing anything at the time, it what my mother was doing and undergoing, and not the color of the pot on the stove, but I can *recall* that color quale.

To this objection, there are several responses Lewis might make. He might insist that if I remember it, then it *was* apperceived, but this sounds to me more like something McDowell would do than the C. I. Lewis I remember from his class in 1949. It is more likely, I believe, that Lewis would have said that the quale *in my present "memory image"* is conceptualized. So focusing on it is still not focusing on the bare "given element in experience." One problem with this should be apparent: if you accept that I do not know what the quale I experienced *then*, approximately seventy-four years ago, was like but only know what the quale in my present "memory image" is like, then an enormous amount of my past experience becomes "ineffable." (In the same way, the qualitative experiences of prelinguistic humans and of nonhuman animals become ineffable for McDowell.)

A second problem is that we do not need to consider long-term memory experiences at all. Do the following: simply walk about the room. Now try to recall what the scene looked like a moment ago. If you are like me, you will be able to recall at least some "peripheral" features, features that you are sure you did not conceptualize at the time. Is it plausible that even short-term memory, when relied on, replaces "ineffable" givens with "effed" experiences?!! But surely the most plausible view is that while apperceptive experiences are indeed different from mere undergoings, they are not different in all respects. Perhaps in some cases recognizing the "quality" of a color (or a color impression) makes a difference to the quality itself, but I see no reason, either phenomenological or scientific to believe that this always happens. I certainly think the table top to the right of this computer that I can recall being in the periphery of my vision when I typed the words "I certainly think" a moment ago looked more or less as it does now. (And not just in the "objective" sense of "looked," I think the experienced quality was the same.) I believe, in short, that while I cannot *focus* on a *present* quale without conceptualizing it, I can *recall* qualia that were not conceptualized at the moment, and that there is thus no reason to concede that there is something *ineffable* about qualia—not in Lewis's sense of "ineffable," anyway.[9]

II. WHY I FIND McDOWELL'S WAY OF MAKING THE PROBLEM "VANISH" UNBELIEVABLE

According to McDowell, as we saw above, the right way to make Lewis's problem vanish is "to see perceptual experience as actualization of conceptual capacities in sensory receptivity." And I said that I find this "unbelievable." For example, there is nothing in current neurological or psychological studies of vision to support in any way the idea that the conceptual capacities involved in conceptual thought are necessary for the mere having of visual experience. I fear that McDowell may reply that experiences, including color experiences, are outside the sphere of brain science altogether, but if that is what he thinks, then I do not agree. I think that neurology and brain science and phenomenology and reflection on the grammar of our psychological terms are *all* relevant to discussions of the nature and etiology of color experiences. Here too, and not only in moral philosophy, I think we should seek for what John Rawls called a "reflective equilibrium," in this case one which will best enable us to accommodate, to interpret, and, to be sure, sometimes to revise, the various things we are inclined to say about perception. And I see no serious reason to think, either *pre* or *post* such reflection, that *conceptualization* is necessary to the having of, say, color experiences. Indeed, if we follow McDowell and see color experiences as "actualizations" of cognitive capacities that we have and animals (and prelinguistic infants) lack, then the color experiences of those animals and those infants must indeed be "ineffable" for us.[10] But there is no good reason to think that they are.

III. WARRANT AND CONCEPTUAL ARTICULATION

McDowell is certainly right that appealing to bare presences cannot provide an answer to the question as to how concepts and experiences are connected, or, in McDowell's terms, how experiences can rationally constrain beliefs. But to get from that observation to the conclusion that "the content of experience is conceptual,"[11] McDowell needs to assimilate sensory impressions themselves to apperceptions, and that is where we disagree.[12] Indeed, there are apperceptions that have *no* accompanying sense quality at all. Suppose I raise my right hand. My awareness that *I raised it* (it did not simply "go up"), is a genuine awareness, a genuine act of apperception, but there is no "sense quality," no "quale" of voluntariness. (I think I remember that Elizabeth Anscombe somewhere describes this kind of awareness as "knowledge without observation," but this seems to me to be a misdescription. I would say that I *did* observe that I raised my hand, but this is observation without any particular sense quality, or, to use a term employed by Alva Noë, an instance of "amodal awareness.") Similarly, my awareness that I am seeing a tomato, something that has a particular sort of other side and a particular inside, and not just a cardboard shell, involves amodal awareness and not only sense qualities. McDowell thinks he has to say that *impressions* warrant beliefs, and that, I think, is why he needs them to be conceptually articulated; my view is that it is *apperceptions* that warrant beliefs. Of course certain sorts of apperceptions are internally related to impressions. But *it is the apperceptions and not the impressions that do the warranting.* Babies and languageless animals do not have apperceptions in the demanding Kantian or McDowellian sense; but I see no reason to deny them sense qualities.

I fear that this will sound to McDowell like Gareth Evans's story,[13] according to which "the informational system" supplies "inputs" which cause (but do not justify) the relevant beliefs.[14] This is a story about how beliefs are *caused* but not about how they are *warranted*. But while this is right as a criticism of Evans's account, it is not right as a criticism of the account I just proposed (and not only because apperceptions can be *rejected*; they do not automatically "trigger" beliefs, although that is an important point about them.) What Evans was doing was speculating about the brain's hardware; thus his account was a *reductionist* account. On my view, talk about what the organism does in *intentional* terms is not reducible to "hardware" talk.[15] To be sure, any intentional state, for example, knowing the meaning of the word "ephebe," or being aware that something is a tomato, has to be realized in "hardware" *somehow*. But intentional states are realizable in a practically infinite number of different ways, and the fact that a particular piece of hardware *is* a realization of a particular intentional state is only visible from the intentional level, not from either the neurological or the computational level by themselves. Apperceiving, being aware of something, is a neither a physicochemical nor a computational "state"; it is an intentional transaction involving a human being and that human being's linguistic and nonlinguistic environment, a "functional" state in a wide sense. And to be aware that something is so is to have a warrant, or putative warrant, for judging it to be so. Whether the awareness (what I have been calling the "apperception") is internally related to an impression or not (to repeat, amodal awarenesses are not internally related to impressions), it is the awareness that is conceptually articulated and not the phenomenal quality of the impression. The phenomenal quality may be such as to make the content of the awareness *true* (in case the awareness is about the phenomenal quality itself; but truth makers do not have to be conceptually articulated; reasons do, but qualia are not reasons.

IV. McDowell's History of the Problem

In McDowell's and my philosophical lifetimes, we have seen the following dialectic play itself out: up to and including Quine, empiricists often offered accounts of perceptual knowledge in which claims to such knowledge were seen as responses to an unconceptualized Given. But such accounts, as McDowell sees it, make our assertions, in effect, mere noises and subvocalizations that are described as "triggered" by impacts on our sense organs, but no genuine account of how they are *warranted* by our experiences is thereby offered. A "solution" suggested by Neurath and embraced by Davidson was to say that knowledge begins with "sentences" and not with experiences; "sentences" (obviously standing in for *judgments*) can be justified only by other "sentences," not by experiences according to these philosophers. But then the threat that everything we take to be meaningful thought is a "frictionless spinning in the void," or, in Kantian language, an "empty play of representations," rears its ugly head. Other philosophers then "recoil" from this unpalatable position back to the Given, and then the whole oscillation repeats. Philosophy does not find peace.

The "oscillation" can be avoided, according to McDowell, by accepting his idea that impressions are themselves conceptualized, an idea with which he credits Kant, even if, in Kant's case, it came with unacceptable metaphysical packaging.

McDowell sees philosophy as having enacted this dialectic, although not with the full consciousness of the problem that we finally see in Neurath and Davidson, ever since the seventeenth century. I neither accept nor reject this historical hypothesis, but I am presently still unconvinced. My problem with it is that I do not see how McDowell's account is supposed to fit the historical facts about the centuries prior to logical positivism. Perhaps McDowell will convince me in the future, but I need to see a much more detailed account of how the dialectic is supposed to have played itself out in the seventeenth, eighteenth, and nineteenth centuries, and not only in the twentieth.

Perhaps I can guess at the beginning of the story McDowell suggests. It is incontestable that British Empiricism, in many ways, set the modern discussion of perception in motion. And in Hume's philosophy, the whole idea of a problem of how the "nonconceptual" can constrain the "conceptual" simply cannot arise. Concepts, in Hume's system, are "ideas" and "ideas" and "impressions" have similar ontological natures; the former are simply "faint copies" of the latter, and they refer to the latter simply by resembling them. So far this can be fitted nicely into McDowell's scheme, because "ideas" are triggered by "impressions" in accordance with psychological laws that Hume himself likens to the laws of physics.[16] This is "scientism" with a vengeance!

Kant also fits, or can be made to fit, something like McDowell's story (without attributing to him a concern with C. I. Lewis's worry about the "ineffability" of the Given), thus: associationist psychology was, in Kant's day, the "scientific" psychology," and Kant realized that in Hume's talk of ideas, impressions, and a pseudoforce of "association" there was nothing that could be called an apperception of *anything*. If we are, as Hume suggests, just congeries of ideas and impressions swirling around under the impact of association, then there is no intentionality present at all; it is indeed just an empty play of representations. "How is it possible that ideas (*Vorstellungen*) have content?" is a question whose answer demanded something more and different than the received associationist psychology. The something more is *apperception*, and Kant has an enormous amount to say about it.

But whatever we take the target of Kant's concern with skepticism to be, whether we take it to be what I just said it was or Lewis's "bind," there is still a gap in the historical record that does not fit McDowell's suggested sequence of oscillation to and away from the Given, followed by the realization that experience is conceptualized, followed by Wittgensteinian peace. The problem is that in the actual history the order is "the myth of the Given (Hume), followed by the realization that experience is conceptualized (Kant), followed (in the second half of the twentieth century!) by the idea that the Given plays no role in warranting our beliefs (Neurath-Davidson)." Kant comes too early (and not obviously as a reaction to a McDowellian "oscillation") and the "frictionless spinning in the void" comes too late. Doubtless McDowell has a different way of telling the story, but I am unable to fill in the details from what he has so far published. Another problem I have with McDowell's diagnosis of the source of our difficulties is that it entirely leaves out what many philosophers saw (and some still see) as the banishment of phenomenal qualities from the physical world—a "banishment" that had its source in the project of the new (seventeenth-century) physics to reduce the number of properties assigned to "primitive matter." This factor in the history does, however, fit McDowell's irenic suggestion that he and I should agree that the deep cause of skeptical worries is scientism.

V. EXTERNALISM, FUNCTIONALISM, AND SCIENTISM

McDowell poses the following question to me: Would I be willing to say that the interface view of perception (what McDowell calls the "received" view) is "just one way the philosophically unhealthy effects of scientism show up"? The answer is an emphatic "yes." I agree, at least on the essential point, when McDowell writes that "The attempt to fit everything real into the mold of the natural sciences [I would prefer to say, "into the mold of *physics*"; I do not believe there is a *single* "mold of the natural sciences"— HP] generates difficulties about mindedness. Central to how this happens is a conception of the mind as an organ—or, in a primitive version of the conception, a para-organ.)" He goes on to say, "On such a conception, the mind is internal to its owner, literally or (in the primitive version) quasi-literally." I am sure that McDowell is aware that the difficulties that arise from the conception of the mind as an internal organ do not only affect the possibility of seeing how *perception* can give us cognitive (as opposed to merely causal) contact with the world; they also affect the possibility of seeing how concepts can help us to have cognitive contact with the world. For once we think of the mind as a thing inside us, for example, the brain, then since concepts (on a non-Platonic view, anyway) are supposed to be in the mind, it follows that concepts are also "inside us." In that case, even seeing impressions as "conceptualized," as McDowell recommends, will not help with the problem of "cognitive access to the 'external' world," the possibility of what is today called "semantic externalism" (that is, the view that our concepts themselves are mostly already informed with worldly content), and the kind of nonreductive functionalism that goes with semantic externalism, is missed from the beginning. (By "the kind of nonreductive functionalism that goes with semantic externalism" I mean the view of our intentional mental states as *world-involving capacities* to do (and, when appropriate, to rationally justify) various things; in a recent publication[17] I referred to mental states so conceived as "long-armed" functional states. In my view, such a view of mental states fits well into *both* philosophy and cognitive science, provided one does not make the mistake (that I once made) of thinking of functional states as "computer programs." To think that *both* philosophy and cognitive science can discuss the same issues is not "scientism," in my view anyway.[18] But reductionism and the idea that

REPLY TO JOHN MCDOWELL   667

all genuine knowledge must employ the supposed "methods of the exact sciences" and resemble knowledge in those sciences *is* scientism, and I agree with McDowell that many of our perplexities can be traced to the baneful influence of those ideas.

H.P.

NOTES

1. James Conant, "Varieties of Skepticism," in *Wittgenstein and Skepticism*, ed. Denis McManus (Abingdon, Oxon and New York: Routledge Press, 2004).

2. Conant, "Varieties of Skepticism."

3. See John McDowell, "Responses," in *Reading McDowell: On Mind and World*, ed. Nicholas Smith (London and New York: Routledge, 1994), 267–305.

4. Collected in my *The Threefold Cord: Mind, Body and World.*

5. See, for example, "Afterword, Part I" in *Mind and World*, for example p. 145 ("In the style of thinking I am advocating, impressions need not be separated from appearings as causes and effects").

6. William James, "Does 'Consciousness' Exist?," in *Essays in Radical Empiricism* (Lincoln, NE: University of Nebraska Press, 1996), 29–30.

7. *The Threefold Cord*, 158.

8. This is suspiciously like Berkeley's worry that I cannot know what a supposed "material object" is like when it is not observed by a "spirit" [that is a mind], only now the problem concerns impressions rather than matter.

9. Ned Block has a different notion of "ineffability" which will not concern us here.

10. McDowell himself writes, "the potential embarrassment I have been discussing does not stop with the denial that mere animals have 'outer experience'. They cannot have 'inner experience' either, on the conception of 'inner experience' I have recommended" (*Mind and World*, 119). He attempts to pacify the reader who finds this unbelievable by granting that they have some sort of "proto-subjectivity."

11. *Mind and World*, 45 and Lecture III.

12. In *Mind and World*, McDowell tells us that sensory impressions have conceptual content in a sense that requires that their subject have self-consciousness and the ability to engage in thinking about the "rational credentials" of those impressions. In my view, there is a vast difference between a mere "impression" or "sense quality" (to use Lewis's term), and an apperception.

13. McDowell discusses Gareth Evans views in the latter's *Varieties of Reference* (Oxford: Clarendon Press, 1982) in Lecture III of *Mind and World.*

14. This is McDowell's interpretation of Evans in *Mind and World*, 46–49.

15. This is argued in *The Threefold Cord*, 119–25.

16. This is what I take Hume to be doing when he writes, "These are therefore the principles of union or cohesion among our simple ideas, and in the imagination supply the place of that inseparable connexion, by which they are united in our memory. Here is a kind of ATTRACTION, which in the mental world will be found to have as extraordinary effects as in the natural, and to shew itself in as many and as various forms. Its effects are every where conspicuous; but as to its causes, they are mostly unknown, and must be resolved into original qualities of human nature, which I pretend not to explain."

Here "ATTRACTION" simultaneously refers to Newton's "gravity" and to Hume's "association"; and the refusal to explain "the original qualities of human nature" exactly imitates Newton's refusal to explain the source of gravitational attraction. *A Treatise of Human Nature* (Oxford: Oxford University Press, 1978), 12–13.

17. The publication in question is chapter 15 (titled simply "Hilary Putnam") in *Mind and Consciousness: 5 Questions*, ed. Patrick Grim (Copenhagen: Automatic Press, an imprint of Vince Inc., 2009).

18. Trying to fit psychology into the model of physics is certainly "scientism." But that sort of scientism can exist even when the mind is not thought of as an inner "organ." As mentioned above, Hume implies that his laws of "association of idea" were comparable to Newton's laws.

18

Pierre Hadot

WORDS IN LIFE: "PHILOSOPHY AS EDUCATION FOR GROWNUPS"

Hilary Putnam wrote: "Philosophy is not only concerned with changing our views, but also with changing our sensibility, our ability to perceive and react to nuances. Philosophers are, ideally, *educators*—not just educators of youth, but of themselves and their peers. Stanley Cavell once suggested that as the definition of philosophy—'education for grown-ups.' I think that is the definition I like best."[1]

For Hilary Putnam, to philosophize is thus not to construct an abstract theory but to construct, to build up, a human being. Such a conception can be inscribed within a very long tradition, going back to Socrates and Plato and honored until the end of antiquity. In the sixth century C.E., the Neoplatonist philosopher Simplicius, commenting on Epictetus and trying to define the role and occupation of the philosopher in the city, declared without hesitation: it is that of a "sculptor of men."[2] The philosopher does not teach humans any particular occupation, he does not prepare them for any particular profession, but he aims at transforming their sensibility, their character, their way of seeing the world or of relating to other humans. We could say that the philosopher teaches them the occupation of being human. Just as, according to Epictetus, we know if a carpenter has benefited from his carpenter's education when we see him build a house, we know if a philosopher has benefited from his philosopher's education when we see him live as a human being must live.[3] The Socrates of the *Apology* already had reproached the Athenians for taking care of their fortune, reputation, and honors instead of trying to better themselves in their thought, their truth, their soul.[4] Quite a few centuries later, Nietzsche will reveal the danger of social and professional life, through which we risk forgetting to live our human life: "How they strut about in a hundred masquerades, as youths, men, graybeards, fathers, citizens, priests, officials, merchants, mindful solely of their collective comedy and not at all of themselves . . . This eternal becoming is a lying puppet-play in beholding which man forgets himself, the actual distraction which disperses the individual to the four winds."[5] For Aristotle, to live as a man is even, paradoxically, to surpass the human condition, for he thinks that philosophy, insofar as it consists in a life devoted to thinking, takes us to the limits of what is human. When man devotes himself entirely to the activity of reflection, "it is not in so far as he is man that he will live so, but in so far as something divine is present in him."[6]

All philosophers of antiquity, each in their own way, tried to get involved in the daily lives of their disciples in order to change their ways of life. For instance, Plato says in his *Seventh Letter*: "Whenever anyone consults me on a question of importance to his life, such as the making of money, or the care of his body or soul, if it appears to me that he follows some plan in his daily life or is willing to listen to reason on the matters he lays before me, I advise him gladly and don't stop at merely discharging my duty."[7] And, in the last book of the *Republic*, Plato affirms that what matters most is to seek the man who will give us both the power and the knowledge required to discern and choose the best way of life.[8] Epicurus, too, was a remarkable guide of conscience; in fact, in the Epicurian school, there existed a treatise written by Philodemus, entitled *On Frank Criticism*.[9] One would read in it that the master must strive to straighten the behavior of his disciple while also empathizing with his difficulties. What will cure the disciple is his courage in admitting errors and the truthfulness of the master, who will make the disciple understand the finality of his reprimands. Thus for the Epicurians, as well as for philosophers of other schools, there was a therapeutic value to words, whether in the avowal of errors, in dialogue, or in exhortation. We know of the famous *Letters* of Seneca to Lucilius, which correspond to a whole program of education for an adult. As for Marcus Aurelius, he says that his master Rusticus would strive to rectify the future emperor's character.

This practice of directing conscience is in fact linked to the realization of the difficulty involved in any choice of conduct or attitude in one's daily life. According to Philodemus, the master's truthfulness is a stochastic art—it is open ended, insofar as one has to take into account moments and circumstances. On their side, the Stoics greatly insisted on the fact that rationally justified choices could only *seem* right, since we do not know what the result of our action will really be.[10]

One could object to what we have said so far by arguing that Hilary Putnam, in speaking of the education for adults, has in mind specifically the self-education of an adult, while the direction of conscience in ancient thought represented a relation between unequal persons, the master and the disciple, the one who knows and the one who does not know.

This is true of the dogmatic philosophers, but Socrates himself, in proclaiming that he did not know anything, was putting forward a kind of relation in which, as Kierkegaard said, "To be a teacher in the right sense is to be a learner."[11] The Socrates of the *Theatetus*, in fact, pretends to be only a midwife, one who helps others to think and decide by themselves. As a matter of fact, antiquity was well aware of the idea of an education of the adult by himself. This self-education is found, for example, in the aphorisms of Marcus Aurelius that the manuscripts name *The Communings with Himself*.[12] This work is not, as has often been thought, a personal journal in which the emperor would relate his private impressions, but a work on himself. Such work consists in formulating the teachings of Stoicism to oneself in a personal and imaginative way, and thereby trying to transform oneself—to create another ethical attitude in order to restrain one's anger or fear of death, to find peace of mind, or to dispose oneself to act in the service of the human community. The *Exercises* of Shaftesbury will have the same finality.[13]

Nonetheless, in antiquity, education, or even the education of oneself by oneself, is conceived as the action of a superior on an inferior, of an adult on a child. Simplicius, for example, defines education in these terms: "Education is strictly speaking the correction of the child in us by the teacher in us."[14] He then explains that he means by this the education of our sensibility by our rational discourse. This idea of the "child who is in us" is inspired by the famous passage in the *Phaedo,* where a participant in the dialogue responds to Socrates: "Maybe there's a child inside us, who has fears of that sort. Try to persuade him, then, to stop being afraid of death, as if it were a bogey-man." To this, Socrates responds: "Well, you must sing spells to him every day, till you've charmed it out of him."[15] But, Socrates adds, to sing spells, there has to be a charmer, and a good one. It is thus finally this good charmer that we have to find. We are thus seeking not theoretical knowledge but a man who can charm us, that is, who has the power of transforming us internally. To Plato's eyes, who could this charmer be other than Socrates?

For Hilary Putnam (and Stanley Cavell, whom he cites), the notion of the "child in us" has a wholly different meaning. According to Stanley Cavell, the "child in us" represents not the irrational part of our being but, to the contrary, that in us which asks us questions and which puts into question what seems acquired, in the way a child can put into question that about which the adult is no longer asking himself any questions: "Why do we eat animals? or Why are some people poor and others rich? or What is God?" and so on.[16] It is finally this putting into question that is the starting point for philosophy, and to try to answer the child who is in us is to begin educating ourselves and thinking by ourselves. Such is, in Putnam's view, all the hope of philosophy: we all have the potentiality to think by ourselves regarding the question "How shall I live?"

There are two important notions in this phrase. First, the question "How shall I live?" appears as the most fundamental philosophical problem. Then, the possibility of thinking by ourselves is considered as a possibility that is inherent in us.

If the question "How shall I live?" is the paradigmatic philosophical problem, one must conclude that philosophy is precisely an education for adults because it is interesting to all persons in general and to each person in particular. This notion of an interest for reason immediately brings to mind the famous Kantian distinction between two concepts of philosophy, the type of philosophy that is of interest to specialists and that which is of interest to each person, a distinction that Hilary Putnam has had the great merit of bringing back to life.[17]

For Kant, the first concept, the type of philosophy that is of interest to specialists, is the "scholarly" or "scholastic type." It aims to realize a system of rational knowledge. The one who practices it is, as Kant says, an "artist of reason" or, as Kant also says, borrowing a statement from Plato in the *Republic* (480a6), a "philodox."[18] By this term, Plato wanted to designate the one who takes interest in the multitude of beautiful things, without taking interest in beauty in itself. For Plato, the philodox is not really a philosopher because he is not interested in the essential. Kant expresses this by saying that the philodox is ignorant of the relevance of knowledge to the ultimate goals of reason—that is, finally, the quest for wisdom and the good. That is why, in fact, the philodox is not really systematic since, staying within the scheme of pure theory and logical skill, he does not see that what unifies philosophy is the universally human interest that animates the whole of philosophical effort.

The philosophy in which each person is interested is what Kant calls the "cosmic" philosophy, that is, philosophy of the "world" as opposed to that of the "school." What each person is interested in is the question "How shall I live?" so it is one's conception of humanity's ultimate aim that, in Kant's eyes, is finally wisdom. The Idea of wisdom or, rather, the Idea of the ideal sage, is the foundation of philosophy. If the Idea of the ideal Sage has never been realized, it nonetheless is the case that all the laws that reason imposes on itself imply this idea. And Kant strongly emphasizes that it is the ancients who came closest to this model of philosophy. The relations that scholarly philosophy and cosmic philosophy bear to each other are, in Kant, complex. Scholarly philosophy has its usefulness. It teaches us to make better judgments. But scholarly philosophy, on its own, is not really philosophy. In fact, if philosophy begins with speculation, it must then elevate itself until it becomes reason's guide towards that which is most interesting to her, man's ultimate aim. One should, in fact, specify that the speculative philosophy that Kant himself practices is, in effect, a critique, which allows one to fix the limits of reason and will open the way to the "philosophy of the world." If it remains pure speculation, it degrades itself. For instance, Kant declares that Wolff, who for him incarnates the scholarly philosophy, was not properly a philosopher.[19] All interest is finally practical, and even that of speculative reason finally refers itself to practical usage. Hilary Putnam explicitly locates himself in the tradition of this Kantian distinction when he refuses to see in philosophy a purely technical discipline and considers as essential the question: "How shall I live?"

Putnam is again faithful to Kant when he identifies philosophy with the effort to think for oneself. "Thinking for oneself" was in fact the definition that Kant gave both of the *Aufklärung* and also of the activity of philosophizing. To think for oneself is precisely to become an adult, to put into question prejudices and trends, but also the imposing arguments of religions and philosophies. In defining the *Aufklärung* as the capacity to "think for oneself," Kant, in fact, effected a vindication of "popular philosophy" in eighteenth-century Germany.[20] They then glorified eclecticism, which they understood as a freedom to choose between the different opinions. Thinking for oneself was not rejecting all traditional culture but was either criticizing or personally assimilating this or that doctrine or attitude which seemed the best in the given circumstance. The philosophy of the Enlightenment was here the heiress of Cicero, himself a witness to the ideas of the Platonic school in the second century B.C.E.: The probabilistic Academy of Arcesilaus and of Carneades: "We, academicians, live for the passing day; we say whatever strikes our minds as probable; and so we alone are free. . . . We are more free and unshackled, because we retain intact our power to judge for ourselves, and are not forced by any compulsion to champion every maxim and almost every word of command which certain men have given us."[21]

If the child in us wants to become an adult, how will he dare to think by himself? We should recognize that this is possible only if he has the means to do it; if he has confidence in himself, that is, in his own rational discourse. He will perhaps not be able to answer questions by himself. He will then perhaps actualize old responses, but having made them his own.

"The most important revolution in the inner life of a human being is 'his exit from his self-incurred immaturity.' Before this he let others think for him . . . Now he ventures to advance, though still shakily, with his own feet on the ground of experience."[22] In saying this in his *Anthropology from a Pragmatic Point of View*, Kant identifies the *Aufklärung* with the maturity of the mind, and he defines this adult kind of thought in three maxims: to think for oneself, to think in place of others (when communicating with others), and at all times, to think in accordance [*einstimmung*] with oneself;[23] these are three maxims, the practice of which, according to another passage in the *Anthropology*, bring one to be the author of one's own wisdom.

The first maxim finally corresponds to this Socratic mind that we already alluded to. Knowledge does not consist in already made formulas that get transferred from the master to the disciple. The master must teach the disciple how to think by himself. The second maxim seems to us to be crucial. It completes and, in a way, corrects the first one. One could in fact worry that thinking for oneself only consists in affirming one's individual point of view. But one must also put oneself in the place of others. Kant says that the second maxim is that of liberal thought, "which adjusts itself to the concepts of others."[24] This attitude consists in recognizing that others also have the right to think by themselves and to think in a way different from ours. If we judge that they are not thinking "in accordance with themselves"—that is, according to Kant, in a logical manner—what will prevent us from expressing our opinion to them and trying to rectify their judgment? One could say that this is about liberalism and tolerance. But these maxims, especially the very crucial second one, will perhaps not suffice for getting one to perceive the "internal revolution" that this attitude represents. For to have real maturity is to be capable of putting oneself in the place of others; it is not only to respect them, it is to free oneself of one's own point of view which is always partial and incomplete; to come to situate oneself in the perspective of the other and to understand the reasons why the other can think otherwise than oneself. To put oneself in the place of others is, finally, to place oneself at the universal point of view represented by rational discourse. It is therefore to detach oneself from oneself to attain objectivity, impartiality, and justice. It is to know how to engage in dialogue while respecting the other's point of view.

We could also wonder whether to put oneself in the place of others is not only to place oneself in the perspective of what is of interest to every man—it is, as we have seen, the point of view of cosmic philosophy. But perhaps it is also to place oneself, through thinking for oneself, in a universal perspective—we are here thinking of the following formulation of the categorical imperative: I am to act "so that I could also will that my maxim should become a universal law."[25]

This concept of universality seems very important. We could say, it seems, that to educate oneself, to become an adult, is to "universalize" oneself, at the same time putting oneself in the place of others, but also, perhaps, resituating oneself in the universe. Kant himself recognizes the following as two constituents of the consciousness of human existence: the starry sky above us and the moral law within us. Is the education of adults only a moral education, or is it not also a radical change in our way of seeing the world?

These reflections on the definition of philosophy proposed by Hilary Putnam aim to show how the originality and modernity of his thought allow him to give a new youthfulness to the ancient tradition of a kind of philosophy that gives meaning to our lives.[26]

PIERRE HADOT

COLLEGE DE FRANCE
NOVEMBER 2002

NOTES

1. Hilary Putnam, "An Interview with Professor Hilary Putnam: The Vision and Argument of a Famous Harvard Philosopher," *Cogito* 3 (1989): 90; reprinted in *Key Philosophers in Conversation: The Cogito Interviews,* ed. Andrew Pyle (London and New York: Routledge, 1999), 52.

2. Simplicius, *Commentary on Epictetus,* xxxii. [This is Hadot's translation of Simplicius. Rather than cite the standard English translation, which does not carry the full sense of Hadot's point, we refer the reader to Pierre Hadot, *What is Ancient Philosophy?* Trans. Michael Chase (Cambridge, MA: Harvard University Press, 2002), xiii.—*Eds.*]

3. Epictetus, *Discourses,* III, 21.

4. Plato, *Apology,* 29d–e.

5. Friedrich Nietzsche, *Untimely Meditations,* ed. Daniel Breazeale, trans. R.J. Hollingdale (Cambridge: Cambridge University Press, 1997), 154–55.

6. Aristotle, *Nicomachean Ethics,* X, 1177b27 in *Complete Works of Aristotle: The Revised Oxford Translation* vol. 2, ed. J. Barnes (Princeton, NJ: Princeton University Press, 1983).

7. Plato, *Seventh Letter,* 331a–b in *Plato: The Complete Works,* ed. John M. Cooper (Indianapolis: Hackett, 1997).

8. Plato, *Republic,* 618c.

9. On this treatise, see M. Gigante, *"Philodeme, Sur la liberte de parole,"* Actes du VIIIe Congres de l'Association Guillaume Bude (1968) (Paris: Belles Lettres, 1970), 196–220.

10. On this theme, see Pierre Hadot, *The Inner Citadel: The Meditations of Marcus Aurelius,* 2nd ed., trans. Micheal Chase (Cambridge, MA: Harvard University Press, 2nd ed. 2001), 190–93.

11. Søren Kierkegaard, *The Point of View for My Work as an Author,* trans. Walter Lowrie (New York: Harper & Brothers, 1962), 29.

12. See Marcus Aurelius, *Meditations.*

13. Hadot is here referring to the works of Webster Edgerly (1852–1926) who, under the pseudonym "Edmund Shaftesbury," penned over 100 books on various techniques in self-cultivation—*Eds.*

14. Simplicius, *On Epictetus' "Handbook 1–26,"* trans. Charles Brittain and Tad Brennan (Ithaca, NY: Cornell University Press, 2002), 74.

15. Plato, *Phaedo,* 77e.

16. Stanley Cavell, *The Claim of Reason: Wittgenstein, Skepticism, Morality, and Tragedy* (Oxford: Clarendon, 1979), 125.

17. James Conant, Introduction to *Realism with a Human Face,* by Hilary Putnam, ed. James Conant (Cambridge, MA: Harvard University Press, 1990).

18. Immanuel Kant, *Lectures on Logic,* ed. J. Michael Young (Cambridge: Cambridge University Press, 2004), 259.

19. Immanuel Kant, *Lessons on the Philosophical Encyclopedia* in *Kant's gesammelte Schriften,* vol. 29 (Berlin: Walter de Gruyter, 1980), 8: *"Der Philosoph ist ein Künstler, wenn er Kenntnisse von allen Sachen hat. Wolff war ein speculativer, aber nicht ein architectonischer Philosoph und Führer der Vernunft. Er war eigentlich gar kein Philosoph, sondern ein grosser Künstler vor die Wissbegierde der Menschen so wie es noch viele sind."* Thanks to Professor Steve Naragon for aid in locating this quotation.

20. See Helmut Holzhey, "Der Philosoph für die Welt—eine Chimäre der deutschen Aufklärung?" in *Esoteric und Exoteric der Philosophie,* ed. H. Holzhey and W. C. Zimmerli (Basel/Stuttgart: Schwabe & Co. Verlag, 1977), 133.

21. Cicero *Tusculan Disputations,* V, 11, 33; *Lucullus,* 3, 8.

22. Immanuel Kant, *Anthropology From a Pragmatic Point of View,* trans. Robert B. Louden in Kant, *Anthropology, History, and Education,* ed. Günter Zöller and Robert B. Louden (Cambridge: Cambridge University Press, 2007), 333/7:229. [Some translations have been slightly modified to accord with Hadot's text.—*Eds.*]

23. Ibid., 308/7:200

24. Ibid., 333/7:228

25. Immanuel Kant, *Groundwork to the Metaphysics of Morals* in *Practical Philosophy,* ed. Mary J. Gregor (Cambridge: Cambridge University Press, 1996), 57/4:402.

26. I am very grateful to Sandra Laugier, for encouraging me to write this essay and for her help and advice regarding Hilary Putnam's work. Many thanks, too, to Arpy Khatchirian and Sandra Laugier for their work on the English version of it.

REPLY TO PIERRE HADOT

To say that I am pleased by what Pierre Hadot wrote for this volume would be carrying understatement to excess; his essay is a great compliment, and I must begin by expressing my heartfelt gratitude. I am grateful not only for the beautiful words that he has written here, but above all for the fact that *this person* wrote them. Pierre Hadot was one of the giants among scholars of ancient philosophy, but more than that, he was a scholar whose *vision* of ancient philosophy as nothing less than a spiritually demanding and spiritually valuable way of life, has been an influence on my own thinking since 1995, when my former student and good friend Arnold Davidson published a selection of translations of writings by Hadot under the title *Philosophy as a Way of Life: Spiritual Exercises from Socrates to Foucault.*[1] I have had students in more than one class whose topic might have seemed far from "ancient philosophy" (including two seminars on Wittgenstein's *Philosophical Investigations*) read substantial sections from that collection of Hadot's writings, because those classes dealt with philosophers who also (or so it seemed to me) saw philosophy as a way of life in the way Hadot describes. That is why I am *so* pleased to find myself becoming the subject of an essay by Hadot on precisely this topic.

To repeat, I admire and have been deeply influenced by Pierre Hadot's conception of "philosophy as a way of life." At the same time, much of my thinking, for many years now, has concerned the foundations of quantum mechanics (much more than one might guess from my nine publications on the subject), as well as the obviously "technical" subjects of philosophy of mathematics and the interpretation of Einstein's General Theory of Relativity. Currently I am also deeply involved with different theories of the nature of *perception*: theories with abstruse names such as "intentionalism," "representationalism," "disquotationalism," and "phenomenism." How can my interest in these scientific (or at least scientifically informed) questions be any part of the conception that Hadot describes as "philosophy as a way of life"? It seems appropriate to devote this reply to Hadot to some thoughts on that question.

I have remarked in more than one place that philosophy needs both a technical side, a side that requires rigorous arguments, and a less technical side, a side that seeks to inspire us to live more fulfilling lives, but not necessarily by offering the sorts of arguments that can be formalized (although the choice of examples by a great moral philosopher can itself represent a form of argument). Without the technical side, philosophy risks becoming homiletics; without the inspirational side, it risks falling prey to the illusion that philosophy can and should become a science. (Moreover, the idea that the inspirational side should disappear today reflects a noncognitivism with respect to values that seems to me bad philosophy, an intellectual mistake.)

That inspiration which cannot be supported by arguments risks becoming *mere* homiletics does not mean that moral insights should or could always be supported by textbook linear arguments. Paul Grice remarked years ago that, for example, rhetoric is a rational form of argument when its function is to get someone to see the *appeal* of a proposed way of life.[2] (If you cannot even understand why anyone would *want* to live that way, you cannot rationally discuss the issue.) Examples, including examples from literature, may be essential to coming to appreciate moral issues (and the "literature" in question may itself be works by philosophers.) In this generous sense of "argument," I do not think it can be denied that even when philosophy seeks to inspire, it also needs arguments. But why did I describe the idea that philosophy can and should become a science (an idea closely identified with "positivism," both in the nineteenth- and the twentieth-century senses of that term) as an "illusion"?

By so describing it, I did not mean to say that philosophy has not in the past and may not in the future contribute to science itself, in a demanding sense of the term "science." When I think about what a reasonable realist interpretation of quantum mechanics might look like, I am thinking about a question about which a number of physicists are also thinking, as well as a number of philosophers and even some mathematicians. And we talk to each other in a common language, and no sharp lines separate our approaches. But the "technical" side of philosophy is not restricted to questions which can also be addressed by scientists qua scientists. (If it were, and if nontechnical philosophy were dismissed as "nonsense," as Carnap and the logical positivists hoped, there would be no justification for the continued existence of philosophy departments.) Trying to construct realist interpretations of quantum mechanics is a scientific task, but arguing that one *should* be a realist in one's philosophy of physics is a task for philosophers (dare I say, for metaphysicians?). And it is, I think, pretty clear that there is not going to be in the foreseeable future any universal agreement on whether one should be a realist in one's philosophy of *mathematics*. In spite of all the attempts to convict metaphysics of being "cognitively meaningless" (or, as the New Wittgensteinians would say, "nonsense" in the literal sense of the term[3]), metaphysical questions do continue to concern us, they will not go away, and to think about them as responsibly and deeply as one can is a part of what Wilfrid Sellars so aptly described as trying to figure out "how things in the broadest possible sense of the term hang together in the broadest possible sense of the term."

If I reject the idea that metaphysics is "cognitively meaningless," it is because, as I wrote many years ago, the idea that it is depends on the claim that philosophers can discover deep truths about language (in this case, about what is and is not "meaningful") that are inaccessible to linguists and to ordinary speakers, and that claim is, on the face of it, a silly one. No doubt philosophers sometimes talk "nonsense" in the sense of saying things that are highly unreasonable, but showing that is a task for other philosophers. The idea of a "metaphilosophy" before which philosophers can be brought to trial to determine whether or not they are "talking nonsense" is a deeply mistaken one (one that I was tempted by for a period of time).

The logical positivists, however, did not only rely on the Verifiability Theory of Meaning to attack metaphysics. Carnap often complained that it led to disputes which are "interminable." When I said, above, that there is not going to be any universal agreement on whether one should be a realist in one's philosophy of mathematics in the foreseeable future, was I not agreeing that this metaphysical question (one about which I have thought almost all my life) is part of an "interminable" dispute? Yes. But what is wrong with saying that some of the questions of the greatest importance (for example, how to live) *are not* questions about which there is going to be universal agreement?

An analogy may be helpful here. One of the things Kant tells us in *The Critique of Judgment*—something which is remarkably little discussed by Kant scholars!—is that it is part of the *value* of art that it provokes interminable discussion. At least that is how I understand him when he writes that "we add to a concept a representation of the imagination that belongs to its presentation, but which *by itself stimulates so much thinking that it can never be grasped in a determinate concept*, hence which aesthetically enlarges the concept itself in an unbounded way . . . in this case the imagination is creative, and sets the faculty of intellectual ideas (reason) into motion."[4] In sum, "interminable discussions" are among the most spiritually valuable and the most characteristically human.

Still, the question I said I would address is: "How can philosophy have two sides?" I have said that it *does* have two sides, but what is their connection? That there *is* a connection is suggested by the fact that philosophy, since as far back as Plato, has concerned itself both with the question of how to live and the question of how to think about the peculiar objectivity and immateriality of mathematical truth. But why?

I am not sure of the answer (how could one be "sure" of any answer to a question about the nature of philosophical reflection itself?), but here are two answers: one which is clearly an oversimplification, and a second which tries to do justice to the complexity of our thinking and feeling.

The oversimplified answer is that, at least at the present time, metaphysical positions tend to lead to broad if somewhat indeterminate ethical positions. Thus "hard" materialists (philosophers who are proud of calling themselves "materialists" or "physicalists," philosophers who think nothing can be called "knowledge" unless it can also be called "science"—think of Quine's saying "philosophy of science is philosophy enough"—or, hyper-reductionist naturalists) are typically noncognitivists in ethics, and, at the same time, are often utilitarians in terms of how they prefer that we actually evaluate our conduct; antireductionist naturalists and nonnaturalists are typically cognitivists in ethics, and typically regard utilitarianism as a dangerously oversimplified answer to our moral dilemmas. Because the objectivity and immateriality of mathematics has always posed a problem for materialists, it is not surprising that it becomes an object of controversy, and that the different attitudes just described divide the two outlooks just mentioned (and already divided them in Plato's day, although both the materialism and the antimaterialism of his time were, naturally, different from the materialism and the antimaterialism of our own time).

The reason I describe this as an oversimplified answer is that it misses an important function of good philosophy, which is to try to break down our rigid dichotomies and to show us that there are more options than those dichotomies suggest. Thus a good philosopher may well try to show that one can be a hard materialist *and* a cognitivist in ethics at the same time, or that one can be an antireductionist naturalist and an expressivist in ethics, or that one can be a physicalist and a realist in one's philosophy of mathematics. This is not to deny that there are the two camps described in the oversimplified answer, but to say that one is not forced to choose sides in the way they suggest. But what remains the case is that any philosopher who shares the Sellarsian holistic aspiration I described will try to unify her reflective commitments; to bring her world view and her evaluations into harmony. From the point of view of that aspiration—which is my own, I confess—philosophy aims at nothing less than a *Weltanschauung* worthy of the name. And seeking such a *Weltanschauung* is itself an ethical obligation, both for me and as it was, I believe, for Sellars himself, as it is also for Stanley Cavell, whose definition of philosophy as "education for grownups" is my favorite definition of the subject (as Hadot points out). It is not, then, that I see philosophy as *just* "having two sides," both of which I *happen* to be interested in; I see the "technical side" as simply the form that the metaphysical impulse takes in me because I live in an age of science, and thinking about metaphysical questions without understanding science generally leads to superficiality or fantasy or both; and I see the concern with the good life as *including* the concern for metaphysical understanding.

H.P.

NOTES

1. Pierre Hadot, *Philosophy as a Way of Life: Spiritual Exercises from Socrates to Foucault*, ed. and trans. Arnold Davidson (Oxford: Blackwell, 1995).

2. I describe hearing Grice say this in a seminar in "Literature, Science and Reflection," in Putnam, *Meaning and the Moral Sciences* (London: Routledge, 1978), 86: "'rhetoric' need not be a mere propaganda device, as it is generally viewed, but may be a legitimate instrument for the purpose of getting someone to imagine vividly what it would be like to live one way rather than another, or at least it may be a way of getting him or her to see vividly what the appeal of one morality is as opposed to the appeal of another."

3. See *The New Wittgenstein*, ed. Alice Crary and Rupert Read (New York: Routledge, 2000).

4. Immanuel Kant, *Critique of the Power of Judgment*, trans. Paul Guyer and Eric Mathews (Cambridge: Cambridge University Press, 2001), §49, 5:315 [emphasis added].

19

John Haldane

PHILOSOPHY, CAUSALITY, AND GOD

I

Some years ago, in a critical study of two books by Hilary Putnam I suggested that the widespread tendency to partition his thought into various stages and phases, as marked by the holding of certain theories or positions, and then to emphasize differences between these commitments, seriously misrepresents the character of his philosophical work and reveals a certain superficiality in thinking about the complex nature of philosophical inquiry.[1] By way of a corrective I proposed the analogy of the career of an artist who might well go through various stages, pursuing different thematic interests and methods of exploration, but whose work nonetheless exhibits a unity of sensibility, conception, and execution. Here differences are more likely to be seen in terms of continuities, for example, as diverse approaches to a common subject or theme.

It may have occurred to some readers that whatever might be true about the description of an artistic career, the analogy is ill chosen for the purpose of evaluating the work of a philosopher and that a better comparison would be with the thought and writings of a scientist. One reason for thinking this is that science *per se*, is a form of intellectual activity directed towards the discovery of truth, and towards the incorporation of limited truths regarding specifics into more general and comprehensive accounts. This too, it is presumed, is the business of the philosopher. By contrast, the artist is concerned with aesthetic ends, and to the extent that integration is an issue for him or her, then the relevant norm is one of aesthetic coherence rather than of logical consistency.

This countersuggestion, however, invites several replies. First, why assume that art is not also interested in truth, or that to the extent that some artists and works may have this interest it can only be *per accidens* and additional to their *per se* aesthetic ends? Equally, why suppose that science and philosophy do not share in aesthetic ends (or moral ones), or, that to the extent that particular scientists or philosophers are concerned with these, then this can only be *per accidens*?

Hilary Putnam is not alone in having attacked the fact/value dichotomy by showing the inextricable entanglement of the descriptive and the evaluative, but he has focused specifically on the case of systematic empirical inquiry. Putnam has shown that scientists qua scientists are concerned with and regulated by values, that truth and truthfulness are interconnected. Moreover, he has shown that the general point of engaging in science, as contrasted with the immediate goal of particular enquiries, is related to an understanding of human flourishing—not as benefitting from the technological application of scientific discoveries but as a form of the actualization of the human power of, and need for, understanding.

There is a further point, and again it is one that Putnam is alert to, namely, the tendency to treat philosophy as a form of scientific inquiry. This was a feature of philosophy in the period in which he first studied it, influenced by the logical positivists who had escaped from Germany and Austria to North America; but while it persisted in somewhat more muted form through Quine's strictures against "first philosophy," the influence of conceptual analysis and ordinary language philosophy (limited as that was in the U.S.) provided some counter to philosophy's scientific self-image. More recently, however, the philosophy-as-science conception has been re-ascendant, particularly in the areas of philosophy of mind and language. In consequence, certain assumptions have become prevalent (if not dominant): first, that the categorical form of philosophical articulation is theoretical; second, that philosophy has a vocabulary of preferred, specialized terms; and third, that the meanings of these are univocal.

So we find: "cause," "condition," "context," "event," "process," "regularity," "relation," "physical," "psychological," "thought," "action," and so on, either taken as terms of art or defined as such. It is also supposed, however, that these meanings are ones that could hold their place within broadly scientific discourse. In the background, and increasingly in the foreground also, are certain ontological presuppositions and one does not have to look hard to see that these are inspired by science, or by what philosophers presume science favors. One mark of this renaissance of "scientific philosophy" is that whereas it used to be assumed (under the influence of Frege, Russell,

Quine, Strawson, and Geach) that the test of ontological admissibility was adequate criteria of identity and individuation (a topic neutral criterion), it is now often assumed that "entities" are only admissible if they can pull their weight in causal explanations, understood in scientific-theoretic terms. This results in the problem of "queerness" for values, minds, and other nonscientific realities.

Returning briefly to the characterization of Putnam's philosophical career seen from the perspective of scientific philosophy, two things will appear dominant: first, his record of rejecting theories or positions he himself proposed or advocated (scientific realism, metaphysical realism, internal realism, functionalism); and second, his rejection of the assumptions mentioned above: the theoretical nature of philosophy, the propriety of privileged and univocal terminology, and the scientific criteria for existence, truth, and intelligibility. In fact, Putnam's reflections on realism (or better "realisms") are largely continuous, taking the form of a dialectical inquiry in which positions are opposed in the service of proceeding to some more satisfactory synthesis, which in turn is tested by being confronted with a contrary or contradictory thesis. I see this not as an expression of contrarianism or restlessness but as a method of inquiry or clarification, and I see the goal of this as *understanding*.

In choosing *understanding* over *truth* I do not mean to suggest that Putnam rejects truth in the style of certain kinds of conceptual relativism or nihilism, nor that, to recall the artist analogy, he prefers some aesthetic end. Rather I have it in mind: first, that what truth amounts to may vary according to the nature of an inquiry (be it scientific, ethical, political, prudential, and so on); second, that what is attained of truth is likely to be partial and conditioned; but third, that what makes truth interesting is that it contributes to understanding. It is common to hear it said that "belief is for the sake of truth," but one should add, I think, that truth is for the sake of belief. This is not to reduce truth to what is believed but only to say that making sense of the value of truth, or better of truth as a value, requires seeing it as answering to a desire for understanding.

The point of the artist analogy was not to substitute one account of the essence of philosophy (as quasi-aesthetic) for another (as quasi-scientific) but a) to pick up features that are common in the career of an artist as he or she explores their themes: trying first one approach then another, developing, refining, and sometimes setting aside certain possibilities, all in search of more satisfactory, because more "true," renderings; and b) to say that these are applicable within philosophical practice and provide a more illuminating, and substantively more appropriate, account of Putnam's philosophical career than does the scientific paradigm. In fact, I do not believe that philosophy has an essence, or not a single one. In general philosophy is, I suggest, an incomplete expression: "_____ philosophy" or "philosophy as _____" where the qualifier spaces are filled by reference to a dominant set of ends and to methods deemed appropriate to the attainment of those ends. While I have no view about how many such completions there might be, one can identify from the history of "philosophy" (now treated as a collective term) four broad categories: *scientific philosophy,* or *philosophy as science*; *artistic philosophy,* or *philosophy as art*; *religious philosophy,* or *philosophy as religion*; and *political philosophy,* or *philosophy as politics.*[2] In the work of an individual, and particularly in the work of the greatest philosophers, most of these often tend to appear intermingled. So for example, Plato's *Republic* involves artistic and political philosophy, and overall Plato pursues all four forms. Again, Kant exemplifies all four.

There is no point in asking which has priority *per se*, for that presumes the idea of a unitary essence which is what my suggestion is intended to combat. Nonetheless I think there is a sense in which whatever mode or form is being practiced, certain issues are either addressed or presumed, issues which one might term *metaphysical*. These include the status of nature and of artifacts, the distinction between reality and appearance, the nature of and relation between persons and social institutions, and the contrast between the divine and the domain of things. Diverse as these may be (and of course it is a philosophical question whether and to what extent they are diverse), there is a concept or family of such that is central to their characterization, affirmation, or elimination; namely that of *causation*. Interestingly this is one that has featured importantly in Putnam's work and which has been implicated in his rejection of certain theories and in his embrace of a pragmatic, realist perspective.

II

There is an interesting trajectory to be traced through Putnam's writings following his discussions of causation and its place in understanding certain issues. In recent decades, the entry point was consideration of a line of reply to his criticism of metaphysical realism as it featured in accounts of the relationship between words and their referents (in cases where referents are at issue). Richard Boyd, Michael Devitt, Jerry Fodor, Clark Glymour, David Lewis, and others had suggested that the reference relation might be determined, fixed, or constituted by causal relations understood either directly or via some notion of counterfactual dependence between the use of a term by a speaker on an occasion and some part of the external world. To this Putnam replied in "Is the Causal Structure of the Physical Itself Something Physical?" One part of his argument is familiar from earlier writings, namely the claim that the world is not self-classifying or self-individuating—there are no elite substances or classes of entities. The other part, however, is what gets the greater emphasis and has developed in later writings into an important positive view. He writes:

> Which is "the cause" and which a "background condition" depends on a *picking out*, an act of *selection*, which depends on what we know and can use in prediction; and this is not written into the physical system itself

> . . . Like counterfactuals, causal statements depend on what we regard as a "normal" state of affairs, what we regard as a state of affairs "similar" to the actual, and so on.

> . . . The causal structure of the world is not physical in the sense of being built into what we conceive of as physical reality. But that doesn't mean that it is pasted onto physical reality by the mind. It means, rather, that "physical reality" *and* "mind" are both abstractions from a world in which things having dispositions, causing one another, having modal properties, are simply matters of course. Like all matters of course, causality can be seen as either the most banal or the most mysterious thing in the world. As is so often the case, each of these ways of seeing it contains a profound insight.[3]

In his 1990 Gifford Lectures published as *Renewing Philosophy*, Putnam developed the theme of the interest- and context-relativity of counterfactuals in response to Fodor's causal theory of reference.[4] Then in Putnam's 1994 John Dewey Lectures, "Sense, Nonsense and the Senses," he deployed similar arguments against Kim's use of counterfactuals in his would be refutation of Davidson's anomalous monism.[5] Kim's contention was that for Davidson mentality *per se* is inefficacious; hence, if mental properties were to be redistributed over physical events, or removed from them, the same network of causal relations would remain, thus counterfactuals expressing these possibilities would be true. Putnam's defense of Davidson is not intended to substantiate anomalous monism but only to show (again) that the evaluation of counterfactuals is subject to a requirement of intelligibility, which is ultimately a matter of our making sense of certain possibilities, and that is not (wholly) determined by the world itself.

Here, however, his discussion goes further towards developing a view (though not a *theory*) of causation. Rather generously he refers approvingly to me as having suggested "that there are as many kinds of cause as there are senses of 'because.' (He [Haldane] added that 'Aristotle's doctrine of four causes was only a preliminary classification.')"[6] Putnam repeats this attribution later in a "first afterword" adding,

But there are a number of ways of understanding this claim. One of them, which I found attractive until quite recently, would be to say that the notion of explanation has priority over the notion of causation. But this formulation now seems to me as wrong as its "opposite," that is, as wrong as the idea that the notion of causation (understood as something that is simply *independent* of our various explanatory practices) has priority over the notion of explanation. The notions of explanation and causation presuppose one another at every point; neither has "priority" in the sense of being reducible to the other.[7]

The remainder of the afterword elaborates on this "no priority" claim and in the course of it he discusses Anscombe, Lewis, and Hume, before in conclusion again quoting and commenting briefly on my "saying." He writes:

> I have explained why that [Haldane's saying] must not be understood as meaning that the notion of explanation has priority over the notion of causation . . . . Nor should Haldane's saying be taken as a claiming or presupposing that the different senses of *because* are literally different *meanings* of the word. . . . I propose to take Haldane's pregnant remark in the following way: what he speaks of as "senses of 'because'" I propose to take as our ever expanding repertoire of explanatory practices.[8]

Here I want to respond briefly to Putnam's qualifications and interpretations, but also (in the next section) to make good on the suggestion that Aristotle's four-cause taxonomy is not exhaustive.

First, then, as regards the matter of priority. The original cue for my remarks was, I think, a passage in Aquinas's *Commentary on Aristotle's Metaphysics* where he notes that "the question, why? seeks a cause."[9] I had then been concerned to apply the point to certain issues in the philosophy of mind. One such was in the context of a debate with Paul Churchland about the explanation of action where I argued that "the analysis of action explanation might be advanced by ditching the Hume/Mill/Davidson view of causation and exploring the possibility of working with a more pluralistic ontology [of causes] including properly rational causes."[10] I then aimed to show how a variety of distinct kinds of cause are implicated in action descriptions, interpretations, and explanations as they arise in connection with certain *why*, *how*, and *what* questions. Later I tried to demonstrate that issues concerning the intentionality of thought and the efficacy of mind could best be resolved by invoking notions of formal and final causality.[11] In this I was thinking both conceptually and ontologically, by which I mean that I was proposing an analysis of the character of certain kinds of (true) descriptions and explanations (I do not regard these as altogether distinct categories), and proposing that they were made true by irreducible features of reality.

One traditional way of interpreting this would be in terms of the distinction between the *ordo cognoscendi* (the order of knowledge) and the *ordo essendi* (the order of being), which stand in opposed priority: thus holding that explanations are epistemically or conceptually prior but that causes are ontologically prior. Putnam's concern, however, seems only to be with the issue of conceptual interdependence, as can be seen above when he writes that "the notions of explanation and causation presuppose one another at every point; neither has "priority" in the sense of being reducible to the other." In the context of his broader pragmatic realist view, however, one might interpret this as saying that neither notion has conceptual priority, and since there is no priority between the conceptual and the real, neither has ontological priority. I suspect that this is Putnam's view, though I doubt that he would wish to express it that way. In any event I want to take something else he says, conjoined with his commendation of Anscombe's argument against Hume on the matter of observing causes, to provide a reconciliation between his thesis of no priority between notions of causation and explanation, and the view that in some sense causes are ontologically prior to explanations.

In "Is the Causal Structure of the Physical Itself Physical?" he wrote, "'physical reality' *and* 'mind' are both abstractions from a world in which things having dispositions, causing one another, having modal properties, are simply matters of course." Perhaps this should be read as uttered from within the context of pragmatic realism in which case dispositions, causings, and modal properties are not treated as existing prior to certain kinds of descriptions and explanations. There is, though, another possibility. What Putnam applauds in Anscombe's "Causality and Determination" (her 1971 Cambridge Inaugural Professorial Lecture)[12] is her rejoinder to Hume's contention that we can never observe causality in the individual case. This comes in two parts. First, she notes that by Hume's own account of what we can observe neither do we perceive bodies in motion, hence we cannot observe constant conjunctions of such bodies and thus his analysis of causation in terms of such observations collapses. Second, having discharged his epistemological premise by implied reductio, Anscombe proceeds to say how we do form the concept of causality on the basis of observation. She writes,

> In learning to speak we learned the linguistic representation of and application of a host of causal concepts. Very many of them were represented by transitive and other verbs of action used in reporting what is observed. Others—a good example is "infect" —form, not observation statements, but rather expressions of causal hypotheses. The word "cause" itself is highly general. How does someone show that he has the concept cause? We wish to say: only by having such a word in his vocabulary. If so, then the manifest possession of

the concept presupposes the mastery of much else in language. I mean: the word "cause" can be *added* to a language in which are already represented many causal concepts. A small selection: *scrape, push, wet, eat, burn* . . . . But if we care to imagine languages in which no special causal concepts are represented, then no description of the use of a word in such a language will be able to present it as meaning *cause*.[13]

Two points here. First, although she does not say so, Anscombe is exclusively concerned with efficient causation, but I suggest that a similar treatment can be given for notions of form, matter, and finality. Thus consider *shape, structure, composition, flesh, metal, liquid, purpose, aim, goal,* and so on, as lower concepts relative to the purely abstract concepts of "formal cause," "material cause," and "final cause." Second, recalling Putnam's remark about a world of things having dispositions and causing one another, one might conjecture the following: the noun expressions "cause," "causality," and "causal condition," used as abstract general terms as they are in philosophical and theoretical contexts, are conceptually on a par and interdependent with certain kinds of descriptive and explanatory forms (and *a fortiori* expressions such as "efficient cause," "material cause," "formal cause," and "final cause"). This, however, leaves open the question of the relationship between a) the specific features and objects from the concepts of which the foregoing higher level notions are abstracted, and b) the kinds of questions and answers in which reference is made to those features. In short, while the notions of causation and explanation may presuppose one another, *both* presuppose specific natures at work in the world, at least some of which are antecedent to human thought and interests. (I write "some of which" because among the things that are explained are artifacts designed in accord with human designs and purposes.) This touches on the question of realism more broadly and that is a large issue that I will not pursue further here, having engaged Putnam's thoughts on it elsewhere.[14]

Next, then, the issue of whether in saying that there are as many kinds of cause as there are senses of "because" I meant to suggest that there are literally many different meanings of the word corresponding to these various senses, or whether, as Putnam interprets it, I would be content to relate the variety to different explanatory practices in which the same word (presumably with the same meaning) is used. Given what has been said by both of us this issue could equally well be raised in relation to the word "cause" and it will be clearer, I think, if I develop my position in relation to that, though equivalent points could be formulated (somewhat more elaborately) with regard to "because."

Accordingly, one way of phrasing the implied question is this: do the various senses of "cause" correspond to one or many meanings? Put like that a dilemma immediately suggests itself. If they are held to correspond to a single meaning, what is to be made of there being several senses of "because" and correspondingly several different kinds of cause? One could relocate plurality at the level of varieties within a single species but in that case it would be misleading to speak of different kinds of causes, and certainly I had something more radical in mind. On the other hand, if one says there really are quite different kinds of cause (not just a diversity within a single kind) and that the expressions naming or describing these have different senses, then it looks as if equivocation threatens. If "cause" in "formal cause," "material cause," "efficient cause," and so on, each has a different meaning, then in what sense can these be said to be different kinds of *cause*? There would be no more reason to do so than to say that the bark of a tree and the bark of a dog are different kinds of *bark*.

My answer, perhaps unsurprisingly, is that we do not have to choose between univocality and equivocality with regard to "cause" since there is also analogicality, that is to say, related but not identical meanings. Earlier I suggested that "philosophy" is an incomplete expression best represented as "_____ philosophy," where what fills the gap determines the nature of the activity. At the same time the common part "philosophy" indicates forms of intelligible connectedness (not just association or extrinsic conjunction) between the various activities. Although causality is widely debated in contemporary Anglo-American philosophy (with discussions ranging far and wide over the relative merits of nominalist as against realist accounts, of conceptual as against empirical approaches, and of regularity, power-based and singularist understandings) it is hardly ever considered whether "cause" is a univocal or an analogical notion and term.

That "cause" is univocal tends to be presumed because of the assumption that all causality is efficient—a case of one thing, event, property instance, and so on, bringing about another—whether as an instance of a nomological generalization, as the expression of active and passive powers, or "free-standingly." According to Aristotelian and Thomistic thought, however, "cause" is an incomplete term whose proper completion distributes it across a range of analogically related notions. It is good to ask what connects these. In "Causality and Determination," Anscombe claimed to have identified this. She wrote: "There is something to observe here, that lies under our noses. It is little attended to, and yet still so obvious as to seem trite. It is this: causality consists in the derivativeness of an effect from its causes. This is the core, the common feature, of causality in its various kinds. Effects derive from, arise out of, come of, their causes."[15]

Given that her essay is rightly highly regarded, has several times been anthologized, and is often cited, it is suprising that this quite major claim, be it in embryonic form, has not received more discussion. Indeed it has barely received any.[16] In that respect it compares very badly with her suggestion in "Modern Moral Philosophy" that ethical theories from Sidgwick to Hare were essentially "consequentialist," or her idea in "The First Person" that "I" is not a referring expression. Certainly her suggestion as to the core of causality deserves consideration, but two points can be noted in passing. First, as previously mentioned, she seems to consider only efficient causation, so the unity in question may be that of what I termed "variations within a single kind" rather than across species (though how these distinctions might be drawn, and whether they should be thought of as strict and invariable is itself a subtle issue). Second, and allowing the restriction to efficiency, one might wonder whether the notion of causality will not have to be reintroduced to distinguish among different forms of derivation. Much the same point might be noted with regard to an account of the common core of causality as *making*: either making to be *simpliciter* (creation), or making to be such and such. I do not have an account of what binds the various uses of "cause," but I hold fast to the idea that analogy is the key to holding together a) the diverse senses of *cause* and *because*, b) the recognition that these may all be literal in primary usage, and c) that these senses and/or uses are not equivocal. At this point then, I turn directly to the issue of the variety of kinds of causes and to the development of the suggestion that Aristotle's doctrine of four causes was only a "preliminary classification."

III

In *Physics*, II, 3, Aristotle writes that cause is spoken of in four ways: first, as referring to that out of which something comes to be and is constituted; second, as the structure, pattern or recipe of something; third, as a source of change; and fourth, as that for the sake of which something occurs or is done. Of this fourfold account (*material, formal, efficient, final*) he then says that it is "a sufficient determination of the number and kinds of cause."[17] Given the previous suggestion, however, about causality as *making* (making to be, or making to be such and such) it is clear that if making *ex nihilo* is to be allowed for, even if only as a logical possibility, then these two—creation and modification—are importantly different. The Aristotelian categories of causality accommodate modification but not creation. Hence it is necessary to add *creative causality* to the list of four. We need, however, to go further.

Consider the following. A teacher is conducting an elementary physics class using a number of basic solids and a range of simple apparatus. One such item is a Newton's cradle: a series of contiguous spherical pendulums each of which is attached to a single frame by two strings of equal length set directly opposite each other. With that arrangement the pendulums' movements are restricted to the same plane. Intending to demonstrate the conservation of momentum and energy, the instructor raises and releases one of the end spheres. Assuming that the impulse propagates through the pendulum set without dispersion, then the opposite end sphere is set in regular motion.

Why did that happen? The motion of the initial sphere produced the motion of the last pendulum via the intermediaries, and hence was an efficient cause of its motion. Anything else? Well, had the shapes or arrangements of the pendulums been different, then so too might have been the result. Hence the effect is also owing to the structure or pattern. What about the material? Again, had the elasticity of the strings, or the rigidity of the frame, or the density and character of the spheres been different, then so might have been the effect. Additionally in the context of a class in which the apparatus has been designed and used with certain purposes, we can and should say that the movement of the initial sphere was for the sake of producing that of the last one. In summary, what happened is not adequately explained if one restricts causal factors to efficient ones: form, matter, and end are also determinants of the outcome. Indeed, for particular explanatory or design purposes one might begin with one of these others (for example, form) and then proceed to the remaining ones.

The example suggests the superiority of Aristotelian causal pluralism and the analogicality of "cause" over present-day causal monism and "cause" univocalism. But does the former go far enough? Another piece of apparatus consists of a pair of parallel, walled inclines each with the same sort of corrugated surface. The teacher takes an iron sphere and a cube of the same material and identical mass and places them at the tops of the inclines. The ball rattles down the slope; the cube remains caught at the top. The experiment is repeated at increasing angles until the point is reached where the cube bounces down. What explains the events and the differences between them? Once again shape or form enters into the explanation, and although the experimental situation is different, it looks as if the four Aristotelian causes serve to explain the effects.

What, though, of why the objects are expected to move at all? Here an appeal to weight is evidently called for, as it is in the more perspicuous demonstration of its efficacy achieved by use of a third piece of apparatus. This is a suspension device consisting of an electromagnet controlled by a variable switch. The preceding sphere and cube along with others of the same material but of different masses are placed in contact with the magnet and the current is lowered to the point where they fall.

Why did the range of events that ensued happen as and when they did? Allowing that we already have an efficient cause in the electromagnet, formal, material, and purposive factors, there remains a need to refer to the weight of the objects as central to their falling. Here a few reminders are called for. First, where the mass of the objects is identical, variability in shape may be irrelevant. Second, where materials of different sorts are introduced but mass and magnetic potential remain equal, the material difference is again irrelevant to what occurs. Third, weight is a cause of an object's falling inasmuch as it is a function of mass times the acceleration of gravity, and the gravitational force is operating on the mass at all times, whatever countervailing forces may be in play. It does not begin to operate and initiate a change as in the manner of an efficient cause. Fourth, the controller of the electromagnet and the magnet itself, when reduced to the point where the objects fall, are not direct causes of their falling; rather they are causes of the removal of an impediment to their falling, namely the degree of countervailing magnetic force.

The weight of the objects is an ineliminable causal factor, but *ex hypothesi* it is not captured either in the monistic scheme that allows only efficient causes, or in the pluralistic one that also recognizes form, matter, and purpose. Aristotle himself tries to account for this sort of causality by claiming that each kind of elementary material has a natural movement it will make when not impeded from doing so, a tendency towards a particular region of the universe: earth towards the center, fire towards the outer. That suggests subsumption under material causality where matter is taken to be intrinsically differently natured or kinded; and on that account he also attributes the particular directions of movement to the different forms and sees this as involving final and efficient causality. Setting aside the details of his theory of nature, the general effort fails because weight is a distinct kind of causal factor from matter, structure, efficient cause, and function. It is an example of what might be termed "physical causality" in the particular sense associated with general physics. At any rate the varieties of causality are several, and greater than four.

They may also be greater than six (*efficient, formal, material, final, physical*, and *creative*). Sometimes the adoption of policies or the performance of actions are justified in terms of independently describable benefits (or are criticized by reference to resultant harms); but sometimes what is at issue is becoming better (or worse) precisely in and through acting in certain morally characterizable ways. Here there is a moral effect but it is an immanent one. It is not an existent distinct from its cause and in general it does not conform to standard and Aristotelian understandings of efficient causation. There are a variety of modes of moral-making relevant to the understanding of culpability, complicity, diminishment, enhancement, recognition, self-respect, and the like, but they have in common a distinctive kind of normative transformation which may relate to material, structural, efficient, functional, and physical causality, but is not as such reducible to any one of them. Accordingly we should recognize in addition a seventh kind: *moral causality*.

This is related to, but distinct from, a further nonefficient, non-Aristotelian mode of causality. As I have described it, moral causality is immanent (not transitive). It may have further effects within and beyond the agent but its proper efficacy is the moral change realized in and by the agent. Compare and contrast this with the case in which someone does something whose effect is realized in and through the act, but where this depends essentially upon another whom it also includes. Pauline marries Peter in saying "I take you to be my husband," thereby making herself a wife and he a husband. Peter and Pauline then complete a legal procedure in respect of orphan Paul by signing an adoption order, thence making themselves parents and he "parented." In due course Pauline, Peter, and Paul immigrate to some other country and in swearing oaths of allegiance to it they become its naturalized subjects. Let it be assumed in each case that the relevant social institutions and the conditions of personal competence are such that these verbal undertakings are necessary and sufficient for the effect to be realized.

Here again the causality operates precisely in and through the act in question. Unlike efficient causality the effect is not a "distinct existence," but it is real and other involving. Let me term this mode of efficacy "performative social causality." Like moral causality this form of making is more akin to creation *ex nihilo* than to modification, since although preexistents are involved, any material changes effected in and through these acts are *per accidens*, whereas the *per se* effect is to bring into being a new creation, though not one distinct from the agent.

Eight causes—and counting? Whatever the actual number, the general lesson is clear: causality is distributed across diverse, but analogically related forms. *Causality* = _____ *cause*, with there being many irreducibly different ways of filling the space and so specifying the kind of causality.[18]

IV

Having begun by discussing the best way to characterize Putnam's philosophical quest and identified different but analogically related conceptions of the nature of philosophy, I am tempted to say that his career has involved a broad movement from scientific philosophy or philosophy as science to some other equally fundamental conception. This, however, does not seem quite right and for two reasons, the first of which looks towards Putnam and the second of which recognizes the aspiration to integration and comprehension that is implicit in philosophy in all its forms. Putnam has not altogether abandoned, let alone rejected, scientific philosophy nor fully embraced some single alternative; rather he has broadened his range of inquiries and objects of concern to embrace philosophy as politics, philosophy as art, and even philosophy as religion. Immediately, however, I have to qualify this in several ways. To begin with, each of these is not a single determinate form but rather a broad orientation. Next, he has not embraced one of them singly or several serially, but has moved to and fro between them and, in doing so, drawn elements of each into the other. Finally, attendant to the diversity of questions technical and conceptual, speculative and practical, proximate and ultimate, that philosophy poses to its practitioners, Putnam practices a kind of "horses-for-courses" or methods-for-tasks pluralism, subsuming this within a broad pragmatism. In a period of increasing academic specialization, technicality, and trade professionalism, this richness and breadth is both an inspiring reminder of what philosophy can be and something of a gently exhibited rebuke to what it has often become.

I want, however, to end with a challenge to Putnam as an occasional or partial practitioner of religious philosophy, and recall that I use this expression, as the others mentioned, in rather broad terms and in a spirit of openness which I hope he will accept. Yet this degree of indeterminacy and openness raises the question of what is "religious," what is "scientific," and what is "political" about "philosophies" to which these terms are conjoined in completion of their diverse but related meanings. Of course there need not be, and indeed there could not be, any single answer to such questions, but a natural place to look for central answers would be with regard to certain attitudes toward the distinctive languages and commitments of these orientations.

So far as religion and philosophy is concerned Putnam first began to reflect on these matters in print in relation to Wittgenstein's *Three Lectures on Religious Belief*. He then proceeded, via consideration of Maimonides's *Guide for the Perplexed* and a commentary on aspects of the Thomistic tradition, to the thoughts and writings of three twentieth-century Jewish religious thinkers: Franz Rosenzweig, Martin Buber, and Emmanuel Levinas. In the case of Rosenzweig, this was conjoined with further reflections on Wittgenstein's ideas about religion as a way of life.[19] In his discussion of Wittgenstein's lectures on religious belief Putnam lays emphasis, as others such as Peter Winch have done, on the following exchange between Wittgenstein and his student Casimir Lewy:

> [*Wittgenstein:*] Suppose someone, before going to China, when he might never see me again, said to me: "We might see one another after death"—would I necessarily say that I didn't understand him? I might say [want to say] simply, "Yes. I *understand* him entirely."

Lewy: In this case you might only mean that he expressed a certain attitude. [*Wittgenstein*:] I would say "No, it isn't the same thing as saying 'I'm very fond of you'"—and it may not be the same as saying anything else. It says what it says. Why should you be able to substitute anything else? Suppose I say: "The man used a picture."[20]

About this Putnam writes as follows:

What I take Wittgenstein to be pointing out [in his reply to Lewy] is that there is a perfectly ordinary notion of expressing an attitude, and what he is doing is contrasting the kind of metaphysical emphasis that non-cognitivists (either about religious language or about ethical language) want to put on the notion of expressing an attitude with the ordinary unemphasised use of that notion.

. . . I believe that what Wittgenstein (in company with Kierkegaard) is saying is this: that religious discourse can be understood in any depth only by understanding the form of life to which it belongs. What characterizes that form of life is not the expressions of belief that accompany it, but a way—a way that includes words and pictures, but is far from just consisting in just words and pictures—of living one's life, of regulating all of one's decisions.[21]

Writing a decade and a half later (in *Jewish Philosophy as a Guide to Life*) Putnam continues to hold to this interpretation of Wittgenstein's position, and sees truth in it as an account of a religious form of life. Yet he also makes clear that while he too is engaged in religious practice he is not a *believer* in the, or at least *a*, familiar understanding of that notion. He writes (first, in the "Introduction [Autobiographical]" and second, in the "Afterword"):

I am still a religious person, and I am still a naturalistic philosopher [. . .] but not a reductionist. Physics indeed describes the properties of matter in motion, but reductive naturalists forget that the world has many levels of form, including the level of morally significant human action, and the idea that all of these can be reduced to the level of physics I believe to be a fantasy. And, like the classical pragmatists, I do not see reality as morally indifferent: reality, as Dewey saw, *makes demands* on us.[22]

[. . .]

Like Dewey, I do not believe in an afterlife, or in God as a supernatural helper who intervenes in the course of history or in the course of our lives to rescue us from disasters. I don't believe in "miracles" in *that* sense.[23]

Let me respond to these points in turn, beginning with the interpretation of Wittgenstein. An individual's use of religious language and imagery (as with aesthetic, political, or scientific language and imagery) depends upon institutions and practices that typically exhibit standards of appropriate and correct usage and also differences with respect to competence and authority. It is, therefore, not within the power of an individual fully to determine the meaning and implications of what he says. Accordingly, it may not be possible to isolate everyday uses from philosophical or theological ones. It would also be a mistake, or at least premature, to suppose that these uses are separable, let alone that they stand in opposition. This being so, the question of whether the speaker is only expressing an attitude or also presupposing a metaphysical possibility cannot be set aside.

Wittgenstein's denial that in saying he understood the speaker he was treating him as having expressed an attitude (rather than as having made a truth-evaluable claim) takes the form of denying that talk of seeing one another after death is equivalent to some expression of affection. It needs to be considered, however, that while a person's hopeful thought that at some point in the future she and her partner might be resurrected and live together forever may be an expression of unconditional love, this fact does not preclude the possibility that part of its content is fixed by a conception of a literal afterlife which she is incapable of articulating but to which she is heir. Putnam treats Wittgenstein's rejection of the equivalence of talk of meeting in an afterlife with an expression of fondness as evidence of his opposition to a reductive account of religious belief (an opposition Putnam shares), but there is more than one kind of reduction.

To begin with, the question of whether saying "We might see one another after death" is equivalent to saying "I'm very fond of you" is one thing; while the question of whether both utterances may be expressions of attitude is another. One could answer "no" to the first and "yes" to the second, but that would still involve one kind of reduction; namely of a content that might be taken to have metaphysical or transcendental import to one that is expressive of an attitude toward the here and now. Furthermore, the two utterances considered as candidates for equivalence are drawn from different logical categories. The second might plausibly be taken to be a description of the speaker's psychological attitude. The first is certainly not that but it nevertheless remains possible that it is an expression of such an attitude.

Rather than try to resolve these matters, however, I am interested in the question as to why the metaphysical interpretation is excluded. It should not be excluded only on the grounds that some other account is possible, since it has not been shown that the metaphysical and the way of life interpretations are incompatible. My own view is that they are individually necessary and jointly complementary. Perhaps a clue to the exclusion of the metaphysical interpretation lies in Putnam's identification of himself as a naturalist philosopher and the associated rejection of the supernatural; but herein may lie a false opposition. Modern uses of the term "supernatural" correspond to what the medievals would have described as the "preternatural," that is, as being outside or contrary to the course of nature, as in someone or something levitating or remaining in a fire while showing no effect of heating. The supernatural, by contrast, belongs to the spiritual order and involves grace, divinely aided personal transformation, and other spiritual effects.

While the preternatural may sit ill with Putnam's naturalism it is not at all clear that the supernatural must also do so. Given his rejection of moral realities to physics he has no reason to exclude the possibility of spiritual realities mediated through the natural order, where that order is understood more expansively than by the materialist. But once the spiritual is allowed as a category of effect, the question cannot be excluded as to whether anything in the natural order is sufficient to produce such effects. In asking that question one is returned to considering the nature of causality, but in doing so there should now be no temptation to insist that this can only involve physical efficient causes.

The most familiar causal proofs of the existence of God begin with natural effects and argue that these depend essentially on a first cause. This is perhaps because proximate causes have to be seen as transmitters of the efficacy of a source of which they are strictly an extended instrument, as in the case of a *per se* ordered causal series. I am sympathetic to such arguments, as to some degree is Putnam, who discusses the issue in his "Thoughts Addressed to an Analytical Thomist." He writes:

> In addition to rejecting the idea that the traditional proofs are "invalid," I reject the idea that they are simply "question begging." On the contrary, even if in the end you reject the view of reason which is implicit in the proofs—that is, the view according to which reason itself tells us that contingent existence requires a cause outside itself, and tells us, moreover, that there have to be necessities which are not simply "conceptual"—you ought, I think, to recognize that that view of reason speaks to and addresses intuitions which are very deep in us (and the idea that those intuitions are ones which have been "refuted" by the modern scientific way of thinking is one which deserves critical examination).[24]

This is refreshingly open, but it prompts a question. Here, I am suggesting a different kind of argument that would begin with personal transformation and come to the view that only something supernatural could be a cause of this. In Christian thought this would be attributable to Grace and the Holy Spirit, but in Judaism there is the category of *teshuva*, "turning" or repentance, the possibility of which depends ultimately on God. Putnam associates his views on religion with those of Dewey, but these stand in some tension: on the one hand asserting against the scientific materialist that reality *makes demands* on us, but on the other rejecting the idea of God as a metaphysical reality and the associated spiritual order on grounds of philosophical naturalism. Yet if naturalism is sufficiently expansive to accord objective standing to the contents of moral and aesthetic experience, on what non-question-begging basis can it refuse recognition to the contents of experiences of spiritual transformation? If it allows these, however, then questions of what? how? and why? immediately arise, and as answers come forward, so too, given the interdependence of "because" and "cause," does the postulation of spiritual causes; and this in turn might suggest a *per se* causal ordering leading to a first spiritual cause, a source to which, as Aquinas would say *"quam omnes Deum nominant,"* everyone gives the name of God.[25]

JOHN HALDANE

UNIVERSITY OF ST. ANDREWS
JUNE 2011

NOTES

1. John Haldane, "Humanism with a Realist Face," *Philosophical Books* 35, no. 1 (1994): 21–29. The books were *Realism with a Human Face*, ed. James Conant (Cambridge, MA: Harvard University Press, 1990) and *Il Pragmatismo: Una Questione Aperta* (Rome: Laterza, 1992) subsequently published in English as *Pragmatism: An Open Question* (Oxford: Blackwell, 1995).

2. For more discussion of these issues see John Haldane, "Has Philosophy Made a Difference and Could It be Expected To?" in *Philosophy at the New Millenium*, ed. Anthony O'Hear (Cambridge: Cambridge University Press, 2001), 155–74.

3. Hilary Putnam, "Is the Causal Structure of the Physical Itself Something Physical?" in *Realism with a Human Face*, 87, 95.

4. See "A Theory of Reference," in Hilary Putnam, *Renewing Philosophy* (Cambridge, MA: Harvard University Press, 1992), 35–59.

5. Hilary Putnam, "Sense, Nonsense and the Senses: An Inquiry into the Powers of the Human Mind," in *Journal of Philosophy* 91, no. 9 (1994): 455–517, and incorporated as Part 1 of *The Threefold Cord: Mind, Body and World* (New York: Columbia University Press, 1999), 3–70.

6. Putnam, *The Threefold Cord*, 77.

7. Ibid., 137.

8. Ibid., 149.

9. See Aquinas, *Commentary on Aristotle's Metaphysics*, Book V, Lesson 2, *"Nam haec quaestio quare, vel propter quid, quaerit de causa"*: to ask why or for what reason is to ask about a cause.

10. John Haldane, "Folk Psychology and the Explanation of Human Behaviour," *Proceedings of the Aristotelian Society*, supp. vol. 62 (1988): 243.

11. See, for example, John Haldane, "A Return to Form in the Philosophy of Mind" in *Form and Matter: Themes in Contemporary Metaphysics*, ed. David S. Oderberg (Oxford: Blackwell, 1999), 40–64.

12. "Causality and Determination," in G. E. M. Anscombe, *Metaphysics and the Philosophy of Mind: Collected Philosophical Papers*, vol. 2 (Oxford: Blackwell, 1981), 133–47.

13. Anscombe, "Causality and Determination," 137; the passage is quoted by Putnam in *The Threefold Cord*, 141–42.

14. See again Haldane, "Humanism with a Realist Face," where I respond to a challenge presented in Putnam's "Aristotle after Wittgenstein" in *Words and Life*, ed. James Conant (Cambridge, MA: Harvard University Press, 1995), and Haldane "Realism with a Metaphysical Skull" in *Hilary Putnam: Pragmatism and Realism*, ed. James Conant and Urszula M. Zeglen (London: Routledge, 1992), 97–104, followed by Putnam's "Comment on John Haldane's paper," 105–8.

15. Anscombe, "Causality and Determination," 136.

16. The two essays I know of that do focus on it are Stephen Makin, "Causality and Derivativeness," in *Logic, Cause and Action*, ed. Roger Teichmann (Cambridge: Cambridge University Press, 2000), 59–71; and Thomas Osborne, "Rethinking Anscombe on Causation," *American Catholic Philosophical Quarterly* 81, no. 1 (2007): 89–107.

17. Aristotle, *Physics*, 195a 27.

18. The foregoing section (III) is drawn from John Haldane, "Gravitas, Moral Efficacy and Social Causes" *Analysis* 68, no. 297 (2008): 34–39.

19. "Wittgenstein on Religious Belief" in *Renewing Philosophy*, 134–57; "On Negative Theology," *Faith and Philosophy* 14, no. 4 (1997): 407–22; "Thoughts Addressed to an Analytical Thomist," *Monist* 80, no. 4 (1997): 487–99; and *Jewish Philosophy as a Guide to Life: Rosenzweig, Buber, Levinas, Wittgenstein* (Bloomington, IN: Indiana University Press, 2008).

20. Ludwig Wittgenstein, *Lectures and Conversations on Aesthetics, Psychology and Religious Belief*, ed. Cyril Barrett (Berkeley: University of California Press, 1996), 53; cited in *Renewing Philosophy*, 152.

21. Putnam, *Renewing Philosophy*, 152–54.

22. Putnam, *Jewish Philosophy as a Guide to Life*, 5–6.

23. Ibid., 102

24. Putnam, "Thoughts Addressed to an Analytical Thomist," 489.

25. For further discussion of various arguments to the existence of God see parts 2, 4, and 6 of J. J. C. Smart and J. J. Haldane, *Atheism and Theism*, 2nd ed. (Oxford: Blackwell, 2003) and Part I of John Haldane, *Reasonable Faith* (London: Routledge, 2010).

REPLY TO JOHN HALDANE

I first met John Haldane in the fall of 1990, when I delivered the Gifford Lectures at the University of St. Andrews. In the preface to the book that grew out of those lectures, I wrote, "The two months that I spent at St. Andrews giving these lectures were a sheer delight, and I profited more than I can say from the companionship and the philosophical conversation of the remarkable group of brilliant and dedicated philosophers there, particularly Peter Clark, Bob Hale, John Haldane, Stephen Read, Leslie Stevenson, John Skorupski, and Crispin Wright."[1] Haldane and Clark, in particular, became almost daily conversation partners, and I often wish that St. Andrews and Cambridge, Massachusetts were not separated by an ocean. Reading Haldane's essay and replying to it is a pleasure, because it is the next best thing to actually walking and talking together as we did in 1990.

I am also pleased that he repeats and elaborates upon an analogy he has previously used about my work, "the analogy of the career of an artist who might well go through various stages, pursuing different thematic interests and methods of exploration, but whose work nonetheless exhibits a unity of sensibility, conception, and execution." There must be *something* to this, because the editors of my most recent collection of papers,[2] Mario De Caro and David Macarthur, use the same analogy in their introduction (they write "artisan," rather than "artist," but the thought seems to be much the same). Moreover, in his essay in the present volume, Cornel West says I am "like a jazzman in the life of the mind"! As I relate in my Intellectual Autobiography in the present volume, as an undergraduate, "if I thought of any profession, it was of becoming a writer like my father, or a poet." Well, I did not become a poet, but I seem to have become an artist nonetheless, if these good friends are to be believed!

I. CAUSATION, EXPLANATION, AND "PRIORITY"

The context sensitivity and interest relativity of notions such as "cause" and "explanation" have long been an interest of mine. (Of course, in saying these notions are context sensitive and interest relative I am *not* saying that "anything goes"; in one context one might say that an accident was "caused by" the bad design of a highway, and in another context one might say it was caused by the driver's error, and each description may be objectively correct given its context (and, of course, it may also be objectively wrong). In *The Threefold Cord* I say that explanation and causation are interdependent notions, and that neither has priority. Commenting on this, Haldane writes,

> Putnam's concern, however, seems only to be with the issue of conceptual interdependence, as can be seen when he writes that "the notions of explanation and causation presuppose one another at every point; neither has 'priority' in the sense of being reducible to the other." In the context of his broader pragmatic realist view, however, one might interpret this as saying that neither notion has conceptual priority and since there is no priority between the conceptual and the real, so neither has ontological priority. I suspect that this is Putnam's view, though I doubt that he would wish to express it that way.

Well, it is not just that I would not wish to express it that way; I have never said, and I do not believe that "there is no priority between the conceptual and the real." I suspect that, like many others, Haldane has taken the unfortunate term (*mea culpa!*) "pragmatic realism" to stand for some shadow of the view that I publicly gave up in 1990 (at the conference in St. Andrews that immediately followed my lectures, in fact) according to which "the mind and the world jointly make up the mind and the world." The reader will see the extent to which I have given up "internal realism" in my replies to Tim Maudlin and to Richard Boyd, among others, in the present volume. In an obvious sense, *of course* the real has "priority" over the conceptual; the explanatory value of concepts lies in their picking out causal structures that are really there. (See also my reply to Cornel West.) Thus I totally agree with Haldane when he goes on to write, "In short, while the notions of causation and explanation may presuppose one another, *both* presuppose specific natures at work in the world at least some of which are antecedent to human thought and interests."

II. Senses and Meanings

At one point in his essay, Haldane raises the question:

> Do the various senses of "cause" correspond to one or many meanings? Put like that a dilemma immediately suggests itself. If they are held to correspond to a single meaning, what is to be made of there being several senses of "because" and correspondingly several different kinds of cause? One could

relocate plurality at the level of varieties within a single species but in that case
it would be misleading to speak of different kinds of causes, and certainly I
had something more radical in mind. On the other hand if one says there really
are quite different kinds of cause (not just a diversity within a single kind) and
that the expressions naming or describing these have different senses, then
it looks as if equivocation threatens. If "cause" in "formal cause," "material
cause," "efficient cause," and so on, each has a different meaning, then in
what sense can these be said to be different kinds of *cause*? There would be
no more reason to do so than to say that the bark of a tree and the bark of a
dog are different kinds of *bark*.

And his response to the dilemma is eminently sensible: "My answer, perhaps unsurprisingly, is that we do not have to choose between univocality
and equivocality with regard to 'cause' since there is also analogicality,
that is to say related but not identical meanings."

While this is not in any sense a disagreement on these particular issues,
I do want to note that my notion of "meaning" is, however, different from
Haldane's. My notion of meaning derives from Austin's remark that "The
question of truth and falsehood does not turn only on what a sentence *is*,
nor yet on what it *means*, but on, speaking very broadly, the circumstances
in which it is uttered,"[3] via Travis's work on "occasion sensitive semantics."[4] On this account, the meaning of a sentence (or better, since there is
no necessity to reify "meanings," what a competent speaker knows when
she "knows the meaning" of a word), is a set of linguistic facts (and "know
hows") that she is expected to have learned/acquired prior to using the
word on any particular occasion. "The Meaning of 'Meaning'" was my
attempt to spell out what those facts are in the case of one important class
of words: the natural kind terms. It is one task of lexical semantics—today
a sadly neglected area of linguistics, in comparison with mathematized
structural linguistics—to find appropriate normal forms for describing
those facts in the case of the many, many other kinds of words there are in
a language. The Austin-Travis thesis is that knowing those facts, "knowing
the meaning" of a word, generally does not mean, is not the same thing as,
knowing the truth-evaluable content of a particular sentence containing
that term. Knowing that content is (in one sense of "sense") knowing the
sense that the word has on a particular occasion. For example,[5] imagine
that John, a bus conductor, allows his friend Jim, to do his job for a day.
John, who is riding along as a passenger, whispers to the person next to
him, "I am the conductor of this bus." Jim says to an unruly passenger, "I
am the conductor of this bus." Each speaks truly, but the truth conditions
for their utterances are different. Different—but both are compatible with
what conductor "means" in English. In Haldane's terminology, Jim and John
use "conductor" with "different but related" meanings; I would say that the

meaning of the word "conductor" is the *same* (in fact, the one any normal speaker of English knows), but the *truth conditions* of their utterances are different but related. (I might also say that "conductor of this bus" has, in this example, different but related *senses*.)

III. Religion

Haldane briefly but accurately (and not unsympathetically) summarizes some of the things I have said in explanation of my own religious stance. If Ruth Anna Putnam had not examined the same writings in her essay in this volume and asked me a number of searching questions about them (to which I respond in my reply to her essay), I would elaborate on those passages now, but as it is I shall simply refer the reader to that reply rather than repeat myself.

As a self-described "analytical Thomist,"[6] Haldane would naturally like to move me away from my avowed naturalism and closer to classical ontotheology. I agree with Haldane that it is a mistake to reject metaphysics, either theological or not, as "meaningless," as Wittgensteinians are prone to do. Thus I can understand why Haldane writes:

> Yet if naturalism is sufficiently expansive to accord objective standing to the contents of moral and aesthetic experience, on what non-question-begging basis can it refuse recognition to the contents of experiences of spiritual transformation? If it allows these, however, then questions of what? how? and why? immediately arise, and as answers come forward, so too, given the interdependence of "because" and "cause," does the postulation of spiritual causes; and this in turn might suggest a per se causal ordering leading to a first spiritual cause, a source to which, as Aquinas would say "*quam omnes Deum nominant,*" everyone gives the name of God.

My situation with respect to Haldane's argument (suggestion?) is, I find, similar to the situation Wittgenstein described on page 55 of *Lectures and Conversations on Aesthetics, Psychology, and Religious Belief.* Wittgenstein wrote,

> If you ask me whether or not I believe in a Judgement Day, in the sense in which religious people have belief in it, I wouldn't say "No. I don't believe there will be such a thing." It would seem to me utterly crazy to say such a thing . . . In one sense, I understand all he says—the English words, "God," "separate," etc. I understand. I could say: "I don't believe in this," and this would be true, meaning I haven't got these thoughts or anything that hangs together with them. But not that I could contradict the thing.[7]

Similarly, I do not have the notion of a "first spiritual cause" or "anything that hangs together with it." But I cannot contradict Haldane, and I feel profound respect for the role that notion plays in his spiritual life.

H.P.

NOTES

1. Hilary Putnam, *Renewing Philosophy* (Cambridge, MA: Harvard University Press, 1992), xi.

2. Hilary Putnam, *Philosophy in an Age of Science: Physics, Mathematics, and Skepticism*, ed. Mario De Caro and David Macarthur (Cambridge, MA: Harvard University Press, 2012).

3. J. L. Austin, *Sense and Sensibilia* (Oxford: Clarendon Press, 1962), 111.

4. See my "Travis on Meaning, Thought and the Ways the World Is," Review of *Unshadowed Thought* by Charles Travis, *Philosophical Quarterly* 52, no. 206 (Jan. 2002): 96–106.

5. I used this example in "Travis on Meaning, Thought and the Ways the World Is," 98–99.

6. Haldane has written, "analytical Thomism involves the bringing into mutual relationship of the styles and preoccupations of recent English-speaking philosophy and the ideas and concerns shared by St. Thomas and his followers" (*Faithful Reason: Essays Catholic and Philosophical* [New York: Routledge, 2004], xii).

7. I discuss this passage, and also give a brief account of what I like and dislike about Wittgenstein's approach to philosophy, in "Wittgenstein: A Reappraisal," in *Philosophy in an Age of Science.*

20

Ruth Anna Putnam

HILARY PUTNAM'S JEWISH PHILOSOPHY

In an early paper in the philosophy of religion, Hilary Putnam recalls a conversation with Elizabeth Anscombe in which "she compared the difference between the atheist view of religion and the view of the believer to the difference between 'seeing the stained glass windows from the outside and seeing them from the inside.'"[1] Reading and rereading Putnam's work in the philosophy of religion, work that spans more than a decade, I find that image, somewhat modified, useful in understanding the limits of philosophy of religion. For, while I have no doubt that Hilary Putnam, the man, sees the stained glass windows from the inside, I am inclined to think that Putnam, the philosopher, and indeed any philosopher *qua philosopher*, can at best stand in the door of the cathedral, able to see the light streaming through the stained glass windows but unable to see the windows themselves. Philosophizing about religion requires a certain intellectual stance that is incompatible with having a religious experience, just as philosophizing about art is incompatible with having an aesthetic experience. Of course, the same person at another moment is capable of having a religious or an aesthetic experience; indeed, I find it difficult to imagine that a person untouched by art or by God could or would philosophize about art or God.

Putnam's writings in the philosophy of religion, particularly in Jewish philosophy of religion, are often exegetical. As a result, I am far from certain that I have identified his exact views. This is especially the case with respect to answers to the second of the three questions to which his philosophy responds. These are the questions: What can we say about God? What can we say about the encounter between God and a human person? What difference does it make?

I. PRELIMINARIES

There is, of course, religious language. Thus arises the question of how it is to be understood. Only when that question has been answered, when we agree that religious discourse is, at least for those who participate in it, meaningful, can we respond to the question, "What can we say about God?"

Putnam's first venture into the philosophy of religion is found in chapters 7 and 8 of his *Renewing Philosophy*.[2] There he offers an interpretation, and a rebuttal of misinterpretations, of Wittgenstein's three lectures on religious belief.[3] The lectures, it seems to me, and Putnam seems to take them so also, are not so much about religious belief as about religious language. Wittgenstein's prime examples are utterances about the Last Judgment, and he notes perceptively various contexts in which religious persons may mention the Last Judgment. But Wittgenstein's and Putnam's main interest is to clarify the idea that an atheist who says, "There is no God," does not contradict the theist who says, "There is a God."

When one imagines a conversation between one who believes in God and one who does not, the utterances one considers belong only marginally to religious language. Ordinary believers in ordinary circumstances do not engage in debates with unbelievers. Ordinary believers use religious language primarily when engaged in religious activities: in prayer, in giving religious instruction, in commenting from a religious point of view on events in their own lives or that of others, etc. I do not deny, of course, that ordinary religious discourse, for example the Psalms, contains many expressions that affirm the existence of God. Rather, I am drawing attention to the fact that these utterances, unlike those addressed to the atheist, are not epistemic. Putnam, using terminology he learned from Stanley Cavell, suggests that believers do not proclaim their knowledge of God's existence but rather acknowledge Him. In any case, I suggest that the use of religious language in theological or philosophical debates is parasitic on the ordinary use of ordinary believers in ordinary circumstances. More precisely, the theist's "There is a God" receives its meaning from the ordinary use of ordinary believers in ordinary circumstances. Thus Putnam writes,

> I believe that Wittgenstein (in company with Kierkegaard) is saying this: that religious discourse can be understood in any depth only by understanding the form of life to which it belongs. What characterizes that form of life is not

the expressions of belief that accompany it, but a way—a way that includes words and pictures, but is far from consisting in just words and pictures—of living one's life, of regulating all one's decisions.[4]

Moreover, Putnam holds that one can understand a religious form of life in any depth only from inside that way of life. This is why the atheist cannot understand and, therefore, cannot contradict the theist.

Here it might be objected that there are many forms of religious life and thus many forms of religious language. Does the view that religious language can be understood only from within a religious life imply that there can be no interfaith dialogue and that a philosopher of religion can speak only to members of his own faith community? This is not Putnam's view; nor is it true. For example, as we shall see shortly, the Jew Maimonides and the Christian Thomas Aquinas both worried about the first of the questions Putnam addresses in his writings in the philosophy of religion, namely, "what can we say about God?" Not only does Putnam believe that his account of religious language as *sui generis* is compatible with interfaith dialogue, he asserts explicitly that "fruitful dialogue between a religious thinker and a secular thinker is possible."[5]

The possibility of fruitful interfaith and even religious/secular dialogue arises, I believe, when the religious life that is home to a particular religious language is embedded in the life of a larger multicultural/multifaith community. Putnam frequently rebuts relativism by pointing out that different cultures are not hermetically sealed off from one another, and this holds clearly for the cultures of communities of faith belonging to or overlapping the same larger community. It holds even more when the different religions share a common root, as do the three Jerusalem-based religions, leading to shared theological problems like the problem of divine predication.

Before turning to the topic of divine predication, it is worthwhile to mention that the sense of the term "belief" in religious contexts differs from the sense it has in ordinary or in scientific contexts. The religious believer, writes Putnam, "is not engaged in the prediction of empirical phenomena, and religious faith is not refuted by this or that empirical happening or scientific discovery."[6] In short, both the atheist who claims that the fact of evolution refutes the Bible and the fundamentalist who claims that the Bible refutes the theory of evolution are deeply confused.

The claim that religious language can be understood in the deepest sense only from inside the way of life to which it belongs gives rise to the question whether is it possible for everyone to enter that way of life. Putnam writes:

I am inclined to say something like this: that while the *potentiality* for religious language, the possibility of making it one's own, is a basic human potentiality, the exercise of that potentiality is not a real possibility for every human being at every time. . . . I myself believe that it requires something *experiential* and not merely intellectual to awaken that possibility in a human being.[7]

This seems correct to me. Indeed, the second question mentioned above— what can we say about the encounter between God and a human being—will speak to that experiential element.

II. WHAT CAN WE SAY ABOUT GOD?

In "On Negative Theology" Putnam points out that the religious believer has two needs: a need for a transcendent deity and a need for an available deity. The latter need causes the believer to wish to say various things about the deity, such as that He is just and merciful, or rules the universe, or loves us. The former makes the believer painfully aware that anything we say about the deity falls woefully short of the truth, indeed must so fall short. For example, God's mercy exceeds not only human mercy but any humanly conceivable mercy. But for medieval theologians— Putnam is concerned particularly with the Jewish philosopher Maimonides but the Christian Thomas Aquinas and others faced the same problem—there are metaphysical reasons that make divine predication problematic.

To put it briefly, the absolute unity of God appeared to these philosophers to prohibit ascribing to the deity more than one attribute, or indeed any attribute. Putnam writes, *"There are no 'propositions' about God that are adequate to God*—that is what one is committed to if one bravely follows out the line of negative theology to the end, as Maimonides did."[8] But I am here not interested in Maimonides's views or Aquinas's views of negative or analogical predication. Nor am I interested in Putnam's reading of Ehud Ben-Or's reading of Maimonides. I am interested in Putnam's own conclusions.

Putnam notes that Maimonides regularly ignores the fact that if we cannot predicate anything of God, then we cannot think of Him as "the unconditioned sufficient reason for the existence of everything conditioned." He adds, "what he [Maimonides] writes seems to me to breathe a deep conviction in the existence of a Ground of the whole created world; and I do not believe that, in his heart of hearts, he regarded this as just an idea that it was good for *him* to have."[9] Putnam speaks for himself here as much as for Maimonides. In "Thoughts Addressed to an Analytical Thomist" he wrote:

Speaking for myself . . . while I do conceive of God as a "Transcendent Be-ing," as a "Necessary Being," "as an unconditioned ground of the existence of everything that is contingent," I feel that insofar as I have any handle on these notions, I have a handle on them as *religious* notions, not as notions that are supported by an independent philosophical *theory*.[10]

Putnam finds medieval, specifically Maimonidean, philosophy of religion profoundly unsatisfactory. It is unable to explain how we can talk about God, but, writes Putnam, "it is possible for us to think about God and to talk about God, but doing so essentially involves uses of language that are *sui generis*."[11] And no scientific theory will explain how it works; neither will any philosophy of language.

In any case, for Putnam and the Jewish philosophers that interest him, "*theorizing* about God is, as it were, beside the point."[12] What then is the point? He quotes Rosenzweig saying that one does not want to say anything about God or about man "but only about an event between the two."[13]

III. What Can We Say about an Event between God and a Human Person?

An event between God and a human being is a religious experience. In "The Depth and Shallows of Experience," Putnam develops his notion of a religious experience. For him, a religious experience is neither wrestling with God nor passively receiving a revelation; rather it is experiencing an event as full of religious significance, say, the birth of a child or even a more ordinary event. The notion of experience entertained by Humean empiricists is too bare to accommodate religious, or for that matter aesthetic or moral, experiences. In fact, experience of the Humean sort is just plainly inadequate. So, Putnam turns to Kant's idea that experience is always already conceptualized. However, not all concepts are determinate. An aesthetic experience involves indeterminate concepts, concepts that require both a sensible subject matter and the application of imagination.

Putnam's point is that we need a deep notion of experience, like Kant's notion of aesthetic experience, in order to appreciate what religious experience consists in. Both aesthetic and religious experience involve the use of indeterminate concepts, concepts that allow for a play of the imagination. This seems to me to be correct. But, he seems to think also that a shared deep notion of experience might enable atheists to communicate with theists. Putnam's remarks on this are quite brief and I find them puzzling. Hoping to provoke some further clarification, I shall suggest that a shared notion of deep experience, exemplified by aesthetic experience, might enable the atheist to understand this: just as aesthetic experiences are not understood as evidence for or proof of the reality or existence of beauty, so religious experiences are not understood as evidence for or proofs of the existence of

God, rather they are direct experiences of beauty or of God. Putnam writes, "One way of overcoming the idea—and we need to overcome it!—that it is simply *obvious* what having a religious faith consists in, is to overcome the idea that it is simply obvious (or if not obvious, obviously irrelevant) what the words 'religious experience' refer to."[14] What then do these words refer to? The short answer is that they refer to an event between God and a human person. What then can we say about that?

In *Jewish Philosophy as a Guide to Life*, Putnam deals with three different answers to this question, those of Rosenzweig, Buber, and Levinas. He will take from each what he finds most congenial. He begins, however, by noting that he is both a religious person and a naturalistic philosopher. The latter requires some clarification. Putnam is not a reductionist; he does not believe, for example, that morally significant human action can be reduced to the level of physics. Instead, he holds:

> Values may be created by human beings and human cultures, but I see them as made in response to demands that we do not create. It is reality that determines whether our responses are adequate or inadequate. Similarly, my friend Gordon Kaufman may be right in saying that "the available God" is a human construct, but I am sure he would agree that we construct our images of God in response to demands that we do not create, and that it is not up to us whether our responses are adequate or inadequate.[15]

So much for the record. The temptation (this is my word) to see a conflict between, as people say, science and religion vanishes when one realizes that theorizing about God is beside the point, that one can theorize only about the relation, or the interaction, between the human person and God, and, it will turn out, the relation between one human person and another.

1. Rosenzweig

Let us turn then to Rosenzweig, or rather to what I think Putnam takes from Rosenzweig. For all their differences—Rosenzweig was a deeply religious Jew and Wittgenstein a man with a complicated relationship to Christianity—Putnam finds important similarities between them. Both reject metaphysics and urge their readers to return to the ordinary use of words, or what Putnam, following Rosenzweig, calls "common sense in action."[16] For Rosenzweig, common sense in action means in particular that our relation to God does not depend on a theory any more than our relation to the world or to other human beings. Putnam recalls that Cavell holds a similar view with respect to our relationship to the world or to other people.

We neither know nor do not know, on Cavell's account, that there is a world and other people. Rather, we acknowledge the world, we acknowledge other people, and, for Rosenzweig and Putnam, we acknowledge God.

Rosenzweig conceived of revelation as an ongoing process in every religious person's life. It is not clear to me whether Putnam shares this notion of revelation. What is clear is that Putnam, like Rosenzweig, believes that we are always in the presence of God, that the only commandment is to love God, and that one should pray only for the strength to meet what Rosenzweig called the "demand[s] of the day."[17] Here, I would like to add that if we, all human beings, are always in the presence of God, then many of us are never, and others only occasionally, aware of this. Moreover, this "being in the presence of God" must be compatible with Putnam's earlier remark that not everyone may be able to enter into a religious form of life. In other words, this claim—that every human being is always in the presence of God—sounds to me like a statement about God, not about an event between God and a human being. That is, it sounds to me like the kind of statement that misleads one into the kind of theologizing that Putnam wants to avoid. Be that as it may, when one is aware of standing in the presence of God, then, if I understand Putnam correctly, one is conscious of God's command, "Love Me!" As we shall see, Putnam does not think that this is the only kind of event between a human being and God.

We are left with the question of what Rosenzweig meant by saying that God commands us to love Him. Putnam approaches an answer indirectly, he turns to Rosenzweig's account of revelation as an event between human beings and God. Or, as Rosenzweig says, "between man and God." When I replace "man" by "human beings," I do not do so for feminist reasons. I find "man" ambiguous. Does it refer to an individual, or to all human beings severally, or to humanity, i.e., all humans collectively? If one thinks of God's revelation to Moses on Mt. Sinai, for example, one can think of it as an event (historical or not) in the life of a particular man, as an event (again historical or not) in the life of the Jewish people, or is revelation something that happens in the life of each Jew, past, present, and future. Once again, I am wondering how this last reading can be compatible with the fact that some people, even some Jews, never have a religious experience. Putnam quotes Rosenzweig writing, "The presentness of the miracle of revelation is and remains its content; its historicity, however, is its ground and warrant."[18] This suggests to me not only that, as mentioned earlier, Rosenzweig regards revelation as an event in each believer's life but also that he sees it as an event in the history of the Jewish people. Putnam, I believe, finds the question of historicity beside the point.

In any case, for Rosenzweig and for the traditional Jew, the historicity of Sinai is only one reason for keeping the commandments and statutes.

Indeed, these "laws" (*Gesetze*) become commandments (*Gebote*) only when they are seen as spelling out the One Commandment, "Love Me!"

Putnam raises several points here. The first concerns Rosenzweig's account of the encounter between God and a human being, not, however, any human being, but rather an exemplary human being, so that the encounter is an exemplary encounter.[19] Of this one can only give a narrative account. Putnam believes that for Levinas the exemplary event is Abraham's response to God, "*hineni*" (I am here, in the sense of I am ready to do whatever you may ask.) More will be said about Levinas and Putnam's response to Levinas. Here, it suffices to say that Rosenzweig's narrative appears to combine two Biblical events. Explicitly, he refers to God calling Adam (in the third chapter of Genesis), but he says that Adam cannot be silent when he is called twice by name and that he then responds "*hineni*." But it is Abraham, not Adam, who is called twice by name and responds, "*hineni*."

I mention this only because it provides a rare glimpse into Putnam's thinking. He finds the idea that the God of all the world fell in love with a particular people "odd," especially that he picked Abraham before Abraham had revealed any particular merit. Yet the picture of God as a lover fascinates him. Of course, love cannot be commanded, but, says Rosenzweig, "love me!" is the only way the lover can declare his love, and when one returns God's love, one seeks "matrimony," that is, redemption. The fact that God loves me should inspire me to love my neighbor. But what does that mean? Clearly, one can love particular people without being inspired by God's love, but Rosenzweig believed, as did Levinas, and, I think, Putnam "that meaningful love of the other, the love that makes one (in Levinas's words, not Rosenzweig's) 'a human being worthy of the name,' cannot be a selective love."[20] In fact, writes Putnam carefully, one must be able to love human beings who do not "appeal" to one.

Putnam concludes his remarks on Rosenzweig with a discussion of his views on redemption, both of how it is experienced by the individual Jew, and of what role the Jewish people play in the world's path to redemption. Redemption, for Rosenzweig, is not something that will happen in an ever receding future, in other words, something that will never be achieved. Rather, the ideal Jew "experiences redemption as something both future *and* present now."[21] Putnam comments: "Speaking now for myself, I can imagine the complex experience to which Rosenzweig refers, but I believe that it is something that can be experienced by a community of faith within any religious tradition that anticipates or hopes for ultimate redemption, at least when that community is a truly spiritual one."[22] Putnam avails himself here of the opportunity to reject Rosenzweig's Jewish (or Jewish-Christian) particularism in favor of a more universalistic and pluralistic position.

2. Buber

I have suggested that Putnam, correctly in my view, evades what might be called the problem of religious knowledge. But what about the problem of evil? How can an omniscient, omnipotent, just, and merciful God allow good people to suffer and bad people to prosper? (Of course, the omniscient, omnipotent, benevolent God is the God of the philosophers. But, an analogous question can be asked with hardly less urgency concerning the God of ordinary believers.) The prophets had suggested that bad things happen to bad people, or bad peoples, and good things to good people, or good peoples, but that view is untenable in the face of experience. The sages of the Talmud reinterpreted it; reward and punishment occur only in eschatological time. But that too is unsatisfactory. Once one considers the possibility that God intervenes in the processes of nature and history, one will inevitably ask such questions as, "Why did He not stop the Nazis before they murdered six million Jews, nearly a million Roma, and millions of others?" Many of us, Putnam included, reject a theology that leads to this sort of question. Instead he turns to Martin Buber, who develops a conception of God—or rather of our relation to God and of His to us—that makes it impossible to formulate the problem of evil; this is, again, an evasion. I take the word "evasion" from Cornel West's title "The American Evasion of Philosophy."[23] I think these evasions are a good thing; they free us from an endless search for answers to unanswerable questions.

To explain Buber's idea, Putnam once again turns to a Cavellian notion—the notion of moral perfectionism. For moral perfectionists the key question one should ask oneself is this: Am I living as I am supposed to live? It is a question that all great Jewish philosophers ask, according to Putnam. It is, in one sense, a question about oneself, a demand one makes on oneself to make one's best effort to "reach (in Cavellian language) my unattained but attainable self."[24] Putnam believes that all the great Jewish philosophers were moral perfectionists in this sense. Thus, in particular, "the famous 'I-Thou' in Buber is a relation that Buber believes is *demanded* of us, and without which no system of moral rules and no institution can have any real value."[25] What, then, is that relation? (From here on, the I-You relation).

Let us begin with an example. An artist who strives selflessly and with undivided attention to realize her conception stands to her work in an I-You relation. I would like to say here, in passing, that it has always seemed to me to be one of the strengths of Buber's vision that he did not restrict the I-You relation to relations between human persons, or between human persons and the divine person, but grants that one could be so related, at least for a brief moment, to a horse, or a tree, or one's work.

The I-You relation is characterized by its total exclusiveness-at-the-moment—which is why it can be/should be only for a brief time—and by the fact that the "You" is not experienced as an object to be used or analyzed.[26] For this second characteristic, an aesthetic experience may serve as an example. Even the I-You relation to God, although, in some sense it encompasses all other I-You relations, can, no, *should*, last only for a brief while. But after an encounter with God one sees the world (the It-World) as God's world, and that has moral implications. Putnam writes:

> In sum, the aim of Buberian philosophy is to teach that the experience of the divine is not an end in itself—but let me put the stress in the right place—the *experience* of the divine is not an end in itself, and the "I-You" relation is not an end in itself, but rather the end is the *transformation* of life *in* the world, life in the *It-world*, through the transforming effect of the recurrent "I-You" relation.[27]

I take it then that standing in an I-You relation to God is one of the ways—another was having a Rosenzweigean revelation—that one becomes aware of being in the presence of God.

Putnam has described his own position as somewhere between Dewey's in *A Common Faith* and Buber's.[28] Here is what he emphasizes in Buber's thought: We cannot theorize about God, but we can speak to God; neither can we theorize about the problem of evil, but we can speak to God and wrestle with God concerning the evils we see. And, having returned to the ordinary world, we can attempt to do something about some of those evils. Putnam writes:

> Moreover—and this is the connection between Buber's theology and his many-sided social concerns—Buber believes that all genuine community, and all genuine moments of transformation in history, require something like a *shared* relation to the ultimate You. . . . If Buber's Zionism involved a lifelong concern with the rights and aspirations of the Palestinians, as it did, it was because for him an immoral Zionism was a doomed Zionism.[29]

What Putnam finds appealing is the fact that Buber has neither a negative nor a positive theology and that the very idea of loving one's neighbor is built into the I-You relationship. Not that all I-You relationships are good; but when they are good, they provide a model of how one should see the other even when the relationship is only one aspect of one's being in the It-World. Putnam found in Buber's *I and Thou* a way of evading not only the epistemological problems raised when one presumes to speak about God but also the problem of evil. Yet one must acknowledge that after the

Holocaust Buber spoke of an "eclipse" of God, and of a "silence" of God. Concerning the silence, having said that the only relation one can have to God is an I-You relation, Buber writes:

> But if man is no longer able to attain this relation, if God is silent toward him, and he toward God, then something has taken place, not in human subjectivity but in Being itself. It would be worthier not to explain it to oneself in sensational and incompetent sayings, such as that of the "death" of God, but to endure it as it is and at the same time to move existentially toward a new happening, toward that event in which the word between heaven and earth will again be heard.[30]

Buber also wrote:

> What is it that we mean when we speak of an eclipse of God which is even now taking place? Through this metaphor we make the tremendous assumption that we can glance up to God with our "mind's eye," or rather being's eye, as with our bodily eye to the sun, and that something can step between our existence and His as between the earth and the sun. That this glance of the being exists . . . is only to be experienced; man has experienced it. And that other, that which steps in between, one also experiences, today.[31]

Yet, Buber affirms, "The eclipse of God is no extinction; even to-morrow that which has stepped in between may give way."[32]

I have added this to Putnam's account of Buber's evasion of the problem of evil for two reasons. First, it adds enormous depth to the earlier account. Abraham pleading with God for Sodom and Gemorrah is one model for dealing with evil; Abraham standing mute with the sacrificial knife lifted is another. And yet "even tomorrow," even now, the silence may be shattered, "Do not touch the boy!" Secondly, I think that the idea of the eclipse of God will help us to understand Levinas.

3. Levinas

Rosenzweig said that one learns to love one's neighbor when one loves God; Buber, I think, believed that one learns to love the ultimate You having experienced the I-You relation with some human beings. For Levinas, or so it seems to me, the relation to the human Other—human yet written with a capital "O"—is neither first nor second, it is absolutely central. For me, the following image, to be found somewhere in the writings of Primo Levi, who, like Levinas, survived the Holocaust, encapsulates everything that Levinas opposed. Here is the image: Primo Levi stands before a Nazi officer, who will assign him to some work brigade, and, says Levi, "He did not look at me as one looks at a man." And, then I imagine Primo Levi standing before Levinas, and Levinas says, "*me voici*," that is, "*hineni*," I am here, I am completely here for you, I am available to you. Levinas looks at Primo Levi "as one looks at a man."

Although this is my image, I believe that it captures what Putnam finds of enormous value in Levinas, namely, Levinas's ethics. For Levinas, ethics is first philosophy. To ask, "Why should I love my neighbor?" may call forth the response, "Because he or she is fundamentally like you." And, that response opens the possibility of another holocaust, because one can always find that some people are not "like us." Or if the answer is, "because they are rational beings," then what about those whose rationality we deny? Although Putnam does not say so, and my knowledge of Levinas is too limited, I believe that "because God loves me" or "because God wants me to love Him" or more traditionally "because we are all made in God's image" are also unacceptable answers, answers that can be misused by religious fanatics, just as the humanist answers can be misused.

Like Rosenzweig and Buber, Levinas is a moral perfectionist, a philosopher who believes that prior to all principles, prior to all legislation, while not denying that those are needed, there is something that gives meaning or value to obeying the principles or laws. For Rosenzweig it was loving God and being loved by Him that turns *Gesetze* into *Gebote*; for Levinas it is what Putnam calls "the fundamental obligation."[33] We noted, when speaking of Buber, that, because of its exclusiveness-at-the-moment, the I-You relation cannot last. Similarly, Levinas knows that one's total availability to the needy Other may have to be modified because there are third parties, but, "Imagine you were in a situation in which your obligations did not conflict with focusing entirely on one other human being. What sort of attitude, what sort of relation, should you strive for toward that other?"[34] Then, as already mentioned, you are to be completely available to the person in front of you, just as Abraham was completely available to God when he said, "*hineni*," I am here. One takes on a fundamental obligation. But does the other not take on the same obligation toward me? No, unlike Buber's I-You relation, this relation is not symmetrical. Of course, the other takes on the same obligation toward me, but the Sages of the Talmud teach that every Israelite is responsible for every Israelite. For Levinas, every human being is responsible for every other. So, I am responsible for you being available to me, and the relation is once again asymmetrical. Levinas wrote, "beyond any responsibility attributed to everyone and for everyone, there is always the additional fact that I am responsible for that responsibility. It is an ideal, but one which is inseparable for the humanity of human beings."[35]

I said that instead of talking about God, which is both beside the point and, in a sense, impossible, the three twentieth-century philosophers Putnam discusses speak about the encounter of a human being with God, and secondarily the encounter of one human being with another. But, Levinas does not speak of an encounter with God, with the utterly Other; he speaks only of an encounter with a human Other, stressing, the utter otherness of that other human being. In fact, Putnam points out, "it is part of Levinas's strategy to regularly transfer predicates to the Other that traditional theology ascribes to God."[36] Thus, for example, he says that it is impossible to see the face of the Other, as we know that a human being cannot see God's face and live.

What happened to the encounter between the human being and God? Putnam doesn't say, but I would like to suggest that for Levinas, even more so than for Buber, because Levinas experienced the horrors of the Holocaust directly, God is eclipsed. Levinas's response to the unavailability of God is to impose availability on himself.

Putnam points out that Levinas addressed his philosophical writings to an audience consisting largely of non-Jews, keeping those writings separate from his writings, addressed to Jewish audiences, on the Talmud. Putnam is interested in the philosopher who seeks to universalize certain themes in Judaism. The first of these is precisely that, in Putnam's words, "every human being should experience him/herself as *commanded* to be available to the neediness, the suffering, the vulnerability of the other person."[37] Secondly, one must know this without there being any philosophical basis, and thirdly, without a personal epiphany.

I have raised several times the question of faith versus reason, although not in those words. Levinas speaks to that issue when he addresses Jewish audiences. He speaks of the Angel of Reason who has, for the past two centuries, called for a universal and homogenous society. Levinas urges his fellow Jews to resist that call. Such resistance does not require rejecting liberal Judaism or clinging to a literal interpretation of the Torah and the Talmud. On these matters Putnam is in full agreement with Levinas. He then turns to Levinas's account of Jewish particularism, which is a problem precisely for Jews who believe in the universality of the fundamental ethical commandment but also in the uniqueness of the Jewish people, thus for Levinas and for Putnam. While Putnam is clear in his rejection of Rosenzweig's conception of Judaism, he fails to make clear, to me at least, whether he finds Levinas's account convincing.

Levinas sees in Judaism, or in ethical monotheism, the inspired human basis for the fundamental obligation and thus for all ethics. But is Judaism just ethical monotheism? Surely what makes the life of an orthodox Jew unique is: the study of Torah and the performance of *mitzvot* (commandments). But, while every religion has some commandments, Putnam points out, "What is characteristic of *mitzvot* is that they form a *system*, a system whose function is to sanctify every possible portion of life. . . .'Keeping *mitzvot'* is an entire way of life, a way which is supposed to glorify God and exemplify justice."[38] Study of Torah, that is study of the Hebrew Bible, of the Talmud, and of the commentaries on these, is itself one of the commandments. Pleading with young liberal Jews not to reject Judaism in favor of Enlightenment universalism, Levinas describes this study as follows:

> The particular type of intellectual life known as study of Torah, that permanent revision and up-dating of the content of Revelation, where every situation within the human adventure can be judged. And it is here precisely that the Revelation is to be found: the die is not cast, the prophets or wise men of the Talmud knew nothing about antibiotics or nuclear energy; but the categories needed to understand these novelties are already available to monotheism. *It is the eternal anteriority of wisdom with respect to science and history. Without it, successs would equal reason, and reason would just be the necessity of living in one's own time.*[39]

Putnam concludes his presentation of Levinas's thought by pointing out that for Levinas the word "God" has no content other than the ethical content that one must always be available for the Other. What then can we learn about Putnam's philosophy from his reaction to Levinas? Putnam agrees that "the indispensable experience"—indispensable for ethics since it has no basis in either metaphysics or psychology—"is the experience of responding to another person, where neither the other person nor my response are seen at that crucial moment as instances of universals."[40] He agrees also that this response must fully respect the other's alterity, and finally, that the ethical relation is asymmetric; I recognize my obligation to the Other without simultaneously regarding the Other as obligated to me.

But Putnam objects when Levinas carries the asymmetry to the point of holding himself responsible for the persecutions he undergoes; he writes, "But the 'asymmetry' of the ethical relation need not be carried as far as Levinas carries it. And—incorrigible Aristotelian that I am—I would not carry it that far. It is, I think, because Levinas thinks of ethics as the *whole* of 'the true life' that he does so. But to be *only* ethical, even if one be ethical to the point of martyrdom, is to live a *one-sided* life."[41] I believe that Putnam is deeply moved by Levinas's notion of one's fundamental obligation to the Other. But for Putnam God is not eclipsed, and his conception of a good life is enriched not only by the ideas of other Jewish philosophers but by the ideas of Aristotle and John Dewey and others.

In a conversation with Philippe Nemo, after saying that he is responsible for the persecutions *he* has suffered, but only for those, Levinas added,

"These are extreme formulas which must not be detached from their context. In the concrete, many other considerations intervene and require justice even for me."[42] Putnam is troubled by the juxtaposition, which he finds more than once in Levinas's writings, of an extreme statement followed by a vague statement that limits the vision of unlimited human responsibility. The vague statement limits my responsibility, but, or so it seems to Putnam, for inadequate reasons, namely, that I am a neighbor of my neighbor. Putnam reminds us that, as Aristotle taught, one must love oneself in order to be able to love others. Levinas is unable to see Buber's I-You relation as another relation that is a basis for the ethical life. Putnam, in contrast, believes that there are "quite a few" big things to be known about the ethical life; Rosenzweig, Buber, and Levinas each contributed their insight.

Putnam wrote *Jewish Philosophy as a Guide to Life* to help a reader of these difficult texts. I have written about Putnam's book, and thus also about these texts, in an effort to discover Putnam's Jewish philosophy and to present my discovery to his critical gaze. But recently Putnam has added an afterword to the book, and there he tells us quite directly what his own religious attitudes are.

He writes, "Like [John] Dewey, I do not believe in an afterlife, or in God as a supernatural helper who intervenes in the course of history or in the course of our lives to rescue us from disasters."[43] He does not believe in miracles in that sense, but there are experiences that are natural and miraculous at the same time, for example, the experience that goes with prayer, the experience of a Buberian I-You relation with another person, or the experience of natural beauty or of art. He thinks of God as a wise, kind, and just person; a thought that need not be taken literally but that he finds more valuable than any philosopher's conception. Indeed, he is in full agreement with Buber that we are not to theorize about God but rather to address him. Thus, when Putnam says that he thinks of God as a wise, kind, and just person he does not speak as a philosopher; he speaks as a man seeing the stained glass windows from the inside.

III. WHAT DIFFERENCE DOES IT MAKE?

Putnam mentions here and there the Greek conception of philosophy as a way of life. What difference does Putnam's Jewish philosophy make to the way of life he recommends to us? Jewish ethics, as already mentioned, appears to give equal weight to the study of Torah and to doing deeds of loving kindness. In his contribution to the *Blackwell Companion to Religious Ethics*, Putnam responds to various objections that have been raised against the traditional Jewish life. Here I want to mention in passing just this. Against the complaint that the traditional Jewish life is too legalistic, he responds that loving one's neighbor and obeying the commandments joyfully are mutually supporting. He mentions Rabbi David Hartman's suggestion that the traditional phrase "the yoke of the *mitzvot*" should be replaced by "the joy of the *mitzvot*."[44] Against the complaint that the Talmud, or the legal code based on it, is too rigid, Putnam points to passages in the Talmud itself in which the sages reinterpret the Torah when it conflicts with their moral sensibility, a process that continues to this day.

There is, however, one persistent moral issue that calls for and receives Putnam's sustained attention, namely, the issue of religious, and thus moral, pluralism. Putnam seeks a middle ground between an antireligious skepticism that seeks to replace religion by something else and the view that religion (one's own religion, of course) is the final court of appeal on questions of morality. Instead, he suggests that religion is one participant in the ongoing process of moral inquiry.

Here is what he takes to be the contribution of the world's great religions to that process. They teach, next to the love of God and inseparable from it that "compassion is *the* all important moral virtue," that love of neighbor and love of the stranger must override all other values.[45] Of course, we know that the great religions have been inconsistent, that they have allowed what they mistook to be the love of God to override compassion. Nevertheless, Putnam holds that universal compassion, Levinas's availability to the suffering Other, is the great teaching of the world religions.

Putnam also holds that the great religions all agree with Rabbi Tarfon's saying, "It is not up to you to finish the work, but neither are you free not to take it up."[46] He sees this as protection against both groundless optimism or total pessimism, as giving one peace of mind. Clearly, if the great monotheistic religions are to avoid the murderous fanaticism to which they have from time to time succumbed, they must at the very least recognize that no tradition has a monopoly on religious value and religious virtue. In fact, Putnam goes further, holding that the voice of God can be heard in the sacred texts of all religions, and that in the words of Jonathan Sachs, Chief Rabbi of the Commonwealth, "The one God, creator of diversity, commands us to honor his creation by respecting diversity."[47]

Respecting other traditions, yes; learning from other traditions, yes; but that does *not* mean giving up one's own tradition. Without disrespecting other traditions, without denying that some of them have similar practices, one can find a unique value in one's own tradition. For Jews it may be that particular activity called studying Torah, or it may be, as Rabbi Hillel said, when challenged to state the content of Torah while standing on one foot, "That which is hateful to thee, do not do onto thy neighbor." Hillel added, "That is the whole of Torah—the rest is commentary—Go study."[48] So that even an exhortation to compassion, truly a universal virtue, leads back to that particular Jewish virtue, the study of Torah.

Putnam's own views on this issue, and with this I will close, are best stated by himself: "I am also convinced that whether one has the right or wrong view on theological questions is far less important to God . . . than whether one shows compassion, cheerfulness, and makes a contribution to enriching human spiritual and material life."[49]

RUTH ANNA PUTNAM

WELLESLEY COLLEGE
MARCH 2002

NOTES

1. Hilary Putnam, "Thoughts Addressed to an Analytical Thomist," *Monist* 80, no. 4 (October 1997): 491.

2. Hilary Putnam, *Renewing Philosophy* (Cambridge, MA: Harvard University Press, 1992).

3. Ludwig Wittgenstein, *Lectures and Conversations on Aesthetics, Psychology and Religious Belief*, Compiled from notes taken by Yorick Smythies, Rush Rhees and James Taylor, ed. Cyril Barret (Berkeley and Los Angeles: University of California Press, 1967).

4. Putnam, *Renewing Philosophy*, 154.

5. Putnam, "Thoughts Addressed to an Analytical Thomist," 492.

6. Hilary Putnam, "On Negative Theology," *Faith and Philosophy* 14, no. 4 (October 1997): 408.

7. Putnam, "Thoughts Addressed to an Analytical Thomist," 492.

8. Putnam, "On Negative Theology," 412.

9. Ibid., 413–14.

10. Putnam, "Thoughts Addressed to an Analytical Thomist," 490.

11. Ibid., 497.

12. Hilary Putnam, *Jewish Philosophy as a Guide to Life: Rosenzweig, Buber, Levinas, Wittgenstein* (Bloomington and Indianapolis: Indiana University Press, 2008), 6. Hereafter: *Jewish Philosophy.*

13. Ibid., 42. Quoted from Franz Rosenzweig, "A Note on Anthropomorphism in Response to the *Encyclopedia Judaica's* Article" in *God, Man, and World: Lectures and Essays*, ed. and trans. Barbara E. Galli (Syracuse: Syracuse University Press, 1998), 138.

14. Hilary Putnam, "The Depths and Shallows of Experience" in *Science, Religion, and the Human Experience*, ed. James D. Proctor (Oxford: Oxford University Press, 2005), 85.

15. Putnam, *Jewish Philosophy*, 6.

16. Ibid., 24.

17. Ibid., 35–36.

18. Franz Rosenzweig, *The Star of Redemption*, trans. William W. Hallo (Notre Dame: University of Notre Dame Press, 1970), 183.

19. Ibid. 175–76. See also Putnam, *Jewish Philosophy,* 42ff.

20. Putnam, *Jewish Philosophy*, 48.

21. Ibid., 51.

22. Ibid., 53.

23. Cornel West, *The American Evasion of Philosophy: A Genealogy of Pragmatism* (Madison: University of Wisconsin Press, 1989).

24. Putnam, *Jewish Philosophy*, 59.

25. Ibid., 59–60.

26. My first example, of the relation of an artist to her work, may seem to contradict my claim that the relation can be only temporary. I understand Buber to say, or, in any case, I say, that total absorption in any one thing or person for prolonged periods of time, would interfere with one's obedience to the command to love one's neighbor.

27. Putnam, *Jewish Philosophy*, 64.

28. John Dewey, *A Common Faith* (New Haven: Yale University Press, 1934).

29. Putnam, *Jewish Philosophy*, 67.

30. Martin Buber, *The Eclipse of God* (Atlantic Highlands, NJ: Humanities Press, 1952, 1988), 68.

31. Ibid., 127.

32. Ibid., 129.

33. Putnam, *Jewish Philosophy*, 73.

34. Ibid.

35. Ibid., 81–82. Quoting Emmanuel Levinas, "The Pact," in *The Levinas Reader*, ed. Seán Hand (Oxford: Blackwell, 1989), 226.

36. Putnam, *Jewish Philosophy*, 80.

37. Ibid., 86.

38. Ibid., 91.

39. Ibid., 92 (my emphasis). Quoting Emmanuel Levinas, "Judaism and the Present" in *The Levinas Reader*, ed. Seán Hand (Oxford: Blackwell, 1989), 257.

40. Putnam, *Jewish Philosophy*, 95.

41. Ibid., 97–98.

42. Ibid., 97. Quoting Emmanuel Levinas, *Ethics and Infinity: Conversations with Philippe Nemo*, trans. Richard A. Cohen (Pittsburgh: Duquesne University Press, 1985), 99–100.

43. Putnam, *Jewish Philosophy*, 102.

44. Hilary Putnam, "Jewish Ethics," in *The Blackwell Companion to Religious Ethics*, ed. William Schweiker (Oxford: Blackwell, 2005), 163.

45. Hilary Putnam, "Monotheism and Humanism," in *Humanity before God: Contemporary Faces of Jewish, Christian, and Islamic Ethics*, ed. William Schweiker et al. (Minneapolis: Fortress Press, 2006), 23.

46. Ibid., 28. Quoting Mishna *Pirke Avot* 2:21.

47. Ibid., 21. Quoting Jonathan Sacks, *The Dignity of Difference* (London and New York: Continuum, 2002, 2003), 200.

48. Putnam, "Jewish Ethics," 162. Quoting Babylonian Talmud Tractate Shabbath 31.

49. Hilary Putnam, "The Pluralism of David Hartman," in *Judaism and Modernity: The Religious Philosophy of David Hartman*, ed. Jonathan Malino (Jerusalem: Shalom Hartman Institute, 2001), 229.

REPLY TO RUTH ANNA PUTNAM

A s I explain in my Intellectual Autobiography, Ruth Anna's and my active interest in Judaism began in 1975 when our oldest son decided he wanted to have a Bar Mitzvah. In the thirty-five years that followed (as of this writing) Ruth Anna and I have learned about Judaism together, and we have each written papers about aspects of Judaism and, in my case, about philosophical issues that concern other religious traditions as well.[1] And together we have wrestled with the flood of new experiences and new learning that all that involved, and read and criticized each other's writing, and I know that I have profited enormously from doing that. So, if Ruth Anna Putnam now voices questions about exactly what I mean by what I have written, that means that I have not thought through what I think to her satisfaction (or, perhaps, it is a sign that I would rather "evade" certain questions, to use her word, than answer them!). I shall try not to be evasive *this* time.

Ruth Anna wants to know if she has correctly identified my answers to three questions: "What can we say about God? What can we say about the encounter between God and a human person? What difference does it make?" and she says that she is especially uncertain about my response to the second question. Before I try to give my best (but, given the nature of the topic, necessarily tentative and imperfect) answers, I want to say something about two preliminary issues: the role of philosophy in religious life, and what she calls my commitment to "pluralism."

I. PHILOSOPHY AND RELIGIOUS LIFE

Ruth Anna Putnam writes, "I am suggesting that philosophizing about religion requires a certain intellectual stance that is incompatible with having a religious experience, just as philosophizing about art is incompatible with having an aesthetic experience."[2] I am not sure I agree with this, and, in any case, I want to add that both religious experience and aesthetic experience can be *enriched* by reflection (and reflection is, after all, what philosophy consists in), rather than impoverished by it. (Moreover, as Pierre Hadot has emphasized, philosophy itself was, for many centuries, *both* a form of reflection *and* a set of spiritual exercises.[3])

To be sure, from the *Euthyphro* on, philosophical reflection has been the enemy of *naïve* religious belief. To some this has seemed a loss; but those who feel that way are making a mistake. In *Religion within the Bounds of Mere Reason*, Kant tells us that the "fanatic" tries to evade the fact that religion concerns a dimension of our existence that is intrinsically uncertain. From the fanatic's point of view, the truth of *his* religion is something he has simply *perceived*. But for Kant—and this seems to me to express a profound insight—to think that "certainty" is the right stance in religious matters is to make a huge mistake. We should not be nostalgic yearners for the supposedly "simple faith" of our childhood; simple faith can easily lead to moral abominations. A more complex faith, a faith that contains many moments of doubt, and a realization that no book and no tradition can be trusted to give the right answer to every moral question, is not inferior to so called "simple faith"; it is something different altogether, and, in the end, something *better*.

II. PLURALISM

Because all three of Ruth Anna Putnam's questions contain the word "God," a reader might assume that I think that having a fulfilling and genuine spiritual dimension to one's life involves thinking in terms of "God," and that is not the case. A traditional Confucian thinks in terms of "the Way of Heaven," but not in so-called "monotheistic" terms; a Taoist thinks in terms of a Way which involves "action through inaction," and harmony with the universe; to a Hindu, it is as true and as false that there is one God as it is that there are six or thirty-three or 3,306,[4] and each of the different varieties of Buddhism has its own religious conceptions and spiritual exercises. My own spiritual life centers on the exercise of asking myself what "God" wants of me; but that does not mean that I think the Confucian or the Taoist or the Buddhist is "making a mistake." They are certainly choosing a different way of manifesting what I see as a fundamental human potentiality, the religious potentiality, but not an inferior way. As I explained in *Jewish Philosophy as a Guide to Life*:

> I understand Dewey to be saying that the kind of reality God has is the reality of an ideal. Some people, we know, feel that this kind of reality is merely

subjective. But Dewey did not believe that ideas and values are "subjective" in the sense of being outside the spheres of rational argument and objective validity. Our values and our ideals are indeed subjective in the sense of being the values of *subjects*, of human individuals and communities. But which values and ideals enable us to grow and flourish is not a mere matter of "subjective opinion"; it is something one can be right or wrong about.[5]

—And I added:

Like John Dewey, I do not believe in an afterlife, or in God as a supernatural helper who intervenes in the course of history or in the course of our lives to rescue us from disasters. I don't believe in "miracles" in *that* sense. But spirituality—in my case, that means praying, meditating, putting myself in touch with the ideals, rituals, ancient texts, that the Jewish people have passed down for more than two millennia, and undergoing the experiences that go with all of these—is miraculous and natural at the same time, just as the contact with another in what Buber calls the "I-You" relation is miraculous and natural, and the contact with natural beauty or with art can be miraculous and natural.[6]

Am I saying then that "all religions are equally good"? I once heard Wilfrid Cantwell Smith[7] answer that question, and I cannot improve on his answer. His answer was, "I am not saying all religions are equally good. I don't believe even *one* religion is equally good."

What Smith meant is that all of the extended groups of people—extended in both space and time in the case of the great religions I have been talking about—consist of many different communities. The communities of faith belonging to a single "religion" may share a common tradition (although they will remember and interpret it differently, if they are live communities and not fossils), but the spiritual and moral content they put into the tradition and the practices they read out of it can vary enormously. Wilfrid Smith himself, with his enormous historical scholarship, made the bold claim that "I could show you as much variety in Methodist communities in London in 1815 as is supposed to exist among the 'world religions.'" Within a single tradition—including the Jewish—there are wonderful communities of faith and there are awful communities of faith and there is a lot in between. Pluralism means recognizing that no tradition has a monopoly on religious value and religious virtue.

Last but not least, I also wrote that "my friend Gordon Kaufman may be right in saying that 'the available God' is a human construct, but I am sure he would agree that we construct our images of God in response to demands that we do not create, and that it is not up to us whether our responses are adequate or inadequate."[8]

To satisfy my pluralist conscience, my responses to Ruth Anna's questions in what follows have to be true to this valorization of diversity, and I will indicate immediately how that is supposed to be the case.

III. WHAT CAN WE SAY ABOUT GOD?

I find what Ruth Anna writes in the section of her essay with this title beautiful and perceptive. She closes this section by remarking: "In any case, for Putnam and the Jewish philosophers that interest him, 'theorizing about God is, as it were, beside the point.' What then is to the point? He quotes Rosenzweig saying that one does not want to say anything about God or about man 'but only about an event between the two.'"

An explicitly pluralistic version of the view she quite rightly ascribes to me might read as follows: "Theorizing about the ontological status of God, or the way of Heaven, or the Tao, or the Hindu Gods who are simultaneously six and thirty-three and 3,306 in number, is beside the point. What one wants to talk about is the ways in which one's life can be informed by asking what God wants of one, or asking how one can be in tune with the way of Heaven, or with the Tao, or with the complex spiritual reality that the "visionary sage" Yajnavalkya described to the student Sakalya in response to the latter's asking "How many Gods are there, Yajnavalkya?" And I want to repeat what I said above, that religious experience can be *enriched* by reflection rather than impoverished by it. How spiritually enriching reflection differs from mere "theorizing" is what Rosenzweig tries to explain, and a large part of what I try to explain in my chapters about Rosenzweig in *Jewish Philosophy as a Guide to Life*.

IV. WHAT CAN WE SAY ABOUT AN EVENT BETWEEN GOD AND A HUMAN PERSON?

As I mentioned above, Ruth Anna says that she is especially uncertain about my response to this question. In fact, this section of her essay contains a number of questions for me, all of them aspects of this large question. But I shall begin with a remark she makes almost in passing that occasioned me much thought. She writes: "Rosenzweig conceived of revelation as an ongoing process in every religious person's life. It is not clear to me whether Putnam shares this notion of revelation. What is clear is that Putnam, like Rosenzweig, believes that we are always in the presence of God, that the only commandment is to love God, and that one should pray only for the strength to meet what Rosenzweig called "the demand of the day."[9]

I think that every religious person's life involves moments of contact, be it with God or the Tao or the Way of Heaven, etc. And I can see how one might think of that, to use the language of Ruth Anna and my tradition, as "revelation," and how one might think of it as an "ongoing process"; but I have to add that I also think that Kierkegaard was right to describe faith as something that is in a dialectical relation with doubt.[10] But what occasioned the lengthy thinking was the phrase "believes that we are always in the presence of God." *Do I* think that?

I can understand very well how someone in a monotheistic tradition may say "We are always in the presence of God," and I can also understand how such a person may say "God is eclipsed." Both the sense of God's availability and the sense of "the absence of God" are moments in the lives of religious people. But because each of them is a moment in one (monotheistic) form of spiritual life (although there are, of course, analogues in the other forms[11] I mentioned earlier), I would not use the language of "belief" here. I do not want to say "I *believe* that we are always in the presence of God," although there are many moments at which I feel that, and I try to live my life as if that were the case.

Some Further Remarks about This

Ruth Anna writes, "this claim—that every human being is always in the presence of God—sounds to me like a statement about God, not about an event between God and a human being, that is, it sounds to me like the kind of statement that misleads one into the kind of theologizing that Putnam wants to avoid." That is absolutely right, and that is why I do not want to make this "statement," or anyway, not make it as a "statement," although it may at times be an appropriate expression of a certain religious feeling.

She continues, "Be that as it may, when one is aware of standing in the presence of God, then, if I understand Putnam correctly, one is conscious of God's command, 'Love Me!' As we shall see, Putnam does not think that this is the only kind of event between a human being and God." Not only do I not think it is the only kind of event between a human being and God, but I do not think that being conscious of the presence of God is the same as *being conscious of* the command to love God, although when the "presence" in question is a positive one[12] it *involves* loving God, just as a positive experience of a friend involves loving the friends, but not normally being conscious of the command to love the friend. Let me place this discussion in its context.

Ruth Anna is referring to my interpretation of Rosenzweig's difficult work, *The Star of Redemption*, an interpretation she describes very well.

For Rosenzweig the one supreme command is to love God, but (as she explains) genuine love of God is, according to Rosenzweig (and, I believe, according to the Jewish tradition) inseparable from the love of the other. (Hillel the Elder expressed this by saying that we are commanded to "love our fellow creatures."[13]) And it is experiencing *this* command that constitutes the "encounter between Man and God" of which Rosenzweig speaks. Ruth Anna writes,

> I find "man" ambiguous. Does it refer to an individual, or to all human beings severally, or to humanity, i.e., all humans collectively? If one thinks of God's revelation to Moses on Mt. Sinai, for example, one can think of it as an event (historical or not) in the life of a particular man, or as an event (again historical or not) in the life of the Jewish people, or is revelation something that happens in the life of each Jew, past, present, and future? Once again I am wondering how this last reading can be compatible with the fact that some people, even some Jews, never have a religious experience.

This is quite a bundle of questions! Let me consider this first as an issue of Rosenzweig interpretation, and then as a bundle of questions addressed to me.

Rosenzweig's prose is an example of what Paul Franks has called "revelatory writing," and Franks suggests the nature of this remarkable genre by prefacing his essay[14] with a quote from Wittgenstein: "You can't hear God speaking to someone else, you can hear him only if you are the addressee.— That is a grammatical remark."[15] Franks's point is that Rosenzweig is not "theorizing" but attempting to *evoke*—to evoke a sense of God's presence in the soul of an individual reader, a reader who will feel himself as the "addressee"—not Rosenzweig's addressee, but God's. If this is right, then here are my answers to Ruth Anna's questions, taken in the first way, that is, as asking what I think Rosenzweig's replies might have been:

(1) "Does it [the idea of an event between Man and God] refer to an individual, or to all human beings severally, or to humanity, i.e., all humans collectively." ANSWER: It refers to *you*, dear reader, the addressee.

(2) "*If* one thinks of God's revelation to Moses on Mt. Sinai, for example, one can think of it as an event (historical or not) in the life of a particular man, or as an event (again historical or not) in the life of the Jewish people, or is revelation something that happens in the life of each Jew, past, present, and future?" ANSWER: I believe that Rosenzweig did not care to speculate, and was not interested in speculating, about the question of the "historicity" of Moses. But the archetype of Moses is an essential part of

the Jewish tradition, even if it does not correspond to whatever is histori-cally true. And I do not think Rosenzweig thought revelation happens in the life of every Jew, although he thought it *should* happen in the life of every Jew, and hoped it *would* someday happen in the life of every Jew.

(3) "Once again I am wondering how this last reading can be compatible with the fact that some people, even some Jews, never have a religious experi-ence." ANSWER: Keep trying to communicate it to them!

—And my own answers: (1) above would also be my answer. But *re* (2) I would agree with Rosenzweig that the historical truth of our myths is not something one has to believe—in fact, I would go further than Rosenzweig, and say that one must take very seriously what text-critical scholarship has come up with if one wants to avoid "fundamentalism" and all its dangers. But as a pluralist, I do not share Rosenzweig's wish that everyone, or even every Jew, should be religious. I do not believe that in spiritual matters "one size fits all," or fits all Jews. There are atheist forms of spirituality as well as conventionally "religious" ones; indeed, that is one of the things Dewey was trying to teach us in *A Common Faith*, and such forms are not to be deplored or patronized. Lastly, with respect to (3), I certainly hope and pray that all human beings will someday rise above selfishness, success worship, and cruelty in all its forms. I do not pray that all human beings will have a "religious experience," although I do think that a life without a spiritual dimension is missing something.

V. A QUESTION ABOUT LEVINAS

Ruth Anna writes that I fail to make clear whether I find Levinas's account of Jewish particularism convincing. Here is my answer to that question: In a conversation, Sidney Morgenbesser once remarked that many philosophers confuse the idea of a universal ethics with the idea of a universal way of life.[16] Like Levinas, I believe that the fundamental moral values are univer-sal (I write "values" in the plural, because I do not agree with Levinas that there is only *one*) but that such obligations as responsibility to the other, compassion, justice, equality, and liberty are compatible with more than one way of life. I also believe that one way of life that is worthy of respect is rooted in the Talmud; but I do not agree with the words that Ruth Anna quotes from Levinas: "the categories needed to understand [antibiotics or nuclear energy] are already available to monotheism." Contrary to Levi-nas, we cannot simply derive a morality for dealing with contemporary biomedical knowledge or with nuclear energy from the Talmud—although we can, of course, *reinterpret* the Talmud in the light of our best ethical thinking, and thus find a way to be both traditional Jews, if that is what we wish to be, *and* modern ethical thinkers. But I do not believe the best ethical thinking is invariably to be found already present in the Talmud. Indeed, on feminist issues, on gay rights, and on respect for the wisdom of non-Jewish traditions, Talmudic sensibility needs to be *corrected* by the sensibility of the Enlightenment.

What Difference Does It Make?

This beautiful section of Ruth Anna Putnam's paper answers her question in a way I totally agree with. I cannot improve on her words. And I am very happy that our way of questioning each other about our ongoing thoughts will be on display in this volume.

H.P.

NOTES

1. For example, "On Negative Theology" (*Faith and Philosophy* 14, no. 4 [October 1997]: 407–22); "God and the Philosophers" (*Midwest Studies in Philosophy* 21, no. 1 [September 1997]: 175–87); "Thoughts Addressed to an Analytical Thomist" (*Monist* 80, no. 4 [October 1997]: 487–99); and "Monotheism and Humanism" (in *Humanity Before God: Contemporary Faces of Jewish, Christian, and Islamic Ethics*, ed. W. Schweiker, M. Johnson, and K. Jung [Minneapolis, MN: Fortress Press, 2006]).

2. "Of course," she adds, "the same person at another moment is capable of having a religious or an aesthetic experience; indeed, I find it difficult to imagine that a person untouched by art or by God could or would philosophize about art or God."

3. An excellent introduction to Hadot's thought is Pierre Hadot and Arnold Davidson, *Philosophy as a Way of Life: Spiritual Exercises from Socrates to Foucault* (Oxford: Blackwell, 1995).

4. See Diana Eck, *Encountering God: A Spiritual Journey from Bozeman to Banaras* (Boston: Beacon Press, 2003), 62.

5. Hilary Putnam, *Jewish Philosophy as a Guide to Life* (Bloomington, IN: Indiana University Press, 2008), 101.

6. Ibid, 102.

7. Smith was the Chairman of the Committee on the Study of Religion at Harvard University for many years, and a world renowned student of the world's religions and their histories.

8. *Jewish Philosophy as a Guide to Life*, 6. The reference is to Gordon Kaufman, *In the Face of Mystery: A Constructive Theology* (Cambridge, MA: Harvard University Press, 1993).

9. Rosenzweig's German readers would have been familiar with the source of the expression "demand of the day": Johann Wolfgang Goethe, *Spruche in Prosa* (Stuttgart:

Verlag freies Geistesleben, 1999), §611 *"Was aber ist deine Pflicht? Die Forderung des Tages?"*

10. In *Concluding Unscientific Postscript*, trans. by David F. Swenson and Walter Lowrie (Princeton: Princeton University Press, 1968). Kierkegaard wrote that faith "has in every moment the infinite dialectic of uncertainty present with it." Ibid., 53.

11. Galia Patt-Shamir, "To Live a Riddle: The Case of the Binding of Isaac," in *Philosophy and Literature* 27, no. 2 (October 2003): 269–83, describes the way in which certain Confucian texts tell us that "Anyone can be a sage" and "No one is a sage." Perhaps these two moments in Confucian spiritual life are a partial analogue to "God is always present" and "God is absent."

12. There can also be terrible experiences of the presence of God, experiences of God as an accuser.

13. *"Ohev et habriot," Pirke Avot*, I:12.

14. Paul Franks, "Everyday Speech and Revelatory Speech in Rosenzweig and Wittgenstein," *Philosophy Today: Special Issue on Jewish Philosophy* (2006): 24–39.

15. Ludwig Wittgenstein, *Zettel*, ed. G. E. M. Anscombe and G. H. von Wright (Oxford: Blackwell, 1981), §717.

16. On this confusion, see my "Pragmatism and Relativism: Universal Values and Traditional Ways of Life," collected in *Words and Life* (Cambridge, MA: Harvard University Press, 1994).

21

Simon Blackburn

PUTNAM ON WITTGENSTEIN AND RELIGIOUS LANGUAGE

> *Wisdom is cold and to that extent stupid. (Faith on the other hand is a passion.)* It might also be said: Wisdom merely *conceals* life from you. (Wisdom is like cold grey ash, covering up the glowing embers.)
> —LUDWIG WITTGENSTEIN, FROM *CULTURE AND VALUE* [1]

In *Renewing Philosophy*, Hilary Putnam included an extended and respectful meditation on Ludwig Wittgenstein's lectures on religious belief. As is well known, these lectures were not written by Wittgenstein, but are transcriptions, mainly by Yorick Smythies, perhaps with the assistance of other students who attended his discussions. Nevertheless, there is no doubt that they represent an aspect of Wittgenstein's thought, and alongside other evidence, they must be taken as indicating at least one important part of it. So in this essay I want to offer some observations both about Wittgenstein's lectures and some of their context in Wittgenstein's other writings, particularly *Culture and Value*, as well as the writings of others. But I also want to venture some remarks about Putnam's sensitive and interesting reaction to them.

I

There is a difficulty at the outset in identifying just what the lectures are about. It is natural to say that they are about religious belief—but one of the questions is going to be whether "belief" is exactly the right word. We might substitute "religious conviction"—but one of the questions may be whether religious practices can properly, and even at their best, coexist with doubt and uncertainty (as Putnam mentions, Kierkegaard was one of Wittgenstein's inspirations, but also someone who thought that a religious way of life could and should include elements of doubt and uncertainty). Religious metaphors, or the use of religious pictures and imaginings, also suggest themselves as the topic, but here too there is a danger of shoehorning the phenomena into a predetermined shape.

Perhaps the most neutral, if cumbersome, description of the topic might be religious frames of mind. One advantage of the plural is that it insulates us from the outset against the danger of presupposing that there is any such thing as *the* religious frame of mind. Perhaps there are many, with only a family resemblance among them. Perhaps in the case of some or many religious and magical ceremonies, the state of mind of the officiant is typically quite different from that of the recipient. And perhaps the state of some religious persons is best characterized not in terms of a frame of mind, but in terms of an oscillation or succession of different frames of mind. We thus characterize the inquiry while leaving it open at the outset how to relate these frames of mind, and the language in which they are voiced, to more familiar psychological and logical categories of belief and expression.

Any account of *the* religious state of mind may simply disguise a normative agenda suggesting that while a *truly* religious state of mind has to be this or that, people unhappily substitute something different and inferior. People advocate positions of this sort in order to distinguish the plane on which *real* religion is found from that of facsimiles, such as mere sectarianism, lip service, superstition, or idolatry. Wittgenstein certainly wants to strike this note: his contempt for superstition as a substitute or distortion of truly religious frames of mind is quite clear. His example of a superstitious person is one Father O'Hara, and Wittgenstein's contempt is evident. He thinks that people who try to show that religious belief is a kind of glorified science, or that it stands up in the light of ordinary canons of confirmation or verification, are "ludicrous," "ridiculous," or "cheating themselves."[2] The whole point is going to be that we are dealing with something special, even when it looks as if the religious believer is talking about ordinary historical events:

> Queer as it sounds: The historical accounts in the Gospels might, historically speaking, be demonstrably false and yet belief would lose nothing by this: *not*, however, because it concerns 'universal truths of reason'! Rather, because historical proof (the historical proof-game) is irrelevant to belief. This message (the Gospels) is seized on by men believingly (i.e. lovingly). *That* is the certainty characterizing this particular acceptance-as-true, not something *else*.

A believer's relation to these narratives is *neither* the relation to historical truth (probability), *nor yet* that to a theory consisting of 'truths of reason'. There is such a thing.—(We have quite different attitudes even to different species of what we call fiction!)[3]

But before we leave "frames of mind" in possession of the territory, we might want to flag another curious aspect of Wittgenstein's discussion: it is fundamentally individualistic (I might have said solipsistic almost). The inquiry is into the state or states of mind of the single individual wrestling with themes of redemption, salvation, sin, judgment, and so on. It is striking how far this is from, say, a social anthropological discussion of religion. Here, for example, is Durkheim: "A religion is a unified system of beliefs and practices relative to sacred things, that is to say, things set apart and forbidden—beliefs and practices which unite into one single moral community called a Church, all those who adhere to them."[4] The social aspects of religious practices are scarcely visible in Wittgenstein. His idea of religion is simply that of one man wrestling with his own soul. Although I consider this a grave weakness, it is not one that actually matters very much to the philosophical thread I want to pursue. I mention it only to register a problem.

II

Wittgenstein begins his discussion with a story:

> An Austrian general said to someone: "I shall think of you after my death, if that should be possible." We can imagine one group who would find this ludicrous, another who wouldn't. . . .

> Suppose that someone believed in the Last Judgment, and I don't, does this mean that I believe the opposite to him, just that there won't be such a thing? I would say: "not at all, or not always."

> Suppose I say that the body will rot, and another says "No. Particles will rejoin in a thousand years, and there will be a Resurrection of you."

> If some said: "Wittgenstein, do you believe in this?" I'd say: "No." "Do you contradict the man?" I'd say: "No." . . .

> Suppose someone were a believer and said: "I believe in a Last Judgment," and I said; "Well, I'm not so sure. Possibly." You would say that there is an

enormous gulf between us. If he said "There is a German aeroplane overhead," and I said "Possibly I'm not so sure," you'd say we were fairly near.

It isn't a question of my being anywhere near him, but on an entirely different plane, which you can express by saying: "You mean something altogether different, Wittgenstein."[5]

The difference might not show up at all in any explanation of meaning. These paragraphs introduce a recurring theme in the lectures, which Putnam unerringly highlights. The first is that the relation between the person advancing this expression of a religious frame of mind and the person who rejects the expression is not one of simple contradiction. It is unlike a case in which a person advances an ordinary belief, and an objector dissents or disagrees. On the other hand, neither is it a simple matter of difference of meaning. It may in some subtle sense be *like* a difference of meaning, but it is also unlike it. Later on, Wittgenstein says:

If you ask me whether or not I believe in a Judgment Day, in the sense in which religious people have belief in it, I wouldn't say: "No. I don't believe there will be such a thing." It would seem to me utterly crazy to say this.

And then I give an explanation: "I don't believe in . . .," but then the religious person never believes what I describe.

I can't say. I can't contradict that person.

In one sense, I understand all he says—the English words "God," "separate," etc. I understand. I could say: "I don't believe in this," and this would be true, meaning I haven't got these thoughts or anything that hangs together with them. But not that I could contradict the thing.[6]

Putnam emphasizes in his discussion that this is not illuminated by casual talk of "incommensurability," which is clearly right, and which I shall not discuss further.

But Putnam also argues that it is not illuminated by talk of noncognitivism, and here I think there is room for puzzlement. He cites the later interchange:

Suppose someone, before going to China, when he might never see me again, said to me: "We might see one another after death"—would I necessarily say that I don't understand him? I might say [want to say] simply, "Yes. I *understand* him entirely."

Lewy[:] "In this case, you might only mean that he expressed a certain attitude."

I would say "No, it isn't the same as saying 'I'm very fond of you'"—and it may not be the same as saying anything else. It says what it says. Why should you be able to substitute anything else?

Suppose I say: "The man used a picture."[7]

After giving this example, Putnam explains that:

What I take Wittgenstein to be pointing out is that there is a perfectly ordinary notion of expressing an attitude, and what he is doing is contrasting the kind of metaphysical emphasis that non-cognitivists (either about religious language or about ethical language) want to put on the notion of expressing an attitude with the ordinary unemphasized use of that notion. . . . Wittgenstein is refusing to say that language is "used to express an attitude" when there is no possibility of replacing the language in question by an explicit expression of the so-called attitude.[8]

And, Putnam continues, his reason for this will be refusal "to turn the distinction between saying something because that is, quite literally, what one means to say, and saying something to express an attitude, into a *metaphysical* distinction."[9]

My puzzle with this diagnosis is, first, that I do not recognize the implied assimilation of saying something to express an attitude and saying something that is not quite literally what one means to say. If I choose my words carefully and mean what I say when I insist that Gordon Brown is pig-headed, do I not thereby express an attitude? I could also say, indeed, that I dislike Gordon Brown's inflexibility of mind, but it is not at all clear that this is a better, more accurate, or revealing way of saying what I wanted to say, or as if I somewhat missed what I wanted to say the first time around. I should say that I very seldom choose to convey an attitude by using a sentence that sounds like a self-description. I do it by careful choice of words, but frequently by intonation and gesture (as Wittgenstein often emphasizes).

Be that as it may, Wittgenstein's rejoinder to Lewy still remains puzzling. It implies that a use of language cannot be said to express an attitude unless it can be substituted by a first-person avowal of some kind (for it would be imposing yet more theory to say that "I'm very fond of you" is simply a *description* of oneself). But it is not at all clear either that this is true, nor that Wittgenstein has any right to say that it is true. To take the second point first, it was Wittgenstein who wrote in connection with other minds: "My attitude towards him is an attitude towards a soul. I am not of the opinion that he has a soul."[10] To think of another person as a person is here placed in the domain of attitude, not that of opinion, theory, or doctrine. But it will not be an attitude that has a simple three-word expression. It will be one that comes out everywhere and in all the innumerably different things that make up a stream of life. Naturalness of English expression has nothing to do with it: indeed, if a context ever arose in which some reassurance was appropriate it would be much more natural and much easier to say "I think you are a person" than "I . . . you," for what exactly could fill in the ellipsis? Any verb that I can think of would be either inadequate or embarrassing, as in the theological-sounding "I respond to you as to a 'thou'" and similar mawkishness. Yet all the same, we are said to be in the domain of attitude.

Furthermore, Wittgenstein was often preoccupied with states of mind that we find difficult to achieve and difficult to express: understanding a piece of music or architecture, for example. An expression of how you feel about Schubert, say, might require a great deal of gesture or facial expression. You will have to search for words, and are very likely discontent with any you find. Wordsworth, for example, required hundreds of poems to express how he felt about nature, and it would be a highly revisionist, or crass, literary critic who thinks he could have got the same effect by writing, in three words, "I love nature." Wittgenstein talks about this too:

> There is a lot to be learned from Tolstoy's bad theorizing about how a work of art conveys 'a feeling.' —You really could call it, not exactly the expression of a feeling, but at least an expression of feeling, or a felt expression. And you could say too that in so far as people understand it, they 'resonate' in harmony with it, respond to it. You might say: the work of art does not aim to convey *something else*, just itself. Just as, when I pay someone a visit, I don't just want to make him have feelings of such and such a sort; what I mainly want is to visit him, though of course I should like to be well received too.[11]

The echo of "it says what it says" is unmistakable. But Wordsworth's feeling for nature is unmistakable as well, and it is no mistake to say that the poems express it.

If I describe, say, someone who has received a disappointment as having reacted modestly or courageously, then I say something about their way of taking what they were told—the posture of their mind, their demeanor or attitude, but there is no implication that they would have been prepared to describe themselves as having felt modest or courageous—indeed, in the first case, they had better not do so.

The rebuttal of Lewy is even more strange in the context in which it is situated. Wittgenstein is evidently trying to describe more adequately a religious frame of mind. Now he himself cites what are naturally (without any metaphysics) described as attitudes and feelings in the course of doing this. At various times, especially in *Culture and Value* he talks of despair, consciousness of sin, love, sorrow, hope, and the two that eventually commend themselves to Putnam, trust and compassion.[12] Wittgenstein writes that "it is my soul with its passions, as it were with its flesh and blood, that has to be saved, not my abstract mind. Perhaps we can say: Only *love* can believe the Resurrection. Or: It is *love* that believes the Resurrection."[13] So he has very little right to jib at words like "passion," "attitude," or "feeling." These are his own words.

So I think that Casimir Lewy (my revered, old teacher) could reasonably have felt aggrieved, and for yet another reason. "It says what it says. Why should you be able to substitute anything else?" sounds nice and plain. No tricky reinterpretations; no rubbing off the bloom. Or, as just described in the context of works of art, no substitutions, nothing that would "do just as well" in order to work as the work of art works. But now consider a sentence such as "the Virgin Mary bore a child." Does it say what it says? It appears to record an historical event. But Wittgenstein has told us that it does not: that even historical disproof of any such event (and after all, do we not have that, in everything that is known about mammalian reproduction?) will not stop people saying it. This is why the lectures have a subject matter: why the saying, as used by the person in the religious frame of mind, needs some additional words, an explanation or interpretation or a "perspicuous representation" of what is going on. Otherwise we might, with just as much right, say that when the Christian says "the Virgin Mary bore a child," and the historian or biologist says that no such event ever happened, then each "says what they say"—in which case, each contradicts the other. But it is the fact that this is not so that sets the lectures in motion.

Talk of any kind of language needing interpretation may raise danger signals, for it was Wittgenstein who taught philosophers the marvellous lesson not to look for meanings as if behind every word or picture there stands "something else"—a private mental device for mapping the words or picture onto the world. But of course that lesson does nothing to undermine ordinary, everyday (we might say, unmetaphysical) activities of interpretation. If we say that religious frames of mind need interpretation, we need not be saying anything more than that we would like to know how "the Virgin Mary bore a child" can be said with passion, feeling, and a sense of grave importance, but without any historical intent or responsibility. How can the historical words, in the past sense, be used so irresponsibly? The problem may not be difficult: it may be that we could simply go along with Richard Braithwaite, and think that the historical sounding declamations are in effect fairy stories, told in order to beef up our behavior, to sprinkle magic dust on our intentions to live good, "agapeistic," lives.[14] Or, it may be no harder than understanding how Romeo can say that Juliet is the sun, and that the sun is 93 million miles away, without inferring that Juliet is 93 million miles away. But there should be something to be said, in each case.

                                    II

> No opinion serves as the foundation for a religious symbol. And only an opinion can involve an error.

> One would like to say: This and that incident have place; laugh, if you can.[15]

It is illuminating to compare Wittgenstein's *Remarks on Frazer's "Golden Bough"* with R. G. Collingwood's reaction to the same work and others like it (it is often illuminating to compare these two). Writing of a previous generation of anthropologists, which included Sir Edward Tylor, James Frazer, and Claude Lévy-Bruhl, Collingwood salutes their real achievements in uncovering magical practices across the world, but then talks of what happened when they tried to explain what magic is for:

> The direction in which they looked for an answer to this question was determined by the prevailing influence of a positivistic philosophy which ignored man's emotional nature and reduced everything in human experience to terms of intellect, and further ignored every kind of intellectual activity except those which, according to the same philosophy, went to the making of natural science. . . . The difference is that the scientist actually possesses scientific knowledge, and consequently his attempts to control nature are successful: the magician possesses none, and therefore his attempts fail.[16]

Collingwood has nothing but contempt for this "explanation" of the function of magic, although perhaps reserving even greater contempt for Freud's theory, in *Totem and Taboo*: that magicians suffer from a neurosis which enables them to believe that things come about merely because they want them to, or because they think of them as happening. Collingwood curtly refutes Freud by noticing that worldwide magic requires special *practices* and *techniques*, themselves shrouded with mysteries and a heightened sense of drama. No shaman or priest thinks he can bring about what he wants just by wishing for it.

Pointing out the kinship between magical practices and artistic activities like dancing, singing, drawing, or modelling, Collingwood interprets magical practices as a species of what he has called art as craft: art produced for an external end. The end is the arousing and control of emotion: when magic emotions are "focused and crystallized, consolidated into effective agents in practical life."[17] He summarizes his view thus:

> Magical activity is a kind of dynamo supplying the mechanism of practical life with the emotional current that drives it. Hence magic is a necessity for every sort and condition of man, and is actually found in every healthy society. A society which thinks, as our own thinks, that it has outlived the need of magic, is either mistaken in that opinion or else it is a dying society, perishing for lack of interest in its own maintenance.[18]

Collingwood has a far more Durkheimian sense than Wittgenstein that the point of religion, together with its mysteries and contradictions and heightened dramas of the "sacred" or untouchable is the cementing and management of social emotions. By contrast, at least at one point in his life, Wittgenstein was implacably hostile to ritual: "Everything ritualistic (everything that, as it were, smacks of the high priest) must be strictly avoided, because it immediately turns rotten."[19]

The other difference between Collingwood and Wittgenstein might be that, for the former, magical art is not "art proper." It is art as craft, which means art at the service of a predetermined end. For Wittgenstein, on the other hand, the religious way of life "stands on its own feet." It says what it says. It is not "for" the arousal or control of emotion any more than my visit to a friend is "for" the arousal or control of emotion (although presumably it sometimes may be). In Wittgenstein the symbol or representation, which for Collingwood provides the emotional current of practical life, has no external end or purpose behind the activities in which it is used. It is not "for" furthering the stream of life, but is part of the stream of life.

However, put thus starkly, the difference between them sounds greater than it is. The previous section showed how closely Wittgenstein's discussion of religious frames of mind ties them to passions, feelings, emotions, and attitudes (let us face it: how could any grown-up discussion of the matter not do so?). Furthermore these emotions and the rest are not alien to us, even when we no longer participate in the practices:

> When Frazer begins by telling us the story of the King of the Wood at Nemi, he does this in a tone which shows that he feels, and wants us to feel, that something strange and dreadful is happening. But the question "why does this happen?" is properly answered by saying: Because it is dreadful. That is, precisely that which makes this incident strike us as dreadful, magnificent, horrible, tragic, etc., as anything but trivial and insignificant, is also *that* which has called this incident to life.[20]

Conversely Collingwood, who was far more ready than Wittgenstein to declare himself a religious person, shows in many ways a more concrete, focused respect for religious practice as an end in itself, than any that is evinced by Wittgenstein's rather abstract and emotional gestures. After describing in sympathetic detail the simple, musical, pious, dignified, gracious, rooted lives of the monks he had stayed with on the island of Santorini, Collingwood ends with a wonderful rhetorical flourish:

> In this way the traveler who began by thinking the men of Santorini ignorant, unenlightened, and superstitious may possibly, unless he is very careful, find within his mind a court sitting wherein the men of Santorini rise up in judgment against his own world and against the protestantism, and secularism, and utilitarianism of which he is so proud; and as judge in that court he may find himself obliged to take their part against his own world; so that if, later on, his own world should accuse him of not worshipping the -isms that it worships, and of corrupting its young men by imparting to them his heresy, he would have to admit that that accusation was just.[21]

I cannot see that Collingwood is less able to attribute an intrinsic value to a way of life or stream of life infused with religious practice than Wittgenstein. Indeed, his sympathy with ritual, and his understanding of the social value of such practice, suggests the reverse.

III

I want to return from these excursions into the nature of religious living to a more pointed philosophical moral, or at least one that concerns me more. In section II I quoted Putnam as hospitable to what we might call a domestic use of the term "attitude" but warning severely against making something "metaphysical" of it. And I think it is clear that what he means is its use by "noncognitivists" to contrast with belief, as part of a package that includes the "metaphysical" contrast, or what he later called a dichotomy between fact and value. So expressivists, of whom I am proud to number myself, are seen not as trying to deflate metaphysics, as our patron saint, David Hume, saw himself as doing, or as desperate to keep it away from subjects it has infected for millennia, including religion and ethics, but as ourselves in the grip of a metaphysics of our own.

I find myself slightly baffled by this charge, since my own endeavors in connection with ethics have always seemed to me to be as antimetaphysical as anything could well be. Roughly, when I started writing, the scene as I saw it was that sides had been taken on a variety of territories, where everyone thought that expressivists "had to" say one kind of thing, and others ("realists") could say other kinds of things. And which of these things you said defined your "metaethics," and put you in one camp or another. But it seemed to me then, and still seems to me now, that none of the pivots on which these debates were supposed to turn was of any use in defining a debate. The character whom I somewhat ineptly called the "quasi-realist" was a dramatization of this thought. Starting off from a position in the sentimentalist or "attitude" camp, he finds himself gradually able to explain and to justify the vocabularies supposedly definitive of realism. In other words, I find myself able to say, justify saying, and indeed revel in saying such things as this: there are duties; it is true that there are duties, and a fact that there are; they are mind independent; we know what many of them are, although we may not yet know what others of them are; we could have been wrong about what they are, but fortunately we are very often not. And similarly for obligations, reasons, or values.

This is not the place to rehearse or defend the various things that enable an expressivist to end up saying these things with a good conscience. The process includes a description of the things we could not do without propositional expression, and hence the pressure to substitute the language we have for any primitive language of ejaculations, commands, or announcings of intent. It includes an "internalist" parsing of mind independency or counterfactual claims, an account of what knowledge claims are that means that expressivism need not labor under the infamous label of noncognitivism, and finally the deployment of a deflationist view of truth—a view that incidentally has the same shape as expressivism in the account it gives of the utility of the truth predicate, and that was itself of course a central doctrine of Wittgenstein's.

The things this journey enables me to say were supposed to be the private property of "moral realists." But in my view, it is the people who think that these things do define an -ism, who put a "metaphysical" gloss on these remarks. By approaching them with a certain picture in mind, they muddy the waters, as they have done since Plato. The picture they have in mind is that in order to say these things you have to conceive of duties or the others as elements in our environment, queer elements or things to be encountered, "intuited," or "tracked." I do not say that this is a coherent picture, any more than the picture of God as having a personality is coherent. But I do say it is to be resisted, and I have tried to resist it, or as Wittgenstein would have said, to combat it. In this I also stand foursquare with Wittgenstein. Wittgenstein thought that in order to get an *übersichtliche Darstellung* of ethics, for instance, you do not rest content with "ethical facts": in many places, indeed in all the places in which he approaches the topic, he insists that "The good is outside the space of facts."[22] I do not go so far as that, but as I read him, it is not that you must not say, as I do say, that it is a fact that you have a duty to your children, for instance. There is a proposition here, and where there is a proposition the language of truth and fact can attach itself perfectly naturally. Rather, the point is that this is only where you end up; it is not *itself* the key to a perspicuous account or understanding of what goes on that you should end up here. The way to do that according to Wittgenstein is to think about how we learned words, and about the word "good," he says:

> A child generally applies a word like 'good' first to food. One thing that is immensely important in teaching is exaggerated gestures and facial expressions. The word is taught as a substitute for a facial expression or a gesture. The gestures, tones of voice, etc., in this case are expressions of approval. What *makes* the word an interjection of approval? It is the game it appears in, not the form of words.[23]

In fact the very beginning of *LAPR* is devoted to Wittgenstein distancing himself from those such as G. E. Moore who think that because "beautiful" and "good" are adjectives, they must function as other adjectives do. This is one place that Wittgenstein wheels out his celebrated comparison of language to a tool chest.[24] Of course aesthetics and ethics grow out of using words just as "interjections of approval," in ways that give the quasi-realist work to do. But they never leave their ancestry behind: the child remains the father of the man.

Wittgenstein thought, as for that matter did Hume, that in grown-up aesthetic judgment it is what you discriminate and notice that counts. Appreciation does not consist in just saying "hooray!" at the right moments. Even what we call "taking delight" in things is complex: not so much expressed in the faces we make as in whether we return to things again and again—the opposite of discontent, disgust, or discomfort. The lectures on aesthetics explore the way the delight or discontent is not an effect separable from its "cause," but an element inside the experience of the object. You cannot get the delight you take in a sonnet by playing a round of golf. All this is surely right and true. In both aesthetics and ethics there is the possibility that Putnam also stresses of increased discrimination and understanding, insight and delicacy. But it is a question of taking delight or not, all the same. And what is the harm in calling that a way of feeling, and improvement in it an education in feeling?

Putnam believes that our values cast their shades of pink over what would otherwise be Quine's pale grey lore, itself a blending of the white of convention and the black of fact. With Wittgenstein in mind we might see it like this: the human activity that we call describing the facts is never free of currents in our stream of life that swirl or tumble according to our values. I am not sure whether I believe that, but suppose it were true. For comparison we might imagine a "hyper-religious" society, in which the picture of the Last Judgment, of life after death, or God as having a personality, is always in peoples' minds. It might dictate their interests, and play a role in determining what they notice, what implications they draw from what they notice, and the exits into action that these implications engender. It might complicate mutual understanding, interpretation, or translation if, as they bring their slightly different pictures to bear, there is some divergence between the interpretations of experience, the inferential paths, and the resulting actions that one or another member of this society offers.

It might be difficult for these hyper-religious people to perceive the omnipresent coloring their pictorial habits bring with them, to understand others who do not color the world the same way, or to accept the contingencies responsible for them coloring as they do, and perhaps, in this respect, they resemble some of us. The question for Putnam is whether Wittgenstein would have to say that in this society there is no use for the kind of investigation his lecture illustrates. Would it indicate that there is no distinction between being in the grip of a picture, for instance, and describing a fact? It is difficult to see why it should. Our imaginings certainly stir our emotions and actions; indeed *all* mental states have an exit into expression and action, and Wittgenstein was the first to insist. But it did not lead him to say that the tool box of language contained only a hammer, nor to suppose that only metaphysical prejudice leads us to notice the patchwork that makes up our language and therefore our minds. It is surely not metaphysics that leads us to want to understand ourselves well enough so that things that might appear puzzling become clear.

IV

Not all the mental descriptions we offer about each other, and therefore about ourselves, describe beliefs. Someone using a metaphor or advancing a picture does not necessarily believe anything, although they may be on the way to doing so. The metaphor or picture is supposed to act as a kind of invitation or signpost. It is a stimulus to the imagination, and hence is often a route to belief and action. But in religious contexts, the route may not lead to actual belief (Hume talks of the "somewhat unaccountable" state of mind of the religious observer), although deploying a picture or even bare imaginings can certainly lead to actions. Involved in the mysteries of magic and religion people are frequently at a loss, bewildered, have their minds in a whirl, are beset by fears, imaginings, distractions, and prejudice; they may be unable to come to an opinion, but also unable to admit that, for they will know to say that faith is a virtue, and the magic depends upon suspension of thought. People may be vacillating and irresolute, and we may describe their states of mind by saying that we do not know where they stand. Western and Middle-Eastern monotheistic religions, with their mysteries, paradoxes, contradictions, and analogies are particularly adapted to such states: mystery and confusion are part of the package.

Hume played off the issue brilliantly by having two, rather than one, religious apologists in his *Dialogues Concerning Natural Religion*. One is the proponent of the Divine Architect—the anthropomorphic, humanoid God of Abraham and Isaac; the other is the Leibnizian proponent of the God of the philosophers, perfect and therefore immutable, atemporal, eternal, and unknowable. The one flirts with idolatry, and the other with mysticism, and by the end of the *Dialogues* each of them has, with complete justice, accused the other of propounding something absolutely useless, no better than atheism. Religious practice—magical practice—could not survive by bringing either of these pictures into focus by itself. It has to revolve or oscillate, and the fact that it finds no stable stopping point is its lifeblood: "Behold I show you a mystery." At the risk of appearing to belittle the awful majesty of the issue, I cannot resist thinking that Lewis Carroll captures this side of it perfectly. When Alice hears the nonsense poem "Jabberwocky" she confesses: "Somehow it seems to fill my head with ideas—only I don't exactly know what they are."

After Durkheim and Collingwood, I do not think we should "combat" people who need to get their heads in a whirl. It is not "stupid," as contemporary, militant atheists think, to invest symbols and rituals with importance. The rituals and practices are things people do, and like other things human beings do, have to be applauded or condemned at the bar of ethics. If we side with Collingwood we would say that the balance sheet is, on the whole, quite favorable. If we side with Hume, we would say that it is not. One side stresses dignity and quiet piety, the sense of awe, the trust and hope and social emotions that make for life going well; the other side stresses the abjection and sense of sin, the fears and terrors, the sectarianism, the fossilizations of dogma, the accusations of heresy and the horrors of theocracy. The one side hears Bach; the other hears car bombs and the madness of crowds. We all have a "particle of the dove kneaded into our frame, along with the elements of the wolf and the serpent," and our religious practices are likely to be no better nor worse than we ourselves are.[25]

SIMON BLACKBURN

UNIVERSITY OF CAMBRIDGE
FEBRUARY 2010

NOTES

1. Ludwig Wittgenstein, *Culture and Value*, trans. Peter Winch (Oxford: Blackwell, 1980), 53.

2. See Ludwig Wittgenstein, *Lectures and Conversations on Aesthetics, Psychology and Religious Belief* (hereafter *LAPR*), ed. Cyril Barrett (Oxford: Blackwell, 1953), 53, 58–59.

3. Wittgenstein, *Culture and Value*, 32.

4. Emile Durkheim, *The Elementary Forms of Religious Life,* trans. K. E. Fields (New York: Simon & Schuster, 1995), 44.

5. Wittgenstein, *LAPR*, 53.

6. Ibid., 55.

7. Ibid., 71.

8. Hilary Putnam, *Renewing Philosophy* (Cambridge, MA: Harvard University Press, 1992), 152–53.

9. Ibid., 153.

10. Ludwig Wittgenstein, *Philosophical Investigations*, trans. E. Anscombe (Oxford: Blackwell, 1953), 178.

11. Wittgenstein, *Culture and Value*, 58.

12. See Putnam, *Renewing Philosophy*, 177–79.

13. Wittgenstein, *Culture and Value*, 33.

14. R. B. Braithwate, "An Empiricist's View of the Nature of Religious Belief," in *The Philosophy of Religion*, ed. Basil Mitchell (Oxford: Oxford University Press, 1971), 86.

15. Ludwig Wittgenstein, *Remarks on Frazer's "Golden Bough,"* in *Philosophical Occasions: 1912–1951*, ed. J. C. Klagge and A. Nordman (Indianapolis: Hackett, 1993), 123.

16. R. G. Collingwood, *The Principles of Art* (Oxford: Oxford University Press, 1938), 58.

17. Ibid., 66.

18. Ibid., 68.

19. Wittgenstein, *Culture and Value*, 8.

20. Wittgenstein, *Remarks on Frazer's "Golden Bough,"* 121.

21. R. G. Collingwood, *Essays in Political Philosophy* (Oxford: Oxford University Press, 1989), 149.

22. Wittgenstein, *Culture and Value*, 3.

23. Wittgenstein, *LAPR*, 2.

24. Ibid., 1–2.

25. David Hume, *An Enquiry concerning the Principles of Morals*, ed. Tom L Beauchamp (Oxford: Oxford University Press, 1998), sec. IX, pt. 1, 4 (p. 147).

REPLY TO SIMON BLACKBURN

S imon Blackburn pays me the compliment of describing my reading of Wittgenstein's lectures on religious belief[1] as "sensitive and interesting," and I am gratified, because he is himself a fine reader of those same lectures, as shows in the present essay. I have been instructed by reading it, and I agree with almost everything he says in the sections of the essay (sections I and II) that he devotes to those lectures (including his criticism of something I said). Sections III and IV briefly explain Blackburn's defense of "quasi-realism," something he and I disagree about, but a matter I am happy to discuss once again.

I. BLACKBURN'S CRITICISM

I said that I agree with *almost* everything Blackburn says in the first two sections of his paper. Indeed, if I have any disagreement with him here at all, it is with something he *fails* to say in those sections. I will come to that later. But first Blackburn's criticism of something I said.

> Putnam explains that "What I take Wittgenstein to be pointing out that there is a perfectly ordinary notion of expressing an attitude, and what he is doing is contrasting the kind of metaphysical[2] emphasis that non-cognitivists (either about religious language or about ethical language) want to put on the notion of expressing an attitude with the ordinary unemphasized use of that notion . . . Wittgenstein is refusing to say that language is 'used to express an attitude' when there is no possibility of replacing the language in question by an explicit expression of the so-called attitude." And, Putnam continues, his reason for this will be refusal "to turn the distinction between saying something because that is, quite literally, what one means to say, and saying something to express an attitude, into a *metaphysical* distinction."

Against this, Blackburn reasonably says, "My puzzle with this diagnosis is firstly that I do not recognize the implied assimilation of saying something to express an attitude and saying something that is not quite literally what one means to say." The second "puzzle with this diagnosis" is that "It implies that a use of language cannot be said to express an attitude unless it can be substituted by a first-person avowal of some kind (for it would be imposing yet more theory to say that 'I'm very fond of you' is simply a *description* of oneself). But it is not at all clear either that this is true, nor that Wittgenstein has any right to say that it is true." And he concludes by saying "I think that Casimir Lewy (my revered old teacher) could reasonably have felt aggrieved," and he is right, and right for all the reasons he gives. Either Wittgenstein was unreasonable here, or the students who took the notes got his meaning wrong. In either case, I was wrong to defend it.

II. BLACKBURN ON "ATTITUDES" AND "REPRESENTATIONS OF HOW THINGS STAND"

The core thesis of "Expressivism," in all its versions, is that the distinctive function of ethical utterances is to express "attitudes" (Blackburn also uses the term "stances"[3]). They may also express beliefs, but, according to other writings by Blackburn, those beliefs vary from speaker to speaker. Contrary to my position in *The Collapse of the Fact/Value Dichotomy*, Blackburn insists that the expressive "load" and the descriptive component [the "representation of how things stand"] of a thick ethical term can be "disentangled."[4] Moreover, he claims that the descriptive component of such a term is extremely variable. According to him, while there may be a fact as to whether or not the descriptive component associated with the term by a particular speaker on a particular occasion fits the world, there is no such thing as an "attitude" fitting or failing to fit the world. "Representations of how things stand must fit the world whereas it is the world that must fit, or be desired to fit, or regretted for not fitting, our attitudes."[5]

What Blackburn *fails* to say in the first two sections of the present essay is that uttering a sentence that Blackburn wants us to understand "realistically" and not "quasirealistically" can *also* "express an attitude." For example, if I show my design for a new model of automobile to an engineer and he says, "It won't go a thousand miles without breaking down," she has clearly expressed an attitude. However, the defining claim of "expressivism" is that the function of ethical, religious, etc., utterances is to express attitudes or "stances"! Perhaps Blackburn might describe the difference he sees between descriptive utterances and, say, ethical utterances, by saying that the descriptive component of "It won't go a thousand miles without breaking down" is fixed by the lexical meaning of the words while the engineer's "attitude" is not, and in the case of an ethical utterance ("John is a cruel father") it is the attitude that is fixed by the lexical meaning of the words, while the descriptive meaning associated with the word "cruel" is not. In my eyes, such a response would leave it more than a little unclear just what an "attitude" is supposed to be, and what a "representation of how things stand" is supposed to be.

III. EXPRESSIVISM AND MORAL REALISM

In the two final sections of the present essay, Blackburn's strategy is to (1) argue that many of the things that it is usually thought only moral realists can say can also be said by expressivists of his variety, and (2) to offer a following rather unflattering description of "moral realism." I take these up in turn.

Re (1): Blackburn writes,

> Starting off from a position in the sentimentalist or "attitude" camp, [the "quasi-realist"] finds himself gradually able to explain and to justify the vocabularies supposedly definitive of realism. In other words, I find myself able to say, justify saying, and indeed revel in saying such things as this: there are duties; it is true that there are duties, and a fact that there are; they are mind independent; we know what many of them are, although we may not yet know what others of them are; we could have been wrong about what they are, but fortunately we are very often not. And similarly for obligations, reasons, or values.

I do not agree with Blackburn's expressivist position on ethical utterances; my own view is that they contain irreducibly normative predicates that resist a "factorization" into a "descriptive component" and an "attitude," but I will not repeat the arguments here.[6] But let us instead consider an utterance that both Blackburn and I might agree to be as purely "expressive" as one is likely to find. Suppose a child, or a childish adult, insists that "Chocolate ice cream is very good" (or, alternatively, that "Whole wheat pasta tastes awful"). I agree that a deflationist about truth should say that when this utterance "fits the speaker's attitude," it is linguistically appropriate for the speaker to say "It is true that chocolate ice cream is very good" (or "it is true that whole wheat pasta tastes terrible," as the case may be). But is the speaker really entitled to say, "it is a *fact* that chocolate ice cream tastes good"? (Or: "it is a *fact* that whole wheat pasta tastes terrible"?).

According to Blackburn, "it is a fact" is just a *synonym* of (disquotational) "true," but this seems dubious. Indeed, if Blackburn is going to treat "is a fact" as simply another way of saying "true," why does he not go all the way and say that "fits the world" is just a synonym for true? He could then talk exactly like a (slightly crazy) value realist. Of course, his "Expressivism" would then become *inexpressible*! In sum, since Blackburn understands "fits the world" in such a way that value expressions do not "fit the world" or "fail to fit the world," then it seems to me he should treat "is a fact" as falling together with "fits the world" and not as falling together with (purely disquotational) "true." And reinterpreting "know" so that the child, or the childish adult, can properly say "I *know* that chocolate ice cream is good" seems to me a bit of sophistry.

Re (2): Blackburn writes,

> The picture ["'moral realists'"] have in mind is that in order to say these things you have to conceive of duties or the others as elements in our environment, queer elements or things to be encountered or "intuited" or "tracked."

The form of "cognitivism" I defend does *not* posit any "queer elements or things to be 'intuited.'" What it posits, as I put in a paper I wrote responding *inter alia* to a lecture of Blackburn's, is that ethics has

> a number of basic interests, including respect for the humanity in the other, equality of moral rights and responsibilities, compassion for suffering and concern to promote human well-being, and not only the desire to be governed by principles for which one can give one another reasons, although that too is one of them. Even though those interests sometimes conflict, I believe that on the whole and over time, promoting any one of them will require promoting the others.[7]

These interests are not, in my view, something that falls from the sky; they have a history. Perhaps the worst error in contemporary thought about ethics is that recognizing that ethics is a historical product is mistakenly believed to imply moral relativism.

To see why it does not, it is useful to consider the history of *racism*. It is true that so-called "racial science" exerted a baneful influence well into the last century, and in the eyes of the German Nazis, provided a "justification" for the holocaust; but today we do know that the claims of "racial science" were both empirically false and profoundly unscientific in their supposed methodology. Generalizing this case, we see that the presuppositions upon which a supposedly ethical form of behavior are based can themselves frequently be rationally criticized, and this is enough to show that the "nihilistic" picture of ethics as just a matter of "conditioning" by one's culture, "conditioning" to value behaviors that are rationally arbitrary, is a naïve oversimplification (as I am sure Blackburn would agree). We are, of course, brought up in cultures and we acquire beliefs from our cultures, but it is possible to ask whether those beliefs are reasonable or unreasonable. For example, the idea that the highest type of human being is a brave male warrior, and that society should therefore be led by brave male warriors—the idea that the standard of human value should be bravery in battle—was one that had already come to seem unreasonable by the time of Plato and Aristotle (which is obviously not to say that they did not value bravery in battle).

Of course, a "nihilist" may retort, "Sure, but what is 'reasonable' and 'unreasonable' is itself just a matter of conditioning." But if judgments of the reasonable and unreasonable are themselves outside of the domain of rational criticism, then, as I pointed out in "The Philosophers of Science's Evasion of Values,"[8] science itself must lie outside the domain of rational criticism. For science is not just a matter of checking "predictions," as the positivists thought; it is also a matter of deciding which hypotheses are worth the time and expense of experimental testing, as the great pragmatist Charles Sanders Peirce already emphasized, and such decisions presuppose *epistemic values.* Indeed, even when a theory is tested experimentally the decision as to which experiments to trust and which to regard as dubious requires judgments of "coherence" and "plausibility" which resemble aesthetic judgments. (This is particularly true of evolutionary theories, by the way, which are always open to the suspicion of being "just so stories.") If all values are regarded as matters of arbitrary conditioning, then science itself should be regarded "nihilistically" as well.

There is much more to be said on this issue, of course. But just as Simon Blackburn believes that an expressivist of his synod does not have to be a logical positivist, so I believe that a reasonable moral realist does not have to believe in "queer elements or things to be encountered or 'intuited' or 'tracked,'" or, indeed, in anything outside the bounds of a liberal naturalism.[9]

H.P.

NOTES

1. The reading in question constitutes chapters 7 and 8 of *Renewing Philosophy.*

2. Here I used "metaphysical" as a term of abuse, something I now regret. Bad metaphysics is a bad thing, and good metaphysics is a good thing. Metaphysics and ethics are the heart of philosophy; the great twentieth-century attempt (Carnap, Heidegger, Wittgenstein) to show that metaphysics is and always was, *von Anfang an,* a disastrous mistake was itself a disastrous error, I believe, and the twenty-first century needs to repudiate it.

3. In this paragraph I draw on Simon Blackburn, "Disentangling Disentangling," delivered at a *"Colloque sur les defis de* Hilary Putnam," *Sorbonne, I, Place de Pantheon 12 and Ecole Normale Superiere*, March 22, 23, 24, 2005. Blackburn's lecture has not yet been published as far as I know.

4. I am quoting from the same lecture of Blackburn's.

5. Again I am quoting the same lecture.

6. The arguments can be found in my *The Collapse of the Fact/Value Dichotomy*, my *Ethics without Ontology*, and my "Capabilities and Two Ethical Theories," in *Philosophy in an Age of Science* (Cambridge, MA: Harvard University Press, 2012), 299–311.

7. "Capabilities and Two Ethical Theories," 305.

8. "The Philosopher of Science's Evasion of Values" is chapter 8 (135–45) of *The Collapse of the Fact/Value Dichotomy*.

9. I take the term "liberal naturalism" from David Macarthur's introduction to *Naturalism in Question*, ed. M. De Caro and D. Macarthur (Cambridge, MA: Harvard University Press, 2004).

22

Cornel West

HILARY PUTNAM AND THE THIRD ENLIGHTENMENT

The golden age of American philosophy is often associated with the Philosophy Department at Harvard University principally owing to the presence of the great and adorable William James and the grand and irritable Josiah Royce. Needless to say, the brief presence of their famous student, George Santayana, on the faculty sealed the case. Yet never in the history of the modern academy have so many philosophic geniuses worked together as in the mid-to-late twentieth century at Harvard University: W. V. Quine, John Rawls, Nelson Goodman, Stanley Cavell, Robert Nozick, and Hilary Putnam. The logical profundity and literary wit of Quine in twentieth-century philosophy are matched only by his Harvard teacher and thesis advisor, Alfred North Whitehead. The moral rigor and social vision of John Rawls generated a paradigm shift in political philosophy comparable to that of Thomas Hobbes and John Locke. The inimitable complexity and understated wisdom of Nelson Goodman have yet to be fully appreciated. The dazzling originality and courageous probing of Stanley Cavell constitute a corpus unmatched by any humanistic philosopher of our time. The sheer power of intellect and intensity of philosophic excavation are found in the youngest of this group, Robert Nozick. What sets Hilary Putnam apart from this contemporary pantheon of philosophic geniuses is the scope, breadth, and depth of his work. No one in contemporary philosophy has published *more, better, deeper*, and *clearer* works than Hilary Putnam in inductive logic, philosophy of mathematics, the logic of quantum mechanics, philosophy of language, philosophy of mind, epistemology, philosophy of science, aesthetics, ethics, morality, social thought, artificial intelligence, and Jewish philosophy. In short, the long shadow cast by the second golden age of American philosophy centered at Harvard has much to do with the vast light provided by the Philosophic Gang of Six, with Hilary Putnam the all purpose ombudsman, making crucial breakthroughs, consolidations, and transgressions.

I have neither the time nor space to defend my major thesis, namely that this diverse yet interdependent Philosophic Gang of Six crystallized what Hilary Putnam called in his acclaimed Spinoza lectures at the University of Amsterdam in 2001 a "Third Enlightenment" that "hasn't at any rate fully happened."[1] This Third Enlightenment is unabashedly *fallibilist*, unapologetically *antiskeptical*, and undeniably committed to the dignity of the everyday, familiar, commonsensical, quotidian, and *democratic* temperaments. The First Enlightenment—Greek in origin and Socratic in conception—institutionalized "the aspiration to justice and the aspiration to critical thinking."[2] The Second Enlightenment—European in origin and liberal in conception—promoted "a new conception of society as a 'social contract' and the new talk of a 'natural rights' as well as a new conception of science as put forward by Newton and others."[3] The Third Enlightenment—American in origin and Deweyan in conception—walks on the slippery tightrope between foundationalism and relativism, between metaphysical realism and wholesale skepticism, between transcendentalism and nihilism. As Putnam puts it "we walk on thin ground, but we do walk."[4]

My more modest aim is to locate and situate the philosophic visions and viewpoints as well as the tones and temperaments of Putnam's contributions to the Third Enlightenment. I do so in light of not only broad (yet selective) readings of his vast corpus, but also personal conversations with him for over forty years. I have been blessed to enroll in a number of classes taught by Hilary Putnam as a Harvard undergraduate student (as well as the other Philosophic Gang of Six). I also was honored to teach with Hilary Putnam in his last course at Harvard in the spring of 2000. Needless to say, teaching that class on "Pragmatism and Neopragmatism" with Hilary Putnam was a high point in my academic career. I also have been fortunate to work with exemplary Putnam friends and students such as the legendary Paul Benacerraf at Princeton.

I

I begin with one of Putnam's favorite novelists—Henry James. James writes to Robert Louis Stevenson on January 12, 1901, "No theory is kind to us that cheats us of seeing." This quip echoes the sixth paragraph in Joseph Conrad's preface to *The Nigger of the 'Narcissus'* (1897), "My task is to make you see . . . a glimpse of truth for which you have forgotten to ask."[5] Hilary

Putnam, the gifted son of Samuel and Riva Putnam, grew up in a deeply literary and political family. His father was an internationally respected translator of literary classics such as *Don Quixote* as well as a crusader for justice in leftist circles. Hilary, like his fellow student at the University of Pennsylvania, Noam Chomsky (another fellow genius), majored in linguistic analysis. He also majored in German literature—in love with the works of Goethe, Schiller, and Rilke. And as an undergraduate at Penn, he studied American philosophy with Morton White, the philosophy of science with C. West Churchman (himself already a kind of pragmatist), and with the ubiquitous Sidney Morgenbesser, then a precocious graduate student. As a graduate student at Harvard in 1948-1949, Putnam studied mathematics and mathematical logic where Quine's protopragmatic views on ontology and the analytic-synthetic distinction pushed him into metaphilosophical pondering. Putnam writes,

> At this point, I was in a mood that is well known to philosophy teachers today: it seemed to me that the great problems of philosophy had turned out to be pseudo-problems, and it was not clear to me that the technical problems that remained to be cleared up possessed anything like the intrinsic interest of the problems in pure logic and mathematics that also interested me. It was a serious question in my mind at this point whether I should go on in philosophy or shift to mathematics.

> Within a few months of my arrival in Los Angeles in the fall of 1949 these philosophical "blahs" had totally vanished (although I did not lose my desire to pursue mathematics in some way, and eventually I succeeded in pursuing both fields simultaneously). What overcame my "philosophy is over" mood, what made the field come alive for me, made it more exciting and more challenging than I had been able to imagine, was Reichenbach's seminar, and his lecture course, on the philosophy of space and time.[6]

And what did Hans Reichenbach do for the young Putnam? He taught Putnam to see, to look at the big picture, to keep track of the large portrait and be intensely aware of the framework that shapes the lens through which we see. Reichenbach had "the sense of a powerful philosophical vision behind . . . . details."[7] Putnam notes, 'A number of times some of my former students (and some who were not my former students) have complimented me on the fact that I have been willing to think and to write about the 'big problems,' and not just about technical problems. But this is something that Reichenbach instilled in me."[8] For the young Putnam, the clarity of big pictures and big problems in philosophy looms large. His metaphilosophical motivations are driven by the search for lucid lenses "that don't cheat us of seeing" and by difficult problems that we too quickly dismiss. Reichenbach's realism (things, not sensations, are epistemologically primary) and fallibilism (probability is the foundation of metaphysics and epistemology) deeply shaped Putnam's philosophic views, yet what was most decisive for Putnam was Reichenbach's own philosophic temperament that led him to treat his own grand logical empiricist framework as a clarifying picture that wrestled with deep problems, not a dogmatic stance that dismissed such problems.[9] Putnam rightly quips, "empiricism, for Reichenbach, was a challenge and not a terminus."[10] One common denominator of Putnam's subsequent philosophic development—from functionalism to internal realism to natural realism or from Marxist to democratic socialist to Deweyan democrat—is his refusal to reach an easy terminus. Putnam is a dynamic learner and genuine seeker for wisdom ever ready for new challenges with lessons to learn and a better life to live. This Emersonian tone makes Putnam a great exemplar of self-criticism across the landscape of twentieth-century philosophy who incessantly recoils from any form of reductionism in the name of pluralism (with elective affinities to Nelson Goodman), rejects all forms of solipsism in the name of holism (here Quine prevails), and abhors all forms of sophomoric relativism in the name of "the *possibility of progress*."[11]

Putnam sees much of the history of philosophy as jumping from the frying pan into the fire, and then into a different frying pan usually in the name of new reductionisms or dogmatisms. If every great philosopher is defined by what he or she fears and hates, for Putnam it would be reductionism, dogmatism, egocentrism, relativism, injustice, and indifference to evil. Let us see how this is manifest in Putnam's relation to and placement in the history of Western philosophy.

Alfred North Whitehead—along with Dewey, Wittgenstein, and Heidegger—was a giant among giants in twentieth-century philosophy. He once wrote that Western philosophy is "a series of footnotes to Plato."[12] For Dewey, this Platonic quest for certainty was misguided and misleading. For Wittgenstein, the aim was to bring this quest to an end and reside in the everyday with a new sense of humility and confidence. For Heidegger, the goal was to restore the primacy of poetry in the face of the Platonic will to power (especially after his support for the Nazi rise to power!). Putnam's contribution to the Third Enlightenment begins with Aristotelian sobriety, not Platonic madness.[13] For Putnam, Aristotle's realism, without his metaphysics, brings together Dewey's experimentalism with Wittgenstein's mature naturalism. In his famous essay written with the distinguished philosopher Martha C. Nussbaum (in reply to Michael Burnyeat), they conclude,

> We suggest that Aristotle's thought really is, properly understood, the fulfillment of Wittgenstein's desire to have a "natural history of man." (It is also, in a different way, the fulfillment of Aquinas' desire to find that our truly natural

being is the being that we live every day, and that God has not screened our real nature behind some arbitrary barrier.) As Aristotelians we do not discover something behind something else, a hidden reality behind the complex unity that we see and are. We find what we are in the appearances.[14]

In this passage, Putnam and Nussbaum are claiming that Aristotelian realism undermines Platonic distinctions between deep reality and surface appearances, and modern dichotomies between mind and body. The Third Enlightenment that begins with Dewey and continues with Wittgenstein has its roots in Aristotle, not Plato. Like Dewey and Wittgenstein, Putnam is a modern flexible and fluid naturalist—who believes that "physics indeed describes the properties of matter in motion"[15]—yet shuns any reductionist naturalism or elimitivism or materialism. "Matter is, in its very nature, just the thing to constitute the functions of life (it is *not* a thing to which the functions of life can be reduced). 'Some things just are this in this, or these parts ordered in such and such a way' (Metaphysics 1036ᵇ22ff). Or, to quote Frank Baum's heroine, 'There's no place like home.'"[16]

For Putnam, the wholesale rejection of reductionism and the piecemeal embrace of pluralism have existential and moral consequences. He notes that we must not

forget that the world has many levels of form, including the level of morally significant human action, and the idea that all of these can be reduced to the level of physics I believe to be a fantasy. And, like the classic pragmatists, I do not see reality as morally indifferent: reality, as Dewey saw, *makes demands* on us. Values may be created by human beings and human cultures, but I see them as made in response to demands that we do not create. It is reality that determines whether our responses are adequate or inadequate.[17]

Putnam here echoes William James's fecund quip that "our opinions about the nature of things belong to our moral life."[18] He also builds on the pragmatic sentiments of Josiah Royce, who once wrote wrote: "Opinions about the universe are counsels as to how to adjust your deeds to the purposes and requirements which a survey of the whole of the life where to your life belongs shows to be genuinely rational purposes and requirements."[19]

II

One interesting lacuna in Putnam's great corpus is the lack of a sustained engagement with the religious Aristotelian influence and imprint during the medieval period (Maimonides in Jewish thought or Aquinas in Christian theology) or the modern age (such as John Henry Newman whose *Grammar of Assent* is a favorite of Putnam's!). Instead, Putnam seems to leap from the premodern pagan Aristotle to the late-modern naturalists Dewey and Wittgenstein in order to get the Third Enlightenment off the ground.

Yet there is one significant detour from the Greek fountainhead to the American and Austrian tributaries—the German lodestar of Kant. Kant occupies a unique place in Putnam's philosophic work. This towering figure of the Second Enlightenment is not only Putnam's brook of fire through which all modern philosophers must pass (as Ludwig Feuerbach was for Marx). The philosophy of Kant is also the crossing of the Rubicon from which there is no return. For Putnam, Kant lays bare the fundamental fissure between precritical metaphysics and postcritical reflections. The modern move to postcritical reflections calls into question all forms of metaphysics and ontology—including Kant's own transcendental idealism and Putnam's earlier metaphysical realism. The three pillars of the Kantian problematic—the problem of synthesis, the problem of moral freedom, and the problem of aesthetic judgment—rightly haunt Putnam's Third Enlightenment.

The problem of synthesis leads to the eclipse of the Cartesian picture of ideas copying or corresponding to things and results in a new conception of the constructive and creative powers of a cohering and integrating schema we impose upon the world. This Copernican revolution in philosophy entangles facts and values, powers and norms, natural capacities and moral freedom. The centrality of Kant to Putnam's naturalism and pragmatism primarily accounts for the role of Charles Sanders Peirce in Putnam's philosophy. Despite Putnam's deep love for William James, whose pragmatism is a species of radical empiricism rooted in John Stuart Mill's legacy, and Putnam's profound respect for John Dewey, whose pragmatism is a form of democratic experimentalism grounded in Left Hegelianism, Charles Sanders Peirce's pragmatism comes out of Kantian critical philosophy. For Kant, Peirce, and Putnam, the problems of determining the status of critical reflection, the role and function of the agent point of view (or the first-person normative point of view) and the appropriate forms of aesthetic judgment loom large. All three are particular kinds of normative reflection on our practice. Putnam writes,

> Kant was right in urging us to realize that reflection on the possibility of gaining knowledge from experience is itself a source of knowledge, even if he was wrong in considering such reflection to be an infallible source (when properly conducted). Kant was further right in supposing that we must reflect not only on the presuppositions of learning from experience, but also on the presuppositions of acting in the ways in which we do act. Most puzzles about the very "possibility" of normative knowledge spring from a too narrowly empiricistic picture of how knowledge is gained and how actions are justified.[20]

For Putnam, the significance of Kant is primarily his rejection of the Cartesian and empiricist pictures and the clarity of the difficult problems to be confronted (not dismissed) in light of Kant's own new transcendental idealist project. Putnam rejects transcendental idealism yet promotes pragmatist conceptions of normative reflection on our practices. In this sense, the Third Enlightenment is deeply shaped by and is an outgrowth of the Second Enlightenment. And if Dewey and Wittgenstein are the best exemplars of the Third Enlightenment (crystallized by the Philosophic Gang of Six) and Socrates and Aristotle are the best embodiments of the First Enlightenment, then Kant (and maybe Locke) are the best enactments of the Second Enlightenment.

III

It is worth noting that Wittgenstein is a strange bedfellow in Putnam's pragmatist Third Enlightenment. First, Wittgenstein's metaphilosophy—to bring philosophy as we know it to an end or stop when we want to—flies in the face of Putnam's Deweyan conception of philosophy as "the critical method of developing methods of criticism."[21] Second, Wittgenstein's cultural pessimism—shaped by Spengler's writings on the decline of the West—stands in stark contrast to Dewey's upbeat attitude toward progress. Third, Wittgenstein's naturalism is so idiosyncratic and iconoclastic in contrast to Dewey's demotic naturalism and democratic experimentalism. Putnam is aware of these tensions between Wittgenstein and Dewey. The crucial issue is whether these tensions are creative or destructive. Putnam rejects any therapeutic conception of philosophy and he also claims that Wittgenstein did not put forward such a conception.[22]

> If one really understands Wittgenstein, then one will see that the need for and the value of escaping the grip of inappropriate conceptual pictures is literally ubiquitous. The pursuit of clarity that Wittgenstein's work was meant to exemplify needs to go on *whenever* we engage in serious reflection. If this idea is grasped, we will see that far from being a way of bringing an end to philosophy, it represents a way to bring philosophical reflection to areas in which we often fail to see anything philosophical at all.[23]

Putnam's creative interpretation of Wittgenstein's metaphilosophy is a fascinating and gallant attempt to move Wittgenstein closer to Dewey and to connect him more closely to the Third Enlightenment.[24] And Wittgenstein's diverse and heterogeneous writings permit a number of contrasting interpretations. Yet I believe Putnam's relations to Aristotle, Kant, Wittgenstein, and the American pragmatists—especially Peirce, Dewey, and James—are complicated. We already observed that it was Reichenbach who rescued Putnam from leaving philosophy. And we are grateful. I surmise that Putnam's most influential intellectual *ancestors* are Aristotle, Kant, Wittgenstein, and Peirce, and his most influential intellectual *relatives* are Dewey, James, Wittgenstein, and Martin Buber. Needless to say, Putnam sharpened his arguments and views against a broad array of historical interlocutors and contemporary colleagues (including the Philosophic Gang of Six and others like Burt Dreben, Israel Scheffler, and Rogers Albritton at Harvard).

Putnam's intellectual ancestors are those deep thinkers who speak to his conception of philosophy in regard to epistemic, scientific, and mathematical issues. To put it bluntly, Aristotle is Putnam's classical philosopher *par excellence*. Kant is his major modern philosophic interlocutor. Wittgenstein is his closest philosophic soulmate—both ancestor and relative. Peirce is Putnam's pragmatist who shares with Wittgenstein "a certain Kantian heritage."

Putnam's intellectual relatives are those deep thinkers whose ideas reinforce his picture of philosophy that speak to existential, ethical, political, and religious issues. To put it crudely, Dewey speaks to Putnam's deep democratic conscience, James speaks to Putnam's generous and adorable heart, and Buber speaks to Putnam's cosmopolitan Jewish soul.[25] And since Wittgenstein is that rare philosophic genius and giant who is religiously musical without being a religious believer, he is both ancestor and relative to Putnam. Another common denominator of Putnam's Emersonian readiness for change—his grand exemplary exercise in critical reflection—is his candor about his radical democratic politics and his nonorthodox Judaic views. This candor has always struck me as a rare kind of courage to enact *parrhesia* (unintimidated, frank, and plain speech) in the midst of the conformity of the Academy. This candor touched me deeply as an undergraduate enrolled in his courses on Marxism or Nonscientific Knowledge where I witnessed his critiques of unfettered capitalism or unchecked scientism. In recent times, it is refreshing to see one of the few philosophic geniuses in our time openly embrace Judaism—no matter how shocking it is to secular colleagues![26]

This Emersonian exemplar—forever young at heart no matter how old he is—stays in motion. This intellectual frontiersman is renewed and revitalized by shattering narrow pictures and by generating new and better ones. This grand prophet of the Third Enlightenment whose passionate pursuit for clarity leads him to wisely learn to live with what is unclear. Ironically, in the end, Putnam is most like Socrates—the founding father of Western philosophy and the First Enlightenment. Putnam is *atopos*—no label can subsume him, no "ism" can define him and no school of thought can contain him. Like a jazzman in the life of the mind, Putnam is forever on the move in search of persuasive pictures of the position of human beings in the world mindful of the wise words of Rabbi Tarphon, "The task is not yours to finish, but neither are you free to desist from it."[27]

CORNEL WEST

PRINCETON UNIVERSITY
JUNE 2011

NOTES

1. Hilary Putnam, *Ethics without Ontology* (Cambridge: Harvard University Press, 2004), 96.

2. Ibid., 92.

3. Ibid., 93–94.

4. Hilary Putnam, *Words and Life*, ed. James Conant (Cambridge, MA: Harvard University Press, 1994), 345.

5. Joseph Conrad, *The Nigger of the 'Narcissus'* (New York: Penguin, 1989), xlix.

6. Putnam, *Words and Life*, 99.

7. Ibid., 100.

8. Ibid.

9. For Putnam's original critique of Reichenbach's vindicatory argument for induction, see his Ph.D. dissertation, *The Meaning of the Concept of Probability in Application to Finite Sequences* (New York: Garland Press, 1990), in the series Harvard Dissertations in Philosophy, edited by Robert Nozick. Putnam notes, "my own attempt, in the dissertation, at a justification for the finite case was invalidated by the discovery of the inconsistency of the Rule of Induction." In *Words and Life*, 146.

10. Ibid., 100.

11. Hilary Putnam, *Ethics without Ontology*, 108.

12. Alfred North Whitehead, *Process and Reality: An Essay in Cosmology* (New York: The Macmillan Company, 1929), 53.

13. For the lovely distinction between Aristotelian sobriety and Platonic madness, see Stanley Rosen, *The Quarrel Between Philosophy and Poetry: Studies in Ancient Thought* (New York: Routledge, 1994), xiii. Rosen also states, "the possibility of philosophy stands or falls upon the possibility of a philosophical madness that is more sober than sobriety." See also Stanley Rosen, *The Ancients and The Moderns: Rethinking Modernity* (South Bend, IN: St. Augustine's Press, 2002), "A Modest Proposal to Rethink Enlightenment": 1–21. For Putnam's fascinating reflections on the relation of philosophy to literature, see Putnam, *Meaning and the Moral Sciences* (Boston: Routledge and Kegan Paul, 1978), 83–94 and Putnam, *Words and Life*, 513–22.

14. Putnam, *Words and Life*, 55.

15. Hilary Putnam, *Jewish Philosophy as a Guide to Life: Rosenzweig, Buber, Levinas, Wittgenstein* (Bloomington: Indiana University Press, 2008), 5.

16. Putnam, *Words and Life*, 56.

17. Putnam, *Jewish Philosophy as a Guide to Life*, 5–6.

18. William James, *Collected Essays and Reviews* (New York: Russell and Russell, 1969), 11.

19. Josiah Royce, *Sources of Religious Insight* (New York: Octagon Books, 1977), 159.

20. Putnam, *Words and Life*, 168–69. For more on Kant in Putnam's work, see *Reason, Truth and History* (Cambridge: Cambridge University Press, 1981), 60–64.

21. John Dewey, *Experience and Nature* (La Salle, IL: Open Court, 1926), 437.

22. Putnam considers this popular interpretation of Wittgenstein to be *"profoundly erroneous"*—an insight he owes to long dialogues with Stanley Cavell and James Conant. See Hilary Putnam, *Jewish Philosophy as a Guide to Life*, 10, 110, n. 6.

23. Ibid., 11.

24. For Putnam's most sustained and subtle effort to connect, compare, and contrast Wittgenstein to pragmatism, see Putnam, *Pragmatism: An Open Question* (Cambridge: Blackwell, 1995), 27–56. He concludes that "even if Wittgenstein was not in the strict sense either a 'pragmatist' or a 'NeoKantian' he shares with pragmatism a certain Kantian heritage (which William James, too, was extremely loathe to acknowledge), and he also shares a central—perhaps *the* central —emphasis with pragmatism: the emphasis on the primacy of practice" (52).

25. Putnam makes it very clear that it is his brilliant and wise wife, Ruth Anna Putnam—a distinguished philosopher in her own right and beloved Professor of Philosophy at Wellesley College for decades—who is responsible for his embrace of pragmatism. He writes, "I want once again to thank my wife, Ruth Anna Putnam, who more than anyone else brought me to an appreciation of American pragmatism in general, and of the significance of John Dewey's contribution to philosophy in particular." Hilary Putnam, *Ethics without Ontology*, ix. See also their two exemplary co-authored essays "Dewey's Logic: Epistemology as Hypothesis" and "Education for Democracy" in Putnam, *Words and Life*, 198–220, 221–41.

26. For Putnam, to be a religious person is to choose to be a certain kind of person in light of particular pictures that ground and guide one's life. To be a religious person is to live a creative tension between a genuine intellectual integrity that leads toward a mature naturalism and a genuine spiritual integrity that leads toward a mature Judaism. Putnam's mature naturalism honors science without granting it a monopoly on truth and knowledge. Putnam's mature Judaism rejects an afterlife and a supernatural God, yet it embraces the miraculous alongside the natural in the practices of everyday life and Judaic rituals. What is God for Putnam? Neither an impersonal God arrived at by logic or metaphysics nor a wholly other God far removed from us. Rather God is visualized "as a supremely wise, kind, just person" in relation to us. Is this God supersensible, supernatural, superontological? Metaphorical? Nonliteral? Can Putnam reconcile his mature naturalism with his mature Judaism? In his Gifford lectures delivered at the University of St. Andrews in 1990, *Renewing Philosophy* (Cambridge, MA: Harvard University Press, 1992), 1, Putnam notes that the religious dimension of his life "is not a dimension that I know how to philosophize about except by indirection." Eighteen years later in his book *Jewish Philosophy as a Guide to Life*, Putnam notes, "I had come to accept that I could have two different 'parts of myself,' a religious part and a purely philosophical part, but I had not truly reconciled them. Some may feel I still haven't reconciled them—in a conversation I recently had with an old friend, I described my current religious standpoint as 'somewhere between John Dewey in *A Common Faith* and Martin Buber.' I am still a religious person, and I am still a naturalistic philosopher." (p. 5). In short, Putnam brings together a Deweyan live or vital ideal with a Buberian live or vital 'You' that generate "deeds of great courage and dedication" (p. 101). He seems to be on the terrain of George Santayana—"Religion is the love of life in the consciousness of impotence"—that miraculously sprouts Hasidic seeds—God can be found in deeds of loving-kindness to others. Yet we die and God does not come to our rescue as a supernatural helper. In conclusion, I suggest that my dear brother Hilary

Putnam is a twenty-first-century Spinoza whose conception of the Third Enlightenment rejects pantheism and determinism yet embraces a God-intoxicated naturalism within the constraints of critical intelligence. Was not Spinoza the great inaugurator of the Second Enlightenment (as the magisterial historian Jonathan Israel has argued) and now Putnam, as part of the Philosophic Gang of Six, helps crystallize the Third Enlightenment? I give Putnam the last word, "although my lectures are not about Spinoza, their central question—what enlightenment means—is one that was close to Spinoza's heart. Moreover, during the three months I spent in Amsterdam I was welcomed to the Sabbath worship services at the "Portuguese-Israelite" synagogue in Amsterdam—ironically, the synagogue from which Spinoza was expelled! . . . And I shall always remember and be grateful for the warm fellowship of the congregation, and the deep spirituality of the previously unfamiliar Sephardic ritual in the beautiful space of one of the oldest and largest of the surviving synagogues of Europe. It is strange to think that Spinoza and I have been members of the same *minyan*!" Hilary Putnam, *Ethics without Ontology*, viii.

    27. Cited in Hilary Putnam, *Words and Life*, 522.

REPLY TO CORNEL WEST

As Cornel West recounts, he took courses from me as an undergraduate. He could have added that those courses led to a friendship and
to discussions between us which have continued to this day! In an essay
about West that I published in 2001,[1] I wrote that in the decades that our
dialogue has been going on "Cornel West has matured from an idealistic
undergraduate to one of the most impressive thinkers (as well as one of the
most impressive human beings) that I know." I am enormously grateful for
the kind things he says about me. (I especially like his description of me
as "like a jazzman in the life of the mind.")

West also mentions that we co-taught a course together (titled "Pragmatism and Neo-Pragmatism") in my final semester of active teaching at
Harvard. His knowledge (and not only of Pragmatism), his moral commitment, and his ability to draw connections between the most diverse areas
of literature and scholarship were on brilliant display in our course. But the
course was not simply a joint course; it was also an occasion for debates,
constructive debates, and never in a contentious spirit. The debates made
it evident that I am more of a realist than a pragmatist. In the present reply
I shall respond to a few sentences in West's essay which will give me an
opportunity to continue our debates.

I. West on "Synthesis" and Schemas We "Impose" upon the World

Here are the sentences in question:

> The problem of synthesis leads to the eclipse of the Cartesian picture of ideas
> copying or corresponding to things and results in a new conception of the
> constructive and creative powers of a cohering and integrating schema we
> impose upon the world. This Copernican revolution in philosophy entangles
> facts and values, powers and norms, natural capacities, and moral freedom.

The centrality of Kant to Putnam's naturalism and pragmatism primarily accounts for the role of Charles Sanders Peirce in Putnam's philosophy.

Where I disagree with West is in not seeing our choices as between describing ourselves as "copying" the world and seeing ourselves as "imposing a schema upon the world." I will devote the remainder of this reply to explaining this disagreement. I will break the explanation into several short sections.

II. Correspondence and "Copying"

West speaks of "the Cartesian picture of ideas copying or corresponding to things." I have trouble with the identification of "corresponding" with *copying*. West may not have meant this as an identification (his "or" may be genuinely disjunctive) but let may say why they *should not* be identified (and, incidentally, why identifying them should not be called "Cartesian").

First of all, it is unfortunate that any theory on which the world determines which statements are true and which are false gets referred to by some authors as a "correspondence theory" of truth. In fact, Aristotle, often cited as the classic source of "the correspondence" theory, does not mention "the world" or "reality," and so on. (Nor does he mention "correspondence.") What he wrote was "To say that [either] that which is is not or that which is not is, is a falsehood; and to say that that which is is and that which is not is not, is true"[2]—and this sounds more like Tarski's "Convention T," often used by "deflationists" about truth to *reject* realist accounts of truth, than a statement that something corresponds to something! But logical niceties aside, if we are to speak that way, what it is to have a "correspondence theory of truth" in this extremely vague sense is simply to think that it is the way things are that determines whether what we say or think or conjecture, and so on, is true or false.[3] The only philosophers I know of who claimed that true ideas literally *resemble* what makes them true, are a small number of empiricists. Locke and Hume, in particular, clearly held such a "copy" theory of truth. Frege famously rejected empiricist talk of "ideas" (by which the empiricists meant subjective representations) as "psychologism," and he *denied* that the predicate "true" denoted a property, although he did say that the terms in a true sentence need to *refer*,[4] and, as is well known, he maintained that some sentences (the true ones) *refer* to the truth-value *truth*. (And while Descartes does say[5] "the word truth, in the strict sense, denotes the conformity of thought with its object"), he never says that "conformity" means *copying*. (In fact, he denies that seeking a definition of truth is either necessary or useful.[6]) Thus accusing either realists in general or Descartes in particular of having a "copy theory of truth" is at best misleading.

•

III. Why Talk of "Imposing" Schemas Is Misleading

Another brilliant former student, Richard Boyd, recently gave a lecture at a conference in honor of my eighty-fifth birthday,[7] in which he gave a beautiful explanation of how it is that the fact that our concepts reflect our interests, and the further fact that those interests reflect our particular biological makeup, evolutionary history, and contingencies of both our history and our environment, does not mean that (when they are not based on errors and illusions, as of course some of them are!) what they describe is not *real*. Although that lecture, titled "How Not to Be Afraid of Correspondence Truth: Evaluating Putnam's Challenges to 'Metaphysical Realism'/ Materialist Naturalism,"[8] has not been published, Boyd has been kind enough to make the PowerPoint presentation available to me, and it is from that that I shall quote.

Boyd illustrates the way in which a concept may be "human" without being in any way incapable of corresponding to something real, by means of an analogy to the calls of "Belding's Ground Squirrels." As Boyd relates, *Spermophilus beldingi* have two distinct relevant kinds of call: one call (a) signals the presence of "aerial predators" (predators on *beldingi*, that is), and the other call (t) signals the presence of "terrestrial predators" (on *beldingi*). These calls, if we think of them as protoconcepts, are as "parochial" as it gets. (They are not, of course, "anthropocentric," but they are "scluridae-centric"[9] with a vengeance, and even "Spermophilus-beldingicentric.") But they correspond to causal factors which are significant for *Spermophilus beldingi* survival, and they help *beldingi* to (in Boyd's terminology) "accommodate their behavior" to those significant causal factors. If we think of (a) and (t) as (proto-)concepts, those (proto-)concepts are "rodential," but they are not *irreducibly* rodential; squirrels are real, and so are the predators.

Applying the analogy to the case of natural kinds, Boyd defends realism by arguing that (the following is one of the slides in his presentation):

- Kinds are human social constructions
- They're "real" if we are and if they correspond to relevant causal structures. Remember Belding's ground squirrels!
- Mind independence?
- Beaver dams are mind-dependent social constructions but they're real, not "merely rodential" or whatever
- Real issue: Do minds/social practices make causal reality?
- Realist answer: Human social practices make no non-causal contribution to causal structures. No one here but us animals!
- Fair play for Humans: Relation to us/our practices does not diminish ontological standing!

*

All of this seems absolutely correct to me, and I see no more reason to say that we "impose" kinds upon the world than to say that *Spermophilus beldingi* "impose" predators upon the world.

I also disagree when West writes that "For Putnam, Kant lays bare the fundamental fissure between precritical metaphysics and postcritical reflections. The modern move to postcritical reflections calls into question all forms of metaphysics and ontology—including Kant's own transcendental idealism and Putnam's earlier metaphysical realism." This is accurate as a description of my views from 1976 through 1989, but not at all what I think now. It is important to note that Kant's own reason for insisting that space and time are "imposed" on reality by the human mind is that (according to him) only thus could we account for the "fact" that the laws of geometry and of mathematics generally are "synthetic a priori," and only thus could we hope for an apodictic proof that our categories possess "objective validity." But we have long seen that the notion of the synthetic a priori was a mistake, and I have argued from "It Ain't Necessarily So" on that we have to live with the fact that our categories are revisable. And, last but not least, I have long repented of having once said that "the mind and the world together *make up* the mind and the world."[10] Kant was a great philosopher, and he asked all the right questions (and Strawson was right to maintain that analytic philosophers can learn from and use material from many of his arguments[11]) but his was a failed, not a successful, "Copernican Revolution."

IV. A (RELEVANT) DIGRESSION

(This section is more relevant to the passage I quoted from Boyd than to anything that West says, but I think that it may deepen our understanding of the issue of the reality of our categories, and how their reality is compatible with their dependence on our human biological and social natures, and the nature of our environments, now and in the past.)

Although I like very much the passage I quoted from Boyd's lecture, I am not particularly happy with his choice of the title "How Not to Be Afraid of Correspondence Truth: Evaluating Putnam's Challenges to 'Metaphysical Realism'/ Materialist Naturalism." Apart from the fact that, contrary to what this suggests, the "Challenges" in question are ones I myself have regarded as mistaken for many years, I think that Boyd misdescribes, or at least unfortunately describes, his own position by calling it "Materialist Naturalism." In the talk, Boyd also described himself as a "nonreductive materialist." I approve of the nonreductionism, and, in particular, of nonreductive *naturalism*, but I sense a tension between "materialist" and "nonreductive." The tension is not that I think there is *more* in the world than matter, in the sense of their being things that consist of something *other* than matter. If denying that is what it takes to be a "materialist," then I too am a materialist. But so are all naturalists (well, all the ones I take seriously). But, although the matter that physics studies is the only matter there is, material objects have many different properties, and most of those properties are compatible with but neither deducible from nor definable in terms of the properties studied by physics and the laws that physics seeks to discover and precisely state. Some material objects are *books*, for example, and when we talk about books the properties that are usually of interest are such properties as the *subject matter*, the *quality of the writing*, the particular *way the author approaches his subjects,* and other "intentional" properties. I am sure Boyd does not disagree with this, and I am also sure that he does not think that such properties as "being a novel that depicts the lives of a number of characters over many years against the background of Napoleon's invasion of Russia" are reducible to physical properties. But if one agrees that what a "physical object" is *about* is not a property that can be *understood* by focusing on the fact that that object obeys the laws obeyed by all matter in motion, then what point is one trying to make by saying one is a "materialist"?[12] It is metaphysically important to always keep in mind that objects have many levels of form, and that explanations seek their own appropriate level.[13] *That is* the point of "nonreductive." "Materialist," with all the ancient ideological baggage it is freighted with, seems to me an unfortunate term to bring into present-day discussions.

V. Realism and Social Constructions, Entanglement, etc.

Let me add that just as (in Boyd's words, quoted above), "Beaver dams are mind-dependent social constructions but they're real, not "merely rodential" or whatever," *referring* to things and situations, actual and nonactual, is a human social practice, and would (probably) not exist if human beings did not exist, but events of referring are real events, not merely "schemas" or "constructs" we "impose" upon reality. Real things and events (including psychological events, social events, and so on) may require human social constructions both for their existence and for their description. But no antirealist consequences flow from that fact.

It may also be the case that applying a concept correctly requires the ability to see things from an ethical point of view. This is, for example, true of the term "courageous": to distinguish (as Plato asked us to do) not just between courage and cowardice, but also between courage and rashness, courage and foolhardiness, and so on, requires such an ability. Courage is an example of a concept that cannot be "disentangled" into a "purely factual" component (in the positivist sense of "factual") and an "evaluative" component. But there are courageous people in the world (and cowardly people, and foolhardy people, and so on.). Courage is something ethical discrimination enables us to *perceive*, not merely something we "project" on the person or action. It may be that courageous people are themselves brought into existence (in part) by social constructions (such as institutions, educational systems, human exemplars, and so on); but that does not make them or their courage less real.

West is right that there is much in Dewey that I admire, in particular in ethics/metaethics (for Dewey there is no sharp line between the two), and much in James that I admire. But the antirealist and/or verificationist views of the classical pragmatists are no part of what I admire in their philosophies.

H.P.

NOTES

1. Hilary Putnam, "Pragmatism Resurgent: A Reading of *The American Evasion of Philosophy*," in *Cornel West: A Critical Reader*, ed. George Yancy (Oxford: Blackwell, 2001), 19–37.

2. Aristotle, *Metaphysics*, 101126b.

3. But I myself prefer not to use the expression "correspondence theory of truth." For more about my reasons, see the final section of my Reply to Fred Stoutland in this volume.

4. In a letter to Russell dated Dec. 28, 1903, Frege writes "Whether the name 'Odysseus' has a reference (or, as one usually says, whether Odysseus is an historical person) doesn't bother us if we only want to enjoy the story. It is when we concern ourselves scientifically (*verhalten sich wissenschaftliche*), the question gains some interest for us at just that moment where we ask, 'Is the story true?'" Thanks to Charles Travis for supplying this reference, and for the translation.

5. Descartes to Mersenne, 16 October 1639, in *The Philosophical Writings of Descartes*, vol. 3: The Correspondence, ed. Cottingham, Stoothoff, Murdoch, and Kenny (Cambridge: Cambridge University Press, 1991), 139.

6. "For my part, I have never had any doubts about truth, because it seems a notion so transcendentally clear that nobody can be ignorant of it. There are many ways of examining a balance before using it, but there is no way to learn what truth is, if one does not know it by nature." Ibid.

7. The Conference on "Philosophy in the Age of Science" in honor of my eighty-fifth birthday was held at Harvard and Brandeis Universities, May 31–June 3, 2011.

8. As the title indicates, Boyd is here criticizing views I held in my "internal realist" period. Unfortunately, he believes that they are views that I hold today!

9. "Scluridae" is the scientific term for the whole family of squirrels.

10. Emphasis added. I said this in *Reason, Truth and History* (Cambridge: Cambridge University Press, 1981), 24. For my reasons for saying that was a mistake, see "From Quantum Mechanics to Ethics and Back Again," in *Philosophy in an Age of Science*, ed. Mario de Caro and David Macarthur (Cambridge, MA: Harvard University Press, 2012), 51–71.

11. P. F. Strawson, *The Bounds of Sense: An Essay on Kant's Critique of Pure Reason* (London: Methuen, 1966).

12. Boyd has been kind enough to look over a draft of this reply, and his response (private communication) was "the point of materialism is, e.g., that such disciplines as cognitive neuroscience are not ruled out as methodological possibilities by any considerations of basic metaphysics even if they might turn out to be too reductionist to work." In the light of this reply, I am not sure that our disagreement is not just a matter of terminological preferences.

13. On this, see my "Reductionism and the Nature of Psychology," in *Words and Life*, ed. James Conant (Cambridge, MA: Harvard University Press, 1994), 428–40.

23

Larry A. Hickman

PUTNAM'S PROGRESS: THE DEWEYAN DEPOSIT IN HIS THINKING

It is a fact, and certainly a value as well, if one happens to be a fan of clasical American philosophy, that during the last thirty years or so Hilary Putnam has gradually embraced many of the central insights of founding pragmatists Charles S. Peirce, William James, and John Dewey. Along with philosophers such as Richard Rorty, Richard Bernstein, Joseph Margolis, and others, Putnam will be remembered for having played a major role in the revival of interest in American pragmatism.

More particularly, thanks to what he has termed the "gentle advocacy" of his wife and frequent collaborator, Ruth Anna Putnam, his recent work has tended to place special emphasis on the work of Dewey. His response to a paper published by Ruth Anna Putnam in 2002 that was clearly guided by the spirit of Dewey's philosophy[1] included the assessment that it was a "statement of almost all the ideas that I take to be of lasting value and vital importance in the legacy of American pragmatism."[2]

What are those ideas, and what is the significance of the cautionary adverb "almost" in that statement? Ruth Anna Putnam answered the second part of this question when she reported that Hilary Putnam has rejected the pragmatist theory of truth. I shall come back to that very important matter in some detail in the last half of this essay.

More positively from the standpoint of Dewey's version of pragmatism, Putnam has argued, first, that philosophers should resist involving themselves in inquiries that lack practical relevance. They should instead focus on the issues that men and women living in a commonsense world find problematic.

This, of course, does not mean that philosophers should not address problems of knowledge and valuation implicated in technical areas such as science, technology, and law, for example, since he agrees with Dewey that the methods of quotidian inquiry and the methods of inquiry in the sciences, technology, and law have evolved on a continuum, distinguishable primarily by their level of abstraction and complexity (as well as certain discipline-specific features) rather than in terms of putative metaphysical or ontological differences. Moreover, the problems of the commonsense world require inquiry into issues such as science policy, medical ethics, food bioethics, and the changing climate, with increasing frequency.[3]

It is thus important to note that Putnam follows the pragmatists in distinguishing between meaning as intelligibility and meaning as pertinent to the real, felt concerns of living human beings. With Dewey, he holds that philosophers have wasted a great deal of energy debating questions that have meaning in the sense of being intelligible but that are not meaning*ful* because irrelevant to life's concerns.[4]

To put the matter somewhat differently, Putnam had earlier taken on the problem of global skepticism in his famous "brain in a vat" paper,[5] arguing among other things that the type of global skepticism involved in the "brain in a vat" thesis is self-defeating. It ignores the constraints of semantic externalism. His current work goes even further. Semantic externalism has been expanded to a thicker contextualism. "In judging the outcome of an inquiry, whether it be an inquiry into what are conventionally considered to be 'facts' or into what are conventionally considered to be 'values,' we always bring to bear a large stock of both valuations and descriptions *that are not in question in that inquiry*."[6] But commitment to contextualism is a matter of degree, as we shall see in Putnam's discussion of his theory of truth.

Putnam has also argued that the traditional problem of "the existence of other minds" has distracted philosophers from a consideration of how real persons relate to one another, and especially how community can be built around institutions such as the various sciences. Peirce said it best, perhaps, but it can certainly be found in Dewey: inquiry is social. The use of inquiry implies an interest in the success of humanity as a whole.[7]

I. Some Criticisms of Dewey

Have there been some detours along the road toward Putnam's current appreciation of Dewey's work? There are in fact some early criticisms of Dewey in *Renewing Philosophy*, for example, where he charged Dewey with (a) having a "dualistic conception of human goods" and (b) being a consequentialist. He suggested at that time that for Dewey there are "fundamentally two, and only two, dominant dimensions to human life: the social dimension, which for Dewey meant the struggle for a better world, for a better society, and for the release of human potential; and the aesthetic dimension."[8] Thus, he argued, Dewey ventured too close to the positivists' bifurcation of prediction and control of experiences, on one side, and the enjoyment of experiences, on the other. The key to this mistake, in his view, was the split between the use of "instrumental rationality," on one side, and the aesthetic appreciation of consummatory experiences, on the other.

This reading of Dewey is hardly what one might have expected given the analytic tradition in which Putnam was trained. It is in fact a reading that is more commonly associated with Dewey's critics among European philosophers such as the first generation of the Frankfurt School, including Max Horkheimer and Theodor Adorno. Perhaps even more remarkably, the split between the instrumental and the consummatory that Putnam ascribed to Dewey at that point in his career is not unlike the split that Dewey himself would surely have found problematic in the work of Habermas.[9] In his early work *Knowledge and Human Interests*, for example, Habermas split what he regarded as the fact-oriented instrumental rationality of the sciences from value-oriented domains of emancipatory and communicative action.

It is worth recalling that these remarks about Dewey's alleged dualism occurred in Putnam's discussion of William James's "existentialism" which, he suggested, treats religious belief as neither rational or irrational (as long as it does not degenerate into superstition). It was in this context that he could charge that Dewey "is not as sensitive to the limits of intelligence as a guide to life as James was," which I take to mean that Dewey neglected important areas of human experience.[10] There may be an element of truth in this. Some of Dewey's critics have pointed out that he had very little to say about suffering, tragedy, or death, for example. But we know that Dewey experienced profound personal tragedy with the death of two of his children and the demise of his wife, Alice. Moreover, he did not neglect the matter of religious belief, although he thought such experience could in most cases be rendered more intelligent.[11] It was just that supernaturalism was for him not an option that was either live, or forced, or momentous.

Regarding Dewey's alleged dualism, however, it would probably be more accurate to say that for Dewey the unproblematic, relatively noncognitive, naively aesthetic appreciation of life's pleasures tends to be interrupted by conflicts of various sorts, and that it is the function of inquiry to address those problematic situations. What Putnam and others have perceived as a split in Dewey's thinking is probably better understood as an articulation of the alternating phases of inquiry—the "perches and flights" that William James thought characterize the career of inquiry.

Then there is the matter of Dewey's alleged consequentialism. Putnam continued to charge Dewey with being a consequentialist as late as 1990. "Like all consequentialist views," he wrote, "Dewey's has trouble doing justice to considerations of right."[12] Of course Putnam has not been alone in identifying Dewey as a consequentialist. Gregory Pappas has provided a list that includes Michael Slote, James Campbell, Matthew Festenstein, Axel Honneth, Andrew Altman, J. E. Tiles, Richard Rorty, Jennifer Welchman, and of course, Hilary Putnam.[13]

But if consequentialism is identified (as Putnam sometimes does)[14] as the view that moral evaluations of acts are based solely on good consequences, then it is clear that Dewey was not a consequentialist. Dewey emphasizes consummations, and he stresses the fact that consummations are not the same as consequences. Unlike mere consequences, consummations involve give and take between means and ends, and they tend to be aesthetically richer.

A key point of Dewey's ethics is that preoccupation with consequences obscures the fact that the means selected to arrive at those consequences are as important as the ends achieved. This is because they will become a part of the equipment, the tools, the habits that will affect future inquiries. This is one of the factors that distinguishes a consequence from a consummation.

In *Human Nature and Conduct*, for example, Dewey writes "For no terminal condition is exclusively terminal. Since it exists in time it has consequences as well as antecedents. In being a *consummation* it is also a force having causal potentialities. It is initial as well as terminal."[15] In his "reintroduction" to *Experience and Nature* in the 1940s, the distinction between consequence and consummation is stated with laserlike precision: "*Only when revolutionary changes are the consummation of actual moral and intellectual changes are their consequences free from internal divisions.*"[16]

It should be noted that by 2002, Putnam had backed off of the notion that Dewey's ethics was instrumentalist "in the classical sense."[17] He admitted that for Dewey, inquiry "involves incessant reconsideration of both means *and* ends; it is not the case that each person's goals are cast in concrete in the form of a 'rational preference function.'"[18] It should also be noted, I suppose, that the charge against Dewey that his view "has trouble doing justice to considerations of right" appears not to take into account the treatment of the relative weight of goods, rights, and virtues in moral inquiry that he spelled out in 1930 in his lecture "Three Independent Factors in Morals."[19]

II. FACTS AND VALUES

Much of Putnam's recent work has focused on the traditional problem of relating facts and values. It is here that his work is, perhaps, most clearly inspired by Dewey's insights. His interest in these matters is hardly new, however. Some thirty years ago, in his discussion of cultural relativism and cultural imperialism,[20] Putnam argued that the claim sometimes mounted against cultural imperialism, that "other cultures are not objectively worse than ours because there is no such thing as objective better and worse . . . therefore they are *just as good as ours*" is self-defeating. It assumes an objective measure or good by which two cultures can be compared. If no such objective measure is available, then values really are arbitrary and there is no argument against destroying another culture.[21]

This strategy of undercutting extreme cultural relativism is just one of the tools in Putnam's toolbox. In *Renewing Philosophy*, for example, he followed Dewey in arguing that even though scientific method furnishes no algorithm, it does teach us some important lessons about how to conduct inquiry, including ethical inquiry.[22] Further, we can know from past inquiries that some practices are valuable, since they have been determined to clarify and sustain values that are required for further inquiry. Other practices should be rejected, since they have been determined to "stunt our nature and capacities." In this formulation we can already see Putnam's emphasis on the "entanglement" of facts and values.

More recently, he has argued that the answer to the question "are values made or discovered" is that "we make ways of dealing with problematical situations and we discover which ones are better and which worse."[23] He reminds us that for pragmatists, experience is not neutral, "that it comes screaming with values," and one of the goals of education is to increase our ability to discriminate among values. Oenophiles will doubtless understand his invitation to consider "the fantastic combinations of fact and value in a wine taster's description of a wine."[24]

In articulating his own position, Putnam appears to adopt a version of Dewey's "objective relativism," or, as Putnam puts it, the view that "certain things are right—*objectively right*—in certain circumstances and wrong—*objectively wrong*—in others, and the culture and the environment constitute relevant circumstances."[25]

That this is a form of objective relativism, there can be little doubt. Here is Putnam: "The idea of ethical objectivity is not the same as and does not presuppose the idea of *a universal way of life*. Dewey supports the former and consistently opposes the latter. Not only individuals but also communities and nations may have different but satisfactory ways of life."[26]

Putnam also appears to accept Dewey's idea that objective relativism is rejection of "bifurcation in nature." By that Dewey meant that both facts and values are natural, and that their separation is not ontological but functional. Their functional separation provides a way of moving inquiry forward. What this means in more concrete terms is that Dewey distinguished between a factual statement that a value is held and what he calls a "valuation judg-ment." "I do not conceive that propositions *about* values already given *as* values are valuation-judgments at all," he writes, "whether they are about value as immediate or about value in the sense of useful, any more than I should wish to term a judgment about a pin a pin-judgment . . . If we call such judgments valuation-judgments, they are on precisely the same logical level as any propositions about matters of established fact."[27]

So what, more precisely, are value judgments? In cases where there is simply no good or value "given to judgment," the situation is genuinely unsettled. "Now it was of this sort of situation and of this only," Dewey writes, "that I contended that valuations aid in determining a new good; and contended that *such* valuations possess a distinctive logical character which the orthodox logics have passed over too lightly."[28] Dewey's remarks here recall a central theme in his theory of inquiry: the fact of prizing, or valuing, is noncognitive and the act of valuation, a value judgment, is cogni-tive. Dewey adds that there may be situations in which no valuing occurs even in what might otherwise have been a problematic situation because values held are "in-valuable," that is, those whose worth is supreme, and thus not the subject of value judgments.

So it should be clear that for Dewey and Putnam alike, facts and values are "entangled." Dewey is clear that ethical deliberation involves examina-tion of accepted values with a view to their reconstruction in the light of novel circumstances. He is also clear that ethical norms are neither discov-ered nor invented, but instead constructed by means of various types of experimentation. Norms are thus objective with respect to the historical cir-cumstances in which they were constructed, and those circumstances may endure for a very long time, provided the problem is stated in sufficiently abstract terms. At the same time, however, objective ethical norms cannot be applied in the abstract: their application requires concrete situations. As Dewey puts the matter in *Theory of Valuation*, "improved valuation must grow out of existing valuations, subjected to critical methods of investiga-tion that bring them into systematic relations with one another."[29]

In his excellent analysis of Putnam's work, Lance P. Hickey has summed up Putnam's solution to the traditional fact/value split. Given the choice between dualistic alternatives of contingent particularism and an absolute perspective, he writes, "The middle path that Putnam and the pragmatists call for consists in lowering the standard for knowledge and truth in sci-ence but raising them in ethics and politics. What results is a more nuanced view where every domain of inquiry is epistemologically on the same level, even if there may still be a difference in degree."[30] It would be difficult to describe the agreement between Putnam and Dewey on the question of facts and values more precisely.

III. Truth—An Unfinished Project?

Putnam does not accept a pragmatic theory of truth. Of course, he knows that there is no single pragmatic theory of truth to accept or reject, since there were significant differences of opinion among Peirce, James, and Dewey regarding such matters. Does this mean that Putnam rejects all of their various formulations? There is a great deal to say about this issue. In terms of the limited scope of this essay, however, I will be limited to a brief discussion of how Putnam's theory of truth differs from that of Dewey.

In *The Threefold Cord*, Putnam makes several key points about the role that his understanding of truth and meaning play in his version of realism. In opposing those metaphysical realists who hold to a mind-independent reality and treat truth as a "substantive property," he is, of course, following a path that Dewey helped to clear. But in addition to some obvious similarities, such as rejecting the idea of truth as correspondence between ideas or statements and mind-independent reality, there are also some striking differences between his position (as articulated in *The Threefold Cord*) and that of Dewey.

First, Putnam asks that we "recognize that empirical statements already make claims about the world—many different sorts of claims about the world—whether or not they contain the words *is true*."[31] "What is right in [truth] deflationism," he continues, "is that if I assert that 'it is true that *p*,' then I assert the same thing as if I simply assert *p*."[32]

There are two parts to this claim. The first, that "empirical statements already make claims about the world" is undeniable in the context of quotidian life, or what Dewey, following Locke, termed "civil" language (as opposed to "philosophical" or "intellectual" language). Dewey thought that such claims tend to give us clues about the purposes of those who make the statements. "When a man is not satisfied, in ordinary intercourse, with saying that two and two make four, but finds it necessary to honor this formula with the title of Truth, we have, as a rule, good grounds for believing that the man is speaking neither as a business man nor as a mathematician, but as a preacher, or at least as an educator."[33]

The second part of the claim, however, because it purports to involve "intellectual" language, is more problematic. The statement "if I assert that 'it is true that *p*,' then I assert the same thing as if I simply assert *p*" makes perfectly good sense in the context of contemporary Anglo-American analytic philosophy, and, of course, in the context of the many logic textbooks that tradition has spawned. But when viewed from the standpoint of Dewey's logic, it is ambiguous.

We have already seen that in the context of quotidian language Dewey thinks that these two statements tend to have different shades of meaning:

one loosely utilitarian, the other didactic. Understood as philosophical, or technical language, however, the situation is different. Here is Dewey in 1911:

> The primary common assumption of both realistic and idealistic conceptions is that a statement by its nature implies an assertion of its own truth. No, replies the pragmatist, a statement, a proposition, in just the degree in which it has a genuinely intellectual quality, implies a doubt concerning its own truth and a *search* for truth, an inquiry for it. The proposition which asserts or assumes its own truth is either a sheer prejudice, a congealed dogmatism; or else it is not an *intellectual* or logical proposition at all, but simply a linguistic memorandum to serve as a direct stimulus of further action. . . . [Further]when the mathematician uses the formula for the value B in his further calculations, there may once have been a genuinely logical proposition involved, but what we have at this time is just a way of directing further action.[34]

The implications of this view for the standard treatment of propositions as either true or false, a treatment that Putnam currently employs, are significant. To get a sense of just how significant, consider the results of applying Dewey's account of propositions to the famous "Gettier Problem." In terms of the way the "problem" is stated, we have either facts which do not stimulate inquiry, and which therefore have no logical import, or else we have hypotheses, the truth of which cannot be said to be asserted until the facts of the case have been determined. In neither case does the idea fit neatly into the disjunctive construction that is the centerpiece of the Gettier "problem." If we take Dewey's characterization of his own pragmatist theory of inquiry seriously, then problems such as the Gettier problem are problems only for realists and idealists, including realists in the Frege-Russell tradition. They are not problems for Dewey's pragmatism.

The pragmatic criticism of both camps, realist and idealist (and this would apparently include Putnam's version of realism), is, Dewey writes, to question the idea

> that every statement by its own nature implies an assertion of its own truth. For that conviction, it substitutes the hypothesis that every proposition (so far as genuinely intellectual in quality, and not mere dogmatic prejudice or memorandum for further guidance) is a hypothesis concerning some state of affairs; that it is of its nature to be doubtful, not assured, of truth; and that its assertion of its own truth is only conditional: that it is a means of setting on foot activities of inquiry which will test the worth of its claim. Truth, then, can *exist* only in the testing of the claim, in making good through the subsequent acts it prescribes.[35]

And of course this involves contexts, which truth tables notoriously exclude. In his essay "Context and Thought" Dewey writes that "the most pervasive fallacy of philosophic thinking goes back to neglect of context."[36]

Second, Putnam argues that what is *mistaken* about verificationism is "the claim that the meaning of an expression like 'things too small to see with the naked eye' depends on there being methods of verifying the existence of such things, and the related claim that the meaning of such an expression changes as these methods of verification change (e.g. with the invention of the microscope.)"[37]

Once again, it seems that Dewey would approach matters differently. Recurring to his treatment of the role of the proposition in inquiry, it seems clear that if we are talking about logic, then he would reject the idea that the proposition "there are things too small to see with the naked eye" is a claim asserted about the physical world (to say nothing of a claim asserted about metaphysics). His view of propositions as affirming, rather than asserting, would locate the proposition squarely within the domain of hypotheses that suggest that something needs to be done.

Before the invention of the microscope the expression "there are things too small to see with the naked eye," was (in most quarters), intelligible enough. It was in fact a mark of its intelligibility that it was capable of being affirmed at some point as provisional, that is, taking on meaning as a hypothesis, and then being submitted to experimental tests. As a proposition, Dewey would tell us, it suggested the type of procedures that would be required to "indicate the types of tests required," which involved improved instrumentation: in this case, the microscope. As means of testing the hypothesis became available, the proposition became *meaningful.*

Of course Dewey did not accept the strong version of verificationism promoted by positivists such as A. J. Ayer. But as a pragmatist, he did accept a weaker version of verification. Dewey would thus, I believe, reject Putnam's claim that the verificationists are *wrong* to hold that "the meaning of such an expression ("there are things too small to see with the naked eye") changes as these methods of verification change (e.g., with the invention of the microscope)." They were wrong, I think he would say, about many things, but not this one in particular. For it is precisely the microscope as means that allows the proposition as hypothesis (which is also a means to an end-in-view) to be tested, that allows the sequence of inquiry to come to fruition, that is, that allows the meaning of the expression to change from a proposition (what is affirmed) to judgment (what is asserted).

To be fair, it should be noted that in the very same paragraph Putnam appears to give back to the verificationists at least some of what he has just taken away. "What is right in verificationism is that a great deal of scientific talk does depend for its full intelligibility on the provision of the kind of thick explanatory detail that is impossible if one has no familiarity with the use of scientific instruments."[38]

Third, Putnam writes that "there are perfectly well-formed declarative sentences that are *neither* true nor false."[39] One class of such sentences, he notes, comprises those that are vague. This statement, which at first glance seems little more than a truism, is in fact quite significant in the context of the present discussion. If it were pursued a bit further, it might lead to the view that propositions as they function in the context of sequences of inquiry are *by their very nature vague*: they are, after all, hypotheses, which are by definition indeterminate. Here, again, is Dewey: "[E]very proposition (so far as genuinely intellectual in quality, not mere dogmatic prejudice or memorandum for further guidance) is a hypothesis concerning some state of affairs . . . it is a means of setting on foot activities of inquiry which will test the worth of its claim."[40] It is here that Putnam's realistic logic coincides, briefly, with Dewey's pragmatic logic. For Putnam, *some* propositions are vague. For Dewey, however, *all* propositions, in their role as hypotheses within sequences of inquiry, are vague in the sense of being incomplete or indeterminate.

One of Putnam's clearest statements of his own position regarding truth can be found in *The Collapse of the Fact/Value Dichotomy*. Seen from the vantage point of Dewey's treatment of truth *as* warranted assertibility, Putnam's position is particularly interesting: he wants to split truth off from warranted assertibility. He seems to argue, for example,[41] that there can be warranted assertibility in ethics precisely *because* judgments about ethics can be objectively true. This, of course, is one aspect of Putnam's "objective relativism" with respect to values, including ethical values.

A few paragraphs later, however, he gets down to the business of discussing the matter of the relationship between truth and warranted assertibility in more detail. He reports that he once believed that "truth could be defined as warranted assertibility under 'ideal' (that is to say, *good enough*) conditions, where what are good enough conditions is itself something that we are able to determine in the course of inquiry."[42] In general terms, that is more or less Dewey's position.

But he also tells us that he no longer thinks this works, or "indeed that one need define truth at all."[43] Why is this so? Because of the problematic nature of verification. For some statements which "could be true," for example, the notion of ideal conditions under which they could be verified does not make sense. For others, such as the statement that "there are chairs in this room," conditions for verification are easily met.

Yet again, Dewey's treatment of propositions appears to avoid this difficulty. If propositions are neither true nor false, but instead valid or invalid, relevant or irrelevant as hypotheses that suggest further action, then statements which "could be true" are just that: hypotheses that suggest further action, even if such action is currently unavailable. (Consider, for example, the marvelously prescient designs of Leonardo.) As for the statement "there are chairs in this room," we once again have to ask whether this is merely a memorandum, and thus not "intellectual in quality," or whether it should be treated as a logical proposition, that is, as a statement that suggests further action as a part of an inquirential situation. And if the latter, then I suppose that we would need to specify the situation in which the proposition is called upon to function. Such a situation might, for example, involve a sight-impaired person who has just entered the room. For the sighted person, this would not involve cognition. For the sight-impaired, it might. So this is another example of an area where Putnam and Dewey appear to be on different pages.

IV. CONCLUSION

Hilary Putnam has been a major player in the revival of classical American pragmatism. Together with his wife, Ruth Anna Putnam (and as a result of her "gentle advocacy"), he has embraced many of the key insights of Dewey's version of pragmatism. We have seen that he has largely revised his earlier criticisms of Dewey as an instrumentalist (in the "classic" sense of the term) and as a consequentialist. His efforts to come to terms with some of the most difficult of the traditional problems of philosophy, including dismantling the hoary fact/value distinction, deserve enormous respect. My motive in pointing to some of the differences between Putnam and Dewey on the matter of truth should in no way be perceived as criticism of his work, implying that one approach is more valuable than the other. This would not be possible in any event, since systematic analysis of Dewey's logic is still in its infancy, or at least its adolescence: it remains to be seen what is valuable in his account. I have instead pointed out these distinctions as a kind of friendly challenge to Hilary Putnam to revisit Dewey's experimental logic, and to contribute to its evaluation, as a part of his response to this essay.

LARRY A. HICKMAN

THE CENTER FOR DEWEY STUDIES
SOUTHERN ILLINOIS UNIVERSITY
SEPTEMBER 2010

LARRY A. HICKMAN

NOTES

1. Ruth Anna Putnam, "Taking Pragmatism Seriously," in *Hilary Putnam: Pragmatism and Realism*, ed. James Conant and Ursula M. Zeglen (London: Routledge, 2002), 7–11.

2. Hilary Putnam, "Comment on Ruth Anna Putnam's Paper," in *Hilary Putnam: Pragmatism and Realism*, 12.

3. Hilary Putnam, *Renewing Philosophy* (Cambridge, MA: Harvard University Press, 1992), 186.

4. Hilary Putnam, *The Threefold Cord: Mind, Body, and World* (New York: Columbia University Press, 1999), 98ff.

5. Hilary Putnam, "Brains in a Vat," in *Reason, Truth and History* (Cambridge: Cambridge University Press, 1981), 1–21.

6. Hilary Putnam, *The Collapse of the Fact/Value Dichotomy: and Other Essays* (Cambridge, MA: Harvard University Press, 2002), 103–4.

7. Hilary Putnam, *Words and Life*, ed. James Conant (Cambridge, MA: Harvard University Press, 1994), 198–220.

8. Putnam, *Renewing Philosophy*, 196.

9. Larry A. Hickman, "Habermas's Unresolved Dualism," in *Perspectives on Habermas*, ed. Lewis Edwin Hahn (Chicago: Open Court, 2000), 501–13.

10. Putnam, *Renewing Philosophy*, 196.

11. See John Dewey, *A Common Faith*, in *The Collected Works of John Dewey, 1882–1953, The Later Works*, vol. 9, ed. Jo Ann Boydston (Carbondale and Edwardsville: Southern Illinois University Press, 1967–1991): 1–58.

12. Putnam, *Renewing Philosophy*, 190.

13. Gregory Fernando Pappas, *John Dewey's Ethics: Democracy as Experience* (Bloomington: Indiana University Press, 2008), 9n19.

14. Putnam, *Words and Life*, 215.

15. John Dewey, *Human Nature and Conduct*, in *The Collected Works of John Dewey, 1882–1953, The Middle Works*, vol. 14, ed. Jo Ann Boydston (Carbondale and Edwardsville: Southern Illinois University Press, 1983), 174 [emphasis added].

16. Dewey, *Experience and Nature*, in *The Collected Works of John Dewey, 1882–1953, The Later Works*, vol. 1, ed. Jo Ann Boydston (Carbondale and Edwardsville: Southern Illinois University Press, 1981), 336 [emphasis added]. See also, ibid., 144, where Dewey writes of "consummatory consequences."

17. Putnam, *The Collapse of the Fact/Value Dichotomy*, 97.

18. Ibid.

19. John Dewey, "Three Independent Factors in Morals," in *The Collected Works of John Dewey, 1882–1953, The Later Works*, vol. 5, ed. Jo Ann Boydston (Carbondale and Edwardsville: Southern Illinois University Press, 1984), 279–88.

20. Hilary Putnam, *Reason, Truth and History* (Cambridge: Cambridge University Press, 1981), 160ff.

21. Ibid., 161–62.

22. Putnam, *Renewing Philosophy*, 186.

23. Putnam, *The Collapse of the Fact/Value Dichotomy*, 97.

24. Ibid., 103.

25. Putnam, *Reason, Truth and History*, 162.

26. Putnam, *Words and Life*, 214–15.

27. John Dewey, "The Objects of Valuation," in *The Collected Works of John Dewey, 1882–1953, The Middle Works*, vol. 11, ed. Jo Ann Boydston (Carbondale and Edwardsville: Southern Illinois University Press, 1982), 4ff.

28. Ibid., 5.

29. John Dewey, *Theory of Valuation*, in *The Collected Works of John Dewey, 1882–1953, The Later Works*, vol. 13, ed. Jo Ann Boydston (Carbondale and Edwardsville: Southern Illinois University Press, 1988), 245.

30. Lance Hickey, *Hilary Putnam* (London: Continuum, 2009), 153.

31. Putnam, *The Threefold Cord*, 55–56.

32. Ibid., 56.

33. John Dewey, "The Problem of Truth," in *The Collected Works of John Dewey, 1882–1953, The Middle Works*, vol. 6, ed. Jo Ann Boydston (Carbondale and Edwardsville: Southern Illinois University Press, 1978), 13. See also John Dewey, *Logic: The Theory of Inquiry*, in *The Collected Works of John Dewey, 1882–1953, The Later Works*, vol. 12, ed. Jo Ann Boydston (Carbondale and Edwardsville: Southern Illinois University Press, 1986), 284.

34. Dewey, "The Problem of Truth," 37.

35. Ibid., 38 [emphasis added].

36. John Dewey, "Context and Thought," in *The Collected Works of John Dewey, 1882–1953, The Later Works*, vol. 6, ed. Jo Ann Boydston (Carbondale and Edwardsville: Southern Illinois University Press,1985), 5.

37. Putnam, *The Threefold Cord*, 56.

38. Ibid., 56–57.

39. Ibid., 65.

40. Dewey, "The Problem of Truth," 38.

41. Putnam, *The Collapse of the Fact/Value Dichotomy*, 106.

42. Ibid., 107.

43. Ibid.

REPLY TO LARRY A. HICKMAN

L arry Hickman ends his essay by saying that his motive in pointing to the differences between myself and Dewey on the subject of truth was not to criticize my work, since "systematic analysis of Dewey's logic is still in its infancy, or at least its adolescence," but was to pose a friendly challenge to "revisit Dewey's experimental logic, and to contribute to its evaluation, as a part of [my] response to this essay." I appreciate the friendly and open-minded spirit of this remark, and I am glad to respond to the issues Hickman raises (all the more so since he is, in my opinion, the greatest living Dewey scholar).

I Am More of a Realist than Hickman Paints Me as Being

To begin with, Hickman is quite right to say that early on in my engagement with Dewey's thought I criticized Dewey for being an instrumentalist "in the classic sense of the term" and a consequentialist (also in the classic sense of the term), and that I later saw the error of both of these descriptions. On these points I have nothing to add to or criticize in what Hickman writes. However, the following five corrections (to points on which Hickman mistakenly thinks Dewey and I are in agreement) are not made for the sake of picking nits, but because as a group they show that I am even farther from Dewey on truth, realism, and the like, than Hickman portrays me as being. Here are the corrections in question:

1. Hickman writes, "Putnam has argued, first, that philosophers should resist involving themselves in inquiries that lack practical relevance." I do not know where I am supposed to have said this, nor do I believe it. Like another of my favorite pragmatists, William James, I believe there are such things as purely intellectual interests. For example, the desire to see Fermat's so-called "Last Theorem" actually proved, and the joy I felt as a mathematician when Andrew Wiles succeeded in proving it, was a purely

intellectual desire/joy. And there are purely intellectual interests in philosophy too; for example, I am interested in the problem of skepticism, about which I continue to think, not only because (as Stanley Cavell has argued) skepticism can sometimes be a real problem (a "practical problem"), but because the issues connected with skepticism are intellectually difficult. What I have said, again and again, is that philosophy has both a practical and a purely intellectual side, and that the subject only flourishes when both sides are nourished, and when each side supports the other.

2. Hickman writes, "With Dewey, [Putnam] holds that philosophers have wasted a great deal of energy debating questions that have meaning in the sense of being intelligible but that are not *meaningful* because irrelevant to life's concerns." The footnote attached to this claim about what I hold sends the reader to pages 98ff of *The Threefold Cord: Mind, Body and World*, in which I argue that the "hypothesis" that other people lack minds (that they are "soulless automata") is "not coherent enough to be described as a possible state of affairs." And the reasons I give in the place cited do not include being "irrelevant to life's concerns."

3. Hickman writes, "Putnam has also argued that the traditional problem of 'the existence of other minds' has distracted philosophers from a consideration of how real persons relate to one another, and especially how community can be built around institutions such as the various sciences." Perhaps Hickman is thinking of my admiration of Cavell's work here? But Cavell himself claims that skepticism about the existence of other minds can be a real problem (an idea which drives his wonderful interpretation of Shakespeare's *Othello*, which takes up all of part IV of *The Claim of Reason*). Cavell's insight can, perhaps, be reformulated thus: philosophers have treated the problem of other minds in abstraction from "a consideration of how real persons relate to one another," but that is different from describing the problem itself as a "distraction," or as somehow incompatible with also being interested in "how community can be built around institutions such as the various sciences." I do not believe there is any such incompatibility, nor do I scoff at the problem of other minds.

4. Referring again to *The Threefold Cord*, Hickman describes me as "opposing those metaphysical realists who hold to a mind-independent reality." What I actually say there is "The traditional metaphysician is perfectly right to insist on the independence of reality."[1] What I oppose is not the idea that reality is mind independent, but the idea that a mind-independent reality must be described in terms of *one preferred ontology* (a distinction also drawn by William James[2]).

5. Hickman speaks of me as "rejecting the idea of truth as correspondence between ideas or statements and mind-independent reality" in *The Threefold Cord*. He is right that in that book I argue that the truth of a

statement is not a matter of a "correspondence" between the statement and reality. In other words, I rejected analyses of truth of the general form:

"S is true $=_{df}$ S corresponds to X (where X is "reality")"

and of the form:

"S is true $=_{df}$ (Ex)(x is a state of affairs & corresponds to x)"

and the like. However, I added that the realist insight that "deflationism" captures is that true empirical statements "already make claims about the world."[3]

The thought was not very well expressed, I admit, but the idea I wanted to convey was that an empirical statement is not something that can be described *apart from* its relation to a "corresponding" state of affairs. Empirical statements are not like paintings.[4] A painting could be described without indicating just who the people in it are, or saying where the scene is supposed to be, and so on (or even described by giving the shapes and colors of the bits of paint and their distribution on the canvas); a statement, as opposed to a painting, or, for that matter, to a mere series of uninterpreted words, would not be the statement that it is, if it did not assert that *those* things have *those* properties and stand in *those* relations. For that reason, it seemed to me that the relation of statements to states of affairs "out there" is too *internal* to be thought of as a "correspondence."

This may or may not be a good objection to the idea that truth must be *defined* in terms of correspondence,[5] but I *did not deny* that there are states of affairs that our true statements describe, and that is surely the fundamental intuition behind the idea of "correspondence truth."

Truth and "Experimental Logic"

Hickman believes that Dewey would disagree with what I said in *The Threefold Cord* when I wrote that we should "recognize that empirical statements already make claims about the world—many different sorts of claims about the world—whether or not they contain the words *is true*. What is right in deflationism is that if I assert that 'it is true that *p*,' then I assert the same thing as if I simply assert *p*." I want to look at the objections to this that Hickman makes on Dewey's behalf.

(But first, let me admit that my assertion was carelessly formulated. Strictly speaking, it is speakers and not "statements" that make claims about the world, and speakers usually do so by making statements. Moreover, I was wrong to suppose that when we use an empirical statement to make a claim about the world—*which* claim is determined by the world involving truth conditions of the sentence we use to make the statement in question—the statement cannot *also* be said to "correspond" to a state of affairs—the one determined by those same truth conditions. In sum, I now think what I called "deflationism" is compatible with holding that true empirical statements *correspond* to states of affairs that hold or fail to hold in the world, and so I would not now set deflation and correspondence truth in *opposition* to each other as I did in the book Hickman cites. But these are not the Dewey/Hickman objections to what I wrote.)

1. Hickman writes, "that 'empirical statements already make claims about the world' is undeniable in the context of quotidian life, or what Dewey, following Locke, termed 'civil' language (as opposed to 'philosophical' or 'intellectual' language). Dewey thought that such claims tend to give us clues about the purposes of those who make the statements. 'When a man is not satisfied, in ordinary intercourse, with saying that two and two make four, but finds it necessary to honor this formula with the title of Truth, we have, as a rule, good grounds for believing that the man is speaking neither as a business man nor as a mathematician, but as a preacher, or at least as an educator.'"

My response: The next Dewey/Hickman objection will show more clearly why Dewey writes this, but at this stage I already want to say that it is not true that we use "is true" only when we engage in theology or pedagogy. Two obvious exceptions: First of all, in *applying* principles of deductive logic, it is frequently necessary to use the word "true." Thus I might say, "If a statement S implies that the negation of T is true, and T is true, then the statement S is false," and one application of this general principle might be to point out that if we can construct a proof that a mathematical statement S implies the negation of "2 + 2 = 4," then, since "2 + 2 = 4" is true, that statement S must be false. Wittgenstein in many places seems to regard the simplest logical truths, for example. "The standard meter stick is the same length as itself" as *nonsense*, but I regard this as a serious failure on his part to appreciate the importance of the deductive logical analysis of inference, a scientific achievement which has already born rich fruits in mathematics and computer science, among other areas. I hope Dewey would not have made the error Wittgenstein made. Secondly, when we use "true" with a universal quantifier we mean to assert all the instances of that quantification: for example, if we say "all the theorems of first-order arithmetic are true" (an important step in many meta-mathematical arguments), and we know that "2 + 2 = 4" is a theorem of first order arithmetic, we mean it to follow that "2 + 2 = 4" is true. And we do not have to worry about whether we are being "business men" (or union organizers) or "preachers" or "educators" when we say "'2 + 2 = 4' is true"; which of these occupations we profess may affect the precise *use* we make of "2 + 2 = 4," but not every difference in use is a difference in truth-conditional meaning.

2. Hickman writes: "the statement 'if I assert that 'it is true that *p*,' then I assert the same thing as if I simply assert *p*' makes perfectly good sense in the context of contemporary Anglo-American analytic philosophy, and, of course, in the context of the many logic textbooks that tradition has spawned. But when viewed from the standpoint of Dewey's logic, it is ambiguous. We have already seen that in the context of quotidian language Dewey thinks that these two statements tend to have different shades of meaning: one loosely utilitarian, the other didactic."

My response: I have already said that I do not agree that "'2 + 2 = 4' is true" is necessarily a "didactic" statement, and, moreover, that even when it is, that does not mean that its truth condition—the state of affairs that has to obtain for it to be true—is any different from its truth condition when its employment is "utilitarian" (for example, when it is used in doing sums). Having more than one use does not mean that this statement is ambiguous. (In fact, it seems to me that Dewey did not think of statements as having *truth conditions* in this sense.)

3. Hickman continues: "Understood as philosophical, or technical language, however, the situation is different. Here is Dewey in 1911: 'The primary common assumption of both realistic and idealistic conceptions is that a statement by its nature implies an assertion of its own truth. No, replies the pragmatist, a statement, a proposition, in just the degree in which it has a genuinely intellectual quality, implies a doubt concerning its own truth and a search for truth, an inquiry for it.'"

My response: In the course of making or designing an experiment, a physicist might well point out that the melting point of tin is 231.9° C, but, in a normal inquiry, the physicist does not *doubt* the statement. Indeed, Dewey himself points out that not every statement *used* in an inquiry is subject to question *in that inquiry* and hence not every statement used in inquiry is one of whose truth we are uncertain.

Perhaps Dewey would say that, when it has the role I just described, "The melting point of tin is 231.9° C" *does not* have "a genuinely intellectual quality." Even so, *both* when it is itself being tested, *and* when it is used as a known fact in the course of testing other propositions, "The melting point of tin is 231.9° C" is true. I see no reason to believe that it does not have the same truth condition when its role with respect to the inquiry changes, but, as I said above, it does not seem that Dewey *has* the realist notion of a truth condition.

4. Dewey (as quoted by Hickman) continued: "The proposition which asserts or assumes its own truth is either a sheer prejudice, a congealed

dogmatism; or else it is not an *intellectual* or logical proposition at all, but simply a linguistic memorandum to serve as a direct stimulus of further action." I do not know what a "proposition which asserts or assumes its own truth" is supposed to be. Probably Dewey means by this that a proposition which is taken to be a conceptual truth is not functioning as a proposition at all. If this is what he means, I find the view absurd. I believe that $2 + 2 = 4$ is a conceptual truth,[6] and it does function as a proposition. Or, to change the example, I agree with Wittgenstein that the statement that the world has existed for a very long time (say, more than a hundred years) serves as a "hinge proposition," that is, as part of a basis on which our whole conceptual system rests, and not something that is subject to test in any inquiry that we can envisage, but I also believe (disagreeing, according to some of Wittgenstein's interpreters with Wittgenstein himself) that it is a *truth* that the world has existed for more than a hundred years.

Dewey continues, "when the mathematician uses the formula for the value B in his further calculations, there may once have been a genuinely logical proposition involved, but what we have at this time is just a way of directing further action."

My response: If in a calculation I use the fact that π is greater than 3.1415 and less than 3.1416, the idea that I am no longer stating a mathematical fact (or "a genuinely logical proposition"), but just "directing" myself to type this or that formula, or whatever the "further action" that my calculation leads to may be, does not, as far as I can see, fit into any coherent account of what mathematics is or of what mathematicians do; I do not find any philosophy of mathematics that I can take seriously, either as a mathematician or as a philosopher, in the whole of Dewey's writings.

5. Hickman continues: "The implications of this view for the standard treatment of propositions as either true or false, a treatment that Putnam currently employs, are significant." His example at this point is the famous Gettier problem, and now I must reply to Hickman himself, because Dewey was not alive when Gettier wrote his famous paper. (I assume that Hickman thinks his reply is one Dewey would have offered, or, perhaps one Dewey *should* have offered, had the Gettier problem been posed in his lifetime.)

What Gettier accomplished in his famous three-page paper[7] was to show that "x knows that p" is not simply analyzable as "x's belief that *p* is warranted by the evidence that x has & *p* is true." A simple example: my car is a red Honda Civic. John sees a red Honda Civic parked in my driveway on several occasions and concludes, reasonably, that my car is a red Honda Civic. But, unknown to John, the red Honda Civic he has seen actually belongs to my cousin, who is visiting me. John's belief that my car is a red Honda Civic is correct, and his belief is warranted, but John does not *know* that I have a red Honda Civic, because one of his assumptions was false, although he had epistemic warrant to believe that assumption. According to Hickman, there is no genuine problem here for pragmatists. Why not? Again, I quote him:

> In terms of the way the "problem" is stated, we have either facts which do not stimulate inquiry, and which therefore have no logical import, or else we have hypotheses, the truth of which cannot be said to be asserted until the facts of the case have been determined. In neither case does the idea fit neatly into the disjunctive construction that is the centerpiece of the Gettier "problem." If we take Dewey's characterization of his own pragmatist theory of inquiry seriously, then problems such as the Gettier problem are problems only for realists and idealists, including realists in the Frege-Russell tradition. They are not problems for Dewey's pragmatism.

But the Gettier problem only depends, in our case, upon its being a fact that my car is a red Honda Civic, and a fact that John had good reason to believe that it is, and the further fact that, unbeknownst to him, one of his assumptions was false. I am not sure what Hickman means by "disjunctive construction"; perhaps what he refers to is the distinction between being known and being warrantedly assertible. (He may be referring to "the standard treatment of propositions as either true or false"; but the example does not actually assume that every proposition is either true or false, but only that these three propositions are true.) And Wittgenstein, who in many places in *On Certainty* seems to me to write like a sophisticated pragmatist, reminds us that "know" is a context sensitive word, but one that (when its context sensitivity is not ignored) is useful and important. And Gettier's observation that "knowledge" is not simply a synonym for "justified true belief" is perfectly compatible with that. Nor does the fact that we should not seek for a simple logical equivalent to the notion of knowing mean that it is foolish to try to say more about when we do and do not use it; indeed this is what Wittgenstein tried to do. I believe that concern with the nature of our concepts, including the concept of knowledge, is something philosophers, including pragmatists, should not attack.[8]—But, as already said, Dewey did not discuss Gettier's problem, so perhaps we should set these remarks of Hickman's aside.

6. Hickman continues: "The pragmatic criticism of both camps, realist and idealist (and this would apparently include Putnam's version of realism), is, Dewey writes, to question the idea 'that every statement by its own nature implies an assertion of its own truth.' [*Comment (HP): Is Dewey attacking the principle that p implies "p is true"? It certainly seems so!*] For that conviction, it substitutes the hypothesis that every proposition (so far as genuinely intellectual in quality, and not mere dogmatic prejudice

or memorandum for further guidance) is a hypothesis concerning some state of affairs [*Comment (HP): Let's grant this for the sake of argument*]; that it is of its nature to be doubtful, not assured, of truth [*Comment (HP): Apparently Dewey thinks that being doubtful—an epistemic status—is incompatible with being true*]; and that its assertion of its own truth is only conditional; that it is a means of setting on foot activities of inquiry which will test the worth of its claim. [*Comment (HP): Does Dewey then think that if p turns out to be false, it is not the case that p implies "p is true"?*] Truth, then, can *exist* only in the testing of the claim, in making good through the subsequent acts it prescribes."

As the comments I have inserted in the above indicate, this seems to me to be a tissue of confusions.

One further remark: in *Logic: The Theory of Inquiry* Dewey writes that "The best definition of truth from the logical standpoint which is known to me is that of Peirce."[9] This is followed by two quotations from Peirce. But Peirce did not think that a *p* which is being tested is not true until inquiry has passed the point at which all real doubt ceases, which is what Dewey seems to think, nor would he ever have said that truth "exists" only in "making good through the subsequent acts."

7. Hickman immediately adds: "*And of course this involves contexts, which truth tables notoriously exclude.* In his essay 'Context and Thought' Dewey writes that 'the most pervasive fallacy of philosophic thinking goes back to neglect of context.'"

My Response: Precisely what the truth-evaluable content of a statement *is* indeed depends on context as I have argued elsewhere.[10] For example, whether an utterance of "There is coffee on the table" means, in the circumstances, that there are cups of coffee on the table, or means that there are cans of coffee beans on the table, and so on, depends on context. What that shows is that the *sentence* "There is coffee on the table" can be used to make a number of different *statements*, depending on the context (including also which table is referred to as "the table," the time of utterance, and so on.). Each of those statements is, apart from cases of vagueness, which I will discuss below, true or false and in such cases classical logic is fully applicable. I have argued that we do also need to work out a logic for inferences that contain vague words, or words that are vague in the relevant context[11]; but to attack the analysis of inference using truth tables as presupposing bad philosophy, as Hickman seems to be doing here, is a mistake. I agree that using truth-table analysis is, indeed, to *idealize* in one respect (by ignoring vagueness), but that kind of analysis does not assume that context is immaterial. Context *is* material to determining just what is being said (and also to determining when vagueness can be ignored).

8. Re "Verificationism," Hickman writes:

Of course Dewey did not accept the strong version of verificationism promoted by positivists such as A. J. Ayer. But as a pragmatist, he did accept a weaker version of verification. Dewey would thus, I believe, reject Putnam's claim that the verificationists are *wrong* to hold that "the meaning of such an expression ("there are things too small to see with the naked eye") changes as these methods of verification change (e.g., with the invention of the microscope.)" They were wrong, I think he would say, about many things, but not this one in particular. For it is precisely the microscope as means that allows the proposition as hypothesis (which is also a means to an end-in-view) to be tested, that allows the sequence of inquiry to come to fruition, that is, that allows the meaning of the expression to change from a proposition (what is affirmed) to judgment (what is asserted).

My Response: Here we simply have to agree to disagree. I think we could already *conceive* of there being things too small to see with the naked eye before microscopes were invented. And I think we could speculate about such things, and that the statement that there are things too small to be seen with the naked eye did not change its *meaning* when it changed its epistemic status from mere conjecture to a testable hypothesis. In fact, I think one of the reasons we *did* look for a way to turn it into a testable hypothesis was precisely that we *could* conceive of its being true. Here it seems to me that the fundamental reason for my lack of sympathy with Dewey's views in this area becomes clear. Dewey's view, it seems to me, makes meaning and truth entirely dependent on our activities, for example our resolutions of problematic situations. In contrast, I see our activities as a very small part of a world that we make many, many conjectures about, only some of which we can actually test. For example, we make conjectures about what happened in the past, some of which we may never be able to verify or even find a way of investigating, and conjectures about what happens at beyond the astronomical "event horizon," that is at distances so great that causal signals from the conjectured events will never reach us. At present such conjectures are neither "hypotheses" that we are testing nor "linguistic memoranda to serve as a direct stimulus of further action." They are statements that describe possible states of affairs that it is of intellectual value to think about, no more and no less than that. (On this sort of realism, I refer the reader to my Reply to Tim Maudlin in the present volume.)

9. Hickman writes:

One class of such sentences [that are neither true nor false], he notes, comprises those that are vague [actually, this is true of only some vague sentences]. This statement, which at first glance seems little more than a truism, is in fact quite significant in the context of the present discussion. If it were pursued a bit further, it might lead to the view that propositions as they function in the context of sequences of inquiry are *by their very nature vague*: they are, after all, hypotheses, which are by definition indeterminate. Here, again, is Dewey: "[E]very proposition (so far as genuinely intellectual in quality, not mere dogmatic prejudice or memorandum for further guidance) is a hypothesis concerning some state of affairs . . . it is a means of setting on foot activities of inquiry which will test the worth of its claim." It is here that Putnam's realistic logic coincides, briefly, with Dewey's pragmatic logic. For Putnam, *some* propositions are vague. For Dewey, however, *all* propositions, in their role as hypotheses within sequences of inquiry, are vague in the sense of being incomplete or indeterminate.

My Response: The sentence of Dewey's quoted by Hickman does not, as far as I can see, support his interpretation that "*all* propositions, in their role as hypotheses within sequences of inquiry, are vague in the sense of being incomplete or indeterminate." But assuming Hickman is right in interpreting Dewey as claiming that it is not only *inquiries* that are incomplete or indeterminate until the problematic situation is resolved, but also the "hypothesis" under test, then again we have to "agree to disagree." If my car will not start, and I look to see whether there is gas in the tank, I do not think the "hypothesis" the tank is empty is *vague*, or that its meaning becomes "determinate" when I find that the tank is or is not empty. Nor, when I find out that filling the tank (if it is empty) does or does not lead to my being able to start the car, does the hypothesis that the car will not start *because* the tank is empty cease to be "vague," because it *was not* vague before; it was only my *knowledge* of its truth value that changed, not that truth value itself.

10. Hickman writes:

> Seen from the vantage point of Dewey's treatment of truth *as* warranted assertibility, Putnam's position is particularly interesting: he wants to split truth off from warranted assertibility. He seems to argue, for example, that there can be warranted assertibility in ethics precisely *because* judgments about ethics can be objectively true. This, of course, is one aspect of Putnam's "objective relativism" with respect to values, including ethical values.

My Response: I do think that a proposition can only be objectively warrentedly assertible if it is capable of being objectively true. But I also say, three pages after the page Hickman cites[12] that for reasons internal to ethics itself, ethical truth cannot be "recognition transcendent"; that is, being truth apt and being capable of being reasonably justified or reasonably rebutted cannot be "split off" from one another in the ethical case.

11. I want to consider one more remark of Hickman's, a remark he makes when he discusses my opposition to verificationism. He writes,

> Yet again, Dewey's treatment of propositions appears to avoid this difficulty. If propositions are neither true nor false, but instead valid or invalid, relevant or irrelevant as hypotheses that suggest further action, then statements which "could be true" are just that: hypotheses that suggest further action, even if such action is currently unavailable.

Again, I wish Hickman had quoted a place where Dewey explicitly says that "propositions are neither true nor false, but instead valid or invalid, relevant or irrelevant as hypotheses that suggest further action." I do wonder whether Hickman has not here exaggerated the extent of Dewey's opposition to what is usually understood as "realism." My reason for doubting that this is really Dewey's view is that this is obviously something that Peirce would *never* have said, and, as I pointed out above, Dewey tells us that "The best definition of *truth* from the logical standpoint which is known to me is that of Peirce." Moreover, Hickman himself writes in one place that "Putnam reports that he once believed that 'truth could be defined as warranted assertibility under "ideal" (that is to say, *good enough*) conditions, where what are good enough conditions is itself something that we are able to determine in the course of inquiry.' In general terms, that is more or less Dewey's position," and this is not consistent with "propositions are neither true nor false."

So Why Do I Think so Highly of Dewey?

Even if Hickman has, in this last point, somewhat exaggerated Dewey's criticism of the classical notion of truth, as I suspect, it is clear from points 1–11 that I am in disagreement with Dewey on a number of fundamental issues. Yet Dewey is one of my philosophical heroes, a thinker from whom I have learned a great deal. The reader may wonder: How can this be?.

The fact is, that while the points Hickman makes on Dewey's behalf (and once again, I thank him for inviting me to confront them) are certainly important, they do not play a conspicuous role in the works of Dewey's that I have been most influenced by. Dewey's *Logic: The Theory of Inquiry* paints a picture of the nature of inquiry that, on the whole,[13] I am very much in agreement with, but the concept of truth is discussed only once, and then in a footnote! I admire and have discussed *The Quest for Certainty*,[14] but I do not find it necessary to agree with the views on truth that Hickman describes in order to appreciate its insights. Similarly with *Art as Experience*, Dewey's chapters in the *Ethics* he coauthored with James Haydn Tufts, and the other books and papers of Dewey's I have commented on in my writings. I regard Dewey's attacks on the fact/value dichotomy as the first of many important criticisms of that dogma, and I regard him and his fellow pragmatists as showing how one can be a *fallibilist* without being a *skeptic*. And the ways in which he relates questions about the possibility of rational inquiry into values to questions about the foundations of democracy[15] are especially important to me.

I said at the outset that Hickman is the greatest living Dewey scholar. And as a scholar he may well want to say, "Putnam, you are *using* Dewey (that is, you do not understand by his writings what he meant you to understand by them)." Well, of course I am using him. An expert in the thought of any great philosopher, be it Aristotle, or Kant, or Dewey, or whoever, will inevitably want to distinguish carefully between the way that philosopher understood his own sentences, and what a later philosopher who finds them inspiring and instructive takes away from reading them. But I believe that one can *legitimately* take away from Dewey's many writings a great deal that is of philosophical importance even if one is not in agreement with Dewey (or with the other pragmatists, for that matter) on this or that metaphysical issue—even if the issue be the nature of truth itself.

H.P.

NOTES

1. Hilary Putnam, *The Threefold Cord: Mind, Body and World* (New York: Columbia University Press, 1999), 8.

2. For my description of James's view on this point, see *The Threefold Cord*, 5. See also my Reply to Tim Maudlin in this volume.

3. Ibid., 55.

4. I confine the discussion here to empirical statements. For my views on logical and mathematical statements, see my replies to Charles Parsons, Geoffrey Hellman, and Steven Wagner in the present volume.

5. As may be inferred from my writing "may or may not be," my views are undergoing modification even as I write these words!

6. By a "conceptual truth" I do *not* mean an "analytic" truth or an "a priori" truth, but simply a framework principle of the science of a given time. See my Reply to Gary Ebbs in the present volume.

7. Edmund L. Gettier, "Is Justified True Belief Knowledge?" *Analysis* 23, no. 6 (1963): 121–23.

8. Ruth Anna Putnam points out to me that a "Gettier case" may well have practical significance. Thus, suppose John recalls the license number of the Honda Civic he believes is mine (he has a fantastic memory for license numbers). And suppose he reads in the newspaper that drugs have been found in a red Honda Civic with that license number,

and, good citizen that he is, he goes to the police and says "I know who that red Honda Civic belongs to; it belongs to Hilary Putnam." Suppose I am tried, and John repeats his assertion on the witness stand. My defense attorney asks: "*How* do you know it belongs to Hilary Putnam?" (That's the sort of thing defense attorneys ask.) John replies that he has seen it parked in front of my house many times (by chance, he has never been to my house when my own car was parked there). My attorney now produces state license records and witnesses to show that the car John saw belonged to my cousin and not to me. Now it is shown that while I do have a red Honda Civic (John's belief that that is the case is correct), he did not *know* that I have a red Honda Civic, and he certainly did not know (because *that* belief is incorrect) that the red Honda Civic with the drugs in it belonged to me. Asking whether "the lemmas are true" is an important way of criticizing knowledge claims, over and above asking whether what is claimed to be known is true and over and above asking whether the belief in question was arrived at reasonably—important *in practice.*

9. John Dewey, *Logic: The Theory of Inquiry* (New York: Henry Holt and Company, 1938); reprinted in *John Dewey, The Later Works*, vol. 12: 1938, ed. Jo Ann Boydston (Carbondale, IL: Southern Illinois University Press, 1986). The note in question is on p. 345 of the Henry Holt & Co edition and on p. 343 of the *Later Works*, vol. 12.

10. See, for example, Hilary Putnam, "Skepticism, Stroud, and the Contextuality of Knowledge," *Philosophical Explorations* 4, no.1 (2001): 2–16.

11. See Hilary Putnam, "Vagueness and Alternative Logic," *Erkenntnis* 19 (1983): 297–314.

12. He cites p. 106 of my *The Collapse of the Fact/Value Dichotomy.*

13. See Hilary Putnam and Ruth Anna Putnam, "Dewey's *Logic*: Epistemology as Hypothesis," in *Words and Life*, ed. James Conant (Cambridge, MA: Harvard University Press), 198–220.

14. See Hilary Putnam, "Dewey's Central Insight," in *John Dewey's Educational Philosophy in International Perspective: A New Democracy for the Twenty-First Century*, ed. Larry A Hickman and Giuseppe Spadafora (Carbondale, IL: Southern Illinois University Press, 2009), 7–21.

15. On these, see Hilary Putnam, "Pragmatism and Moral Objectivity," in *Words and Life*, 151–81.

24

Harvey Cormier

WHAT IS THE USE OF CALLING PUTNAM A PRAGMATIST?

But you aren't a pragmatist? No. For I am not saying that a proposition is true if it is useful.
—LUDWIG WITTGENSTEIN, *REMARKS ON THE PHILOSOPHY OF PSYCHOLOGY*

Sometimes Hilary Putnam sounds like a pragmatist, sometimes not. For one of the fairly long periods between his famous changes of mind, he described his philosophical outlook as "pragmatic realism,"[1] but even during that time he argued against positions associated with both historical and contemporary figures who have called themselves pragmatists, and since then he has undergone another change of outlook. He still cites John Dewey as an influence, and as recently as 2007 he has remarked that he is "not unhappy" to be called a pragmatist as long as his views are not being assimilated to Richard Rorty's;[2] but he has compared his outlook as much with the views of the later Wittgenstein as with those of Dewey or William James,[3] and there are good reasons not to think of Wittgenstein as a pragmatist.[4]

Of course, it is hard to say whether any given thinker is a pragmatist because different "pragmatists" have said different things. But since Putnam has had a fair amount to say about William James's philosophy, we can compare Putnam's and James's views, and then, at least, we can find out whether Putnam is a *Jamesian* pragmatist. I try to do this in what follows. In the end it seems to me that even though he has been right to resist the label, Putnam could call himself a Jamesian pragmatist if he wanted to. He has actually been quite explicit in his rejection of James's pragmatic theory of truth, and I will examine this rejection here, arguing that Putnam's logical approach to the issue of truth leads him to misunderstand how James's pragmatism works in a fundamental way. I think that if he reconsidered that theory, he might well feel welcome in The Metaphysical Club.

I

To argue for this conclusion I need to do two things: First, I have to spell out a key tenet of Jamesian pragmatism that Putnam seems to me to have trouble with; then I have to explain why Putnam's logically-based approach to philosophical issues causes that trouble.

Thing one I can do in a few words: Putnam seems to me not quite to have broken with what John Dewey used to call "the spectator theory of knowledge," though criticism of this "theory" was at the heart of James's pragmatism. Here, in an underappreciated 1878 essay criticizing Herbert Spencer—an essay Ralph Barton Perry described both as "perhaps the key to all of James's later thought" and "the germinal idea of James's psychology, epistemology, and philosophy of religion"[5]—James describes and rejects the spectator theory:

> The knower is not simply a mirror floating with no foot-hold anywhere, and passively reflecting an order that he comes upon and finds simply existing. The knower is an actor, and coefficient of the truth on one side, whilst on the other he registers the truth which he helps to create. Mental interests, hypotheses, postulates, so far as they are bases for human action—action which to a great extent transforms the world—help to *make* the truth which they declare. In other words, there belongs to mind, from its birth upwards, a spontaneity, a vote. It is in the game, and not a mere looker-on; and its judgments of the *should-be*, its ideals, cannot be peeled off from the body of the *cogitandum* as if they were excrescences or meant, at most, survival.[6]

Our true knowledge and the minds that contain it are not items that passively reflect a world of objective realities distinct from them. Knowing is not, or is at least not "simply," a matter of mirroring, copying, or corresponding to *something else* apart from the knowing subject, something "simply existing" that the knower finds waiting and then passively records in theories.

We knowers live and do things *in the world*—we are "in the game"—and our active, goal-driven lives are among the things that shape and reshape both the world and the truth we know about it. Our knowledge is a thing not just for finding but also for making. It is our fur, fangs, and claws, our toolkit for survival—and not by any means *just* for survival, since we individuals have developed for ourselves over the centuries, and we continue to develop, lots of new interests that we use knowledge to serve. Those interests start out subjective, but they can spread widely, and some have even begun to seem like *human* interests, or things no thinking, feeling human being could fail to care about.

James insisted over the years that our understanding of both knowers and known things must take into account this contingent, observable fact about the way knowledge actually exists and works in the world. And this is the pragmatic idea that Putnam does not quite appreciate or accept. In the end, Putnam holds on to the spectator theory.

II

This will seem unlikely, to say the least. Putnam has often, in more than one period of his thinking, criticized the picture of the mind and the world as items found always on distant, opposite ends of a quasivisual copying, correspondence, or mirroring relation. In the introduction to one of his best known books, he claimed that:

> the mind does not simply 'copy' a world which admits of description by One True Theory. But my view is not a view in which the mind *makes up* the world, either. . . . [T]he mind and the world jointly make up the mind and the world. (Or, to make the metaphor even more Hegelian, the Universe makes up the Universe—with minds—collectively—playing a special role in the making up.)[7]

The mind would seem to be "in the game" according to this story, as it plays a "special role" in making the reality of which it is a part. Putnam is introducing here his middle period view, according to which "'objects' themselves are as much made as discovered, as much products of our conceptual invention as of the 'objective' factor in experience, the factor independent of our will."[8] This story, "internal" or "pragmatic" realism, features objects of knowledge reminiscent of the "objects as they appear," as opposed to the "objects as they are in themselves," found in Kant's first *Critique*.[9] But Putnam does not argue, as Kant at least sometimes seems to, that there are two worlds, one internal, mind dependent, and knowable while the other is external, mind independent, and unknowable. Instead, Putnam rejects the very idea "that there is a coherent 'external' perspective, a theory which is simply true 'in itself', apart from all possible observers."[10] He wants, more Hegelianly, to challenge any effort to draw the traditional distinction between mind and world, inner and outer, subjective and objective. Thus he seems to be trying even harder than Kant did to close any transcendental gap across which knowers might look at the known world. How could this effort be compatible with the spectator theory?

Moreover, the preceding quotes are from Putnam's middle period. Since then he has left "internal" realism behind for "direct" or "natural" realism, an even more hands-on account that he attributes more directly to William James himself. Even as he explicitly rejects James's pragmatic theory of truth, he endorses James's affirmation of the everyday real objects that we perceive and interact with. For example, James argues:

> I am a natural realist. The world *per se* may be likened to a cast of beans on a table. By themselves they spell nothing. An onlooker may group them as he likes.... Whatever he does, so long as he *takes account* of them, his account is neither false nor irrelevant. If neither, why not call it true? It *fits* the beans-*minus*-him and *expresses* the total fact, of beans-*plus*-him.... All that Schiller and I contend for is that there is *no* "truth" without some interest, and that non-intellectual interests [that is, interests in things apart from mapping and counting] play a part as well as intellectual ones. Whereupon we are accused of denying the beans, or denying being in any way constrained by them! It's too silly![11]

Putnam endorses this remark, according to which mind-independent reality has to be out there beyond our language, interests, and knowledge, doing its part to make truths true and to constrain what we say.

Objects for middle-period Putnam were something like Kant's empirically real, representation objects; they did not exist only subjectively, in the minds of particular observers, but they were *relative* to the perceptions and conceptually organized knowledge of beings like us. There would be no such things if there were no human observers or if our theories and perceptions were entirely different. (Think of constellations of stars.) But prephilosophically we think of "real" objects as existences on which our true thoughts depend, not as things that depend on our thoughts for existence. That independence of human thinking and acting is the distinctive characteristic of the (nonmental) real, and without the real we have nothing to point to in explanation of our scientific success or in support of our moral praise and criticism. There are real gold coins and fake, real moral exemplars and real moral monsters, and the truth about all of them depends on their being independent of what we individuals think or say. Or, at least, so say the ordinary persons on the street. (Unless they are on their way to their first freshman philosophy class, where they are just as likely to say the opposite, in my experience.)

Putnam in his latest period wants to return to these ordinary intuitions, and he has therefore renounced his middle period Kantianism. He says that he has undertaken a journey from the familiar to the familiar and entered a second naïveté.[12] In no sense of "dependent" are all real objects dependent on our thinking and perceiving, but neither are real objects unknowable denizens of the world beyond an "interface" of perception or conception. We cannot so much as make sense of either of these possibilities. Instead, our cognitive powers reach all the way to independent real things.

As Putnam has held during all three of his philosophical periods, intentionality "ain't in the head."[13] We can speak or know about things only if we have perceptual contacts with them; and in those events of perception, we do not perceive mental *perceptions that copy objects*, we perceive *objects*. External objects do cause perceptions or brain-states "inside" individual thinkers, but both inner and outer objects also play roles in public, social relations among individuals, relations into which we are initiated when we learn what we should say of those objects. And now Putnam has given up the sophisticated Kantian idea that the objects we speak of *depend for their being* on our perceptions, or conceptually organized batches of them. In his second naïveté, Putnam holds that mind-independent things in the world not only cause perceptions but exert what John McDowell calls "*rational* control" over them and our perceptual judgments. Because of this we can make genuinely *correct or incorrect* judgments about the world we perceive.[14] Our perceptions are "conceptualized"; like our sentences and thoughts, they are best understood not as hidden, inner mental things but rather in terms of their roles in our later-Wittgensteinian forms of life. We are initiated into perception just as much as we are into our languages, and this initiation takes place in ways that involve public contact with extra-mental things. Perceptions, the real perceptions that are intrinsically different from illusions and hallucinations, are less like passively received mirror images and more like parts of games, which are norm-governed, public *activities* containing representations and objects alike.[15]

Considering all this, how can I charge either middle- or latest-period Putnam with having a spectator theory of knowledge? All along, as he has tried to keep subjectivism and skepticism at bay, Putnam has tried to picture knowers as being in cognitive touch with the things they know. And especially in his new explicitly Jamesian phase, that cognitive connection has been an active connection, one described in terms of what we human beings do and how we live. How is any of this compatible with the spectator theory as it is opposed by Dewey and James?

III

To appreciate Putnam the spectator theorist, we have to think not of his praise of James but his criticisms. He has described James's pragmatism as having a "fatal" flaw; in James's theory, "the truth value of every statement about the past *depends on what happens in the future*—and that cannot be right."[16] We can see this clearly, says Putnam, if we draw a connection—disregarding James's explicit warning to avoid doing this[17]—between James's idea of pragmatic truth and his metaphysical and epistemological position, "radical empiricism."[18]

James's pragmatic truths are, according to Putnam, the ideas or judgments that meet and are verified—actually, manifestly verified—by what radical empiricism identifies as "conjunctive relations" or "conjunctive experiences." They connect what we have imagined, thought, or believed with the experiential realities we encounter as we act. If my thoughts of and beliefs about Memorial Hall on the Harvard campus allow me to take someone there and have, as we walk around, only satisfying experiences of similarity to what I imagine and remember, then my earlier mental pictures and thoughts count as cognitions, and my beliefs are verified. But disconcerting experiences would have shown that those thoughts were not cognitions of an external object but rather subjective parts of my own internal mental processes. Those earlier ideas would have wound up a lot of "flat psychological surface" unconnected to an outer world.[19] Thus, thanks to this experiential verification process, some truth about Memorial Hall is, as James would say, "made." However, if nothing like this verification process actually takes place, then my ideas are not *made* true and thus cannot *be* true.[20]

Obviously, nothing like this can happen to many beliefs about the past. Putnam offers the example of a belief concerning whether Lizzie Borden killed her parents. James distinguishes between what *was real in* the past and what *is true about* the past, so that Borden either did kill her parents or did not, irrespective of what anybody may experience in the future.[21] If there arises irresistible future evidence that Borden did commit the murders, then, on James's pragmatic theory, "'L. B. is the killer' is true" itself "becomes" or is "made" true, even if Borden did not really kill anyone and "L. B. is the killer" is still false. Or it might be that she did it, thus making "L. B. is the killer" true, even if the judgment that she did never "becomes true" by getting verified, and "'L. B. is the killer' is true" turns out to be false. Either way, James's theory winds up "contradicting the principle that, for any judgment *p, p* is equivalent to the judgment that *p* is true."[22]

And surely there are also judgments like this about the present. In another paper, Putnam argues that since "we cannot have any causal interaction of any kind with space-time regions outside our light cone (i.e., with regions such that a signal from those regions would have to travel faster than light to reach us)" it follows that, concerning even the present moment, "We can *know* that there are some things which are possible . . . but which are such that if they are the case, then we cannot know that they are the case."[23] For example: "There do not happen to be any stars arranged as the vertices of a regular 100-gon (in a region of space otherwise free of stars)."[24] This "statement" may or may not be true, but we know as well as we know any scientific thing that we will never be able to verify it.

It follows that James's kind of pragmatic verificationism can be no more than partly right. Pragmatists are right to connect "empirical concepts" with perceptual justifications, so that a concept like "chair" could not be explained to a being that lacked a body to sit or perceive with; but "our conceptual powers" extend beyond the verifiable. Thanks to logical quantifiers, we can conceive of realities that exist out beyond our verification processes, and we know of truths that cannot possibly be verified or shown to "work." We cannot know that these truths are true, but, thanks to logic alone, we know that they are out there, with the realities, independent of our verifications.

IV

James was admittedly not much of a logician himself; he called himself "almost blind mathematically and logically."[25] But he described our "great systems of logical and mathematical truth" as composing an "ideal order" or abstract reality with which our ideas must agree "under penalty of endless inconsistency and frustration."[26] Logical principles were as real as anything else we human beings had to use or to struggle with. Still, his biggest target for pragmatic criticism was what he called "diseased abstractionism," or the tendency among some philosophers to picture logical principles, truth, and meanings as if they were knowable and real independently of the struggles of human life.[27]

His preeminent rationalistic opponents in this struggle were Hegel and Hegelians like Royce, whom he took to describe a Parmenidean "block universe," or a world without real individuality or future possibility. Their view seemed to James to treat all the messy, painful, and plural experiences of individual human beings as insignificant and even illusory by contrast with the unified, rational, rationally knowable, and eternally good universe that seemed to contain them. Nothing could, and nothing should, really change in such a rational, orderly world.[28] James's pragmatism thus exists mainly as an anti-Hegelianism.

In this contest James is debating philosophers, and he therefore uses the language of traditional philosophy. But it is a mistake to evaluate his theories exclusively by the standards of epistemology and metaphysics. Instead of attempts to lay out what is undeniably real in the universe,

James's writings, many of which originated as popular public lectures, are a rallying cry. James wants to help individuals to acknowledge the evils of their circumstances, to stop hating their own mistakes and fallibilities, to overcome their despair, and to see how, especially if they think of themselves as free and work to share their ideas and motivations with others, they can develop power to change the world around them.[29] Living in an open universe with a changeable future, and in societies that amplify their efforts, individual human beings can *fight*, can be pivot-points of history, and can make genuinely bad things *better*.

James's single most famous remark is probably the one he made in his diary describing the beginning of his recovery from the obsessive thought that his acts were ineffectual. He wrote on April 30, 1870, as he realized that at least his attention was in his control:

> My first act of free will shall be to believe in free will. I will . . . voluntarily cultivate the feeling of moral freedom. . . . I will go a step further with my will, not only act with it, but believe as well; believe in my individual reality and creative power.[30]

James will henceforth think of himself as a free human agent, focusing his attention on his volitions and their results. This theory will change what he is, and this change will then result in more and more powerful volitions. And pragmatism is the philosophical self-understanding of this developing and struggling organism. It is James's way of seeing his thoughts and beliefs as tools that he has made for himself in his struggles to make real changes in the real world.

But though the Hegelians were his main opponents, James also had to battle a brand new group of in-some-ways abstractionist thinkers, the "analytic" philosophers. G. E. Moore, in "Professor James' 'Pragmatism,'" criticized James's verificationism:

> One historian thinks that a certain event took place, and another that it did not; and both may admit that they cannot verify their idea. Subsequent historians may, no doubt, sometimes be able to verify one or the other. . . . But is it certain that this will *always* happen? . . . Surely the probability is that in the case of an immense number of events, with regard to which we should like to know whether they happened or not, it never will be possible for any man to verify either the one hypothesis or the other. Yet it may be certain that either the events in question did happen or did not.[31]

The ideas we generate and verify for our own benefit are one thing, the reality we sometimes know by means of those ideas is another. There is no necessary connection between the two. Getting truth is finding something that somehow matches that reality, not creating "verified" idea/tools. As Bertrand Russell observes,

> the truth 'A exists', if it is a truth, is concerned with A, who in that case is a fact; and to say that 'A exists' may be true [because useful or verifiable] even if A does not exist is to give a meaning to 'truth' which robs it of all interest. Dr Schiller [James's fellow pragmatist] is fond of attacking the view that truth must correspond with reality; we may conciliate him by agreeing that *his* truth, at any rate, need not correspond with reality. But we shall have to add that reality is to us more interesting than such truth.[32]

Ultimately the analytics think that by analyzing the logical meanings of truth, knowledge, and reality, we can learn all we philosophically need to know about the real and its relations to our theories. In particular we will see that details about which beliefs benefit us and how are entirely beside the point.

V

James wrote rather impatiently to Peirce in 1909 that "I am *a*-logical, if not illogical, and glad to be so when I find Bertie Russell trying to excogitate what true knowledge means, in the absence of any concrete universe surrounding the knower and the known. Ass!"[33] James was unrelentingly critical of Russell's effort to define truth as a matter of pure abstract logic:

> He attempts this feat by limiting the discussion to three terms only, a proposition, its content, and an object, abstracting from the whole context of associated realities in which such terms are found in every case of actual knowing. . . . There is no problem at all in truth and falsehood; . . . "some propositions are true and some false, just as some roses are red and some white; . . . belief is a certain attitude towards propositions, which is called knowledge when they are true, error when they are false"—and he seems to think that when once this insight is reached the question may be closed forever![34]

James thought that the *what* of these philosophical abstractions, however rigorously investigated, answers no interesting questions without an account of their *how* or their *why*. Why bother getting truths? How do we use them in the fight to make our lives worth living? The logical meaning of "truth" is only interesting if it helps us see the practical meaning—the significance, the value in life—of the thing called by that name.

James was especially skeptical regarding Russell's abstract "propositions":

I do not say that for certain logical purposes it may not be useful to treat propositions as absolute entities, with truth or falsehood inside of them respectively, or to make of a complex like 'that-Caesar-is-dead' a single term and call it a 'truth.' But the 'that' here . . . sometimes . . . means the *fact* that, and sometimes the *belief* that, Caesar is no longer living. When I then call the belief true, I am told that the truth means the fact; when I claim the fact also, I am told that my definition has excluded the fact. . . .[35]

If propositional logic is helpful, propositions are as real as anything else; but we will not understand truth if we get confused about where propositions come from and how they work. Is a proposition something we generate as we are driven by circumstances to think? That is, is it some kind of belief?[36] Or is it a "fact," a reality, part of the circumstances driving us to believe? Or is the bearer of truth something else entirely, a being of pure logic that exists, waiting to have its truth or falsity discovered, in a timeless realm independent of both human thinkers and the world of objects and events those thinkers live in? In his battle with Russell, James is most critical of the last alternative. What is true is not a "bare logical entity" but a "belief" or an "idea," a "postulate," or, perhaps most tellingly, a "hypothesis." James uses all of these terms at different times to mean the same thing, namely, a "rule for action" or a guide to making life better, a thing that we *create* and then test as we try to remake our world.[37] When these things work or provide good results, we have truths. Before we create those real-life guides to action, there *is* no truth because there is nothing to work this way or to *be* true.

VI

Putnam's critique of James's verificationism is strikingly similar to Russell's and Moore's criticisms, though he does acknowledge that James rejected the idea of purely abstract propositions, and he accordingly puts his antipragmatic criticisms in terms of "judgments" and "statements" that presumably have actually been made by someone on the basis of some kind of evidence. And there was, of course, evidence in the case of Lizzie Borden: there were well known family quarrels over money; the ashes of one of Borden's dresses were found in the furnace a few days after the killings; the maid was seen departing with a mysterious parcel. Borden was acquitted, but there was evidence enough so that her neighbors in Fall River *did* something, namely, ostracize Lizzie for the rest of her life.

But if we turn back to Putnam's giant stellar polygons beyond all our possible perceptions, do we really find "judgments" and "statements" about *that*? Who made them and why? Surely there are no *hypotheses* about any such things. Why would anyone produce any? How would it help anything? And there are no "beliefs" in this vicinity, at least as pragmatists understand belief. What would anyone *do* to show that she or he believed or disbelieved in unknowable vast stellar polygons? What kind of "rule for action" would *that* be? Thus, it is simply not true that there are any vast stellar polygons beyond our light cone—*because there is no "it" to be true.*[38] "It" is not false, either, for the obvious analogous reason. The idea that there might be such a truth, a true judgment, or a true proposition, existing apart from all our real-life verification efforts or our efforts to make the world better, is nothing less than a Russellian case of "diseased abstractionism."

The Lizzie Borden situation is, once again, a little better. Since there actually was and is some evidence, there actually were and are people with hypotheses or beliefs about the Borden murders. Back then there were Lizzie's appalled neighbors, and today there are feminist historians who think that Borden was acquitted only because a sexist, all-male jury of that period could not believe a woman capable of those particular killings even after looking at the evidence.[39] The neighbors and the historians alike have convincing empirical and historical evidence of their shared hypothesis, and, more important, they have found a use for that hypothesis in the future-oriented project of improving their lives and their society. Thus there really are hypotheses or beliefs about Lizzie Borden that might be true or false. And Putnam, channeling Russell and Moore, argues that James's account of those beliefs runs afoul of the logic of truth. In James's picture, our thoughts could wind up being "true" of events that never happened. Pragmatic verificationism is thus a kind of dualism, putting up an "interface" partition between reality and our "true" thoughts.

However, it is really Putnam who is doing the dualistic world-dividing here, not James. Even, or maybe especially, in his latest period, Putnam is implacably committed to dividing the world into us thinkers and our interests, on the one hand, and a realm of things mostly independent of and unaffected by our thoughts and interests, on the other. Putnam's dualism is not the dualism of a (stereotypical) Cartesian, who sees spirits on one side of an ontological gap and material things on the other, with sensory qualia as an interface. Nor is it that of a materialist who sees brain-representations as coming between us sociable neural systems and the world around us. But it is resolutely a dualism dividing the *made* from the *found*. In Putnam's world there are things and events we human beings produce through willed choices, and there is a different and vastly larger amount of stuff that is just *there* whether we like it or not, stuff that would just go its own way even if we were not here. We have some control over ourselves—*some*—and we can change a few pitiful things—not by any means everything—on earth and in its spatial vicinity; but the vast preponderance of the realities in spacetime, including quite a lot of the stuff we know as part of the local human environment and even human nature, is as it is no matter what we want or can possibly do. There are also logical principles that we have no choice about, like "For any p, p is equivalent to 'p is true'"; and even the languages we have created have meanings that "ain't in the head" and depend on features of that world beyond our control. The logical and physical universe around our tiny demesne is just *there*, not to be wrestled with but only to be found and then appreciated . . . that is, to be looked upon passively. Putnam's picture of our relationship to the world is a kind of spectator theory of knowledge.

Our thinking usually is and always should be *controlled* by the stuff that is just *there*. When it is not, what results is a "disaster" like James's pragmatic theory of truth, according to which human thinking is free to go wherever human desires might take it. Pragmatic thinkers can think and say anything they find satisfying and no other person or thing can stop them. Anything goes, in their world—or so the pragmatic thinkers think, anyway. Of course they are wrong; some thoughts are irrational and dangerous. They lead us into bad social and physical situations. We should avoid such thoughts and pursue and develop thoughts with good consequences, ideas that make our lives better. Sometimes ideas can even make our lives better or worse in ways we have not anticipated; not only are we not omnipotent, we are also not omniscient. We have to go along using our tentative hypotheses, things that we believe to be true only as long as they keep satisfying us and that we toss away when they let us down. But we can, do, and should go along this way, and that is in fact how we have successfully advanced in our understanding of the world, how we have developed lives that feature fewer and fewer bad surprises. We have scientific, logical, moral, and even religious ideas that seem to help us in life, and we use our ongoing experiences to improve and expand that ever more powerful arsenal of intellectual weapons.

All of which is to say, of course, that Putnam's worries about the looming disaster of pragmatic truth seem misplaced. James only wants us to do what Putnam himself wants us to do, namely, pay attention to life and the way it really works when we develop our philosophical self-understanding.[40] Putnam thinks that pragmatism's "anything goes" theory of truth will impede our efforts to do this, but, as Stanley Fish has pointed out, James's theory entails not that anything goes but that "*anything that can be made to go goes.*"[41] James is telling us not to ignore the world outside ourselves but rather to pay attention to all and only things, wherever they might be, that we have a *reason* to pay attention to.[42]

Concepts do not become an "interface" between two realms in James's story. Tools are not an interface, or at least not always. If I use my opposable thumbs to pick up an object, I am not (necessarily) using my thumbs to represent the object to myself or creating a representation that comes between me and the thing. I am literally—*literally*—in direct touch with it. If I deal with that object with forceps or a hammer, I am no longer literally in direct touch, but neither am I interposing a *representation* between myself and the object. And James, once again, treats concepts as tools, not unlike hammers and forceps, for dealing with objects, for managing them and trying to get from them what we want and need for life. Concepts are extraordinarily useful tools that can change the world we live in. They can even work at a distance; the ideas of fertilizer and irrigation, for the kind of mundane example Dewey might have pointed to, have spread all around the world and changed many lives. And, just like some physical tools, ideas can be used to horrible effect. The idea of racial superiority has killed millions more human beings than any species of physical weapon. When ideas lead to consequences we understand as bad, we call them false and try to get rid of them, whether they are scientific, religious, or of any other kind.

Future ideas will even work to help us deal with past events. Gavin Stevens, a character in a William Faulkner fiction, famously observes that "The past is never dead. It's not even past."[43] This imaginary person has a point. Past events can have left world shaping consequences, and our hypotheses about those events can help us navigate those consequences. Moreover, if this were not true, we would not develop any such hypotheses. They originate in our need to deal with the past and we hold on to them only as long as they keep proving helpful. We may later find out that a newer idea of the past is better than the idea that we started with, and then we will say that that new idea was always true even before we knew it, but what we will mean is that the new idea would always have proven useful, just as hammers or bows and arrows would have proven useful before they were invented. This will not commit us to the idea that there is or was always some pure, ideal abstraction called the truth, unrelated to the rule-for-action beliefs and hypotheses we have *made*, waiting out there with the rest of the realities to be *found*. And that is a good thing, for that is an idea that only a logician could love.

VII

The made versus the found: this may *really* be the last dogma of empiricism—that is, of "logical empiricism" or what became analytic philosophy. Maybe, indeed, the other "dogmas," the dualisms of analysis and synthesis (according to Quine),[44] scheme and content (Davidson),[45] and value and fact (Putnam)[46] are in the end all variations of this Über-dogma, a distinction between what we human beings make up in our own minds and what is just *there* for our minds to work on. Obviously this is not a distinction marked by empiricists alone; almost all philosophical thinkers of almost all varieties have taken something like it for granted. Nonphilosophers usually do, too, though half-heartedly at most. (Again, think of day one in Philosophy 101.) But it is especially bad for empiricist philosophers to assume the reality of this distinction if there is no empirical evidence for it, or no principled, non-question-begging way to mark it in experiential terms. And the distinction seems especially important to empiricists, who typically make a point of basing their thinking on the evidence they scientifically *find* (or are "given") rather than on a priori ideas that thinkers willfully *make* to suit their personal tastes. (At least this is C. S. Peirce's polemical picture of the a priori method in "The Fixation of Belief.")[47] But what kind of empirical evidence is there that the made is distinct from the found? What kind of evidence could there be?

If this is the last pillar of the empiricist temple, it may fall, like those other empiricist articles of faith, to an assault by pragmatism. It seems clear that James wants to challenge the made/found distinction as he tries to transcend both empiricism and rationalism. Especially in the chapter of *Pragmatism* called "Pragmatism and Humanism," James says things that Putnam the natural realist will find obnoxious, including: "Does the river make its banks, or do the banks make the river? Does a man walk with his right leg or with his left leg more essentially? Just as impossible may it be to separate the real from the human factors in the growth of our cognitive experience,"[48] and "We create the subjects of our true as well as of our false propositions."[49] It seems hard to square passages like these with the story of the beans, which let us count them and put them into bean constellations but are nevertheless *there* to be found, in their beanhood, controlling what we think about them and setting a discernible limit beyond which we cannot truthfully go.

However, one important thing to notice about these antirealist sounding passages, and the whole *Pragmatism* lecture in which we find them, is that James is not discussing his own view. Here, in some of his best-known remarks, he is actually describing and defending the "humanism" of F. C. S. Schiller. Schiller saw himself as a pragmatist, but while his general philosophical views were compatible with James's pragmatism, they were not all contained in it. Schiller held that the world we think about is an Aristotelian ὕλη *(hȳlē)* or prime matter with no essence, no *is,* apart from what "*is* what is made of it. Hence . . . the world is *plastic*" or ours to shape in our truth making processes.[50] But while pragmatism is *compatible* with this picture of reality as "a mere unresisting ὕλη,"[51] *it does not entail it.* James says that:

> Other pragmatists may reach more positive beliefs about the sensible [that is, experienceable] core of reality. . . . They may make theories that tell us all about it; and if these theories work satisfactorily they will be true. The transcendental idealists say there is no core, the finally completed wrapping being

reality and truth in one. Scholasticism still teaches that the core is 'matter'.
. . . Messrs. Dewey and Schiller treat it as a 'limit.' Which is the truer of all
these diverse accounts, or of others comparable with them, unless it be the
one that finally proves the most satisfactory?[52]

And perhaps James might have added that his own radical empiricism treats
the "core" of reality as sensations and memories in changing experienced
conjunctive relations. Radical empiricism is one more epistemological and
metaphysical theory that is compatible with, but not either entailed or presupposed by, pragmatism. Pragmatism, by making sense of truth in verificationist terms, makes it *possible* for James to theorize a reality of plural
facts and experienced conjunctions among them; but it does not require in
advance that this or any other story of reality be the true one. That would
be dogmatic, not pragmatic.

Thus Putnam is mistaken to treat James's pragmatic truths as ideas that
must be occurrently verified by conjunctive experiences. Pragmatic truths
may wind up putting us in touch with a kind of reality entirely different
from James the radical empiricist's world—or with no reality at all. We
cannot say now; we have to wait and see what works out. The truth about
the nature of reality is just like the truth about anything else.

And, thus, we have another reason to think that there is no special difficulty connected with pragmatic truth about the past. To say that the truth
is what works is not necessarily to say that a particular truth has to provide
actual events of satisfying contact with any "reality," perceptual or otherwise.[53] This is good; it means the pragmatist need have no special trouble
with truth about fictions, for one thing. There are beliefs about Sherlock
Holmes or Gavin Stevens that work and there are beliefs that do not, and
that is all there is to it. And, what is more, while it is perfectly reasonable to
think that the kind of perceptual contact with the past that James is talking
about is possible—the kind that involves profitable use in lived experience
of an idea of Julius Caesar, Martin Luther King, Jr., or the first nanoseconds
of the Big Bang—if one wants both to insist that the past is utterly gone and
still believe that pragmatic truth about the past is possible, that particular
metaphysical position can work out, too.

Moreover, if someone is also convinced that there is a real world entirely
beyond what we say and think, an objective world that justifies us—somehow, in some way unrelated to what we happen to find evident or helpful—in
our beliefs, then there is room under the pragmatist tent for that person,
too. I *think* this accurately describes Hilary Putnam, and I therefore think
that while Putnam will not want to be a Schillerian humanist, he may well
find Jamesian pragmatism, properly understood as a thing independent of
James's radical empiricism, to be congenial.

According to James's pragmatism, we do not need to appeal to any purely objective realities to make sense of our truth-seeking process, and we had better not try dogmatically to spell out now what things are out there in the purely objective world. The history of scientific and other investigative surprises is a long one, and it shows our need to stay open to future evidence. (Who knows: someday some evidence may show us that it was not such a good idea to call those particular legumes "beans.") But is any objective world of things out there at all? Thanks to the same pragmatic investigations we make into nonmetaphysical matters, we can give this question the confident answer: We shall see.

HARVEY CORMIER

STONY BROOK UNIVERSITY
JUNE 2011

NOTES

1. He renames the "internal realism" of his middle-period "pragmatic realism" at Hilary Putnam, *The Many Faces of Realism* (LaSalle, IL: Open Court, 1987), 17.
2. Hilary Putnam, 2007 University College Dublin Ulysses Medal Lecture, "The Fact/Value Dichotomy and its Critics," unpublished. Thanks to Professor Putnam for generously sending me a copy.
3. For example, in "The Face of Cognition," Part One, Lecture Three of Hilary Putnam, *The Threefold Cord: Mind, Body and World* (New York: Columbia University Press, 1999), Putnam argues that his new "naïve" or natural realism, a practical position between reductionism or verificationism and the embrace of metaphysics, parallels Wittgenstein's treatment of language in terms of the variety of practices in which our terms play different roles.
4. Russell Goodman's excellent book *Wittgenstein and William James* (Cambridge: Cambridge University Press, 2007) describes both the large influence James had on Wittgenstein and the significant differences between the two thinkers' views.
5. "Remarks" is found at William James, *Collected Essays and Reviews*, ed. Ralph Barton Perry (Boston: Longmans, Green, 1920), 43–68. Perry offers these two appreciations of the paper at p. viii and p. 43, respectively. This article is also reprinted in William James, *Essays in Philosophy*, ed. F. H. Burkhardt, F. Bowers, and I. Skrupskelis (Cambridge, MA: Harvard University Press, 1978).
6. James, *Collected Essays and Reviews*, 67.
7. Hilary Putnam, *Reason, Truth and History* (Cambridge: Cambridge University Press, 1981), xi.
8. Ibid., 54.
9. Putnam argues at *Reason, Truth and History*, 60–62 that he and Kant both try to show the meaninglessness of talk about a world beyond thought and perception. He argues that Kant is best read as his kind of "internal realist."
10. Ibid., 55. Of course, it is not perfectly clear that Kant is trying to establish the existence of two worlds when he distinguishes the empirical or phenomenal from the noumenal. Henry Allison's *Kant's Transcendental Idealism: An Interpretation and Defense* (New

Haven: Yale University Press, 1983) offers a well known argument for the idea that Kant understands these realms to be two aspects of one world or reality.

11. James's letter to Dickinson S. Miller, dated August 5, 1907, in *The Letters of William James*, vol. 2 (Boston: Atlantic Monthly, 1920), 295; cited at Putnam, *The Threefold Cord*, 5.

12. Putnam, *The Threefold Cord*, 15.

13. See Hilary Putnam, *Mind, Language and Reality: Philosophical Papers*, vol. 2 (Cambridge: Cambridge University Press, 1975), 215–71. That paper, "The Meaning of 'Meaning,'" lays out Putnam's "externalism," according to which linguistic meaning is tied to real objects in the natural world rather than being a matter of internal mental states or states of the brain.

14. John McDowell, *Mind and World* (Cambridge, MA: Harvard University Press, 1996) is mainly a theory of experience that allows the facts that constitute the world to exert rational control on human thought.

15. Cf. Putnam, *The Threefold Cord*, 153–54, for a discussion of McDowell's "disjunctive" theory of perception.

16. See Hilary Putnam, "James's Theory of Truth," in *The Cambridge Companion to William James*, ed. Ruth Anna Putnam (Cambridge: Cambridge University Press, 1997), 182.

17. William James, *Pragmatism and the Meaning of Truth* (Cambridge: Harvard University Press, 1978), 6. (This text is hereafter cited as *PMT*.)

18. This paragraph and a number of the ones following it are adapted from Harvey Cormier, *The Truth Is What Works* (Lanham, MD: Rowman and Littlefield, 2000), 130–50.

19. James, *PMT*, 272, cited at Putnam, "James's Theory of Truth," 174.

20. Putnam, "James's Theory of Truth," 172–79.

21. Putnam, "James's Theory of Truth," 182–83. James, at *PMT* 108, 272–73, and 320–25, among other places, draws a general distinction between the real and the true, and he accuses some of his critics of confusing the two in their criticisms.

22. Putnam, "James's Theory of Truth," 182–83.

23. Hilary Putnam, "Pragmatism," *Proceedings of the Aristotelian Society* 95 (1995): 291–306. The passage cited is from 294.

24. Putnam, "Pragmatism," 294.

25. William James, *Some Problems of Philosophy* (New York: Longmans, Green & Co., 1940), 183.

26. James, *PMT*, 101.

27. James describes Russell's view as displaying "diseased abstractionism" at *PMT*, 318.

28. The opening chapter of James's *Pragmatism* (*PMT*, 9–26) establishes this theme.

29. Cormier, *The Truth Is What Works*, is an exploration of this idea.

30. William James, *The Letters of William James*, vol. I., edited by his son, Henry James (Boston: Atlantic Monthly Press, 1920), 148.

31. G. E. Moore, *Philosophical Studies* (London: Routledge & Kegan Paul, 1951), 103.

32. Bertrand Russell, *Philosophical Essays* (New York: Simon and Schuster, 1966), 123.

33. Cited at Ralph Barton Perry, *The Thought and Character of William James* (Nashville: Vanderbilt University Press, 1996), 368.

34. James, *PMT*, 318.

35. James, *PMT*, 317.

36. At William James, *Principles of Psychology* (New York: Dover, 1950), 2:286–87, James agrees with Franz Brentano that "conception and belief . . . are two different fundamental psychic phenomena" and that "the mere thought of the object may exist as something quite distinct from the belief in its reality." He goes on to allow that the content or object of thought is a "proposition," a combination of ideas by means of a copula that can be believed or disbelieved. But James also says of the propositional objects of our thought,

"Any object which remains uncontradicted is ipso facto believed and posited as absolute reality." (James, *Principles of Psychology*, 2:289; emphasis in original.) That is, unbelieved "propositions" are no more than beliefs at odds with other beliefs—beliefs about things in an inner world of imaginings rather than the outer spatial world. Again: *"all propositions . . . are believed through the very fact of being conceived, unless they clash with other propositions believed at the same time. . . ."* (James, *Principles of Psychology*, 2: 290; emphasis in original, once again.) Propositions are not pure logical entities distinct from the psychic activities of real human thinkers.

37. James adopts Peirce's "principle of pragmatism" and his related idea that beliefs are rules for action at *PMT*, 29.

38. From James, *PMT*, 322:

> PRAG:—Then I beg you again to tell me in what this truth consists, all by itself, this *tertium quid* intermediate between the facts *per se*, on the one hand, and all knowledge of them, actual or potential, on the other. What is the shape of it in this third estate? Of what stuff, mental, physical, or 'epistemological,' is it built? What metaphysical region of reality does it inhabit?

> ANTI-PRAG:—What absurd questions! Isn't it enough to say that it *is true* that the facts are so-and-so, and false that they are otherwise?

> PRAG:—'*It*' is true that the facts are so-and-so–I won't yield to the temptation of asking you *what* is true; but I do ask you whether your phrase that 'it is true that' the facts are so-and-so really means anything really additional to the bare *being* so-and-so of the facts themselves.

> ANTI-PRAG:—It seems to mean more than the bare being of the facts. It is a sort of mental equivalent for them, their epistemological function, their value in noetic terms.

> PRAG:—A sort of spiritual double or ghost of them, apparently! If so, may I ask you *where* this truth is found.

James is challenging the idea that the "it" in "it is true that" refers to some entity existing somehow in between real things and our true beliefs (theories, hypotheses) about those things.

39. I was unaware of the feminists when I considered this case at *The Truth Is What Works*, 133–39. One such writer argues:

> The jury, twelve middle-aged, middle class New England gentlemen, proved unable to accept [the prosecutor Hosea] Knowlton's radical reinterpretation of nineteenth-century sex roles, unable to accept the notion that women might be like men, and perhaps, most importantly, unable to envision the possibility that if Lizzie Borden could commit parricide might not [*sic*] their own wives and daughters be capable of the same act? Within an hour they returned a verdict of not guilty.

From Ann Schofield, "Lizzie Borden Took an Axe: History, Feminism, and American Culture," *American Studies* 34, no. 1 (1993): 99.

40. Putnam concludes his Dewey Lectures with the observation that "if there was one great insight in pragmatism, it was the insistence that what has weight in our lives should also have weight in philosophy." Putnam, *The Threefold Cord*, 70.

41. Stanley Fish, "Truth and Toilets," in *The Trouble with Principle* (Cambridge, MA: Harvard University Press, 1999), 307.

42. Can we really rest content with "verified" truths that are not intrinsically connected to reality? Should we? In the case of Lizzie Borden, we will be failing to investigate *what really happened*—a bloody murder!—and paying attention instead to what we just happen to find it helpful or convincing to believe. Can that be the right thing to do? It is if there is no difference between trying to find out what happened and trying to find out what it is best to believe about what happened. In the course of a real life inquiry, *the evidence is always exactly the same in both cases.*

43. From William Faulkner, *Requiem for a Nun* (New York: Vintage, 1975), Act I, Scene III.

44. See W. V. Quine, "Two Dogmas of Empiricism," in *From a Logical Point of View* (Cambridge, MA: Harvard University Press, 1980), 20–46.

45. See Donald Davidson, "On the Very Idea of a Conceptual Scheme," in *Inquiries into Truth and Interpretation* (Oxford: Oxford University Press, 2001), 183–98.

46. See Hilary Putnam, *The Collapse of the Fact-Value Dichotomy and Other Essays* (Cambridge, MA: Harvard University Press, 2002), esp. 135–45.

47. Found at Peirce, *Collected Papers,* vol. 2, 4.358–4.387.

48. James, *PMT,* 120.

49. James, *PMT,* 122.

50. F. C. S. Schiller, *Personal Idealism: Philosophical Essays by Eight Members of the University of Oxford,* ed. Henry Sturt (London: Macmillan, 1902), 60. Cited at James, *PMT,* 117.

51. James, *PMT,* 120. Actually, James is being a little unfair to Schiller in this particular description. James himself has just noted, at *PMT* 117, the "resistance" provided by reality in Schiller's picture. At *Personal Idealism,* 59, Schiller says, "Let it be observed, therefore, that our activity always meets with resistance, and that in consequence we often fail in our experiments." *Even plastic things can put up some resistance.*

52. James, *PMT,* 120.

53. Actually, James can treat verifications just as subjunctively as Peirce, and it is important to recognize that he makes a point of doing so. Truth is, for him, a "habit"; it is the *disposition or tendency* of beliefs to provide good experienced consequences, not the manifest provision of those good experiences. At James, *PMT,* 106, we find:

> The scholastics, following Aristotle, made much of the distinction between habit and act. Health *in actu* means, among other things, good sleeping and digesting. But a healthy man need not always be sleeping, or always digesting, any more than a wealthy man need be always handling money, or a strong man always lifting weights. All such qualities sink to the status of 'habits' between their times of exercise; and similarly truth becomes a habit of certain of our ideas and beliefs in their intervals of rest from their verifying activities. But those activities are the root of the whole matter, and the condition of there being any habit to exist in the intervals.

REPLY TO HARVEY CORMIER

Harvey Cormier belongs to a very different academic generation than did Richard Rorty; Rorty was only slightly younger than I, while Cormier was one of my students as recently as 1992. Nevertheless, there are strong similarities between these two philosophers. They both are associated with strong pragmatist-influenced views, they both strongly oppose realism (Rorty once said to me, "commonsense realism is just as bad as metaphysical realism [which he regarded as unquestionably bad], one leads to the other"), and they both express their views with verve and rhetorical effectiveness. Although our disagreements were clearly not going to go away, Rorty and I always enjoyed and profited from our debates, and I am sure that the same will be the case with Cormier—at least, I am sure that *I* have profited from seeing this interpretation and defense of a "Jamesian" view laid out so clearly, and I hope that he will feel the same way about this reply.

Cormier is an expert on the history of pragmatism (which does not prevent it from being the case that he and I disagree on the right interpretation of William James—perhaps no two James experts agree completely on the interpretation of that endearing but elusive thinker!). I will end this reply with a description of that disagreement. But I do not disagree with Cormier's description of *my* successive positions (apart from one slip that does not affect his main argument.)[1] In sum, I plead "guilty" to all his charges. In fact, not only am I guilty of what he calls a "spectator view" of knowledge (although I think it is wrong to call it that, nevertheless, *as Cormier defines what such a view is*, I am indeed guilty). Moreover, I am *unrepentantly* guilty. I think my view is right and I think Cormier's is wrong, just as I thought Rorty's views were wrong, although they were not the same as Cormier's.[2]

The nub of my disagreement with Cormier is this. As Cormier correctly says, on the view I have held since I gave up "internal realism" in 1990 (Cormier calls this my "latest period"):

(1) "In no sense of 'dependent' are all real objects dependent on our thinking and perceiving, but neither are real objects unknowable denizens of the world beyond an 'interface' of perception or conception. . . . our cognitive powers reach all the way to independent real things."

(2) I believe that there are truths (for example, about exactly what there is in regions of spacetime outside our light cone) that "we know as well as we know any scientific thing that we will never be able to verify."

(3) I do believe, as Cormier charges, that the things there are can be divided into us and the things we affect, on the one hand, and " a realm of things mostly independent of and unaffected by our thoughts and interests on the other."

[The reason I think that it is wrong to call this a "spectator view of knowledge" is that (1)–(3) are a view of the nature of the universe and not a view of knowledge. A spectator view of knowledge, as I would use the term, claims that we can know about the world by a priori reasoning, without interacting with it. Holding that a great deal of reality is independent of us and rejecting a spectator view of knowledge in *this* sense, are not incompatible.]
In contrast, what Cormier holds is that:

(4) A belief or idea that can be true (or false) is "a 'rule for action' or a guide to making life better, a thing that we *create* and then test as we try to remake our world."

(5) Such a "rule of action" is true if and only if it is useful in making life better. "When these things work or provide good results, we have truths."

(6) This also applies to beliefs about the past: "We may later find out that a newer idea of the past is better than the idea that we started with, and then we will say that that new idea was always true even before we knew it, but what we will mean is that the new idea would always have proven useful, just as hammers or bows and arrows would have proven useful before they were invented. This will not commit us to the idea that there is or was always some pure, ideal abstraction called the truth, unrelated to the rule-for-action beliefs and hypotheses we have *made*, waiting out there with the rest of the realities to be *found*. And that is a good thing, for that is an idea that only a logician could love."

(7) As a consequence, the idea that anything really exists beyond what we have "made"—namely (3) above— has to be rejected, as do (1) and (2). "[It] is simply not true that there are any vast stellar polygons beyond our light

cone." (A vast stellar polygon was simply an example I used of something that, consistent with our best physical theory, might or might not exist somewhere outside our light cone. The proposition that there is any such thing is not a rule for action that can be useful or not useful, and conjectures about such things are cases of "diseased abstractionism," according to Cormier.)

So there you have it! As total a disagreement as two philosophers who are still able to talk to one another and address one another's arguments can have. So how do we decide between (1)–(3) and (4)–(6)?

I believe that one should accept (1)–(3), because they express, in broad outlines, the picture of the universe, a universe we did not make (*pace* Cormier and *pace* the late Nelson Goodman), and a picture of thinkers like ourselves as a very small part of that universe, that informs *all* of modern science. As I have repeatedly argued through the years, that picture is the only picture we know of that does not make the success of science a miracle. It is not an accident that successive scientific theories lead to better and better "rules for action"; they do that because they are approximately true, and they lead to better rules for action as the approximation gets better. There is *no* scientific picture of the universe according to which nothing exists except human beings and things that human beings do or "make," in *any* sense of "make." And it is just plain false that there is nothing outside the light cone of the human species. There is lots of stuff out there, and lots of truths about that stuff. Saying this is not "diseased abstractionism" as Cormier contends; it is a recognition that we are not the makers of the universe.

If I appeal to science here it is not, as I am sure Cormier knows, that I think only the exact sciences are worthy of the name "knowledge." We have historical knowledge and social knowledge too, and those knowledges presuppose that there are better and worse interpretations of human sayings, writings, and doings—knowledge of products of human intentionality cannot be relegated to some sort of second-class status, as Quine sought to do. And we also have warranted beliefs about values of various kinds; the positivists' fact/value dichotomy is untenable. All the different sorts of tools, including conceptual ones, that we find indispensable in our lives need to be taken seriously by philosophers. That is the sound legacy of pragmatism. But a "pragmatism" that would turn the very physical universe into a human tool is not a pragmatism I can take seriously.

I. Cormier's Bashing of Analytic Philosophy

Given that Cormier was an excellent student at Harvard University, where he learned a great deal of analytic philosophy, I am surprised that he presents a caricature of it in the present essay. Here is his description:

Ultimately the analytics think that by analyzing the logical meanings of truth, knowledge, and reality, we can learn all we philosophically need to know about the real and its relations to our theories. In particular we will see that details about which beliefs benefit us and how are entirely beside the point.

In addition, Cormier attacks Russell and Moore for quantifying over propositions (which many analytic philosophers have also attacked, including Quine and Davidson). The alternative, Cormier says, is to talk only about judgments in the sense of hypotheses that people actually make as guides to action. If someone conjectures that there may be intelligent extraterrestrials that we will never know of (certainly an *interesting* conjecture, from a purely intellectual point of view—and James never scorned purely intellectual interests, by the way), then since this conjecture is not a "rule of action" it is a *nothing* to Cormier, just as the conjecture that there may be a vast stellar polygon outside our light cone is dismissed by him as a nothing, a mere "case of diseased abstractionism."

I have already said why I think this last claim is wrong. But the whole picture of analytical philosophy as a single position, a position which thinks "that by analyzing the logical meanings of truth, knowledge, and reality, we can learn all we philosophically need to know about the real and its relations to our theories" is also wrong.

Here is why I say it is wrong: different present-day analytic philosophers hold many *different* theories of truth, including neopragmatist theories (Robert Brandom), deflationist theories (Paul Horwich, Hartry Field, Stephen Leeds, and many others), correspondence theories of various kinds, and theories which do not have "classical" names. But all contemporary work on the topic in the analytic tradition starts from Tarski's "semantical conception," and all of it responds in one way or another to Quine's philosophical writings (which are hard to classify, because Quine sometimes writes like a deflationist, and at other times, as he himself says, like a "robust realist"). But Quine is only mentioned (in one sentence!) as having rejected the analytic/synthetic dichotomy, and Tarski is not mentioned at all.

The reason this matters is that neither Tarski, nor Quine, nor any of the philosophers I have just named (with the possible exception of Horwich), thinks that philosophy can proceed by simply "analyzing the logical meanings" of terms (whatever that is supposed to mean). Both Tarski and Quine rejected the whole notion of "analysis of meanings," and the philosophers I have listed follow them in being concerned with giving an account of the function of the locution "true" that does justice to its role in both science and ordinary language. Taking what our best scientific theories say seriously (and, I would add, taking what we find indispensable in our lives seriously), not the "analysis of meaning," is what is most characteristic of post–Logical Empiricist analytic philosophy.

II. Cormier's Appeal to Evidence

Cormier asks, "But what kind of empirical evidence is there that the made is distinct from the found? What kind of evidence could there be?" But this question assumes that we can make sense of the claim that we "make" everything that we speak of, and, as illustrated by the difficulties Nelson Goodman had in defending his notorious claim that "We make the stars,"[3] that is not obvious. Like Goodman, I am sure that Cormier will say "we do not make stars as we make bricks."[4] But then how, or better, in what sense, do we "make" stars? Goodman's answer was that we make "versions," that is, texts and discourses, in which the term "star" appears, but that is not making stars at all.

If I am to pretend to understand the claim that "the made is not distinct from the found," I can only say that, judging from what Cormier says in this essay, it sounds as if what he is defending is an ontological claim according to which there is *nothing* outside our light cone (and, more generally, no objects except those that we interact with in some way relevant to our interest in leading better lives), and the whole of present day cosmology is evidence against *that* claim. Or more likely, he is defending a verificationist claim to the effect that talk of such objects is cognitively meaningless; the evidence against that claim is the whole of the accumulated evidence that verificationism does not give an acceptable picture of scientific theory and practice (or of ordinary language either, as Wittgensteinians have seen). Of course, that this is so is a matter of philosophical judgment and argument, and there is no one single piece of conclusive "evidence" to be had for such a philosophical claim. That does not make it a "dogma."

III. Cormier's James Interpretation and Mine

Above, I described Cormier as making the following claim:

(5) Such a "rule of action" [a belief or idea] is true if and only if it is useful in making life better. "When these things work or provide good results, we have truths."

He also says of truths that they "benefit us." I do not agree that James thought all beliefs were to be judged in the light of the moral interest in making life better or benefiting us. Cormier quotes one of my favorite passages from James's letters:

I am a natural realist. The world *per se* may be likened to a cast of beans on a table. By themselves they spell nothing. An onlooker may group them as he likes. . . . Whatever he does, so long as he *takes account* of them, his account is neither false nor irrelevant. If neither, why not call it true? It *fits* the beans-*minus*-him and *expresses* the *total* fact, of beans-*plus*-him. . . . All that Schiller and I contend for is that there is *no* "truth" without *some* interest, and that non-intellectual interests [that is, interests in things apart from mapping and counting] play a part as well as intellectual ones. Whereupon we are accused of denying the beans, or denying being in anyway constrained by them! It's too silly![5]

I repeat this passage because I think it shows that James did *not* agree with Cormier's claim that "a 'belief' or an 'idea'" that can be true (or false) is "a 'rule for action' or *a guide to making life better*" (emphasis added). Cormier and I agree that James thought that a truth must answer to some interests. But James says here, "why not call it true?" if the idea fits the reality (the beans) *and* answers the "onlooker's" interests. And concerning those interests he says "he may group them as he likes." This is the opposite of saying "as long as he groups them in a way that makes life better." In addition, James says that answering to the onlooker's interests is not sufficient. The grouping must also fit the "beans." And in his printed work, as opposed to his letters, he spells this out even more explicitly. For example, in James's replies to his critics in *The Meaning of Truth*, he writes that the idea that satisfactions are *sufficient* for truth is a "misunderstanding" of his doctrine.[6]

"Such anti-pragmatism as this," James says, "seems to me a tissue of confusions. To begin with, when the pragmatist says 'indispensable,' it confounds this with 'sufficient.' The pragmatist calls satisfactions indispensable for truth-building, but I have everywhere called them insufficient *unless reality be also incidentally led to*. If the reality assumed were cancelled from the pragmatist's universe of discourse, he would straightway give the name falsehood to the beliefs remaining in spite of all their satisfactoriness."

H.P.

NOTES

1. The slip occurs when Cormier writes that according to my views in my "internal realist" period (for example, in *Reason, Truth and History*), "There would be no such things if there were no human observers or if our theories and perceptions were entirely different." What things we say there are depends on which theory we choose, and according to "internal realism," if there is more than one "ideal theory," there is no fact of the matter as to which of those theories is true, or which objects "really exist," but according to none of our theories is the counterfactual "those things (for example, the stars) would not exist if we did not exist" true.

2. In fact, as Brandom's work came to exert an increasing influence on Rorty, those views changed considerably, and were still in flux when he passed away.

3. See *Starmaking: Realism, Anti-Realism and Irrealism,* ed. Peter J. McCormick (Cambridge, MA: MIT Press, 1996), for a collection of the principal papers by Goodman and his critics.

4. Nelson Goodman, "On Starmaking," in *Starmaking; Realism, Anti-Realism and Irrealism*, 145.

5. James to Dickinson S. Miller, 5 August, 1907, in *The Letters of William James,* vol. 2 (Boston: Atlantic Monthly, 1920), 295; cited at Putnam, *The Threefold Cord,* 5.

6. Cf. ch. VIII of *The Meaning of Truth*, "The Pragmatist Account of Truth and its Misunderstanders," James's reply to what he calls the "fourth misunderstanding." The "fourth misunderstanding" is "No pragmatist can be a realist in his epistemology." William James, *Pragmatism and the Meaning of Truth* (Cambridge, MA: Harvard University Press, 1977), 270 ff.

25

Marcin Kilanowski

TOWARD A RESPONSIBLE AND RATIONAL ETHICAL DISCUSSION— A CRITIQUE OF PUTNAM'S PRAGMATIC APPROACH

Hilary Putnam's philosophy is deeply rooted in pragmatism. As Putnam says, there are ideas in pragmatism that deserve to be part of the future of philosophy[1] and there are many things that we can learn from pragmatism.[2] He admits that he does not normally call himself a pragmatist, but he is not unhappy when he is described as one. Although, in saying this, he makes one reservation: that even though he might be described as a pragmatist, he does not want his views to be assimilated with the views of his friend and philosophical opponent Richard Rorty.[3] However, I hope that Professor Putnam will not be very unhappy as I would like to suggest that he does think in a similar manner to Rorty and Habermas on the issue of democratic politics. Presenting this issue is important for an understanding of pragmatism as a whole, not only for an understanding of classical pragmatism, but also for an understanding of contemporary pragmatism, and for an appreciation of the very important message that pragmatism delivers. I strongly believe—as does Putnam—that pragmatism can be "part of the future of philosophy." But for this to happen, certainly much more needs to be said and new steps must be taken. I believe an important step for the future of philosophy is to broaden our understanding of the role of ethics, and Putnam is taking this step. To understand his position on ethics, it is important to first present the commonalities of his philosophical thinking with that of Rorty and Habermas, to then look at where they differ—Putnam's criticism of certain philosophical points made by

Rorty and Habermas—and later to examine Putnam's perspective on the objectivity of ethics.

I. ON POLITICS—SHARING PERSPECTIVE WITH RORTY AND HABERMAS

Putnam is, like Rorty and Habermas, in favor of democracy. This democratic position shapes his approach in dealing with practical problems. This is why Putnam wants to defend a democratic (rather than metaphysical) answer to the question of how we should make decisions. This is—as he says—a "Deweyan" answer and he would be happy to call for, as Dewey does, "deliberative democracy" characterized by "application of intelligence to problems." We should investigate, discuss, and try things out in a cooperative, democratic, and fallibilistic way. We should rely on critical and independent thinking, without which, as he points out, the search for justice can so easily become a cover for fanaticism.[4] Putnam holds that the alternative to fanaticism is that we settle on, in practice, seeking arguments that will convince substantial majorities—arguments that we hope will produce an "overlapping consensus," to use Rawls's term.[5] He believes in the power of argumentation and conversation, not in the possibility of referring to and discovering some reality in itself. This is why Putnam admits that Rorty is right when he criticizes the idea that one could stand outside of one's own thoughts and concepts to compare "reality as it is in itself" with those thoughts and concepts. A consequence of this is that Putnam argues that he does not possess a metaphysical story that will explain how he knows that his concerns for the welfare of others, their freedom of speech, and freedom of thought (regardless of national, ethnic, or religious boundaries) are better than alternative forms of social life. However, these freedoms are not better in the way that he would be able to explain how ethical knowledge is possible in "absolute" terms. Such an idea seems to Putnam to be ridiculous. These concerns are better because Putnam is able to offer arguments that people with no metaphysically liberal convictions can and do offer.[6]

Putnam also shares a common view with Habermas and Rorty on the question of conversation. Like them, he points out the necessary conditions for such conversations to be possible. He holds, for example, that policy recommendations should be a consequence of informed discussion that respects discourse ethics and attempts to understand and make explicit the concerns of all affected.[7] Putnam says that Habermas is right on this point. But, at the same time, Putnam points out that the outcomes of the discussions (whether agreements or decisions) are not necessarily going to be right or reasonable. As Putman says, he will not give "necessary and sufficient conditions for 'right' and 'wrong,' for 'reasonable,' 'well being,' or for any other important value concept."[8] But, to be clear, he means that he is against giving necessary conditions for what is *necessarily* right or *necessarily* wrong.

The outcomes will not be "necessarily right," but they can still be "right." Putnam holds that our conclusions will not always be right, will not always be justified, but we can add that they *might* be the right ones, as far as we will inquire carefully, test our proposals in an experimental spirit, discuss them thoroughly, and so on, while always—at the same time—being conscious that our inquiries are fallible. This is so because for Putnam fallibilism is an inseparable part of the methodology of rational inquiry in general—and the same should apply to us. Putnam praises fallibilism because, like Rorty and Habermas, he denies that there is a set of substantive necessary truths that we can discover once and for all. This is why he claims that if the process of inquiry is right, we will be reasonable more often than if we rely on any foundational philosophical theory, dogma, or fixed method in advance that would not be part of the process of revision in the course of inquiry.[9] According to Putnam we should continue reviewing our "knowledge," keeping in mind that not everything we presently believe can be revised. Doing that allows us, after careful evaluation, to invent new concepts, to develop new descriptions of experience, and to introduce these new concepts and descriptions to general use. This process is an essential part of the "language game" that we play in science, ethics, and law.[10] These new concepts create the possibility of formulating new truths, as Putnam says. Rorty would call such a process an invention of new languages. In this process no one is granted intellectual superiority. This is why Putnam believes that we should avoid established hierarchies and intellectual dependence during the process of inquiry so that every question and objection can be raised. He praises the course of history in which we have rejected aristocratic and patriarchal ethics as empirically false, pointing at claims of intellectual superiority and of some superior "reasonableness." We have also rejected them—as he states—because we have started to appreciate what Dewey calls "the democratic way of life" characterized by compassionate and pluralistic visions of human well-being.[11]

This pluralistic vision relies on an appreciation for pluralism. Putnam calls his vision of pluralism "pragmatic pluralism." He is in favor of pluralisms like those of Rorty and Habermas, who are also following in the footsteps of John Dewey. His pragmatic pluralism "does not require us to find mysterious and supersensible objects *behind* [the] language games" that we actually play, in which truth can be told when language is working.[12] Putnam places pragmatic pluralism in the place of Ontology and points to different discourses that function in everyday language, which are subject to different logical and grammatical standards and possess different sorts of applications. These different discourses and interactions, between them, are the basis for the learning processes that we have achieved in history. Like Habermas, Putnam believes that there can be further learning in the future.[13] This is why, like Habermas and Rorty, he shares a belief in the possibility of progress. But, such a belief in the *possibility* of progress means something different than just a belief in progress. Putnam does not think that progress is inevitable. Progress would then just be a secular version of eschatology. The progress that Putnam is thinking about will be possible *if* we make it happen. It will happen *if* we rely on fallible rational inquiry, the outcomes of which will serve to undertake our future decisions. During this inquiry we have to use human intelligence that holds good for such inquiry by not blocking its paths. All questions and objections should be raised, if possible. We should avoid relationships of hierarchy and dependence. Such inquiry should also insist upon experimentation and be based on a careful evaluation of experience and an invention of new descriptions of such experience.[14] In other words, such inquiry should obey the principles of what Habermas calls "discourse ethics."[15]

All of the above characterizes—as Putnam says—fallibilistic democratic experimentalism, and he admits that this is the worst approach to *expedient* decision making in the public sphere that has ever been devised. The same was said about democracy by Winston Churchill. But democracy as well as fallibilistic democratic experimentalism—even though they are not great—are the best among those approaches that have been tried so far. Putnam claims that democratic experimentalism is the worst approach "*except* for those others that have been tried from time to time."[16]

Summing up, we can say that Putnam believes in pluralism, the possibility of progress, and the learning process in history, beliefs that also characterize the philosophical thinking of Rorty and Habermas. These beliefs are crucial because they form a vision of how society and politics should look. But Putnam goes further and points out that this is not all that should be said and that "*Habermasian* discourse ethics, can and should be seen . . . as spelling out in more detail what rational inquiry worthy of the name requires."[17]

II. Putnam on Habermas and Rorty— A Critical Approach

Putnam believes in the value of discourse ethics because it is identified with the binding power of rational thought and communication, concepts which Putnam admires. But, as he says, there are many points at which he has a difficulty recognizing himself in the picture that Habermas paints.[18]

Putnam believes that there must be more to discourse ethics. However, it is worth noting that his criticism in no way diminishes the importance of discourse ethics.

In the first place, Putnam does not hold Habermas's belief that we can talk about a valid ethical judgment if it is, or follows from, a maxim that is binding on all rational beings, which would be accepted by all persons affected at the end of a sufficiently prolonged discussion that was conducted according to norms of discourse ethics—a modification of a Kantian idea. As Putnam states, this position rests on an epistemological and metaphysical idea which he does not hold. That "the matter will be decided" on the basis of a discovery procedure. The ethical question will be decided by following the norms of communicative action. The metaphysical idea here refers to the validity of ethical statements and the possibility of reaching for the truth. Such truth is what we would agree on after sufficiently prolonged discussion conducted according to the norms of ideal communicative action. Putnam rejects such a metaphysical idea. He claims that the idea that truth is that on which we would agree after sufficiently prolonged discussion conducted according to the norms of ideal communicative action and on which the whole community would come into agreement—is simply false.

Putnam considers Habermas to be a "Kantian" who is haunted by the idea of "universal agreement." Habermas perceives a continuation of discussion until everyone affected is in agreement as a utopian idea.[19] In the real world, agreement of this sort never happens, Putnam claims, even when the discussion is long enough. Even if the speech situation would be ideal "there will never be consensus," even if everyone was speaking honestly, trying to say what was true and justified.[20] This is why we should not expect that the results will be unanimous agreement among the experts any more than among the voters.[21] Because of this problem of unanimous agreement, Putnam believes that it is not possible to repair Habermas's "consent of all" formula, and he considers Habermas's philosophy to be ultimately unrealistic and to have little to do with actual democratic politics.

At this point, one may ask if Habermas really thinks that "consent of all" will be finally reached. When asked, Habermas says that in the real world we can only "hope" for universal agreement and adds that in his *Theory of Communicative Action* he only deals with the issue of communication on the "theoretical level." In other words, Habermas presents only a philosophical theory. And at one point Putnam sees this when he writes:

> One way of understanding Habermas "discourse ethics" is to think of it as precisely such a "middle way," a way in which philosophy can be a "valuable and distinctive participant" in our ethical discussions without pretending to the authority of "final court of appeal." (Many, perhaps most of the silly

criticisms of discourse ethics that I have run across depend on the double mistake of supposing that Habermas believes that an "ideal speech situation" will actually be *reached* at some particular time in the future and supposing that such a situation is precisely the "final court of appeal.") . . . Rather than undertake the task of producing a "final" ethical system, a final set of rules of conduct, what Habermas offers us instead is a rule for how to conduct our inevitable disagreements.[22]

Putnam is right in this passage—that Habermas does not think that in practice an ideal speech situation will finally be reached—rather it is something that we constantly work toward, so that the speech situation will be as undisturbed as possible. And—as I understand Putnam—he also points out that Habermas does not present a final set of rules that will guide us to reach the final truth. Indeed, Habermas presents the rules of how to communicate and he presents formal rules of conduct. But one has also to remember that these rules are strongly connected with something that, for Habermas, is universal—validity claims that are present in every communication. This reference to universal validity is something that differentiates Habermas from Rorty in the way they perceive communication.

Apart from criticizing the consent of all based on the Kantian idea of "universal agreement," Putnam also criticizes the fact/value dichotomy in Habermas's thinking. In his opinion, such a dichotomy blocks the path of inquiry. The worst thing about the fact/value dichotomy is that it functions as a discussion-stopper and a thought-stopper in practice.[23] Besides, such a dichotomy, according to Putnam, also denies such a thing as "responsible and rational ethical discussion."[24] Putnam desires to defend it and the possibility of discussion and the examination of any ethical issue. Ethical issues should not be put aside with the claim that "value judgment" is just a matter of subjective preference. In his opinion, the right approach to our ethical problems is not to give up on the very possibility of intelligent discussion but to stop looking for a metaphysical foundation outside or "above" all problematic situations.[25] He considers providing reasons which are not part of ethics for the truth of ethical statements as deeply misguided, as an attempt to provide an ontological explanation of the objectivity of ethics. Putnam is neither in favor of an ontological explanation of the objectivity of ethics nor a subjective explanation of it. But he is in favor of a certain kind of objectivity of ethics. Unfortunately, both Habermas and Rorty support a subjective explanation.

As Putnam says, Rorty disagrees with any references to "objectivity" or to "objective reality." "Rorty argues that the notion of 'objective reality' is empty since we cannot stand outside of our skins and compare our notions with (supposed) objective reality as it is 'in itself.'"[26] Putnam points out that the idea of reality as it is "in itself," is apparently "the only possible meaning that Rorty sees for the notion of "objective reality." In claiming that the metaphysical sort of realism that posits "things in themselves" with an "intrinsic nature" makes no sense, Rorty goes on to say that neither does the notion of objectivity. We should drop all talk of objectivity and we should talk about "solidarity" instead. We should also understand that the solutions or resolutions that we find to our problematical situations are, at best, according to Rorty, solutions or resolutions proposed in accordance with standards of our culture and not with some supposed further standard or standards of "objectivity."

Rorty does not stop here. He goes further to be skeptical about the possibility of representation in a "perfectly everyday sense." His conclusion is that there is no metaphysically innocent way to say that our words represent things outside themselves.[27] But, Putnam rightly points out that if it is impossible to say (that is, unintelligible) that we sometimes succeed in representing things as they are, it is also unintelligible to say that we never succeed. Moreover, Putnam does not agree with Rorty that what is true and false is determined completely by the norms of "our" culture, nor with Rorty's willingness "to say that what is *justified* to believe in other cultures is decided by the sociological facts about those cultures."[28] For Putnam, Rorty's view is self-refuting. He believes that Rorty's position presupposes a naïve realism about sociological facts and norms of "our" culture, which is contrary to his position as a whole.

Putnam admits that he joins Rorty in rejecting certain metaphysical notions, but Putnam does not believe that giving them up requires us to draw the conclusions that Rorty does. Putnam agrees that the idea of comparing thoughts and beliefs with "things in themselves" makes no sense. But even though we cannot rely on an idea of "things in themselves," we can still think that there are objects that are not part of our thought or language, and we can still think that what we say about these objects "sometimes *gets the facts right*." Putnam further points out that the Rortian notion of solidarity requires exactly what he is talking about: "commonsense realism about the objective existence of the people one is in 'solidarity' with."[29] Because of that, we should not confuse a metaphysical notion of objectivity (that we can make sense of talk about things "as they are in themselves") with the "ordinary idea that our thoughts and beliefs refer to things in the world."[30]

In light of the above we can ask: what is the meaning of Putnam's statement that "we should not confuse a metaphysical notion of objectivity . . . with the ordinary idea"?[31] Is it that "we should not" because there are things in the world to which we refer, or is it that we have to assume that they exist and that this assumption is a requirement of our commonsense realism? It seems that for Putnam the latter is correct. However, we might be confused when Putnam later says that language can represent something that is itself outside of language and that, in this case, Rorty is giving up a "perfectly obvious fact."[32] But by saying this it seems that Putnam goes too far, because after the criticism of Rorty's position and his categorical claim that we cannot succeed in representing something that is outside of language, and instead of saying that we should assume that we might succeed, Putnam claims that it is a "perfectly obvious fact" that we might succeed in representing something outside of language. Additionally, when we ask on what ground Putnam makes such a statement about a "perfectly obvious fact," he would answer that it is on the grounds of common sense. Putnam would add that he is taking up the true task of philosophy to illuminate the ordinary notion of representation (and of the world of things to be represented). But, relying here on "common sense" and the "ordinary notion of representation" can also raise our doubts. I would say that we should be careful about using such terms because old uses of the terms "common sense" and "representation" were the philosophic basis for crusades and totalitarian regimes. One would have to say more about these terms to be able to rely on them today.[33]

Let us now turn to Habermas. Values in Habermas's philosophy are also treated "naturalistically," as Putnam would say. They are seen as contingent social products which vary as the different life worlds vary.[34] Putnam considers it fatal to Habermas's own philosophical/political project to make any concessions to what we might call sociology about values—"to treat value disputes as, in effect, mere social conflicts to be resolved (although they are frequently that too) and not as *rational disagreements calling for a decision as to where the better reasons lie.*"[35] Putnam points out that we can engage in discussion with the aim of getting to a common vocabulary and a common understanding of how that vocabulary should be applied, but unless there is a correct answer to those questions, "that discussion cannot really be an effort to find the answer for which there are *better reasons.*"[36]

If Habermas is going in that direction, that value claims possess only a relative sort of validity, then he is in favor of "minimalist ethics"—he is in favor of validity in "some social world." On the basis of such a minimalist position we can tell, as Putnam says, "how to behave in the absence of such a thing as a universally valid claim about value."[37] But in this case, if the words that we use like "kindness" or "cruelty" are regarded as possessing denotation only relative to particular communities, then the laws that "reason" legislates would possess formal universality but their content would not be universal. This is why Putnam says that, "relativism of any kind with respect to values cannot leave 'norms' . . . unaffected."[38] In such a case making ethical maxims into universal laws would be problematic—"in any view according to which *what the extensions of those ethical concepts are* is a question that has no universally intelligible answer."[39] Such questions would make sense only within some social world. Even "do not be cruel" would not be universally valid if we considered that criteria of cruelty are simply subjective or contingent social products that differ from community to community. If so, then the maxim that we should avoid cruelty would not take us far. We could only discuss, in the way that discourse ethics prescribes, whether or not we should be cruel and what counts as cruelty.[40] The only universally valid ethical rule then would be *"keep talking."* But all of this, Putnam believes, Habermas would be unwilling to accept, and again, asks the question "Jürgen, are you really a minimalist?"[41]

III. PUTNAM ON PUTNAM

There are many things on the table after presenting critical comments of Putnam on Habermas's and Rorty's philosophies. I have touched upon the issues of a "correct answer," "formal rules," and "content of ethical claims" to which Putnam refers. I will now deal with them in more detail, to attempt to present Putnam's position. While doing this, I will be referring more to his thoughts in reference to Habermas's because Putnam himself does that when he talks about such issues. But we will see that there are other inspirations that are present in this thought, such as a capabilities approach, or Aristotle's and Levinas's philosophy.

On the basis of the above, we can say that we have to assume that there is such a thing as a "correct answer." But, by assuming that there is a correct answer, we would have to agree that there is some reference point, otherwise we could only talk; however, that would not take us far. One could say that the only reason to "keep talking" would be to keep us busy so that we would not fight. Our temporary answers would be relative to our communities and would not be better than others in any way. Contrary to this, it is Putnam's view that we need to think and act as if there is a "correct answer," and only then can we look for "reasons better" than the other reasons, and for something more than just relative claims. But what does this mean? Does it mean that we should assume the existence of a "correct answer" as an idealized reference point that we need to have if we want to discuss issues? I do not believe that this is the case, because even though Putnam supported the necessity of referring to idealizations for some time, he now thinks that he was wrong.[42] In light of that, we can ask if our judgments are going to be better because they will more correctly refer to the issues discussed, be these issues related to the cruelty of behavior or to its kindness. If so, then we would also have to assume that there is such a thing as "cruelty" that we can get to "know" more correctly than other people. In such a case, when talking about better judgments, or better reasons, we would be referring to something more than just an acknowledgment that it is better inside some particular community—supported by the arguments presented on the basis of some social world and characteristic of it. Of course, we would have to be conscious that reaching for that "correct answer" will always be difficult and we would not know "for certain" if we have reached it for some time, given the fallibility of our knowledge. But Putnam—as I understand him—would not support such an answer because he rejects talking about reference to something "more." There is, however, a third option—at least it seems to be another option—namely, the one that is against minimalistic ethics and defends the idea of a "correct answer" by referring to the "objectivity of ethics." Putnam believes that we can talk about the objectivity or universality of values. Objective values would rest on the "ordinary" or "commonsense" notion of representation. Illuminating that ordinary notion is what Putnam considers the true task of philosophy to be. Philosophy should not be frozen in the gesture of repudiation.[43]

We should certainly investigate Putnam's position on the objectivity of ethics and check if its defense is convincing. But, before we go into that in more detail, we should refer at this point to his arguments considering the formal universality of "discourse ethics." Putnam also criticizes Habermas in this regard. As stated above, Putnam points out that if words like "kindness" or "cruelty" are regarded as possessing denotation only relative to particular communities, then the laws that "reason" legislates would possess formal universality, but their content would be anything but universal. In other words, formal rules would have a universal character but not the issues discussed or the outcomes of the discussions. But, one can say that this is exactly Habermas's point—he wants to show the rules of communication and not the rules leading to correct answers. He believes that the norms of "discourse ethics" are, when they are followed accordingly, quite enough for creating the conditions for communication. I mentioned "quite" because the attitude of those involved is important—treating each disputant equally is necessary, for example. It seems that there is nothing wrong in Habermas's understanding that the words used will have denotation relative to a particular community. These words are certainly rooted in our particular languages which are used in certain social worlds—but that still does not constrain us from looking for agreements among ourselves.

For Putnam, however, formal rules of discourse ethics are not enough—and this is why Putnam is critical of them. Following these formal rules would not bring us closer to the "correct verdict." In addition, he says that even if, during the ethical dispute, disputants were *"ideally morally sensitive, imaginative, impartial,"* and if they came up with the correct verdict, then it would be purely a "grammatical" one.[44] It would provide "no content to the notion of a 'correct verdict in an ethical dispute' that such a notion did not independently possess."[45] And this is the objection raised when Kantian ethics is discussed, and it is also raised when discourse ethics is discussed by Putnam. As Putnam claims, Kantian ethics, as well as discourse ethics, are empty formalism—they are empty and formal unless we supply them with content from Levinasian and Aristotelian thought, and concerns with democracy, toleration, or pluralism. In other words, the notion of an "ideal speech situation" is, for Putnam, empty due to the absence of thick ethical concepts.[46] Putnam is more focused on these thick concepts than Habermas.

On the basis of the above, we can see that the content of an ethical dispute is important for Putnam when he talks about Habermas's discourse ethics. We should focus for a moment on this issue. While doing this, we should notice that when we talk about the content of an ethical discussion, the formal rules of conduct and communication that Habermas describes are based on some values that have to be considered as commonly shared (for Rorty shared inside a certain community and for Habermas shared because they are common for every communication). Because of this assumption of value we can say that in Habermas's philosophy the whole process of communication is not ethically neutral. Further, we can also claim that the discussion was already finished to some extent when certain conditions for its appearance were acknowledged. When the parties involved in the process of communication agree on such conditions they have already taken a position, a position which might be questioned by others who do not share the values that form such a basis for communication.[47] On the basis of this we can say that the formal rules do not contain specific content, but we should also say that their use is based on content. Not seeing that content certainly strips discourse ethics from its ethical position which is already there. In other words, one has to see that Habermas's position is already based on content and that it is based on values of tolerance, equality, or pluralism.

But Putnam seems to agree with the above and Habermas's response to Lyotard that the norms of discourse ethics are not everything. Certain content is necessary and is already present in Habermas's perspective.[48] We need a certain ethical attitude or, in other words, we need to take the ethical position when undertaking the dialogue. Habermas in this way answers Lyotard's criticism that discourse ethics marginalizes or excludes the "inarticulate." Putnam understands this criticism to mean that Lyotard points out that the less articulate and less intelligent might not be able to participate in the dialogue. But even though—according to Habermas— these marginalized people might not participate, they are also members of the group because they are supposed to be affected by the dialogue. Further, every member in that group must have a nonmanipulative attitude toward each other and consider the positions of others.[49] In other words, referring to the above, it seems right to say that there is content in Habermas's "discourse ethics"—that there is a certain ethical position that plays a role in the ethical dialogue. This is why we cannot say that there is no content in it at all.

Putnam sees such content in Habermas's position not only when Habermas is answering Lyotard but also when Putnam rightly points out that Habermas assumes that we have a minimum prerequisite for an ethical life at all, when Habermas assumes that we have a community of human beings who "*do* regard the ends of others as important, and who do not simply assume that their own ends should override."[50] In another place, Putnam mentions also that "the Habermasian norm of 'communicative action' requires us to *defend* our values by means of communicative action—fundamentally, this means in the spirit of recognizing the other as an end and not only as a means."[51] On the basis of this we can say that in Habermas's discourse ethics there is an additional value which is the basis for his ethics—this is the value of a human being. And, again, because of these values, we should see that Habermas's discourse ethics is not empty of content.

However, we can certainly say that Putnam is right to a large extent when he points out the necessity of content in an ethical dispute, because when different parties come together to discuss some particular issues they will need "content." This content—as I pointed out—is already to a certain extent present in Habermas's communicative action, but the discussants will need "more content" to discuss particular cases and to look for the agreement among themselves.

IV. FROM THICK ETHICAL WORDS TO THE OBJECTIVITY OF ETHICS

As Putnam says, "ideally morally sensitive" and other such concepts that are present in Habermas's "discourse ethics" are themselves *ethical* concepts—and in this way he admits what I have said above—but he adds that giving them content in any actual dispute will require "thickening" them, replacing them with terms that are still value terms but that have more descriptive content.[52] And, for those who are wondering what Putnam means by the term "thick ethical concepts," he points out that in literature such concepts like "cruel" that simply "ignore the supposed fact/value dichotomy and cheerfully allow themselves to be used sometimes for a normative purpose and sometimes as a descriptive term" are often referred to as "thick ethical concepts."[53]

In Putnam's view, thick ethical concepts defy all the traditional fact/value dichotomies. Such is the case with the norm/value dichotomy which reduces all questions of existential choice to mere subjective preferences.

He is against such dichotomies and promotes simple reflection, and says that our ethical maxims, norms, and the laws that we impose upon ourselves by universalizing them, themselves contain value terms, in particular the so-called "thick ethical words."[54] They contain entangled terms such as "kind," "cruel," or "sensitive." This is why he believes that "without our human manifold of *values* there is no vocabulary for *norms* . . . to be stated *in*."[55]

Unfortunately, such is not the case with Habermas, whose position seems to be characterized—as Putnam says—by a positivistic desire to treat talk about values, outside narrow limits of discourse ethics, as a mere negotiation of differences between "life worlds" and positivistic reason that Putnam fears denies any objectivity that goes beyond such negotiations. He fears that such a concession would not be compatible with "modernity." But, Putnam wants to go further, and by referring to "thick ethical concepts" he wants to reject the widespread belief that ethical judgments lack objectivity. He believes that "ethics do possess objectivity without being about sublime or intangible objects such as 'Platonic forms' or 'abstract entities,'"[56] but rather about emphasis on alleviating suffering regardless of the class or gender of the sufferer. In fact, as he says, "what I call 'ethics' is precisely the morality that Nietzsche deplored."[57] Such "ethics" is for him universal so far as it is concerned with the alleviation of *everyone's* suffering, or so far as it is concerned with *everybody's* positive well-being.[58] By that, as he says, he is not "accepting apriorism or authoritarianism with respect to values."[59] And, he assures that the moral realism that he is in favor of "need not and should not represent a commitment to the idea that there is some final set of moral truths . . . all of which can be expressed in the same fixed moral and legal vocabulary."[60] He just wants to oppose the rejection of "substantive value realism" and argues that skepticism about "value realism" is fatally self-undermining.

In the course of a dialogue Habermas finally, as Putnam mentions, concedes that certain values are objective.[61] Not only are norms then objective but also certain values—the ones that appear in moral norms. Habermas admitted—in reply to Putnam's comments, as Putnam mentions—that the objective validity of Kantian "norms" presupposes the objective applicability of the value terms that these norms contain. But the problem is that Habermas considers only some values as objective—universalizable values. There are others that he considers merely subjective to individual or group projects—they are nonuniversalizable values, which are not prohibited by a valid "norm." In consequence, as Putnam comments, most values are, for Habermas, still culturally relative.

Putnam would be happy if Habermas would say that discourse ethics is a part of ethics, a valuable and important part, but not one that can stand on its own, "not the foundation . . . of all the 'validity' that ethics can possess."[62]

Putnam does not believe that conformity to the norms of discourse ethics is a sufficient condition for arriving at justified ethical beliefs. This is why he believes that we need something more to arrive at such a belief. We need "moral perception"—the ability to see that someone is suffering unnecessarily or that suffering is something that is part of the process of growing up, the ability to distinguish between someone who is compassionate and someone who is only whining. And even though "there is no *science* that can teach one to make these distinctions,"[63] it is always possible "to *improve one's understanding* of a concept like 'impertinence' or 'cruelty'" if it is not sufficient.[64] We also need to see that ethics rests on a variety of different interests, one could say on every human interest. These interests are fundamentally different than the interests of the past. And, the justification for these interests has to come from within morality, "not from outside or from a foundation prior to morality."[65] Putnam goes in that direction because he does not want to concede to the skeptic that we have no irreducibly ethical knowledge, and believes that we can rationally discuss ethical values. Putnam asks "what is, what could be *more* irreducible than my knowledge, face to face with a needy human being?"[66] Even if, on reflection, he would decide "that other *ethical* obligations override that first obligation, this does not change his awareness of something absolutely fundamental and irreducible."[67] And, he is aware of the demands made upon us. He believes that "our imperfect but indefinitely perfectible ability to recognize the demands made upon us by various values is precisely what provides "Kantian" (or "discourse") ethics with *content*."[68] He would certainly also say that we have an ability to recognize real human needs.

In other words, we can recognize demands made upon us. These demands, as Putnam says, are made upon us by various values. If I am correct, this means that we can see other values as crucial in our conduct in the processes of inquiry—they play a vital role. This is the content that is missing in Habermas's philosophy—his discourse ethics—according to Putnam's understanding. But what does it mean that we see other values and that we recognize the demands made upon us by them? This can mean that we are socialized in such a way that values play a role in our lives when undertaking actions and creating plans. Yet, the values employed can be different ones depending on the culture or society that we are from. Or even if there is no cultural difference, various values can be understood differently among the members of a group. In other words, we can differ about the "content" and how it should be understood and about what is important or what is not when we try to describe it. But, if this difference is not about socialization, as Putnam certainly would say, but about some values that make a demand upon us, that are there and that cannot be ignored, and that make us aware of something important, then I would ask: What are they?

The dignity of other human beings? The equality of men and women?[69] By looking at different clashes of cultures, or even at clashes within our own ethically unstable cultures, we see that there is a problem with that recognition—with the recognition of the values "that make demands upon us." I should say that this is a crucial problem—to recognize them as making demands upon us or to recognize what "real human needs" are. When we have problems with such a recognition then we also have problems with recognizing what is "absolutely fundamental and irreducible."[70]

Putnam is trying to help in this regard by bringing up the issue of central human capabilities. He says that Kantian ethics is empty and formal unless we supply it with content precisely from our other values. Among these values we should also include a concern with central human capabilities.[71] In other words, when Putnam talks about the content that is so needed, he means that we need "other values" and "capabilities." Above, I have referred to the issue of values, so at this point I would like to focus on capabilities and see if Putnam's perspective on them will bring us closer to overcoming the difficulties in understanding his position on what is "absolutely fundamental and irreducible."

V. More to Objectivity—Toward Capabilities

Putnam believes that seeking sexual satisfaction, seeking to cultivate an appreciation of the arts, or seeking personal property belong to the capabilities that are part of human flourishing. And, by saying this, he does not mean that everyone ought to possess all of these capabilities. Judgments that they are important are meant not as universalizable judgments, but as judgments pointing out that they are important and valuable for the flourishing of many, many human lives. But he adds that "any society in which some groups lack these capabilities, or possess them to a level that is below any acceptable minimum, is stunting some human lives."[72]

The previous claim can seem puzzling, because on the one hand he mentions "that not everyone ought to possess all of them" but on the other he says that they are so important that if they are not present in one's life then one's life is stunted. In other words these capabilities are so important in people's lives that if they are missing one of these capabilities, they are not able to develop properly as human beings. However, mentioning these capabilities as the ones that people need does not explain a great deal because we can then only say that people do need them, but we know from experience that different people need different capabilities on the basis of their personal desire. What is important in such a case is that these capabilities will be recognized by others as important for other human beings and respected.

This is why Putnam writes that "what makes concerns with capabilities universalizable is not that everyone is under the obligation to exercise each of the central capabilities, but that everyone is under an obligation to do what they can to bring about a situation in which everyone enjoys, at least to a reasonable minimum level, the *freedom* to exercise them."[73]

But can this be achieved without problems arising? Would we agree that those for whom a central capability in their life is obeying the rules of a tradition or religion can live freely among us if, in their understanding, that capability is connected with securing traditional inequality between men and women or physical punishment for not obeying sacred rules? Why should we be obliged to do what we can in order for them to freely exercise their desired capability? Certainly they will not agree with our argumentation that our capabilities are the ones that they should look for because, thanks to them, they may live in a better way—in a right way. They will not agree that it is not appropriate for them to say "that 'they' . . . 'don't really want' these capabilities [like ours] as long as they never had the *option* of developing the capabilities in question."[74] They will not be convinced that they should first cut the forest in which they hunt and kill, set up the garden and plant vegetables, and that it will then be possible for them to see that gardening is better and planting vegetables is right. If that happens they will have no way to come back to what they praise at the moment—it will be too late. The claim that "you do not want that but you would like it if you knew how good it is" would not be convincing for them.

So it is hard, if not impossible, to talk about universalizable concerns with capabilities and our obligation to do what we can to create a situation in which everyone enjoys them. We can be against some of them as others can be against ours.[75] We may not—and I would say we should not—be in favor of unlimited freedom to exercise capabilities. And this is certainly why Putnam writes that everyone should enjoy them to a "reasonable" minimum level. But I think Putnam goes too far in saying that we are "obliged to do what we can"—that we are under an obligation. I would say that we should be concerned with capabilities—but at the same time be reasonable about them and critical—taking under consideration the context of the situation in which they should be present or the consequences of exercising them.

On the basis of the above, we can see that judgments—such as those that claim that capabilities are important—are not, for Putnam, universalizable. But, Putnam considers concern about them as universalizable. That would mean that we should have a universalizable attitude toward capabilities. To the question of whether we should agree about the necessity of being concerned about them, the answer would be "yes." We should all agree that these capabilities are important, which seems to mean that such an answer should become universalizable. But can that be the case when in so many places we read that Putnam is against universalizable answers? He says that there may be, and indeed he thinks that there usually is, an objective right answer to the question, but "it would be absurd to suppose that there is a universalizable answer to the question."[76] Because of that Putnam also suggests that we should overcome the difficulty in recognizing that an objective value need not be universalizable. In the same spirit Putnam writes that there are objective ethical questions that are not about whether one should or should not universalize some proposed norms. In other words, on the basis of such a statement, we can say that it would be absurd to think that there could be an answer or a value that everyone should agree and act upon—that would be universalizable. In reality it is not possible to get into a universal agreement, as Putnam would say. After all of this we are still left with the question: universalizable or not? With this puzzling case it would be good to ask Putnam how to justify the idea that concerns about human capabilities should be universalizable, taking under consideration issues that were raised above—that he is against universalizable answers or universalizable norms.

VI. True? False? Right or Wrong?

As we can see, Putnam is against universalizability and the claim that at some certain point everyone will agree. However, on the basis of the aforementioned, it seems that he cannot be completely against it, because he is in favor of the universality of capabilities. He believes that we should not perceive granting capabilities that he refers to in his texts as contrary to universality, even though not everyone will wish to exercise them. And, I read Putnam's work as supportive of considering capabilities as universal, even though I see no justification for that. As stated above, he is also in favor of objectivity and he believes that there are objective right answers and objective ethical questions. He says that we should recover our common sense in these areas.[77] But, when seeing such statements we can ask: how can we say that a certain answer, or judgment, can be right or wrong, that it can be true or false? Putnam touches on this issue and he refers to the issue of warranted assertibility.

He admits that we often face many judgments of value, such as those judgments where we claim that a particular act is kind or cruel. These judgments are under discussion and, in practice, are regarded as true or false. And, as Putnam says, they "should" be so regarded. He says this because he wants to uphold the truth even though, as he says, his view is strongly fallibilistic. He considers that one of the most difficult things for philosophy to do is to uphold truth and not give up the game to skepticism.[78] Putnam is not talking about transcendent truth here. We need no reasons for the truth of ethical statements that are not part of ethics. Any attempt to provide an ontological explanation of the objectivity of ethics he considers as deeply misguided.[79] We need to recover our common sense in these areas.[80] Putnam writes that one can be a moral realist in metaethics and hold that some "value judgments" are true as a matter of objective fact "without holding that moral facts are or can be recognition transcendent facts."[81] He argues that "we need no better ground for treating 'value judgments' as capable of truth and falsity than the fact that we can and do treat them as capable of warranted assertibility and warranted deniability."[82] We do not need a special "sense organ," but criticism of our valuations from which an objective value arises. These valuations are incessant and inseparable from all of our activities. And, it is by "intelligent reflection on our valuations, intelligent reflection of the kind Dewey calls 'criticism,' that we conclude that some of them are warranted while others are unwarranted."[83]

On the basis of the above, we know what we should not look for and what we need in order to state that our valuation is warranted or not (namely, critical thinking). But when is it warranted and what does it mean that it is warranted? The answer "when we are critical and use intelligent reflection" would not take us far if the method of our conduct was taken by us as a goal, no matter what the outcome was. One could answer that a valuation would be warranted when it fulfilled certain criteria, but then we would ask what those criteria are. Why "should," as Putnam might say, certain judgments be regarded as true and others as false?

We face the same problem when we ask Putnam by what criteria we can tell what is right when we have an ethical disagreement? In his lecture *Pragmatism and the Future of Philosophy*, he makes some points regarding this issue. Concerning the question about what the criteria are on the basis of which we can decide who is right when we have an ethical disagreement, Putnam replies by saying that we do not have, nor do we need, one single "criterion" or decision method for judging warranted assertibility in ethics any more than we do in any other area. Rather, we need commitment to the ethical life and the authority of intelligence, of criticism.[84] So, we again only hear about the method that we should apply, about critical thinking, and not about any criteria. Putnam is not giving a clear answer. We can suspect that he is in favor of many criteria; and we would be glad to hear what they are and how to choose among them. Instead, Putnam says that "there is no reason that it should be impossible to discover in individual problematical situations—however fallibly—that one putative resolution is superior to another."[85] In other words, for Putnam, it is possible to point at a "superior resolution." But, we would like to be convinced about that. We would like to be convinced that our judgments can be right, even though they "won't always be right,"[86] and even though the community will not come to agreement about that.[87] We would like to be convinced that warranted assertibility is not just a culturally relative matter and that truth has to agree with reality,[88] and that our ethical concepts can be "true as a matter of objective facts," be "valid," be right and not just be reasonably shared by a particular community.[89]

In the above explanation, what Putnam means by true and false, right and wrong, or valid and invalid does not seem to be sufficient. And, because of this insufficiency, the issue of the objectivity of ethics and values still does not seem to be explained. What does Putnam mean when he says that they can be objective when they refer to real human needs?

VII. SUMMING UP—ENLIGHTENMENT AND RESPONSIBILITY

Summing up, we can say that all of the above characterizes Putnam's pragmatist "Enlightenment." For him the idea that "there is such a thing as the *situated* resolution of political and ethical problems and conflicts (of what Dewey calls 'problematical situations'), and that claims concerning evaluations of—and proposals for the resolution of—problematical situations can be more and less *warranted* without being *absolute*."[90] As he says, situated resolutions of problems always require ideas but they are not "free of contingent historical perspective." In this case, Putnam follows Dewey who stressed that problematical situations are contingent and their resolutions are also contingent. The primary aim is, in Dewey's as in Putnam's philosophy, not to produce a "system," a fixed set of rules and principles, but to contribute to the solution of practical problems, and such solutions are always provisional and fallible.[91] But "there is still a difference," as Putnam says, "an all-important difference, between *thinking* that a claim concerning the resolution of a situation is a warranted claim and its actually *being* warranted."[92]

Putnam believes that there have been two enlightenments, with the third possibly close. The third, however, has not yet come fully to fruition, but it can with pragmatism—with its fallibilistic and antimetaphysical approach, and without lapsing into skepticism. What was characteristic for enlightenments so far, and what we can see in pragmatism these days, is a critical approach in how to use intelligence in dealing with ethical and political problems, propositions of revisions and reforms. Every time in enlightenments—Putnam says—"there is the same aspiration for reflective transcendence, the same willingness to criticize conventional beliefs and institutions, and to propose radical reforms."[93] They "simultaneously [bring] revolutions in our epistemological thinking and in our ethical thinking."[94]

When saying the above—that Putnam believes that we are entering a Third Enlightenment—we can ask if this can be the case when we are taking under consideration problems I have raised. Certainly, on the basis of the above analysis we can say that there are issues on which Putnam would have to elaborate more to let his readers know what he means. But it is also certain that there is a goal in his philosophical thinking—this goal is "more responsibility." This goal is connected with a certain perception of ethics. I say "certain perception of ethics" because when Putnam is talking about ethics, he is not thinking about "a systems of principles—although principles . . . are certainly a part of ethics—but a system of interrelated concerns, concerns which I see as mutually supporting but also in partial tension."[95] In other words, Putnam is against thinking about ethics as being based upon "one single concern," such as a Kantian concern with universalizable maxims or a Utilitarian concern with maximizing pleasures. Ethics for him is not a noble statue standing on top of a single pillar. Ethics is like a table with many legs and these legs represent many concerns upon which ethics is based. Because of these concerns, our thinking about ethics should not be distorted by a tendency to dichotomize and we should perceive concerns with human flourishing and concerns with norms as interdependent parts of a system of concerns that are the basis for responsible ethical consciousness.[96] In this regard, as Putnam states, we should perceive the Categorical Imperative of Kant as a useful test but not as a sublime foundation for all of ethics.

Putnam believes that in ethics we need both an Aristotelian concern with human flourishing as well as Kantian insights. But, does the consciousness of many concerns upon which ethics is based make us more responsible? Putnam would answer positively. He believes that through this consciousness, there is a possibility for a responsible and rational ethical discussion. That will happen if the path of inquiry is not blocked. The path of inquiry is blocked by the fact/value dichotomy which denies such a responsible and rational ethical discussion.[97] And, this is a "terrible thing," as he says. In this regard his goal is like the goal of Habermas and Rorty—a responsible use of our freedom. But, Putnam takes another step in presenting a justification for it. Taking such a step can lead us to different social relations and a different politics.

Certainly, Rorty is skeptical of the way Putnam wants to take "another step." Rorty says in reaction that Putnam wants to preserve pure commonsense realist convictions even though in the past Putnam shared Rorty's doubts about representationalism. Rorty considers Putnam's position as a "throwback to Cartesianism, . . . an unfortunate throwback to pre-Hegelian attempts to find something ahistorical to which philosophers may pledge allegiance."[98] And, Habermas is not convinced of the use of the notions of realism and objectivity while talking about ethics, and still holds on to certain distinctions that Putnam is criticizing. However, both agree on Putnam's goal and both share an important pragmatic insight that makes them form a common front for "a responsible and rational ethical discussion." And I believe that they could all agree on the possibility of a Third Enlightenment even though trying to reach it, to a certain extent, by different means. Nevertheless, their doubts, as well as my own doubts, trigger questions. I have questions concerning Putnam's philosophy that need to be answered, all of which I have mentioned above, and I am very much looking forward to the answers.

MARCIN KILANOWSKI

UNIWERSYTET MIKOLAJA KOPERNIKA
TORUŃ, POLAND
JANUARY 2010

NOTES

1. Hilary Putnam, "Pragmatism and the Future of Philosophy" (David Ross Lecture at the University of Oklahoma [Lecture III], Norman, OK, October 28, 2005), 1.

2. Hilary Putnam, "From Quantum Mechanics to Ethics and Back" in *Philosophy in an Age of Science*, ed. M. De Caro and D. Macarthur (Cambridge, MA: Harvard University Press, 2012), 70.

3. Ibid.

4. Hilary Putnam, *Ethics without Ontology* (Cambridge, MA: Harvard University Press, 2004), 92.

5. Hilary Putnam, "Capabilities and Two Ethical Theories," *Journal of Human Development and Capabilities* 9, no. 3 (November 2008): 387. Putnam refers to John Rawls, *Political Liberalism*, rev. ed. (New York: Columbia University Press, 1993, 1996), 133–72.

6. And, he adds that what follows from the failure of philosophy to come up with an explanation in "absolute terms" is only perhaps a senselessness of a certain sort of metaphysics. Cf. Hilary Putnam, *The Collapse of the Fact/Value Dichotomy, and Other Essays* (Cambridge, MA: Harvard University Press, 2002), 45.

7. Putnam, "Capabilities and Two Ethical Theories," 388.

8. Ibid.

9. Putnam is answering the question: "how *do* we decide?" (Ibid.)

10. Hilary Putnam, "Are Values Made or Discovered?" in *The Collapse of the Fact/Value Dichotomy*, 109. Also cf. Putnam, "Pragmatism and the Future of Philosophy," 8.

11. Putnam, "Capabilities and Two Ethical Theories," 387.

12. Putnam, *Ethics without Ontology*, 22.

13. See: ibid., 107, 110.

14. See: "Pragmatism and the Future of Philosophy," 8.

15. Putnam, "Are Values Made or Discovered?" 105.

16. Putnam, "Capabilities and Two Ethical Theories," 388.

17. Hilary Putnam, "Values and Norms," in *The Collapse of the Fact/Value Dichotomy and Other Essays*, 133.

18. Putnam, "Antwort auf Jürgen Habermas" in *Hilary Putnam und die Tradition des americanischen Pragmatismus*, ed. Marie-Luise Raters and Marcus Willaschek (Frankfurt am Main: Suhrkamp, 2002), 306.

19. Putnam, "Capabilities and Two Ethical Theories," 388.

20. Putnam, "Values and Norms," 127. Also see Putnam, "Concluding Remarks and Reply to Jürgen Habermas," (unpublished), 1.

21. Putnam, "Capabilities and Two Ethical Theories," 9. Putnam also refers many times to the example of the father who is cruel. Putnam writes that we can perfectly *imagine* that the father and others like him will never "get it" that they are cruel.

22. Putnam, "Values and Norms," 116.

23. Putnam, *The Collapse of the Fact/Value Dichotomy*, 44.

24. The fact/value dichotomy or dualism also impoverished "the welfare economics' ability to evaluate what it was supposed to evaluate—economic wellbeing" (Putnam, "Pragmatism and the Future of Philosophy," 8).

25. Ibid.

26. Putnam, "Are Values Made or Discovered?" 99.

27. Ibid., 101.

28. Putnam, *Ethics without Ontology*, 121.

29. Putnam, "Are Values Made or Discovered?" 100.

30. Ibid.

31. Ibid.

32. Ibid., 101.

33. I could probably defend Putnam's idea of representation by saying that we do not face a collapse of representation. Indeed we do not, but we do face a collapse of a certain metaphor in which language mirrors reality and in which we can get to know things in themselves as they really are. We start to think too much inside this metaphor and constrain our thinking against the position that we do not need to agree on skepticism when we realized that we cannot function according to this metaphor. We should just try to describe our processes of conduct in a different way and, at the same time, we should try to understand the process of representation in a different way. Of course one could still say that talking about the rejection of the old metaphor of mirroring, and talking about some "commonsense realism" comes from a cultural position, but that would still indicate being trapped by the old metaphor. But after saying this, I wonder if Putnam would agree with that or what he would perhaps add.

34. Putnam, "Values and Norms," 112.

35. Ibid., 121. And, Putnam adds that in the case of ethics, the true view cannot differ from the view for which there are the best reasons.

36. Ibid.

37. Ibid., 123.

38. Ibid., 120.

39. Ibid.

40. Putnam, *"Antwort auf Jürgen Habermas,"* 307.

41. Ibid., 308.

42. Putnam, "Values and Norms," 124. Putnam writes: "Although I myself tried for a number of years to defend the idea that truth can be identified with 'idealized rational acceptability,' I am today convinced that this was an error."

43. Putnam, "Are Values Made or Discovered?" 101. It seems that it would be better not to talk about a correct answer but about a better answer. Putnam already talks about better reasons. "Correct" has different cultural connotations and using this term blurs the one that Putnam wants to present. Using the term "correct" unfortunately takes the discussion to the

second option I have described, and to thinking that there must be a correct reason, a reason more correct than others because it would be touching on something more substantial, that would mirror something real even though we would not know certainly when that would be happening.

44. Putnam, "Values and Norms," 130. Also cf. Putnam, "For Ethics and Economics without the Dichotomies," *Review of Political Economy* 15, no. 3 (July 2003): 410.

45. Putnam, "For Ethics and Economics without the Dichotomies," 410.

46. Ibid., 407. Putnam says that we have to understand that we valuate when we describe.

47. And this is probably the biggest problem with Habermas's and Rorty's perspective: how can we justify tolerance, equality, and freedom for free communication which would allow the resolution of the problems of men when we do not want to agree on tolerance, equality, and freedom? The problem is not whether agreement can be partial or common, but rather the problem is how to get different parties together and to make them start discussing issues.

48. Putnam, "Values and Norms," 130.

49. Saying that Putnam adds that in such a process we should be "listening to the cries of the wounded."

50. Ibid., 115. And as we have said before—the assumption of such a minimum is a problem in itself. We can assume such a minimum, and we can further create conceptions of communication filled up with disagreements as to what the ethical life really requires from us, but how to achieve such a minimum—people treating each other equally—is a problem.

51. Ibid., 112. In this regard Habermas follows Kant and his Categorical Imperative.

52. Ibid., 129. Also see Putnam, "For Ethics and Economics without the Dichotomies," 410.

53. Putnam, *The Collapse of the Fact/Value Dichotomy,* 35. As Putnam says in judging the outcome of an inquiry, we always bring both valuations and descriptions.

54. Putnam, "Values and Norms," 118.

55. Ibid., 119.

56. Putnam, *Ethics without Ontology*, 2.

57. Ibid., 23.

58. Putnam, "For Ethics and Economics without the Dichotomies," 410. In light of this Putnam writes that Kant's great achievement in the area of moral philosophy was his Categorical Imperative—not as a practical guide, not as a discovery procedure or a test that the maxims that we propose to ourselves have to pass—"but as a powerful statement of the idea that ethics is *universal*, that, insofar as ethics is concerned with the alleviation of suffering, it is concerned with the alleviation of *everyone's* suffering, or if it is concerned with positive well-being, it is concerned with *everybody's* positive well-being" (Putnam, *Ethics without Ontology*, 25). In another place we read that we should look at universalizability as just *one* among many interests that ethics subserves (Putnam, "For Ethics and Economics without the Dichotomies," 408).

59. Putnam, "Values and Norms," 133.

60. Putnam, "Are Values Made or Discovered?" 109.

61. Putnam, "For Ethics and Economics without the Dichotomies," 407.

62. Putnam, "Values and Norms," 129.

63. Ibid., 128.

64. Putnam, *The Collapse of the Fact/Value Dichotomy*, 40. In another place he writes that one has to be able to identify imaginatively with evaluative points of view.

65. Putnam, "Capabilities and Two Ethical Theories," 387.

66. Putnam, "Values and Norms," 132.

67. Ibid.

68. Ibid., 134.

69. When Habermas asks Putnam about an example of value which would represent more than preference or the preference of some life world, Putnam does not give a clear answer. He only says that "values do not have to be global,"that he is in favor of a diversity of ideals, and that such a diversity is better. And Putnam stops answering the question that Habermas had posited; but the question remains unanswered. Cf. Ibid., 112.

70. Ibid., 132.

71. Putnam, "For Ethics and Economics without the Dichotomies," 409.

72. Ibid., 408.

73. Ibid., 411.

74. Ibid., 408.

75. They may not accept freedom of speech, for example.

76. Ibid., 407.

77. Putnam, *Ethics without Ontology*, 3.

78. Ibid., 16. A combination of fallibilism with antiskepticism is, indeed as Putnam says, one of the chief characteristics of American pragmatism.

79. In the context of these words, I believe, Putnam writes that "he no longer thinks that one needs to defend truth at all." Putnam, "Are Values Made or Discovered?" 107.

80. Putnam, *Ethics without Ontology,* 4.

81. Putnam, "Are Values Made or Discovered?" 108.

82. Ibid., 110.

83. Ibid., 103.

84. Putnam, "Pragmatism and the Future of Philosophy," 8.

85. Putnam, "Are Values Made or Discovered?" 106–7.

86. Putnam, "Capabilities and Two Ethical Theories," 388.

87. By saying that Putnam refers to Wittgenstein, Putnam is pointing out that Wittgenstein was quite reasonable when he said that judgments on which the community does not come to agreement may nevertheless be right (Putnam, "Values and Norms," 126).

88. Hilary Putnam, "The Story of Pragmatism" (David Ross Lecture at the University of Oklahoma [Lecture I], Norman, OK, October 24, 2005), 6. Putnam mentions in his lecture what Dewey's perspective was, at the same time we can easily see that this is also his own.

89. Putnam, "For Ethics and Economics without the Dichotomies," 407.

90. Putnam, *Ethics without Ontology,* 129.

91. Putnam believes that in approaching all practical problems, reason and emotions should work together—they should work together and inform one another in approaching all practical problems.

92. Putnam, *Ethics without Ontology*, 129.

93. Ibid., 94. This reflective transcendence Dewey called, as Putnam points out, "*criticism of criticisms*" or "the authority of intelligence, of criticism." See: John Dewey, *Experience and Nature*, in *The Later Works of John Dewey: 1925–1953*, vol.1, ed. Jo Ann Boydston (Carbondale, IL: Southern Illinois University Press, 1981), 298.

94. Ibid., 5.

95. Ibid., 22.

96. See: Putnam, "For Ethics and Economics without the Dichotomies," 411.

97. Putnam, "Pragmatism and the Future of Philosophy," 8.

98. Richard Rorty, "Response to Putnam," in *Rorty and His Critics*, ed. B. R. Brandom (Malden, MA: Blackwell, 2000), 90.

REPLY TO MARCIN KILANOWSKI

I believe there is such a thing as objective truth. Kilanowski suggests that belief in objective truth is dangerous because it could lead to totalitarianism. There are, it seems to me, two things wrong with this worry. The first is that it is not (unless a missing premise be supplied) an argument against the correctness of my view at all. Even if it is a fact that it would have bad effects if people came to believe that *p*, that fact is, prima facie, not an argument against the *truth* of *p*. It becomes an argument against the truth of *p* only if the following premise be supplied: *if p is such that it would have bad effects if people believed it, then p is false.*

The second thing wrong is that history does not actually support Kilanowski's suggestion. Marxist-Leninists do, of course, think they have the objective truth about society, but so do pacifists. Marxism-Leninism led to several totalitarian regimes,[1] and pacifism did not. What produced Marxist-Leninist totalitarianism was not the belief in objective truth, but the substantive content of the propositions about how society could allegedly be changed for the better that the Marxist-Leninists believed and the pacifists did not. Secondly, the leading *fascist* thinkers in the twentieth century did *not*, in fact, believe in objective truth; their favorite philosopher (if we discount Mussolini's admiration for William James![2]) was probably Nietzsche, and Nietzsche, on their reading, had shown that all the traditional Western values, *including truth*, represent forms of "slave morality" or (equally bad, in their eyes) the values of the "last men." Both truth and goodness, in the eyes of facists, are created by the will of the stronger. So it turns out that *disbelief* in objective truth is no protection against totalitarianism at all. It is the substantive political and moral values to which thinkers commit themselves (as well as their willingness or unwillingness to be fallibilistic about the things that they claim to be true, as opposed to their philosophical *theories* of truth), that determine whether they favor democracy or dictatorship, peace or war, respect for other cultures or attempts to destroy them. Although the claim that belief in objective truth tends to lead to totalitarianism is one that Rorty makes, there is no real evidence for it, and I am sorry that Kilanowski takes it so seriously.

I. KILANOWSKI ON RORTY AND MYSELF

In one place, Kilanowski writes that I *admit* "that Rorty is right when he criticizes the idea that one could stay outside of one's thoughts and concepts and compare 'reality as it is in itself' with those thoughts and concepts." This is probably only a slip, because subsequently Kilanowski does refer to what I actually say, which is that Rorty makes the *claim* that one cannot stand outside of one's thoughts and concepts and compare reality as it is in itself with those thoughts and concepts, but, in fact, both this claim and its denial are *unintelligible*. (This is hardly a case of "admitting that Rorty is right.") Here, for example, is one way in which I have spelled this out in the past:

> As John McDowell likes to put it, you can't view your language "from side-ways on" in the way that the idea of looking at one's language and looking at the world and comparing the two suggests. But it doesn't follow that language and thought do not describe something outside themselves, even if that something can only be described by describing it (that is, by employing language and thought); and, as Rorty ought to have seen, the belief that they do plays an essential role *within* language and, more important, within our lives.[3]

And I continued:

> In stating [the argument of Rorty's that I just criticized], I said that it is impossible to stand outside and compare our thought and language, on the one hand, with the world on the other; and, indeed, this is the way in which Rorty puts matters. But if we agree that it is *unintelligible* to say, 'We sometimes succeed in comparing language and thought with reality as it is in itself,' then we should realize that it is also unintelligible to say, 'It is *impossible* to stand outside and compare our thought and language with the world.' . . . Rorty seems to be telling us of an impotence, in the way in which a physicist tells us of an impotence when he says "You can't build a perpetual motion machine," but it turns out on examination that the impotence is a mirage, or even less than a mirage—that it is *chimerical*. [emphasis added][4]

At any rate, what Kilanowski is disturbed by is my saying that "it is a perfectly obvious fact" that we sometimes succeed in representing things outside of language and thought. (It is here that he makes the claim that I discussed above, that "we should be careful about using such terms because old uses of the terms 'common sense' and 'representation' *were the philosophic basis for crusades and totalitarian regimes.*" But I did not ever simply *rest* with an appeal to "common sense." For example, in "Richard Rorty on Reality and Justification," I point out that Rorty says, "Using those vocables [the words and sentences of 'our language'] is *as direct as contact with reality can get* (as direct as kicking rocks, for instance). The fallacy comes in thinking that the relationship between vocables and reality has to be piecemeal (like the relation between individual kicks and individual rocks), a matter of discrete component capacities to get in touch with discrete hunks of reality." [5] And I asked, "Is Rorty claiming that kicking the rock involves a particular rock, but describing the rock does not involve that same particular rock? How can *that* be? How can Rorty so much as use *words* to tell us that kicking a rock involves a particular rock if those very words do not relate particularly to kicks and to rocks?" [6] This was an effort to show that there is something incoherent about what Rorty says, and not a mere appeal to "common sense."

It is not, by the way, as if Rorty *always* wanted to say that reality talk is meaningless, although his essay in the present volume might suggest that, and it is not as if he had proposed an *account* of how we can talk about rocks, and so forth, *without* "representing" them in language. Kilanowski makes it sound as if saying that, for example, "most if not all languages contain a term for *stones*" is a piece of dogmatism verging on totalitarianism and religious crusades.

II. KILANOWSKI ON ME AND "REPRESENTATION"

I am disturbed when Kilanowski writes: "Putnam believes that we can talk about the objectivity or universality of values. *Objective values would rest on the 'ordinary' or 'commonsense' notion of representation*" (emphasis added—HP). In fact, I have never claimed that the objectivity or universality of values (objectivity and universality are *not* the same thing, by the way! [7]), or of truths about any other subject matter, "rests on" the notion of representation. I believe that there are objective truths in *set theory*, as it happens; is that supposed to be because I think that the truths of set theory "rest on the notion of representation"? I believe that many, many different sorts of statements are objectively true; am I supposed to believe that all of these different sorts of truth "rest on" the semantical claim that there is a relation of representation (more, precisely, of reference, or, to use Tarski's term for the converse of the reference relation, a relation of "satisfaction") between terms and particular entities, ordered pairs of entities, ordered triples of entities, and so on?

But let us look a little earlier in this part of Kilanowski's essay. Kilanowski is discussing my belief that most value questions have a correct answer. He is puzzled by this, and he offers three possible interpretations. (I have inserted the numerals 1, 2, 3 just before each of his the three interpretations.)

> it is Putnam's view that we need to think and act as if there is a "correct answer" and only then can we look for "reasons better" than the other reasons, and for something more than just relative claims. But what does this mean? Does it mean [1] that we should assume the existence of a "correct answer" as an idealized reference point that we need to have if we want to discuss issues? I do not believe that this is the case, because even though Putnam supported the necessity of referring to idealizations for some time, he now thinks that he was wrong. In light of that, [2] we can ask if our judgments are going to be better because they will more correctly refer to the issues discussed, be these issues related to the cruelty of behavior or to its kindness. If so, then we would also have to assume that there is such a thing as "cruelty" that we can get to "know" more correctly than other people. In such a case, when talking about better judgments, or better reasons, we would be referring to something more than just an acknowledgment that it is better inside some particular community—supported by the arguments presented on the basis of some social world and characteristic of it. Of course, we would be conscious that reaching for that "correct answer" will always be difficult and we would never know "for certain" if we have reached it for some time, given the fallibility of our knowledge. But Putnam—as I understand him—would not support such an answer because he rejects talking about reference to something "more." There is however a third option—at least it seems to be another option—[3] namely, the one that is against minimalistic ethics and defends the idea of a "correct answer" by referring to the "objectivity of ethics." Putnam believes that we can talk about objectivity or universality of values. Objective values would rest on the "ordinary" or "commonsense" notion of representation. Illuminating that ordinary notion is what Putnam considers the true task of philosophy to be. Philosophy should not be frozen in the gesture of repudiation.

Contrary to Kilanowski, (3) is *not* the correct alternative. In my view, "referring to the objectivity of ethics" just *is* referring to the fact that ethical questions (generally) have a correct answer, or better, an answer which is sufficiently correct for the problematic situation at hand. The idea that the objectivity of ethics is something that *guarantees* the existence of correct answers (as opposed to just *consisting in* the existence of correct answers) makes no sense to me, and the idea that the objectivity of ethics "rests on" the existence of a words/world relation of reference (or "representation") is also a confusion, as I explained above. The alternative that is *closest* to correct is (2). But (2) as it stands also will not quite do, because it makes the puzzling assumption that true sentences "more correctly refer" than false ones. In general, this is not the case. If I mistakenly say that George W. Bush was born in Texas, there is nothing "incorrect" about the *reference* of "George W. Bush" or "Texas," or the two-place predicate "was born in." The statement is false, but the terms in it refer to determinate individuals and relations. Perhaps this is just an unfortunate choice of words on Kilanowski's part. But it is hard to know which words *should* replace the ones Kilanowski used. If he had written, for example, "(2) we can ask if our judgments are going to be better because they will be *true, or closer to the truth*, about the issue discussed be it the cruelty of a behavior or the kindness of it," then this would be a tautology, and Kilanowski clearly does not intend it to be a tautology. It really does seem as if his interpretation (2), like his interpretation (3), is an attempt to saddle me with the view that "reference" is what ethics rest on.[8]

I also do not understand my supposed objection to interpretation (2): "Of course we would be conscious that reaching for that 'correct answer' will always be difficult and we would never know 'for certain' if we have reached it for some time, given the fallibility of our knowledge. *But Putnam—as I understand him—would not support such an answer because he rejects talking about reference to something 'more'*" (emphasis added—HP). Of course, I am a fallibilist, and of course a naturalistic fallibilist like myself believes that we may find out that there is more—a lot more—to say about a particular issue than we now know. That notion of knowing "more" is essential to fallibilism. So I do not know why Kilanowski says that "he rejects talking about reference to something 'more'" (unless, perhaps this refers to something I have said somewhere about not needing any sort of inflationary metaphysics in ethics or in philosophy of language?).

III. KILANOWSKI ON MY DISAGREEMENT WITH HABERMAS

I deeply admire Jürgen Habermas, not only as a thinker but as a public intellectual who has made an extremely significant contribution to the struggle to interpret, explain, and to further democracy and democratic values in Germany and in the whole world.[9] We have been friends for several decades, and we have had a number of productive exchanges. However, the validity of Habermas's "norms/values" dichotomy is one on which we continue to disagree.

Kilanowski rightly points out that, in "Values and Norms,"[10] I made two incompatible criticisms of that dichotomy[11]: at times I claim that by accepting that dichotomy, Habermas renders his own "discourse ethics" "empty" (or purely "formal"); at other times I write as if I agree that discourse ethics does have substantive implications for how democratic polities should be constituted, and, more broadly, for those areas of ethics that are within the scope of absolutely universalizable that is, exceptionless) moral laws. But I argue that there are important political and ethical issues that are inherently contextual—that concern what Habermas calls "values" as opposed to "norms"—and that those issues too can and usually do have what Dewey called "objective resolutions."[12] Habermas claims that judgments about what is right (or what is good, or what is better, or what is bad, or worse, and so forth to do) cannot be objectively true or false if the disagreement is over "values"; there is only a fact of the matter as to whether a particular community's *way of discussing* what they want their "values" to be satisfies the norms of discourse ethics. (Those norms are, of course, supposed to be objectively valid.) As he himself puts it:

> Norms inform decisions as to what one ought to do, values inform decisions as to what conduct is desirable. . . . Norms raise a binary validity claim in virtue of which they are said to be either valid or invalid. . . .Values, by contrast, fix relations of preference that signify that certain goods are more attractive than others; hence, we can assent to evaluative statements to a greater or lesser degree. The obligatory force of norms has the absolute meaning of an unconditional and universal duty. . . . The attractiveness of values reflects on evaluation and a transitive ordering of goods that has become established in particular cultures or has been adopted by particular groups.[13]

My two criticisms are indeed incompatible because, if discourse ethics does yield substantive universal norms, then even if my second criticism (that those norms do not exhaust the whole writ of objective truth in ethics) be right, it must still be the case that discourse ethics is not "empty" or merely "formal." Kilanowski is right that I need to modify or abandon at least one of these criticisms. My response (which should not come as a surprise to anyone who has read my "For Ethics and Economics Without the Dichotomies"), is to maintain the second criticism, and to change the first criticism to a dilemma for Habermas.

IV. The Case of the Cruel (but Well-Intentioned) Father

In my discussions with Habermas, I asked him to imagine the following case: a father engages in psychological cruelty by teasing his child, while sincerely denying that the child's tears and the like, are really "serious." "He has to learn to take it," the father says.[14] As I argued in *The Collapse of the Fact/Value Dichotomy*, "cruel" and its relatives (for example, "psychological cruelty") are typical value terms; their descriptive content and normative force are, in my view, inextricably entangled. So, if we regard the statement that the father's actions are a form of psychological cruelty as a judgment of *value* in Habermas's sense, then the conclusion must be that if the judgment that what the father does *is not* "cruelty" has "become established" in the father's "particular culture," then for *us* to insist that it is would be "ethnocentric." Perhaps all cultures can accept the maxim *Do not use cruel methods to educate children*, but what constitutes "using cruel methods" will vary from culture to culture. As a "universal norm," "Do not use cruel methods to educate children" will have no objective content whatsoever. It will be "empty and formal." (This is one horn of the dilemma which replaces my first criticism.)

The second horn is the following: If Habermas denies that the statement that the father's actions are a form of psychological cruelty is a judgment of *value* in his sense, it is hard to see why it is not. As I just said, "cruel" is a *typical* value expression. If judgments of cruelty can be objectively right *even when they contradict* the "evaluation and . . . transitive ordering of goods that has become established in particular cultures or has been adopted by particular groups," why should this not go for *all* value judgments? In a discussion with me that took place a few years ago,[15] Habermas replied to my example by saying:

> Values that meet the condition of universalizibility become the defining elements of moral norms. The same holds for the moral conflict over the behavior of the teasing father, that reflects a somewhat authoritarian socialization pattern. Again, entering moral discourse the father will first reproduce the prevailing virtues of community that praises rigor, toughness, etc. (*"Ein deutscher Junge weint nicht"* ["A German boy doesn't cry"]). And the opponents will confront him with what equalizes such a lack of sensitivity [as] 'cruel,' with regard to the suffering soul of a vulnerable child. In this case, the matter will be decided *as* soon as everyone comes to see, as a result of a metalinguistic or hermeneutic discussion, that the term "cruel" applies to this kind of teasing. That cruelty falls under the moral norm, not to harm anyone, is—as well as this norm itself, I suppose—beyond dispute.

Thus Habermas's way of trying to "go between the horns" of the dilemma I described was to subdivide the realm of "values" into two subrealms: a subrealm of universalizable values, whose "validity"[16] is not culture relative, and another subrealm of nonuniversalizable values, whose validity is still held by him to be culture relative. (Kilanowski rightly describes this as Habermas's concession to me in the course of a long series of discussions.) In my view, this idea is weak philosophically and unacceptable ethically.

It is weak philosophically because the criterion for being a "universal-izable" value is itself problematic. For example, the norm "Do not harm anyone" is held to be one of those norms that "[have] the absolute meaning of an unconditional and universal duty," a judgment that very few moral philosophers would accept. (If an officer is forced to sacrifice the life of a soldier under his command to avoid the loss of a whole platoon, has he not *harmed* that soldier? Yet there are situations where it is morally obligatory for an officer to do that.) Likewise, "Do not do anything cruel" is similarly supposed to be a norm that "has the absolute meaning of an unconditional and universal duty," because it follows from the norm of not harming, and, assuming all this, that teasing a child, even for the purpose of teaching the child to be more stoical (which is the father's justification) is supposed to follow from the norm of not being cruel, even if the father's culture does not agree that teasing a child for that purpose and in that way *is* an instance of cruelty. This is supposed to be so because "the matter will be decided *as* soon as everyone comes to see, as a result of a metalinguistic or hermeneutic discussion, that the term 'cruel' applies to this kind of teasing."

But what does "the matter will be decided" mean? Does it mean that, *as a matter of empirical fact* everyone—*everyone!*—will sooner or later come to agree? And not just everyone in Habermas's and my "wet liberal" culture, but in a culture soaked with such ideas as "spare the rod and spoil the child," and *"Ein deutscher Junge weint nicht"*? That is clearly false. (I take it that Kilanowski agrees with me on this, and he interprets Habermas as agreeing with me too that this is not an empirical claim, but I do not find Habermas's different writings consistent on this point.)

On the other hand, if it means that *if the member of the community that conducts the envisaged discussion are ideal discourse theoretic partners* then they will come to agree, as I wrote in "For Ethics and Economics without the Dichotomies,"

> if the claim that the correct verdict in an ethical dispute will be arrived at in an ideal speech situation just means that it will be arrived at if the disputants are ideally morally sensitive, imaginative, impartial, etc, then the claim is a purely "grammatical" one; it provides no content to the notion of a "correct verdict in an ethical dispute" that that notion did not independently possess. Indeed, not only are 'ideally morally sensitive', etc, themselves ethical concepts, but giving them content in any actual dispute will require 'thickening' them, replacing them by terms (which are still value terms, but) which have more descriptive content.[17]

Kilanowski seems to agree with this claim, but it may be worthwhile to un-pack it. My objection in this passage was not that we do not have a decision method (a "criterion") for finding what the outcome of an "ideal" case of "communicative action" would be; I do not believe in *decision* methods in ethics. All we have are fallible procedures; discussion is one of them, but, as Dewey reminded us, *democratic experimentation* is another. But even a community that is democratic and idealistic in the best sense and that possesses the pragmatist virtues of experimentalism and fallibilism may make mistakes. Nonetheless, those procedures are the best we have, and the best we have is good enough. Rather, my objection was that those procedures are needed to determine the extension of *every* value term; they neither reflect nor support the idea that only "universalizable" values possess more than culture-relative "validity."

I also said that the idea that the nonuniversalizable values possess only culture-relative validity is unacceptable ethically. To see why, consider the values represented by Martha Nussbaum's list of "Central Human Capabilities."[18] Among them are freedom to make sexual and reproductive choices, freedom to enjoy and/or participate in making works of art, and freedom to own personal property. According to supporters of the "capabilities" conception of freedom (including myself, Amartya Sen, and Martha Nussbaum) every society *ought* to make those capabilities available to those of its members who do wish to enjoy them to the extent reasonably possible given its means. But that does *not* mean, contrary to what Kilanowski writes, that I believe that "If [those capabilities] are not present in one's life, then this life is stunted." Some people can and do flourish without any given one of those capabilities, and to judge that those people are living stunted lives would be grossly unfair. I have no idea why Kilanowski attributes such a judgment to me. It is precisely because I *do not* hold that view that I can consistently say that the judgment that any of those capabilities is important *to enormously many people* is not a universally valid norm in Habermas's sense. From Habermas's point of view, since making the enjoyment of any one of these freedoms part of one's personal conception of the good life is *not* a universalizable value (not a "norm"), it follows that a culture that that denies one or more of them altogether is doing nothing wrong, provided the decision was not reached undemocratically. It is not clear, in fact, why even a society in which women are denied higher education would be in violation of Habermasian ethics, provided that the women "agreed" that they should not have it. (No doubt Habermas would respond that the society *would not* agree to such an inequality "as soon as everyone comes to see" that it is wrong, but the disagreement with that inequality that he would predict might well depend on the development of capacities for "communicative action" which, in the real world, depend on egalitarian *education*. Communicative action is itself, in fact, a capability that not all possess to an equal degree, and certainly not independently of the support or lack of support provided by the community. That is one of the reasons why educational opportunities belong in the list of Central Human Capabilities.)[19]

V. What Really Worries Kilanowski

What really worries Kilanowski is the idea that questions can have correct, or even rationally warranted, answers if there is not a "criterion" by which we can tell which answers are true or at least warrantedly assertible. This profound skepticism about the ideas of truth and warranted assertibility (in the absence of such a criterion) is more and more strongly expressed toward the end of Kilanowski's essay, for example:

(1) Would we agree that those for whom a central capability in their life is obeying the rules of a tradition or religion can live freely among us if, in their understanding, that capability is connected with securing traditional inequality between men and women or physical punishment for not obeying sacred rules?[20] Why should we be obliged to do what we can in order for them to freely exercise their desired capability?[21] Certainly they will not agree with our argumentation that our capabilities are the ones that they should look for because, thanks to them, they may live in a better way—in a right way.[22]

(2) Kilanowski quotes me as saying, that it is by "intelligent reflection on our valuations, intelligent reflection of the kind Dewey calls 'criticism,' that we conclude that some of them are warranted while others are unwarranted," and responds: "On the basis of the above, we know what we should not look for and what we need in order to state that our valuation is warranted or not (namely, critical thinking). But when is it warranted and what does it mean that it is warranted? The answer 'when we are critical and use intelligent reflection' would not take us far if the method of our conduct was taken by us as a goal, no matter what the outcome was. One could answer that a valuation would be warranted when it fulfilled certain criteria, but then we would ask what those criteria are. Why, 'should,' as Putnam might say, certain judgments be regarded as true and others as false?"

(3) "Concerning the question about what the criteria are on the basis of which we can decide who is right when we have an ethical disagreement, Putnam replies by saying that we do not have, nor do we need, one single 'criterion' or decision method for judging warranted assertibility in ethics any more than we do in any other area. Rather, we need commitment to the ethical life and the authority of intelligence, of criticism. So, we again only hear about the method that we should apply, about critical thinking, and not about any criteria. Putnam is not giving a clear answer."

(4) "In the above explanation, what Putnam means by true or false, right and wrong, or valid or invalid does not seem to be sufficient. And, because

of this insufficiency, the issue of the objectivity of ethics and values still does not seem to be explained. What does Putnam mean when he says that they can be objective when they refer to real human needs?"

Of course, Kilanowski does not only mean that I have failed to "sufficiently" and "clearly" explain what truth and warranted assertibility are. He is casting doubt on the notions of truth, warranted assertibility, and (while he is at it) common sense and reference themselves, and not merely on what I have written about them. But I see no reason whatsoever to give up these notions, or any possibility of doing so.

VI. A Closing Remark

I know from our conversations that Kilanowski himself is farther from Rortian skepticism than his essay might lead a reader to think, and that his purpose here was to force me to respond to that skepticism, not to defend it. I have, however, not drawn on this "insider knowledge" in the present reply, and I have answered just as I would have done if the essay were written by a committed "Rortian." I look forward to learning from Kilanowski's future writings how he himself would defend democratic and fallibilistic ethics.

H.P.

NOTES

1. I write "Marxism-Leninism" and not "Marxism," because I agree with Shlomo Avineri that the former was not an inevitable development out of the latter. See Avineri's *The Social and Political Thought of Karl Marx* (Cambridge: Cambridge University Press, 1968).

2. "In April 1926, Mussolini gave an interview to the press in which he named James, along with Nietzsche and Sorel, among his philosophical masters. . . . James taught me that an action should be judged by its results rather than by its doctrinary basis. I learnt from James that faith in action, that ardent will to live and fight, to which Fascism owes a great part of its success." Ralph Barton Perry, *The Thought and Character of William James: As Revealed in Unpublished Correspondence and Notes, Together with his Published Writings*, vol. II (Boston: Little, Brown, and Company, 1935), 575.

3. Hilary Putnam, "The Question of Realism," in *Words and Life*, ed. James Conant (Cambridge, MA: Harvard University Press, 1994), 297

4. Ibid., 299.

5. Hilary Putnam, "Richard Rorty on Reality and Justification," in *Rorty And His Critics*, ed. Robert Brandom (Oxford: Blackwell, 2000), 81.

6. Ibid., 83–84.

7. On the danger of confusing the two see Hilary Putnam, "Pragmatism and Relativism: Universal Values and Traditional Ways of Life," in *Words and Life*, 182–97.

8. Another possibility is that Kilanowski thinks that there is no such property as *cruelty*, or that there is such thing as coming to understand better what cruelty consists in; but if

he thinks that, then that is an objection that does not depend on any particular account of what *referring* involves.

9. Kilanowski, perhaps because he is not a native speaker of English, fails to hear the sarcasm in Churchill's saying democracy is the "worst" of all systems—"except for those others that have actually been tried." Thus he makes the mistake of writing that "[Putnam] admits that this is the worst approach to decision making in the public sphere that has ever been devised." Of course, I believe passionately in democratic values, and I admire those who are devoted to them, as Habermas and Kilanowski are.

10. "*Werte und Normen,*" in *Die Öffentlichkeit der Vernunft und die Vernunft der Öffentlichkei. Festschrift für Jürgen Habermas,* ed. Lutz Wingert and Klaus Günther (Frankfurt am Main: Suhrkamp, 2001), 280–313. English version published as "Values and Norms" in Hilary Putnam, *The Collapse of the Fact/Value Dichotomy and Other Essays* (Cambridge, MA: Harvard University Press, 2002), 111–34.

11. Kilanowski also refers to a later paper of mine: "For Ethics and Economics without the Dichotomies," *Review of Political Economy* 15, no. 3 (July 2003): 395–412.

12. John Dewey, *Logic: The Theory of Inquiry, The Later Works, 1925–1953,* ed. Jo Ann Boydston, vol. 12 (Carbondale, IL: Southern Illinois University Press, 1984), 287. Dewey's phrase is "objective resolutions of problematic situations."

13. Jürgen Habermas, "Reconciliation through the Public use of Reason: Remarks on John Rawls' *Political Liberalism,*" *Journal of Philosophy* 92, no. 3 (1995): 114–15.

14. Putnam, *The Collapse of the Fact/Value Dichotomy,* 127.

15. Our discussion took place on November 13, 2003 at Northwestern University (Habermas was kind enough to provide me with a written text).

16. Habermas restricts the terms "true" and "false" to empirical statements; ethical norms (and mathematical statements as well) can be "valid" or "invalid" but not true or false. I criticize this view in "*Antwort auf Jürgen Habermas*" in *Hilary Putnam und die Tradition des Pragmatismus,* ed. Marie-Luise Raters and Marcus Willaschek (Frankfurt am Main: Suhrkamp, 2002), 306–21.

17. Putnam, "For Ethics and Economics without the Dichotomies," 410.

18. See "For Ethics and Economics without the Dichotomies," 402 for the list in question.

19. One might also criticize Habermas's "universalizable/nonuniversalizable" dichotomy from a different direction, by arguing that *every* value is "universalizable" in the sense that if V is a genuine value, that there must be circumstances C such that "an agent has morally good reasons to value V in circumstances C" is an exceptionless "maxim." (This is suggested in Scanlon's recent Locke Lectures, which are still unpublished as of this writing.) But I am not persuaded that the relevant circumstances *can* always be explicitly and exhaustively described in our language, as Scanlon assumes.

20. If someone claims that their way of life was dictated to some prophet by God, then the answer given by Kant in *Religion within the Bounds of Mere Reason*—that when one believes that God commanded something, one is always in fact relying on some human being or group of human beings who told one that this is what God commanded, and that sort of reliance is inferior to reliance on rational criticism—is exactly right.

21. Capability theorists do not claim we have an obligation to help everyone "to freely exercise their desired capability," no matter what it is; we claim that we can reach reasonable, if fallible, decisions as to which capabilities are morally important.

22. Yes, I claim that the right answer to an ethical question (or any other sort of question) may not be one that everyone accepts!

26

Richard Rorty

PUTNAM, PRAGMATISM, AND PARMENIDES

I. PRAGMATISM AND INSTRUMENTALISM

Hilary Putnam and I have been disagreeing for the last twenty years about what lessons to draw from the writings of William James and John Dewey.[1] We both use weapons borrowed from these authors when attacking our favorite targets: for example, the fact/value distinction, the idea that physical science has a privileged relation to reality, and the assumption that intuition is, as Putnam puts it, "not just a mode of access to our culture's inherited picture of the world."[2] But Putnam thinks that my radical version of pragmatism gives rise to pointless paradox—that it saves us from the frying pan he calls "metaphysical realism" only to throw us into the fires of relativism. He thinks his moderate version returns us to what he calls the "natural realism" of common sense.

I think that Putnam's version does not do justice to the possibility that James was right when he compared the movement's importance to that of the Protestant Reformation.[3] Whereas Putnam sees the so-called "classical" pragmatists as helping us return to "the ordinary," I see them as heralding a new, and extraordinary, change in humanity's self-image. Putnam thinks that they had no wish to throw the baby of common sense out with the philosophical bathwater. I see them as hoping to change common sense by changing some of the images embedded in our picture of the world—the one our culture inherited from Parmenides and Plato.

Putnam thinks that "there is a way to do justice to our sense that knowledge claims are responsible to reality without recoiling into metaphysical fantasy."[4] I do not. On my view, the claim that human beings are responsible to reality is as hopeless as the idea that true sentences correspond to reality. I read James and Dewey as saying that we have no responsibilities except to fellow players of what Sellars and Brandom call "the game of giving and asking for reasons." My slogan is: if it does not talk, we are not answerable to it. I think of that slogan as summing up the cash value of Hegel's thesis that "Spirit never confronts anything other than itself."[5] Most of this essay will be a defense of this claim about our responsibilities against Putnam's objections to it.

Before turning to this defense, however, I want to take up another topic, and to abjure some things that I have said about pragmatism in the past, things that Putnam was right to criticize. He has argued in various places that I distort the classical pragmatists by emphasizing and reiterating James's claim that the true is the expedient in the way of belief, and by taking this instrumentalist claim as central to the pragmatist message. Putnam thinks that instrumentalism is too bad an idea to be attributed to James. Robert Brandom has recently intervened in this debate. Brandom agrees with me that James and Dewey were in fact instrumentalists, and that this instrumentalism was central to their work, but he agrees with Putnam that instrumentalism is wrong headed. Brandom finds the value of pragmatism in other parts of James's and Dewey's work—notably in those parts of Dewey that are most clearly reminiscent of Hegel. Brandom agrees with Putnam that instrumentalism is the wrong handle by which to pick up pragmatism.

After trying for years to evade Brandom's point, I now agree with him that there is "a major tension" in what I have written between a "robust appreciation of the transformative potential of new vocabularies" and an "appeal to instrumental models for thinking and talking about them."[6] Brandom's argument is that if such transformations are as thoroughgoing as I should like them to be, they cannot be judged in terms of how well they satisfy antecedent goals. For new vocabularies give us new self-images, and new self-images give us new goals.[7] This means that we should not try to put the process of transformation in a larger context, reference to which might help us determine which transformations have been good and which bad. In particular, we should not try to put the pragmatists's suggested transformation in such a context. We should not ask what pragmatism is good for, nor why it would be expedient to adopt it.

It is often said that the only trouble with pragmatism is that it does not work. But that is as if one had said to Luther and Calvin that their movement would not work—that the idea of the priesthood of all believers was too counterintuitive to be pressed into useful service. The Reformers, however, wanted to change our ends as well as our means, and so did the pragmatists. There is no overarching framework by reference to which we can judge either the workability or the value of a large-scale, revolutionary proposal for change in the human self-image. Religious movements like the Reformation and philosophical movements like pragmatism resemble artistic breakthroughs of the sort made by Cervantes, Turner, and Beethoven. There are no criteria in place by which to evaluate them. They create, as Wordsworth said, the taste by which they are judged.

Putnam thinks Brandom's polemic against the idea that we should "evaluate beliefs by their tendency to promote success at the satisfaction of wants"[8] is right on target. On his view, however, Brandom's polemic should be directed exclusively against me, since, contrary to common opinion, this idea was not held by James or Dewey. I continue to disagree with Putnam about the interpretation of these authors. There are plenty of passages in their works that support Brandom's and my instrumentalist reading of James and Dewey, just as there are plenty that support Putnam's "natural realist" reading. Putnam views my favorite passages as rhetorical hyperbole, and I regard his favorite passages as momentary backsliding. In what follows, however, I shall set aside exegetical questions. Instead, I shall try to explain why I now agree with Putnam that it was a mistake on my part to try to assimilate the quest for truth to the quest for happiness.

In the past, I have suggested that James and Dewey gave us a way of reconciling Nietzsche's Darwinian description of human beings as "clever animals" with Hegel's description of them, belonging to a realm of Spirit, as having freed themselves from Nature through successive self-redescriptions. I thought that the way to naturalize Hegel was to view language as a tool developed by a certain species of animal to increase its pleasure and diminish its pain. So I suggested we think of language and culture as analogous to the spider's web and the beaver's dam. But, as Brandom has made me realize, describing language as a tool misleadingly suggests that there is something by reference to which we can evaluate the utility of playing the game of giving and asking for reasons—something for the sake of which this game is played. He has convinced me that Heidegger was right in saying that it would be merely a barren inversion of Platonism to describe the point of language and culture as the satisfaction of animal desire. To make this mistake, as Nietzsche sometimes did, amounts to casting animal desires in the role previously played by Plato's and Kant's ideals of reason.

It would be better to say that nothing should be cast in this role—to just stop asking questions like "what is the point of inquiry?" Only the social practices that constitute what Brandom calls "being sapient" permit us to isolate means/end relations. There is no point in trying to step outside the ensemble of those practices in order to see sapience itself as a means to some larger end.

Abandoning the idea that sapience has a function would chime with Dewey's polemics against what he called "fixed ends." In Dewey's sense of the term, discovering The Meaning of Human Life and discovering The True Nature of Physical Reality are fixed ends. By contrast, curing cancer, fixing a leaky faucet, sending a spaceship to Arcturus, and achieving world peace, are what Dewey called "ends-in-view." These are ends toward which we know how to devise means, and are such that we can tell whether or not we have attained them.

By contrast, fixed ends of the sort that philosophers have envisaged are designed to be unattainable. Unlike Kant, Dewey did not think that we needed any limit concepts, any regulative ideas, to lure us on. He agreed with Hegel that the dialectical tensions between inherited social practices would always suffice to nudge the present into creating a novel future. The finitude and achievability of ends-in-view, however, enables pursuit of them to contribute to what Dewey called "growth." "Growth" he said, "is the only moral end.'" [9] That dictum amounts to saying that it is the journey that matters—the ever renewed ability of the species to surprise itself by turning itself into something new. Dewey learned from Hegel that human communities grow when, and only when, they revise their own ends-in-view, rather than remaining faithful to the goals their ancestors cherished.

One reason I made the mistake of calling language a tool was that I was concerned to defend Davidsonian disquotationalism against Crispin Wright's charge that it neglects the fact that truth and warranted assertibility are distinct goals.[10] My argument was that justification to a particular audience is the end-in-view of inquiry, and that Wright's claim that inquiry has, in addition, a fixed end called "truth" is one that can make no practical difference. We would pursue the same inquiries in the same ways, I argued, if the idea of truth as a goal had never crossed our minds. This led me to say that we should think of ourselves as having only one goal—happiness—rather than two, happiness and truth.

I still want to defend Davidson against Wright, but I no longer want to say that the pursuing justification—taking part in the game of giving and asking for reasons—has happiness as its goal. Thanks to Brandom's criticisms, I now think that my quasi-Nietzschean and pseudo-Darwinian attempt to assimilate what we do to what the animals do was on the wrong track. For "happiness" is a vacuous term that serves only to obscure the difference between hoping for the cessation of an itch and hoping to write immortal lyrics, just as "truth" is a vacuous term that obscures the difference between true sentences like "This is red" and true sentences like "The Protestant Reformation helped liberate the human mind." To propose, as I did, that happiness should replace truth as the goal of inquiry is to propose replacing one vacuity by another.

The reason these notions are vacuous is that neither the injunction to seek truth, nor that to seek happiness, provides any guidance. A goal should be something you can judge your distance from. There are ways of figuring out when you have veered from it and when you are closer to it. In the case of fixed ends such as truth and happiness there are no such ways. We can never know, for example, whether a science has become "mature." Nor can we know whether what seems to us the best possible political regime may not strike our descendants as one more excuse for oppressing the weak. Aristotelian mechanics and the Roman Republic are reminders that we can never infer from current justifiability to justification simpliciter. Justification is a relative notion, whereas truth is an absolute notion. Efforts to tie them together will always fail.

It is one thing to deny that truth is a goal distinct from justification, and another to propose an alternative goal for inquiry. I still want to do the former, but I should not have done the latter. Nor should I have focused on the passages in which James identifies the true with the expedient, and on his attempt to ally his pragmatism with John Stuart Mill's utilitarianism—a doctrine whose vacuity was effectively criticized by Dewey. To say that inquiry aims at human happiness is as pointless as saying that goodness is what answers to our interests. That latter response is not exactly false, but, like the sentence "everything is identical with itself," it is a good example of language going on holiday. Anybody who, having asked what goodness is, receives that response, will rightly feel that her question has been evaded rather than answered. For she was, implicitly, asking what interests she should have—which of her projects should be pursued and which abandoned. She wants to know if she should change her life, and if so, how.

The Greeks suggested that we might find out whether and how to change our lives by attempting to pin down both the nature of truth and the nature of happiness. James and Dewey reminded us that such attempts have not paid off. So I suggest we read James's claim that the true is the expedient in the way of belief not as an attempt to answer the question "what is truth?" but as a way of mocking that question. On that reading, James was being therapeutic rather than constructive. He was trying to cure people of Platonism—of the temptation to think about fixed ends rather than about ends-in-view. He was not proposing expediency as a goal in order to redirect our inquiries. He was just urging us to conduct those inquiries without reference to an ahistorical context of the sort in which Plato hoped to put them.

Plato argued that there was an analogy between knowing how to be a good carpenter or physician and knowing how to be a good human being. On the view that Dewey took over from Hegel, there is no analogy. Carpenters and physicians have ends-in-view, but humanity does not. Humanity makes itself up as it goes along, changing its ends-in-view as it changes its self-image. There is no way to step outside the wavering and unpredictable course of history—the realm that Plato called "opinion"—and make contact with the really real. If you drop Plato's analogy you will no longer try to place your scientific, political, or other deliberations within a larger context called "our relation to Reality" or "our relation to Truth." You will read James and Dewey as trying to move us back to the rough ground, and to eschew the slick and seductive abstractions that were Plato's legacy.

When, in the past, I emphasized what Brandom calls "the transformative potential of new vocabularies," I thought of myself as making an anti-Platonist point. When I have appealed to instrumental models when describing such transformations, I was thinking of myself as making another anti-Platonist point. But actually, I now realize, I was just succumbing to the same temptation to which Plato succumbed—the temptation to draw an analogy between a particular human activity and human life in general. I was trying to pin down the goal of human life by describing it in terms of the gratification of desire, and thinking of desire on the model of what Brandom, following Hegel, calls *sinnliche Neigungen*: simple animal urges like the need to stop itching. Brandom's article "Pragmatics and Pragmatisms" finally succeeded in making me see that my analogy between the ideal beaver dam and the ideal set of human beliefs would be appropriate only if I were trying to develop a reductionist view of human beings of the sort currently being pursued by people like Steven Pinker and E. O. Wilson, who are dismissive of the idea that "culture" is of any great importance in understanding human beings. That is about the last thing I want to do.

II. PUTNAM AND THE SUPERTHING

But although Brandom has made me see the point, and acknowledge the justice, of some of Putnam's criticisms, I am not yet ready to go over to Putnam's side when it comes to the question of whether we need the notion of being responsible to reality as well as that of being responsible to our fellow humans. Putnam long ago described me as holding that "there is only the dialogue; no ideal end can be posited or should be needed." In his *Reason, Truth and History* he said that that view amounted to a "self-refuting relativism," because, as he went on to say "The very fact that we speak of our different conceptions as different conceptions of *rationality* posits a *Grenzbegriff*, a limit concept of the ideal truth."[11] On my reading of Dewey, that is exactly what he denied. So I think myself no more of a relativist than Dewey was, or than a good pragmatist should be.

Reason, Truth and History was published in 1980, and Putnam has changed his mind on many issues since then. But he still describes me, in his most recent books, as a relativist.[12] He still thinks it important for philosophers to take seriously what I describe as Platonist vacuities. However, he has now repudiated the notion of "ideal truth." In an essay of 1990 criticizing Bernard Williams he wrote that "To say, as Williams sometimes does, that convergence to one big picture is required by the very concept of knowledge is sheer dogmatism." He goes on to say that "without the postulate that science converges to a single definite theoretical picture . . . the whole notion of 'absoluteness' collapses. It is, indeed, the case that ethical knowledge cannot claim absoluteness; but that is because the notion of absoluteness is incoherent."[13] Recently he has said that he not only no longer thinks that truth can be defined in terms of warranted assertibility under ideal conditions, but that he now sees no "need [to] define truth at all."[14]

I should have thought that giving up on absoluteness and coming to agree with Davidson about the indefinability of truth would lead Putnam to have more sympathy with my view that "there is only the dialogue." But he still sees me as occupying an extreme position. In the opening pages of his Dewey Lectures of 1994, reprinted in *The Threefold Cord*, he tries to stake out a position intermediate between Williams's and mine. In a passage I have already quoted, he says that he wants to "do justice to our sense that knowledge claims are responsible to reality without recoiling into metaphysical fantasy."[15] Williams and other philosophers whom Putnam describes as "celebrating materialism cum cognitive science" are the metaphysical fantasists, whereas Nelson Goodman and I are among those who have given up on the idea that "knowledge claims are responsible to reality." The result of doing the latter, Putnam says, is "linguistic idealism," which he regards as so paradoxical as to be merely frivolous.[16]

Putnam says that he agrees "with the [realist] critic [of James] that the world is as it is independently of the interests of describers." He goes on to say that "James's suggestion that the world we know is to an indeterminate extent the product of our own minds is one I deplore."[17] In a footnote to this passage he quotes, as an example of a deplorable Jamesian doctrine, the claim that "We create the subjects of our true as well as of our false propositions." He goes on to say "I myself regret having spoken of 'mind dependence' in connection with those issues in my *Reason, Truth and History*."[18]

But Putnam thinks that "the realist critic of James" goes wrong insofar as she believes that "there is one definite totality of objects that can be classified and one definite totality of all 'properties.'"[19] He calls this totality a "superthing." He denounces "the common philosophical error of supposing that the term reality must refer to a single superthing instead of looking at the ways in which we endlessly renegotiate—and are forced to renegotiate—our notion of reality as our language and our life develop."[20]

My problem with Putnam's attempt to find a position intermediate between Williams's and mine is that I cannot see why, once he has denied that the word "reality" refers to a single superthing, he should still object to James's claim that "we create the subjects as well of our true as of our false propositions." Obviously Putnam does not think that James intended "create" to mean "cause to come into existence," any more than he himself meant to describe causal relations when he wrote, in *Reason, Truth and History*, that "the mind and the world jointly make up the mind and the world."[21] So I would read James's claim about the subjects of our true propositions as saying simply that we create what Ian Hacking calls "truth-candidates." When James says that "the world stands really malleable" and that "man engenders truth upon the world," I take him to be agreeing with Putnam that no superthing determines which of our truth-candidates are somehow legitimate and which not. For legitimation is not given by something non-human but by the relative utility of various competing truth-candidates for the attainment of human ends-in-view.

Envisaging such a superthing amounts to an attempt to put the process of discarding old truth-candidates and dreaming up new ones, the process that Hegel thought of as the self-realization of Spirit, in the context of a relation between two things, "mind" and "world," that can be examined independently of one another. Inquiry, in this context, is what brings these two things into closer relation with one another.[22] Putnam and I agree that James and Dewey wanted us to reject this picture, but Putnam seems to want to retain just enough of its elements to enable him to say that the subjects of our true propositions are not created by us.

I imagine James replying to Putnam as follows: All I meant by the sentence you deplore was that we create subjects of both true and false propositions by dreaming up new topics of discourse (such as "phlogiston," "electron," "original sin," "mauve," and "moral obligation"). There is no point in asking which of the predicates we employ when we formulate these propositions to match up with properties of reality. Since you yourself say that there is no superthing that contains "a totality of properties fixed once and for all," what do we disagree about? How do you propose to hang onto what you call "the real insight" of my pragmatism—"the insight that 'description' is never a mere copying and that we constantly add to the ways in which language can be responsible to reality"[23] while still rejecting the sentence you call 'deplorable'? My claim was that once we give up on copying we can substitute "coping with reality" for "being responsible to reality." Without a superthing, how are we supposed to distinguish between successful coping and fulfilled responsibility? Once we dispense with a superthing, what is there left to be responsible to save our fellow inquirers?

James could press this line of questioning further by asking how, having given up on a superthing, Putnam can still object to the claim that "there is no such thing as one language game being better than another, there is only *being better relative to this, that, or the other interest*."[24] Putnam thinks that claim absurd, since he thinks it entails that "we cannot say . . . that

Newton's physics is superior to Aristotle's physics, or that there are things that Aristotle's physics got wrong and that Newton's physics got right."[25] But it is not clear why he should think this, for he agrees with James that "the trail of the human serpent is over all." He says, for example, that we humans are beings "who cannot have a view of the world that does not reflect our interests and values."[26] Without a superthing to authenticate some of our topics of discourse and not others by having properties corresponding to Newtonian but not to Aristotelian predicates, how are we to give sense to the claim that Newton was superior in some sense that is *not* interest relative?

James quoted with approval W. S. Franklin's definition of physics as "the science of the ways of taking hold of bodies and pushing them." Newton was much better at helping us push bodies around then Aristotle had been. But to say that this was because he got some things right is a vacuous compliment unless it is spelled out in terms of matching up to a superthing. What, exactly, is he supposed to have gotten right? Newton did not get what Aristotle was talking about—natural motion—right. He did not think that there was such a thing. Aristotle did not get force and mass wrong. He had never heard of them. Such considerations led Kuhn to say that these two scientists lived in different worlds. But it would be better to say that we do not need the notion of "the world"—either singular or plural—to explain Newton's superiority. We can just list all the ends-in-view that Newton helped us realize that Aristotle did not.

The world as superthing is what metaphysical realists believe in. They want to leave room for the possibility that we might become able to push bodies around to our heart's content while still being clueless about what the world is *really* like. Putnam and I agree that this skeptical suggestion is empty. But whereas I think that rejecting metaphysical realism should lead us to drop the realism/antirealism issue altogether, Putnam wants to say that the realists were right about something and their critics wrong.

For many years, Putnam described his alternative view as "internal realism," but, like many others, I could never get the hang of what that was. I am glad that Putnam has now dropped that term,[27] but my interpretive problems remain pretty much the same. I cannot see that he has given what he would call "full intelligibility" to a notion he says "plays a deep role in our lives and is to be respected," namely that "our words and life are constrained by a reality not of our own invention"—constraint that is not causal but rational.[28] Putnam, like McDowell, thinks that we need, in addition to the idea of constraint by social norms, ideas like "objective purport" and "answerability to the world." James, on my reading of him, would argue that the latter notions do not work.

This is not to say that James would not happily grant that, given our present social norms, we recognize an obligation to say things like "the tumor is malignant" and "I cannot replicate the experiment," even when we would rather not. Those norms determine when it is appropriate for us to believe things that we wish we were able to disbelieve. But the reason belief is not under the control of our will is not that Nature, as well as Spirit, constrains us. It is that we have internalized those norms. We have no faculties which enable us to break away from them in the way that Plato thought that *nous* might enable us to break away from *doxa*. As the dialogue goes along, we continually change those norms, but we do not do so because we are answerable to some superthing called "the world."

Nobody denies that we invent predicates. If one believes in a superthing, one can give sense to the question "which of the predicates we have invented signify properties, properties we have not invented?" But if one does not, one will treat a property as simply the reification of a predicate. Such reification is harmless enough in itself, but not when it leads us to ask bad questions, such as whether to be "realist" about moral obligations as well as about atoms. That question can only be a question about the properties of a superthing. Putnam wants to be realist about both, but by denying the existence of a superthing he deprives himself of the resources to explain what his realism amounts to.

The best argument for dropping the question about the properties of a superthing, as well as the question about what we invented and what we did not, is just the irrelevance of both questions to practice. Neither subjectivism nor realism about some entities, or about some area of culture, will ever have any effects on our nonphilosophical inquiries. To adopt either attitude is merely to strike a philosophical pose, one which can be adopted or abandoned without affecting anything else we do. The notion that some predicates correspond to properties and others do not serves no purpose except to let philosophers pay empty compliments to areas of culture that they particularly prize (as Plato prized mathematics, and Hobbes prized particle physics).

The question of relevance to practice arises also in connection with another issue about which Putnam and I differ. I agree with Davidson and Brandom that nothing save a belief can justify, or infirm, a belief. Putnam and McDowell disagree. They think that experiences, as opposed to judgments, can also justify and infirm. McDowell says that "we cannot make sense of discourse-governing social norms prior to and independently of objective purport . . . answerability to the world and answerability to each other have to be understood together."[29]

The big difference between Brandom and McDowell is that Brandom wants to disjoin the notion of talking about objects from that of answerability to them. He argues that we can milk the notion of "object" out of the social practices that make up our use of singular terms. For on his account, to understand what it is to be an object it is sufficient to know how to make *de re* ascriptions, a know how that is acquired by internalizing social norms. Making such descriptions does not require anything like McDowellian cognitive contact with objects, but only by finding ways to integrate one's linguistic and other behavior with those of one's peers.

How does one decide the central issue that divides McDowell and Putnam from Brandom and Davidson? Not, I think, by looking more closely at our notions of "objective purport" and "empirical content," nor by asking which view rescues more of our antecedent intuitions than its rival. The issue should rather be viewed as a practical one—a question of whether the notions that one side wishes to preserve and the other to discard are paying their way, doing us enough good to compensate for having created seemingly endless philosophical disputes. Putnam, addressing just that question, says: "It is of course true that such general terms as *reality, reason,* (and one might add *language, meaning, reference* . . .) are sources of deep philosophical puzzlement. Yet, the solution is not simply to jettison these words. The notion that our words are constrained by a reality not of our own invention plays a deep role in our lives, and is to be respected."[30]

He goes on to say that we can continue to let these words play a deep role in our lives, but get rid of the philosophical puzzlement, if we just get rid of the notion that reality is a superthing. My argument has been that once we get rid of the notion of a superthing—of the idea that we are responsible for matching up our predicates with the superthing's properties—our lives will be changed. The words that Putnam rightly says play a deep role in our lives will no longer do so. The intuitions to which Putnam appeals, and which he agrees are nothing more than "a mode of access to our cultures' inherited picture of the world," will no longer hold us captive. We will no longer feel discomfited by James's claim that "we create the subjects of our true as well of our false propositions."

III. Perception

In this section I shall apply what I have just been saying to perception, another topic on which Putnam and I hold sharply contrasting views. I am one of those whom Putnam describes as wanting "to dismiss traditional problems in the philosophy of perception" because "too much time has been wasted on them," and who regard a return to these problems as "a re-infantilization of philosophy."[31] While I agree with Putnam that J. L. Austin did a beautiful job of disposing of sense data and of A. J. Ayer's phenomenalism, I do not think that Austin's achievement has much extra-Oxonian significance.

Putnam and McDowell both see perception as an important topic because both believe that what McDowell calls "answerability of the world" needs to be preserved. Without it, they both think, inquiry would be "frictionless." Brandom, on the other hand, thinks that we can say everything we need to about rationality without ever using the word "experience." We can, as Sellars did, treat perceptual reports as "language-entry transitions"— learned linguistic reactions to environmental or neural states. Since I share this view, I think of James's book *Radical Empiricism* and Dewey's book *Experience and Nature* as irrelevant to pragmatism, and as having been made obsolete by Sellars's essay "Empiricism and the Philosophy of Mind."

McDowell disagrees with me and Brandom about how to interpret that essay; he thinks that Sellars had a view rather like his own. On my interpretation, however, Sellars taught us how to avoid a view, enunciated by James, endorsed by Putnam, and resurrected by McDowell: the view that perception is "thought and sensation *fused*."[32] Brandom and I read Sellars as urging that we think of sensation in purely causal terms and of thought in purely intentional terms, and thus give up the idea of fusing them. By contrast, Putnam and McDowell want us, in Putnam's words to "think of hearing and seeing as accessing information from the environment." Only thus, they think, will we be able to do justice to the natural realism of common sense. I agree, but since I want to change common sense, I think we should follow Sellars in thinking of thought and sensation—norm-governed social practices and physiological states—as capable of standing only in causal relations to one another. We should stop looking for a fusion of the two, or for a middle ground between them called "perception," or for a way of "reducing" one to the other.

Putnam says that "The 'how does language hook onto the world?' issue is, at bottom, a replay of the old 'how does perception hook onto the world?' issue."[33] He sees the latter question as arising from the seventeenth-century idea that there must be an "interface between the mind and the 'external' objects we perceive."[34] He argues that James, in *Radical Empiricism*, and Austin, in *Sense and Sensibilia*, showed us what was wrong with the idea of such interface. By doing so, they enabled us to believe that "in perception we are in unmediated contact with our environment."[35]

I disagree about which question is a replay of which. The question of how *perception* hooks on to the world did indeed, as Putnam says, become important in the seventeenth century as a result of our realization that Democritus had been on the right track. That discovery made it seem that we needed a replacement for the Aristotelian account of the sensitive soul becoming identical with the properties of the sensed object. The idea of inner representations of outer objects was an obvious candidate. But neither Aristotelian notions of identity nor Cartesian notions of mental representation would have been of interest had Plato not induced us to think of knowledge as a word/world relation rather than as a relation between participants in a conversation.[36] The question of whether perception puts us in direct or in indirect contact with objects would never have seemed important, for the notion of a "cognitive relation to the world" would not have been available.

Plato, following up on Parmenides, saddled us with the idea that knowledge should be thought of in terms of a noncausal relation between humans and what they are talking about that somehow lies behind, and makes possible, such talk. Pursuing that line of thought will lead one to say, as Putnam does, that *"sentences cannot be true or false of an external reality if there are no justificatory connections between things we say in language and any aspects of that reality whatsoever."*[37] I read James and Dewey as disposed to agree with Brandom that no such connection is necessary or possible. It was only the Greek way of talking about knowledge as a word/world relation, rather than as a matter of the justification of beliefs by other beliefs, that made such connections seem necessary. It is a matter for regret that attempts to locate such connections dominated Western philosophy up to the time of Hegel, the first thinker who suggested that we stop thinking of the attainment of knowledge as a matter of building bridges between subject and object.

Putnam thinks of me as answering the question "how does knowledge hook on to the world" by saying "causally," and thus, as he puts it, "treating causality as Kant treated his pseudocausal relation of 'ground'"—as a "transcendental relation connecting the story which we and our cultural peers make up with a world in itself." Hence, he says, "Rorty's picture is, in this respect, a materialist version of Kant's transcendental metaphysics."[38] But Putnam here elides a distinction upon which I have insisted: that between "the world" (a notion which, I argued, we would be better off without) and the collection of entities such as stars, people, beavers, numbers, poems, governments, and positrons. This is the difference between something we can never be sure that we are in touch with and an assortment of things that nobody has ever been able to doubt that we are in touch with.

The difference between the two is what Kant would call the difference between the unconditioned and the conditioned. It is the difference between questions that make a difference to practice—particular questions about the stars and the people and the numbers—and questions that cannot make such a difference—questions about the nature of reality. Parmenides made it possible for us to ask the latter sort of question by scooping all the particular things together and compressing them into a well-rounded and impermeable sphere, standing over and against the fallible, human mind. The Parmenidean One was the original superthing, and its descendants still linger within the common sense of the West.

Heidegger was right that questions about our relation to "the world" are not inevitable, that they were first introduced in the West by Parmenides and Plato. He was also right that the popularity of these questions among Western intellectuals was a misfortune, and that pursuing them in subsequent centuries was what landed us with Nietzsche's inverted Platonism. Hegel was right that pursuing these Greek questions has made us unable to appreciate that Spirit is sufficient unto itself—that it does not have to answer to Nature, that the dialogue it conducts with itself is enough. Dewey was right that pursuing those questions was a pointless, and harmful, distraction from the problems of the day. If one puts together these Heideggerian, Hegelian, and Deweyan theses, one gets a sense of how James and Dewey hoped the common sense of the West might change. One begins to see the point of the analogy James drew with the Protestant Reformation—an earlier movement that helped free us from the idea that we were responsible to something powerful, authoritative, and mysterious.

IV. LINGUISTIC IDEALISM

In this concluding section I shall take up Putnam's claim that I am a relativist. His application of the term "relativist" is not restricted to those who want to reduce truth to justification, as he and I both were once tempted to do. In *Reason, Truth and History* he gives the epithet a wider, and, I think more interesting sense, one in which it is more or less the same as what he once called "linguistic idealism." There he says that

> The whole *purpose* of relativism, its very defining characteristic, is . . . to *deny* the existence of any intelligible notion of *objective* "fit." Thus the relativist cannot understand talk about truth in terms of *objective* justification-conditions. . . . The relativist must end by denying that any thought is *about* anything in either a realist or non-realist sense; for he cannot distinguish between thinking one's thought is about something and actually thinking about that thing. In short, what the relativist fails to see is that it is a presupposition of thought itself that some kind of objective 'rightness' exists.[39]

If linguistic idealism is defined as denying the utility of the notions of "objective justification-conditions" and of "objective rightness," then I am indeed a linguistic idealist. I think that if James and Dewey had replaced talk of experience with talk of language, as they would have been wise to have done, they would have been linguistic idealists too.

One would think of the purely negative claim made by linguistic idealism as amounting to relativism only if one thought that the only alternative to objective rightness was subjective rightness, and therefore inferred from justifiability to a particular community, and the absence of objective rightness, to truth. But there is no reason to make this inference. All that is necessary to deny the utility of the notion of "objective rightness" is to accept what Brandom calls "the essential point of a theory such as James's," namely, "to treat calling something true as doing something more like praising it than like describing it." This means, as Brandom goes on to say, ceasing to ask what property "true" signifies and asking instead for "the practical significance of the act we are performing in attributing that property."[40]

The notions of "objective rightness" and "objective justification-conditions" were invented in order to answer the question "what property does 'true' signify?" The temptation to answer that question brings with it the temptation to contrast merely local and parochial cultural justification-conditions with the justification-conditions invoked by a superculture at the Peircean end of inquiry, or with those that would be invoked by someone who, having been vouchsafed a vision of a superthing, can tell which predicates in our culture's language correspond to properties the world actually has. Putnam, it seems to me, has almost freed himself from belief in either a superculture or a superthing, but not quite. He still wants to say that in perception we have access to, and thus hook on to, something called "the world," something that is what it is ahistorically and transculturally.

Putnam's claim that linguistic idealists cannot distinguish between thinking about something and merely thinking that one is thinking about it presupposes that genuine aboutness requires something like access—that simply talking about X in norm-governed ways, exchanging reasons for one's beliefs about X, is not enough. But for Hegelians, who hold that there is only the dialogue, that is all one could possibly ask for. To be thinking about beavers or about phlogiston is just to be able to talk about these things. So the question is not "Are we talking about something real?" but rather "Should we continue talking about X, or would it be more profitable to change the subject?" We know how to give reasons to back up our answers to the latter question, but not our answers to the former.

Terms like "the world" and "reality" stand to terms like "stars," "numbers," "phlogiston," and "beavers" as the "fixed ends" that Dewey denounced stand to the "ends-in-view" he praised. You know when you have made progress in your study of phlogiston or of beavers, but you never know when you have made progress in understanding the true nature of reality. You know when a culture has become better able to take hold of bodies and push them around than it was before, but you will never know whether you have grasped The True Nature of the Physical Universe. You can tell when you have achieved more socio-economic equality, but you will never know when you have achieved understanding of The True Meaning of Human Life.

James wanted to follow his friend F. C. S. Schiller in calling the movement they pioneered "humanism," and only later, in tribute to Peirce, decided on pragmatism. We shall only be humanists in Schiller's sense if we resist the temptation to which Parmenides and Plato succumbed—to think that the goal of inquiry is to get in closer touch with something not merely human. To become humanist in this sense requires becoming what Putnam calls a "linguistic idealist." Putnam thinks of this sort of idealism as recent, French, and ephemeral. He describes it as "largely a fashionable 'put-on.'"[41] I think of it as two hundred years old, German in origin, and of world historical significance. As I suggested earlier, it is summed up in Hegel's thesis that Spirit's consciousness of its own freedom culminates in the realization that it is answerable to nothing save itself.

For most of the two hundred years since Hegel wrote, this thesis has been interpreted in terms of Descartes's distinction between immaterial and material substance, with Hegel's "Spirit" being construed as the name of something that has no causal connections with matter. That is why Hegel's idealism has so often been construed (by Royce, for example) as a fancier version of Berkeley's. The de-Cartesianizing of Hegel currently being practiced by Brandom, Pinkard, Pippin, and other recent commentators has let us see that Hegel and Berkeley have nothing in common. We are also coming to see that Hegel's sympathy for the monism common to Parmenides and Spinoza was incompatible with his onward and upward story about Spirit's endless proliferation. Dewey's attempt to synthesize Hegel and Darwin required him to reject the idea of convergence to unity and to welcome unceasing diversification.

I think of Putnam as Deweyan enough to want to get rid of the notion of getting in touch with a superthing, but still Kantian enough to think that there we need fixed ends, regulative ideals, and lofty *Grenzbegriffe*. The common sense of contemporary analytic philosophy is still, alas, largely Kantian. But Hegel is gradually regaining the position he held in the days of Royce and Croce, the days before Russell and Popper convinced us that he was not worth reading. If he manages to displace Kant once and for all, the silver cord that connects Putnam with Parmenides will finally have been cut.

RICHARD RORTY

STANFORD UNIVERSITY
APRIL 2006

NOTES

1. See "Solidarity or Objectivity?" (1984), reprinted in my *Objectivity, Relativism and Truth* (Cambridge: Cambridge University Press, 1991); and "Putnam and the Relativist Menace" (1993), reprinted in my *Truth and Progress* (Cambridge: Cambridge University Press, 1998). The present essay tries to take account of Putnam's publications which post-date the latter article, especially his Dewey Lectures of 1994.

2. Hilary Putnam, *Realism with a Human Face* (Cambridge, MA: Harvard University Press, 1990), 65.

3. "I shouldn't be surprised if ten years hence it [James's forthcoming book, *Pragmatism*] should be rated as 'epoch-making,' for of the definitive triumph of that general way of thinking I can entertain no doubt whatever—I believe it to be something quite like the protestant reformation" (Letter to Henry James, Jr. of May 4, 1907). See also a letter of April 7, 1906 to F. C. S. Schiller, in which James says that he has been led, after reading Papini and Dewey, to grasp the true importance of the movement that Schiller called "humanism" and James called "pragmatism": "I confess that it is only after reading these things [Papini's and Dewey's articles] that I seem to have grasped the full import for life and regeneration, the *great* perspective of the programme, and the renovating character *for all things*, of Humanism."

4. Hilary Putnam, *The Threefold Cord: Mind, Body, and World* (New York: Columbia University Press, 2000), 4.

5. G. W. F. Hegel, *Encyclopedia* (New York: Philosophical Library, 1959), paragraph 377, Zusatz: "*Ein durchaus Anderes is fuer den Geist gar nicht vorhanden.*"

6. Robert Brandom, "Pragmatics and Pragmatisms" in *Hilary Putnam: Pragmatism and Realism*, ed. James Conant and Urszula M. Zeglen (London: Routledge, 2002), 215 [note]. Putnam replies to Brandom, but confines himself to exegetical remarks (59–65).

7. I have developed this Hegelian point at tedious length in various writings. So I was startled to find Putnam saying that I "see language games as virtually automatic performances" (*Pragmatism: An Open Question* [Cambridge: Blackwell, 1995], 34). Ever since I read Sellars as a graduate student, I have been insisting, as he did, on the difference between conformity to norms and quasi-mechanical automaticity. See, for example, my "Pragmatism, Categories and Language," *Philosophical Review* 70, no. 2 (April 1961): 197–223. I do not think that I have ever attempted the task Putnam rightly describes as hopeless: "trying to show that the referential directedness of our thinking at the objects we think about can be constituted out of, or in some way 'reduced to,' the *causal* impacts of those objects upon us" (Putnam, *The Threefold Cord*, 43–44).

8. Putnam, "Reply to Brandom," in *Hilary Putnam: Pragmatism and Realism*, 59.

9. See John Dewey, *Reconstruction in Philosophy*, in *The Middle Works of John Dewey*, vol. 12 (Carbondale, IL: Southern Illinois University Press, 1982), 181: "the process of growth, of improvement and progress, rather than the static outcome and result, becomes the significant thing. . . . The end is no longer a terminus or limit to be reached. It is the active process of transforming the existent situation. Not perfection as a final goal, but the ever-enduring process of perfecting, maturing, refining is the aim in living. . . . Growth itself is the only moral end." For a sample polemic against "fixed ends," see *Reconstruction*, 119–20.

10. See "Is Truth a Goal of Inquiry?: Davidson vs. Wright," a review article about Wright's *Truth and Objectivity*, reprinted in my *Truth and Progress*.

11. This and the previous quotation are from Hilary Putnam, *Reason, Truth and History* (Cambridge: Cambridge University Press, 1980), 216.

12. See Putnam, *The Collapse of the Fact/Value Dichotomy and Other Essays* (Cambridge, MA: Harvard University Press, 2002), 143; and *Pragmatism and Realism*, 74.

13. Putnam, *Realism with a Human Face*, 171.

14. Putnam, *The Collapse of the Fact/Value Dichotomy*, 107.

15. Putnam, *The Threefold Cord*, 4.

16. Putnam, *Pragmatism*, 75. I return to the topic of "linguistic idealism" in the final section of this paper.

17. Putnam, *The Threefold Cord*, 6.

18. Ibid., 178.

19. Ibid., 7.

20. Ibid., 9.

21. Putnam, *Reason, Truth and History*, xi.

22. This picture of inquiry shared by all those who agree with Ernest Sosa that: once everything intentional and semantic is settled, once it is settled what people are believing through their brain or mind or soul states and what people are saying through their utterances, but without it being settled which are true and which are not, and once it is settled what reality is nonintentionally and nonsemantically like, that is, what individuals exist and how they are propertied and interrelated—once all this is antecedently settled, surely it must follow, as a supervenient necessary consequence of all this, which beliefs or sayings are true and which are not true. (Sosa, "Epistemology and Primitive Truth" in *The Nature of Truth: Classic and Contemporary Perspectives*, ed. Michael Lynch (Cambridge, MA: MIT Press, 2001), 659–60. Philosophy of mind and language is divided, these days, into two camps. Philosophers in the former camp hold that one can "in principle" settle all intentional and semantic questions independently of finding out what individuals exist and how they are propertied and interrelated, and conversely. The smaller camp, containing Putnam, Davidson, Brandom, and their followers do not think that one can do that.

23. Putnam, *The Threefold Cord*, 9.

24. Putnam, *Pragmatism*, 38.

25. Ibid.

26. Putnam, *Realism with a Human Face*, 178.

27. Putnam, *The Threefold Cord*, 182.

28. Ibid., 9.

29. McDowell says this in the course of responding to Robert Pippin in *Reading McDowell* (New York: Routledge, 2002), 275. Hegelians like Pippin and Brandom are wrong, McDowell says, to think that "we can make sense of discourse-governing social norms prior to and independently of objective purport." For Brandom, it is enough to explain how the notion of "talking about the same thing" comes into the language. If one has that notion, one does not also need that of "objective purport." The former notion is applied to familiar things (physical objects, number, moral obligations), whereas the latter requires explication by reference to a superthing—the sort of superthing that makes impressions on what McDowell calls "our faculty of receptivity." Hegelians do not believe that we have such a faculty, and Pippin and Brandom do not see that McDowell's notion of that faculty being "conceptualized" by "second nature" helps. At p. 69 of *Reading McDowell*, Pippin articulates the Herderian side of Hegelianism by saying "Given the unbelievable variety in human culture, it seems safe to say that first nature radically underdetermines, even when it conditions, any second nature." The Hegelian strategy is to contrast cultures with other cultures, rather than Culture as a whole with Nature as a whole.

30. Putnam, *The Threefold Cord*, 9.

31. Ibid., 13.

32. Putnam [quoting William James], *Pragmatism*, 67.

33. Putnam, *The Threefold Cord*, 12.

34. Ibid., 43.

35. Ibid., 44.

36. Here is Brandom's description of it in the latter terms: "Treating an assertion as expressing knowledge—attributing to the asserter entitlement to the commitment undertaken thereby and endorsing that commitment oneself—is the response that constitutes the practical recognition of the authority that is implicitly claimed by the assertion. For that is the authority to license undertakings of commitment to that same claim by those in the audience, in virtue of the asserter's entitlement to the commitment" (*Making It Explicit* [Cambridge, MA: Harvard University Press, 1994], 203).

37. Putnam, *Pragmatism*, 65.

38. Putnam, *Words and Life* (Cambridge, MA: Harvard University Press, 1994), 287.

39. Putnam, *Reason, Truth and History*, 123–24.

40. Brandom, *Making It Explicit*, 287–88.

41. Putnam, *Pragmatism*, 75.

REPLY TO RICHARD RORTY

On Feb. 8, 2007, four months to the day before he died, I received the following heartbreaking message from Richard Rorty:

> I had hoped to do one last revision of the paper for your LLP volume before sending it off to Auxier, but when I got diagnosed I gave up such plans. It's a bit rambling, but I hope it contains some points that you will enjoy discussing. It's nice to think of your reading it out loud.

Richard referred to my reading his paper out loud because I had told him that as soon as I received it I did just that: I read it out loud to Ruth Anna. He was, over many years, both a personal friend and a philosopher with whom I loved to argue. I do not think either of us ever succeeded in changing the other's mind, but I know that thinking about the issues he raised was enormously valuable for me, and I believe he would say the same about me were he alive today. And if he *were* alive, I would certainly reply to his essay by marshalling the best arguments against what he says in it that I could think of, and I know we would both enjoy the "combat." But he is not alive, and I simply cannot bring myself to "reply" in the conventional way in his absence. Instead, I will mainly reflect in a general way on the kind of philosopher he was, and on the differences between our philosophical outlooks. As far as the arguments in his present essay are concerned, I will confine myself to pointing out a few places where his description of my views might mislead the unwary reader. (But I will try to keep those discussions brief.) Mainly, I want to describe Rorty as I knew him—a truly unique philosopher and a "gadfly" in the best tradition of the term. I doubt that there was or will be another like him.

I. RORTY'S CARNAPIAN BEGINNINGS AND THEIR INFLUENCE

Richard Rorty was Carnap's student at the University of Chicago, where he received his Ph.D. in 1956. When I wrote a memorial minute about

Rorty for the *Proceedings of the American Philosophical Society*[1] (not to be confused with the American Philosophical Association), I wrote that he "did not repudiate [that influence] until his famous 'turn' against the idea of 'scientific philosophy' in 1972."[2] Recently, however, I find myself thinking about the parts of Carnap's philosophy, or perhaps I should say "the aspects of Carnap's philosophical spirit," that Rorty did *not* "repudiate." (Perhaps part of the reason is that I also knew and was influenced by Carnap, and I have found myself thinking about him a good deal in recent years.) Carnap was an opponent of metaphysics from his time as a graduate student at Jena (which does not mean there was no metaphysics in his views; but it does mean there is nothing he *recognized* as metaphysics in them); that opposition to metaphysics is something that Rorty shared with his old teacher. Moreover, questions of the form "Are so and sos *real*" were often cited by Carnap as examples of metaphysical "nonsense," and the notion of "reality" is precisely Rorty's target in the present essay. Even a distrust of the notion of *truth* was something that Carnap exhibited, until Tarski convinced Carnap that a purely deflationary notion of truth was acceptable.[3] What changed with "The World Well Lost" was that Rorty broke with the idea that sticking to scientific language is the way to avoid "metaphysics." But I think it is important to see that breaking with Logical Positivism on *that* issue only reinforced Rorty's belief in the sheer awfulness of metaphysics, a belief he shared with Carnap. And, although this is not as much appreciated as it should be, even the claim that metaphysics is bad not just for intellectual reasons, but because it leads to evil and authoritarian politics was a feature of Carnap's thought, as well as of the other two signers of the manifesto of "the Vienna Circle."[4] However, for Rorty it was not scientific language that would liberate us, but *creative* language. We should not try to be "scientific socialists," as Rorty's Trotskyist father had thought, but ironic poetic democrats, creators of new visions for ourselves and for society.

II. BUT . . .

But Rorty's talk of irony, poetry, "new metaphors," and the like, did not mean that he was politically irresponsible. He rejected revolutionary leftism as, on the whole, a disaster ("Lenin and Trotsky did more harm than good"[5]), but he also rejected the political posturing of his fellow Derrida-admirers, writing about the so-called "culture wars" of the eighties and nineties, "I am distrusted by both the 'orthodox' side . . . and the 'postmodern' side . . . because I think that the 'postmoderns' are philosophically right though politically silly, and that the 'orthodox' are philosophically wrong as well as politically dangerous." These two aspects of Rorty's thought, the raging against the idea of objective truth, and the appeal for political responsibility (which do not seem to *me* to be particularly compatible) are especially prominent in a book much of which I like very much, Rorty's *Achieving Our Country*.[6] In that book, not only did Rorty accuse the cultural left of abandoning economic issues at precisely the time when they are most important, but he poured scorn on claims for the political relevance of what the postmoderns were calling "theory": "Recent attempts to subvert social institutions by problematizing concepts have produced a few very good books. They have also produced many thousands of books which represent scholastic philosophizing at its worse."[7] Even authors who normally receive high praise from Rorty—Nietzsche, Heidegger, Foucault, and Derrida—are criticized. For, although Rorty sympathizes with what he sees as the antimetaphysical thrust of their writing, he adds that "insofar as these antimetaphysical, anti-Cartesian philosophers offer a quasi-religious form of spiritual pathos, they should be related to private life and not taken as guides to political deliberation. . . . Emphasizing the impossibility of meaning, or of justice, as Derrida sometimes does, is a temptation to Gothicize—to view democratic politics as ineffectual, because unable to cope with preternatural forces."[8] And once again, Rorty appeals for a Left that is willing to be pragmatic, to form alliances, to engage in electoral politics and to eschew the rhetoric of revolution.

Not surprisingly, Rorty frames all of this in terms of his own version of pragmatism. "The culminating achievement of Dewey's philosophy," Rorty tells us, "was to treat evaluative terms such as 'true' and 'right' not as signifying a relation to some antecedently existing thing—such as God's Will, or Moral Law, or the Intrinsic Nature of Objective Reality—but as expressions of satisfaction at having found a solution to a problem: a problem which may someday seem obsolete, and a satisfaction which may someday seem misplaced."[9] But Rorty misreads Dewey here. First of all, Dewey insists that "satisfaction" by itself is not a good criterion for being valuable; what *is* a good criterion, Dewey argues, is *intelligently evaluated* satisfaction.[10] Secondly, although Rorty insists that "although objectivity is a useful goal when one is trying to calculate means to ends by predicting consequences of action, it is of little relevance when deciding what sort of person or nation to be," it was Dewey who claimed that "plans of remedial procedure [for 'moral evils'] can be projected in objective terms."[11] No notion is more central or more insistent in Dewey's writing than the notion of the *objective* resolution of a problematical situation.

If Rorty's views do not really derive from Dewey, from whence do they derive? In effect, Rorty argues as follows:

1. There is no God whose Will we should try to realize.
2. Belief in objective moral prescriptions is just another form of the yearning for a transcendent authority to tell us what to do.
3. Belief in objective truth (equated by Rorty with belief in an "intrinsic nature of things") is just another form of the same yearning.

The problem with this is that the alternatives are manifestly not exhaustive. Thus, a theological liberal will reject Rorty's assumption that belief in God is the same as belief that one has infallible knowledge of God's Will. Not all religious people are fundamentalists. Similarly, Rorty's equation of *trying to find an answer to the question "what human beings should be like"* with *hoping for "authoritative guidance"*[12] ignores the possibility of trying to find an answer to that question without hoping for authoritative guidance. And likewise the belief most of us share, that one can sometimes say what the facts are (and that their being the facts is independent of our will) without believing in a metaphysics of "intrinsic natures." If Rorty found that the "postmoderns" are philosophically right though politically silly, and that the "orthodox" are philosophically wrong as well as politically dangerous, I found Rorty himself to be philosophically wrong but politically hard-headed.

III. Rorty's Description of My View of Reality

After a fascinating description of the ways in which Brandom's criticisms led Rorty to change certain views, Rorty turns to things that I said in *The Threefold Cord: Mind, Body and World.* In particular, he writes,

> My problem with Putnam's attempt to find a position intermediate between Williams's and mine is that I cannot see why, once he has denied that the word "reality" refers to a single superthing, he should still object to James's claim that "we create the subjects as well of our true as of our false propositions." Obviously Putnam does not think that James intended "create" to mean "cause to come into existence," any more than he himself meant to describe causal relations when he wrote, in *Reason, Truth and History*, that "the mind and the world jointly make up the mind and the world." So I would read James's claim about the subjects of our true propositions as saying simply that we create what Ian Hacking calls "truth-candidates." When James says that "the world stands really malleable" and that "man engenders truth upon the world," I take him to be agreeing with Putnam that no superthing determines which of our truth-candidates are somehow legitimate and which not. For legitimation

is not given by something nonhuman, but by the relative utility of various competing truth-candidates for the attainment of human ends-in-view.

A comment on this: as I explained in *The Threefold Cord*, I believe that our notion of reality is an extendible one, in much the way that the hierarchy of levels of language familiar from Tarski is intrinsically extendible, as is the hierarchy of sets familiar from Zermelo and his successors. (I find nothing contradictory in the notion that some concepts are essentially extendible.) I also continue to defend the idea of "ontological relativity"; as I explain in my reply to Ben-Menahem, at the beginning of my "internal realist" period (1976–1990) I used the existence of equivalent descriptions that have different "ontologies" as an argument against realism and for "verificationist semantics," but my present view is that it is perfectly possible to be a metaphysical realist, in a wide sense of the term, and to accept the existence of such pairs of descriptions. I do still agree with William James that reality does not dictate one unique ontology to us is; as he once put it:

> The world *per se* may be likened to a cast of beans on a table. By themselves they spell nothing. An onlooker may group them as he likes. He may simply count them all and map them. He may select groups and name these capriciously, or name them to suit certain extrinsic purposes of his. Whatever he does, so long as he *takes account of them*, his account is neither false nor irrelevant. If neither, why not call it true? It *fits* the beans-*minus*-him, and expresses the *total* fact, of beans-*plus*-him. Truth in this total sense is partially ambiguous, then. If he simply counts or maps, he obeys a subjective interest as much as if he traces figures. Let that stand for pure "intellectual" treatment of the beans, while grouping them variously stands for non-intellectual interests. All that . . . I contend for is that there is *no* "truth" without *some* interest, and that non-intellectual interests play a part as well as the intellectual ones. Whereupon we are accused of denying the beans, or denying being in anyway constrained by them! It's too silly![13]

It seems to me that Rorty was one who thought that James denies being in any way constrained by "the beans"! But James is partly to blame for the misleading formulation that Rorty quoted; what we create are conceptual schemes, not the "subjects of our propositions." Because I describe my view more fully on this question in my reply to Ben-Menahem, I will not expand on this here, but I will repeat one sentence from that reply which compactly summarizes my present view: "even if 'bosons' and 'fermions' are sometimes artifacts of the representation of a quantum mechanical system that we choose, as many physicists contend, the system is mind-independently real, for all that, and each of its states is a mind-independently real condition, albeit one that can be represented in each of these different ways."

IV. RORTY'S DESCRIPTION OF MY VIEW OF PERCEPTION

Rorty's description of my view of perception in section III of his essay is correct. One comment: at one point in the section he writes, "Putnam here elides a distinction upon which I have insisted: that between 'the world' (a notion which, I argued, which we would be better off without) and the collection of entities such as stars, people, beavers, numbers, poems, governments, and positrons. This is the difference between something we can never be sure that we are in touch with and an assortment of things that nobody has ever been able to doubt that we are in touch with." The admission that we are "in touch with" all the objects Rorty lists sounds surprisingly realist for Rorty. However, I cannot understand how Rorty thought he could *say* that we are "in touch" with people, beavers, numbers, poems, governments, and positrons if the words in the very sentence I just quoted do not stand in any relation to those very objects; or if they do, why was "representationalism" supposed to be a "no-no"?

V. RORTY ON LINGUISTIC IDEALISM AND RELATIVISM

I do not simply identify "relativism" and "linguistic idealism." But I *have* accused Rorty of both. Here is a brief explanation of my reasons (which I wish to clarify, not to argue for, in this reply):

(1) *Relativism.* Years ago, I mistakenly accused Rorty of "relativism" with respect to *truth* (in the same paper, I spoke of "cultural imperialism," and that is the term I should have used[14]). One of my arguments was that if "true" is simply an adjective of commendation (like "thanks"), and what we care about is admitted to be "ethnocentric," then cross-cultural comparisons are also ethnocentric: what the other culture values, believes, and so on is simply what it comes out valuing, believing, and so on according to *our* translation scheme, and there is no objective rightness to that translation scheme (to our "social norms," in the Brandomesque language Rorty preferred in the present essay).

With respect to *justification*, on the other hand, Rorty was a textbook example of a "relativist." (His formulation was "I view warrant as a sociological matter, to be ascertained by observing the reception of S's statements by her peers."[15])

(2) *Linguistic idealism*. Rorty's account of my alternative to linguistic idealism is based on a single sentence in *Reason, Truth and History*, and not on anything I have written since 1981.[16] He writes: "I think of Putnam as Deweyan enough to want to get rid of the notion of getting in touch with a superthing, but still Kantian enough to think that there we need fixed ends, regulative ideals, and lofty *Grenzbegriffe*." I think we are "in touch," not only causally but also semantically with all the things Rorty lists ("stars, people, beavers, numbers, poems, governments, and positrons") and much more besides. What I was not willing to say in my "internal realist period" was that the notion of making true and approximately true statements about such things does not need to be cashed out in terms of justification, and certainly not in terms of converging to what would be justified under "ideal conditions." Rorty thinks of our perceptual reports as "learned linguistic reactions to environmental or neural states" and our theoretical judgments as linguistic reactions that help us "cope." I see them as descriptions of a world we often succeed in both perceiving and theorizing about.

I feel sad at ending this paper, because it is, in a way, my last conversation with Richard Rorty, even if it has to be a one-sided one.

H.P.

NOTES

1. Hilary Putnam, "Richard Rorty," *Proceedings of the American Philosophical Society* 153, no. 2, (June 2009).

2. The reference is to Rorty's address to the American Philosophical Association in 1972 titled "The World Well Lost." It was published in the *Journal of Philosophy* 69 (1972): 649–65.

3. As I point out in a note to my reply to Gary Ebbs's essay, Thomas Ricketts has denied that Carnap once thought that the notion of truth was metaphysical (in his "Carnap: From Logical Syntax to Semantics" in *Origins of Logical Empiricism*, ed. Ronald N. Giere, Alan W. Richardson [Minneapolis: University of Minnesota Press, 1996], 231–50), however I feel sure that Ricketts is wrong about this.

4. The other signers were Herbert Feigl and Otto Neurath. For details, see Peter Galison, "Aufbau/Bauhaus: Logical Positivism and Architectural Modernism," *Critical Inquiry* 16 (1990): 709–52. For the text of the manifesto, see: "The Scientific Conception of the World: The Vienna Circle" in *The Emergence of Logical Empiricism: From 1900 to the Vienna Circle*, ed. Sahotra Sarkar (New York: Garland Publishing, 1996), 321–40.

5. Richard Rorty, "Trotsky and the Wild Orchids," in *Philosophy and Social Hope* (London: Penguin, 1992), 18.

6. Richard Rorty, *Achieving Our Country: Leftist Thought in Twentieth-Century America* (Cambridge, MA: Harvard University Press, 1988).

7. Ibid., 93.

8. Ibid., 97.

9. Ibid., 28.

10. See my "Dewey's Central Insight" in *John Dewey's Educational Philosophy in International Perspective*, ed. Larry A Hickman and Giuseppe Spadafora, *A New Democracy for the Twenty-First Century* (Carbondale, IL: Southern Illinois University Press, 2009), 7–21.

11. John Dewey, *Logic: The Theory of Inquiry* (New York: Henry Holt and Co., 1938), 495.

12. Rorty, *Achieving Our Country*, 23.

13. *The Letters of William James*, vol. 2, ed. Henry James (Boston: *Atlantic Monthly Press*, 1920), 295–96.

14. The paper in question is my, "Why Reason Can't Be Naturalized," in *Realism and Reason: Philosophical Papers*, vol. 3 (Cambridge: Cambridge University Press, 1983).

15. Richard Rorty, "Putnam and the Relativist Menace," *Journal of Philosophy* 90 (1993): 443–61, 449.

16. The sentence, which occurs on page 216 of *Reason, Truth and History*, is "The very fact that we speak of our different conceptions as different conceptions of rationality posits a *Grenzbegriff*, a limit-concept of the ideal truth."

PART THREE

BIBLIOGRAPHY OF THE WRITINGS OF HILARY PUTNAM

Compiled and Edited by
JOHN R. SHOOK

with the assistance of
HILARY PUTNAM AND JOSEPH PALENCIK

BIBLIOGRAPHY OF THE WRITINGS OF HILARY PUTNAM

This bibliography lists books and then shorter writings, in chronological order of their first publication. Chapters of books are accompanied by a year of first publication; those chapters lacking a year were first published in that book. Only selected reprintings of shorter writings are mentioned, to clarify multiple versions. A translation of a shorter item is included if that was its first publication; any later publication in English is mentioned.

BOOKS

The Meaning of the Concept of Probability in Application to Finite Sequences. Ph.D. dissertation, University of California, Los Angeles, 1951. New York: Garland, 1990. The 1990 reprinting includes "Introduction Some Years Later," 1–12.

Philosophy of Mathematics: Selected Readings. Edited with Paul Benacerraf. Englewood Cliffs, NJ: Prentice Hall, 1964. Includes an "Introduction" with Paul Benacerraf, 1–27. The 2nd edition (Cambridge, UK: Cambridge University Press, 1983) adds two chapters by Putnam: "Mathematics without Foundations" (1967), 295–313; and "Models and Reality" (1980), 421–45.

Philosophy of Logic. New York: Harper and Row, 1971. London: George Allen and Unwin, 1972. Translated into Italian (1975), Japanese (1975), Chinese (1984). Repr. in *Mathematics, Matter and Method*, 2nd ed. (1985), 323–57. Repr., London: Routledge, 2010.

CONTENTS

Preface, vii
1. What Logic Is, 3–7
2. The Nominalism-Realism Issue, 9–23
3. The Nominalism-Realism Issue and Logic, 25–32
4. Logic versus Mathematics, 33–34
5. The Inadequacy of Nominalistic Language, 35–43
6. Predicative versus Impredicative Conceptions of "Sets," 45–51
7. How Much Set Theory is Really Indispensable for Science?, 53–56
8. Indispensability Arguments, 57–74
9. Unconsidered Complications, 75–76

Mathematics, Matter and Method. Philosophical Papers, volume 1. Cambridge, MA: Cambridge University Press, 1975. The 2nd edition (Cambridge, UK: Cambridge University Press, 1979) adds "Philosophy of Logic" (1971), 323–57. Translated into Italian (1993).

CONTENTS

Mind, Language and Reality. Philosophical Papers, volume 2. Cambridge, MA: Cambridge University Press, 1975. Translated into Japanese (1975), Italian (1987), Chinese (2012). Chapters 6, 12, 14, 18, 20, 21, and *Philosophy of Logic* (1971) were translated into Russian as *Filosofija soznanija* (1999).

CONTENTS

Meaning and the Moral Sciences. London: Routledge and Kegan Paul, 1978. Translated into Italian (1982), Japanese (1984), Spanish (1991). Repr., London: Routledge, 2010.
CONTENTS
Preface, vii–ix
Introduction, 1–6
1. Meaning and Knowledge, 7–80
2. Literature, Science and Reflection (1976), 83–94
3. Reference and Understanding, 97–119
4. Realism and Reason (1977), 123–38

Reason, Truth and History. Cambridge, MA: Cambridge University Press, 1981. Translated into German (1982), French (1984), Italian (1985), Chinese (1988), Spanish (1988), Japanese (1994), Chinese (1997).
CONTENTS
Preface, ix–xii
1. Brains in a Vat, 1–21
2. A Problem about Reference, 22–48
3. Two Philosophical Perspectives, 49–74
4. Mind and Body, 75–102
5. Two Conceptions of Rationality, 103–26
6. Fact and Value, 127–49
7. Reason and History, 150–73
8. The Impact of Science on Modern Conceptions of Rationality (1981), 174–200
9. Values, Facts and Cognition, 201–16
Appendix (the Permutation Theorem), 217–18

Realism and Reason. Philosophical Papers, volume 3. Cambridge, UK: Cambridge University Press, 1983. Translated into Japanese (1992).
CONTENTS
Introduction: An Overview of the Problem, vii–xviii
1. Models and Reality (1980), 1–25
2. Equivalence (1978), 26–45
3. Possibility and Necessity (1980), 46–68
4. Reference and Truth (1980), 69–86
5. 'Two Dogmas' Revisited (1976), 87–97
6. There Is at Least One *A Priori* Truth (1978), 98–114
7. Analyticity and Apriority: Beyond Wittgenstein and Quine (1979), 115–38
8. Computational Psychology and Interpretation Theory, 139–54
9. Reflections on Goodman's *Ways of Worldmaking* (1979), 155–69
10. Convention: A Theme in Philosophy (1981), 170–83
11. Philosophers and Human Understanding (1981), 184–204
12. Why There Isn't a Ready-made World (1982), 205–28
13. Why Reason Can't Be Naturalized (1982), 229–47
14. Quantum Mechanics and the Observer (1981), 248–71
15. Vagueness and Alternative Logic (1983), 271–86
16. Beyond Historicism, 287–303

Methodology, Epistemology, and Philosophy of Science: Essays in Honour of Wolfgang Stegmüller. Edited with Wilhelm K. Essler and Carl G. Hempel. *Erkenntnis* 19, no. 1–3 (Dordrecht: D. Reidel, May 1983).
Epistemology, Methodology, and Philosophy of Science: Essays in Honour of Carl G. Hempel. Edited with Wilhelm K. Essler and Wolfgang Stegmüller. *Erkenntnis* 22, no. 1 (Dordrecht: D. Reidel, January 1985).

The Many Faces of Realism. La Salle, IL: Open Court, 1987. Translated into Italian (1991), Spanish (1994), Chinese (2005), Polish (2013).

CONTENTS

Representation and Reality. Cambridge, MA: MIT Press, 1988. Translated into French (1990), German (1991), Italian (1993), Spanish (1995), Japanese (1997).

CONTENTS

Realism with a Human Face. Edited by James Conant. Cambridge, MA: Harvard University Press, 1990. Translated into French (1994), Italian (1995), Polish (1998).

CONTENTS

Définitions. Pourquoi ne peut on pas « naturaliser » la raison. Combas, France: Éditions de l'Éclat, 1992. Consists of a translation of "Why Reason Can't Be Naturalized" (in *Philosophical Papers*, vol. 3), accompanied by a nearly fifty-page interview titled "Les voies de la raison. Entretien avec Hilary Putnam par Christian Bouchindhomme."

Renewing Philosophy. Cambridge, MA: Harvard University Press, 1992. Translated into Spanish (1994), German (1997), Italian (1998).

CONTENTS

Pursuits of Reason: Essays in Honor of Stanley Cavell. Edited with Ted Cohen and Paul Guyer. Lubbock: Texas Tech University Press, 1993. Includes two items by Putnam: "Preface: Introducing Cavell," vii–xii; and "Pope's *Essay on Man* and Those 'Happy Pieties'," 513–22.

Von einem realistischen Standpunkt: Schriften zu Sprache und Wirklichkeit. Selected essays translated by Vincent C. Müller. Reinbek and Hamburg: Rowohlt Taschenbuch Verlag, 1993.

Words and Life. Edited by James Conant. Cambridge, MA: Harvard University Press, 1994. Chapters 1–3 and 8–11 were translated into Spanish as *La herencia del pragmatismo* (1997).

CONTENTS

Pragmatism: An Open Question. Oxford: Blackwell, 1995. These lectures delivered in Rome in March 1992 were first published as *Il Pragmatismo: una questione aperta* (1992). Translated into German (1995), Spanish (1999), Dutch (2001).

CONTENTS

The Threefold Cord: Mind, Body, and World. New York: Columbia University Press, 1999. Part One consists of the March 1994 Dewey Lectures at Columbia University, and Part Two consists of the November 1997 Royce Lectures at Brown University. Translated into Spanish (2000), Italian (2003), Japanese (2005). Most of the text of the Royce Lectures was published in Portuguese in two parts as "O Mental e o Físico" and "Correlação Mente-Corpo," trans. Pedro Santosin, *Disputatio: International Journal of Philosophy* (Lisbon) 5 (November 1998): 4–22, 23–46.

CONTENTS

First Afterword. Causation and Explanation, 137–50
Second Afterword. Are Appearances "Qualia"?, 151–75

Enlightenment and Pragmatism. Assen: Koninklijke Van Gorcum, 2001. Repr. in *Ethics without Ontology* (2004), 87–129.

The Collapse of the Fact/Value Dichotomy and Other Essays. Cambridge, MA: Harvard University Press, 2002. Translated into French (2004), Italian (2004), Spanish (2004), Japanese (2006), Portuguese (2008).

CONTENTS

Ethics without Ontology. Cambridge, MA: Harvard University Press, 2004. Translated into Italian (2005), Korean (2006), Japanese (2007), Chinese (2008), Spanish (2013).

CONTENTS

Jewish Philosophy as a Guide to Life: Rosenzweig, Buber, Levinas, Wittgenstein. Bloomington: Indiana University Press, 2008. Translated into French (2011), Italian (2011), Spanish (2011), Hebrew (2012), Japanese (2013).

CONTENTS

The End of Value-Free Economics. Edited with Vivian Walsh. London and New York: Routledge, 2012. This volume includes these chapters by Putnam:

Philosophy in an Age of Science: Physics, Mathematics and Skepticism. Edited by Mario De Caro and David Macarthur. Cambridge, MA: Harvard University Press, 2012. Translated into Italian (2012).

CONTENTS

Strawson and Skepticism (1998), 535–51
Philosophy as the Education of Grownups: Stanley Cavell and Skepticism (2006), 552–64
PART SIX. Experience and Mind
The Depths and Shallows of Experience (2005), 567–83
Aristotle's Mind and the Contemporary Mind (2000), 584–607
Functionalism: Cognitive Science or Science Fiction? (1997), 608–23
How to Be a Sophisticated "Naïve Realist," 624–39

SHORTER WRITINGS

1954

1954a. "Synonymity, and the Analysis of Belief Sentences." *Analysis* 14.5 (April 1954): 114–22.

1955

1956

1956a. "A Definition of Degree of Confirmation for Very Rich Languages." *Philosophy of Science* 23.1 (January 1956): 58–62.
1956b. "Mathematics and the Existence of Abstract Entities." *Philosophical Studies* 7.6 (December 1956): 81–88.
"Red, Greens, and Logical Analysis." *Philosophical Review* 65.2 (April 1956): 206–17.

1957

1957a. "Arithmetic Models for Consistent Formulae of Quantification Theory." Abstract. *Journal of Symbolic Logic* 22.1 (March 1957): 110–11.
1957b. "Decidability and Essential Undecidability." *Journal of Symbolic Logic* 22.1 (March 1957): 39–54.
1957c. "Eine Unableitbarkeitsbeweismethode für den Intuitionistischen Aussagenkalkül." With Georg Kreisel. *Archiv für Mathematische Logik und Grundlagenforschung* 3.1–2 (1957): 74–78.
1957d. "Psychological Concepts, Explication, and Ordinary Language." *Journal of Philosophy* 54.4 (14 February 1957): 94–100.
1957e. "Red and Green All Over Again: A Rejoinder to Arthur Pap." *Philosophical Review* 66.1 (January 1957): 100–103.
1957f. "Review of Hugues Leblanc's *An Introduction to Deductive Logic*." *Philosophical Review* 66.4 (October 1957): 551–54.
1957g. "Review of Rupert Crawshay-Williams, 'Equivocal Confirmation'." *Journal of Symbolic Logic* 22.4 (December 1957): 406–7.
1957h. "Three-Valued Logic." *Philosophical Studies* 8.5 (October 1957): 73–80. Repr. in *Mathematics, Matter and Method* (1975), 166–73.

1958

1958a. "Elementary Logic and Foundations of Set Theory." *Philosophy in the Mid-Century*, ed. Raymond Klibansky (Florence: La Nuova Italia Editrice, 1958), 56–61.

1958b. "Feasible Computational Methods in the Propositional Calculus." With Martin Davis. Troy, N.Y.: Rensselaer Polytechnic Institute, Research Division (October 1958).

1958c. "Formalization of the Concept 'About'." *Philosophy of Science* 25.2 (April 1958): 125–30.

1958d. "Reductions of Hilbert's Tenth Problem." With Martin Davis. *Journal of Symbolic Logic* 23.2 (June 1958): 183–87.

1958e. "Review of John E. Freund, 'On the Problem of Confirmation'." *Journal of Symbolic Logic* 23.1 (March 1958): 76–77.

1958f. "Review of Philipp Frank, *Philosophy of Science: The Link between Science and Philosophy.*" *Science* n.s. 127.3301 (4 April 1958): 750–51.

1958g. "Review of Thomas Storer, 'On Defining "Soluble"—Reply to Bergmann'." *Journal of Symbolic Logic* 23.1 (March 1958): 75–76.

1958h. "Unity of Science as a Working Hypothesis." With Paul Oppenheim. *Concepts, Theories and the Mind-Body Problem*, Minnesota Studies in the Philosophy of Science, vol. 2, ed. Herbert Feigl, Michael Scriven, and Grover Maxwell (Minneapolis: University of Minnesota Press, 1958), 3–36.

1959

1959a. "Memo on 'Conventionalism'." Minnesota Center for the Philosophy of Science (22 March 1959). Repr. in *Mathematics, Matter and Method* (1975), 206–14.

1959b. "Review of Norwood Russell Hanson, *Patterns of Discovery: An Inquiry into the Conceptual Foundations of Science.*" *Science* n.s. 129.3364 (19 June 1959): 1666–67.

1959c. "Review of Raphael M. Robinson, 'Arithmetical Representation of Recursively Enumerable Sets'." *Journal of Symbolic Logic* 24.2 (June 1959): 170–71.

1960

1960a. "A Computing Procedure for Quantification Theory." With Martin Davis. *Journal of the Association for Computing Machinery* 7.3 (July 1960): 201–15.

1960b. "An Unsolvable Problem in Number Theory." *Journal of Symbolic Logic* 25.3 (September 1960): 220–32.

1960c. "Exact Separation of Recursively Enumerable Sets within Theories." With Raymond Smullyan. *Proceedings of the American Mathematical Society* 11.4 (August 1960): 574–77.

1960d. "Minds and Machines." In *Dimensions of Mind*, ed. Sidney Hook (New York: New York University Press, 1960), 138–64. Repr. in *Mind, Language and Reality* (1975), 362–85.

1960e. "Review of Max Black, *Problems of Analysis: Philosophical Essays.*" *Journal of Philosophy* 57.1 (7 January 1960): 38–44.

1960f. "Review of Gustav Bergmann, *Philosophy of Science.*" *Philosophical Review* 69.2 (April 1960): 276–77.

"Review of Ernest Nagel and James R. Newman, *Gödel's Proof.*" *Philosophy of Science* 27.2 (April 1960): 205–7.

1961

1961a. "Comments on the Paper of David Sharp." *Philosophy of Science* 28.3 (July 1961): 234–37.

1961b. "The Decision Problem for Exponential Diophantine Equations." With Martin Davis and Julia Robinson. *Annals of Mathematics* 2nd series 74.3 (November 1961): 425–36.

1961c. "Some Issues in the Theory of Grammar." In *Structure of Language and Its Mathematical Aspects. Proceedings of Symposium in Applied Mathematics*, vol. 12 (Providence, RI: American Mathematical Society, 1961), 25–42. Repr. in *Mind, Language and Reality* (1975), 85–106.

1961d. "Uniqueness Ordinals in Higher Constructive Number Classes." *Essays on the Foundations of Mathematics dedicated to A. A. Fraenkel on his Seventieth Anniversary*, ed. Yoshua Bar-Hillel and others (Jerusalem: Magness Press, The Hebrew University, 1961), 190–206.

1962

1962a. "The Analytic and the Synthetic." In *Scientific Explanation, Space, and Time. Minnesota Studies in the Philosophy of Science*, vol. 3, ed. Herbert Feigl and Grover Maxwell (Minneapolis: University of Minnesota Press, 1962), 358–97. Repr. in *Mind, Language and Reality* (1975), 33–69.

1962b. "Dreaming and 'Depth Grammar'." In *Analytical Philosophy, First Series*, ed. R. J. Butler (Oxford: Basil Blackwell, 1962), 211–35. Repr. in *Mind, Language and Reality* (1975), 304–24.

1962c. "It Ain't Necessarily So." *Journal of Philosophy* 59.22 (25 October 1962): 658–71. Repr. in *Mathematics, Matter and Method* (1975), 237–49.

1962d. "On Families of Sets Represented in Theories." *Archiv für Mathematische Logik und Grundlagenforschung* 6.1–2 (1962): 66–70.

1962e. "Review of Hakan Törnebohm, 'On Two Logical Systems Proposed in the Philosophy of Quantum-Mechanics'." *Journal of Symbolic Logic* 27.1 (March 1962): 115.

1962f. "Review of Hans Reichenbach, *The Direction of Time*." *Journal of Philosophy* 59.8 (12 April 1962): 213–16.

1962g. "Review of R. M. Martin, *The Notion of Analytic Truth*." *Philosophy of Science* 29.3 (July 1962): 318–20.

1962h. "What Theories Are Not." *Logic, Methodology and Philosophy of Science*, ed. Ernest Nagel, Patrick Suppes, and Alfred Tarski (Stanford, CA: Stanford University Press, 1962), 240–51. Repr. in *Mathematics, Matter and Method* (1975), 215–27.

1963

1963a. "A Note on Constructible Sets of Integers." *Notre Dame Journal of Formal Logic* 4.4 (October 1963): 270–73.

1963b. "An Examination of Grünbaum's Philosophy of Geometry." In *Philosophy of Science. The Delaware Seminar vol. 2, 1962–1963*, ed. Bernard Baumrin (New York: Interscience/John Wiley, 1963), 205–55. Repr. in *Mathematics, Matter and Method* (1975), 93–129.

1963c. "Brains and Behavior." In *Analytical Philosophy, Second Series*, ed. R. J. Butler (Oxford: Basil Blackwell, 1963), 1–19. Repr. in *Mind, Language and Reality* (1975), 325–41.

1963d. "'Degree of Confirmation' and Inductive Logic." In *The Philosophy of Rudolf Carnap*, ed. Paul A. Schilpp (La Salle, IL: Open Court, 1963), 761–83. Repr. in *Mathematics, Matter and Method* (1975), 270–92.

1963e. "Diophantine Sets over Polynomial Rings." With Martin Davis. *Illinois Journal of Mathematics* 7.2 (June 1963): 251–56.

1963f. "Probability and Confirmation." *The Voice of America Forum Lectures, Philosophy of Science Series*, No. 10 (Washington, D.C.: United States Information Agency, 1963), 1–11. Repr. in *Mathematics, Matter and Method* (1975), 293–304.

1963g. "Review of Georg Henrik von Wright, *Logical Studies.*" *Philosophical Review* 72.2 (April 1963): 242–49.

1963h. "Review of Norwood Russell Hanson, *The Concept of the Positron: A Philosophical Analysis.*" *Science* n.s. 139.3556 (22 February 1963): 745.

1964

1964a. "The Compleat Conversationalist: A 'Systems Approach' to the Philosophy of Language." *Views on General Systems Theory. Proceedings of the Second Systems Symposium at Case Institute of Technology*, ed. Mihajlo D. Mesarovic (New York: John Wiley and Sons, 1964), 89–105.

1964b. "Discussion: Comments on Comments on Comments: A Reply to Margenau and Wigner." *Philosophy of Science* 31.1 (January 1964): 1–6. Repr. in *Mathematics, Matter and Method* (1975), 159–65.

1964c. "Introduction." With Paul Benacerraf. *Philosophy of Mathematics: Selected Readings*, ed. Hilary Putnam and Paul Benacerraf (New York: Prentice-Hall, 1964), 1–27.

1964d. "On Hierarchies and Systems of Notations." *Proceedings of the American Mathematical Society* 15.1 (February 1964): 44–50.

1964e. "Robots: Machines or Artificially Created Life?" *Journal of Philosophy* 61.21 (12 November 1964): 668–91. Repr. in *Mind, Language and Reality* (1975), 386–407.

1965

1965a. "A Philosopher Looks at Quantum Mechanics." *Beyond the Edge of Certainty: Essays in Contemporary Science and Philosophy*, ed. Robert G. Colodny (Englewood Cliffs, NJ: Prentice-Hall, 1965), 75–101. Repr. in *Mathematics, Matter and Method* (1975), 130–58.

1965b. "Craig's Theorem." *Journal of Philosophy* 62.10 (13 May 1965): 251–60. Repr. in *Mathematics, Matter and Method* (1975), 228–36.

1965c. "How Not to Talk about Meaning: Comments on J. J. C. Smart." *Boston Studies in the Philosophy of Science*, vol. 2, ed. Robert S. Cohen and Marx R. Wartofsky (New York: Humanities Press, 1965), 205–22. Repr. in *Mind, Language and Reality* (1975), 117–31.

1965d. "More about 'About'." With Joseph S. Ullian. *Journal of Philosophy* 62.12 (10 June 1965): 305–10.

1965e. "On Minimal and Almost-Minimal Systems of Notations." With David Luckham. *Transactions of the American Mathematical Society* 119.1 (July 1965): 86–100.

1965f. "On the Notational Independence of Various Hierarchies of Degrees of Unsolvability." With Gustav Hensel. *Journal of Symbolic Logic* 30.1 (March 1965): 69–86.

1965g. "Philosophy of Physics." *Aspects of Contemporary American Philosophy*, ed. Franklin H. Donnell, Jr. (Würzburg, Germany: Physica-Verlag, Rudolf Liebing K. G., 1965), 27–40. Repr. in *Mathematics, Matter and Method* (1975), 79–92.

1965h. "Recursively Enumerable Classes and their Application to Recursive Sequences of Formal Theories." With Marian Boykan Pour-El. *Archiv für Mathematische Logik und Grundlagenforschung* 8 (1965): 104–21.

1965i. "Trial and Error Predicates and the Solution to a Problem of Mostowski." *Journal of Symbolic Logic* 30.1 (March 1965): 49–57.

1966

1967

1967a. "The Craig Interpolation Lemma." With Burton Dreben. *Notre Dame Journal of Formal Logic* 8.3 (July 1967): 229–33.

1967b. "The 'Innateness Hypothesis' and Explanatory Models in Linguistics." *Synthese* 17.1 (March 1967): 12–22. Repr. in *Mind, Language and Reality* (1975), 107–16.

1967c. "Mathematics without Foundations." *Journal of Philosophy* 64.1 (19 January 1967): 5–22. Repr. in *Mathematics, Matter and Method* (1975), 43–59. Repr. in *Philosophy of Mathematics: Selected Readings*, 2nd ed. (1983), 295–313.

1967d. "The Mental Life of Some Machines." *Intentionality, Minds and Perception*, ed. Hector-Neri Castañeda (Detroit, MI: Wayne State University Press, 1967), 177–200. Repr. in *Mind, Language and Reality* (1975), 408–28.

1967e. "Psychological Predicates." *Art, Mind and Religion*, ed. William H. Capitan and Daniel D. Merrill (Pittsburgh, PA: University of Pittsburgh Press, 1967), 37–48. Repr. as "The Nature of Mental States" in *Mind, Language and Reality* (1975), 429–40. Repr. in *The Many Faces of Realism* (1987), 150–61.

1967f. "Rejoinder." To Alvin Plantinga. *Intentionality, Minds and Perception*, ed. Hector-Neri Castañeda (Detroit, MI: Wayne State University Press, 1967), 206–13.

1967g. "The Thesis That Mathematics Is Logic." *Bertrand Russell: Philosopher of the Century*, ed. Ralph Schoenman (London: Allen and Unwin, 1967), 273–303. Repr. in *Mathematics, Matter and Method* (1975), 12–42.

1967h. "Time and Physical Geometry." *Journal of Philosophy* 64.8 (27 April 1967): 240–47. Repr. in *Mathematics, Matter and Method* (1975), 198–205.

1968

1968a. "Degrees of Unsolvability of Constructible Sets of Integers." With George Boolos. *Journal of Symbolic Logic* 33.4 (December 1968): 497–513.

1968b. "Is Logic Empirical?" *Boston Studies in the Philosophy of Science*, vol. 5, ed. Robert S. Cohen and Marx W. Wartofsky (Dordrecht: D. Reidel, 1968), 216–41. Repr. as "The Logic of Quantum Mechanics" in *Mathematics, Matter and Method* (1975), 174–97.

1969

1969a. "Logical Positivism and the Philosophy of Mind." *The Legacy of Logical Positivism: Studies in Philosophy of Science*, ed. Peter Achinstein and Samuel Barker (Baltimore, MD: Johns Hopkins Press, 1969), 211–25. Repr. in *Mind, Language and Reality* (1975), 441–51.

1969b. "Normal Models and the Field Σ_1^*." With Gustav Hensel. *Fundamenta Mathematicae* 64 (1969): 231–40.

1969c. "A Recursion-Theoretic Characterization of the Ramified Analytical Hierarchy." With Gustav Hensel and Richard Boyd. *Transactions of the American Mathematical Society* 141 (July 1969): 37–62.

1970

1970a. "A Note on the Hyperarithmetical Hierarchy." With Herbert B. Enderton. *Journal of Symbolic Logic* 35.3 (September 1970): 429–30.

1970b. "Is Semantics Possible?" *Metaphilosophy* 1.3 (July 1970): 187–201. Revised version in *Language, Belief and Metaphysics. Contemporary Philosophic Thought: The International Philosophy Year Conferences at Brockport*, vol. 1, ed. Howard E. Kiefer and Milton K. Munitz (Albany: State University of New York Press, 1970), 50–63. Repr. in *Mind, Language and Reality* (1975), 139–52.

1970c. "Liberalism, Radicalism and Contemporary 'Unrest'." *Metaphilosophy* 1.1 (January 1970): 71–74.

1970d. "On Properties." *Essays in Honor of Carl G. Hempel: A Tribute on the Occasion of his Sixty-Fifth Birthday*, ed. Nicholas Rescher et al. (Dordrecht: D. Reidel, 1970), 235–54. Repr. in *Mathematics, Matter and Method* (1975), 305–22.

1971

1971a. "An Intrinsic Characterization of the Hierarchy of Constructible Sets of Integers." With Stephen Leeds. *Logic Colloquium '69*, ed. Robin O. Grandy and Charles E. M. Yates (Amsterdam: North-Holland, 1971), 311–50.

1972

1972a. "Other Minds." *Logic and Art: Essays in Honor of Nelson Goodman*, ed. Richard Rudner and Israel Scheffler (Indianapolis: Bobbs-Merrill, 1972), 78–99. Repr. in *Mind, Language and Reality* (1975), 342–61.

1973

1973a. "Explanation and Reference." *Conceptual Change*, ed. Glenn Pearce and Patrick Maynard (Dordrecht: D. Reidel, 1973), 199–221. Repr. in *Mind, Language and Reality* (1975), 196–214.

1973b. "Meaning and Reference." *Journal of Philosophy* 70.19 (8 November 1973): 699–711. Expanded version published as "The Meaning of 'Meaning'" (1975).

1973c. "Recursive Functions and Hierarchies." *American Mathematical Monthly, Supplement: Papers in the Foundations of Mathematics* 80.6 part 2 (June-July 1973): 68–86.

1973d. "Reductionism and the Nature of Psychology." *Cognition* 2.1 (1973): 131–46. Repr. in *Words and Life* (1994), 428–40.

1974

1974a. "Comment on Wilfrid Sellars." *Synthese* 27.3–4 (July-August 1974): 445–55.

1974b. "The 'Corroboration' of Theories." *The Philosophy of Karl Popper*, ed. Paul A. Schilpp (La Salle, IL: Open Court, 1974), vol. 1, 221–40. Repr. in *Mathematics, Matter and Method* (1975), 250–69.

1974c. "Discussion." On "Hilary Putnam's 'Scientific Explanation'," in the same volume. With Patrick Suppes, I. B. Cohen, Peter Achinstein, Sylvain Braunberger, Dudley Shapere, Carl Hempel, Thomas Kuhn, and Bas van Fraassen. *The Structure of Scientific Theories*, ed. Frederick Suppes (Urbana: University of Illinois Press, 1974), 437–58.

1974d. "Foreword." To Norman Daniels, *Thomas Reid's 'Inquiry': The Geometry of Visibles and the Case for Realism* (Stanford, CA: Stanford University Press, 1974), i–vii.

1974e. "Hilary Putnam's 'Scientific Explanation'." An Editorial Summary-Abstract. *The Structure of Scientific Theories*, ed. Frederick Suppes (Urbana: University of Illinois Press, 1974), 424–33.

1974f. "How to Think Quantum-Logically." *Synthese* 29.1–4 (December 1974): 55–61.

1974g. "The Refutation of Conventionalism." *Noûs* 8.1 (March 1974): 25–40. Revised version in *Semantics and Philosophy*, ed. Milton K. Munitz and Peter K. Unger (New York: New York University Press, 1974), 215–55. Repr. in *Mind, Language and Reality* (1975), 153–91.

1974h. "Reply to Lugg." *Cognition* 3.3 (1974-75): 295–98.

1974i. "Solution to a Problem of Gandy's." With Stephen Leeds. *Fundamenta Mathematicae* 81.2 (1974): 99–106.

1974j. "Systems of Notations and the Ramified Analytical Hierarchy." With Joan D. Lukas. *Journal of Symbolic Logic* 39.2 (June 1974): 243–53.

1975

1975a. "The Meaning of 'Meaning'." *Language, Mind and Knowledge. Minnesota Studies in the Philosophy of Science*, vol. 7, ed. Keith Gunderson (Minneapolis: University of Minnesota Press, 1975), 131–93. Repr. in *Mind, Language and Reality* (1975), 215–71. Translated into German (1979). Reprinted in *The Twin Earth Chronicles: Twenty Years of Reflection on Hilary Putnam's "The Meaning of 'Meaning',"* ed. Andrew Pessin and Sanford Goldberg (Armonk, NY: M. E. Sharpe, 1996), 3–52.

1975b. "What Is Mathematical Truth?" *Historia Mathematica* 2 (1975): 529–33. Repr. in *Mathematics, Matter and Method* (1975), 60–78.

1976

1976a. "Literature, Science and Reflection." *New Literary History* 7.3 (Spring 1976), 483–91. Repr. in *Meaning and the Moral Sciences* (1978), 83–94.

1976b. "Philosophy of Language and Philosophy of Science." *PSA 1974: Proceedings of the 1974 Biennial Meeting of the Philosophy of Science Association. Boston Studies in the Philosophy of Science*, vol. 32, ed. Robert S. Cohen and Marx W. Wartofsky (Dordrecht: D. Reidel, 1976), 603–10.

1976c. "'Two Dogmas' Revisited." *Contemporary Aspects of Philosophy*, ed. Gilbert Ryle (London: Oriel Press, 1976), 202–13. Repr. in *Realism and Reason* (1983): 87–97.

1976d. "What Is 'Realism'?" *Proceedings of the Aristotelian Society* 76 (1976): 177–94. Portions used in *Meaning and the Moral Sciences* (1978).

1977

1977a. "A Note on 'Progress'." *Erkenntnis* 11.1 (May 1977): 1–4.

1977b. "Realism and Reason." *Proceedings and Addresses of the American Philosophical Association* 50.6 (August 1977): 483–98. Repr. in *Meaning and the Moral Sciences* (1978), 123–38.

1978

1978a. "Deduzione/prova." Trans. A. Collo. *Enciclopedia*, vol. 4 (Torino, Italy: Giulio Einaudi Editore, 1978), 485–501.

1978b. "Equivalenza." Trans. P. Odifreddi. *Enciclopedia*, vol. 5 (Torino, Italy: Giulio Einaudi Editore, 1978), 547–64. English version published as "Equivalence" in *Realism and Reason* (1983), 26–45.

1978c. "Meaning, Reference and Stereotypes." *Meaning and Translation: Philosophical and Linguistic Approaches*, ed. F. Guenthner and M. Guenthner-Reutter (New York: New York University Press; London: Duckworth, 1978), 61–81.

1978d. "The Philosophy of Science: Dialogue with Hilary Putnam." *Men of Ideas: Some Creators of Contemporary Philosophy*, ed. Brian Magee (London: British Broadcasting Corporation, 1978), 224–39.

1978e. "Quantum Logic, Conditional Probability, and Interference." With Michael Friedman. *Dialectica* 32.3–4 (1978): 305–15.

1978f. "Reference and Understanding." *Meaning and the Moral Sciences* (1978), 97–119. Also published in *Meaning and Use*, ed. Avishai Margalit (Dordrecht: D. Reidel, 1979), 199–217.

1978g. "There Is at Least One A Priori Truth." *Erkenntnis* 13.1 (July 1978): 153–70. Repr. in *Realism and Reason* (1983), 98–114.

1979

1979a. "Analyticity and Apriority: Beyond Wittgenstein and Quine." *Studies in Metaphysics. Midwest Studies in Philosophy,* vol. 4, ed. Peter French, Theodore Uehling, and Howard Wettstein (Minneapolis: University of Minnesota Press, 1979), 423–41. Repr. in *Realism and Reason* (1983), 115–38.

1979b. "Comment on 'Empirical Realism and Other Minds'." *Philosophical Investigations* 2 (Fall 1979): 71–72.

1979c. "Formalizzazione." Trans. M. Mamiani. *Enciclopedia*, vol. 6 (Torino, Italy: Giulio Einaudi Editore, 1979), 324–41.

1979d. "Logica." Trans. A. Conte. *Enciclopedia*, vol. 8 (Torino, Italy: Giulio Einaudi Editore, 1979), 491–550.

1979e. "Philosophy of Mathematics: A Report." *Current Research in Philosophy of Science: Proceedings of the P.S.A. Critical Research Problems Conference*, ed. Peter D. Asquith and Henry E. Kyburg, Jr. (East Lansing, MI: Philosophy of Science Association, 1979), 386–98. Repr. as "Philosophy of mathematics: why nothing works" in *Words and Life* (1994), 499–512.

1979f. "The Place of Facts in a World of Values." *The Nature of the Physical Universe: 1976 Nobel Conference*, ed. Douglas Huff and Omer Prewett (New York: John Wiley and Sons, 1979), 113–40. Repr. in *Realism with a Human Face* (1990), 142–62.

1979g. "Reflections on Goodman's *Ways of Worldmaking*." *Journal of Philosophy* 76.11 (November 1979): 603–18. Repr. in *Realism and Reason* (1983), 155–69.

1979h. "Reply to Dummett's Comment." *Meaning and Use*, ed. Avishai Margalit (Dordrecht: D. Reidel, 1979), 226–28.

1979i. "Retrospective Note (1978): A Critic Replies to his Philosopher." *Philosophy as It Is*, ed. Ted Honderich and Myles Burnyeat (Harmondsworth, UK: Penguin, 1979), 377–80.

1980

1980a. "Comments on Chomsky's and Fodor's Replies." *Language and Learning: The Debate between Jean Piaget and Noam Chomsky*, ed. Massimo Piattelli-Palmarini (Cambridge, MA: Harvard University Press; London: Routledge and Kegan Paul, 1980), 335–40.

1980b. "How to Be an Internal Realist and a Transcendental Idealist (at the Same Time)." *Sprache, Logik und Philosophie: Akten des vierten internationalen Wittgenstein Symposiums*, ed. Rudolf Haller and Wolfgang Grassl (Vienna: Hölder-Pichler-Tempski, 1980), 100–108.

1980c. "Models and Reality." *Journal of Symbolic Logic* 45.3 (September 1980): 464–82. Repr. in *Realism and Reason* (1983), 1–25. Repr. in *Philosophy of Mathematics: Selected Readings*, 2nd ed. (1983), 421–45.

1980d. "Possibilità/necessità." Trans. G. Millone. *Enciclopedia*, vol. 10 (Torino, Italy: Giulio Einaudi Editore, 1980), 976–95. English version published as "Possibility and Necessity" in *Realism and Reason* (1983), 46–68.

1980e. "Referenza/verità." Trans. G. Millone. *Enciclopedia*, vol. 11 (Torino, Italy: Giulio Einaudi Editore, 1980), 725–41. English version published as "Reference and Truth" in *Realism and Reason* (1983), 69–86.

1980f. "'Si Dieu est Mort, alors tout est Permi'... (réflexions sur la philosophie du langage)." Trans. Denis Bansard. *Critique* 36 (1980): 791–801.

1980g. "What is Innate and Why: Comments on the Debate." *Language and Learning: The Debate between Jean Piaget and Noam Chomsky*, ed. Massimo Piattelli-Palmarini (Cambridge, MA: Harvard University Press; London: Routledge and Kegan Paul, 1980), 287–309.

1981

1981a. "Answer to a Question from Nancy Cartwright." *Erkenntnis* 16.3 (November 1981): 407–10.

1981b. "Convention: A Theme in Philosophy." *New Literary History* 13.1 (Autumn 1981): 1–14. Repr. in *Realism and Reason* (1983), 170–83.

1981c. "The Impact of Science on Modern Conceptions of Rationality." *Synthese* 46.3 (March 1981): 359–82. Repr. in *Reason, Truth and History* (1981), 174–200.

1981d. "Philosophers and Human Understanding." *Scientific Explanation: Papers Based on Herbert Spencer Lectures Given in the University of Oxford*, ed. A. F. Heath (Oxford: Clarendon Press, 1981), 99–120. Repr. in *Realism and Reason* (1983), 184–204.

1981e. "Quantum Mechanics and the Observer." *Erkenntnis* 16.2 (July 1981): 193–219. Repr. in *Realism and Reason* (1983), 248–70.

1981f. "Ricorsività." Trans. G. Millone. *Enciclopedia*, vol. 12 (Torino, Italy: Giulio Einaudi Editore, 1981), 33–61.

1982

1982a. "Beyond the Fact-Value Dichotomy." *Crítica: Revista Hispanoamericana de Filosofía* (Mexico City) 14.2 (no. 41) (August 1982): 3–11. Repr. as "Beyond the Fact/Value Dichotomy" in *Realism with a Human Face* (1990), 135–41.

1982b. "Comment on Fodor's 'Cognitive Science and the Twin Earth Problem'." *Notre Dame Journal of Formal Logic* 23.3 (July 1982): 294–95.

1982c. "Peirce the Logician." *Historia Mathematica* 9 (1982): 290–301. Repr. in *Realism with a Human Face* (1990), 252–60.

1982d. "Reply to Two Realists." *Journal of Philosophy* 69.10 (October 1982): 575–77. Revised version published as 1982e. "A Defense of Internal Realism" in *Realism with a Human Face* (1990), 30–42.

1982f. "Review of Burleigh Taylor Wilkins, *Has History any Meaning?*" *CLIO: A Journal of Literature, History and the Philosophy of History* 11.3 (Spring 1982): 291–93.

1982g. "Semantical Rules and Misinterpretations: Reply to R. M. Martin." *Philosophy and Phenomenological Research* 42.4 (June 1982): 604–9.

1982h. "Three Kinds of Scientific Realism." *Philosophical Quarterly* 32.4 (July 1982): 195–200. Repr. in *Words and Life* (1994), 492–98.

1982i. "Why Reason Can't Be Naturalized." *Synthese* 52.1 (July 1982): 3–23. Repr. in *Realism and Reason* (1983), 229–47. Translated into French (1992).

1982j. "Why There Isn't a Ready-Made World." *Synthese* 51.2 (May 1982): 141–67. Repr. in *Realism and Reason* (1983), 205–28.

1983

1983a. "Explanation and Reduction." In Hebrew. *Iyyun: The Jerusalem Philosophical Quarterly* 32 (July 1983): 123–37.

1983b. "Foreword to the Fourth Edition." *Fact, Fiction, and Forecast*, by Nelson Goodman (Cambridge, MA: Harvard University Press, 1979), vii–xvi. Repr. as "Nelson Goodman's *Fact, Fiction, and Forecast*" in *Realism with a Human Face* (1990), 303–8.

1983c. "How Not To Solve Ethical Problems." The Lindley Lecture, University of Kansas, March 10, 1983. Lawrence: Department of Philosophy, University of Kansas, 1983. Repr. in *Realism with a Human Face* (1990), 179–92.

1983d. "Is There a Fact of the Matter about Fiction?" *Poetics Today* 4.1 (1983): 77–81. Repr. in *Realism with a Human Face* (1990), 209–13.

1983d. "On Truth." *How Many Questions? Essays in Honor of Sidney Morgenbesser*, ed. Leigh S. Cauman, Isaac Levi, et al. (Indianapolis: Hackett, 1983), 35–56. Repr. in *Words and Life* (1994), 315–29.

1983e. "Probability and the Mental." *Human Meanings and Existence. Jadavpur Studies in Philosophy*, vol. 5, ed. D. P. Chattopadhyaya (New Delhi: Macmillan India, 1983), 163–73. Repr. in *Words and Life* (1994), 376–88.

1983f. "Taking Rules Seriously: A Reply to Martha Nussbaum." *New Literary History* 15.1 (Autumn 1983): 193–200. Repr. as "Taking Rules Seriously" in *Realism with a Human Face* (1990), 193–200.

1983g. "Vagueness and Alternative Logic." *Erkenntnis* 19.1–3 (May 1983): 297–314. Repr. in *Realism and Reason* (1983), 271–86.

1984

1984a. "After Ayer, After Empiricism." Review of A. J. Ayer, *Philosophy in the Twentieth Century. Partisan Review* 51.2 (Spring 1984): 265–75. Revised version published as "After Empiricism" in *Post-Analytic Philosophy*, ed. John Rajchman and Cornel West (New York: Columbia University Press, 1985), 20–30. Repr. in *Realism with a Human Face* (1990), 43–53.

1984b. "The Craving for Objectivity." *New Literary History* 15.2 (Winter 1984): 229–39. Repr. in *Realism with a Human Face* (1990), 120–31.

1984c. "Is the Causal Structure of the Physical Itself Something Physical?" *Causation and Causal Theories. Midwest Studies in Philosophy*, vol. 9, ed. Peter French, Theodore Uehling and Howard Wettstein (Minneapolis: University of Minnesota Press, 1984), 3–16. Repr. in *Realism with a Human Face* (1990), 80–95.

1984d. "Models and Modules." Review of Jerry Fodor's *The Modularity of Mind. Cognition* 17.3 (August 1984): 253–64. Repr. as "Models and Modules: Fodor's *The Modularity of Mind*" in *Words and Life* (1994), 403–15.

1984e. "Proof and Experience." *Proceedings of the American Philosophical Society* 128.1 (March 1984): 31–34.

1984f. *"Realismo e relativismo concettuale: il problema del fatto e del valore."* *Livelli di realtà*, ed. Massimo Piatelli-Palmarini (Milan, Italy: Feltrinelli, 1984), 39–53. This essay is followed by "Discussione" with Bas van Fraassen, A. J. Ayer, R. L. Gregory, André Green, Nelson Goodman, Thomas Bever, and Dan Sperber, 53–65.

1985

1985a. "A Comparison of Something with Something Else." *New Literary History* 17.1 (Autumn 1985): 61–79. Repr. in *Words and Life* (1994), 330–50.

1985b. "A Quick Read Is a Wrong Wright." *Analysis* 45.4 (October 1985): 203.
1985c. "Reflexive Reflections." *Erkenntnis* 22.1 (January 1985): 143–53. Repr. in *Words and Life* (1994), 416–27.

1986

1986a. "Hilary Putnam's Response." *Meaning and Cognitive Structure: Issues in the Computational Theory of Mind*, ed. Zenon W. Pylyshyn and William Demopoulos (Norwood, NJ: Ablex Publishing, 1986), 217–24. "General Discussion of Putnam's Paper" follows, 225–54.
1986b. "How Old Is the Mind?" *Exploring the Concept of Mind*, ed. Richard M. Caplan (Iowa City: University of Iowa Press, 1986), 31–49. Repr. in *Words and Life* (1994), 3–21.
1986c. "Information and the Mental." *Truth and Interpretation: Perspectives on the Philosophy of Donald Davidson*, ed. Ernie Lepore (Oxford: Blasil Blackwell, 1986), 262–71.
1986d. "Meaning and Our Mental Life." *The Kaleidoscope of Science. The Israel Colloquium: Studies in History, Philosophy, and Sociology of Science, vol. 1*, ed. Edna Ulman-Margalit (Dordrecht: D. Reidel, 1986), 17–32.
1986e. "Meaning Holism." *The Philosophy of W. V. Quine*, ed. Lewis E. Hahn and Paul A. Schilpp (La Salle, IL: Open Court, 1986), 405–26. Repr. in *Realism with a Human Face* (1990), 278–302.
1986f. "Rationality in Decision Theory and in Ethics." *Crítica: Revista Hispanoamericana de Filosofía* (Mexico City) 18.3 (no. 54) (December 1986): 3–14. Revised version in *Rationality in Question*, ed. Shlomo Biderman and Ben-Ami Scharfstein (Leiden: E. J. Brill, 1989), 19–28.
1986e. "The Realist Picture and the Idealist Picture." *Philosophie et Culture: Actes de XVIIe Congrès Mondial de Philosophie*, ed. Venant Cauchy (Montréal: Montmorency, 1986), vol. 1, 205–11.

1987

1987a. "The Diversity of the Sciences: Global versus Local Methodological Approaches." *Metaphysics and Morality: Essays in Honor of J. J. C. Smart*, ed. Philip Pettit, Richard Sylan, and Jean Norman (Oxford: Basil Blackwell, 1987), 137–53. Repr. as "The Diversity of the Sciences" in *Words and Life* (1990), 463–80.
1987b. "Meaning Holism and Epistemic Holism." *Theorie der Subjektivität*, ed. Konrad Cramer et al. (Frankfurt am Main: Suhrkamp, 1987), 251–77.
1987c. "Scientific Liberty and Scientific License." *Grazer Philosophische Studien* 13 (1987): 43–51. Repr. in *Realism with a Human Face* (1990), 201–8.
1987d. "Truth and Convention: On Davidson's Refutation of Conceptual Relativism." *Dialectica* 41.1-2 (June 1987): 69–77. Repr. as "Truth and Convention" in *Realism with a Human Face* (1990), 96–104.

1988

1988a. "After Metaphysics, What?" *Metaphysik nach Kant? Stuttgarter Hegel-Kongress 1987*, ed. Dieter Henrich and Rolf-Peter Horstmann (Stuttgart: Klett-Cotta, 1988), 457–66. Repr. as part 2 of "Realism with a Human Face" in *Realism with a Human Face* (1990), 18–29.
1988b. "Review of W. V. O. Quine, *Quiddities: An Intermittently Philosophical Dictionary.*" *London Review of Books* 10.8 (21 April 1988): 11–13. Repr. as "The Greatest Logical Positivist" in *Realism with a Human Face* (1990), 268–77.

1988c. "La objetividad y la distinción ciencia/ética." *Diánoia: Anuario de Filosofía* (Mexico City) 34 (1988): 7–25. English version published as "Objectivity and the Science/Ethics Distinction" in *Realism with a Human Face* (1990), 163–78.

1988d. "Much Ado about Not Very Much." *Daedalus* 117.1 (Winter 1988): 269–81. Repr. as "Artificial Intelligence: Much Ado about Not Very Much" in *Words and Life* (1994), 391–402.

1989

1989a. "Afterthoughts on My Carus Lectures: Philosophy as Anthropology." *Lyceum* (Saint Anselm College) 1.2 (Fall 1989): 40–42.

1989b. "Aloft with Freedom's Banner." *Times Higher Education Supplement*, no. 852 (3 March 1989): 13, 15.

1989c. "An Interview with Professor Hilary Putnam: The Vision and Arguments of a Famous Harvard Philosopher." *Cogito* 3.2 (Summer 1989): 85–91. Repr. in *Key Philosophers in Conversation: The Cogito Interviews*, ed. Andrew Pyle (London and New York: Routledge, 1999), 44–54.

1989d. "Model Theory and the 'Factuality' of Semantics." *Reflections on Chomsky*, ed. Alex George (Oxford: Basil Blackwell, 1989), 213–32. Repr. in *Words and Life* (1994), 351–75.

1989e. "Why Is a Philosopher?" *The Institution of Philosophy: A Discipline in Crisis?* ed. Avner Cohen and Marcello Dascal (La Salle, IL: Open Court, 1989), 61–75. Repr. in *Realism with a Human Face* (1990), 105–19.

1989f. "William James's Ideas." With Ruth Anna Putnam. *Raritan* 8.3 (Winter 1989): 27–44. Repr. in *Realism with a Human Face* (1990), 217–31.

1990

1990a. "A Reconsideration of Deweyan Democracy." *Southern California Law Review* 63.6 (September 1990) 1671–97. Putnam participates in the "Afterword" discussion, 1911–28. Shorter version in *Renewing Philosophy* (1992), 180–200.

1990b. "Epistemology as Hypothesis." With Ruth Anna Putnam. *Transactions of the Charles S. Peirce Society* 26.4 (Fall 1990): 407–33. Repr. as "Dewey's *Logic*: Epistemology as Hypothesis" in *Words and Life* (1994), 198–220.

1990c. "Introduction Some Years Later." *The Meaning of the Concept of Probability in Application to Finite Sequences* (New York: Garland, 1990), 1–12.

1990d. "The Idea of Science." *The Philosophy of the Human Sciences. Midwest Studies in Philosophy*, vol. 15, ed. Peter French, Theodore Uehling, and Howard Wettstein (Notre Dame, IN: University of Notre Dame Press, 1990), 57–64. Repr. in *Words and Life* (1994), 481–91.

1990e. "Preface." *Medical Choices, Medical Chances*, 2nd ed., ed. Harold J. Bursztajn (London and New York: Routledge, 1990), ix–xix.

1990f. "Rorty e Wittgenstein." Trans. Alessandro Pagnini. *Iride: Filosofia e Discussione Pubblica* (Bologna, Italy) 4/5 (January-December 1990): 313–17.

1991

1991a. "Does the Disquotational Theory Really Solve All Philosophical Problems?" *Metaphilosophy* 22.1-2 (January-April 1991): 1–13. Repr. as "Does the Disquotational Theory of Truth Solve All Philosophical Problems?" in *Words and Life* (1994), 264–78.

1991b. "The French Revolution and the Holocaust: Can Ethics Be Ahistorical?" *Culture and Modernity: East-West Philosophical Perspectives*, ed. Eliot Deutsch (Honolulu: University of Hawaii Press, 1991), 299–312. Repr. as "Pragmatism and Relativism: Universal Values and Traditional Ways of Life" in *Words and Life* (1994), 182–97.

1991c. "Il principio di indeterminazione e il progresso scientifico." *Iride: Filosofia e Discussione Pubblica* (Bologna, Italy) 7 (July-December 1991): 9–27.

1991d. "Logical Positivism and Intentionality." *A. J. Ayer Memorial Essays. Philosophy* 30 Supplement (1991): 105–16. Repr. in *Words and Life* (1994), 85–98.

1991e. "Philosophical Reminiscences with Reflections on Firth's Work." *Philosophy and Phenomenological Research* 51.1 (March 1991): 143–47.

1991f. "Preface." To Special Issue on Putnam's Philosophy. *Erkenntnis* 34.3 (May 1991): 269.

1991g. "Reichenbach's Metaphysical Picture." *Erkenntnis* 35.1–3 (July 1991): 61–75. Also published as "Introduction" in Hans Reichenbach, *The Direction of Time* (Berkeley: University of California Press, 1991), ix–xix. Repr. in *Words and Life* (1994), 99–114.

1991g. "Replies and Comments." In Special Issue on Putnam's Philosophy. *Erkenntnis* 34.3 (May 1991): 401–24.

1991h. "Wittgenstein on Religious Belief." *On Community*, ed. Leroy S. Rouner (Notre Dame, IN: University of Notre Dame Press, 1991), 56–75. Repr. in *Renewing Philosophy* (1992), 134–57.

1992

1992a. "Atando Cabos." Trans. Gabriela Montes de Oca Vega and ed. Margarita M. Valdés. *Diánoia: Anuario de Filosofía* (Mexico City) 38 (1992): 1–15. English version published as "Realism without Absolutes," *International Journal of Philosophical Studies* 1.2 (September 1993): 179–92. Repr. in *Words and Life* (1994), 279–94.

1992b. "Changing Aristotle's Mind." With Martha Nussbaum. *Essays on Aristotle's "De Anima,"* ed. Martha C. Nussbaum and Amélie Rorty (Oxford: Oxford University Press, 1992), 27–56. Repr. in *Words and Life* (1994), 22–61.

1992c. "Comments on the Lectures." *Reasoning and the Logic of Things* by Charles S. Peirce, ed. Kenneth Laine Ketner (Cambridge, MA: Harvard University Press, 1992), 55–102.

1992d. "Introduction: The Consequences of Mathematics." With Kenneth Laine Ketner. *Reasoning and the Logic of Things*, by Charles S. Peirce, ed. Kenneth Laine Ketner (Cambridge, MA: Harvard University Press, 1992), 1–54.

1992e. "Replies." In special issue on The Philosophy of Hilary Putnam. *Philosophical Topics* 20.1 (Spring 1992): 347–408.

1992f. "Truth, Activation Vectors and Possession Conditions for Concepts." *Philosophy and Phenomenological Research* 52.2 (June 1992): 431–47.

1992g. "Why Functionalism Didn't Work." *Inference, Explanation and Other Philosophical Frustrations*, ed. John Earman (Berkeley: University of California Press, 1992), 255–70. This paper covers the same ground as, and includes some sentences from, the fifth chapter of *Representation and Reality* (1988). Repr. as "Why Functionalism Didn't Work" in *Words and Life* (1994), 441–59.

1993

1993a. "Aristotle after Wittgenstein." *Modern Thinkers and Ancient Thinkers*, ed. Robert W. Shaples (Boulder, CO: Westview; London: UCL Press, 1993), 117–37. Repr. in *Words and Life* (1994), 62–81.

1993b. "Education for Democracy." With Ruth Anna Putnam. *Educational Theory* 43.4 (Fall 1993): 361–76. Repr. in *Words and Life* (1994), 221–41.

1993c. "Hat Philosophie noch eine Zukunft?" Trans. Constantin Schölkopf. *Philosophie der Gegenwart, Gegenwart der Philosophie*, ed. Herbert Schnädelbach and Geert Keil (Hamburg: Junius, 1993), 21–39.

1993d. "Pope's *Essay on Man* and Those 'Happy Pieties'." *Pursuit of Reason: Essays in Honor of Stanley Cavell* (Lubbock, TX: Texas Tech University Press, 1993), 13–20. Repr. as "The Cultural Impact of Newton: Pope's *Essay on Man* and Those 'Happy Pieties'" in *Words and Life* (1994), 513–22.

1993e. "Preface: Introducing Cavell." *Pursuit of Reason: Essays in Honor of Stanley Cavell* (1993), vii–xii.

1994

1994a. "Afterthoughts on 'Models and Reality'." *Diálogos* 63 (1994): 41, 43, 45. Spanish translation: 40, 42, 44.

1994b. "The Best of All Possible Brains?" Review of Roger Penrose, *Shadows of the Mind*. *New York Times Book Review* 144 (20 November 1994): 7. A longer version was published in 1995.

1994c. "Comments and Replies." *Reading Putnam*, ed. Bob Hale and Peter Clark (Oxford: Blackwell, 1994), 242–95.

1994d. "The Limits of Vindication." *Proceedings of the Ninth International Congress of Logic, Methodology, and Philosophy of Science, Uppsala, Sweden, August 7–14, 1991*, ed. Dag Prawitz, Brian Skyrms, and Dag Westerståhl (Amsterdam: Elsevier Science Publishers, 1994), 867– 82. Repr. as "Reichenbach and the Limits of Vindication" in *Words and Life* (1994), 131–48.

1994e. "Logic and Psychology." *The Logical Foundations of Cognition. Vancouver Studies in Cognitive Science*, vol. 4, ed. John Macnamara and Gonzalo E. Reyes (Oxford: Oxford University Press, 1994), 35–42.

1994f. "Pragmatism and Moral Objectivity." In *Words and Life* (1994), 151–81. Also published in *Women, Culture, and Development: A Study of Human Capabilities*, ed. Martha Nussbaum and Jonathan Glover (Oxford: Oxford University Press, 1995), 199–224.

1994g. "Rethinking Mathematical Necessity." In *Words and Life* (1994), 245–63. Also published as "Mathematical Necessity Reconsidered" in *On Quine: New Essays*, ed. Paolo Leonardi and Marco Santambrogio (Cambridge, UK: Cambridge University Press, 1995), 267–82.

1994h. "Putnam, Hilary." *A Companion to the Philosophy of Mind*, ed. Samuel Guttenplan (Oxford: Blackwell, 1994), 507–13.

1994i. "Sense, Nonsense, and the Senses: An Inquiry into the Powers of the Human Mind." The Dewey Lectures at Columbia University, March 1994. *Journal of Philosophy* 91.9 (September 1994): 445–517. Repr. in *The Threefold Cord* (1999), 3–70. Translated into Spanish as *Sentido, sinsentido y los sentidos*, trans. Norma B. Goethe (Barcelona: Paidós, 2000).

1995

1995a. "Are Moral and Legal Values Made or Discovered?" *Legal Theory* 1.1 (March 1995): 5–19. Revised version published as "Are Values Made or Discovered?" in *The Collapse of the Fact/Value Dichotomy and Other Essays* (2002), 96–110.

1995b. "Further Adventures of Wigner's Friend." With David Z. Albert. *Topoi* 14.1 (March 1995): 17–22.

1994c. "Logical Positivism, the Kantian Tradition, and the Bounds of Sense." *The Philosophy of P. F. Strawson*, ed. Pranab Kumar Sen and Roop Rekha Verma (New Delhi: Indian Council of Philosophical Research, 1995), 145–60.

1994d. "Peirce's Continiuum." *Peirce and Contemporary Thought: Philosophical Inquiries*, en Kenneth L. Ketner (New York: Fordham University Press, 1995), 1–22.

1994e. "Pragmatism." *Proceedings of the Aristotelian Society* 95.3 (March 1995): 291–306.

1994f. "Replies." *Legal Theory* 1.1 (March 1995): 69–80.

1994g. "Review of Roger Penrose, *Shadows of the Mind.*" *Bulletin of the American Mathematical Society* 32.3 (July 1995): 370–73.

1996

1996a. "Introduction." In *The Twin Earth Chronicles: Twenty Years of Reflection on Hilary Putnam's "The Meaning of 'Meaning',"* ed. Andrew Pessin and Sanford Goldberg (Armonk, NY: M. E. Sharpe, 1996), xv–xxii.

1996b. "Must We Choose Between Patriotism and Universal Reason?" *For Love of Country*, ed. Joshua Cohen (Boston: Beacon Press, 1996), 91–97.

1996c. "On Wittgenstein's Philosophy of Mathematics." *Proceedings of the Aristotelian Society* 70 Supplement (1996): 243–64. An expanded version was published as "Was Wittgenstein *Really* an Anti-Realist about Mathematics?" in 2001.

1996d. "Pragmatism and Realism." *Cardozo Law Review* 18.1 (September 1996): 153–70. Repr. in *The Revival of Pragmatism: New Essays on Social Thought, Law, and Culture*, ed. Morris Dickstein (Durham, NC: Duke University Press, 1998), 37–53.

1996e. "The Quarrel between Poetry and Philosophy." With Ruth Anna Putnam. *Bulletin of the Santayana Society* 15 (1996): 1–14.

1996f. "Über die Rationalität von Präferenzen." Trans. Astrid Wagner. *Allgemeine Zeitschrift für Philosophie* 21.3 (1996): 209–28. English version published as "On the Rationality of Preferences" in *The Collapse of the Fact/Value Dichotomy and Other Essays* (2002), 79–95.

1996g. "What-it's-like-ness." Review of Galen Strawson, *Mental Reality*. London Review of Books 18.3 (8 February 1996): 11.

1996h. "What the Spilled Beans Can Spell: The Difficult and Deep Realism of Williams James." With Ruth Anna Putnam. *Times Literary Supplement*, no. 4864 (21 June 1996): 14–15.

1997

1997a. "A Half Century of Philosophy, Viewed from Within." *Daedalus: Proceedings of the American Academy of Arts and Sciences* 126.1 (Winter 1997): 175–208.

1997b. "An Interview with Hilary Putnam." With Giancarlo Marchetti. *Cogito* 11.3 (November 1997): 149–57.

1997c. "Functionalism: Cognitive Science or Science Fiction?" *The Future of the Cognitive Revolution*, ed. David M. Johnson and Christina E. Erneling (Oxford: Oxford University Press, 1997), 32–44. Repr. in *Philosophy in an Age of Science* (2012), 608–23.

1997d. "God and the Philosophers." *Philosophy of Religion. Midwest Studies in Philosophy*, vol. 21, ed. Peter French, Theodore Uehling and Howard Wettstein (Notre Dame, IN: University of Notre Dame Press, 1997), 175–87.

1997e. "James's Theory of Truth." *The Cambridge Companion to William James*, ed. Ruth Anna Putnam (Cambridge, UK: Cambridge University Press, 1997), 166–85.

1997f. "La Importancia del conocimiento no-científico." Trans. Angel García Rodríguez. *Limbo*, supplement to *Revista Teorema* 16.2 (1997): 1–17. A revised version was later published as "Pragmatism and Nonscientific Knowledge" in 2002.

1997g. "On Negative Theology." *Faith and Philosophy* 14.4 (October 1997): 407–22.
1997h. "Review of John McDowell, *Mind and World.*" *Philosophical Review* 106.2 (April 1997): 267–69.
1997i. "Thoughts Addressed to an Analytical Thomist." *Monist* 80.4 (October 1997): 487–99.

1998

1998a. "A Politics of Hope." Review of Richard Rorty, *Achieving Our Country. Times Literary Supplement*, no. 4964 (22 May 1998): 10.
1998b. "Floyd, Wittgenstein and Loneliness." *Loneliness*, ed. Leroy S. Rouner (Notre Dame, IN: University of Notre Dame Press, 1998), 109–14.
1998c. "Kripkean Realism and Wittgenstein's Realism." *The Story of Analytical Philosophy: Plot and Heroes*, ed. Anat Biletzki and Anat Matar (London and New York: Routledge, 1998), 241–52.
1998d. "Skepticism." *Philosophie in Synthetischer Absicht*, ed. Marcelo Stamm (Stuttgart: Klett-Cotta, 1998), 239–68. Revised version published as "Skepticism and Occasion-sensitive Semantics" in *Philosophy in an Age of Science* (2012), 514–34.
1998e. "Strawson and Skepticism." *The Philosophy of P. F. Strawson*, ed. Lewis Hahn (La Salle, IL: Open Court, 1998), 273–87. Most of this essay is contained within "Skepticism" (1998). Repr. in *Philosophy in an Age of Science* (2012), 535–51.
1998f. "The Real William James: Response to Robert Meyers." With Ruth Anna Putnam. *Transactions of the Charles S. Peirce Society* 34.2 (Spring 1998): 366–81.
1998g. "Why Fraternity Cannot be Cloned." *Times Higher Education Supplement*, no. 1317 (30 January 1998): 18–19.

1999

1999a. "Cloning People." *The Genetic Revolution and Human Rights*, ed. Justine Burley (Oxford: Oxford University Press, 1999), 1–13. Repr. in *Philosophy in an Age of Science* (2012), 327–36.
1999b. "Ein Deutscher Dewey." *Neue Züricher Zeitung* 12.133 (13 June 1999): 77.
1999c. "Introduction." *Understanding the Sick and the Healthy: A View of World, Man, and God* by Franz Rosenzweig, trans. Nahum Norbert Glatzer (Cambridge, MA: Harvard University Press, 1999), 1–20. Portions repr. in "Rosenzweig and Wittgenstein" in *Jewish Philosophy as a Guide to Life* (2008), 9–36.

2000

2000a. "A Note on Wittgenstein's 'Notorious Paragraph' about the Gödel Theorem." With Juliet Floyd. *Journal of Philosophy* 97.11 (November 2000): 624–32.
2000b. "Aristotle's Mind and the Contemporary Mind." *Aristotle and Contemporary Science*, ed. Demetra Sfendoni-Mentzou, Jagdish Hattiangadi, and David M. Johnson (New York: Peter Lang, 2000), vol. 1, 7–28. Repr. in *Philosophy in an Age of Science* (2012), 584–607.
2000c. "Carta al lector Espanōl." Preface to the Spanish publication of the 1994 Dewey Lectures as *Sentido, sinsentido y los sentidos*, trans. Norma B. Goethe (Barcelona: Paidós, 2000), 9–16.
2000d. "Das modelltheoretische Argument und die Suche nach dem Realismus des Common Sense" in *Realismus*, ed. Marcus Willaschek (Padeborn, Germany: Ferdinand

Schöningh, 2000), 125–42. Repr. as "Nonstandard Models and Kripke's Proof of the Gödel Theorem" in *Philosophy in an Age of Science* (2012), 263–69.

2000e. "Foreword." To *Kierkegaard, Religion, and Existence* by Avi Sagi (Amsterdam: Editions Rodopi, 2000), vii.

2000f. "Nonstandard Models and Kripke's Proof of the Gödel Theorem." *Notre Dame Journal of Formal Logic* 41.1 (2000): 53–58. Repr. in *Philosophy in an Age of Science* (2012), 263–69.

2000g. "Paradox Revisited I: Truth." *Between Logic and Intuition: Essays in Honor of Charles Parsons*, ed. Gila Sherr and Richard Tieszen (Cambridge, UK: Cambridge University Press, 2000), 3–15. Repr. as "Revisiting the Liar Paradox" in *Philosophy in an Age of Science* (2012), 202–16.

2000h. "Paradox Revisited II: Sets." *Between Logic and Intuition: Essays in Honor of Charles Parsons*, ed. Gila Sherr and Richard Tieszen (Cambridge, UK: Cambridge University Press, 2000), 16–26.

2000i. "Philosophie als umgestaltende Tätigkeit. William James über Moralphilosophie." *Die Renaissance des Pragmatismus: Aktuelle Verflechtungen zwischen analytischer und kontinentaler Philosophie*, ed. Mike Sandbothe (Weilerswist, Germany: Velbrück Wissenschaft, 2000), 234–52. English version published as "Philosophy as a Reconstructive Activity: William James on Moral Philosophy" in *The Pragmatic Turn in Philosophy: Contemporary Engagements Between Analytic and Continental Thought*, ed. William Egginton and Mike Sandbothe (Albany, NY: State University of New York Press, 2004), 31–46.

2000j. "Richard Rorty on Reality and Justification." *Rorty and His Critics*, ed. Robert Brandom (Oxford: Blackwell, 2000), 81–87.

2000k. "Thoughts about Domestic Tranquility / Bne Brak." *Joshua Neustein: Five Ash Cities*, illustrated by Joshua Neustein (Chicago: Academy Chicago Publishers, 2000), 100–108.

2000l. "To Think with Integrity." *Harvard Review of Philosophy* 8 (Spring 2000): 4–13.

2001

2001a. "A Reply by Hilary Putnam." To John Searle's "On Hilary Putnam's Farewell Lecture." *Harvard Review of Philosophy* 9 (Spring 2001): 6.

2001b. "Hans Reichenbach: Realist and Verificationist." *Future Pasts: The Analytic Tradition in Twentieth-Century Philosophy*, ed. Juliet Floyd and Sanford Shieh (Oxford: Oxford University Press, 2001), 277–87.

2001c. "Pragmatism Resurgent: A Reading of *The American Evasion of Philosophy*." *Cornel West: A Critical Reader*, ed. George Yancy (Oxford: Blackwell, 2001), 19–37.

2001d. "Reply to Bernard Williams' 'Philosophy As a Humanistic Discipline'." *Philosophy* 76.4 (October 2001): 605–14.

2001e. "Reply to Charles Travis." *Revue Internationale de Philosophie* 55.4 (December 2001): 525–33.

2001f. "Reply to Jean-Pierre Cometti." *Revue Internationale de Philosophie* 55.4 (December 2001): 457–69.

2001g. "Reply to Jennifer Case." *Revue Internationale de Philosophie* 55.4 (December 2001): 431–38.

2001h. "Reply to Michael Devitt." *Revue Internationale de Philosophie* 55.4 (December 2001): 495–502.

2001i. "Rules, Attunement, and 'Applying Words to the World': The Struggle to Understand Wittgenstein's Vision of Language." *The Legacy of Wittgenstein: Pragmatism or*

Deconstruction, ed. Chantal Mouffe and Ludwig Nagl (New York: Peter Lang, 2001), 9–23. Repr. in *Philosophy in an Age of Science* (2012), 404–20.

2001j. "Skepticism, Stroud and the Contextuality of Knowledge." *Philosophical Explorations* 4.1 (January 2001): 2–16. Repr. in *Philosophy in an Age of Science* (2012), 495–513.

2001k. "Was Wittgenstein *Really* an Anti-Realist about Mathematics?" *Wittgenstein in America*, ed. Timothy McCarthy and Sean C. Stidd (Oxford: Oxford University Press, 2001), 140–94. Repr. in *Philosophy in an Age of Science* (2012), 355–403.

2001l. "Werte und Normen." *Die Öffentlichkeit der Vernunft und die Vernunft der Öffentlichkei. Festschrift für Jürgen Habermas*, ed. Lutz Wingert and Klaus Günther (Frankfurt am Main: Suhrkamp, 2001), 280–313. English version published as "Values and Norms" in *The Collapse of the Fact/Value Dichotomy and Other Essays* (2002), 111–34.

2001m. "When 'Evidence Transcendence' Is Not Malign: A Reply to Crispin Wright." *Journal of Philosophy* 98.11 (November 2001): 594–600.

2002

2002a. "Antwort auf Jürgen Habermas." *Hilary Putnam und die Tradition des americanishen Pragmatismus*, ed. Marie-Luise Raters and Marcus Willaschek (Frankfurt am Main: Suhrkamp, 2002), 306–21.

2002b. "Comment on Charles Travis's Paper." *Hilary Putnam: Pragmatism and Realism*, ed. James Conant and Urszula M. Żegleń (London and New York: Routledge, 2002), 209–10.

2002c. "Comment on Gary Ebb's Paper." *Hilary Putnam: Pragmatism and Realism*, ed. James Conant and Urszula M. Żegleń (London and New York: Routledge, 2002), 186–87.

2002d. "Comment on John Haldane's Paper." *Hilary Putnam: Pragmatism and Realism*, ed. James Conant and Urszula M. Żegleń (London and New York: Routledge, 2002), 105–8.

2002e. "Comment on John Heil's Paper." *Hilary Putnam: Pragmatism and Realism*, ed. James Conant and Urszula M. Żegleń (London and New York: Routledge, 2002), 143.

2002f. "Comment on Nicholas Rescher's Paper." *Hilary Putnam: Pragmatism and Realism*, ed. James Conant and Urszula M. Żegleń (London and New York: Routledge, 2002), 80–85.

2002g. "Comment on Richard Warner's Paper." *Hilary Putnam: Pragmatism and Realism*, ed. James Conant and Urszula M. Żegleń (London and New York: Routledge, 2002), 38–39.

2002h. "Comment on Robert Brandom's Paper." *Hilary Putnam: Pragmatism and Realism*, ed. James Conant and Urszula M. Żegleń (London and New York: Routledge, 2002), 59–65

2002i. "Comment on Ruth Anna Putnam's Paper." *Hilary Putnam: Pragmatism and Realism*, ed. James Conant and Urszula M. Żegleń (London and New York: Routledge, 2002), 12–13.

2002j. "Comment on Tadeusz Szubka's Paper." *Hilary Putnam: Pragmatism and Realism*, ed. James Conant and Urszula M. Żegleń (London and New York: Routledge, 2002), 125–27.

2002k. "Comment on Wolfgang Künne's Paper." *Hilary Putnam: Pragmatism and Realism*, ed. James Conant and Urszula M. Żegleń (London and New York: Routledge, 2002), 166.

2002l. "Introduction." *The Correspondence of William James*, vol. 10, ed. John J. McDermott, Ignas K. Skrupskelis, and Elizabeth M. Berkeley (Charlottesville: University Press of Virginia, 2002), xxv–xlvii.

2002m. "Levinas and Judaism." *The Cambridge Companion to Levinas*, ed. Simon Critchley and Robert Bernasconi (Cambridge, UK: Cambridge University Press, 2002), 33–62. Revised version as "Levinas on What Is Demanded of Us" in *Jewish Philosophy as a Guide to Life* (2008), 68–99.

2002n. "McDowell's Mind and McDowell's World." *Reading McDowell on Mind and World*, ed. Nicholas H. Smith (London and New York: Routledge, 2002), 174–90.

2002o. "Nachwort." To *Die Unheimlichkeit des Gewöhnlichen und andere philosophische Essays* by Stanley Cavell, ed. Davide Sparti and Espen Hammer (Frankfurt am Main: Fischer, 2002), 265–79.

2002p. "Pragmatism and Nonscientific Knowledge." *Hilary Putnam: Pragmatism and Realism*, ed. James Conant and Urszula M. Żegleń (London and New York: Routledge, 2002), 14–24.

2002q. "Quine." *Common Knowledge* 8.2 (April 2002): 273–79.

2002r. "Travis on Meaning, Thought and the Ways the World Is." Review of Charles Travis, *Unshadowed Thought*. *Philosophical Quarterly* 52.2 (January 2002): 96–106.

2002s. "Wittgenstein, le réalisme et les mathématiques." *Wittgenstein, dernières pensées*, ed. Jacques Bouveresse, Sandra Laugier, and Jean-Jacques Rosat (Marseilles, France: Agone, 2002), 289–313. English version in *Philosophy in an Age of Science* (2012), 421–40.

2003

2003a. "For Ethics and Economics without the Dichotomies." *Review of Political Economy* 15.3 (July 2003): 395–412. Repr. in *The End of Value-Free Economics* (2012), 111–29.

2003b. "Out of Our Heads." *What Philosophers Think*, ed. Julian Baggini (London: Continuum Press, 2003), 226–36.

2003c. "Plädoyer für die Verabschiedung des Begriffs 'Idolatrie'." *Religion nach der Religionskritik*, ed. by Ludwig Nagl (Vienna: Oldenbourg Verlag; Berlin: Akademie Verlag, 2003), 49–59.

2004

2004a. "The Chosen People." Review of *The Jewish Political Tradition, vol. 2, Membership*, ed. Michael Walzer, Menachem Lorberbaum, and Noam J. Zohar. *Boston Review* 29.1 (February-March 2004): 45–46.

2004b. "The Content and Appeal of 'Naturalism'." *Naturalism in Question*, ed. Mario De Caro and David Macarthur (Cambridge, MA: Harvard University Press, 2004), 59–70. Repr. in *Philosophy in an Age of Science* (2012), 109–25.

2004c. "Philosophy as a Reconstructive Activity: William James on Moral Philosophy" in *The Pragmatic Turn in Philosophy: Contemporary Engagements between Analytic and Continental Thought*, ed. William Egginton and Mike Sandbothe (Albany, NY: State University of New York Press, 2004), 31–46. First published in German in 2000.

2004d. "The Pluralism of David Hartman." *Judaism and Modernity*, ed. Jonathan Malino (Aldershot, UK: Ashgate, 2004), 237–48.

2004e. "Sosa on Internal Realism and Conceptual Relativity." *Ernest Sosa and His Critics*, ed. John Greco (Malden, MA: Blackwell, 2004), 233–48.

2004f. "What Is Pragmatism?" With Richard Rorty and James Conant. *Think: Philosophy for Everyone* 8 (Autumn 2004): 71–88.

2004g. "The Uniqueness of Pragmatism." *Think: Philosophy for Everyone* 8 (Autumn 2004): 89–106.

2005

2005a. "A Philosopher Looks at Quantum Mechanics (Again)." *British Journal for the Philosophy of Science* 56.4 (December 2005): 615–34. Repr. in *Philosophy in an Age of Science* (2012), 126–47.

2005b. "The Depths and Shallows of Experience." *Science, Religion, and the Human Experience*, ed. James D. Proctor (Oxford: Oxford University Press, 2005), 71–86. Repr. in *Philosophy in an Age of Science* (2012), 567–83.

2005c. "James on Truth (Again)." *William James and the Varieties of Religious Experience: A Centenary Celebration*, ed. Jeremy R. Carrette (London and New York: Routledge, 2005), 172–82.

2005d. "Jewish Ethics?" *The Blackwell Companion to Religious Ethics*, ed. William Schweiker (Malden, MA: Blackwell, 2005), 159–65.

2005e. "Philosophy Should Not Be Just an Academic Discipline: A Dialogue with Hilary Putnam." Interview with János Boros. *Common Knowledge* 11.1 (Winter 2005): 126–35.

2006

2006a. "After Gödel." *Logic Journal of the IGPL* 14.5 (October 2006): 745–59. Repr. in *Philosophy in an Age of Science* (2012), 256–62.

2006b. "A Philosophical Puzzle: Who Was This Guy Spinoza Anyway?" Review of *Betraying Spinoza: The Renegade Jew Who Gave Us Modernity* by Rebecca Goldstein. *New York Observer* (18 December 2006): 25.

2006c. "Bays, Steiner, and Wittgenstein's 'Notorious' Paragraph About the Gödel Theorem." With Juliet Floyd. *Journal of Philosophy* 103.2 (February 2006): 101–10.

2006d. "The Epistemology of Unjust War." *Political Philosophy*, ed. Anthony O'Hear. *Royal Institute of Philosophy Supplements*, vol. 58 (Cambridge, UK: Cambridge University Press, 2007), 173–88. Repr. in *Philosophy in an Age of Science* (2012), 312–26.

2006e. "Intelligence and Ethics." *A Companion to Pragmatism*, ed. John R. Shook and Joseph Margolis (Malden, MA: Blackwell, 2006), 267–77.

2006f. "Monotheism and Humanism." *Humanity before God*, ed. William Schweiker, Michael A. Johnson, and Kevin Jung (Minneapolis, MN: Augsburg Fortress Press, 2006), 19–30.

2006g. "Philosophy as the Education of Grownups: Stanley Cavell and Skepticism." *Reading Cavell*, ed. Alice Crary and Sanford Shieh (London and New York: Routledge, 2006), 119–30. Repr. in *Philosophy in an Age of Science* (2012), 552–64.

2006h. "Replies to Commentators." *Contemporary Pragmatism* 3.2 (December 2006): 67–98.

2006i. "Respuestas a 'Needs, Values and Truth', de David Wiggins." Trans. Moris Polanco. *Utopìa y Praxis Latinoamericana* (Maracaibo, Venezuela) 11.32 (January-March 2006): 39–53.

2006j. "Science and (Some) Philosophers." *Ontology Studies: Cuadernos de Ontología* 6 (2006): 5–6, 11–19.

2007

2007a. "Between Scylla and Charybdis: Does Dummett Have a Way Through?" *The Philosophy of Michael Dummett*, ed. Randall E. Auxier and Lewis Edwin Hahn (Chicago: Open Court, 2007), 155–67.

2007b. "Facts, Theories, Values and Destitution in the Works of Sir Partha Dasgupta." With Vivian C. Walsh. *Review of Political Economy* 19.2 (2007): 181–202. Repr. in *The End of Value-Free Economics* (2012), 150–71.

2007c. "Metaphysical/Everyday Use: A Note on a Late Paper by Gordon Baker." *Wittgenstein and His Interpreters: Essays in Memory of Gordon Baker*, ed. Guy Kahane, Edward Kanterian, and Oskari Kuusela (Malden, MA: Blackwell, 2007), 169–73.
2007d. "Response to Dasgupta." With Vivian C. Walsh. *Economics and Philosophy* 23.3 (November 2007): 359–64.
2007e. "Science and (Some) Philosophers." *Ontology Studies: Cuadernos de Ontología* (Spain) 7 (2007): 12–26.
2007f. "What James' Pragmatism Offers Us (A Reading of the First Chapter of *Pragmatism*)." *Scopus: Časopis za filozofiju studenata Hrvatskih studija* (Zagreb, Croatia) 11.24 (2007): 7–12.
2007g. "Wittgenstein and the Real Numbers." *Wittgenstein and the Moral Life*, ed. Alice Crary (Cambridge, MA: MIT Press, 2007), 235–50. Repr. in *Philosophy in an Age of Science* (2012), 441–57.

2008

2008a. "12 Philosophers—and Their Influence on Me." *Proceedings and Addresses of the American Philosophical Association* 82.2 (November 2008): 101–15.
2008b. "A Note on Steiner on Wittgenstein, Gödel, and Tarski." *Iyyun: The Jerusalem Philosophical Quarterly* 57 (January 2008): 83–93.
2008c. "Capabilities and Two Ethical Theories." *Journal of Human Development* 9.3 (November 2008): 377–388. Repr. in *Philosophy in an Age of Science* (2012), 299–311.
2008d. "Wittgenstein and Realism." *International Journal of Philosophical Studies* 16.1 (February 2008): 1–14. Repr. in *Philosophy in an Age of Science* (2012), 339–54.
2008e. "Wittgensteins 'berüchtigter' Paragraph über das Gödel-Theorem: Neuere Diskussionen." With Juliet Floyd. *Prosa oder Beweis? Wittgensteins 'berüchtigte' Bemerkungen zu Gödel: Texte und Dokumente*, ed. Esther Ramharter (Berlin: Parerga Verlag, 2008), 75–97. Longer version, incorporating material from "A Note on Steiner on Wittgenstein, Gödel and Tarski" (2008), was published as "Wittgenstein's 'Notorious' Paragraph about the Gödel Theorem: Recent Discussions" in *Philosophy in an Age of Science* (2012), 458–81.

2009

2009a. "Dewey's Central Insight." *John Dewey's Educational Philosophy in International Perspective: A New Democracy for the Twenty-first Century*, ed. Larry A. Hickman and Giuseppe Spadafora (Carbondale: Southern Illinois University Press, 2009), 7–21.
2009b. "Entanglement throughout Economic Science: The End of a Separate Welfare Economics." With Vivian Walsh. *Review of Political Economy* 21.2 (2009): 291–97. Repr. in *The End of Value-Free Economics* (2012), 207–13.
2009c. "Hilary Putnam." *Mind and Consciousness: 5 Questions*, ed. Patrick Grim (Copenhagen: Automatic Press, 2009), 145–54. Enlarged version published as "How to Be a Sophisticated 'Naïve Realist'" in *Philosophy in an Age of Science* (2012), 624–39.
2009d. "Richard Rorty." *Proceedings of the American Philosophical Society* 53.2 (June 2009): 229–32.

2010

2010a. "Between Dolev and Dummett: Some Comments on 'Antirealism, Presentism and Bivalence'." *International Journal of Philosophical Studies* 18.1 (February 2010): 91–96.

2010b. "Science and Philosophy." *Naturalism and Normativity*, ed. Mario De Caro and David Macarthur (New York: Columbia University Press, 2010), 89–99. Repr. in *Philosophy in an Age of Science* (2012), 39–50.

2011

2011a. "The Fact/Value Dichotomy and Its Critics." *Stanley Cavell and the Education of Grownups*, ed. Naoko Saito and Paul Standish (New York: Fordham University Press, 2011), 37–54. Repr. in *Philosophy in an Age of Science* (2012), 283–98.
2011b. "The Gödel Theorem and Human Nature." *Kurt Gödel and the Foundations of Mathematics: Horizons of Truth*, ed. Matthias Baaz (Cambridge, UK: Cambridge University Press, 2011), 325–38. Repr. in *Philosophy in an Age of Science* (2012), 239–55.
2011c. "Reflections on Pragmatism." *Dewey's Enduring Impact: Essays on America's Philosopher*, ed. John R. Shook and Paul Kurtz (Amherst, NY: Prometheus Books, 2011), 43–56.

2012

2012a. "Comments on Richard Boyd." *Reading Putnam*, ed. Maria Baghramian (London: Routledge, 2012), 95–100.
2012b. "Comments on Michael Devitt." *Reading Putnam*, ed. Maria Baghramian (London: Routledge, 2012), 121–26.
2012c. "Comments on David Macarthur." *Reading Putnam*, ed. Maria Baghramian (London: Routledge, 2012), 140–42.
2012d. "Comments on Axel Mueller." *Reading Putnam*, ed. Maria Baghramian (London: Routledge, 2012), 179–81.
2012e. "Comments on Charles Parsons." *Reading Putnam*, ed. Maria Baghramian (London: Routledge, 2012), 202–4.
2012f. "Comments on Russell Goodman." *Reading Putnam*, ed. Maria Baghramian (London: Routledge, 2012), 219–24.
2012g. "Comments on David Albert." *Reading Putnam*, ed. Maria Baghramian (London: Routledge, 2012), 237–39.
2012h. "Comments on Ruth Anna Putnam." *Reading Putnam*, ed. Maria Baghramian (London: Routledge, 2012), 257–60.
2012i. "Comments on Tyler Burge." *Reading Putnam*, ed. Maria Baghramian (London: Routledge, 2012), 272–74.
2012j. "Comments on Ned Block." *Reading Putnam*, ed. Maria Baghramian (London: Routledge, 2012), 319–21.
2012k. "Comments on Travis and McDowell." *Reading Putnam*, ed. Maria Baghramian (London: Routledge, 2012), 347–58.
2012l. "From Quantum Mechanics to Ethics and Back Again." *Reading Putnam*, ed. Maria Baghramian (London and New York: Routledge, 2012), 19–36. Repr. in *Philosophy in an Age of Science* (2012), 51–71.
2012m. "On Mathematics, Realism, and Ethics." Interview by Bill Kowalsky. *Harvard Review of Philosophy* 18.1 (Spring 2012): 143–60.
2012n. "Quantum Mechanics and Ontology." *Analysis and Interpretation in the Exact Sciences: Essays in Honour of William Demopoulos*, ed. Mélanie Frappier, Derek H. Brown, and Robert DiSalle (Dordrecht: Springer, 2012), 179–90. Repr. in *Philosophy in an Age of Science* (2012), 148–61.
2012o. "Realismo e senso commune." Italian translation of "Commonsense Realism." *Bentornata realtà: Il nuovo realismo in discussione*, ed. Mario De Caro and Maurizio Ferraris (Turin, Italy: Giulio Einaudi Editore, 2012), 5–20.

20120p. "Sensation and Apperception." *Consciousness and Subjectivity*, ed. Sofia Miguens and Gerhard Preyer (Berlin: Ontos Verlag, 2012), 39–50.

2013

2013a. "The Development of Externalist Semantics." *Theoria* 79.3 (2013): 192–203.
2013b. "The Revival of Naïve Realism." *Rivista di filosofia* 104.3 (2013): 505–22.

2014

2014a. "Not Very Much." *Understanding Moral Sentiments: Darwinian Perspectives*, ed. Hilary Putnam, Susan Neimann, and Jefffey Schloss (New Brunswick, NJ: Transaction Publishers, 2014), 203–11.
2014b. "Needlessness of Adverbialism, Attributeism and its Compatibility with Cognitive Science." With Hilla Jacobson. *Philosophia* 42.3 (September 2014): 555–70.

INDEX